FINANCIAL INSTITUTIONS MANAGEMENT

A RISK MANAGEMENT APPROACH

FIFTH CANADIAN EDITION

Anthony Saunders
Stern School of Business
New York University

Marcia Millon Cornett
Bentley University

Patricia A. McGraw
Ted Rogers School of Management
Ryerson University

Mc Graw Hill Education | McGraw-Hill Ryerson

McGraw-Hill Ryerson

Financial Institutions Management
Fifth Canadian Edition

ISBN-13: 978-0-07-105159-0
ISBN-10: 0-07-105159-7

3 4 5 6 7 8 9 0 WEB 1 9 8 7 6 5 4

Printed and bound in Canada.

Director of Product Management: Rhondda McNabb
Senior Product Manager: Kimberley Veevers
Marketing Manager: Jeremy Guimond
Group Product Development Manager: Kelly Dickson
Product Developer: Sarah Fulton
Photo/Permissions: Sarah Fulton
Senior Product Team Associate: Christine Lomas
Supervising Editor: Joanne Limebeer
Copy Editor: Karen Rolfe
Proofreader: Julia Cochrane
Plant Production Coordinator: Scott Morrison
Manufacturing Production Coordinator: Emily Hickey
Cover and Interior Design: Dave Murphy/Valid Design & Layout
Cover Image: Pierre Tremblay/Masterfile
Composition: Aptara®, Inc.
Printer: Webcom

Library and Archives Canada Cataloguing in Publication

Saunders, Anthony, author
Financial institutions management : a risk management approach/Anthony Saunders, Stern School of Business, New York University, Marcia Millon Cornett, Bentley University, Patricia McGraw, Ted Rogers School of Management, Ryerson University.—Fifth Canadian edition.

Includes bibliographical references and index.
ISBN 978-0-07-105159-0 (pbk.)

1. Financial institutions—Canada—Management—Textbooks. 2. Risk management—Canada—Textbooks. I. Cornett, Marcia Millon, author II. McGraw, Patricia A. (Patricia Anne), 1951–, author III. Title.

To all my co-authors over the years.

Anthony Saunders

To my parents, Tom and Sue.

Marcia Millon Cornett

To my family, Gary, Bryan, Andrea, Tyler, Lavon, Doreen, Joanna, Cameron, Lachlan, and Lilly.

Patricia A. McGraw

About the Authors

Anthony Saunders

Anthony Saunders is the John M. Schiff Professor of Finance and former Chair of the Department of Finance at the Stern School of Business at New York University. Professor Saunders received his Ph.D. from the London School of Economics and has taught both undergraduate- and graduate-level courses at NYU since 1978. Throughout his academic career, his teaching and research have specialized in financial institutions and international banking. He has served as a visiting professor all over the world, including INSEAD, the Stockholm School of Economics, and the University of Melbourne.

Professor Saunders has held positions on the Board of Academic Consultants of the Federal Reserve Board of Governors and the Council of Research Advisors for the Federal National Mortgage Association. In addition, Dr. Saunders has acted as a visiting scholar at the Comptroller of the Currency and at the Federal Reserve Banks of Philadelphia and New York. He also held a visiting position in the research department of the International Monetary Fund. He is editor of *Financial Markets, Instruments and Institutions.* His research has been published in all the major money and banking and finance journals and in several books. In addition, he has authored or coauthored several professional books, the most recent of which is *Credit Risk Measurement: New Approaches to Value at Risk and Other Paradigms*, 3rd edition, John Wiley and Sons, New York, 2010. In 2008, he was ranked as the most published author in the last 50 years in the top seven journals in finance.

Marcia Millon Cornett

Marcia Millon Cornett is a Professor of Finance at Bentley University, in Waltham, Massachusetts. She received her B.S. degree in Economics from Knox College in Galesburg, Illinois, and her M.B.A. and Ph.D. degrees in Finance from Indiana University in Bloomington, Indiana. Dr. Cornett has written and published several articles in the areas of bank performance, bank regulation, and corporate finance. Articles authored by Dr. Cornett have appeared in academic journals such as the *Journal of Finance*, the *Journal of Money, Credit and Banking*, the *Journal of Financial Economics*, *Financial Management*, and the *Journal of Banking & Finance*. In 2008, she was ranked as the 124th most published author in the last 50 years in the top seven journals in finance. Dr. Cornett served as an associate editor of *Financial Management* and is currently an associate editor for the *Journal of Financial Services Research*, *FMA Online*, the *Multinational Finance Journal*, and the *Review of Financial Economics*. She has served as a member of the Board of Directors, the Executive Committee, and the Finance Committee of the SIU Credit Union. Dr. Cornett has also taught at the University of Colorado, Boston College, Southern Methodist University, and Southern Illinois University at Carbonale. She is a member of the Financial Management Association, the American Finance Association, and the Western Finance Association.

Patricia A. McGraw

Patricia A. McGraw is Associate Professor, Finance, at the Ted Rogers School of Management, Ryerson University. Dr. McGraw received a B.Sc. degree in Geology and Chemistry from McGill University, an M.Sc. in Geology from Dalhousie University, an M.B.A. in Finance and Accounting from the University of Toronto, and a Ph.D. in Interdisciplinary Studies from Dalhousie University. She has taught at Dalhousie University and Ryerson University in Canada; at Lincoln University in New Zealand; and at Universiti Tenaga Nasional in Kuala Lumpur, Malaysia.

Dr. McGraw has worked as an exploration geologist and as a corporate banker specializing in lending to resource companies. She has also consulted to the offshore natural gas industry. Her research and publications focus on financial intermediation, capital markets, and capital structure in emerging markets.

Acknowledgements

When considering the efforts of contributors, I am indebted and offer special thanks to the following reviewers, whose constructive suggestions have been incorporated as much as possible into the development of the fifth Canadian edition:

Pan Zhang, Northern Alberta Institute of Technology
Young Cheol Jung, University of New Brunswick—Saint John
Eldon Gardner, University of Lethbridge
Zaidong Dong, University of Northern British Columbia

I would also like to thank McGraw-Hill Higher Education and McGraw-Hill Ryerson for their professional contributions, including Kimberley Veevers, Senior Product Manager; Sarah Fulton, Product Developer; Joanne Limebeer, Supervising Editor; Karen Rolfe, Copy Editor; Pan Zhang, Technical Checker; and many others.

Patricia A. McGraw
Ted Rogers School of Management
Ryerson University

BRIEF CONTENTS

Preface *xiv*

PART 1
The Financial Services Industry *1*

1 Why Are Financial Institutions Special? *2*
2 Deposit-Taking Institutions *21*
3 Finance Companies *40*
4 Securities, Brokerage, and Investment Banking *55*
5 Mutual Funds, Hedge Funds, and Pension Funds *75*
6 Insurance Companies *102*
7 Risks of Financial Institutions *126*

PART 2
Measuring Risk *146*

8 Interest Rate Risk I *147*
9 Interest Rate Risk II *164*
10 Credit Risk: Individual Loans *194*
11 Credit Risk: Loan Portfolio and Concentration Risk *237*
12 Liquidity Risk *252*
13 Foreign Exchange Risk *277*
14 Sovereign Risk *302*
15 Market Risk *325*
16 Off-Balance-Sheet Risk *357*
17 Technology and Other Operational Risks *380*

PART 3
Managing Risk *412*

18 Liability and Liquidity Management *413*
19 Deposit Insurance and Other Liability Guarantees *431*
20 Capital Adequacy *457*
21 Product and Geographic Expansion *493*
22 Futures and Forwards *528*
23 Options, Caps, Floors, and Collars *563*
24 Swaps *598*
25 Loan Sales *622*
26 Securitization *638*

Index *I-1*

Chapter Appendices
Available on Connect

connect

CONTENTS

Preface *xiv*

PART 1
THE FINANCIAL SERVICES INDUSTRY *1*

CHAPTER 1
Why Are Financial Institutions Special? *2*

Introduction *2*
Financial Institutions' Specialness *3*
FIs Function as Brokers 4
FIs Function as Asset Transformers 5
Information Costs 5
Liquidity and Price Risk 6
Other Special Services 7
Other Aspects of Specialness *8*
The Transmission of Monetary Policy 8
Credit Allocation 9
Intergenerational Wealth Transfers or Time Intermediation 9
Payment Services 9
Denomination Intermediation 9
Specialness and Regulation *9*
Safety and Soundness Regulation 10
Monetary Policy Regulation 12
Credit Allocation Regulation 12
Consumer Protection Regulation 12
Investor Protection Regulation 13
Entry Regulation 13
The Changing Dynamics of Specialness *13*
Trends in Canada 14
Risk Measurement and the Financial Crisis 15
Global Issues *17*

Questions and Problems *19*

CHAPTER 2
Deposit-Taking Institutions *21*

Introduction *21*
Banks *23*
Size, Structure, and Composition of the Industry 23
Balance Sheet and Recent Trends 25
Other Activities 30
Regulation 31
Industry Performance 33
Credit Unions and Caisses Populaires *34*
Size, Structure, and Composition of the Industry and Recent Trends 34
Regulation 36
Industry Performance 36
Global Issues: The Financial Crisis *36*

Questions and Problems *39*

CHAPTER 3
Finance Companies *40*

Introduction *40*
Size, Structure, and Composition of the Industry *41*
Balance Sheet and Recent Trends *45*
Assets 45
Liabilities and Equity 49
Industry Performance 50
Regulation *51*
Government Financing Entities *52*
Crown Corporations in Canada 52
Global Issues *53*

Questions and Problems *54*

CHAPTER 4
Securities, Brokerage, and Investment Banking *55*

Introduction *55*
Size, Structure, and Composition of the Industry *56*

Balance Sheet and Recent Trends 66
Recent Trends 66
Balance Sheet 66
Regulation 69
Global Issues 72
Questions and Problems 73

CHAPTER 5
Mutual Funds, Hedge Funds, and Pension Funds 75

Introduction 75
Mutual Funds 76
Size, Structure, and Composition of the Industry 76
Different Types of Mutual Funds 79
Mutual Fund Objectives 80
Investor Returns from Mutual Fund Ownership 80
Mutual Fund Costs 82
Regulation 84
Global Issues 86
Hedge Funds 86
History, Size, Structure, and Composition of the Industry 86
Types of Hedge Funds 89
Fees on Hedge Funds 94
Offshore Hedge Funds 94
Regulation 95
Pension Funds 95
Size, Structure, and Composition of the Industry 95
Balance Sheet and Recent Trends 97
Regulation 99
Global Issues 100
Questions and Problems 101

CHAPTER 6
Insurance Companies 102

Introduction 102
Life Insurance Companies 103
Size, Structure, and Composition of the Industry 103
Balance Sheet and Recent Trends 108
Regulation 110
Property and Casualty Insurance 111
Size, Structure, and Composition of the Industry 112
Balance Sheet and Recent Trends 114
Regulation 121
Global Issues 122
Questions and Problems 124

CHAPTER 7
Risks of Financial Institutions 126

Introduction 126
Interest Rate Risk 127
Credit Risk 129
Liquidity Risk 131
Foreign Exchange Risk 132
Country or Sovereign Risk 134
Market Risk 135
Off-Balance-Sheet Risk 137
Technology and Operational Risks 139
Insolvency Risk 140
Other Risks and the Interaction of Risks 141
Questions and Problems 142

PART 2
MEASURING RISK 146

CHAPTER 8
Interest Rate Risk I 147

Introduction 147
The Level and Movement of Interest Rates 148
The Repricing Model 150
RSAs 153
RSLs 153
Equal Changes in Rates on RSAs and RSLs 154
Unequal Changes in Rates on RSAs and RSLs 155
Weaknesses of the Repricing Model 158
Market Value Effects 158
Overaggregation 158
The Problem of Runoffs 159
Cash Flows from OBS Activities 159
Questions and Problems 161

CHAPTER 9
Interest Rate Risk II 164

Introduction 164
Duration: A Simple Introduction 165
A General Formula for Duration 167
The Duration of Interest-Bearing Bonds 168
The Duration of a Zero-Coupon Bond 170
The Duration of a Consol Bond (Perpetuities) 171
Features of Duration 171
Duration and Maturity 172
Duration and Yield 172
Duration and Coupon Interest 173

The Economic Meaning of Duration *173*
Semiannual Coupon Bonds 176
Duration and Interest Rate Risk *177*
Duration Management on a Single Security 178
Duration Management on the Whole Balance Sheet 181
Immunization and Regulatory Considerations *185*
Difficulties in Applying the Duration Model *186*
Duration Matching Can Be Costly 186
Immunization Is a Dynamic Problem 187
Large Interest Rate Changes and Convexity 187

Questions and Problems *189*

CHAPTER 10
Credit Risk: Individual Loans *194*

Introduction *194*
Credit Quality Problems *195*
Types of Loans *197*
Business Loans 197
Mortgage Loans 199
Personal (Consumer) Loans 200
Other Loans 202
Calculating the Return on a Loan *202*
The Contractually Promised Return on a Loan 202
The Expected Return on a Loan 205
Retail and Wholesale Credit Decisions *206*
Retail (Consumer) 206
Wholesale (Business) 206
Measurement of Credit Risk *208*
Default Risk Models *209*
Qualitative Models 209
Quantitative Models 211
Newer Models of Credit Risk Measurement and Pricing *215*
Term Structure Derivation of Credit Risk 215
Mortality Rate Derivation of Credit Risk 221
RAROC Models 223
Option Models of Default Risk 226

Questions and Problems *232*

CHAPTER 11
Credit Risk: Loan Portfolio and Concentration Risk *237*

Introduction *237*
Simple Models of Loan Concentration Risk *237*
Portfolio Theory and Loan Diversification *239*
Moody's Analytics' Portfolio Manager Model 242
Partial Applications of Portfolio Theory 245
Loan Loss Ratio–Based Models 248
Regulatory Models 249

Questions and Problems *250*

CHAPTER 12
Liquidity Risk *252*

Introduction *252*
Causes of Liquidity Risk *253*
Liquidity Risk at Deposit-Taking Institutions *253*
Liability-Side Liquidity Risk 253
Asset-Side Liquidity Risk 257
Measuring a DTI's Liquidity Exposure 259
Liquidity Risk, Unexpected Deposit Drains, and Bank Runs 268
Bank Runs, the Bank of Canada, and Deposit Insurance 269
Liquidity Risk and Life Insurance Companies *269*
Liquidity Risk and Property and Casualty Insurers *270*
Investment Funds *271*

Questions and Problems *274*

CHAPTER 13
Foreign Exchange Risk *277*

Introduction *277*
Foreign Exchange Rates and Transactions *277*
FX Rates 277
FX Transactions 278
Sources of Foreign Exchange Risk Exposure *280*
FX Rate Volatility and FX Exposure 283
Foreign Currency Trading *284*
FX Trading Activities 285
Foreign Asset and Liability Positions *286*
The Return and Risk of Foreign Investments 287
Risk and Hedging 289
Multicurrency Foreign Asset–Liability Positions 293
Interest Rate, Inflation, and Exchange Rate Interactions *294*
PPP 295
IRP Theorem 296

Questions and Problems *298*

CHAPTER 14
Sovereign Risk *302*

Introduction *302*
Credit Risk versus Sovereign Risk *306*
Debt Repudiation versus Debt Rescheduling *307*
Country Risk Evaluation *309*
Outside Evaluation Models 309
Internal Evaluation Models 312
Using Market Data to Measure Risk: The Secondary Market for Sovereign Debt 319

Questions and Problems *323*

CHAPTER 15
Market Risk *325*

Introduction *325*
Calculating Market Risk Exposure *328*
The RiskMetrics Model *329*
The Market Risk of Fixed-Income Securities 330
FX 332
Equities 333
Portfolio Aggregation 334
Historic (Back Simulation) Approach *337*
The Historic (Back Simulation) Model versus RiskMetrics 340
The Monte Carlo Simulation Approach *341*
Expected Shortfall Approach *343*
Regulatory Models: The Bank for International Settlements Standardized Framework *346*
Partial Risk Factor Approach 347
Fuller Risk Factor Approach 348
The Bank for International Settlements Regulations and Large Bank Internal Models *351*

Questions and Problems *353*

CHAPTER 16
Off-Balance-Sheet Risk *357*

Introduction *357*
Off-Balance-Sheet Activities and Financial Institution Solvency *358*
Returns and Risks of Off-Balance-Sheet Activities *361*
The Major Types of Off-Balance-Sheet Activities *363*
Loan Commitments 363
Commercial LCs and SLCs 367
Derivative Contracts: Futures, Forwards, Swaps, and Options 369
Forward Purchases and Sales of WI Securities 373
Loans Sold 374
Other Off-Balance-Sheet Risks *375*
Settlement Risk 375
Affiliate Risk 376
The Role of Off-Balance-Sheet Activities in Reducing Risk *377*

Questions and Problems *378*

CHAPTER 17
Technology and Other Operational Risks *380*

Introduction *380*
What Are the Sources of Operational Risk? *382*
Technological Innovation and Profitability *383*
Technology and Financial Services *385*
Wholesale Financial Services 385
Retail Financial Services 387
Advanced Technology Requirements 388
The Effect of Technology on Revenues and Costs *390*
Technology and Revenues 391
Technology and Costs 392
Testing for Economies of Scale and Economies of Scope *396*
The Production Approach 396
The Intermediation Approach 396
Empirical Findings on Economies of Scale and Scope *396*
Economies of Scale and Scope and X-Inefficiencies 397
Technology and the Evolution of the Payments System *398*
Risks That Arise in an Electronic Transfer Payment System 400
Other Operational Risks *407*
Regulatory Issues and Technology and Operational Risks *408*

Questions and Problems *410*

PART 3
MANAGING RISK *412*

CHAPTER 18
Liability and Liquidity Management *413*

Introduction *413*
Liquid Asset Management *414*
The Composition of the Liquid Asset Portfolio *415*
Return–Risk Trade-off for Liquid Assets *416*
Liability Management *417*
- Funding Risk and Cost 417

Choice of Liability Structure *418*
- Demand Deposits 418
- Interest-Bearing Chequing Accounts 420
- Savings Accounts 421
- Retail Term Deposits and GICs 421
- Wholesale Fixed-Term Deposits and CDs 422
- Interbank Funds 423
- Repurchase Agreements (Repos) 424
- Other Borrowings 425

Deposit-Taking Institutions and Liquidity Risk *426*
Insurance Companies and Liquidity Risk *427*
Other Financial Institutions and Liquidity Risk *428*
The Role of Central Banks and Regulators *429*

Questions and Problems *430*

CHAPTER 19
Deposit Insurance and Other Liability Guarantees *431*

Introduction *431*
- The Canadian Experience with Deposit Insurance 432
- The U.S. Experience with Bank Deposit Insurance 434

Causes of Deposit Insurance Insolvency *435*
- The Financial Environment 435
- Moral Hazard 436

Panic Prevention versus Moral Hazard *437*
Controlling Risk Taking *438*
- Stockholder Discipline 438
- Depositor Discipline 442

Federal Deposit Insurance Corporation's Policies *445*
- Regulatory Discipline 447

Deposit Insurance Systems Globally *448*
Lender of Last Resort *449*
- Deposit Insurance versus the Central Bank 449
- The Bank of Canada's Lender of Last Resort Policies 449
- The U.S. Federal Reserve 450

Other Guarantee Programs *452*
- Autorité des marchés financiers (FMA) 452
- CUs and CPs 453
- Assuris 453
- PACICC 454
- CIPF 454

Questions and Problems *455*

CHAPTER 20
Capital Adequacy *457*

Introduction *457*
Capital and Insolvency Risk *458*
- Capital 458
- The Market Value of Capital 458
- The Book Value of Capital 459
- The Discrepancy between the Market and Book Values of Equity 460
- Arguments against Market Value Accounting 462

Capital Adequacy for Deposit-Taking Institutions *463*
- The Assets to Capital Multiple 463
- Risk-Based Capital Ratios: The Basel Agreement 464
- Minimum Capital Requirements 468
- Calculating Risk-Based Capital Ratios 469

Capital Requirements for Other Financial Institutions *487*
- Securities Firms 487
- Life Insurance Companies 487
- Property and Casualty Insurance Companies 488

Questions and Problems *490*

CHAPTER 21
Product and Geographic Expansion *493*

Introduction *493*
Product Diversification *494*
Segmentation in the Financial Services Industry *494*
- Banking and Investment Banking 494
- Banking and Insurance 495
- Nonbank Financial Services Firms and Banking 496

Diversification in Other Countries *498*
Issues Involved in the Diversification of Product Offerings *499*
- Safety and Soundness 500
- Economies of Scale and Scope 501
- Conflicts of Interest 502
- Deposit Insurance 504
- Regulatory Oversight 504
- Competition 505

Geographic Expansions: Canada and the United States *508*
Regulatory Factors Impacting Geographic Expansion *509*
- Insurance Companies 509
- Banks 509
- U.S. Commercial Banks 509

Synergies of Geographic Expansion *511*
- Cost Synergies 511
- Revenue Synergies 511
- Merger Guidelines 512

Other Factors Impacting Geographic Expansion *515*
International Expansions *516*
- Canadian and U.S. Banks Abroad 517
- Foreign Banks in North America 520

Advantages and Disadvantages of International Expansion *523*
- Advantages 524
- Disadvantages 524

Questions and Problems *525*

CHAPTER 22
Futures and Forwards *528*

Introduction *528*
Forward and Futures Contracts *531*
- Spot Contracts 532
- Forward Contracts 532
- Futures Contracts 533

Forward Contracts and Hedging Interest Rate Risk *534*
Hedging Interest Rate Risk with Futures Contracts *535*
- Microhedging 536
- Macrohedging 536
- Routine Hedging versus Selective Hedging 536
- Macrohedging with Futures 537
- The Problem of Basis Risk 544

Hedging Foreign Exchange Risk *546*
- Forwards 546
- Futures 547
- Estimating the Hedge Ratio 550

Hedging Credit Risk with Futures and Forwards *553*
- Credit Forward Contracts and Credit Risk Hedging 554
- Futures Contracts and Catastrophe Risk 556

Regulation of Derivative Securities *557*

Questions and Problems *558*

CHAPTER 23
Options, Caps, Floors, and Collars *563*

Introduction *563*
Basic Features of Options *563*
- Buying a Call Option on a Bond 564
- Writing a Call Option on a Bond 565
- Buying a Put Option on a Bond 566
- Writing a Put Option on a Bond 567

Writing versus Buying Options *568*
- Economic Reasons for Not Writing Options 568
- Regulatory Reasons 570
- Futures versus Options Hedging 570

The Mechanics of Hedging a Bond or Bond Portfolio *571*
- Hedging with Bond Options Using the Binomial Model 572

Actual Bond Options *575*
Hedging Interest Rate Risk with Options *577*
Hedging Foreign Exchange Risk with Options *582*
Hedging Credit Risk with Options *583*
Hedging Catastrophe Risk with Call Spread Options *584*
Caps, Floors, and Collars *585*
- Caps 586
- Floors 588
- Collars 589
- Caps, Floors, Collars, and Credit Risk 592

Questions and Problems *593*

CHAPTER 24
Swaps *598*

Introduction *598*
Swap Markets *599*
Interest Rate Swaps *600*
Realized Cash Flows on an Interest Rate Swap 604
Macrohedging with Swaps 605
Currency Swaps *608*
Fixed–Fixed Currency Swaps 608
Fixed–Floating Currency Swaps 610
Credit Swaps *611*
Total Return Swaps 613
Pure Credit Swaps 614
CDS Indexes 615
Swaps and Credit Risk Concerns *615*
Netting and Swaps 617
Payment Flows Are Interest and Not Principal 618
Standby Letters of Credit 618

Questions and Problems *618*

CHAPTER 25
Loan Sales *622*

Introduction *622*
The Bank Loan Sales Market *623*
Definition of a Loan Sale 623
Types of Loan Sales 624
Types of Loan Sales Contracts 625
Trends in Loan Sales *627*
The Buyers and the Sellers 628
Why Banks and Other Financial Institutions Sell Loans *632*
Reserve Requirements 632
Fee Income 632
Capital Costs 633
Liquidity Risk 633
Factors Affecting Loan Sales Growth *633*
Access to the CP Market 633
Customer Relationship Effects 633
Legal Concerns 633
BIS Capital Requirements 634
Market Value Accounting 634
Asset Brokerage and Loan Trading 634
Government Loan Sales 635
Credit Ratings 635
Purchase and Sale of Foreign Bank Loans 635
The Global Credit and Liquidity Crisis, 2008–2009 *635*

Questions and Problems *636*

CHAPTER 26
Securitization *638*

Introduction *638*
Converting On-Balance-Sheet Assets to a Securitized Asset *639*
The Pass-Through Security *643*
CMHC 643
GNMA 644
FNMA 644
FHLMC 645
The Incentives and Mechanics of Pass-Through Security Creation 645
Prepayment Risk on Pass-Through Securities 650
Prepayment Models 655
NHA MBS Pools 661
U.S. Government Sponsorship and Oversight of FNMA and FHLMC 663
The Collateralized Mortgage Obligation *664*
Creation of CMOs 665
Class A, B, and C Bond Buyers 667
Other CMO Classes 667
The Mortgage-Backed (Covered) Bond *668*
Innovations in Securitization *670*
Mortgage Pass-Through Strips 670
Securitization of Other Assets 673
Can All Assets Be Securitized? *674*
The Canadian Market for Asset-Backed Securities *676*
ABCP Market Freeze: August 2007 676
The Canadian Securitization Market 676

Questions and Problems *678*

Index *I-1*

CHAPTER APPENDICES

All appendices are available on Connect.

Appendix 1A: The Financial Crisis: The Failure of Financial Services Institution Specialness

Appendix 2A: Financial Statement Analysis Using a Return on Equity (ROE) Framework

Appendix 2B: Who Regulates Bank Financial Groups in Canada?

Appendix 2C: Technology in Commercial Banking

Appendix 8A: The Maturity Model

Appendix 8B: Term Structure of Interest Rates

Appendix 9A: The Basics of Bond Valuation

Appendix 9B: Incorporating Convexity into the Duration Model

Appendix 10A: Credit Analysis

Appendix 10B: Black–Scholes Option Pricing Model

Appendix 11A: CreditMetrics

Appendix 11B: CreditRisk+

Appendix 12A: Illustrative Template for the LCR

Appendix 14A: Mechanisms for Dealing with Sovereign Risk Exposure

Appendix 16A: A Letter of Credit Transaction

Appendix 19A: Deposit Insurance Coverage for Commercial Banks in Various Countries

Appendix 20A: Internal Ratings–Based Approach to Measuring Credit Risk–Weighted Assets

Appendix 20B: Methodology Used to Determine G-SIBs Capital Surcharge

Appendix 21A: EU and G-10 Countries: Regulatory Treatment of the Mixing of Banking, Securities, and Insurance Activities and the Mixing of Banking and Commerce

Appendix 22A: Microhedging with Futures

Appendix 23A: Black–Scholes Option Pricing Model

Appendix 23B: Microhedging with Options

Appendix 24A: Setting Rates on an Interest Rate Swap

PREFACE TO THE FIFTH CANADIAN EDITION

The last 25 years have been dramatic for the financial services industry. In the 1990s and 2000s boundaries between the traditional industry sectors, such as commercial banking and investment banking, broke down, and competition became increasingly global in nature. Many forces contributed to this breakdown in interindustry and intercountry barriers, including financial innovation, technology, taxation, and regulation. Then, in 2008–2009, the financial services industry experienced the worst financial crisis since the Great Depression. The global financial industry has not yet recovered from this crisis, and it is in this context that this resource is written. Although the traditional nature of each sector's product activity is analyzed, a greater emphasis is placed on new areas of activities, such as asset securitization, off-balance-sheet banking, international banking, and regulatory changes occurring as a result of the financial crisis.

The fifth Canadian edition of this text focuses on managing return and risk in modern financial institutions (FIs). *Financial Institutions Management*'s central theme is that the risks faced by FI managers and the methods and markets through which these risks are managed are similar whether an institution is a bank or an insurance company. As in any stockholder-owned corporation, the goal of FI managers should always be to maximize the value of the FI. However, pursuit of value maximization does not mean that risk management can be ignored.

Modern FIs are in the risk management business. As we discuss in this book, in a world of perfect and frictionless capital markets, FIs would not exist and individuals would manage their own financial assets and portfolios. But since real-world financial markets are not perfect, FIs bear and manage risk on behalf of their customers through the pooling of risks and the sale of their services as risk specialists. The purpose of this text is to examine the risk management techniques used by FIs in Canada. As well, this fifth Canadian edition focuses on the response of Canadian FIs and their regulators to global events.

What's New in the Fifth Canadian Edition

Each chapter in this edition has been revised to reflect the most up-to-date information available. End-of-chapter questions and problems have been expanded and updated to provide a complete selection of testing material. The following are some of the new features of this edition:

- Tables and figures in all chapters have been revised to include the most recent available data.
- Updates on the major changes proposed for the regulation of FIs are included where appropriate throughout the resource along with new material detailing how the financial crisis has affected risk management in FIs.
- The Internet Exercises and Integrated Minicases have been moved to the Instructors Manual. New Minicases have been added for Chapters 9, 13, 16, and 24.
- The material on finance companies has been moved to Chapter 3 in order to contrast the lending activities of this relatively unregulated industry with the highly regulated FIs (banks) in Chapter 2.

- Insurance companies are now discussed in Chapter 6.
- Chapters 2, 7, and 14 include discussions of the effects of the European debt crisis on the risks and returns of FIs.
- Chapter 4 includes a new section on venture capital.
- Chapter 5 includes an expanded discussion of ETFs and an update on the regulation of hedge funds.
- In Part 2, Measuring Risk, the chapters have been reordered to reflect the relative importance of the risks. Interest Rate Risk (Chapters 8 and 9), Credit Risk (Chapters 10 and 11), and Liquidity Risk (Chapter 12) are covered first, followed by Foreign Exchange Risk (Chapter 13), Sovereign Risk (Chapter 14), Market Risk (Chapter 15), Off-Balance-Sheet Risk (Chapter 16), and Technology and Other Operational Risks (Chapter 17).
- Chapter 15 introduces a discussion of and examples of the newest market risk measures enacted as a result of Basel III.
- Chapter 17 includes a new section on advanced technologies in banking.
- Chapter 20 includes a detailed discussion of Basel III capital adequacy rules as they are being implemented by the Office of the Superintendent of Financial Institutions (OSFI). The new leverage ratio for banks and the additional capital required of domestic and globally significant FIs (D-SIBs and G-SIBs) are discussed.
- Former Chapters 21 and 22 have been combined into one chapter (Product and Geographic Expansion). The combined Chapter 21 includes a new section on shadow banks.
- Chapter 26 (Securitization) includes a new section on synthetic collateralized debt obligations (CDOs).

Organization

Since the focus is on return and risk and the sources of that return and risk, this resource relates ways in which the managers of FIs can expand return with a managed level of risk to achieve the best, or most favourable, return–risk outcome for FI owners.

Part 1: Introduction

Chapter 1 introduces the special functions of FIs and takes an analytical look at how financial intermediation benefits the Canadian and the global economies. Chapters 2 through 6 provide an overview describing the key balance sheet and regulatory features of the major sectors of the Canadian financial services industry. Deposit-taking institutions are discussed in Chapter 2; finance companies in Chapter 3; securities firms and investment banks in Chapter 4; mutual funds, hedge funds, and pension funds in Chapter 5; and insurance companies in Chapter 6. Chapter 7 previews the risk measurement and management sections with an overview of the risks facing FIs.

Part 2: Risk Measurement

Chapters 8 and 9 start the risk measurement section by investigating the net interest margin as a source of profitability and risk, with a focus on the effects of interest rate volatility and the mismatching of asset and liability durations on FI risk exposure.

Chapter 10 looks at the measurement of credit risk of individual loans and bonds and how this risk adversely affects an FI's profits through losses and provisions against the loan and debt security portfolio. Chapter 11 looks at the risk of loan (asset) portfolios and the effects of loan concentrations on risk exposure. In addition, as a byproduct of the provision of their interest rate and credit intermediation services, FIs face liquidity risk. The special nature of this risk is analyzed in Chapter 12.

FIs do more than generate returns and bear risk through traditional maturity mismatching and credit extensions. They also engage in foreign exchange activities and overseas financial investments (Chapter 13) and participate in sovereign lending and securities activities (Chapter 14). Chapter 15 analyzes market risk, a risk incurred by FIs in trading assets and liabilities due to changes in interest rates, exchange rates, and other asset prices.

FIs engage in off-balance-sheet activities to generate fee income (Chapter 16) and make technological investments to reduce costs (Chapter 17). Each of these has implications for the size and variability of an FI's profits and/or revenues.

Part 3: Risk Management

Chapter 18 begins the risk management section by looking at ways in which FIs can insulate themselves from liquidity risk. Chapter 19 looks at the role that deposit insurance and other guarantee programs play in reducing liquidity risk. The size and adequacy of the owners' capital or equity investment in the FI is the focus of Chapter 20. Chapter 21 analyzes how and why product diversification and geographic expansion—both domestic and international—can improve an FI's return–risk performance and the impact of regulation on opportunities for diversification. Chapters 22 through 26 review various markets and instruments that have been innovated or engineered to allow FIs to better manage three important types of risk: interest rate risk, credit risk, and foreign exchange risk. These markets and instruments and their strategic use by FIs include futures and forwards (Chapter 22); options, caps, floors, and collars (Chapter 23); swaps (Chapter 24); loan sales (Chapter 25); and securitization (Chapter 26).

Main Features

Throughout the text, special features have been integrated to encourage students' interaction with the text and to aid them in absorbing the material. Some of these features include:

In-chapter examples, which provide numerical demonstrations of the analytics described in various chapters.

EXAMPLE 5-1
Effect of Capital Appreciation on NAV

Suppose a mutual fund contains 1,000 shares of Canadian Tire currently trading at $37.75, 2,000 shares of Encana currently trading at $43.70, and 1,500 shares of CIBC currently trading at $46.67. The mutual fund currently has 15,000 shares outstanding held by investors. Thus, today, the NAV of the fund is calculated as

$$NAV = [(1{,}000 \times \$37.75) + (2{,}000 \times \$43.70) + (1{,}500 \times \$46.67)] \div 15{,}000 = \$13.01$$

If next month Canadian Tire shares increase to $45, Encana shares increase to $48, and CIBC shares increase to $50, the NAV (assuming the same number of shares outstanding) would increase to

$$NAV = [(1{,}000 \times \$45) + (2{,}000 \times \$48) + (1{,}500 \times \$50)] \div 15{,}000 = \$14.40$$

Bold key terms and marginal glossary, which emphasize the main terms and concepts throughout the chapter and aid in studying.

economies of scale The concept that the cost reduction in trading and other transaction services results from increased efficiency when FIs perform these services.

asset transformer An FI issues financial claims that are more attractive to household savers than the claims directly issued by corporations.

primary securities Securities issued by corporations and backed by the real assets of those corporations.

secondary securities Securities issued by FIs and backed by primary securities

investment research and make investment recommendations for their retail (or household) clients as well as conduct the purchase or sale of securities for commission or fees. Discount brokers (e.g., E'Trade) carry out the purchase or sale of securities at better prices and with greater efficiency than household savers could achieve by trading on their own. This efficiency results in reduced costs of trading, or **economies of scale** (see Chapter 21 for a detailed discussion). Similarly, independent insurance brokers identify the best types of insurance policies household savers can buy to fit their savings and retirement plans. In fulfilling a brokerage function, the FI plays an extremely important role by reducing transaction and information costs or imperfections between households and corporations. Thus, the FI encourages a higher rate of savings than would otherwise exist.

FIs Function as Asset Transformers

The second function is the asset-transformation function. In acting as an **asset transformer**, the FI issues financial claims that are far more attractive to household savers than the claims directly issued by corporations. That is, for many households, the financial claims issued by FIs dominate those issued directly by corporations as a result of lower monitoring costs, lower liquidity costs, and lower price risk. In acting as asset transformers, FIs purchase the financial claims issued by corporations—equities, bonds, and other debt claims called **primary securities**—and finance these purchases by selling financial claims to household investors and other sectors in the form of deposits, insurance policies, and so on. The financial claims of FIs may be considered **secondary securities** because these assets are backed by the primary securities issued by commercial corporations that in turn invest in real assets. Specifically, FIs are independent market parties that create financial products whose value added to their clients is the transformation of financial risk.

How can FIs purchase the direct or primary securities issued by corporations and profitably transform them into secondary securities more attractive to household savers? This question strikes at the very heart of what makes FIs special and important to the economy. The answer lies in the ability of FIs to better resolve the three costs facing a saver who chooses to invest directly in corporate securities.

Global Issues highlights, which call out material relating to North American and global issues.

GLOBAL ISSUES

The disruptions in the global capital markets in 2007 and 2008 reshaped the investment banking industry in the United States and globally. As mentioned earlier in the chapter, Canada went through a "Big Bang" in 1987 that resulted in revisions to the Bank Act and the formation of OSFI. The largest securities firms were bought by the Big Six banks, the trust companies were also consolidated, and Canadian financial institutions moved toward universal banking. The model thus saw investment activities supported by merging with a bank funded by a stable source of deposits. By the time of the credit crisis in 2007, Canada had 20 years of experience with this model. The United States, however, didn't replace

Concept Questions, which aid in studying by allowing students to test themselves on the main concepts within each major chapter section.

CONCEPT QUESTIONS

1. How are liquidity and liability management related?
2. Describe the trade-off faced by an FI manager in structuring the liability side of the balance sheet.

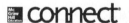

McGraw-Hill Connect ™ is a web-based assignment and assessment platform that gives students the means to better connect with their coursework, with their instructors, and with the important concepts that they will need to know for success now and in the future. With Connect, instructors can easily deliver assignments, quizzes, and tests online. Students can practise important skills at their own pace and on their own schedule. With Connect, students also get 24/7 online access to an eBook—an online edition of the text—to aid them in successfully completing their work, wherever and whenever they choose.

Instructor's Supplements

Instructor's Solutions Manual Prepared by the textbook author and adapted to reflect this latest Canadian edition, this manual includes worked-out solutions to all of the exercises in the text.

Computerized Test Bank Prepared by the textbook author, the computerized test bank has been extensively revised and technically checked for accuracy. The computerized test bank contains a variety of questions, including true/false, multiple-choice, and short-answer questions requiring analysis and written answers. The computerized test bank is available through EZ Test Online—a flexible and easy-to-use electronic testing program that allows instructors to create tests from book-specific items. EZ Test accommodates a wide range of question types and allows instructors to add their own questions. Test items are also available in Word format (rich text format). For secure online testing, exams created in EZ Test can be exported to WebCT and Blackboard. EZ Test Online is supported at mhhe.com/eztest, where users can download a *Quick Start Guide*, access FAQs, or log a ticket for help with specific issues.

Microsoft® PowerPoint® Lecture Slides Prepared by Patrick O'Meara of Centennial College, the PowerPoint slides draw on the highlights of each chapter and provide an opportunity for the instructor to emphasize the most relevant visuals in class discussions.

Connect questions were authored by Pan Zhang of Northern Alberta Institute of Technology.

Superior Learning Solutions and Support

The McGraw-Hill Ryerson team is ready to help you assess and integrate any of our products, technology, and services into your course for optimal teaching and learning performance. Whether it's helping your students improve their grades, or putting your entire course online, the McGraw-Hill Ryerson team is here to help you do it. Contact your Learning Solutions Consultant today to learn how to maximize all of McGraw-Hill Ryerson's resources!

For more information on the latest technology and Learning Solutions offered by McGraw-Hill Ryerson and its partners, please visit us online: www.mcgrawhill.ca/he/solutions.

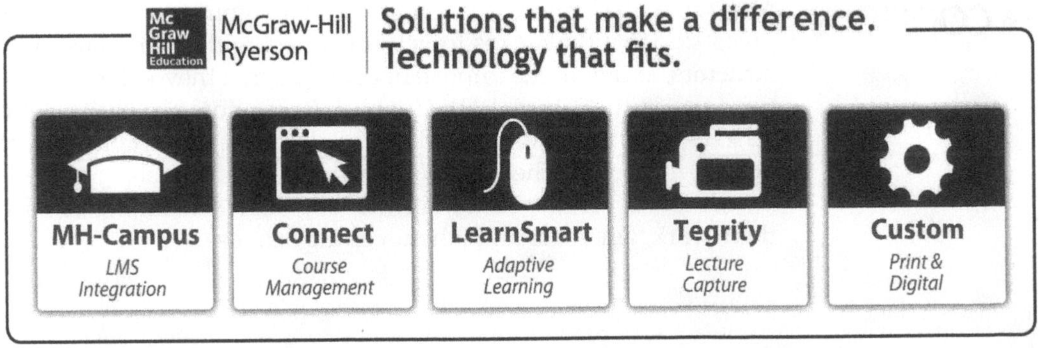

PART 1

THE FINANCIAL SERVICES INDUSTRY

1 ▸ Why Are Financial Institutions Special? 2

2 ▸ Deposit-Taking Institutions 21

3 ▸ Finance Companies 40

4 ▸ Securities, Brokerage, and Investment Banking 55

5 ▸ Mutual Funds, Hedge Funds, and Pension Funds 75

6 ▸ Insurance Companies 102

7 ▸ Risks of Financial Institutions 126

CHAPTER 1

WHY ARE FINANCIAL INSTITUTIONS SPECIAL?

After studying this chapter you should be able to:

LO1 Discuss the special functions that financial institutions provide.

LO2 Illustrate how financial institutions act as brokers and asset transformers.

LO3 Explain the types of regulations that are applied to financial institutions as a result of their specialness.

LO4 Discuss the impact of the financial crisis on financial institutions.

LO5 Discuss the actions taken by governments to support the financial system during the financial crisis.

INTRODUCTION

LO1

Bank Act
Federal legislation in Canada governing deposit-taking FIs.

four pillars
A term used to describe the separation of financial intermediation into four functions: banking, trust (fiduciary), insurance, and investment banking (securities).

universal bank
An FI that is permitted by regulators to offer a full range of financial services.

Prior to 1992, when the **Bank Act**, which determines which organizations may operate as a bank in Canada and in which activities, was revised, financial institutions (FIs) in Canada were divided by function into **four pillars**: chartered banks, trust companies, insurance companies, and investment dealers. These FIs were prevented from providing services "cross-pillar." For example, prior to 1954, Canadian banks could not offer residential mortgages. In the 1970s and 1980s, new, relatively unregulated financial service industries sprang up (including mutual funds, brokerage funds, etc.) that separated financial services functions even further. However, in the 21st century, regulatory barriers, technology, and financial innovations are changing so that, eventually, a full set of financial services may be offered by a single firm or **universal bank**. Now, the boundaries between industry sectors are blurred, and competition is global. As the competitive environment changes, attention to profit and, more than ever, risk becomes increasingly important. The major themes of this book are the measurement and management of the risks of FIs. FIs (e.g., banks, credit unions, insurance companies, and mutual funds) perform the essential function of channelling funds from those with surplus funds (suppliers of funds) to those with shortages of funds (users of funds). At the beginning of 2013, the assets of just the banks in Canada were greater than $3.8 trillion. By comparison, at the beginning of 2013, the market capitalization of the 364 mining companies listed on the Toronto Stock Exchange (TSX) was $381.1 billion. The market capitalization of the 76 financial services firms listed on the TSX was $515.1 billion.

Although we might categorize or group FIs as life insurance companies, banks, finance companies, and so on, they face many common risks. Specifically, all FIs described in this chapter and Chapters 2 through 6 (1) hold some assets that are potentially subject to default or credit risk and (2) tend to mismatch the maturities

TABLE 1–1 Areas of FIs' Specialness in the Provision of Services

Information costs	The aggregation of funds in an FI provides greater incentive to collect information about customers (such as corporations) and to monitor their actions. The relatively large size of the FI allows this collection of information to be accomplished at a lower average cost (so-called economies of scale) than would be the case for individuals.
Liquidity and price risk	FIs provide financial claims to household savers with superior liquidity attributes and with lower price risk.
Transaction cost services	Similar to economies of scale in information production costs, an FI's size can result in economies of scale in transaction costs.
Maturity intermediation	FIs can better bear the risk of mismatching the maturities of their assets and liabilities.
Transmission of monetary policy	DTIs are the conduit through which monetary policy actions by the country's central bank (such as the Bank of Canada) affect the rest of the financial system and the economy.
Credit allocation	FIs are often viewed as the major, and sometimes only, source of financing for a particular sector of the economy, such as farming, small business, and residential real estate.
Intergenerational wealth transfers	FIs, especially life insurance companies and pension funds, provide savers with the ability to transfer wealth from one generation to the next.
Payment services	The efficiency with which DTIs provide payment services such as cheque clearing directly benefits the economy.
Denomination intermediation	FIs, such as mutual funds, allow small investors to overcome constraints to buying assets imposed by large minimum denomination size.

of their balance sheet assets and liabilities to a greater or lesser extent and are thus exposed to interest rate risk. Moreover, all FIs are exposed to some degree of liability withdrawal or liquidity risk, depending on the type of claims they have sold to liability holders. In addition, most FIs are exposed to some type of underwriting risk, whether through the sale of securities or the issue of various types of credit guarantees on or off the balance sheet. Finally, all FIs are exposed to operating risks because the production of financial services requires the use of real resources and back-office support systems (labour and technology combined to provide services).

Because of these risks and the special role that FIs play in the financial system, FIs are singled out for special regulatory attention. In this chapter, we first examine questions related to this specialness. In particular, what are the special functions provided by FIs, both deposit-taking institutions (DTIs; banks, credit unions, and caisses populaires) and non-deposit-taking institutions (insurance companies, securities firms, investment banks, finance companies, and mutual funds)? These special functions are summarized in Table 1–1. How do these functions benefit the economy? Second, we investigate what makes some FIs more special than others. Third, we look at how unique and long-lived the special functions of FIs really are. As part of this discussion, we briefly examine how changes in the way FIs deliver services played a major part in the events leading up to the severe financial crisis of the late 2000s. A more detailed discussion of the causes of, major events during, and regulatory and industry changes resulting from the financial crisis is provided in Appendix 1A to the chapter.

FINANCIAL INSTITUTIONS' SPECIALNESS

LO2

To understand the important economic function of FIs, imagine a simple world in which FIs do not exist. In such a world, households generating excess savings by consuming less than they earn would have a basic choice: They could hold cash as an asset or invest in the securities issued by corporations. In general, corporations issue securities to finance their investments in real assets and cover the gap

FIGURE 1–1
Flow of Funds in a World without FIs

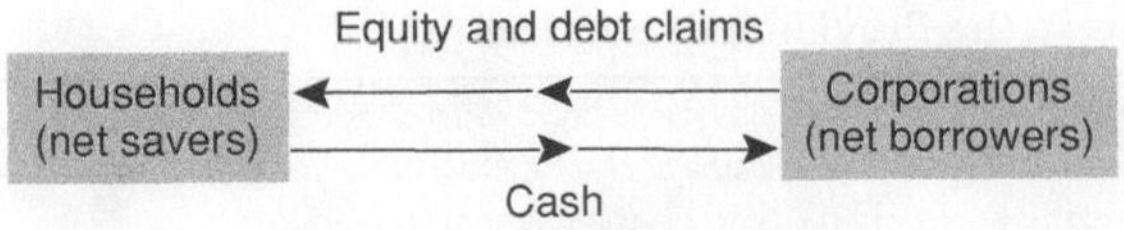

between their investment plans and their internally generated savings, such as retained earnings.

As shown in Figure 1–1, in such a world, savings would flow from households to corporations. In return, financial claims (equity and debt securities) would flow from corporations to household savers.

In an economy without FIs, the level of fund flows between household savers and the corporate sector is likely to be quite low. There are several reasons for this. Once they have lent money to a firm by buying its financial claims, households need to monitor, or check, the actions of that firm. They must be sure that the firm's management neither absconds with nor wastes the funds on any projects with low or negative net present values. Such monitoring actions are extremely costly for any given household because they require considerable time and expense to collect sufficiently high quality information relative to the size of the average household saver's investments. Given this, it is likely that each household would prefer to leave the monitoring to others. In the end, little or no monitoring would be done. The resulting lack of monitoring would reduce the attractiveness and increase the risk of investing in corporate debt and equity.

liquidity
The ease of converting an asset into cash.

The relatively long term nature of corporate equity and debt, and the lack of a secondary market in which households can sell these securities, creates a second disincentive for household investors to hold the direct financial claims issued by corporations. Specifically, given the choice between holding cash and holding long-term securities, households may well choose to hold cash for **liquidity** reasons, especially if they plan to use savings to finance consumption expenditures in the near future.

price risk
The risk that the sale price of an asset will be lower than the purchase price of that asset.

Finally, even if financial markets existed (without FIs to operate them) to provide liquidity services by allowing households to trade corporate debt and equity securities among themselves, investors would also face a **price risk** on sale of securities, and the secondary market trading of securities involves various transaction costs.

Because of (1) monitoring costs, (2) liquidity costs, and (3) price risk, the average household saver may view direct investment in corporate securities as an unattractive proposition and prefer either not to save or to save in the form of cash. However, the economy has developed an alternative and indirect way to channel household savings to the corporate sector. This is to channel savings via FIs. Because of costs of monitoring, liquidity, and price risk, as well as for some other reasons explained later, savers often prefer to hold the financial claims issued by FIs rather than those issued by corporations. Consider Figure 1–2, which is a closer representation than Figure 1–1 of the world in which we live and the way funds flow in our economy. Notice how FIs or intermediaries are standing, or intermediating, between the household and corporate sectors. These intermediaries fulfill two functions. Any given FI might specialize in one or the other or might do both simultaneously.

FIs Function as Brokers

The first function is the brokerage function. When acting as a pure broker, an FI acts as an agent for the saver by providing information and transaction services. For example, full-service securities firms (e.g., RBC Dominion Securities) carry out

FIGURE 1–2
Flow of Funds in a World with FIs

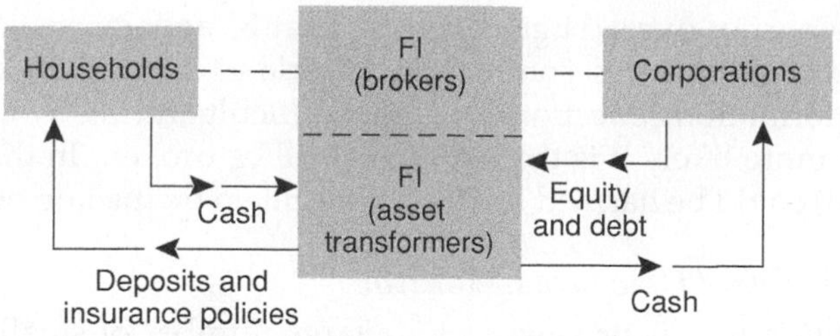

investment research and make investment recommendations for their retail (or household) clients as well as conduct the purchase or sale of securities for commission or fees. Discount brokers (e.g., E*Trade) carry out the purchase or sale of securities at better prices and with greater efficiency than household savers could achieve by trading on their own. This efficiency results in reduced costs of trading, or **economies of scale** (see Chapter 21 for a detailed discussion). Similarly, independent insurance brokers identify the best types of insurance policies household savers can buy to fit their savings and retirement plans. In fulfilling a brokerage function, the FI plays an extremely important role by reducing transaction and information costs or imperfections between households and corporations. Thus, the FI encourages a higher rate of savings than would otherwise exist.

economies of scale
The concept that the cost reduction in trading and other transaction services results from increased efficiency when FIs perform these services.

FIs Function as Asset Transformers

The second function is the asset-transformation function. In acting as an **asset transformer**, the FI issues financial claims that are far more attractive to household savers than the claims directly issued by corporations. That is, for many households, the financial claims issued by FIs dominate those issued directly by corporations as a result of lower monitoring costs, lower liquidity costs, and lower price risk. In acting as asset transformers, FIs purchase the financial claims issued by corporations—equities, bonds, and other debt claims called **primary securities**—and finance these purchases by selling financial claims to household investors and other sectors in the form of deposits, insurance policies, and so on. The financial claims of FIs may be considered **secondary securities** because these assets are backed by the primary securities issued by commercial corporations that in turn invest in real assets. Specifically, FIs are independent market parties that create financial products whose value added to their clients is the transformation of financial risk.

asset transformer
An FI issues financial claims that are more attractive to household savers than the claims directly issued by corporations.

primary securities
Securities issued by corporations and backed by the real assets of those corporations.

secondary securities
Securities issued by FIs and backed by primary securities.

How can FIs purchase the direct or primary securities issued by corporations and profitably transform them into secondary securities that are more attractive to household savers? This question strikes at the very heart of what makes FIs special and important to the economy. The answer lies in the ability of FIs to better resolve the three costs facing a saver who chooses to invest directly in corporate securities.

Information Costs

One problem faced by an average saver directly investing in a commercial firm's financial claims is the high cost of information collection. Household savers must monitor the actions of firms in a timely and complete fashion after purchasing securities. Failure to monitor exposes investors to **agency costs**, that is, the risk that the firm's owners or managers will take actions with the saver's money contrary to the promises contained in the covenants of its securities contracts. Monitoring

agency costs
Costs relating to the risk that the owners and managers of firms that receive savers' funds will take actions with those funds contrary to the best interests of the savers.

costs are part of overall agency costs. That is, agency costs arise whenever economic agents enter into contracts in a world of incomplete information and thus costly information collection. The more difficult and costly it is to collect information, the more likely it is that contracts will be broken. In this case, the saver (the principal) could be harmed by the actions taken by the borrowing firm (the agent).

An FI's Role as Delegated Monitor

One solution to this problem is for a large number of small savers to place their funds with a single FI. This FI groups these funds together and invests in the direct or primary financial claims issued by firms. This agglomeration of funds resolves a number of problems. First, the large FI now has a much greater incentive to collect information and monitor actions of the firm because it has far more at stake than does any small individual household. In a sense, small savers have appointed the FI as a **delegated monitor** to act on their behalf. Not only does the FI have a greater incentive to collect information, but also the average cost of collecting information is lower. For example, the cost to a small investor of buying a $100 broker's report may seem inordinately high for a $10,000 investment. For an FI with $10 million under management, however, the cost seems trivial. Such economies of scale of information production and collection tend to increase the advantages to savers of using FIs rather than directly investing themselves.

delegated monitor
An economic agent appointed to act on behalf of smaller agents in collecting information and/or investing funds on their behalf.

An FI's Role as Information Producer

Second, associated with the greater incentive to monitor and the costs involved in failing to monitor appropriately, FIs may develop new secondary securities that enable them to monitor more effectively. Thus, a richer menu of contracts may improve the monitoring abilities of FIs. Perhaps the classic example of this is the bank loan. Bank loans are generally shorter-term debt contracts than bond contracts. This short-term nature allows the FI to exercise more monitoring power and control over the borrower. In particular, the information the FI generates regarding the firm is frequently updated as its loan renewal decisions are made. When bank loan contracts are sufficiently short term, the banker becomes almost like an insider to the firm regarding informational familiarity with its operations and financial conditions. This more frequent monitoring often replaces the need for the relatively inflexible and hard-to-enforce covenants found in bond contracts. Thus, by acting as a delegated monitor and producing better and more timely information, FIs reduce the degree of information imperfection and asymmetry between the ultimate suppliers and users of funds in the economy.

Liquidity and Price Risk

In addition to improving the flow and quality of information, FIs provide financial or secondary claims to household and other savers. Often, these claims have superior liquidity attributes compared with those of primary securities such as corporate equity and bonds. For example, banks and other DTIs issue transaction account deposit contracts with a fixed principal value (and often a guaranteed interest rate) that can be withdrawn immediately on demand by household savers. Money market mutual funds issue shares to household savers that allow those savers to enjoy almost fixed principal (depositlike) contracts while often earning interest rates higher than those on bank deposits. Even life insurance companies allow policyholders to borrow against their policies held with the company at very short notice. The real puzzle is how FIs such as DTIs can offer highly liquid and low price risk contracts to savers on the liability side of their balance sheets while investing in relatively illiquid and higher price risk securities issued by corporations on the asset side. Furthermore, how can FIs be confident enough to guarantee that they can provide liquidity services to investors and savers when they themselves invest in risky asset portfolios? And why should savers and investors believe FIs' promises regarding the liquidity of their investments?

diversify
Reduce risk by holding a number of securities in a portfolio.

The answers to these questions lie in the ability of FIs to **diversify** away some but not all of their portfolio risks. The concept of diversification is familiar to all students of finance: Basically, as long as the returns on different investments are not perfectly *positively* correlated, by exploiting the benefits of size, FIs diversify away significant amounts of portfolio risk—especially the risk specific to the individual firm issuing any given security. Indeed, experiments have shown that equal investments in as few as 15 securities can bring significant diversification benefits to FIs and portfolio managers. Further, as the number of securities in an FI's asset portfolio increases beyond 15 securities, portfolio risk falls, albeit at a diminishing rate. Therefore, FIs exploit the law of large numbers in their investments, achieving a significant amount of diversification, whereas because of their small size, many household savers are constrained to holding relatively undiversified portfolios. This risk diversification allows an FI to predict more accurately its expected return on its asset portfolio. A domestically and globally diversified FI may be able to generate an almost risk free return on its assets. As a result, it can credibly fulfill its promise to households to supply highly liquid claims with little price or capital value risk. A good example of this is the ability of a bank to offer highly liquid demand deposits—with a fixed principal value—as liabilities, while at the same time investing in risky loans as assets. As long as an FI is sufficiently large to gain from diversification and monitoring, its financial claims are likely to be viewed as liquid and attractive to small savers compared with direct investments in the capital market.

Other Special Services

The preceding discussion has concentrated on three general or special services provided by FIs: reducing household savers' monitoring costs, increasing their liquidity, and reducing their price-risk exposure. Next, we discuss two other special services provided by FIs: reduced transaction costs and maturity intermediation.

Reduced Transaction Costs

Just as FIs provide potential economies of scale in information collection, they also provide potential economies of scale in transaction costs. For example, small retail buyers face higher commission charges or transaction costs than do large wholesale buyers. By grouping their assets in FIs that purchase assets in bulk—such as in mutual funds and pension funds—household savers can reduce the transaction costs of their asset purchases. In addition, bid–ask (buy–sell) spreads are normally lower for assets bought and sold in large quantities.

Maturity Intermediation

An additional dimension of FIs' ability to reduce risk by diversification is that they can better bear the risk of mismatching the maturities of their assets and liabilities than can small household savers. Thus, FIs offer maturity intermediation services to the rest of the economy. Specifically, through maturity mismatching, FIs can produce long-term contracts, such as fixed-rate mortgage loans to households, while still raising funds with short-term liability contracts. Further, while such mismatches can subject an FI to interest rate risk (see Chapters 8 and 9), a large FI is better able to manage this risk through its superior access to markets and instruments for hedging such as loan sales and securitization (Chapters 25 and 26); futures (Chapter 22); swaps (Chapter 24); and options, caps, floors, and collars (Chapter 23).

CONCEPT QUESTIONS

1. **What are the three major risks to household savers from direct security purchases?**
2. **What are two major differences between brokers (such as security brokers) and DTIs (such as banks)?**
3. **What are primary securities and secondary securities?**
4. **What is the link between asset diversification and the liquidity of deposit contracts?**

OTHER ASPECTS OF SPECIALNESS

The theory of the flow of funds points to three principal reasons for believing that FIs are special, along with two other associated reasons. In reality, academics, policymakers, and regulators identify other areas of specialness relating to certain specific functions of FIs or groups of FIs. We discuss these next.

The Transmission of Monetary Policy

The highly liquid nature of bank and other FI deposits has resulted in their acceptance by the public as the most widely used medium of exchange in the economy. Indeed, at the core of the three most commonly used definitions of the money supply—M1, M2, and M3[1]—lie DTIs' deposit contracts. Because the liabilities of DTIs are a significant component of the money supply that influences the rate of inflation, they play a key role in the *transmission of monetary policy* from the central bank to the rest of the economy. That is, chartered banks and other DTIs are the conduits through which monetary policy actions affect the rest of the financial sector and the economy in general. A major reason the United States and other countries bailed out many FIs during the financial crisis in 2008–2009 was so that the central banks could implement aggressive monetary policy actions to combat collapsing financial markets. In Canada, the aim of monetary policy is to protect the value of the dollar by controlling the level of inflation. The Bank of Canada carries out monetary policy primarily through setting the target overnight rate (the rate at which FIs lend money to each other for one day in the overnight interbank market). The target overnight rate in turn influences the loan rates and deposit rates offered by the DTIs.

bankofcanada.ca

[1] The Bank of Canada defines the money supply as M1+ (gross)—($669.99 billion January 2013) the "currency outside banks plus all chequable deposits held at chartered banks, trust and mortgage loan companies, credit unions and caisses populaires (excluding the deposits of these institutions) plus continuity adjustments (to 'smooth' a time series when there are structural breaks)"; M2 (gross)—($1.161 trillion January 2013) the "currency outside banks plus bank personal deposits, bank non-personal demand and notice deposits; less interbank deposits; plus continuity adjustments"; and M3 (gross)—($1.623 trillion January 2013) equal to "M2 (gross) plus bank non-personal term deposits and foreign currency deposits of residents; less interbank deposits; plus continuity adjustments."

Credit Allocation

A further reason FIs are often viewed as special is that they are the major and sometimes the only source of finance for a particular sector of the economy pre-identified as being in special need of finance. Policymakers in Canada, the United States, and a number of other countries, such as the United Kingdom, have identified *residential real estate* as needing special subsidies. For example, Canada Mortgage and Housing Corporation (CMHC) insures residential mortgage loans where the down payment is less than 20 percent. This has enhanced the specialness of FIs that most commonly service the needs of that sector. In a similar fashion, farming is an especially important area of the economy in terms of the overall social welfare of the population. Farm Credit Canada (FCC) provides loans to members of the agricultural industry who are unable to get credit elsewhere.

cmhc.ca

www.fcc-fac.ca

Intergenerational Wealth Transfers or Time Intermediation

The ability of savers to transfer wealth across generations is also of great importance to the social well-being of a country. Because of this, life insurance companies (see Chapter 6) and pension funds (see Chapter 5) are often especially encouraged, via special taxation relief and other subsidy mechanisms, to service and accommodate those needs.

Payment Services

DTIs such as banks, credit unions, and caisses populaires (see Chapter 2) are special in that the efficiency with which they provide payment services directly benefits the economy. Important payment services are cheque-clearing, debit and credit transactions, and wire transfer services. For example, on any given day, billions of dollars' worth of payments are effected through the Large Value Transfer System (LVTS) operated by the Canadian Payments Association (see Chapter 17). Any breakdowns in this system would probably produce gridlock in the payment system, with resulting harmful effects to the economy.

Denomination Intermediation

Both money market and debt-equity mutual funds (Chapter 5) are special because they provide services relating to denomination intermediation. Because they are sold in very large denominations, many assets are either out of reach of individual savers or would result in savers' holding highly undiversified asset portfolios. For example, the minimum size of a negotiable CD is $100,000, and commercial paper (short-term corporate debt) is often sold in minimum packages of $250,000 or more. Individually, a saver may be unable to purchase such instruments. However, by buying shares in a money market mutual fund along with other small investors, household savers overcome the constraints to buying assets imposed by large minimum denomination sizes. Such indirect access to these markets may allow small savers to generate higher returns on their portfolios as well.

SPECIALNESS AND REGULATION

LO3

In the preceding section, FIs were shown to be special because of the various services they provide to sectors of the economy. Failure to provide these services or a breakdown in their efficient provision can be costly to both the ultimate sources

negative externalities Actions by an economic agent imposing costs on other economic agents.

(households) and users (firms) of savings. The **negative externalities**[2] affecting firms and households when something goes wrong in the FI sector of the economy make a case for regulation. That is, FIs are regulated to protect against a disruption in the provision of the services discussed above and the costs this would impose on the economy and society at large. For example, bank failures may destroy household savings and at the same time restrict a firm's access to credit. Insurance company failures may leave households totally exposed in old age to catastrophic illnesses and sudden drops in income on retirement. Further, individual FI failures may create doubts in savers' minds regarding the stability and solvency of FIs in general and cause panics and even runs on sound institutions. This possibility provided the reasoning in 2009 for the U.S. Federal Deposit Insurance Corporation (FDIC) to increase the deposit insurance cap to US$250,000 per person per bank. At this time, the FDIC was more concerned about the possibility of contagious runs as a few major DTIs (e.g., IndyMac, Washington Mutual) failed or nearly failed. At this point, the FDIC wanted to instill confidence in the banking system and made the change to avoid massive depositor runs from many of the troubled DTIs and a collapse of the U.S. and global financial systems. Canada Deposit Insurance Corporation (CDIC) did not follow the same path, as Canadian FIs showed remarkable stability during the financial crisis, as we will discuss throughout the book.

cdic.ca

This type of market failure is often corrected by regulation. Although regulation may be socially beneficial, it also imposes private costs, or a regulatory burden, on individual FI owners and managers. Consequently, regulation is an attempt to improve the social welfare benefits and mitigate the social costs of the provision of FI services. The private costs of regulation relative to its private benefits, for the producers of financial services, is called the **net regulatory burden**.

net regulatory burden The difference between the private costs of regulations and the private benefits for the producers of financial services.

Six types of regulation seek to increase the net social welfare benefits of FIs' services: (1) safety and soundness regulation, (2) monetary policy regulation, (3) credit allocation regulation, (4) consumer protection regulation, (5) investor protection regulation, and (6) entry and chartering regulation. Regulations are imposed differentially on the various types of FIs. For example, DTIs are the most heavily regulated of the FIs. Finance companies, on the other hand, are subject to fewer regulations. Regulation can also be imposed at the federal or the provincial/territorial level and occasionally at the international level, as in the case of bank capital requirements (see Chapter 20). Finally, some of these regulations are functional in nature, covering all FIs that carry out certain functions, such as payment services, while others are institution specific.

Safety and Soundness Regulation

To protect depositors and borrowers against the risk of FI failure due, for example, to a lack of diversification in asset portfolios, regulators have developed layers of protective mechanisms. These mechanisms are intended to ensure the safety and soundness of the FI and thus to maintain the credibility of the FI in the eyes of its borrowers and lenders. Indeed, even during the worst of the financial crisis, deposit runs at banks, credit unions, and caisses populaires in Canada did not occur.

[2] A good example of a negative externality is the costs faced by small businesses in a one-bank town if the bank that owns that branch closes or fails. These businesses could find it difficult to get financing elsewhere, and their customers could be similarly disadvantaged. As a result, the closure or failure of the bank may have a negative or contagious effect on the economic prospects of the whole community, resulting in lower sales, production, and employment.

This is because the safety and soundness regulations in place protected virtually all depositors from losing their money.

In the first layer of protection are requirements encouraging FIs to diversify their assets. Thus, regulations prohibit banks from making loans to individual borrowers that exceed 25 percent of their total capital even though the loans may have a positive net present value to the bank. (see Chapter 10).

The second layer of protection concerns the minimum level of capital or equity funds that the owners of an FI need to contribute to the funding of its operations (see Chapter 20). For example, FI regulation is concerned with the minimum ratio of capital to (risk) assets. The higher the proportion of capital contributed by owners, the greater the protection against insolvency risk to outside liability claimholders such as depositors and insurance policyholders. This is because losses on the asset portfolio due, for example, to the lack of diversification are legally borne by the equity holders first, and only after equity is totally wiped out by outside liability holders. Consequently, by varying the required degree of equity capital, FI regulators can directly affect the degree of risk exposure faced by nonequity claimholders in FIs. For example, the six largest Canadian banks are required to hold additional capital as their stability and interconnectedness are seen as integral to the operation of the Canadian financial system. (See Chapter 20 for more discussion on the role of capital in FIs.)

cdic.ca

The third layer of protection is the provision of guaranty funds such as Canada Deposit Insurance Corporation (CDIC) to meet insolvency losses to small claimholders (see Chapter 19). By protecting FI claimholders, these funds create a demand for regulation of the insured institutions to protect the funds' resources when an FI collapses and owners' equity or net worth is wiped out (see Chapter 19 for more discussion).

The fourth layer of regulation is monitoring and surveillance itself. Regulators subject all FIs, whether banks, securities firms, or insurance companies, to varying degrees of monitoring and surveillance. This involves on-site examination as well as an FI's production of accounting statements and reports on a timely basis for off-site evaluation. Just as savers appoint FIs as delegated monitors to evaluate the behaviour and actions of ultimate borrowers, society appoints regulators to monitor the behaviour and performance of FIs. Many of the regulatory changes proposed in reaction to the financial crisis included significant increases in the monitoring and surveillance of any financial institution (e.g., the six largest Canadian banks, as noted above) whose failure could have serious systemic effects.

Finally, note that regulation is not without costs for those regulated. For example, society's regulators may require FIs to have more equity capital than private owners believe is in their own best interests. Similarly, producing the information requested by regulators is costly for FIs because it involves the time of managers, lawyers, and accountants. Again, the socially optimal amount of information may differ from an FI's privately optimal amount.[3]

As noted earlier, the differences between the private benefits to an FI from being regulated—such as insurance fund guarantees—and the private costs it faces from adhering to regulation—such as examinations—is called the *net regulatory burden*. The higher the net regulatory burden on FIs, the more inefficiently they

[3] Also, a social cost rather than a social benefit from regulation is the potential risk-increasing behaviour (often called moral hazard) that results if deposit insurance and other guaranty funds provide coverage to FIs and their liability holders at less than the actuarially fair price (see Chapter 19 for further discussion).

produce any given set of financial services from a private (FI) owner's perspective.

Monetary Policy Regulation

bankofcanada.ca

outside money
The part of the money supply directly produced by the government or central bank, such as notes and coin.

inside money
The part of the money supply produced by the private banking system.

Another motivation for regulation concerns the special role banks play in the transmission of monetary policy from the Bank of Canada (the central bank) to the rest of the economy. The problem is that the central bank directly controls only the quantity of notes and coin in the economy—called **outside money**—whereas the bulk of the money supply consists of deposits—called **inside money**. In theory, a central bank can vary the quantity of cash or outside money and directly affect a bank's reserve position as well as the amount of loans and deposits a bank can create without formally regulating the bank's portfolio. In practice, regulators have chosen to impose formal controls. Since 1994, banks in Canada have not been subject to reserve requirements, but in many countries, including the United States, regulators commonly impose a minimum level of required cash reserves to be held against deposits (see Chapter 18). Some argue that imposing such reserve requirements makes the control of the money supply and its transmission more predictable. Such reserves also add to an FI's net regulatory burden if they are more than the institution believes are necessary for its own liquidity purposes. In general, whether banks or insurance companies, all FIs would choose to hold some cash reserves—even non-interest-bearing—to meet the liquidity and transaction needs of their customers directly. For well-managed FIs, however, this optimal level is normally low, especially if the central bank (or other regulatory body) does not pay interest on required reserves. As a result, FIs often view required reserves as similar to a tax and as a positive cost of undertaking intermediation.

Credit Allocation Regulation

Credit allocation regulation supports the FI's lending to socially important sectors such as housing and farming. Canada does not have this type of regulation, but in the United States these regulations may require an FI to hold a minimum amount of assets in one particular sector of the economy or to set maximum interest rates, prices, or fees to subsidize certain sectors. Examples of asset restrictions include insurance regulations that set maximums on the amount of foreign or international assets in which insurance companies can invest. Examples of interest rate restrictions are the usury laws on the maximum rates that can be charged on loans. The Criminal Code of Canada defines a criminal rate as an effective annual rate greater than 60 percent.

Such price and quantity restrictions may have justification on social welfare grounds—especially if society has a preference for strong (and subsidized) housing and farming sectors. However, they can also be harmful to FIs that have to bear the private costs of meeting many of these regulations. To the extent that the net private costs of such restrictions are positive, they add to the costs and reduce the efficiency with which FIs undertake intermediation.

Consumer Protection Regulation

fcac-acfc.gc.ca

In 2001, Bill C-8 was passed by the federal government to reform the financial services industry in Canada. The Financial Consumer Agency of Canada (FCAC) was created to protect consumers of financial services by ensuring that FIs adhered to the consumer protection regulation in Canada. For example, the FCAC provides information for consumers on services such as bank accounts and investment products. The FCAC also examines and imposes fines on FIs that violate consumer protection laws.

In addition, on July 21, 2003, eight Canadian FIs renewed a public commitment to provide low-cost banking services to Canadians. Thus, it can be argued that consumer protection laws impose a considerable net regulatory burden on FIs, but the offsetting benefit is the provision of equal access to mortgage and lending markets. As deregulation proceeds, it is likely that such laws will be extended beyond banks to other financial services providers such as insurance companies.

Investor Protection Regulation

A considerable number of laws protect investors who use investment firms directly to purchase securities and/or indirectly to access securities markets through investing in mutual or pension funds. Various laws protect investors against abuses such as insider trading, lack of disclosure, outright malfeasance, and breach of fiduciary responsibilities (see Chapter 4). As with consumer protection legislation, compliance with these acts can impose a net regulatory burden on FIs.[4]

Entry Regulation

The entry and activities of FIs are also regulated (e.g., new bank chartering regulations). Increasing or decreasing the cost of entry into a financial sector affects the profitability of firms already competing in that industry. Thus, the industries heavily protected against new entrants by high direct costs (e.g., through required equity or capital contributions) and high indirect costs (e.g., by restricting individuals who can establish FIs) of entry produce bigger profits for existing firms than those in which entry is relatively easy (see Chapter 21). In addition, regulations (such as the Bank Act) define the scope of permitted activities under a given charter. The broader the set of financial service activities permitted under a given charter, the more valuable that charter is likely to be. Thus, barriers to entry and regulations pertaining to the scope of permitted activities affect the *charter value* of an FI and the size of its net regulatory burden.

CONCEPT QUESTIONS

1. **Why should more regulation be imposed on FIs than on other types of private corporations?**
2. **Define the concept of net regulatory burden.**
3. **What six major types of regulation do FIs face?**

THE CHANGING DYNAMICS OF SPECIALNESS

LO4

At any moment in time, each FI supplies a set of financial services (brokerage-related, asset transformation–related, or both) and is subject to a given net regulatory burden. As the demands for the special features of financial services change

[4] There have been a number of moves to extend these regulations to hedge funds, which have traditionally been outside regulations and the securities acts as long as they have fewer than 100 "sophisticated" investors. It has been believed that large sophisticated investors do not need such protections. However, scandals and failures relating to hedge funds and their investments—such as the failure of Long-Term Capital Management in 1998 and its subsequent bailout—appear to be changing lawmakers' and regulators' perceptions, as we discuss in Chapter 5.

as a result of changing preferences and technology, one or more areas of the financial services industry become less profitable. Similarly, changing regulations can increase or decrease the net regulatory burden faced in supplying financial services in any given area. These demand, cost, and regulatory pressures are reflected in changing market shares in different financial service areas as some contract and others expand. Clearly, an FI seeking to survive and prosper must be flexible enough to move to growing financial service areas and away from those that are contracting. If regulatory activity restrictions inhibit or reduce the flexibility with which FIs can alter their product mix, this will reduce their competitive ability and the efficiency with which financial services are delivered. That is, activity barriers within the financial services industry may reduce the ability to diversify and potentially add to the net regulatory burden faced by FIs.

Trends in Canada

Figure 1–3 shows the percentage distribution of the financial sector assets held in Canada at the beginning of 2013 by banks, trust and mortgage loan companies, investment funds (including mutual funds), life insurers (including accident and sickness branches and segregated funds), nondepository credit intermediation, and credit unions/caisses populaires. The banks are highest at 66 percent of total assets, followed by investment fund companies at 13 percent. The effect of investment fund companies is understated in Figure 1–3 as the data for the banks, insurance companies, and credit unions/caisses populaires include the assets of investment fund activities (e.g., the segregated funds of life insurance companies). The dominance of the Canadian banks in the financial services industry in Canada is apparent, but investment fund assets have increased over the years, as have the assets of nondepository financial intermediation, including shadow banking, discussed below.

Traditional services provided by DTIs (payment services, transaction cost services, and information costs) have become relatively less significant as a portion of all services provided by FIs. In particular, FIs engaged in securities functions such as the sale of mutual funds and other investment products differ from banks and insurance companies in that they give savers cheaper access to the direct securities markets. They do so by exploiting the comparative advantages of size and diversification, with the transformation of financial claims, such as maturity transformation, a lesser concern. Thus, mutual funds and other investment funds buy stocks, bonds, commercial paper, and Treasury bills directly in financial markets and then issue to savers shares whose value is linked in a direct pro rata fashion to the

FIGURE 1–3
Financial Services Assets in Canada by Sector, 2013

Source: *Bank of Canada Banking and Financial Statistics*, June 2013, bankofcanada.ca

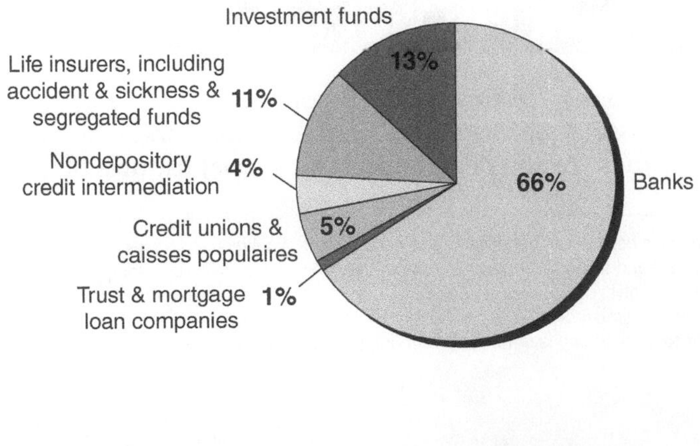

value of the investment fund's asset portfolio. To the extent that these funds efficiently diversify, they also offer price-risk protection and liquidity services. The maturity and return characteristics of the financial claims issued by investment funds closely reflect the maturities of the direct equity and debt securities portfolios in which they invest. In contrast, banks, credit unions, and insurance companies have lower correlations between their asset portfolio maturities and the promised maturity of their liabilities. Thus, banks may partially fund a 7-year business loan with demand deposits, and a credit union may fund 25-year conventional mortgages with 3-month term deposits.

To the extent that the financial services market is efficient and these changes reflect the forces of demand and supply, they indicate a trend: Savers have increasingly preferred the denomination intermediation and information services provided by investment funds. These FIs provide investments that closely mimic diversified investments in the *direct* securities markets over the transformed financial claims offered by traditional FIs. This trend may also indicate that the net regulatory burden on traditional FIs—such as banks and insurance companies—is higher than that on investment companies. As a result, traditional FIs are unable to produce their services as cost efficiently as they could previously.

In addition to a decline in the use of traditional services provided by DTIs and insurance companies and an increase in the services provided by investment funds, there has also been an overall weakening of public trust and confidence in the ethics followed by FIs. Specifically, tremendous publicity was generated concerning conflicts of interest in a number of FIs between analysts' research recommendations on stocks to buy or not buy and whether these firms played a role in underwriting the securities of the firms the analysts were recommending. As a result, several highly publicized securities violations resulted in criminal cases brought against securities law violators in the United States. Such allegations of securities law violations also reached across the U.S.–Canada border and led to a loss in public trust and confidence in many sectors of the financial services industry.

Risk Measurement and the Financial Crisis

The growth of investment funds coupled with the weakening of public trust and confidence (amid a multitude of regulatory investigations into the practices of investment advisors, brokers, and banks), as well as investors' recent focus on direct investments in primary securities, may signal the beginning of a trend away from intermediation as the most efficient mechanism for savers to channel funds to borrowers. While this trend may reflect changed investors' preferences toward risk and return, it may also reflect a decline in the relative costs of direct securities investment versus investment via FIs. Nevertheless, since the late 1980s, Canada's experiment with universal banking has been relatively successful. Canada's experience contrasts with that of the United States, where the Financial Services Modernization Act, which allowed the FI industry to consolidate, was not enacted until 1999. Certainly, a major event that changed and reshaped the financial services industry in North America was the financial crisis of the late 2000s. As FIs adjusted to regulatory changes, there was a dramatic increase in the systemic risk of the financial system, caused in large part by a shift in the banking model from that of "originate and hold" to "originate to distribute." In the traditional model, banks take short-term deposits and other sources of funds and use them to fund longer-term loans to businesses and consumers. Banks typically hold these loans to maturity and thus have an incentive to screen and monitor borrower activities even after a loan is made. However, the traditional banking model exposes the institution to potential liquidity, interest rate, and credit risks. In attempts to avoid these risk exposures and generate improved return–risk trade-offs, banks shifted to an underwriting model in which they originated or warehoused loans and then quickly sold them.

More recently, activities of shadow banks, nonfinancial service firms that perform banking services, have facilitated the change from the originate-and-hold model of commercial banking to the originate-and-distribute banking model. Participants in the shadow banking system include structured investment vehicles (SIVs), special-purpose vehicles (SPVs), asset-backed paper vehicles, credit hedge funds, asset-backed commercial paper (ABCP) conduits, limited-purpose finance companies, money market mutual funds (MMMFs), and credit hedge funds (see Chapter 21 for a detailed discussion of these FIs). In the shadow banking system, savers place their funds with money market mutual and similar funds, which invest in the liabilities of other shadow banks. Borrowers get loans and leases from shadow banks such as finance companies rather than from banks. Like the traditional banking system, the shadow banking system intermediates the flow of funds between net savers and net borrowers. However, instead of the bank serving as the intermediary, it is the nonbank financial service firm, or shadow bank, that intermediates. Further, unlike the traditional banking system, where the complete credit intermediation is performed by a single bank, in the shadow banking system it is performed through a series of steps involving many nonbank financial service firms.

These innovations removed risk from the balance sheet of FIs and shifted risk to other parts of the financial system. Since the FIs, acting as underwriters, were not exposed to the credit, liquidity, and interest rate risks of traditional banking, they had little incentive to screen and monitor the activities of borrowers to whom they originated loans. Thus, FIs failed to act as specialists in risk measurement and management.

Adding to FIs' move away from risk measurement and management was the boom ("bubble") in the U.S. housing markets, which began building in 2001. The U.S. Federal Reserve lowered the short-term money market rate. Canadian interest rates declined as well. Perhaps not surprisingly, low interest rates resulted in a rapid expansion in consumer, mortgage, and corporate debt financing. Demand for residential mortgages and credit card debt rose dramatically. As the demand for mortgage debt grew, especially among those who had previously been excluded from participating in the market because of their poor credit ratings, U.S. FIs began lowering their credit quality cut-off points. Moreover, to boost their earnings, in the market now popularly known as the "subprime market," banks and other mortgage-supplying institutions often offered relatively low "teaser" rates on adjustable or variable rate mortgages (ARMs or VRMs), i.e., exceptionally low initial interest rates, but, if market rates rose in the future, substantial increases in rates after the initial rate period expired two or three years later. Under the traditional originate-and-hold banking model, banks might have been reluctant to so aggressively pursue low credit quality borrowers for fear that the loans would default. However, under the originate-to-distribute model of banking, asset securitization and loan syndication allowed banks to retain little or no part of the loans, and hence to shift the default risk on loans that they originated to other market participants. Thus, as long as the borrower did not default within the first months after a loan's issuance and the loans were sold or securitized without recourse back to the bank, the issuing bank could ignore longer-term credit risk concerns. The result was a deterioration in credit quality, at the same time as there was a dramatic increase in consumer and corporate leverage.

Eventually, in 2006, U.S. housing prices started to fall. At the same time, the U.S. Federal Reserve started to raise interest rates in the money market as it began to fear inflation. Since many U.S. subprime mortgages originating in the 2001–2005 period had floating rates, the cost of meeting mortgage commitments rose to unsustainable levels for many low-income households. The confluence of falling house prices, rising interest rates, and rising mortgage costs led to a wave of mortgage defaults in the subprime market and foreclosures that only reinforced the downward trend in house prices. The number of U.S. subprime mortgages that were more than 60 days behind on their payments was 17.1 percent in June 2007 and over 20 percent in August 2007. As this happened, the poor quality of the collateral and credit quality underlying subprime mortgage pools became apparent, with default rates far exceeding those apparently anticipated by the rating agencies in setting their initial subprime mortgage securitizations ratings. These effects built throughout 2006 and through the middle of 2007. By February 2007, the percentage of U.S. subprime mortgage-backed securities delinquent by 90 days or more was 10.09 percent, substantially higher than the 5.37 percent rate in May 2005. As borrowers had difficulty repaying their existing mortgages, they found it impossible to refinance their existing loans prior to the higher step-up interest rate's kicking in. By the fall of 2007, there was a decline in sales of new homes and existing homes. The financial crisis, which started in the United States and spread globally, had begun. Appendix 1A to the chapter provides a detailed discussion of the causes of, major events during, and regulatory and industry changes resulting from the financial crisis.

The economy relies on FIs to act as specialists in risk measurement and management. The importance of this was demonstrated in the aftermath of the FIs' failure to perform this critical function during the global financial crisis. The result was a worldwide breakdown in credit markets, as well as an enhanced level of equity market volatility. When FIs failed to perform their critical risk measurement and management functions, the result was a crisis of confidence that disrupted financial markets.

GLOBAL ISSUES

LO5

The turmoil in credit markets started in August 2007 when FIs (commercial banks, investment banks, hedge funds, pension funds, governments) around the world began to experience losses related to subprime mortgage–backed securities that originated in the United States. These mortgages had been transformed through securitization and sold to investors around the world. However, 2007 was just the beginning. In 2008, financial markets experienced disruptions of credit that resulted in **deleveraging**, a decline of confidence in the markets, runs on FIs, and failures of insurance companies and commercial and investment banks worldwide. Stock exchanges around the world experienced declines in value on the order of 40 percent, and FIs lost close to US$1 trillion in asset value.

deleveraging
A decline in a company's debt-to-equity ratio, either through asset shrinkage or through a decline in debt and an increase in owner's equity.

Regulators acted internationally to support the financial system by providing (1) liquidity injections, (2) collateral changes to central bank borrowing facilities,

TABLE 1–2 Central Banks' and Regulators' Actions to Stabilize the Global Financial System

Liquidity injection *Provision of term funding by central banks*	The Bank of Canada increased the size of term PRAs*, increased their frequency to weekly, and introduced new facilities, e.g., a Term Loan Facility (TLF) for LVTS participants. The United States, the United Kingdom, and the Eurozone saw increased liquidity provided by the central banks. As well, the Federal Reserve increased the U.S. dollar swap agreements with other central banks to increase liquidity worldwide.
Collateral changes *Broadening the list of assets eligible as collateral for central banks' lending operations*	The central banks of Canada, the United States, the United Kingdom, and the Eurozone broadened the type of collateral acceptable for borrowing from central banks' lending facilities. For example, in Canada, ABCP was accepted as collateral for term PRAs.
Deposit insurance *Increase in the amount of customer deposits insured by the government*	The deposit insurance provided by the CDIC remained unchanged at $100,000. However, the United States, the United Kingdom, and the European Union (EU) increased the amounts in order to prevent bank runs and stabilize the banking system. In some cases, e.g., Ireland, deposit insurance was extended to all bank deposits.
Guarantees of bank liabilities *Introduction of government guarantee on interbank lending, bank debt, and/or other bank liabilities*	Federally (and some provincially) regulated deposit-taking FIs were provided with up to three years' insurance on some types of unsecured debt through the Canadian Lenders Assurance Facility (CLAF). The United States, the United Kingdom, and the Eurozone (e.g., Germany, Greece, Ireland, and Spain) provided debt guarantees.
Capital injection *Injection of public funds into the capital of banks or other major financial intermediaries*	Canada did not provide capital injections. The United States set up the Troubled Asset Relief Program (TARP), which allowed the United States Treasury to purchase nonvoting, cumulative preferred shares from FIs. The United Kingdom provided equity and preferred shares to banks. The Eurozone injected capital into its largest FIs as well.
Asset purchases *Purchase of various assets from FIs, including impaired assets*	The Canadian government set up a facility to purchase, via auctions, up to $75 billion in insured mortgage pools through CMHC. The U.S. Treasury agreed to purchase mortgage-backed securities through TARP and unsecured commercial paper and ABCP through a Commercial Paper Funding Facility. The U.S. Federal Reserve Term Asset-Backed Securities Loan Facility (TALF) was set up to purchase asset-backed securities. The United Kingdom and the Eurozone set up asset purchase programs as well.

*PRAs are purchase and resale agreements whereby an FI sells securities to the central bank and agrees to repurchase them at a set time in the future.

Source: Bank of Canada, *Financial System Review*, December 2008, p. 13.

(3) increased deposit insurance, (4) guarantees of bank liabilities, (5) capital injections, and (6) asset purchases. Table 1–2 summarizes the six major measures taken by governments, central banks, and regulators to stem the crisis starting in 2008. The largest initiative was the US$700 billion Troubled Assets Relief Program (TARP) passed by the U.S. government in September 2008 after the failure of Lehman Brothers investment bank and the near-failure of the U.S. insurance company American International Group Inc. (AIG). AIG received a separate US$85 million support package. The TARP was designed to purchase impaired assets in order to remove them from the balance sheets of FIs and allow the FIs to begin lending again. Australia, China, and other countries also brought in their own initiatives to fight their liquidity issues and potential FI failures. These support measures show the importance and the specialness of FIs to the global economy as well as the cost to the global financial system when the market and regulatory systems fail. As well, the deleveraging of FI, company, and consumer balance sheets was carried out by leveraging the balance sheets of governments. As a result, debt-to-GDP ratios for governments (e.g., the United States and the EU countries) increased. The sovereign debt crisis in the Eurozone (see Chapter 14) is a result of governments' overleveraging and, with a global economic slowdown, being unable to meet their debt obligations.

While other countries undertook FI bailouts in 2008, Canada experienced less disruption. Canadian banks claimed losses of only $12 billion in the first three quarters of 2008. There were no failures and no need to bail out any of Canada's major FIs. The situation was much like the Great Depression from 1929 to 1933, when over 5,000 U.S. banks failed but no Canadian banks did.

www.financialstabilityboard.org

As a result of the crisis, the Financial Stability Board (FSB) was created in 2009 to replace the Financial Stability Forum. Mark Carney, now Governor of the Bank of England, was appointed head of the FSB, which reports to the leaders of the G20. Its mandate is to examine the causes of the crisis and to recommend changes in the global regulations to reduce systemic risk in the financial system. The new regulations will touch on all areas of the balance sheets of FIs, including capital budgeting (investment) decisions, working capital decisions, capital structure decisions, and dividend decisions. As we work through the chapters in this book, we will be examining companies whose specialness, as we have previously discussed, results in regulations that set limits on the decision-making of the firm. This emphasizes how important FIs are to the global economy and helps us to understand why FIs are special. Although we might categorize or group FIs and label them as life insurance companies, banks, finance companies, and so on, in fact, they face risks that are more common than different. Specifically, all the FIs described in this and the next five chapters (1) hold some assets that are potentially subject to default or credit risk and (2) tend to mismatch the maturities of their balance sheets to a greater or lesser extent and are thus exposed to interest rate risk. Moreover, all are exposed to some degree of saver withdrawal or liquidity risk depending on the type of claims sold to liability holders. And most are exposed to some type of underwriting risk, whether through the sale of securities or by issuing various types of credit guarantees on or off the balance sheet. Finally, all are exposed to operating cost risks because the production of financial services requires the use of real resources and back-office support systems. In Chapters 7 through 26 of this textbook, we investigate the ways managers of FIs are measuring and managing this inventory of risks to produce the best return–risk trade-off for shareholders in a competitive market environment.

CONCEPT QUESTIONS

1. **What were the causes of the financial crisis?**
2. **What actions did governments and regulators take to support the domestic and global financial systems?**
3. **Can you think of any companies whose capital budgeting, working capital, capital structure, and dividend decisions are made by regulations?**

Questions and Problems

1. What are five risks common to FIs?
2. Explain how economic transactions between household savers of funds and corporate users of funds would occur in a world without FIs.
3. Identify and explain three economic disincentives that would probably damp the flow of funds between household savers of funds and corporate users of funds in an economic world without FIs.
4. Identify and explain the two functions in which FIs may specialize that would enable the smooth flow of funds from household savers to corporate users.
5. In what sense are the financial claims of FIs considered *secondary securities*, while the financial claims of commercial corporations are considered *primary securities*? How does the transformation process, or intermediation, reduce the risk, or economic disincentives, to savers?

6. Explain how FIs act as delegated monitors. What secondary benefits often accrue to the entire financial system because of this monitoring process?
7. What are five general areas of FI specialness that are caused by providing various services to sectors of the economy?
8. What are *agency costs*? How do FIs solve the information and related agency costs when household savers invest directly in securities issued by corporations?
9. How do large FIs solve the problem of high information collection costs for lenders, borrowers, and financial markets?
10. How do FIs alleviate the problem of liquidity risk faced by investors who wish to buy securities issued by corporations?
11. How do FIs help individual savers diversify their portfolio risks? Which type of financial institution is best able to achieve this goal?
12. How can FIs invest in high-risk assets with funding provided by low-risk liabilities from savers?
13. How can individual savers use FIs to reduce the transaction costs of investing in financial assets?
14. What is *maturity intermediation*? What are some of the ways the risks of maturity intermediation are managed by FIs?
15. What are five areas of institution-specific FI specialness, and which types of institutions are most likely to be the service providers?
16. How do DTIs such as banks assist in the implementation and transmission of monetary policy?
17. What is meant by *credit allocation regulation*? What social benefit is this type of regulation intended to provide?
18. Which intermediaries best fulfill the intergenerational wealth transfer function? What is this wealth transfer process?
19. What are two of the most important payment services provided by FIs? To what extent do these services efficiently provide benefits to the economy?
20. What is *denomination intermediation*? How do FIs assist in this process?
21. What is *negative externality*? In what ways does the existence of negative externalities justify the extra regulatory attention received by FIs?
22. If financial markets operated perfectly and costlessly, would there be a need for FIs?
23. Why are FIs among the most regulated sectors in the world? When is the net regulatory burden positive?
24. What forms of protection and regulation do the regulators of FIs impose to ensure their safety and soundness?
25. How do regulations regarding barriers to entry and the scope of permitted activities affect the *charter value* of FIs?
26. What six extraordinary actions were taken by central banks and governments during the financial crisis? Explain why these actions were necessary.
27. What events resulted in banks' shift from the traditional banking model of "originate and hold" to a model of "originate and distribute"?

Appendix 1A The Financial Crisis: The Failure of Financial Services Institution Specialness

View Appendix 1A on Connect.

CHAPTER 2

DEPOSIT-TAKING INSTITUTIONS

After studying this chapter you should be able to:

LO1 Discuss the size, structure, and composition of the banking industry in Canada.

LO2 Discuss the nature and importance of off-balance-sheet assets and liabilities for Canadian banks.

LO3 Explain the types of regulations that are applied to banks in Canada.

LO4 Explain how credit unions and caisses populaires differ from banks.

INTRODUCTION

A theme of this book is that the products sold and the risks faced by modern financial institutions (FIs) are becoming increasingly similar, as are the techniques used to measure and manage those risks. To illustrate this, Tables 2–1A and 2–1B contrast the products sold by the financial services industry before the Bank Act revisions of the 1980s with those sold in 2013. Between 1990 and 2008, FIs developed that could engage in banking activities (payments, savings, fiduciary, and lending), securities activities (underwriting debt and equity), and insurance activities. Legislation enacted as a result of the financial crisis, however, represents a partial reversal of this trend. For example, the "Volcker rule" provision of the Wall Street Reform and Consumer Protection Act prohibits bank holding companies operating in the United States from engaging in proprietary trading and limits their investments in hedge funds, private equity, and related vehicles. As well, it has been concluded that the models of finance and investing used by FIs globally had become too risky. The result has been tighter regulations and much closer supervision by bank examiners. The new regulations require deposit-taking institutions (DTIs) to be subject to more disclosure, hold higher levels of capital, and take less risk.

In this chapter we begin by describing the major FI groups—banks, trusts and loans, credit unions (CUs), and caisses populaires (CPs)—which are also called DTIs because significant amounts of their funding come from customer deposits. Historically, banks have operated as more diversified institutions, having a large concentration of residential mortgage assets but holding business and consumer loans as well. Savings institutions have concentrated on residential mortgages. Credit unions have historically focused on consumer loans funded with member deposits. In Chapters 3 through 6, other (non-deposit-taking) FIs will be described. We focus on four major characteristics of each group: (1) size, structure, and composition of the industry group; (2) balance sheet and recent trends; (3) regulation; and (4) industry performance.

Figure 2–1 presents a very simplified product-based balance sheet for DTIs. Notice that DTIs offer products to their customers on both sides of their balance sheets (loans on the asset side and deposits on the liability side). This joint-product nature of the DTI business creates special challenges for management in dealing

TABLE 2–1A Products Sold by the Financial Services Industry, Pre-1985

	Function							
				Lending		Underwriting Issuance of		
Institution	Payment Services	Savings Products	Fiduciary Services	Business	Consumer	Equity	Debt	Insurance and Risk Management Products
DTIs	X	X	X	X	X			
Insurance companies		X		*				X
Finance companies				*	X			
Securities firms		X	X			X	X	
Pension funds		X						
Mutual funds		X						

*Minor involvement.

TABLE 2–1B Products Sold by the Financial Services Industry, 2013

	Function							
				Lending		Underwriting Issuance of		
Institution	Payment Services	Savings Products	Fiduciary Services	Business	Consumer	Equity	Debt	Insurance and Risk Management Products
DTIs	X	X	X	X	X	X	X	X
Insurance companies	X	X	X	X	X	X	X	X
Finance companies	X	X	X	X	X	†	†	X
Securities firms	X	X	X	X	X	X	X	X
Pension funds		X	X	X				X
Mutual funds	X	X	X					X

†Selective involvement via affiliates.

FIGURE 2–1
A Simple DTI Balance Sheet

DTI

Assets	Liabilities and Equity
Loans	Deposits
Other assets	Other liabilities and equity

commercial bank
A bank that accepts deposits and makes consumer, business, and real estate loans.

Big Six
The six largest banks in Canada (Bank of Montreal, Bank of Nova Scotia, Canadian Imperial Bank of Commerce, National Bank of Canada, Royal Bank of Canada, and TD Canada Trust).

with the many risks facing these institutions. These risks will be discussed in Chapters 7 through 26.

Table 2–2 lists the largest Canadian DTIs in 2013 ranked by their total on-balance-sheet assets. All but two (Desjardins Group, a caisse populaire, and Vancouver City Savings, a credit union) of the 11 FIs in Table 2–2 are **commercial banks**, demonstrating the concentration of deposit-taking services in Canada and the dominance of the **Big Six** banks (Bank of Montreal, Bank of Nova Scotia, Canadian Imperial Bank of Commerce, National Bank of Canada, Royal Bank of Canada,

TABLE 2–2 The Largest Canadian DTIs by Asset Size, Year-End 2012 ($ billions)

Source: 2012 Company Annual Reports.

Company	Assets
Royal Bank of Canada	$825.1
Toronto-Dominion Bank	811.1
Bank of Nova Scotia	668.0
Bank of Montreal	525.4
Canadian Imperial Bank of Commerce	393.4
Desjardins Group Inc.*	196.7
National Bank of Canada	177.9
HSBC Bank Canada*	80.7
Laurentian Bank Canada	34.9
Canadian Western Bank	16.9
Vancouver City Savings*	16.1

*As of December 31, 2012; all others as of October 31, 2012.

and TD Canada Trust). These are financial services powerhouses, that is, what may be called "full-service" FIs that operate in other financial services areas (e.g., investment banking and security brokerage) in addition to lending and deposit-taking. Many of the Canadian banks have significant assets outside Canada. For example, TD Bank was the ninth-largest DTI in the United States in September 2012. TD Bank had US$195.9 billion in banking assets and $212.5 billion in total holding company assets. TD Bank competes in the United States with several U.S. DTIs whose banking assets at September 30, 2012, totalled more than US$1 trillion (JPMorgan Chase—US$1.8 trillion, Bank of America—US$1.5 trillion, Citigroup—US$1.3 trillion, Wells Fargo—US$1.2 trillion).

BANKS

LO1

Size, Structure, and Composition of the Industry

www.osfi-bsif.gc.ca

bank
A federally regulated deposit-taking financial institution governed by the Bank Act and requiring a charter or letter of patent to operate.

Office of the Superintendent of Financial Institutions (OSFI)
The main regulator of federally chartered FIs in Canada.

FIs that are allowed to operate as **banks** in Canada are governed by the Bank Act and regulated at the federal level by the **Office of the Superintendent of Financial Institutions (OSFI)**. OSFI provides a list of all of the banks that are currently allowed to operate in Canada on its website at www.osfi-bsif.gc.ca. Banks are divided into domestic chartered banks (**Schedule I banks**, 26 companies in 2013) and foreign banks, whose activities are restricted as follows: (1) subsidiaries of foreign banks (**Schedule II banks**, 24 companies); (2) foreign bank full-service branches (**Schedule III banks**, 23 companies), which may accept only deposits over $150,000 (wholesale deposits); and (3) foreign bank lending branches (4 companies), which are allowed only to provide lending services in Canada. In addition, there are 21 foreign bank representative offices that are not allowed to accept deposits and that are primarily focused on facilitating banking business for their clients from their home country. Large Canadian banks (equity > $5 billion) must be widely held; no one person may hold more than 20 percent of the voting shares. Of the total assets of $3.87 trillion reported to OSFI at April 30, 2013 (see Table 2–4), $3.67 trillion (95%) represented the domestic banks and the remaining 5% was reported by foreign banks. The intent of regulators has been to maintain Canadian supervision of the financial services sector and to provide a safe and sound banking system.

Schedule I bank
A domestic Canadian FI, widely held, chartered to conduct business under the Bank Act.

Schedule II bank
A subsidiary, usually closely held, of a foreign bank that is authorized to conduct business in Canada under the Bank Act.

Schedule III bank
A foreign bank branch that is authorized under the Bank Act to accept deposits only in amounts over $150,000.

contagion
Asset withdrawals from FIs because of financial system uncertainty and destabilization resulting from the failure of another FI.

Compared to the United States and other countries, the concentration of assets, the payments system, and the coast-to-coast branch banking system have meant that the Canadian banking industry has been remarkably stable. The 1980s saw the first bank failures since the failure of the Home Bank in 1923. The Canadian Commercial Bank and the Northland Bank of Canada, which both operated in Western Canada and had major exposure to real estate and oil and gas loans, failed in 1985. However, their assets were only 0.75 percent of the total assets of the banking system at the time. When these two banks got into trouble early in 1985, the Big Six banks worked together with the Bank of Canada and the Inspector General of Banks, the regulator at the time, to provide a rescue package, but the Canadian Commercial and Northland banks ultimately failed and **contagion** effects resulted in the merger of two other smaller banks, the Bank of British Columbia and the Continental Bank of Canada, with other banks. This stability contrasts with the reorganization and failures in the U.S. banking system, which has had a turbulent history. The Savings and Loan (S&L) crisis of the mid-1980s saw the failure of almost 400 commercial banks in 1984 alone. As well, during the financial crisis that started in 2008, 115 U.S. banks had failed by early November 2009.

At the time of the FI failures in the 1980s, the Canadian and U.S. financial systems were still based on the concept of the "four pillars" (banking, trust or fiduciary functions, investment banking activities, and insurance). Each financial institution was prohibited from offering services outside its own pillar. In Canada, this changed with the revision of the Bank Act in the 1980s. The shift toward universal banking started with the purchase of almost all of the independent investment dealers by the Big Six by the early 1990s. This was followed by the movement of banks into trust functions when the 1991 Bank Act revisions permitted them to own trust companies. As a result, the trust pillar was virtually eliminated as a stand-alone function by the end of the 1990s. Banks have been permitted to own insurance subsidiaries since 1991, but they are still not permitted to sell insurance products (property and casualty and life insurance policies) side by side with banking services (e.g., mortgages and chequing accounts) and investment services (e.g., mutual funds) in their branches. However, online insurance sales were permitted by OSFI but vetoed by the Minister of Finance in 2009.

spread
The difference between lending and deposit rates.

LIBOR
London interbank offered rate.

CDOR
Canadian Dealer Offered Rate, which is an average rate for bankers' acceptances calculated daily from a survey of market participants.

cost of funds
The market cost of all sources of capital used as the base rate in pricing loans.

The history of the financial services industry in Canada since the 1980s and the United States since the mid-1990s can thus be viewed as a move to universal banking. In Canada, this has resulted in the creation of the eleven large DTIs that are listed in Table 2–2. The consolidation of the financial services industry as a whole continues with issues related to banks' selling insurance products in their branches, and the perennial question of whether the Canadian banks should be allowed to merge with each other to create a larger concentration of banking assets in Canada and result in stronger FIs that are better able to operate in the global marketplace. The question of bank mergers, a political issue as much as an economic one in Canada, is discussed in more detail in Chapter 21.

Canadian banks fund themselves in the national markets and in the international interbank markets, and they lend to larger corporations. This means that their **spreads** (i.e., the differences between lending and deposit rates) are subject to both North American market and global market conditions. To the extent that their lending is based on **LIBOR** or **CDOR**, the interest rates charged to larger customers represent an estimate of the market-based **cost of funds**. This has an effect on the return on equity (ROE) and the return on assets (ROA) as reported along with the average interest rate spread in Table 2–3 for the Big Six banks from 1999 to 2012. As well, the switch from Canadian Generally Accepted Accounting Principles (GAAP) to International Financial Reporting Standards (IFRS) by Canadian FIs in 2011 means that the ROE is not strictly comparable in every year. IFRS require Canadian FIs to re-recognize securitized assets over which they still had some control or risk. Under GAAP, Canadian FIs had removed many securitized assets from their balance sheets. The ROA averages less than 1 percent in every year. However, the return on common shareholders' equity (ROE) is positive in every year and less than 10 percent only in 2002. The average interest rate spread for all currencies for the six Canadian banks varies over the time period and has decreased slightly from 2.75 percent in 1999 to 2.70 percent in 2012. Appendix 2A shows how a bank's ROE can be decomposed to examine the different underlying sources of profitability. This decomposition is often referred to as DuPont analysis. However, the use of balance sheet items for FI analysis has become less valuable as FIs, particularly banks, have participated in more off-balance-sheet activities. The trend by both FIs and their regulators has thus been to a risk-based analysis.

Balance Sheet and Recent Trends

Assets

The four principal earning asset areas of banks are Canadian securities, business loans, mortgages, and personal loans. One important long-term influence on the asset structure of banks has been the growth of the commercial paper market,

TABLE 2–3 ROA, ROE, and Selected Indicators of the Big Six Canadian Banks, 1999–2012

For the Fiscal Year Ended Oct. 31	Return on Average Assets (ROA) (%)	Return on Average Common Shareholders' Equity (ROE) (%)	Net Interest Income/ Average Total Assets (%)	Loan Loss Provisions/ Average Total Assets (%)	AVERAGE INTEREST RATE SPREAD (percentages, all currencies)		
					Earned On Loans*	Paid On Deposits*	Average Spread**
1999	0.71	17.50	1.83	0.23	7.03	4.29	2.75
2000	0.72	16.81	1.83	0.27	7.64	4.77	2.86
2001	0.66	15.14	1.92	0.39	7.13	4.15	2.98
2002	0.44	9.90	2.01	0.56	5.36	2.37	2.99
2003	0.69	15.88	1.88	0.22	5.24	2.15	3.09
2004	0.79	18.07	1.78	0.06	5.03	1.96	3.07
2005	0.67	15.32	1.67	0.09	5.01	2.28	2.73
2006	0.96	22.96	1.52	0.09	5.78	3.08	2.70
2007	0.55	21.08	1.45	0.12	6.01	3.58	2.44
2008	0.49	11.78	1.52	0.22	5.39	3.02	2.37
2009	0.54	12.07	1.65	0.42	4.52	1.67	2.85
2010	0.77	15.21	1.69	0.24	4.04	1.26	2.79
2011	1.00	17.13	1.72	0.21	4.50	1.14	3.36
2012	0.88	18.72	1.66	0.20	3.86	1.15	2.70

*Includes all currencies
**Interest Earned on Loans less Interest Paid on Deposits
The banks include BMO Financial Group, CIBC, National Bank of Canada, RBC Financial Group, Scotiabank, and TD Bank Financial Group.

Source: Canadian Bankers Association, cba.ca.

disintermediation
The process by which firms go directly to the financial markets to raise funds without using an FI.

securitization
The removal of assets from the balance sheet by creating a contract that is sold in the financial marketplace.

which has become an alternative funding source that substitutes for bank loans for major corporations. This is an example of **disintermediation**, whereby companies that have their own credit ratings are able to bypass an FI and go directly to the market to raise funds. Another has been the **securitization** of mortgages and other assets—the pooling and packaging of mortgage and other loans for sale in the form of bonds (see Chapter 26). As noted above, IFRS now make it harder for loans to be removed from an FI's balance sheet through securitization. As well, the demand for asset-backed securities (ABSs), particularly those backed by U.S. subprime mortgages, declined worldwide following the global financial crisis in 2008–2009.

Look at the detailed balance sheet for all banks reporting to OSFI as of April 30, 2013 (Table 2–4). As noted previously, personal and business loans, as well as mortgages, make up a major portion of the assets. Hard assets (i.e., land, building, and equipment) make up less than 1 percent of total assets. The securities are

TABLE 2–4 Consolidated Monthly Balance Sheet—All Banks Reporting to OSFI, as at April 30, 2013

ASSETS	($ billions)	(%)
Cash and equivalent	$178.5	4.6%
Securities:		
Government:*		
Treasury bills, other short-term paper	104.9	2.7%
Other government securities	138.9	3.6%
Nongovernment:**		
Debt	330.0	8.5%
Shares	214.0	5.5%
Nonmortgage loans:**		
Call loans	12.2	0.3%
To regulated FIs	45.6	1.2%
To Canadian governments***	3.9	0.1%
To foreign governments	13.4	0.3%
Lease receivables	14.5	0.4%
To individuals, nonbusiness purposes	507.1	13.1%
Reverse repurchase agreements	388.7	10.1%
To individuals and others, business purposes	421.2	10.9%
Mortgage loans:**		
Residential, insured	384.0	9.9%
Residential, NHA MBS pooled and unsold	159.0	4.1%
Residential, uninsured	382.4	9.9%
Residential reverse mortgages	1.1	–
Nonresidential	58.8	1.5%
Customers' liability under acceptances**	61.8	1.6%
Land, buildings, equipment, net of depreciation	14.0	0.4%
Other assets:		
Insurance-related assets	4.7	0.1%
Goodwill and intangibles	47.1	1.2%
Deferred tax assets	8.4	0.2%
Derivative-related assets	274.3	7.1%
Other	98.1	2.5%
Total assets	$3,866.6	100%

LIABILITIES	($ billions)	(%)
Demand and notice deposits:		
Federal, provincial, municipal, and school	$23.3	1%
DTIs	23.1	1%
Individuals	673.9	17%
Other	518.5	13%
Fixed-term deposits:		
Federal, provincial, municipal, and school	3.7	–
DTIs	88.1	2%
Individuals	354.5	9%
Other	715.5	19%
Cheques, items in transit	2.1	–
Advances from the Bank of Canada		–
Acceptances	61.9	2%
Other liabilities:		
Insurance-related amounts	21.3	1%
Mortgages and loans payable	254.9	7%
Income taxes	4.4	–
Obligations related to borrowed securities	175.7	5%
Obligations: assets sold under repurchase agreements	246.9	6%
Derivative-related amounts	280.5	7%
Other****	160.5	4%
Subordinated debt	38.9	1%
Shareholders' equity:		
Preferred shares	19.0	–
Common shares	76.4	2%
Contributed surplus	1.5	–
Retained earnings	108.7	3%
Noncontrolling interests	7.7	–
Accumulated other comprehensive income (loss)	5.9	–
Total liabilities and shareholders' equity	$3,866.6	100%

*Securities issued or guaranteed by the Government of Canada, Canadian Provincial or Territorial governments, and Canadian municipalities or School Corporations.
**Less allowance for impairment
***Loans to the Government of Canada, Canadian Provincial or Territorial governments, and Canadian municipalities or School Corporations.
****Includes liabilities of subsidiaries other than deposits, accrued interest, deferred income, and other liabilities.

Source: OSFI, osfi-bsif.gc.ca.

composed of those issued or guaranteed by the Canadian federal government, province/territory, or municipality, as well as other debt securities and shares. Foreign assets reported to OSFI make up $1.31 trillion (34 percent of the total assets, an indication of the international nature of the operations). It is notable that insurance-related assets make up only 0.1 percent of the total, demonstrating that so far this cross-pillar diversification is small for these FIs.

A major inference that we can draw from this asset structure is that, with loans and mortgages at over 50 percent of the assets, credit or default risk exposure is a major risk faced by bank managers (see Chapters 10 and 11). Because banks are highly leveraged and therefore hold little equity (see next section) compared with

demand deposits
Deposits held at an FI that can be withdrawn by the depositor without notice.

notice deposits
Deposits held at an FI that require notification to the FI before withdrawal. If the notice period is not met, the depositor could be denied access to the funds.

fixed-term deposits
Deposits held at an FI that cannot be withdrawn by the depositor prior to the maturity date. Often these deposits may be withdrawn prior to maturity with a penalty being paid by the depositor.

Canada Deposit Insurance Corporation (CDIC)
The corporation that insures eligible deposits of federally regulated deposit-taking FIs in Canada, cdic.ca.

interbank borrowings
Short-term loans (demand, notice, and fixed-term deposits), often overnight, received from other FIs.

total assets, even a relatively small number of loan defaults could decrease the equity of a bank, moving it toward insolvency. Losses such as those due to defaults are charged off against the earnings and therefore ultimately decrease the equity (shareholders' stake) in a bank. Loans are carried on the balance sheet net of an allowance for impairment, which is calculated according to criteria set by OSFI. The intent is to cause the bank to recognize potential loan losses on a timely basis and so not overstate the balance sheet position.

Liabilities

Banks have two major sources of funds other than the equity provided by owners: deposits and borrowed or other liability funds. A major difference between banks and other firms is the banks' high leverage. For example, the six largest Canadian banks had an average ratio of total shareholders' equity to total assets of 5.5 percent in 2012; this implies that 94.5 percent of their assets were funded by debt, either deposits or borrowed funds.

Note in Table 2–4 that deposits amounted to $2.4 trillion or 62 percent of total liabilities and equity. Subordinated debt represented just 1 percent. Note also that **demand deposits** and **notice deposits** represent 32 percent of total liabilities and shareholders' equity and **fixed-term deposits** provide 30 percent. A good portion of these will be accounts insured by **Canada Deposit Insurance Corporation (CDIC)**, the deposit insurance company for DTIs. Deposit insurance is discussed in greater detail in Chapter 19. Insurance liabilities are small, at 1 percent of the total.

Overall, the liability structure of bank balance sheets tends to reflect a shorter maturity structure than does the asset portfolio, with relatively more liquid instruments such as deposits and **interbank borrowings** used to fund less liquid assets such as loans. Thus, maturity mismatch or interest rate risk and liquidity risk are key exposure concerns for bank managers (see Chapters 8, 9, 12, and 18).

Equity

Bank equity capital (5.0 percent of total liabilities and shareholders' equity at April 30, 2013) consists mainly of preferred and common shares and retained earnings. Contributed surplus is a minor amount, representing the difference between a share's stated par value and what the original shareholders paid when they bought the newly issued stock. OSFI requires banks to hold a minimum level of equity capital to act as a buffer against losses from their on- and off-balance-sheet activities (see Chapter 20). Because of the relatively low cost of deposit funding, banks may tend to hold equity close to the minimum levels set by regulators. As we discuss in subsequent chapters, this impacts banks' exposures to risk and their ability to grow—both on and off the balance sheet—over time.

Off-Balance-Sheet Activities

LO2

The balance sheet itself does not reflect the total scope of bank activities. Banks conduct many fee-related activities off the balance sheet. Off-balance-sheet (OBS) activities are important in terms of their dollar value and the income they generate for banks. OBS activities include issuing various types of guarantees (such as letters of credit), which often have a strong insurance underwriting element, and making future commitments to lend. Both services generate additional fee income for banks. OBS activities also involve engaging in derivative transactions—futures, forwards, options, and swaps.

off-balance-sheet (OBS) asset
An item that moves onto the asset side of the balance sheet when a contingent event occurs.

off-balance-sheet (OBS) liability
An item that moves onto the liability side of the balance sheet when a contingent event occurs.

capital adequacy requirements
Levels of equity capital that an FI is required by regulators to maintain in order to be allowed to continue in operation.

Under current accounting standards, some of these activities are not shown on the current balance sheet. Rather, an item or activity is an **off-balance-sheet (OBS) asset** if, when a contingent event occurs, the item or activity moves onto the asset side of the balance sheet or an income item is realized on the income statement. Conversely, an item or activity is an **off-balance-sheet (OBS) liability** if, when a contingent event occurs, the item or activity moves onto the liability side of the balance sheet or an expense item is realized on the income statement.

By moving activities off the balance sheet, banks hope to earn additional fee income to complement the margins or spreads on their traditional lending business. At the same time, they can avoid regulatory costs or "taxes" since deposit insurance premiums are not levied on OBS activities (see Chapter 16). As well, the **capital adequacy requirements** for on-balance-sheet loans differ from those for OBS items and in some cases may make the OBS activity more profitable (see Chapter 20). Thus, the banks have both earnings and regulatory incentives to undertake activities off their balance sheets.

OBS activities, however, can involve risks that add to the overall insolvency exposure of an FI. Indeed, at the very heart of the financial crisis were losses associated with OBS mortgage-backed securities created and held by FIs. Losses resulted in the failure, acquisition, or bailout of some of the largest FIs and a near meltdown of the world's financial and economic systems. However, OBS activities and instruments have both risk-reducing and risk-increasing attributes, and, when used appropriately, they can reduce or hedge an FI's interest rate, credit, and foreign exchange risks.

Canadian banks engage in OBS credit-related activities such as loan commitments and letters of credit. They also participate in derivatives activities that include interest rate contracts, foreign exchange contracts, credit derivatives, and equity-linked contracts, both exchange-traded and over the counter (see Table 16–5). Canadian banks' derivatives are reported to OSFI on a quarterly basis. For Quarter 1, 2013, the total notional amount of derivative contracts reported was $20.1 trillion, an amount that is five times the total on-balance-sheet assets of $3.9 trillion reported in Table 2–4. It should be noted that the notional, or face, value of OBS activities does not accurately reflect the risk to the bank of undertaking such activities. The potential for the bank to gain or lose is based on the possible change in the market value over the life of the contract rather than the notional, or face, value of the contract, normally less than 3 percent of the notional value of an OBS contract. For example, the market value of a swap today is the difference between the present value of the cash flows expected to be received minus the present value of the cash flows expected to be paid (see Chapter 24).

The growth in the use of derivative securities activities by banks has been a direct response to the increased interest rate risk, credit risk, and foreign exchange risk exposures they have faced, both domestically and internationally. In particular, these contracts offer banks a way to hedge these risks without having to make extensive changes on the balance sheet. However, of the total notional amount of $20.1 billion derivatives contracts reported, $19.0 trillion or 94.5 percent were held for trading purposes, indicating that this is likely a profitable source of income for the banks. The exposure is limited since 41 percent of the contracts have a maturity of less than one year. As well, many of the contracts are over the counter rather than exchange traded, an indication of the market-making function of the banks as well as a market risk.

Although the simple notional dollar amount of OBS items overestimates their risk exposure amounts, the increase in these activities has been phenomenal and has pushed regulators into imposing capital requirements on such activities to explicitly recognize an FI's solvency risk exposure from pursuing such activities, as described in Chapter 20. As we discuss in detail in Chapters 22 through 24, the significant growth in derivative securities activities by commercial banks has been a direct response to the increased interest rate risk, credit risk, and foreign exchange risk exposures they have faced, both domestically and internationally. In particular, these contracts offer banks a way to hedge these risks without having to make extensive changes on the balance sheet. However, these assets and liabilities also introduce unique risks that must be managed. The failure or near failure of some of the largest U.S. FIs during the financial crisis can be attributed to risks associated with OBS activities (e.g., Citigroup). As mortgage borrowers defaulted on their mortgages, FIs that held these "toxic" mortgages and "toxic" credit derivatives (in the form of mortgage-backed securities) started announcing huge losses on them. Losses from the falling value of OBS securities reached over US$1 trillion worldwide through 2009.

Other Activities

Banks engage in other fee-generating activities that cannot easily be identified from analyzing their on- and off-blance-sheet accounts.

Trust Services

Federally regulated trusts are governed by OSFI under the Trust and Loans Companies Act (48 firms were listed in 2013). There are also some provincially regulated trusts. Trusts offer similar services to banks (i.e., deposit-taking, loans), as well as fiduciary activities such as administering estates, trusts, and pension plans. Since banks are prohibited from providing these fiduciary services directly, the banks offer these types of services through their subsidiaries. For example, TD Waterhouse, the securities arm of TD Canada Trust, the result of a merger of Toronto-Dominion Bank with Canada Trust, offers estate planning, tax planning, and other trust services. TD's banking customers can access TD Waterhouse directly from its website, an advantage of a full-service FI. The larger trust companies are owned by the banks (for example, The Bank of Nova Scotia Trust Company, CIBC Mellon Trust Company, and The Canada Trust Company). The total assets of federally regulated trusts were $157.5 billion at April 30, 2013. In many cases, the deposits of trust companies are covered by deposit insurance from CDIC. The advantage for banks of offering deposit services, investment services, and trust services is the **cross-selling** of services to customers, providing banks with additional revenue. As well, with online access to accounts, a bank client may be less likely to move to another institution because of the inconvenience of establishing accounts with another FI.

cross-selling
The marketing of other services such as mutual funds or insurance to a customer along with traditional banking.

Loan Companies

In addition to operating trust subsidiaries, the banks also participate in loan companies, of which there were 19 listed by OSFI in 2013. A loan company may be federally (falling under the Trust and Loan Companies Act) or provincially regulated, may offer deposit-taking services that are covered by CDIC's deposit insurance, and may conduct other activities similar to a bank. The total assets of the loan companies regulated by OSFI were $170.1 billion at April 30, 2013. The 19 loan companies supervised by OSFI primarily represent the mortgage arms of the chartered banks (e.g., Bank of Montreal Mortgage Corporation, TD Mortgage Corporation). These subsidiaries would be included in the consolidated financial statements of their parents.

Correspondent Banking

Correspondent banking is the provision of banking services to other banks that do not have the staff resources to perform the services themselves. These services include cheque-clearing and collection, foreign exchange trading, hedging services, and participation in large loan and security issuances. The nature of the Canadian economy means that firms rely heavily on both exporting and importing, which implies a risk of nonpayment and also foreign exchange risk. In addition to supplying over-the-counter foreign exchange contracts (forwards), the banks also provide **letters of credit** that allow a seller to be guaranteed that they will be paid in an exporting agreement with an unknown party (Chapter 13).

letters of credit
Letters from a bank to an exporter (importer) stating that it will pay the amount of the contract on the completion of certain conditions.

Regulation

LO3

Figure 2–2 shows the regulatory system for FIs operating in Canada. The current regulatory system for banks in Canada dates back to July 1987 when the government enacted the Financial Institutions and Deposit Insurance Amendment Act and the Office of the Superintendent of Financial Institutions Act. The Department of Insurance and the Office of the Inspector General of Banks joined to form one national regulator, OSFI, to supervise federally regulated DTIs. OSFI's role has, since then, been to ensure the safety and soundness of the financial system in Canada under the Bank Act. As a member of global committees that determine capital requirements for international banks (set by the Bank for International Settlements, BIS, and discussed in detail in Chapter 20), OSFI enforces those rules through its reporting requirements and inspection of the FIs under its jurisdiction. OSFI also sets rules for FIs related to their liquidity and the safety and soundness of their transactions sent through the domestic and international payments systems (Chapter 12).

The Bank of Canada is responsible for ensuring the integrity of the financial markets system in Canada, primarily through its monetary policy. It participates in the payments system through the Canada Payments Association (CPA). As such, the Bank of Canada participates indirectly in the regulation of banks, primarily by producing research on capital markets and identifying global and

FIGURE 2–2
The Canadian Regulatory System

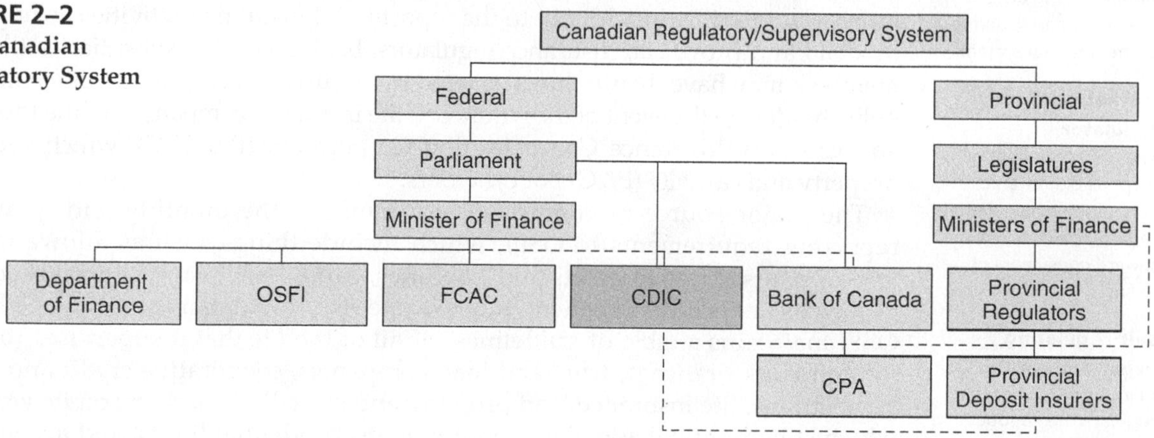

bankofcanada.ca
www.financialstabilityboard.org
bis.org
www.fcac-acfc.gc.ca

Financial Consumer Agency of Canada (FCAC)
A federal government agency reporting to the Minister of Finance that monitors federally regulated FIs and enforces consumer protection acts with respect to financial services.

national trends that may affect different aspects of the financial services industry. As well, the Bank of Canada and OSFI have representation on the Financial Stability Board (FSB) and the Basel Committee for Banking Supervision (BCBS). Depositors are protected by the CDIC, which insures specified deposits of both federal and provincial DTIs. Canadian consumers of banking products are also protected by the **Financial Consumer Agency of Canada (FCAC)**, which was established in 2001 to enforce consumer protection laws related to FIs in Canada. One of the initiatives related to consumers was the commitment of eight Canadian FIs to provide low-cost accounts for consumers. A list of the acts and regulations that the FCAC is responsible for enforcing is available at the FCAC's website.

Regulations

Banks are among the most regulated firms in the global economy. Because of the inherent special nature of banking and banking contracts, as discussed in Chapter 1, regulators impose numerous restrictions on their product and geographic activities. In Canada, the division of powers between the federal government and the provinces/territories under the British North America (BNA) Act means that there are additional national, territorial, and provincial regulatory agencies that come into play. The creation of one federal regulator (OSFI) was intended to simplify the regulatory framework and reduce the regulatory burden for FIs, as well as to firmly establish responsibility for the implementation of the BIS capital adequacy regulations (the Basel Accord; see Chapter 20). In addition, the move cross-pillar to include insurance and securities functions means that, although banks are primarily governed by the Bank Act administered by OSFI at the federal level, the provincial and territorial regulators also have jurisdiction. A table outlining the federal and provincial/territorial regulators in Canada is provided in Appendix 2B.

cdnpay.ca
iiac.ca
mfda.ca
cdic.ca
fintrac.gc.ca
assuris.ca
pacicc.com

At the federal level, OSFI is the **prudential regulator**, responsible for monitoring the solvency and risk management of an FI. FCAC is the **market conduct regulator**, charged with ensuring that consumers of financial services are treated ethically and fairly. In addition, there are many **self-regulatory organizations (SROs)**, such as the CPA, the Investment Industry Association of Canada (IIAC), and the Mutual Fund Dealers Association of Canada (MFDA), which are industry associations that police their members. Other regulators at the federal level are CDIC, which establishes deposit insurance coverage, and the Financial Transactions and Reports Analysis Centre of Canada (FINTRAC), which oversees the reporting of terrorist activities as well as money laundering. In addition to the reporting of insurance activities as required by OSFI and provincial insurance regulators, bank insurance subsidiaries that are members may have their policies covered by Assuris, which protects life insurance policyholders in the event of the failure of a life insurance company, and the Property and Casualty Insurance Compensation Corporation (PACICC), which protects property and casualty (P&C) policyholders.

prudential regulator
The government agency responsible for ensuring compliance with good management practices within an FI to ensure the safety and soundness of the financial system.

market conduct regulator
The government agency responsible for enforcing adherence to regulations regarding FIs' behaviour toward consumers of financial services.

self-regulating organizations (SROs)
FI industry groups that regulate the conduct and business practices of their members.

The major source of compliance for banks is the monthly and quarterly reporting requirements to OSFI, which include things such as allowance for impairments, average assets and liabilities, capital adequacy, and market risk, as well as an income statement, interest rate risk, and details of mortgage loans. OSFI maintains a table of guidelines for all of the FIs that it supervises (banks, foreign bank branches, trust and loan companies, cooperative credit and retail associations, life insurance, and property and casualty insurance) on its website, which covers capital adequacy requirements, prudential limits, and accounting guidelines.

Industry Performance

Table 2–3 on page 25 presents selected performance ratios for six members of the Canadian Bankers Association (the Big Six Banks), which represent more than 90 percent of the assets of banks in Canada. The ROA was below 1 percent in every year, a low amount compared to U.S. banks, which achieved an ROA higher than 1 percent (ranging from 1.15 in 2001 to 1.40 in 2003). The return on total shareholders' equity (ROE) exceeded 10 percent in every year except 2002, a year associated with the highest loan loss provision to average total assets, which was equal to 0.56 percent. As well, the loan loss provision to average total assets was equal to 0.22 and 0.06 percent in 2003 and 2004, likely reflecting the low interest rate climate. When interest rates start to climb, then the **provision for loan losses** should also be expected to increase as borrowers feel the financial stress and become less able to meet their interest obligations. This ratio shows an increase in 2007 and again in 2008 and 2009. **Net interest income** as a percentage of average total assets (also called net interest margin or NIM) also showed declines in 2006 and 2007.

provision for loan losses
Bank management's recognition of expected bad loans for the period.

net interest income
Total interest income less total interest expense before provision for credit losses.

During the early 2000s, Canadian banks showed a strong performance. There are several reasons for this. First, lower interest rates made debt cheaper to service and kept many households and small firms borrowing. Second, lower interest rates made home purchasing more affordable. Thus, the housing market boomed throughout the period. Third, the development of new financial instruments, such as credit derivatives and mortgage-backed securities, helped banks shift credit risk from their balance sheets to financial markets and other FIs such as insurance companies. Finally, improved information technology helped banks manage their risk better.

However, as shown in Table 2–3, in 2007 the effect of the credit crisis was starting to be felt at the Canadian banks. The ROA was down, as were ROE and other income. As well, loan loss provisions were up, reflecting the spread of the global recession that carried over into 2008 and 2009. Housing prices started to drop, the global credit crisis had an impact on liquidity, and securitization markets dried up, putting a further strain on banks' balance sheets.

As mentioned in Chapter 1, during the financial crisis, there was a weakening in the public trust and confidence in the ethics followed by FIs. Many banks have dealt with ethical issues over the years. For example, in 2003, JPMorgan Chase, Citigroup, and CIBC settled with the New York District Attorney over allegations that the banks wrongly helped Enron hide its debt prior to the energy company's filing for bankruptcy in 2001. Also, ethical issues related to the trading of mutual funds in the United States caused the Ontario Securities Commission to review the trading practices of Ontario mutual fund managers from November 2003 to December 2004. The commission's report discussed **late trading** and **market timing** issues and resulted in fines of $205.6 million levied against five fund managers. Related to the ethical issues are conflicts of interest that can arise between the market-oriented trading culture of the securities subsidiaries of the banks and the gatekeeper role of the traditional banker.

late trading
Illegally buying or selling mutual fund securities after the close of trading at the current price rather than at the next day's price as required by law.

market timing
Frequent short-term trading of mutual fund securities by a fund manager to take advantage of changes in price that are not in the best interests of the funds' investors.

Also certain to affect the future performance of banks as well as credit unions and caisses populaires is the extent to which banks adopt the newest technology (Chapter 17), including the extent to which industry participants embrace online and mobile banking. Early entrants into online and mobile banking have introduced new technology in markets with demographic and economic characteristics that help ensure customer acceptance. In addition, keeping up to date with advances in technology helps FIs to provide better customer service, both for retail customers and for business customers, which ultimately helps FIs to retain customers (see Appendix 2C).

CONCEPT QUESTIONS

1. **What are the major assets held by banks?**
2. **What are the major sources of funding for banks?**
3. **Describe the responsibilities of the regulatory agencies responsible for banks in Canada.**
4. **What has the trend in ROA and ROE been in the banking industry?**

CREDIT UNIONS AND CAISSES POPULAIRES

LO4

credit unions (CUs)
Cooperative deposit-taking FIs that are owned by their members.

caisses populaires (CPs)
Cooperative deposit-taking FIs similar to credit unions that are owned by their members and operate primarily in Quebec.

cooperative financial institutions
Generic term used for FIs owned by their members.

mutual organizations
Savings banks in which the depositors are also the legal owners of the bank.

Credit unions (CUs) and **caisses populaires (CPs)** (which primarily operate in Quebec) are **cooperative financial institutions** that are owned by their members (depositors). The shares are covered by share and deposit insurance, and the owner of the shares may receive dividends from the CU or CP. These cooperatives are also called **mutual organizations**. The cooperative credit movement has been important globally as it is based on the principle that a local community can provide banking services. In developed countries like Canada and the United States, credit cooperatives account for a relatively small proportion of the financial services industry. However, in many less developed countries they play an important role in mobilizing savings at the rural level. One very important CU-type FI, first developed in Bangladesh and extended to other developing countries, has been the Grameen Bank. As well, credit cooperatives still provide deposit functions and lending to rural areas of China. These small FIs are part of the regulatory challenge facing China as it modernizes its financial architecture.

Cooperatives in Canada have been an alternative to the major banks, which were seen as unfriendly to retail customers and small borrowers by providing low deposit rates paired with high interest rates on loans. Thus, universities, labour unions, cultural organizations, and even towns formed credit cooperatives to pool the resources of the community. This was particularly important in Quebec and British Columbia, where two of these independent FIs (Desjardins Group Inc. and Vancouver City Savings, respectively) now rank in the top ten of the deposit- taking Canadian FIs based on asset size (see Table 2–2). CUs and CPs, both large and small, will have a role to play in the issue of bank mergers (see Chapter 21) as they are an integral part of small towns and remote communities in Canada and will continue to provide banking services even if bank mergers result in branch closings.

The primary objective of financial cooperatives is to satisfy the deposit-taking and lending needs of their members. CU and CP member deposits (shares) are used to provide loans to other members in need of funds. Any earnings from these loans are used to pay higher rates on member deposits, charge lower rates on member loans, and attract new members. Because cooperatives do not issue common stock, the members are legally the owners.

Size, Structure, and Composition of the Industry and Recent Trends

www.cucentral.ca

CUs and CPs are the most numerous of the deposit-taking FIs in Canada. However, like other FIs, they have declined in number from over 2,000 in 1999 to 740 in 2013. CUs and CPs are regulated at the provincial level. As well,

Credit Union Central of Canada (CUCC) does not provide financial services; it acts as a trade association for the Canadian CU system. Six provincial cooperative credit associations (CCAs) receive oversight from OSFI, primarily in terms of liquidity. The CCAs do not take deposits but primarily provide liquidity to their members. Table 2–5 presents statistics on the CUs and CPs in Canada for the first quarter of 2013. As can be seen from Table 2–5, the total membership of CUs and CPs in Canada in 2013 was 10.2 million, roughly 30 percent of the Canadian population. British Columbia and Ontario had the largest number of CU members, but almost 44 percent of the members (4.5 million) live in Quebec, a demonstration of the strength of the cooperative movement in Quebec and the source of the success of Desjardins Group Inc., presented in Table 2–2 on page 23 as one of the largest deposit-taking FIs in Canada. In addition, the total assets of $298.7 billion are made up of $247.2 billion in loans (82.8 percent). Total members' deposits of $246.9 billion funded 82.7 percent of assets.

TABLE 2–5 Statistics for CUs and CPs, First Quarter 2013*

($ millions) Province	Total Savings/ Deposits	Total Loans	Total Assets	Total CUs	Total Locations	Total Members
AFFILIATED CUs & CPs						
CU						
Central Class						
British Columbia	$50,362	$49,293	$57,362	43	370	1,878,369
Alberta	18,373	17,381	20,481	33	206	639,933
Saskatchewan	15,443	13,166	17,383	55	295	501,004
Manitoba	20,133	17,710	21,770	40	190	590,235
Ontario	26,847	26,299	31,310	97	508	1,320,866
New Brunswick	818	697	897	10	31	71,698
Nova Scotia	1,811	1,516	2,012	29	80	155,637
Prince Edward Island	753	595	825	9	15	55,500
Newfoundland & Labrador	920	801	988	10	40	51,947
SUBTOTAL	$135,460	$127,458	$152,958	326	1,735	5,265,189
Federation Class						
Ontario-L'Alliance	1,128	1,046	1,286	13	25	62,099
TOTAL	$136,588	$128,504	$154,244	339	1,760	5,327,288
NONAFFILIATED CUs & CPs						
CPs						
CPs outside Quebec (MB, ON, NB)	$6,948	$6,618	$7,992	34	158	355,548
Quebec	102,995	111,845	135,998	358	1,159	4,460,587
TOTAL (All)	$109,943	$118,463	$143,990	392	1,317	4,816,135
CUs						
Ontario	$390	$288	$437	9	22	42,023
TOTAL	$110,333	$118,751	$144,427	401	1,339	4,858,158
COMBINED CANADIAN CU & CP SYSTEM RESULTS						
TOTAL	$246,921	$247,255	$298,671	740	3,099	10,185,446

*Above figures do not include affiliated companies of the CU system, such as Concentra Financial Inc., The CUMIS Group Ltd., The Co-operators Group Ltd., Credential Financial Inc., and NEI Investments.

Source: Credit Union Central of Canada, www.cucentral.ca.

To attract and keep customers, CUs and CPs have expanded their services to compete with banks. For example, CUs and CPs offer products and services ranging from mortgages and auto loans to credit lines and automated teller machines. In addition, CUCC lists other cooperatives operating in Canada, such as Agrifinance, which provides agricultural loans; Co-operative Trust Company of Canada, providing fiduciary and trust services; The Co-operators Group Limited, a property and casualty insurance company; Credential Financial Inc., which provides wealth management services; and Northwest and Ethical Investments, a mutual fund company.

Regulation

The regulation of CUs and CPs is primarily at the provincial/territorial level. The provincial/territorial regulators are charged with ensuring that the CUs and CPs follow sound financial practices and, in most provinces and territories, require that external auditors prepare their annual financial statements. In addition, each firm is inspected by the regulator on an annual basis. Each province has legislation that defines the *statutory liquidity* that a CU must maintain at its central CU (CCA).

Depositors' funds are protected at varying levels by provincial and territorial organizations. These may take the form of deposit insurance, deposit guarantee corporations, stabilization funds, or a central CU or CP.

Industry Performance

Given the mutual-ownership status of this industry, growth in ROA (or profits) is not necessarily the primary goal of CUs and CPs. Rather, as long as capital or equity levels are sufficient to protect a CU or CP against unexpected losses on its credit portfolio as well as other financial and operational risks, this not-for-profit industry has a primary goal of serving the deposit and lending needs of its members. This contrasts with the emphasis placed on profitability by shareholder-owned banks.

CONCEPT QUESTIONS

1. **How do CUs and CPs differ from banks?**
2. **Why have CUs and CPs prospered in recent years?**
3. **What is the major asset held by CUs and CPs?**

GLOBAL ISSUES: THE FINANCIAL CRISIS

Very soon after it hit the United States, the financial crisis spread worldwide. As the crisis spread, banks worldwide saw losses driven by their portfolios of structured finance products and securitized exposures to the subprime mortgage market. Losses were magnified by illiquidity in the markets for those instruments. As with U.S. banks, this led to substantial losses in their marked-to-market valuations. In Europe, the general picture of bank performance in 2008 was similar to that in the United States. That is, net income fell sharply at all banks. The largest banks in the Netherlands, Switzerland, and the United Kingdom had net losses for the year. Banks in Ireland, Spain, and the United Kingdom were especially hard hit as they had large investments in mortgages and mortgage-backed securities, both U.S.

and domestic. Because they focused on domestic retail banking, French and Italian banks were less affected by losses on mortgage-backed securities. Continental European banks, in contrast to U.K. banks, partially cushioned losses through an increase in their net interest margins.

A number of European banks averted outright bankruptcy thanks to direct support from their central banks and national governments. During the last week of September and first week of October 2008, the German government guaranteed all consumer bank deposits and arranged a bailout of Hypo Real Estate, the country's second-largest commercial property lender. The United Kingdom nationalized mortgage lender Bradford & Bingley (the country's eighth-largest mortgage lender) and raised deposit guarantees. Ireland guaranteed deposits and debt of its six major FIs. Iceland rescued its third-largest bank with the US$860 million purchase of 75 percent of the bank's stock and a few days later seized the country's entire banking system. The Netherlands, Belgium, and Luxembourg central governments together agreed to inject US$16.37 billion into Fortis NV (Europe's first ever cross-border financial services company) to keep it afloat. However, five days later this deal fell apart, and the bank was split up. The Dutch bought all assets located in the Netherlands for approximately US$23 billion. The central bank in India stepped in to stop a run on the country's second-largest bank, ICICI Bank, by promising to pump in cash. Central banks in Asia injected cash into their banking systems as banks' reluctance to lend to each other led the Hong Kong Monetary Authority to inject liquidity into its banking system after rumours led to a run on Bank of East Asia Ltd. South Korean authorities offered loans and debt guarantees to help small and midsize businesses with short-term funding. Canada, the United Kingdom, Belgium, Italy, and Ireland were just a few of the countries to pass an economic stimulus plan and/or bank bailout plan. The Bank of England lowered its target interest rate to a record low of 1 percent, hoping to help the British economy out of a recession. The Bank of Canada, Bank of Japan, and Swiss National Bank also lowered their main interest rate to 1 percent or less. All of these actions were a result of the spread of the U.S. financial market crisis to world financial markets.

However, the worldwide economic slowdown experienced in the later stages of the crisis meant that bank losses have become more closely connected to macroeconomic performance. Countries around the world saw companies scrambling for credit and cutting their growth plans. Additionally, consumers worldwide reduced their spending. Even China's booming economy slowed more than had been predicted, from 10.1 percent in the second quarter of 2008 to 9 percent in the third quarter. This was the first time since 2002 that China's growth was below 10 percent and dimmed hopes that Chinese demand could help keep world economies growing. In late October, the global crisis hit the Persian Gulf as Kuwait's central bank intervened to rescue Gulf Bank, the first bank rescue in the oil-rich Gulf. Until this time, the area had been relatively immune to the world financial crisis. However, plummeting oil prices (which had dropped over 50 percent between July and October 2008) left the area's economies vulnerable. In this period, the majority of bank losses were more directly linked to a surge in borrower defaults and to anticipated defaults, as evidenced by the increase in the amount and relative importance of loan loss provision expenses.

International banks' balance sheets continued to shrink during the first half of 2009 (although at a much slower pace than in the preceding six months) and, as in the United States, began to recover in the latter half of the year. In the fall of 2009, a steady stream of mostly positive macroeconomic news reassured investors that the global economy had turned around, but investor confidence remained fragile. For example, in late November 2009, security prices worldwide dropped sharply as investors reacted to news that government-owned Dubai World had asked for a delay in some payments on its debt.

Further, throughout the spring of 2010 Greece struggled with a severe debt crisis. Early on, some of the healthier European countries tried to step in and assist the debt-ridden country. Specifically, in March 2010 a plan led by Germany and France to bail out Greece with as much as US$41 billion in aid began to take shape. However, in late April 2010 Greek bond prices dropped dramatically as traders began betting a debt default was inevitable, even if the country received a massive bailout. The selloff was the result of still more bad news for Greece, which showed that the 2009 budget deficit was worse than had been previously reported, and, as a result, politicians in Germany began to voice opposition to a Greek bailout. Further, Moody's Investors Service downgraded Greece's debt rating and warned that additional cuts could be on the way. Greece's debt created heavy losses across the Greek banking sector. A run on Greek banks ensued. Initially, between €100 million and €500 million per day was being withdrawn from Greek banks. At its peak, the run on Greek banks produced deposit withdrawals of as high as €750 million a day, nearly 0.5 percent of the entire €170 billion deposit base in the Greek banking system.

Problems in the Greek banking system then spread to other European nations with fiscal problems, such as Portugal, Spain, and Italy. The risk of a full-blown banking crisis arose in Spain where the debt ratings of 16 banks and four regions were downgraded by Moody's Investor Service. Throughout Europe, some of the biggest banks announced billions of euros lost from writedowns on Greek loans. In 2011, Crédit Agricole reported a record quarterly net loss of €3.07 billion ($US4.06 billion) after a €220 million charge on its Greek debt. The United Kingdom's Royal Bank of Scotland revalued its Greek bonds at a 79 percent loss—or £1.1 billion ($US1.7 billion)—for 2011. Germany's Commerzbank's fourth-quarter 2011 earnings decreased by €700 million due to losses on Greek sovereign debt. The bank needed to find €5.3 billion to meet the stricter new capital requirements set by Europe's banking regulator. Bailed-out Franco-Belgian bank Dexia warned it risked going out of business due to losses of €11.6 billion from its break-up and exposure to Greek debt and other toxic assets such as U.S. mortgage-backed securities. While Canadian exposure to the European crisis was small, in late 2010, U.S. banks had sovereign risk exposure to Greece totalling US$43.1 billion. In addition, exposures to Ireland totalled US$113.9 billion, to Portugal US$47.1 billion, and to Spain US$187.5 billion. Worldwide, bank exposure to these four countries totalled US$2,512.3 billion. Default by a small country such as Greece cascaded into something that threatened the world's financial system.

Worried about the effect a Greek debt crisis might have on the European Union, other European countries tried to step in and assist Greece. On May 9, 2010, in return for huge budget cuts, Europe's finance ministers and the International Monetary Fund approved a rescue package worth US$147 billion and a safety net of US$1 trillion aimed at ensuring financial stability across Europe. Through the rest of 2010 and into 2012, Eurozone leaders agreed on more measures designed to prevent the collapse of Greece and other member economies. In return, Greece continued to offer additional austerity reforms and agreed to reduce its budget deficits. At times, the extent of these reforms and budget cuts led to worker strikes and protests (some of which turned violent), as well as changes in Greek political leadership. In December 2011, the leaders of France and Germany agreed on a new fiscal pact that they said would help prevent another debt crisis. Then–French President Nicolas Sarkozy outlined the basic elements of the plan to increase budget discipline after meeting with German Chancellor Angela Merkel in Paris. The pact, which involved amending or rewriting the treaties that govern the European Union, was presented in detail at a meeting of European leaders and was approved. Efforts by the EU and reforms enacted by the Greek and other European country governments appear to have worked: on December 18, 2012, Standard & Poor's (S&P) raised its rating on Greek debt by six notches to B minus from selective default. S&P cited a strong and clear commitment from members of the Eurozone to keep Greece in the common currency bloc as the main reason for the upgrade. After the bailout, the market price of Greek debt rose: some hedge funds made huge profits by betting on this bailout effect.

Questions and Problems

1. What are the differences between Schedule I, Schedule II, and Schedule III banks?
2. What changes have banks implemented to deal with changes in the financial services environment?
3. What are the major uses of funds for banks in Canada? What are the primary risks to a bank caused by each use of funds? Which of these risks is most critical to the continuing operation of a bank?
4. What are the major sources of funds for banks in Canada? How is the landscape for these funds changing and why?
5. How does the liability maturity structure of a bank's balance sheet compare with the maturity structure of the asset portfolio? What risks are created or intensified by these differences?
6. a. What types of activities are normally classified as OBS activities?
   b. How does an OBS activity move onto the balance sheet as an asset or liability?
   c. What are the benefits of OBS activities to a bank?
   d. What are the risks of OBS activities to a bank?
7. How is mobile and online banking expected to provide benefits in the future?
8. What factors are given credit for the strong performance of banks in the early 2000s?
9. How does the asset structure of CUs compare with the asset structure of banks?
10. Compare and contrast the performance of the Canadian DTI industry with U.S. and global FIs during and after the financial crisis.
11. Who are the major regulators of banks in Canada?
12. What is a *prudential regulator*?
13. What is a *market conduct regulator*?
14. What is an *SRO*?

Appendix 2A Financial Statement Analysis Using a Return on Equity (ROE) Framework

Appendix 2B Who Regulates Bank Financial Groups in Canada?

Appendix 2C Technology in Commercial Banking

View Appendices 2A, 2B, and 2C on Connect.

CHAPTER 3

FINANCE COMPANIES

After studying this chapter you should be able to:

LO1 Discuss the size, structure, and composition of finance companies in Canada and the United States.

LO2 Discuss the types of lending done by finance companies.

LO3 Discuss the differences in the regulation of banks and finance companies.

LO4 Discuss the types of specialized services provided by Crown corporations in Canada.

INTRODUCTION

Our discussions now move from the highly regulated DTIs (Chapter 2) to the credit intermediation provided by finance companies. The finance company industry, with the exception of the leasing arms of major banks, is basically unregulated in Canada. The Financial Stability Board (FSB) classifies finance companies as part of the shadow banking system since these companies are nonbank FIs (NBFIs) whose chief purpose is to provide credit to consumers and business. In addition, since many of the major players are private companies, it is difficult to measure the scope of the industry and its effect on the Canadian and North American economies. However, their role is important for small and medium-sized businesses and in supporting troubled companies. For example, GE Capital provided loans to keep Air Canada flying during its restructuring between 2003 and 2004 and provided refinancing as it came out of bankruptcy.

Finance companies provide consumer lending, business lending, and mortgage financing. Some finance company loans are similar to bank loans, such as consumer and car loans, but others are more specialized, such as aircraft and equipment leasing. The assets of finance companies are subject to credit risk, but this risk is mitigated because their loans are usually backed by collateral. As well, finance companies often lend to customers that banks find too risky. This can lead to losses and even failure if the high risk does not pay off. Since many of their assets are loans for capital expenditures, finance companies are dependent on expansion in the economy for asset growth.

Finance companies differ from banks in that they are not permitted to accept deposits but instead rely on short- and long-term debt (e.g., commercial paper) as a source of funds, often raising these funds in international markets. Their ability to offer loans is therefore affected by their own ability to borrow, and, with the right credit conditions, they are able to closely match the maturities of their assets with those of their liabilities, controlling for liquidity risk. However, the market meltdown in 2008 and the economic slowdown in 2009 resulted in downsizing and reshaping of the industry. The liquidity crisis in 2008 shut off the commercial paper market as a source of funds, and many U.S. finance companies converted into bank holding companies, exchanging market liquidity risk for withdrawal risk. Many received funding and guarantees from the U.S. government. For example, CIT Group, based in New York, was a major lender to small businesses in the United States and to the National Hockey League (Edmonton Oilers, Ottawa Senators), infrastructure projects (roads), and hospitals in Canada. In 2008, CIT became a U.S. bank holding company. Some finance companies suffered as a result of the problems of their parent companies. For example, GMAC Financial, owned by General Motors Corporation and Cerberus Capital Management, was a major provider of car loans and home loans. When credit markets seized up in 2008, GMAC experienced a liquidity crisis, applied for bank status, and received a bailout from the U.S. government. GMAC Financial, now known as Ally Financial, accepts FDIC-insured deposits in the United States. Royal Bank of Canada purchased the car financing business of Ally Financial in Canada in 2013.

In this chapter we discuss the size, structure, and composition of the industry; the services finance companies provide; and the competitive and financial position and regulation of the industry. We conclude the chapter with a look at some global issues.

SIZE, STRUCTURE, AND COMPOSITION OF THE INDUSTRY

LO1

asset-based financing (ABF)/asset-based lending (ABL)
A loan extended to a borrower based on the assets held as collateral.

structured finance
A unique loan and/or equity financing tailored to meet the specific needs of the borrower.

Crown corporation
A corporation owned by the federal government or by a provincial or territorial government.

Finance companies offer lending services similar to banks, such as mortgages (residential and commercial), loans (e.g., **asset-based financing (ABF)** or **asset-based lending (ABL), structured finance**, consumer loans), equipment leasing (e.g., automobile, aircraft), and credit cards. Finance companies in Canada are dominated by the unregulated institutions that are wholly owned subsidiaries (and therefore private companies) of U.S.-based firms. For example, Ford Credit Canada is the financing arm of the automobile manufacturer that provides new car loans in Canada. In addition, some **Crown corporations** (e.g., Export Development Canada) also offer financing. Also, the major Canadian banks offer some asset-based financing through their commercial lending operations. Finance companies are less transparent in their activities, but they perform more traditional, asset-based lending and provide competition for the large Canadian FIs that were discussed in Chapter 2. The size of the sector in Canada is small, so we look to the United States for statistics (see Tables 3–1, 3–2, and 3–3) and insight regarding the operations and regulation of these participants in the shadow banking (i.e., non-deposit-taking FIs) sector of the financial markets.

The history of finance companies in North America has been the provision of loans to a clientele that is unable to get credit elsewhere. The first major finance company originated during the Great Depression in the United States when General Electric Corp. created General Electric Capital Corp. as a means of financing appliance sales to cash-constrained customers who were unable to get instalment credit from banks. Instalment credit is a loan that is paid back to the lender with periodic payments (instalments) consisting of varying amounts of interest and principal (e.g., car loans and home mortgages). By the late 1950s banks were more willing to make instalment loans, so finance companies began looking outside their parent companies for business. GE Capital's consumer finance and banking businesses today provide millions of customers worldwide with loans including credit cards, personal loans, auto financing, and real estate. GE Capital Real

TABLE 3–1 Assets and Liabilities of U.S. Finance Companies, 2012

Source: *Federal Reserve Bulletin*, December 2012, federalreserve.gov.

	Billions of U.S. Dollars	Percentage of Total Assets
Assets		
Accounts receivable, gross	$1,300.8	74.8%
Consumer	578.3	33.3
Business	429.2	24.7
Real estate	293.3	16.8
Less reserves for unearned income	(24.3)	(1.4)
Less reserves for losses	(26.5)	(1.5)
Accounts receivable, net	1,250.0	71.9
All other	488.0	28.1
Total assets	1,738.0	100.0
Liabilities and Capital		
Bank loans	76.5	4.4
Commercial paper	61.8	3.6
Debt due to parent	256.6	14.8
Debt not elsewhere classified	771.5	44.4
All other liabilities	322.4	18.5
Capital, surplus, and undivided profits	249.2	14.3
Total liabilities and capital	$1,738.0	100.0%

TABLE 3–2 Assets and Liabilities of U.S. Finance Companies on December 31, 1977

Source: *Federal Reserve Bulletin*, June 1978, p. A39, federalreserve.gov.

	Billions of U.S. Dollars	Percentage of Total Assets
Assets		
Accounts receivable, gross	$ 99.2	95.1%
Consumer	44.0	42.2
Business	55.2	52.9
Less reserves for unearned income and losses	(12.7)	(12.2)
Accounts receivable, net	86.5	82.9
Cash and bank deposits	2.6	2.5
Securities	0.9	0.9
All others	14.3	13.7
Total assets	104.3	100.0
Liabilities and Capital		
Bank loans	5.9	5.7
Commercial paper	29.6	28.4
Debt		
Short-term	6.2	5.9
Long-term	36.0	34.5
Other	11.5	11.0
Capital, surplus, and undivided profits	15.1	14.5
Total liabilities and capital	$104.3	100.0%

Estate's assets total US$73 billion, while GE Energy Financial Services' assets total US$21 billion. GE Capital also now performs commercial lending and leasing in a number of industries, including aviation, healthcare, energy, fleet, franchise, and middle-market corporate finance. In the United States, Canada, and Mexico, GE

TABLE 3–3
Largest U.S. Consumer and Commercial Finance Companies, 2012 (U.S. $ millions)

Source: Insurance Information Institute and Authors' Research.

Company Name	Total receivables ($ millions)	Type of Finance Company	Ownership
General Electric Capital Corporation	285,395	Sales finance and business credit	Captive of GE
Capital One Financial	203,132	Personal credit	NYSE-listed independent that also owns Capital One Bank
SLM Corp.	167,166	Personal credit	NYSE-listed independent
JPMorgan Chase (credit card business)	124,537	Personal credit	Part of JPMorgan Chase
Ally Financial	121,259	Sales finance	Owned by consortium of investors including the U.S. Treasury, Cerberus Capital Management, and GM
American Express	117,380	Personal credit	NYSE-listed independent that also owns American Express Bank
Citigroup (credit card business)	108,819	Personal credit	Part of Citigroup
Bank of America (credit card business)	108,659	Personal credit	Part of Bank of America
HSBC Finance Corp.	86,680	Personal credit	Subsidiary of HSBC Holdings
Ford Motor Credit Company	71,517	Sales finance	Captive of Ford

Capital is a leading provider of business lending and leasing for companies of all sizes in a wide array of industries. In Europe, GE Capital has over 350,000 customers, while in Asia GE Capital provides services for over 15 million businesses and consumers. Services include acquisition finance, inventory and working capital financing, leveraged and sponsor finance, equity capital, equipment leasing, and fleet management. GE Aviation is a world-leading provider of commercial and military jet engines and components. GE Aviation owns and manages over 1,800 aircraft for over 245 customers in 75 countries.

GE Capital's exposure to the financial crisis resulted in General Electric Corp.'s market value falling by more than half during 2008. In order to reassure investors and help the GE Capital unit compete with banks that already had government protection behind their debt, the FDIC approved GE Capital's application for designation as an eligible entity under the FDIC's Temporary Liquidity Guarantee Program (TLGP). Under the TLGP, as much as US$139 billion in debt issued by GE Capital was guaranteed and backed by the full faith and credit of the United States. Granting this finance company access to the FDIC program was possible because GE Capital also owns a federal savings bank and an industrial loan company, both of which qualified for FDIC assistance.

Ally Financial (formerly GMAC) is another major finance company, founded in 1919 as the General Motors Acceptance Corporation (GMAC), a provider of financing to automotive customers. The company lost US$8 billion in 2007–2008. In light of the impact GMAC's losses were having on the financial markets, to help ensure the survival of the company, U.S. federal regulators permitted the financing arm of General Motors to become a bank holding company. The move allowed GMAC access to as much as US$6 billion in government bailout money. As of November 2012, the U.S. Treasury owned 73.8 percent of GMAC, followed by General Motors (9.9 percent), Cerberus (8.7 percent), and other third-party investors (7.6 percent).

ally.com
credit.ford.ca
gecapital.ca

GMAC (Ally) still operates and provides financial services mainly as a finance company but is in the process of selling its worldwide operations. On February 1, 2013, Royal Bank of Canada acquired the automobile financing business of Ally Financial Inc. (Ally Credit Canada Limited) and Ally's deposit business in Canada (ResMor Trust Company) for US$4.1 billion. Ally has been selling its international operations, including insurance in Mexico and auto financing in Europe and Latin America. As part of the restructuring of General Motors (GM), GMAC's parent company, the Government of Ontario provided $3.5 billion, taking a 3.8 percent ownership of GM, and the Canadian federal government provided $10.6 billion.

Because of the attractive rates that finance companies offer on some loans (such as the 0 percent financing offered on new car loans), their willingness to lend to riskier borrowers than DTIs, their often direct affiliation with manufacturing firms, and the relatively limited amount of regulation imposed on these firms, finance companies were one of the fastest-growing FI groups in North America prior to the financial crisis. Data collected by the U.S. Federal Reserve show the assets of U.S. finance companies equalled US$1,738.0 billion in 2012, as shown in Table 3–1, compared to US$104.3 billion in 1977, as shown in Table 3–2, a growth in assets of almost 1,566 percent over a 35-year period.

sales finance institutions
Institutions that specialize in making loans to the customers of a particular retailer or manufacturer.

personal credit institutions
Institutions that specialize in making instalment and other loans to consumers.

business credit institutions
Institutions that specialize in making business loans.

factoring
The process of purchasing accounts receivable from corporations (often at a discount), usually with no recourse to the seller if the receivables go bad.

captive finance company
A finance company that is wholly owned by a parent corporation.

The three major types of finance companies are (1) sales finance institutions, (2) personal credit institutions, and (3) business credit institutions. **Sales finance institutions** (e.g., Ford Motor Credit) specialize in making loans to the customers of a particular retailer or manufacturer. Because sales finance institutions can frequently process loans faster and more conveniently (generally at the location of purchase) than DTIs, this sector of the industry competes directly with DTIs for consumer loans. **Personal credit institutions** (e.g., HSBC Finance) specialize in making instalment and other loans to consumers whom DTIs deem too risky to lend to (due to low income or a bad credit history). These institutions compensate for the additional risk by charging higher interest rates than DTIs and/or accepting collateral (e.g., used cars) that DTIs do not find acceptable. **Business credit institutions** (e.g., CIT Group) are companies that provide financing to corporations, especially through equipment leasing and **factoring**, in which the finance company purchases accounts receivable from corporate customers. These accounts are purchased at a discount from their face value, and the finance company specializes in and assumes the responsibility for collecting the accounts receivable. As a result, the corporate customer no longer has to worry whether the accounts receivable will be delayed and thus receives cash for sales faster than the time it takes customers to pay their bills. Many finance companies perform more than one of these three services.

The industry is quite concentrated, with the 20 largest North American firms accounting for more than 65 percent of its assets. In addition, many of the largest finance companies, such as Ford Credit Canada, tend to be wholly owned or captive subsidiaries of major manufacturing companies. A major role of a **captive finance company** is to provide financing for the purchase of products manufactured by the parent, as Ford does for cars. In turn, the parent company is often a major source of debt finance for the captive finance company. A benefit of the captive finance company to the parent company is diversification in revenue streams. For example, as the car industry suffered from a lack of sales in the mid-2000s, Ford Motor Credit Company (FMCC) was producing record profits, as much as 80 percent of the overall profits of Ford Motor Corporation. This can also work in reverse.

As noted previously, disruptions in the credit markets, particularly the commercial paper markets, stressed the finance subsidiaries as well as the parent companies (General Motors and General Electric) in 2009.

Table 3–3 lists the top U.S. finance companies in terms of total receivables as of 2012. GE Capital was the largest, with receivables totalling US$285.4 billion. Note that six of the ten finance companies are subsidiaries of U.S. financial services holding companies. Thus, while banks such as Citibank in the United States cannot make high-risk, high-interest-rate loans due to bank regulations that restrict credit risk, banks can indirectly make these loans through a finance subsidiary or joint venture.

CONCEPT QUESTIONS

1. **What are the three major types of finance companies? What types of customers does each serve?**
2. **What is a captive finance company?**

BALANCE SHEET AND RECENT TRENDS

LO2

Assets

As mentioned above, finance companies provide three basic lending services: customer lending, consumer lending, and business lending. In Table 3–1 we showed the balance sheet of U.S. finance companies in 2012. As you can see, business and consumer loans (called *accounts receivable*) are the major assets held by finance companies, accounting for 58.0 percent of total assets, while real estate loans account for 16.8 percent of total assets. Comparing the figures in Table 3–1 to those in Table 3–2 for 1977, we see that 95.1 percent of total assets were consumer and business loans in 1977, yet no real estate loans were listed. Over the last 35 years, finance companies have replaced consumer and business loans with increasing amounts of real estate loans and other assets, although these loans have not become dominant, as is the case with DTIs. However, like DTIs, these activities create credit risk, interest rate risk, and liquidity risk that finance company managers must evaluate and manage. The financial crisis was a period that saw the downside of these risks, producing losses in all lending areas for the industry.

Table 3–4 shows the breakdown of the industry's loans in the United States from 1995 and 2012 for consumer, real estate, and business lending. In recent years, the fastest-growing areas of asset business have been in the nonconsumer finance areas, especially leasing and business lending. In 2012, consumer loans constituted 58.5 percent of all finance company loans, mortgages represented 12.8 percent, and business loans made up 28.7 percent.

Consumer Loans

Consumer loans consist of motor vehicle loans and leases, other consumer loans, and securitized loans from each category. Motor vehicle loans and leases are typically the major type of consumer loan (53.1 percent = (294.6 + 139.9 + 11.0)/839.4 of the consumer loan portfolio in 2012). Historically, finance companies have charged higher rates than banks for automobile loans. Nevertheless, sometimes these rates are lowered dramatically. For example, because new-car sales in the late 1990s and early 2000s were lower than normal, the auto finance companies owned by the major U.S. auto manufacturers slashed interest rates on new-car

TABLE 3–4
Finance Company Loans Outstanding, 1995–2012[1] (U.S. $ billions)

Source: Federal Reserve Board, *Flow of Fund Accounts*, various issues, federalreserve.gov.

	1995	Percent of Total, 1995	2012	Percent of Total, 2012
Consumer	$285.8	41.5%	$ 839.4	58.5%
Motor vehicle loans	81.1	11.8	294.6	20.5
Motor vehicle leases	80.8	11.7	139.9	9.7
Revolving[2]	28.5	4.1	74.2	5.2
Other[3]	42.6	6.2	312.2	21.8
Securitized assets				
Motor vehicle loans	34.8	5.1	11.0	0.8
Motor vehicle leases	3.5	0.5	0.0	0.0
Revolving	n.a.	n.a.	0.0	0.0
Other	14.7	2.1	7.4	0.5
Real estate	72.4	10.5	183.5	12.8
One- to four-family	n.a.	n.a.	134.0	9.3
Other	n.a.	n.a.	49.4	3.5
Securitized real estate assets[4]				
One- to four-family	n.a.	n.a.	0.0	0.0
Other	n.a.	n.a.	0.1	0.0
Business	331.2	48.0	411.8	28.7
Motor vehicles	66.5	9.6	127.5	8.9
Retail loans	21.8	3.1	23.7	1.7
Wholesale loans[5]	36.6	5.3	73.0	5.1
Leases	8.0	1.2	30.8	2.1
Equipment	188.0	27.3	202.6	14.1
Loans	58.6	8.5	120.6	8.4
Leases	129.4	18.8	82.0	5.7
Other business receivables[6]	47.2	6.8	81.7	5.7
Securitized assets[4]				
Motor vehicles	20.6	3.0	0.0	0.0
Retail loans	1.8	0.3	0.0	0.0
Wholesale loans	18.8	2.7	0.0	0.0
Equipment	8.1	1.2	0.0	0.0
Loans	5.3	0.8	0.0	0.0
Leases	2.8	0.4	0.0	0.0
Other business receivables[6]	0.8	0.1	0.0	0.0
Total	$689.5	100.0%	$1,434.7	100.0%

[1]Owned receivables are those carried on the balance sheet of the institution. Managed receivables are outstanding balances of pools upon which securities have been issued; these balances are no longer carried on the balance sheets of the loan originator.
[2]Excludes revolving credit reported as held by depository institutions that are subsidiaries of finance companies.
[3]Includes personal cash loans; mobile home loans; and loans to purchase other types of consumer goods, such as appliances, apparel, boats, and recreation vehicles.
[4]Outstanding balances of pools on which securities have been issued; these balances are no longer carried on the balance sheets of the loan originator.
[5]Credit arising from transactions between manufacturers and dealers, that is, floor plan financing.
[6]Includes loans on commercial accounts receivable, factored commercial accounts, and receivable dealer capital; small loans used primarily for business or farm purposes; and wholesale and lease paper for mobile homes, campers, and travel trailers.

loans, some to 0.0 percent. The financial crisis saw the resurrection of 0 percent car loan rates as auto manufacturers tried to boost slumping car sales. The difference between new car loans at commercial banks and those at finance companies continued to widen throughout the early 2000s. By 2002 finance companies were charging more than 3.3 percentage points less on new car loans than commercial banks, mainly due to the zero interest rates offered by the major auto manufacturers' captive finance company loans to new car buyers. However, other than for new car loans, these types of low rates are fairly rare.

subprime lender
A finance company that lends to high-risk customers.

loan sharks
Subprime lenders that charge unfairly exorbitant rates to desperate subprime borrowers.

criminal rate
Under section 347 of the Criminal Code of Canada, an effective annual rate of interest that is greater than 60 percent of the amount advanced, including fees, charges, and other expenses.

payday loans
Short-term, small-sum, unsecured consumer loans.

cpla-acps.ca

The higher rates finance companies charge for consumer loans are mostly due to the fact that finance companies attract riskier customers than banks. Customers who seek individual (or business) loans from finance companies are often those judged too risky to obtain loans from banks. We look at the analysis of borrower credit risk in Chapter 10. It is, in fact, possible for individuals to get a loan from a **subprime lender** finance company (a finance company that lends to high-risk customers) even with a bankruptcy on their records. For example, Jayhawk Acceptance Corp., one of a group of U.S. finance companies that lent money to used-car buyers with poor or no credit, began marketing loans for tummy tucks, hair transplants, and other procedures. Jayhawk entered into contracts with doctors to lend money to their patients who were seeking cosmetic surgery or some types of dental procedures. Borrowers who paid the loans within a year paid an annual rate of 9.9 percent, but those who repaid within the maximum of two years paid 13.9 percent per year. Left unanswered, however, was what Jayhawk could repossess if a borrower defaulted on a loan: Jayhawk eventually declared bankruptcy. Banks would rarely make these types of risky loans. Most finance companies that offer these types of loans charge rates commensurate with the higher risk, and there are a few **loan shark** companies that prey on desperate consumers, charging exorbitant rates. This has meant that in the past, the industry has had to fight a reputation for engaging in loansharking and charging usurious rates, a criminal offence in Canada. A class action suit brought against Easyhome Ltd., which sells appliances and furniture on credit, alleged that it charged its customers a **criminal rate** in excess of 60 percent.

Other consumer loans are **payday loans**, which are short-term, small-sum, unsecured loans to people who would not qualify for a bank loan or a bank line of credit. A payday loan is typically 10 days, provided with proof of a regular paycheque. The Canadian Payday Loan Association (CPLA) has a code of ethics and listed 19 companies (e.g., Money Mart) providing loans in Canada in 2013. Payday loans are governed by provincial legislation for consumer protection. For example, in Ontario, the cost of a payday loan is limited to $21 for each $100 borrowed.

Mortgages

high-ratio residential mortgage
A mortgage loan in which the down payment is less than 20 percent.

Residential and commercial mortgages have become an important component in finance company portfolios. However, since finance companies are not subject to as extensive regulations as are banks, they are often willing to issue mortgages to riskier borrowers than are banks, and they compensate for this additional risk by charging higher interest rates and fees. Because they have an irregular source of income, entrepreneurs have trouble qualifying for a regular or high-ratio mortgage from a DTI. Genworth MI Canada Inc., a private company, and Canada Mortgage and Housing Corporation (CMHC), a Crown corporation, provide mortgage insurance for **high-ratio residential mortgages**. CMHC also informs consumers about real estate prices, mortgages, and other housing-related issues. FIs (such as banks, credit unions, and caisses populaires) that are on the list of CMHC's approved lenders are able to provide mortgages to homebuyers that are insured by CMHC, reducing the default risk for the lender.

lien
A legal charge on real property to secure a loan such as a mortgage loan.

securitized mortgage assets
Mortgages packaged and used as assets backing secondary-market securities.

home equity line of credit (HELOC)
A loan that lets customers borrow on a line of credit secured with a second mortgage on their home.

Mortgages include all loans secured by **liens** on any type of real estate. Mortgages can be made directly or as **securitized mortgage assets.** Securitization in mortgages involves the pooling of a group of mortgages with similar characteristics, the removal of these mortgages from the balance sheet, and the subsequent sale of interest in the pool to secondary-market investors. Securitization of mortgages results in the creation of mortgage-backed securities (e.g., collateralized mortgage obligations) that can be traded in secondary mortgage markets, as we discuss in more detail in Chapter 26.

Mortgages in the loan portfolio of a finance company can be first mortgages or second mortgages in the form of home equity loans. A **home equity line of credit (HELOC)** allows customers to borrow on a line of credit secured with a second mortgage on their home. The bad-debt expense and administrative costs on home equity loans are lower than those on other finance company loans. As discussed below, in 2007–2008, a sharp rise in late payments and defaults by U.S. subprime and even relatively strong credit mortgage and home equity loan borrowers caused large losses for mortgage lenders and mortgage-backed securities investors, and ultimately was the root cause of the global financial crisis of 2008–2009.

Business Loans

Business loans represent the largest portion of the loan portfolio of finance companies. Finance companies have several advantages over banks in offering services to small-business customers. First, as mentioned earlier, they are not subject to regulations that restrict the types of products and services they can offer. Second, because finance companies do not accept deposits, they have no bank-type regulators looking directly over their shoulders.[1] Third, being in many cases subsidiaries of corporate-sector holding companies, finance companies often have substantial industry and product expertise. Fourth, as mentioned in regard to consumer loans, finance companies are more willing to accept risky customers than are banks. Fifth, finance companies generally have lower overheads than banks have. For example, they do not need tellers or branches for taking deposits.

The major subcategories of business loans are retail and wholesale motor vehicle loans and leases (US$127.5/US$411.8 = 31.0 percent of all business loans in 2012), equipment loans (49.2 percent), other business loans (19.8 percent), and securitized business assets (0.0 percent) (Table 3–4). Motor vehicle loans consist of retail loans that assist in transactions between the retail seller of the product and the ultimate consumer (i.e., passenger car fleets and commercial land vehicles for which licences are required). Wholesale loans are loan agreements between parties other than the companies' consumers. For example, FMCC provides wholesale financing to Ford dealers for inventory floor plans in which FMCC pays for Ford dealers' auto inventory received from Ford. FMCC puts a lien on each car on the showroom floor. Although the dealer pays periodic interest on the floor plan loan, it is not until the car is sold that the dealer pays for the car. These activities extend to retail and wholesale leasing of motor vehicles as well.

Business-lending activities of finance companies also include equipment loans, with the finance company either owning or leasing the equipment directly to its industrial customer or providing the financial backing for a leveraged lease, a working capital loan, or a loan to purchase or remodel the customer's facility.

[1] Finance companies do, of course, have market participants looking over their shoulders and monitoring their activities.

Finance companies often prefer to lease equipment rather than sell and finance the purchase of equipment. One reason for this is that repossession of the equipment in the event of default is less complicated when the finance company retains its title (by leasing). Further, a lease agreement generally requires no down payment, making a lease more attractive to the business customer. Finally, when the finance company retains ownership of the equipment (by leasing), it receives a tax deduction in the form of depreciation expense on the equipment.

cfla-acfl.ca

The Canadian Finance and Leasing Association (CFLA) estimated that in 2009, the assets of the asset-based financing industry totalled $87.7 billion ($34.4 billion commercial equipment financing, $6.9 billion commercial vehicle financing, and $46.4 billion retail vehicle financing). This was a decline in the industry's assets of 15 percent from $103.5 billion in 2008.

Other business loans include loans to finance accounts receivable; factored commercial accounts; small-farm loans; and wholesale and lease paper for mobile homes, campers, and trailers. As well, finance companies provide credits such as **revolvers** and **term loans**, construction loans, secured and unsecured credits, and equipment financing. For example, in 2004, GE Commercial Finance, Bank of America, CIT Business Credit Canada Inc., and HSBC Bank Canada arranged a $650 million revolving asset-based facility for Hudson's Bay Company that was secured by the company's merchandise inventory. As well, asset-backed lending and leasing provide a way to extend credit to companies that are in a troubled industry or engaged in bankruptcy proceedings. For example, Stelco, the steelmaker based in Hamilton, Ontario, which entered protection from its creditors under the **Companies' Creditors Arrangement Act (CCAA)** in 2004, was given a $500 million secured loan by Deutsche Bank and CIT Business Credit Canada as part of its restructuring. Stelco was acquired by U.S. Steel Corp. in 2007.

revolver
A credit facility that can be drawn down and repaid over the term of the loan.

term loan
A credit facility that, once it is drawn down, must be repaid according to a schedule set out in the loan agreement.

Companies' Creditors Arrangement Act (CCAA)
Legislation that allows a company that owes its creditors more than $5 million to operate under protection from its creditors while it undergoes restructuring.

Liabilities and Equity

To finance asset growth, finance companies have relied primarily on short-term commercial paper and other debt (longer-term notes and bonds). Thus, management of liquidity risk is quite different from that in banks that mostly rely on deposits (see Chapter 2). As reported in Table 3–1, in 2012 commercial paper amounted to US$61.8 billion (3.6 percent of total assets), while other debt (debt due to parents and debt not elsewhere classified) totalled US$1,028.1 billion (59.2 percent) and bank loans totalled US$76.5 billion (4.4 percent). Comparing these figures with those for 1977 (in Table 3–2), commercial paper was used more in 1977 (28.4 percent of total liabilities and capital), while other debt (short and long term) was less significant as a source of financing (40.4 percent). Finance companies also now rely less on bank loans and commercial paper for financing. In 1977, bank loans accounted for 5.7 percent of total financing. Much of the change in funding sources is due to the strong economy and low interest rates in the U.S. long-term debt markets in the early and mid-2000s and the continued low interest rates during the financial crisis of 2008–2009. Finally, in 2012, finance companies' capital-to-assets ratio was 14.3 percent, only slightly lower than the 14.5 percent in 1977.

To finance assets, finance companies rely on short-term commercial paper, with many having direct sale programs in which commercial paper is sold directly to mutual funds and other institutional investors on a continuous day-by-day basis. Most commercial paper issues have maturities of 30 days or less, although they can be issued with maturities of up to 270 days. As well, companies also have bank lines of credit as backup to commercial paper. These became common in Canada in the

1980s when the commercial paper market developed and corporate customers became able to access the capital markets directly. A standby fee is usually charged by the banks to make this facility available to their customers. The freeze in the asset-backed commercial paper markets in 2007 and 2008 required these FIs to switch to another source of short-term financing, as we discuss in Chapter 26.

Industry Performance

In the early 2000s, the outlook for the industry in North America as a whole was bright. Interest rates were at historic lows. Mortgage refinancing grew, and loan demand among lower- and middle-income consumers was strong. Because many of their potential borrowers had very low savings, no major slowdown in the demand for finance company services was expected. The largest finance companies—those that lend to less risky individual and business customers and with few subprime borrowers (e.g., HSBC Finance)—experienced strong profits and loan growth and became takeover targets for other financial services firms as well as industrial firms. For example, in 2003 Household International was acquired by British commercial bank HSBC Holdings for US$14.9 billion, one of the largest mergers and acquisitions of any kind in 2003.

hsbc.com

Nevertheless, in the mid-2000s, problems for industry participants that specialize in loans to relatively lower quality customers created large losses in the industry and a very big problem for the U.S. and the global economy. As U.S. home prices fell in 2005 and 2006 and borrowers faced rising interest rates, more people defaulted on their mortgages. At the end of 2006, the percentage of subprime mortgage loans on which payments were at least 60 days late was 14 percent, up from 6 percent in early 2005, and forecasts estimated that 19 percent of subprime mortgages originating in 2005 and 2006 would end in foreclosure. With delinquencies and defaults by borrowers rising, finance companies started a sharp pullback in subprime lending. Originations of subprime mortgages declined 30 to 35 percent in 2007 from 2006, when they totalled approximately US$600 billion, or about one-fifth of the entire U.S. mortgage market. For example, Countrywide Financial, a leading U.S. mortgage lender, lost over half its market value in the summer and fall of 2007 as it announced continued losses in its subprime mortgage portfolio. Only a US$2 billion equity investment by Bank of America in 2007 and then an acquisition offer in 2008 kept this finance company alive. Other leaders in the subprime mortgage lending market were units of some of the biggest financial services holding companies, including HSBC (the number-one subprime mortgage lender, which took a US$10.6 million charge for bad loans in 2006), General Electric, Wells Fargo, and Washington Mutual.

This crash in the subprime mortgage market created serious problems in the global economy. The U.S. housing boom of the early 2000s held defaults to very low levels because borrowers who fell behind on payments could easily sell their homes or refinance into a loan with easier terms. Further, roughly two-thirds of mortgages were packaged into securities and sold to investors worldwide. That and other innovations made credit cheaper and more available, helping more people afford a home. But as home prices flattened and dropped, more borrowers fell behind on their mortgage payments and more than 7.2 million U.S. mortgage loans fell behind on payments. As the financial crisis developed and spread, other areas of lending saw increased losses. Small business loan failure rates hit the double digits, at 11.9 percent, in 2009. Finance company performance suffered along with these decreases in loan performance.

As noted earlier, the crisis resulted in the failure of Countrywide Financial and the forced conversion of GMAC Financial Services to a bank holding company in order to prevent its failure. Another notable failure is that of CIT Group, which filed for Chapter 11 bankruptcy in November 2009. In 2008, CIT was a lender to nearly a million mostly small and medium-size businesses and companies. As the financial crisis hit, many of its borrowers became delinquent or defaulted on their loans. While CIT's failure would not affect financial markets to the same extent as the failure of a large commercial bank such as Citigroup, it could hurt the flow of credit to many businesses to which banks traditionally did not lend. At the time of its bankruptcy, CIT had assets of US$71 billion and liabilities of US$65 billion, making it one of the largest filings ever of a U.S. company—trailing only Lehman Brothers, Washington Mutual, and General Motors.

CONCEPT QUESTIONS

1. **How have the major assets held by finance companies changed over time?**
2. **How do subprime lender finance company customers differ from consumer loan customers at banks?**
3. **What advantages do finance companies offer over commercial banks to small-business customers?**

REGULATION

LO3

The Bank of Canada includes statistics on finance companies with "non-depository credit intermediaries and other institutions," the FSB defines finance companies very broadly as "non-bank financial entities that provide loans to other entities," and the U.S. Federal Reserve defines a finance company as "a firm (other than a depository institution) whose primary assets are loans to individuals and businesses," whereas a bank is defined as an institution that *both* accepts deposits and makes loans. Finance companies, like DTIs, are FIs that borrow funds for relending, making a profit on the difference between the interest rate on borrowed funds and the rate charged on the loans. Also, like DTIs, finance companies are subject to any usury ceilings on the maximum loan rate assigned to any individual customer and are regulated as to the extent to which they can collect on delinquent loans (e.g., legal mechanisms to be followed). However, because finance companies do not accept deposits, they are not subject to extensive oversight by any specific federal, state, or provincial/territorial regulators as are banks—even though they offer services that compete directly with those of DTIs (e.g., consumer instalment loans and mortgages). The lack of regulatory oversight for these companies enables them to offer a wide scope of "banklike" services and yet avoid the expense of regulatory compliance.

However, because of the impact that NBFIs, including finance companies, had on the U.S. economy during the financial crisis, and as a result of the need for the U.S. Federal Reserve to rescue several NBFIs, U.S. regulators proposed that NBFIs receive more oversight. At the height of the financial crisis, the Federal Reserve stepped in to rescue numerous finance companies, including GMAC, GE Capital, and CIT Group. Credit card lenders American Express and Discover Financial (as well as investment banks Goldman Sachs and Morgan Stanley) also became bank holding companies in 2008. As a result, as part of the 2010 Financial Services Regulatory

Overhaul Bill, the U.S. government was provided with a new regime to resolve NBFIs whose failure could have serious systemic effects.

Since finance companies are heavy borrowers in the capital markets and do not enjoy the same regulatory "safety nets," such as deposit insurance and borrowing from the central bank, they need to signal their solvency and safety to investors. Signals of solvency and safety are usually sent by holding higher equity or capital–asset ratios—and therefore lower leverage ratios—than banks hold. For example, in 2012 the aggregate balance sheet (Table 3–1) shows a capital–assets ratio of 14.3 percent for finance companies. This can be compared to the capital–assets ratio for Canadian banks of 5.7 percent reported in Table 2–4 and 11.5 percent for U.S. banks. Larger, captive finance companies also use default protection guarantees from their parent companies and/or guarantees such as letters of credit or lines of credit purchased for a fee from high-quality commercial or investment banks as additional protection against insolvency risk and as a device to increase their ability to raise additional funds in the capital and money markets. Thus, this group will tend to operate with lower capital-to-asset ratios than smaller finance companies. Given that there is little regulatory oversight of this industry, having sufficient capital and access to financial guarantees is critical to their continued ability to raise funds. Thus, finance companies operate more like nonfinancial, nonregulated companies than other types of FIs.

CONCEPT QUESTIONS

1. **Since finance companies seem to compete in the same lending markets as banks, why aren't they subject to the same regulations as banks?**
2. **How do finance companies signal solvency and safety to investors?**

GOVERNMENT FINANCING ENTITIES

LO4

Crown Corporations in Canada

Additional financing and export-related services to business are provided by Crown corporations, which are government entities that provide complementary services to support business in Canada. None of these organizations are large, but they do provide services to areas of the Canadian economy—small and medium-sized businesses, farmers, and home buyers—that may not be served by the other FIs previously discussed, either because they are too small or because they are too risky. Each has a different mandate, as discussed below.

Business Development Bank of Canada

bdc.ca

The Business Development Bank of Canada (BDC) was created in 1944 by an act of Parliament to provide loans to Canadian companies. While its initial focus was on manufacturing, it has evolved over the years into support for small and medium-sized businesses in Canada by providing consulting services, financing, and **venture capital**. In 1995, the Business Development Bank of Canada Act was passed, giving the BDC the mandate to support the development of exporting and technology. For example, during the credit crisis in 2008, the BDC provided additional support and advice for small businesses. Prior to 2008, BDC issued its own short- and long-term debt in the financial markets. This debt was guaranteed by the Government of Canada. Since 2008, the BDC has been funded by borrowing directly from the Government of Canada.

venture capital
Business development financing provided in exchange for an equity position and some level of management control.

Canada Mortgage and Housing Corporation

cmhc.ca

The mandate of Canada Mortgage and Housing Corporation (CMHC) is the promotion of housing in Canada. It was formed in 1946 to provide housing for veterans of World War II. Over the years, its mandate has expanded to developing housing programs for low-income housing and first-time homebuyers, as well as supporting quality housing. CMHC performs a major role by providing mortgage insurance for high-ratio residential mortgages extended by approved lenders under the National Housing Act. CMHC also insures mortgage-backed securities, as discussed in detail in Chapter 26.

Export Development Canada

edc.ca

Export Development Canada (EDC) supports export and import companies by providing services such as insurance, financing, and bonding, as well as advice on doing business outside Canada. EDC is different from the other Crown corporations discussed here, as it is self-financing. Its focus is on international business, so it has offices in seven countries that provide local support for Canadian exporters. EDC's business is primarily small and medium-sized exporters, so it provides advice as well as online risk management tools.

Farm Credit Canada

www.fcc-fac.ca

Farm Credit Canada (FCC) completed 50 years in business in 2009. It was created in 1959 to support the agriculture sector in Canada and reports to the minister of agriculture. FCC provides services such as loans, life and accident insurance, and venture capital to farmers and others in the agricultural business in Canada, including equipment manufacturers and dealers, sawmills, wholesalers, and processors. Similar to the BDC, as discussed above, FCC came under the Consolidated Borrowing Program in April 2008, which allows it to borrow directly from the Canadian government. Therefore, it no longer issues its own debt.

GLOBAL ISSUES

While commercial banks are the most important source of credit supply in many foreign countries, particularly emerging market economies, NBFIs (finance companies, credit unions, and building societies) account for a substantial part of the outstanding credit by all FIs. The 2012 survey of practices in 25 countries done by the FSB indicated that the amount of nonbank financial intermediation and the level of regulation varies across countries. Figure 3–1 shows the share of assets of NBFIs for 20 countries and the Eurozone that participated in the survey. Note that at the end of 2011 the U.S. and Eurozone NBFIs had the highest percentage of financial sector assets (of banks, insurance companies and pension funds, public FIs, and central bank assets) at 35 percent and 33 percent, respectively. While the U.S. shadow banking industry was the largest in the world at US$23 billion, this sector's share of the market had decreased significantly since year-end 2005. In other countries, such as Canada, Australia, and Switzerland, which have strong banking sectors, shadow banking constituted just 1 percent of the total assets. Therefore, in many jurisdictions, the regulation of these FIs is not considered crucial to the stability of the financial system.

FIGURE 3–1
Share of Assets of NBFIs

Source: Global Shadow Banking Monitoring Report 2012, p. 10. Financial Stability Board, www.financialstabilityboard.org.

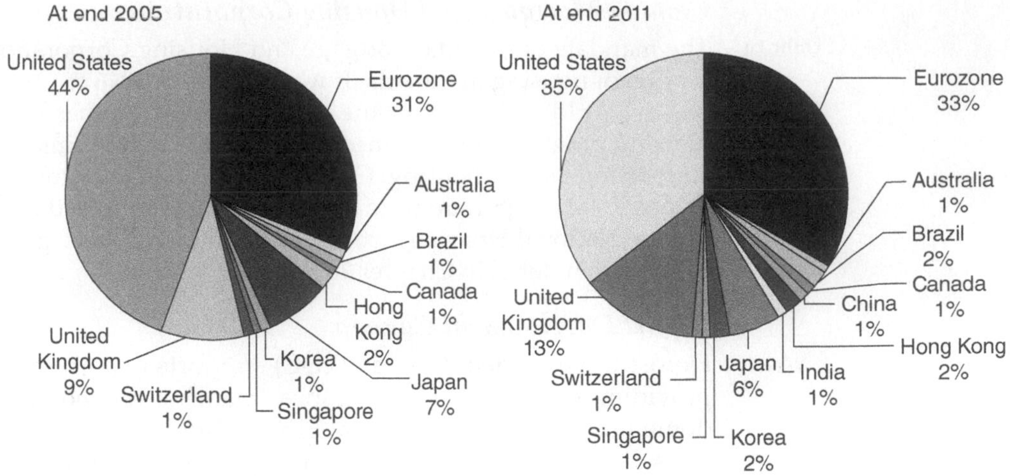

Source: National flow of funds data.

www.financialstabilityboard.org
worldbank.org

An issue related to financial services and global FIs is the development of a sound global financial system, which means sound financial infrastructure, particularly in developing countries. Monetary and technical support for this development is provided by the World Bank Group, an international organization owned by its member countries. The World Bank provides loans, technical assistance, and advice through the International Bank for Reconstruction and Development (IBRD), the International Development Association (IDA), the International Finance Corporation (IFC), the Multilateral Investment Guarantee Agency (MIGA), and the International Centre for Settlement of Investment Disputes (ICSID).

Questions and Problems

1. What is the primary function of finance companies? How do finance companies differ from DTIs?
2. What are the three major types of finance companies? To which market segments do each of these types of companies provide service?
3. What are the major types of consumer loans? Why are the rates charged by consumer finance companies typically higher than those charged by commercial banks?
4. Why have home equity loans become popular? What are securitized mortgage assets?
5. What advantages do finance companies have over commercial banks in offering services to small-business customers? What are the major subcategories of business loans? Which category is the largest?
6. What have been the primary sources of financing for finance companies?
7. How do finance companies make money? What risks does this process entail? How do these risks differ for a finance company versus a commercial bank?
8. How does the amount of equity as a percentage of total assets compare for finance companies and banks? What accounts for this difference?

CHAPTER 4

SECURITIES, BROKERAGE, AND INVESTMENT BANKING

After studying this chapter you should be able to:

LO1 Discuss the size, structure, and composition of companies in the securities industry in Canada.

LO2 Explain the difference between integrated firms, institutional firms, and retail firms.

LO3 Discuss the eight activities that securities firms engage in.

LO4 Discuss balance sheet and revenue trends for securities firms.

INTRODUCTION

LO1

Securities firms and investment banks help net suppliers of funds (e.g., households) transfer funds to net users of funds (e.g., businesses) at a low cost and with a maximum degree of efficiency. Unlike other types of FIs, securities firms and investment banks do not transform the securities issued by the net users of funds into claims that may be "more" attractive to the net suppliers of funds (e.g., banks and their creation of bank deposits and loans). Rather, they serve as brokers intermediating between fund suppliers and users.

The securities industry in Canada performs two functions: (1) the raising of debt and equity securities, including the origination, underwriting, and placement of securities in money and capital markets for corporate or government issuers, and (2) assistance in the trading of securities in the secondary markets, including brokerage services and/or market-making. Firms in the securities industry that specialize in the purchase, sale, and brokerage of existing securities (the retail side of the business) are called **broker-dealers**, whereas firms that specialize in originating, underwriting, and distributing issues of new securities are called **investment banks**.

broker-dealers
Securities firms that assist in the trading of existing securities.

investment banks
Firms that specialize in originating, underwriting, and distributing issues of new securities.

Investment banking also includes corporate finance activities such as advising on mergers and acquisitions (M&As), as well as advising on the restructuring of existing corporations. Merger activity in Canada parallels that of the United States. Canadian investment banks (e.g., RBC Capital Markets, Scotia Capital) are in direct competition domestically with the major Wall Street investment firms (e.g., J. P. Morgan, Goldman Sachs), which lead the world in terms of size, experience, research capability, and relationships. In fact, the history of the investment industry since the 1980s can be viewed as one of consolidation within Canada and increasing competition with globally dominant firms. M&A activity follows the economy, reaching US$4.5 trillion worldwide in 2007. As the financial crisis hit, worldwide M&A activity fell to US$2.9 trillion in 2008, US$1.8 trillion in 2009, and US$1.7 trillion in 2010. As the global economy started to recover in 2011 and 2012, worldwide M&A activity rose to US$2.33 trillion and US$2.04 trillion, respectively.

integrated firm
A securities firm offering a full range of investment services to retail, institutional, and corporate customers.

underwriting
Assisting in the issue of new securities.

Much like other sectors of the financial system, the global investment banking industry has undergone substantial structural changes since the financial crisis, particularly in the United States. Some of these consolidations include the acquisition of Bear Stearns by JPMorgan Chase, the bankruptcy of Lehman Brothers, and the acquisition of Merrill Lynch by Bank of America. Indeed, the U.S. investment banking industry has seen the failure or acquisition of all but two of its major firms (Goldman Sachs and Morgan Stanley), which converted to commercial bank holding companies in 2008.

In this chapter we present an overview of (1) the size, structure, and composition of the industry; (2) the balance sheet and recent trends; and (3) the regulation of the industry.

SIZE, STRUCTURE, AND COMPOSITION OF THE INDUSTRY

LO2

regulatory capital
Capital and margin requirements, including shareholders' equity and subordinated debt, as defined by the Investment Industry Association of Canada for its members.

Investment Industry Association of Canada (IIAC)
The national association representing the investment industry's position on securities regulation, public policy, and industry issues on behalf of 166 IIROC-regulated investment dealer Member firms in the Canadian securities industry.

The current structure of the securities industry dates back to the late 1980s when the federal government changed the Bank Act to allow banks, trust companies, and foreign firms to operate in the industry. This resulted in many securities firms, previously wholly owned and operated by partnerships, being taken over by the major banks, creating the six largest integrated bank-owned firms (BMO Nesbitt Burns, CIBC World Markets, National Bank Financial, RBC Dominion Securities Limited, Scotia Capital, and TD Securities). The global stock market crash of 1987 accelerated the consolidation by making investment dealers cheap to acquire. Table 4–1 shows the investment firms acquired and the year of acquisition for the largest investment dealers in Canada ranked by their revenue in 2012.

As shown in Figure 4–1 and Table 4–2, the Canadian securities industry can be divided into integrated, institutional, and retail firms based on their activities as follows:

1. **Integrated firms:** The integrated firms service retail customers (especially in acting as broker-dealers, assisting in the trading of existing securities) and corporate customers (such as **underwriting**, assisting in the issue of new securities), as well as institutional customers (servicing other FIs, such as insurance companies, mutual funds, banks, trust companies, and pension funds). The 11 integrated firms generated 74.0 percent of the total operating revenue of the securities industry in 2012 and, as well, represented 69.7 percent of the total shareholders' equity of $17.1 billion and 72.3 percent of the **regulatory capital** (shareholders' equity and subordinated debt as defined by Regulation 100 of the **Investment Industry**

TABLE 4–1
Canadian Bank Investment Firm Acquisitions, 1987–1996

Firm	2012 Revenue ($ millions)	Company Acquired, Year of Acquisition
1. RBC Capital Markets	$6,188.0	Dominion Securities, 1988 Pemberton Willoughby Investment Co., 1989 McNeil Mantha, 1991 Richardson Greenshields, 1996
2. Scotia Capital	3,582.0	McLeod, Young, Weir, 1987
3. BMO Nesbitt Burns	2,265.0	Nesbitt Thomson, 1987 Burns Fry, 1994
4. TD Securities	2,654.0	Marathon Brokerage, 1993
5. CIBC World Markets	2,060.0	Wood Gundy Inc., 1988
6. National Bank Financial	1,365.0	Lévesque Beaubien Geoffrion, 1988 First Marathon Securities, 1993

Source: Company websites and 2012 annual reports.

FIGURE 4–1
Securities Industry Employment in Canada, 2013

Source: Investment Industry Association of Canada, "Securities Industry Performance Q1 2013," iiac.ca.

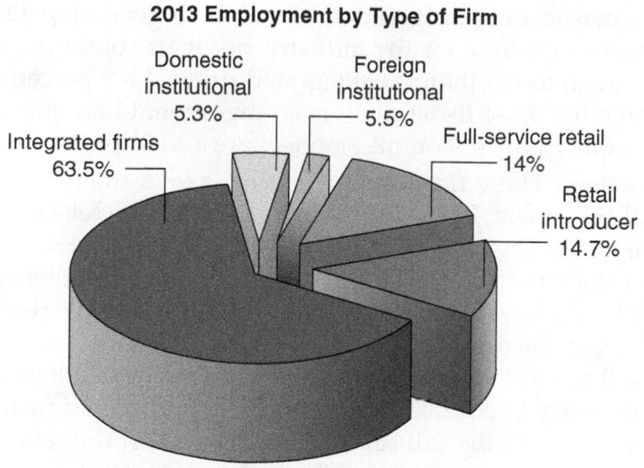

Association of Canada (IIAC) for its members). They derived 31.7 percent of their revenue from mutual fund and other commissions. Fee income represented 21.1 percent of their operating revenue in 2012. The integrated firms had the highest return at 16.6 percent.

institutional firm
A securities firm offering services only to other FIs, such as insurance companies, mutual funds, banks, trust companies, and pension funds.

2. **Institutional firms:** These firms offer investment services primarily to other FIs. They may be domestic (e.g., Maison Placements Canada Inc.) or subsidiaries of U.S. or European firms (e.g., Deutsche Bank Securities). As shown in Table 4–2,

TABLE 4–2 Structure and Statistics of the Securities Industry in Canada, 2012 ($ millions)

	Industry Totals	Integrated Firms	Total Institutional	Full-Service Retail Firms	Retail Introducer Firms
Number of firms	196	11	79	33	73
Number of employees	39,555	25,146	3,115	5,547	5,747
Shareholders' equity	$17,087	$ 11,902	$ 3,982	$ 643	$ 559
Regulatory capital	34,343	24,989	7,735	838	782
Client cash holdings	38,684	33,018	1,756	2,783	1,127
Client margin debt outstanding	14,432	n.a.	n.a.	n.a.	n.a.
Annual return					
(net profit/shareholders' equity)	12.6%	16.6%	6.9%	−7.9%	−8.7%
Revenue					
Commission	$ 5,117	$ 3,597	$ 558	$ 503	$ 458
Investment banking:					
New equity issues	1,782	1,325	315	88	54
New debt issues	816	659	103	45	8
Corporate advisory fees	967	612	338	9	8
Fixed-income trading	1,176	1,031	93	29	22
Equity trading	118	166	(61)	3	10
Net interest	1,131	942	63	64	62
Fees	3,206	2,400	190	340	276
Other	1,020	618	263	64	75
Total revenue	$15,332	$ 11,350	$ 1,863	$ 1,146	$ 973
Percentage of industry total revenue	100.0%	74.0%	12.2%	7.5%	6.3%

Source: Investment Industry Association of Canada, *Securities Industry Performance 2013, Q1,* iiac.ca.

retail firm
A securities firm offering investment services only to retail investors, either on a full-service or on a discount basis.

full-service retail
A securities firm that provides all services to clients, including back-office functions.

retail introducer
A securities firm that contracts with a full-service firm to carry out specified trading functions on its behalf.

discount brokers
Stockbrokers that conduct trades for customers but do not offer investment advice.

79 domestic and foreign institutional firms generated 12.2 percent of the total operating revenue for the industry, but their combined annual return in 2012 was much lower than the integrated firms at 6.9 percent. The major source of income for these firms came from investment banking activities, particularly new equity issues. Commission fees are also important.

3. **Retail firms:** These firms act primarily as investment advisors and brokers for retail customers. Retail firms can be divided into **full-service retail** and **retail introducer** firms. They also include specialized **discount brokers**, who carry out trades for customers online or offline without offering investment advice or tips and usually charge lower commissions than do full-service retail firms. As shown in Table 4–2, the revenue of retail firms comes from commissions on mutual funds as well as other securities. Retail firms provided 13.8 percent of the revenue of the industry in 2012, ranking behind the integrated firms. As well, the annual return for both the full-service retail firms and the retail introducer firms was negative (–7.9 percent and –8.7 percent, respectively) in 2013.

In addition, specialized electronic trading securities firms (such as Scotiabank's iTRADE) provide a platform for customers to trade online without the use of a broker. Also, venture capital firms pool money from individual investors and other FIs (e.g., hedge funds, pension funds, and insurance companies) to fund relatively small new businesses (e.g., in biotechnology). Venture capital firms generally play an active management role in the firms in which they invest and hold significant equity stakes. This differentiates them from traditional banking and securities firms.

LO3

Securities firms engage in as many as eight key activity areas: investment banking, venture capital, market-making, trading, investing, cash management and banking services, M&As, and back-office and other service functions. As we describe each of these below, note that while each activity is available to a firm's customers independently, many of these activities can be and are conducted simultaneously (such as M&As financed by new issues of debt and equity underwritten by the M&A advising firm) for a firm's customers.

IPO
An initial, or first-time, public offering of debt or equity by a corporation.

1. Investment Banking

Investment banking refers to activities related to underwriting and distributing new issues of debt and equity. New issues can be either primary, the first-time issues of companies (sometimes called **IPOs** [initial public offerings]), or secondary issues (the new issues of seasoned firms whose debt or equity is already trading).

tsx.com

Figure 4–2 shows the dollar value of new common equity issues (secondary issues, IPOs, conventional and convertible preferred shares) from 2001 to 2012. The disruptions in the global capital markets in 2007 and 2008 resulted in significant declines in common equity financings (Figure 4–2) and the issuance of corporate debt, as shown in Figure 4–3. Much of the equity activity after the crisis came from banks that were raising capital to meet their capital adequacy requirements (see Chapter 20). However, the issue of debt by governments (federal and provincial crown corporations and federal, provincial, and municipal governments) increased to a high of $201.9 billion in 2011.

As shown in Tables 4–1 and 4–2, the large integrated firms in Canada (which include the investment banking subsidiaries of the Big Six Canadian banks) were profitable in 2012 and captured the largest portion of revenue from the investment

FIGURE 4–2
Common Equity Financings in Canada, 2001–2012

Source: Investment Industry Association of Canada, *IIAC Annual New Issues,* iiac.ca.

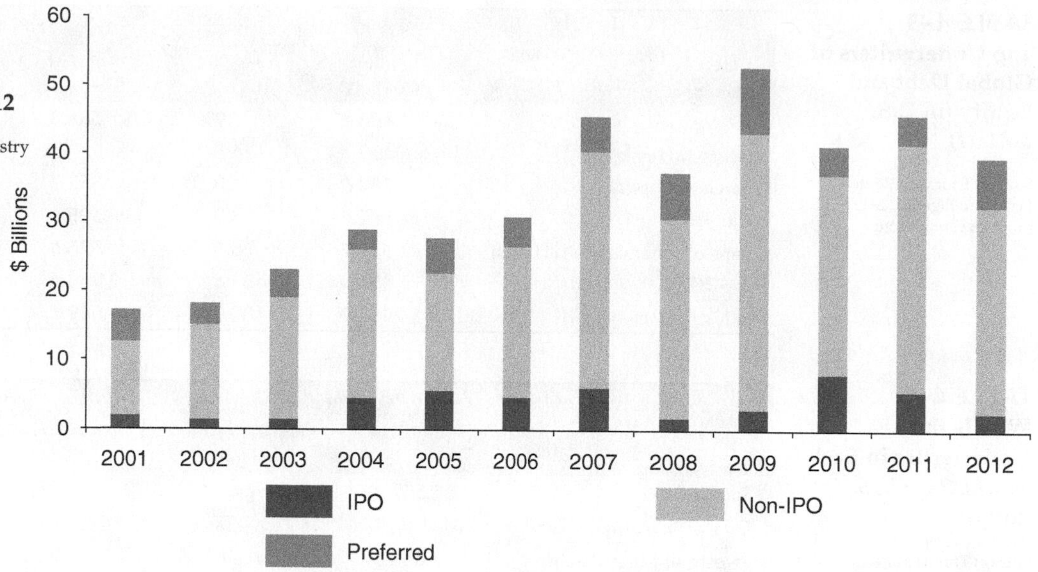

banking activities of new equity and debt issues and fees. Table 4–3 shows the top five underwriters of global debt and equity in 2011 and 2012. The $289.8 billion total for Canadian debt and equity issues of Figures 4–2 and 4–3 is significantly less than the US$6.2 trillion for the industry globally in 2012. The top five common stock underwriters represented 32.2 percent and the top ten firms represented more than 50 percent of the industry total, suggesting that the industry is dominated globally by a handful of top-tier underwriting firms. Top-tier rating and the implied reputation this brings have a huge effect in this business. At times, investment banks have refused to participate in an issue because their name would not be placed where they desired it on the "tombstone" advertisement announcing the issue and its major underwriters.

FIGURE 4–3
Government and Corporate Debt Annual New Issues 2001–2012

Source: Investment Industry Association of Canada, *IIAC Annual New Issues,* iiac.ca.

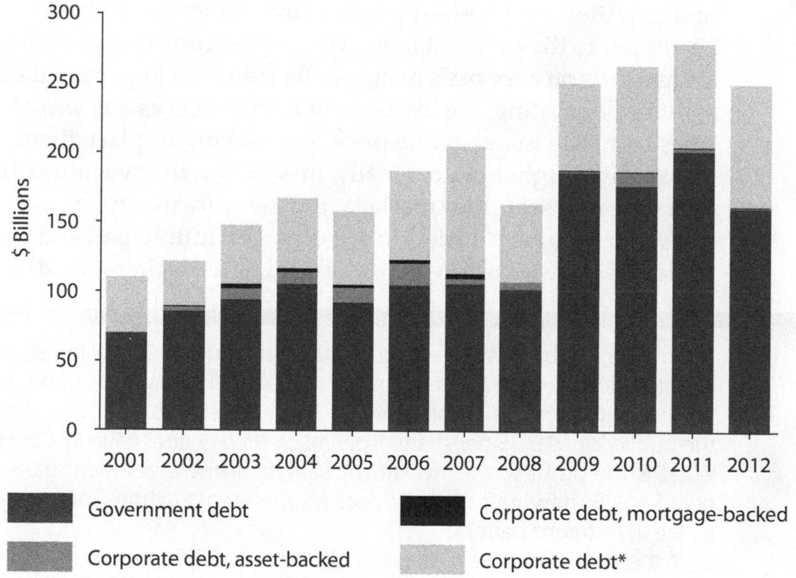

*Conventional, convertible, and medium-term notes.

TABLE 4–3
Top Underwriters of Global Debt and Equity (in U.S. dollars)

Source: Thomson Reuters Deals Intelligence, 2013, thomsonreuters.com

	Full Year 2012		Full Year 2011		
Manager	Amount ($ billions)	Market Share (%)	Amount ($ billions)	Rank	Market Share (%)
J.P. Morgan	$ 488.6	7.9%	$ 384.8	1	6.9%
Deutsche Bank	409.7	6.6	371.3	2	6.7
Barclays Capital	384.6	6.2	365.9	3	6.6
Citigroup	373.6	6.0	305.6	5	5.5
Bank of America Merrill Lynch	339.1	5.5	325.6	4	5.9
Top 10	3,323.2	53.6	2,958.4		53.2
Industry total	$6,191.7	100.0%	$5,569.7		100.0%

TABLE 4–4
Who Is the Lead Underwriter in Each Market? (in U.S. dollars)

Source: Thomson Reuters Deals Intelligence, 2013, thomsonreuters.com

	Full Year 2012		Full Year 2011	
Type	Amount ($ billions)	Top-Ranked Manager	Amount ($ billions)	Top-Ranked Manager
Total debt	$5,557.2	J.P. Morgan	$4,952.2	Barclays Capital
Convertible debt	64.2	Deutsche Bank	65.4	Goldman Sachs
Investment-grade debt	2,655.3	J.P. Morgan	2,258.7	J.P. Morgan
Mortgage-backed securities	462.0	Deutsche Bank	521.5	Bank of America Merrill Lynch
Asset-backed securities	321.0	J.P. Morgan	243.0	Bank of America Merrill Lynch
Common stock	566.2	Goldman Sachs	551.9	Goldman Sachs
IPOs	117.4	Morgan Stanley	163.8	Goldman Sachs
Syndicated loans	3,226.8	J.P. Morgan	3,934.0	J.P. Morgan

private placement
A securities issue placed with one or a few large institutional investors.

Securities underwritings can be undertaken through either public offerings or private offerings. In a private offering, the investment banker acts as a **private placement** agent for a fee, placing the securities with one or a few large institutional investors, such as life insurance companies. In a public offering, the securities may be underwritten on a best-efforts or a firm commitment basis, and the securities may be offered to the public at large. With best-efforts underwriting, investment bankers act as *agents* on a fee basis related to their success in placing the issue. In firm commitment underwriting, the investment banker acts as a *principal*, purchasing the securities from the issuer at one price and seeking to place them with public investors at a slightly higher price. Finally, in addition to investment banking operations in the corporate securities markets, the investment banker may participate as an underwriter (primary dealer) in government, municipal, and asset-backed securities. Table 4–4 shows the top-ranked global underwriters for 2012 and 2013.

EXAMPLE 4–1
Best-Efforts versus Firm Commitment Securities Offering

An investment bank agrees to underwrite an issue of 20 million shares of stock for Murray Construction Corp. on a firm commitment basis. The investment bank pays $15.50 per share to Murray Construction Corp. for the 20 million shares of stock. It then sells those shares to the public for $16.35 per share. How much money does Murray Construction Corp. receive? What is the profit to the investment banker? If the investment bank can sell the shares for only $14.75, how much money does Murray Construction Corp. receive? What is the profit to the investment bank?

If the investment bank sells the stock for $16.35 per share, Murray Construction Corp. receives $15.50 × 20,000,000 shares = $310,000,000. The profit to the investment bank is

(\$16.35 − \$15.50) × 20,000,000 shares = \$17,000,000. The stock price of Murray Construction Corp. is \$16.35 since that is what the public agrees to pay. From the perspective of Murray Construction Corp., the \$17 million represents the commission that it must pay to issue the stock.

If the investment bank sells the stock for \$14.75 per share, Murray Construction Corp. still receives \$15.50 × 20,000,000 shares = \$310,000,000. The profit to the investment bank is (\$14.75 − \$15.50) × 20,000,000 shares = −\$15,000,000. The stock price of Murray Construction Corp. is \$14.75 since that is what the public agrees to pay. From the perspective of the investment bank, the −\$15 million represents a loss for the firm commitment it made to Murray Construction Corp. to issue the stock.

Suppose, instead, that the investment bank agrees to underwrite the 20 million shares on a best-efforts basis. The investment bank is able to sell 18.4 million shares for \$15.50 per share, and it charges Murray Construction Corp. \$0.375 per share sold. How much money does Murray Construction Corp. receive? What is the profit to the investment bank? If the investment bank can sell the shares for only \$14.75, how much money does Murray Construction Corp. receive? What is the profit to the investment bank?

If the investment bank sells the stock for \$15.50 per share, Murray Construction Corp. receives (\$15.50 − \$0.375) × 18,400,000 shares = \$278,300,000, the investment bank's profit is \$0.375 × 18,400,000 shares = \$6,900,000, and the stock price is \$15.50 per share since that is what the public pays.

If the investment bank sells the stock for \$14.75 per share, Murray Construction Corp. receives (\$14.75 − \$0.375) × 18,400,000 shares = \$264,500,000, the investment bank's profit is still \$0.375 × 18,400,000 shares = \$6,900,000, and the stock price is \$14.75 per share since that is what the public pays.

2. *Venture Capital*

A difficulty for new and small firms in obtaining debt financing from commercial banks is that these FIs are generally not willing or able to make loans to new companies with no assets or business history. In this case, new and small firms often turn to investment banks (and other firms) that make venture capital investments to get capital financing as well as advice. **Venture capital** is a professionally managed pool of money used to finance new and often high-risk firms. Venture capital is generally provided to back an untried company and its managers in return for an equity investment in the firm. Venture capital firms do not make outright loans. Rather, they purchase an equity interest in the firm that gives them the same rights and privileges as are associated with an equity investment made by the firm's other owners. The terms *venture capital* and *private equity* are often used interchangeably. However, in Canada, venture capital is a subset of private equity. **Private equity** can consist of buyout capital for an established firm that is restructuring. **Mezzanine capital** is the same as buyout capital, but it is often provided in the form of subordinated debt or preferred shares. Venture capital firms, generally using the pooled investment resources of institutions and wealthy individuals, concern themselves more with startup business concerns, while private equity firms acquire the investment funds they use from sources such as equity securities and nonpublicly traded stocks as well as the institutional and individual investment pooling used by venture capital firms. Further, venture capital firms tend to utilize teams of either scientific or business professionals to help identify new and emerging technologies in which to place their money. Private equity firms deal more with existing companies that have already proven themselves in the business field. As a result of the financial crisis, the differences between venture capital firms and private equity firms have become less distinct. With fewer new ventures being

venture capital
A professionally managed pool of money used to finance new and often high-risk firms.

private equity
A professionally managed pool of money that provides buyout, mezzanine, and venture capital

mezzanine capital
Equity capital provided in the form of subordinated debt and preferred shares.

brought forth, there has been greater competition between the two types of investment institutions, with both types searching for and funding the same kinds of new and small firms.

institutional venture capital firms
Business entities whose sole purpose is to find and fund the most promising new firms.

There are many types of venture capital firms. **Institutional venture capital firms** are business entities whose sole purpose is to find and fund the most promising new firms. Private-sector institutional venture capital firms include venture capital limited partnerships (which are established by professional venture capital firms, acting as general partners in the firm, organizing and managing the firm and eventually liquidating their equity investment), financial venture capital firms (subsidiaries of investment or commercial banks), and corporate venture capital firms (subsidiaries of nonfinancial corporations that generally specialize in making start-up investments in high-tech firms). Limited-partner venture capital firms dominate the industry. In addition to these private-sector institutional venture capital firms, there are government-sponsored venture capital funds such as those provided by the Business Development Corporation (BDC), discussed in Chapter 3. In contrast to institutional venture capital firms, **angel venture capitalists (or angels)** are wealthy individuals who make equity investments. Angel venture capitalists have invested much more in new and small firms than institutional venture capital firms. Detailed information about the Canadian venture capital market is available from the Canadian Venture Capital and Private Equity Association (CVCA), which had over 1,900 members in 2012.

angel venture capitalists (or angels)
Wealthy individuals who make equity investments.

cvca.ca

Venture capital firms receive many unsolicited proposals for funding from new and small firms. A majority of these requests are rejected. Venture capital firms look for two things in making their decisions to invest in a firm. The first is a high return. Venture capital firms are willing to invest in high-risk new and small firms. However, they require high levels of returns (sometimes as high as 700 percent within five to seven years) to take on these risks. The second is an easy exit. Venture capital firms realize a profit on their investments by eventually selling their interests in the firm. They want a quick and easy exit opportunity when it comes time to sell. Basically, venture capital firms provide equity funds to new, unproven, and young firms. This separates venture capital firms from commercial banks, which prefer to invest in existing, financially secure businesses.

3. Market-Making

Market-making involves creating a secondary market in an asset by a securities firm or investment bank. Thus, in addition to being primary dealers in government securities and underwriters of corporate bonds and equities, investment bankers make a secondary market in these instruments. Market-making can involve either agency or principal transactions. *Agency* transactions are two-way transactions on behalf of *customers*, for example, acting as a *stockbroker* or dealer for a fee or commission. On the TSX, a market-maker in a stock may, upon the placement of orders by its customers, buy the stock at $78 from one customer and immediately resell it at $79 to another customer. The $1 difference between the buy and sell price is usually called the bid–ask spread and represents a large portion of the market-maker's profit.

In *principal* transactions, the market-maker seeks to profit on the price movements of securities and takes either long or short inventory positions for its own account. (Or an inventory position may be taken to stabilize the market in the securities.) In the example above, the market-maker would buy the stock at $78 and hold it in its own portfolio in expectation of a price increase later on.

Normally, market-making can be a fairly profitable business; however, in periods of market stress or high volatility, these profits can rapidly disappear. For example, on the New York Stock Exchange (NYSE), market-makers, in return for having monopoly power in market-making for individual stocks (e.g., IBM), have an affirmative obligation to buy stocks from sellers even when the market is crashing. This caused a number of actual and near bankruptcies for NYSE market-makers at the time of the October 1987 market crash when liquidity was significantly impaired and many firms withdrew from market-making.

4. Trading

Trading is closely related to the market-making activities just described, where a trader takes an active net position in an underlying instrument or asset. There are at least six types of trading activities:

1. *Position trading* involves purchasing large blocks of securities on the expectation of a favourable price move. Position traders maintain long or short positions for intervals of up to several weeks or even months. Rather than attempting to profit from very short term movements in prices, as day traders do, position traders take relatively longer views of market trends. Such positions also facilitate the smooth functioning of the secondary markets in such securities.
2. *Pure arbitrage* entails buying an asset in one market at one price and selling it immediately in another market at a higher price. Pure arbitrage "locks in" profits that are available in the markets. This profit position usually occurs with no equity investment, the use of only very short term borrowed funds, and reduced transaction costs for securities firms. Pure arbitrageurs often attempt to profit from price discrepancies that may exist between the spot, or cash, price of a security and its corresponding futures price. Some important theoretical pricing relationships in futures markets should exist with spot markets and prices. When these relationships get out of line, pure arbitrageurs enter the market to exploit them.
3. *Risk arbitrage* involves buying securities in anticipation of some information release, such as a merger or takeover announcement or an interest rate announcement. It is termed *risk arbitrage* because if the event does not actually occur—for example, if a merger does not take place or the Bank of Canada does not change interest rates—the trader stands to lose money.
4. *Program trading* is defined as the simultaneous buying and selling of a large portfolio of different stocks using computer programs to initiate such trades. Program trading is often associated with seeking a risk arbitrage between a cash market price and the *futures* market price of that instrument, for example, buying the cash S&P index and selling futures contracts on the S&P index. Because computers are used to continuously monitor stock and futures prices—and can even initiate buy or sell orders—these trades are classified separately as *program trading*.
5. *Stock brokerage* involves the trading of securities on behalf of individuals who want to transact in the money or capital markets. To conduct such transactions, individuals contact their broker (such as CIBC Capital Markets), which then sends the orders to its representative at the exchange to conduct the trades. Large brokerage firms often have several licences on the floor of a stock exchange (e.g., TSX), through which their commission brokers trade orders from the firm's clients or for the firm's own account.

6. *Electronic brokerage*, offered by major brokers, involves direct access, via the Internet, to the trading floor, thereby bypassing traditional brokers. Many securities firms and investment banks offer online trading services to their customers as well as direct access to a client representative (stockbroker). Thus, customers may now conduct trading activities from their homes and offices through their accounts at securities firms. Because services provided by a typical brokerage firm are bypassed, the cost per share is generally lower and the price may be advantageous compared with trading directly on the exchanges. Users of the system can often use the network to discover existing sizes and quotes of offers to buy or sell. Interested parties can then negotiate with each other using the system's computers.

As with many activities of securities firms, such trading can be conducted on behalf of a customer as an agent (or broker), or on behalf of the firm as a principal. When trading at the retail level occurs on behalf of customers, it is often called *brokerage* (or stock brokering).

5. *Investing*

Investing involves managing not only pools of assets such as closed- and open-end mutual funds but also pension funds in competition with life insurance companies. Securities firms can manage such funds either as agents for other investors or as principals for themselves. The objective in funds management is to choose asset allocations to beat some return–risk performance benchmark such as the S&P TSX Composite Index or the S&P 500 index. Since this business generates fees that are based on the size of the pool of assets managed, it tends to produce a more stable flow of income than does either investment banking or trading.

6. *Cash Management and Banking Services*

Retail investment firms offer their customers the ability to invest in shares through a cash account, or to borrow on margin. As shown in Table 4–2, 2012 client cash holdings in the industry equalled \$38.684 billion, and margin debt outstanding, a credit risk for the securities firms, equalled \$14.432 billion. The integrated firms owned by the major banks are able to offer their retail, business, and corporate clients online access to banking and investment accounts in addition to services such as investment advice, **private banking** (domestic and global), trust services, investment management, and financial planning.

private banking
The provision of wealth management services for high-net-worth clients.

7. *M&As*

Investment banks are frequently involved in providing advice or assisting in M&As. For example, they will assist in finding merger partners, underwriting new securities to be issued by the merged firms, assessing the value of target firms, recommending terms of the merger agreement, and even helping target firms prevent a merger (for example, seeing that poison-pill provisions are written into a potential target firm's securities contracts). Panel A of Table 4–5 lists the top 10 investment bank merger advisors ranked by U.S. dollar volume of U.S. M&A activity in which they were involved. Panel B of Table 4–5 lists the top 10 investment banks ranked by U.S. dollar volume of worldwide M&A activity. While U.S. and foreign firms rank in the top 10 worldwide, the 5 largest Canadian bank-owned integrated firms also have a presence in M&A advising, particularly for cross-border deals. However, ranking and market share each year depend on the

TABLE 4–5 Ten Largest M&A Firms Ranked by Value of Mergers, 2012 (in U.S. dollars)

Source: Thomson Reuters Deals Intelligence, 2013, thomsonreuters.com

Panel A: Mergers Completed in the United States			
Rank	**Investment Bank**	**Value ($ billions)**	**Number of Deals**
1	Goldman Sachs	$299.8	140
2	J.P. Morgan	241.5	114
3	Barclays Capital	229.9	120
4	Credit Suisse	216.7	86
5	Morgan Stanley	175.2	95
6	Evercore Partners	140.9	65
7	Citigroup	134.1	72
8	Bank of America Merrill Lynch	131.5	91
9	Lazard	124.8	91
10	Deutsche Bank	101.3	66
	Industry total	$882.1	6,951
Panel B: Worldwide Mergers			
Rank	**Investment Bank**	**Credit Lent ($ billions)**	**Number of Deals**
1	Goldman Sachs	$ 570.2	352
2	J.P. Morgan	406.4	247
3	Morgan Stanley	379.4	320
4	Credit Suisse	354.5	231
5	Barclays Capital	321.6	235
6	Bank of America Merrill Lynch	274.2	192
7	Deutsche Bank	265.0	216
8	Citigroup	238.1	184
9	Lazard	220.0	223
10	Rothschild	164.6	234
	Industry total	$2,040.6	28,454

size and the number of deals in which investment advisors are able to participate. Canadian deals are often small compared to the worldwide completed M&As of US$2.04 trillion in 2012. The bank-owned integrated firms (e.g., CIBC World Markets) are active participants on Wall Street, providing expertise in resource financing, particularly oil and gas and mining.

8. Back-Office and Other Service Functions

These functions include custody and escrow services, clearance and settlement services, and research and other advisory services—for example, giving advice on divestitures and asset sales. In addition, investment banks are making increasing inroads into traditional bank service areas, such as small-business lending and the trading of loans (see Chapter 21). In performing these functions, a securities firm normally acts as an agent for a fee. As mentioned above, fees charged are often based on the total bundle of services performed for the client by the firm.

CONCEPT QUESTIONS

1. **Describe the difference between brokerage services and underwriting services.**
2. **What are the key areas of activities for securities firms?**
3. **Describe the difference between a best-efforts offering and a firm commitment offering.**
4. **What are the trading activities performed by securities firms?**

BALANCE SHEET AND RECENT TRENDS

LO4

Recent Trends

Trends in this industry depend heavily on the state of the stock market. For example, a major effect of the 1987 stock market crash was a sharp decline in stock market trading volume and thus in commissions earned by securities firms over the 1987–1991 period. Commission income began to recover only after 1992, with record equity trading volumes being achieved in 1995–2000 when stock market indexes hit new highs. As stock market values declined in 2001 and 2002, so did commission income. The overall level of commissions has declined from 58 percent of total revenues in 1987 to 33 percent in 2012 (Table 4–6). This reflects the greater competition in the industry for customers, particularly after the banks formed the large integrated firms, whose effect was felt from the early 1990s, as well as the introduction of discount brokers.

Between 1990 and 2001, however, the securities industry generally showed a growth in profitability. For example, revenue grew from $2.4 billion in 1990 to $10.1 billion in 2001. The principal reasons for this were improved trading profits and increased growth in new issue underwritings. Corporate debt issues became highly attractive to corporate treasurers because of relatively low long-term interest rates. Another sign of the resurgence in this industry during the 1990s appears in employment figures. Annual employment in the securities industry increased from 29,636 in 1996 to 37,121 in 2001.

As can be seen from Table 4–6, the investment industry showed a trend of increasing operating revenues and profits from 2003 through to 2007. However, the world economy entered a recession in late 2008, causing industry profits to reach their lowest since 2005. The TSX showed an annual decline of 35 percent in 2008, a loss in value of approximately $700 billion. Industry revenues peaked at $17.1 billion in 2007 and declined to $14.6 billion in 2008. As the world economy recovered from the financial crisis, revenues in the Canadian industry slowly recovered as well. Table 4–6 provides a summary of the operating revenue for the industry from 1987 to 2012, and Table 4–7 provides a summary of statistics for the industry from 1996 to 2012.

Balance Sheet

reverse repurchase agreements (reverse repos)
Securities purchased under agreement to resell.

A balance sheet for investment services firms, the retail brokers discussed previously (including stockbrokers and investment managers), is shown in Table 4–8. Investments and accounts with affiliates as well as portfolio investments make up 56 percent of total assets. **Reverse repurchase agreements (reverse repos)**, securities purchased under agreement to resell (i.e., the broker gives a short-term loan to the repurchase agreement reseller), are included in the total assets. Because of the extent to which this industry's balance sheet consists of financial market securities, the industry is subjected to particularly high levels of market risk (see Chapter 15) and interest rate risk (see Chapters 8 and 9). Further, to the extent that many of these securities are foreign-issued securities, FI managers must also be concerned with foreign exchange risk (see Chapter 13) and sovereign risk (see Chapter 14).

TABLE 4–6 **Securities Industry Total Operating Revenue by Source, 1987–2012**

	2012	2011	2010	2009	2008	2007	2006	2005	2004	2003	2002	2001	2000	1995	1990	1987
Total Revenue ($ millions)	**$15,332**	**$16,136**	**$15,878**	**$16,306**	**$14,593**	**$17,123**	**$15,879**	**$13,485**	**$12,469**	**$10,618**	**$9,805**	**$10,133**	**$12,260**	**$5,139**	**$2,403**	**$3,247**
Op. Expenses	**7,249**	**7,355**	**6,826**	**6,555**	**6,528**	**6,279**	**5,711**	**5,279**	**5,187**	**4,447**	**4,666**	**4,683**	**4,723**	**2,484**	**1,591**	**1,677**
Op. Profit	**3,806**	**4,723**	**4,789**	**5,987**	**3,914**	**6,382**	**5,765**	**4,315**	**3,553**	**3,321**	**2,735**	**2,793**	**3,565**	**961**	**85**	**477**
Revenue Source																
Commissions	33%	36%	35%	31%	38%	37%	38%	39%	38%	38%	40%	41%	48%	45%	41%	58%
Investment banking	23	25	25	24	21	27	25	27	25	25	22	21	17	19	18	20
Fixed-income trading	8	7	7	13	7	4	5	5	5	7	9	10	5	14	20	6
Equity trading	1	0	2	3	0.1	3	5	4	5	6	3	4	9	5	−2	6
Net interest	7	9	7	6	13	10	10	9	8	10	10	11	10	10	15	6
Other	28	24	23	24	21	19	17	16	18	13	16	13	10	8	7	5
Total	**100%**	**100%**	**100%**	**100%**	**100%**	**100%**	**100%**	**100%**	**100%**	**100%**	**100%**	**100%**	**100%**	**100%**	**100%**	**100%**
Mutual fund commissions as a percentage of total	14%	13%	12%	10%	13%	13%	12%	13%	11%	10%	12%	12%	12%	9%	3%	2%

Source: Investment Industry Association of Canada, iiac.ca.

TABLE 4–7 Securities Industry Statistics, 1996–2012 ($ millions unless otherwise noted)

	2012	2011	2010	2009	2008	2007	2006	2005	2004	2003	2002	2001	2000	1999	1998	1997	1996
Highlights																	
Number of employees	39,555	40,427	39,917	39,894	40,086	42,329	40,919	39,174	37,739	37,262	37,949	37,121	39,433	36,175	34,445	32,990	29,636
Number of firms	196	201	201	200	202	203	198	201	205	207	206	198	191	188	186	187	182
Operating revenue	$15,332	$16,136	$15,878	$16,306	$14,593	$17,123	$15,879	$13,485	$12,469	$10,613	$9,807	$10,133	$12,260	$8,812	$7,725	$8,478	$7,472
Operating expenses	7,249	7,355	6,826	6,555	6,528	6,279	5,711	5,279	5,187	4,477	4,666	4,683	4,723	3,990	3,753	3,456	2,815
Operating profit	3,806	4,723	4,789	5,987	3,914	6,382	5,765	4,315	3,934	3,321	2,735	2,793	3,565	1,946	1,345	2,070	2,061
Net profit (loss)	2,155	2,036	2,395	2,869	1,875	2,771	2,515	1,752	1,773	1,484	1,257	1,011	1,183	582	395	769	850
Shareholders' equity	17,807	15,269	16,988	15,225	13,507	12,655	11,103	8,593	8,372	7,076	6,995	5,681	5,526	4,850	3,745	3,526	3,344
Regulatory capital	34,343	30,383	31,647	29,559	27,197	23,413	19,804	17,430	15,108	13,962	12,968	12,454	10,557	8,667	7,458	8,143	7,158
Client cash holdings	38,684	39,304	37,952	36,816	36,777	28,500	25,281	23,156	22,109	20,615	18,750	21,102	18,501	14,941	14,283	11,500	10,799
Client margin debt outstanding	14,432	13,458	13,731	11,048	8,846	14,001	11,710	11,580	9,478	7,615	7.019	7,833	10,696	na	na	na	na
Productivity ($000s) (annual revenue per employee)	388	399	398	409	367	405	388	347	330	285	258	273	311	244	224	257	252
Annual return (net profit/shareholders' equity)	13%	13%	14%	19%	14%	22%	23%	21%	18%	21%	18%	18%	21%	12%	11%	22%	25%

Source: Investment Industry Association of Canada, iiac.ca.

TABLE 4–8
Balance Sheet for Investment Services (Including Stockbrokers and Investment Dealers), 2012 ($ millions)

Source: Statistics Canada, statcan.gc.ca.

	2012	Percent of Total Assets
Assets	**$405,333**	
Cash and deposits	67,184	16.6
Accounts receivable and accrued revenue	41,814	10.3
Investments and accounts with affiliates	102,598	25.3
Portfolio investments	124,969	30.8
Loans	18,166	4.5
Mortgage	10,378	2.6
Nonmortgage	7,788	1.9
Allowance for losses on investments and loans	−213	
Net capital assets	25,469	6.3
Other assets	25,344	6.3
Liabilities	**$210,444**	51.9
Deposits	0	0
Accounts payable and accrued liabilities	58,140	14.3
Loans and accounts with affiliates	76,524	18.9
Borrowings	44,113	10.9
Loans and other borrowings	32,740	8.1
Bankers' acceptances and paper	1,004	0.2
Bonds and debentures	7,504	1.8
Mortgages	2,865	0.7
Future income tax	171	0.04
Other liabilities	31,495	7.8
Equity	**$194,889**	48.1
Share capital	87,162	21.5
Contributed surplus and other	24,670	6.1
Accumulated other comprehensive income	689	0.2
Retained earnings	82,368	20.3

With respect to liabilities, loans and accounts with affiliates accounted for 18.9 percent of total liabilities. Borrowings (loans and other borrowings, bankers' acceptances and paper, bonds and debentures, and mortgages) accounted for 10.9 percent of total liabilities. Equity capital (share capital, contributed surplus, and retained earnings) represented 48.1 percent of total assets. The level of capital maintained by securities firms is governed by the rules of the securities regulators and by the IIAC for its member firms, as noted previously.

CONCEPT QUESTIONS

1. **Describe the trend in profitability in the securities industry over the last 10 years.**
2. **What are the major assets held by broker-dealers?**

REGULATION

The regulation of the securities industry in Canada is a provincial and territorial responsibility. The securities regulators of Canada's ten provinces and three territories coordinate regulation through the Canadian Securities Administrators (CSA, www.csa-acvm.ca) via a passport system that allows market participants to issue a prospectus or register in their home province or territory and be recognized by all other jurisdictions in Canada.

The growth of the securities industry, plus the globalization of securities trading (particularly cross-border issues that arise as a result of companies cross-listing on the Canadian and U.S. exchanges), has meant that the securities industry in Canada needs to have consistent regulation across the country. As well, the financial crisis in 2008 revealed how risks can be transferred quickly throughout the domestic and global financial systems. With this in mind, the Canadian government proposed a Canadian Securities Act in 2010. In 2011 the Supreme Court ruled the proposed Act unconstitutional since securities regulation is considered primarily a provincial responsibility. Currently, the provincial and territorial regulators establish legislation in their own jurisdictions, but they allow self-regulatory organizations to carry out certain aspects of regulation. For example, the exchanges are **self-regulatory organizations (SROs)**. Each SRO has a particular role in the regulation of securities firms. The Investment Industry Regulatory Organization of Canada (IIROC) regulates its member firms for capital adequacy, as well as code of conduct, and provides details of the current regulations at its website. Also, since mutual funds have become such a large source of revenue for securities firms, having grown from 2 percent of commission income in 1987 to 14 percent in 2012, securities dealers are also members of the Mutual Fund Dealers Association of Canada (MFDA), which is an SRO recognized in several provinces.

self-regulatory organization (SRO)
Industry-owned organization designated by a provincial securities regulator to regulate its members.

In addition to the regulators, consumer protection is provided by the Canadian Investor Protection Fund (CIPF), which is a trust fund organized by the TSX Group, the IIROC, and the Montréal Exchange (MX) to provide investor protection of up to $1 million if a dealer were to become insolvent. Also, the Centre for Financial Services OmbudsNetwork (CFSON) provides dispute resolution for consumers free of charge.

cipf.ca

cfson.org

While Canadian regulators have been unable to establish a national securities regulator, the primary regulator of the securities industry in the United States, the Securities and Exchange Commission (SEC), spurred on by the corporate governance scandals of Enron, Global Crossings, Tyco, and WorldCom in the early 2000s, moved to limit U.S. state regulators' ability to control securities firms. The primary roles of the SEC are administration of securities laws, review and evaluation of registrations of new securities offerings (ensuring that all relevant information is revealed to potential investors), review and evaluation of annual and semiannual reports summarizing the financial status of all publicly held corporations, and the prohibition of any form of security market manipulation.

The SEC has instituted rules requiring Wall Street analysts to guarantee that their stock picks are not influenced by investment banking colleagues and that analysts disclose details of their compensation that would alert investors to any possible conflicts. If evidence surfaces that the analysts have falsely attested to the independence of their work, it could be used to bring enforcement actions. Violators could face a wide array of sanctions, including fines and other penalties, such as a suspension or a ban from the securities industry. In addition, the SEC proposed that top officials from all public companies sign off on financial statements.

SEC regulations, the Sarbanes-Oxley Act, the U.S. Patriot Act, and the 2010 Wall Street Reform and Consumer Protection Act all have cross-border impacts on Canadian FIs. The financial crisis reshaped much of the U.S. securities firms and investment banking industry. In response, regulators were charged with reshaping regulations to prevent events similar to those that led to the market collapse and the near collapse of this industry. The Wall Street Reform and Consumer Protection Act (also called the Dodd-Frank Act) set forth many changes in the way securities firms and investment banks are regulated. This has an impact on Canadian FIs' securities activities in the United States. The bill's Financial Services Oversight Council of financial regulators was given oversight of the industry in its charge to identify emerging systemic risks. Also under the act, effective July 21, 2011, the dollar threshold for determining whether an investment advisor must register under federal or state law increased. Generally, all advisors with assets under management of under US$100 million must register with state regulators and those with over US$100 million under management must register with the SEC. The bill also gave new authority for the U.S. Federal Reserve to supervise all firms that could pose a threat to financial stability and called for stronger capital and other prudential standards for all financial firms, and even higher standards for large, interconnected firms. Investment banks also saw stricter oversight as the bill called for the regulation of securitization markets; stronger regulation of credit rating agencies; a requirement that issuers and originators retain a financial interest in securitized loans; comprehensive regulation of all over-the-counter derivatives; and new authority for the Federal Reserve to oversee payment, clearing, and settlement systems. Finally, the bill gave authority to the U.S. government to resolve NBFIs whose failure could have serious systemic effects and revised the Federal Reserve's emergency lending authority to improve accountability.

One of the most publicized "missteps" by global securities firms and investment banks over the course of the financial crisis was related to executive compensation. Top executives received millions of dollars in bonuses for taking risks that in some cases paid off and in others cases left taxpayers to bail out the firms. As a result, at U.S. FIs receiving government support, a "pay czar" was given a say over compensation packages given to top executives. While meant to curb what was seen by many as excessive pay, others argued that these restrictions would make it difficult to attract and retain talent sufficient to keep U.S. FIs on a competitive footing with their global peers. No such regulations to cap executive compensation have been introduced in Canada.

Securities firms and banks have historically been strongly supportive of efforts to combat money laundering, and the industry has been subject to laws that impose extensive reporting and record-keeping requirements. However, the Patriot Act, passed in response to the September 11, 2001, terrorist attacks, included additional provisions that financial services firms operating in the United States must implement. The new rules, in effect since October 1, 2003, imposed three requirements. First, firms must verify the identity of any person seeking to open an account. Second, firms must maintain records of the information used to verify the person's identity. Third, firms must determine whether a person opening an account appears on any list of known or suspected terrorists or terrorist organizations. The new rules are intended to deter money laundering without imposing undue burdens that would constrain the ability of firms to serve their customers.

Canadian securities firms have been required to identify money laundering since 1993, and, in response to global concerns following September 11, 2001, amendments to the Proceeds of Crime (Money Laundering) and Terrorist Financing Act 2001 require firms to report suspicious transactions, report large cash transactions, and obtain clear identification of their clients. IIROC maintains a section for its members on money laundering on its website similar to that provided by OSFI for federally regulated banks and insurance companies.

CONCEPT QUESTIONS

1. **How does the regulation of the securities industry differ between Canada and the United States?**
2. **How and why does the regulatory framework differ for DTIs and securities firms?**

GLOBAL ISSUES

Much more so than other sectors of the FI industry, securities firms and investment banks operate globally. This can be seen in Table 4–3, as three of the top five (and five of the top ten) underwriters of global debt and equity are U.S. investment banks (JPMorgan Chase, Bank of America Merrill Lynch, Citigroup) and the rest European banks (Barclays Capital, Deutsche Bank). Further, U.S. investment banks held six of the top ten spots on M&A deals in Europe and held the top five spots on deals in Asia.

The disruptions in the global capital markets in 2007 and 2008 reshaped the investment banking industry in the United States and globally. As mentioned earlier in the chapter, Canada went through a "Big Bang" in 1987 that resulted in revisions to the Bank Act and the formation of OSFI. The largest securities firms were bought by the Big Six banks, the trust companies were also consolidated, and Canadian FIs moved toward universal banking. The model thus saw investment activities supported by merging with a bank funded by a stable source of deposits. By the time of the credit crisis in 2007, Canada had 20 years of experience with this model. The United States, however, didn't replace the Glass-Steagall Act (1933) with the Financial Services Modernization Act until 1999, so the U.S. system was 10 years behind the Canadian system in consolidating. Markets are now more globally connected and more complex, which makes them more opaque and increases the potential for global systemic risk. At the time of the crisis in 2007, the U.S. investment banks were standalone. As well, their high debt levels and reliance on short-term market funding made their model a risky strategy when liquidity dried up in the global capital markets.

One result of the financial crisis in the late 2000s was that large investment banks around the world became more concerned than ever with capital, liquidity, and leverage. However, they did not want to lose ground in the global competition for clients. The result was that global investment banks looked for strategic alliances that would allow them to compete in foreign markets, or they exited foreign markets altogether. For example, in 2008, Morgan Stanley, in need of capital to bolster its balance sheet, sold a 21 percent stake in the firm to Japanese FI Mitsubishi UFJ. In March 2009, the two announced plans to form a joint venture that combined the two firms' Japan-based securities businesses. Morgan Stanley took 40 percent ownership and managerial control of the institutional business, and Mitsubishi took the remaining ownership and control of the retail operations. This kind of arrangement provides U.S.-based investment banks with a foothold alongside a domestic firm in the foreign market. In contrast, Citigroup—which during the financial crisis had to deal with growing U.S. government ownership, a deteriorating credit environment, and an unwieldy structure—decided to abandon several foreign markets. Citigroup sold its Japanese domestic securities unit and its Japanese asset management unit, Nikko Asset Management, to subsidiaries of Sumitomo Mitsui Financial Group. It also sold NikkoCiti Trust and Banking Corp. to Nomura Trust & Banking Co. Moves such as the sale of international properties, originally acquired to allow the investment bank to expand globally, will likely continue to play a part in the reshaping of the global investment banking industry.

One of the more grievous actions by some global investment banks during the financial crisis was the manipulation of the LIBOR interest rate. LIBOR is the interest rate at which banks can borrow from each other. It is also used to price, among other things, mortgage and business loans and derivative securities. LIBOR is the average of the interest rates submitted by major banks in the United States, Europe, and the United Kingdom in a variety of major currencies such as the dollar, euro, and yen. The scandal arose when it was discovered that banks had been manipulating the LIBOR rate either to make profits on their derivative positions such as interest rate swaps or to make the banks look stronger for reputational reasons. It is estimated that the banks involved made at least US$75 billion on the manipulations. The scandal became widely public in June 2012 when British investment bank Barclays agreed to pay US$450 million to settle allegations by U.S. and British authorities that some of its traders attempted to manipulate LIBOR rates to increase the bank's profits and reduce concerns about its stability during the financial crisis.

Concerns were also raised about the failure of British and U.S. regulators to stop the manipulation of LIBOR when there was evidence that both were aware of it. In July 2012, a former trader stated that LIBOR manipulation had been occurring since at least 1991. In July 2012, the U.S. Federal Reserve Bank of New York released documents dated as far back as 2007 showing that they knew that banks were misreporting their borrowing costs when setting LIBOR. Yet, no action was taken. Similarly, documents from the Bank of England indicated that the bank knew as early as November 2007 that the LIBOR rate was being manipulated. It was not until June 2012 that Barclays was the first bank to agree to settle LIBOR manipulation allegations. In December 2012, UBS agreed to pay about $1.5 billion to settle charges that it manipulated LIBOR. In February 2013, the Royal Bank of Scotland also decided to settle at a cost of US$610 million. Also in early 2013, Deutsche Bank stated that it had set aside money to cover potential fines associated with its role in the manipulation of LIBOR.

CONCEPT QUESTION

1. Why is LIBOR important to international financial markets?

Questions and Problems

1. Explain how securities firms differ from investment banks. In what ways are they financial intermediaries?
2. What are the different types of firms in the securities industry, and how does each type differ from the others?
3. What are the key activity areas for securities firms? How does each activity area assist in the generation of profits, and what are the major risks for each area?
4. What is the difference between an IPO and a secondary issue?
5. What is the difference between a private placement and a public offering?
6. What are the risk implications to an investment bank from underwriting on a best-efforts basis versus a firm commitment basis? If you operated a company issuing stock for the first time, which type of underwriting would you prefer? Why? What factors might cause you to choose the alternative?

7. An investment bank agrees to underwrite an issue of 15 million shares of stock for Looney Landscaping Corp.
   a. If the investment bank underwrites the stock on a firm commitment basis, it agrees to pay $12.50 per share to Looney Landscaping Corp. for the 15 million shares of stock. It can then sell those shares to the public for $13.25 per share. How much money does Looney Landscaping Corp. receive? What is the profit to the investment bank? If the investment bank can sell the shares for only $11.95, how much money does Looney Landscaping Corp. receive? What is the profit to the investment bank?
   b. Suppose, instead, that the investment bank agrees to underwrite the 15 million shares on a best-efforts basis. The investment bank is able to sell 13.6 million shares for $12.50 per share, and it charges Looney Landscaping Corp. $0.275 per share sold. How much money does Looney Landscaping Corp. receive? What is the profit to the investment bank? If the investment bank can sell the shares for only $11.95, how much money does Looney Landscaping Corp. receive? What is the profit to the investment bank?
8. An investment banker agrees to underwrite a $500 million, 10-year, 8 percent semiannual bond issue for KDO Corporation on a firm commitment basis. The investment banker pays KDO on Thursday and plans to begin a public sale on Friday. What type of interest rate movement does the investment bank fear while holding these securities? If interest rates rise 0.05 percent, or 5 basis points, overnight, what will be the impact on the profits of the investment banker? What if the market interest rate falls 5 basis points?
9. An investment bank pays $23.50 per share for 4 million shares of JCN Company. It then sells those shares to the public for $25 per share. How much money does JCN receive? What is the profit to the investment bank? What is the stock price of JCN?
10. XYZ Inc. has issued 10 million new shares. An investment bank agrees to underwrite these shares on a best-efforts basis. The investment bank is able to sell 8.4 million shares for $27 per share, and it charges XYZ $0.675 per share sold. How much money does XYZ receive? What is the profit to the investment bank? What is the stock price of XYZ?
11. What is venture capital?
12. What are the different types of venture capital firms? How do institutional venture capital firms differ from angel venture capital firms?
13. What are the advantages and disadvantages to a new or small firm of getting capital funding from a venture capital firm?
14. How do agency transactions differ from principal transactions for market-makers?
15. One of the major activity areas of securities firms is trading.
    a. What is the difference between pure arbitrage and risk arbitrage?
    b. What is the difference between position trading and program trading?
16. If an investor observes that the price of a stock trading in one exchange is different from the price in another exchange, what form of arbitrage is applicable, and how can the investor participate in that arbitrage?
17. An investor notices that an ounce of gold is priced at US$318 in London and US$325 in New York.
    a. What action could the investor take to try to profit from the price discrepancy?
    b. Under which of the four trading activities would this action be classified?
    c. If the investor is correct in identifying the discrepancy, what pattern should the two prices take in the short-term future?
    d. What may be some impediments to the success of this transaction?
18. What factors are given credit for the steady decline in brokerage commissions as a percentage of total revenues over the period beginning in 1987 and ending in 1991?
19. What factors are given credit for the resurgence of profitability in the securities industry beginning in 1991? Are firms that trade in fixed-income securities more or less likely to have volatile profits? Why?
20. How did the financial crisis affect the performance of securities firms and investment banks?
21. How do the operating activities, and thus the balance sheet structures, of securities firms differ from the operating activities of DTIs, such as banks and insurance firms? How are the balance sheet structures of securities firms similar to those of other FIs?
22. Based on the data in Table 4–8, what were the second-largest single asset and the largest single liability of securities firms in 2012? Are these asset and liability categories related? Exactly how does a repurchase agreement work?
23. Identify the major regulatory organizations that are involved in the daily operations of the securities industry, and explain their role in providing smoothly operating markets.

CHAPTER 5

MUTUAL FUNDS, HEDGE FUNDS, AND PENSION FUNDS

After studying this chapter you should be able to:

- **LO1** Discuss the size, structure, and composition of companies in the mutual fund industry in Canada.
- **LO2** Explain the differences between mutual funds, hedge funds, and pension funds.
- **LO3** Calculate the NAV for a mutual fund.
- **LO4** Discuss the size, structure, and composition of the hedge fund industry.

INTRODUCTION

fund
A financial institution whose primary purpose is to acquire and manage financial assets for its owners.

mutual funds
FIs that pool the financial resources of individuals and companies and invest in diversified portfolios of assets, targeting a specific level of risk.

hedge funds
FIs that pool the financial resources of sophisticated investors and invest in a diversified pool of assets, usually high risk.

pension funds
FIs that pool the retirement savings of individuals, invest in a diversified portfolio of assets, and pay an income to their owners after retirement.

When the term *fund* is mentioned, most people automatically add the term *mutual* as an adjective. However, a **fund** can be defined more generally as an FI whose primary purpose is to acquire and manage financial assets (e.g., bonds, shares, money market securities) for its owners. The types of funds that will be discussed in this chapter are **mutual funds**, **hedge funds**, and **pension funds**. For example, an open-ended mutual fund (the major type of mutual fund) continuously stands ready to sell new shares to investors and to redeem outstanding shares on demand at their fair market value. Thus, by pooling the financial resources of individuals and companies and investing in diversified portfolios of assets, funds provide opportunities for small savers to invest in financial securities and to diversify risk. Funds may also be able to generate greater economies of scale by incurring lower transaction costs and commissions than are incurred when individual investors buy securities directly. In this respect, funds are similar to deposit-taking FIs in converting savings into income-earning assets. However, while the 1990s saw savings transferred from banks and other DTIs into funds, these funds differ for investors in the increased risk of a loss of capital, a market risk not present with government-insured deposits. Many investors saw their retirement savings devastated by the market downturn of 2001 and again in 2008.

The growth in savings, as a result of an employment benefit (a pension fund, firm-operated or government-operated) or through individual efforts (often within a legal shelter such as a **registered retirement savings plan (RRSP)** or a **registered education savings plan (RESP)**), created FIs whose liability side is essentially all owners' equity. The fiduciary nature of pension funds was recognized early, and regulations were established to govern them. Mutual funds were left to self-regulatory organizations (SROs) for their control, and hedge funds, a product offered to knowledgeable investors, were left unregulated. The history of the last decade is thus one of growth in size and in regulation for these three types of FIs, whose

registered retirement savings plan (RRSP)
A retirement savings plan that allows Canadians to defer tax until retirement.

registered education savings plan (RESP)
A savings plan that allows Canadians to earn income for their children that is not taxed if used for educational purposes when withdrawn.

wealth management
The provision of professional portfolio management, tax planning, and retirement planning services to individuals and companies.

primary service is **wealth management**, the provision of professional asset management to individual investors and companies.

By providing wealth management services, mutual funds, hedge funds, and pension funds are subject to interest rate risk, market risk, foreign exchange risk, and possibly off-balance-sheet (OBS) risk on the asset side of their balance sheet. With the exception of capital adequacy rules, the risk management of funds parallels that of other FIs.

In this chapter we first provide an overview of the services offered by mutual funds and highlight their rapid growth over the last two decades. Then we look at the size, structure, and composition of the industry. This section highlights historical trends in the industry, the different types of mutual funds, mutual fund objectives, investor returns from mutual fund ownership, and mutual fund costs. We also look at the industry's balance sheets and recent trends, the regulations and regulators governing the industry, and global issues for this industry. We then discuss investment pools organized as hedge funds. Because hedge funds are limited to only the wealthiest investors, they are examined separately from the mutual funds discussed elsewhere in the chapter. Lastly, we look at pension funds, which differ from mutual funds and hedge funds in that a pension fund's assets are managed in trust for its beneficiaries.

MUTUAL FUNDS

LO1, LO2

An open-ended mutual fund (the major type of mutual fund) continuously stands ready to sell new shares to investors and to redeem outstanding shares on demand at their fair market value. As a result of the tremendous increase in the market value of financial assets, such as equities, in the 1990s (for example, the S&P TSX Composite Index saw a return of over 25 percent in 1993, 1996, and 1999) and the relatively low cost opportunity that mutual funds provide to investors (particularly small investors) who want to hold such assets (through either direct mutual fund purchases or contributions to their RRSPs), the mutual fund industry boomed in size and number of customers in the 1990s. Shareholder services offered by mutual funds include free exchanges of investments between a mutual fund company's funds, automatic investing, automatic reinvestment of dividends, and automatic withdrawals.

Size, Structure, and Composition of the Industry

Historical Trends

Figure 5–1 presents information about the growth of the net assets under management (AUM) of the mutual fund industry in Canada from 2000 to 2013 provided by the Investment Funds Institute of Canada (IFIC). Figure 5–1 shows that net assets have grown from $439.7 billion at year-end 2000 to $907.0 billion at June 30, 2013. Over the same time period, the number of funds has increased from over 1,600 in 2000 to 2,895 in 2013. Net mutual fund assets decreased only in 2002, when the return on the S&P TSX Composite Index was –14 percent, and again in 2008, when the index declined by 35 percent.

Because of the financial market crisis, the net new sales of mutual funds was only $100.2 million in 2008 and $106.7 million in 2009, compared to $3.6 billion in

FIGURE 5–1
Mutual Fund AUM 2000–2013 ($ billions)

Source: The Investment Funds Institute of Canada, 2013, ific.ca.

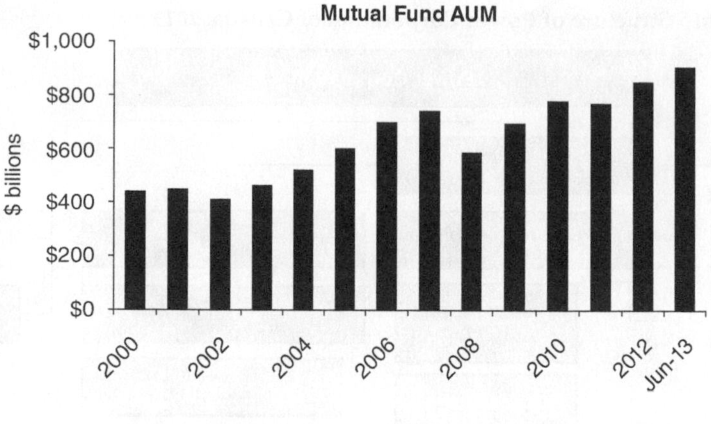

RRSP-eligible
A mutual fund or other security that meets the criteria of CRA for inclusion in an RRSP.

clone fund
A Canadian mutual fund that creates returns equivalent to a foreign stock portfolio or, generically, that mimics the strategy of another fund, often using derivatives.

fund of funds
A mutual fund that invests in other mutual funds.

ific.ca
iiac.ca
osfi-bsif.gc.ca
sedar.com

2007. However, comparison of these statistics year over year may be misleading due to changes in the regulations governing **RRSP-eligible** funds. For example, the limit on foreign content in RRSPs was 10 percent in 1990, 30 percent in 2001, and eliminated in 2005. In addition, some foreign **clone funds** were created, which increased the foreign content of a mutual fund by using derivatives to emulate the returns of a foreign securities portfolio. In Canada, clone funds refer to funds created to increase the foreign content of a mutual fund. More generally, the term is also used for any fund that mimics the strategy of another, usually larger, fund without investing directly in the same securities.

Industry participants consist of those who manufacture mutual funds, those who distribute funds, and those who do both, such as banks, insurance companies, and investment management firms. As well, there are **funds of funds**, which invest in other mutual funds.

Mutual funds represent an investment security and are therefore regulated at the provincial/territorial level in Canada. A provincial/territorial regulator's goal is the protection of the investor by ensuring disclosure of information and market transparency. In order to sell mutual funds, individuals must meet the licensing requirements of their home province or territory, which include training in the products sold. As well, training in the evaluation of the clients' investment goals, their risk tolerance, and their investment knowledge is included in order to ensure that the funds recommended are appropriate. Each dealer must be a member of a self-regulating organization such as the Investment Industry Association of Canada (IIAC). However, in addition to specific securities laws, the sale of funds by DTIs and others regulated by the OSFI means that the Bank Act, The Insurance Companies Act, the Trust and Loan Companies Act, and other federal and provincial/territorial statutes may also apply. The majority of Canadian mutual funds are regulated by the OSC, which is involved with other provincial/territorial securities regulators in harmonizing the regulations through the CSA. As well, information about publicly traded companies and mutual funds is available at SEDAR, the System for Electronic Document Analysis and Retrieval.

The mutual fund industry has many large firms. The MFDA lists 121 members, 29 of which have assets under administration greater than $1 billion. The investment subsidiaries of the Big Six banks (TD Asset Management, CIBC Asset Management, BMO Investments, Scotia Asset Management, RBC

FIGURE 5–2 Ownership Structure of Power Corporation of Canada, 2013

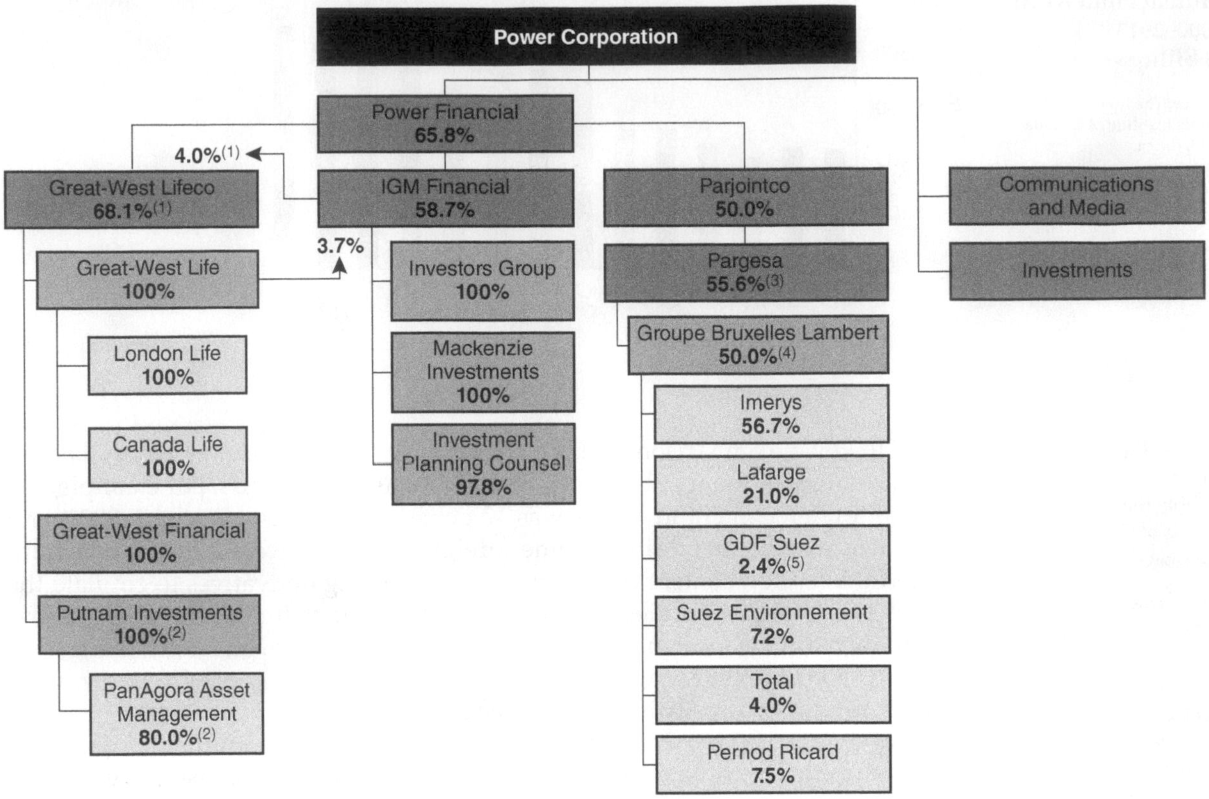

Source: Power Corporation of Canada website, powercorporation.com.

Percentages denote equity interest as at March 31, 2013.
(1) Together, approximately 65% direct and indirect voting interest.
(2) Denotes voting interest.
(3) Parjointco held a voting interest of 74.4% in Pargesa.
(4) Pargesa held a voting interest of 52.0% in Groupe Bruxelles Lambert.
(5) As of May 14, 2013.

Global Asset Management, National Bank Securities) are large fund managers and offer all types of mutual funds to meet investors' needs. Each investment fund can be found on SEDAR's website. For example, CIBC reported AUM of $88.8 billion at year-end 2012 and recorded net sales of mutual funds of $3.9 billion. Banks distribute mutual funds through their branch networks, provided their salespeople have been certified by the appropriate provincial or territorial regulator. In addition, banks' clients are able to buy and sell mutual funds online from the same website where they conduct their other banking, giving banks an advantage in selling mutual funds.

Insurance companies (Manulife Asset Management, Sun Life Financial) are also large participants in the mutual fund industry, as is IGM Financial Inc., part of Power Corporation of Canada. Power Corporation of Canada is a financial conglomerate whose controlling shareholder is the Desmarais family of Quebec. As shown in Figure 5–2, Power Corporation has expanded into two areas of financial intermediation. Its assets include life insurance (Great-West

Life, London Life, Canada Life) and mutual funds (IGM Financial, Investors Group, Mackenzie Financial, Investment Planning Counsel Group of Funds). Through its website, IGM Financial sells mortgages, insurance, and other banking products.

AGF Investments Inc. is an independent Canadian-owned fund. Invesco Trimark, Fidelity Investments Canada, and Franklin Templeton are owned by large U.S.-based companies. Fonds Desjardins is owned by a CP based in Québec. Each mutual fund offered by these large firms is listed with SEDAR, and up-to-date information on asset size and performance is available from Morningstar and Globefunds.

bond funds
Funds that contain fixed-income capital market debt securities.

equity funds
Funds that contain primarily common stock securities.

balanced funds
Funds that contain bond and stock securities.

cifsc.org

Different Types of Mutual Funds

The assets of the mutual fund industry can be divided into two sectors: long-term funds and short-term funds. These are reported on an aggregate basis by the Bank of Canada as non-money market mutual funds and money market mutual funds as part of the money supply. Long-term funds include **bond funds** (composed of fixed-income securities with a maturity over one year), **equity funds** (composed of primarily common stock securities), **balanced funds** (composed of common and preferred shares and bonds), and specialty funds. Short-term funds include money market mutual funds that are invested in short-term paper, usually with maturities of less than six months. As well, the Canadian Investment Funds Standards Committee (CIFSC) has developed a classification system for investment funds based on its holdings.

As can be seen from Table 5–1, of the total $907.0 billion of net AUM at June 30, 2013, 73.5 percent ($666.5 billion) was stand-alone funds and the remaining 26.5 percent was funds of funds. The long-term funds dominate, with the short-term money market funds making up only 3.1 percent of total AUM in June 2013. Of the $878.5 billion of long-term funds, equity represented 31.3 percent, balanced funds were 47.6 percent, bond funds were 15 percent, and specialty funds were 3 percent. The total industry grew by 13.7 percent from June 30, 2012, to June 30, 2013, a dollar value increase of $109.1 billion.

TABLE 5–1
Canadian Mutual Fund Assets by Fund Type, June 30, 2013

Source: The Investment Funds Institute of Canada, 2013, www.ific.ca.

Asset Class	Net Assets Month-End ($ thousands)	Market Share (%)	Change in Assets Yr. to Yr. (%)
Stand-alone vs. fund-of-funds			
Stand-alone funds	$666.5	73.5%	8.7%
Fund-of-funds	240.5	26.5	30.4
Total	907.0	100.0	13.7
Long-term funds: Broad asset classes			
Equity funds	283.5	31.3	10.7
Balanced funds	431.3	47.6	19.5
Bond funds	136.1	15.0	13.8
Specialty funds	27.6	3.0	−4.8
Total long-term funds	878.5	96.9	14.8
Short-term funds	28.5	3.1	−12.3
Total industry	$907.0	100.0%	13.7%

Mutual Fund Objectives

Mutual funds are legally required to provide investors with a prospectus that outlines the fund's investment strategy and its costs. In addition, each fund produces an annual report that provides details of its activities, and also maintains a website to provide monthly and quarterly information, and, in some cases, a copy of the fund's prospectus. The goal is to fully inform existing and potential investors of its activities so that they can evaluate the risks and returns. Investment advisors and sellers of mutual funds must meet provincial/territorial requirements, which include a duty to ensure that the investor is informed and that the fund is appropriate for a particular client.

Investor Returns from Mutual Fund Ownership

LO3

marked-to-market
When asset and balance sheet values are adjusted to reflect current market prices.

net asset value (NAV) or **net asset value per share (NAVPS)**
The market value of the assets in a mutual fund portfolio divided by the number of shares outstanding.

The return an investor gets from investing in mutual fund shares reflects three aspects of the underlying portfolio of mutual fund assets. First, income and dividends are earned on those assets. Second, capital gains occur when assets are sold by a mutual fund at prices higher than the purchase price. Third, capital appreciation in the underlying values of the assets held in a fund's portfolio adds to the value of mutual fund shares. With respect to capital appreciation, mutual fund assets are normally **marked-to-market** daily. This means that the managers of the fund calculate the current value of each mutual fund share by computing the daily market value of the fund's total asset portfolio and then dividing this amount by the number of mutual fund shares outstanding. The resulting value is called the **net asset value (NAV)** or **net asset value per share (NAVPS)** of the fund. This is the price the investor gets when selling shares back to the fund that day or buying any new shares in the fund on that day.

EXAMPLE 5–1
Effect of Capital Appreciation on NAV

Suppose a mutual fund contains 1,000 shares of Canadian Tire currently trading at \$37.75, 2,000 shares of Encana currently trading at \$43.70, and 1,500 shares of CIBC currently trading at \$46.67. The mutual fund currently has 15,000 shares outstanding held by investors. Thus, today, the NAV of the fund is calculated as

$$\text{NAV} = [(1{,}000 \times \$37.75) + (2{,}000 \times \$43.70) + (1{,}500 \times \$46.67)] \div 15{,}000 = \$13.01$$

If next month Canadian Tire shares increase to \$45, Encana shares increase to \$48, and CIBC shares increase to \$50, the NAV (assuming the same number of shares outstanding) would increase to

$$\text{NAV} = [(1{,}000 \times \$45) + (2{,}000 \times \$48) + (1{,}500 \times \$50)] \div 15{,}000 = \$14.40$$

open-end mutual funds
Funds in which the supply of shares is not fixed but can increase or decrease daily with purchases and redemptions of shares.

Most mutual funds are **open-end mutual funds** in that the number of shares outstanding fluctuates daily with the amount of share redemptions and new purchases. With open-end mutual funds, investors buy and sell shares from and to the mutual fund company. Thus, the demand for shares determines the number outstanding and the NAV of shares is determined solely by the market value of the underlying securities held in the mutual fund divided by the number of shareholders outstanding.

EXAMPLE 5-2

Effect of Investment Size on NAV

Consider the mutual fund in Example 5–1, but suppose that today 1,000 additional investors buy into the mutual fund at the current NAV of \$13.01. This means that the fund manager now has \$13,010 in additional funds to invest. Suppose the fund manager decides to use these additional funds to buy additional shares in Canadian Tire. At today's market price, he or she can buy \$13,010 ÷ \$37.75 = 344 additional shares of Canadian Tire. Thus, the mutual fund's new portfolio of shares would be 1,344 in Canadian Tire, 2,000 in Encana, and 1,500 in CIBC. At the end of the month, the NAV of the portfolio would be

$$\text{NAV} = [(1{,}344 \times \$45) + (2{,}000 \times \$48) + (1{,}500 \times \$50)] \div 16{,}000 = \$14.47$$

given the appreciation in value of all three stocks over the month.

Note that the fund's value changed over the month due to both capital appreciation and investment size. A comparison of the NAV in Example 5–1 with the one in this example indicates that the additional shares alone enabled the fund to gain a slightly higher NAV than if the number of shares had remained static (\$14.47 versus \$14.40).

closed-end investment companies
Specialized investment companies that invest in securities and assets of other firms but have a fixed supply of shares outstanding themselves.

income trusts
Income funds/trusts set up to own assets whose earnings (income) are passed on to the unitholders monthly or quarterly and taxed in their hands.

real estate investment trust (REIT)
A closed-end investment company that specializes in investing in mortgages, property, or real estate company shares.

Open-end mutual funds can be compared to most regular corporations traded on stock exchanges and to **closed-end investment companies**, both of which have a fixed number of shares outstanding at any given time. For example, **income trusts** are closed-end funds, as are **real estate investment trusts (REITs)**, which specialize in investment in real estate company shares and/or in buying mortgages. With closed-end funds, investors must buy and sell the investment company's shares on a stock exchange similar to the trading of corporate stock. Since the number of shares available for purchase at any moment in time is fixed, the NAV of the fund's shares is determined not only by the value of the underlying shares but also by the demand for the investment company's shares themselves. When demand is high, the shares can trade at more than the NAV of the securities held in the fund. In this case, the fund is said to be *trading at a premium*, that is, at more than the fair market value of the securities held. When the value of the closed-end fund's shares are less than the NAV of its assets, its shares are said to be *trading at a discount*, that is, at less than the fair market value of the securities held.

EXAMPLE 5-3

Market Value of Closed-End Mutual Fund Shares

Because of high demand for a closed-end investment company's shares, the 50 shares (N_S) are trading at \$20 per share (P_S). The market value of the equity-type securities in the fund's asset portfolio, however, is \$800, or \$16 (\$800 ÷ 50) per share. The market value balance sheet of the fund is shown below:

Assets		Liabilities and Equity	
Market value of asset portfolio	\$800	Market value of closed-end fund shares ($P_S \times N_S$)	\$1,000
Premium	\$200		

The fund's shares are trading at a premium of \$4 (200 ÷ 50) per share.

Because of low demand for a *second* closed-end fund, the 100 shares outstanding are trading at $25 per share. The market value of the securities in this fund's portfolio is $3,000, or each share has a NAV of $30 per share. The market value balance sheet of this fund is as follows:

Assets		Liabilities and Equity	
Market value of asset portfolio	$3,000	Market value of closed-end fund shares (100 × $25)	$2,500
Discount	−$500		

Exchange-Traded Funds

exchange-traded funds (ETFs)
Funds that track a specific index or basket of shares on a stock exchange. They can be bought and sold at any time during a trading day.

Similar to closed-end funds in that a fixed number of shares are outstanding at any point in time, an **exchange-traded fund (ETF)** is an investment company with shares that trade intraday on stock exchanges at market-determined prices. ETFs may be bought or sold through a broker or in a brokerage account, like trading shares of any publicly traded company. While ETFs are registered with a provincial/territorial securities regulator as investment companies, they differ from traditional mutual funds both in how their shares are issued and redeemed and in how their shares or units are traded. Specifically, ETF shares are created by an institutional investor's depositing of a specified block of securities with the ETF. In return for this deposit, the institutional investor receives a fixed amount of ETF shares, some or all of which may then be sold on a stock exchange. The institutional investor may obtain its deposited securities by redeeming the same number of ETF shares it received from the ETF. Individual investors can buy and sell the ETF shares only when they are listed on an exchange. Unlike an institutional investor, a retail investor cannot purchase or redeem shares directly from the ETF, as with a traditional mutual fund.

Mutual Fund Costs

Mutual funds charge shareholders a price or fee for the services they provide (i.e., management of a diversified portfolio of financial securities). Two types of fees are incurred by investors: sales loads and fund operating expenses. We discuss these next. The total cost to the shareholder of investing in a mutual fund is the sum of the annualized sales load and other fees charged.

Load versus No-Load Funds

load fund
A mutual fund with an up-front sales or commission charge that has to be paid by the investor.

no-load funds
Mutual funds that do not charge up-front fees or commission charges on the sale of mutual fund shares to investors.

An investor who buys a mutual fund share may be subject to a sales charge, sometimes as high as 8.5 percent. In this case, the fund is called a **load fund**. Another kind of load, called a *back-end load*, is sometimes charged when mutual fund shares are sold by investors. Back-end loads, also referred to as *deferred sales charges*, are an alternative way to compensate the fund managers or sales force for their services. Other funds that directly market shares to investors do not use sales agents working for commissions and have no up-front commission charges. These are called **no-load funds**.

The argument in favour of load funds is that their managers provide investors with more personal attention and advice than managers of no-load funds. However, the cost of this increased attention may not be worthwhile.

Fund Operating Expenses

In contrast to one-time up-front load charges on the initial investment in a mutual fund, annual fees are charged to cover all fund-level expenses experienced as a percentage of the fund assets. One type of fee (called a *management fee*) is charged

TABLE 5–2 A Selection of the Largest Mutual Funds Ranked by Assets Held, July 2013

Source: *Morningstar*, July 2013, www.morningstar.ca.

Fund Name	Category	Assets ($ millions)	MER (%)
RBC Canadian Dividend Series A	Canadian Dividend & Income Equity	$15,049.17	1.79%
RBC Canadian Dividend Series F	Canadian Dividend & Income Equity	15,049.17	0.94
RBC Canadian Dividend Series Adv	Canadian Dividend & Income Equity	15,049.17	1.77
RBC Canadian Dividend Series T5	Canadian Dividend & Income Equity	15,049.17	1.82
RBC Canadian Dividend Series T8	Canadian Dividend & Income Equity	15,049.17	1.76
RBC Canadian Dividend Series D	Canadian Dividend & Income Equity	15,049.17	1.22
RBC Canadian Dividend Series I	Canadian Dividend & Income Equity	15,049.17	0.52
Investors Dividend A	Canadian Equity Balanced	14,486.89	2.46
Investors Dividend B	Canadian Equity Balanced	14,486.89	2.58
Investors Dividend C	Canadian Equity Balanced	14,486.89	2.83
RBC Select Conservative Portfolio F	Global Neutral Balanced	11,702.40	0.81
RBC Bond Adv	Canadian Fixed Income	11,050.77	1.17
TD Canadian Bond A	Canadian Fixed Income	10,810.63	1.37
RBC Select Balanced Portfolio Series F	Canadian Fixed Income	9,441.75	0.90
Fidelity Monthly Income Series A	Canadian Neutral Balanced	9,421.28	2.29

management fee
The amount paid to an investment manager for operating a mutual fund.

management expense ratio (MER)
A mutual fund's operating costs expressed as a percentage of its total average assets.

trailer fee
A commission paid monthly or quarterly to the investment advisor who sells a fund. It is payable as a percentage of the assets for as long as the investor owns the fund.

investment advisor
A person licensed to sell investment products to the public.

to meet operating costs (such as administration and shareholder services). In addition, mutual funds generally require a small percentage (or fee) of investable funds to meet fund-level marketing and distribution costs.

The amount the investor pays to the fund for investment management and administrative costs (excluding brokerage fees) is reported as a **management fee**. As shown in Table 5–2, the level of management fees is expressed as the **management expense ratio (MER)**, which is the ratio of all the costs to operate a fund as a percentage of the average total assets in the fund.

The MER is often increased by the inclusion of a **trailer fee** (also called a *trailer commission*), which is an amount paid monthly or quarterly to the **investment advisor** (i.e., the person who sells the fund to the investor) as long as the investor owns the fund. These fees are controversial as they may amount to 50 basis points or 0.5 percent per year of the amount of assets owned by the investor and, since they are essentially a sales commission, do not relate to the actual management of the funds year to year. The payment of trailer fees is included in the fund's prospectus, but many investors rely on their advisor's recommendations. The advisor has a conflict of interest and could recommend those funds for which he or she would receive a trailer fee. Since mutual fund pricing is done on funds whose values and number of units outstanding may change on a daily basis, calculating the returns can be a difficult exercise, and the results subject to interpretation.

EXAMPLE 5–4

Calculation of Mutual Fund Costs

The cost of mutual fund investing to the shareholder includes both the one-time sales load and any annual fees charged. Because the sales load is a one-time charge, it must be converted to an annualized payment incurred by the shareholder over the life of his or her investment. With this conversion, the total shareholder cost of investing in a fund is the sum of the annualized sales load and any annual fees.

For example, suppose an investor purchases fund shares with a 4 percent front-end load and expects to hold the shares for 10 years. The annualized sales load[1] incurred by the investor is

4 percent/10 years = 0.4 percent per year

[1] Convention in the industry is to annualize the sales load without adjusting for the time value of money.

Further, suppose the fund has a management expense ratio of 1 percent per year. The annual total shareholder cost for this fund is calculated as

0.4 percent + 1 percent = 1.4 percent per year

Funds sold through financial professionals such as brokers have recently adopted alternative payment methods. These typically include an annual fee based on asset values that also may be combined with a front-end or back-end sales charge. In many cases, funds offer several different share classes (all of which invest in the same underlying portfolio of assets), but each share class may offer investors different methods of paying for broker services and therefore have different MERs. For example, a fund could be sold to offer investors three payment plans through three share classes (A, B, and C), each having different mixes of sales loads and management fees. Class A shares could represent the traditional means for paying for investment advice. That is, class A shares carry a front-end load that is charged at the time of purchase as a percentage of the sales price. The front-end load on class A shares would be charged on new sales and not generally incurred when class A shares are exchanged for another mutual fund within the same fund family. In addition to the front-end load, class A shares could have annual management fees that are used to compensate brokers and sales professionals for ongoing assistance and service provided to fund shareholders. As an example, the management fees for class A shares could typically be between 25 and 35 basis points of the portfolio's assets. Unlike class A shares, class B shares would be offered for sale at the NAV without a front-end load. Class B share investors would pay for advice and assistance from brokers through a combination of annual management fees and a back-end load. The back-end load would be charged when shares are redeemed (sold) and would typically be based on the lesser of the original cost of the shares and the market value at the time of sale. After six to eight years, class B shares typically convert to class A shares, lowering the level of the annual management fees from 1 percent to that of A shares. Class C shares would be offered at the NAV with no front-end load, and they typically would recover distribution costs through a combination of annual management fees of 1 percent and a back-end load, set at 1 percent in the first year of purchase. After the first year, no back-end load is charged on redemption. Class C shares would not usually convert to class A shares, and thus the annual 1 percent payment to the broker continues throughout the period of time that the shares are held. As can be seen from Table 5–2, RBC's Canadian Dividend Fund comes in seven different series with seven different MERs, reflecting the level and type of fees paid. The Investors Dividend Fund comes in ten different series, but of the three shown in Table 5–2, the MER increases from A to B to C as we discussed in the example above. This reflects the type of fees that apply. Details would be provided in the fund's prospectus, available at Investors' website. Since returns are net of the MER, Investors Dividend C would have a lower return than A or B because the expenses paid by the investor are higher.

CONCEPT QUESTIONS

1. **Describe the difference between short-term and long-term mutual funds.**
2. **Describe the difference between open-end and closed-end mutual funds.**
3. **What is the difference between a mutual fund and an exchange-traded fund?**

Regulation

The mutual fund industry is regulated by the provincial and territorial securities commissions (e.g., the OSC) and thus is subject to the rules regarding securities sales and distribution. In addition, each mutual fund is a member of an SRO such as the

mfda.ca

Mutual Fund Dealers Association of Canada (MFDA)
An SRO governing issues related to mutual funds in Canada.

market timing
Excessive buying and selling of securities to take advantage of arbitrage opportunities between different markets.

late trading (or backward pricing)
Illegally buying or selling securities submitted after the closing time at that day's price.

directed brokerage fees
Fees paid to brokerage firms for promoting a stock or mutual fund.

forward pricing
Execution of a security trade received after market hours at the following day's price.

IIAC or the **Mutual Fund Dealers Association of Canada (MFDA)**. However, Canadian FIs and investors are globally oriented, and integration of the Canadian and the U.S. financial markets means that cross-border issues are important for both Canadian FIs and Canadian regulators. The actions of the SEC, including the Sarbanes-Oxley Act of 2002, and the prosecution of brokers for insider trading and market timing have implications for Canadian markets and have focused global attention on corporate governance and stable and efficient capital markets.

In the early 2000s, the SEC investigated securities violations by the mutual fund industry. The market for mutual funds was rocked by charges of **market timing, late trading (or backward pricing)**, and **directed brokerage fees.**

Market timing involves short-term trading of mutual funds that seeks to take advantage of short-term discrepancies between the price of a mutual fund's shares and out-of-date values on the securities in the fund's portfolio. It is especially common in international funds, as traders can exploit differences in time zones. Typically, market timers hold a fund for only a few days. For example, when Asian markets close with losses but are expected to rebound the following day, market timers can buy a mutual fund, investing in Asian securities after the loss on that day, and then sell the shares for a profit the next day. This single-day investment dilutes the profits of the fund's long-term investors, while market timers profit without much risk.

The U.S. late trading allegations involved cases in which some investors were able to buy or sell mutual fund shares long after the price had been set at 4:00 PM Eastern time each day (i.e., after the close of the exchange). Under existing rules, investors have to place an order with their broker or another FI by 4:00 PM. If the mutual fund company has not received the order until much later, it legally must be **forward priced**, that is, processed at the next trading day's price. However, because of this time delay, some large U.S. investors had been able to illegally call their broker back after the market closed and alter or cancel their orders. The Canadian system differs in that most orders are processed through the banks (or through a clearing agency, FundSERV Inc.), which automatically time-stamps the order and places it in the queue for next-day pricing. This makes late trading difficult in Canada.

Directed brokerage involves arrangements between mutual fund companies and brokerage houses and whether those agreements improperly influenced which funds brokers recommended to investors. The U.S. investigation examined whether some mutual fund companies agreed to direct orders for stock and bond purchases and sales to brokerage houses that agreed to promote sales of the mutual fund company's products.

The U.S. investigations resulted in some of the largest names in the U.S. securities industry (Bank of America, Charles Schwab, Citigroup, Merrill Lynch) being disciplined, destroying investor confidence in the fairness of the markets. In 2003, in response to the U.S. situation, an investigation in Canada was set up with the securities regulators, the Investment Dealers Association (IDA), and the MFDA. From late 2003 to 2004, Canadian mutual funds were questioned about market timing (which is not illegal in Canada but is not in the interests of all investors in the funds) and late trading. The report was released in March 2005, and agreements were made with CI Mutual Funds, AGF Funds, IG Investment Management, and AIC to repay $156.5 million to investors harmed by the trading practices.

The result of both the Canadian and the U.S. investigations is the increased and ongoing scrutiny of the industry by investors and the movement toward more regulation in order to ensure a transparent system that is fair for investors and promotes efficient markets.

CONCEPT QUESTION

Who regulates mutual funds in Canada?

GLOBAL ISSUES

As discussed throughout the chapter, mutual funds have been a fast-growing sector in the Canadian FI industry throughout the 1990s and into the 2000s. Only the worldwide financial crisis and the worst worldwide recession since the Great Depression curtailed the growth in this industry. Worldwide, investments in mutual funds (Table 5–3) have increased from US$21.8 trillion in 2006 to US$26.8 trillion in 2012 but declined to US$18.9 trillion in 2008. In contrast, as this industry developed in countries throughout the world, the number of mutual funds increased from 61,855 in 2006 to 73,243 in 2012.

HEDGE FUNDS

LO4

History, Size, Structure, and Composition of the Industry

Hedge funds are a type of investment pool that solicits funds from wealthy individuals and other investors (e.g., banks, insurance companies) and invests these funds on their behalf. Hedge funds are similar to mutual funds in that they are pooled investment vehicles that accept investors' money and generally invest it on a collective basis.

Hedge funds are, however, not subject to the numerous regulations that apply to mutual funds for the protection of individuals, such as regulations requiring a certain degree of liquidity, regulations requiring that mutual fund shares be redeemable at any time, regulations protecting against conflicts of interest, regulations to ensure fairness in the pricing of funds shares, disclosure regulations, and regulations limiting the use of leverage. Further, hedge funds do not have to disclose their activities to third parties. Therefore, hedge funds are usually sold without a prospectus and generally are not required to publish financial statements on SEDAR. Thus, hedge funds offer a high degree of privacy for their investors.

Historically, U.S. hedge funds avoided regulations by limiting the number of investors to fewer than 100 individuals (below the number required for SEC registration), who must be deemed "accredited investors." To be accredited, an investor must have a net worth of over US$1 million or have an annual income of at least US$200,000 (US$300,000 if married). These stiff financial requirements allowed hedge funds to avoid regulation under the theory that individuals with such wealth should be able to evaluate the risk and return on their investments. According to the SEC, these types of investors should be expected to make more informed decisions and take on higher levels of risk. However, as a result of some heavily publicized hedge fund failures and near failures (the result of fraud by fund managers, e.g., Bernard L. Madoff Investment Securities, and the financial

TABLE 5–3 Worldwide Total Net Assets of Mutual Funds, Year-End 2006–Year-End 2012 (U.S. $ millions)*

	2006	2007	2008	2009	2010	2011	2012
World	**$21,808,884**	**$26,131,496**	**$18,920,057**	**$22,945,623**	**$24,710,398**	**$23,796,672**	**$26,837,407**
Americas	**11,470,489**	**13,423,089**	**10,581,988**	**12,578,593**	**13,598,071**	**13,530,122**	**15,139,998**
Argentina	6,153	6,789	3,867	4,470	5,179	6,808	9,185
Brazil	418,771	615,365	479,321	783,970	980,448	1,008,928	1,070,998
Canada	566,298	698,397	416,031	565,156	636,947	753,606	856,504
Chile	17,700	24,444	17,587	34,227	38,243	33,425	37,900
Costa Rica	1,018	1,203	1,098	1,309	1,470	1,266	1,484
Mexico	62,614	75,428	60,435	70,659	98,094	92,743	112,201
Trinidad and Tobago	N/A	N/A	N/A	5,832	5,812	5,989	6,505
United States	10,397,935	12,001,463	9,603,649	11,112,970	11,831,878	11,627,357	13,045,221
Europe	**7,803,877**	**8,934,861**	**6,231,116**	**7,545,535**	**7,903,389**	**7,220,298**	**8,230,061**
Austria	128,236	138,709	93,269	99,628	94,670	81,038	89,125
Belgium	137,291	149,842	105,057	106,721	96,288	81,505	81,651
Bulgaria	N/A	N/A	226	256	302	291	324
Czech Republic	6,488	7,595	5,260	5,436	5,508	4,445	5,001
Denmark	95,601	104,083	65,182	83,024	89,800	84,891	103,506
Finland	67,804	81,136	48,750	66,131	71,210	62,193	73,985
France	1,769,258	1,989,690	1,591,082	1,805,641	1,617,176	1,382,068	1,473,085
Germany	340,325	372,072	237,986	317,543	333,713	293,011	327,640
Greece	27,604	29,807	12,189	12,434	8,627	5,213	6,011
Hungary	8,472	12,573	9,188	11,052	11,532	7,193	8,570
Ireland	855,011	951,371	720,486	860,515	1,014,104	1,061,051	1,276,601
Italy	452,798	419,687	263,588	279,474	234,313	180,754	181,720
Liechtenstein	17,315	25,103	20,489	30,329	35,387	32,606	31,951
Luxembourg	2,188,278	2,685,065	1,860,763	2,293,973	2,512,874	2,277,465	2,641,964
Malta	N/A	N/A	N/A	N/A	N/A	2,132	3,033
Netherlands	108,560	113,759	77,379	95,512	85,924	69,156	76,145
Norway	54,075	74,709	41,157	71,170	84,505	79,999	98,723
Poland	28,959	45,542	17,782	23,025	25,595	18,463	25,883
Portugal	31,214	29,732	13,572	15,808	11,004	7,321	7,509
Romania	247	390	326	1,134	1,713	2,388	2,613
Russia	5,659	7,175	2,026	3,182	3,917	3,072	N/A
Slovakia	3,168	4,762	3,841	4,222	4,349	3,191	2,952
Slovenia	2,486	4,219	2,067	2,610	2,663	2,279	2,370
Spain	367,918	396,534	270,983	269,611	216,915	195,220	191,284
Sweden	176,968	194,955	113,331	170,277	205,449	179,707	205,733
Switzerland	159,517	176,282	135,052	168,260	261,893	273,061	310,686
Turkey	15,462	22,609	15,404	19,426	19,545	14,048	16,478
United Kingdom	755,163	897,460	504,681	729,141	854,413	816,537	985,517
Asia and Pacific	**2,456,492**	**3,678,325**	**2,037,536**	**2,715,234**	**3,067,323**	**2,921,276**	**3,322,198**
Australia	864,234	1,192,988	841,133	1,198,838	1,455,850	1,440,128	1,667,128
China	N/A	434,063	276,303	381,207	364,985	339,037	437,449
Hong Kong	631,055	818,421	N/A	N/A	N/A	N/A	N/A
India	58,219	108,582	62,805	130,284	111,421	87,519	114,489
Japan	578,883	713,998	575,327	660,666	785,504	745,383	738,488
Korea, Rep. of	251,930	329,979	221,992	264,573	266,495	226,716	267,582
New Zealand	12,892	14,925	10,612	17,657	19,562	23,709	31,145
Pakistan	2,164	4,956	1,985	2,224	2,290	2,984	3,159
Philippines	1,544	2,090	1,263	1,488	2,184	2,363	3,566
Taiwan	55,571	58,323	46,116	58,297	59,032	53,437	59,192
Africa	**78,026**	**95,221**	**69,417**	**106,261**	**141,615**	**124,976**	145,150
South Africa	78,026	95,221	69,417	106,261	141,615	124,976	**145,150**

* Funds of funds are not included except for France, Italy, and Luxembourg. Data include home-domiciled funds, except for Hong Kong, the Republic of Korea, and New Zealand, which include home- and foreign-domiciled funds.

N/A = not available

Note: Components may not add to the total because of rounding.

Source: Investment Company Institute, ICI Fact Book, 2012, ici.org.

TABLE 5–4
Largest Hedge Fund Firms by Assets Managed, 2012

Source: Institutional Investor, January 2013, institutionalinvestor.com

Name of Fund	Country	Total Assets (in U.S. $ billions)
Bridgewater Associates	United States	$76.1
J.P. Morgan Asset Management	United States	53.6
Man Group	United Kingdom	38.5
Brevan Howard Asset Management	United Kingdom	34.2
Winton Capital Management	United Kingdom	30.0
Och-Ziff Capital Management Group	United States	28.8
BlackRock	United States	28.8
BlueCrest Capital Management	United Kingdom	28.6
Baupost Group	United States	25.2
AQR Capital Management	United States	23.2
Paulson & Co.	United States	22.6

crisis, e.g., Bear Stearns High Grade Structured Credit Strategies Fund), in 2010 U.S. federal regulators increased the oversight of hedge funds.

Because hedge funds have been exempt from many of the rules and regulations governing mutual funds, they can use aggressive strategies that are unavailable to mutual funds, including short selling, leveraging, program trading, arbitrage, and derivatives trading. Further, since hedge funds that do not exceed US$100 million in AUM do not register with the SEC, their actual data cannot be independently tracked. Therefore, much hedge fund information is self-reported. It is estimated that in 2013 there were over 8,000 hedge funds in the world, with managed assets estimated at US$2.25 trillion. Table 5–4 lists the largest hedge funds by total assets managed in 2012.

Hedge funds grew in popularity in the 1990s as investors saw returns of over 40 percent after management fees (often more than 25 percent of the fund's profits). They came to the forefront in the news in the late 1990s when one large hedge fund, Long-Term Capital Management (LTCM), nearly collapsed. LTCM's troubles not only hurt its investors, but also arguably came close to damaging the world's financial system through the credit risk exposure of other FIs. LTCM had lines of credit from FIs such as banks and brokerages that were used to increase the size of its investment pool and to exploit arbitrage opportunities. At its peak, LTCM had only approximately US$5 billion in capital supporting US$120 billion in investments, a debt-to-equity ratio of 24 times. To prevent LTCM's collapse, the U.S. Federal Reserve intervened by brokering a US$3.6 billion bailout by a consortium of some of the world's largest FIs.

The Canadian hedge fund industry is much smaller than the global market. The industry was estimated to be approximately $30 billion in 2011. The industry association, the Alternative Investment Management Association (AIMA), provides support for the industry. Scotia Capital produces the Canadian Hedge Fund Performance Index, which tracks open and closed funds with a minimum of $15 million in AUM. The list of 75 funds on which the data are based is available at www.gbm.scotiabank.com. Figure 5–3 shows the monthly performance of the hedge funds from December 2004 to March 2013.

Some hedge funds take positions (using sophisticated computer models) speculating that some prices will rise faster than others. For example, a hedge fund may buy (take a long position in) a bond expecting that its price will rise. At the same time, the fund will borrow (take a short position in) another bond and sell it, promising to

FIGURE 5–3

Scotia Capital's Canadian Hedge Fund Performance Index, Historical Monthly Performance, December 2004–May 2013

Source: Scotia Capital, scotiacapital.com/hfpi, May 2013.

return the borrowed bond in the future. Generally, bond prices tend to move up and down together. Thus, if prices go up as expected, the hedge fund will gain on the bond it purchased while losing money on the bond it borrowed. The hedge fund will make a profit if the gain on the bond it purchased is larger than the loss on the bond it borrowed. If, contrary to expectations, bond prices fall, the hedge fund will make a profit if the gains on the bond it borrowed are greater than the losses on the bond it bought. Thus, regardless of the change in prices, the simultaneous long and short positions in bonds will minimize the risk of overall losses for the hedge fund. This strategy is sometimes called **nondirectional** since the direction of market movement is irrelevant and so the market risk exposure for the hedge fund is low.

nondirectional strategy
An arbitrage position that allows a hedge fund to benefit whether market prices go up or down.

Types of Hedge Funds

Most hedge funds are highly specialized, relying on the specific expertise of the fund manager(s) to produce a profit. Hedge fund managers follow a variety of investment strategies, some of which use leverage and derivatives, while others use more conservative strategies and involve little or no leverage. Generally, hedge funds are set up with specific parameters so that investors can forecast a risk–return profile. Figure 5–4 shows the general categories of hedge funds by risk classification.

FIGURE 5–4 Classification of Hedge Funds

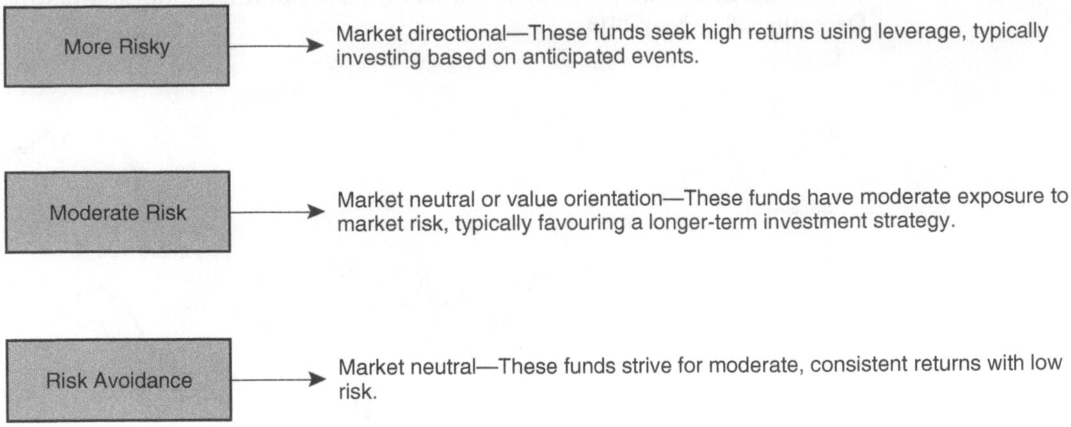

More Risky
Market directional—These funds seek high returns using leverage, typically investing based on anticipated events.
Moderate Risk
Market neutral or value orientation—These funds have moderate exposure to market risk, typically favouring a longer-term investment strategy.
Risk Avoidance
Market neutral—These funds strive for moderate, consistent returns with low risk.

More risky funds are the most aggressive and may produce profits in many types of market environments. Funds in this group are classified by objectives such as aggressive growth, emerging markets, macro, market timing, and short selling. Aggressive growth funds invest in equities expected to experience acceleration in growth of earnings per share. Generally, low- or no-dividend companies with high price-to-earnings ratios are included. These funds hedge by shorting equities where earnings disappointment is expected, or by shorting stock indexes. Emerging market funds invest in equity or debt securities of emerging markets, which tend to have higher inflation and volatile growth. Macro funds aim to profit from changes in global economies, typically brought about by shifts in government policy that impact interest rates. These funds include investments in equities, bonds, currencies, and commodities. They use leverage and derivatives to accentuate the impact of market moves. Market timing funds allocate assets among different asset classes depending on the manager's view of the economic or market outlook. Thus, portfolio emphasis may swing widely between asset classes. The unpredictability of market movements and the difficulty of timing entry and exit from markets add significant risk to this strategy. Short-selling funds sell securities in anticipation of being able to buy them back in the future at a lower price based on the manager's assessment of the overvaluation of the securities or in anticipation of earnings disappointments.

Moderate risk funds are more traditional funds, similar to mutual funds, with only a portion of the portfolio being hedged. Funds in this group are classified by objectives such as distressed securities; funds of funds; and opportunistic, multistrategy, and special situations. Distressed securities funds buy equity, debt, or trade claims, at deep discounts, of companies in or facing bankruptcy or reorganization. Profit opportunities come from the market's lack of understanding of the true value of these deep-discount securities and from the fact that the majority of institutional investors cannot own below-investment-grade securities. Funds of funds mix hedge funds and other pooled investment vehicles. This blending of different strategies and asset classes aims to provide a more stable long-term investment return than any of the individual funds. Returns and risk can be controlled by the mix of underlying strategies and funds. Capital preservation is generally an important consideration for these funds. Opportunistic funds change their investment strategy as opportunities arise to profit from events such as IPOs, sudden price changes resulting from a disappointing earnings announcement, and hostile takeover bids. These funds may utilize several investing styles at any point in time and are not restricted to any particular investment approach or asset class. Multistrategy funds take a diversified investment approach by implementing various strategies simultaneously to realize short- and long-term gains. This style of investment allows the manager to overweight or underweight different strategies to best capitalize on current investment opportunities. Special-situation funds invest in event-driven situations such as mergers, hostile takeovers, reorganizations, and leveraged buyouts. These funds may undertake the simultaneous purchase of stock in a company being acquired and sale of stock in its bidder, hoping to profit from the spread between the current market price and the final purchase price of the company.

Risk-avoidance funds are also more traditional funds, emphasizing consistent but moderate returns while avoiding risk. Funds in this group are classified by objectives such as income, market-neutral arbitrage, market-neutral securities hedging, and value. Income funds invest with the primary focus on yield or current income rather than solely on capital gains. These funds use leverage to buy bonds and some fixed-income derivatives, profiting from principal appreciation and interest income. Market-neutral arbitrage funds attempt to hedge market risk by taking offsetting positions, often in different securities of the same issuer. For example, a fund could hold a position that is long a firm's convertible bonds and short a firm's equity. Their focus is on obtaining returns with low or no correlation to both equity and bond markets. Market-neutral securities hedging funds invest equally in long and short equity portfolios in particular market sectors. Market risk is reduced, but effective stock analysis is critical to obtaining a profit. These funds use leverage to magnify their returns. They also sometimes use market index futures to hedge systematic risk. Value funds invest in securities perceived to be selling at deep discounts relative to their intrinsic values. Securities include those that may be out of favour or underfollowed by analysts.

Using traditional risk-adjusted measures of performance (such as Sharpe ratios), the performance of hedge funds has been very strong compared to that of traditional financial investments like stocks and bonds.[2] Many hedge funds posted strong returns during the early 2000s even as stock returns were plummeting. A few hedge funds even performed well during the financial crisis. Table 5–5 lists the top U.S. hedge fund managers and their hedge fund company by 2009 earnings. The average hedge fund lost 15.7 percent in 2008, the worst performance on record. Nearly three-quarters of all hedge funds experienced losses. Nevertheless, many funds outperformed many of the underlying markets, such as the S&P 500 index. Note that two of the hedge funds listed in Table 5–5 earned positive returns for 2008 as well as 2009 and one, BlueGold Global Fund, earned 209.4 percent in 2008, a year where the S&P 500 index earned a return of −37.0 percent. Indeed, only two of the listed hedge funds performed worse during the beginning of the financial crisis than the S&P 500 index. Performance improved significantly in 2009 with the average fund earning over 20 percent for the year, the highest level since 2003 and the second-best return in 10 years. However, the 2009 return on the S&P 500 index was 26.46 percent. Note that while mutual fund performance is generally measured by

---

[2] However, data deficiencies in the reporting and collection of hedge fund returns somewhat reduce confidence in all measures of hedge fund performance. Further, the inability to explain returns of individual hedge funds with standard multifactor risk models leaves open the possibility that it is not possible to properly measure the risk associated with at least some hedge fund strategies. If so, risk-adjusted returns earned by hedge funds may be overstated.

TABLE 5–5
Largest U.S. Hedge Funds by Fund Earnings, 2008–2009

Source: Bloomberg, 2009. www.bloomberg.com.

Fund, Manager Name(s)	Fund Company	2009 Return	2008 Return
Appaloosa Investment I, David Tepper	Appaloosa Mgmt.	117.3%	−26.7%
Redwood Capital Master, Jonathan Kolatch	Redwood Captial Mgmt.	69.1	−33.0
Glenview Institutional Partners, Larry Robbins	Glenview Capital Mgmt.	67.1	−49.0
PARS IV, Changhong Zhu	Pacific Investment Mgmt.	61.0	−17.0
Tennenbaum Opportunities V, TCP Investment Committee	Tennenbaum Capital Partners	58.5	−51.2
Kensington Global Strategies, Kenneth Griffin	Citadel Investment Group	57.0	−55.0
BlueGold Global, Pierre Andurand, Dennis Crema	BlueGold Capital Mgmt.	54.6	209.4
Waterstone Market Neutral Master, Shawn Bergerson	Waterstone Capital Mgmt.	50.3	12.0
Canyon Value Realization, Mitchell Julis, Joshua Friedman	Canyon Partners	49.6	−29.0
Discovery Global Opportunity, Robert Citrone	Discovery Capital Mgmt.	47.9	−31.0

returns relative to some benchmark (and therefore can perform "well" even by losing 10 percent if the benchmark loses 10.5 percent), performance of hedge funds is measured by the growth in total assets managed. AUM in the U.S. hedge fund industry fell by nearly 30 percent (to US$1.5 trillion) in 2008. The decline was the largest on record and was attributed to a combination of negative performance, a surge in redemptions, and liquidations of funds.

Hedge fund performance continued to lag into the 2010s. In 2010, the average hedge fund earned 10.3 percent. In 2011 the average was 5.0 percent and in 2012 the average was 6.2 percent. The returns on the S&P 500 Index for these three years were 15.1 percent, 2.0 percent, and 14.5 percent, respectively. As discussed below, hedge funds generally charge fees of 2 percent of the money they manage whether the fund makes money or not. Further, managers may take up to 20 percent of any profit the hedge fund earns. With performance as seen in the last four years, the question for the industry is whether investors will start to lose faith in hedge funds and start liquidating their sizeable investments in these funds. In 2012, the U.S. industry saw net outflows of funds invested of US$31 billion. Man Group, the world's biggest publicly traded hedge fund, has seen its stock drop by 40 percent through mid-2012 after its AUM fell by almost one-third. Table 5–6 lists the top U.S. hedge fund managers and their hedge fund company for 2012.

event-driven strategy
A hedge designed to take advantage of a potential occurrence in the market such as the purchase of shares of a merger target or an investment in distressed debt.

opportunistic strategy
A hedge designed to take advantage of temporary pricing discrepancies in markets.

Despite their name, hedge funds do not always "hedge" their investments to protect the fund and its investors against market price declines and other risks. Some may use an **event-driven strategy** (e.g., potential mergers), and others use an **opportunistic strategy**, designed to take advantage of discrepancies in global macroeconomic conditions or markets. For example, although bond prices generally move in the same direction, the risk in hedge funds is that bond prices may unexpectedly move faster in some markets than in others. In 1997 and 1998, computer models used by LTCM detected a price discrepancy between U.S. Treasury markets and other bonds (including high-yield corporate bonds, mortgage-backed securities, and European government bonds). LTCM consequently shorted U.S. Treasury securities (betting that their prices would fall) and took long positions in

TABLE 5–6
Largest Hedge Funds by Fund Earnings, 2011–2012

Source: Bloomberg, 2013, bloomberg.com.

Fund, Manager Name(s)	Fund Company	2012 Return*	2011 Return
Metacapital Mortgage Opportunities, Deepak Narula	Metacapital Mgmt.	37.8%	23.6%
Pine River Fixed Income, Steve Kuhn	Pine River Capital Mgmt.	32.9	4.8
CQS Directional Opportunities, Michael Hintze	CQS	28.9	−10.4
Pine River Liquid Mortgage, Steve Kuhn/Jiayi Chen	Pine River Capital Mgmt.	28.0	7.2
Omega Overseas Partners A, Leon Cooperman	Omega Advisors	24.4	−1.4
Odey Europen, Crispin Odey	Odey Asset Mgmt.	24.1	−20.3
Marathon Securitized Credit, Bruce Richards/ Louis Hanover	Marathon Asset Mgmt.	24.0	−4.2
Palomino, David Tepper	Appaloosa Mgmt.	24.0	−3.5
BTG Pactual GEMM, Team managed	BTG Pactual Global Asset Mgmt.	23.1	3.4
Third Point Ultra, Daniel Loeb	Third Point	22.1	−2.3

* Through three quarters.

other types of bonds (betting their prices would rise). However, unexpectedly, in 1998 large drops in many foreign stock markets caused money to pour into the U.S. Treasury markets, driving Treasury security prices up and yields down. This drop in U.S. Treasury yields drove rates on mortgages down, which pushed down the prices of many mortgage-backed securities. Further, the flight to U.S. Treasury security markets meant a drop in funds flowing into European bond markets and high-yield corporate bond markets. With all of its positions going wrong, LTCM experienced huge losses. A major reason for LTCM's large loss was that it was two to four times as leveraged as the typical fund.

Similarly, the failures of two of Bear Stearns' hedge funds (Bear Stearns High-Grade Structured Credit Fund and Bear Stearns High-Grade Structured Credit Enhanced Leveraged Fund) were the result of managers' failure to accurately predict how the subprime bond market would behave under extreme circumstances. The market moved against them, and their investors lost US$1.6 billion when the funds, heavily invested in mortgage securities, collapsed in the summer of 2007. The failures were the first sign of the upcoming financial crisis that would eventually cripple financial markets and the overall economy.

The strategy employed by the Bear Stearns funds was quite simple. Specifically, the funds purchased collateralized debt obligations (CDOs) that paid an interest rate over and above the cost of borrowing. Thus, every incremental unit of leverage added to the hedge funds' total expected return. To capitalize on this, fund managers used as much leverage as they could raise. Because the use of leverage increased the portfolio's exposure, fund managers purchased insurance on movements in credit markets. The insurance instruments, called credit default swaps (CDSs), were designed to cover losses during times when credit concerns cause the bonds to fall in value, effectively hedging away some of the risk. In instances when credit markets (or the underlying bonds' prices) remained relatively stable, or even when they behaved in line with historically based expectations, this strategy generated consistent, positive returns with very little deviation.

Unfortunately, as the problems with subprime debt began to appear, the subprime mortgage-backed securities market behaved well outside of what the portfolio managers expected. This started a chain of events that imploded the funds. The subprime mortgage market began to see substantial increases in delinquencies from homeowners, which caused sharp decreases in the market values of these types of bonds. Since the Bear Stearns hedge fund managers failed to expect these sorts of extreme price movements, they failed to purchase sufficient credit insurance to protect against these losses. Because they had leveraged their positions substantially, the funds began to experience large losses. The large losses made the creditors who provided the debt financing uneasy. The lenders required Bear Stearns to provide additional cash on their loans because the collateral (subprime bonds) was rapidly falling in value. However, the funds had no cash holdings. Thus, fund managers needed to sell bonds in order to generate cash. Quickly, it became public knowledge that Bear Stearns was in trouble, and competing funds moved to drive the prices of subprime bonds lower to force Bear Stearns into an asset fire-sale. As prices on bonds fell, the fund experienced losses, which caused it to sell more bonds, which lowered the prices of the bonds, which caused it to sell more bonds. It did not take long before the funds had experienced a complete loss of capital.

Fees on Hedge Funds

Hedge fund managers generally charge two type of fees: management fees and performance fees. As with mutual funds, the management fee is computed as a percentage of the total AUM and typically runs between 1.5 and 2.0 percent. Performance fees are unique to hedge funds. Performance fees give the fund manager a share of any positive returns on a hedge fund. The average performance fee on hedge funds is approximately 20 percent but varies widely. For example, SAC Capital Partners charges a performance fee of 50 percent. Performance fees are paid to the hedge fund manager before returns are paid to the fund investors. Hedge funds often specify a *hurdle rate*, which is a minimum annualized performance benchmark that must be realized before a performance fee can be assessed. Further, a *high-water mark* is usually used for hedge funds in which the manager does not receive a performance fee unless the value of the fund exceeds the highest NAV that it has ever achieved. High-water marks are used to link the fund manager's incentives more closely to those of the fund investors and to reduce the manager's incentive to increase the risk of trades.

Offshore Hedge Funds

Many offshore financial centres encourage hedge funds to locate in their countries. The major centres are the Cayman Islands, Bermuda, Dublin, and Luxembourg. The Cayman Islands are estimated to be the location of approximately 75 percent of all hedge funds. Offshore hedge funds are regulated in that they must obey the rules of the host country. However, the rules in most of these countries are not generally burdensome and provide anonymity to fund investors.

When compared to domestic hedge funds, offshore hedge funds have been found to trade more intensely, due to the low or zero capital gains tax for offshore funds. Further, offshore hedge funds tend to engage less often in positive feedback trading (rushing to buy when the market is booming and rushing to sell when the market is declining) than domestic hedge funds. Finally, offshore hedge funds have been found to herd (mimic each other's behaviour when trading while ignoring information about the fundamentals of valuation) less than domestic hedge funds. Many hedge fund managers maintain both domestic and offshore hedge funds. Given the needs of their client investors, hedge fund managers want to have both types of funds to attract all types of investors.

Regulation

While mutual funds are very highly regulated, hedge funds have generally been unregulated. However, their role in global capital markets has come under scrutiny in recent years, particularly as they are participants in the shadow banking sector. It is thought that no one fund is likely to pose a systemic risk since, after LTCM, the amount of borrowing that banks extend to any one hedge fund client is far more carefully monitored by bank regulators. But, given the copycat nature of hedge fund management, there is concern that similar fund strategies by many hedge funds are combining to create potential LTCM-type problems. Along with the use of similar investment strategies, many hedge funds are using the same risk models. These models are often historically based and are subject to similar errors in predicting the future.

iosco.org
www.financialstabilityboard.org
bankofcanada.ca

The International Organization of Securities Commissions (IOSCO), whose members represent securities regulators around the world, including Canada and the United States, as well as the FSB and the BIS (which includes the Bank of Canada), are currently evaluating the policy actions that must be taken to ensure that the shadow banking system does not pose a significant systemic risk. In Canada, as hedge funds expand from targeting the sophisticated large investor to targeting the smaller "retail" customer, securities regulators are starting to be concerned, hence the 2005 report by IDA (now IIAC), *Regulatory Analysis of Hedge Funds*. Unlike mutual funds, hedge funds are not required to report their holdings and they are usually organized as limited partnerships and structured to be exempt from securities laws governing their marketing practices, conflicts of interest, and disclosure of financials. Since September 2009, however, they are required to be registered. Discussions about regulating hedge funds have been spurred on by the scandal surrounding Portus Alternative Asset Management Inc., a hedge fund that has caused losses for investors and other FIs who referred investors such as Manulife Securities International Ltd., a unit of Manulife Financial that sells mutual funds. The global impact of hedge funds means that disclosure and regulation of their activities can be expected to increase in the future.

CONCEPT QUESTIONS

1. **What is the difference between a mutual fund and a hedge fund?**
2. **What are the performance fees charged by hedge funds?**
3. **How is the regulatory status of hedge funds changing?**

PENSION FUNDS

Size, Structure, and Composition of the Industry

Growth of mutual funds and hedge funds may be driven by retirement savings as previously discussed, but pension funds are directly driven by government regulations regarding retirement savings in Canada, and represent the biggest funds in Canada. Retirement savings in Canada come from:

trusteed pension funds
Registered pension plans (RPPs) usually sponsored by employers for the benefit of their employees and governed by a trust agreement.

1. Government-funded or -sponsored plans, e.g., the Canada Pension Plan and Quebec Pension Plan
2. Employer-sponsored pension plans, e.g., **trusteed pension funds**, profit-sharing plans, group RRSPs
3. Individual savings, e.g., RRSPs

TABLE 5–7 Top 20 Pension Funds in Canada by Asset Size, December 31, 2012 ($ millions)

Source: Benefits Canada, Top 100 Pension Funds, June 2013, benefitscanada.com.

Rank	Organization	Change (%) 2011–2013	2012 ($ millions)	2011 ($ millions)
1	Ontario Teachers' Pension Plan	▲ 9.5%	$127,263.0	$116,258.0
2	Ontario Municipal Employees Retirement System	▲ 10.3	60,767.0	55,083.0
3	Healthcare of Ontario Pension Plan	▲ 17.6	47,400.0	40,300.0
4	Public Service Pension Plan	▲ 11.4	47,128.0	42,310.0
5	Quebec Government & Public Employees Retirement Plan	▲ 7.5	45,140.6	41,981.8
6	B.C. Municipal Pension Fund	▲ 10.8	31,014.4	27,998.3
7	Alberta Local Authorities Pension Plan	▲ 16.2	22,800.0	19,615.2
8	B.C. Public Service Pension Plan	▲ 8.5	20,213.8	18,635.0
9	Ontario Pension Board	▲ 9.8	18,964.1	17,269.9
10	B.C. Teachers Pension Fund	▲ 8.4	18,308.8	16,886.3
11	BCE Master Trust Fund	▲ 8.2	17,727.0	16,384.0
12	Canada Post Corp.	▲ 8.8	16,743.5	15,383.3
13	Hydro-Quebec	▲ 10.2	16,414.0	14,897.0
14	Canadian National Railways	▲ 8.5	15,811.0	14,574.0
15	OPSEU Pension Trust	▲ 7.1	14,686.0	13,707.0
16	Quebec Construction Industry	▲ 10.1	14,469.2	13,142.7
17	Canadian Forces Pension Plan	▲ 10.1	12,438.0	11,300.0
18	Air Canada Pension Investments	▲ 10.9	12,737.7	11,120.6
19	General Motors of Canada Ltd.	▲ 2.3	11,132.0	10,877.0
20	Ontario Power Generation Inc.	▲ 7.2	10,299.0	9,605.0

vested assets
Contributions to a pension plan that are legally owned by the employee and may be withdrawn prior to retirement and transferred to another registered plan in which the assets are locked in until retirement.

defined contribution plan
A pension plan that sets up a separate account for each employee. A certain percentage is contributed each year and is made available to the employee on retirement.

defined benefit plan
A pension plan that pays benefits to retirees based on a formula.

vesting
Granting of a legal right to an employee to receive funds in a pension plan regardless of whether the employee leaves the company or the pension plan is dissolved.

The top 100 pension funds in Canada had total assets of $877.15 billion in 2012, an increase of almost 11 percent over 2011. The top 20 funds are shown in Table 5–7. The dollar value of pension assets is the next largest source of FI assets after the Big Six banks, but, in 2012, that was equal to approximately 23 percent of the reported $3.8 trillion in assets of the banks that reported to OSFI. While the focus of hedge funds and mutual funds is the market and returns in order to attract investors, pension funds are focused on return and risk in order to meet their liabilities to their beneficiaries at retirement. With the exception of **vested assets**, which may be withdrawn by an employee and placed into a restricted RRSP, the assets of pension funds are withdrawn only to meet payments to beneficiaries. The risk for pension funds is that their asset growth, which comes from both investment returns and new contributions, will not meet their liabilities to their beneficiaries.

As shown in Table 5–7, the 10 largest pension funds in Canada are employer sponsored by provincial governments for civil servants (e.g., teachers, hospital workers), who usually negotiate a pension plan and its benefits as part of a union contract. Plans may be employer sponsored, union sponsored, or jointly sponsored. Pensions can be a significant portion of the benefit package of an employee, and may be classified as a **defined contribution plan**, by which an employer contributes a certain percentage each year (e.g., a percentage of profits) for the benefit of the employee, whose payments on retirement depend on the amount in the plan, or a **defined benefit plan**, whose payments to employees on retirement are known and employer contributions are determined by actuarial calculations based on factors such as mortality rates and investment returns. A plan's assets are held in trust for the benefit of employees, but **vesting**, which gives the employee the legal right to the funds, may occur after a specified period.

Balance Sheet and Recent Trends

The importance of pension funds as FIs in Canada comes from their ability to hold significant ownership of both corporate debt and corporate equity. This differs from the banks, which are precluded from having significant equity holdings in any one company. Thus, pension funds can be significant lenders to domestic and foreign corporations through investments in corporate bonds. They are also shareholders of domestic and foreign corporations through public share purchases and private placements. The growth of pension funds and their significant contribution to the capital of corporations, both in Canada and in the United States, has led to the growth of shareholder activism and the push for pension funds to have representation on companies' boards of directors.

Table 5–8 shows the allocation of assets of trusteed pension funds in Canada at the end of 2011 and 2012. Note that the largest asset categories are bonds (37.1 percent of total assets in 2012) and stocks (31.2 percent in 2012). Unlike the mutual funds and the hedge funds, the liabilities of the pension funds are easier to forecast and have a longer time horizon, resulting in a smaller investment (3.5 percent in 2012) in short-term assets. However, liquidity must be balanced with returns to meet their liabilities. The investment in assets exposes pension funds to interest rate risk, market risk, and foreign exchange risk. As well, the aging of Canada's population means that pension payments to retirees will increase in the coming years, making it even more important to improve on higher returns. Some pension funds, therefore, are moving into alternative assets, such as infrastructure. However, the financial crisis has led many pension funds to turn away from the risk of equities even though low interest rates have reduced the returns on fixed-income assets.

The search for returns along with the growth in size of pension fund assets has fuelled professional fund management in Canada. The management styles of pension funds vary from in-house to a mix of in-house and outside specialist to specialist only. In addition, the assets may be actively or passively managed. The top 40 money managers in Canada in 2012 are listed in Table 5–9. From the last column, it can be seen that while some managers specialize in pension funds so that their pension assets equal their total assets, most funds manage pensions as well

TABLE 5–8
Trusteed Pension Funds: Market Value of Assets by Type, 2011 and 2012

Source: Statistics Canada, July 2013, www.statcan.gc.ca

	Fourth Quarter 2011	Fourth Quarter 2011	Fourth Quarter 2012^P	Fourth Quarter 2012^P	Fourth Quarter 2011 to Fourth Quarter 2012
	millions of dollars	% of total assets	millions of dollars	% of total assets	% change
Total assets	**1,091,507**	**100.0**	**1,193,445**	**100.0**	**9.3**
Bonds	424,418	38.9	443,295	37.1	4.4
Stocks	336,894	30.9	372,931	31.2	10.7
Mortgages	12,135	1.1	12,993	1.1	7.1
Real estate	83,345	7.6	95,786	8.0	14.9
Short-term*	36,288	3.3	41,501	3.5	14.4
Other assets**	191,999	17.6	219,500	18.4	14.3
Assets, funds under $10 million***	6,426	0.6	7,439	0.6	15.8

^P Preliminary.
* Includes cash, deposits, guaranteed investment certificates, and short-term securities.
** Includes investments in foreign and miscellaneous pooled vehicles, as well as accruals and receivables.
*** Assets of small pension funds not broken out in detail.

TABLE 5–9 Top 40 Money Managers, 2012

Top 40 Money Managers			As of December 31, 2012 ($ millions)			
			Total Pension Assets		Change	Total Assets
2012	2011	Company	2012	2011	(%)	2012
1	1	TD Asset Management Group*[1,5]	$ 69,812.0	$62,399.0	11.9%	$194,901.0
2	2	Blackrock	54,182.7	49,931.7	8.5	134,381.5
3	3	Phillips, Hager & North Investment Management Ltd. (RBC Global Asset Management)[1]	45,743.1	42,307.0	8.1	193,670.2
4	5	Beutel Goodman & Company Ltd.	28,016.0	21,766.0	28.7	32,742.0
5	5	State Street Global Advisors Ltd.*	25,209.9	22,406.4	12.5	38,991.1
6	9	Connor, Clark & Lunn Financial Group.	21,001.9	18,267.3	15.0	42,779.1
7	6	Greystone Managed Investments Inc.[2]	20,638.8	21,607.1	−4.5	32,975.4
8	13	Fiera Capital Corp.*[3]	19,219.1	13,629.0	41.0	58,138.3
9	7	MFS McLean Budden Ltd.	19,088.6	20,508.0	−6.9	24,079.7
10	11	CIBC Global Asset Management Inc.[1,2]	17,703.9	16,185.6	9.4	86,606.4
11	10	Standard Life Investments Inc.	16,098.4	16,424.8	−2.0	34,375.4
12	15	Brookfield Asset Management	15,554.0	13,408.0	16.0	17,497.0
13	16	J. P. Morgan Asset Management[1]	15,268.0	12,401.0	23.1	20,643.0
14	8	Jarislowsky, Fraser Ltd.	15,202.0	18,876.9	−19.5	32,373.0
15	12	Letko, Brosseau & Associates Inc.	14,204.0	14,246.0	−0.3	22,302.0
16	17	GLC Asset Management Group Ltd.	12,684.7	11,537.8	9.9	33,663.5
17	19	Pyramis Global Advisors (a Fidelity Investments company)	12,316.6	11,210.6	9.9	69,589.6
18	18	BNY Mellon Asset Management Ltd.	12,313.9	11,523.8	6.9	16,698.4
19	20	Bentall Kennedy (Canada) LP	11,696.0	10,692.0	9.4	19,809.0
20	27	Wellington Management Company, LLP	10,877.9	7,430.0	46.4	13,288.0
21	21	Franklin Templeton Institutional	10,798.0	8,291.0	30.2	37,469.0
22	14	Addenda Capital Inc.	10,483.9	13,597.7	−22.9	25,520.8
23	21	Manulife Asset Management	9,923.5	9,135.0	8.6	37,549.0
24	24	Sprucegrove Investment Management Ltd.	9,887.4	8,528.3	15.9	11,913.0
25	26	Leith Wheeler Investment Counsel Ltd.*[5]	9,795.4	8,673.0	12.9	12,515.8
26	23	Morguard Investments Ltd.	9,605.5	8,586.0	11.9	12,870.6
27	22	PIMCO Canada Corp.	9,085.0	8,906.0	2.0	14,207.0
28	35	Aberdeen Asset Management PLC	7,418.9	4,586.9	61.7	10,764.8
29	30	UBS Global Asset Management (Canada) Inc.[1,2]	6,704.9	5,348.6	25.4	11,815.9
30	32	Guardian Capital LP	5,990.5	4,917.8	21.8	17,005.5
31	36	Baillie Gifford Overseas Ltd.	5,451.0	4,112.7	32.5	7,527.0
32	29	Foyston, Gordon & Payne Inc.	5,384.0	5,664.3	−4.9	11,658.0
33	31	GE Asset Management Canada Company	4,878.5	5,143.3	−5.1	5,368.3
34	34	Russell Investments Canada Ltd.[2]	4,768.8	4,706.5	1.3	13,919.8
35	n/a	Sun Life Global Investments[2,4]	4,541.6	2,749.3	65.2	5,489.9
36	38	SEI[1,2]	4,375.8	3,895.6	12.3	9,193.5
37	37	Invesco	4,114.8	4,011.6	3.3	28,762.7
38	40	Canso Investment Counsel, Ltd.	4,008.5	3,326.0	20.5	9,461.1
39	n/a	Mawer Investment Management Ltd.	3,977.0	1,924.7	106.6	14,316.6
40	n/a	Burgundy Asset Management Ltd.	3,889.9	2,847.8	36.6	10,568.8
		2012 Total:	$591,944.3			
		2011 Total:	$535,709.1			
		% Variance:	10.5%			

Notes:
*2011 value has been restated.
1. Includes overlay strategies.
2. Includes assets managed by third-party managers.
3. Formerly listed as Fiera Sceptre. Merged with Natcan Investment Management to form Fiera Capital Corp., effective April 2, 2012.
4. Sun Life acquired a portion of McLean Budden assets, September 2011.
5. 2011 pension numbers restated due to the reallocation of "Insurance co. segregated" into pension assets.

Figures in this report are based on responses provided by the survey participants. *Benefits Canada* assumes no responsibility for the accuracy of the data provided. All totals are subject to a +/− variance due to rounding.

Source: Carolyn Cakebread, *2013 Top 40 Managers Report: Time to Retool, May 2013*, Benefits Canada, www.benefitscanada.com.

TABLE 5–10
Revenue and Expenditures of Trusteed Pension Funds in Canada, 2012 ($ millions)

Source: Statistics Canada, July 2013, www.statcan.gc.ca.

	Fourth Quarter 2012*	Percentage of Revenue
Revenue:		
Revenue from contributions	$15,898	44.0%
Investment income	10,945	30.3
Net profit on sale of securities	8,371	23.2
Miscellaneous revenue	925	2.6
Total revenue	$36,138	100.0%
Expenditures:		
Pension payments out of funds	$11,770	32.6%
Cost of pension purchased	163	0.5
Cash withdrawals	2,038	5.6
Administration costs	1,169	3.2
Net loss on sale of securities	309	0.9
Other	632	1.7
Total expenditures	$16,081	45.0%

*Preliminary numbers

as other funds, earning a return on their investment in employees and their expertise. The largest manager of pension funds is TD Asset Management, which manages $69.8 billion in pension assets, 35.8 percent of the $194.9 billion in assets under its management. Other asset managers are a mix of U.S. (e.g., State Street Global Advisors, Ltd.) and other Canadian FIs (e.g., Standard Life Investment Inc.). The top 40 money managers in Canada had $591.94 billion in pension AUM in 2012, an increase of 10.5 percent from 2011.

Table 5–10 shows the revenue and expenditures of trusteed pension funds in Canada for 2012. Investment income represents 30.3 percent of the total revenue of the funds, a significant source of the long-term growth in assets of the funds. Contributions from employers and employees provided 44.0 percent of revenues. The major expenditures come from cash withdrawals, at 5.6 percent of revenue, and disbursements to pensioners, at 32.6 percent. Disbursement to pensioners can be expected to increase over the coming years as the population shifts and retirees start drawing benefits. This demographic shift is of global significance, as it represents a switch from savings to consumption for global capital markets.

Regulation

Regulation of pension funds is entirely focused on the best interests of the owners or beneficiaries of the pensions' assets; the regulation, therefore, has not been left to SROs as is the case for mutual funds. Some private pension plans are regulated by and report to OSFI and are subject to the Pension Benefits Standards Act of 1985. Others report to provincial or territorial bodies (e.g., Ontario Pension Board). Regulators are concerned with protecting the retirement savings of funds that may be in danger in the event of insolvency or bankruptcy proceedings, such as the reorganization of Air Canada in the early 2000s and the bankruptcy of Nortel. OSFI may inspect the funds under its jurisdiction and, as well, provides guidelines for recommended industry practice that focuses on proper governance and accountability, as well as appropriate risk management practices.

CONCEPT QUESTIONS

1. **Why are mutual funds and hedge funds primarily self-regulated, whereas pension funds are regulated federally and provincially/territorially?**
2. **Compare the investment practices of mutual funds, hedge funds, and pension funds. Why might they differ?**

GLOBAL ISSUES

The growth in pension funds worldwide was significant between 2002 and 2007. With an average compound annual growth rate of 22.06 percent, Canada was second only to Australia, which had a growth rate of 27.34 percent. Canada's pension assets in 2007 represented 5.9 percent of the top 300 global pension funds tracked by *Pensions & Investments*/Watson Wyatt and 5.3 percent in 2012, as shown in Figure 5–5. Relative to size, in 2007, the total global investment in pension funds was estimated at US$22.6 trillion and mutual funds at US$21.8 trillion. **Sovereign wealth funds**, e.g., Abu Dhabi Investment Authority, had total assets of US$2.5 trillion in 2007, while hedge fund assets were only estimated at US$1.5 trillion.

sovereign wealth funds
Pools of capital owned by sovereign governments that are managed separately from official reserves.

After growth in total assets at global pension funds of 14.4 percent in 2007, pension funds suffered losses during the credit crisis of 2008. Canadian pension funds showed the worst year on record with assets dropping 15.9 percent for the year. In the United States, the top 1,000 funds lost close to US$1 trillion in 2008. Globally, all funds face volatile equity markets and lower interest rates that may hamper their ability to earn sufficient returns on their investments.

FIGURE 5–5 Percentage of the Assets of the *Pensions & Investments/Watson Wyatt World 300* Domiciled in Each Country

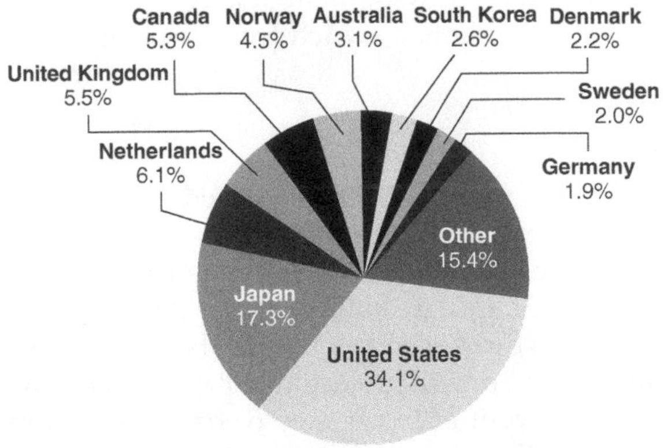

Note: Other includes the following countries: Belgium, Brazil, Chile, China, Colombia, Finland, France, India, Ireland, Kuwait, Luxembourg, Malaysia, Mexico, New Zealand, Philippines, Poland, Portugal, Russia, Singapore, South Africa, Spain, Switzerland, Taiwan, and Thailand.

Source: *Pensions & Investments*, December 24, 2012, pionline.com.

Questions and Problems

1. What is a mutual fund? In what sense is it an FI?
2. What are money market mutual funds? In what assets do these funds typically invest?
3. What are long-term mutual funds? In what assets do these funds usually invest?
4. How might investors' preferences for long-term versus short-term mutual funds have changed since the global market meltdown in 2008?
5. How does the risk of short-term funds differ from the risk of long-term funds?
6. What are the economic reasons for the existence of mutual funds; that is, what benefits do mutual funds provide for investors? Why do individuals rather than corporations hold most mutual fund shares?
7. What are the three possible components reflected in the return an investor receives from a mutual fund?
8. An investor purchases a mutual fund for $60. The fund pays dividends of $1.75, distributes a capital gain of $3, and charges a fee of $3 when the fund is sold one year later for $67.50. What is the net rate of return from this investment?
9. How is the NAV of a mutual fund determined? What is meant by the term *marked-to-market daily*?
10. A mutual fund owns 400 shares of Fiat, currently trading at $7, and 400 shares of Microsoft, currently trading at $70. The fund has no liabilities and has 100 shares outstanding.
    a. What is the NAV of the fund?
    b. If investors expect the price of Fiat shares to increase to $9 and the price of Microsoft shares to decrease to $55 by the end of the year, what is the expected NAV at the end of the year?
    c. Assume that the expected price of the Fiat shares is realized at $9. What is the maximum price decrease that can occur to the Microsoft shares to realize an end-of-year NAV equal to the NAV estimated in part (a)?
11. What is the difference between open-end and closed-end mutual funds? Which type of fund tends to be more specialized in asset selection? How does a closed-end fund provide another source of return from which an investor may either gain or lose?
12. Suppose today a mutual fund contains 2,000 shares of National Bank, currently trading at $46.75; 1,000 shares of Royal Bank, currently trading at $70.10; and 2,500 shares of Barrick, currently trading at $27.50. The mutual fund has no liabilities and 10,000 shares outstanding held by investors.
    a. What is the NAV of the fund?
    b. Calculate the change in the NAV of the fund if tomorrow National Bank's shares increase to $50, Royal Bank's shares increase to $73, and Barrick's shares increase to $30.
    c. Suppose that today 1,000 additional investors buy one share each of the mutual fund at the NAV of $23.235. This means that the fund manager has $23,235 in additional funds to invest. The fund manager decides to use these additional funds to buy additional shares in National Bank. Calculate tomorrow's NAV given the same rise in share values as assumed in part (b).
13. Open-end Fund A owns 165 shares of Bell valued at $35 each and 50 shares of Rogers valued at $45 each. Closed-end Fund B owns 75 shares of Bell and 120 shares of Rogers. Each fund has 1000 shares of stock outstanding.
    a. What are the NAVs of both funds using these prices?
    b. Assume that in one month the price of Bell stock has increased to $36.25 and the price of Rogers stock has decreased to $43.375. How do these changes impact the NAV of both funds? If the funds were purchased at the NAV prices in part (a) and sold at month-end, what would be the realized returns on the investments?
    c. Assume that another 155 shares of Bell are added to Fund A. What is the effect on Fund A's NAV if the stock prices remain unchanged from the original prices?
14. What is the difference between a load fund and a no-load fund?
15. Suppose an individual invests $10,000 in a load mutual fund for two years. The load fee entails an up-front commission charge of 4 percent of the amount invested and is deducted from the original funds invested. In addition, annual fund operating expenses are 0.85 percent. The annual fees are charged on the average NAV invested in the fund and are recorded at the end of each year. Investments in the fund return 5 percent each year paid on the last day of the year. If the investor reinvests the annual returns paid on the investment, calculate the annual return on the mutual fund over the two-year investment period.
16. Who are the primary regulators of the mutual fund industry in Canada? How do their regulatory goals differ from those of other types of FIs?
17. How and why does the regulation of mutual funds, hedge funds, and pension funds differ?
18. What is a hedge fund and how is it different from a mutual fund?
19. What are the different categories of hedge funds?
20. What is the difference between a defined benefit pension plan and a defined contribution pension plan?

CHAPTER 6

INSURANCE COMPANIES

After studying this chapter you should be able to:

LO1 Discuss the size, structure, and composition of companies in the life insurance industry in Canada.

LO2 Discuss the size, structure, and composition of the property and casualty insurance industry in Canada.

INTRODUCTION

The primary function of insurance companies is to protect individuals and corporations (policyholders) from adverse events. By accepting premiums, insurance companies promise policyholders compensation if certain specified events occur. These policies represent financial liabilities to the insurance company. With the premiums collected, insurance companies invest in financial securities such as corporate bonds and stocks. The industry is classified into two major groups: life, and property and casualty (P&C). Life insurance provides protection against the possibility of untimely death, illnesses, and retirement. P&C insurance protects against personal injury and liability such as accidents, theft, and fire. Many FIs offer both life and P&C services. Further, many FIs that offer insurance services also sell a variety of investment products in a similar fashion to other financial service firms, such as mutual funds (Chapter 5) and DTIs (Chapter 2).

The financial crisis showed just how much risk the insurance companies can present to FIs and the global financial system. Specifically, as the U.S. subprime mortgage market began to fail in the summer of 2008, subprime mortgage pools and the securities written on them that FIs bought ended up falling precipitously in value as foreclosures and defaults rose on the underlying mortgage pools. Many credit default swaps (CDSs) were written on these subprime mortgage securities. CDS contracts offer credit protection (insurance) against default on the mortgage securities. As mortgage security losses started to rise, buyers of the CDS contracts wanted to be paid for these losses. AIG was a major writer of these CDS securities. So when mortgage-backed securities started to fall in value, AIG had to make good on billions of dollars of CDSs. Soon it became clear that AIG was not going to be able to cover its CDS market losses. The result was a significant increase in the risk exposure of banks, investment banks, and insurance companies that had purchased AIG CDS insurance contracts. Indeed, the reason the U.S. federal government stepped in and bailed out AIG was that the insurer was a dominant player in the CDS market. Had AIG defaulted, every FI that had bought a CDS contract from the company would have suffered substantial losses.

In this chapter we describe the main features of life insurance and P&C insurance companies, concentrating on (1) the size, structure, and composition of the industry in which they operate; (2) balance sheets and recent trends; and (3) regulations for each. We also look at global competition and trends in this industry.

LIFE INSURANCE COMPANIES

LO1

Life insurance allows individuals and their beneficiaries to protect against losses in income through premature death or retirement. By pooling risks, life insurance transfers income-related uncertainties from the insured individual to a group.

Size, Structure, and Composition of the Industry

demutualization
Conversion from a mutual insurance company owned by policyholders to a stockholder-controlled insurance firm.

As competition in the insurance industry increased in the late 1990s, many of the largest global insurance firms converted from being mutual companies owned by their policyholders to stockholder-controlled companies, a process called **demutualization.** Figure 6–1 illustrates the difference between a mutual insurer and a stock insurance company. Demutualization allows an insurance firm to gain access to the equity markets in order to raise additional capital for future business expansions and compete with the much larger banking industry. The ability to raise capital is also important from a regulatory standpoint since a mutual company cannot readily raise capital to offset a decline in asset values. Because a mutual company is owned by its policyholders, the existing capital and reserves (equal to accumulated past profits) have to be distributed to the insurer's policyholders.

In 1957, the Canadian and British Insurance Companies Act was amended to allow insurance companies to mutualize in order to prevent U.S. takeovers of Canadian companies. As a result, in the 1960s, Mutual of Canada (a mutual since 1870) and North American Life Insurance (which mutualized in 1931) were joined by Canada Life, Sun Life, Equitable Life, Confederation Life, and Manufacturers Life as federally regulated mutual companies. This process was reversed in the 1990s, and firms demutualized. Demutualization in Canada (e.g., Manulife and Sun Life), the United States (e.g., Metropolitan Life and Prudential), and other countries (e.g., Australia and the United Kingdom) set the stage for global consolidation as well as bank–insurance company mergers (e.g., Citibank and Travelers in the United States), although these are not yet permitted in Canada.

In Canada, the number of firms declined from 163 in 1990 to 102 in 2008. In 2009, 88 firms were regulated by OSFI, composed of 46 Canadian and 42 foreign life insurance companies. The consolidation has taken the form of Canadian insurers' acquiring the assets of other Canadian companies, such as Great-West Life's acquisition of London Life and Canada Life (see Chapter 5, Figure 5–2) and Sun Life's acquisition of Clarica Life Insurance in 2002. In addition, Canadian companies have

FIGURE 6–1
Mutual versus Stock Insurance Companies

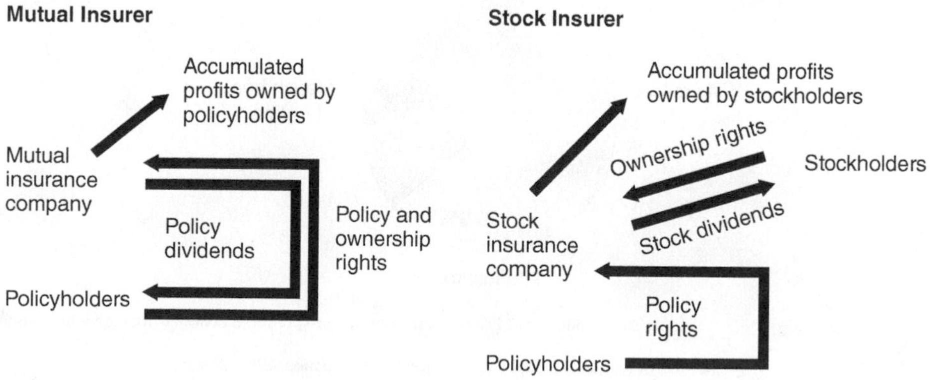

TABLE 6–1
Largest North American Publicly Traded Insurers Ranked by Assets (U.S. $ billions), 2012

Source: Best's Review, July 2013. © A.M. Best Company. Used with permission.

Rank	Insurance Company	2012 Assets	2011 Assets	% Change	2012 Revenue	2011 Revenue	% Change
1	MetLife Inc.	$836.781	$796.226	5.1	68.150	70.241	−3.0
2	Prudential Financial Inc.	709.298	620.244	14.4	84.815	49.030	73.0
3	American International Group	548.633	553.054	−0.8	65.656	59.812	9.8
4	Manulife Financial Corporation	487.704	453.061	5.2	28.939	49.017	−42.3
5	Berkshire Hathaway Inc.	427.452	392.647	8.9	162.463	145.792	11.4
6	Hartford Financial Services Group Inc.	298.513	302.609	−1.4	26.412	21.859	20.8
7	Great-West Lifeco Inc.	254.578	234.160	6.3	30.163	29.321	0.5
8	Sun Life Financial Inc.	226.547	214.042	3.4	17.673	19.509	−11.5
9	Lincoln National Corporation	218.869	201.491	8.6	11.532	10.641	8.4
10	Principal Financial Group Inc.	161.926	147.362	9.9	9.215	8.671	6.3

greatwestlife.com
sunlife.ca
manulife.ca

expanded their operations abroad. Of note was the US$11 billion merger of Manulife Financial with U.S. company John Hancock in April 2004. Table 6–1 shows the top 10 publicly traded North American life and health insurance companies ranked by assets at December 31, 2012. Three of the top 10 (Manulife Financial, Great-West Lifeco, and Sun Life Financial) are Canadian companies. As well, several large U.S. mutual companies (New York Life, assets of US$237.98 billion; Northwestern Mutual, assets of US$202.53 billion) are not included with the publicly listed insurers in Table 6–1. Note that Canadian life insurance companies report using IFRS. U.S. companies use Generally Accepted Accounting Principles (U.S. GAAP), so the numbers may not be strictly comparable.

Life insurance allows individuals and their beneficiaries to protect against losses in income through premature death or retirement. By pooling risks, life insurance transfers income-related uncertainties from the insured individual to a group. While life insurance may be the core activity area, life insurance companies also sell annuity contracts, manage pension plans, and provide accident and health insurance. Figure 6–2 shows the distribution of premium income for the various lines of insurance in 2011. Note that annuities provide the largest income at 44.2 percent, followed by health benefit plans at 36.5 percent.

FIGURE 6–2 **Distribution of Premium Income, 2011**

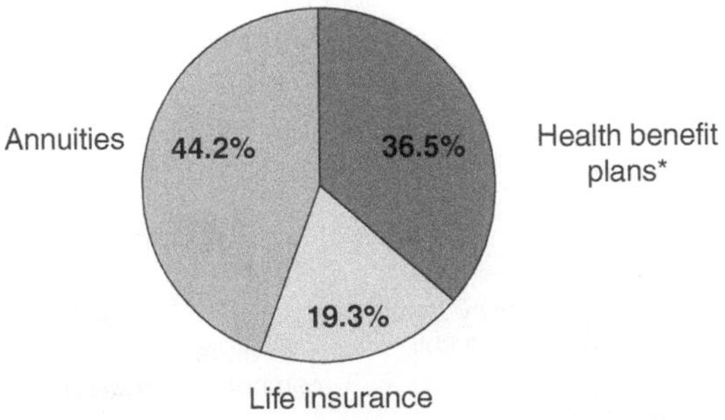

*Includes $9.805 billion (12.1%) uninsured employer-sponsored contracts that are administered by life insurance companies.

Source: Canadian Life and Health Insurance Association, 2013, clhia.ca.

moral hazard
The loss exposure faced by an insurer when the provision of insurance encourages the insured to take more risks.

adverse selection
The tendency for higher-risk individuals to carry higher levels of insurance, making the overall risk in the insurance pool higher than in the general population.

actuarially priced insurance premiums
Insurance premiums based on the perceived risk of the insured.

Two problems that face life insurers and P&C insurers are moral hazard and adverse selection. **Moral hazard** occurs when the insured person or company is encouraged to take more risks because the downside risk has been transferred to the insurer. **Adverse selection** is a problem in that customers who apply for insurance policies are more likely to be those most in need of insurance (e.g., someone with chronic health problems is more likely to purchase a life insurance policy than someone in perfect health). Thus, in calculating the probability of having to pay out on an insurance contract and, in turn, determining the insurance premium to charge, insurance companies' use of health (and other) statistics representing the overall population may not be appropriate (since the insurance company's pool of customers is more prone to health problems than the overall population). Insurance companies deal with the adverse selection problem by establishing different pools of the population based on health and related characteristics (such as income). By altering the pool used to determine the probability of losses to a particular customer's health characteristics, the insurance company can more accurately determine the probability of having to pay out on a policy and can adjust the insurance premium accordingly. These premiums are said to be **actuarially priced insurance premiums.** In a broader sense, an insurance contract can be thought of as a put option that can be exercised by the insured only if an adverse event occurs. The insurer is the seller of the option, paying out if a bad event occurs and the option is exercised.

As the various types of insurance policies and services offered are described below, notice that some policies (such as universal life policies and annuities) provide not only insurance features but also savings components. For example, universal life policy payouts are a function of the interest earned on the investment of the policyholder's premiums.

Types of Life Insurance

The four basic classes or lines of life insurance are distinguished by the manner in which they are sold or marketed to purchasers. These classes are (1) individual life, (2) group life, (3) industrial life, and (4) credit life. According to the Canadian Life and Health Insurance Association Inc. (CLHIA), of the total life insurance coverage of $334.1 billion that Canadians purchased during 2011, $217.8 billion or 65.2 percent was for individual life insurance. The remaining $116.2 billion was for group life insurance.

Individual Life Individual life insurance involves policies marketed on an individual basis, usually in units of $1,000, on which policyholders make periodic premium payments. Despite the enormous variety of contractual forms, there are essentially five basic contractual types. The first three are traditional forms of life insurance, and the last two are newer contracts that originated in the 1970s and 1980s as a result of increased competition for savings from other segments of the financial services industry. The three traditional contractual forms are term life, whole life, and endowment life. The two newer forms are variable life and universal life. The key features of each of these contractual forms are as follows:

- *Term life.* A term life policy is the closest to pure life insurance, with no savings element attached. Essentially, the individual receives a payout contingent on death during the coverage period. The term of coverage can vary from as little as 1 year to 40 years or more.

- *Whole life.* A whole life policy protects the individual over an entire lifetime. In return for periodic or level premiums, the individual's beneficiaries receive the face value of the life insurance contract on death. Thus, there is certainty that if the policyholder continues to make premium payments, the insurance company will make a payment—unlike term insurance. As a result, whole life has a savings element as well as a pure insurance element.
- *Endowment life.* An endowment life policy combines a pure (term) insurance element with a savings element. It guarantees a payout to the beneficiaries of the policy if death occurs during some endowment period (e.g., prior to reaching retirement age). An insured person who lives to the endowment date receives the face amount of the policy.
- *Variable life.* Unlike traditional policies that promise to pay the insured the fixed or face amount of a policy if a contingency arises, variable life insurance invests fixed premium payments in mutual funds of stocks, bonds, and money market instruments. Usually, policyholders can choose mutual fund investments to reflect their risk preferences. Thus, variable life provides an alternative way to build savings compared with the more traditional policies such as whole life because the value of the policy increases or decreases with the asset returns of the mutual fund in which the premiums are invested.
- *Universal life and variable universal life.* Universal life allows both the premium amounts and the maturity of the life contract to be changed by the insured, unlike traditional policies, which maintain premiums at a given level over a fixed contract period. In addition, for some contracts, insurers invest premiums in money, equity, or bond mutual funds—as in variable life insurance—so that the savings or investment component of the contract reflects market returns. In this case, the policy is called *variable universal life.*

Group Life Group life insurance covers a large number of insured persons under a single policy. Usually issued to corporate employers, these policies may be either contributory (where both the employer and the employee cover a share of the employee's cost of the insurance) or noncontributory (where the employee does not contribute to the cost of the insurance) for the employees. Cost economies represent the principal advantage of group life over ordinary life policies. Cost economies result from mass administration of plans, lower costs for evaluating individuals through medical screening and other rating systems, and reduced selling and commission costs.

Industrial Life Industrial life insurance currently represents a very small area of coverage. Industrial life usually involves weekly payments directly collected by representatives of the companies. To a large extent, the growth of group life insurance has led to the demise of industrial life as a major activity class.

Credit Life Credit life insurance is sold to protect lenders against a borrower's death prior to the repayment of a debt contract such as a mortgage or car loan. Usually, the face amount of the insurance policy reflects the outstanding principal and interest on the loan. Credit life insurance can also be sold by DTIs in their branches in Canada.

Other Life Insurer Activities

The other major activities of life insurance companies involve the sale of investment and retirement products (annuities, pension plans, RRSPs, RRIFs) and accident and health insurance.

Investment Annuities represent the reverse of life insurance activities. Whereas life insurance involves different contractual methods of *building up* a fund, annuities involve different methods of *liquidating* a fund, such as paying out a fund's proceeds. Many different types of annuity contracts have been developed. Specifically, they can be sold to an individual or a group on a fixed or variable basis by being linked to the return on some underlying investment portfolio. Individuals can purchase annuities with a single payment or with payments spread over a number of years. The annuity builds up a fund whose returns are tax deferred; that is, they are not subject to capital gains taxes on their investments. Payments may be structured to start immediately, or they can be deferred (at which time taxes are paid based on the tax rate of the annuity receiver). These payments may cease on death or continue to be paid to beneficiaries for a number of years after death. While the traditional life insurance products described above remain an important part of life insurance firms' business, these lines are not the primary business of many companies in the life insurance industry whose major area of business has shifted to annuities. Payments received by individuals from annuity contracts are declared as income that may or may not be taxable as determined by the Income Tax Act, available from the CRA at www.cra-arc.gc.ca. Annuity premiums in Canada were $35.8 billion in 2011 compared with $34.7 billion in 2008, representing 44.2 percent of the total premium income, as shown in Figure 6–2. Although annuities were the largest source of premium income, primarily from the growth in retirement products such as pension plans and **registered retirement savings plans (RRSPs)**, premium income from annuities has declined from 47.8 percent of total premium income in 2000 as life insurers faced increased competition from banks in the annuity product market. Life insurance premiums were 19.3 percent (versus 22.7 percent in 2000), whereas health insurance premium income has increased from 29.5 percent in 2000 to 36.5 percent in 2011.

registered retirement savings plans (RRSPs)
Retirement savings funds that allow Canadians to shield a portion of their income from tax, but must be converted into an RRIF by age 71.

Annuity premiums include group retirement plans, such as private pension plans, which are known as registered pension plans in Canada (pension plans are covered in more detail in Chapter 5). According to the CLHIA, individual annuities amounted to $15.3 billion in 2011, whereas group annuities were $20.5 billion. Individual premiums come from demand for assets placed in an RRSP, and from **registered retirement income funds (RRIFs)**. Individuals in Canada are able to shelter income from tax during their earning years via RRSPs, but must transfer the funds to an RRIF and pay the tax on withdrawal during retirement.

registered retirement income funds (RRIFs)
Funds that are designed to provide a regular income to an individual and allow the individual to defer payment and tax on money withdrawn from an RRSP.

Accident and Health Insurance Although life insurance protects against mortality risk, accident and health insurance protects against morbidity, or ill health, risk. Canada's public health system provides coverage for many medical services, but health insurance provides additional coverage, often through supplementary health insurance plans provided by employers as benefits to their employees. These include dental plans, travel insurance, disability insurance, and accidental death and dismemberment insurance. At year-end 2011, 23.2 million people in Canada were insured for extended health care, and total health insurance premiums were $29.5 billion, 36.5 percent of total premium income. Life insurers provide over 90 percent of the supplementary health insurance in Canada, and the remainder is provided by P&C insurers. In many respects, the loss exposures faced by insurers in health insurance are more similar to those faced under P&C insurance than to those faced under traditional life insurance, as discussed below.

Balance Sheet and Recent Trends

Assets

Because of the long-term nature of their liabilities (as a result of the long-term nature of life insurance policyholders' claims) and the need to generate competitive returns on the savings elements of life insurance products, life insurance companies concentrate their asset investments at the longer end of the maturity spectrum (e.g., bonds, equities, and government securities). Look at Table 6–2, where we show the consolidated Canadian life insurance companies balance sheet as of Quarter 4, 2012, as submitted to OSFI. The total assets reported were $980.3 billion, roughly 25 percent of the total on-balance-sheet assets reported by the Canadian banks.

As you can see, at the end of Quarter 4 in 2012, for the firms reporting to OSFI, 31.2 percent of life insurance assets were invested in bonds and debentures, 7.0 percent in mortgage loans, 3.2 percent in preferred and common shares, and 4.4 percent in reinsurance assets, discussed below. The debt securities expose the companies to credit risk as well as interest rate risk. **Policy loans** (loans made to policyholders using their policies as collateral) made up 1.3 percent of the remainder. While banks are the major issuers of new mortgages (sometimes keeping the mortgages on their books and sometimes selling them to secondary market investors), insurance companies hold mortgages as investment securities. That is, they purchase many mortgages in the secondary markets (see Chapters 25 and 26). Thus, insurance company managers must be able to measure and manage the credit risk, interest rate risk, and other risks associated with these assets.

policy loans
Loans made by an insurance company to its policyholders, using their policies as collateral.

In Canada, life and health insurance companies offer shares in investment funds called **segregated funds**, which are similar to the mutual funds offered by other FIs, and which are similarly invested in equities, bonds, and money market instruments. These funds have been popular since the early 2000s when many investors saw their retirement savings in stocks and mutual funds reduced by the downturn in the market. Segregated funds must return a minimum percentage (usually 75 percent or more) of the capital invested to the investor at maturity, reducing the risk of capital loss. Also, segregated funds are a means of **creditor-proofing** assets, a feature of interest to small-business owners. Segregated funds must be managed separately from the other assets of the firm, and insurance companies report the market value of their assets held as segregated funds to OSFI. Table 6–2 shows that segregated fund assets of $391.45 billion are exactly offset on the liabilities side by segregated fund liabilities, indicating that the funds are owned by the investors, but are held in trust. Segregated funds have increased from $186.8 billion in 2001, reflecting the growth of individual and group pension plans.

segregated funds
Investment funds held and managed separately by life and health insurance companies in Canada.

creditor-proofing
The placing of assets in a vehicle that cannot be claimed by creditors in the event of the owners' bankruptcy.

Liabilities

The liabilities and shareholders' equity side of the consolidated balance sheet for Canadian life insurance companies at Quarter 4, 2012, is shown in Table 6–2. Looking at the liability side, we see that 42.3 percent represent **actuarial liabilities** for insurance contracts. These are based on actuarial assumptions regarding the insurers' expected future liability commitments to pay out on present contracts, including death benefits, matured endowments (lump sum or otherwise), and the cash

actuarial liabilities
A liability item for insurers that reflects their expected payment commitment on existing policy contracts.

TABLE 6–2
Consolidated Canadian Life Insurance Companies Balance Sheet, Q4, 2012 ($ thousands)

Source: OSFI, osfi-bsif.gc.ca.

Assets	Q4, 2012	% of Assets
Cash and cash equivalents	$17,015,597	1.7
Short-term investments	9,435,243	1.0
Accrued investment income	3,888,171	0.4
Accounts receivable	7,725,270	0.8
Policy/certificate loans	13,072,794	1.3
Bonds and debentures	305,609,452	31.2
Mortgage loans	68,453,894	7.0
Preferred shares	1,299,306	0.1
Common shares	29,960,350	3.1
Investment properties	18,631,727	1.9
Derivative financial instruments	17,856,657	1.8
Reinsurance assets	42,966,955	4.4
Property and equipment	2,144,725	0.2
Interests in associates & joint ventures	3,516,103	0.4
Segregated funds net assets	391,448,775	39.9
Other loans and invested assets	15,672,196	1.6
Current and deferred tax assets	3,773,575	0.4
Goodwill	9,654,717	1.0
Intangible assets	3,800,259	0.4
Other assets	14,414,157	1.5
Total assets	$980,339,833	100.0
Liabilities		**% of Total**
Actuarial liabilities for insurance contracts	415,108,961	42.3
Other contract liabilities	34,410,550	3.5
Trust and banking deposits	18,904,685	1.9
Accounts payable	17,155,117	1.7
Mortgage loans and other real estate encumbrances	547,113	0.1
Derivative financial instruments	11,561,393	1.2
Provisions and other liabilities	11,774,033	1.2
Segregated fund liabilities	391,448,775	39.9
Current and deferred tax liabilities	3,629,130	0.3
Subordinated debt	3,831,929	0.4
Other debt	3,615,410	0.4
Total liabilities	$911,987,096	93.0
Nonparticipating account-accumulated other comprehensive income (loss)	240,311	0.1
Total policyholders' equity	3,791,100	0.4
Shareholders' equity		
Capital stock	36,962,720	3.8
Contributed surplus and other capital	5,412,558	0.5
Retained earnings net of accumulated other comprehensive income (loss)	21,469,521	2.2
Total shareholders' equity	$63,844,799	6.5
Noncontrolling interests	716,838	0.1
Total equity	68,352,737	7.0
Total liabilities and equity	$980,339,833	100.0

surrender values of policies
The cash values of policies received from the insurer if a policyholder surrenders the policy before maturity. The cash surrender value is normally only a portion of the contract's face value.

surrender values of policies (the cash value paid to the policyholder if the policy is surrendered before it matures). Even though the actuarial assumptions underlying policy reserves are normally very conservative, unexpected fluctuations in future required payouts can occur; thus, underwriting life insurance is risky. For example, mortality rates—and life insurance payouts—might unexpectedly increase above those defined by historically based mortality tables as a result of a catastrophic epidemic illness such as widespread influenza. To meet unexpected future losses, the life insurer holds a capital fund with which to meet such losses (and reduce insolvency risk). The total of policyholders' and shareholders' equity at Quarter 4, 2012, was $67.6 billion, 6.9 percent of the total liabilities and equity. The equity accounts provide a surplus to meet unexpected underwriting losses, as do the insurer's investment income from its asset portfolio and any new premium income flows.

Recent Trends

The life insurance industry was very profitable in the early and mid-2000s, and capital levels for the industry remained strong. However, the financial crisis took a toll on this industry. The value of stocks and bonds in insurers' asset portfolios dropped as financial markets deteriorated. Further losses were experienced on life insurers' positions in commercial mortgage-backed securities, commercial loans, and lower-grade corporate debt as bond default rates increased and U.S. mortgage markets froze. Lower equity market values also reduced asset-based fees earned from balances on equity-linked products, such as variable annuities. As a result, life insurers were particularly hard hit with declining earnings from equities. Furthermore, as investors fled to the safety of government bonds during the financial crisis, government bond yields (which are generally a significant source of investment income for life insurers) fell. Additionally, historically low short-term interest rates prevented life insurers from lowering minimum rates on new policies, which encouraged higher surrender rates on existing policies that were already at minimum credit rates. The results were huge losses in 2008 for the North American life insurance industry. Realized and unrealized capital losses from bonds, preferred stocks, and common stocks topped US$35 billion in 2008, and net investment income fell by 3.5 percent in 2008. Net after-tax income for the year was less than half of that in 2007. The large drop in the value of stocks and bonds that the insurers held made it harder for the companies to pay out money due to their policyholders, and the falling value of their assets made it harder for the insurers to raise capital. The U.S. Treasury Department provided bailout funds to a number of struggling life insurance companies, the most notable being US$127 billion to AIG.

As shown in Table 6–1, revenues declined for both Manulife Financial Corporation (–42.3 percent) and Sun Life Financial Inc. (–11.5 percent) between 2011 and 2012, primarily from declines in net investment income.

Regulation

At the federal level, Canadian health and life insurers and branches of foreign-owned life insurance companies are regulated by OSFI under the Insurance Companies Act. These companies hold more than 95 percent of the industry's assets. Total assets in Canada of foreign life insurance companies reporting to OSFI were only $22.9 billion compared to the $980.34 billion of the Canadian life insurers at Quarter 4, 2012. However, on a global basis, the foreign insurance companies operating in Canada represent some of the largest life insurers in the world, including the AXA Group of France, Metropolitan Life of the United

States, and Prudential Assurance of the United Kingdom. OSFI's regulatory approach is primarily prudential, meaning that its focus is on the safety and soundness of the health and life insurers so that these FIs do not pose a risk to the Canadian financial system. To this end, OSFI provides guidelines for health and life insurers on its website. These guidelines include minimum capital and surplus requirements (which will be discussed in detail in Chapter 20) as well as guidelines for innovative instruments, large exposure limits, securities lending, asset securitization, derivatives best practices, and outsourcing. As well, accounting guidelines and reporting requirements are specified; these include standards for sound business and financial practices that address capital management, credit risk management, foreign exchange risk management, interest rate risk management, and liquidity management, among others—risks that will be addressed for FIs in subsequent chapters.

Health and life insurers are also regulated at the provincial/territorial level. In each province/territory in which they do business, insurers must abide by the market conduct regulation and licensing requirements. For Canadian insurers with operations in the United States, regulation is established at the state level. In addition to chartering, state insurance commissions supervise and examine insurance companies. As well, the Wall Street Reform and Consumer Protection Act of 2010 (or Dodd-Frank) established the Federal Insurance Office (FIO), which reports to the U.S. Congress and the President on matters pertaining to the insurance industry. While the industry's main regulator continues to be the states in which firms operate, the FIO has the authority to monitor the insurance industry, identify regulatory gaps or systemic risk, deal with international insurance matters, and monitor the extent to which underserved communities have access to affordable insurance products. The Wall Street Reform and Consumer Protection Act also established the Financial Stability Oversight Council (FSOC), which can subject any FI (including insurance companies) that presents a systemic risk to the economy to greater regulation.

assuris.ca

The Canadian Life and Health Insurance Compensation Corporation (Assuris) is a private, nonprofit corporation that is financed by the life and health insurance companies. Assuris provides a guarantee, subject to limits, of existing life insurance policies, accident and sickness policies, and annuity contracts in the event of the bankruptcy of an insurance company. Assuris insures up to 85 percent of insurance benefits on the bankruptcy of an insurer, and up to $100,000 for deposit-type products. In addition, the OmbudService for Life and Health Insurance (OLHI) provides support for consumers who have concerns about life and health insurance companies.

olhi.ca

CONCEPT QUESTIONS

1. **What is the difference between a life insurance contract and an annuity contract?**
2. **Describe the different forms of life insurance.**
3. **Why do life insurance companies invest in long-term assets?**
4. **Who are the main regulators of the life insurance industry?**

PROPERTY AND CASUALTY INSURANCE

LO2

Property insurance covers the loss of real and personal property. Casualty—or, perhaps more accurately, liability—insurance concerns protection against legal liability exposures. However, the distinctions between the two broad areas of property and liability insurance are increasingly becoming blurred. This is due to the tendency of P&C insurers to offer multiple-activity line coverage combining features of property and liability insurance into single policy packages, for example, homeowners' multiple-peril insurance.

Size, Structure, and Composition of the Industry

Table 6–3 lists the gross written premiums in Canada for the leading P&C and life insurance companies in 2011. While the dollar amounts of premiums are similar for the top companies in both categories, the products provided by the two industries are different. The P&C insurance industry performs the important function of spreading the risk of personal or business loss over many policyholders. The industry is much less concentrated than the life and health insurance industry, and, because it does not have a savings function, it is much smaller in size. However, estimates of the Insurance Bureau of Canada (IBC) place the industry employment at over 115,400 people spread across Canada and divided among primary insurers and reinsurers, brokers, independent adjusters, and appraisers. **Primary insurers** are the originators of a policy, whereas **reinsurance** provides "insurance for insurers" by spreading the risk across many insurers. The major reinsurers are large international companies, so that a major catastrophe such as the 2011 earthquakes in New Zealand and Japan, which caused large insured losses, could result in an increase in property insurance premiums in Canada and globally.

primary insurers
Originators of insurance policies.

reinsurance
The payment of a premium to transfer the risk of a part of a claim to another insurer, called a *reinsurer*.

TABLE 6–3
Leading P&C and Life Insurance Companies in Canada, 2011, Ranked by Gross Written Premiums ($ millions)

Source: Insurance Information Institute, *III International Insurance Fact Book 2012*, iii.org.

Leading P&C Insurance Companies, 2011	
Company	**Gross Written Premiums**
Intact Financial	$3,652.1
Aviva Canada	2,439.5
Wawanesa Mutual	2,380.9
Co-Operators Group	2,310.9
AXA Canada	2,034.0
Lloyd's	1,873.5
Economical Insurance Group	1,710.0
Security National Insurance	1,512.6
State Farm Mutual Auto	1,425.9
Dominion of Canada General	1,266.6
Leading Life Insurance Companies, 2011	
Company	**Gross Written Premiums**
Munich Reinsurance Co.	$8,010.8
Great-West Life Assurance Company	4,082.2
Manufacturers life Insurance Co.	3,365.3
Desjardins Financial Security Life Assurance	3,264.0
London Life Insurance Company	2,825.3
Industrial Alliance Insurance & Financial Services	2,527.5
Sun Life Assurance Co. of Canada	2,464.5
Sun Life Insurance (Canada) Ltd.	1,539.4
Canada Life Insurance Company of Canada	1,150.3
Canada Life Assurance Company	1,142.4

Like the life and health insurance industry, the P&C industry is regulated jointly by provincial bodies with respect to marketing and licensing issues, and by OSFI with respect to solvency issues. In 2013, OSFI listed 172 companies authorized to operate in Canada: 92 Canadian firms and 80 foreign firms. Many of the Canadian firms are subsidiaries of large, global firms such as Allianz, Allstate, Munich Reinsurance, and Swiss RE. Assets of the Canadian firms totalled $97.9891 billion at December 31, 2012. This represented just 2.6 percent of the $3.85 trillion on-balance-sheet assets of the Canadian banks and 10 percent of the $980.3 billion assets of the Canadian life insurance companies that OSFI supervises. At the present time, some Canadian banks have insurance subsidiaries that report to OSFI, but they are allowed to sell insurance through their branch networks, a regulation that has been challenged by the banks but that has so far limited their expansion into this field. This issue will be discussed under product diversification in Chapter 21.

Types of P&C Insurance

In this section we describe the key features of the main P&C lines. Note, however, that some insurance lines are marketed to both individuals and commercial firms (e.g., automobile insurance) and other lines are marketed to one specific group (e.g., boiler and machinery insurance targeted at commercial purchasers). To understand the importance of each line in terms of premium income and losses incurred, look at Figure 6–3, which shows the **net written premiums (NWP)** (the entire amount of premiums on insurance contracts written) for major P&C lines. Major insurance lines include the following:

net written premiums (NWP)
The entire amount of premiums on insurance contracts written.

- *Property insurance.* Protects personal and commercial property against fire, lightning, and other damage (33.2 percent of NWPs in 2011; 27.8 percent in 1990).
- *Automobile insurance.* Provides protection against (1) losses resulting from legal liability due to the ownership or use of a vehicle (auto liability) and (2) theft of or damage to vehicles (auto physical damage). Auto insurance represents the largest category of premiums of all types of insurance (47.3 percent of NWPs in 2011 versus 59.2 percent in 1990).
- *Liability insurance (other than auto).* Provides either individuals or commercial firms with protection against non-automobile-related legal liability. For commercial

FIGURE 6–3
NWPs in Canada by Line of Business, 2011 ($000,000)

Source: Insurance Bureau of Canada, *Facts of the Property & Casualty Insurance Industry in Canada 2013*, ibc.ca.

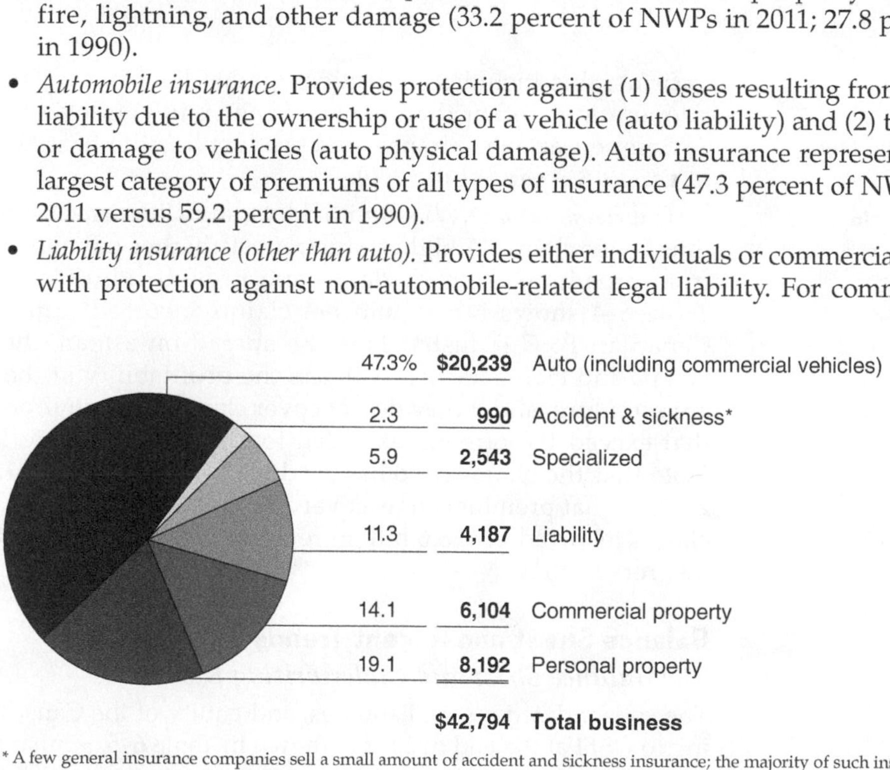

* A few general insurance companies sell a small amount of accident and sickness insurance; the majority of such insurance, however, is sold by life and health insurers.

TABLE 6–4
NWPs, Net Claims Incurred, and Claims Ratio of P&C Insurers in Canada, 1990–2011 ($ millions)

Source: The Insurance Bureau of Canada, *Facts of the Property & Casualty Insurance Industry in Canada, 2013*, ibc.ca.

	NWPs	Net Claims Incurred	Claims Ratio
1990	13,215	10,163	1.30
1991	13,844	10,645	1.30
1992	14,439	11,121	1.30
1993	15,203	11,469	1.33
1994	16,465	12,087	1.36
1995	18,014	12,820	1.41
1996	18,624	13,226	1.41
1997	18,573	13,168	1.41
1998	18,559	13,768	1.35
1999	18,728	13,483	1.39
2000	20,178	14,790	1.36
2001	21,242	16,161	1.31
2002	27,507	19,494	1.41
2003	31,413	20,388	1.54
2004	33,275	20,161	1.65
2005	33,864	21,568	1.57
2006	24,964	20,326	1.23
2007	36,095	21,817	1.65
2008	36,698	25,003	1.47
2009	38,187	26,338	1.45
2010	40,285	27,288	1.48
2011	42,794	28,567	1.50

firms, this includes protection against liabilities relating to their business operations (other than personal injury to employees covered by Workers' Compensation insurance) and product liability hazards (11.3 percent in 2011 versus 8.8 percent in 1990).

claims ratio
Ratio of premiums written to claims paid out.

The **claims ratio** (NWPs divided by claims incurred) shows how well premiums cover claims. A higher ratio reflects higher payouts and a smaller surplus from premiums to cover claims and provide a buffer against loss of capital. Table 6–4 shows NWPs and net claims incurred from 1990 to 2011 for the Canadian P&C industry. Like the spread on a loan, the difference between NWPs and claims incurred affects the profitability of the industry. Premiums are estimates, and if they do not cover claims (e.g., environmental cleanup costs that exceed the original expected loss), then the insurer's capital is affected. Note that the claims ratio has gradually increased from 1.30 in 1990 to 1.50 in 2011, so that premiums now cover a higher level of claims. Nevertheless, the net claims incurred of $28.6 billion represented 54 percent of the revenues of P&C insurers in 2011.

Balance Sheet and Recent Trends

The Balance Sheet and Underwriting Risk

The consolidated assets, liabilities, and equity of the Canadian P&C firms reporting to OSFI at the end of 2012 is shown in Table 6–5. Similar to life insurance companies, P&C insurers invest the majority of their assets in long-term securities,

TABLE 6–5
Consolidated Assets, Liabilities, and Equity for Canadian P&C Companies, Q4, 2012 ($ thousands)

Source: OSFI, www.osfi-bsif.gc.ca

Assets		% of Total Assets
Cash	$2,265,300	2.3%
Investment income due and accrued	364,631	0.4%
Investments:		
Short-term investments	2,122,837	2.2%
Bonds and debentures	51,345,330	53.4%
Mortgage loans	522,427	0.5%
Preferred shares	3,388,633	3.5%
Common shares	7,587,163	7.7%
Investment properties	15,830	0.0%
Other loans and invested assets	1,785,122	1.8%
Total investments	$66,767,342	68.1%
Receivables:		
Agents, brokers, and policyholders	1,515,440	1.5%
Instalment premiums	7,576,923	7.7%
Other receivables	1,068,528	1.0%
Recoverable from reinsurers	9,801,843	10.0%
Other recoverables on unpaid claims	591,115	0.6%
Interests in subsidiaries, affiliates, and joint ventures	921,880	0.9%
Property and equipment	266,475	0.23%
Deferred policy acquisition expenses	3,233,947	3.3%
Current and deferred tax assets	1,257,386	1.3%
Goodwill and intangible assets	1,917,534	1.9%
Other assets	441,068	0.4%
Total assets	$97,989,412	100.0%
Liabilities		**% of Total**
Overdrafts and borrowed money	$256,595	0.2%
Payables	1,657,173	1.7%
Expenses and other taxes due and accrued	1,467,023	1.5%
Unearned premiums and commissions	19,518,933	19.9%
Unpaid claims and adjustment expenses	44,612,544	45.5%
Current and deferred tax liabilities	786,113	0.8%
Provisions and other liabilities	2,564,004	2.6%
Total liabilities	$70,862,385	72.3%
Equity		**% of Total**
Share capital issued and paid	10,739,634	11.0%
Contributed surplus	1,593,261	1.6%
Retained earnings	12,967,172	13.2%
Reserves and other	361,589	0.4%
Accumulated other comprehensive income (loss)	1,465,371	1.5%
Total policyholders/shareholders' equity	27,127,027	27.7%
Noncontrolling interests	0	0.0%
Total equity	$27,127,027	27.7%
Total liabilities and equity	$97,989,412	100.0%

thus subjecting them to credit and interest rate risks. Bonds and debentures ($51.3 billion), preferred shares ($3.4 billion), and common shares ($7.6 billion) constituted 64.6 percent of total assets in 2012. P&C insurers, unlike life insurers, have more uncertain payouts on their insurance contracts (i.e., they incur greater levels of liquidity risk). Thus, their asset structure includes many assets with relatively fixed returns that can be liquidated easily and at low cost. Looking at their liabilities, we can see that major components are the unpaid claims and adjustment expenses item ($44.6 billion), which relates to pending claims and the expected administrative and related costs of adjusting (settling) these claims. This item constitutes 45.5 percent of total liabilities and equity. **Unearned premiums** (a reserve set aside that contains the portion of a premium that has been paid before insurance coverage has been provided) are also a major liability, representing 19.9 percent of total liabilities and capital.

unearned premiums
Reserve set aside that contains the portion of a premium that has been paid before insurance coverage has been provided.

To understand how and why a loss reserve on the liability side of the balance sheet is established, we need to understand the risks of underwriting P&C insurance. In particular, P&C underwriting risk results when the premiums generated on a given insurance line are insufficient to cover (1) the claims (losses) incurred insuring against the peril and (2) the administrative expenses of providing that insurance (legal expenses, commissions, taxes, etc.) after taking into account (3) the investment income generated between the time premiums are received and the time claims are paid. Thus, underwriting risk may result from (1) unexpected increases in loss rates, (2) unexpected increases in expenses, and/or (3) unexpected decreases in investment yields or returns. Next, we look more carefully at each of these three areas of P&C underwriting risk.

Loss Risk The key feature of claims loss exposure is the actuarial *predictability* of losses relative to premiums earned. This predictability depends on a number of characteristics or features of the perils insured, specifically:

- *Property versus liability.* In general, the maximum levels of losses are more predictable for property lines than for liability lines. For example, the monetary value of the loss of, or damage to, an auto is relatively easy to calculate, while the upper limit to the losses an insurer might be exposed to in a product liability line—for example, asbestos damage to workers' health under other liability insurance—may be difficult, if not impossible, to estimate.
- *Severity versus frequency.* In general, loss rates are more predictable on low-severity, high-frequency lines than they are on high-severity, low-frequency lines. For example, losses in fire, auto, and homeowners' peril lines tend to involve events expected to occur with a high frequency and to be independently distributed across any pool of the insured. Furthermore, the dollar loss on each event in the insured pool tends to be relatively small. Applying the law of large numbers, insurers can estimate the expected loss potential of such lines—the **frequency of loss** times the size of the loss (**severity of loss**)—within quite small probability bounds. Other lines, such as earthquake, hail, and financial guaranty insurance, tend to insure very low probability (frequency) events. Here the probabilities are not always stationary, the individual risks in the insured pool are not independent, and the severity of the loss could be enormous. For example, according to the IBC, property insurance claims for severe weather damage have increased, and Environment Canada notes that the extreme weather events that could be expected to occur every 40 years are now expected to occur every 6 years. This means that estimating expected loss rates

frequency of loss
The probability that a loss will occur.

severity of loss
The size of the loss.

(frequency times severity) is extremely difficult in these coverage areas. For example, in the United States, since the September 11, 2001, terrorist attacks, coverage for high-profile buildings in big cities, as well as other properties considered potential targets, remains expensive. This higher uncertainty of losses forces P&C firms to invest in more short-term assets and hold a larger percentage of capital and reserves than life insurance firms hold.

long-tail loss
A claim that is made some time after a policy was written.

- *Long tail versus short tail.* Some liability lines suffer from a long-tail risk exposure phenomenon that makes the estimation of expected losses difficult. This **long-tail loss** arises in policies in which the insured event occurs during a coverage period but a claim is not filed or reported until many years later. The delay in filing of a claim is in accordance with the terms of the insurance contract and often occurs because the detrimental consequences of the event are not known for a period of time after the event actually occurs. Losses incurred but not reported have caused insurers significant problems in lines such as medical malpractice and other liability insurance where product damage suits occur years after the event and the coverage period has expired. For example, in 2002 Halliburton, a major U.S. corporation, agreed to pay US$4 billion in cash and stock and to seek bankruptcy protection for a subsidiary to settle more than 300,000 asbestos claims. Questions still remain about how much insurance companies will be required to reimburse Halliburton for the cost of asbestos case settlements. The company had only US$1.6 billion of expected insurance on its books for asbestos claims since the nature of the risk being covered was not fully understood at the time the policies were written.
- *Product inflation versus social inflation.* Loss rates on all P&C property policies are adversely affected by unexpected increases in inflation. Such increases were triggered, for example, by the oil price shocks of 1973 and 1978. However, in addition to a systematic unexpected inflation risk in each line, there may be line-specific inflation risks. The inflation risk of property lines is likely to reflect the approximate underlying inflation risk of the economy. Liability lines may be subject to social inflation, as reflected in the courts' willingness to award punitive and other liability damages at rates far above the underlying rate of inflation. Such social inflation has been particularly prevalent in commercial liability and medical malpractice insurance in the United States.

Reinsurance An alternative to managing risk on a P&C insurer's balance sheet is to purchase reinsurance from a reinsurance company. *Reinsurance* is essentially insurance for insurance companies. Note from Table 6–5 that 10.0 percent of total assets was made up of recoverables from reinsurers (unearned premiums and unpaid claims and adjustment expenses). Reinsurance is a way for primary insurance companies to protect against unforeseen or extraordinary losses. Depending on the contract, reinsurance can enable the insurer to improve its capital position, expand its business, limit losses, and stabilize cash flows, among other things. In addition, the reinsurer, drawing information from many primary insurers, will usually have a far larger pool of data for assessing risks. Reinsurance takes a variety of forms. It may represent a layer of risk, such as losses within certain limits, say, $5 million to $10 million, that will be paid by the reinsurer to the primary insurance company for which a premium is paid, or a sharing of both losses and profits for certain types of business. Reinsurance is an international business. About 75 percent of the reinsurance business that comes from U.S. insurance companies is written by non-U.S. reinsurers such as Munich Re.

Insurers and reinsurers also typically issue catastrophe bonds. The bonds pay high interest rates and diversify an investor's portfolio because natural disasters occur randomly and are not associated with (are independent of) economic factors. Depending on how the bond is structured, if losses reach the threshold specified in the bond offering, the investor may lose all or part of the principal or interest. For example, a deep-discount or zero-coupon catastrophe bond would pay $100(1 - \alpha)$ on maturity, where α is the loss rate due to the catastrophe. Thus, Munich Re issued a US$250 million catastrophe bond in 2009, where α (the loss rate) reflected losses incurred on all reinsurer policies over a 24-hour period should an event (such as a flood or hurricane) occur and losses exceed a certain threshold. The required yield on these bonds reflected the risk-free rate plus a premium reflecting investors' expectations regarding the probability of the event occurring.

loss (claims) ratio
Ratio that measures losses incurred to premiums earned.

premiums earned
Premiums received and earned on insurance contracts because time has passed with no claim being filed.

Measuring Loss Risk The **loss (claims) ratio** measures the actual losses incurred on a line. It measures the ratio of losses incurred to **premiums earned** (premiums received and earned on insurance contracts because time has passed with no claim being filed). Thus, a loss ratio less than 100 percent means that premiums earned were sufficient to cover losses incurred on that line. For example, referring back to Table 6–4, NWPs by the Canadian P&C industry in 2011 were $42.794 billion and claims incurred were $28.567 billion, resulting in a loss ratio, also called an *earned loss ratio,* of 67 percent ($28.567/42.794). For 2006, NWPs were $24.964 billion and claims incurred were $20.326 billion, resulting in a loss ratio of 81 percent ($20.326/$24.964). From 2006 to 2011, the loss ratio declined, reflecting an increase in premiums written that was greater than the increase in claims incurred, resulting in an increase in profitability for the insurance companies. However, the earned loss ratio does not tell the whole story, as the expense of providing insurance coverage must also be considered.

combined ratio
Ratio that measures the overall underwriting profitability of a line; it is equal to the loss ratio plus the ratios of loss adjustment expenses to premiums earned and commission and other acquisition costs to premiums written as a proportion of premiums earned.

Expense Risk The two major sources of expense risk to P&C insurers are (1) loss adjustment expenses (LAEs) and (2) commissions and other expenses. LAEs relate to the costs surrounding the loss settlement process. For example, many P&C insurers employ adjusters who determine the liability of the insurer and the size of the adjustment or settlement to be made. The other major area of expense occurs in the commission costs paid to insurance brokers and sales agents, and other expenses related to the acquisition of new business. The underwriting loss/gain is calculated as NWPs less claims and expenses incurred. A common measure of the overall underwriting profitability of a line, which includes both loss and expense experience, is the **combined ratio**. The combined ratio is equal to the earned loss ratio plus the operating expense ratio. If the combined ratio is less than 100, premiums alone are sufficient to cover both losses and expenses related to the line and there is an underwriting profit; if the combined ratio is greater than 100, then there is an underwriting loss. Table 6–6 shows the yearly underwriting loss/gain for Canadian P&C insurers for the period from 1990 to 2011. With a combined ratio of 87.5 percent in 2006, P&C insurers experienced their largest underwriting profit over the period, as well as underwriting profits in every year from 2003 to 2007 and 2009 to 2011. Clearly, increasing insurance broker commissions and other operating costs can rapidly render an insurance line unprofitable.

If premiums are insufficient and the combined ratio exceeds 100 percent, the P&C insurer must rely on investment income earned on premiums for overall profitability. As shown in Table 6–6, the underwriting losses (combined ratio greater than 100 percent) from 1990 to 2002 were offset by investment income (return on

TABLE 6–6 P&C Industry Return on Equity, Return on Investment, and Underwriting Ratios, 1990 to 2011

Source: The Insurance Bureau of Canada, *Facts of the Property & Casualty Insurance Industry in Canada, 2013*, ibc.ca.

	Return on Equity	Return on Investment	Earned Loss Ratio	Operating Expense Ratio	Combined Ratio
1990	9.7%	10.8%	79.1%	31.4%	110.4%
1991	9.6%	10.9%	78.6%	32.5%	111.2%
1992	8.5%	10.4%	77.7%	32.9%	110.6%
1993	9.5%	10.7%	77.1%	32.8%	109.9%
1994	6.8%	8.0%	75.7%	31.3%	107.0%
1995	11.7%	9.1%	73.3%	30.8%	104.1%
1996	13.6%	10.3%	72.7%	30.7%	103.4%
1997	13.1%	10.4%	71.4%	31.1%	102.6%
1998	6.8%	8.5%	74.9%	32.9%	107.8%
1999	6.5%	7.3%	72.6%	33.2%	105.9%
2000	6.3%	9.0%	75.9%	32.7%	108.7%
2001	2.6%	7.5%	80.0%	31.0%	111.0%
2002	1.7%	5.4%	76.9%	28.9%	105.8%
2003	11.6%	6.2%	69.9%	28.6%	98.4%
2004	18.1%	5.6%	62.7%	28.2%	91.0%
2005	17.2%	5.9%	64.7%	28.7%	93.4%
2006	16.9%	5.9%	59.5%	28.1%	87.5%
2007	14.1%	5.5%	62.5%	28.5%	91.0%
2008	6.0%	3.9%	70.3%	30.0%	100.3%
2009	6.9%	4.2%	69.5%	30.0%	99.6%
2010	7.6%	4.3%	69.1%	30.2%	99.4%
2011	8.0%	4.2%	68.2%	30.3%	98.4%

A note about terminology:
Earned loss ratio is the ratio of claims incurred to net premiums earned.
Operating expense ratio is the ratio of operating expenses to net premiums earned.
Combined ratio is the ratio of claims and expenses to net premiums earned.
When the combined ratio is 100% or more, it signifies an underwriting loss. When the combined ratio is less than 100%, it signifies an underwriting profit.

investment) in each year. In 2011, the return on investment for the industry was 4.2 percent on total investments (bonds, shares, real estate, mortgages, term deposits, and other investments) of $9.393 billion. The profitability of the industry thus depends on identifying the risks and setting appropriate premiums, as well as on investment skills. Bad years for the investment portfolios shown in Table 6–6 may also result in poor profitability for the P&C insurers. Declines in the value of the investment portfolio would be reflected in an erosion of capital. However, Canadian P&C companies have less exposure to equity investments than do U.S. and European firms and, while showing a decline in profitability, did not experience as large an impact on their income statements and balance sheets from the global recession in 2008.

The effects of the global liquidity crisis for P&C insurers were felt in Canada by some consolidation of the industry. For example, the Dutch bank ING Group was forced to sell most of its interest in ING Canada.

Investment Yield/Return Risk As discussed above, when the combined ratio is more than 100 percent, overall profitability can be ensured only by a sufficient investment return on premiums earned. That is, P&C firms invest premiums in assets between the time they are received and the time they are paid out to meet claims. Thus, the effect of interest rates and default rates on P&C insurers' investments is crucial to P&C insurers' overall profitability. That is, measuring and managing credit and interest rate risk are key concerns of P&C managers.

Consider the following example. Suppose an insurance company's projected earned loss ratio is 79.8 percent, its expense ratio is 27.9 percent, and it pays 2 percent of its premiums earned to policyholders as dividends. The combined ratio (after dividends) for this insurance company is equal to:

Loss Ratio	+	Expense Ratio	+	Dividend Ratio	=	Combined Ratio after Dividends
79.8%	+	27.9%	+	2.0%	=	109.7%

Thus, expected losses on all P&C lines and expenses exceeded premiums earned by 9.7 percent.

operating ratio
A measure of the overall profitability of a P&C insurer; it equals the combined ratio minus the investment yield.

If the company's investment portfolio, however, yielded 12 percent, the **operating ratio** and overall profitability of the P&C insurer would be:

Operating Ratio = Combined Ratio after Dividends − Investment Yield
= 109.7% − 12.0%
= 97.7%

and

Overall Profitability = 100% − Operating Ratio
= 100% − 97.7%
= 2.3%

As can be seen, the high investment returns (12 percent) make the P&C insurer profitable overall.

Finally, if losses, expenses, and other costs are higher and investment yields are lower than expected so that operating losses are incurred, P&C insurers carry reserves (0.4 percent of total assets in 2011) to reduce the risk of insolvency.

Recent Trends Figure 6–4 shows the catastrophic losses in Canada from 1983 to 2011, and the trend in those losses in 2011 dollars. The major source for insurance company losses came from storms (hail, flooding, winds, and tornadoes) across Canada. The ice storm of 1998, which affected southern Québec ($1.48 billion) and eastern Ontario ($165.56 million), is the only incident in Canada where total payouts have exceeded $1 billion. By way of contrast, insurance incidents in the United States regularly

FIGURE 6–4
Catastrophic Losses in Canada ($000,000,000, 2011 dollars) from 1983 to 2011

Source: Insurance Bureau of Canada, *Facts of the Property & Casualty Insurance Industry in Canada, 2011*, ibc.ca.

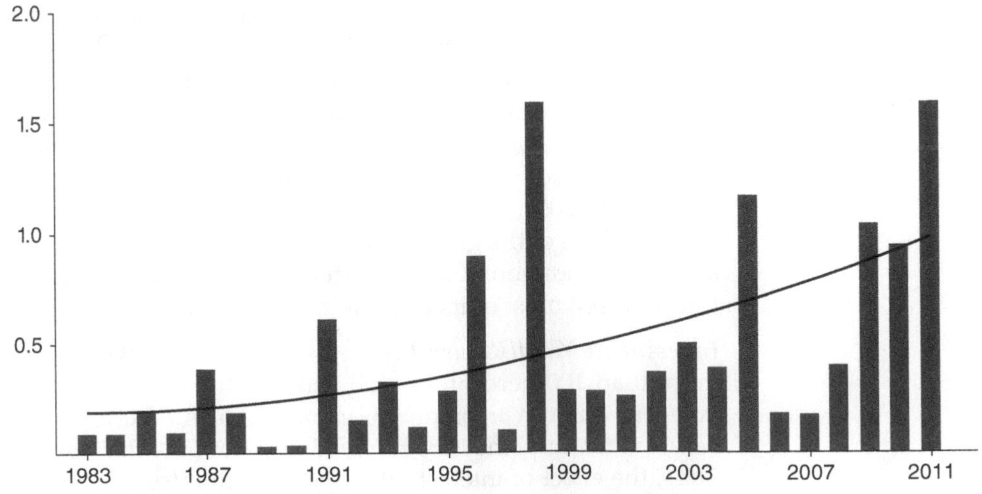

exceed US$1 billion. Reinsurance means that large payouts affect global insurance rates and therefore rates in Canada. For example, Hurricane Katrina in 2005 cost insurers over US$35 billion, and Manulife's reinsurance losses were estimated at US$135 million.

Although catastrophes should be random, the period 1983–2011 was characterized by a number of catastrophes of historically high severity. A succession of catastrophes, including the tsunami and nuclear reactor disaster in Japan and the earthquakes in New Zealand in 2011, meant that, in the terminology of P&C insurers, the global industry was in the trough of an underwriting cycle, or underwriting conditions were hard. These cycles are characterized by periods of rising premiums leading to increased profitability. Following a period of solid but not spectacular rates of return, the industry enters a down phase in which premiums soften as the supply of insurance products increases. As a result, the period 1983–2011 was not very profitable for the P&C industry, with combined ratios exceeding 90 percent (Table 6–6) in every year except 2006. (Remember that a combined ratio higher than 100 percent is bad in that it means that losses, expenses, and dividends totalled more than premiums earned.)

The year 2001 saw a big blow to the insurance industry and the world with the terrorist attacks on the World Trade Center and the Pentagon. Because of the tremendous impact these attacks had on the health of the U.S. insurance industry, the U.S. government paid some of the industry's losses due to the attacks, capping insurers' 2002 liabilities at US$12 billion, 2003 liabilities at US$23 billion, and 2004 liabilities at US$36 billion. Despite this bailout of the industry, many insurers did not survive and those that did were forced to increase premiums significantly.

In summary, the traditional reaction to losses or poor profit results has been exit from the industry—through failure or acquisition—of less profitable firms and a rapid increase in premiums among the remaining firms.

Regulation

Similar to life insurance companies, regulation of the P&C insurance industry is shared by the provincial/territorial and federal governments. P&C insurers may be incorporated federally or provincially/territorially. OSFI provides a *Table of Guidelines* that are specific to P&C insurers, including investment concentration limits, securities lending, asset securitization, derivatives best practices, earthquake exposure, outsourcing, impaired loans, and accounting guidelines. Provincial and territorial regulators govern the marketing and licensing of P&C insurers.

Canadian P&C policyholders are protected from the insolvency of their insurers, up to certain limits, by the Property and Casualty Insurance Compensation Corporation (PACICC), which is industry run. All Canadian provinces and territories require PACICC coverage prior to licensing. In addition, foreign insurers are required to vest assets in Canada so that their policyholders are protected.

pacicc.ca

CONCEPT QUESTIONS

1. **Why do P&C insurers hold more capital and reserves than do life insurers?**
2. **Why are life insurers' assets, on average, longer in maturity than those of P&C insurers?**
3. **Describe the main lines of insurance offered by P&C insurers.**
4. **What are the components of the combined ratio?**
5. **How does the operating ratio differ from the combined ratio?**
6. **Why does the combined ratio tend to behave cyclically?**

GLOBAL ISSUES

Like the other sectors of the FI industry, the insurance sector is global. Table 6–7 lists the top 10 countries in terms of total premiums written in 2011 (in U.S. dollars) and their percentage share of the world market. Table 6–8 lists the top 10 insurance companies worldwide by total revenues. Panel A lists the data for life insurance, while panel B lists the data for non-life insurance (called P&C in Canada and the United States). While North America, Japan, and Western Europe dominate the global market, all regions are engaged in the insurance business and many insurers are engaged internationally. Worldwide, 2011 was a bad year for life and P&C insurers. Catastrophic losses were the worst on record. The earthquake and tsunami in Japan and earthquakes in New Zealand, along with tornadoes in the United States, contributed to US$350 billion in global disaster losses. Japan's earthquake and tsunami (insured losses of US$40 billion), earthquakes in New Zealand (insured losses of US$13 billion), floods in Thailand (insured losses of US$10 billion), and severe tornadoes in the United States (US$14.2 billion) all contributed to insured losses. Insurance losses from these disasters would have been far greater had the governments in these countries not picked up a large portion of the loss coverage. Worldwide insured losses in 2012 were 36 percent higher than the 10-year average (US$72 billion versus US$53 billion), mainly due to events in the United States. However, except for the earthquake in Italy (with insured losses topping US$1.6 billion), no major catastrophes occurred outside the United States. Insured losses in Europe, Asia, and Canada were far below their 10-year averages.

TABLE 6–7 The World's Top Countries by Life and Nonlife Insurance Premiums Written, 2011[1] (direct premiums written, U.S. $ billions)

Source: Swiss Re, *sigma* 3/2012, 2013 International Insurance Fact Book, iii.org.

Rank	Country	Life Premiums Written (US$ billions)	Non-Life Premiums Written[2] (US$ billions)	Total Premiums Written (US$ billions)	Share of World Market (%)
1	United States[3,4]	$ 537.6	667.1	$1,204.7	26.2
2	Japan[4,6]	524.7	130.7	655.4	14.26
3	United Kingdom[4]	210.1	109.5	319.6	6.95
4	France[4]	174.8	98.4	273.1	5.94
5	Germany[5]	113.9	131.3	245.1	5.34
6	PR China[5]	134.5	87.3	221.9	4.83
7	Italy	105.1	55.4	160.5	3.49
8	South Korea[6]	79.2	51.2	130.4	2.84
9	Canada[4,7]	52.2	69.0	121.2	2.64
10	Netherlands	31.2	79.7	110.9	2.41
	Top 10 Total	**$ 1,963.1**	**$1,479.7**	**$3,442.8**	**74.9%**
	World Total	**$2,627.2**	**1,969.5**	**4,596.7**	**100.0%**

1. Before reinsurance transactions
2. Includes accident and health insurance.
3. Life premiums include an estimate of group pension business; nonlife premiums include state funds.
4. Estimated.
5. Provisional
6. April 1, 2011, to March 31, 2012.
7. Life insurance premiums are net premiums.

TABLE 6–8 Top 10 Global Insurance Companies by Revenues, 2011[1] (U.S. $ millions)

Source: Insurance Information Institute, *International Insurance Fact Book*, 2011, iii.org.

Panel A: Life/Health Insurance			
Rank	**Company**	**Revenues**	**Country**
1	Japan Post Holdings	$211,019	Japan
2	AXA	142,712	France
3	Assicurazioni Generali	112,628	Italy
4	Nippon Life Insurance	90,783	Japan
5	Meiji Yasuda Life Insurance	77,463	Japan
6	MetLife	70,641	United States
7	China Life Insurance	67,274	China
8	Dai-ichi Life Insurance	62,462	Japan
9	Aviva	61,754	United Kingdom
10	Prudential	58,527	United Kingdom
Panel B: P&C Insurance			
Rank	**Company**	**Revenues[2]**	**Country**
1	Berkshire Hathaway	$143,688	United States
2	Allianz	134,168	Germany
3	Munich Re Group	90,137	Germany
4	American International Group	61,730	United States
5	State Farm Insurance Companies	64,305	United States
6	Zurich Financial Services	52,983	Switzerland
7	MS&AD Insurance Group Holdings	47,684	Japan
8	Tokio Marine Holdings	43,264	Japan
9	People's Insurance Co. of China	36,549	China
10	NKSJ Holdings	35,343	Japan

[1] Based on an analysis of companies in the Global Fortune 500. Includes stock and mutual companies.
[2] Revenues include premium and annuity income, investment income and capital gains or losses, but exclude deposits; includes consolidated subsidiaries, excludes excise taxes.

directors and officers (D&O) insurance
Insurance that protects corporate directors and senior managers from legal claims.

monoline insurers
Companies that act as guarantors of the debt or equity obligations of other firms.

However, like the other sectors of the financial services industry, the insurance sector has been impacted by the global financial crisis. Insurance companies can be exposed to the credit crisis on the asset side through holding subprime mortgage-backed securities. On the liability side, insurance companies provide mortgage insurance, financial guarantees such as CDSs, and **directors and officers (D&O) insurance**. Losses in these areas affect their profitability and result in declines in capital. In September 2008, the world's largest P&C insurer, American International Group Inc. (AIG), received a US$85 billion rescue package and became 79.9 percent owned by the U.S. government. The stress placed on insurance companies globally has resulted in further consolidation of the markets, sometimes to the benefit of Canadian banks. For example, Scotiabank acquired ING's P&C insurance arm, ING Canada Inc., and BMO Financial Group acquired AIG Life Insurance, renaming it BMO Life Assurance Company, in 2009. As well, the global market disruptions have caused problems for **monoline insurers**, which act as guarantors of corporate and municipal debt and other securities. This issue is important as a credit enhancement for off-balance-sheet (OBS) items.

Questions and Problems

1. What is the primary function of an insurance company? How does this function compare with the primary function of a DTI?
2. What is moral hazard?
3. What is the adverse selection problem? How does adverse selection affect the profitability of an insurance company?
4. What are the similarities and differences among the four basic lines of life insurance products?
5. Explain how annuity activities represent the reverse of life insurance activities.
6. Explain how life insurance and annuity products can be used to create a steady stream of cash disbursements and payments to avoid paying or receiving a single lump-sum cash amount.
7. a. Calculate the annual cash flows from a $1 million, 20-year fixed-payment annuity earning a guaranteed 10 percent per annum if payments are to begin at the end of the current year.
   b. Calculate the annual cash flows from a $1 million, 20-year fixed-payment annuity earning a guaranteed 10 percent per annum if payments are to begin at the end of year 5.
   c. What is the amount of the annuity purchase required if you wish to receive a fixed payment of $200,000 for 20 years? Assume that the annuity will earn 10 percent per annum.
8. You deposit $10,000 annually into a life insurance fund for the next 10 years, after which time you retire.
   a. If the deposits are made at the beginning of the year and earn an interest rate of 8 percent, what will be the amount of retirement funds at the end of year 10?
   b. Instead of a lump sum, you wish to receive annuities for the next 20 years (years 11 through 30). What is the constant annual payment you expect to receive at the beginning of each year if you assume an interest rate of 8 percent during the distribution period?
   c. Repeat parts (a) and (b) above assuming earning rates of 7 percent and 9 percent during the deposit period and earning rates of 7 percent and 9 percent during the distribution period. During which period does the change in the earning rate have the greatest impact?
9. You deposit $12,000 annually into a life insurance fund for the next 10 years, at which time you plan to retire. Instead of a lump sum, you wish to receive annuities for the next 20 years. What is the annual payment you expect to receive beginning in year 11 if you assume an interest rate of 6 percent for the whole time period?
10. a. Suppose a 65-year-old person wants to purchase an annuity from an insurance company that would pay $20,000 per year until the end of that person's life. The insurance company expects this person to live for 15 more years and would be willing to pay 6 percent on the annuity. How much should the insurance company ask this person to pay for the annuity?
    b. A second 65-year-old person wants the same $20,000 annuity, but this person is much healthier and is expected to live for 20 years. If the same 6 percent interest rate applies, how much should this healthier person be charged for the annuity?
    c. In each case, what is the difference in the purchase price of the annuity if the distribution payments are made at the beginning of the year?
11. Contrast the balance sheet of a life insurance company with the balance sheet of a bank. Explain the balance sheet differences in terms of the differences in the primary functions of the two organizations.
12. How do life insurance companies earn a profit?
13. How would the balance sheet of a life insurance company change if it offered to run a private pension fund for another company?
14. How does the regulation of insurance companies differ from the regulation of DTIs?
15. How do guarantee funds for life insurance companies compare with deposit insurance for banks?
16. What are the two major activity lines of P&C insurance firms?
17. Contrast the balance sheet of a P&C insurance company with the balance sheet of a bank. Explain the balance sheet differences in terms of the differences in the primary functions of the two organizations.
18. What are the three sources of underwriting risk in the P&C insurance industry?
19. How do unexpected increases in inflation affect P&C insurers?
20. Identify the four characteristics or features of the perils insured against by P&C insurance. Rank the features in terms of actuarial predictability and total loss potential.

21. Insurance companies will charge a higher premium for which of the insurance lines listed below? Why?
    a. Low-severity, high-frequency lines versus high-severity, low-frequency lines.
    b. Long-tail lines versus short-tail lines.
22. What does the loss ratio measure? What has been the long-term trend of the loss ratio? Why?
23. What does the expense ratio measure? Identify and explain the two major sources of expense risk to a P&C insurer.
24. How is the combined ratio defined? What does it measure?
25. What is the investment yield on premiums earned? Why has this ratio become so important to P&C insurers?
26. How is investment yield related to the interest rate risk and credit risk faced by a P&C insurer?
27. An insurance company's projected loss ratio is 77.5 percent, and its LAE ratio is 12.9 percent. The company estimates that commission payments will be 16 percent. What must be the minimum yield on investments to achieve a positive operating ratio?
28. a. What is the combined ratio for a property insurer that has a simple loss ratio of 73 percent, an LAE of 12.5 percent, and a ratio of commissions and other acquisition expenses of 18 percent?
    b. What is the combined ratio adjusted for investment yield if the company earns an investment yield of 8 percent?
29. An insurance company collected $3.6 million in premiums and disbursed $1.96 million in losses. Loss adjustment expenses amounted to 6.6 percent. The total income generated from the company's investments was $170,000 after all expenses were paid. What is the net profitability in dollars?
30. A P&C insurer brings in $6.25 million in premiums on its homeowners multiple peril line of insurance. The line's losses amount to $4,343,750, expenses are $1,593,750, and dividends are $156,250. The insurer earns $218,750 in the investment of its premiums. Calculate the line's loss ratio, expense ratio, dividend ratio, combined ratio, investment ratio, operating ratio, and overall profitability.

CHAPTER 7

RISKS OF FINANCIAL INSTITUTIONS

After studying this chapter you should be able to:

LO1 Define and identify interest rate risk, market risk, credit risk, OBS risk, foreign exchange risk, country or sovereign risk, technology and operational risk, liquidity risk, and insolvency risk for an FI.

LO2 Discuss the interaction of risks for an FI.

INTRODUCTION

LO1

A major objective of FI management is to increase the FI's returns for its owners. This often comes, however, at the cost of increased risk. This chapter is an overview of the various risks facing FIs: interest rate risk, credit risk, liquidity risk, foreign exchange risk, country or sovereign risk, market risk, off-balance-sheet (OBS) risk, technology and operational risk, and insolvency risk. Table 7–1 presents a brief definition of each of these risks. By the end of this chapter, you will have a basic understanding of the variety and complexity of the risks facing managers of modern FIs. In the remaining chapters of the text, we look at the measurement and management of the most important of these risks. As will become clear, the effective management of these risks is central to an FI's performance.

TABLE 7–1 **Risks Faced by FIs**

1. **Interest rate risk** The risk incurred by an FI when the maturities of its assets and liabilities are mismatched.
2. **Credit risk** The risk that promised cash flows from loans and securities held by FIs may not be paid in full.
3. **Liquidity risk** The risk that a sudden surge in liability withdrawals may require an FI to liquidate assets in a very short period of time and at less than fair market prices.
4. **Foreign exchange risk** The risk that exchange rate changes can affect the value of an FI's assets and liabilities denominated in nondomestic currencies.
5. **Country or sovereign risk** The risk that repayments to foreign tenders or investors may be interrupted because of restrictions, intervention, or interference from foreign governments.
6. **Market risk** The risk incurred from assets and liabilities in an FI's trading book due to changes in interest rates, exchange rates, and other prices.
7. **OBS risk** The risk incurred by an FI as a result of activities related to its contingent assets and liabilities held off the balance sheet.
8. **Technology risk** The risk incurred by an FI when its technological investments do not produce anticipated cost savings.
9. **Operational risk** The risk that existing technology, auditing, monitoring, and other support systems may malfunction or break down.
10. **Insolvency risk** The risk that an FI may not have enough capital to offset a sudden decline in the value of its assets.

INTEREST RATE RISK

interest rate risk
The risk incurred by an FI when the maturities of its assets and liabilities are mismatched.

Chapter 1 discussed asset transformation as a key special function of financial intermediation. Asset transformation involves an FI buying primary securities or assets and issuing secondary securities or liabilities to fund asset purchases. The primary securities purchased by FIs often have maturity and liquidity characteristics different from those of the secondary securities FIs sell. In mismatching the maturities of assets and liabilities as part of their asset-transformation function, FIs potentially expose themselves to **interest rate risk.**

EXAMPLE 7–1

Effect of an Interest Rate Increase on an FI's Profits When the Maturity of Its Assets Exceeds the Maturity of Its Liabilities

Consider an FI that issues $100 million of liabilities of one-year maturity to finance the purchase of $100 million of assets with a two-year maturity. We show this situation in the following time lines:

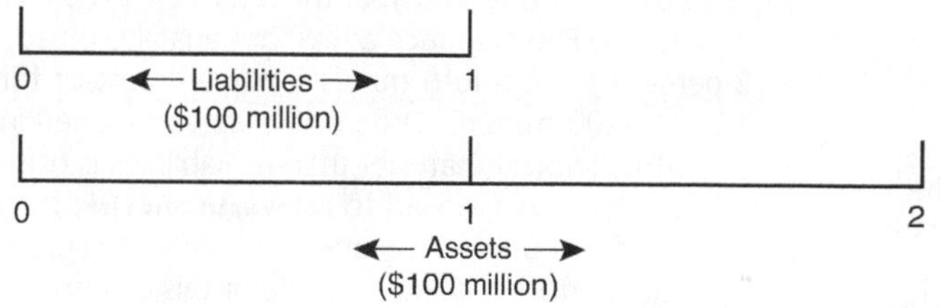

In these time lines the FI can be viewed as being "short-funded." That is, the maturity of its liabilities is less than the maturity of its assets.

Suppose the cost of funds (liabilities) for the FI is 9 percent per year and the interest return on an asset is 10 percent per year. Over the first year the FI can lock in a profit spread of 1 percent (10 percent − 9 percent) times $100 million by borrowing short term (for one year) and lending long term (for two years). Thus, its profit is $1 million (0.01 × $100 million).

However, its profit for the second year is uncertain. If the level of interest rates does not change, the FI can *refinance* its liabilities at 9 percent and lock in a 1 percent, or $1 million, profit for the second year as well. There is always a risk, however, that interest rates will change between years 1 and 2. If interest rates were to rise and the FI could borrow new one-year liabilities only at 11 percent in the second year, its profit spread in the second year would actually be negative; that is, 10 percent − 11 percent = −1 percent, or the FI's loss is $1 million (−0.01 × $100 million). The positive spread earned in the first year by the FI from holding assets with a longer maturity than its liabilities would be offset by a negative spread in the second year. Note that if interest rates were to rise by more than 1 percent in the second year, the FI would stand to take losses over the two-year period as a whole. As a result, when an FI holds longer-term assets relative to liabilities, it potentially exposes itself to **refinancing risk**. This is the risk that the cost of rolling over or reborrowing funds could be more than the return earned on asset investments. During the 2008 financial crisis, FIs that had funded their long-term assets with short-term commercial paper or interbank funds found that, as the credit crisis intensified, the interest rates on their liabilities increased, reducing their interest rate spreads.

refinancing risk
The risk that the cost of rolling over or reborrowing funds will rise above the returns being earned on asset investments.

EXAMPLE 7–2

Impact of an Interest Rate Decrease When the Maturity of an FI's Liabilities Exceeds the Maturity of Its Assets

An alternative balance sheet structure would have the FI borrowing $100 million for a longer term than the $100 million of assets in which it invests. In the time lines below the FI is "long-funded." The maturity of its liabilities is longer than the maturity of its assets. Using a similar example, suppose the FI borrowed funds at 9 percent per annum for two years and invested the funds in an asset that yields 10 percent for one year. This situation is shown as follows:

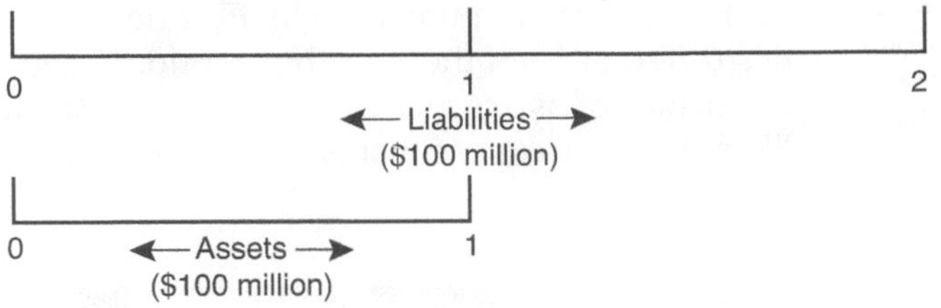

In this case, the FI is also exposed to an interest rate risk: By holding shorter-term assets relative to liabilities, it faces uncertainty about the interest rate at which it can reinvest funds in the second period. As before, the FI locks in a one-year profit spread of 1 percent, or $1 million. At the end of the first year, the asset matures and the funds that have been borrowed for two years have to be reinvested. Suppose interest rates fall between the first and second years so that in the second year the return on $100 million invested in new one-year assets is 8 percent. The FI would face a loss, or negative spread, in the second year of 1 percent (that is, 8 percent asset return minus 9 percent cost of funds), so the FI would lose $1 million ($-0.01 \times$ $100 million). The positive spread earned in the first year by the FI from holding assets with a shorter maturity than its liabilities is offset by a negative spread in the second year. Thus, the FI is exposed to **reinvestment risk**; by holding shorter-term assets relative to liabilities, it faces uncertainty about the interest rate at which it can reinvest funds borrowed for a longer period. A good example of this exposure has been provided by banks that have borrowed fixed-rate deposits while investing in floating-rate loans, that is, loans whose interest rates are changed or adjusted frequently.

reinvestment risk
The risk that the returns on funds to be reinvested will fall below the cost of funds.

In addition to a potential refinancing or reinvestment risk that occurs when interest rates change, an FI faces *market value* risk as well. Remember that the market (or fair) value of an asset or liability is conceptually equal to the present value of current and future cash flows from that asset or liability. Therefore, rising interest rates increase the discount rate on those cash flows and reduce the market value of that asset or liability. Conversely, falling interest rates increase the market values of assets and liabilities. Moreover, mismatching maturities by holding longer-term assets than liabilities means that when interest rates rise, the market value of the FI's assets falls by a greater amount than its liabilities. This exposes the FI to the risk of economic loss and, potentially, the risk of insolvency.

If holding assets and liabilities with mismatched maturities exposes FIs to reinvestment (or refinancing) and market value risks, FIs can seek to hedge, or protect against, interest rate risk by matching the maturity of their assets and liabilities.[1] This has resulted in the general philosophy that matching maturities is somehow the best policy to hedge interest rate risk for FIs that are averse to risk. Note, however, that matching maturities is not necessarily consistent with an active asset-transformation function for FIs. That is, FIs cannot be asset transformers

[1] This assumes that FIs can directly control the maturities of their assets and liabilities. As interest rates fall, many mortgage borrowers seek to *prepay* their existing loans and refinance at a lower rate. This prepayment risk—which is directly related to interest rate movements—can be viewed as a further interest rate–related risk. Prepayment risk is discussed in detail in Chapter 26.

(e.g., transform short-term deposits into long-term loans) and direct balance sheet matchers or hedgers at the same time. While reducing exposure to interest rate risk, matching maturities may also reduce the FI's profitability because returns from acting as specialized risk-bearing asset transformers are reduced. As a result, some FIs emphasize asset–liability maturity mismatching more than others. For example, banks traditionally hold longer-term assets than liabilities, whereas life insurance companies tend to match the long-term nature of their liabilities with long-term assets. Finally, matching maturities hedges interest rate risk only in a very approximate rather than complete fashion. The reasons for this are technical, relating to the difference between the average life (or duration) and maturity of an asset or liability and whether the FI partly funds its assets with equity capital as well as debt liabilities. In the preceding simple examples, the FI financed its assets completely with borrowed funds. In the real world, FIs use a mix of debt liabilities and shareholders' equity to finance asset purchases. When assets and debt liabilities are not equal, hedging risk (i.e., insulating the FI shareholders' equity values) may be achieved by not exactly matching the maturities (or average lives) of assets and liabilities. We discuss the causes of interest rate risk and methods used to measure interest rate risk in detail in Chapters 8 and 9. We discuss the methods and instruments used to hedge interest rate risk in Chapters 22 through 24.[2]

CONCEPT QUESTIONS

1. **What is refinancing risk?**
2. **Why does a rise in the level of interest rates adversely affect the market value of both assets and liabilities?**
3. **Explain the concept of maturity matching.**

CREDIT RISK

credit risk
The risk that the promised cash flows from loans and securities held by FIs may not be paid in full.

Credit risk arises because of the possibility that promised cash flows on financial claims held by FIs, such as loans or bonds, will not be paid in full. Virtually all types of FIs face this risk. However, in general, FIs that make loans or buy bonds with long maturities are more exposed than are FIs that make loans or buy bonds with short maturities. This means, for example, that banks and life insurance companies are more exposed to credit risk than are money market mutual funds and P&C insurance companies. If the principal on all financial claims held by FIs was paid in full on maturity and interest payments were made on the promised dates, FIs would always receive back the original principal lent plus an interest return. That is, they would face no credit risk. If a borrower defaults, however, both the principal loaned and the interest payments expected to be received are at risk. As a result, many financial claims issued by corporations and held by FIs promise a limited or fixed upside return (principal and interest payments to the lender) with a high probability and a large downside risk (loss of loan principal and promised interest) with a much smaller probability. Good examples of financial claims issued with these return–risk trade-offs are fixed-income coupon bonds issued by corporations and bank loans. In both cases, an FI holding these claims as assets earns the coupon on the bond or the interest promised on the loan if no borrower

[2] We assume in our examples that interest payments are paid only at the end of each year and can be changed only then. In reality, many loan and deposit rates are adjusted frequently or float as market rates change.

default occurs. In the event of default, however, the FI earns zero interest on the asset and may lose all or part of the principal lent, depending on its ability to lay claim to some of the borrower's assets through legal bankruptcy and insolvency proceedings. Accordingly, a key role of FIs involves screening and monitoring loan applicants to ensure that FI managers fund the most creditworthy loans (see Chapter 10).

The effects of credit risk are shown by impairment charges at Spanish banks from 2006 to mid-2012. Global economic conditions deteriorated, resulting in increases in loan defaults, particularly on real estate loans. Spain's economy, along with the economies of Greece, Ireland, Italy, and Portugal, was hard hit by the global recession. The economic downturn is reflected in loan defaults at Spanish banks. Total impairment as a percentage of total domestic loans for Spanish banks climbed from less than 0.5 percent in 2006 to almost 3.0 percent in 2012. By July 2012, the total amount of impairment charges reached close to €70 billion. Because the probability of partial or complete default on bond and loan interest and principal exists, an FI must estimate expected default risk on these assets and demand risk premiums commensurate with the perceived risk exposure. For example, when a business customer applies for a loan, the loan officer must determine whether the default risk is low enough to grant the loan and, if so, the interest rate to charge for this risk.

The potential loss an FI can experience from lending suggests that FIs need to monitor and collect information about borrowers whose assets are in their portfolios and to monitor those borrowers over time. Thus, managerial monitoring efficiency and credit risk management strategies directly affect the return and risks of the loan portfolio. Moreover, one of the advantages FIs have over individual household investors is the ability to diversify some credit risk away by exploiting the law of large numbers in their asset investment portfolios (see Chapter 1). Diversification across assets, such as loans exposed to credit risk, reduces the overall credit risk in the asset portfolio and thus increases the probability of partial or full repayment of principal and/or interest. FIs earn the maximum dollar return when all bonds and loans pay off interest and principal in full. In reality, some loans or bonds default on interest payments, principal payments, or both. Thus, the mean return on the asset portfolio would be less than the maximum possible in a risk-free, no-default case. The effect of risk diversification is to truncate or limit the probabilities of the bad outcomes in the portfolio. In effect, diversification reduces individual **firm-specific credit risk**, such as the risk specific to holding the debt of Air Canada, while leaving the FI still exposed to **systematic credit risk**, such as factors that simultaneously increase the default risk of all firms in the economy (e.g., an economic recession). We describe methods to measure the default risk of individual corporate claims such as bonds and loans in Chapter 10. In Chapter 11, we investigate methods of measuring the risk in portfolios of such claims. Chapter 25 discusses various methods—for example, loan sales, reschedulings, and a good bank–bad bank structure—to manage and control credit risk exposures better, while Chapters 22 to 24 and Chapter 26 discuss the role of the credit derivative markets in hedging credit risk.

firm-specific credit risk
The risk of default of the borrowing firm associated with the specific types of project risk taken by that firm.

systematic credit risk
The risk of default associated with general economywide or macroconditions affecting all borrowers.

CONCEPT QUESTIONS

1. **Why does credit risk exist for FIs?**
2. **How does diversification affect an FI's credit risk exposure?**

LIQUIDITY RISK

liquidity risk
The risk that a sudden surge in liability withdrawals may leave an FI in a position of having to liquidate assets in a very short period of time and at low prices.

Liquidity risk arises when an FI's liability holders, such as depositors or insurance policyholders, demand immediate cash for the financial claims they hold with an FI or when holders of OBS loan commitments (or credit lines) suddenly exercise their right to borrow (draw down their loan commitments). When liability holders demand cash immediately—that is, "put" their financial claims back to the FI—the FI must either borrow additional funds or sell assets to meet the demand for the withdrawal of funds. The most liquid asset of all is cash, which FIs can use to directly meet liability holders' demands to withdraw funds. Although FIs limit their cash asset holdings because cash earns no interest, low cash holdings are usually not a problem. Day-to-day withdrawals by liability holders are generally predictable, and FIs can normally expect to borrow additional funds to meet any sudden shortfalls of cash on the money and financial markets.

However, there are times when an FI can face a liquidity crisis. Because of a lack of confidence by liability holders in the FI or some unexpected need for cash, liability holders may demand *larger* withdrawals than normal. When all, or many, FIs face abnormally large cash demands, the cost of additional purchased or borrowed funds rises and the supply of such funds becomes restricted. As a consequence, FIs may have to sell some of their less-liquid assets to meet the withdrawal demands of liability holders. This results in a more serious liquidity risk, especially as some assets with "thin" markets generate lower prices when the asset sale is immediate than when the FI has more time to negotiate the sale of an asset. As a result, the liquidation of some assets at low or fire-sale prices (the price an FI receives if an asset must be liquidated immediately at less than its fair market value) could threaten an FI's profitability and solvency. For example, the 2008 global credit crisis resulted in runs on banks in the United Kingdom (Northern Rock) and the United States (Countrywide Financial) and disrupted money markets, causing hedge funds and other FIs funded with short-term commercial paper to search for other sources of funding. In the summer of 2008, the U.S. bank IndyMac failed partly due to a bank run that continued for several days. The bank had announced on July 7 that, due to its deteriorating capital position, its mortgage operations would stop and it would operate only as a retail bank. News reports over the weekend highlighted the possibility that IndyMac would become the largest U.S. bank failure in over 20 years. Worried that they would not have access to their money, bank depositors rushed to withdraw money from IndyMac even though their deposits were insured up to US$100,000 by the FDIC. The run was so large that within a week of the original announcement, the FDIC stepped in and took over the bank. IndyMac was eventually acquired by OneWest Bank Group.

EXAMPLE 7–3

Impact of Liquidity Risk on an FI's Equity Value

Consider the simple FI balance sheet in Table 7–2. Before deposit withdrawals, the FI has $10 million in cash assets and $90 million in nonliquid assets (such as small business loans). These assets were funded with $90 million in deposits and $10 million in owner's equity. Suppose that depositors unexpectedly withdrew $15 million in deposits (perhaps due to the release of negative news about the profits of the FI) and the FI receives no new deposits to replace them. To meet these deposit withdrawals, the FI first uses the $10 million it has in cash assets and then seeks to sell some of its nonliquid assets to raise an additional $5 million

TABLE 7–2
Adjusting to a Deposit Withdrawal Using Asset Sales (in millions)

Before the Withdrawal				After the Withdrawal			
Assets		**Liabilities/Equity**		**Assets**		**Liabilities/Equity**	
Cash assets	$ 10	Deposit	$ 90	Cash assets	$ 0	Deposits	$75
Nonliquid assets	90	Equity	10	Nonliquid assets	80	Equity	5
	$100		$100		$80		$80

in cash. Assume that the FI cannot borrow any more funds in the short-term money markets, and because it cannot wait to get better prices for its assets in the future (as it needs the cash now to meet immediate depositor withdrawals), the FI has to sell any nonliquid assets at 50 cents on the dollar. Thus, to cover the remaining $5 million in deposit withdrawals, the FI must sell $10 million in nonliquid assets, incurring a loss of $5 million from the face value of those assets. The FI must then write off any such losses against its capital or equity funds. Since its capital was only $10 million before the deposit withdrawal, the loss on the fire-sale of assets of $5 million leaves the FI with $5 million.

We examine the nature of normal, abnormal, and run-type liquidity risks and their impact on banks, insurance companies, and other FIs in more detail in Chapter 12. In addition, we look at ways an FI can better manage liquidity and liability risk exposures in Chapter 18. Chapter 19 discusses the roles of deposit insurance and other liability guarantee schemes in deterring deposit (liability) runs.

CONCEPT QUESTIONS

1. **Why might an FI face a sudden liquidity crisis?**
2. **What circumstances might lead an FI to liquidate assets at fire-sale prices?**

FOREIGN EXCHANGE RISK

Increasingly, FIs have recognized that both direct foreign investment and foreign portfolio investments can extend the operational and financial benefits available from purely domestic investments. For example, the Bank of Nova Scotia invested over $1 billion in Grupo Financiero Inverlat, a Mexican bank, between 1996 and 2004, creating Scotiabank Inverlat. As well, other Canadian FIs have significant investments in the United States (Bank of Montreal, TD Canada Trust) and in Asia (Sun Life Financial). To the extent that the returns on domestic and foreign investments are imperfectly correlated, there are potential gains for an FI that expands its asset holdings and liability funding beyond the domestic border.

The returns on domestic and foreign direct investing and portfolio investments are not perfectly correlated for two reasons. The first is that the underlying technologies of various economies differ, as do the firms in those economies. For example, one economy may be based on agriculture while another is industry based. Given different economic infrastructures, one economy could be expanding while another is contracting. The second reason is that exchange rate changes are not perfectly correlated across countries. This means the dollar–euro exchange rate may be appreciating while the dollar–yen exchange rate may be falling.

One potential benefit from an FI's becoming increasingly global in its outlook is an ability to expand abroad directly through branching or acquisitions or by

FIGURE 7–1
The Foreign Asset and Liability Position: Net Long Asset Position in Pounds

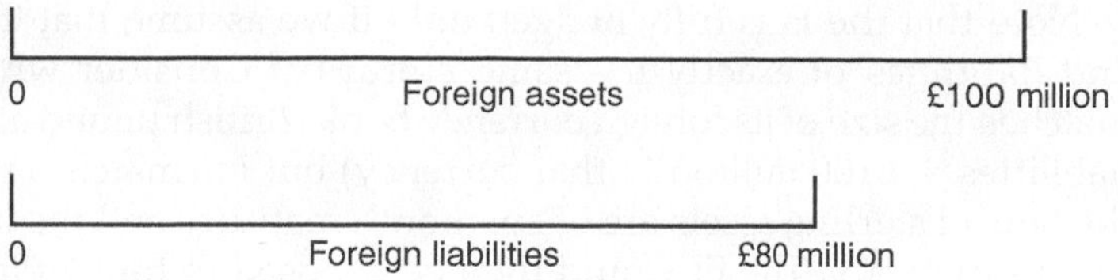

FIGURE 7–2
The Foreign Asset and Liability Position: Net Short Asset Position in Pounds

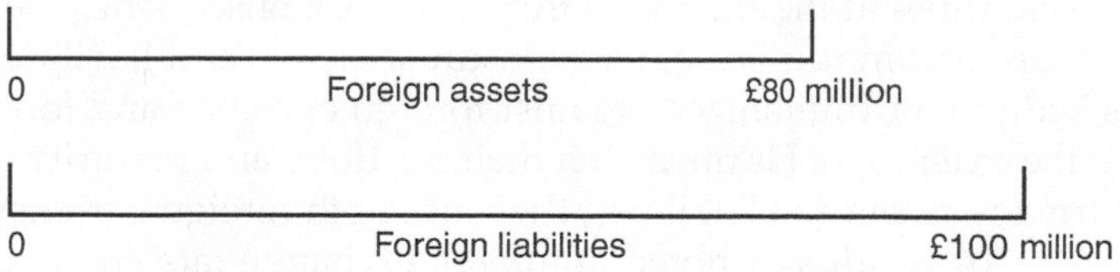

developing a financial asset portfolio that includes foreign securities as well as domestic securities. For example, the removal of the limits on foreign assets in pension funds in 2005 changed the composition of their portfolios and eliminated clone funds and the use of derivatives to circumvent the restriction. Even so, foreign investment exposes an FI to **foreign exchange risk.** Foreign exchange risk is the risk that exchange rate changes can adversely affect the value of an FI's assets and liabilities denominated in foreign currencies.

foreign exchange risk
The risk that exchange rate changes can affect the value of an FI's assets and liabilities denominated in foreign currencies.

To understand how foreign exchange risk arises, suppose that an FI makes a loan to a British company in pounds sterling (£). Should the British pound depreciate in value relative to the dollar, the principal and interest payments received by investors would be devalued in dollar terms. If the British pound fell far enough over the investment period, when cash flows were converted back into dollars, the overall return could be negative. That is, on the conversion of principal and interest payments from sterling into dollars, foreign exchange losses can offset the promised value of local currency interest payments at the original exchange rate at which the investment occurred.

In general, an FI can hold assets denominated in a foreign currency and/or issue foreign liabilities. Consider an FI that holds £100 million loans as assets and funds £80 million of them with British pound certificates of deposit. The difference between the £100 million in pound loans and £80 million in pound CDs is funded by dollar CDs (i.e., £20 million worth of dollar CDs). See Figure 7–1. In this case, the FI is *net long* £20 million in British assets; that is, it holds more foreign assets than liabilities. The FI suffers losses if the exchange rate for pounds falls or depreciates against the dollar over this period. In dollar terms, the value of the British pound loan assets falls or decreases in value by more than the British pound CD liabilities do. That is, the FI is exposed to the risk that its net foreign assets may have to be liquidated at an exchange rate lower than the one that existed when the FI entered into the foreign asset–liability position.

Instead, the FI could have £20 million more foreign liabilities than assets; in this case, it would be holding a *net short* position in foreign assets, as shown in Figure 7–2. Under this circumstance, the FI is exposed to foreign exchange risk if the pound appreciates against the dollar over the investment period. This occurs because the value of its British pound liabilities in dollar terms rose faster than the return on its pound assets. Consequently, to be approximately hedged, the FI must match its assets and liabilities in each foreign currency.

Note that the FI is fully hedged only if we assume that it holds foreign assets and liabilities of exactly the same maturity.[3] Consider what happens if the FI matches the size of its foreign currency book (British pound assets = British pound liabilities = £100 million in that currency) but mismatches the maturities so that the pound sterling assets are of six-month maturity and the liabilities are of three-month maturity. The FI would then be exposed to foreign interest rate risk—the risk that British interest rates would rise when it has to roll over its £100 million in CD liabilities at the end of the third month. Consequently, an FI that matches both the size and maturities of its exposure in assets and liabilities of a given currency is hedged, or immunized, against foreign currency and foreign interest rate risk. To the extent that FIs mismatch their portfolio and maturity exposures in different currency assets and liabilities, they face both foreign currency and foreign interest rate risks. As already noted, if foreign exchange rate and interest rate changes are not perfectly correlated across countries, an FI can diversify away part, if not all, of its foreign currency risk. We discuss the measurement and evaluation of an FI's foreign currency risk exposure in depth in Chapter 13.

CONCEPT QUESTIONS

1. **Explain why the returns on domestic and foreign portfolio investments are not, in general, perfectly correlated.**
2. **A Canadian FI is net long in euro-denominated assets. If the euro appreciates against the dollar, will the FI gain or lose?**

COUNTRY OR SOVEREIGN RISK

country or sovereign risk
The risk that repayments from foreign borrowers may be interrupted because of interference from foreign governments.

As we noted in the previous section, a globally oriented FI that mismatches the size and maturities of its foreign assets and liabilities is exposed to foreign currency and foreign interest rate risks. Even beyond these risks, and even when investing in dollars, holding assets in a foreign country can expose an FI to an additional type of foreign investment risk called **country or sovereign risk**. Country or sovereign risk is a different type of credit risk that is faced by an FI that purchases assets such as the bonds and loans of foreign corporations. For example, when a domestic corporation is unable or unwilling to repay a loan, an FI usually has recourse to the domestic bankruptcy courts and may eventually recoup at least a portion of its original investment when the assets of the defaulted firm are liquidated or restructured. By comparison, a foreign corporation may be unable to repay the principal or interest on a loan even if it would like to. Most commonly, the government of the country in which the corporation is headquartered may prohibit or limit debt payments because of foreign currency shortages and adverse political reasons.

For example, in 2001, the government of Argentina, which had pegged its peso to the dollar on a one-to-one basis since the early 1990s, had to default on its government debt largely because of an overvalued peso and the adverse effect this had on its exports and foreign currency earnings. In December 2001, Argentina ended up defaulting on US$130 billion in government-issued debt and, in 2002, passed legislation that led to defaults on US$30 billion of corporate debt owed to foreign creditors. As Argentina's economic problems continued, it defaulted on a

[3] Technically speaking, hedging requires matching the durations (average lives of assets and liabilities) rather than simple maturities (see Chapter 9).

US$3 billion loan repayment to the International Monetary Fund (IMF) in 2003 and in 2005 announced that it was offering its creditors about 30 cents on the dollar from its debt restructuring of US$103 billion. More recently, despite massive injections of bailout funds by the Eurozone and the IMF, in March 2012, Greek government debtholders lost 53.5 percent of their US$265 billion investment as Greece restructured much of its sovereign debt, the largest ever sovereign debt default.

In the event of such restrictions, reschedulings, or outright prohibitions on the payment of debt obligations by sovereign governments, the FI claimholder has little, if any, recourse to the local bankruptcy courts or an international civil claims court. The major leverage available to an FI to ensure or increase repayment probabilities and amounts is its control over the future supply of loans or funds to the country concerned. However, such leverage may be very weak in the face of a country's collapsing currency and government. Chapter 14 discusses how country or sovereign risk is measured and considers possible financial market solutions to the country risk exposure problems of a globally oriented FI.

CONCEPT QUESTIONS

1. **Can an FI be subject to sovereign risk if it lends only to the highest-quality foreign corporations?**
2. **What is one major way an FI can discipline a country that threatens not to repay its loans?**

MARKET RISK

market risk
The risk incurred in the trading of assets and liabilities due to changes in interest rates, exchange rates, and other asset prices.

Market risk arises when FIs actively trade assets and liabilities (and derivatives) rather than holding them for longer-term investment, funding, or hedging purposes. Market risk is closely related to interest rate risk, credit risk, and foreign exchange risk in that as these risks increase or decrease, the overall risk of the FI is affected. However, market risk adds another dimension resulting from its trading activity. Market risk is the incremental risk incurred by an FI when interest rate, foreign exchange, and equity return risks are combined with an active trading strategy, especially one that involves short trading horizons, such as a day. Conceptually, an FI's trading portfolio can be differentiated from its investment portfolio on the basis of time horizon and secondary market liquidity. The trading portfolio contains assets, liabilities, and derivative contracts that can be quickly bought or sold on organized financial markets. The investment portfolio (banking book) contains assets and liabilities that are relatively illiquid and held for longer holding periods. Table 7–3 shows a hypothetical breakdown between banking book and trading book assets and liabilities. As can be seen, the banking book contains the majority of loans and deposits plus other illiquid assets. The trading book contains long and short positions in instruments such as bonds, commodities, foreign exchange, equities, and derivatives.

With the increasing securitization of bank loans (e.g., mortgages), more and more assets have become liquid and tradable. Of course, with time, every asset and liability can be sold. While bank regulators have normally viewed tradable assets as those being held for horizons of less than one year, private FIs take an even shorter term view. In particular, FIs are concerned about the fluctuation in value of their trading account assets and liabilities for periods as short as one day, especially if such fluctuations pose a threat to their solvency.

TABLE 7–3
The Investment (Banking) Book and Trading Book of a Bank

	Assets	Liabilities
	Cash	Deposits
Banking book	Loans	Capital
	Premises and equipment	
	Other illiquid assets	Other illiquid borrowed funds
Trading book	Bonds (long)	Bonds (short)
	Commodities (long)	Commodities (short)
	Foreign exchange (long)	Foreign exchange (short)
	Equities (long)	Equities (short)
	Derivatives* (long)	Derivatives* (short)

*Derivatives are OBS items, as discussed in Chapter 16.

An extreme case of the type of risk involved in active trading is, of course, the market meltdown of 2008–2009. As mortgage borrowers defaulted on their mortgages, FIs that held these mortgages and mortgage-backed securities started announcing huge losses on them. It is these securitized loans, and particularly securitized subprime mortgage loans, that led to huge financial losses resulting from market risk. Investment banks and securities firms were major purchasers of mortgage originators in the early 2000s, which allowed them to increase their business of packaging the loans as securities. As more borrowers defaulted, the securitized mortgage market froze up and FIs were left to hold these "toxic" assets at deeply reduced market values. Investment banks were particularly hard hit with huge losses on the mortgages and securities backing them. On Monday, September 15, 2008, Lehman Brothers (the 158-year-old U.S. investment bank) filed for bankruptcy, Merrill Lynch was bought by Bank of America, AIG (one of the world's largest insurance companies) met with federal regulators to raise desperately needed cash, and Washington Mutual (the largest savings institution in the United States) was acquired by JPMorgan Chase. A sense of foreboding gripped Wall Street. The Dow fell more than 500 points, the largest drop in over seven years. World stock markets saw huge swings in value as investors tried to sort out who might survive and markets from Russia to Europe were forced to suspend trading as stock prices plunged. By the end of September, financial markets had frozen and banks had stopped lending to each other at anything but exorbitantly high rates. Banks that were active traders faced extreme market risk.

The financial market crisis illustrates that market, or trading, risk is present whenever an FI takes an open or unhedged long (buy) or short (sell) position in bonds, equities, and foreign exchange (as well as in commodities and derivative products), and prices change in a direction opposite to that expected. As a result, the more volatile are asset prices in the markets in which these instruments trade, the greater are the market risks faced by FIs that adopt open trading positions. This requires FI management (and regulators) to establish controls to limit positions taken by traders as well as to develop models to measure the market risk exposure of an FI on a day-to-day basis. These market risk measurement models are discussed in Chapter 15.

CONCEPT QUESTIONS

1. **What is market, or trading, risk?**
2. **What modern conditions have led to an increase in this particular type of risk for FIs?**

OFF-BALANCE-SHEET RISK

off-balance-sheet (OBS) risk
The risk incurred by an FI due to activities related to contingent assets and liabilities.

One of the most striking trends for many modern FIs has been the growth in their OBS activities and thus their **off-balance-sheet (OBS) risk**. While all FIs to some extent engage in OBS activities, most attention has been drawn to the activities of banks, especially large banks. By contrast, OBS activities have been less of a concern to smaller DTIs and many insurance companies. An OBS activity, by definition, does not appear on an FI's current balance sheet since it does not involve holding a *current primary* claim (asset) or the issuance of a *current secondary* claim (liability). Instead, OBS activities affect the *future* shape of an FI's balance sheet in that they involve the creation of contingent assets and liabilities that give rise to their potential (future) placement on the balance sheet.

standby letter of credit (LC or L/C)
An irrevocable credit guarantee that the issuing FI will pay a third party should its customer default on its obligation.

commercial letter of credit
A written undertaking that the issuing FI will pay a third party on the presentation of specified documents evidencing the shipment of goods.

A good example of an OBS activity is the issuance of a **standby letter of credit (LC or L/C)** by a bank to support the import activities of one of its customers. For example, the foreign seller of goods to a Canadian importing company may require the importer to provide a standby letter of credit by which the bank guarantees that it will pay for the goods only in the event that its customer defaults. A **commercial letter of credit**, also called a *documentary letter of credit*, requires the bank to pay the foreign seller on presentation of the appropriate documents as specified in the letter of credit. In either case, the bank charges a fee that it includes in its income statement, but does not record the transaction on the balance sheet. Canadian banks show the dollar value of letters of credit in notes to their annual financial statements. The bank will conduct a credit analysis of its customer before issuing the letter of credit, but, if the bank pays the commercial letter of credit when the seller of the goods presents the documents and its customer does not pay, the bank may experience a credit loss on the transaction. Thus, a standby letter of credit guarantees payment should a bank's customer face financial problems in paying the promised amount to the supplier. If the customer's cash flow is sufficiently strong so as to pay the supplier directly, the standby letter of credit issued by the FI expires unused. Nothing appears on the FI's balance sheet today or in the future. However, the fee earned for issuing the letter of credit appears on the FI's income statement.

As a result, the ability to earn fee income while not loading up or expanding the balance sheet has become an important motivation for FIs to pursue OBS business. Unfortunately, this activity is not risk-free. If the customer does not pay the supplier, then the contingent liability or guarantee that the FI issued becomes an actual liability that appears on the FI's balance sheet. That is, the FI has to use its own equity to compensate the supplier. Significant losses in OBS activities can cause an FI to fail, just as major losses due to balance sheet default and interest rate risks can cause an FI to fail.

Letters of credit are just one example of OBS activities. Others are loan commitments and positions in forwards, futures, swaps, and other derivative securities. While some of these activities are structured to reduce an FI's exposure to credit, interest rate, or foreign exchange risks, mismanagement or speculative use of these instruments can result in major losses to FIs. Indeed, as seen during the financial crisis of 2008–2009, significant losses in OBS activities (e.g., CDSs) can cause an FI to fail.

EXAMPLE 7–4

Impact of OBS Risk on an FI's Equity Value

Consider Table 7–4. In Panel A, the value of the FI's net worth (E) is calculated in the traditional way as the difference between the market values of its on-balance-sheet assets (A) and liabilities (L):

$$E = A - L$$

$$10 = 100 - 90$$

Under this calculation, the market value of the stockholders' equity stake in the FI is 10 and the ratio of the FI's capital to assets is 10 percent. Regulators and FIs often use the latter ratio as a simple measure of solvency (see Chapter 20 for more details).

A more accurate picture of the FI's economic solvency should consider the market values of both its on-balance-sheet and OBS activities (Panel B of Table 7–4). Specifically, the FI manager should value contingent or future asset and liability claims as well as current assets and liabilities. In our example, the current market value of the FI's contingent assets (CA) is 50; the current market value of its contingent liabilities (CL) is 55. Since CL exceeds CA by 5, this difference is an additional obligation, or claim, on the FI's net worth. That is, stockholders' true net worth (E) is really

$$E = (A - L) + (CA - CL)$$
$$= (100 - 90) + (50 - 55) = 5$$

rather than 10 when we ignored OBS activities. Thus, economically speaking, contingent assets and liabilities are contractual claims that directly impact the economic value of the equity holders' stake in an FI. Indeed, from both the stockholders' and regulators' perspectives, large increases in the value of OBS liabilities can render the FI economically insolvent just as effectively as losses due to mismatched interest rate gaps and default or credit losses from on-balance-sheet activities.

TABLE 7–4 Valuation of an FI's Net Worth with and without Consideration of OBS Activities

Panel A: Traditional Valuation of an FI's Net Worth			
Market value of assets (A)	100	Market value of liabilities (L)	90
		Net worth (E)	10
	100		100
Panel B: Valuation of an FI's Net Worth with On- and Off-Balance-Sheet Activities Valued			
Market value of assets (A)	100	Market value of liabilities (L)	90
		Net worth (E)	5
Market value of contingent assets (CA)	50	Market value of contingent liabilities (CL)	55
	150		150

We detail the specific nature of the risks of OBS activities more fully in Chapter 16. We look at how some of these instruments (forwards, futures, options, and swaps) can be used to manage risks in Chapters 23, 24, and 26.

CONCEPT QUESTIONS

1. **Why are letter of credit guarantees an OBS item?**
2. **Why are FIs motivated to pursue OBS business? What are the risks?**

TECHNOLOGY AND OPERATIONAL RISKS

Technology and operational risks are closely related and in recent years have caused great concern to FI managers and regulators alike. The Bank for International Settlements (BIS), the principal organization of central banks of the major economies of the world, defines operational risk (inclusive of technological risk) as "the risk of loss resulting from inadequate or failed internal processes, people, and systems or from external events."[4] A number of FIs add reputational risk and strategic risk (e.g., due to a failed merger) as part of a broader definition of operational risk.

bis.org

Technological innovation was a major growth area of FIs in the 1990s and 2000s. Banks, insurance companies, and investment companies all sought to improve operational efficiency with major investments in internal and external communications, computers, and an expanded technological infrastructure. For example, most Canadian FIs provide depositors with the capability to check account balances, transfer funds between accounts, manage finances, pay bills, and perform other functions from their home computers, tablets, or smart phones. The clearing of both electronic funds and paper-based transactions is conducted through the national clearing and settlement system that is operated by the Canadian Payments Associations (CPA). The Automated Clearing Settlement System (ACSS) clears cheques, wire transfers, direct deposits, preauthorized debits, bill payments, and point-of-sale transactions, while the Large Value Transfer System (LVTS) provides real-time transfer of irrevocable payments across Canada.

economies of scale
The degree to which an FI's average unit costs of producing financial services fall as its outputs of services increase.

economies of scope
The degree to which an FI can generate cost synergies by producing multiple financial service products.

technology risk
The risk incurred by an FI when technological investments do not produce the cost savings anticipated.

The major objectives of technological expansion are to lower operating costs, increase profits, and capture new markets for the FI. In current terminology, the objective is to allow the FI to exploit, to the fullest extent possible, better potential economies of scale and economies of scope in selling its products. **Economies of scale** refer to an FI's ability to lower its average costs of operations by expanding its output of financial services. **Economies of scope** refer to an FI's ability to generate cost synergies by producing more than one output with the same inputs. For example, an FI could use the same information on the quality of customers stored in its computers to expand the sale of both loan products and insurance products. That is, the same information (e.g., age, job, size of family, income) can identify both potential loan and potential life insurance customers.

Technology risk occurs when technological investments do not produce the anticipated cost savings in the form of economies of either scale or scope. Diseconomies of scale, for example, arise because of excess capacity, redundant technology, and/or organizational and bureaucratic inefficiencies (red tape) that become worse as an FI grows in size. Diseconomies of scope arise when an FI fails to generate perceived synergies or cost savings through major new technology investments. We describe the measurement and evidence of economies of scale and scope in FIs in Chapter 17. Technological risk can result in major losses in the competitive efficiency of an FI and, ultimately, in its long-term failure. Similarly, gains from technological investments can produce performance superior to an FI's rivals as well as allow it to develop new and innovative products, enhancing its long-term survival chances.

---

[4] See Basel Committee on Bank Supervision, Sound Practices for the Management and Supervision of Operational Risk, July 2002, p. 2, Basel, Switzerland.

operational risk
The risk that existing technology or support systems may malfunction or break down.

Operational risk is partly related to technology risk and can arise whenever existing technology malfunctions or back-office support systems break down. For example, the summer of 2004 saw a string of computer glitches that affected customer accounts and transactions at three major banks. In June, a programming error at the Royal Bank of Canada held up millions of customer transactions from coast to coast for a week. In July, a computer malfunction created duplicate debits, and over 60,000 customers at the Canadian Imperial Bank of Commerce overdrew their accounts. At TD Bank, a computer problem made automated teller machines and online banking unavailable to customers for three hours. Even though such computer breakdowns are rare, their occurrence can cause major dislocations in the FIs involved and potentially disrupt the financial system in general.

Operational risk is not exclusively the result of technological failure. For example, employee fraud and errors constitute a type of operational risk that often negatively affects the reputation of an FI (see Chapter 17). For example, human error at the Canadian Imperial Bank of Commerce in 2004 resulted in confidential customer information being faxed to a scrapyard dealer in the United States. This incident led to an investigation by the Privacy Commissioner. Another good example involves trading losses incurred in 2012 by a J. P. Morgan trader, Bruno Iksil, also known as "the London Whale," who had taken large CDS positions in expectation that the financial crisis in Europe would cause anxiety in financial markets. Instead, bailouts, austerity measures, and interventions prevented any major events in Europe. To maintain the proper balance and deal with expiring contracts, Iksil needed to continually make new trades. But the CDS market was too small and the amounts Iksil was trading were too large to let J. P. Morgan operate in secrecy. Once the story got out, hedge fund traders took positions designed to gain from the trades that Iksil had to make to keep the position going. That activity negatively altered prices on the CDSs that Iksil needed. Eventually the only choice was to close the position and take the loss. These activities by employees resulted in an overall loss in reputation and, in turn, business for the FI employer.

CONCEPT QUESTIONS

1. **What is the difference between economies of scale and economies of scope?**
2. **How is operational risk related to technology risk?**
3. **How does technological expansion help an FI better exploit economies of scale and economies of scope? When might technology risk interfere with these goals?**

INSOLVENCY RISK

insolvency risk
The risk that an FI may not have enough capital to offset a sudden decline in the value of its assets relative to its liabilities.

Insolvency risk is a consequence or outcome of one or more of the risks described above: interest rate, credit, liquidity, foreign exchange, sovereign, market, OBS, technology, and operational risks. Technically, insolvency occurs when the capital or equity resources of an FI's owners are driven to or near zero because of losses incurred as a result of one or more of the risks described above. Consider the 1985 failures of the Canadian Commercial Bank (CCB) and the Northland Bank of Canada (NBC), which were the last Canadian banks to fail. Both FIs concentrated their operations in western Canada, investing in oil and gas and in real estate loans. A decline in the Canadian dollar and increases in interest rates caused the loan portfolios of both banks to deteriorate and led to difficulties in rolling over deposits (liquidity risk). Despite interim support from the other chartered banks and borrowings from the Bank of Canada, the capital of both banks deteriorated (solvency risk) and they were eventually allowed to fail. We can contrast CCB's and NBC's failures with the case of Washington Mutual (WaMu), which incurred heavy losses from its on- and off-balance-sheet holdings during the financial crisis. By early September 2008, WaMu's market capital was worth only US$3.5 billion, down from US$43 billion at the end of 2006. In September 2008, the bank was taken over by the FDIC and sold to JPMorgan Chase. In March 2009, Citigroup's stock price fell to below US$1 per share, and the once largest bank in the United States was near failure. Proving that some banks are too big to fail, Citigroup received a substantial government guarantee against losses and an injection of cash to prevent failure. Through December 2009, over 700 U.S. banks had received a total of US$200 billion in federal government funds in an effort to prop up bank capital and support lending.

In 2008 and 2009, liquidity problems resulting from the ongoing credit crisis led to insolvency and caused the failure of U.S. investment banks (e.g., Lehman Brothers) or their conversion to bank holding companies (e.g., Goldman Sachs). Globally, the threat to financial stability that would result from the failure of large FIs has led regulators to nationalize banks by purchasing their preferred and common shares. Canadian banks suffered losses in 2008, but the Canadian financial system and its FIs were remarkably stable and no government capital injections were required. In general, the more equity capital to borrowed funds an FI has—that is, the lower its leverage—the better able it is to withstand losses, whether due to adverse interest rate changes, unexpected credit losses, or other reasons. Thus, both management and regulators of FIs focus on an FI's capital (and adequacy) as a key measure of its ability to remain solvent and grow in the face of a multitude of risk exposures. The issue of what is an adequate level of capital to manage an FI's overall risk exposure is discussed in Chapter 20.

CONCEPT QUESTIONS

1. **When does insolvency risk occur?**
2. **How is insolvency risk related to the other risks discussed in this chapter?**

OTHER RISKS AND THE INTERACTION OF RISKS

LO2

In this chapter we have concentrated on 10 major risks that continuously impact an FI manager's decision-making process and risk management strategies. These risks were interest rate risk, credit risk, liquidity risk, foreign exchange risk, country or sovereign risk, market risk, OBS risk, technology risk, operational risk, and insolvency risk. Even though the discussion described each independently, in reality, these risks are often interdependent. For example, when interest rates rise, corporations and consumers find maintaining promised payments on their debt more difficult. Thus, over some range of interest rate movements, credit, interest rate, and OBS risks are positively correlated. Furthermore, the FI may have been counting on the funds from promised payments on its loans for liquidity management purposes. Thus, liquidity risk is also correlated with interest rate and credit risks. The inability of a customer to make promised payments also affects the FI's income and profits and, consequently, its equity or capital position. Thus, each risk and its interaction with other risks ultimately affects solvency risk. Similarly, foreign exchange rate changes and interest rate changes are also highly correlated. When the Bank of Canada changes the target overnight rate, exchange rates are also likely to change.

Various other risks, often of a more discrete or event type, also impact an FI's profitability and risk exposure, although, as noted earlier, many view discrete or event risks as part of operational risks. Discrete risks might include events external to the FI, such as a sudden change in taxation. Such changes can affect the attractiveness of some types of assets over others, as well as the liquidity of an FI's balance sheet.

Changes in regulatory policy constitute another type of external, discrete, or event risk. These include lifting the regulatory barriers to lending or to entry or on products offered (see Chapter 21). Other discrete or event risks involve sudden and unexpected changes in financial market conditions due to war, revolution, or sudden market collapse, such as the 1929 and 1987 stock market crashes or the financial crisis of 2008–2009. These can have a major impact on an FI's risk exposure. Other event risks include fraud, theft, earthquakes, storms, malfeasance, and breach of fiduciary trust; all of these can ultimately cause an FI to fail or be severely harmed. Yet each is difficult to model and predict.

Finally, more general macroeconomic or systemic risks, such as increased inflation, inflation volatility, and unemployment, can directly and indirectly impact an FI's level of interest rate, credit, and liquidity risk exposure. For example, inflation was very volatile in the 1979–1982 period in Canada and the United States. Interest rates reflected this volatility. During periods in which FIs face high and volatile inflation and interest rates, interest rate risk exposure from mismatching balance sheet maturities tends to rise. Credit risk exposure also rises because borrowing firms with fixed-price product contracts often find it difficult to keep up their loan payments when inflation and interest rates rise abruptly. As well, consumers facing unemployment are more likely to default on their mortgages, consumer loans, and credit card payments.

CONCEPT QUESTIONS

1. **What is meant by the term *event risk*?**
2. **What are some examples of event and general macroeconomic risks that impact FIs?**

Questions and Problems

1. What is the process of *asset transformation* performed by an FI? Why does this process often lead to the creation of *interest rate risk*? What is interest rate risk?
2. What is *refinancing risk*? How is refinancing risk part of interest rate risk? If an FI funds long-term assets with short-term liabilities, what will be the impact on earnings of an increase in the rate of interest? A decrease in the rate of interest?
3. What is *reinvestment risk*? How is reinvestment risk part of interest rate risk? If an FI funds short-term assets with long-term liabilities, what will be the impact on earnings of a decrease in the rate of interest? An increase in the rate of interest?
4. The sales literature of a mutual fund claims that the fund has no risk exposure since it invests exclusively in federal government securities that are free of default risk. Is this claim true? Explain why or why not.
5. How can interest rate risk adversely affect the economic or market value of an FI?
6. Consider an FI that issues $100 million of liabilities with one year to maturity to finance the purchase of $100 million of assets with a two-year maturity. Suppose that the cost of funds (liabilities) for the FI

is 5 percent per year and the interest return on the assets is 8 percent per year.

a. Calculate the FI's profit spread and dollar value of profit in year 1.
b. Calculate the profit spread and dollar value of profit in year 2 if the FI can refinance its liabilities at 5 percent.
c. If interest rates rise and the FI can borrow new one-year liabilities at 9 percent in the second year, calculate the FI's profit spread and dollar value of profit in year 2.
d. If interest rates fall and the FI can borrow new one-year liabilities at 3 percent in the second year, calculate the FI's profit spread and dollar value of profit in year 2.

7. Consider an FI that issues $200 million of liabilities with two years to maturity to finance the purchase of $200 million of assets with a one-year maturity. Suppose that the cost of funds (liabilities) for the FI is 5 percent per year and the interest return on the assets is 9 percent per year.
   a. Calculate the FI's profit spread and dollar value of profit in year 1.
   b. Calculate the profit spread and dollar value of profit in year 2 if the FI can reinvest its assets at 9 percent.
   c. If interest rates fall and the FI can invest in one-year assets at 6 percent in the second year, calculate the FI's profit spread and dollar value of profit in year 2.
   d. If interest rates rise and the FI can invest in one-year assets at 11 percent in the second year, calculate the FI's profit spread and dollar value of profit in year 2.
8. An FI has the following market value balance sheet structure:

Assets	
Cash	$ 1,000
Bond	10,000
Total assets	$11,000
Liabilities and Equity	
Term deposit	$10,000
Equity	1,000
Total liabilities and equity	$11,000

   a. The bond has a 10-year maturity and a fixed-rate coupon of 10 percent paid at the end of each year. The term deposit has a 1-year maturity and a 6 percent fixed rate of interest. The FI expects no additional asset growth. What will be the net interest income (NII) at the end of the first year? *Note:* NII equals interest income minus interest expense.
   b. If at the end of year 1, market interest rates have increased 100 basis points (1 percent), what will be the NII for the second year? Is this result caused by reinvestment risk or refinancing risk?
   c. Assuming that market interest rates increase 1 percent, the bond will have a value of $9,446 at the end of year 1. What will be the market value of equity for the FI? Assume that all of the NII in part (a) is used to cover operating expenses or dividends.
   d. If market interest rates had decreased 100 basis points by the end of year 1, would the market value of equity have been higher or lower than $1,000? Why?
   e. What factors have caused the changes in operating performance and market value for this firm?
9. How does the policy of matching the maturities of assets and liabilities work (a) to minimize interest rate risk and (b) against the asset-transformation function of FIs?
10. Corporate bonds usually pay interest semiannually. If a company decided to change from semiannual to annual interest payments, how would this affect the bond's interest rate risk?
11. Two 10-year bonds are being considered for an investment that may have to be liquidated before the maturity of the bonds. The first bond is a 10-year premium bond with a coupon rate higher than its required rate of return, and the second bond is a zero-coupon bond that pays only a lump-sum payment after 10 years with no interest over its life. Which bond would have more interest rate risk? That is, which bond's price would change by a larger amount for a given change in interest rates? Explain your answer.
12. Consider again the two bonds in problem 11. If the investment goal is to leave the assets untouched until maturity, such as for a child's education or for retirement, which of the two bonds has more interest rate risk? What is the source of this risk?
13. A mutual fund bought $1,000,000 of two-year government notes six months ago. During this time, the value of the securities has increased, but for tax reasons the mutual fund wants to postpone any sale for two more months. What type of risk does the mutual fund face for the next two months?
14. A bank invested $50 million in a two-year asset paying 10 percent interest per annum and simultaneously issued a $50 million, one-year liability paying

8 percent interest per year. The liability will be rolled over after one year at the current market rate. What will be the impact on the bank's net interest income (NII) if at the end of the first year all interest rates have increased by 1 percent (100 basis points)?

15. What is *credit risk*? Which types of FIs are more susceptible to this type of risk? Why?
16. What is the difference between *firm-specific credit risk* and *systematic credit risk*? How can an FI alleviate firm-specific credit risk?
17. Two banks, Canadian Commercial Bank (CCB) and Northland Bank of Canada (NBC), which failed in the 1980s in Canada, had made mortgage loans to homeowners in Alberta. When oil prices fell, oil companies, the regional economy, the homeowners, and the banks all experienced financial problems. What types of risk were inherent in the loans that were made by these banks?
18. What is *liquidity risk*? What routine operating factors allow FIs to deal with this risk in times of normal economic activity? What market reality can create severe financial difficulty for an FI in times of extreme liquidity crises?
19. Consider the simple FI balance sheet below (in millions of dollars):

Before the Withdrawal

Assets		Liabilities/Equity	
Cash assets	$ 20	Deposit	$150
Nonliquid assets	155	Equity	25
	$175		$175

Suppose that depositors unexpectedly withdraw $50 million in deposits and the FI receives no new deposits to replace them. Assume that the FI cannot borrow any more funds in the short-term money markets, and because it cannot wait to get better prices for its assets in the future (as it needs the cash now to meet immediate depositor withdrawals), the FI has to sell any nonliquid assets at 75 cents on the dollar. Show the FI's balance sheet after adjustments are made for the $50 million of deposit withdrawals.

20. What two factors provide potential benefits to FIs that expand their asset holdings and liability funding sources beyond their domestic borders?
21. What is *foreign exchange risk*? What does it mean for an FI to be *net long* in foreign assets? What does it mean for an FI to be *net short* in foreign assets? In each case, what must happen to the foreign exchange rate to cause the FI to suffer losses?
22. If the euro is expected to depreciate in the near future, would a Canadian-based FI in Paris prefer to be net long or net short in the euro in its asset positions? Discuss.
23. If international capital markets are well integrated and operate efficiently, will FIs be exposed to foreign exchange risk? What are the sources of foreign exchange risk for FIs?
24. If an FI has the same amount of foreign assets and foreign liabilities in the same currency, has that FI necessarily reduced to zero the risk involved in these international transactions? Explain.
25. An insurance company invests $1 million in a private placement of British bonds. Each bond pays £300 in interest per year for 20 years. If the current exchange rate is $1.564/£, what is the nature of the insurance company's exchange rate risk? Specifically, what type of exchange rate movement concerns this insurance company?
26. Assume that a bank has assets located in London that are worth £150 million on which it earns an average of 8 percent per year. The bank has £100 million in liabilities on which it pays an average of 6 percent per year. The current spot rate is $1.50/£.
    a. If the exchange rate at the end of the year is $2.00/£, will the dollar have appreciated or depreciated against the pound?
    b. Given the change in the exchange rate, what is the effect in dollars on the net interest income (NII) from the foreign assets and liabilities? *Note:* NII is interest income minus interest expense.
    c. What is the effect of the exchange rate change on the value of assets and liabilities in dollars?
27. Six months ago, Maple Leaf Bank Ltd. issued a $100 million, one-year maturity deposit denominated in euros (€). On the same date, $60 million was invested in a euro-denominated loan and $40 million was invested in a Government of Canada note. The exchange rate on this date was $1.5675/€. Assume no repayment of principal and an exchange rate today of $1.2540/€.
    a. What is the current value of the deposit (in dollars and euros)?
    b. What is the current value of the euro-denominated loan principal (in dollars and euros)?
    c. What is the current value of the Government of Canada note (in dollars and euros)?
    d. What is Maple Leaf Bank's profit/loss from this transaction (in dollars and euros)?
28. Suppose you purchase a 10-year, AAA-rated Swiss bond for par that is paying an annual coupon of 6 percent. The bond has a face value of 1,000 Swiss francs (Sf). The spot rate at the time of purchase is

$1.15/Sf. At the end of the year, the bond is downgraded to AA and the yield increases to 8 percent. In addition, the Sf depreciates to $1.05/Sf.

a. What is the loss or gain to a Swiss investor who holds this bond for a year? What portion of this loss or gain is due to foreign exchange risk? What portion is due to interest rate risk?

b. What is the loss or gain to a Canadian investor who holds this bond for a year? What portion of this loss or gain is due to foreign exchange risk? What portion is due to interest rate risk?

29. What is *country or sovereign risk*? What remedy does an FI realistically have in the event of a collapsing country or currency?
30. What is *market risk*? How does this risk affect the operating performance of FIs? What actions can be taken by an FI's management to minimize the effects of this risk?
31. What is the nature of an OBS activity? How does an FI benefit from such activities? Identify the various risks that these activities generate for an FI, and explain how these risks can create varying degrees of financial stress for the FI at a later time.
32. What is *technology risk*? What is the difference between *economies of scale* and *economies of scope*? How can these economies create benefits for an FI? How can these economies prove harmful to an FI?
33. What is the difference between technology risk and *operational risk*? How does internationalizing the payments system among banks increase operational risk?
34. Why can *insolvency risk* be classified as a consequence or outcome of any or all of the other types of risks?
35. Discuss the interrelationships among the different sources of bank risk exposure. Why would the construction of a bank risk management model to measure and manage only one type of risk be incomplete?
36. Characterize the risk exposure(s) of the following FI transactions by choosing one or more of the risk types listed below:

a. Interest rate risk

b. Credit risk

c. OBS risk

d. Technology risk

e. Foreign exchange risk

f. Country or sovereign risk

(i) A bank finances a $10 million, six-year fixed-rate corporate loan by selling one-year certificates of deposit.

(ii) An insurance company invests its policy premiums in a long-term government bond portfolio.

(iii) A French bank sells two-year fixed-rate notes to finance a two-year fixed-rate loan to a British entrepreneur.

(iv) A Japanese bank acquires an Austrian bank to facilitate clearing operations.

(v) A mutual fund completely hedges its interest rate risk exposure by using forward contingent contracts.

(vi) A Canadian bond dealer uses his own equity to buy Greek government bonds.

(vii) A securities firm sells a package of mortgage loans as mortgage-backed securities.

PART 2

MEASURING RISK

8 ▸ Interest Rate Risk I 147

9 ▸ Interest Rate Risk II 164

10 ▸ Credit Risk: Individual Loans 194

11 ▸ Credit Risk: Loan Portfolio and Concentration Risk 237

12 ▸ Liquidity Risk 252

13 ▸ Foreign Exchange Risk 277

14 ▸ Sovereign Risk 302

15 ▸ Market Risk 325

16 ▸ Off-Balance-Sheet Risk 357

17 ▸ Technology and Other Operational Risk 380

CHAPTER 8

INTEREST RATE RISK I

After studying this chapter you should be able to:

LO1 Discuss the Bank of Canada's role in setting monetary policy and influencing the level and movement of interest rates

LO2 Discuss the repricing model and apply it to the balance sheet of an FI.

LO3 Discuss the weaknesses of the repricing model.

INTRODUCTION

net worth
The value of an FI to its owners; this is equal to the difference between the market value of assets and that of liabilities.

In Chapter 7 we established that while performing their asset-transformation functions, FIs often mismatch the maturities of their assets and liabilities. In so doing, they expose themselves to interest rate risk and could become economically insolvent (if the **net worth** or equity of their owners was eradicated) if interest rates change unexpectedly. All FIs tend to mismatch their balance sheet maturities to some degree. However, measuring interest rate risk exposure by looking only at the size of the maturity mismatch can be misleading. The next two chapters present techniques used by FIs to measure their interest rate risk exposure.

bankofcanada.ca

This chapter begins with a discussion of the Bank of Canada's monetary policy, a key determinant of interest rate risk. The chapter also analyzes the simpler method used to measure an FI's interest rate risk: *the repricing model*. The repricing, or funding gap, model concentrates on the impact of interest rate changes on an FI's net interest income (NII = interest income − interest expense). As explained later in this chapter, however, the repricing model has some serious weaknesses. Appendix 8A compares and contrasts this model with the market value–based maturity model, which, while rarely used any more, includes the impact of interest rate changes on the market value of an FI's assets and liabilities.

The major banks in Canada report their interest rate gap in their annual reports, and also use the more sophisticated duration (Chapter 9) and value-at-risk (VaR) (Chapter 15) models. For example, in its 2012 Annual Report, the Bank of Montreal used market value exposure (MVE), earnings volatility (EV), simulations, sensitivity analysis, stress testing, and gap analysis to understand and manage its interest rate risk. The Office of the Superintendent of Financial Institutions (OSFI) requires gap analysis to be reported quarterly for federally regulated DTIs, but has issued a guideline that supports the Bank for International Settlements (BIS) recommendation that market value accounting and the duration model be applied by internationally active banks and their regulators to their banking book.

bmo.com
osfi-bsif.gc.ca
bis.org

THE LEVEL AND MOVEMENT OF INTEREST RATES

LO1

While many factors influence the level and movement of interest rates, the most direct factor is the central bank's monetary policy strategy. Interest rates, in turn, affect an FI's cost of funds and return on assets (ROA).

Since 1991, the Bank of Canada, Canada's central bank, has carried out monetary policy actions based on a target range for inflation. The inflation measure used is the **consumer price index (CPI)**, which is calculated by Statistics Canada. The target inflation range has been set at 1 to 3 percent to the end of 2016. The Bank of Canada adjusts the target for the **overnight rate**, the rate that FIs charge each other for one-day funds, to achieve its inflation target, which is the range midpoint, 2 percent. The **bank rate**, the rate the Bank of Canada charges for one-day loans it makes to FIs, is always the upper limit of the **operating band**, which is 0.5 percent wide. The overnight rate is at the middle of the band. The lower limit of the operating band is the rate the Bank of Canada will pay on funds deposited with the Bank. A target overnight rate of 1 percent means that the bank rate is 1¼ percent and the deposit rate is ¾ percent.

consumer price index (CPI)
A measure of the cost of living tracked monthly by Statistics Canada based on changes in the retail prices of a basket of consumer goods and services.

overnight rate
The rate that major FIs charge on one-day funds borrowed and lent to each other. It is at the middle of the operating band.

bank rate
The rate charged by the Bank of Canada on overnight loans to FIs.

operating band
The range (0.5 percent wide) of the overnight rates charged by the Bank of Canada. The bottom of the band is the rate the Bank of Canada will pay on deposits. The top of the band is the rate charged by the Bank of Canada on loans (the bank rate).

federal funds rate
The rate charged by the U.S. Federal Reserve on overnight loans to FIs.

The target overnight rate is the main instrument used by the Bank of Canada to carry out monetary policy. If the Bank of Canada forecasts that production will be below capacity and so it expects that inflation will be below its target rate, it may lower the target overnight rate so that money is cheaper. Companies and consumers will respond by increasing their borrowing and production, and spending in Canada will rise. If the opposite is true and inflation is expected to rise above the target rate, then the target for the overnight rate will be set higher, putting pressure on companies and consumers to decrease their borrowing, and bringing inflation levels back into line. The Bank of Canada recognizes that rate changes will not have immediate effects, so the Bank forecasts 18 to 24 months into the future. The Bank schedules eight fixed days every year on which it will set the bank rate. In addition, the Bank publishes quarterly monetary policy reports in January, April, July, and October giving its view of the economy and an indication of where it expects rates to be.

Global financial integration requires the Bank of Canada to pay attention to the actions of other central banks, particularly the U.S. Federal Reserve. Since 1993, the Federal Reserve has used interest rates—the **federal funds rate**—as its main target variable to guide monetary policy. Under this regime the Federal Reserve simply announces after each monthly meeting whether the federal funds rate target has been increased, decreased, or left unchanged. It should also be noted that although Federal Reserve actions are targeted mostly at short-term rates (especially the federal funds rate), changes in short-term rates usually feed through to the whole term structure of interest rates. The linkages between short-term rates and long-term rates and the theories of the term structure of interest rates are discussed in Appendix 8B.

federalreserve.gov

Figure 8–1 shows a comparison of the bank rate with the U.S. federal funds rate for the period from 1965 to 2013. The rates in both countries vary over time, declining to their lowest levels in 2012. In addition, the bank rate is generally higher than the Federal Reserve funds rate. This reflects the Bank of Canada's focus on the U.S.–Canadian dollar exchange rate and the flow of funds between the two countries as a result of interest rate differentials. Until 2009, the Canadian government worked to eliminate its deficit, while the U.S. deficit widened. This caused

FIGURE 8–1
Comparison of the Bank Rate and the U.S. Federal Funds Rate, 1965–2013

Source: Bank of Canada, bankofcanada.ca

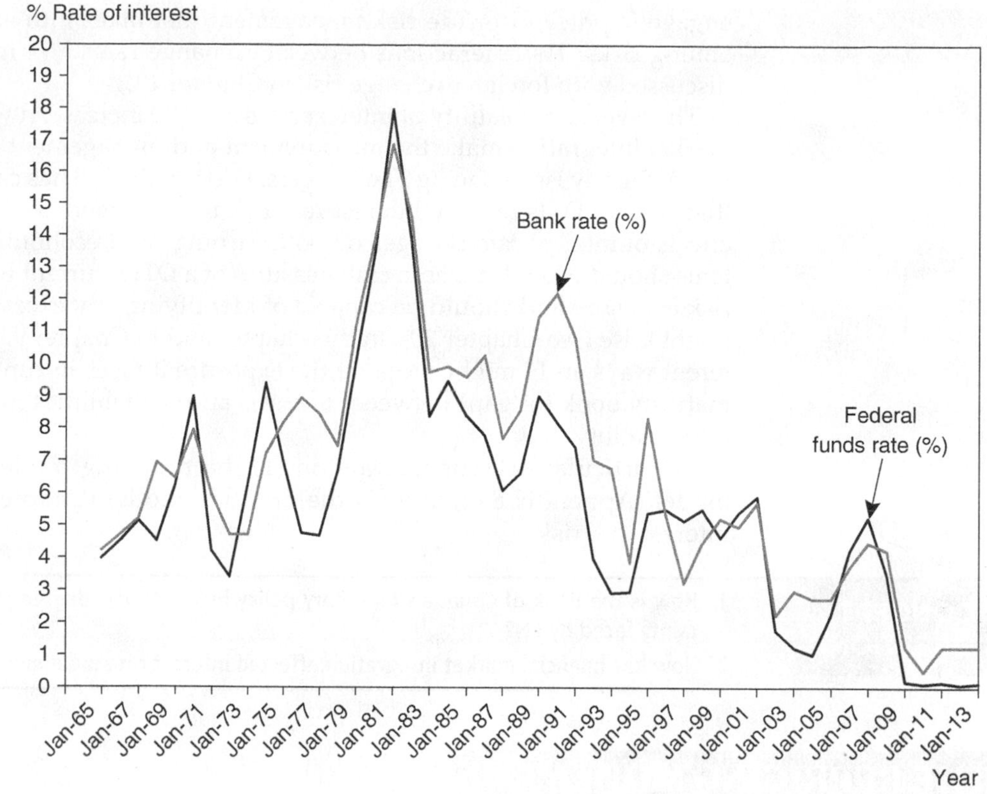

the Canadian dollar to rise in value relative to the U.S. dollar, which is used globally to price commodities such as metals, oil, and gas. Of note in Figure 8–1 is the large decline in the Canadian bank rate from 4.50 percent in January 2007 to 0.50 percent in January 2010. The U.S. federal funds rate fell as well, from 5.27 percent in January 2007 to 0.12 percent in January 2010. These rates reflect the efforts of the central banks to get the credit markets and the economy moving again after the market meltdowns in September and October 2008. Central banks were facing the prospect of stagnating economies and deflation. As a result, interest rates around the world (in the United States, Australia, the United Kingdom, and the Eurozone, for example) reached historically low levels. At the same time, as noted in Chapter 1, around the world, central banks provided liquidity to the markets and governments ran deficits, raising the prospect of higher inflation in the longer term. However, the focus at the time was on stabilizing the global financial system to allow the world to work its way out of a recession.

Financial market integration increases the speed with which interest rate changes and associated volatility are transmitted among countries. The increased globalization of financial market flows in recent years has made the measurement and management of interest rate risk a prominent concern facing FI managers. For example, investors around the world carefully evaluate the statements made by the chairman of the Federal Reserve. Changes in U.S. interest rates can have a major effect on world interest rates, foreign exchange rates, and stock prices. This emphasizes that, although we isolate risks in our discussions here, complex FIs engage in enterprisewide risk management that takes into account interactions among risks. The interactions between exchange rates and monetary policy are discussed with foreign exchange risk in Chapter 13.

The level and volatility of interest rates and the increase in worldwide financial market integration make the measurement and management of interest rate risk one of the key issues facing FI managers. Further, the BIS has called for regulations that require DTIs to have interest rate risk measurement systems that assess the effects of interest rate changes on both earnings and economic value. These systems should provide meaningful measures of a DTI's current levels of interest rate risk exposure and should be capable of identifying any excessive exposures that might arise (see Chapter 20). In this chapter and in Chapter 9, we analyze the different ways an FI might measure the exposure it faces in running a mismatched maturity book (or gap) between its assets and its liabilities in a world of interest rate volatility.

In particular, we concentrate on (1) the repricing model, (2) the maturity model (Appendix 8A), and (3) the duration model (Chapter 9) for measuring interest rate risk.

CONCEPT QUESTIONS

1. **How is the Bank of Canada's monetary policy linked to the degree of interest rate uncertainty faced by FIs?**
2. **How has financial market integration affected interest rate movements?**

THE REPRICING MODEL

LO2

repricing gap
The difference between assets whose interest rates will be repriced or changed over some future period (rate-sensitive assets) and liabilities whose interest rates will be repriced or changed over some future period (rate-sensitive liabilities).

rate-sensitive assets or liabilities
Assets or liabilities that are repriced at or near current market interest rates within a maturity bucket.

The repricing, or funding gap, model is essentially a book value accounting cash flow analysis of the **repricing gap** between the interest revenue earned on an FI's assets and the interest expense paid on its liabilities (or its NII) over a particular period of time. The assets or liabilities are **rate-sensitive**, that is, the interest rate charged or earned will change (i.e., be repriced) over that period. This contrasts with the market value–based maturity and duration models discussed in Appendix 8A and in Chapter 9. Under the repricing gap approach, banks report the repricing gap for assets and liabilities with various maturities:[1]

1. One day
2. More than one day to three months
3. More than three months to six months
4. More than 6 months to 12 months
5. More than one year to five years
6. More than five years

A bank reports the gaps in each maturity bucket by calculating the rate sensitivity of each asset (RSA) and each liability (RSL) on its balance sheet. *Rate sensitivity* here means that the asset or liability is repriced at or near current market interest

[1] OSFI requires FIs to report quarterly and to use 10 maturity buckets for their floating-rate assets and liabilities: 1 day to 1 month, 1 month to 3 months, 3 months to 6 months, 6 months to 12 months, 1 year to 2 years, 2 years to 3 years, 3 years to 4 years, 4 years to 5 years, 5 years to 7 years, and greater than 7 years. For illustration purposes, we consider only six periods.

TABLE 8–1
Repricing Gap (in millions of dollars)

	1 Assets	2 Liabilities	3 Gaps	4 Cumulative Gap
1. One day	$ 20	$ 30	−$10	−$10
2. More than one day–three months	30	40	−10	−20
3. More than three months–six months	70	85	−15	−35
4. More than 6 months–12 months	90	70	+20	−15
5. More than one year–five years	40	30	+10	−5
6. Over five years	10	5	+5	0
	$ 260	$ 260		

rates within a certain time horizon (or maturity bucket). Repricing can be the result of a rollover of an asset or liability (e.g., a loan is paid off at or prior to maturity, and the funds are used to issue a new loan at current market rates), or it can occur because the asset or liability is a variable-rate instrument (e.g., a floating-rate mortgage whose interest rate is reset every quarter based on movements in a prime rate).

Table 8–1 shows the asset and liability repricing gaps of an FI, categorized into each of the six previously defined maturity buckets. The advantage of the repricing model lies in its information value and its simplicity in pointing to an FI's *NII exposure* (or profit exposure) to interest rate changes in different maturity buckets.

refinancing risk
The risk that the cost of rolling over or reborrowing funds will rise above the returns being earned on asset investments.

reinvestment risk
The risk that the returns on funds to be reinvested will fall below the cost of the funds.

For example, suppose that an FI has a negative $10 million difference between its assets and liabilities being repriced in one day (one-day bucket). Assets and liabilities that are repriced each day are likely to be interbank borrowings or repurchase agreements (see Chapter 2). Thus, a negative gap (RSA < RSL) exposes the FI to **refinancing risk**, in that a rise in these short-term rates would lower the FI's *NII* since the FI has more RSLs than RSAs in this bucket. In other words, assuming equal changes in interest rates on RSAs and RSLs, interest expense will increase by more than interest revenue. Conversely, if the FI has a positive $20 million difference between its assets and liabilities being repriced in 6 months to 12 months, it has a positive gap (RSA > RSL) for this period and is exposed to **reinvestment risk**, in that a drop in rates over this period would lower the FI's NII; that is, interest income would decrease by more than interest expense. Specifically, let

ΔNII_i = Change in NII in the *i*th bucket
GAP_i = Dollar size of the gap between the book value of RSAs and RSLs in maturity bucket *i*
ΔR_i = Change in the level of interest rates impacting assets and liabilities in the *i*th bucket

Then

$$\Delta NII_i = (GAP_i)\Delta R_i = (RSA_i - RSL_i)\Delta R_i$$

In this first bucket, if the gap is negative $10 million and short-term interest rates rise 1 percent, the annualized change in the FI's future NII is

$$\Delta NII_i = (-\$10 \text{ million}) \times 0.01 = -\$100{,}000$$

TABLE 8–2
Simple FI Balance Sheet (in millions of dollars)

Assets		Liabilities	
1. Short-term consumer loans (one-year maturity)	$ 50	1. Equity capital (fixed)	$ 20
2. Long-term consumer loans (two-year maturity)	25	2. Demand deposits	40
3. Three-month Treasury bills	30	3. Savings deposits	30
4. Six-month Treasury bills	35	4. Three-month GICs	40
5. Three-year Government of Canada bonds	70	5. Three-month bankers' acceptances	20
6. 10-year fixed-rate mortgages	20	6. Six-month commercial paper	60
7. 25-year floating-rate mortgages (rate adjusted every six months)	40	7. One-year term deposits	20
	$270		
		8. Two-year term deposits	40
			$270

This approach is very simple and intuitive. Remember, however, from Chapter 7 and our overview of interest rate risk that capital or market value losses also occur when rates rise. The capital loss effect that is measured by both the maturity and duration models developed in Appendix 8A and in Chapter 9 is not accounted for in the repricing model. The reason is that in the book value accounting world of the repricing model, asset and liability values are reported at their *historic* values or costs. Thus, interest rate changes affect only current interest income or interest expense—that is, NII on the FI's income statement—rather than the market value of assets and liabilities on the balance sheet.[2]

The FI manager can also estimate cumulative gaps (CGAPs) over various repricing categories or buckets. A common CGAP of interest is the one-year repricing gap (in millions) estimated from Table 8–1 as

$$CGAP = (-\$10) + (-\$10) + (-\$15) + \$20 = -\$15$$

If ΔR_i is the average interest rate change affecting assets and liabilities that can be repriced within a year, the cumulative effect on the bank's NII is[3]

$$\begin{aligned}\Delta NII_i &= (CGAP)\Delta R_i \\ &= (-\$15 \text{ million})(0.01) = -\$150{,}000 \end{aligned} \tag{8.1}$$

We can now look at how an FI manager would calculate the cumulative one-year gap from a balance sheet. Remember that the manager asks: Will or can this asset or liability have its interest rate changed within the next year? If the answer is yes, it is an RSA or an RSL. If the answer is no, it is not rate sensitive.

Consider the simplified balance sheet facing the FI manager in Table 8–2. Instead of the original maturities, the maturities are those remaining on different assets and liabilities at the time the repricing gap is estimated.

---

[2] For example, a 30-year bond purchased 10 years ago when rates were 13 percent would be reported as having the same book (accounting) value as when rates are 7 percent. Using market value, gains and losses to asset and liability values would be reflected in the balance sheet as rates changed.

[3] Note that a change in the dollar value and mix of RSAs and RSLs (or a change in CGAP) also affects the FI's net income.

RSAs

Looking down the asset side of the balance sheet in Table 8–2, we see the following one-year RSAs:

1. *Short-term consumer loans: $50 million.* These are repriced at the end of the year and just make the one-year cutoff.
2. *Three-month T-bills: $30 million.* These are repriced on maturity (rollover) every three months.
3. *Six-month T-bills: $35 million.* These are repriced on maturity (rollover) every six months.
4. *25-year floating-rate mortgages: $40 million.* These are repriced (i.e., the mortgage rate is reset) every six months. Thus, these long-term assets are rate-sensitive assets in the context of the repricing model with a one-year repricing horizon.

Summing these four items produces total one-year RSAs of $155 million. The remaining $115 million of assets are not rate sensitive over the one-year repricing horizon—that is, a change in the level of interest rates will not affect the size of the interest revenue generated by these assets over the next year.[4] Although the $115 million in long-term consumer loans, 3-year Government of Canada bonds, and 10-year fixed-rate mortgages generates interest revenue, the size of revenue generated will not change over the next year, since the interest rates on these assets are not expected to change (i.e., they are fixed over the next year).

RSLs

Looking down the liability side of the balance sheet in Table 8–2, we see that the following liability items clearly fit the one-year rate or repricing sensitivity test:

1. *Three-month GICs: $40 million.* These mature in three months and are repriced on rollover.
2. *Three-month bankers' acceptances: $20 million.* These also mature in three months and are repriced on rollover.
3. *Six-month commercial paper: $60 million.* These mature and are repriced every six months.
4. *One-year term deposits: $20 million.* These are repriced right at the end of the one-year gap horizon.

Summing these four items produces one-year RSLs of $140 million. The remaining $130 million is not rate sensitive over the one-year period. The $20 million in equity capital and $40 million in demand deposits (see the following discussion) do not pay interest and are therefore classified as non-interest-paying. The $30 million in savings deposits (see the following discussion) and $40 million in two-year term deposits generate interest expense over the next year, but the level of the interest expense generated will not change if the general level of interest rates changes. Thus, we classify these items as rate-insensitive liabilities.

[4] We are assuming that the assets are noncallable over the year and that there will be no prepayments (runoffs; see below) on the mortgages within a year.

Note that demand deposits (or transaction accounts in general) were not included as RSLs. We can make strong arguments for and against their inclusion as RSLs.

Against Inclusion

Although explicit interest is paid on transaction accounts such as chequing/savings accounts, the rates paid by FIs may not fluctuate with changes in the general level of interest rates, particularly when rates are rising. Moreover, many demand deposits act as **core deposits**, a long-term source of funds.

core deposits
Those deposits that act as an FI's long-term source of funds.

For Inclusion

If interest rates rise, individuals draw down (or run off) their demand deposits, forcing the FI to replace them with higher-yielding, interest-bearing, rate-sensitive funds. This is most likely to occur when the interest rates on alternative instruments are high. In such an environment, the opportunity cost of holding funds in demand deposit accounts is likely to be larger than it is in a low-interest-rate environment.

Similar arguments for and against inclusion of retail savings accounts can be made. Banks adjust these rates infrequently. However, savers tend to withdraw funds from these accounts when rates rise, forcing banks into more expensive fund substitutions. The Interest Rate Risk and Maturities Matching Return submitted by DTIs in Canada to OSFI every quarter includes deposits as RSAs. The four repriced liabilities (\$40 + \$20 + \$60 + \$20) sum to \$140 million, and the four repriced assets (\$50 + \$30 + \$35 + \$40) sum to \$155 million. Given this, the cumulative one-year repricing gap (CGAP) for the bank is

$$\begin{aligned} CGAP &= \text{One-year RSAs} - \text{one-year RSLs} \\ &= RSA - RSL \\ &= \$155 \text{ million} - \$140 \text{ million} = \$15 \text{ million} \end{aligned}$$

Interest rate sensitivity can also be expressed as a percentage of assets (A):

$$\frac{CGAP}{A} = \frac{\$15 \text{ million}}{\$270 \text{ million}} = 0.056 = 5.6\%$$

Expressing the repricing gap in this way is useful since it tells us (1) the direction of the interest rate exposure (positive or negative CGAP) and (2) the scale of that exposure as indicated by dividing the gap by the asset size of the institution. In our example the bank has 5.6 percent more RSAs than RSLs in one-year-and-less buckets as a percentage of total assets. Alternatively, FIs calculate a gap ratio defined as RSAs divided by RSLs. A gap ratio greater than 1 indicates that (similar to a gap > 0) there are more RSAs than RSLs. Thus, the FI will see increases in net interest income when interest rates increase. A gap ratio less than 1 indicates that (similar to a gap < 0) there are more RSLs than RSAs. Thus, the FI will see increases in NII when interest rates decrease. In our example, the gap ratio is 1.107, meaning that, in the one-year-and-less time bucket, the FI has \$1.107 of RSAs for every \$1 of RSLs.

Equal Changes in Rates on RSAs and RSLs

The CGAP provides a measure of an FI's interest rate sensitivity. Table 8–3 highlights the relationship between CGAP and changes in NII when interest rate changes for RSAs are equal to interest rate changes for RSLs. For example, when

TABLE 8–3 The Impact of CGAP on the Relationship between Changes in Interest Rates and Changes in NII, Assuming Rate Changes for RSAs Equal Rate Changes for RSLs

Row	CGAP	Change in Interest Rates	Change in Interest Revenue		Change in Interest Expense	Change in NII
1	>0	⇑	⇑	$>$	⇑	⇑
2	>0	⇓	⇓	$>$	⇓	⇓
3	<0	⇑	⇑	$<$	⇑	⇓
4	<0	⇓	⇓	$<$	⇓	⇑

CGAP is positive (or the FI has more RSAs than RSLs), NII will rise when interest rates rise (row 1, Table 8–3), since interest revenue increases more than interest expense does.

EXAMPLE 8–1

Impact of Rate Changes on NII When CGAP Is Positive

Suppose that interest rates rise by 1 percent on both RSAs and RSLs. The CGAP would project the expected annual change in NII (ΔNII) of the bank as approximately

$$\begin{aligned}\Delta NII &= (RSA \times \Delta R) - (RSL \times \Delta R) = CGAP \times \Delta R \\ &= (\$155 \text{ million} \times 0.01) - (\$140 \text{ million} \times 0.01) = (\$15 \text{ million} \times 0.01) \\ &= (\$1.55 \text{ million} - \$1.40 \text{ million}) = \$150{,}000\end{aligned}$$

Similarly, if interest rates fall equally for RSAs and RSLs (row 2, Table 8–3), NII will fall when CGAP is positive. As rates fall, interest revenue falls by more than interest expense. Thus, NII falls. Suppose that for our FI, rates fall by 1 percent. The CGAP predicts that NII will fall by:

$$\begin{aligned}\Delta NII &= (\$155 \text{ million} \times (-0.01)) - (\$140 \text{ millon} \times (-0.01)) = (\$15 \text{ million}) \times -0.01 \\ &= -\$1.55 \text{ million} - (-\$1.40 \text{ million}) = -\$150{,}000\end{aligned}$$

It is evident from this equation ($\Delta NII = CGAP \times \Delta R$) that the larger the absolute value of CGAP, the larger the expected change in NII (i.e., the larger the increase or decrease in the FI's interest revenue relative to interest expense). In general, when CGAP is positive, the change in NII is positively related to the change in interest rates. Thus, an FI would want its CGAP to be positive when interest rates are expected to rise. Conversely, when CGAP is negative, if interest rates rise by equal amounts for RSAs and RSLs (row 3, Table 8–3), NII will fall since the FI has more RSLs than RSAs. If interest rates fall equally for RSAs and RSLs (row 4, Table 8–3), NII will increase when CGAP is negative. As rates fall, interest expense decreases by more than interest revenue. In general, then, when CGAP is negative, the change in NII is negatively related to the change in interest rates. Thus, an FI would want its CGAP to be negative when interest rates are expected to fall. We refer to these relationships as **CGAP effects.**

CGAP effects
The relationships between changes in interest rates and changes in NII.

Unequal Changes in Rates on RSAs and RSLs

The previous section considered changes in NII as interest rates changed, assuming that the change in rates on RSAs was exactly equal to the change in rates on RSLs (in other words, assuming the interest rate spread between rates on RSAs and RSLs remained unchanged). This is not often the case. Rather, rate changes on

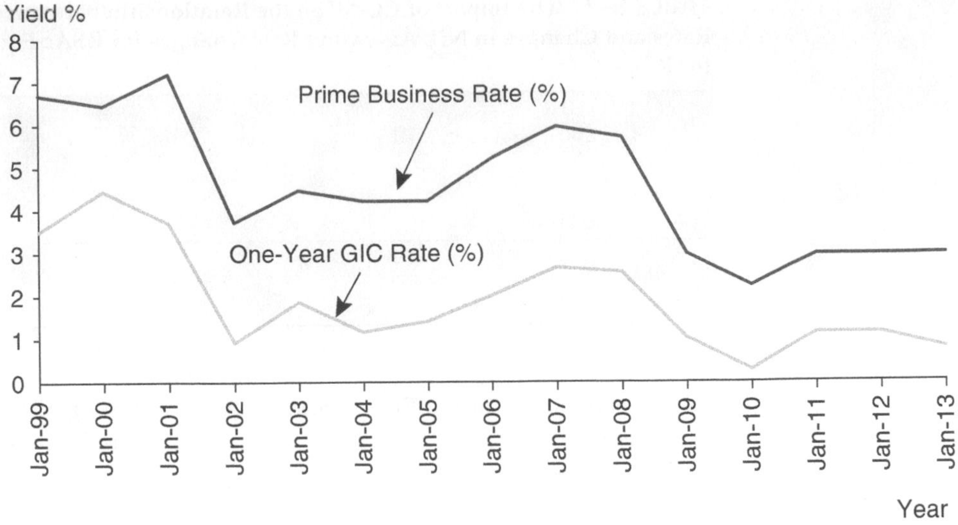

FIGURE 8–2 **Comparison of One-Year Guaranteed Investment Certificate Rates and the Prime Business Rate, January 1999–January 2013**

Source: Bank of Canada, bankofcanada.ca

spread effect The effect that a change in the spread between rates on RSAs and RSLs has on NII as interest rates change.

RSAs generally differ from those on RSLs (i.e., the spread between interest rates on assets and liabilities changes along with the levels of these rates). See Figure 8–2, which plots one-year GIC rates (liabilities) and prime lending rates (assets) for the period 1999–2013. Notice that although the rates generally move in the same direction, they are not perfectly correlated. In this case, as we consider the effect of rate changes on NII, we have a **spread effect** in addition to the CGAP effects.[5]

EXAMPLE 8–2 *Impact of Spread Effect on NII*

To understand spread effect, assume for a moment that RSAs equal RSLs equal \$155 million. Suppose that rates rise by 1.2 percent on RSAs and by 1 percent on RSLs (i.e., the spread between the rates on RSAs and RSLs increases by 1.2 percent − 1 percent = 0.2 percent). The resulting change in NII is calculated as

$$\begin{aligned}\Delta NII &= (RSA \times \Delta R_{RSA}) - (RSL \times \Delta R_{RSL})\\ &= \Delta\text{Interest revenue} - \Delta\text{Interest expense}\\ &= (\$155\text{ million} \times 1.2\%) - (\$155\text{ million} \times 1.0\%)\\ &= \$155\text{ million}(1.2\% - 1.0\%)\\ &= \$310{,}000\end{aligned}$$

Table 8–4 shows combinations of CGAP and spread changes and their effects on NII. The first four rows consider an FI with a positive CGAP; the last four rows consider an FI with a negative CGAP. Notice in Table 8–4 that both the CGAP and spread effects can have the same effect on NII. For example, in row 6,

[5] The spread effect therefore presents a type of basis risk for the FI. The FI's NII varies as the difference (basis) between interest rates on RSAs and interest rates on RSLs varies. We discuss basis risk in detail in Chapter 23.

TABLE 8–4 **Impact of CGAP on the Relationship between Changes in Interest Rates and Changes in NII, Allowing for Different Rate Changes for RSAs and RSLs**

Row	CGAP	Change in Interest Rates	Change in Spread	NII
1	>0	⇑	⇑	⇑
2	>0	⇑	⇓	⇑⇓
3	>0	⇓	⇑	⇑⇓
4	>0	⇓	⇓	⇓
5	<0	⇑	⇑	⇑⇓
6	<0	⇑	⇓	⇓
7	<0	⇓	⇑	⇑
8	<0	⇓	⇓	⇑⇓

if CGAP is negative and interest rates increase, the CGAP effect says NII will decrease. If, at the same time, the spread between RSAs and RSLs decreases as interest rates increase, the spread effect also says NII will decrease. In these cases, FI managers can accurately predict the direction of the change in NII as interest rates change. When the two work in opposite directions, however, the change in NII cannot be predicted without knowing the size of the CGAP and expected change in the spread. For example, in row 5, if CGAP is negative and interest rates increase, the CGAP effect says NII will decrease. If, at the same time, the spread between RSAs and RSLs increases as interest rates increase, the spread effect says NII will decrease.

EXAMPLE 8–3

Combined Impact of CGAP and Spread Effect on NII

Suppose that for the FI in Table 8–2, interest rates fall by 1 percent on RSAs and by 1.2 percent on RSLs. Now the change in NII is calculated as

$$\begin{aligned}\Delta NII &= [\$155 \text{ million} \times (-0.01)] - [\$140 \text{ million} \times (-0.012)] \\ &= -\$1.55 \text{ million} - (-\$1.68 \text{ million}) \\ &= \$0.13 \text{ million or } \$130{,}000\end{aligned}$$

Even though the CGAP effect (i.e., RSA > RSL) is putting negative pressure on NII (in Example 8–1, the CGAP effect of a 1 percent decrease in the rate on both RSAs and RSLs produced a *decrease* in NII of \$150,000), the increase in the spread, and the resulting spread effect, is so big that NII *increases* by \$130,000.

The repricing gap is the measure of interest rate risk historically used by FIs, and it is still the main measure of interest rate risk used by small FIs. In contrast to the market value–based models of interest rate risk discussed in Appendix 8A and in Chapter 9, the repricing gap model is conceptually easy to understand and can easily be used to forecast changes in profitability for a given change in interest rates. The repricing gap can be used to allow an FI to structure its assets and liabilities or to go off the balance sheet to take advantage of a projected interest rate change. However, the repricing gap model has some major weaknesses that have resulted in regulators calling for the use of more comprehensive models (e.g., the duration gap model) to measure interest rate risk. We next discuss some of these major weaknesses.

CONCEPT QUESTIONS

1. **Why is it useful to express the repricing gap in terms of a percentage of assets? What specific information does this provide?**
2. **How can banks change the size and the direction of their repricing gap?**

WEAKNESSES OF THE REPRICING MODEL

LO3

The repricing model has four major shortcomings: (1) it ignores market value effects of interest rate changes, (2) it is overaggregative, (3) it fails to deal with the problem of rate-insensitive asset and liability runoffs and prepayments, and (4) it ignores cash flows from OBS activities. In this section we discuss each of these weaknesses in more detail.

Market Value Effects

As was discussed in the overview of FI risks (Chapter 7), interest rate changes have a market value effect in addition to an income effect on asset and liability values. That is, the present values of the cash flows on assets and liabilities change, in addition to the immediate interest received or paid on them, as interest rates change. In fact, the present values (and where relevant, the market prices) of virtually all assets and liabilities on an FI's balance sheet change as interest rates change. The repricing model ignores the market value effect—implicitly assuming a book value accounting approach. As such, the repricing gap is only a *partial* measure of the true interest rate exposure of an FI. We discuss market value–based measures of interest rate risk in Appendix 8A and Chapter 9.

Overaggregation

The problem of defining buckets over a range of maturities ignores information regarding the distribution of assets and liabilities within those buckets. For example, the dollar values of RSAs and RSLs within any maturity bucket range may be equal; however, on average, liabilities may be repriced toward the end of the bucket's range, while assets may be repriced toward the beginning, in which case a change in interest rates will have an effect on asset and liability cash flows that will not be accurately measured by the repricing gap approach.

Look at the simple example for the three-month to six-month bucket in Figure 8–3. Note that \$50 million more RSAs than RSLs are repriced between months 3 and 4, while \$50 million more RSLs than RSAs are repriced between months 5 and 6. The bank would show a zero repricing gap for the three-month to six-month bucket [+50 + (−50) = 0]. But the bank's assets and liabilities are *mismatched* within the bucket. Clearly, the shorter the range over which bucket gaps are calculated, the smaller this problem is. If an FI manager calculated one-day bucket gaps out into the future, this would give a more accurate picture of the NII exposure to rate changes. Reportedly, many large banks have internal systems that indicate their repricing gaps on any given day in the future (252 days' time, 1,329 days' time, etc.). This suggests that although regulators require the reporting of repricing gaps over only relatively wide maturity bucket ranges, FI managers could set in place internal information systems to report the daily future patterns of such gaps.

FIGURE 8–3
The Overaggregation Problem: The Three-Month to Six-Month Bucket)

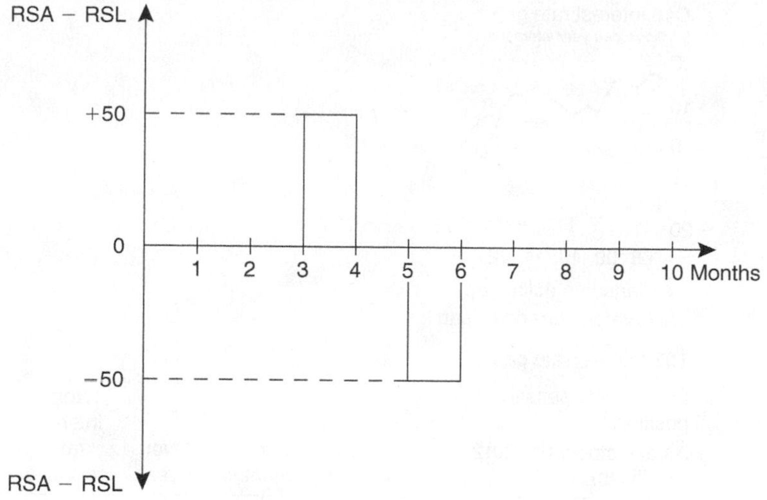

The Problem of Runoffs

In the simple repricing model discussed above, we assumed that all consumer loans matured in 1 year or that all conventional mortgages matured in 25 years. In reality, the FI continuously originates and retires consumer and mortgage loans as it creates and retires deposits. For example, today, some 25-year original maturity mortgages may have only 1 year left before they mature; that is, they are in their 24th year. In addition, these loans will sometimes be prepaid early as mortgage holders refinance their mortgages and/or sell their houses. Thus, the resulting proceeds will be reinvested at current market rates within the year. In addition, even if an asset or liability is rate insensitive, virtually all assets and liabilities (e.g., long-term mortgages) pay some principal and/or interest back to the FI in any given year. As a result, the FI receives a **runoff** cash flow from its rate-insensitive portfolio that can be reinvested at current market rates; that is, this runoff cash flow component of a rate-insensitive asset or liability is itself rate sensitive. The FI manager can easily deal with this in the repricing model by estimating the cash flow that will run off within the next year and adding these amounts to the value of RSAs and RSLs.

runoff
Periodic cash flow of interest and principal amortization payments on long-term assets, such as conventional mortgages, that can be reinvested at market rates.

Cash Flows from OBS Activities

The RSAs and RSLs used in the basic repricing model include only the assets and liabilities listed on the balance sheet. Changes in interest rates will affect the cash flows on many OBS instruments as well. For example, an FI might have hedged its interest rate risk with an interest rate futures contract (see Chapter 22). As interest rates change, these futures contracts—as part of the marking-to-market process—produce a daily cash flow (either positive or negative) for the FI that may offset any on-balance-sheet gap exposure. These offsetting cash flows from futures contracts are ignored by the simple repricing model but are included in the model used by the Canadian banks in their reporting to OSFI.

Figure 8–4 shows the interest rate sensitivity position report by Scotiabank in its 2012 Annual Report with a repricing gap for 0 to 3 months, 3 to 12 months, and

FIGURE 8–4
Scotiabank's 2012 Interest Rate Gap and Interest Rate Sensitivity Position

Source: 2012 Scotiabank Annual Report, page 64, scotiabank.com.

C45 Interest rate gap
$ billions, one-year interest gap

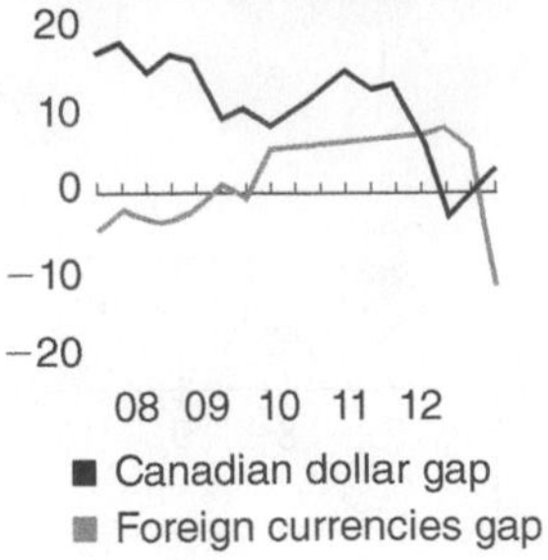

T37 Interest rate gap

Interest rate sensitivity position(1) As at October 31, 2012 ($ billions)	Within 3 months	3 to 12 months	Over 1 year	Non-interest rate sensitive	Total
Canadian dollars					
Assets	$206.8	$ 22.9	$108.4	$ 9.2	$347.3
Liabilities	191.5	49.6	95.6	10.6	347.3
Gap	15.3	(26.7)	12.8	(1.4)	–
Foreign currencies					
Assets	$243.0	$ 19.4	$ 30.7	$ 27.6	$320.7
Liabilities	247.0	12.9	15.6	45.2	320.7
Gap	(4.0)	6.5	15.1	(17.6)	–
Total Gap	$ 11.3	$(20.2)	$ 27.9	$ (19.0)	$ –
As at October 31, 2011: Gap	$ 28.3	$ (8.0)	$ 1.9	$ (22.2)	$ –

(1) The above figures reflect the inclusion of off-balance sheet instruments, as well as an estimate of prepayments on consumer and mortgage loans and cashable GICs. The off-balance sheet gap is included in liabilities.

scotiabank.com

over 1 year for both its Canadian and foreign currency assets and liabilities. Scotiabank modifies the simple repricing model to include OBS instruments and an estimate of prepayments on consumer loans, mortgages, and cashable GICs. The interest rate risk exposure depends on asset size and a rate forecast, as shown in the plot of Scotiabank's one-year Canadian dollar and foreign currencies gaps by year. For example, in its 2008 Annual Report, Scotiabank showed a cumulative one-year gap on Canadian dollar assets and liabilities of $17.3 billion and on foreign currency assets and liabilities of −$4.5 billion, for a total positive cumulative one-year gap of $12.8 billion. At year-end October 31, 2012, the cumulative one-year Canadian dollar gap was −$11.4 billion ($15.3 billion + (−$26.7 billion)) and the cumulative one-year foreign currencies gap was $2.5 billion (−$4.0 billion + 6.5 billion) for a total negative cumulative one-year gap of −$8.9 billion. Scotiabank estimated that a 100-basis-point (bp) increase in rates would decrease its net income after tax by $23 million, based on its 2012 year-end interest rate position.

CONCEPT QUESTIONS

1. **What are four major weaknesses of the repricing model?**
2. **What does "runoff" mean?**

Questions and Problems

1. How do monetary policy actions made by the Bank of Canada impact interest rates?
2. How has the increased level of financial market integration affected interest rates?
3. What is the repricing gap? What is meant by rate sensitivity?
4. What is a maturity bucket in the repricing model? Why is the length of time selected for repricing assets and liabilities important in using the repricing model?
5. What is the CGAP effect? According to the CGAP effect, what is the relationship between changes in interest rates and changes in NII when CGAP is positive? When CGAP is negative?
6. Which of the following is an appropriate change to make on a bank's balance sheet when GAP is negative, spread is expected to remain unchanged, and interest rates are expected to rise?
   a. Replace fixed-rate loans with rate-sensitive loans.
   b. Replace marketable securities with fixed-rate loans.
   c. Replace fixed-rate GICs with rate-sensitive deposits.
   d. Replace equity with demand deposits.
   e. Replace cash with marketable securities.
7. If a bank manager was quite certain that interest rates were going to rise within the next six months, how should the bank manager adjust the bank's six-month repricing gap to take advantage of this anticipated rise? What if the manager believed rates would fall in the next six months?
8. Consider the following balance sheet positions for an FI:
   - RSAs = $200 million
     RSLs = $100 million
   - RSAs = $100 million
     RSLs = $150 million
   - RSAs = $150 million
     RSLs = $140 million

   a. Calculate the repricing gap and the impact on NII of a 1 percent increase in interest rates for each position.
   b. Calculate the impact on NII of each of the above situations, assuming a 1 percent decrease in interest rates.
   c. What conclusion can you draw about the repricing model from these results?
9. Consider the following balance sheet for BAT Bank (in millions of dollars):

Assets		Liabilities and Equity	
1. Cash & equivalents	$ 6.25	1. Equity capital (fixed)	$ 25.00
2. Consumer loans (one-year maturity)	62.50	2. Demand deposits, (non-interest-bearing)	50.00
3. Consumer loans (two-year maturity)	31.25	3. Savings deposits	37.50
4. Three-month T-bills	37.50	4. Three-month GICs	50.00
5. Six-month T-notes	43.75	5. Three-month bankers' acceptances	25.00
6. Three-year Canada bonds	75.00	6. Six-month commercial paper	75.00
7. 10-year, fixed-rate mortgages	25.00	7. One-year term deposits	25.00
8. 25-year, floating-rate mortgages	50.00	8. Two-year term deposits	50.00
9. Premises & equipment	6.25		$337.50
	$337.50		

   a. Calculate the value of BAT's RSAs, RSLs, and repricing gap over the next year.
   b. Calculate the expected change in the NII for the bank if interest rates rise by 1 percent on both RSAs and RSLs. Do the same if interest rates fall by 1 percent on both RSAs and RSLs.
   c. Calculate the expected change in the NII for the bank if interest rates rise by 1.2 percent on RSAs and by 1 percent on RSLs. Do the same if interest rates fall by 1.2 percent on RSAs and by 1 percent on RSLs.
10. Banks in Canada include interest-bearing demand deposits in their calculation of RSLs. What are the reasons for not including demand deposits as RSLs in the repricing analysis for a commercial bank? What is the reason for including demand deposits in the total of RSLs?
11. What is the gap to total assets ratio? What is the value of this ratio to interest rate risk managers and regulators?
12. Which of the following assets or liabilities fit the one-year rate or repricing sensitivity test?
    a. 3-month Treasury bills
    b. 1-year Government of Canada notes
    c. 20-year Government of Canada bonds
    d. 20-year floating-rate corporate bonds with annual repricing

e. 25-year floating-rate mortgages with repricing every two years
f. 25-year floating-rate mortgages with repricing every six months
g. Overnight borrowing from the Bank of Canada
h. 9-month fixed-rate GICs
i. 1-year fixed-rate GICs
j. 5-year floating-rate GICs with annual repricing
k. Common stock

13. What is the spread effect?
14. A bank manager is quite certain that interest rates are going to fall within the next six months. How should the bank manager adjust the bank's six-month repricing gap and spread to take advantage of this anticipated rise? What if the manager believed rates would rise in the next six months?
15. Consider the following balance sheet for WatchoverU Credit Union (in millions of dollars):

Assets		Liabilities and Equity	
Floating-rate mortgages (currently 10% annually)	$ 50	1-year term deposits (currently 6% annually)	$ 70
25-year fixed-rate mortgages (currently 7% annually), repriced every 5 years	50	3-year term deposits (currently 7% annually)	20
		Equity	10
Total assets	$100	Total liabilities and equity	$100

a. What is WatchoverU's expected NII at year-end?
b. What will NII be at year-end if interest rates rise 2 percent?
c. Using the cumulative repricing gap model, what is the expected NII for a 2 percent increase in interest rates?
d. What will NII be at year-end if interest rates on RSAs increase by 2 percent but interest rates on RSLs increase by 1 percent? Is it reasonable for changes in interest rates on RSAs and RSLs to differ? Why?

16. Use the following information about a hypothetical government security dealer named Barclays Merrill Burns Canada. Market yields are in parentheses, and amounts are in millions.

Assets		Liabilities and Equity	
Cash	$ 10	Overnight repos	$170
1-month T-bills (7.05%)	75	Subordinated debt	150
3-month T-bills (7.25%)	75	7-year fixed rate (8.55%)	
2-year Canada bonds (7.50%)	50		
8-year Canada bonds (8.96%)	100		
5-year provincial government debt (floating rate) (8.20% reset every 6 months)	25	Equity	15
Total assets	$335	Total liabilities and equity	$335

a. What is the repricing gap if the planning period is 30 days? 3 months? 2 years? Recall that cash is a non-interest-earning asset.
b. What is the impact over the next 30 days on NII if interest rates increase 50 bp? Decrease 75 bp?
c. The following one-year runoffs are expected: $10 million for two-year Canada bonds and $20 million for eight-year Canada bonds. What is the one-year repricing gap?
d. If runoffs are considered, what is the effect on NII at year-end if interest rates increase 50 bp? Decrease 75 bp?

17. A bank has the following balance sheet:

Assets		Avg. Rate	Liabilities/Equity		Avg. Rate
Rate-sensitive	$ 550,000	7.75%	Rate-sensitive	$ 375,000	6.25%
Fixed rate	755,000	8.75	Fixed rate	805,000	7.50
Nonearning	265,000		Nonpaying	390,000	
Total	$1,570,000		Total	$1,570,000	

Suppose interest rates rise such that the average yield on RSAs increases by 45 bp and the average yield on RSLs increases by 35 bp.

a. Calculate the bank's CGAP, gap to total assets ratio, and gap ratio.
b. Assuming the bank does not change the composition of its balance sheet, calculate the resulting change in the bank's interest income, interest expense, and NII.
c. Explain how the CGAP and spread effects influenced this increase in NII.

18. A bank has the following balance sheet:

Assets		Avg. Rate	Liabilities/Equity		Avg. Rate
Rate-sensitive	$ 550,000	7.75%	Rate-sensitive	$ 575,000	6.25%
Fixed rate	755,000	8.75	Fixed rate	605,000	7.50
Nonearning	265,000		Nonpaying	390,000	
Total	$1,570,000		Total	$1,570,000	

Suppose interest rates fall such that the average yield on RSAs decreases by 15 bp and the average yield on RSLs decreases by 5 bp.

a. Calculate the bank's CGAP, gap to total assets ratio, and gap ratio.

b. Assuming the bank does not change the composition of its balance sheet, calculate the resulting change in the bank's interest income, interest expense, and NII.

c. The bank's CGAP is negative and interest rates decreased, yet NII decreased. Explain how the CGAP and spread effects influenced this decrease in NII.

19. The balance sheet of A. G. Fredwards, a security dealer, is listed below. Market yields are in parentheses, and amounts are in millions of dollars:

Assets		Liabilities and Equity	
Cash	$ 20	Overnight repos	$ 340
1-month T-bills (7.05%)	150	Subordinated debt	
3-month T-bills (7.25%)	150	7-year fixed rate (8.55%)	300
2-year Canada notes (7.50%)	100		
8-year Canada notes (8.96%)	200		
5-year municipal notes (floating rate) (8.20% reset every 6 months)	50	Equity	30
Total assets	$ 670	Total liabilities and equity	$ 670

a. What is the repricing gap if the planning period is 30 days? 3 months? 2 years?

b. What is the impact over the next three months on NII if interest rates on RSAs increase 50 bp and interest rates on RSLs increase 75 bp?

c. What is the impact over the next two years on NII if interest rates on RSAs increase 50 bp and interest rates on RSLs increase 75 bp?

d. Explain the difference in your answers to parts (b) and (c). Why is one answer a negative change in NII, while the other is positive?

20. A bank has the following balance sheet:

Assets		Avg. Rate	Liabilities/Equity		Avg. Rate
Rate-sensitive	$ 225,000	6.35%	Rate-sensitive	$300,000	4.25%
Fixed rate	550,000	7.55	Fixed rate	505,000	6.15
Nonearning	120,000		Nonpaying	90,000	
Total	$895,000		Total	$895,000	

Suppose interest rates rise such that the average yield on RSAs increases by 45 bp and the average yield on RSLs increases by 35 bp.

a. Calculate the bank's repricing GAP.

b. Assuming the bank does not change the composition of its balance sheet, calculate the NII for the bank before and after the interest rate changes. What is the resulting change in NII?

c. Explain how the CGAP and spread effects influenced this increase in NII.

21. What are some of the weaknesses of the repricing model? How have large banks solved the problem of choosing the optimal time period for repricing? What is runoff cash flow, and how does this amount affect the repricing model's analysis?

Appendix **8A** The Maturity Model

Appendix **8B** Term Structure of Interest Rates

View Appendices 8A and 8B on Connect.

CHAPTER 9

INTEREST RATE RISK II

After studying this chapter you should be able to:

LO1 Calculate duration for zero-coupon and interest-bearing bonds.

LO2 Discuss the features of duration and the economic meaning of duration.

LO3 Discuss the relationship between duration and interest rate risk.

LO4 Apply the duration gap model to an FI's balance sheet to calculate changes in owner's equity with changes in interest rates.

LO5 Discuss the difficulties in applying the duration gap model to immunize the balance sheet of an FI.

INTRODUCTION

book value accounting
An accounting method in which the assets and liabilities of the FI are recorded at historic values.

market value accounting
An accounting method in which the assets and liabilities of the FI are revalued according to the current level of interest rates.

marking to market
Valuing securities at their current market price.

As mentioned in Chapter 8, a weakness of the repricing model is its reliance on book values rather than market values of assets and liabilities. Indeed, in most countries, FIs report their balance sheets by using **book value accounting.** This method records the historic values of securities purchased, loans made, and liabilities sold. For example, for banks, investment assets (i.e., those expected to be held to maturity) are recorded at book values, while those assets expected to be used for trading are reported according to market value so that assets and liabilities are revalued to reflect current market conditions. Thus, if a fixed-coupon bond is purchased at $100 per $100 of face value in a low-interest-rate environment, a rise in current market rates reduces the present value of the cash flows from the bond to the investor. Such a rise also reduces the price—say to $97—at which the bond could be sold in the secondary market today. That is, the **market value accounting** approach reflects economic reality, or the true values of assets and liabilities if the FI's portfolio were to be liquidated at today's securities prices rather than at the prices when the assets and liabilities were originally purchased or sold. Valuing securities at their market value is referred to as **marking to market.** We discuss book value versus market value accounting in Chapter 20. Appendix 9A reviews bond pricing and volatility.

In this second chapter on measuring interest rate risk, we present a market value–based model of managing interest rate risk: the duration gap model. We explain the concept of *duration* and see that duration and the duration gap are more accurate measures of an FI's interest rate risk exposure than is the repricing gap model described in Chapter 8. Unlike the repricing gap model, duration gap considers market values and the maturity distributions of an FI's assets and liabilities. Further, duration gap considers the degree of leverage on an FI's balance sheet as well as the timing of the payment or arrival of cash flows of assets and liabilities. Thus, duration gap is a more comprehensive measure of an FI's interest rate risk. As a result, regulators are increasingly focusing on this model in determining an appropriate level of capital for an FI exposed to interest rate risk.

First we present the basic arithmetic needed to calculate the duration of an asset or liability. Then we analyze the economic meaning of duration. Duration, which measures the average life of an asset or liability, also has *economic* meaning as the interest rate sensitivity (or interest elasticity) of that asset's or liability's value. Next, we show how duration can be used to protect an FI against interest rate risk. Finally, we examine some problems in applying the duration measure to real-world FIs' balance sheets. For more advanced issues, see Appendix 9B.

DURATION: A SIMPLE INTRODUCTION

LO1

Duration is a more complete measure of an asset's or liability's interest rate sensitivity than is maturity because duration takes into account the time of arrival (or payment) of all cash flows as well as the asset's (or liability's) maturity. Consider a loan with a 15 percent interest rate and required repayment of half the $100 in principal at the end of six months and the other half at the end of the year. The loan is financed with a one-year Guaranteed Investment Certificate (GIC) paying 15 percent interest per year. The promised cash flows (*CF*) received by the FI from the loan at the end of one-half year and at the end of the year appear in Figure 9–1.

$CF_{1/2}$ is the $50 promised repayment of principal plus the $7.50 promised interest payment ($100 × ½ × 15%) received after six months. CF_1 is the promised cash flow at the end of the year and is equal to the second $50 promised principal repayment plus $3.75 promised interest ($50 × ½ × 15%). To compare the relative sizes of these two cash flows, we should put them in the same dimensions. This is the case because $1 of principal or interest received at the end of a year is worth less to the FI in terms of the time value of money than $1 of principal or interest received at the end of six months. Assuming that the current required interest rates are 15 percent per annum, we calculate the present values (*PV*) of the two cash flows (*CF*) shown in Figure 9–2 as

$$CF_{1/2} = \$57.50 \qquad PV_{1/2} = \$57.5/(1.075) = \$53.49$$
$$CF_1 = \$53.75 \qquad PV_1 = \$53.75/(1.075)^2 = \$46.51$$
$$CF_{1/2} + CF_1 = \$111.25 \qquad PV_{1/2} + PV_1 = \$100.00$$

Note that since $CF_{1/2}$, the cash flows received at the end of one-half year, are received earlier, they are discounted at $(1 + \frac{1}{2}R)$, where R is the current annual interest rate on the loan. This is smaller than the discount rate on the cash flow received at the end of the year $(1 + \frac{1}{2}R)^2$. Figure 9–2 summarizes the present values of the cash flows from the loan.

duration
The weighted-average time to maturity of an investment.

Technically speaking, **duration** is the *weighted-average* time to maturity on the loan using the relative present values of the cash flows as weights. On a time value of money basis, duration measures the period of time required to recover the initial investment on the loan. Any cash flows received prior to the loan's duration reflect recovery of the initial investment, while cash flows received after the

FIGURE 9–1
Promised Cash Flows on the One-Year Loan

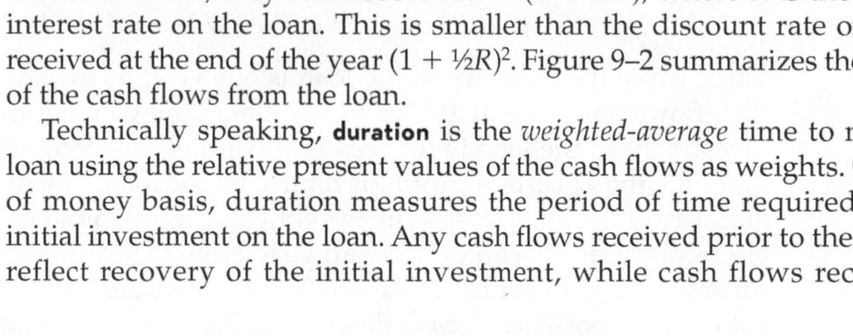

FIGURE 9–2
Present Values of the Cash Flows from the Loan

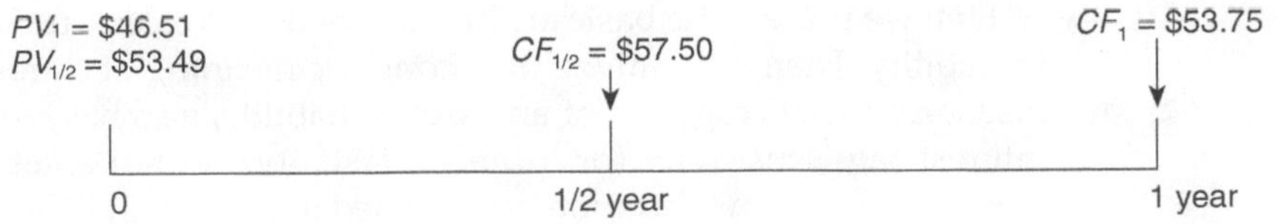

period of the loan's duration and before its maturity are the profits, or return, earned by the FI. As Figure 9–2 shows, the FI receives some cash flows at one-half year and some at one year. Duration analysis weights the time at which cash flows are received by the relative importance in present value terms of the cash flows arriving at each point in time. In present value terms, the relative importance of the cash flows arriving at time $t = ½$ year and time $t = 1$ year are as follows:

Time (t)	Weight (X)			
1/2 year	$X_{1/2} = \frac{PV_{1/2}}{PV_{1/2} + PV_1}$	$= \frac{53.49}{100.00}$	= 0.5349	= 53.49%
1 year	$X_1 = \frac{PV_1}{PV_{1/2} + PV_1}$	$= \frac{46.51}{100.00}$	= 0.4651	= 46.51%
			1.0	100%

That is, in present value terms, the FI receives 53.49 percent of cash flows on the loan with the first payment at the end of six months ($t = ½$) and 46.51 percent with the second payment at the end of the year ($t = 1$). By definition, the sum of the (present value) cash flow weights must equal 1:

$$X_{1/2} + X_1 = 1$$

$$0.5349 + 0.4651 = 1$$

We can now calculate the duration *(D)*, or the weighted-average time to maturity, of the loan using the present value of its cash flows as weights:

$$D_1 = X_{1/2}(1/2) + X_1(1)$$

$$= 0.5349(1/2) + 0.4651(1) = 0.7326 \text{ years}$$

Thus, while the maturity of the loan is one year, its duration, or average life in a cash flow sense, is only 0.7326 years. On a time value of money basis, the initial investment in the loan is recovered (albeit not realized) after 0.7326 years. After that time the FI earns a profit, or return, on the loan. The duration is less than the maturity of the loan because in present value terms, 53.49 percent of the cash flows are received at the end of one-half year. Note that duration is measured in years since we weight the time (t) at which cash flows are received by the relative present value importance of cash flows ($X_{1/2}$, X_1, etc.).

We next calculate the duration of the one-year, \$100, 15 percent GIC. The FI promises to make only one cash payment to depositors at the end of the year; that is, CF_1 = \$115, which is the promised principal (\$100) and interest repayment (\$15) to the depositor. Since weights are calculated in present value terms:

$$CF_1 = \$115, \text{ and } PV_1 = \$115/1.15 = \$100$$

FIGURE 9–3
Present Value of the Cash Flows of the Deposit

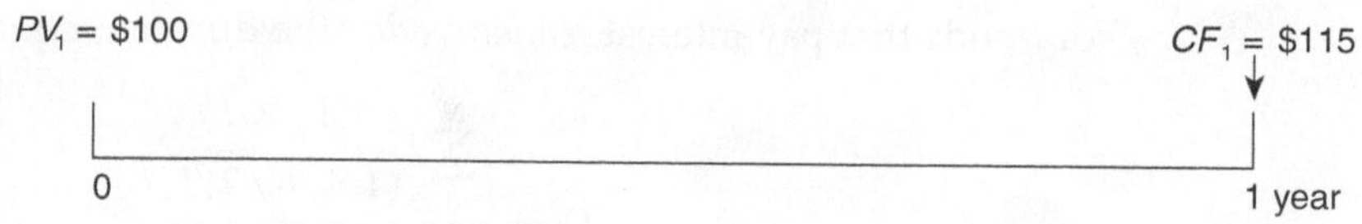

We show this in Figure 9–3. Because all cash flows are received in one payment at the end of the year, $X_1 = PV_1/PV_1 = 1$, the duration of the deposit is

$$D_D = X_1 \times (1)$$
$$D_D = 1 \times (1) = 1 \text{ year}$$

Thus, only when all cash flows are limited to one payment at the end of the period with no intervening cash flows does duration equal maturity. This example also illustrates that while the maturities on the loan and the deposit are both one year (and thus the difference or gap in maturities is zero), the duration gap is negative:

$$M_L - M_D = 1 - 1 = 0$$
$$D_L - D_D = 0.7326 - 1 = -0.2674 \text{ years}$$

As will become clearer, to measure and to hedge interest rate risk, the FI needs to manage its duration gap rather than its maturity gap.

CONCEPT QUESTIONS

1. **Why is duration considered a more complete measure of an asset's or liability's interest rate sensitivity than maturity?**
2. **When is the duration of an asset equal to its maturity?**

A GENERAL FORMULA FOR DURATION

You can calculate duration (also called Macaulay duration) for any fixed-income security that pays interest *annually* using the following general formula:

$$D = \frac{\sum_{t=1}^{N} CF_t \times DF_t \times t}{\sum_{t=1}^{N} CF_t \times DF_t} = \frac{\sum_{t=1}^{N} PV_t \times t}{\sum_{t=1}^{N} PV_t} \tag{9.1}$$

where

D = Duration measured in years
CF_t = Cash flow received on the security at the end of period t
N = Last period in which the cash flow is received
DF_t = Discount factor $= 1/(1 + R)^t$, where R is the annual yield or current level of interest rates in the market

$\sum_{t=1}^{N}$ = Summation sign for addition of all terms from $t = 1$ to $t = N$

PV_t = Present value of the cash flow at the end of period t, which equals $CF_t \times DF_t$

For bonds that pay interest *semiannually,* the duration equation becomes:[1]

$$D = \frac{\sum_{t=1/2}^{N} \frac{CF_t \times t}{(1 + R/2)^{2t}}}{\sum_{t=1/2}^{N} \frac{CF_t}{(1 + R/2)^{2t}}} \tag{9.2}$$

where $t = ½, 1, 1½, \ldots, N$.

A key assumption of the simple Macaulay duration model is that the yield curve or the term structure of interest rates is flat and that when rates change, the yield curve shifts in a parallel fashion. Further, the simple duration equation assumes that the issuer of a security or the borrower of a loan pays the interest and principal as promised. That is, the equation assumes no default risk. As we go through the theory and analysis of the duration model and interest rate risk in the body of the chapter, we use the simple Macaulay duration model and these assumptions. In Appendix 9B, we relax these assumptions, allowing for something other than a flat yield curve and default risk. Relaxing these assumptions changes the formulas in the body of the chapter slightly. However, the intuition and general trends remain the same as those seen in the body of the chapter.

Notice that the denominator of the duration equation is the present value of the cash flows on the security (which in an efficient market will be equal to the current market price). The numerator is the present value of each cash flow received on the security multiplied or weighted by the length of time required to receive the cash flow. To help you fully understand this formula, we next look at some examples. Table 9–1 summarizes duration and its features, which we illustrate in the examples.

The Duration of Interest-Bearing Bonds

TABLE 9–1 Duration: Definition and Features

Definition of Duration
1. The weighted-average time to maturity on a security.
2. The interest elasticity of a security's price to small interest rate changes.
Features of Duration
1. Duration increases with the maturity of a fixed-income security, but at a decreasing rate.
2. Duration decreases as the yield on a security increases.
3. Duration decreases as the coupon or interest payment increases.
Risk Management with Duration
1. Duration is equal to the maturity of an immunized security.
2. Duration gap is used by FIs to measure and manage the interest rate risk of an overall balance sheet.

[1] In general, the duration equation is written as

$$D = \frac{\sum_{t=1/m}^{N} \frac{CF_t \times t}{(1 + R/m)^{mt}}}{\sum_{t=1/m} \frac{CF_t}{(1 + R/m)^{mt}}}$$

where m = number of times per year interest is paid.

EXAMPLE 9-1

The Duration of a Six-Year Eurobond

Eurobonds pay coupons *annually*. Suppose the annual coupon is 8 percent, the face value of the bond is $1,000, and the current yield to maturity (R) is also 8 percent. We show the calculation of its duration in Table 9–2.

As the calculation indicates, the duration or weighted-average time to maturity on this bond is 4.993 years. In other words, on a time value of money basis, the initial investment of $1,000 is recovered after 4.993 years. Between 4.993 years and maturity (6 years), the bond produces a profit or return to the investor.

TABLE 9–2 The Duration of a Six-Year Eurobond with 8 Percent Coupon and Yield

t	CF_t	DF_t	$CF_t \times DF_t$	$CF_t \times DF_t \times t$
1	80	0.9259	74.07	74.07
2	80	0.8573	68.59	137.18
3	80	0.7938	63.51	190.53
4	80	0.7350	58.80	235.20
5	80	0.6806	54.45	272.25
6	1,080	0.6302	680.58	4,083.48
			1,000.00	4,992.71

$$D = \frac{4{,}992.71}{1{,}000} = 4.993 \text{ years}$$

EXAMPLE 9-2

The Duration of a Two-Year Government of Canada Bond

Government of Canada bonds and U.S. Treasury bonds pay coupon interest semiannually. Suppose the annual coupon is 8 percent, the face value is $1,000, and the annual yield to maturity (R) is 12 percent. See Table 9–3 for the calculation of the duration of this bond. As the calculation indicates, the duration, or weighted-average time to maturity, on this bond is 1.883 years. Table 9–4 shows that if the annual coupon is lowered to 6 percent, duration rises to 1.909 years. Since 6 percent coupon payments are lower than 8 percent, it takes longer to recover the initial investment in the bond. In Table 9–5 duration is calculated for the original 8 percent bond, assuming that the yield to maturity increases to 16 percent. Now duration falls from 1.883 years (in Table 9–3) to 1.878 years. The higher the yield to maturity on the bond, the more the investor earns on reinvested coupons and the shorter the time needed to recover the initial investment. Finally, when the maturity on a bond decreases to 1 year (see Table 9–6), its duration falls to 0.980 years. Thus, the shorter the maturity on the bond, the more quickly the initial investment is recovered.

TABLE 9–3 The Duration of a Two-Year Government of Canada Bond with 8 Percent Coupon and 12 Percent Yield

t	CF_t	DF_t	$CF_t \times DF_t$	$CF_t \times DF_t \times t$
1/2	40	0.9434	37.74	18.87
1	40	0.8900	35.60	35.60
1 1/2	40	0.8396	33.58	50.37
2	1,040	0.7921	823.78	1,647.56
			930.70	1,752.40

$$D = \frac{1{,}752.40}{930.70} = 1.883 \text{ years}$$

TABLE 9–4
Duration of a Two-Year Government of Canada Bond with 6 Percent Coupon and 12 Percent Yield

t	CF_t	DF_t	$CF_t \times DF_t$	$CF_t \times DF_t \times t$
1/2	30	0.9434	28.30	14.15
1	30	0.8900	26.70	26.70
1 1/2	30	0.8396	25.19	37.78
2	1,030	0.7921	815.86	1,631.71
			896.05	1,710.34

$$D = \frac{1{,}710.34}{896.05} = 1.909 \text{ years}$$

TABLE 9–5
Duration of a Two-Year Government of Canada Bond with 8 Percent Coupon and 16 Percent Yield

t	CF_t	DF_t	$CF_t \times DF_t$	$CF_t \times DF_t \times t$
1/2	40	0.9259	37.04	18.52
1	40	0.8573	34.29	34.29
1 1/2	40	0.7938	31.75	47.63
2	1,040	0.7350	764.43	1,528.86
			867.51	1,629.30

$$D = \frac{1{,}629.30}{867.51} = 1.878 \text{ years}$$

TABLE 9–6
Duration of a One-Year Government of Canada Bond with 8 Percent Coupon and 12 Percent Yield

t	CF_t	DF_t	$CF_t \times DF_t$	$CF_t \times DF_t \times t$
1/2	40	0.9434	37.74	18.87
1	1,040	0.8900	925.60	925.60
			963.34	944.47

$$D = \frac{944.47}{963.34} = 0.980 \text{ years}$$

Next, we look at two other types of bonds that are useful in understanding duration.

The Duration of a Zero-Coupon Bond

The Government of Canada and the U.S. Treasury have created zero-coupon bonds that allow securities firms and other investors to strip individual coupons and the principal from regular bonds and sell them to investors as separate securities. In the Eurobond markets, corporations have issued discount or zero-coupon bonds denominated in both Canadian and U.S dollars. Canadian and U.S. T-bills and commercial paper are usually issued on a discount basis and are additional examples of discount bonds. These bonds sell at a discount from face value on issue; pay the face value (e.g., $1,000) on maturity; and have no intervening cash flows, such as coupon payments, between issue and maturity. The current price an investor is willing to pay for such a bond is equal to the present value of the single, fixed (face value) payment on the bond that is received on maturity (here, $1,000), or

$$P = \frac{1{,}000}{(1 + R)^N}$$

where R is the required annually compounded yield to maturity, N is the number of years to maturity, and P is the price. Because there are no intervening cash flows such as coupons between issue and maturity, the following must be true:

$$D_B = M_B$$

That is, the duration of a zero-coupon bond equals its maturity. Note that only for zero-coupon bonds are duration and maturity equal. Indeed, for any bond that pays some cash flows prior to maturity, its duration will always be less than its maturity.

The Duration of a Consol Bond (Perpetuities)

consol bond
A bond that pays a fixed coupon each year forever.

Although consol bonds have yet to be issued in Canada, they are of theoretical interest in exploring the differences between maturity and duration. A **consol bond** pays a fixed coupon each year. This bond *never* matures; that is, it is a perpetuity:

$$M_c = \infty$$

In fact, consol bonds that were issued by the British government in the 1890s to finance the Boer Wars in South Africa are still outstanding. However, while its maturity is theoretically infinity, the formula for the duration of a consol bond is

$$D_c = 1 + \frac{1}{R}$$

where R is the required yield to maturity. Suppose that the yield curve implies $R = 5$ percent annually; then the duration of the consol bond is

$$D_c = 1 + \frac{1}{0.05} = 21 \text{ years}$$

Thus, while maturity is infinite, duration is finite. Specifically, on the basis of the time value of money, recovery of the initial investment on this perpetual bond takes 21 years. After 21 years, the bond produces profit for the bondholder. Moreover, as interest rates rise, the duration of the consol bond falls. Consider the 1979–1982 period, when some yields rose to around 20 percent on long-term government bonds. Then,

$$D_c = 1 + \frac{1}{0.2} = 6 \text{ years}$$

CONCEPT QUESTIONS

1. **What does the denominator of the duration equation measure?**
2. **What does the numerator of the duration equation measure?**
3. **Calculate the duration of a one-year, 8 percent coupon, 10 percent yield bond that pays coupons quarterly.**
4. **What is the duration of a zero-coupon bond?**
5. **What feature is unique about a consol bond compared with other bonds?**

FEATURES OF DURATION

LO2

From the preceding examples, we derive three important features of duration relating to the maturity, yield, and coupon interest of the security being analyzed.

TABLE 9–7
Duration of a Three-Year Government of Canada Bond with 8 Percent Coupon and 12 Percent Yield (coupon interest paid semiannually)

t	CF_t	DF_t	$CF_t \times DF_t$	$CF_t \times DF_t \times t$
1/2	40	0.9434	37.74	18.87
1	40	0.8900	35.60	35.60
1 1/2	40	0.8396	33.58	50.37
2	40	0.7921	31.68	63.36
2 1/2	40	0.7473	29.89	74.72
3	1,040	0.7050	733.16	2,199.48
			901.65	2,442.40

$$D = \frac{2{,}442.40}{901.65} = 2.709 \text{ years}$$

FIGURE 9–4
Duration versus Maturity

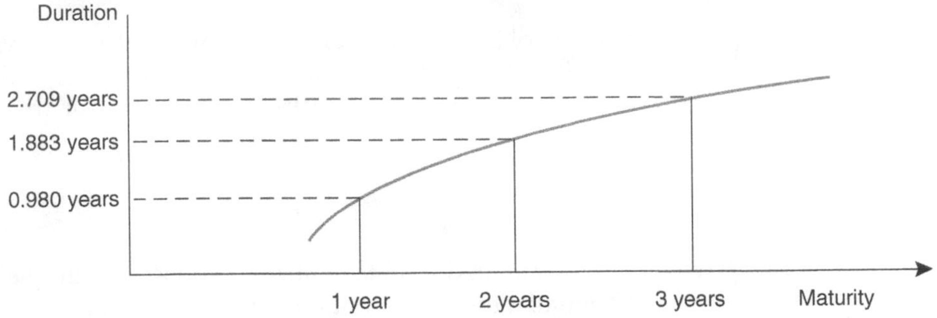

Duration and Maturity

A comparison of Tables 9–6, 9–3, and 9–7 indicates that duration *increases* with the maturity of a fixed-income asset or liability, but at a *decreasing* rate:[2]

$$\frac{\partial D}{\partial M} > 0 \qquad \frac{\partial^2 D}{\partial M^2} < 0$$

To see this, look at Figure 9–4, where we plot duration against maturity for a three-year, a two-year, and a one-year bond using the *same yield of 12 percent* for all three and assuming an annual coupon of 8 percent (with semiannual payments of 4 percent) on each bond. As the maturity of the bond increases from one year to two years (Tables 9–6 and 9–3), duration increases by 0.903 years, from 0.980 years to 1.883 years. Increasing maturity an additional year, from two years to three years (Tables 9–3 and 9–7), increases duration by 0.826, from 1.883 years to 2.709 years.

Duration and Yield

A comparison of Tables 9–3 and 9–5 indicates that duration decreases as yield increases:

$$\frac{\partial D}{\partial R} < 0$$

As the yield on the bond increased from 12 percent to 16 percent (Tables 9–3 and 9–5), the duration on the bond decreased from 1.883 years to 1.878 years. This makes sense intuitively because higher yields discount later cash flows more

[2] This is the case for the vast majority of securities. It needs to be noted, however, that for bonds selling below par, duration increases at a decreasing rate up to a point. At long maturities (e.g., 50 years), duration starts to decline.

heavily, and the relative importance, or weights, of those later cash flows decline when compared with earlier cash flows on an asset or liability.

Duration and Coupon Interest

A comparison of Tables 9–4 and 9–3 indicates that the higher the coupon or promised interest payment on the security, the lower its duration:

$$\frac{\partial D}{\partial C} < 0$$

As the coupon rate on the Government of Canada bond increased from 6 percent to 8 percent in Tables 9–4 and 9–3, the duration on the bond decreased from 1.909 years to 1.883 years. This is because the larger the coupons or promised interest payments, the more quickly cash flows are received by investors and the higher are the present value weights of those cash flows in the duration calculation. On a time value of money basis, the investor recoups the initial investment faster when coupon payments are larger.

CONCEPT QUESTIONS

1. **Which has the longer duration, a 30-year, 8 percent, zero-coupon bond or an 8 percent consol bond?**
2. **What is the relationship between duration and yield to maturity on a financial security?**
3. **Do high-coupon bonds have high or low durations?**

THE ECONOMIC MEANING OF DURATION

So far we have calculated duration for a number of different fixed-income assets and liabilities. Now we are ready to make the direct link between the number measured in years we call duration and the interest rate sensitivity of an asset or liability or of an FI's entire portfolio.

In addition to being a measure of the average life, in a cash flow sense, of an asset or liability, duration is also a *direct* measure of the interest rate sensitivity, or elasticity, of an asset or liability. In other words, the larger the value of D, the more sensitive the price of that asset or liability is to changes or shocks in interest rates.

Consider the following equation showing that the current price of a bond is equal to the present value of the coupons and principal payment on the bond:

$$P = \frac{C}{(1+R)} + \frac{C}{(1+R)^2} + \cdots + \frac{C+F}{(1+R)^N} \tag{9.3}$$

where

P = Price on the bond
C = Coupon (annual)
R = Yield to maturity
N = Number of periods to maturity
F = Face value of the bond

We want to find out how the price of the bond (P) changes when yields (R) rise. We know that bond prices fall, but we want to derive a direct measure of the size of this fall (i.e., its degree of price sensitivity).

Taking the derivative of the bond's price (P) with respect to the yield to maturity (R), we can show that[3]

$$\frac{dP}{dR} = -\frac{1}{1+R}[P \times D]$$

By cross-multiplying,

$$\frac{dP}{dR} \times \frac{1+R}{P} = -D$$

or, recognizing that interest rate changes tend to be discrete:[4]

$$\frac{\dfrac{\Delta P}{P}}{\dfrac{\Delta R}{(1+R)}} = -D \qquad (9.4)$$

interest elasticity
The percentage change in the price of a bond for any given change in interest rates.

The economic meaning of equation 9.4 is that the number D is the **interest elasticity,** or sensitivity, of the security's price to small interest rate changes. That is, D describes the percentage price fall of the bond ($\Delta P/P$) for any given (present value) increase in required interest rates or yields ($\Delta R/(1+R)$).

---

[3] The first derivative of the bond's price in equation 9.3 with respect to the yield to maturity (R) is

$$\frac{dP}{dR} = \frac{-C}{(1+R)^2} + \frac{-2C}{(1+R)^3} + \cdots + \frac{-N(C+F)}{(1+R)^{N+1}}$$

By rearranging, we get

$$\frac{dP}{dR} = -\frac{1}{1+R}\left[\frac{C}{(1+R)} + \frac{2C}{(1+R)^2} + \cdots + \frac{N(C+F)}{(1+R)^N}\right] \qquad (9A)$$

We have shown that duration (D) is the weighted-average time to maturity using the present value of cash flows as weights; that is, by definition,

$$D = \frac{1 \times \dfrac{C}{(1+R)} + 2 \times \dfrac{C}{(1+R)^2} + \cdots + N \times \dfrac{(C+F)}{(1+R)^N}}{\dfrac{C}{(1+R)} + \dfrac{C}{(1+R)^2} + \cdots + \dfrac{(C+F)}{(1+R)^N}}$$

Since the denominator of the duration equation is simply the price (P) of the bond that is equal to the present value of the cash flows on the bond, then

$$D = \frac{1 \times \dfrac{C}{(1+R)} + 2 \times \dfrac{C}{(1+R)^2} + \cdots + N \times \dfrac{(C+F)}{(1+R)^N}}{P}$$

Multiplying both sides of this equation by P, we get

$$P \times D = 1 \times \frac{C}{(1+R)} + 2 \times \frac{C}{(1+R)^2} + \cdots + N \times \frac{C+F}{(1+R)^N} \qquad (9B)$$

The term on the right side of equation 9B is the same term as that in square brackets in equation 9A. Substituting equation 9B into equation 9A, we get

$$\frac{dP}{dR} = -\frac{1}{1+R}[P \times D]$$

[4] In what follows, we use the Δ (change) notation instead of d (derivative notation) to recognize that interest rate changes tend to be discrete rather than infinitesimally small. For example, in real-world financial markets, the smallest observed rate change is usually one basis point (bp), or 1/100th of 1 percent.

Equation 9.4 can be rearranged in another useful way for interpretation regarding interest sensitivity:

$$\frac{\Delta P}{P} = -D\left[\frac{\Delta R}{1 + R}\right] \tag{9.5}$$

Equation 9.5 shows that for small changes in interest rates, bond prices move *in an inversely proportional* fashion according to the size of D. Clearly, for any given change in interest rates, long-duration securities suffer a larger capital loss (or receive a higher capital gain) should interest rates rise (fall) than do short-duration securities. By implication, gains and losses under the duration model are *symmetric*. That is, if we repeated the above examples but allowed interest rates to *decrease* by one basis point (bp) annually (or 1/2 bp semiannually), the percentage increase in the price of the bond ($\Delta P/P$) would be proportional to D. Further, the capital gains would be a mirror image of the capital losses for an equal (small) increase in interest rates.

modified duration
Duration divided by 1 plus the interest rate.

The duration equation can be rearranged, combining D and $(1 + R)$ into a single variable, $D/(1 + R)$, to produce what practitioners call **modified duration** (MD). For annual compounding of interest,

$$\frac{\Delta P}{P} = -MD\Delta R$$

where

$$MD = \frac{D}{1 + R}$$

This form is more intuitive because we multiply MD by the simple change in interest rates rather than the discounted change in interest rates as in the general duration equation.

dollar duration
The dollar value change in a security's price to a 1 percent change in the return on the security.

Duration is a measure of the *percentage change* in the price of a security for a 1 percent change in the return on the security. **Dollar duration** is the *dollar value change* in the price of a security to a 1 percent change in the return on the security. The dollar duration is defined as the modified duration times the price of a security:

$$\text{Dollar duration} = MD \times P$$

Thus, the total dollar change in value of a security will increase by an amount equal to the dollar duration times the change in the return on the security:

$$\Delta P = -\text{Dollar duration} \times \Delta R$$

Like the modified duration, the dollar duration is intuitively appealing in that we multiply the dollar duration by the change in the interest rate to get the actual dollar change in the value of a security to a change in interest rates.[5] Next, we use duration to measure the interest sensitivity of an asset or liability.

[5] Another measure of interest sensitivity is spread duration. Spread duration is the sensitivity of the price of a bond to a change in its option-adjusted spread (OAS). OAS is the required interest spread of a pass-through or mortgage-backed security over a Treasury rate when prepayment risk is taken into account. Since mortgage payers tend to exercise their right to prepay when it is favourable for them, buying a pass-through or mortgage-backed security partly involves selling an option. This is the source of the OAS. Thus, spread duration is the price sensitivity of the pass-through or mortgage-backed security to a change in the OAS. A change in the OAS of a pass-through or mortgage-backed security does not affect the cash flows that the security pays to the investor. Thus, spread duration is the impact of these cash flows at varying interest rates, as discussed in Chapter 26.

EXAMPLE 9–3
The Six-Year Eurobond

Consider Example 9–1 for the six-year Eurobond with an 8 percent coupon and 8 percent yield. We determined in Table 9–2 that its duration was approximately $D = 4.993$ years. The modified duration is

$$MD = D/(1 + R) = 4.993/1.08 = 4.623$$

That is, the price of the bond will increase by 4.623 percent for a 1 percent decrease in the interest rate on the bond. Further, the dollar duration is

$$\text{Dollar duration} = 4.623 \times \$1{,}000 = \$4{,}623$$

or a 1 percent (or 100-bp) change in the return on the bond would result in a change of \$46.23 in the price of the bond.

To see this, suppose that yields were to rise by 1 bp (1/100th of 1 percent) from 8 to 8.01 percent. Then

$$\frac{\Delta P}{P} = -(4.993)\left[\frac{0.0001}{1.08}\right]$$
$$= -0.0004623$$
$$\text{or } -0.04623\%$$

The bond price had been \$1,000, which was the present value of a 6-year bond with an 8 percent coupon and an 8 percent yield. However, the duration model predicts that the price of the bond would fall to \$999.5377 after the increase in yield by 1 bp. That is, the price would change by:

$$\Delta P = -\text{Dollar duration} \times \Delta R$$
$$= -\$4{,}623 \times 0.0001 = -\$0.4623$$

EXAMPLE 9–4
The Consol Bond

Consider a consol bond with an 8 percent coupon paid annually, an 8 percent yield, and a calculated duration of 13.5 years ($D_c = 1 + 1/0.08 = 13.5$). Thus, for a 1-bp change in the yield (from 8 percent to 8.01 percent),

$$\frac{\Delta P}{P} = -(13.5)\left[\frac{0.0001}{1.08}\right]$$
$$= -0.00125$$
$$\text{or } -0.125\%$$

As you can see, for any given change in yields, long-duration securities suffer a greater capital loss or receive a greater capital gain than do short-duration securities.

Semiannual Coupon Bonds

For fixed-income assets or liabilities whose interest payments are received semiannually or more frequently than annually, the formula in equation 9.5 has to be modified slightly. For semiannual payments,

$$\frac{\Delta P}{P} = -D\left[\frac{\Delta R}{1 + \frac{1}{2}R}\right] \tag{9.6}$$

The only difference between equation 9.6 and equation 9.5 is the introduction of a ½ in the discount rate term 1 + ½*R* to take into account the semiannual payments of interest.

EXAMPLE 9–5

Semiannual Coupon, Two-Year Maturity Treasury Bonds

Recall from Example 9–2 the two-year bond with semiannual coupons whose duration we derived in Table 9–3 as 1.883 years when annual yields were 12 percent. The modified duration is

$$MD = D/(1 + R) = 1.883/1.06 = 1.776$$

That is, the price of the bond will increase by 1.776 percent for a 1 percent decrease in the interest rate on the bond. Further, the dollar duration is

$$\text{Dollar duration} = 1.776 \times \$930.70 = \$1{,}653$$

or a 1 percent (or 100-bp) change in the return on the bond would result in a change of \$16.53 in the price of the bond.

Thus, a 1-bp rise in interest rates would have the following predicted effect on its price:

$$\frac{\Delta P}{P} = -1.883\left[\frac{0.0001}{1.06}\right]$$
$$= -0.0001776$$

or the price of the bond would fall by 0.01776 percent from \$930.6979 to \$930.5326. That is,

$$\Delta P = -\text{Dollar duration} \times \Delta R$$
$$= -\$1{,}653 \times 0.0001 = -\$0.1653$$

CONCEPT QUESTIONS

1. **What is the relationship between the duration of a bond and the interest elasticity of a bond?**
2. **How would the formula in equation 9.6 have to be modified to take into account quarterly coupon payments? Monthly coupon payments?**

DURATION AND INTEREST RATE RISK

LO3

So far, we have calculated duration and discussed the fact that duration has economic meaning because it indicates the interest sensitivity, or elasticity, of an asset's or liability's value. For FIs, duration is used for managing interest rate risk exposure. Duration also allows an FI to reduce or eliminate interest rate risk on its balance sheet. In the following sections we consider two examples of how FIs can use the duration measure to manage interest rate risk. The first is its use by insurance company and pension fund managers to help meet promised cash flow payments to policyholders or beneficiaries at a particular time in the future. The second is its use to reduce interest rate risk or to immunize the whole balance sheet of an FI against interest rate risk.

Duration Management on a Single Security

Frequently, pension fund and life insurance company managers face the problem of structuring their asset investments so they can pay out a given cash amount to policyholders in some future period, such as an insurance policy that pays the holder some lump sum on reaching retirement age. The risk to the life insurance company is that interest rates on the funds generated from investing the holder's premiums could fall. Thus, the accumulated returns on the premiums invested would not meet the target or promised amount and the insurance company would be forced to draw down its reserves and net worth to meet its commitments.

Suppose that we are in 2016 and the insurer has to make a guaranteed payment to a policyholder in five years, 2021. For simplicity, we assume that this target guaranteed payment is $1,469, a lump-sum policy payout on retirement, equivalent to investing $1,000 at an annually compounded rate of 8 percent over five years. Of course, realistically, this payment would be much larger, but the underlying principles of the example do not change by scaling the payout amount up or down.

To immunize, or protect, itself against interest rate risk, the insurer needs to determine which investments would produce a cash flow of exactly $1,469 in five years regardless of what happens to interest rates in the immediate future. The FI investing either in a five-year maturity and duration zero-coupon bond or in a coupon bond with a five-year duration would produce a $1,469 cash flow in five years no matter what happened to interest rates in the immediate future. Next, we consider the two strategies: buying five-year-maturity and -duration deep-discount bonds and buying five-year-duration coupon bonds.

Buying Five-Year-Maturity Discount Bonds

Given a $1,000 face value and an 8 percent yield and assuming annual compounding, the current price per five-year discount bond would be $680.58:

$$P = 680.58 = \frac{1,000}{(1.08)^5}$$

If the insurer bought 1.469 of these bonds at a total cost of $1,000 in 2016, these investments would produce exactly $1,469 on maturity in five years ($\$1,000 \times (1.08)^5 = \$1,469$). The reason is that the duration of this bond portfolio exactly matches the target horizon for the insurer's future liability to its policyholder. Intuitively, since no intervening cash flows or coupons are paid by the issuer of the zero-coupon discount bonds, future changes in interest rates have no reinvestment income effect. Thus, the return would be unaffected by intervening interest rate changes.

Buying a Five-Year-Duration Coupon Bond

Suppose no five-year discount bonds exist. Then the portfolio manager may seek to invest in appropriate-duration coupon bonds to hedge interest rate risk. In this example the appropriate investment would be in five-year-duration coupon-bearing bonds.

We demonstrated earlier in Table 9–2 that a six-year-maturity Eurobond paying 8 percent coupons with an 8 percent yield to maturity had a duration of 4.993 years, or approximately five years. If we buy this six-year-maturity, five-year-duration bond in 2016 and hold it for five years, until 2021, the term exactly matches the target horizon of the insurer. The cash flows generated at the end of five years will be $1,469 whether interest rates stay at 8 percent or instantaneously (immediately) rise to 9 percent or fall to 7 percent. Thus, buying a coupon bond whose duration exactly matches the time horizon of the insurer also immunizes the insurer against interest rate changes.

EXAMPLE 9–6

Interest Rates Remain at 8 Percent

The cash flows received by the insurer on the bond if interest rates stay at 8 percent throughout the five years are:

1. Coupons, 5 × $80	$ 400
2. Reinvestment income	69
3. Proceeds from sale of bond at end of fifth year	1,000
	$1,469

We calculate each of the three components of the insurer's income from the bond investment as follows:

1. *Coupons.* The $400 from coupons is simply the annual coupon of $80 received in each of the five years.
2. *Reinvestment income.* Because the coupons are received annually, they can be reinvested at 8 percent as they are received, generating an additional cash flow of $69.[6]
3. *Bond sale proceeds.* The proceeds from the sale are calculated by recognizing that the six-year bond has just one year left to maturity when it is sold by the insurance company at the end of the fifth year. That is

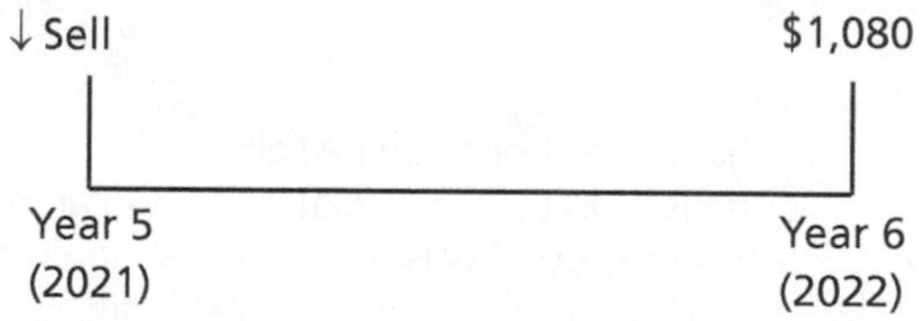

What fair market price can the insurer expect to get when selling the bond at the end of the fifth year with one year left to maturity? A buyer would be willing to pay the present value of the $1,080—final coupon plus face value—to be received at the end of the one remaining year (i.e., in 2022), or

$$P_5 = \frac{1,080}{1.08} = \$1,000$$

Thus, the insurer would be able to sell the one remaining cash flow of $1,080, to be received in the bond's final year, for $1,000.

---

[6] Receiving annual coupons of $80 is equivalent to receiving an annuity of $80. The terminal value of receiving $1 a year for five years and reinvesting at 8 percent can be determined from the future value of an annuity (FVA) formula:

$$FVA_{n,R} = \left[\frac{(1 + R)^n - 1}{R}\right]$$

In our example,

$$FVA_{5,8\%} = \left[\frac{(1 + 0.08)^5 - 1}{0.08}\right] = 5.867$$

Thus, the reinvestment income for $80 of coupons per year is

$$\text{Reinvestment income} = (80 \times 5.867) - 400 = 469 - 400 = 69$$

Note that we take away $400 since we have already counted the simple coupon income (5 × $80).

Next, we show that since this bond has a duration of five years, matching the insurer's target period, even if interest rates were to instantaneously fall to 7 percent or rise to 9 percent, the expected cash flows from the bond would still exactly sum to $1,469. That is, the coupons + reinvestment income + principal at the end of the fifth year would be immunized and the cash flows protected against interest rate changes.

EXAMPLE 9-7

Interest Rates Fall to 7 Percent

In this example with falling interest rates, the cash flows over the five years are:

1. Coupons, 5 × $80	$ 400
2. Reinvestment income	60
3. Bond sale proceeds	1,009
	$1,469

The total proceeds over the five years are unchanged from what they were when interest rates were 8 percent. To see why this occurs, consider what happens to the three parts of the cash flow when rates fall to 7 percent:

1. *Coupons.* These are unchanged since the insurer still gets five annual coupons of $80 = $400.
2. *Reinvestment income.* The coupons can now be reinvested only at the lower rate of 7 percent. Reinvestment income is only $60, which is $9 less than it was when rates were 8 percent.[7]
3. *Bond sale proceeds.* When the six-year maturity bond is sold at the end of the fifth year with one cash flow of $1,080 remaining, investors are now willing to pay more:

$$P_5 = \frac{1{,}080}{1.07} = 1{,}009$$

That is, the bond can be sold for $9 more than it could have when rates were 8 percent. The reason for this is that investors can get only 7 percent on newly issued bonds, while this older bond was issued with a higher coupon of 8 percent.

A comparison of reinvestment income with bond sale proceeds indicates that the fall in rates has produced a *gain* on the bond sale proceeds of $9. This exactly offsets the loss of reinvestment income of $9 due to reinvesting at a lower interest rate. Thus, total cash flows remain unchanged at $1,469.

EXAMPLE 9-8

Interest Rates Rise to 9 Percent

In this example with rising interest rates, the proceeds from the bond investment are:

1. Coupons, 5 × $80	$ 400
2. Reinvestment income [(5.985 × 80) − 400]	78
3. Bond sale proceeds (1,080/1.09)	991
	$1,469

Notice that the rise in interest rates from 8 percent to 9 percent leaves the terminal cash flow unaffected at $1,469. The rise in rates has generated $9 extra reinvestment income ($78 − $69), but the price at which the bond can be sold at the end of the fifth year has declined from $1,000 to $991, equal to a capital loss of $9. Thus, the gain in reinvestment income is exactly offset by the capital loss on the sale of the bond.

[7] This reinvestment income is calculated as follows.

$$FVA_{5,7\%} = \left[\frac{(1 + 0.07)^5 - 1}{0.07}\right] = 5.751$$

Reinvestment income = (5.751 × 80) − 400 = 60

These examples demonstrate that matching the duration of a coupon bond—or any other fixed-interest-rate instrument, such as a loan or mortgage—to the FI's target or investment horizon *immunizes* the FI against instantaneous shocks to interest rates. The gains or losses on reinvestment income that result from an interest rate change are exactly offset by losses or gains from the bond proceeds on sale.

Duration Management on the Whole Balance Sheet

LO4

So far we have looked at the durations of individual instruments and ways to select individual fixed-income securities to protect FIs such as life insurance companies and pension funds with precommitted liabilities such as future pension plan payouts. The duration model can also evaluate the overall interest rate exposure for an FI, that is, measure the **duration gap** on its balance sheet.

duration gap
A measure of overall interest rate risk exposure for an FI.

The Duration Gap for an FI

To estimate the overall duration gap of an FI, we determine first the duration of an FI's asset portfolio (A) and the duration of its liability portfolio (L). These can be calculated as

$$D_A = X_{1A}D_1^A + X_{2A}D_2^A + \cdots + X_{nA}D_n^A$$

and

$$D_L = X_{1L}D_1^L + X_{2L}D_2^L + \cdots + X_{nL}D_n^L$$

where

$$X_{1j} + X_{2j} + \cdots + X_{nj} = 1 \qquad \text{and} \qquad j = A, L$$

The X_{nj}'s in the equation are equal to the market value proportions of each asset or liability held in the respective asset and liability portfolios. Thus, if new 30-year Government of Canada bonds are 1 percent of a life insurer's portfolio and D_1^A (the duration of those bonds) is equal to 9.25 years, then $X_{1A}D_1^A = 0.01(9.25) = 0.0925$. More simply, the duration of a portfolio of assets or liabilities is a market value weighted average of the individual durations of the assets or liabilities on the FI's balance sheet.

Consider an FI's simplified market value balance sheet:

Assets ($)	Liabilities ($)
$A = 100$	$L = 90$
	$E = 10$
100	100

From the balance sheet,

$$A = L + E$$

and

$$\Delta A = \Delta L + \Delta E$$

or

$$\Delta E = \Delta A - \Delta L$$

That is, when interest rates change, the change in the FI's equity or net worth (E) is equal to the difference between the change in the market values of assets and liabilities on each side of the balance sheet.

Since $\Delta E = \Delta A - \Delta L$, we need to determine how ΔA and ΔL—the changes in the market values of assets and liabilities on the balance sheet—are related to duration.

From the duration model (assuming annual compounding of interest),

$$\frac{\Delta A}{A} = -D_A \frac{\Delta R}{(1+R)}$$

$$\frac{\Delta L}{L} = -D_L \frac{\Delta R}{(1+R)}$$

Here we have simply substituted $\Delta A/A$ or $\Delta L/L$, the percentage change in the market values of assets or liabilities, for $\Delta P/P$, the percentage change in any single bond's price, and D_A or D_L, the duration of the FI's asset or liability portfolio, for D_i, the duration on any given bond, deposit, or loan. The term $\Delta R/(1 + R)$ reflects the shock to interest rates, as before.[8] To show dollar changes, these equations can be rewritten as

$$\Delta A = -D_A \times A \times \frac{\Delta R}{(1+R)} \tag{9.7}$$

and

$$\Delta L = -D_L \times L \times \frac{\Delta R}{(1+R)} \tag{9.8}$$

We can substitute these two expressions into the equation $\Delta E = \Delta A - \Delta L$. Rearranging and combining this equation[9] results in a measure of the change in the market value of equity:

$$\Delta E = -[D_A - D_L k] \times A \times \frac{\Delta R}{1+R} \tag{9.9}$$

---

[8] We assume that the level of rates and the expected shock to interest rates are the same for both assets and liabilities, which means that the FI's spread (the difference between the rate on earning assets and interest-bearing liabilities) is zero. However, as long as the FI has more earning assets than interest-bearing liabilities, it will have a positive level for net interest income. This assumption is standard in Macaulay duration analysis. While restrictive, this assumption can be relaxed. However, if this is done, the duration measure changes, as is discussed in Appendix 9B.

[9] We do this as follows:

$$\Delta E = \left[-D_A \times A \times \frac{\Delta R}{(1+R)}\right] - \left[-D_L \times L \times \frac{\Delta R}{(1+R)}\right]$$

Assuming that the level of rates and the expected shock to interest rates are the same for both assets and liabilities,

$$\Delta E = [-D_A A + D_L L] \frac{\Delta R}{(1+R)}$$

or

$$\Delta E = -[D_A A - D_L L] \frac{\Delta R}{(1+R)}$$

To rearrange the equation in a slightly more intuitive fashion, we multiply and divide both $D_A A$ and $D_L L$ by A (assets):

$$\Delta E = -\left[D_A \frac{A}{A} - D_L \frac{L}{A}\right] \times A \times \frac{\Delta R}{(1+R)}$$

$$\text{or } \Delta E = -[D_A - D_L K] \times A \times \frac{\Delta R}{(1+R)}$$

where $k = L/A$ is a measure of the FI's leverage, that is, the amount of borrowed funds or liabilities rather than owners' equity used to fund its asset portfolio. The effect of interest rate changes on the market value of an FI's equity or net worth (ΔE) breaks down into three effects:

1. *The leverage-adjusted duration gap* $= [D_A - D_L k]$. This gap is measured in years and reflects the degree of duration mismatch in an FI's balance sheet. Specifically, the larger this gap is *in absolute terms*, the more exposed the FI is to interest rate shocks.
2. *The size of the FI.* The term A measures the size of the FI's assets. The larger the scale of the FI, the larger the dollar size of the potential net worth exposure from any given interest rate shock.
3. *The size of the interest rate shock* $= \Delta R/(1 + R)$. The larger the shock, the greater the FI's exposure.

Given this, we express the exposure of the net worth of the FI as

$$\Delta E = -[\text{Leverage-adjusted duration gap}] \times \text{Asset size} \times \text{Interest rate shock}$$

Interest rate shocks are largely external to the FI and often result from changes in the Bank of Canada's monetary policy (as discussed in the first section of Chapter 8). The size of the duration gap and the size of the FI, however, are under the control of management.

Equation 9.9 and the duration model provide an FI manager with a benchmark measure of the FI's performance for various interest rate changes and therefore the extent to which the FI is exposed to interest rate risk. If, for an expected change in interest rates, managers find the change in equity will be small or negative, the duration model can be used to identify changes needed on or off the FI's balance sheet to reduce or even immunize the FI against interest rate risk. The next section explains how a manager can use information on an FI's duration gap to limit losses and immunize stockholders' net worth against interest rate risk by setting the balance sheet up *before* a change in interest rates, so that ΔE is nonnegative for an expected change in interest rates. Chapters 22 through 24 look at ways a manager can use OBS derivatives to reduce interest rate risk.

EXAMPLE 9-9

Interest Rates Rise to 9 Percent

Suppose the FI manager calculates that

$$D_A = 5 \text{ years}$$
$$D_L = 3 \text{ years}$$

Then the manager learns from an economic forecasting unit that rates are expected to rise from 10 to 11 percent in the immediate future; that is,

$$\Delta R = 1\% = 0.01$$
$$1 + R = 1.10$$

The FI's initial balance sheet is assumed to be:

Assets ($ millions)	Liabilities ($ millions)
$A = 100$	$L = 90$
	$E = 10$
100	100

The FI's manager calculates the potential loss to equity holders' net worth (E) if the forecast of rising rates proves true as follows:

$$\Delta E = -(D_A - kD_L) \times A \times \frac{\Delta R}{(1+R)}$$

$$= -(5 - (0.9)(3)) \times \$100 \text{ million} \times \frac{0.01}{1.1} = -\$2.09 \text{ million}$$

The FI could lose \$2.09 million in net worth if rates rise 1 percent. Since the FI started with \$10 million in equity, the loss of \$2.09 million is almost 21 percent of its initial net worth. The market value balance sheet after the rise in rates by 1 percent would look like this:[10]

Assets ($ millions)	Liabilities ($ millions)
A = 95.45	L = 87.54
	E = 7.91
95.45	95.45

Even though the rise in interest rates would not push the FI into economic insolvency, it reduces the FI's net worth–to–assets ratio from 10 percent (10/100) to 8.29 percent (7.91/95.45). To counter this effect, the manager might reduce the FI's duration gap. In an extreme case, the gap might be reduced to zero:

$$\Delta E = -[0] \times A \times \Delta R/(1 + R) = 0$$

To do this, the FI should not directly set $D_A = D_L$, which ignores the fact that the FI's assets (A) do not equal its borrowed liabilities (L) and that k (which reflects the ratio L/A) is not equal to 1. To see the importance of factoring in leverage, suppose the manager increased the duration of the FI's liabilities to five years, the same as D_A. Then

$$\Delta E = -[5 - (0.9)(5)] \times \$100 \text{ million} \times (0.01/1.1) = -\$0.45 \text{ million}$$

The FI is still exposed to a loss of \$0.45 million if rates rise by 1 percent. An appropriate strategy would involve changing D_L until

$$D_A = kD_L = 5 \text{ years}$$

For example,

$$\Delta E = -[5 - (0.9)5.55] \times \$100 \text{ million} \times (0.01/1.1) = 0$$

In this case the FI manager sets $D_L = 5.55$ years, or slightly longer than $D_A = 5$ years, to compensate for the fact that only 90 percent of assets are funded by

[10] These values are calculated as follows:

$$\Delta A/A = -5(0.01/1.1) = -0.04545 = -4.545\%$$
$$100 + (-0.04545)100 = 95.45$$

and

$$\Delta L/L = -3(0.01/1.1) = -0.02727 = -2.727\%$$
$$90 + (-0.02727)90 = 87.54$$

borrowed liabilities, with the other 10 percent funded by equity. Note that the FI manager has at least three other ways to reduce the duration gap to zero:

1. *Reduce D_A.* Reduce D_A from 5 years to 2.7 years (equal to kD_L or (0.9)3) such that

$$[D_A - kD_L] = [2.7 - (0.9)(3)] = 0$$

2. *Reduce D_A and increase D_L.* Shorten the duration of assets and lengthen the duration of liabilities at the same time. One possibility would be to *reduce* D_A to 4 years and to *increase* D_L to 4.44 years such that

$$[D_A - kD_L] = [4 - (0.9)(4.44)] = 0$$

3. *Change k and D_L.* Increase k (leverage) from 0.9 to 0.95 and increase D_L from 3 years to 5.26 years such that

$$[D_A - kD_L] = [5 - (0.95)(5.26)] = 0$$

CONCEPT QUESTIONS

1. **Refer to the example of the insurer in Examples 9–6 through 9–8. Suppose rates fell to 6 percent. Would the FI's portfolio still be immunized? What if rates rose to 10 percent?**
2. **How is the overall duration gap for an FI calculated?**
3. **How can a manager use information on an FI's duration gap to restructure, and thereby immunize, the balance sheet against interest rate risk?**
4. **Suppose D_A = 3 years, D_L = 6 years, k = 0.8, and A = \$100 million. What is the effect on owners' net worth if $\Delta R/(1 + R)$ rises 1 percent? (ΔE = \$1,800,000)**

IMMUNIZATION AND REGULATORY CONSIDERATIONS

In the above section we assumed that the FI manager wants to structure the duration of assets and liabilities to immunize the equity or net worth stake (E) of the FI's equity owners from interest rate shocks. However, regulators periodically monitor the solvency or capital position of FIs. As we discuss in greater detail in Chapter 20 on capital adequacy, regulators set minimum target ratios for an FI's capital (or net worth) to assets. The simplest is the ratio of FI capital to its assets, or

$$\frac{E}{A} = \text{Capital (net worth) ratio}$$

Given the regulations imposed on the minimum level of the capital ratio, if an FI's asset levels change significantly through time, FI managers may be most interested in immunizing against changes in the capital ratio [$\Delta(E/A)$] due to interest rate risk rather than changes in the level of capital (ΔE). For example, suppose the FI manager is close to the minimum regulatory required E/A (or capital) ratio and wants to immunize the FI against any fall in this ratio if interest rates rise.[11] That is, the immunization target is no longer $\Delta E = 0$ when rates change but $\Delta(E/A) = 0$.

Obviously, immunizing ΔE against interest rate risk cannot result in the same management strategy as immunizing $\Delta(E/A)$. A portfolio constructed to immunize

[11] OSFI requires federally regulated DTIs to have an assets to capital multiple (ACM) that is less than or equal to 20 ($A/E \leq 20$). Basel III will require a leverage ratio (E/A) to be reported (see Chapter 20).

ΔE would have a different duration match from that required to immunize $\Delta(E/A)$. Or, more simply, the manager could satisfy either the FI's stockholders or the regulators *but not both* simultaneously.

More specifically, when the objective is to immunize equity capital against interest rate risk, that is, to set $\Delta E = 0$, the FI manager should structure the balance sheet so that the leverage-adjusted duration gap is zero:

$$\Delta E = 0 = D_A - kD_L$$

or set

$$D_A = kD_L$$

By comparison, to immunize the capital ratio, that is, to set $\Delta(E/A) = 0$, the manager needs to set

$$D_A = D_L$$

In this scenario, the leverage-adjustment effect (k) drops out. If $D_A = 5$, then immunizing the capital ratio would require setting $D_L = 5$.

CONCEPT QUESTION

Is immunizing a bank's net worth the same as immunizing its net worth–assets ratio? If not, why not?

In the next section, we analyze weaknesses of the duration model. Specifically, there are several practical problems in estimating duration and duration gaps for real-world FIs.

DIFFICULTIES IN APPLYING THE DURATION MODEL

LO5

bis.org

Critics of the duration model have often claimed that it is difficult to apply in real-world situations. However, duration measures and immunization strategies are useful in real-world situations. The model proposed by the BIS and supported by OSFI for Canadian banks for monitoring bank interest rate risk is based on the duration model. This section examines criticisms of the duration model and discusses ways that an FI would deal with them in practice. Appendix 9B discusses advanced issues associated with these weaknesses.

Duration Matching Can Be Costly

Critics charge that although in principle an FI manager can change D_A and D_L to immunize the FI against interest rate risk, restructuring the balance sheet of a large and complex FI can be both time-consuming and costly. Although this argument may have been true historically, the growth of purchased funds, asset securitization, and loan sales markets has considerably eased the speed and lowered the transaction costs of major balance sheet restructurings. (See Chapters 25 and 26 for a discussion of these strategies.) Moreover, an FI manager could still manage risk exposure using the duration model by employing techniques other than direct portfolio rebalancing to immunize against interest rate risk. Managers can get many of the same results of direct duration matching by taking hedging positions in the markets for derivative securities, such as futures and forwards (Chapter 22); options, caps, floors, and collars (Chapter 23); and swaps (Chapter 24).

Immunization Is a Dynamic Problem

Immunization is an aspect of the duration model that is not well understood. Let's go back to the earlier immunization example in which an insurer sought to buy bonds to provide an accumulated cash flow of $1,469 in five years no matter what happened to interest rates. We showed that buying a six-year maturity, 8 percent coupon bond with a five-year duration immunizes the insurer against an instantaneous change in interest rates. The word *instantaneous* is very important here; it means a change in interest rates immediately after purchasing the bond. However, interest rates can change at any time over the holding period. Further, the duration of a bond changes as time passes, that is, as it approaches maturity or the target horizon date. In addition, duration changes at a different rate than does real or calendar time.

To understand this time effect, consider the initially hedged position in which the insurer bought the five-year-duration (six-year-maturity), 8 percent coupon bond in 2016 to match its cash flow target of $1,469 in 2021. Suppose the FI manager puts the bond in the bottom drawer of a desk and does not think about it for a year, believing that the insurance company's position is fully hedged. After one year has passed (in 2017), suppose interest rates (yields) have fallen from 8 percent to 7 percent and the manager opens the drawer of the desk and finds the bond. Knowing the target date is now only four years away, the manager recalculates the duration of the bond. Imagine the manager's shock on finding that the same 8 percent coupon bond with a 7 percent yield and only five years left to maturity has a duration of 4.33 years. This means the insurance company is no longer hedged; the 4.33-year duration of this bond portfolio *exceeds* the investment horizon of four years. As a result, the manager has to restructure the bond portfolio to remain immunized. One way to do this is to sell some of the five-year bonds (4.33-year duration) and buy some bonds of shorter duration so that the overall duration of the investment portfolio is four years.

For example, suppose the insurer sold 50 percent of the five-year bonds with a 4.33-year duration and invested the proceeds in 3.67-year-duration and -maturity zero-coupon bonds. Because duration and maturity are the same for discount bonds, the duration of the asset portfolio is

$$D_A = [4.33 \times 0.5] + [3.67 \times 0.5] = 4 \text{ years}$$

This simple example demonstrates that immunization based on duration is a dynamic strategy. In theory, the strategy requires the portfolio manager to rebalance the portfolio continuously to ensure that the duration of the investment portfolio exactly matches the investment horizon (i.e., the duration of liabilities). Because continuous rebalancing may not be easy to do and involves costly transaction fees, most portfolio managers seek to be only approximately dynamically immunized against interest rate changes by rebalancing at discrete intervals, such as quarterly. That is, there is a trade-off between being perfectly immunized and the transaction costs of maintaining an immunized balance sheet dynamically.

Large Interest Rate Changes and Convexity

Duration accurately measures the price sensitivity of fixed-income securities for small changes in interest rates of the order of 1 bp. But suppose interest rate shocks are much larger, of the order of 2 percent, or 200 bp. Then duration becomes a less accurate predictor of how much the prices of securities will change and therefore a less accurate measure of interest rate sensitivity. Looking at Figure 9–5, you can see the reason for this. Note first the change in a bond's price due to yield changes

FIGURE 9–5
Duration versus True Relationship

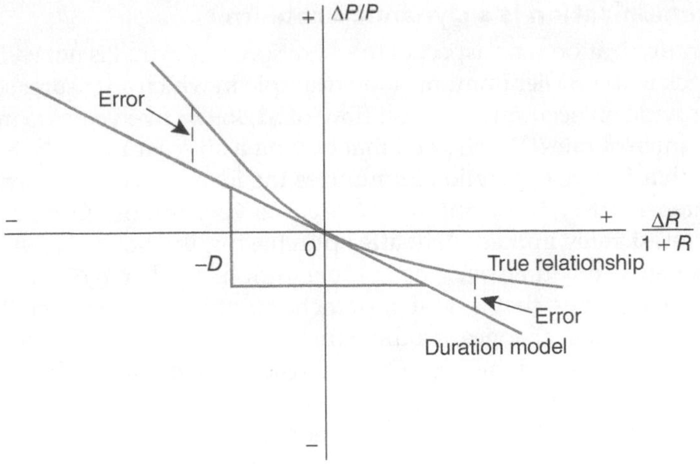

according to the duration model and second, the true relationship, as calculated directly, using the exact present value calculation for bond valuation.

The duration model predicts that the relationship between interest rate shocks and bond price changes will be proportional to D (duration). However, by precisely calculating the true change in bond prices, we find that for large interest rate increases, duration overpredicts the *fall* in bond prices, while for large interest rate decreases, it underpredicts the *increase* in bond prices. That is, the duration model predicts symmetric effects for rate increases and decreases on bond prices. As Figure 9–5 shows, in actuality, for rate increases, the *capital loss effect* tends to be smaller than the *capital gain effect* is for rate decreases. This is the result of the bond price–yield relationship exhibiting a property called *convexity* rather than *linearity,* as assumed by the basic duration model.

convexity
The degree of curvature of the price-yield curve around some interest rate level.

Note that **convexity** is a desirable feature for an FI manager to capture in a portfolio of assets. Buying a bond or a portfolio of assets that exhibits a lot of convexity, or curvature, in the price–yield curve relationship is similar to buying partial interest rate risk insurance. Specifically, high convexity means that for equally large changes of interest rates up and down (e.g., plus or minus 2 percent), the capital gain effect of a rate decrease more than offsets the capital loss effect of a rate increase. Appendix 9B shows that all fixed-income assets or liabilities exhibit some convexity in their price–yield relationships.

To see the importance of accounting for the effects of convexity in assessing the impact of large rate changes on an FI's portfolio, consider the six-year Eurobond with an 8 percent coupon and yield. According to Table 9–2, its duration is 4.993 years and its current price, P_0, is \$1,000 at a yield of 8 percent:

$$P_0 = \frac{80}{(1.08)} + \frac{80}{(1.08)^2} + \frac{80}{(1.08)^3} + \frac{80}{(1.08)^4} + \frac{80}{(1.08)^5} + \frac{1{,}080}{(1.08)^6} = \$1{,}000$$

This is point A on the price–yield curve in Figure 9–6.

If rates rise from 8 to 10 percent, the duration model predicts that the bond price will fall by 9.2463 percent; that is,

$$\frac{\Delta P}{P} = -4.993\left[\frac{0.02}{1.08}\right] = -9.2463\%$$

FIGURE 9–6
The Price–Yield Curve for the Six-Year Eurobond

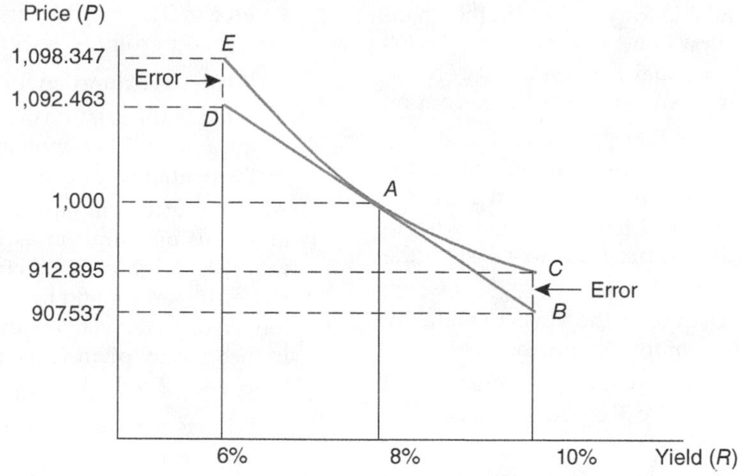

or, from a price of $1,000 to $907.537 (see point *B* in Figure 9–6). However, calculating the exact change in the bond's price after a rise in yield to 10 percent, we find that its true value is

$$P_0 = \frac{80}{(1.10)} + \frac{80}{(1.10)^2} + \frac{80}{(1.10)^3} + \frac{80}{(1.10)^4} + \frac{80}{(1.10)^5} + \frac{1{,}080}{(1.10)^6} = \$912.895$$

This is point *C* in Figure 9–6. As you can see, the true or actual fall in price is less than the predicted fall by $5.358. This means that there is more than a 0.5 percent error using the duration model. The reason for this is the natural convexity of the price–yield curve as yields rise.

Reversing the experiment reveals that the duration model would predict the bond's price to rise by 9.2463 percent if yields fell from 8 to 6 percent, resulting in a predicted price of $1,092.463 (see point *D* in Figure 9–6). By comparison, the true or actual change in price can be computed as $1,098.347 by estimating the present value of the bond's coupons and its face value with a 6 percent yield (see point *E* in Figure 9–6). The duration model has underpredicted the bond price increase by $5.884, or by over 0.5 percent of the true price increase.

Questions and Problems

1. What is the difference between book value accounting and market value accounting?
2. What are the two different general interpretations of the concept of duration, and what is the technical definition of this term? How does duration differ from maturity?
3. A one-year, $100,000 loan carries a market interest rate of 12 percent. The loan requires payment of accrued interest and one-half of the principal at the end of six months. The remaining principal and the accrued interest are due at the end of the year.
   a. What will be the cash flows at the end of six months and at the end of the year?
   b. What is the present value of each cash flow discounted at the market rate? What is the total present value?
   c. What proportion of the total present value of cash flows occurs at the end of six months? What proportion occurs at the end of the year?
   d. What is the duration of this loan?

4. Two bonds are available for purchase in the financial markets. The first bond is a two-year, $1,000 bond that pays an annual coupon of 10 percent. The second bond is a two-year, $1,000 zero-coupon bond.
   a. What is the duration of the coupon bond if the current yield to maturity (R) is 8 percent? 10 percent? 12 percent? (*Hint:* You may wish to create a spreadsheet program to assist in the calculations.)
   b. How does the change in the yield to maturity affect the duration of this coupon bond?
   c. Calculate the duration of the zero-coupon bond with a yield to maturity of 8 percent, 10 percent, and 12 percent.
   d. How does the change in the current yield to maturity affect the duration of the zero-coupon bond?
   e. Why does the change in the yield to maturity affect the coupon bond differently than it affects the zero-coupon bond?
5. What is the duration of a five-year, $1,000 Government of Canada bond with a 10 percent semiannual coupon selling at par? Selling with a yield to maturity of 12 percent? 14 percent? What can you conclude about the relationship between duration and yield to maturity? Plot the relationship. Why does this relationship exist?
6. Consider three Government of Canada bonds, each of which has a 10 percent semiannual coupon and trades at par.
   a. Calculate the duration for a bond that has a maturity of four years, three years, and two years.
   b. What conclusions can you reach about the relationship between duration and the time to maturity? Plot the relationship.
7. A six-year, $10,000 term deposit pays 6 percent interest annually. What is the duration of the term deposit? What would be the duration if interest were paid semiannually? What is the relationship of duration to the relative frequency of interest payments?
8. What is a consol bond? What is the duration of a consol bond that sells at a yield to maturity of 8 percent? 10 percent? 12 percent? Would a consol trading at a yield to maturity of 10 percent have a greater duration than a 20-year zero-coupon bond trading at the same yield to maturity? Why?
9. Maximum Pension Fund is attempting to balance one of the bond portfolios under its management. The fund has identified three bonds that have five-year maturities and trade at a yield to maturity of 9 percent. The bonds differ only in that the coupons are 7 percent, 9 percent, and 11 percent.
   a. What is the duration for each bond?
   b. What is the relationship between duration and the amount of coupon interest that is paid? Plot the relationship.
10. An insurance company is analyzing three bonds and is using duration as the measure of interest rate risk. All three bonds trade at a yield to maturity of 10 percent and have $10,000 par values, and have five years to maturity. The bonds differ only in the amount of annual coupon interest they pay: 8, 10, and 12 percent.
    a. What is the duration for each five-year bond?
    b. What is the relationship between duration and the amount of coupon interest that is paid?
11. You can obtain a loan for $100,000 at a rate of 10 percent for two years. You have a choice of (i) paying the principal at the end of the second year and (ii) amortizing the loan, that is, paying interest (10 percent) and principal in equal payments each year. The loan is priced at par.
    a. What is the duration of the loan under both methods of payment?
    b. Explain the difference in the two results.
12. How is duration related to the interest elasticity of a fixed-income security? What is the relationship between duration and the price of the fixed-income security?
13. You have discovered that the price of a bond rose from $975 to $995 when the yield to maturity fell from 9.75 percent to 9.25 percent. What is the duration of the bond?
14. A 10-year, 10 percent annual coupon $1,000 bond trades at a yield to maturity of 8 percent. The bond has a duration of 6.994 years. What is the modified duration of this bond? What is the practical value of calculating modified duration? Does modified duration change the result of using the duration relationship to estimate price sensitivity?
15. What is dollar duration? How is dollar duration different from duration?
16. Calculate the duration of a two-year, $1,000 bond that pays an annual coupon of 10 percent and trades at a yield of 14 percent. What is the expected change in the price of the bond if interest rates fall by 0.50 percent (50 bp)?
17. The duration of an 11-year, $1,000 Government of Canada bond paying a 10 percent semiannual coupon and selling at par has been estimated at 6.763 years.

a. What is the modified duration of the bond [modified duration = $D/(1 + R)$]?

b. What will be the estimated price change of the bond if market interest rates increase 0.10 percent (10 bp)? If rates decrease 0.20 percent (20 bp)?

c. What would the actual price of the bond be under each rate change situation in part (b) using present value bond pricing techniques? What is the amount of error in each case?

18. Suppose you purchase a five-year, 15 percent coupon bond (paid annually) that is priced to yield 9 percent. The face value of the bond is $1,000.

a. Show that the duration of this bond is equal to four years.

b. Show that if interest rates rise to 10 percent within the next year and your investment horizon is four years from today, you will still earn a 9 percent yield on your investment.

c. Show that a 9 percent yield will also be earned if interest rates fall next year to 8 percent.

19. Suppose you purchase a five-year, 13.76 percent bond that is priced to yield 10 percent.

a. Show that the duration of this annual payment bond is equal to four years.

b. Show that if interest rates rise to 11 percent within the next year and your investment horizon is four years from today, you will still earn a 10 percent yield on your investment.

c. Show that a 10 percent yield will also be earned if interest rates fall next year to 9 percent.

20. Consider the case in which an investor holds a bond for a period of time longer than the duration of the bond, that is, longer than the original investment horizon.

a. If interest rates rise, will the return that is earned exceed or fall short of the original required rate of return? Explain.

b. What will happen to the realized return if interest rates decrease? Explain.

c. Recalculate parts (b) and (c) of problem 19 above, assuming that the bond is held for all five years, to verify your answers to parts (a) and (b) of this problem.

d. If either calculation in part (c) is greater than the original required rate of return, why would an investor ever try to match the duration of an asset with his or her investment horizon?

21. Two banks are being examined by the regulators to determine the interest rate sensitivity of their balance sheets. Bank A has assets composed solely of a 10-year, 12 percent $1 million loan. The loan is financed with a 10-year, 10 percent $1 million GIC. Bank B has assets composed solely of a seven-year, 12 percent zero-coupon bond with a current (market) value of $894,006.20 and a maturity (principal) value of $1,976,362.88. The bond is financed with a 10-year, 8.275 percent coupon $1,000,000 face value GIC with a yield to maturity of 10 percent. The loan and the GICs pay interest annually, with principal paid at maturity.

a. If interest rates increase 1 percent (100 bp), how do the market values of the assets and liabilities of each bank change? That is, what will be the net effect on the market value of the equity for each bank?

b. What accounts for the differences in the changes in the market value of equity between the two banks?

c. Verify your results above by calculating the duration for the assets and liabilities of each bank, and estimate the changes in value for the expected change in interest rates. Summarize your results.

22. If an FI uses only duration to immunize its portfolio, what factors affect changes in the net worth of the FI when interest rates change?

23. Financial Institution XY has assets of $1 million invested in a 30-year, 10 percent semiannual coupon Government of Canada bond selling at par. The duration of this bond has been estimated at 9.94 years. The assets are financed with equity and a $900,000, two-year, 7.25 percent semiannual coupon capital note selling at par.

a. What is the leverage-adjusted duration gap of Financial Institution XY?

b. What is the impact on equity value if the relative change in all market interest rates is a decrease of 20 bp? (*Note:* The relative change in interest rates is $\Delta R/(1 + R/2) = -0.0020$.)

c. Using the information you calculated in parts (a) and (b), infer a general statement about the desired duration gap for an FI if interest rates are expected to increase or decrease.

d. Verify your inference by calculating the change in market value of equity assuming that the relative change in all market interest rates is an increase of 30 bp.

e. What would the duration of the assets need to be to immunize the equity from changes in market interest rates?

24. The balance sheet for Gotbucks Bank Inc. (GBI) is presented below ($ millions):

Assets		Liabilities and Equity	
Cash	$ 30	Core deposits	$ 20
Loans (floating)	125	Euro deposits	180
Loans (fixed)	65	Equity	20
Total assets	$220	Total liabilities and equity	$220

Notes to the balance sheet: The floating loan rate is LIBOR + 4 percent, and currently LIBOR is 11 percent. Fixed-rate loans have five-year maturities, are priced at par, and pay 12 percent annual interest. The principal is repaid at maturity. Core deposits are fixed rate for two years at 8 percent paid annually. Euro deposits currently yield 9 percent.

a. What is the duration of the fixed-rate loan portfolio of GBI?
b. If the duration of the floating-rate loans is 0.36 year, what is the duration of GBI's assets?
c. What is the duration of the core deposits if they are priced at par?
d. If the duration of the Euro deposits is 0.401 year, what is the duration of GBI's liabilities?
e. What is GBI's duration gap? What is its interest rate risk exposure?
f. What is the impact on the market value of equity if the relative change in all market interest rates is an increase of 1 percent (100 bp)? Note that the relative change in interest rates is $\Delta R/(1 + R) = 0.01$.
g. What is the impact on the market value of equity if the relative change in all interest rates is a decrease of 0.5 percent (−50 bp)?
h. What variables can be used to immunize GBI? How much would each variable need to change to get DGAP to equal zero?

25. Hands Insurance Company issued a $90 million, one-year zero-coupon note at 8 percent add-on annual interest (paying one coupon at the end of the year). The proceeds were used to fund a $100 million, two-year corporate loan at 10 percent annual interest. Immediately after these transactions were simultaneously closed, all market interest rates increased 1.5 percent (150 bp).

a. What is the true market value of the loan investment and the liability after the change in interest rates?
b. What impact did these changes in market value have on the market value of the FI's equity?
c. What was the duration of the loan investment and the liability at the time of issuance?
d. Use these duration values to calculate the expected change in the value of the loan and the liability for the predicted increase of 1.5 percent in interest rates.
e. What was the duration gap of Hands Insurance Company after the issuance of the asset and note?
f. What was the change in equity value forecasted by this duration gap for the predicted increase in interest rates of 1.5 percent?
g. If the interest rate prediction had been available during the time period in which the loan and the liability were being negotiated, what suggestions would you have offered to reduce the possible effect on the equity of the company? What are the difficulties in implementing your ideas?

26. The following balance sheet information is available (amounts in thousands of dollars and duration in years) for an FI:

	Amount	Duration
T-bills	90	0.50
T-notes	55	0.90
Government bonds	176	x
Loans	2,724	7.00
Deposits	2,092	1.00
Bank of Canada funds	238	0.01
Equity	715	

The government bonds are five-year maturities paying 6 percent semiannually and selling at par.

a. What is the duration of the government bond portfolio?
b. What is the average duration of all the assets?
c. What is the average duration of all the liabilities?
d. What is the leverage-adjusted duration gap? What is the interest rate risk exposure?
e. What is the forecasted impact on the market value of equity caused by a relative upward shift in the entire yield curve of 0.5 percent [i.e., $\Delta R/(1 + R) = 0.0050$]?
f. If the yield curve shifts downward 0.25 percent [i.e., $\Delta R/(1 + R) = -0.0025$], what is the forecasted impact on the market value of equity?
g. What variables are available to the FI to immunize the balance sheet? How much would each variable need to change to get DGAP to equal 0?

27. Assume that a goal of a regulatory agency of an FI is to immunize the ratio of equity to total assets, that is, $\Delta(E/A) = 0$. Explain how this goal changes the desired duration gap for the institution. Why does this differ from the duration gap necessary to immunize the total equity? How would your answers to part (h) in problem 24 and part (g) in problem 26 change if immunizing equity to total assets was the goal?

28. Identify and discuss three criticisms of using the duration model to immunize the portfolio of an FI.
29. In general, what changes have occurred in the financial markets that would allow FIs to restructure their balance sheets more rapidly and efficiently to meet desired goals? Why is it critical for an FI manager who has a portfolio immunized to match a desired investment horizon to rebalance the portfolio periodically? What is convexity? Why is convexity a desirable feature to capture in a portfolio of assets?
30. An FI has an investment horizon of two years 9.33 months (or 2.777 years). The FI has converted all assets into a portfolio of 8 percent, $1,000 three-year bonds that are trading at a yield to maturity of 10 percent. The bonds pay interest annually. The portfolio manager believes that the assets are immunized against interest rate changes.
    a. Is the portfolio immunized at the time of the bond purchase? What is the duration of the bonds?
    b. Will the portfolio be immunized one year later?
    c. Assume that one-year, 8 percent zero-coupon bonds are available in one year. What proportion of the original portfolio should be placed in these bonds to rebalance the portfolio?

Appendix 9A The Basics of Bond Valuation

Appendix 9B Incorporating Convexity into the Duration Model

View Appendices 9A and 9B on Connect.

CHAPTER 10

CREDIT RISK: INDIVIDUAL LOANS

After studying this chapter you should be able to:

LO1 Discuss the differences between business, real estate, and consumer loans

LO2 Calculate the return on a loan.

LO3 Compare retail and wholesale credit decisions.

LO4 Discuss the models used to measure credit risk for individual loans.

LO5 Discuss the newer models of credit risk measurement and pricing.

INTRODUCTION

As discussed in Chapter 1, FIs are special because of their ability to efficiently transform financial claims of household savers into claims issued to corporations, individuals, and governments. An FI's ability to evaluate information and to control and monitor borrowers allows it to transform these claims at the lowest possible cost to all parties. Through credit allocation FIs transform the claims (deposits) of household savers into loans issued to corporations, individuals, and governments. The FI accepts the credit risk on these loans in exchange for a fair return sufficient to cover the cost of funding (e.g., covering the costs of borrowing or issuing deposits) to household savers and the credit risk involved in lending.

In this chapter we discuss various approaches to analyzing and measuring the credit or default risk on *individual* loans (and bonds). In the next chapter, we consider methods for evaluating the risk of *the overall loan portfolio*, or loan concentration risk. Methods for hedging and managing an FI's credit risk are left to Chapters 22 to 26. Measurement of the credit risk on individual loans or bonds is crucial if an FI manager is to (1) price a loan or value a bond correctly and (2) set appropriate limits on the amount of credit extended to any one borrower or the loss exposure it accepts from any particular counterparty, since the default of one major borrower can have a significant impact on the value and reputation of an FI. For example, both Nortel Networks and Canwest Global filed for bankruptcy protection in Canada and the U.S. in 2009. Canadian FIs had exposure to US$4.5 billion of Nortel's debt and to $3.9 billion of Canwest's debt. Thus, an FI needs to protect itself from the failure of a single borrower.

Management of the overall loan portfolio is equally important. For example, in 2005 Hurricanes Katrina and Rita resulted in over US$1.3 billion in bad loans for banks operating in areas hit by the storms. And, of course, the financial market crisis of the late 2000s resulted in the largest ever credit risk–related losses for FIs around the world. Losses from the falling value of on- and off-balance-sheet credit instruments (e.g., mortgages, mortgage-backed securities, credit cards) topped US$2.3 trillion worldwide. In 2013, banks around the globe continue to monitor their exposure to the sovereign, business, and consumer debt of European countries, particularly the debt of Greece, Italy, Spain, and Portugal. In an economic recession all types of loans become subject to greater scrutiny by FIs as they try to limit their exposure to credit risk. Poor economic conditions can lead to defaults on consumer loans, such as lines of credit, mortgages, and credit card debt, and on business and government loans as well. Defaults ultimately reduce an FI's operating profits. Thus, it is important to remember that economic conditions have a significant impact on the ability (based on liquidity and capital adequacy) and willingness (based on the assessed credit risk) of FIs to lend to consumers and businesses.

We begin this chapter with a look at the types of loans (business, real estate, individual (consumer), and others), as well as the characteristics of these loans, made by FIs. We then look at how both interest and fees determine the return on a loan. This is followed by a discussion of how the return on a loan versus the quantity of credit made available for lending is used by FIs to make decisions on wholesale (business) versus retail (consumer) lending. Finally, we examine various models used to measure credit risk, including qualitative and quantitative models (credit scoring models and newer models of credit risk measurement). Appendix 10A discusses the cash flow and financial ratio analysis used in analyzing mortgage, consumer, and commercial loans.

CREDIT QUALITY PROBLEMS

junk bond
A bond rated as speculative or less than investment grade by bond-rating agencies such as DBRS.

dbrs.com
moodys.com
standardandpoors.com

nonperforming loans
loans that are 90 days or more past due or are not accruing interest.

Over the past three decades the credit quality of many FIs' lending and investment decisions has attracted a great deal of attention. In the 1980s there were tremendous problems with bank loans to less-developed countries. In the early 1990s attention switched to the problems of commercial real estate loans (to which banks and insurance companies were exposed) as well as **junk bonds** (rated as speculative or less than investment grade securities by bond-rating agencies (e.g., Dominion Bond Rating Service (DBRS), Moody's, and Standard & Poor's (S&P)). In the late 1990s and early 2000s, attention was focused on problems with telecommunications companies; new-technology companies; and a variety of sovereign countries, including at various times Argentina, Brazil, Russia, and South Korea. In 2007 and 2008, FIs started to struggle with the deterioration of credit conditions related to the financial crisis and global economic downturn. All types of assets, including subprime loans and credit card receivables, had been securitized, as we discuss in detail in Chapter 26.

Figure 10–1 shows **nonperforming loans** as a percentage of total loans for Canada, the United States, the euro area, and the United Kingdom from 2006 to 2012. The credit quality of the loans of all major Canadian banks has varied over the last two decades but, as shown in Figure 10–1, the credit crisis that began in 2008 resulted in higher nonperforming loans for FIs from the United Kingdom, the euro area, and the United States than for Canadian FIs.

Consumer loans and mortgages in arrears in Canada are shown in Figure 10–2. Personal bankruptcy rates and residential mortgage loans in arrears (three months or more) rise during economic downturns, and defaults on personal loans and credit card debt can have a significant impact on an FI's profitability. The impact of residential mortgage loans is not as significant since many mortgages carry insurance

FIGURE 10–1
Nonperforming Loans as a Percentage of Total Loans for Canada, the United States, the Euro Area, and the United Kingdom, 2006–2012

Source: The Bank of Canada, *Financial System Review,* December 2012, page 12.

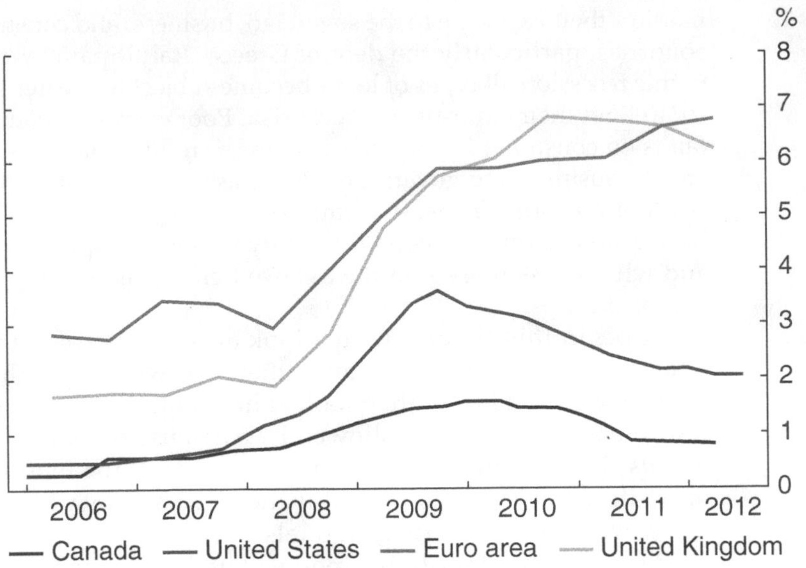

Note: The sample includes 6 Canadian banks 8 U.S. banks, 9 euro-area banks, and 5 U.K. banks.
Sources: Regulatory filings of Canadian banks and Bloomberg.

Last observations: Canada, July 2012; United States, September 2012; other countries, June 2012.

FIGURE 10–2
Household Loans More Than 90 days in Arrears as a Percentage of Loans Outstanding

Source: The Bank of Canada, *Financial System Review,* December 2012, page 23.

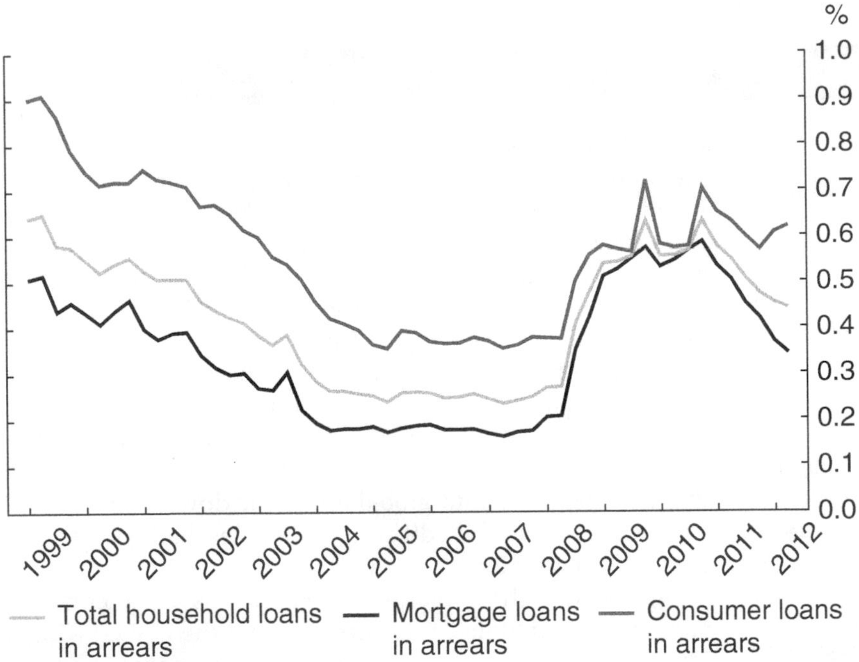

Sources: Regulatory filings of Canadian banks and Bank of Canada calculations.

Last observations: February 2012.

provided by CMHC. However, household debt reached historically high levels in Canada from 2007 to 2012, causing a tightening of the rules for mortgages in order to protect Canada from a housing bubble and price collapse as experienced in the United States, Spain, and China. For example, the maximum amortization period for mortgages insured by government-backed mortgage insurance decreased from 40 years in 2008 to 25 years in 2012.

Credit quality problems, in the worst case, can cause an FI to become insolvent or can result in such a significant drain on capital[1] and net worth that they adversely affect its growth prospects and ability to compete with other domestic and international FIs. However, credit risk does not apply only to traditional areas of lending and bond investing. As banks and other FIs have expanded into credit guarantees and other OBS activities (see Chapter 16), new types of credit risk exposure have arisen, causing concern among managers and regulators. Thus, credit risk analysis is now important for a whole variety of contractual agreements between FIs and counterparties.

CONCEPT QUESTION

What are some of the credit quality problems faced by FIs over the last two decades?

TYPES OF LOANS

LO1

Although most FIs make loans, the types of loans made and the characteristics of these loans differ considerably. This section analyzes the major types of loans made by Canadian banks. Remember from Chapters 2 through 6, however, that other FIs, such as trust and mortgage loan companies, life insurance companies, credit unions (CUs), and caisses populaires (CPs), also engage in lending, especially in the real estate area.

Table 10–1 shows a recent breakdown of the aggregate loan portfolio of Canadian banks into four broad classes: business, mortgages, personal, and all others. We look briefly at each of these loan classes in turn.

Business Loans

The figures in Table 10–1 disguise a great deal of heterogeneity in the business loan portfolio. Business loans can be made for periods as short as a few weeks to as long as eight years or more. Traditionally, short-term business loans (those with an original maturity of one year or less) are used to finance firms' working capital needs and other short-term funding needs, while long-term commercial loans are used to finance credit needs that extend beyond one year, such as the purchase of real assets (machinery), new venture start-up costs, and permanent increases in working capital. They can be made in quite small amounts, such as $100,000, to small businesses or in excess of $100 million or more to major corporations. Large loans are often **syndicated loans** provided by a group of FIs. A syndicated loan is structured by the lead FI (or agent) and the borrower. Once the terms (rates, fees,

syndicated loan
A loan provided by a group of FIs as opposed to a single lender.

[1] Losses drain capital through the income statement item "provision for loan losses." The provision for loan losses is a noncash, tax-deductible expense representing the FI management's prediction of loans at risk of default for the current period. As credit quality problems arise, the FI recognizes its expected bad loans by recording this expense, which reduces net income and, in turn, the FI's capital. The provision for loan losses is then allocated to the allowance for loan losses listed on the balance sheet. The allowance for loan and lease losses is a cumulative estimate by the FI's management of the percentage of the gross loans (and leases) that will not be repaid to the FI. Although the maximum amount of the provision of loan losses and the reserve for loan losses is influenced by tax laws, the FI's management actually sets the level based on loan growth and recent loan loss experience. The allowance for loan losses is an accumulated reserve that is adjusted each period as management recognizes the possibility of additional bad loans and makes appropriate provisions for such losses. Actual losses are then deducted from, and recoveries are added to (referred to as *net write-offs*), their accumulated loans and lease loss reserve balance. See Appendix 2A, "Financial Statement Analysis Using a Return on Equity (ROE) Framework" (on Connect), for a more detailed discussion of these items.

TABLE 10–1
Loans of All Banks Reporting to OSFI as at December 31, 2012: Net of Allowance for Impairment ($ billions)

Source: Office of the Superintendent of Financial Institutions Canada, osfi-bsif.gc.ca.

	Amount	Percent
Business loans*	$ 794.8	34.2
Mortgages		
Residential, insured	532.4	22.9
Residential, uninsured	384.1	16.5
Nonresidential	58.1	2.5
Personal loans	494.6	21.2
Other**	63.0	2.7
Total loans	$2,327.0	100.0
Total assets	$3,849.6	
Loans/total assets (%)	60.4	

* Includes lease receivables and reverse purchase agreements.
** Includes interbank loans, reverse purchase mortgages, and loans to domestic and foreign governments.

and covenants) are set, pieces of the loan are sold to other FIs. In addition, business loans can be secured or unsecured. A **secured loan** (or asset-backed loan) is backed by specific assets of the borrower; if the borrower defaults, the lender has a first lien or claim on those assets. In the terminology of finance, a secured debt is senior to an **unsecured loan** (or junior debt), which has only a general claim on the assets of the borrower if default occurs. There is normally a trade-off between the security or collateral backing of a loan and the loan interest rate or risk premium charged by the lender on a loan.

secured loan
A loan that is backed by a first claim on certain assets (collateral) of the borrower if default occurs.

unsecured loan
A loan that has only a general claim on the assets of the borrower if default occurs.

In addition, business loans can be made at either fixed or floating rates of interest. A fixed-rate loan has the rate of interest set at the beginning of the contract period. This rate remains in force over the loan contract period no matter what happens to market rates. Suppose, for example, Encana borrowed $100 million at 10 percent for one year, but the FI's cost of funds rose over the course of the year. Because this is a fixed-rate loan, the FI bears all the interest rate risk. This is why many loans have floating-rate contractual terms. That is, Encana borrows $100 million at a floating rate of LIBOR plus 5 percent for one year. The loan rate can be periodically adjusted according to a formula so that the interest rate risk is transferred in large part from the FI to the borrower. As might be expected, longer-term loans are more likely to be made under floating-rate contracts than are relatively short-term loans. However, floating-rate loans have higher credit risk than fixed-rate loans, holding all other contractual features the same. This is because floating-rate loans pass the risk of all interest rate changes on to borrowers. In rising interest rate environments, floating-rate borrowers may be unable to pay the interest and be forced to default.

Finally, loans can be made either spot or under commitment. A **spot loan** is made by the FI, and the borrower uses or takes down the entire loan amount immediately. With a **loan commitment**, or line of credit, the lender makes an amount of credit available, such as $10 million; the borrower has the option to draw down any amount up to the $10 million at any time over the commitment period. In a fixed-rate loan commitment, the interest rate to be paid on any drawdown is established when the loan commitment contract originates. In a floating-rate commitment, the borrower pays the loan rate in force when the loan is actually drawn down. For example, suppose the $100 million Encana loan was made under a one-year loan commitment. When the loan commitment was originated (say, January 2014), Encana borrows nothing.

spot loan
A loan where the loan amount is withdrawn by the borrower immediately.

loan commitment
A credit facility with a maximum size and a maximum period of time over which the borrower can withdraw funds; a line of credit.

Instead, it waits until six months have passed (say, July 2014) before it draws down the entire $100 million. Encana pays the loan rate in force as of July 2014. Loan commitments are an OBS risk that is discussed in Chapter 16.

commercial paper
An unsecured short-term debt instrument issued by corporations.

Finally, as we noted in Chapter 2, there has been a rise in nonbank loan substitutes, especially commercial paper. **Commercial paper** is an unsecured short-term debt instrument issued by corporations either directly or via an underwriter to purchasers in the financial markets. By using commercial paper, a corporation can sidestep banks and the loan market to raise funds, often at rates below those that banks charge.

Mortgage Loans

home equity loans
Loans where borrowers use the equity they have in their homes as collateral.

variable-rate mortgage (VRM)
A mortgage whose interest rate adjusts with movements in an underlying market index interest rate.

Real estate loans at Canadian FIs are primarily mortgage loans and some revolving **home equity loans.** Table 10–2 shows the residential (insured and uninsured) mortgage credit for banks, trusts, and loan companies. As shown in Table 10–1, residential mortgage loans are the largest component of the mortgage portfolio for Canadian banks. The characteristics of these loans can differ widely, including the size of the loans, the ratio of the loan to the property's price (the loan–price or loan–value ratio), the maturity of the mortgage, and the mortgage interest rate. The mortgage rate differs according to whether the mortgage has a fixed rate or a floating rate, also called a *variable* or *adjustable rate.* **Variable-rate mortgages (VRMs)** have their contractual rates periodically adjusted to some underlying index, usually the FI's prime lending rate. The proportion of fixed-rate mortgages to VRMs in FI portfolios varies with the interest rate cycle. In low-interest-rate periods, borrowers prefer fixed-rate mortgages. As a result, the proportion of VRM to fixed-rate mortgages can vary considerably over the rate cycle.

Residential mortgages are long-term loans, usually based on an amortization period of 25 years. House prices can fall below the amount of the loan outstanding—that is, the loan-to-value ratio rises—and the residential mortgage portfolio can also be susceptible to default risk. For example, from 1979 to 1982, a period of volatility in the economy, Canadian five-year mortgage rates varied from 11.05 percent to 21.46 percent, housing prices declined, and mortgage defaults increased, as did mortgage foreclosures. As well, following the economic downturn in 2008, which led to rising unemployment, housing prices in both Canada and the United States declined significantly in some markets, despite lower interest

TABLE 10–2 Residential Mortgage Credit in Canada, 2008–2012 ($ millions)

	2008	2009	2010	2011	2012
			$ millions		
Total outstanding balances	**858,031**	**921,568**	**984,911**	**1,058,466**	**1,132,232**
Chartered banks	463,162	442,518	478,790	580,162	839,730
Trust and mortgage loan companies	9,842	10,228	11,120	28,823	30,223
Life insurance company policy loans	15,336	15,343	14,360	14,860	15,121
Pension funds	15,309	15,649	14,361	13,360	12,703
National Housing Act mortgage-backed securities	189,494	273,908	301,526	236,987	41,231
CUs and CPs	110,523	117,298	121,902	131,579	139,924
Special-purpose corporations (securitization)	22,529	16,817	13,808	12,080	10,122

Note: Figures may not add to totals due to rounding.
Source: Statistics Canada, CANSIM, table 176-0069; Bank of Canada.

rates. Mortgage arrears started to increase as well, as shown in Figure 10–2. As shown in Table 10–2, Canadian banks reported residential mortgage loans of $840.2 billion in 2011. This represented 79 percent of the total residential mortgage loans reported. The credit risk of these loans for FIs was reduced since approximately 40 percent of the mortgage loans carried mortgage insurance. Table 10–2 shows the trends in total outstanding residential mortgage credit from 2007 to 2011. At December 31, 2011, the total outstanding residential mortgage credit was $1.06 trillion, with 79 percent held by the chartered banks. An additional 13 percent was held by CUs and CPs. Note the significant decline in National Housing Act mortgage-backed securities from $301.5 billion in 2009 to $35.9 billion in 2011.

As we will see in Chapter 26, from 2001 to 2006, the market for mortgage-backed securities in Canada did not grow as fast as the U.S. subprime market. In 2006, the subprime mortgage market was less than 5 percent of mortgage originations in Canada. In comparison, U.S. subprime mortgages reached over 20 percent of all mortgages originated in 2006 and 2007. U.S. housing policy, which was intended to increase the number of lower-income Americans who owned their own homes, encouraged FIs to issue mortgages to higher-risk individuals. As a result, almost 8 percent of U.S. subprime mortgages were in arrears over 90 days or in foreclosure in 2006. The Canadian experience was much less than 2 percent in the same time period.

Personal (Consumer) Loans

personal lines of credit
Revolving loans that allow a consumer to borrow and pay back an amount up to the approved credit limit.

personal loan plans
Consumer loans that have a fixed rate, a fixed term, and amortized payments.

revolving loan
A credit line on which a borrower can both draw and repay many times over the life of the loan contract.

Another major type of loan is the individual, or consumer, loan, such as personal loans and car loans. Commercial banks, finance companies, retailers, savings institutions, CUs, CPs, and oil companies also provide consumer loan financing through credit cards, such as Visa, MasterCard, and proprietary credit cards issued by, for example, Sears and Canadian Tire. According to the Canadian Bankers Association (CBA), the largest credit card issuers in Canada, Visa and MasterCard, had 74.5 million cards issued and a net retail volume of $301.86 billion in 2011.

Table 10–3 shows the major types of personal, nonmortgage loans at Canadian chartered banks reported for November 2008 and 2012. This nonmortgage debt increased by 45 percent over the four-year period. **Personal lines of credit**, revolving loans that allow consumers to borrow and repay up to the approved amount or credit limit, are the major source of consumer credit, followed by **personal loan plans**, which are generally fixed-rate, fixed-term loans, and then credit cards. Credit cards and lines of credit are revolving loans. With a **revolving loan** the borrower has a credit line on which to draw as well as to repay up to a maximum over the life of the credit contract.

TABLE 10–3
Personal Loans of Chartered Banks, Monthly Average November 2008 and 2012 ($ millions)

Source: Bank of Canada, *Monthly Statistics*, February 2013, bankofcanada.ca.

	2008		2012	
Personal loan plans	$ 50,475	17.1%	$ 76,190	17.7%
Credit cards	50,687	17.2%	73,704	17.2%
Personal lines of credit	175,180	59.4%	260,002	60.8%
Other	18,707	6.3%	18,020	4.2%
Total	$295,048	100%	$ 427,915	100%

cba.ca

The delinquency rate (90 days and over) on Visa and MasterCard year-end outstanding amounts reported by the CBA declined from 1.34 percent at January 31, 2010, to 0.87 percent at October 31, 2012. The CBA also reported that the percentage of the total number of mortgages in arrears (three or more months) declined from 0.45 percent (18,059 mortgages) in December 2009 to 0.32 percent (14,002 mortgages) in November 2012. Consumer credit, excluding mortgages, from chartered banks, trust and mortgage loan companies, life insurance companies, CUs, and CPs grew by 37 percent from 2000 to 2004.

Loss rates on credit cards in Canada have historically been less than 4 percent. However, a survey of credit card issuers in Canada conducted by accounting firm Deloitte found that by October 2008, delinquencies had jumped and were expected to increase further. Residential mortgages in the United State are nonrecourse to other assets. This makes it easier for consumers to default on their mortgages, forcing FIs to foreclose on houses. In contrast, residential mortgages in Canada are recourse to consumer's other assets and so Canadian consumers were found to default on their credit card debt and car loans first rather than to stop making payments on their homes. The Canadian ratio of debt to disposable income for households reported by Statistics Canada has been steadily increasing since 1990. As shown in Figure 10–3, aggregate household debt to income in the United States exceeded 160 percent in 2008. Canadian household debt to income surpassed the United States in 2011, but as of 2012, had not reached the levels of the United States during the financial crisis.

Table 10–4 shows indicative interest rates on car, mortgage, line of credit, and credit card loans in February 2013. These rates differ depending on features such as collateral backing, maturity, default rate experience, and non-interest-rate fees.

FIGURE 10–3 Aggregate Household Debt-to-Income Ratio, Canada and the United States, 1990–2012

Source: Bank of Canada *Financial System Review*, December 2012, p. 22.

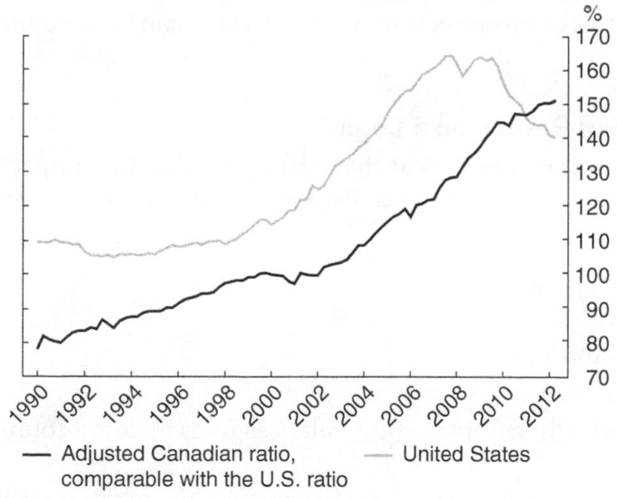

Note: U.S. calculations include the unincorporated business sector.

Sources: Statistics Canada, U.S. Federal Reserve, and Bank of Canada calculations. Last observation: 2012Q2.

TABLE 10–4 Interest Rates on Consumer Loans, February 2013

48-month car loan	4.00–7.89%
5-year closed mortgage	3.10–5.24%
Unsecured line of credit	5.50–12.60%
Secured line of credit	4.00–8.25%
Bank credit card	11.90–19.99%

Source: Various financial institutions' websites.

In addition, competitive conditions in each market as well as usury ceilings (60 percent effective annual rate in Canada) all affect the rate structure for consumer loans. Declines in interest rates decrease the funding costs for banks and, to the extent that these rate decreases are passed on, help ease the debt service ratios for businesses and consumers.

Other Loans

The "other" loans category can include a wide variety of borrowers and types, including secured call loans (also called *demand loans*), broker margin loans (loans financing a percentage of an individual's investment portfolio), loans to the federal and provincial/territorial governments, loans to municipalities and schools, loans to other financial institutions, and loans to foreign (sovereign) governments. Sovereign loans are discussed in Chapter 14.

CONCEPT QUESTIONS

1. **What are the major types of loans made by Canadian banks? What are the basic distinguishing characteristics of each type of loan?**
2. **Will more VRMs be originated in high- or low-interest-rate environments? Explain your answer.**
3. **In Table 10–4, explain why credit card loan rates are much higher than car loan, mortgage, and line of credit rates.**

CALCULATING THE RETURN ON A LOAN

LO2

An important element in the credit management process, once the decision to make a loan has been made, is its pricing. This includes adjustments for the perceived credit risk or default risk of the borrower and any fees and collateral backing the loan. FIs also offer relationship discounts on interest rates for customers based on the total amount of fee-based services used and investments held at the FI. This section demonstrates one method used to calculate the return on a loan: the *return on assets (ROA) approach*. Although we demonstrate the return calculations using examples of business loans, the technique can be used for other loans as well.

The Contractually Promised Return on a Loan

The previous description of loans makes it clear that a number of factors impact the promised return an FI achieves on any given dollar loan (asset) amount. These factors include the following:

1. The interest rate on the loan
2. Any fees relating to the loan
3. The credit risk premium on the loan
4. The collateral backing of the loan
5. Other nonprice terms (especially compensating balances and, in some countries, reserve requirements)

First, let us consider an example of how to calculate the promised return on a business loan. Suppose that an FI makes a spot one-year, $1 million loan. The loan rate is set as follows:

$$\text{Base lending rate } (BR) = 12\%$$
$$+ \text{ Credit risk premium or margin } (\phi) = \underline{\ 2\%}$$
$$BR + \phi = 14\%$$

LIBOR
The London Interbank Offered Rate, which is the rate for interbank dollar loans of a given maturity in the offshore or Eurodollar market.

Canadian Dealer Offered Rate (CDOR)
A floating rate based on Canadian bankers' acceptances, determined daily from a survey of Canadian FIs and used for pricing of Canadian dollar loans.

prime lending rate
The base lending rate periodically set by banks.

compensating balance
A percentage of a loan that a borrower is required to hold on deposit at the lending institution.

The base lending rate (*BR*) could reflect the FI's weighted-average cost of capital or its marginal cost of funds, such as the commercial paper rate, or **LIBOR**—the London Interbank Offered Rate, which is the rate for interbank U.S. dollar loans of a given maturity in the Eurodollar market. The centre of the Eurodollar market is London, United Kingdom. A floating rate similar to LIBOR is the **Canadian Dealer Offered Rate (CDOR)**, which is a rate based on Canadian bankers' acceptances that is determined daily from a survey of Canadian FIs. Higher LIBOR or CDOR rates result in higher borrowing costs for businesses, while lower rates can make FIs hesitant to lend. In addition to business loans, some bonds and interest rate swaps also use LIBOR or CDOR as their benchmark. There is evidence that several large banks tried to manipulate the LIBOR rate during the financial crisis. Because of the extensive use of LIBOR as a base rate on business loans, even a small bit of manipulation can cause massive redistribution of resources. In addition to the Canadian government, the U.S. Justice Department and officials in Switzerland and the United Kingdom are involved in the investigation. In June 2012, U.K. bank Barclays agreed to pay US$453 million to U.S. and U.K. authorities to settle allegations that it manipulated the LIBOR rate.

As an alternative to LIBOR or CDOR, the base lending rate could be the **prime lending rate**. Traditionally, the prime rate has been the rate charged to the FI's lowest-risk customers. Now, it is more of a base rate to which positive or negative risk premiums can be added. In other words, the best and largest borrowers now commonly pay below prime rate to be competitive with the commercial paper market.

Direct and indirect fees and charges relating to a loan generally fall into three categories:

1. A loan origination fee (*of*) charged to the borrower for processing the application.
2. A compensating balance requirement (*b*) to be held as non-interest-bearing demand deposits. A **compensating balance** is a percentage of a loan that a borrower cannot actively use for expenditures. Instead, this balance must be kept on deposit at the FI. For example, a borrower facing a 10 percent compensating balance requirement on a $100 loan would have to place $10 on deposit (traditionally a demand deposit) with the FI and could use only $90 of the $100 borrowed. This requirement raises the effective cost of loans for the borrower since less than the full loan amount ($90 in this case) can actually be used by the borrower and the deposit rate earned on compensating balances is less than the borrowing rate. Thus, compensating balance requirements act as an additional source of return on lending for an FI.[2]
3. A reserve requirement (*RR*) imposed by the central bank on the FI's demand deposits, including any compensating balances. The Bank of Canada has not imposed reserve requirements on Canadian DTIs since 1991, but the U.S. Federal Reserve still imposes reserve requirements on banks operating in the United States.

[2] Compensating balances also create a more stable supply of deposits and thus mitigate liquidity problems. Further, compensating balances are sometimes used as an offset to fees charged on the loan. That is, loans with a compensating balance requirement often have lower fees than loans without a compensating balance. In this case, the additional revenue from the compensating balances is offset by the loss in fee income.

While credit risk may be the most important factor ultimately affecting the return on a loan, these other factors should not be ignored by FI managers in evaluating loan profitability and risk. FIs can compensate for high credit risk in a number of ways other than charging a higher explicit interest rate or risk premium on a loan or restricting the amount of credit available. In particular, higher fees, high compensating balances, and increased collateral backing all offer implicit and indirect methods of compensating an FI for lending risk.

The contractually promised gross return on the loan, k, per dollar lent—or ROA per dollar lent—equals[3]

$$1 + k = 1 + \frac{of + (BR + \phi)}{1 - [b(1 - RR)]}$$

In this formula, the numerator is the promised gross cash inflow to the FI per dollar, reflecting direct fees (of) plus the loan interest rate ($BR + \phi$). In the denominator, for every \$1 in loans the FI lends, it retains b as non-interest-bearing compensating balances. Thus, $1 - b$ is the net proceeds of each \$1 of loans received by the borrower from the FI, ignoring reserve requirements. However, since b (compensating balances) is held by the borrower at the FI as demand deposits, the central bank may require DTIs to hold non-interest-bearing reserves at the rate RR against these compensating balances. Thus, the FI's net benefit from requiring compensating balances must consider the cost of holding additional non-interest-bearing reserve requirements. The net outflow by the FI per \$1 of loans is $1 - [b(1 - RR)]$ or 1 minus the reserve adjusted compensating balance requirement. With $RR = 0$ in Canada, the denominator reduces to $1 - b$.

EXAMPLE 10-1

Calculation of ROA on a Loan

Suppose a bank does the following:

1. Sets the loan rate on a prospective loan at 10 percent (where $BR = 6\%$ and $\phi = 4\%$).
2. Charges a 1/8 percent (or 0.125 percent) loan origination fee to the borrower.
3. Imposes an 8 percent compensating balance requirement to be held as non-interest-bearing demand deposits.
4. Sets aside reserves, at a rate of 10 percent of deposits.

Plugging the numbers from our example into the return formula, we have[4]

$$1 + k = 1 + \frac{0.00125 + (0.06 + 0.04)}{1 - [(0.08)(0.90)]}$$

$$1 + k = 1 + \frac{0.10125}{0.928}$$

$$1 + k = 1.1091 \text{ or } k = 10.91\%$$

This is, of course, greater than the simple promised interest return on the loan, $BR + \phi = 10\%$.

[3] This formula ignores present value aspects that could easily be incorporated. For example, fees are earned in up-front undiscounted dollars, while interest payments and risk premiums are normally paid on loan maturity and thus should be discounted by the FI's cost of funds.

[4] If we take into account the present value effects on the fees and the interest payments and assume that the bank's discount rate (d) was 10½ percent, then the $BR + \phi$ term needs to be discounted by $1 + d = 1.105$, while fees (as up-front payments) are undiscounted. In this case, k is 9.89 percent.

In the special case where fees (of) are zero and the compensating balance (b) is zero,

$$of = 0$$
$$b = 0$$

the contractually promised return formula reduces to

$$1 + k = 1 + (BR + \phi)$$

That is, the credit risk premium or margin (ϕ) is the fundamental factor driving the promised return on a loan once the base rate on the loan is set.

Note that as commercial and corporate lending markets have become more competitive, both origination fees (of) and compensating balances (b) are becoming less important. For example, where compensating balances are still charged, the bank may now allow them to earn interest. As a result, borrowers' opportunity losses from compensating balances have been reduced to the difference between the loan rate and the compensating balance deposit rate. Further, compensating balance requirements are very rare on international loans, such as Eurodollar loans.[5] Finally, note that for a given promised gross return on a loan, k, FI managers can use the pricing formula to find various combinations of fees, compensating balances, and risk premiums they may offer their customers that generate the same returns.

The Expected Return on a Loan

default risk
The risk that the borrower is unable or unwilling to fulfill the terms promised under the loan contract.

The promised return on the loan ($1 + k$) that the borrower and lender contractually agree on includes both the loan interest rate and non-interest-rate features such as fees. The promised return on the loan, however, may well differ from the expected and, indeed, actual return on a loan because of default risk. **Default risk** is the risk that the borrower is unable or unwilling to fulfill the terms promised under the loan contract. Default risk is usually present to some degree in all loans. Thus, at the time the loan is made, the expected return [$E(r)$] per dollar lent is related to the promised return as follows:

$$1 + E(r) = p(1 + k) + (1 - p)(0)$$

where p is the probability of complete repayment of the loan (such that the FI receives the principal and interest as promised) and $(1 - p)$ is the probability of default (in which the FI receives nothing, i.e., 0). Rearranging this equation, we get

$$E(r) = p(1 + k) - 1$$

To the extent that p is less than 1, default risk is present. This means the FI manager must (1) set the risk premium (ϕ) sufficiently high to compensate for this risk and (2) recognize that setting high risk premiums as well as high fees and base rates may actually reduce the probability of repayment (p). That is, k and p are not independent. Indeed, over some range, as fees and loan rates increase, the

[5] If compensating balances held as deposits paid interest at 2 percent (r_d = 2 percent), then the numerator (cash flow) of the bank in the example would be reduced by $b \times r_d$, where $r_d = 0.02$ and $b = 0.08$. In this case, k = 10.74 percent. This assumes that the reserve requirement on compensating balances held as time deposits (RR) is 10 percent. However, while U.S. reserve requirements on demand deposits are currently 10 percent, the reserve requirement on time deposits is 0 percent (zero). Recalculating but assuming $RR = 0$ and interest of 2 percent on compensating balances, we find k = 10.83 percent. In Canada, reserve requirements are always equal to zero.

probability that the borrower pays the promised return may decrease (i.e., k and p may be negatively related). As a result, FIs usually have to control for credit risk along two dimensions: the price or promised return dimension $(1 + k)$ and the quantity or credit availability dimension. Further, even after adjusting the loan rate (by increasing the risk premium on the loan) for the default risk of the borrower, there is no guarantee that the FI will actually receive the promised payments. The measurement and pricing approaches discussed in this chapter consider credit risk based on probabilities of receiving promised payments on the loan. The actual payment or default on a loan once it is issued may vary from the probability expected.

In general, compared with business loans, the quantity dimension controls credit risk differences on retail (e.g., consumer) loans more than the price dimension does. We discuss the reasons for this in the next section. That is followed by a section that evaluates various ways FI managers can assess the appropriate size of ϕ, the risk premium on a loan. This is the key to pricing loan risk exposures correctly.

CONCEPT QUESTIONS

1. **Calculate the promised return (k) on a loan if the base rate is 13 percent, the risk premium is 2 percent, the compensating balance requirement is 5 percent, fees are ½ percent, and reserve requirements are 10 percent. (16.23%)**
2. **What is the expected return on this loan if the probability of default is 5 percent? (10.42%)**

RETAIL AND WHOLESALE CREDIT DECISIONS

LO3

Retail (Consumer)

Because of the small dollar size of the loans in the context of an FI's overall asset portfolio and the higher costs of collecting information on household borrowers (consumer loans), most loan decisions made at this level tend to be accept or reject decisions. Regardless of their credit risk, borrowers who are accepted are often charged the same rate of interest and by implication the same credit risk premium. For example, a wealthy individual borrowing from a credit union to finance the purchase of a Rolls-Royce is likely to be charged the same auto loan rate as a less-wealthy individual borrowing from that credit union to finance the purchase of a Honda. In the terminology of finance, retail customers (consumer loans) are more likely to be sorted or rationed by loan quantity restrictions than by price or interest rate differences. That is, at the consumer level, an FI controls its credit risks by **credit rationing** rather than by using a range of interest rates or prices. Thus, the FI may offer the wealthy individual a loan of up to $80,000, while the same FI may offer the less-wealthy individual a loan of up to $20,000, both at the same interest rate. Residential mortgage loans provide another good example. While two borrowers may be accepted for mortgage loans, an FI discriminates between them according to the loan-to-value ratio—the amount the FI is willing to lend relative to the market value of the house being acquired—rather than by setting different mortgage rates.

credit rationing
Restricting the quantity of loans made available to individual borrowers.

Wholesale (Business)

In contrast to retail lending, at the business level FIs use both interest rates and credit quantity to control credit risk. Thus, when FIs quote a prime lending rate (BR) to business borrowers, lower-risk borrowers may be charged a lending rate below the prime lending rate. Higher-risk borrowers are charged a markup on the prime rate, or a credit (default) risk premium (ϕ), to compensate the FI for the additional credit risk involved.

As long as they are compensated with sufficiently high interest rates (or credit risk premiums), over some range of credit demand, FIs may be willing to lend funds to high-risk borrowers. However, as discussed earlier, increasing loan interest rates (k) may decrease the probability (p) that a borrower will pay the promised return. For example, a borrower who is charged 15 percent for a loan—a prime rate of 6 percent plus a credit risk premium of 9 percent—may be able to make the promised payments on the loan only by using the funds to invest in high-risk investments with some small chance of a big payoff. However, by definition, high-risk projects have relatively high probabilities that they will *fail* to realize the big payoff. If the big payoff does not materialize, the borrower may have to default on the loan. In an extreme case, the FI receives neither the promised interest and fees on the loan nor the original principal lent. This suggests that very high contractual interest rate charges on loans may actually reduce an FI's expected return on loans because high interest rates induce the borrower to invest in risky projects.[6] Alternatively, only borrowers that intend to use the borrowed funds to invest in high-risk projects (high-risk borrowers) may be interested in borrowing from FIs at high interest rates. Low-risk borrowers drop out of the potential borrowing pool at high-rate levels. This lowers the average quality of the pool of potential borrowers. We show these effects in Figure 10–4.

At very low contractually promised interest rates (k), borrowers do not need to take high risks in their use of funds, and those with relatively safe investment projects use FI financing. As interest rates increase, borrowers with fairly low risk, low return projects no longer think it is profitable to borrow from FIs and drop out of the pool of potential borrowers. Alternatively, borrowers may switch their use of the borrowed funds to high-risk investment projects to have a (small) chance of

FIGURE 10–4
Relationship between the Promised Loan Rate and the Expected Return on the Loan

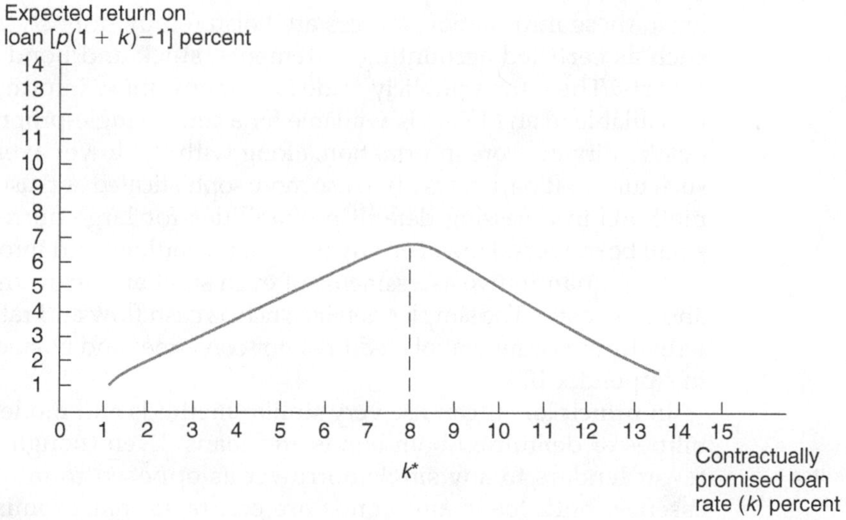

[6] A high k on a loan with a high base rate (BR) and risk premium (ϕ) can lead to a lower probability of repayment (p) and lower $E(r)$ on the loan, where $E(r) = p(1 + k) - 1$. For a very high k, the expected return on the loan becomes negative.

being able to pay off the loan. In terms of Figure 10–4, when interest rates rise above k^* (8 percent), the additional expected return earned by the FI through higher contractually promised interest rates (k) is increasingly offset by a lower probability of repayment on the loan (p). In other words, because of the potential increase in the probability of default when contractually promised loan rates are high, an FI charging wholesale borrowers loan rates in the 9 to 14 percent region can earn a *lower* expected return than will an FI charging 8 percent.

This relationship between contractually promised interest rates and the expected returns on loans suggests that beyond some interest rate level, it may be best for the FI to *credit ration* its loans, that is, to not make loans or to make fewer loans. Rather than seeking to ration by price (by charging higher and higher risk premiums to borrowers), the FI can establish an upper ceiling on the amounts it is willing to lend to maximize its expected returns on lending. In the context of Figure 10–4, borrowers may be charged interest rates up to 8 percent, with the most risky borrowers also facing more restrictive limits or ceilings on the amounts they can borrow at any given interest rate.

CONCEPT QUESTIONS

1. **Can an FI's return on its loan portfolio increase if it cuts its loan rates?**
2. **What might happen to the expected return on a business (wholesale) loan if an FI eliminates its fees and compensating balances in a low-interest-rate environment?**

MEASUREMENT OF CREDIT RISK

LO4

To calibrate the default risk exposure of credit and investment decisions as well as to assess the credit risk exposure in OBS contractual arrangements such as loan commitments, an FI manager needs to measure the probability of borrower default. The ability to do this depends largely on the amount of information the FI has about the borrower. At the consumer level, much of the information needs to be collected internally or purchased from external credit agencies. At the business level, these information sources are bolstered by publicly available information, such as certified accounting statements, stock and bond prices, and analysts' reports. Thus, for a publicly traded company, more information is produced and is available to an FI than is available for a small, single-proprietor corner store. The availability of more information, along with the lower average cost of collecting such information, allows FIs to use more sophisticated and usually more quantitative methods in assessing default probabilities for large borrowers compared with small borrowers. However, advances in technology and information collection are making quantitative assessments of even smaller borrowers increasingly feasible and less costly. The simpler details (such as cash flow and ratio analysis) associated with the measurement of credit risk for consumer and business loans are discussed in Appendix 10A.

In principle, FIs can use very similar methods and models to assess the probabilities of default on both bonds and loans. Even though loans tend to involve fewer lenders to any single borrower as opposed to multiple bondholders, in essence, both loans and bonds are contracts that promise fixed (or indexed) payments at regular intervals in the future. Loans and bonds stand ahead of the borrowing firm's equity holders in terms of the priority of their claims if things go wrong. Also, bonds, like loans, include **covenants** restricting or encouraging

covenants
Restrictions written into bond and loan contracts, either limiting or encouraging the borrower's actions, that affect the probability of repayment.

various actions to enhance the probability of repayment. Covenants can include limits on the type and amount of new debt, investments, and asset sales the borrower may undertake while the loans or bonds are outstanding. Financial covenants are also often imposed restricting changes in the borrower's financial ratios, such as its leverage ratio or current ratio. For example, a common restrictive covenant included in many bond and loan contracts limits the amount of dividends a firm can pay to its equity holders. Clearly, for any given cash flow, a high dividend payout to stockholders means that less is available for repayments to bondholders and lenders. Moreover, bond yields, like wholesale loan rates, usually reflect risk premiums that vary with the perceived credit quality of the borrower and the collateral or security backing of the debt. Given this, FIs can use many of the following models that analyze default risk probabilities either in making lending decisions or when considering investing in corporate bonds offered either publicly or privately.

CONCEPT QUESTIONS

1. **Is it more costly for an FI manager to assess the default risk exposure of a publicly traded company or a small, single-proprietor firm? Explain your answer.**
2. **How do loan covenants help protect an FI against default risk?**

DEFAULT RISK MODELS

Economists, analysts, and FI managers have employed many different models to assess the default risk on loans and bonds. These vary from relatively qualitative to highly quantitative models. Further, these models are not mutually exclusive; an FI manager may use more than one model to reach a credit pricing or loan quantity rationing decision. As will be discussed below in more detail, a great deal of time and effort has recently been expended by FIs in building highly technical credit risk evaluation models. Many of these models use ideas and techniques similar to the market risk models discussed in Chapter 15. We analyze a number of models in three broad groups: qualitative models, credit scoring models, and newer models.

Qualitative Models

In the absence of publicly available information on the quality of borrowers, the FI manager has to assemble information from private sources—such as credit and deposit files—and/or purchase such information from external sources—such as credit rating agencies. This information helps a manager make an informed judgment on the probability of default of the borrower and price the loan or debt correctly.

In general, the amount of information assembled varies with the size of the potential debt exposure and the costs of collection. However, a number of key factors enter into the credit decision. These include (1) *borrower-specific* factors, which are idiosyncratic to the individual borrower, and (2) *market-specific* factors, which have an impact on all borrowers at the time of the credit decision. The FI manager then weights these factors subjectively to come to an overall credit decision. Because of their reliance on the subjective judgment of the FI manager, these models are often called *expert systems*. Commonly used borrower-specific and market-specific factors are discussed next.

Borrower-Specific Factors

Reputation The borrower's reputation involves the borrowing–lending history of the credit applicant. If, over time, the borrower has established a reputation for prompt and timely repayment, this enhances the applicant's attractiveness to the FI. A long-term customer relationship between a borrower and a lender forms an **implicit contract** regarding borrowing and repayment that extends beyond the formal explicit legal contract on which borrower–lender relationships are based. The importance of reputation, which can be established only over time through repayment and observed behaviour, works to the disadvantage of small, newer borrowers. This is one of the reasons initial public offerings of debt securities by small firms often require higher yields than do offerings of older, more seasoned firms.

implicit contract
A long-term customer relationship between a borrower and a lender, based on reputation.

Leverage A borrower's **leverage** or capital structure—the ratio of debt to equity—affects the probability of its default because large amounts of debt, such as bonds and loans, increase the borrower's interest charges and pose a significant claim on its cash flows. As shown in Figure 10–5, relatively low debt–equity ratios may not significantly impact the probability of debt repayment. Yet beyond some point, the risk of bankruptcy increases, as does the probability of some loss of interest or principal for the lender. Thus, highly leveraged firms may find it necessary to pay higher risk premiums on their borrowings if they are not rationed in the first place.

leverage
The ratio of a borrower's debt to equity.

Volatility of Earnings As with leverage, a highly volatile earnings stream increases the probability that the borrower cannot meet fixed interest and principal charges for any given capital structure. Consequently, newer firms or firms in high-tech industries with a high earnings variance over time are less attractive credit risks than are those with long and more stable earnings histories.

Collateral As discussed earlier, a key feature in any lending and loan-pricing decision is the degree of collateral, or assets backing the security of the loan. Many loans and bonds are backed by specific assets should a borrower default on repayment obligations. Mortgage bonds give the bondholder first claim to some specific piece of property of the borrower, normally machinery or buildings; debentures give a bondholder a more general and more risky claim to the borrower's assets. Subordinated debentures are even riskier because their claims to the assets of a defaulting borrower are junior to those of both mortgage bondholders and debenture bondholders. Similarly, loans can be either secured (collateralized) or unsecured (uncollateralized). Collateralized loans are still subject to some default risk unless these loans are significantly overcollateralized, that is, if assets are pledged with market values exceeding the face value of the debt instrument. The best borrowers often do not need to post collateral since they are good credit risks. Posting collateral may be a signal of more rather than less credit risk.

FIGURE 10–5 Relationship between the Cost of Debt, the Probability of Default, and Leverage

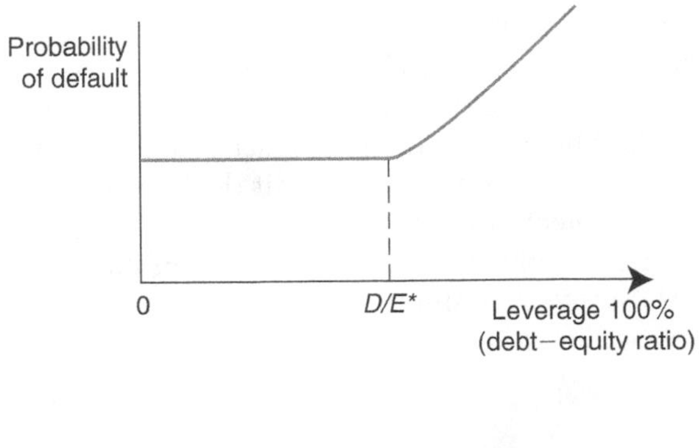

Market-Specific Factors

The Business Cycle The position of the economy in the business cycle phase is enormously important to an FI in assessing the probability of borrower default. For example, during recessions, firms in the consumer durable goods sector that produce autos, refrigerators, or houses do badly compared with those in the nondurable goods sector producing tobacco and foods. People cut back on luxuries during a recession but are less likely to cut back on necessities such as food. Thus, corporate borrowers in the consumer durable goods sector of the economy are especially prone to default risk. For example, the major U.S. car companies, Chrysler and General Motors, as well as Toyota and other international companies, suffered from declines in sales in 2008. The Canadian, U.S., Japanese, and Korean governments were asked to provide support. Because of cyclical concerns, FIs are more likely to increase the relative degree of credit rationing during a recession. This has especially adverse consequences for smaller borrowers with limited or no access to alternative credit markets such as the commercial paper market.

bankofcanada.ca

The Level of Interest Rates High interest rates indicate restrictive monetary policy actions by the Bank of Canada. FIs not only find funds to finance their lending decisions scarcer and more expensive but also must recognize that high interest rates are correlated with higher credit risk in general. As discussed earlier, high interest rates may encourage borrowers to take excessive risks and/or encourage only the most risky customers to borrow.

So far, we have delineated just a few of the qualitative borrower- and economy-specific factors an FI manager may take into account in deciding on the probability of default on any loan or bond. Five Cs of credit should be included in any subjective (qualitative) credit analysis (see Appendix 10A): character (willingness to pay), capacity (cash flow), capital (wealth), collateral (security), and conditions (economic conditions). Rather than letting such factors enter into the decision process in a purely subjective fashion, the FI manager may weight these factors in a more objective or quantitative manner. We discuss quantitative credit scoring models used to measure credit risk next. One frequently used source of much of this information is the Risk Management Association (RMA). RMA has become a standard reference for thousands of commercial lenders by providing average balance sheet and income data for more than 400 industries, common ratios computed for each size of group and industry, five-year trend data, and financial statement data for more than 100,000 commercial borrowers.

rmahq.org

CONCEPT QUESTIONS

1. **Make a list of 10 key borrower characteristics you would assess before making a mortgage loan.**
2. **How would a loan's risk premium be affected if a borrower reduced its leverage?**

LO5

Quantitative Models

Credit Scoring Models

credit scoring models Mathematical models that use observed loan applicant characteristics either to calculate a score representing the applicant's probability of default or to sort borrowers into different default risk classes.

Credit scoring models are quantitative models that use observed borrower characteristics either to calculate a score representing the applicant's probability of default or to sort borrowers into different default risk classes. By selecting and combining different economic and financial borrower characteristics, an FI manager may be able to

1. Numerically establish which factors are important in explaining default risk.
2. Evaluate the relative degree or importance of these factors.
3. Improve the pricing of default risk.
4. Be better able to screen out bad loan applicants.
5. Be in a better position to calculate any reserves needed to meet expected future loan losses.

The primary benefit from credit scoring is that credit lenders can more accurately predict a borrower's performance without having to use more resources. Using these models means fewer defaults and write-offs for lenders.

To use credit scoring models, the manager must identify objective economic and financial measures of risk for any particular class of borrower. For consumer debt, the objective characteristics in a credit scoring model might include income, assets, age, occupation, and location. For commercial debt, cash flow information and financial ratios such as the debt–equity ratio are usually key factors. After data are identified, a statistical technique quantifies, or scores, the default risk probability or default risk classification.

Credit scoring models include these three broad types: (1) linear probability models, (2) logit models, and (3) linear discriminant analysis. Appendix 10A looks at credit scoring models used to evaluate mortgages and consumer loans. In this section we look at credit scoring models used to evaluate commercial and corporate loans.

Linear Probability Model and Logit Model The linear probability model uses past data, such as financial ratios, as inputs into a model to explain repayment experience on old loans. The relative importance of the factors used in explaining past repayment performance then forecasts repayment probabilities on new loans. That is, factors explaining past repayment performance can be used for assessing *p*, the probability of repayment discussed earlier in this chapter (a key input in setting the credit premium on a loan or determining the amount to be lent), and the probability of default (*PD*).

Briefly, we divide old loans (*i*) into two observational groups: those that defaulted ($PD_i = 1$) and those that did not default ($PD_i = 0$). Then we relate these observations by linear regression to a set of *j* causal variables (X_{ij}) that reflect quantitative information about the *i*th borrower, such as leverage or earnings. We estimate the model by linear regression of this form:

$$PD_i = \sum_{j=1}^{n} \beta_j X_{ij} + \text{error}$$

where β_j is the estimated importance of the *j*th variable (e.g., leverage) in explaining past repayment experience.

If we then take these estimated β_js and multiply them by the observed X_{ij} for a prospective borrower, we can derive an expected value of PD_i for the prospective borrower. That value can be interpreted as the probability of default for the borrower: $E(PD_i) = (1 - p_i)$ = Expected probability of default, where p_i is the probability of repayment on the loan.

EXAMPLE 10-2

Estimating the Probability of Repayment on a Loan Using Linear Probability Credit Scoring Models

Suppose there were two factors influencing the past default behaviour of borrowers: the leverage or debt–equity ratio (*D/E*)and the sales–asset ratio (*S/A*). Based on past default (repayment) experience, the linear probability model is estimated as

$$PD_i = 0.5(D/E_i) - 0.0525(S/A_i)$$

Assume a prospective borrower has a $D/E = 0.3$ and an $S/A = 2.0$. Its expected probability of default (PD_i) can then be estimated as

$$PD_i = 0.5(0.3) - 0.0525(2.0) = 0.045 \text{ or } 4.5\%$$

While this technique is straightforward as long as current information on the X_{ij} is available for the borrower, its major weakness is that the estimated probabilities of default can often lie outside the interval 0 to 1. The logit model overcomes this weakness by restricting the estimated range of default probabilities from the linear regression model to lie between 0 and 1. Essentially this is done by plugging the estimated value of PD_i from the linear probability model (in our example, $PD_i = 0.45$) into the following formula:

$$F(PD_i) = \frac{1}{1 + e^{-PD_i}}$$

where e is the exponential (equal to 2.718) and $F(PD_i)$ is the logistically transformed value of PD_i.

Linear Discriminant Models While linear probability and logit models project a value for the expected probability of default if a loan is made, discriminant models divide borrowers into high or low default risk classes contingent on their observed characteristics (X_j). Similar to these models, however, linear discriminant models use past data as inputs into a model to explain repayment experience on old loans. The relative importance of the factors used in explaining past repayment performance then forecasts whether the loan falls into the high or low default class.

Consider the discriminant analysis model developed by E. I. Altman for publicly traded manufacturing firms in the United States. The indicator variable Z is an overall measure of the default risk classification of a commercial borrower and is a default indicator, not a direct probability of default (PD) measure. The Z score in turn depends on the values of various financial ratios of the borrower (X_j) and the weighted importance of these ratios based on the past observed experience of defaulting versus nondefaulting borrowers derived from a discriminant analysis model.[7]

Altman's discriminant function (credit-classification model) takes the form

$$Z = 1.2X_1 + 1.4X_2 + 3.3X_3 + 0.6X_4 + 1.0X_5$$

where

X_1 = Working capital/total assets ratio, where working capital equals current assets minus current liabilities
X_2 = Retained earnings/total assets ratio
X_3 = Earnings before interest and taxes/total assets ratio
X_4 = Market value of equity/book value of long-term debt ratio
X_5 = Sales/total assets ratio

According to Altman's credit scoring model, any firm with a Z score of less than 1.81 should be considered a high default risk firm; between 1.81 and 2.99, an indeterminant default risk firm; and greater than 2.99, a low default risk firm.

[7] E. I. Altman, "Managing the Commercial Lending Process," in *Handbook of Banking Strategy,* R. C. Aspinwall and R. A. Eisenbeis, eds. (New York: John Wiley & Sons, 1985), pp. 473–510.

EXAMPLE 10-3

Calculation of Altman's Z Score

Suppose that the financial ratios of a potential borrowing firm took the following values:

$X_1 = 0.2$
$X_2 = 0$
$X_3 = -0.20$
$X_4 = 0.10$
$X_5 = 2.0$

The ratio X_2 is zero and X_3 is negative, indicating that the firm has had negative earnings or losses in recent periods. Also, X_4 indicates that the borrower is highly leveraged. However, the working capital ratio (X_1) and the sales/assets ratio (X_5) indicate that the firm is reasonably liquid and is maintaining its sales volume. The Z score provides an overall score or indicator of the borrower's credit risk since it combines and weights these five factors according to their past importance in explaining borrower default. For the borrower in question:

$$
\begin{aligned}
Z &= 1.2(0.2) + 1.4(0) + 3.3(-0.20) + 0.6(0.10) + 1.0(2.0) \\
&= 0.24 + 0 - 0.66 + 0.06 + 2.0 \\
&= 1.64
\end{aligned}
$$

With a Z score less than 1.81 (i.e., in the high default risk region), the FI should not make a loan to this borrower until it improves its earnings.

There are a number of problems in using the discriminant analysis model to make credit risk evaluations. Most of these criticisms also apply to the linear probability and logit models. The first problem is that these models usually discriminate only between two extreme cases of borrower behaviour: no default and default. As discussed in Chapter 7, in the real world, various gradations of default exist, from nonpayment or delay of interest payments (nonperforming assets) to outright default on all promised interest and principal payments. This problem suggests that a more accurate or finely calibrated sorting among borrowers may require defining more classes in the discriminant analysis model.

The second problem is that there is no obvious economic reason to expect that the weights in the discriminant function—or, more generally, the weights in any credit scoring model—will be constant over any but very short periods. The same concern also applies to the variables X_j. Specifically, because of changing real and financial market conditions, other borrower-specific financial ratios may come to be increasingly relevant in explaining default risk probabilities. Moreover, the linear discriminant model assumes that the X_j variables are independent of one another.

The third problem is that these models ignore important, hard-to-quantify factors that may play a crucial role in the default or no-default decision. For example, the reputation of the borrower and the nature of long-term borrower–lender relationships could be important borrower-specific characteristics, as could macrofactors such as the phase of the business cycle. These variables are often ignored in credit scoring models. Moreover, traditional credit scoring models rarely use publicly available information, such as the prices of outstanding public debt and equity of the borrower.

A fourth problem relates to default records kept by FIs. Currently, no centralized database on defaulted business loans for proprietary and other reasons exists. Some task forces set up by consortiums of commercial banks, insurance companies, and consulting firms are currently seeking to construct such databases largely in response to proposed reforms to bank capital requirements (see Chapter 20). However, it may well be many years before they are developed. This constrains the ability of many FIs to use traditional credit scoring models (and quantitative models in general) for larger business loans—although their use for smaller consumer loans, such as credit card loans, where much better centralized databases exist, is well established.

The newer credit risk models use *financial theory* and more widely available *financial market* data to make inferences about default probabilities on debt and loan instruments. Consequently, these models are most relevant in evaluating loans to larger borrowers in the corporate sector. This is the area in which a great deal of current research by FIs is taking place, as noted in Appendices 10A and 10B. Below we consider a number of these newer approaches or models of credit risk, including

1. Term structure of credit risk approach.
2. Mortality rate approach.
3. Risk-adjusted return on capital (RAROC) models.
4. Option models, including the KMV credit monitor model (also called *structural models* since they are based on an economic model of why firms default).

While some of these models focus on different aspects of credit risk, they are all linked by a strong reliance on modern financial theory and financial market data.[8]

CONCEPT QUESTIONS

1. **Suppose the estimated linear probability model looked like this: $Z = 0.3X_1 + 0.1X_2 +$ error, where**

   X_1 = Debt/equity ratio and X_2 = Total assets/working capital ratio

   Suppose, for a prospective borrower, $X_1 = 1.5$ and $X_2 = 3.0$. What is the projected probability of default for the borrower? (7.5%)
2. **Suppose $X_3 = 0.5$ in Example 10–3. Show how this would change the default risk classification of the borrower. ($Z = 3.95$)**
3. **What are two problems in using discriminant analysis to evaluate credit risk?**

NEWER MODELS OF CREDIT RISK MEASUREMENT AND PRICING

Term Structure Derivation of Credit Risk

standardandpoors.com

One market-based method of assessing credit risk exposure and default probabilities is to analyze the risk premiums inherent in the current structure of yields on corporate debt or loans to similar risk-rated borrowers. Rating agencies such as S&P categorize corporate bond issuers into at least seven major classes according

[8] For further details on these newer models, see A. Saunders and L. Allen, *Credit Risk Management: In and Out of the Financial Crisis,* 3rd ed. (John Wiley and Sons: New York, 2010).

FIGURE 10–6
Corporate and Government Discount Bond Yield Curves

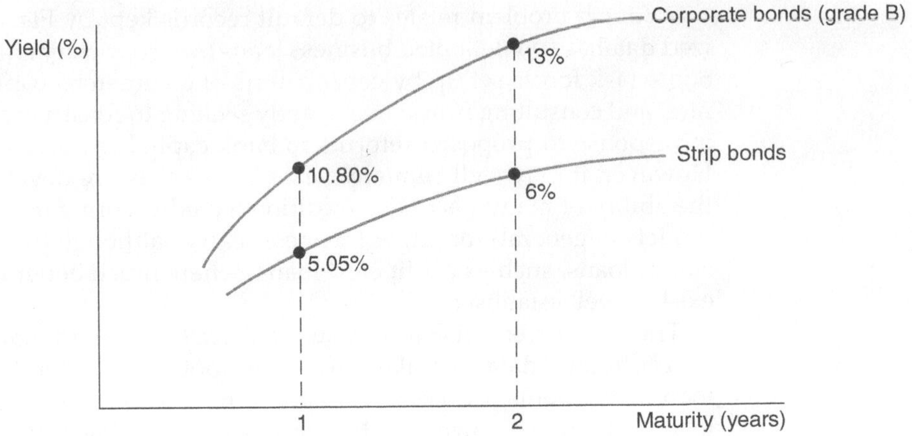

to perceived credit quality.[9] The first four quality ratings—AAA, AA, A, and BBB—indicate investment-quality borrowers. Non-investment-grade securities with ratings such as BB, B, and CCC are known as high-yield or junk bonds. Different quality ratings are reflected in the degree to which corporate bond yields exceed those implied by the strip bond (credit risk–free) yield curve.

strip bonds and zero-coupon corporate bonds
Bonds that are created or issued bearing no coupons and only a face value to be paid on maturity. As such, they are issued at a large discount from face value (also called "deep-discount bonds").

Look at the spreads shown in Figure 10–6 for zero-coupon corporate (grade B) bonds over similar maturity zero-coupon government debt (called *strip bonds*). Because **strip bonds** and **zero-coupon corporate bonds** are single-payment discount bonds, it is possible to extract required credit risk premiums and implied probabilities of default from actual market data on interest rates. That is, the spreads between risk-free discount bonds issued by the Government of Canada and discount bonds issued by corporate borrowers of differing quality reflect perceived credit risk exposures of corporate borrowers for single payments at different times in the future. FIs can use these credit risk probabilities on existing debt to decide whether or not to issue additional debt to a particular credit risk borrower. Note that in market-based models of assessing default risk, FIs use information on credit quality processed by rating agencies rather than by the FI itself. Thus, the use of market-based models abstracts the FI's role as an information processor. Rather, the unique role played by the FI is to process market-based information to assess default probabilities.

Next, we look at the simplest case of extracting an implied probability of default for an FI considering buying one-year bonds from or making one-year loans to a risky borrower. Then, we consider multiyear loans and bonds. In each case, we show that we can extract a market view of the credit risk—the expected probability of default—of an individual borrower.

Probability of Default on a One-Period Debt Instrument

Assume that the FI requires an expected return on a one-year (zero-coupon) corporate debt security equal to at least the risk-free return on one-year (zero-coupon) strip bonds. Let p be the probability that the corporate debt, both principal and interest, will be repaid in full; therefore, $1 - p$ is the probability of default. If the

[9] Rating agencies use many factors to assign a credit rating on a bond. For example, financial analysis is conducted of the issuer's operations, financing needs, position in the industry, financial strength, and ability to pay the interest and principal. Rating agencies analyze the issuer's liquidity, profitability, debt capacity, and corporate governance structure. Then for each particular issue, rating agencies evaluate the nature and provisions of the debt issue (e.g., covenants) and the protection afforded by, and relative position of, the debt issue in the event of bankruptcy or reorganization.

borrower defaults, the FI is (for now) assumed to get nothing (i.e., the recovery rate is zero or the loss given default is 100 percent).[10] By denoting the contractually promised return on the one-year corporate debt security as $1 + k$ and on the credit risk–free one-year strip security as $1 + i$, the FI manager would just be indifferent between corporate and strip securities when[11]

$$p(1 + k) = 1 + i$$

or the expected return on corporate securities is equal to the risk-free rate.

EXAMPLE 10–4

Calculating the Probability of Default on a One-Year Bond (Loan) Using Term Structure Derivation of Credit Risk

Suppose, as shown in Figure 10–6, the interest rates in the market for one-year zero-coupon government bonds and for one-year zero-coupon grade B corporate bonds are, respectively,

$$i = 5.05\%$$

and

$$k = 10.8\%$$

This implies that the probability of repayment on the security as perceived by the market is

$$p = \frac{1 + i}{1 + k} = \frac{1.0505}{1.1080} = 0.948$$

If the probability of repayment is 0.948, this implies a probability of default $(1 - p)$ equal to 0.052. Thus, in this simple one-period framework, a probability of default of 5.2 percent on the corporate bond (loan) requires the FI to set a risk premium (ϕ) of 5.75 percent:[12]

$$\phi = k - i = 5.75\%$$

Clearly, as the probability of repayment (p) falls and the probability of default $(1 - p)$ increases, the required spread, ϕ, between k and i increases.

This analysis can easily be extended to the more realistic case in which the FI does not expect to lose all interest and all principal if the corporate borrower defaults. Realistically, the FI lender can expect to receive some partial repayment even if the borrower goes into bankruptcy. For example, Altman estimated that when firms defaulted on their bonds in 2011, the investor lost on average 63.3 cents on the dollar (i.e., recovered around 36.7 cents on the dollar).[13] Table 10–5 gives recovery rates on defaulted debt by seniority from 1988 to 2010. As discussed earlier in this chapter, many loans and bonds are secured or collateralized by first liens on various pieces of property or real assets should a borrower default. Note that secured loans experienced the highest recovery rates among the corporate bonds listed.

[10] This is a key assumption. If the recovery rate is nonzero (which in reality is true, since in recent years banks have recovered on average up to 80 percent of a defaulted loan and 60 percent of a senior secured bond), then the spread between the corporate bond return and the strip bond return will reflect both the probability of default and the loss given default (LGD, equal to 1 minus the recovery rate). To disentangle the probability of default from the LGD, we need to make assumptions about the size of the LGD or the statistical process that either the PD or the LGD follows, such as the Poisson process.

[11] This assumes that the FI manager is not risk averse; that is, this is a risk-neutral valuation method and the probabilities so derived are called *risk-neutral probabilities*. In general, these will differ from probabilities estimated from historic data on defaults. See Saunders and Allen, *Credit Risk Management*, Chapter 5.

[12] A bank could partially capture this required spread in higher fees and compensating balances rather than only in the risk premium.

[13] E. I. Altman, Current Conditions and Outlook on Global Sovereign and Corporate Credit Markets, Working paper, New York University Salomon Center, February 2012.

TABLE 10–5
Recovery Rates (RR) on Defaulted Debt, 1988–2010

Source: E. I. Altman, Default Recovery Rates and LGD in Credit Risk Modeling and Practice, Working paper, New York University Salomon Center, January 2012.

Type of Debt	Recovery Rate	Number of Observations
Bank debt	82.24%	1,156
Revolving loans	85.63	1,034
Term loans	56.34	122
Senior secured bonds	62	320
Senior unsecured bonds	43.8	863
Senior subordinated bonds	30.5	489
Subordinated bonds	28.8	399

Let γ be the proportion of the loan's principal and interest that is collectible on default, where in general γ is positive. The FI manager would set the expected return on the loan to equal the risk-free rate in the following manner:

$$[(1 - p)\gamma(1 + k)] + [p(1 + k)] = 1 + i$$

The new term here is $(1 - p)\gamma(1 + k)$; this is the payoff the FI expects to get if the borrower defaults.

As might be expected, if the loan has collateral backing such that $\gamma > 0$, the required risk premium on the loan will be less for any given default risk probability $(1 - p)$. Collateral requirements are a method of controlling default risk; they act as a direct substitute for risk premiums in setting required loan rates. To see this, solve for the risk premium ϕ between k (the required yield on risky corporate debt) and i (the risk-free rate of interest):

$$k - i = \phi = \frac{(1 + i)}{(\gamma + p - p\gamma)} - (1 + i)$$

If $i = 5.05$ percent and $p = 0.948$ as before but the FI can expect to collect 90 percent of the promised proceeds if default occurs ($\gamma = 0.9$), then the required risk premium is $\phi = 0.55$ percent.

Interestingly, in this simple framework, γ and p are perfect substitutes for each other. That is, a bond or loan with collateral backing of $\gamma = 0.95$ and $p = 0.9$ would have the same required risk premium as one with $\gamma = 0.9$ and $p = 0.95$. An increase in collateral, γ, is a direct substitute for an increase in default risk (i.e., a decline in p).

Probability of Default on a Multiperiod Debt Instrument

We can extend this type of analysis to derive the credit risk or default probabilities occurring in the market for longer-term loans or bonds (e.g., two-year bonds). To do this, the manager must estimate the probability that the bond will default in the second year conditional on the probability that it does not default in the first year. The probability that a bond will default in any given year is clearly conditional on the fact that the default has not occurred earlier. The probability that a bond will default in any given year, t, is the **marginal default probability** for that year, $1 - p_t$. However, for, say, a two-year loan, the marginal probability of default in the second year $(1 - p_2)$ can differ from the marginal probability of default in the first year $(1 - p_1)$. If we use these marginal default probabilities, the **cumulative default probability** at some time between now and the end of year 2 is

marginal default probability
The probability that a borrower will default in any given year.

cumulative default probability
The probability that a borrower will default over a specified multiyear period.

$$C_p = 1 - [(p_1)(p_2)]$$

EXAMPLE 10-5

Calculating the Probability of Default on a Multiperiod Bond (Loan)

Suppose the FI manager wanted to find out the probability of default on a two-year loan. For the one-year loan, $1 - p_1 = 0.05$ is the marginal and total or cumulative probability (C_p) of default in year 1. Later in this chapter we discuss ways in which p_2 can be estimated by the FI manager, but for the moment suppose that $1 - p_2 = 0.07$. Then

$$1 - p_1 = 0.05 = \text{Marginal probability of default in year 1}$$
$$1 - p_2 = 0.07 = \text{Marginal probability of default in year 2}$$

The probability of the borrower surviving (not defaulting at any time between now (time 0) and the end of period 2) is $p_1 \times p_2 = (0.95)(0.93) = 0.8835$.

$$C_p = 1 - [(0.95)(0.93)] = 0.1165$$

There is an 11.65 percent probability of default over this period.

We have seen how to derive the one-year probability of default from yield spreads on one-year bonds. We now want to derive the probability of default in year 2, year 3, and so on. Refer back to Figure 10–6; as you can see, yield curves are rising for both government issues and corporate bond issues. We want to extract from these yield curves the *market's expectation* of the multiperiod default rates for corporate borrowers classified in the grade B rating class.[14]

Look first at the government yield curve. The condition of efficient markets and thus **no arbitrage** profits by investors requires that the return on buying and holding the two-year government discount bond to maturity just equals the expected return from investing in the current one-year discount government bond and reinvesting the principal and interest in a new one-year discount government bond at the end of the first year at the expected one-year **forward rate**. That is,

no arbitrage
The inability to make a profit without taking risk.

forward rate
A one-period rate of interest expected on a bond issued at some date in the future.

$$(1 + i_2)^2 = (1 + i_1)(1 + f_1) \tag{10.1}$$

The term on the left side is the return from holding the two-year discount bond to maturity. The term on the right side results from investing in two successive one-year bonds, where i_1 is the current one-year bond rate and f_1 is the expected one-year bond rate or forward rate next year. Since we can observe directly from the government bond yield curve the current required yields on one- and two-year government bonds, we can directly infer the market's expectation of the one-year government bond rate next period, or the one-year forward rate, f_1:

$$1 + f_1 = \frac{(1 + i_2)^2}{(1 + i_1)} \tag{10.2}$$

We can use the same type of analysis with the corporate bond yield curve to infer the one-year forward rate on corporate bonds (grade B in this example). The one-year rate expected on corporate securities (c_1) one year into the future reflects the

[14] To use this model, one has to place borrowers in a rating class. One way to do this for unrated firms is to use the *Z* score model to calculate a *Z* ratio for this firm. E. I. Altman has shown that there is a high correlation between *Z* scores and S&P and Moody's bond ratings. Once a firm is placed in a bond rating group (e.g., B) by the *Z* score model, the term structure model can be used to infer the expected (implied) probabilities of default for the borrower at different times in the future.

market's default risk expectations for this class of borrower as well as the more general time value factors also affecting f_1:

$$1 + c_1 = \frac{(1 + k_2)^2}{(1 + k_1)} \tag{10.3}$$

The expected rates on one-year bonds can generate an estimate of the expected probability of repayment on one-year corporate bonds in one year's time, or what we have called p_2. Since

$$p_2(1 + c_1) = 1 + f_1$$

then

$$p_2 = \left[\frac{1 + f_1}{1 + c_1}\right] \tag{10.4}$$

Thus, the expected probability of default in year 2 is

$$1 - p_2 \tag{10.5}$$

In a similar fashion, the one-year rates expected in two years' time can be derived from the strip bond and corporate term structures so as to derive p_3, and so on.

EXAMPLE 10–6

Calculating the Probability of Default on a Multiperiod Bond Using Term Structure Derivation of Credit Risk

From the government bond yield curve in Figure 10–6, the current required yields on one- and two-year strip bonds are i_1 = 5.05 percent and i_2 = 6 percent, respectively. If we use equation 10.2, the one-year forward rate, f_1, is given by

$$1 + f_1 = \frac{(1.06)^2}{1.0505} = 1.0696\%$$

or

$$f_1 = 6.96\%$$

The expected rise in one-year rates from 5.05 percent (i_1) this year to 6.96 percent (f_1) next year reflects investors' perceptions regarding inflation and other factors that directly affect the time value of money.

Further, the current yield curve in Figure 10–6 indicates that appropriate one-year discount bonds are yielding k_1 = 10.80 percent and two-year bonds are yielding k_2 = 13 percent. Thus, if we use equation 10.3, the one-year rate expected on corporate securities, c_1, is

$$1 + c_1 = \frac{(1.13)^2}{1.1080} = 1.1524$$

or

$$c_1 = 15.24\%$$

We summarize these calculations in Table 10–6. As you can see, the expected spread between one-year corporate bonds and government bonds in one year's time is higher than the spread for current one-year bonds. Thus, the default risk premium increases with the maturity on the corporate (risky) bond.

From these expected rates on one-year bonds, if we use equations 10.4 and 10.5, the expected probability of repayment on one-year corporate bonds in one year's time, p_2, is

$$p_1 = \frac{1.0696}{1.1524} = 0.9281$$

and the expected probability of default in year 2 is

$$1 - 0.9281 = 0.0719$$

or

$$7.19\%$$

TABLE 10–6
Government and Corporate Rates and Rate Spreads

	Current One-Year Rate	Expected One-Year Rate
Government	5.05%	6.96%
Corporate (B)	10.80	15.24
Spread	5.75	8.28

The probabilities we have estimated are marginal probabilities conditional on default not occurring in a prior period. We also discussed the concept of the *cumulative probability* of default that would tell the FI the probability of a loan or bond investment defaulting over a particular time period. In the example developed earlier, the cumulative probability that corporate grade B bonds would default over the next two years is

$$C_p = 1 - [(p_1)(p_2)]$$
$$C_p = 1 - [(0.948)(0.9281)] = 12.02\%$$

As with the credit scoring approach, this model creates some potential problems. Its principal advantages are that it is clearly forward looking and based on market expectations. Moreover, if there are liquid markets for government and corporate discount bonds—such as strip bonds and corporate zero-coupon bonds—then we can easily estimate expected future default rates and use them to value and price loans. However, while the market for strip bonds is now quite deep, the market for corporate discount bonds is quite small. Although a discount yield curve for corporate bonds could be extracted mathematically from the corporate bond coupon yield curve, these bonds are often not very actively traded and prices are not very transparent. Given this, the FI manager might have to consider an alternative way to use bond or loan data to extract default rate probabilities for all but the very largest corporate borrowers. We consider a possible alternative next.

CONCEPT QUESTIONS

1. **What is the difference between the marginal default probability and the cumulative default probability?**
2. **How should the posting of collateral by a borrower affect the risk premium on a loan?**

Mortality Rate Derivation of Credit Risk

mortality rate
The historic default rate experience of a bond or loan.

marginal mortality rate (MMR)
The probability of a bond or loan defaulting in any given year after issue.

Rather than extracting *expected* default rates from the current term structure of interest rates, the FI manager may analyze the *historic* or past default risk experience, the **mortality rates**, of bonds and loans of a similar quality. Consider calculating p_1 and p_2 using the mortality rate model. Here p_1 is the probability of a grade B bond or loan surviving the first year of its issue; thus $1 - p_1$ is the **marginal mortality rate (MMR)**, or the probability of the bond or loan defaulting in the first year of issue. While p_2 is the probability of the loan surviving in the second year given that default has not occurred during the first year, $1 - p_2$ is the MMR for the second year. Thus, for each grade of corporate borrower quality, an MMR curve can show the historical default rate experience of bonds in any specific quality class in each year after issue on the bond or loan.

Note in Figure 10–7 that as grade B bonds age, their probability of dying increases in each successive year. Of course, in reality, any shape to the mortality curve is possible. It is possible that MMRs can be flat, decline over time, or show

FIGURE 10–7
Hypothetical MMR Curve for Grade B Corporate Bonds

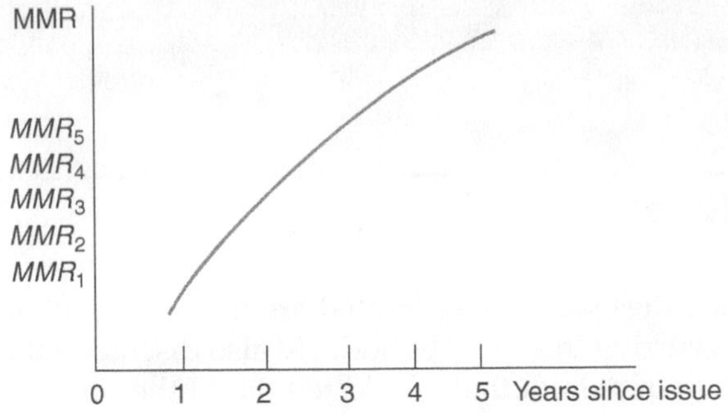

a more complex functional form. These MMRs can be estimated from actual data on bond and loan defaults. Specifically, for grade B quality bonds (loans):

$$MMR_1 = \frac{\text{Total value of grade B bonds defaulting in year 1 of issue}}{\text{Total value of grade B bonds outstanding in year 1 of issue}}$$

$$MMR_2 = \frac{\text{Total value of grade B bonds defaulting in year 2 of issue}}{\text{Total value of grade B bonds outstanding in year 2 of issue adjusted for defaults, calls, sinking fund redemptions, and maturities in the prior year}}$$

Table 10–7 shows the estimated mortality and cumulative default rates for samples of 2,644 rated corporate bonds over the 1971–2011 period. From Table 10–7 it can be seen that mortality rates are higher the lower the rating of the bond. For example, between 1971 and 2011, there was a 1.15 percent probability that A-rated bonds would default over the 10 years after issue and a 37.51 percent probability that B-rated bonds would default over the 10 years after issue.

TABLE 10–7 Mortality Rates by Original Rating—All Rated* Corporate Bonds, 1971–2011

		Years after Issuance									
		1	2	3	4	5	6	7	8	9	10
AAA	Marginal	0.00%	0.00%	0.00%	0.00%	0.02%	0.02%	0.01%	0.00%	0.00%	0.00%
	Cumulative	0.00%	0.00%	0.00%	0.00%	0.02%	0.04%	0.05%	0.05%	0.05%	0.05%
AA	Marginal	0.00%	0.00%	0.25%	0.11%	0.02%	0.02%	0.01%	0.01%	0.03%	0.01%
	Cumulative	0.00%	0.00%	0.25%	0.36%	0.38%	0.40%	0.41%	0.42%	0.45%	0.46%
A	Marginal	0.01%	0.06%	0.16%	0.17%	0.14%	0.10%	0.04%	0.30%	0.11%	0.07%
	Cumulative	0.01%	0.07%	0.23%	0.40%	0.54%	0.64%	0.68%	0.98%	1.09%	1.15%
BBB	Marginal	0.38%	2.49%	1.37%	1.05%	0.58%	0.27%	0.30%	0.17%	0.16%	0.36%
	Cumulative	0.38%	2.86%	4.19%	5.20%	5.75%	6.00%	6.28%	6.44%	6.59%	6.93%
BB	Marginal	1.01%	2.07%	3.95%	2.00%	2.42%	1.47%	1.51%	1.10%	1.50%	3.20%
	Cumulative	1.01%	3.06%	6.89%	8.75%	10.96%	12.27%	13.59%	14.54%	15.82%	18.52%
B	Marginal	2.96%	7.86%	7.95%	7.93%	5.84%	4.58%	3.66%	2.15%	1.83%	0.82%
	Cumulative	2.96%	10.59%	17.70%	24.22%	28.65%	31.92%	34.41%	35.82%	36.99%	37.51%
CCC	Marginal	8.30%	12.65%	18.28%	16.35%	4.82%	11.78%	5.45%	4.95%	0.70%	4.41%
	Cumulative	8.30%	19.90%	34.54%	45.24%	47.88%	54.02%	56.53%	58.68%	58.97%	60.78%

*Rated by S&P at issuance. Based on 2,644 issues.

Source: E. I. Altman and B. J. Kuehne, Special Report on Default and Returns in the High-Yield Bond and Distressed Debt Market: The Year 2011 in Review and Outlook, Working paper, New York University Salomon Center, February 2012.

The mortality rate approach has a number of conceptual and applicability problems. Probably the most important of these is that, like the credit scoring model, it produces historic, or backward-looking, measures. Also, the estimates of default rates and therefore implied future default probabilities tend to be highly sensitive to the period over which the FI manager calculates the MMRs. For example, WorldCom had an S&P rating of BBB just prior to its defaulting on its debt in 2002. Note in Table 10–7 the second year's marginal mortality rate for BBB bonds (2.49 percent) is much higher than those of years 3 and 4 (1.37 and 1.05 percent, respectively) and is even higher than that of the second-year mortality rate for BB bonds (2.07 percent). This is primarily due to the default of WorldCom in 2002. In addition, the estimates tend to be sensitive to the number of issues and the relative size of issues in each investment grade.[15]

CONCEPT QUESTIONS

1. **In Table 10–7, the cumulative mortality rate over three years for CCC-rated corporate bonds is 34.54 percent. Check this calculation using the individual-year MMRs.**
2. **Why would any FI manager buy loans that have a cumulative mortality rate of 34.54 percent? Explain your answer.**

RAROC Models

RAROC
Risk-adjusted return on capital.

A popular model used to evaluate (and price) credit risk based on market data is the RAROC model. The **RAROC** (risk-adjusted return on capital) was pioneered by Bankers Trust (acquired by Deutsche Bank in 1998) and has now been adopted by some Canadian banks and virtually all the large banks in the United States and Europe, although with some significant proprietary differences between them.

The essential idea behind RAROC is that rather than evaluating the actual or contractually promised annual ROA on a loan, (that is, net interest and fees divided by the amount lent), the lending officer balances expected interest and fee income less the cost of funds against the loan's expected risk. Thus, the numerator of the RAROC equation is net income (accounting for the cost of funding the loan) on the loan. Further, rather than dividing annual loan income by assets lent, it is divided by some measure of asset (loan) risk or what is often called *capital at risk*, since (unexpected) loan losses have to be written off against an FI's capital:[16]

$$RAROC = \frac{\text{One-year net income on a loan}}{\text{Change in loan's market value}}$$

A loan is approved only if RAROC is sufficiently high relative to a benchmark return on capital (ROE) for the FI, where ROE measures the return stockholders require on their equity investment in the FI. The idea here is that a loan should be made only if the risk-adjusted return on the loan adds to the FI's equity value as measured by the ROE required by the FI's stockholders. Thus, for example, if an FI's ROE is 10 percent, a loan should be made only if the estimated RAROC is higher than the 10 percent required by the FI's stockholders as a reward for their investment in the FI. Alternatively, if the RAROC on an existing loan falls below

[15] For example, even though the estimates in Table 10–7 are based on 2,644 observations of bonds, these estimates still have quite wide confidence bands. See Saunders and Allen, *Credit Risk Measurement*.

[16] Traditionally, expected loan losses are covered by a bank's loss reserve (or provisions), while unexpected or extreme loan losses are met by a bank's capital reserves.

an FI's RAROC benchmark, the lending officer should seek to adjust the loan's terms to make it "profitable" again. Therefore, RAROC serves as both a credit risk measure and a loan-pricing tool for the FI manager.

The numerator of the RAROC equation is relatively straightforward to estimate. Specifically,

$$\text{One-year net income on loan} = (\text{Spread} + \text{Fees}) \times \text{Dollar value of the loan outstanding}$$

FIs may deduct any overhead and tax expenses as well to get the one-year net income on the loan. However, a more difficult problem in estimating RAROC is the measurement of loan risk (the denominator in the RAROC equation). Two methods of estimating loan risk involve the use of a duration model and the use of loan default rates.

Using Duration to Estimate Loan Risk

Chapter 9, on duration, showed that the percentage change in the market value of an asset such as a loan ($\Delta LN/LN$) is related to the duration of the loan and the size of the interest rate shock ($\Delta R/(1 + R)$), where R is the base rate, BR, plus the credit risk premium, ϕ:

$$\frac{\Delta LN}{LN} = -D_{LN}\frac{\Delta R}{1 + R}$$

The same concept is applied here, except that (assuming that the base rate remains constant) interest rate shocks are the consequence of credit quality (or credit risk premium) shocks (i.e., shocks to ϕ). We can thus rewrite the duration equation with the following interpretation to estimate the loan risk or capital at risk on the loan:

$$\Delta LN = -D_{LN} \times LN \times (\Delta R/(1 + R))$$

ΔLN	$=$	$-D_{LN}$	$\times$	LN	$\times$	$(\Delta R/(1 + R))$
(change in loan's market value)		(duration of the loan)		(risk amount or size of loan)		(expected maximum change in the loan rate due to a change in the credit premium (ϕ) or risk factor on the loan)

EXAMPLE 10-7

Calculation of RAROC on a Loan

Suppose an FI wants to evaluate the credit risk of a \$1 million loan with a duration of 2.7 years to a AAA borrower. Assume there are currently 400 publicly traded bonds in that class (i.e., bonds issued by firms of a rating type similar to that of the borrower). The first step is to evaluate the actual changes in the credit risk premiums ($R_i - R_G$) on each of these bonds for the past year (in this example, the year 2015). These (hypothetical) changes are plotted in the frequency curve of Figure 10–8. They range from a fall in the risk premiums of 2 percent to an increase of 3.5 percent. Since the largest increase may be a very extreme (unrepresentative) number, the 99 percent worst-case scenario is chosen (i.e., only 4 bonds out of 400 had risk premium increases exceeding the 99 percent worst case). For the example shown in Figure 10–8, this is equal to 1.1 percent.

The estimate of loan (or capital) risk, assuming that the current average level of rates (R) on AAA bonds is 5 percent, is

FIGURE 10–8
Hypothetical Frequency Distribution of Yield Spread Changes for All AAA Bonds in 2012

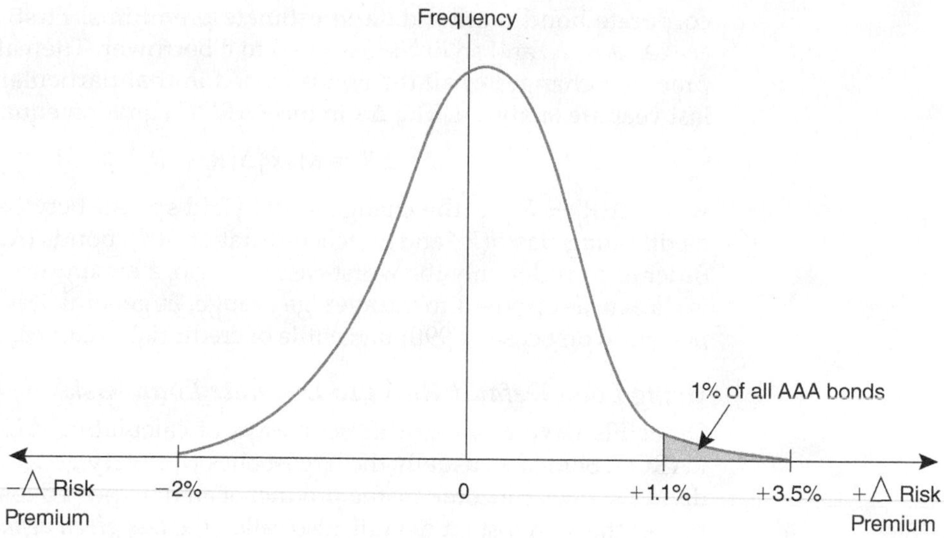

$$\Delta LN = -D_{LN} \times LN \times \frac{\Delta R}{1+R}$$

$$= -(2.7)(\$1 \text{ million})(0.011/1.05)$$

$$= -\$28,286$$

Thus, while the face value of the loan amount is \$1 million, the risk amount, or change in the loan's market value due to a decline in its credit quality, is \$28,826.

To determine whether the loan is worth making, the estimated loan risk is compared with the loan's income (spread over the FI's cost of funds plus fees on the loan). Suppose the projected (one-year) spread plus fees is as follows:

$$\text{Spread} = 0.2\% \times \$1 \text{ million} = \$2,000$$

$$\text{Fees} = 0.1\% \times \$1 \text{ million} = \underline{\$1,000}$$

$$\$3,000$$

The loan's RAROC is

$$RAROC = \frac{\text{One-year net income on loan}}{\text{Loan risk (or capital risk) } (\Delta LN)} = \frac{\$3,000}{\$28,286} = 10.61\%$$

Note that RAROC can be either forward looking, comparing the projected income over the next year on the loan with ΔLN, or backward looking, comparing the actual income generated on the loan over the past year with ΔLN. If the 10.61 percent exceeds the FI's internal RAROC benchmark (based on its cost of capital, or ROE), the loan will be approved. If it is less, the loan will be rejected outright or the borrower will be asked to pay higher fees and/or a higher spread to increase the RAROC to acceptable levels.

While the loan's duration (2.7 years in our example) and the loan amount (\$1 million) are easily estimated, it is more difficult to estimate the maximum change in the credit risk premium on the loan over the next year. Since publicly available data on loan risk premiums are scarce, we turn to publicly available corporate bond market data to estimate premiums. First, an S&P credit rating (AAA, AA, A, and so on) is assigned to a borrower. Thereafter, the available risk premium changes of all the bonds traded in that particular rating class over the last year are analyzed. The ΔR in the RAROC equation equals

$$\Delta R = \text{Max}\,[\Delta(R_i - R_G) > 0]$$

where $\Delta(R_i - R_G)$ is the change in the yield spread between corporate bonds of credit rating class $i(R_i)$ and matched-duration strip bonds (R_G) over the last year. In order to consider only the worst-case scenario, a maximum change in yield spread is chosen, as opposed to the average change. In general, it is common to pick the 1 percent worst case or 99th percentile of credit risk changes.

Using Loan Default Rates to Estimate Loan Risk

Other FIs have adopted different ways of calculating ΔLN in their versions of RAROC. Some FIs, usually the largest ones with very good loan default databases, divide one-year income by the product of an unexpected loss rate and the proportion of the loan lost on default, also called the *loss given default (LGD)*. Thus,

$$RAROC = \frac{\text{One-year net income per dollar loaned}}{\text{Unexpected default rate} \times \text{Proportion of loan lost on default (LGD)}}$$

Suppose expected income per dollar lent is 0.3 cents, or 0.003. The 99th percentile historic (extreme case) default rate for borrowers of this type is 4 percent, and the dollar proportion of loans of this type that cannot be recaptured is 80 percent. Then[17]

$$RAROC = \frac{0.003}{(0.04)(0.8)} = \frac{0.003}{(0.032)} = 9.375\%$$

CONCEPT QUESTION

Describe the basic concept behind RAROC models.

Option Models of Default Risk

Theoretical Framework

Following the pioneering work of Nobel Prize winners Merton, Black, and Scholes, we now recognize that when a firm raises funds by issuing bonds or increasing its bank loans, it holds a very valuable default or repayment option.[18] That is, if a borrower's investment projects fail so that it cannot repay the bondholder or

[17] Calculating the unexpected default rate commonly involves calculating the standard derivation (σ) of annual default rates on loans of this type and then multiplying σ by a factor such that 99 percent (or higher) of defaults are covered by capital. For example, if the loss distribution was normally distributed, then the σ of default rates would be multiplied by 2.33 to get the extreme 99 percent default rate. For many FIs, default rates are skewed and have fat tails, suggesting a multiplier much larger than 2.33. For example, to get coverage of 99.97 percent of defaults, Bank of America has historically used a multiplier of 6. Finally, the denominator can also be adjusted for the degree of correlation of the loan with the rest of the FI's portfolio. See, for example, Edward Zaik et al., "RAROC at Bank of America: From Theory to Practice," *Journal of Applied Corporate Finance,* Summer 1996, pp. 83–93.

[18] R. C. Merton, "On the Pricing of Corporate Debt: The Risk Structure of Interest Rates," *Journal of Finance* 29 (1974), pp. 449–470; and F. Black and M. Scholes, "The Pricing of Options and Corporate Liabilities," *Journal of Political Economy* 81 (1973), pp. 637–659.

the bank, it has the option of defaulting on its debt repayment and turning any remaining assets over to the debt holder. Because of limited liability for equity holders, the borrower's loss is limited on the downside by the amount of equity invested in the firm. On the other hand, if things go well, the borrower can keep most of the upside returns on asset investments after the promised principal and interest on the debt have been paid. The KMV Corporation (which was purchased by Moody's in 2002 and is now part of Moody's Analytics Enterprise Risk Solutions) turned this relatively simple idea into a credit monitoring model. Many of the largest FIs are now using this model to determine the expected default risk frequency (EDF) of large corporations.[19] Before we look at the Moody's Analytics Credit Monitor model, we will take a closer look at the theory underlying the option approach to default risk estimation. Appendix 10B reviews the Black–Scholes option pricing model.

moodysanalytics.com

The Borrower's Payoff from Loans

Look at the payoff function for the borrower in Figure 10–9, where S is the size of the initial equity investment in the firm, B is the value of outstanding bonds or loans (assumed for simplicity to be issued on a discount basis), and A is the market value of the assets of the firm.

If the investments in Figure 10–9 turn out badly such that the firm's assets are valued at point A_1, the limited-liability stockholders–owners of the firm will default on the firm's debt, turn its assets (such as A_1) over to the debt holders, and lose only their initial stake in the firm (S). By contrast, if the firm does well and the assets of the firm are valued highly (A_2), the firm's stockholders will pay off the firm's debt and keep the difference ($A_2 - B$). Clearly, the higher A_2 is relative to B, the better off are the firm's stockholders. Given that borrowers face only a limited downside risk of loss of their equity investment but a very large potential upside return if things turn out well, equity is analogous to buying a call option on the assets of the firm (see also Chapter 23 on options).

FIGURE 10–9
Payoff Function to Corporate Borrowers (Stockholders)

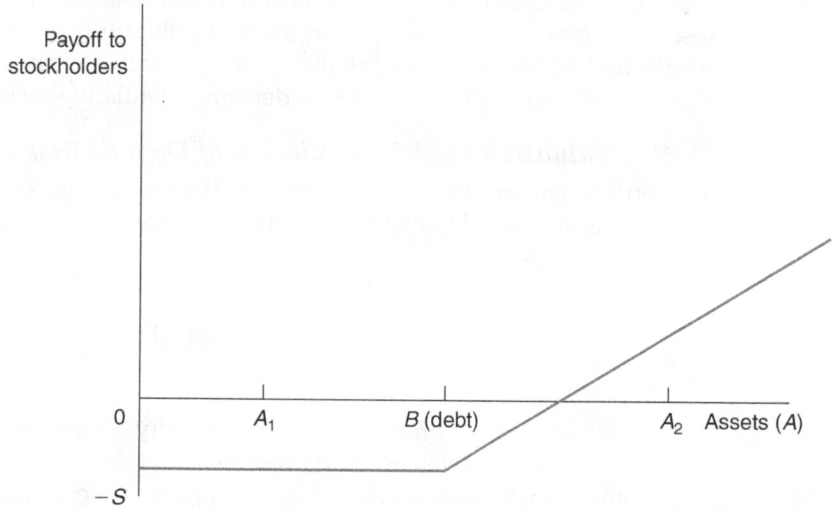

[19] See *KMV Corporation Credit Monitor,* KMV Corporation, San Francisco, 1994; and Saunders and Allen, *Credit Risk Measurement,* Chapter 4.

FIGURE 10–10
Payoff Function to the Debt Holder (the FI) from a Loan

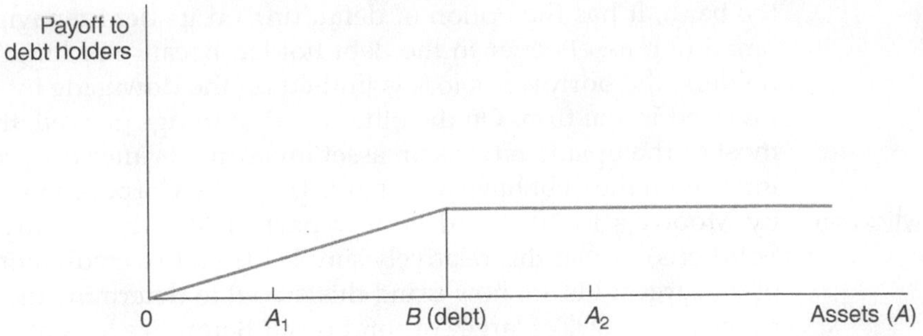

The Debt Holder's Payoff from Loans

Consider the same loan or bond issue from the perspective of the FI or bondholder. The maximum amount the FI or bondholder can get back is B, the promised payment. However, the borrower who possesses the default or repayment option would rationally repay the loan only if $A > B$, that is, if the market value of assets exceeds the value of promised debt repayments. A borrower whose asset value falls below B would default and turn over any remaining assets to the debt holders. The payoff function to the debt holder is shown in Figure 10–10.

After investment of the borrowed funds has taken place, if the value of the firm's assets lies to the right of B—such as A_2—the debt holder or FI will be paid off in full and receive B, the face value of the debt. On the other hand, if asset values fall in the region to the left of B—such as A_1—the debt holder will receive back only those assets remaining as collateral, thereby losing $B - A_1$. Thus, the value of the loan from the perspective of the lender is always the minimum of B and A, or min $[B, A]$. That is, the payoff function to the debt holder is similar to writing a put option on the value of the borrower's assets with B, the face value of debt, as the *exercise price*. If $A > B$, the loan is repaid and the debt holder earns a small fixed return (similar to the premium on a put option), which is the interest rate implicit in the discount bond. If $A < B$, the borrower defaults and the debt holder stands to lose both interest and principal. In the limit, default for a firm with no assets left results in debt holders' losing all their principal and interest. In actuality, if there are also costs of bankruptcy, the debt holder can potentially lose even more than this.

Option Valuation Model Calculation of Default Risk Premiums

Merton has shown that in the context of the preceding options framework, it is quite straightforward to express the market value of a risky loan made by a lender to a borrower as[20]

$$F(\tau) = Be^{-i\tau}[(1/d)N(h_1) + N(h_2)] \tag{10.6}$$

where

τ = Length of time remaining to loan maturity; that is, $\tau = T - t$, where T is the maturity date and time t is today.

d = Borrower's leverage ratio measured as $Be^{-i\tau}/A$, where the market value of debt is valued at the rate i, the risk-free rate of interest.

[20] See Merton, "On the Pricing of Corporate Debt."

$N(h)$ = Value computed from the standardized normal distribution statistical tables. This value reflects the probability that a deviation exceeding the calculated value of h will occur.

$$h_1 = -\left[\frac{1}{2}\sigma^2\tau - \ln(d)\right]/\sigma\sqrt{\tau}$$

$$h_2 = -\left[\frac{1}{2}\sigma^2\tau + \ln(d)\right]/\sigma\sqrt{\tau}$$

σ^2 = Measures the asset risk of the borrower. Technically, it is the variance of the rate of change in the value of the underlying assets of the borrower.

More important, written in terms of a yield spread, this equation reflects an equilibrium default risk premium that the borrower should be charged:

$$k(\tau) - i = (-1/\tau)\ln[N(h_2) + (1/d)N(h_1)]$$

where

$k(\tau)$ = Required yield on risky debt (the contractually promised return from earlier)
ln = Natural logarithm
i = Risk-free rate on debt of equivalent maturity (here, one period)

Thus, Merton has shown that the lender should adjust the required risk premium as d and σ^2 change, that is, as leverage and asset risk change.

EXAMPLE 10-8

Calculating the Value of and Interest Rate on a Loan Using the Option Model

Suppose that

B = \$100,000
τ = 1 year
i = 5 percent
d = 90% or 0.9
σ = 12%

That is, suppose we can measure the market value of a firm's assets (and thus $d = Be-^{i\tau}/A$) as well as the volatility of those assets (σ). Then, substituting these values into the equations for h_1 and h_2 and solving for the areas under the standardized normal distribution, we find that

$$N(h_1) = 0.174120$$
$$N(h_2) = 0.793323$$

where

$$h_1 = -[1/2(0.12)^2(1) - \ln(0.9)]/0.12 = -0.938$$

and

$$h_2 = -[1/2(0.12)^2(1) + \ln(0.9)]/0.12 = +0.818$$

The current market value of the loan is

$$L(t) = Be^{-i\tau}[N(h_2) + (1/d)N(h_1)]$$
$$= \frac{\$100{,}000}{1.05127}[0.793323 + (1.1111)(0.17412)]$$
$$= \frac{\$100{,}000}{1.05127}[0.986788]$$
$$= \$93{,}866$$

and the required risk spread or premium is

$$k(\tau) - i = \left(\frac{-1}{\tau}\right) \ln\,[N(h_2) + (1/d)N(h_1)]$$
$$= (-1)\ln\,[0.986788]$$
$$= 1.33\%$$

Thus, the risky loan rate $k(\tau)$ should be set at 6.33 percent when the risk-free rate (i) is 5 percent.

Theoretically, this model is an elegant tool for extracting premiums and default probabilities; it also has important conceptual implications regarding which variables to focus on in credit risk evaluation [e.g., the firm's market value of assets (A) and asset risk (σ^2)]. Even so, this model has a number of real-world implementation problems. Probably the most significant is the fact that neither the market value of a firm's assets (A) nor the volatility of the firm's assets (σ^2) is directly observed.

Moody's Analytics Option Model and Expected Default Frequency

moodysanalytics.com

The Moody's Analytics model in fact recognizes this problem by using an option pricing model (OPM) approach to extract the implied market value of assets (A) and the asset volatility of a given firm's assets (σ^2). The Moody's Analytics model uses the value of equity in a firm (from a stockholder's perspective) as equivalent to holding a call option on the assets of the firm (with the amount of debt borrowed acting similarly to the exercise price of the call option). From this approach, and the link between the volatility of the market value of the firm's equity and that of its assets, it is possible to derive the asset volatility (risk) of any given firm (σ) and the market value of the firm's assets (A).[21] Using the implied value of σ for assets and A, the market value of assets, the likely distribution of possible asset values of the firm relative to its current debt obligations can be calculated over the next year. As shown in Figure 10–11, the expected default frequency (EDF) that is calculated reflects the probability that the market value of the firm's assets (A) will fall below the promised repayments on its short-term debt liabilities (B) in one year. If the value of a firm's assets falls below its debt liabilities, it can be viewed as being economically insolvent.

Suppose the value of the firm's assets (A) at time zero is \$100 million and the value of its short-term debt is \$80 million. Suppose that the implied volatility (σ) of asset values is estimated at \$12.12 million, and it is assumed that asset-value changes are normally distributed. The firm becomes distressed only if the value of its assets falls to \$80 million or below (falls by \$20 million). Such a fall is equal to 1.65σ, i.e., $1.65 \times \$12.12$ million = \$20 million. From statistics, we know that the

---

[21] More specifically, it does this by using the equity (stock market) value of the firm's shares (E) and the volatility of the value of the firm's shares (σ_E). Since equity can be viewed as a call option on the firm's assets, and the volatility of a firm's equity value will reflect the leverage-adjusted volatility of its underlying assets, we have in general form

$$\bar{E} = f(A, \sigma, \bar{B}, \bar{r}, \bar{\tau})$$

and

$$\bar{\sigma}_E = g(\sigma)$$

where the bars denote values that are directly measurable. Since we have two equations and two unknowns (A, σ), we can directly solve for both A and σ and use these, along with the firm's outstanding short-term liabilities or current liabilities, to calculate the EDF (expected default frequency).

FIGURE 10–11
EDF Using the Moody's Analytics Model

Source: *KMV Corporation Credit Monitor.* Reprinted by permission of Moody's Analytics Corporation, moodysanalytics.com.

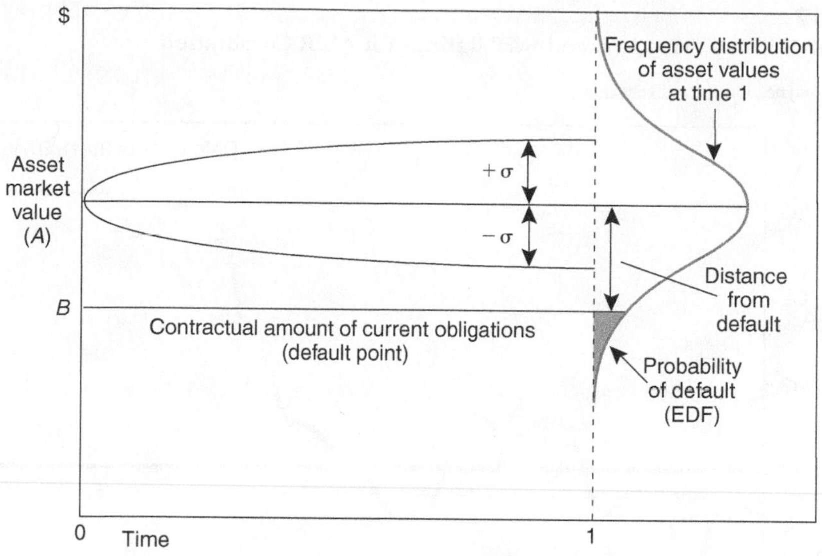

area of the normal distribution (in each tail) lying $\pm 1.65\sigma$ from the mean is theoretically 5 percent. Thus, the Moody's Analytics model would suggest a theoretical 5 percent probability of the firm's going into distress over the next year (by time 1). However, Moody's Anlytics calculates empirical EDFs, since we do not know the true distribution of asset values (A) over time. Essentially, it asks this question: In practice, how many firms that started the year with asset values 1.65σ distance from default (see Figure 10–11) actually defaulted at the end of the year? This value may or may not equal 5 percent.

Simulations by Moody's Analytics have shown that EDF models outperform both *Z* score–type models and S&P rating changes as predictors of corporate failure and distress.[22]

An example for AMR Corp., which filed for Chapter 11 bankruptcy protection in the United States on November 29, 2011, is shown in Figure 10–12. Note that the Moody's Analytics EDF score is rising faster than the rating agencies are downgrading the firm's debt. Indeed, the rating agency ratings are very slow to react to, if not totally insensitive to, the increase in AMR Corp.'s risk. The Moody's Analytics EDF score starts to rise almost a year prior to AMR Corp.'s bankruptcy and suggests a C rating by July 2011. Thus, the Moody's Analytics EDF score gives a better early warning of impending default. Credit rating firms have been under scrutiny from global regulators for their role in rating securitizations in 2007–2008. We discuss this issue further in Chapter 26.

CONCEPT QUESTIONS

1. **Which is the only credit risk model discussed in this section that is really forward looking?**
2. **How should the risk premium on a loan be affected if there is a reduction in a borrower's leverage and the underlying volatility of its earnings?**
3. **What is the link between the implied volatility of a firm's assets and its EDF?**

[22] Moody's Analytics database contains 30 years of information on over 6,000 public and 220,000 private company default events for a total of 60,000 public and 2.8 million private companies, healthy and distressed, around the world.

FIGURE 10–12
Moody's Analytics EDF, Moody's, and S&P Ratings for AMR Corporation

Source: Moody's Analytics, moodysanalytics.com.

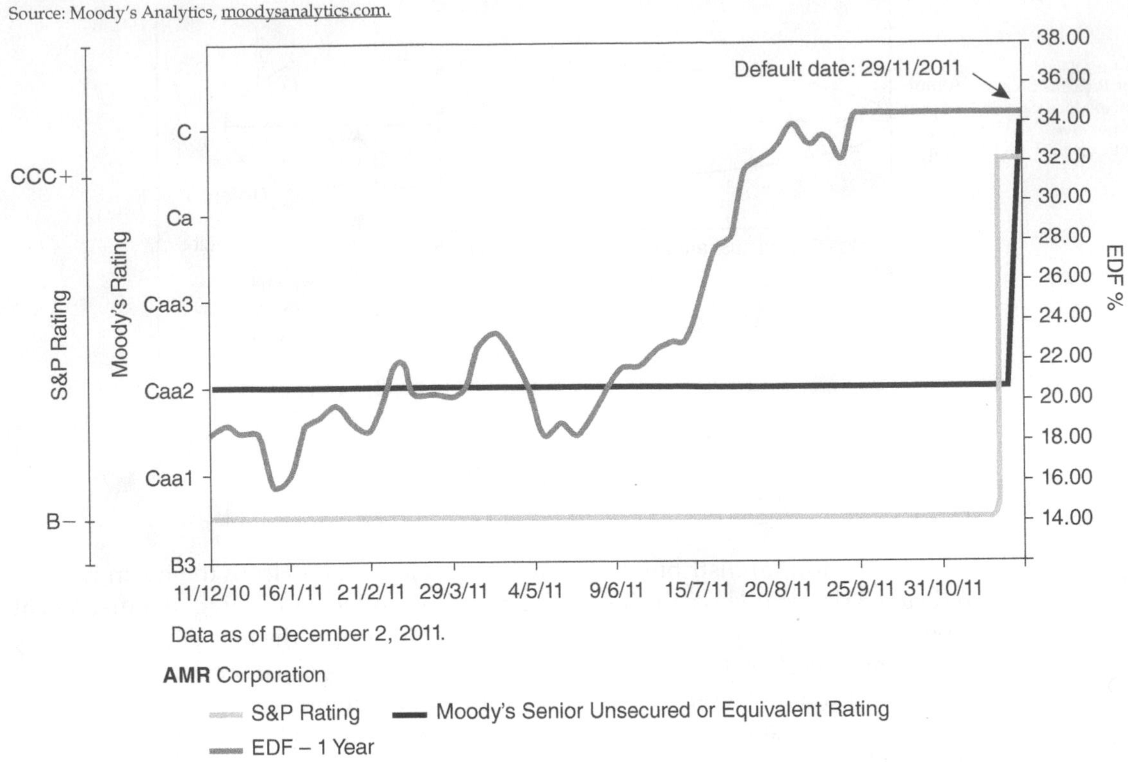

Questions and Problems

1. Why is credit risk analysis an important component of an FI's risk management? What recent activities by FIs have made the task of credit risk assessment more difficult for both FI managers and regulators?
2. Differentiate between a secured loan and an unsecured loan. Who bears most of the risk in a fixed-rate loan? Why would FI managers prefer to charge floating rates, especially for longer-maturity loans?
3. How does a spot loan differ from a loan commitment? What are the advantages and disadvantages of borrowing through a loan commitment?
4. Why is commercial and corporate lending declining in importance in Canada and the United States? What effect did this decline have on overall business lending activities?
5. What are the primary characteristics of residential mortgage loans? Why does the ratio of variable-rate mortgages to fixed-rate mortgages in the economy vary over the interest rate cycle? When would the ratio be highest?
6. What are the two major classes of consumer loans at Canadian banks? How do revolving loans differ from nonrevolving loans?
7. Why are rates on credit cards generally higher than rates on car loans?
8. What are compensating balances? What is the relationship between the amount of compensating balance requirement and the return on the loan to the FI?
9. Suppose that the bank does the following:
   - Sets a loan rate on a prospective loan at 8 percent (where BR = 5% and $\phi = 3\%$).

- Charges a 1/10 percent (or 0.10 percent) loan origination fee to the borrower.
- Imposes a 5 percent compensating balance requirement to be held as non-interest-bearing demand deposits.

Calculate the bank's ROA on this loan.

10. Canada Bank offers one-year loans with a stated rate of 9 percent but requires a compensating balance of 10 percent. What is the true cost of this loan to the borrower? How does the cost change if the compensating balance is 15 percent? If the compensating balance is 20 percent?
11. West Coast Bank offers one-year loans with a 9 percent stated or base rate, charges a 0.25 percent loan origination fee, and imposes a 10 percent compensating balance requirement and must pay a 6% reserve requirement. The loans are typically repaid at maturity.
    a. If the risk premium for a given customer is 2.5 percent, what is the simple promised interest return on the loan?
    b. What is the contractually promised gross return on the loan per dollar lent?
    c. Which of the fee items has the greatest impact on the gross return?
12. Why are most consumer loans charged the same rate of interest, implying the same risk premium or class? What is credit rationing? How is it used to control credit risks with respect to loans?
13. Why could a lender's expected return be lower when the risk premium is increased on a loan? In addition to the risk premium, how can a lender increase the expected return on a commercial or corporate loan? A consumer loan?
14. What are covenants in a loan agreement? What are the objectives of covenants? How can these covenants be negative? Positive?
15. Identify and define the borrower-specific and market-specific factors that enter into the credit decision. What is the impact of each type of factor on the risk premium?
    a. Which of these factors is more likely to adversely affect small businesses rather than large businesses in the credit assessment process by lenders?
    b. How does the existence of a high debt ratio typically affect the risk of the borrower?
    c. Why is the volatility of the earnings stream of a borrower important to a lender?
16. Why is the degree of collateral as specified in the loan agreement of importance to the lender? If the book value of the collateral is greater than or equal to the amount of the loan, is the credit risk of the lender fully covered? Why or why not?
17. Why are FIs consistently interested in the expected level of economic activity in the markets in which they operate? Why is the monetary policy of the Bank of Canada important to FIs?
18. What are the purposes of credit scoring models? How do these models assist an FI manager in better administering credit?
19. Suppose there were two factors influencing the past default behaviour of borrowers: the leverage or debt–assets ratio (D/A) and the profit margin ratio (PM). Based on past default (repayment) experience, the linear probability model is estimated as

$$PD_i = 0.105(D/A_i) - 0.35(PM_i)$$

    Prospective borrower A has a $D/A = 0.65$ and a $PM = 5\%$ and prospective borrower B has a $D/A = 0.45$ and a $PM = 1\%$. Calculate the prospective borrowers' expected probabilities of default (PD_i). Which borrower is the better loan candidate? Explain your answer.
20. Suppose the estimated linear probability model is $PD = 0.03X_1 + 0.02X_2 - 0.05X_3 + \text{error}$, where X_1 is the borrower's debt–equity ratio, X_2 is the volatility of the borrower earnings, and X_3 is the borrower's profit ratio. For a particular loan applicant, $X_1 = 0.75$, $X_2 = 0.25$, and $X_3 = 0.10$.
    a. What is the projected probability of default for the borrower?
    b. What is the projected probability of repayment if the debt–equity ratio is 2.5?
    c. What is a major weakness of the linear probability model?
21. Describe how a linear discriminant analysis model works. Identify and discuss the criticisms that have been made regarding the use of this type of model to make credit risk evaluations.
22. Suppose that the financial ratios of a potential borrowing firm take the following values:
    - Working capital/total assets ratio (X_1) = 0.75
    - Retained earnings/total assets ratio (X_2) = 0.10
    - Earnings before interest and taxes/total assets ratio (X_3) = 0.05
    - Market value of equity/book value of long-term debt ratio (X_4) = 0.10
    - Sales/total assets ratio (X_5) = 0.65

    Calculate the Altman Z-score for the borrower in question. How is this number a sign of the borrower's default risk?

23. MNO Inc., a publicly traded manufacturing firm, has provided the following financial information in its application for a loan. All numbers are in thousands of dollars:

Assets	
Cash	$ 20
Accounts receivable	90
Inventory	90
Plant and equipment	500
Total assets	$ 700
Liabilities and Equity	
Accounts payable	$ 30
Notes payable	90
Accruals	30
Long-term debt	150
Equity (retained earnings = $22)	400
Total liabilities and equity	$700

Also assume sales = $500,000, cost of goods sold = $360,000, taxes = $56,000, interest payments = $40,000, dividend payout ratio = 50 percent, and the market value of equity is equal to the book value.

a. What is the Altman discriminant function value for MNO Inc.? Recall that

Net working capital = Current assets − current liabilities

Current assets = Cash + Accounts receivable + Inventories

Current liabilities = Accounts payable + Accruals + Notes payable

EBIT = Revenues − Cost of goods sold − Depreciation

EBT = EBIT − Interest

Net income = EBIT − Interest − Taxes

Retained earnings = Net income(1 − Dividend payout ratio)

b. Based only on the Altman Z-score, should you approve MNO Inc.'s application for a $500,000 capital expansion loan?

c. If sales for MNO were $300,000, the market value of equity were only half of book value, and all other values were unchanged, would your credit decision change?

d. Would the discriminant function change for firms in different industries? Would the function be different for retail lending in different geographic sections of the country? What are the implications for the use by FIs of these types of models?

24. Consider the coefficients of the Altman Z score. Can you tell by the size of the coefficients which ratio appears most important in assessing the creditworthiness of a loan applicant? Explain.

25. If the rate on one-year strips bonds is currently 6 percent, what is the repayment probability for each of the following two securities? Assume that if the loan is defaulted, no payments are expected. What is the market-determined risk premium for the corresponding probability of default for each security?

a. One-year AA-rated zero-coupon bond yielding 9.5 percent.

b. One-year BB-rated zero-coupon bond yielding 13.5 percent.

26. A bank has made a loan charging a base lending rate of 10 percent. It expects a probability of default of 5 percent. If the loan is defaulted, the bank expects to recover 50 percent of its money through the sale of its collateral. What is the expected return on this loan?

27. Assume that a one-year strip bond is currently yielding 5.5 percent and an AAA-rated discount bond with similar maturity is yielding 8.5 percent.

a. If the expected recovery from collateral in the event of default is 50 percent of principal and interest, what is the probability of repayment of the AAA-rated bond? What is the probability of default?

b. What is the probability of repayment of the AAA-rated bond if the expected recovery from collateral in the case of default is 94.47 percent of principal and interest? What is the probability of default?

c. What is the relationship between the probability of default and the proportion of principal and interest that may be recovered in case of default on the loan?

28. What is meant by the phrase *marginal default probability*? How does this term differ from *cumulative default probability*? How are the two terms related?

29. Suppose the FI manager wants to find out the probability of default on a two-year loan. For the one-year loan, $1 - p_1 = 0.03$ is the marginal and total or cumulative probability (C_p) of default in year 1. For the second year, suppose that $1 - p_2 = 0.05$. Calculate the cumulative probability of default over the next two years.

30. From the strip bond yield curve, the current required yields on one- and two-year strip bonds are $i_1 = 4.65$ percent and $i_2 = 5.50$ percent, respectively. Further, the current yield curve indicates

that appropriate one-year discount bonds are yielding $k_1 = 8.5$ percent and two-year bonds are yielding $k_2 = 10.25$ percent.

a. Calculate the one-year forward rate on the strip bonds and the corporate bond.

b. Using the current and forward one-year rates, calculate the marginal probability of repayment on the corporate bond in years 1 and 2, respectively.

c. Calculate the cumulative probability of default on the corporate bond over the next two years.

31. Calculate the term structure of default probabilities over three years using the following spot rates from the Government of Canada strip and corporate bond (pure discount) yield curves. Be sure to calculate both the annual marginal and the cumulative default probabilities.

	Spot 1 Year	Spot 2 Year	Spot 3 Year
Government bonds	5.0%	6.1%	7.0%
BBB-rated bonds	7.0	8.2	9.3

32. The bond equivalent yields for Government of Canada and A-rated corporate bonds with maturities of 93 and 175 days are given below:

	93 Days	175 Days
Government	8.07%	8.11%
A-rated corporate	8.42	8.66
Spread	0.35	0.55

a. What are the implied forward rates for both an 82-day Government of Canada and an 82-day A-rated bond beginning in 93 days? Use daily compounding on a 365-day year basis.

b. What is the implied probability of default on A-rated bonds over the next 93 days? Over 175 days?

c. What is the implied default probability on an 82-day A-rated bond to be issued in 93 days?

33. What is the mortality rate of a bond or loan? What are some of the problems with using a mortality rate approach to determine the probability of default of a given bond issue?

34. The first table below is a schedule of historical defaults (yearly and cumulative) experienced by an FI manager on a portfolio of commercial and mortgage loans.

a. Complete the blank spaces in the first table below.

b. What are the probabilities that each type of loan will not be in default after five years?

c. What is the measured difference between the cumulative default (mortality) rates for commercial and mortgage loans after four years?

35. The second table below shows the dollar amounts of outstanding bonds and corresponding default amounts for every year over the past five years. The default figures are in millions and the outstanding amounts are in billions. The outstanding figures reflect default amounts and bond redemptions. Calculate the annual and cumulative default rates of the bonds.

36. How does the RAROC model use the concept of duration to measure the risk exposure of a loan? How is the expected change in the credit premium measured? What is ΔLN in the RAROC equation?

	Years after Issuance				
Loan Type	**1 Year**	**2 Years**	**3 Years**	**4 Years**	**5 Years**
Commercial:					
Annual default	0.00%	______	0.50%	______	0.30%
Cumulative default	______	0.10%	______	0.80%	______
Mortgage: Annual default	0.10%	0.25%	0.60%	______	0.80%
Cumulative default	______	______	______	1.64%	______

	Years after Issuance				
Loan Type	**1 Year**	**2 Years**	**3 Years**	**4 Years**	**5 Years**
A-rated: Annual default ($ millions)	0	0	0	1	2
Outstanding ($ billions)	100	95	93	91	88
B-rated: Annual default ($ millions)	0	1	2	3	4
Outstanding ($ billions)	100	94	92	89	85
C-rated: Annual default ($ millions)	1	3	5	5	6
Outstanding ($ billions)	100	97	90	85	79

37. An FI wants to evaluate the credit risk of a $5 million loan with a duration of 4.3 years to an AAA borrower. There are currently 500 publicly traded bonds in that class (i.e., bonds issued by firms with an AAA rating). The current average level of rates (*R*) on AAA bonds is 8 percent. The largest increase in credit risk premiums on AAA loans, the 99 percent worst-case scenario, over the last year was equal to 1.2 percent (i.e., only 5 bonds out of 500 had risk premium increases exceeding the 99 percent worst case). The projected (one-year) spread on the loan is 0.3 percent, and the FI charges 0.25 percent of the face value of the loan in fees. Calculate the capital at risk and the RAROC on this loan.
38. A bank is planning to make a loan of $5,000,000 to a firm in the steel industry. It expects to charge a servicing fee of 50 basis points. The loan has a maturity of 8 years and a duration of 7.5 years. The cost of funds (the RAROC benchmark) for the bank is 10 percent. Assume the bank has estimated the maximum change in the risk premium on the steel manufacturing sector to be approximately 4.2 percent, based on two years of historical data. The current market interest rate for loans in this sector is 12 percent.
    a. Using the RAROC model, determine whether the bank should make the loan.
    b. What should be the duration in order for this loan to be approved?
    c. Assuming that duration cannot be changed, how much additional interest and fee income would be necessary to make the loan acceptable?
    d. Given the proposed income stream and the negotiated duration, what adjustment in the risk premium would be necessary to make the loan acceptable?
39. Calculate the value of and interest rate on a loan using the option model and the following information.
    Face value of loan (B) = $500,000
    Length of time remaining to loan maturity (τ) = 4 years
    Risk-free rate (i) = 4%
    Borrower's leverage ratio (d) = 60%
    Standard deviation of the rate of change in the value of the underlying assets = 15%
40. A firm is issuing a two-year loan in the amount of $200,000. The current market value of the borrower's assets is $300,000. The risk-free rate is 4 percent, and the standard deviation of the rate of change in the underlying assets of the borrower is 20 percent. Using an options framework, determine the following:
    a. The current market value of the loan.
    b. The risk premium to be charged on the loan.
41. A firm has assets of $200,000 and total debts of $175,000. With an option pricing model, the implied volatility of the firm's assets is estimated at $10,730. Under the Moody's Analytic method, what is the EDF (assuming a normal distribution for assets)?
42. Carman County Bank (CCB) has a $5 million face value outstanding adjustable-rate loan to a company that has a leverage ratio of 80 percent. The current risk-free rate is 6 percent, and the time to maturity on the loan is exactly ½ year. The asset risk of the borrower, as measured by the standard deviation of the rate of change in the value of the underlying assets, is 12 percent. The normal density function values are given below:

h	N(*h*)	*h*	N(*h*)
−2.55	0.0054	2.50	0.9938
−2.60	0.0047	2.55	0.9946
−2.65	0.0040	2.60	0.9953
−2.70	0.0035	2.65	0.9960
−2.75	0.0030	2.70	0.9965

    a. Use the Merton option valuation model to determine the market value of the loan.
    b. What should be the interest rate for the last six months of the loan?

Appendix 10A Credit Analysis

Appendix 10B Black–Scholes Option Pricing Model

View Appendices 10A and 10B on Connect.

CHAPTER 11

CREDIT RISK: LOAN PORTFOLIO AND CONCENTRATION RISK

After studying this chapter you should be able to:

LO1 Discuss the benefits of measuring loan portfolio risk and apply simple models of loan concentration risk.

LO2 Discuss diversification, modern portfolio theory, and other models as applied to loan portfolios.

INTRODUCTION

The models discussed in the previous chapter describe alternative ways by which an FI manager can measure the default risks of *individual* debt instruments, such as loans and bonds. Rather than looking at credit risk one loan at a time, this chapter concentrates on the ability of an FI manager to measure credit risk in a loan (asset) *portfolio context* and the benefit from loan (asset) diversification. We discuss and illustrate several models that are used by FI managers to assess the risk of a loan portfolio. The risk–return characteristics of each loan in its portfolio are a concern for an FI, but the risk–return of the overall loan portfolio, with some of the risk of the individual loans diversified, affects an FI's overall credit exposure. Additionally, we look at the use of loan portfolio models in setting maximum concentration (borrowing) limits for certain business or borrowing sectors.

osfi-bsif.gc.ca

Since 1994, the Office of the Superintendent of Financial Institutions (OSFI) has allowed banks, foreign bank branches, and federal trust and loan companies to self-assess their credit risks and to develop their own approaches. We discuss Moody's Analytics in the chapter and other models (CreditMetrics and CreditRisk+ in the appendices.

SIMPLE MODELS OF LOAN CONCENTRATION RISK

LO1

dbrs.com
standardandpoors.com
moodys.com

migration analysis
A method to measure loan concentration risk by tracking credit ratings of firms in particular sectors or rating classes for unusual declines.

FIs employ two simple models to measure credit risk concentration in the loan portfolio beyond the purely subjective model of "we have already lent too much to this borrower." The first is **migration analysis**, where lending officers track DBRS, S&P, Moody's, or their own internal credit ratings of certain pools of loans or certain sectors, for example, oil and gas. If the credit ratings of a number of firms in a sector or rating class decline faster than has been historically experienced, FIs curtail lending to that sector or rating class.

A **loan migration matrix** (or transition matrix) seeks to reflect the historic experience of a pool of loans in terms of their credit rating migration over time. As such, it can be used as a benchmark against which the credit migration patterns of any new pool of loans can be compared. Table 11–1 shows a hypothetical

TABLE 11–1 A Hypothetical Rating Migration, or Transition, Matrix

		Risk Rating at End of Year			
		AAA-A	BBB-B	CCC-C	D*
Risk Rating at Beginning of Year	AAA-A	0.85	0.10	0.04	0.01
	BBB-B	0.12	0.83	0.03	0.02
	CCC-C	0.03	0.13	0.80	0.04

*D = default.

loan migration matrix
A measure of the probability of a loan being upgraded, being downgraded, or defaulting over some period.

credit migration matrix, or table, in which loans are assigned to one of three rating classes (most FIs use 10 to 13 rating classes). The rows in Table 11–1 list the S&P rating at which the portfolio of loans began the year and the columns list the rating at which the portfolio ended the year. The numbers in the table are called *transition probabilities*, reflecting the average experience (proportions) of loans that began the year, say, as rating BBB-B remaining at BBB-B at the end of the year, being upgraded to AAA-A, being downgraded to CCC-C, or defaulting (D).

For example, for loans that began the year at rating BBB-B, historically (on average), 12 percent have been upgraded to AAA-A, 83 percent have remained at BBB-B, 3 percent have been downgraded to CCC-C, and 2 percent have defaulted by the end of the year. Suppose that the FI is evaluating the credit risk of its current portfolio of loans of borrowers rated BBB-B and that over the last few years, a much higher percentage (say, 5 percent) of loans has been downgraded to CCC-C and a higher percentage (say, 3 percent) has defaulted than is implied by the historic transition matrix. The FI may then seek to restrict its supply of lower-quality loans (e.g., those rated BBB-B and CCC-C), concentrating more of its portfolio on grade AAA-A loans. At the very least, the FI should seek higher credit risk premiums on lower-quality (rated) loans. Migration analysis is not only used to evaluate commercial loan portfolios, but also widely used to analyze credit card portfolios and consumer loans.

concentration limits
External limits set on the maximum loan size that can be made to an individual borrower.

The second simple model requires the FI to set a limit on the maximum amount of loans that will be made to an individual borrower or sector. The FI determines **concentration limits** on the proportion of the loan portfolio that can go to any single customer by assessing the borrower's current portfolio, its operating unit's business plans, its economists' economic projections, and its strategic plans. Typically, FIs set concentration limits to reduce exposures to certain industries and increase exposures to others. When two industry groups' performances are highly correlated, an FI may set an aggregate limit of less than the sum of the two individual industry limits. FIs also typically set geographic limits. They may set aggregate portfolio limits or combinations of industry and geographic limits.

EXAMPLE 11–1
Calculating Concentration Limits for a Loan Portfolio

Suppose management is unwilling to permit losses exceeding 10 percent of an FI's capital to a particular sector. If management estimates that the amount lost per dollar of defaulted loans in this sector is 40 cents, the maximum loans to a single sector as a percentage of capital, defined as the concentration limit, is

$$\text{Concentration limit} = \text{Maximum loss as a percentage of capital} \times \frac{1}{\text{Loss rate}}$$

$$= 10\% \times \frac{1}{0.4}$$

$$= 25\%$$

large exposure limit
The maximum amount of credit or investment exposure a federally regulated FI may have to a single entity.

In recent years, regulators have limited loan concentrations to *individual borrowers* to a certain percentage of the FI's capital. OSFI applies a "prudent person approach" and requires each FI to have written investment and lending policies. OSFI also has **large exposure limits** on credit risk for Canadian banks, federally regulated trust and loan companies, and foreign bank branches. The exposure is limited to a maximum of 25 percent of the FI's total capital as defined in calculating its risk-based capital adequacy ratio. The FI is expected to set lower internal limits and reach the maximum only on an exception basis. Canadian life insurance companies regulated by OSFI are also subject to a maximum exposure of 25 percent of their capital. The aggregate book value of investments of a property and casualty (P&C) insurance company to an entity or group cannot exceed 5 percent of the company's assets.

CONCEPT QUESTIONS

1. **In Example 11–1, what would the concentration limit be if the loss rate on bad loans was 25 cents on the dollar? (40%)**
2. **In Example 11–1, what would the concentration limit be if the maximum loss (as a percentage of capital) was 15 percent instead of 10 percent? (60%)**

Next we look at the use of more sophisticated portfolio theory–based models These models have a great deal of potential, but data availability and other implementation problems have hindered their use.

PORTFOLIO THEORY AND LOAN DIVERSIFICATION

LO2

To the extent that an FI manager holds widely traded loans and bonds as assets or, alternatively, can calculate loan or bond returns, portfolio diversification models can be used to measure and control the FI's aggregate credit risk exposure. Suppose the manager can estimate the expected returns of each loan or bond ($\overline{R}_i$) in the FI's portfolio.

After calculating the individual security return series, the FI manager can compute the expected return ($\overline{R}_p$) on a portfolio of assets as

$$\overline{R}_p = \sum_{i=1}^{N} X_i \overline{R}_i \tag{11.1}$$

In addition, the variance of returns or risk of the portfolio (σ_i^2) can be calculated as

$$\sigma_p^2 = \sum_{i=1}^{n} X_i^2 \sigma_i^2 + \sum_{i=1}^{n} \sum_{\substack{j=1 \\ i \neq j}}^{n} X_i X_j \sigma_{ij} \tag{11.2}$$

or

$$\sigma_p^2 = \sum_{i=1}^{n} X_i^2 \sigma_i^2 + \sum_{i=1}^{n} \sum_{\substack{j=1 \\ i \neq j}}^{n} X_i X_j \rho_{ij} \sigma_i \sigma_j \tag{11.3}$$

where

$\overline{R}_p$ = Expected or mean return on the asset portfolio
Σ = Summation sign
$\overline{R}_i$ = Mean return on the *i*th asset in the portfolio
X_i = Proportion of the asset portfolio invested in the *i*th asset (the desired concentration amount)

σ_i^2 = Variance of returns on the *i*th asset

σ_{ij} = Covariance of returns between the *i*th and *j*th assets

ρ_{ij} = Correlation between the returns on the *i*th and *j*th assets[1]

The fundamental lesson of modern portfolio theory (MPT) is that by taking advantage of its size, an FI can diversify credit risk as long as the returns on different assets are imperfectly correlated with respect to their default risk–adjusted returns.[2]

Consider the σ_p^2 in equation 11.3. If many loans have negative covariances or correlations of returns (ρ_{ij} are negative)—that is, when one borrower's loans do badly and another's do well—then combining loans to both borrowers may reduce the FI's overall risk exposure. That is, if there is negative correlation across borrower default probabilities, then a portfolio of loans may have less risk than an individual loan, all else being equal. Thus, the sum of the individual credit risks of loans viewed independently overestimates the risk of the whole portfolio. Because correlation is constrained to lie between plus and minus one, we can evaluate the effect of a change in ρ_{ij} on asset portfolio risk. For example, in the two-asset case, if ρ_{ij} is negative, the second term in equation 11.3 is also negative and offsets the first term, which is always positive. By appropriately exploiting correlation relationships among assets, an FI can significantly reduce risk in the asset portfolio and improve the portfolio's risk–return trade-off. This is what we meant in Chapter 5 when we stated that by pooling funds, FIs can reduce risk by taking advantage of the law of large numbers in their investment decisions.

EXAMPLE 11-2

Calculation of Return and Risk on a Two-Asset Portfolio

Loan *i*	X_i	$\bar{R}_i$	σ_i	σ_i^2	
1	0.40	10%	0.0857	0.007344	$\rho_{12} = -0.84$
2	0.60	12	0.0980	0.009604	$\sigma_{12} = -0.007058$

The return on the loan portfolio is

$$R_p = 0.4(10\%) + 0.6(12\%) = 11.2\%$$

while the risk (variance, σ^2, measured in percent squared) of the portfolio is

$$\sigma_p^2 = (0.4)^2(0.007344) + (0.6)^2(0.009604) + 2(0.4)(0.6)(-0.84)(0.0857)(0.0980)$$
$$= 0.0012462$$

Thus, $\sigma_p = \sqrt{0.0012462} = 0.0353 = 3.53\%$.

Notice that the risk (or standard deviation of returns) of the portfolio, σ_p (3.53 percent), is less than the risk of either individual asset (8.57 percent and 9.8 percent, respectively). The negative correlation between the returns of the two loans (−0.84) results in an overall reduction of risk when they are put together in an FI's portfolio.

[1] The correlation coefficient, ρ, reflects the joint movement of asset returns or default risks in the case of loans and lies between the values −1 and +1. As can be seen from equations 11.2 and 11.3, the covariance between any two assets (σ_{ij}) is related to the correlation coefficient (ρ_{ij}) by $\sigma_{ij} = \rho_{ij}\sigma_i\sigma_j$.

[2] One objection to using MPT for loans is that the returns on individual loans are not normally or symmetrically distributed. Most loans have limited upside returns and long-tail downside risks (see Appendix 11A and Chapter 9 in A. Saunders and L. Allen, *Credit Risk Measurements: In and Out of the Financial Crisis,* 3rd ed. (New York: John Wiley & Sons, 2010)). Also, concerns about relationships with traditional customers may limit diversification. This relationship limit is called the "paradox of credit." FIs specialize in monitoring and generating information about their key customers (see Chapter 1) that may lead to a highly concentrated loan portfolio.

FIGURE 11–1
FI Portfolio Diversification

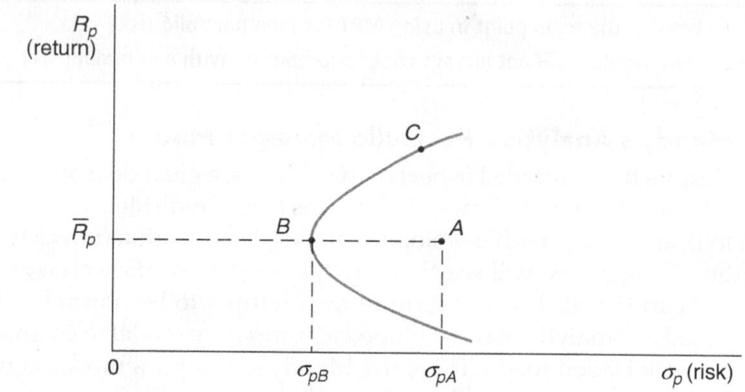

To see the advantages of diversification, consider Figure 11–1. *A* is an undiversified portfolio with heavy investment concentration in just a few loans or bonds. By fully exploiting diversification potential with bonds or loans whose returns are negatively correlated or have a low positive correlation with those in the existing portfolio, the FI manager can lower the credit risk on the portfolio from σ_{pA} to σ_{pB} while earning the same expected return. That is, portfolio *B* is the efficient (lowest-risk) portfolio associated with portfolio return level $\bar{R}_p$. By varying the proportion of the asset portfolio invested in each asset (in other words, by varying the required portfolio return level $\bar{R}_p$ up and down), the manager can identify an entire frontier of efficient portfolio mixes (weights) of loans and bonds. Each portfolio mix is efficient in the sense that it offers the lowest risk level to the FI manager at each possible level of portfolio returns. However, as you can see in Figure 11–1, of all possible efficient portfolios that can be generated, portfolio *B* produces the lowest possible risk level for the FI manager. That is, it maximizes the gains from diversifying across all available loans and bonds so that the manager cannot reduce the risk of the portfolio below σ_{pB}. For this reason, σ_{pB} is labelled the **minimum-risk portfolio**.

minimum-risk portfolio
The combination of assets that reduces the variance of portfolio returns to the lowest feasible level.

Even though *B* is clearly the minimum-risk portfolio, it does not generate the highest returns. Consequently, portfolio *B* may be chosen only by the most risk-averse FI managers, whose sole objective is to minimize portfolio risk regardless of the portfolio's return. Most portfolio managers have some desired risk–return trade-off in mind; they are willing to accept more risk if they are compensated with higher expected returns. One such possibility would be portfolio *C* in Figure 11–1. This is an efficient portfolio in that the FI manager has selected loan proportions (X_i) to produce a portfolio risk level that is a minimum for that higher expected return level. This portfolio dominates all other portfolios that can produce the same expected return level.[3]

Portfolio theory is attractive, but the question arises as to its applicability for banks, insurance companies, credit unions (CUs), and caisses populations (CPs), which often hold significant amounts of regionally specific nontraded or infrequently traded loans and bonds.

---

[3] Instead of a point on the efficient frontier for loans (e.g., Figure 11–1, point *C*), the FI would pick a point that maximizes firm value. This would be the point where the return of the portfolio minus the risk-free rate divided by the standard deviation of portfolio returns is maximized, that is, the maximum of $[(\bar{R}_p - \bar{R}_f)/\sigma_p)]$. This is the *Sharpe ratio*, a point on the efficient frontier where a straight line drawn from the vertical axis, from a point equal to $\bar{R}_f$, is just tangential to the efficient frontier. At this tangency point, it is impossible to improve upon the risk–return trade-off.

CONCEPT QUESTIONS

1. **What is the main point in using MPT for loan portfolio risk?**
2. **Why would an FI not always choose to operate with a minimum-risk portfolio?**

Moody's Analytics' Portfolio Manager Model

moodysanalytics.com

Moody's Analytics' Portfolio Manager
A model that applies MPT to the loan portfolio.

Despite the nontraded aspect of many loans, a great deal of recent research has gone into developing MPT models for loans (e.g., CreditMetrics, CreditRisk+). Below we look at one approach developed by KMV Corporation (now Moody's) called Portfolio Manager. We will see that **Moody's Analytics' Portfolio Manager** model differs from MPT in that it does not require loan returns to be normally distributed. Further, Moody's Analytics has developed a proprietary model to estimate the value of infrequently traded loans. Thus, the Moody's Analytics model is unique in the way it estimates the return, risk, and correlations between loans in an FI's loan portfolio. Once these variables are estimated in the Portfolio Manager model, they are then incorporated into the standard MPT equations to get an estimate of the risk and return of the loan portfolio. The Moody's Analytics' Credit Monitor model examines Moody's Analytics' method of evaluating default risk on an individual loan (so-called expected default frequency, or EDF). The Moody's Analytics' Portfolio Manager model, examined in this chapter, uses the default probability on each loan in a portfolio to identify the overall risk of the portfolio.

Any model that seeks to estimate an efficient frontier for loans, as in Figure 11–1, and thus the optimal or best proportions (X_i) in which to hold loans made to different borrowers, needs to determine and measure three things (see equations 11.1, 11.2, and 11.3): the expected return on a loan to borrower i (R_i), the risk of a loan to borrower i (σ_i), and the correlation of default risks between loans made to borrowers i and j (ρ_{ij}). Specifically, in the Moody's Analytics' Portfolio Manager model, portfolio return and risk are a function of the extent to which loan (exposure) values can change over a one-year horizon and how these value changes move together across different loans in the loan portfolio (correlations). Changes in loan values are determined by changes in the borrower's credit quality (measured as the EDF, discussed in Chapter 10) and the amount of the loan not recovered (i.e., the loss given default [LGD] on the loan). To calculate correlations, Moody's Analytics considers the joint impact of 120 different systematic factors, which reflect the global economy, region, industry, and country.

In its simplest model, Moody's Analytics measures each of these as follows:

$$R_i = AIS_i - E(L_i) = AIS_i - [EDF_i \times LGD_i] \tag{11.4}$$

$$\sigma_i = UL_i = \sigma_{Di} \times LGD_i = \sqrt{EDF_i(1 - EDF_i)} \times LGD_i \tag{11.5}$$

ρ_{ij} = Correlation between the systematic return components of the asset returns of borrower i and borrower j

Each of these needs some explanation.

Return on the Loan (R_i)

The return on a loan is measured by the *annual all-in-spread* (AIS), which measures annual fees earned on the loan by the FI plus the annual spread between the loan rate paid by the borrower and the FI's cost of funds. Deducted from this is the expected loss on the loan [$E(L_i)$]. This expected loss is equal to the product of the expected probability of the borrower defaulting over the next year, or its EDF (EDF_i)—as discussed in Chapter 10—times the amount lost by the FI if the borrower defaults (the LGD, or LGD_i). Also, if desired, the return on the loan can be expressed in excess return form by deducting the risk-free rate on a security of equivalent maturity.

We looked at Altman's estimates of recovery rates (1 – LGD) on defaulted bonds in Chapter 10. Altman's research consistently finds that approximately 90 percent of bond recovery rates can be explained and estimated using regressions that include default rates on bonds, one-year changes in bond default rates, and the amount of high-yield bonds outstanding in a particular year (which represents the potential supply of defaulted bonds). Macroeconomic factors are found to be insignificant in explaining recovery rates on defaulted bonds (much of this effect is captured in bond default rates).[4] Different types of debt instruments have different recovery rates. For example, more senior securities tend to have higher recovery rates than subordinated securities, all else being equal. Moody's Analytics' research has found that the highest and lowest LGD is for preferred stock and junior subordinated bonds, and industrial revenue bonds, senior secured bonds, and senior secured loans, respectively. Because of seniority, recovery rates are higher on bank loans. The Basel Committee assessed a fixed 45 percent LGD on secured loans if fully secured by physical, non–real estate collateral and 40 percent if fully secured by receivables. However, there is evidence suggesting that these fixed LGD rates may be too high for bank loans.

Risk of the Loan (σ_i)

The risk of the loan reflects the volatility of the loan's default rate (σ_{Di}) around its expected value times the amount lost given default (LGD_i). The product of the volatility of the default rate and the LGD is called the *unexpected loss on the loan* (UL_i) and is a measure of the loan's risk, or σ_i. To measure the volatility of the default rate, assume that loans can either default or repay (no default); then defaults are binomially distributed, and the standard deviation of the default rate for the *i*th borrower (σ_{Di}) is equal to the square root of the probability of default times 1 minus the probability of default [$\sqrt{(EDF)(1 - EDF)}$].

Correlation (ρ_{ij})

To measure the unobservable default risk correlation between any two borrowers, the Moody's Analytics' Portfolio Manager model uses the systematic asset return components of the two borrowers—as discussed in Chapter 10—and calculates a correlation that is based on the historical comovement between those returns. The model decomposes asset returns into systematic and unsystematic risk using the three-level structural model illustrated in Figure 11–2. Asset returns are extracted from equity returns using Moody's Analytics' Credit Manager's approach for imputing firm asset values. Using a time series of these asset values, asset returns are calculated. Once asset returns are estimated, the first-level decomposition into risk factors is a single-index model that regresses asset returns on a composite market factor that is constructed individually for each firm. The composite market factor used in the first-level analysis is composed of a weighted sum of country and industry factors. These factors are estimated at the second level of analysis and may be correlated with each other. The second level separates out the systematic component of industry and country risk, each of which is further decomposed into three sets of independent factors at a third level. These third-level factors are (1) two global economic factors—a market-weighted index of returns for all firms and the return index weighted by the log of market values; (2) five regional factors—Europe, North

[4] See E. I. Altman, Loss Given Default: The Link between Default and Recovery Rates, Recovery Ratings and Recent Empirical Evidence, Working paper, New York University Salomon Center, May 2008.

FIGURE 11–2
Moody's Analytics' Asset Level Correlation

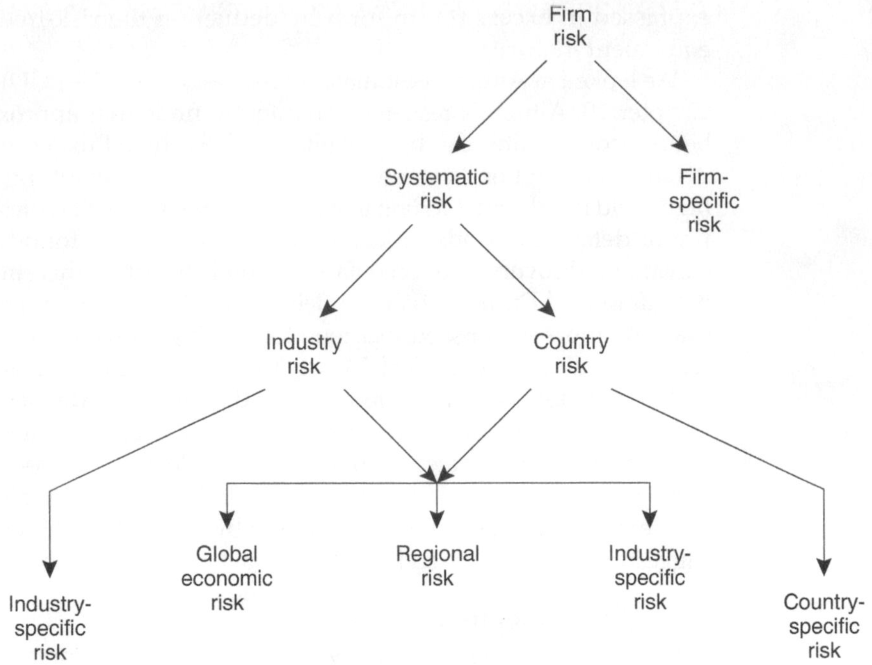

America, Japan, Southeast Asia, and Australia/New Zealand; (3) seven sector factors—interest sensitive (banks, real estate, and utilities), extraction (oil and gas, mining), consumer nondurables, consumer durables, technology, medical services, and other (materials processing, chemicals, paper, steel production).

According to Moody's Analytics, default correlations tend to be low and lie between 0.002 and 0.15. This makes intuitive sense. For example, what is the probability that both IBM and General Motors will go bankrupt at the same time? For both firms, their asset values would have to fall below their debt values at the same time over the next year. The likelihood of this is small except in a very severe or extreme recession or extremely high growth in each firm's short-term debt obligations. The generally low (positive) correlations between the default risks of borrowers is also good news for FI managers in that it implies that by spreading loans across many borrowers, they can reduce portfolio risk significantly.[5]

[5] The Portfolio Manager model of Moody's Analytics can also be used to assess the risk of extending more loans to any one borrower, which means that fewer loans can be made to others (assuming a fixed amount of loans). Technically, since the variance of the loan portfolio is

$$UL_p^2 = \sum_{i=1}^{n} X_i^2 UL_i^2 + \sum_{i=1}^{n} \sum_{\substack{j=1 \\ i \neq j}}^{n} X_i X_j UL_i UL_j \rho_{ij}$$

the marginal risk contribution of a small amount of additional loans to borrower i can be calculated as

$$\text{Marginal risk contribution} = \frac{dUL_p}{dX_i}$$

where UL_p is the standard deviation (in dollars) of the loan portfolio. Clearly, the marginal risk contribution (dUL_p) of an additional amount of loans to borrower i (dX_i), will depend not just on the risk of loan i on a stand-alone basis, but also on (1) the correlation of loan i with j other loans, (2) the risk of the j other loans, and (3) where the funds to increase loan i come from. In particular, if $dX_i > 0$, then the sum of the proportion of all remaining loans must decrease unless new funds are raised. Indeed, in the presence of a binding funding constraint $\sum_{i=1}^{n} dx_i < 0$ where $j \neq i$, the key insight is that a loan to a BBB-rated borrower may well be more valuable to an FI (in an MPT sense) if it has a lower correlation with other loans than a loan to an A-rated borrower; that is, it is the loan's marginal risk contribution to total portfolio risk that is important, not its stand-alone risk.

EXAMPLE 11-3

Calculation of Return and Risk on a Two-Asset Portfolio Using Moody's Analytics' Portfolio Manager

Suppose that an FI holds two loans with the following characteristics:

Loan i	X_i	Annual Spread between Loan Rate and FI's Cost of Funds	Annual Fees	LGD to FI	EDF	
1	0.60	5%	2%	25%	3%	$\rho_{12} = -0.25$
2	0.40	4.5	1.5	20	2	

The return and risk on loan 1 are

$$R_1 = (0.05 + 0.02) - [0.03 \times 0.25] = 0.0625 \text{ or } 6.25\%$$
$$\sigma_1 = [\sqrt{0.03(0.97)}] \times 0.25 = 0.04265 \text{ or } 4.265\%$$

The return and risk on loan 2 are

$$R_2 = (0.045 + 0.015) - [0.02 \times 0.20] = 0.056 \text{ or } 5.60\%$$
$$\sigma_2 = [\sqrt{0.02(0.98)}] \times 0.20 = 0.028 \text{ or } 2.80\%$$

The return and risk of the portfolio are then

$$R_p = 0.6(6.25\%) + 0.4(5.60\%) = 5.99\%$$
$$\sigma_p^2 = (0.6)^2(0.04265)^2 + (0.4)^2(0.028)^2 + 2(0.6)(0.4)(-0.25)(0.04265)(0.028)$$
$$= 0.0006369$$

Thus, $\sigma_p = \sqrt{0.0006369} = 0.0252 = 2.52\%$.

FIs use the Moody's Analytics model to actively manage their loan portfolios.

CONCEPT QUESTIONS

1. **How does Moody's Analytics measure the return on a loan?**
2. **If *EDF* = 0.1 percent and *LGD* = 50 percent, what is the unexpected loss (σ_i) on the loan? (1.58%)**
3. **How does Moody's Analytics calculate loan default correlations?**

Partial Applications of Portfolio Theory

Loan Volume–Based Models

As discussed above, direct application of MPT is often difficult for FIs lacking information on market prices of assets because many of the assets—such as loans—are not bought and sold in established markets. However, sufficient loan volume data may be available to allow managers to construct a modified or partial application of MPT to analyze the overall concentration or credit risk exposure of the FI. Such loan volume data include:

1. *Bank regulatory reports.* Federally regulated DTIs report monthly to the Bank of Canada and classify their loans as business, personal, and residential and nonresidential mortgages, as well as those to FIs and to domestic and foreign governments. They report geographically for inside and outside Canada, as well as reporting their impaired assets to OSFI. The information is available on an aggregate basis and can be used to estimate the notional allocation of loans among categories or types. Data are published monthly by the Bank of

bankofcanada.ca
osfi-bsif.gc.ca

Canada on an aggregate basis and quarterly by OSFI for the DTIs under its supervision.

2. *Data on shared national credits.* A U.S. database on large commercial and industrial loans categorizes loan volume by two-digit Standard Industrial Classification (SIC) codes. For example, loans made to businesses in SIC Code 49 are loans to public utilities. Because this database provides a picture of the allocation of large loans across sectors, it is analogous to the market portfolio or basket of commercial and industrial loans and, given the interconnection between the Canadian and U.S. economies, could provide a surrogate database for Canadian lending.
3. *Commercial databases.* These are data on 100,000-plus loans by bank and by borrower on the *Loan Pricing Corporation's DealScan* database. Data on over 1,800 Canadian companies are available.

loanpricing.com

These data therefore provide *market benchmarks* against which an individual FI can compare its own internal allocations of loans across major lending sectors such as real estate and oil and gas.

By comparing its own allocation, or the proportions (X_{ij}), of loans in any specific area with the national allocations across borrowers (X_i, where i designates different loan groups), the jth FI can measure the extent to which its loan portfolio deviates from the market portfolio benchmark. This indicates the degree to which the FI has developed *loan concentrations* or relatively undiversified portfolios in various areas.

Consider Table 11–2, which evaluates the first level of the loan asset allocation problem: the amount to be lent to each major loan sector or type. Here we show hypothetical numbers for four types of loans: real estate, business, consumer, and others. Column (1) shows the loan allocation proportions at the national level for all banks; this is the market portfolio allocation. Column (2) lists the allocations assumed to be chosen by Bank A, and column (3) shows the allocations chosen by Bank B.

Note that Bank A has concentrated loans more heavily in real estate lending than the national average, while Bank B has concentrated loans more heavily in lending to consumers. To calculate the extent to which each bank deviates from the national benchmark, we use the standard deviation of Bank A's and Bank B's loan allocations from the national benchmark. We calculate the relative measure of loan allocation deviation as[6]

$$\sigma_j = \sqrt{\frac{\sum_{i=1}^{N}(X_{ij} - X_i)^2}{N}} \qquad (11.6)$$

where

σ_j = Standard deviation of Bank j's asset allocation proportions from the national benchmark

X_{ij} = Asset allocation proportions of the jth bank

X_i = National asset allocations

N = Number of observations or loan categories, $N = 4$

[6] For small samples such as this, it may be more appropriate for the divisor of equation 12.6 to be $N - 1$ rather than N.

TABLE 11-2
Allocation of the Loan Portfolio to Different Sectors

	(1) National	(2) Bank A	(3) Bank B
Real estate	45%	65%	10%
Business	30	20	25
Consumer	15	10	55
Others	10	5	10
	100%	100%	100%

EXAMPLE 11-4

Calculating Loan Allocation Deviation

Refer again to Table 11-2. Applying equation 11.6 to Bank A's loan portfolio, we get the deviation in its loan portfolio allocation as follows:

$$(X_{1A} - X_1)^2 = (0.65 - 0.45)^2 = 0.0400$$
$$(X_{2A} - X_2)^2 = (0.20 - 0.30)^2 = 0.0100$$
$$(X_{3A} - X_3)^2 = (0.10 - 0.15)^2 = 0.0025$$
$$(X_{4A} - X_4)^2 = (0.05 - 0.10)^2 = \underline{0.0025}$$

and

$$\sum_{i=1}^{4} (X_{iA} - X_i)^2 = 0.0550$$

Therefore, $\sigma_A = \sqrt{(0.0550/4)} = 11.73\%$. Repeating this process for Bank B's loan portfolio, we get

$$(X_{1B} - X_1)^2 = (0.10 - 0.45)^2 = 0.1225$$
$$(X_{2B} - X_2)^2 = (0.25 - 0.30)^2 = 0.0025$$
$$(X_{3B} - X_3)^2 = (0.55 - 0.15)^2 = 0.1600$$
$$(X_{4B} - X_4)^2 = (0.10 - 0.10)^2 = \underline{0.0000}$$

and

$$\sum_{i=1}^{4} (X_{iB} - X_i)^2 = 0.2850$$

Therefore, $\sigma_B = \sqrt{(0.2850/4)} = 26.69\%$. As you can see, Bank B deviates more significantly from the national benchmark than Bank A because of its heavy concentration on loans to individuals.

Deviation from the national benchmark is not necessarily bad. An FI could have comparative advantages that are not required or available to other FIs. For example, an FI could generate high returns by serving specialized markets or product niches that are not well diversified. An FI may specialize in this area of lending because of its comparative advantage in information collection and monitoring of personal loans (perhaps due to its size or location). Additionally, an FI could specialize in only one product, such as mortgages, but be well diversified within this product line by investing in several different types of mortgages that are distributed both nationally and internationally. This would still enable it to obtain portfolio diversification benefits that are similar to the national average. The standard deviation simply provides a manager with a measure of the degree to which an FI's loan portfolio composition deviates from the national average or benchmark. Nevertheless, to the extent that the national composition of a loan portfolio represents a more diversified market portfolio, because it aggregates across all banks, the asset proportions derived nationally (the X_i) are likely to be closer to the *most efficient portfolio composition* than the X_{ij} of the individual bank. This partial use of MPT provides an FI manager with a sense of the relative degree of loan concentration carried in the asset portfolio. Finally, although the preceding analysis has referred to the loan portfolio of banks, any FI can use this portfolio theory for any asset group or, indeed, the whole asset portfolio, whether the asset is traded or not. The key data needed are the allocations of a peer group of FIs faced with similar investment decision choices.

Loan Loss Ratio-Based Models

systematic loan loss risk
A measure of the sensitivity of loan losses in a particular business sector relative to the losses in an FI's loan portfolio.

A second partial application of MPT is a model based on historic loan loss ratios. This model involves estimating the **systematic loan loss risk** of a particular sector or industry relative to the loan loss risk of an FI's total loan portfolio. This systematic loan loss can be estimated by running a time-series regression of quarterly losses of the *i*th sector's loss rate on the quarterly loss rate of an FI's total loans:

$$\left(\frac{\text{Sectoral losses in the } i\text{th sector}}{\text{Loans to the } i\text{th sector}}\right) = \alpha + \beta_i\left(\frac{\text{Total loan losses}}{\text{Total loans}}\right)$$

where α measures the loan loss rate for a sector that has no sensitivity to losses on the aggregate loan portfolio (i.e., its $\beta = 0$) and β_i measures the systematic loss sensitivity of the *i*th sector loans to total loan losses. For example, regression results showing that the consumer sector has a β of 0.2 and the real estate sector has a β of 1.4 suggest that loan losses in the real estate sector are systematically higher than the total loan losses of the FI (by definition, the loss rate β for the whole loan portfolio is 1). Similarly, loan losses in the consumer sector are systematically lower than the total loan losses of the FI. Consequently, it may be prudent for the FI to maintain lower concentration limits for the real estate sector as opposed to the consumer sector, especially as the economy moves toward a recession and total loan losses start to rise. The implication of this model is that sectors with lower βs could have higher concentration limits than high-β sectors—since low-β loan sector risks (loan losses) are less systematic, that is, are more diversifiable in a portfolio sense.

EXAMPLE 11-5
Calculating Loan Loss Ratios

Over the last 10 years, a finance company has experienced the following loan losses on its business loans, consumer loans, and total loan portfolio:

Year	Business Loans	Consumer Loans	Total Loans
2015	0.02175	0.03625	0.0250
2014	0.02318	0.03862	0.0269
2013	0.02340	0.03900	0.0272
2012	0.02535	0.04225	0.0298
2011	0.02437	0.04062	0.0285
2010	0.02415	0.04025	0.0282
2009	0.02400	0.04000	0.0280
2008	0.02370	0.03950	0.0276
2007	0.02325	0.03875	0.0270
2006	0.02212	0.03688	0.0255

Using regression analysis on these historical loan losses, a finance company has estimated the following:

$$X_B = 0.003 + 0.75X_L \quad \text{and} \quad X_h = 0.005 + 1.25X_L$$

where X_B = the loss rate in the business loan sector, X_h = the loss rate in the consumer (household) loan sector, and X_L = the loss rate for the finance company's loan portfolio. If the finance company's total loan loss rate increases by 15 percent, the expected loss rate increase in the business loan sector will be

$$X_B = 0.0030 + 0.750(0.15) = 11.55\%$$

and in the consumer loan sector will be

$$X_h = 0.005 + 1.25(0.15) = 19.25\%$$

To protect against this increase in losses, the finance company should consider reducing its concentration of consumer loans.

Regulatory Models

The board of directors of a Canadian FI has a legal obligation to develop and follow "investment and lending policies, standards and procedures that a reasonable and prudent person would apply in respect of a portfolio of investments and loans to avoid undue risk of loss and obtain a reasonable return," according to OSFI. OSFI's B-1 (1993) and B-2 (1994) guidelines for Canadian DTIs and federally regulated insurance companies set limits for concentrations, allow FIs to use in-house models to measure credit risk subject to approval by OSFI, and also require them to ensure that the staff assigned to monitor the risks are appropriately trained. In June 2006 the Bank for International Settlements (BIS) released guidance on sound credit risk assessment and valuation for loans. The guidance addresses how common data and processes related to loans may be used for assessing credit risk, accounting for loan impairment, and determining regulatory capital requirements and is structured around 10 principles that fall within two broad categories: supervisory expectations concerning sound credit risk assessment and valuation for loans, and supervisory evaluation of credit risk assessment for loans, controls, and capital adequacy.

osfi-bsif.gc.ca

bis.org

CONCEPT QUESTIONS

1. **If the loan returns are independent, are there gains from diversification?**
2. **How would you find the minimum-risk loan portfolio in an MPT framework?**
3. **Should FI managers select the minimum-risk loan portfolio? Why or why not?**

Questions and Problems

1. How do loan portfolio risks differ from individual loan risks?
2. What is *migration analysis*? How do FIs use it to measure credit risk concentration? What are its shortcomings?
3. What does *loan concentration risk* mean?
4. A manager decides not to lend to any firm in sectors that generate losses in excess of 5 percent of equity.
   a. If the average historical losses in the automobile sector total 8 percent, what is the maximum loan a manager can make to a firm in this sector as a percentage of total capital?
   b. If the average historical losses in the mining sector total 15 percent, what is the maximum loan a manager can make to a firm in this sector as a percentage of total capital?
5. An FI has set a maximum loss of 2 percent of total capital as a basis for setting concentration limits on loans to individual firms. If it has set a concentration limit of 25 percent to a firm, what is the expected loss rate for that firm?
6. Explain how MPT can be applied to lower the credit risk of an FI's portfolio.
7. Suppose that an FI holds two loans with the following characteristics:

Loan i	X_i	R_i	σ_i	σ_i^2	
1	0.55	8%	8.55%	73.1025%	$\rho_{12} = 0.24$
2	0.45	10	9.15	83.7225	$\sigma_{12} = 18.7758$

   Calculate the return and risk of the portfolio.
8. The Bank of Tinytown has two $20,000 loans with the following characteristics: loan A has an expected return of 10 percent and a standard deviation of returns of 10 percent. The expected return and standard deviation of returns for loan B are 12 percent and 20 percent, respectively.
   a. If the correlation between A and B is 0.015 (1.5 percent), what are the expected return and the standard deviation of this portfolio?
   b. What is the standard deviation of the portfolio if the correlation is −0.015 (−1.5 percent)?
   c. What role does the covariance, or correlation, play in the risk-reduction attributes of MPT?
9. Why is it difficult for FIs to measure credit risk using MPT?
10. What is the *minimum-risk portfolio*? Why is this portfolio usually not the portfolio chosen by FIs to optimize the risk–return trade-off?
11. The obvious benefit to holding a diversified portfolio of loans is to spread risk exposures so that a single event does not result in a great loss to the bank. Are there any benefits to not being diversified?
12. A bank vice-president is attempting to rank, in terms of the risk–return trade-off, the loan portfolios of three loan officers. Information on the portfolios is noted below. How would you rank the three portfolios?

Expected Portfolio	Standard Return	Deviation
A	10%	8%
B	12	9
C	11	10

13. Suppose that an FI holds two loans with the following characteristics:

Loan	X_i	Annual Spread between Loan Rate and FI's Cost of Funds	Annual Fees	LGD to FI	EDF	
1	0.45	5.5%	2.25%	30%	3.5%	$\rho_{12} = -0.15$
2	0.55	3.5	1.75	20	1.0	

   Calculate the return and risk on the two-asset portfolio using Moody's Analytics' Portfolio Manager.
14. Countrywide uses Moody's Analytics' Portfolio Manager model to evaluate the risk–return characteristics of the loans in its portfolio. A specific $10 million loan earns 2 percent per year in fees, and the loan is priced at a 4 percent spread over the cost of funds for the FI. Because of collateral considerations, the loss to the FI if the borrower defaults will be 20 percent of the loan's face value. The expected probability of default is 3 percent. What is the anticipated return on this loan? What is the risk of the loan?
15. Suppose that an FI holds two loans with the following characteristics:

Loan	X_i	Annual Spread between Loan Rate and FI's Cost of Funds	Annual Fees	LGD to FI	EDF	
1	?	4.0%	1.50%	?%	4.0%	$\rho_{12} = -0.10$
2	?	2.5	1.15	?	1.5	

   The return on loan 1 is $R_1 = 6.25\%$, the risk on loan 2 is $\sigma_2 = 1.8233\%$, and the return of the portfolio is $R_p = 4.555\%$. Calculate the LGD on loans 1 and 2; the proportions of loans 1 and 2 in the portfolio; and the risk of the portfolio, σ_p, using Moody's Analytics' Portfolio Manager.

16. What data are available to an FI on loan information? How can these data be used to analyze credit concentration risk?
17. Information concerning the allocation of loan portfolios to different market sectors is given below:

Allocation of Loan Portfolios in Different Sectors

Sector	National Average	Bank A	Bank B
Corporate & commercial	30%	50%	10%
Consumer	40	30	40
Real estate	30	20	50

Bank A and Bank B would like to estimate how much their portfolios deviate from the national average.

a. Which bank is farther away from the national average?
b. Is a large standard deviation necessarily bad for a bank using this model?

18. Assume that, on average, FIs engaged in mortgage lending have their assets diversified in the following proportions: 60 percent residential, 15 percent commercial, 5 percent international, and 20 percent mortgage-backed securities. A bank has the following distribution of mortgage loans: 50 percent residential, 30 percent commercial, and 20 percent international. How does this bank differ from the average?
19. Over the last 10 years, a bank has experienced the following loan losses on its business loans, consumer loans, and total loan portfolio:

Year	Business Loans	Consumer Loans	Total Loans
2015	0.0080	0.0165	0.0075
2014	0.0088	0.0183	0.0085
2013	0.0100	0.0210	0.0100
2012	0.0120	0.0255	0.0125
2011	0.0104	0.0219	0.0105
2010	0.0084	0.0174	0.0080
2009	0.0072	0.0147	0.0065
2008	0.0080	0.0165	0.0075
2007	0.0096	0.0201	0.0095
2006	0.0144	0.0309	0.0155

Using regression analysis on these historical loan losses, the bank has estimated the following:

$$X_B = 0.002 + 0.8X_L \quad \text{and} \quad X_h = 0.003 + 1.8X_L$$

where X_B = loss rate in the commercial sector, X_h = loss rate in the consumer (household) sector, and X_L = loss rate for its total loan portfolio.

a. If the bank's total loan loss rates increase by 10 percent, what are the expected loss rate increases in the business and consumer sectors?
b. In which sector should the bank limit its loans and why?

20. What guidelines on credit concentrations has OSFI provided for federally regulated FIs?
21. An FI is limited to holding no more than 8 percent of the securities of a single issuer. What is the minimum number of securities it should hold to meet this requirement? What if the requirements are 2 percent, 4 percent, and 7 percent?

Appendix 11A CreditMetrics

Appendix 11B CreditRisk+

View Appendices 11A and 11B on Connect.

CHAPTER 12

LIQUIDITY RISK

After studying this chapter you should be able to:

LO1 Identify the causes of liquidity risk on an FI's balance sheet, both on the asset and on the liability side.

LO2 Discuss the methods used to measure an FI's liquidity risk exposure.

LO3 Discuss regulatory mechanisms used to prevent runs on FIs.

LO4 Discuss the consequences of extreme liquidity risk, including deposit liability drains and bank runs.

LO5 Discuss the reasons liquidity risk differs among banks, life insurance companies, mutual funds, pension funds, and property and casualty insurance companies.

INTRODUCTION

This chapter looks at the problems created by liquidity risk. Unlike other risks that threaten an FI's solvency, liquidity risk is a normal aspect of the everyday management of an FI. For example, DTIs must manage liquidity so they can pay out cash as deposit holders request withdrawals of their funds. Only in extreme cases do liquidity risk problems develop into solvency risk problems, where an FI cannot generate sufficient cash to pay creditors as promised. This chapter identifies the causes of liquidity risk on the liability side of an FI's balance sheet as well as on the asset side. We discuss methods used to measure an FI's liquidity risk exposure and consequences of extreme liquidity risk (such as deposit liability drains and runs) and examine regulatory mechanisms put in place to ease liquidity problems and prevent runs on FIs. Moreover, some FIs are more exposed to liquidity risk than others. At one extreme, DTIs are highly exposed; in the middle, life insurance companies are moderately exposed; and at the other extreme, mutual funds, hedge funds, pension funds, and property and casualty (P&C) insurance companies generally have relatively low exposure.

The global financial crisis of 2008–2009 was, in part, due to liquidity risk. As mortgage and mortgage-backed securities markets started to experience large losses, credit markets froze and banks stopped lending to each other at anything but high overnight rates. The overnight U.S. dollar London Interbank Offered Rate (LIBOR), the benchmark that reflects the rate at which banks lend to one another in international markets, more than doubled, rising from 2.57 percent on September 29, 2008, to an all-time high of 6.88 percent on September 30, 2009. Banks generally rely on each other for cash needed to meet their daily liquidity needs. Interest rates on interbank borrowings are generally low because of confidence that FIs will repay each other. However, this confidence broke down in

August 2009. Without interbank funding, banks became reluctant to lend to other credit markets, resulting in a more general and widespread global liquidity crisis. The freezing up of money markets, interbank lending, and bank loan markets led to the insolvency of Lehman Brothers and other highly leveraged FIs worldwide.

CAUSES OF LIQUIDITY RISK

LO1

Liquidity risk arises for two reasons: a liability-side reason and an asset-side reason. The liability-side reason occurs when an FI's liability holders, such as depositors or insurance policyholders, seek to cash in their financial claims immediately. When liability holders demand cash by withdrawing deposits, the FI needs to borrow additional funds or sell assets to meet the withdrawal. The most liquid asset is cash; FIs use this asset to pay claimholders who seek to withdraw funds. However, FIs tend to minimize their holdings of cash because it is an asset that pays little or no interest. To generate interest revenues, most FIs invest in less liquid and/or longer-maturity assets. While most assets can be turned into cash eventually, for some assets this can be done only at a high cost when the asset must be liquidated immediately. The price the asset holder must accept for immediate sale may be far less than it would receive with a longer horizon over which to negotiate a sale. Thus, some assets may be liquidated only at low **fire-sale prices**, thus threatening the solvency of the FI. Alternatively, rather than liquidating assets, an FI may seek to purchase or borrow additional funds.

fire-sale prices
Prices received for an asset that has to be liquidated (sold) immediately.

The second cause of liquidity risk is asset-side liquidity risk, such as the ability to fund the exercise of off-balance-sheet (OBS) loan commitments. As we will describe in Chapter 16, a loan commitment allows a customer to borrow (draw down) funds from an FI (over a commitment period) on demand. When a borrower draws on its loan commitment, the FI must fund the loan on the balance sheet immediately; this creates a demand for liquidity. As it can with liability withdrawals, an FI can meet such a liquidity need by running down its cash assets, selling off other liquid assets, or borrowing additional funds.

To analyze the differing degrees of importance of liquidity risk across FIs, we next consider liquidity risk problems faced by DTIs, insurance companies, and mutual and pension funds.

CONCEPT QUESTIONS

1. **What are the sources of liquidity risk?**
2. **Why is cash more liquid than loans for an FI?**

LIQUIDITY RISK AT DEPOSIT-TAKING INSTITUTIONS

Liability-Side Liquidity Risk

As discussed in Chapter 2, a DTI's balance sheet typically has a large amount of short-term liabilities, such as demand deposits and other transaction accounts, which fund relatively long term assets. Demand deposit accounts and other transaction accounts are contracts that give the holders the right to put their claims back to the DTI on any given day and demand immediate repayment of the face value of their deposit claims in cash. DTIs typically liquidate deposit account contracts immediately upon request of the customer. Many savings account contracts, however, give a DTI some powers to delay withdrawals by requiring notification of withdrawal a certain number of days before withdrawal or by imposing penalty fees such as loss of interest. An individual demand deposit account holder with a balance of $10,000 can demand cash to be repaid immediately, as can a corporation with $100 million in its demand deposit account. In theory, at least, a DTI that has 20 percent of its liabilities in demand deposits and other transaction accounts must stand ready to pay out that amount by liquidating an equivalent amount of assets on any banking day. Table 12–1 shows the aggregate balance sheet of the assets and liabilities of Canadian banks and other DTIs. As seen in this table, total deposits are 67.7 percent of total liabilities. By comparison, cash assets are only 2.4 percent of total assets. Also note that borrowed funds are 7.4 percent of total liabilities.

core deposits Those deposits that provide a DTI with a long-term funding source.

In reality, a DTI knows that normally only a small proportion of its deposits will be withdrawn on any given day. Most demand deposits act as consumer **core deposits** on a day-by-day basis, providing a relatively stable or long-term source of savings and time deposit funds for the DTI. Moreover, deposit withdrawals may in part be offset by the inflow of new deposits and income generated from the DTI's on- and off-balance-sheet activities. The DTI manager must monitor the resulting net deposit withdrawals or net deposit drains.[1] Specifically, over time, a DTI manager can normally predict—with a good degree of accuracy—the probability distribution of **net deposit drains** (the difference between deposit withdrawals and deposit additions) on any given normal banking day.[2]

net deposit drains The amount by which cash withdrawals exceed additions; a net cash outflow.

Consider the two possible distributions shown in Figure 12–1. In Panel (a) of Figure 12–1, the distribution is assumed to be strongly peaked at the 5 percent net deposit withdrawal level—this DTI expects approximately 5 percent of its net deposit funds to be withdrawn on any given day with the highest probability. In Panel (a) a net deposit drain means that the DTI is receiving insufficient additional deposits (and other cash inflows) to offset deposit withdrawals. The DTI in Panel (a) has a mean, or expected, net positive drain on deposits, so its new deposit funds and other cash flows are expected to be insufficient to offset deposit withdrawals. The liability side of its balance sheet is contracting. Table 12–2 illustrates an actual 5 percent net drain of deposit accounts (or, in terms of dollars, a drain of $5 million).

TABLE 12–1
Assets and Liabilities of Canadian DTIs, Q4, 2012

Source: Statistics Canada, statcan.gc.ca.

Assets*	$ billions	Percentage	Liabilities**	$ billions	Percentage
Total cash assets	$ 73.5	2.4%	Total deposits	$1,948.2	67.7%
Total investments	644.9	20.8	Borrowings	212.9	7.4
Total loans	2,022.4	65.2	Other liabilities	716.9	24.9
Other assets	362.8	11.7	**Total liabilities**	**$2,878.0**	**100.0%**
Total assets	**$3,103.6**	**100.0%**			

* Includes chartered banks, trust companies, deposit-accepting mortgage companies, and credit unions (CUs).
** Excludes bank equity capital.

[1] Also a part of liquidity risk (although not as likely to cause an FI to fail) is an unexpected inflow of funds. For example, in the early 2000s as stock prices fell, investors liquidated their mutual fund shares and deposited these funds in their banks, credit unions (CUs), and caisses populaires (CPs). With interest rates at historic lows, DTIs faced a problem of finding sufficiently attractive (in a return sense) loans and securities in which to invest these funds.

[2] Apart from predictable daily seasonality to deposit flows, there are other seasonal variations, many of which are, to a greater or lesser degree, predictable. For example, many retail DTIs face above-average deposit outflows around the end of the year and in the summer (due to Christmas and the vacation season).

FIGURE 12–1
Distribution of Net Deposit Drains

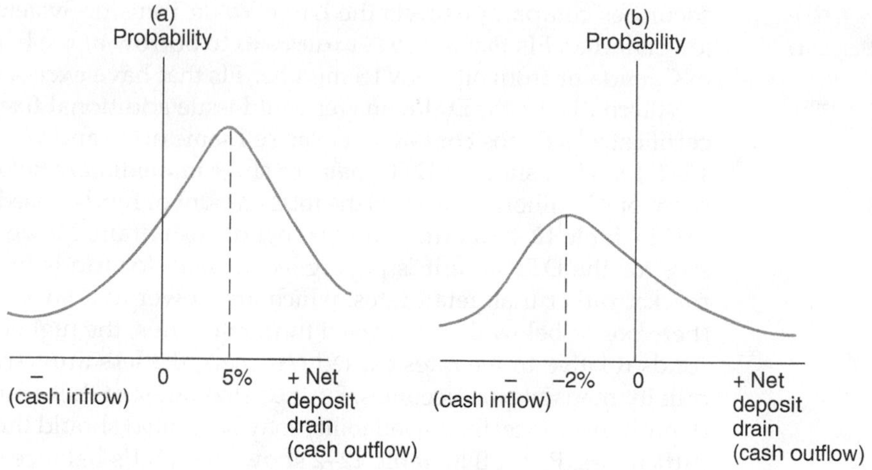

For a DTI to be growing, it must have a mean or average deposit drain such that new deposit funds more than offset deposit withdrawals. Thus, the peak of the net deposit drain probability distribution must be at a point to the left of zero. See the −2 percent in Panel (b) in Figure 12–1, where the distribution of net deposit drains peaks at −2 percent, or the FI is receiving net cash inflows with the highest probability.

A DTI can manage a drain on deposits in two major ways: (1) purchased liquidity management and/or (2) stored liquidity management. Traditionally, DTI managers have relied on stored liquidity management as the primary mechanism of liquidity management. Today, many DTIs—especially the largest banks with access to the money market and other nondeposit markets for funds—rely on purchased liquidity (or liability) management to deal with the risk of cash shortfalls. A more extensive discussion of liability management techniques is left to Chapter 18. Here we briefly discuss the alternative methods of liquidity risk management.

Purchased Liquidity Management

A DTI manager who purchases liquidity may turn to the markets for short-term funds. These could be the repurchase agreement markets used extensively by

TABLE 12–2
Effect of Net Deposit Drains on the Balance Sheet ($ millions)

Panel A: Balance Sheet Immediately before and after Deposit Drain

Before the Drain				After the Drain			
Assets		**Liabilities**		**Assets**		**Liabilities**	
Assets	100	Deposits	70	Assets	100	Deposits	65
		Borrowed funds	10			Borrowed funds	10
		Other liabilities	20			Other liabilities	20
	100		100		100		95

Panel B: Adjusting to a Deposit Drain through Purchased Liquidity Management

Assets		**Liabilities**	
Assets	100	Deposits	65
		Borrowed funds	15
		Other liabilities	20
	100		100

LVTS participants
Members of the Canadian Payments Association that settle directly with the Bank of Canada and participate in the LVTS.

securities companies, or via the Large Value Transfer System (LVTS) used by major Canadian FIs that are **LVTS participants** to borrow at the bank rate from the Bank of Canada or from other LVTS member FIs that have excess funds.

Alternatively, the DTI manager could issue additional fixed-maturity wholesale certificates of deposit or GICs or even sell some notes and bonds. For example, Table 12–2, Panel A, shows a DTI's balance sheet immediately before and after a deposit drain of $5 million. As long as the total amount of funds raised equals $5 million, the DTI in Table 12–2 can fully fund its net deposit drain. However, this can be expensive for the DTI since it is paying *market rates* for funds in the wholesale money market rather than retail rates, which are slower to adjust to market changes and therefore lie below the purchased fund rate. Thus, the higher the cost of purchased funds relative to the rates earned on assets, the less attractive this approach to liquidity management becomes. Further, since most of these funds are not covered by deposit insurance, their availability may be limited should the DTI incur insolvency difficulties. Panel B in Table 12–2 shows the DTI's balance sheet if it responds to deposit drains by using purchased liquidity management techniques.

purchased liquidity management
An adjustment to a deposit drain that occurs on the liability side of the balance sheet.

Note that **purchased liquidity management** has allowed the DTI to maintain its overall balance sheet size of $100 million without disturbing the size and composition of the asset side of its balance sheet—that is, the complete adjustment to the deposit drain occurs on the liability side of the balance sheet. In other words, purchased liquidity management can insulate the asset side of the balance sheet from normal drains on the liability side of the balance sheet. This is one of the reasons for the enormous growth in recent years of FI-purchased liquidity management techniques and associated purchased fund markets, such as borrowings from the Bank of Canada, repurchase agreements, and wholesale GICs, which we discuss in more detail in Chapter 18. In the event of a liquidity crunch, additional wholesale funds could be hard to obtain. This occurred during the global liquidity crisis in September to October 2008.

Stored Liquidity Management

stored liquidity management
An adjustment to a deposit drain that occurs on the asset side of the balance sheet.

Instead of meeting the net deposit drain by purchasing liquidity in the wholesale money markets, the DTI could use **stored liquidity management**. That is, the FI could liquidate some of its assets, utilizing its stored liquidity. Traditionally, DTIs have held stored cash at the Bank of Canada and in their vaults for this very purpose as reserve requirements. Canada and the United Kingdom now have no official central bank–designated cash reserve requirements, while the U.S. Federal Reserve sets minimum reserve requirements for the cash reserves that U.S. banks must hold.[3] Even so, DTIs still tend to hold cash in excess of the minimum required to meet liquidity drains.

Suppose, in our example, that on the asset side of the balance sheet the DTI normally holds $9 million of its assets in cash. We depict the situation before the net drain in liabilities in Table 12–3, Panel A. As depositors withdraw $5 million in deposits, the DTI can meet this directly by using the excess cash stored in its vaults or held on deposit at other DTIs or at the Bank of Canada. If the reduction of $5 million in deposit liabilities is met by a $5 million reduction in cash assets held by the DTI, its balance sheet will be as shown in Table 12–3, Panel B.

bankofcanada.ca

[3] The U.S. Federal Reserve requires 3 percent on the first US$71 million and 10 percent on the rest of a DTI's demand deposit and transaction account holdings. The first US$11.5 million of the US$71 million is not subject to reserve requirements (as of July 2012).

TABLE 12–3
Composition of the DTI's Balance Sheet ($ millions)

Panel A: Balance Sheet Immediately before Deposit Drain			
Assets		**Liabilities**	
Cash	9	Deposits	70
Other assets	91	Borrowed funds	10
		Other liabilities	20
	100		100
Panel B: Adjusting to a Deposit Drain through Stored Liquidity Management			
Assets		**Liabilities**	
Cash	4	Deposits	65
Other assets	91	Borrowed funds	10
		Other liabilities	20
	95		95

When the DTI uses its cash as the liquidity adjustment mechanism, both sides of its balance sheet contract. In this example, the DTI's total assets and liabilities shrink from $100 million to $95 million. The cost to the DTI from using stored liquidity, apart from decreased asset size, is that it must hold excess non-interest-bearing assets in the form of cash on its balance sheet. These could be highly liquid interest-bearing assets such as T-bills, but these are still less liquid than cash, and immediate liquidation may result in some small capital value losses. Thus, the cost of using cash to meet liquidity needs is the forgone return (or opportunity cost) of being unable to invest these funds in loans and other higher-income-earning assets.

Note that while stored liquidity management and purchased liquidity management are alternative strategies for meeting deposit drains, a DTI can combine the two methods by using some purchased liquidity management and some stored liquidity management to meet liquidity needs.

Asset-Side Liquidity Risk

Just as deposit drains can cause a DTI liquidity problems, so can the exercise by borrowers of their loan commitments and other credit lines. During the credit crisis in 2008, as the money markets and interbank markets shut down, many borrowers drew down their credit lines at banks, exacerbating the liquidity problems for many global FIs. Table 12–4, Panel A, shows the effect of a $5 million exercise of a loan commitment by a borrower. As a result, the DTI must fund $5 million in additional loans on the balance sheet. Consider Panel A (the balance sheet before the loan commitment is exercised) and Panel B (the balance sheet after the loan commitment is exercised) in Table 12–4. In particular, the exercise of the loan commitment means that the DTI needs to provide $5 million in loans immediately to the borrower (other assets rise from $91 to $96 million). This can be done either by purchased liquidity management (borrowing an additional $5 million in the money market and lending these funds to the borrower) or by stored liquidity management (decreasing the DTI's cash assets from $9 million to $4 million). We present these two policies in Table 12–4, Panel B.

Another type of asset-side liquidity risk arises from the FI's investment portfolio. Specifically, unexpected changes in interest rates can cause investment portfolio values to fluctuate significantly. If interest rates increase, the value of the investment securities portfolio falls and large losses in portfolio value can occur

TABLE 12–4
Effects of a Loan Commitment Exercise ($ millions)

Panel A: Balance Sheet Immediately before and after Exercise

(a) Before Exercise				(b) After Exercise			
Cash	9	Deposits	70	Cash	9	Deposits	70
Other assets	91	Borrowed funds	10	Other assets	96	Borrowed funds	10
		Other liabilities	20			Other liabilities	20
	100		100		105		100

Panel B: Adjusting the Balance Sheet to a Loan Commitment Exercise

(a) Purchased Liquidity Management				(b) Stored Liquidity Management			
Cash	9	Deposits	70	Cash	4	Deposits	70
Other assets	96	Borrowed funds	15	Other assets	96	Borrowed funds	10
		Other liabilities	20			Other liabilities	20
	105		105		100		100

(see Chapter 15 on market risk). Further, there is the risk that liquidity in a particular market will deteriorate because market traders want to sell and no one wants to buy. It has been argued that technological and other developments have led to a steady improvement in the liquidity of financial markets. However, this is questionable in that there is an increasing tendency toward "herd" behaviour, where most traders want to make the same type of trade (such as a sale) at a particular time. During the sell-off, liquidity dries up and investment securities can be sold only at fire-sale prices. The result is a reduction in the value of the investment portfolio and increased liquidity risk for the FI.

In Table 12–5, Panel A shows an FI's balance sheet immediately before and after a $5 million decrease in the market value of its investment portfolio. In addition to a loss in equity value, the FI must fund the $5 million loss in value on the balance sheet such that loan requests and deposit withdrawals can be met. The FI must replace the loss in value of the investment portfolio. This can be done either by purchased liquidity management (borrowing an additional $5 million in deposits or purchased funds) or by stored liquidity management (purchasing an additional

TABLE 12–5 Effects of a Drop in the Value of the Investment Securities Portfolio ($ millions)

Panel A: Balance Sheet Immediately before and after Drop in Portfolio Value

Before Drop in Value				After Drop in Value			
Cash	$ 9	Deposits	$ 60	Cash	$ 9	Deposits	$60
Investment portfolio	40	Borrowed funds	10	Investment portfolio	35	Borrowed funds	10
Other assets	51	Other liabilities	20	Other assets	51	Other liabilities	20
		Equity	10			Equity	5
	$100		$100		$95		$95

Panel B: Adjusting the Balance Sheet for a Drop in Investment Portfolio Value

(a) Purchased Liquidity Management				(b) Stored Liquidity Management			
Cash	$ 9	Deposits	$ 65	Cash	$ 4	Deposits	$60
Investment portfolio	40	Borrowed funds	10	Investment portfolio	40	Borrowed funds	10
Other assets	51	Other liabilities	20	Other assets	51	Other liabilities	20
		Equity	5			Equity	5
	$100		$100		$95		$95

$5 million in assets).[4] Panel B of Table 12–5 shows the effect of these two strategies on the balance sheet. Notice, in both cases, that the FI has lost $5 million in equity.

Measuring a DTI's Liquidity Exposure

LO2

Sources and Uses of Liquidity

As discussed above, a DTI's liquidity risk arises from ongoing conduct of business, such as a withdrawal of deposits, or from new loan demand, and the subsequent need to meet those demands through liquidating assets or borrowing funds. Therefore, a DTI's manager must be able to measure its liquidity position on a daily basis, if possible. A useful tool is a *net liquidity statement*, which lists sources and uses of liquidity and thus provides a measure of a DTI's net liquidity position. Such a statement for a hypothetical bank is presented in Table 12–6.

The DTI can obtain liquid funds in three ways. First, it can sell its liquid assets such as T-bills immediately with little price risk and low transaction cost. Second, it can borrow funds in the money/purchased funds market up to a maximum amount (this is an *internal* guideline based on the manager's assessment of the credit limits that the purchased or borrowed funds market is likely to impose on the DTI). Third, it can use any excess cash. In Table 12–6 the DTI's *sources* of liquidity total $14,500 million. Compare this with the DTI's *uses* of liquidity, in particular the amount of borrowed or purchased funds it has already utilized and the amount of cash it has already borrowed from the Bank of Canada. These total $7,000 million. As a result, the DTI has a positive net liquidity position of $7,500 million. These liquidity sources and uses can be easily tracked on a day-by-day basis.

The net liquidity position in Table 12–6 lists management's expected sources and uses of liquidity for a hypothetical bank. All FIs report their historical sources and uses of liquidity in their annual and quarterly reports. As an FI manager deals with liquidity risk, historical sources and uses of liquidity statements can assist the manager in determining where future liquidity issues may arise.

Peer Group Ratio Comparisons

Another way to measure a DTI's liquidity exposure is to compare certain key ratios and balance sheet features of the DTI—such as its loans to deposits, borrowed funds to total assets, and commitments to lend to assets ratios—with those of DTIs of a similar size and geographic location. Table 12–7 shows these

TABLE 12–6
Net Liquidity Position ($ millions)

Sources of Liquidity	
1. Total cash-type assets	$ 2,000
2. Maximum borrowed funds limit	12,000
3. Excess cash	500
Total	$14,500
Uses of Liquidity	
1. Funds borrowed	$ 6,000
2. Bank of Canada borrowing	1,000
Total	$ 7,000
Total net liquidity	$ 7,500

[4] Note that the FI could raise an additional $5 million in equity, e.g., through a common stock issue. However, this is likely to be more costly than adjusting to the loss via purchased liquidity management or stored liquidity management.

TABLE 12–7 Liquidity Ratios for Canadian Banks, 2012

	Loans and Acceptances/ Assets	Loans and Credit Commitments/ Assets	Loans and Acceptances/ Deposits	Loans and Credit Commitments/ Deposits	Cash and Securities/ Total Assets
BMO	48.8%	60.3%	79.3%	98.8%	29.4%
CIBC	64.2	94.9	101.9	150.5	18.7
National Bank	51.1	73.5	97.5	140.3	32.7
RBC	47.0	65.8	76.3	106.9	22.4
Scotiabank	55.9	72.4	80.6	104.3	28.2
TD Bank	31.3	61.4	85.3	102.1	27.7
Average	53.1%	71.4%	86.8%	117.0%	26.5%

Source: Authors' calculations from company 2012 annual reports.

ratios for the six largest Canadian banks for 2012. A high ratio of loans to deposits (and loans and loan commitments to deposits) means that the DTI relies heavily on the short-term money market rather than on core deposits to fund loans. This could mean future liquidity problems if the DTI is at or near its borrowing limits in the purchased funds market. As noted previously, Canadian banks rely on the commercial paper market for funding. Similarly, a high ratio of loans and loan commitments to assets indicates the need for a high degree of liquidity to fund any unexpected drawdowns of these loans—high-commitment DTIs (e.g., CIBC, National Bank, and RBC, from Table 12–7) often face more liquidity risk exposure than do low-commitment FIs (e.g., BMO).

bmo.com
cibc.com
nbc.ca
rbc.com
scotiabank.com
td.com

Liquidity Index

liquidity index
A measure of the potential losses an FI could suffer as the result of sudden (or fire-sale) disposal of assets.

A third way to measure liquidity risk is to use a **liquidity index**. Developed by Jim Pierce at the U.S. Federal Reserve, this index measures the potential losses an FI could suffer from a sudden or fire-sale disposal of assets compared with the amount it would receive at a fair market value established under normal market (sale) conditions—which might take a lengthy period of time as a result of a careful search and bidding process. The greater the differences between immediate fire-sale asset prices (P_i) and fair market prices (P_i^*), the less liquid is the DTI's portfolio of assets. Define an index I such that

$$I = \sum_{i=1}^{N} [(w_i)(P_i / P_i^*)]$$

where w_i is the percentage of each asset in the FI's portfolio:

$$\sum_{i=1}^{N} w_i = 1$$

EXAMPLE 12-1

Calculation of the Liquidity Index

Suppose that a DTI has two assets: 50 percent in one-month Treasury bills and 50 percent in real estate loans. If the DTI must liquidate its T-bills today (P_1), it receives \$99 per \$100 of face value; if it can wait to liquidate them on maturity (in one month's time), it will receive \$100 per \$100 of face value (P_1^*). If the DTI has to liquidate its real estate loans today, it receives \$85 per \$100 of face value (P_2); liquidation at the end of one month (closer to maturity) will produce \$92 per \$100 of face value (P_2^*). Thus, the one-month liquidity index value for this DTI's asset portfolio is

$$
\begin{aligned}
I &= \frac{1}{2}\left(\frac{0.99}{1.00}\right) + \frac{1}{2}\left(\frac{0.85}{0.92}\right) \\
&= 0.495 + 0.462 \\
&= 0.957
\end{aligned}
$$

Suppose, alternatively, that a slow or thin real estate market caused the DTI to be able to liquidate the real estate loans at only $65 per $100 of face value ($P_2$). The one-month liquidity index for the DTI's asset portfolio is

$$
\begin{aligned}
I &= \frac{1}{2}\left(\frac{0.99}{1.00}\right) + \frac{1}{2}\left(\frac{0.65}{0.92}\right) \\
&= 0.495 + 0.353 \\
&= 0.848
\end{aligned}
$$

The value of the one-month liquidity index decreases as a result of the larger discount on the fire-sale price—from the fair (full-value) market price of real estate—over the one-month period. The larger the discount from fair value, the smaller the liquidity index and the higher the liquidity risk the DTI faces.

The liquidity index will always lie between 0 and 1. The liquidity index for this DTI could also be compared with similar indexes calculated for a peer group of similar DTIs.

Financing Gap and the Financing Requirement

A fourth way to measure liquidity risk exposure is to determine the DTI's financing gap. As we discussed earlier, even though demand depositors can withdraw their funds immediately, they do not do so in normal circumstances. On average, most demand deposits stay at DTIs for quite long periods—often two years or more. Thus, a DTI manager often thinks of the average deposit base, including demand deposits, as a core source of funds that over time can fund a DTI's average amount of loans.

financing gap
The difference between a DTI's average loans and average (core) deposits.

We define a **financing gap** as the difference between a DTI's average loans and average (core) deposits, or

Financing gap = Average loans − Average deposits

If this financing gap is positive, the DTI must fund it by using its cash and liquid assets and/or borrowing funds in the money market. Thus,

Financing gap = −Liquid assets + Borrowed funds

We can write this relationship as

Financing gap + Liquid assets = Financing requirement (borrowed funds)

financing requirement
The financing gap plus a DTI's liquid assets.

As expressed in this fashion, the liquidity and managerial implications of the **financing requirement** (the financing gap plus a DTI's liquid assets) are that the level of core deposits and loans as well as the amount of liquid assets determines the DTI's borrowing or purchased fund needs. In particular, the larger a DTI's financing gap and liquid asset holdings, the larger the amount of funds it needs to borrow in the money markets and the greater is its exposure to liquidity problems from such a reliance.

The balance sheet in Table 12–8 indicates the relationship between the financing gap, liquid assets, and the borrowed fund financing requirement. The following equation also shows this relationship:

Financing gap	+	Liquid assets	=	Financing requirement
($5 million)		($5 million)		($10 million)

TABLE 12–8
Financing Requirement of a DTI ($ millions)

Assets		Liabilities	
Loans	$ 25	Core deposits	$ 20
Liquid assets	5	Financing requirement (borrowed funds)	10
Total	$ 30	Total	$ 30
		Financing gap	$ 5

A widening financing gap can warn of future liquidity problems since it may indicate increased deposit withdrawals (core deposits falling below $20 million in Table 12–8) and increasing loans due to increased exercise of loan commitments (loans rising above $25 million). If the DTI does not reduce its liquid assets—they stay at $5 million—the manager must resort to more money market borrowings. As these borrowings rise, sophisticated lenders in the money market may be concerned about the DTI's creditworthiness. They may react by imposing higher risk premiums on borrowed funds or establishing stricter credit limits by not rolling over funds lent to the DTI. If the DTI's financing requirements exceed such limits, it may become insolvent. A good example of an excessive financing requirement was Continental Bank of Canada. Following the failure of Canadian Commercial Bank and Northland Bank of Canada in 1985, financial markets in Canada were jittery, and short-term wholesale funds moved out of the smaller FIs into larger, safer institutions. This loss of wholesale deposits forced Continental Bank, whose assets were of good quality, to seek a six-month $1.4 billion loan from the Bank of Canada, and then to arrange a $1.5 billion three-month standby line of credit with the other major banks that cost $750,000 in facility fees. Despite these efforts, Continental never regained the confidence of the market, and it ultimately merged with Lloyds Bank International, becoming a Schedule B bank (the equivalent of today's Schedule II banks).

BIS Liquidity Risk Measures

LO3

During the 2008 financial crisis, many DTIs struggled to maintain adequate liquidity. As discussed in Chapter 1, extraordinary levels of liquidity assistance were required from central banks and governments in order to maintain the stability of the global financial system. Even with this extensive support, a number of DTIs failed or were forced into mergers or government ownership. Recognizing the need for DTIs to improve their liquidity risk management and control their liquidity risk exposures, BIS's Basel Committee on Banking Supervision (BCBS) developed two regulatory standards for liquidity risk supervision. The standards are intended to "enhance tools, metrics, and benchmarks that supervisors can use to assess the resilience of banks' liquidity cushions and constrain any weakening in liquidity maturity profiles, diversity of funding sources, and stress testing practices."[5] The two liquidity ratios to be maintained by DTIs are the liquidity coverage ratio (LCR), to be implemented in 2015, and the net stable funding ratio (NSFR), to be implemented in 2018.

bis.org

LCR. The LCR aims to ensure that a DTI maintains an adequate level of high-quality assets that can be converted into cash to meet liquidity needs for a 30-day time horizon under an "acute liquidity stress scenario" specified by supervisors.

[5] *International Framework for Liquidity Risk Measurement, Standards and Monitoring*, Bank for International Settlements, December 2009, bis.org.

The specified scenario incorporates both institution-specific and systemic shocks that are based on actual circumstances experienced in the global financial crisis. Thus, maintenance of the LCR is intended to ensure that DTIs can survive a severe liquidity stress scenario for at least 30 days. The LCR will be reported to DTI supervisors monthly starting in 2015:

$$LCR = \frac{\text{Stock of high-quality liquid assets}}{\text{Total net cash outflows over the next 30 calendar days}} \geq 100\%$$

The stock of high-quality liquid assets (the numerator of the LCR) is defined as follows:

- Liquid assets must remain liquid in times of stress (i.e., convertible into cash at little loss of value and usable at the central bank discount window as collateral).
- The liquid assets must be "unencumbered."
- Liquid assets are divided into Level 1 and Level 2. The Level 1 amount has no cap; the Level 2 amount is capped at 40 percent of total liquid assets:

  Level 1 = Cash + Central bank reserves + Sovereign debt

  Level 2 = Mortgage-backed securities that are government guaranteed + Corporate bonds (plain vanilla) rated at least AA−

- A minimum 15 percent "haircut" has to be applied to the value of each Level 2 asset.

Total net cash outflows (the denominator of the ratio) is defined as

$$\text{Total } \textit{net} \text{ cash outflows over the next 30 calendar days} = \text{Outflows} - \min(\text{inflows; } 75\% \text{ of outflows})$$

where cash outflows and inflows are defined in Table 12–9. Appendix 12A presents the template provided by the BIS used to calculate the LCR.

EXAMPLE 12-2

Calculation of the LCR

CanBank has the following balance sheet (in millions of dollars):

Assets		Liquidity Level	Liabilities and Equity		Run-off Factor
Cash	$ 10	Level 1	Stable retail deposits	$ 95	5%
Deposits at the Bank of Canada	15	Level 1	Less stable retail deposits	40	10
Govt. of Canada securities	100	Level 1	Unsecured wholesale funding from:		
NHA-MBS*	75	Level 2	Stable small business deposits	100	5
Loans to A-rated corporations	110	Level 2	Less stable small business deposits	80	10
Loans to B-rated corporations	85		Nonfinancial corporates	50	75
Premises	15		Equity	45	
Total	$410			$410	

*National Housing Act mortgage-backed securities.

Cash inflows over the next 30 days from the bank's performing assets are $5 million.

The LCR for CanBank is calculated as follows:

Level 1 assets	$10 + $15 + $100 =	$125
Level 2 assets	(75 + 110) × 0.85 =	157.25
Capped at 40% of Level 1	125 × 0.40 =	50
Stock of highly liquid assets		$175
Cash outflows:		
Stable retail deposits	$95 × 0.05 =	$4.75
Less stable retail deposits	40 × 0.10 =	4.00
Stable small business deposits	100 × 0.05 =	5.00
Less stable small business deposits	80 × 0.10 =	8.00
Nonfinancial corporates	50 × 0.75 =	37.50
Total cash outflows over next 30 days		59.25
Total cash inflows over next 30 days		5.00
Total net cash outflows over next 30 days		$54.25

LCR = $175/$54.25 = 322.58%. The bank is in compliance with liquidity requirements based on the LCR.

NSFR The NSFR takes a longer-term look at liquidity on a DTI's balance sheet. The NSFR evaluates liquidity over the entire balance sheet and provides incentives for DTIs to use stable sources of financing. This longer-term liquidity ratio requires a minimum amount of stable funding to be held over a one-year time horizon based on liquidity risk factors assigned to liquidity exposures of on- and off-balance-sheet assets. The NSFR is intended to ensure that long-term assets are funded with a minimum amount of stable liabilities. It limits reliance on short-term wholesale funding, which was a major problem in the financial crisis.

TABLE 12–9 Cash Outflows and Inflows Used in the LCR

Cash outflows included in the LCR:

- Retail deposits = stable + less stable
  Stable = deposits covered by deposit insurance (receive a minimum run-off factor of 5%)
  Less stable = deposits not covered by deposit insurance (receive a minimum run-off factor of 10%)
- Retail deposits with maturity > 30 days and no early withdrawal (0% run-off factor)
- All unsecured wholesale funds with < 30 days maturity (i.e., callable by funds provider) (100% run-off factor)
- Secured funds backed by Level 1 assets (0% run-off factor); backed by Level 2 assets (15% run-off factor)
- Loss of funding on commercial paper if maturity < 30 days (100% run-off factor)
- All debt maturing with 30 days (100% run-off factor)
- Loan commitment (drawdown) factors:
  5% drawdowns on committed credit and liquidity facilities to retail and small business customers
  10% drawdowns on committed credit facilities to nonfinancial corporates, sovereigns, central banks, public-sector entities, and multilateral development banks
  100% drawdowns on committed liquidity facilities to nonfinancial corporates, sovereigns, central banks, public-sector entities, and multilateral development banks
  100% drawdowns on committed credit and liquidity facilities to other legal entities; these entities include FIs (including banks, securities firms, and insurance companies), conduits and special-purpose vehicles, fiduciaries, and beneficiaries
- Cash outflows related to operating costs (0% run-off factor)

Cash inflows included in the LCR:

- Include other inflows for sources where no default is expected in next 30 days.
- There is a 75% cap on inflows meeting outflows so DTIs do not just rely on inflows for liquidity.
- Assume that no lines of credit on other banks can be drawn on (0% inflow).
- 100% inflow received on wholesale loans and 50% inflow on retail loans from counterparties.
- Assume 100% inflow on known derivative payments.

Source: Basel Committee on Banking Supervision, Basel III: The Liquidity Coverage Ratio and Liquidity Risk Monitoring Tools, January 2013, www.bis.org.

TABLE 12–10 Components of ASF and Associated ASF Factors

ASF Factor	Components of ASF Category
100%	The total amount of capital, including both Tier 1 and Tier 2 as defined in existing global capital standards issued by the Committee. The total amount of any preferred stock not included in Tier 2 that has an effective remaining maturity of one year or greater taking into account any explicit or embedded options that would reduce the expected maturity to less than one year. The total amount of secured and unsecured borrowings and liabilities (including term deposits) with effective remaining maturities of one year or greater excluding any instruments with explicit or embedded options that would reduce the expected maturity to less than one year. Such options include those exercisable at the investor's discretion within the one-year horizon.
90%	"Stable" nonmaturity (demand) deposits and/or term deposits (as defined in the LCR) with residual maturities of less than one year provided by retail customers and small business customers.
80%	"Less stable" (as defined in the LCR) nonmaturity (demand) deposits and/or term deposits with residual maturities of less than one year provided by retail and small business customers.
50%	Unsecured wholesale funding, nonmaturity deposits, and/or term deposits with a residual maturity of less than one year, provided by nonfinancial corporates, sovereigns, central banks, multilateral development banks, and PSEs.
0%	All other liabilities and equity categories not included in the above categories.

Source: Basel Committee on Banking Supervision, Basel III: The Liquidity Coverage Ratio and Liquidity Risk Monitoring Tools, January 2013, www.bis.org.

Basically, stable funding is sought for all illiquid assets and securities held, where stable funding is defined as equity and liability financing expected to be reliable sources of funds over a one-year time horizon. The NSFR ratio will be reported to DTI supervisors quarterly starting in 2018:

$$NSFR = \frac{\text{Available amount of stable funding}}{\text{Required amount of stable funding}} > 100\%$$

Available stable funding (the numerator of the ratio) includes:

- Bank capital
- Preferred stock with a maturity > 1 year
- Liabilities with maturities > 1 year
- The portion of retail deposits and wholesale deposits expected to stay with the bank during a period of idiosyncratic stress

The available amount of stable funding (ASF) is calculated by first assigning the value of a DTI's equity and liabilities to one of five categories as presented in Table 12–10. The amount assigned to each category is multiplied by an ASF factor. The total ASF is the sum of the weighted amounts.

Required stable funding (RSF; the denominator of the ratio) is measured using supervisory assumptions on the characteristics of the liquidity risk profiles of a DTI's assets, OBS exposures, and other selected activities. The required amount of stable funding is calculated as the sum of the value of the on-balance-sheet assets held and funded by the DTI, multiplied by a specific RSF factor assigned to each particular asset type, plus the amount of OBS activities (or potential liquidity exposure) multiplied by the associated RSF factor. The RSF factor applied to the reported values of each asset or OBS exposure is the amount of that item that supervisors believe should be supported with stable funding. The RSF factors assigned to various types of assets are intended to approximate the amount of a particular asset that could not be sold or used as collateral in a secured borrowing during a severe liquidity event lasting one year. Table 12–11 summarizes the specific types of assets to be assigned to each asset category and their associated RSF factor.

TABLE 12–11 Detailed Composition of Asset Categories and Associated RSF Factors

Components of RSF Category	RSF Factor
• Cash immediately available to meet obligations, not currently encumbered as collateral, and not held for planned use (as contingent collateral, as salary payments, or for other reasons). • Unencumbered short-term unsecured instruments and transactions with outstanding maturities of less than one year. • Unencumbered securities with slated remaining maturities of less than one year with no embedded options that would increase the expected maturity to more than one year. • Unencumbered securities held where the institution has an offsetting reverse repurchase transaction when the security on each transaction has the same unique identifier (e.g., ISIN* or CUSIP). • Unencumbered loans to financial entities with effective maturity of less than one year that are not renewable and for which the lender has an irrevocable right to call.	0%
• Unencumbered marketable securities with residual maturities of one year or greater representing claims on or claims guaranteed by sovereigns, central banks, BIS, IMF, EC, non-central government PSEs, or multilateral development banks that are assigned a 0% risk weight under the Basel II standardized approach, provided that active repo or sale markets exist for these securities. • OBS exposures require little long-term funding. Thus, revocable and irrevocable credit and liquidity facilities to any client have an RSF ratio = 5%.	5%
• Unencumbered corporate bonds or covered bonds rated AA− or higher with residual maturities of one year or greater satisfying all of the conditions for Level 2 assets in the LCR. • Unencumbered marketable securities with residual maturities of one year or greater representing claims on or claims guaranteed by sovereigns, central banks, and noncentral government PSEs that are assigned a 20% risk weight under the Basel II standardized approach, provided that they meet all of the conditions for Level 2 assets in the LCR.	20%
• Unencumbered gold. • Unencumbered equity securities, not issued by FIs or their affiliates, listed on a recognized exchange and included in a large cap market index. • Unencumbered corporate bonds and covered bonds that satisfy all of the following conditions: - Central bank eligibility to intraday liquidity needs and overnight liquidity shortages in relevant jurisdictions. - Not issued by FIs or their affiliates (except in the case of covered bonds). - Not issued by the respective firm itself or its affiliates. - Low credit risk: assets have a credit assessment by a recognized ECAI of A+ to A−, or do not have a credit assessment by a recognized ECAI and are internally rated as having a PD corresponding to a credit assessment of A+ to A−. - Traded in large, deep, and active markets characterized by a low level of concentration. • Unencumbered loans to nonfinancial corporate clients, sovereigns, central banks, and PSEs having a remaining maturity of less than one year.	50%
• Unencumbered residential mortgages of any maturity that would qualify for the 35% or lower risk weight under the Basel II Standardized Approach for credit risk. • Other unencumbered loans, excluding loans to FIs, with a remaining maturity of one year or greater, that would qualify for the 35% or lower risk weight under the Basel II Standardized Approach for credit risk.	65%
• Unencumbered loans to retail customers (i.e., natural persons) and small business customers (as defined in the LCR) having a remaining maturity of less than one year (other than those that qualify for the 65% RSF above).	85%
• All other assets not included in the above categories.	100%

*Definitions of abbreviations in the table are as follows: CUSIP, Committee on Uniform Security Identification Procedures; EC, European Community; ECAI, External Credit Assessment Institution; IMF, International Monetary Fund; ISIN, International Securities Identification Number; PSE, Public Sector Entity; PD, Probability of Default.

Source: Basel Committee on Banking Supervision, Basel III: The Liquidity Coverage Ratio and Liquidity Risk Monitoring Tools, January 2013, www.bis.org.

EXAMPLE 12-3

Calculation of the NSFR

CanBank has the following balance sheet (in millions of dollars).

Assets		RSF Factor	Liabilities and Equity		ASF Factor
Cash	$ 10	0%	Stable retail deposits	$ 95	90%
Deposits at the Bank of Canada	15	5	Less stable retail deposits	40	80
Govt. of Canada securities	100	5	Unsecured wholesale funding from:		
NHA-MBS	75	20	Stable small business deposits	100	90
Loans to A-rated corporations (maturity > 1 year)	110	65	Less stable small business deposits	80	80
Loans to B-rated corporations (maturity < 1 year)	85	50	Nonfinancial corporates	50	50
Premises	15	100	Equity	45	100
Total	$410			$410	

The NSFR for CanBank is calculated as follows:

Available amount of stable funding = $45 × 1.00 + ($95 + $100) × 0.90 + ($40 + $80) × 0.80 + $50 × 0.50 = $341.5

Required amount of stable funding = $10 × 0.00 + ($15 + $100) × 0.05 + $75 × 0.20 + $110 × 0.65 + $85 × 0.50 + $15 × 1.00 = $149.75

NSFR = $341.5/$149.75 = 228.05%. The bank is in compliance with liquidity requirements based on the NSFR.

Other Liquidity Risk Control Measures. In addition to the LCR and NSFR described above, regulators will monitor several additional DTI and systemwide trends. These additional metrics capture specific information related to a bank's cash flows, balance sheet structure, available unencumbered collateral, and certain market indicators. The additional monitoring measures include:

Contractual maturity mismatch. Compare assets with liabilities in time bands based on maturity e.g., overnight; 7 and 14 days; 1, 2, 3, 4, and 9 months; 1, 2, 3, and 5 years; and beyond. Data on maturity mismatches are to be provided to DTI supervisors on frequent basis.

Concentration of funding. Identify those sources of wholesale funding that are of such significance that withdrawal of these funds could trigger liquidity problems.

Available unencumbered asset. Identify the quantity and key characteristics, including currency denomination and location, of banks' available unencumbered assets. These assets have the potential to be used as collateral to raise additional secured funding in secondary markets and/or are eligible at central banks and as such may potentially be additional sources of liquidity for the bank.

LCR by significant currency. Monitor the LCR in significant currencies. This will allow DTIs and supervisors to track potential currency mismatch issues that could arise.

Market-related monitoring tools. Monitor high-frequency market data (including marketwide data and information on the financial sector) with little or no time lag. These measures can be used as early warning indicators in monitoring potential liquidity difficulties at banks.

Liquidity Risk, Unexpected Deposit Drains, and Bank Runs

LO4

Under normal conditions and with appropriate management planning, neither net deposit withdrawals nor the exercise of loan commitments pose significant liquidity problems for DTIs because borrowed funds availability or excess cash reserves are adequate to meet anticipated needs. For example, even in December and the summer vacation season, when net deposit withdrawals are high, DTIs anticipate these *seasonal* effects by holding greater than normal amounts of cash or borrowing more than normal on the wholesale money markets.

Major liquidity problems can arise, however, if deposit drains are *abnormally large* and unexpected. Abnormal deposit drains (shocks) may occur for a number of reasons, including:

1. Concerns about a DTI's solvency relative to that of other DTIs.
2. Failure of a related DTI leading to heightened depositor concerns about the solvency of other DTIs (the contagion effect).
3. Sudden changes in investor preferences regarding holding nonbank financial assets (such as T-bills or mutual fund shares) relative to deposits.

bank run
A sudden and unexpected increase in deposit withdrawals from a DTI.

In such cases, any sudden and unexpected surges in net deposit withdrawals risk triggering a **bank run** that could eventually force a bank into insolvency. Government actions can exacerbate the situation, but in Canada, actions by the Bank of Canada and regulators have, in the past, forestalled this type of bank run.

Deposit Drains and Bank Run Liquidity Risk

At the core of bank run liquidity risk is the fundamental and unique nature of the *demand deposit contract*. Specifically, demand deposit contracts are first-come, first-served contracts in the sense that a depositor's place in line determines the amount he or she will be able to withdraw from a DTI. In particular, a depositor either gets paid in full or gets nothing.[6] Because demand deposit contracts pay in full only a certain proportion of depositors when a DTI's assets are valued at less than its deposits—and because depositors realize this—any line outside a DTI encourages other depositors to join the line immediately even if they do not need cash today for normal consumption purposes. Thus, even the DTI's core depositors rationally seek to withdraw their funds immediately when they observe a sudden increase in the lines at their DTI.

As a bank run develops, the demand for net deposit withdrawals grows. The DTI may initially meet this by decreasing its cash reserves, selling off liquid or readily marketable assets such as T-bills and Government of Canada and U.S. government bonds, and seeking to borrow in the money markets. As a bank run increases in intensity, more depositors join the withdrawal line, and a liquidity crisis develops. Specifically, the DTI finds it difficult, if not impossible, to borrow from the money markets at virtually any price. Also, it has sold all its liquid assets, cash, and bonds as well as any saleable loans (see Chapter 25). The DTI is likely to have left only relatively illiquid loans on the asset side of the balance sheet to meet depositor claims for cash. However, these loans can be sold or liquidated only at

[6] We are assuming no deposit insurance exists that guarantees payments of deposits and no borrowing from the Bank of Canada is available to fund a temporary liquidity need. The presence of deposit insurance and Bank of Canada funds alters the incentives to engage in a bank run as we describe later in this chapter and in Chapter 19. There have been no documented occurrences of contagion while deposit insurance has been in place in Canada, even during the market turmoil of 2007 and 2008. FIs in other countries (Northern Rock in the United Kingdom and Countrywide Financial in the United States) did experience bank runs.

very large discounts from face value. A DTI needing to liquidate long-term assets at fire-sale prices to meet continuing deposit drains faces the strong possibility that the proceeds from such asset sales will be insufficient to meet depositors' cash demands. The DTI's liquidity problem then turns into a solvency problem; that is, the DTI must close its doors.

The incentives for depositors to run first and ask questions later creates a fundamental instability in the banking system in that an otherwise sound DTI can be pushed into insolvency and failure by unexpectedly large depositor drains and liquidity demands. This is especially so in periods of contagious runs, or **bank panics**, when depositors lose faith in the banking system as a whole and engage in a run on all DTIs by not materially discriminating among them according to their asset qualities.

bank panic
A systemic or contagious run on the deposits of the banking industry as a whole.

Bank Runs, the Bank of Canada, and Deposit Insurance

Regulators have recognized the inherent instability of the banking system due to the all-or-nothing payoff features of the deposit contract. As a result, regulatory mechanisms are in place to ease DTIs' liquidity problems and to deter bank runs and panics. The two major liquidity risk insulation devices are *deposit insurance* and *borrowing from the Bank of Canada*. Because of the serious social welfare effects that a contagious run on DTIs could have, government regulators of DTIs have established guarantee programs offering deposit holders varying degrees of insurance protection to deter runs. Specifically, if a deposit holder believes a claim is totally secure, even if the DTI is in trouble, the holder has no incentive to run. The deposit holder's place in line no longer affects his or her ability to obtain the funds. Deposit insurance deters runs as well as contagious runs and panics.

In addition to deposit insurance, central banks such as the Bank of Canada have traditionally provided overnight lending facilities to meet DTIs' short-term nonpermanent liquidity needs. The Bank of Canada has three roles as **lender of last resort (LLR)** in providing liquidity to the financial system. As previously noted, through the LVTS, the Bank of Canada provides daily and overnight funds to cover temporary shortfalls of an FI. The Bank can also provide emergency lending assistance (ELA) to solvent deposit-taking FIs for a longer time period, as it did for Continental Bank of Canada. During extreme conditions, the Bank of Canada can also buy securities issued by financial and nonfinancial Canadian or foreign firms and government entities. As mentioned in Chapter 1, many central banks, including the Bank of Canada, expanded their programs of providing liquidity to FIs during the credit crisis in 2008.

lender of last resort (LLR)
The role of a central bank in providing funds to a country's FIs during a liquidity crisis.

CONCEPT QUESTIONS

1. **List two benefits and two costs of using (a) purchased liquidity management and (b) stored liquidity management to meet a deposit drain.**
2. **What are the three major sources of DTI liquidity? What are the two major uses?**
3. **What are the measures of liquidity risk used by FIs?**

LIQUIDITY RISK AND LIFE INSURANCE COMPANIES

LO5

DTIs are not the only FIs exposed to liquidity risk or run problems. Like DTIs, life insurance companies hold cash reserves and other liquid assets to meet policy cancellations (surrenders) and other working capital needs that arise in the course of writing insurance. The early cancellation of an insurance policy

surrender value
The amount received by an insurance policyholder when cashing in a policy early.

results in the insurer's having to pay the insured the **surrender value** of that policy.[7] In the normal course of business, premium income and returns on an insurer's asset portfolio are sufficient to meet the cash outflows required when policyholders cash in or surrender their policies early. As with DTIs, the distribution or pattern of premium income minus policyholder liquidations is normally predictable. When premium income is insufficient to meet surrenders, however, a life insurer can sell some of its relatively liquid assets, such as government bonds. In this case, bonds act as a buffer or reserve asset source of liquidity for the insurer.

Nevertheless, concerns about the solvency of an insurer can result in a run in which new premium income dries up and existing policyholders seek to cancel their policies by cashing them in early. To meet exceptional demands for cash, a life insurer could be forced to liquidate the other assets in its portfolio, such as commercial mortgage loans and other securities, potentially at fire-sale prices. As with DTIs, forced asset liquidations can push an insurer into insolvency.[8]

CONCEPT QUESTIONS

1. **What is likely to be a life insurance company's first source of liquidity when premium income is insufficient?**
2. **Can a life insurance company be subjected to a run? If so, why?**

LIQUIDITY RISK AND PROPERTY AND CASUALTY INSURERS

As discussed in Chapter 6, P&C insurers sell policies insuring against certain contingencies impacting either real property or individuals. Unlike those of life insurers, P&C contingencies (and policy coverages) are relatively short term, often one to three years. With the help of mortality tables, claims on life insurance policies are generally predictable. P&C claims (such as those associated with natural disasters such as the tsunami and nuclear reactor meltdown in Japan and the earthquake in New Zealand in 2011), however, are virtually impossible to predict. As a result, P&C insurers' assets tend to be shorter term and more liquid than those of life insurers. P&C insurers' contracts and premium-setting intervals are usually relatively short term as well, so problems caused by policy surrenders are less severe. P&C insurers' greatest liquidity exposure occurs when policyholders cancel or fail to renew policies with an insurer because of insolvency risk, pricing, or competitive reasons. This may cause an insurer's premium cash inflow, when added to its investment returns, to be insufficient to meet policyholders' claims.

Alternatively, large unexpected claims may materialize and exceed the flow of premium income and income returns from assets, causing severe liquidity crises and failures among smaller P&C insurers.[9] Insurance giant AIG came close to failure in the late summer of 2008 when it was hit by US$18 billion in losses from

[7] A surrender value is usually some proportion or percentage less than 100 percent of the face value of the insurance contract. The surrender value continues to grow as funds invested in the policy earn interest (returns). Earnings to the policyholder are taxed if and when the policy is actually surrendered or cashed in before the policy matures.

[8] Life insurers also provide loan commitments, especially in the commercial property area. As a result, they face asset-side loan commitment liquidity risk in a fashion similar to that of DTIs.

[9] Claims may arise in long-tail lines when a contingency occurs during the policy period but a claim is not lodged until many years later, for example, the claims regarding asbestos damage (Chapter 6).

credit default swaps (CDSs, which are credit guarantees) it wrote on mortgage derivatives. As the mortgage debt securities' values declined, AIG was forced to post more collateral to signal to CDS contract counterparties that it could pay off the mortgage guarantees it wrote. Despite these actions by AIG, S&P announced that it would downgrade AIG's credit rating. The rating downgrade required AIG to post up to an additional US$4.5 billion in collateral, funds it did not have. AIG made an unprecedented approach to the U.S. Federal Reserve seeking US$40 billion in short-term financing. The company announced that a financing entity—funded by the Federal Reserve Bank of New York and AIG—had purchased US$46.1 billion of the complex debt securities insured by AIG. The deal also included a broader restructuring of the U.S. federal government's bailout, which originally included a US$85 billion bridge loan and US$37.8 billion in financing.

CONCEPT QUESTIONS

1. **What is the greatest cause of liquidity exposure faced by P&C insurers?**
2. **Is the liquidity risk of P&C insurers in general greater or less than that of life insurers?**

INVESTMENT FUNDS

closed-end fund
An investment fund that sells a fixed number of shares in the fund to outside investors.

open-end fund
An investment fund that sells an elastic or nonfixed number of shares in the fund to outside investors.

net asset value (NAV)
The price at which investment fund shares are sold (or can be redeemed). It equals the total market value of the assets of the fund divided by the number of shares in the funds outstanding.

Investment funds such as mutual funds and hedge funds sell shares as liabilities to investors and invest the proceeds in assets such as bonds and equities. These funds are open-end or closed-end. **Closed-end funds** issue a fixed number of shares as liabilities; unless the issuing fund chooses to repurchase them, the number of outstanding shares does not change. As discussed in Chapter 5, by far the majority of Canadian investment funds are **open-end funds**; that is, they can issue an unlimited supply of shares to investors. Open-end funds must also stand ready to buy back previously issued shares from investors at the current market price for the fund's shares. Thus, at a given market price, *P*, the supply of open-end fund shares is perfectly elastic. The price at which an open-end investment fund stands ready to sell new shares or redeem existing shares is the **net asset value (NAV)** of the fund. NAV is the current or market value of the fund's assets less any accrued liabilities divided by the number of shares in the fund. An investment fund's willingness to provide instant liquidity to shareholders while it invests funds in equities, bonds, and other long-term instruments could expose it to liquidity problems similar to those banks and life insurance companies face when the number of withdrawals (or fund shares cashed in) rises to abnormally and unexpectedly high levels. Investment funds can be subject to dramatic liquidity runs if investors become nervous about the NAV of the funds' assets. However, the fundamental difference in the way investment fund contracts are valued compared with the valuation of DTI deposit and insurance policy contracts mitigates the incentives for fund shareholders to engage in runs. Specifically, if a fund were to be liquidated, its assets would be distributed to fund shareholders on a pro rata basis rather than the first-come, first-served basis employed under deposit and insurance contracts.

To illustrate this difference, we can directly compare the incentives for mutual fund and hedge fund investors to engage in a run with those of DTI depositors. Table 12–12 shows a simple balance sheet of an open-end investment

TABLE 12–12 Run Incentives of DTI Depositors versus Mutual Fund Investors

DTI				Investment Fund			
Assets		Liabilities		Assets		Liabilities	
Assets	$90	Deposits (100 depositors with $1 deposits)	$100	Assets	$90	Shares (100 shareholders with $1 shares)	$100

fund and a DTI. When they perceive that a DTI's assets are valued below its liabilities, depositors have an incentive to engage in a run on the DTI to be first in line to withdraw. In the example in Table 12–12, only the first 90 bank depositors would receive $1 back for each $1 deposited. The last 10 would receive nothing at all.

Now consider the investment fund with 100 shareholders who invested $1 each for a total of $100, but whose assets are worth $90. If these shareholders tried to cash in their shares, *none* would receive $1. Instead, a fund values its balance sheet liabilities on a market value basis; the price of any share liquidated by an investor is

$$P = \frac{\text{Value of assets}}{\text{Shares outstanding}} = NAV$$

Thus, unlike deposit contracts that have fixed face values of $1, the value of a fund's shares reflects the changing value of its assets divided by the number of shares outstanding.

In Table 12–12, the value of each shareholder's claim is

$$P = \frac{\$90}{100} = \$0.9$$

That is, each investment fund shareholder participates in the fund's loss of asset value on a *pro rata*, or proportional, basis. Technically, whether first or last in line, each fund shareholder who cashes in shares on any given day receives the same NAV per share of the fund. In this case, it is 90 cents, representing a loss of 10 cents per share. All fund shareholders realize this and know that investors share asset losses on a pro rata basis; being the first in line to withdraw has no overall advantage as it has at DTIs.

This is not to say that investment funds bear no liquidity risk, but that the incentives for fund shareholders to engage in runs that produce the extreme form of liquidity problems faced by DTIs and life insurance companies are generally absent. A sudden surge of investment fund shareholder redemptions might require a fund manager to sell some of its less marketable bonds and equities at fire-sale prices. Money market mutual funds (MMMFs) experienced tremendous liquidity at the start of the financial crisis. On September 16, 2008, one day after Lehman Brothers filed for bankruptcy, Reserve Primary Fund, the oldest MMMF in the United States, saw its shares fall to 97 cents (below the $1.00 book value) after writing off debt issued by Lehman Brothers. Resulting investor anxiety about Reserve Primary Fund spread to other funds, and investors industrywide liquidated their MMMF shares. In just one week investors liquidated US$170 billion of the industry total US$4 trillion invested in MMMFs. The U.S. Department of Treasury opened the Temporary Guarantee

Program for MMMFs, which provided up to US$50 billion in coverage to MMMF shareholders for amounts they held in the funds as of close of business that day. The guarantee was triggered if a participating fund's NAV fell below $0.995. The program was designed to address the severe liquidity strains in the industry and immediately stabilized the industry and stopped the outflows.

Some of the biggest liquidity crises recently experienced by FIs have occurred with hedge funds, which are highly specialized investment funds with a limited number of wealthy investors, usually 100 or fewer. For example, in the summer of 2007, two Bear Stearns hedge funds suffered heavy losses on investments in the subprime mortgage market. The two funds filed for bankruptcy in the fall of 2007. Bear Stearns' market value was hurt badly from these losses. The losses became so great that by March 2008 Bear Stearns was struggling to finance its day-to-day operations. Rumours of Bear Stearns' liquidity crisis became a reality as investors began quickly selling off their stock and draining what little liquid assets the firm had left—the first major run on a U.S. FI since the Great Depression. Bear Stearns had no choice but to basically sell itself to the highest bidder to avoid declaring bankruptcy or completely closing down and leaving investors totally empty-handed. JPMorgan Chase purchased the company for US$236 million; Bear Stearns' skyscraper in New York was worth over US$2 billion alone. However, in 2008, some mortgage-backed securities markets (see Chapter 26) were insufficiently deep to be able to absorb the massive sale of hedge fund assets without major price dislocations. As well, during the liquidity crisis in 2007 and 2008, the requirement of many hedge funds for investors to provide three months' notice before withdrawing their funds helped to mitigate the risk of fire sales of assets. A greater liquidity risk for hedge funds came from their high levels of short-term debt funding. Hedge funds were forced to sell assets quickly to meet margin calls from their primary dealers as the global financial system underwent deleveraging.

Despite these recent crises, the incentives for mutual fund shareholders to engage in runs that produce the extreme form of liquidity problems faced by DTIs are generally absent. This situation has led some academics to argue for deposit contracts to be restructured in a form more similar to mutual fund or equity contracts. This might also obviate the need for deposit insurance to deter bank runs.[10]

CONCEPT QUESTIONS

1. **What would be the impact on their liquidity needs if DTIs offered deposit contracts of an open-end mutual fund type rather than the traditional all-or-nothing demand deposit contract?**
2. **How do the incentives of investment fund investors to engage in runs compare with the incentives of DTI depositors?**

[10] An argument against this is that since deposits are money and money is the unit of account in the economy, equity-type contracts could pose a problem if the value of a deposit were to fluctuate from day to day. However, note that MMMFs offer depositlike contracts as well. As their NAV varies, they solve the fluctuating share value problem by setting the value of each share at $1 but allowing the number of shares an individual holds to fluctuate so that the value of the individual's overall holdings moves in line with asset values, while each MMMF share remains at $1. A similar policy could be adopted for deposits at DTIs.

Questions and Problems

1. How does the degree of liquidity risk differ for different types of FIs?
2. What are the two reasons liquidity risk arises? How does liquidity risk arising from the liability side of the balance sheet differ from liquidity risk arising from the asset side of the balance sheet? What is meant by *fire-sale prices*?
3. What are *core deposits*? What role do core deposits play in predicting the probability distribution of net deposit drains?
4. The probability distribution of the net deposit drain of a DTI has been estimated to have a mean of 2 percent and a standard deviation of 1 percent. Is this DTI increasing or decreasing in size? Explain.
5. How is a DTI's distribution pattern of net deposit drains affected by the following?
   a. The holiday season.
   b. Summer vacations.
   c. A severe economic recession.
   d. Double-digit inflation.
6. What are two ways a DTI can offset the liquidity effects of a net deposit drain of funds? How do the two methods differ? What are the operational benefits and costs of each method?
7. What are two ways a DTI can offset the effects of asset-side liquidity risk, such as the drawing down of a loan commitment?
8. A DTI with the following balance sheet ($ millions) expects a net deposit drain of $15 million:

Assets		Liabilities and Equity	
Cash	$ 10	Deposits	$ 68
Loans	50	Equity	7
Securities	15		
Total assets	$ 75	Total liabilities and equity	$ 75

Show the DTI's balance sheet if the following conditions occur:

   a. The DTI purchases liabilities to offset this expected drain.
   b. The stored liquidity management method is used to meet the expected drain.

9. Manitoba Bank has the following balance sheet ($ millions):

Assets		Liabilities and Equity	
Cash	$ 30	Deposits	$ 110
Loans	90	Borrowed funds	40
Securities	50	Equity	20
Total assets	$ 170	Total liabilities and equity	$ 170

Manitoba Bank's largest customer decides to exercise a $15 million loan commitment. How will the new balance sheet appear if Manitoba Bank uses the following liquidity risk strategies?

   a. Stored liquidity management.
   b. Purchased liquidity management.

10. A DTI has assets of $10 million consisting of $1 million in cash and $9 million in loans. The DTI has core deposits of $6 million, subordinated debt of $2 million, and equity of $2 million. Increases in interest rates are expected to cause a net drain of $2 million in core deposits over the year.
    a. The average cost of deposits is 6 percent, and the average yield on loans is 8 percent. The DTI decides to reduce its loan portfolio to offset this expected decline in deposits. What will be the effect on net interest income (NII) and the size of the DTI after the implementation of this strategy?
    b. If the interest cost of issuing new short-term debt is expected to be 7.5 percent, what would be the effect on NII of offsetting the expected deposit drain with an increase in interest-bearing liabilities?
    c. What will be the size of the DTI after the drain if the DTI uses this strategy?
    d. What dynamic aspects of DTI management would further support a strategy of replacing the deposit drain with interest-bearing liabilities?
11. Define each of the following four measures of liquidity risk. Explain how each measure would be implemented and utilized by a DTI.
    a. Sources and uses of liquidity.
    b. Peer group ratio comparisons.
    c. Liquidity index.
    d. Financing gap and financing requirement.
12. A DTI has $10 million in T-bills and a $5 million line of credit to borrow in the repo market. The DTI currently has borrowed $6 million in interbank funds and $2 million from the Bank of Canada to meet seasonal demands.
    a. What is the DTI's total available (sources of) liquidity?
    b. What is the DTI's current total uses of liquidity?
    c. What is the net liquidity of the DTI?
    d. What conclusions can you derive from the result?

13. A DTI has the following assets in its portfolio: $10 million in cash, $25 million in T-bills, and $65 million in mortgage loans. If the DTI has to liquidate the assets today, it will receive only $98 per $100 of face value of the T-bills and $90 per $100 of face value of the mortgage loans. Liquidation at the end of one month (closer to maturity) will produce $100 per $100 of face value of the T-bills and $97 per $100 of face value of the mortgage. Calculate the one-month liquidity index for this DTI using the above information.

14. A DTI has the following assets in its portfolio: $20 million in cash on deposit with the Bank of Canada, $20 million in T-bills, and $50 million in mortgage loans. If the assets need to be liquidated at short notice, the DTI will receive only 99 percent of the fair market value of the T-bills and 90 percent of the fair market value of the mortgage loans. Liquidation at the end of one month (closer to maturity) will produce $100 per $100 of face value of the T-bills and the mortgage loans. Calculate the liquidity index using the above information.

15. Conglomerate Corporation has acquired Acme Corporation. To help finance the takeover, Conglomerate will liquidate the overfunded portion of Acme's pension fund. The face values and current and one-year future liquidation values of the assets that will be liquidated are given below:

		Liquidation Values	
Asset	**Face Value**	$t = 0$	$t = 1$
BCE stock	$10,000	$9,900	$10,500
RBC bonds	5,000	4,000	4,500
Government of Canada securities	15,000	13,000	14,000

Calculate the one-year liquidity index of these securities.

16. Quebec Bank has $10 million in cash and equivalents, $30 million in loans, and $15 million in core deposits.
    a. Calculate the financing gap.
    b. What is the financing requirement?
    c. How can the financing gap be used in the day-to-day liquidity management of the bank?

17. How can an FI's liquidity plan help reduce the effects of liquidity shortages? What are the components of a liquidity plan?

18. CAN Bank has the following balance sheet (in millions of dollars):

Assets		Liabilities and Equity	
Cash	$ 20	Stable retail deposits	$ 190
Deposits at the Bank of Canada	30	Less stable retail deposits	70
Treasury bonds	145	GICs maturing in 6 months	100
Qualifying marketable securities	50	Unsecured wholesale funding from:	
NHA-MBS mortgage bonds	60	Stable small business deposits	125
Loans to AA-rated corporations	540	Less stable small business deposits	100
Mortgages	285	Nonfinancial corporates	450
Premises	35	Equity	130
Total	$1,165	Total	$1,165

Cash inflows over the next 30 days from the bank's performing assets are $7.5 million. Calculate the LCR for CAN Bank.

19. Sask Bank has the following balance sheet (in millions of dollars):

Assets		Liabilities and Equity	
Cash	$ 12	Stable retail deposits	$ 55
Deposits at the Bank of Canada	19	Less stable retail deposits	20
Treasury securities	125	Unsecured wholesale funding from:	
NHA-MBS securities	94	Stable small business deposits	80
Loans to AA-rated corporations	138	Less stable small business deposits	49
Loans to BB-rated corporations	106	Nonfinancial corporates	250
Premises	20	Equity	60
Total	$514	Total	$514

Cash inflows over the next 30 days from the bank's performing assets are $5.5 million. Calculate the LCR for Sask Bank.

20. Alberta Bank has the following balance sheet (in millions of dollars):

Assets		Liabilities and Equity	
Cash	$ 12	Stable retail deposits	$ 55
Deposits at the Bank of Canada	19	Less stable retail deposits	20
Govt. of Canada securities	125	Unsecured wholesale funding from:	
CMHC mortgage securities	94	Stable small business deposits	80
Loans to A-rated corporations (maturity > 1 year)	138	Less stable small business deposits	49
		Nonfinancial corporates	250
Loans to B-rated corporations (maturity < 1 year)	106		
Premises	20	Equity	60
Total	$514	Total	$514

Calculate the LCR for Alberta Bank.

21. What is a bank run? What are some possible withdrawal shocks that could initiate a bank run? What feature of the demand deposit contract provides deposit withdrawal momentum that can result in a bank run?

22. The following is the balance sheet of a DTI ($ millions):

Assets		Liabilities and Equity	
Cash	$ 2	Demand deposits	$ 50
Loans	50		
Plant and equipment	3	Equity	5
Total	$ 55	Total	$ 55

The asset–liability management committee has estimated that the loans, whose average interest rate is 6 percent and whose average life is three years, will have to be discounted at 10 percent if they are to be sold in less than two days. If they can be sold in four days, they will have to be discounted at 8 percent. If they can be sold later than a week from now, the DTI will receive the full market value. Loans are not amortized; that is, the principal is paid at maturity.

a. What will be the price received by the DTI for the loans if they have to be sold in two days? In four days?

b. In a crisis, if depositors all demand payment on the first day, what amount will they receive? What will they receive if they demand to be paid within the week? Assume no deposit insurance.

23. What government safeguards are in place to reduce liquidity risk for DTIs?

24. What are the levels of defence against liquidity risk for a life insurance company? How does liquidity risk for a P&C insurer differ from that for a life insurance company?

25. How is the liquidity problem faced by mutual funds different from that faced by DTIs and insurance companies?

26. A mutual fund has the following assets in its portfolio: $40 million in fixed-income securities and $40 million in stocks at current market values. In the event of a liquidity crisis, the fund can sell the assets at 96 percent of market value if they are disposed of in two days. The fund will receive 98 percent if the assets are disposed of in four days. Two shareholders, A and B, own 5 percent and 7 percent of equity (shares), respectively.

a. Market uncertainty has caused shareholders to sell their shares back to the fund. What will the two shareholders receive if the mutual fund must sell all the assets in two days? In four days?

b. How does this situation differ from a bank run? How have bank regulators mitigated the problem of bank runs?

27. A mutual fund has $1 million in cash and $9 million invested in securities. It currently has 1 million shares outstanding.

a. What is the NAV of this fund?

b. Assume that some of the shareholders decide to cash in their shares of the fund. How many shares at its current NAV can the fund take back without resorting to a sale of assets?

c. As a result of anticipated heavy withdrawals, the fund sells 10,000 shares of stock currently valued at $40. Unfortunately, it receives only $35 per share. What is the NAV after the sale? What are the cash assets of the fund after the sale?

d. Assume that after the sale of stock, 100,000 shares are sold back to the fund. What is the current NAV? Is there a need to sell more securities to meet this redemption?

Appendix 12A Illustrative Template for the LCR

View Appendix 12A on Connect.

CHAPTER 13

FOREIGN EXCHANGE RISK

After studying this chapter you should be able to:

- **LO1** Discuss the difference between spot and forward foreign exchange transactions.
- **LO2** Discuss the sources of foreign exchange risk exposure for FIs.
- **LO3** Calculate an FI's net foreign exchange exposure.
- **LO4** Discuss the four foreign exchange trading activities of FIs.
- **LO5** Discuss the return and risk of foreign exchange positions and on-balance-sheet and off-balance-sheet hedging.
- **LO6** Discuss the interaction of interest rates, inflation, and exchange rates.

INTRODUCTION

The globalization of the financial services industry has meant that FIs are increasingly exposed to foreign exchange (FX) risk. FX risk can occur as a result of trading in foreign currencies, making foreign currency loans (such as a loan in sterling to a corporation), buying foreign-issued securities (U.K. sterling–denominated gilt-edged bonds or German euro-government bonds), or issuing foreign currency–denominated debt (sterling certificates of deposit) as a source of funds. Canadian FIs and their business customers may be particularly exposed to exchange rate risk relative to the U.S. dollar both for trade and the pricing of commodities such as oil and gas, metals, and forest products. In particular, exchange rate movements are related to the Bank of Canada's monetary policy and, therefore, interest rate risk (as discussed in Chapters 8 and 9). Exchange rate movements have been particularly important for Canadian FIs as the U.S. dollar has become more volatile relative to other world currencies.

This chapter looks at how FIs evaluate and measure the risks faced when their assets and liabilities are denominated in foreign (as well as in domestic) currencies and when they take major positions as traders in the spot and forward foreign currency markets.

FOREIGN EXCHANGE RATES AND TRANSACTIONS

FX Rates

direct quote
Canadian dollars received for one unit of the foreign currency exchanged.

An FX rate is the price at which one currency (e.g., the Canadian dollar) can be exchanged for another currency (e.g., the Swiss franc). Table 13–1 lists the closing exchange rates between the Canadian dollar and other currencies as of 16:30, Eastern Standard Time, on March 19, 20, and 21, 2013. FX rates are listed in two ways: Canadian dollars received for one unit of the foreign currency exchanged, or a **direct quote** ("Canadian $ equivalent"), and foreign currency received for each

TABLE 13–1
Foreign Currency Exchange Rates

Source: Bank of Canada, bankofcanada.ca.

Daily closing FX rates

Nominal quotations based on official parities or market rates, in terms of U.S. dollars converted into Canadian dollars. Updated at about 16:30 ET the same business day.

Currency	19/3/13	20/3/13	21/3/13
U.S. dollar (close)	1.0270	1.0254	1.0243
Australian dollar (close)	1.0652	1.0643	1.0691
Danish krone (close)	0.1776	0.1780	0.1772
European euro (close)	1.3235	1.3271	1.3208
Hong Kong dollar (close)	0.132305	0.132099	0.131942
Japanese yen (close)	0.01081	0.01068	0.01080
Mexican peso (close)	0.08251	0.08291	0.08240
New Zealand dollar (close)	0.8466	0.8435	0.8514
Norwegian krone (close)	0.1761	0.1754	0.1754
Swedish krona (close)	0.1590	0.1586	0.1577
Swiss franc (close)	1.0839	1.0859	1.0813
U.K. pound sterling (close)	1.5507	1.5491	1.5540

indirect quote
Foreign currency received for each Canadian dollar exchanged.

Canadian dollar exchanged, or an **indirect quote** ("currency per Canadian $"). For example, the closing exchange rate of U.S. dollars for Canadian dollars on March 21, 2013, was $1.0243 (CDN$/US$), or CDN$1.0243 could be received for each U.S. dollar exchanged. Conversely, the exchange rate of U.S. dollars for each Canadian dollar was US$0.9763 (US$/CDN$), or US$0.9763 could be received for each Canadian dollar exchanged.

FX Transactions

LO1

spot foreign exchange transactions
FX transactions involving the immediate exchange of currencies at the current (or spot) exchange rate.

There are two basic types of FX rates and FX transactions: spot and forward. **Spot foreign exchange transactions** involve the immediate exchange of currencies at the current (or spot) exchange rate—see Figure 13–1. Spot transactions can be conducted through the FX division of banks or a nonbank foreign currency dealer. For example, a Canadian investor wanting to buy U.K. pounds through a local bank on March 21, 2013, essentially had the dollars transferred from his or her bank account to the dollar account of a pound seller at a rate of $1 per 0.6435 pound (or $1.5540 per pound).[1] Simultaneously, pounds are transferred from the seller's account into an account designated by the Canadian investor. If the dollar depreciates in value relative to the pound (e.g., $1 per 0.6046 pound or $1.6540 per pound), the value of the pound investment, if converted back into Canadian dollars, increases. If the dollar appreciates in value relative to the pound (e.g., $1 per 0.6876 pound or $1.4543 per pound), the value of the pound investment, if converted back into Canadian dollars, decreases.

Historically, the exchange of a sum of money into a different currency required a trader to first convert the money into U.S. dollars and then convert it into the desired currency. More recently, cross-currency trades allow currency traders to bypass this step of initially converting into U.S. dollars. Cross-currency trades are a pair of currencies traded in FX markets that do not involve the U.S. dollar. For example, UKP/JPY cross-exchange trading was created to allow individuals in the

[1] In actual practice, settlement—exchange of currencies—normally occurs two days after a transaction.

FIGURE 13–1
Exchange Rate of U.S. $ with Various Foreign Currencies

Source: www.bloomberg.com/markets/currencies.

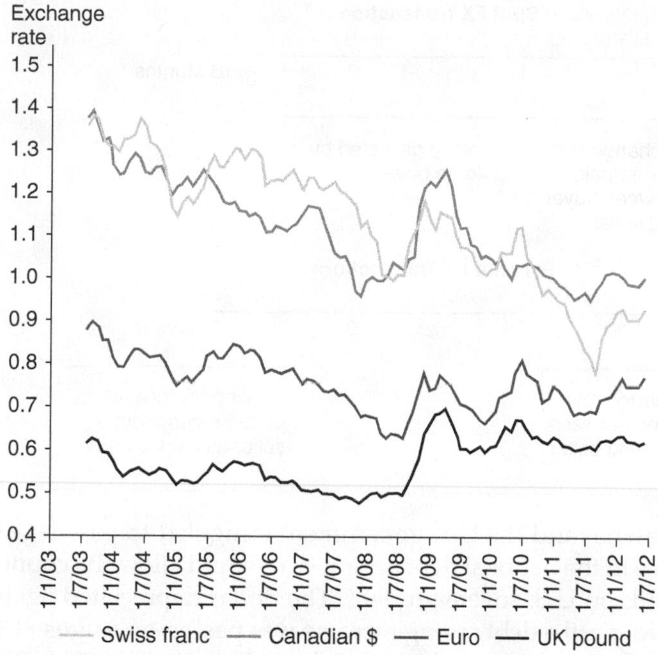

United Kingdom and Japan who wanted to convert their money into the other currency to do so without having to bear the cost of first converting into U.S. dollars. Cross-currency exchange rates for eight major countries are listed by Bloomberg.

bloomberg.com/markets/currencies

The appreciation of a country's currency (or a rise in its value relative to other currencies) means that the country's goods are more expensive for foreign buyers and that foreign goods are cheaper for foreign sellers (all else being constant). Thus, when a country's currency appreciates, domestic manufacturers find it harder to sell their goods abroad and foreign manufacturers find it easier to sell their goods to domestic purchasers. Conversely, depreciation of a country's currency (or a fall in its value relative to other currencies) means the country's goods become cheaper for foreign buyers and foreign goods become more expensive for domestic buyers.

Figure 13–1 shows the pattern of exchange rates between the U.S. dollar and several foreign currencies (the Canadian dollar, the Swiss franc, the euro, and the U.K. pound sterling) from January 2003 through June 2012. Notice the significant swings in the exchange rates of foreign currencies relative to the U.S. dollar during the financial crisis. Between September 2008 and mid-2010, exchange rates went through three trends. During the first phase, from September 2008 to March 2009, the U.S. dollar appreciated relative to most foreign currencies (foreign currencies depreciated relative to the dollar) as investors sought a safe haven in U.S. Treasury securities. During the second phase, from March 2009 through November 2009, much of the appreciation of the dollar relative to foreign currencies was reversed as worldwide confidence returned. Between November 2009 and June 2010, countries (particularly those in the euro area) began to see depreciation relative to the dollar resume (the dollar appreciated relative to the euro) amidst concerns about the euro, due to problems in various EU countries (such as Portugal, Ireland, Iceland, Greece, and Spain). From June 2010 through August 2011 worries about Europe subsided

FIGURE 13–2
Spot versus Forward FX Transaction

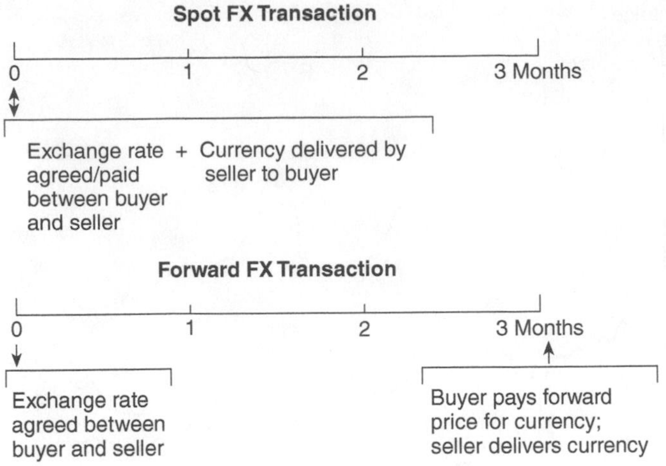

somewhat and the U.S. government struggled to pass legislation allowing an increase in the national debt ceiling that would allow the country to avoid a potential default on U.S. sovereign debt. The dollar depreciated against many foreign currencies until a debt ceiling increase was passed on August 2, 2011. Despite a downgrade in the rating on the U.S. debt by Standard & Poor's (S&P) on August 5, 2011 (resulting from the inability of the U.S. Congress to work to stabilize the U.S. debt deficit situation in the long term), the dollar again appreciated relative to most foreign currencies in the period after August 2011 as fears of escalating problems in Europe, including a possible dissolution of the euro, led investors to again seek safe haven in U.S. Treasury securities.

Further, from 1994 to 2000, U.S. banks had more liabilities to than claims (assets) on foreigners. Thus, if the dollar depreciated relative to foreign currencies, more dollars (converted into foreign currencies) would be needed to pay off the liabilities and U.S. banks would experience a loss due to FX risk. However, the reverse was true in 2005 through 2012; i.e., as the dollar depreciated relative to foreign currencies, U.S. banks experienced a gain from their FX exposures.

forward foreign exchange transaction
The exchange of currencies at a specified exchange rate (or forward exchange rate) at some specified date in the future.

A **forward foreign exchange transaction** is the exchange of currencies at a specified exchange rate (or forward exchange rate) at some specified date in the future, as illustrated in Figure 13–2. An example is an agreement today (at time 0) to exchange dollars for pounds at a given (forward) exchange rate three months in the future. Forward contracts are typically written for one-, three-, or six-month periods, but in practice they can be written over any given length of time.

CONCEPT QUESTION

What is the difference between a spot and a forward FX market transaction?

SOURCES OF FOREIGN EXCHANGE RISK EXPOSURE

LO2

Canadian banks are the major players in foreign currency trading and dealing in Canada. They take significant positions in foreign currency assets and liabilities (see also Chapter 15 on market risk, where we look at methods of calculating value at risk on FX contracts). Table 13–2 shows the annual outstanding dollar value of Canadian

TABLE 13–2 Foreign Currency Assets and Liabilities Reported by Canadian Banks, 2004–2012 ($ millions, as at December 31)

	2004	2005	2006	2007	2008	2009	2010	2011	2012
Liabilities & shareholders' equity	665,448	740,004	949,927	977,072	1,332,588	949,988	1,022,025	1,335,435	1,504,636
Cash, near-cash	67,720	77,723	93,650	100,160	130,132	115,951	130,424	176,562	179,469
Securities	248,143	282,229	342,963	286,142	310,612	304,758	324,691	327,747	369,684
Loans	206,000	240,860	308,675	352,519	476,032	397,769	471,795	558,550	657,670
Derivative-related	73,121	75,572	46,928	134,667	361,070	0	−16,697	112,703	74,141
Other assets	50,454	35,630	132,987	64,112	61,375	115,111	61,366	103,040	159,236
Total foreign assets	645,438	712,014	925,203	937,599	1,339,221	940,060	978,541	1,278,602	1,440,200
Net foreign assets	−20,010	−27,990	−24,724	−39,473	6,634	−9,928	−43,484	−56,833	−64,436
Total assets	1,898,703	2,052,203	2,388,192	2,596,667	3,183,169	2,856,537	3,085,455	3,662,711	3,849,487
Foreign assets/ Total assets	34%	35%	39%	36%	42%	33%	32%	35%	37%

Source: Office of Superintendent of Financial Institutions, osfi-bsif.gc.ca.

domestic banks' on-balance-sheet foreign assets and liabilities for the period 2004 to 2012. The 2008 figure for foreign assets (claims) was $1.339 trillion, with foreign liabilities and shareholders' equity of $1.333 trillion, giving a net foreign asset exposure of $6.63 billion, meaning that the reporting domestic banks were net long in foreign assets. As you can see, Canadian banks reported negative net foreign assets (meaning they are net short foreign currency, as explained below) in every year except 2008. Foreign assets made up an average of 36 percent of the reporting domestic banks' total on-balance-sheet assets over the time period. In 2012, foreign loans were the highest dollar amount at $657.7 billion, followed by securities at $369.7 billion and cash and near-cash at $179.5 billion. The reported on-balance-sheet derivative-related amounts declined significantly between 2008 and 2012.

The Bank for International Settlements (BIS) conducts a survey of the FX and over-the-counter (OTC) derivatives markets activity triennially in April. As well, the Canadian Foreign Exchange Committee (CFEC) conducts a similar survey of the Canadian FX market semiannually in April and October. The seven banks participating in the CFEC's October 2012 survey were Bank of Nova Scotia, BMO Capital Markets, CIBC World Markets, HSBC Bank Canada, National Bank of Canada, RBC Capital Markets, and TD Securities.

Table 13–3 summarizes the foreign currency exchange turnover in Canada as reported to the CFEC's October 2012 survey. The results, by instrument, demonstrate that FX swaps in U.S. dollars against the Canadian dollar constituted the largest amount of FX transactions in Canada. U.S.–Canadian dollar transactions represent 58.3 percent of the $1.12 trillion total monthly turnover reported for business days covered by the survey. Transactions in Canada of the U.S. dollar against currencies other than the Canadian dollar were the next-largest category. The average daily turnover globally was US$4.0 trillion in April 2010, a growth of 20 percent from April 2007. This compares with an average daily turnover of US$51.0 billion in Canada of traditional FX products for October 2012.

Table 13–4 gives the categories of foreign currency positions (or investments) of a hypothetical FI in major currencies. Columns (1) and (2) refer to the assets and liabilities denominated in foreign currencies that are held in the portfolios.

TABLE 13–3 **FX Turnover in Canada, October 2012 (US$ millions)**

Summary by Instrument	Canadian $ vs. U.S. $	U.S. $ vs. Currencies Other Than Canadian $	Canadian $ vs. Currencies Other Than U.S. $	All Other Currency Pairs	Total All Currencies
Spot	147,709	102,452	9,792	7,061	267,013
Outright forwards	77,346	63,256	15,999	2,065	158,685
FX swaps	428,771	241,953	19,181	5,417	695,321
Total	653,825	407,661	44,972	14,562	1,121,019

Source: Canadian Foreign Exchange Committee, *Canadian Foreign Exchange Volume Survey*, Table 3, p. 6, October 2012.

TABLE 13–4 **Sample FI Positions in Foreign Currencies and Foreign Assets and Liabilities (in currency of denomination)**

	(1) Assets	(2) Liabilities	(3) FX Bought*	(4) FX Sold*	(5) Net Position**
U.S. dollars (thousands)	158,058	149,893	901,521	934,328	−24,642
Japanese yen (millions)	59,620	54,591	471,248	481,227	−4,950
Swiss francs (thousands)	142,614	105,387	1,091,408	1,132,886	−4,251
U.K. pounds (thousands)	621,761	516,453	1,579,274	1,626,368	58,214
Euros (thousands)	2,278,375	2,212,581	6,816,463	6,840,067	42,190

* Includes spot, future, and forward contracts.
** Net position = (Assets − Liabilities) + (FX bought − FX sold).

spot foreign exchange
Foreign currency traded for immediate delivery.

forward foreign exchange
Foreign currency traded for future delivery.

net position exposure
The degree to which an FI is net long (positive) or net short (negative) in a given currency.

Columns (3) and (4) refer to foreign currency trading activities (the **spot foreign exchange** and **forward foreign exchange** contracts bought—a long position—and sold—a short position—in each major currency). Foreign currency trading dominates this FI's direct portfolio investments. Even though the aggregate trading positions appear very large—for example, ¥471,248 million—the overall or net exposure position can be relatively small (e.g., the net position in yen was −¥4,950 million).

An FI's overall FX exposure in any given currency can be measured by the **net position exposure**, which is measured in column (5) of Table 13–4 as

$$\begin{aligned}\text{Net exposure}_i &= (\text{FX assets}_i - \text{FX liabilities}_i) + (\text{FX bought}_i - \text{FX sold}_i)\\ &= \text{Net foreign assets}_i + \text{Net FX bought}_i\end{aligned}$$

where

$$i = i\text{th currency}$$

LO3

Clearly, an FI could match its foreign currency assets to its liabilities in a given currency and match buys and sells in its trading book in that foreign currency to reduce its FX net exposure to zero and thus avoid FX risk. It could also offset an imbalance in its foreign asset–liability portfolio by an opposing imbalance in its trading book so that its net exposure position in that currency would be zero.

net long in a currency
Holding more assets than liabilities in a given currency.

net short in a currency
Holding less in assets than in liabilities in a given currency.

Notice in Table 13–4 that this FI had a positive net FX exposure in two of the five major currencies, U.K. pounds and euros. A *positive* net exposure position implies the FI is overall **net long in a currency** (i.e., the FI has bought more foreign currency than it has sold) and faces the risk that the foreign currency will fall in value against the dollar, the domestic currency. A *negative* net exposure position implies that the FI is **net short in a currency** (i.e., the FI has sold more foreign currency than it has purchased) and faces the risk that the foreign currency could rise in value against the dollar. Thus, failure to maintain a fully balanced position in any given currency exposes an FI to fluctuations in the FX rate of that currency against the dollar. The greater the volatility of FX rates given any net exposure position, the greater the fluctuations in value of an FI's FX portfolio. (See Chapter 15, where we discuss market risk.)

Table 13–2 shows the FX exposures only for Canadian banks, but most nonbank FIs also have some FX exposure through either asset–liability holdings or currency trading, for their own account or for their customers. The absolute sizes of these exposures are smaller for three reasons: smaller asset sizes, prudent person concerns,[2] and regulations. For example, the Canada Pension Plan Investment Board's annual report states that as at March 31, 2012, 40.2 percent ($65.1 billion) of its assets was invested in Canada. Of the remaining 59.8 percent, 29.0 percent was invested in North America, excluding Canada; 16.8 percent in the United Kingdom and Europe; 11.1 percent in Japan, Asia, and Australia; and 2.9 percent in other countries.[3]

carry trade
The purchase by an investor of a currency in a country with high interest rates funded by borrowing in a currency with low interest rates.

momentum trading
Taking a large position in a currency (or other financial asset) in order to take advantage of long-term increases in exchange rates.

The levels of claims and positions in foreign currencies held by financial institutions have increased in recent years. Higher volatility in the markets resulted in increased hedging, pushing up the volume of trading. Also, interest rate differentials played a part as **carry trades** were popular, whereby a money manager would buy a higher-interest-rate currency such as the Australian or New Zealand dollar and fund the trade by borrowing a lower-interest-rate currency such as the U.S. dollar, the Japanese yen, or the Swiss franc, thus betting that the exchange rate would not change and wipe out the interest rate differential. In addition, traders also engaged in and profited from **momentum trading** by holding long positions in currencies that were experiencing long-run swings in exchange rates.

FX Rate Volatility and FX Exposure

We can measure the potential size of an FI's FX exposure by analyzing the asset, liability, and currency trading mismatches on its balance sheet and the underlying volatility of exchange rate movements. Specifically, we can use the following equation:

$$\text{Dollar loss (gain) in currency } i = [\text{Net exposure in foreign currency } i \text{ measured in dollars}] \times \text{Shock (volatility) to the \$/Foreign currency } i \text{ exchange rate}$$

The larger the FI's net exposure in a foreign currency and the larger the foreign currency's exchange rate volatility, the larger is the potential dollar loss or gain to an FI's earnings (i.e., the greater its daily value at risk). As we discuss in more detail later in the chapter, the underlying causes of FX volatility reflect fluctuations in the demand for and supply of a country's currency. That is, conceptually, an FX rate is like the price of any good and will appreciate in value relative to other currencies when demand is high or supply is low, and will depreciate in value when demand is low or supply is high. For example, in August 2011, the Swiss National Bank announced that it was considering a plan to fix the country's exchange rate at 1.20 Swiss francs per euro and indicated it was prepared to buy an unlimited amount of euros regardless of the risk to maintain that value. The plan was confirmed on

[2] Prudent person concerns are especially important for pension funds.

[3] Canada Pension Plan Investment Board 2012 Annual Report, page 10, cppib.ca.

September 6, 2011. During the summer of 2011, as the magnitude of the European crisis became apparent and the United States grappled with a looming debt default, Switzerland was one of the few countries with a safe and robust financial system and secure fiscal conditions. Investors bought Swiss francs as a safe-haven currency. The purchases led to large appreciation of the currency: from September 2010 to September 2011, the Swiss franc appreciated by 14.8 percent against the U.S. dollar, 7.7 percent against the euro, 20.7 percent against the Japanese yen, and 14.8 percent against the U.K. pound (see Figure 13–1). This appreciation in the Swiss franc led to lower import costs and more expensive exports. In this export-oriented country, substantial appreciation led to unexpected pressures on export margins that officials worried would weaken the economy and lead to deflationary conditions. With the announcement, the Swiss franc depreciated significantly against most currencies: from August 5 to August 11, 2011, the Swiss franc depreciated by 6.5 percent against the U.S. dollar, 6.1 percent against the euro, 3.7 percent against the Japanese yen, and 7.3 percent against the U.K. pound.

CONCEPT QUESTIONS

1. **How is the net foreign currency exposure of an FI measured?**
2. **If a bank is long in U.K. pounds, does it gain or lose if the dollar appreciates in value against the pound?**
3. **A bank has £10 million in assets and £7 million in liabilities. It has also bought £52 million in foreign currency trading. What is its net exposure in pounds? (£55 million)**

FOREIGN CURRENCY TRADING

LO4

The FX markets of the world have become one of the largest of all financial markets. Trading turnover has averaged as high as US$4.7 trillion a day in recent years, 70 times the daily trading volume on the New York Stock Exchange. Of the over US$4.7 trillion in average daily trading volume in the FX markets in 2011, $1.57 trillion (33.5 percent) involved spot transactions while $3.13 trillion (66.5 percent) involved forward and other transactions. This compares to 1989, when average daily trading volume was $590 billion, $317 billion (53.7 percent) of which was spot FX transactions and $273 billion (46.3 percent) forward and other FX transactions. The main reason for this increase in the use of forward relative to spot FX transactions is the increased ability to hedge FX risk with forward FX contracts (see below). Indeed, FX trading has continued to be one of the few sources of steady income for global banks during the late 2000s and early 2010s.

London is the largest market with 34 percent of global FX trading, followed by New York (17 percent), Switzerland, and Tokyo (6 percent). Canada's share is approximately 1 percent. Table 13–5 lists the top foreign currency traders as of June 2012. The top four banks operating in these markets make up almost half of all foreign currency trading.

FX trading has been called the fairest market in the world because of its immense volume and the fact that no single institution can control the market's direction. Although professionals refer to global FX trading as a market, it is not really one in the traditional sense of the word. There is no central location where FX trading takes place. Moreover, the FX market is essentially a 24-hour market,

TABLE 13–5
Top Currency Traders by Percent of Overall Volume

Source: 2013 Foreign Exchange Survey, Euromoney, euromoney.com.

Rank	Name	Market Share
1	Deutsche Bank	15.18%
2	Citigroup	14.90
3	Barclays	10.24
4	UBS	10.11
5	HSBC	6.93
6	JP Morgan Chase	6.07
7	RBS	5.62
8	Credit Suisse	3.70
9	Morgan Stanley	3.15
10	Bank of America Merrill Lynch	3.08

moving among Tokyo, London, and New York throughout the day. Therefore, fluctuations in exchange rates and thus FX trading risk exposure continue into the night even when other FI operations are closed. This clearly adds to the risk from holding mismatched FX positions. Most of the volume is traded among the top international banks, which process currency transactions for everyone from large corporations to governments around the world. Online FX trading is increasing. Electronic FX trading volume has topped 60 percent of overall global FX trading. The transnational nature of the electronic exchange of funds makes secure, Internet-based trading an ideal platform. Online trading portals—terminals where currency transactions are executed—are a low-cost way of conducting spot and forward FX transactions.

FX Trading Activities

An FI's position in the FX markets generally reflects four trading activities:

1. The purchase and sale of foreign currencies to allow customers to partake in and complete international commercial trade transactions.
2. The purchase and sale of foreign currencies to allow customers (or the FI itself) to take positions in foreign real and financial investments.
3. The purchase and sale of foreign currencies for hedging purposes to offset customer (or FI) exposure in any given currency.
4. The purchase and sale of foreign currencies for speculative purposes through forecasting or anticipating future movements in FX rates.

In the first two activities, the FI normally acts as an *agent* of its customers for a fee but does not assume the FX risk itself. In the third activity, the FI acts defensively as a hedger to reduce FX exposure. For example, it may take a short (sell) position in the FX of a country to offset a long (buy) position in the FX of that same country. Thus, FX risk exposure essentially relates to **open positions** taken as a principal by the FI for speculative purposes, the fourth activity. An FI usually creates an open position by taking an unhedged position in a foreign currency in its FX trading with other FIs. FIs can make speculative trades directly with other FIs or arrange them through specialist FX brokers. Speculative trades can be instituted through a variety of FX instruments. Spot currency trades are the most common, with FIs seeking to make a profit on the difference

open position
An unhedged position in a particular currency.

TABLE 13–6 **FX Trading Revenue of the Big Six Banks, as Reported for Year-End October 31 ($ millions)**

	2004	2005	2006	2007	2008	2009	2010	2011	2012
Bank of Montreal	85	89	204	273	379	362	247	288	269
Bank of Nova Scotia	171*	295*	301*	323*	384*	534*	478*	181	232
CIBC	169	169	163	190	264	291	265	276	290
National Bank	30	28	25	−7	114	85***	91***	92***	73***
Royal Bank*	278	235	300	355	584	641	407	351***	391***
TD Bank	230	248	306	312	481	573	418	428	374

* Includes precious metals trading.
** Includes all FX revenue.
*** Includes commodities.

Sources: Bank annual reports.

between buy and sell prices (i.e., on movements in the bid–ask prices over time). However, FIs can also take speculative positions in FX forward contracts, futures, and options.

Most profits or losses on foreign trading come from taking an open position or speculating in currencies. Revenues from market making—the bid–ask spread—or from acting as agents for retail or wholesale customers generally provide only a secondary or supplementary revenue source.

Note the trading income from FX trading for the six large Canadian banks in Table 13–6. As can be seen, total trading revenue is variable, but generally grew for each FI between 2004 and 2012. The level of operations is not large compared to the rest of the banks' operations, and is small relative to the major U.S. banks. For example, Citigroup and JPMorgan Chase, the dominant FX trading banks in the United States, reported FX trading income of US$1,871.0 million and US$1,043.0 million, respectively, at December 2011.

citigroup.com
jpmorganchase.com

CONCEPT QUESTIONS

1. **What are the four major FX trading activities?**
2. **In which trades do FIs normally act as agents, and in which trades as principals?**
3. **What is the source of most profits or losses on FX trading? What foreign currency activities provide a secondary source of revenue?**

FOREIGN ASSET AND LIABILITY POSITIONS

LO5

The second dimension of an FI's FX exposure results from any mismatches between its foreign financial asset and foreign financial liability portfolios. As discussed earlier, an FI is long a foreign currency if its assets in that currency exceed its liabilities, while it is short a foreign currency if its liabilities in that currency exceed its assets. Foreign financial assets might include Swiss franc–denominated bonds, U.K. pound–denominated gilt-edged securities, or Mexican peso-denominated bonds. Foreign financial liabilities might include issuing U.K. pound CDs or a yen-denominated bond in the Euromarkets to raise yen funds. The globalization of financial markets has created an enormous range of possibilities for raising funds in currencies other than the home currency. This is important for FIs that wish to not only diversify their source and use of funds but also exploit imperfections in foreign banking markets that create opportunities for higher returns on assets or lower funding costs.

The Return and Risk of Foreign Investments

This section discusses the extra dimensions of return and risk from adding foreign currency assets and liabilities to an FI's portfolio. Like domestic assets and liabilities, profits (returns) result from the difference between contractual income from or costs paid on a security. With foreign assets and liabilities, however, profits (returns) are also affected by changes in FX rates.

EXAMPLE 13-1

Calculating the Return of FX Transactions

Suppose that an FI has the following assets and liabilities:

Assets	Liabilities
$100 million loans (one-year) in dollars	$200 million GICs (one-year) in dollars
$100 million-equivalent U.K. loans (one-year) (loans made in sterling)	

The FI is raising all of its $200 million liabilities in dollars (one-year GICs) but investing 50 percent in dollar assets (one-year maturity loans) and 50 percent in U.K. pound sterling assets (one-year maturity loans).[4] In this example, the FI has matched the duration of its assets and liabilities ($D_A = D_L = 1$ year) but has mismatched the currency composition of its asset and liability portfolios. Suppose the promised one-year GIC rate is 8 percent, to be paid in dollars at the end of the year, and that one-year, default risk–free loans in Canada are yielding only 9 percent. The FI would have a positive spread of 1 percent from investing domestically. Suppose, however, that default risk–free one-year loans are yielding 15 percent in the United Kingdom.

To invest in the United Kingdom, the FI decides to take 50 percent of its $200 million in funds and make one-year-maturity U.K. sterling loans while keeping 50 percent of its funds to make dollar loans. To invest $100 million (of the $200 million in GICs issued) in one-year loans in the United Kingdom, the FI engages in the following transactions (illustrated in Panel (a) of Figure 13–3).

1. At the beginning of the year, sells $100 million for pounds on the spot currency markets. If the exchange rate is $1.60 to £1, this translates into $100 million/($1.6/£) = £62.5 million.
2. Takes the £62.5 million and makes one-year U.K. loans at a 15 percent interest rate.
3. At the end of the year, sterling revenue from these loans will be £62.5(1.15) = £71.875 million.
4. Repatriates these funds back to Canada at the end of the year. That is, the FI sells the £71.875 million in the FX market at the spot exchange rate that exists at that time, the end of the year spot rate.

---

[4] For simplicity, we ignore the leverage or net worth aspects of the FI's portfolio.

FIGURE 13–3
Time Line for an FX Transaction

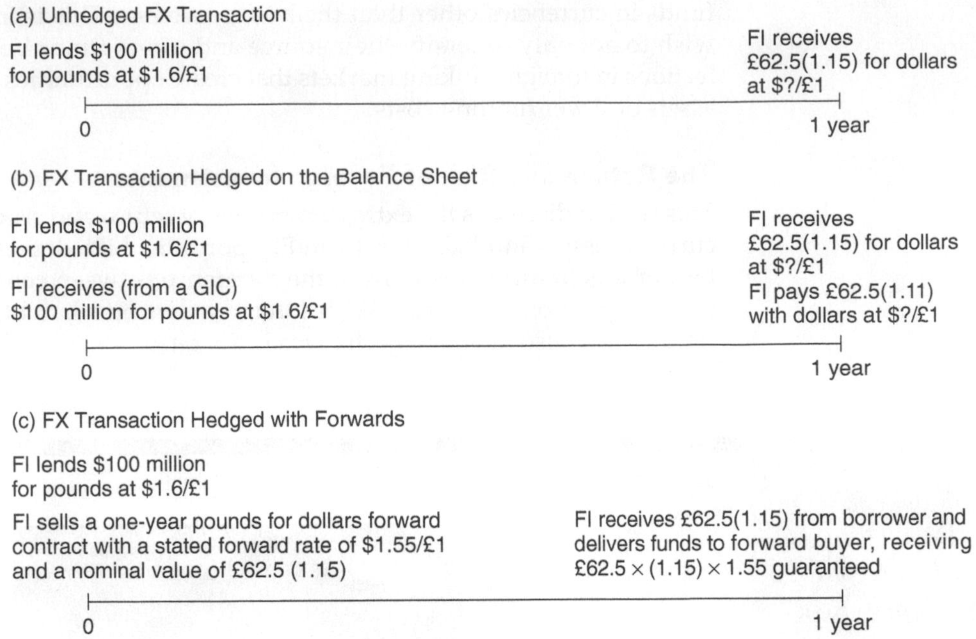
(a) Unhedged FX Transaction
FI lends $100 million for pounds at $1.6/£1
FI receives £62.5(1.15) for dollars at $?/£1
0
1 year
(b) FX Transaction Hedged on the Balance Sheet
FI lends $100 million for pounds at $1.6/£1
FI receives (from a GIC) $100 million for pounds at $1.6/£1
FI receives £62.5(1.15) for dollars at $?/£1
FI pays £62.5(1.11) with dollars at $?/£1
0
1 year
(c) FX Transaction Hedged with Forwards
FI lends $100 million for pounds at $1.6/£1
FI sells a one-year pounds for dollars forward contract with a stated forward rate of $1.55/£1 and a nominal value of £62.5 (1.15)
FI receives £62.5(1.15) from borrower and delivers funds to forward buyer, receiving £62.5 × (1.15) × 1.55 guaranteed
0
1 year

Suppose the spot FX rate has not changed over the year; it remains fixed at $1.60/£1. Then the dollar proceeds from the U.K. investment will be

$$£71.875 \text{ million} \times \$1.60/£1 = \$115 \text{ million}$$

or, as a return,

$$\frac{\$115 \text{ million} - \$100 \text{ million}}{\$100 \text{ million}} = 15\%$$

Given this, the weighted return on the bank's portfolio of investments would be

$$(0.5)(0.09) + (0.5)(0.15) = 0.12 \text{ or } 12\%$$

This exceeds the cost of the FI's GICs by 4 percentage points (12% − 8%).

Suppose, however, that at the end of the year the U.K. pound had fallen in value relative to the dollar, or the dollar had appreciated in value relative to the pound. The returns on the U.K. loans could be far less than 15 percent even in the absence of interest rate or credit risk. For example, suppose the exchange rate had fallen from $1.60/£1 at the beginning of the year to $1.45/£1 at the end of the year when the FI needed to repatriate the principal and interest on the loan. At an exchange rate of $1.45/£1, the pound loan revenues at the end of the year translate into

$$£71.875 \text{ million} \times \$1.45/£1 = \$104.22 \text{ million}$$

or a return on the original dollar investment of

$$\frac{\$104.22 - \$100}{\$100} = 0.0422 = 4.22\%$$

The weighted return on the FI's asset portfolio would be

$$(0.5)(0.09) + (0.5)(0.0422) = 0.0661 = 6.61\%$$

In this case, the FI actually has a loss or has a negative interest margin (6.61% − 8% = −1.39%) on its balance sheet investments.

The reason for the loss is that the depreciation of the pound from \$1.60 to \$1.45 has offset the attractive high yield on U.K. pound sterling loans relative to domestic loans. If the pound had instead appreciated (risen in value) against the dollar over the year—say, to \$1.70/£1—then the Canadian FI would have generated a dollar return from its U.K. loans of

$$£71.875 \times \$1.70/£ = \$122.188 \text{ million}$$

or a percentage return of 22.188 percent. Then the FI would receive a double benefit from investing in the United Kingdom: a high yield on the domestic U.K. loans plus an appreciation in sterling over the one-year investment period.

Risk and Hedging

Since a manager cannot know in advance what the pound/dollar spot exchange rate will be at the end of the year, a portfolio imbalance or investment strategy in which the FI is *net long* \$100 million in pounds (or £62.5 million) is risky. As we discussed, the U.K. loans would generate a return of 22.188 percent if the pound appreciated from \$1.60 to \$1.70 but would produce a return of only 4.22 percent if the pound depreciated in value against the dollar to \$1.45.

In principle, an FI manager can better control the scale of its FX exposure in two major ways: on-balance-sheet hedging and off-balance-sheet (OBS) hedging. On-balance-sheet hedging involves making changes in the on-balance-sheet assets and liabilities to protect FI profits from FX risk. OBS hedging involves no on-balance-sheet changes but rather involves taking a position in forward or other derivative securities to hedge FX risk.

On-Balance-Sheet Hedging

The following example illustrates how an FI manager can control FX exposure by making changes on the balance sheet.

EXAMPLE 13-2

Hedging on the Balance Sheet

Suppose that instead of funding the \$100 million investment in 15 percent U.K. loans with dollar GICs, the FI manager funds the U.K. loans with \$100 million–equivalent one-year pound sterling GICs at a rate of 11 percent (as illustrated in Panel (b) of Figure 13–3). Now the balance sheet of the bank would look like this:

Assets	Liabilities
\$100 million Cdn. loans (9%)	\$100 million Cdn. GICs (8%)
\$100 million U.K. loans (15%) (loans made in sterling)	\$100 million U.K. GICs (11%) (deposits raised in sterling)

In this situation, the FI has both a matched maturity and a matched currency foreign asset–liability book. We might now consider the FI's profitability or spreads between the return on assets and the cost of funds under two scenarios: first, when the pound depreciates in value against the dollar over the year from \$1.60/£1 to \$1.45/£1 and, second, when the pound appreciates in value over the year from \$1.60/£1 to \$1.70/£1.

The Depreciating Pound

When the pound falls in value to \$1.45/£1, the return on the U.K. loan portfolio is 4.22 percent. Consider now what happens to the cost of \$100 million in pound liabilities in dollar terms:

1. At the beginning of the year, the FI borrows $100 million equivalent in sterling GICs for one year at a promised interest rate of 11 percent. At an exchange rate of $1.60/£, this is a sterling equivalent amount of borrowing of $100 million/($1.6/£) = £62.5 million.
2. At the end of the year, the bank has to pay back the sterling GIC holders their principal and interest, £62.5 million(1.11) = £69.375 million.
3. If the pound had depreciated to $1.45/£ over the year, the repayment in dollar terms would be £69.375 million × $1.45/£1 = $100.59 million, or a dollar cost of funds of 0.59 percent.

Thus, at the end of the year the following occurs:

Average return on assets:

$$(0.5)(0.09) + (0.5)(0.0422) = 0.0661 = 6.61\%$$

Canadian asset return + U.K. asset return = Overall return

Average cost of funds:

$$(0.5)(0.08) + (0.5)(0.0059) = 0.04295 = 4.295\%$$

Canadian cost of funds + U.K. cost of funds = Overall cost

Net return:

Average return on assets − Average cost of funds

$$6.61\% - 4.295\% = 2.315\%$$

The Appreciating Pound

When the pound appreciates over the year from $1.60/£1 to $1.70/£1, the return on U.K. loans is equal to 22.188 percent. Now consider the dollar cost of U.K. one-year GICs at the end of the year when the FI has to pay the principal and interest to the GIC holder:

£69.375 million × $1.70/£1 = $117.9375 million

or a dollar cost of funds of 17.9375 percent. Thus, at the end of the year:

Average return on assets:

$$(0.5)(0.09) + (0.5)(0.22188) = 0.15594 \text{ or } 15.594\%$$

Average cost of funds:

$$(0.5)(0.08) + (0.5)(0.179375) = 0.12969 \text{ or } 12.969\%$$

Net return:

$$15.594\% - 12.969\% = 2.625\%$$

Note that even though the FI locked in a positive return when setting the net FX exposure on the balance sheet to zero, net return is still volatile. Thus, the FI is still exposed to FX risk. However, by directly matching its foreign asset and liability book, an FI can lock in a positive return or profit spread no matter which direction exchange rates change over the investment period. For example, even if domestic banking is a relatively low profit activity (i.e., there is a low spread between the return on assets and the cost of funds), the FI could be quite profitable overall. Specifically, it could lock in a large positive spread—if it exists—between deposit rates and loan rates in foreign markets.

In our example, a 4 percent positive spread existed between U.K. one-year loan rates and deposit rates compared with only a 1 percent spread domestically.

Note that for such imbalances in domestic spreads and foreign spreads to continue over long periods of time, financial service firms would have to face significant barriers to entry in foreign markets. Specifically, if real and financial capital is free to move, FIs would increasingly withdraw from the Canadian market and reorient their operations toward the United Kingdom. Reduced competition would widen loan deposit interest spreads in Canada, and increased competition would contract U.K. spreads, until the profit opportunities from foreign activities disappeared. We further discuss FIs' abilities, and limits on their abilities, to engage in cross-border financial and real investments in Chapter 21.[5]

Hedging with Forwards

forward exchange rate
The exchange rate agreed to today for future (forward) delivery of a currency.

Instead of matching its $100 million foreign asset position with $100 million of foreign liabilities, the FI might have chosen to remain unhedged on the balance sheet.[6] As a lower-cost alternative, it could hedge by taking a position in the forward market for foreign currencies—for example, the one-year forward market for selling sterling for dollars. We discuss the nature and use of forward contracts by FI managers more extensively in Chapter 22; however, here we introduce them to show how they can insulate the FX risk of the FI in our example. Any forward position taken would not appear on the balance sheet; it would appear as a contingent OBS claim, which we describe in Chapter 16 as an item below the bottom line. The role of the forward FX contract is to offset the uncertainty regarding the future spot rate on sterling at the end of the one-year investment horizon. Instead of waiting until the end of the year to transfer sterling back into dollars at an unknown spot rate, the FI can enter into a contract to sell forward its *expected* principal and interest earnings on the loan, at today's known **forward exchange rate** for dollars/pounds, with delivery of sterling funds to the buyer of the forward contract taking place at the end of the year. Essentially, by selling the expected proceeds on the sterling loan forward, at a known (forward FX) exchange rate today, the FI removes the future spot exchange rate uncertainty and thus the uncertainty relating to investment returns on the U.K. loan.

---

[5] In the background of the previous example was the implicit assumption that the FI was also matching the durations of its foreign assets and liabilities. In our example, it was issuing one-year-duration sterling GICs to fund one-year-duration sterling loans. Suppose instead that it still had a matched book in size ($100 million) but funded the one-year 15 percent U.K. loans with three-month 11 percent sterling GICs:

$$D_{£A} - D_{£L} = 1 - 0.25 = 0.75 \text{ years}$$

Thus, sterling assets have a longer duration than do sterling liabilities.

If U.K. interest rates were to change over the year, the market value of sterling assets would change by more than the market value of sterling liabilities. This effect should be familiar from Chapter 9. More important, the FI would no longer be locking in a fixed return by matching the size of its foreign currency book since it would have to take into account its potential exposure to capital gains and losses on its sterling assets and liabilities due to shocks to U.K. interest rates. In essence, an FI is hedged against both FX rate risk and foreign interest rate risk only if it matches both the size and the durations of its foreign assets and liabilities in a specific currency.

[6] An FI could also hedge its on-balance-sheet FX risk by taking OBS positions in futures, options, and swaps on foreign currencies. Such strategies are discussed in detail in Chapters 22 through 24.

EXAMPLE 13–3

Hedging with Forwards

Consider the following transactional steps when the FI hedges its FX risk immediately by selling its expected one-year sterling loan proceeds in the forward FX market (illustrated in Panel (c) of Figure 13–3).

1. The FI sells \$100 million for pounds at the *spot* exchange rate *today* and receives \$100 million/(\$1.6/£) = £62.5 million.
2. The FI then immediately lends the £62.5 million to a U.K. customer at 15 percent for one year.
3. The FI also sells the expected principal and interest proceeds from the sterling loan forward for dollars at today's forward rate for one-year delivery. Let the current forward one-year exchange rate between dollars and pounds stand at \$1.55/£1, or at a 5 cent discount to the spot pound; as a percentage discount, we have

   $$(\$1.55 - \$1.60)/\$1.6 = -3.125\%$$

   This means that the forward buyer of sterling promises to pay

   $$£62.5 \text{ million}(1.15) \times \$1.55/£1 = £71.875 \text{ million} \times \$1.55/£1 = \$111.406 \text{ million}$$

   to the FI (the forward seller) in one year when the FI delivers the £71.875 million proceeds of the loan to the forward buyer.
4. In one year, the U.K. borrower repays the loan to the FI plus interest in sterling (£71.875 million).
5. The FI delivers the £71.875 million to the buyer of the one-year forward contract and receives the promised \$111.406 million.

Barring the sterling borrower's default on the loan or the forward buyer's reneging on the forward contract, the FI knows from the very beginning of the investment period that it has locked in a guaranteed return on the U.K. loan of

$$\frac{\$111.406 - \$100}{\$100} = 0.11406 = 11.406\%$$

Specifically, this return is fully hedged against any dollar/pound exchange rate changes over the one-year holding period of the loan investment. Given this return on U.K. loans, the *overall expected return* on the FI's asset portfolio is

$$(0.5)(0.09) + (0.5)(0.11406) = 0.10203 \text{ or } 10.203\%$$

Since the cost of funds for the FI's \$200 million GICs is an assumed 8 percent, it has been able to lock in a risk-free return spread over the year of 2.203 percent regardless of spot exchange rate fluctuations between the initial foreign (loan) investment and repatriation of the foreign loan proceeds one year later.

In the preceding example, it is profitable for the FI to increasingly drop domestic loans and invest in hedged foreign U.K. loans, since the hedged dollar return on foreign loans of 11.406 percent is higher than 9 percent domestic loans. As the FI seeks to invest more in U.K. loans, it needs to buy more spot sterling. This drives up the spot price of sterling in dollar terms to more than \$1.60/£1. In addition, the FI would need to sell more sterling forward (the proceeds of these sterling loans) for dollars, driving the forward rate to below \$1.55/£1. The outcome would widen the dollar forward–spot exchange rate spread on sterling, making forward hedged sterling investments less attractive than before. This process would continue until the Canadian cost of FI funds just equalled the forward hedged return on U.K. loans. That is, the FI could make no further profits by borrowing in dollars and making forward contract–

hedged investments in U.K. loans (see also the discussion below on the interest rate parity theorem).

Multicurrency Foreign Asset-Liability Positions

So far, we have used a one-currency example of a matched or mismatched foreign asset–liability portfolio. Many FIs, including banks, mutual funds, and pension funds, hold multicurrency asset–liability positions. As for multicurrency trading portfolios, diversification across many asset and liability markets can potentially reduce the risk of portfolio returns and the cost of funds. To the extent that domestic and foreign interest rates or stock returns for equities do not move closely together over time, potential gains from asset–liability portfolio diversification can offset the risk of mismatching individual currency asset–liability positions.

real interest rate
The difference between a nominal interest rate and the expected rate of inflation.

Theoretically speaking, the one-period nominal interest rate (r_i) on fixed-income securities in any particular country has two major components. First, the **real interest rate** reflects underlying real sector demand and supply for funds in that currency. Second, the *expected inflation rate* reflects an extra amount of interest lenders demand from borrowers to compensate the lenders for the erosion in the principal (or real) value of the funds they lend due to inflation in goods prices expected over the period of the loan. Formally,[7]

$$r_i = rr_i + i_i^e$$

where

r_i = Nominal interest rate in country i
rr_i = Real interest rate in country i
i_i^e = Expected one-period inflation rate in country i

If real savings and investment demand and supply pressures, as well as inflationary expectations, are closely linked or integrated across countries, we expect to find that nominal interest rates are highly correlated across financial markets. For example, if, as a result of a strong demand for investment funds, German real interest rates rise, there may be a capital outflow from other countries toward Germany. This may lead to rising real and nominal interest rates in other countries as policymakers and borrowers try to mitigate the size of their capital outflows. On the other hand, if the world capital market is not very well integrated, quite significant nominal and real interest deviations may exist before equilibrating international flows of funds materialize. Foreign asset or liability returns are likely to be relatively weakly correlated, and significant diversification opportunities exist.

Table 13–7 lists the correlations among the returns in major stock indices before and during the financial crisis of 2007–2008. Looking at correlations between foreign stock market returns and Canadian and U.S. stock market returns, you can see that all are positive. Further, relative to the pre-crisis period, stock market return correlations increased during the financial crisis. In the pre-crisis period, correlations across markets vary from a high of 0.778 between the United

[7] This equation is often called the *Fisher equation* after Irving Fisher, the economist who first publicized this hypothesized relationship among nominal rates, real rates, and expected inflation. As shown, we ignore the small cross-product term between the real rate and the expected inflation rate.

TABLE 13–7
Correlation of Returns on Stock Markets before and during the Financial Crisis

Source: R. Horvath and P. Poldauf, "International stock market co-movements: What happened during the financial crisis?" *Global Economy Journal*, March 2012.

Panel A: Pre-crisis 19/12/2000–12/09/2008				
	United States	**United Kingdom**	**Japan**	**Hong Kong**
United States	1.000	0.456	0.132	0.135
United Kingdom	0.456	1.000	0.294	0.302
Japan	0.131	0.294	1.000	0.506
Hong Kong	0.135	0.302	0.506	1.000
Australia	0.085	0.281	0.488	0.500
Brazil	0.553	0.354	0.132	0.174
Canada	0.663	0.460	0.176	0.220
Germany	0.538	0.778	0.283	0.285
Panel B: Crisis 15/09/2008–15/12/2010				
	United States	**United Kingdom**	**Japan**	**Hong Kong**
United States	1.000	0.631	0.138	0.216
United Kingdom	0.631	1.000	0.273	0.351
Japan	0.138	0.273	1.000	0.573
Hong Kong	0.216	0.351	0.573	1.000
Australia	0.160	0.340	0.640	0.611
Brazil	0.702	0.514	0.112	0.301
Canada	0.777	0.574	0.213	0.302
Germany	0.663	0.865	0.271	0.327

Kingdom and Germany to a low of 0.085 between the United States and Australia. In the crisis period, correlations across markets vary from a high of 0.865 between the United Kingdom and Germany to a low of 0.112 between Japan and Brazil.[8]

CONCEPT QUESTIONS

1. **The cost of one-year Canadian dollar GICs is 8 percent, one-year Canadian dollar loans yield 10 percent, and U.K. pound loans yield 15 percent. The dollar/pound spot exchange is \$1.50/£1, and the one-year forward exchange rate is \$1.48/£1. Are one-year Canadian dollar loans more or less attractive than U.K. pound loans?**
2. **What are two ways an FI manager can control FX exposure?**

INTEREST RATE, INFLATION, AND EXCHANGE RATE INTERACTIONS

LO6

As global financial markets have become increasingly interlinked, so have interest rates, inflation, and FX rates. For example, higher domestic interest rates may attract foreign financial investment and impact the value of the domestic currency. In this section, we look at the effect that inflation in one country has on its foreign currency exchange rates—purchasing power parity (PPP). We also examine the

[8] From the Fisher relationship, high correlations may be due to high correlations of real interest rates over time and/or inflation expectations.

links between domestic and foreign interest rates and spot and forward FX rates—interest rate parity (IRP).

PPP

One factor affecting a country's foreign currency exchange rate with another country is the relative inflation rate in each country (which, as shown below, is directly related to the relative interest rates in these countries). Specifically,

$$r_{CAN} = i_{CAN} + rr_{CAN}$$

and

$$r_S = i_S + rr_S$$

where

r_{CAN} = Interest rate in Canada
r_S = Interest rate in Switzerland (or another foreign country)
i_{CAN} = Inflation rate in Canada
i_S = Inflation rate in Switzerland (or another foreign country)
rr_{CAN} = Real rate of interest in Canada
rr_S = Real rate of interest in Switzerland (or another foreign country)

Assume that real rates of interest (or rates of time preference) are equal across countries:

$$rr_{CAN} = rr_S$$

Then

$$r_{CAN} - r_S = i_{CAN} - i_S$$

The (nominal) interest rate spread between Canada and Switzerland reflects the difference in inflation rates between the two countries.

As relative inflation rates (and interest rates) change, foreign currency exchange rates that are not constrained by government regulation should also adjust to account for relative differences in the price levels (inflation rates) between the two countries. One theory that explains how this adjustment takes place is the theory of **purchasing power parity (PPP)**. According to PPP, foreign currency exchange rates between two countries adjust to reflect changes in each country's price levels (or inflation rates and, implicitly, interest rates) as consumers and importers switch their demands for goods from relatively high inflation (interest) rate countries to low inflation (interest) rate countries. Specifically, the PPP theorem states that the change in the exchange rate between two countries' currencies is proportional to the difference in the inflation rates in the two countries. That is,

purchasing power parity (PPP)
The theory explaining the change in foreign currency exchange rates as inflation rates in the countries change.

$$i_{Domestic} - i_{Foreign} = \Delta S_{Domestic/Foreign} / S_{Domestic\,/\,Foreign}$$

where

$S_{Domestic/Foreign}$ = Spot exchange rate of the domestic currency for the foreign currency (e.g., Canadian dollars for Swiss francs)
$\Delta S_{Domestic/Foreign}$ = Change in the one-period FX rate

Thus, according to PPP, the most important factor determining exchange rates is the fact that in open economies, differences in prices (and, by implication, price level changes with inflation) drive trade flows and thus demand for and supplies of currencies.

EXAMPLE 13-4

Application of PPP

Suppose that the current spot exchange rate of Canadian dollars for Russian rubles, $S_{CAN/R}$, is 0.17 (i.e., 0.17 dollar, or 17 cents, can be received for 1 ruble). The price of Russian-produced goods increases by 10 percent (i.e., inflation in Russia, i_R, is 10 percent), and the Canadian price index increases by 4 percent (i.e., inflation in Canada, i_{CAN}, is 4 percent). According to PPP, the 10 percent rise in the price of Russian goods relative to the 4 percent rise in the price of Canadian goods results in a depreciation of the Russian ruble (by 6 percent). Specifically, the exchange rate of Russian rubles to Canadian dollars should fall, so that[9]

$$\text{Canadian inflation rate} - \text{Russian inflation rate} = \frac{\text{Change in spot exchange rate of Canadian dollars for Russian rubles}}{\text{Initial spot exchange rate of Canadian dollars for Russian rubles}}$$

or

$$i_{CAN} - i_R = \Delta S_{CAN/R}/S_{CAN/R}$$

Plugging in the inflation and exchange rates, we get

$$0.04 - 0.10 = \Delta S_{CAN/R}/S_{CAN/R} = \Delta S_{CAN/R}/0.17$$

or

$$-0.06 = \Delta S_{CAN/R}/0.17$$

and

$$\Delta S_{CAN/R} = -(0.06) \times 0.17 = -0.0102$$

Thus, it costs 1.02 cents less to receive a ruble (i.e., 1 ruble costs 15.98 cents: 17 cents − 1.02 cents), or 0.1598 of \$1 can be received for 1 ruble. The Russian ruble depreciates in value by 6 percent against the Canadian dollar as a result of its higher inflation rate.[10]

IRP Theorem

interest rate parity theorem (IRPT)
The relationship in which the discounted spread between domestic and foreign interest rates equals the percentage spread between forward and spot exchange rates.

We discussed earlier that FX spot market risk can be reduced by entering into forward FX contracts. In general, spot rates and forward rates for a given currency differ. The forward exchange rate is determined by the spot exchange rate and the interest rate differential between the two countries. The specific relationship that links spot exchange rates, interest rates, and forward exchange rates is described as the **interest rate parity theorem (IRPT)**. Intuitively, the IRPT implies that by hedging in the forward exchange rate market, an investor realizes the same returns whether investing domestically or in a foreign country. This is a *no-arbitrage relationship* in the sense that the investor cannot make a risk-free return by taking offsetting positions in the domestic and foreign markets. That is, the hedged dollar return on foreign investments just equals the return on domestic investments. The eventual equality between the cost of domestic funds and the hedged return on foreign assets, or the IRP, can be expressed as

$$1 + r_i^D = \frac{1}{S_t} \times [1 + r_{ukt}^L] \times F_t$$

[9] This is the relative version of the PPP theorem. There are other versions of the theory (such as the absolute PPP and the law of one price). However, the version shown here is the one most commonly used.

[10] A 6 percent fall in the ruble's value translates into a new exchange rate of 0.1598 dollars per ruble if the original exchange rate between dollars and rubles was 0.17.

or

Rate on domestic investment = Hedged return on foreign (U.K.) investment

where

$1 + r_t^D$ = 1 plus the interest rate on GICs for the FI at time t
S_t = \$/£ spot exchange rate at time t
$1 + r_{ukt}^L$ = 1 plus the interest rate on U.K. loans at time t
F_t = \$/£ forward exchange at time t

EXAMPLE 13-5

An Application of the IRPT

Suppose r_t^D = 8 percent and r_{ukt}^L = 15 percent, as in Example 13–3. As the FI moves into more U.K. loans, suppose the spot exchange rate for buying pounds rises from \$1.60/£1 to \$1.63/£1. In equilibrium, the forward exchange rate would have to fall to \$1.5308/£1 to completely eliminate the attractiveness of U.K. investments to the FI manager. That is,

$$(1.08) = \left(\frac{1}{1.63}\right)[1.15](1.5308)$$

This is a *no-arbitrage* relationsip in the sense that the hedged dollar return on foreign investments just equals the FI's dollar cost of domestic GICs. Rearranging, the IRP can be expressed as

$$\frac{r_t^D - r_{ukt}^L}{1 + r_{ukt}^L} \simeq \frac{F_t - S_t}{S_t}$$

$$\frac{0.08 - 0.15}{1.15} \simeq \frac{1.5308 - 1.63}{1.63}$$

$$-0.0609 \simeq -0.0609$$

That is, the discounted spread between domestic and foreign interest rates is, in equilibrium, approximately equal to ($\simeq$) the percentage spread between forward and spot exchange rates.

Suppose that in the preceding example, the annual rate on domestic deposits is 8.1 percent (rather than 8 percent). In this case, it would be profitable for the investor to put excess funds in domestic rather than U.K. deposits. In fact, the arbitrage opportunity that exists results in a flow of funds out of U.K. time deposits into domestic time deposits. According to the IRPT, this flow of funds would quickly drive up the dollar–U.K. pound exchange rate until the potential profit opportunities from domestic deposits are eliminated. The implication of IRPT is that in a competitive market for deposits, loans, and FX, the potential profit opportunities from overseas investment for the FI manager are likely to be small and fleeting.[11] Long-term violations of IRPT are likely to occur only if there are major imperfections in international deposit, loan, and other financial markets, including barriers to cross-border financial flows.

CONCEPT QUESTIONS

1. **What is PPP?**
2. **What is the IRP condition? How does it relate to the existence or nonexistence of arbitrage opportunities?**

[11] Note that in a fully competitive market for loans and deposits (and free movement of exchange rates), not only would the domestic deposit rate equal the hedged return on U.K. loans (8 percent in our example), but also the domestic loan rate (for risk-free loans) would be driven into equality with the domestic GIC rate, that is, it would fall from 9 percent to 8 percent.

Questions and Problems

1. What are the four FX risks faced by FIs?
2. What is the spot market for FX? What is the forward market for FX? What is the position of being net long in a currency?
3. Refer to Table 13–1.
   a. What was the spot exchange rate of Canadian dollars for U.S. dollars as a direct quote on March 21, 2013? As an indirect quote?
   b. What was the spot exchange rate of Canadian dollars for U.K. pounds sterling as a direct quote on March 19, 2013? As an indirect quote?
4. Refer to Table 13–1.
   a. On February 19, 2013, Credit Union Jack purchased a U.K. pound–denominated interbank certificate of deposit (CD) by converting $1 million into pounds at a rate of 0.6400 pound per Canadian dollar. It is now March 19, 2013. Has the Canadian dollar appreciated or depreciated in value relative to the pound?
   b. Using the information in part (a), what is Credit Union Jack's FX gain or loss on the investment in the CD? Assume that no interest has been paid on the CD.
5. On March 19, 2013, Olympic Bank converts $500,000 into U.S. dollars in the spot FX market and purchases a one-month forward contract to convert U.S. dollars into Canadian dollars. If the forward rate is US$0.9767 per Canadian dollar, how much will Olympic receive in Canadian dollars at the end of the month? Use the data in Table 13–1 for the spot rate.
6. X-IM Bank has ¥14 million in assets and ¥23 million in liabilities and has sold ¥8 million in foreign currency trading. What is the net exposure for X-IM? For what type of exchange rate movement does this exposure put the bank at risk?
7. What two factors directly affect the profitability of an FI's position in a foreign currency?
8. The following are the foreign currency positions of an FI, expressed in dollars:

Currency	Assets	Liabilities	FX Bought	FX Sold
Swiss franc (Sf)	$125,000	$50,000	$10,000	$15,000
U.K. pound (£)	50,000	22,000	15,000	20,000
Japanese yen (¥)	75,000	30,000	12,000	88,000

   a. What is the FI's net exposure in Swiss francs?
   b. What is the FI's net exposure in U.K. pounds?
   c. What is the FI's net exposure in Japanese yen?
   d. What is the expected loss or gain if the Sf exchange rate appreciates by 1 percent?
   e. What is the expected loss or gain if the £ exchange rate appreciates by 1 percent?
   f. What is the expected loss or gain if the ¥ exchange rate appreciates by 2 percent?
9. What are the four FX trading activities undertaken by FIs? How do FIs profit from these activities?
10. CB Bank issued $200 million of one-year GICs in Canada at a rate of 6.50 percent. It invested part of this money, $100 million, in the purchase of a one-year bond issued by a Canadian firm at an annual rate of 7 percent. The remaining $100 million was invested in a one-year Brazilian government bond paying an annual interest rate of 8 percent. The exchange rate at the time of the transactions was Brazilian real 0.5/$1.
    a. What will be the net return on this $200 million investment in bonds if the exchange rate between the Brazilian real and the Canadian dollar remains the same?
    b. What will be the net return on this $200 million investment if the exchange rate changes to real 0.4167/$1?
    c. What will be the net return on this $200 million investment if the exchange rate changes to real 0.40/$1?
11. Atlantic Bank has purchased a €16 million one-year loan that pays 12 percent interest annually. The spot rate of Canadian dollars per euro is $1.25/€1. Atlantic Bank has funded this loan by accepting a U.K. pound (£)–denominated deposit for the equivalent amount and maturity at an annual rate of 10 percent. The current spot rate of the U.K. pound is $1.60/£1.
    a. What is the net interest income (NII) earned in dollars on this one-year transaction if the spot rates of Canadian dollars per euro and Canadian dollars per U.K. pound at the end of the year are 1.35 and 1.70?
    b. What should be the spot rate of Canadian dollars per U.K. pound at the end of the year in order for the bank to earn a net interest margin of 4 percent?
    c. Does your answer to part (b) imply that the dollar should appreciate or depreciate against the pound?

d. What is the total effect on NII and principal of this transaction given the end-of-year spot rates in part (a)?

12. Newfoundland Bank just made a one-year $10 million loan that pays 10 percent interest annually. The loan was funded with a Swiss franc–denominated one-year deposit at an annual rate of 6 percent. The current spot rate is Sf1.05/$1.
    a. What will be the NII in dollars on the one-year loan if the spot rate at the end of the year is Sf1.03/$1?
    b. What will be the net interest return on assets?
    c. What is the total effect on NII and principal of this transaction given the end-of-year spot rates in part (a)?
    d. How far can the Sf/$1 appreciate before the transaction will result in a loss for the Newfoundland Bank?
13. What motivates FIs to hedge foreign currency exposures? What are the limitations to hedging foreign currency exposures?
14. What are the two primary methods of hedging FX risk for an FI? What two conditions are necessary to achieve a perfect hedge through on-balance-sheet hedging? What are the advantages and disadvantages of OBS hedging in comparison to on-balance-sheet hedging?
15. Suppose that a Canadian FI has the following assets and liabilities:

Assets	Liabilities
$100 million C$ loans (one year) in dollars	$200 million C$ GICs (one year) in dollars
$100 million–equivalent U.K. loans (one year) (loans made in pounds)	

The promised one-year Canadian dollar GIC rate is 5 percent, to be paid in Canadian dollars at the end of the year; the one-year, default risk–free loans in Canada are yielding 6 percent; and default risk–free one-year loans are yielding 12 percent in the United Kingdom. The exchange rate of dollars for pounds at the beginning of the year is $1.6/£1.

a. Calculate the dollar proceeds from the U.K. investment at the end of the year, the return on the FI's investment portfolio, and the net interest margin for the FI if the spot FX rate has not changed over the year.
b. Calculate the dollar proceeds from the U.K. investment at the end of the year, the return on the FI's investment portfolio, and the net interest margin for the FI if the spot FX rate falls to $1.45/£1 over the year.
c. Calculate the dollar proceeds from the U.K. investment at the end of the year, the return on the FI's investment portfolio, and the net interest margin for the FI if the spot FX rate rises to $1.70/£1 over the year.

16. Suppose that instead of funding the $100 million investment in 12 percent U.K. loans with Canadian dollar GICs, the FI manager in question 15 funds the U.K. loans with $100 million–equivalent one-year pound GICs at a rate of 8 percent. Now the balance sheet of the FI would be as follows:

Assets	Liabilities
$100 million C$ loans (6%) $100 million	$100 million C$ GICs (5%) $100 million
U.K. loans (12%) (loans made in pounds)	U.K. GICs (8%) (deposits raised in pounds)

a. Calculate the return on the FI's investment portfolio, the average cost of funds, and the net interest margin for the FI if the spot FX rate falls to $1.45/£1 over the year.
b. Calculate the return on the FI's investment portfolio, the average cost of funds, and the net interest margin for the FI if the spot FX rate rises to $1.70/£1 over the year.

17. Suppose that instead of funding the $100 million investment in 12 percent U.K. loans with GICs issued in the United Kingdom, the FI manager in question 16 hedges the FX risk on the U.K. loans by immediately selling its expected one-year pound loan proceeds in the forward FX market. The current forward one-year exchange rate between dollars and pounds is $1.50/£1, or a 5 cent discount to the spot pound.
    a. Calculate the return on the FI's investment portfolio (including the hedge) and the net interest margin for the FI over the year.
    b. Will the net return be affected by changes in the dollar for pound spot FX rate at the end of the year?
18. Suppose that a Canadian FI has the following assets and liabilities:

Assets	Liabilities
$300 million C$ loans (one year) in dollars	$500 million C$ GICs (one year) in dollars
$200 million–equivalent German loans (one year) (loans made in euros)	

The promised one-year Canadian GIC rate is 4 percent, to be paid in dollars at the end of the year; the one-year, default risk–free loans in Canada are yielding 6 percent; and default risk–free one-year loans are yielding 10 percent in Germany. The exchange rate of dollars to euros at the beginning of the year is $1.25/€1.

a. Calculate the dollar proceeds from the German loan at the end of the year, the return on the FI's investment portfolio, and the net interest margin for the FI if the spot FX rate has not changed over the year.

b. Calculate the dollar proceeds from the German loan at the end of the year, the return on the FI's investment portfolio, and the net interest margin for the FI if the spot FX rate falls to $1.15/€1 over the year.

c. Calculate the dollar proceeds from the German loan at the end of the year, the return on the FI's investment portfolio, and the net interest margin for the FI if the spot FX rate rises to $1.35/€1 over the year.

19. Suppose that instead of funding the $200 million investment in 10 percent German loans with Canadian dollar GICs, the FI manager in question 18 funds the German loans with $200 million–equivalent one-year euro GICs at a rate of 7 percent. Now the balance sheet of the FI would be as follows:

Assets	Liabilities
$300 million C$ loans (6%) $200 million	$300 million C$ GICs (4%) $200 million
German loans (10%) (loans made in euros)	German CDs (7%) (deposits raised in euros)

a. Calculate the return on the FI's investment portfolio, the average cost of funds, and the net interest margin for the FI if the spot FX rate falls to $1.15/€1 over the year.

b. Calculate the return on the FI's investment portfolio, the average cost of funds, and the net interest margin for the FI if the spot FX rate rises to $1.35/€1 over the year.

20. Suppose that instead of funding the $200 million investment in 10 percent German loans with GICs issued in Germany, the FI manager in question 19 hedges the FX risk on the German loans by immediately selling its expected one-year euro loan proceeds in the forward FX market. The current forward one-year exchange rate between dollars and euros is $1.20/€1.

a. Calculate the return on the FI's investment portfolio (including the hedge) and the net interest margin for the FI over the year.

b. Will the net return be affected by changes in the dollar for euro spot FX rate at the end of the year?

21. North Bank has been borrowing in the U.S. markets and lending abroad, thus incurring FX risk. In a recent transaction, it issued a one-year US$2 million GIC at 6 percent and funded a loan in euros at 8 percent. The spot rate for the euro was €1.45/US$ at the time of the transaction.

a. Information received immediately after the transaction closing indicated that the euro will depreciate to €1.47/US$ by year-end. If the information is correct, what will be the realized spread on the loan? What should the bank interest rate on the loan have been to maintain the 2 percent spread?

b. The bank had an opportunity to sell one-year forward euros at €1.46. What would the spread on the loan have been if the bank had hedged forward its FX exposure?

c. What would an appropriate change in loan rates have been to maintain the 2 percent spread if the bank intended to hedge its exposure using forward contracts?

22. A bank purchases a six-month US$1 million eurodollar deposit at an annual interest rate of 6.5 percent. It invests the funds in a six-month Swedish krone bond paying 7.5 percent per year. The current spot rate is US$0.18/SK.

a. The six-month forward rate on the Swedish krone is being quoted at US$0.1810/SK. What is the net spread earned on this investment if the bank covers its FX exposure using the forward market?

b. What forward rate will cause the spread to be only 1 percent per year?

c. Explain how forward and spot rates will both change in response to the increased spread.

d. Why will a bank still be able to earn a spread of 1 percent knowing that IRP usually eliminates arbitrage opportunities created by differential rates?

23. How does the lack of perfect correlation of economic returns between international financial markets affect the risk–return opportunities for FIs holding multicurrency assets and liabilities? Refer to Table 13–7. Which country pairings seem to have the highest correlation of stock returns before and during the financial crisis?

24. What is the PPP theorem?
25. Suppose that the current spot exchange rate of Canadian dollars for Australian dollars, $S_{C\$/A\$}$, is 1.0277 (i.e., $1.0277 can be received for 1 Australian dollar). The price of Australian-produced goods increases by 5 percent (i.e., inflation in Australia, i_A, is 5 percent), and the Canadian price index increases by 3 percent (i.e., inflation in Canada, i_C, is 3 percent). Calculate the new spot exchange rate of Canadian dollars for Australian dollars that should result from the difference in inflation rates.
26. Explain the concept of IRP. What does this concept imply about the long-run profit opportunities from investing in international markets? What market conditions must prevail for the concept to be valid?
27. Assume that annual interest rates are 8 percent in Canada and 4 percent in Japan. An FI can borrow (by issuing GICs) or lend (by purchasing GICs) at these rates. The spot rate is $0.60/¥.
    a. If the forward rate is $0.64/¥, how could the FI arbitrage using a sum of $1 million? What is the expected spread?
    b. What forward rate will prevent an arbitrage opportunity?
28. What is the relationship between the real interest rate, the expected inflation rate, and the nominal interest rate on fixed-income securities in any particular country? Refer to Table 13–7. What factors may be the reasons for the relatively high correlation coefficients?
29. What is economic integration? What impact does the extent of economic integration of international markets have on the investment opportunities for FIs?
30. An FI has $100,000 of net positions outstanding in U.K. pounds (£) and –$30,000 in Swiss francs (Sf). The standard deviation of the net positions as a result of exchange rate changes is 1 percent for the Sf and 1.3 percent for the £. The correlation coefficient between the changes in exchange rates of the £ and the Sf is 0.80.
    a. What is the risk exposure to the FI of fluctuations in the £/$ rate?
    b. What is the risk exposure to the FI of fluctuations in the Sf/$ rate?
    c. What is the risk exposure if both the £ and the Sf positions are combined?
31. A mutual fund manager is looking for some profitable investment opportunities and observes the following one-year interest rates on government securities and exchange rates: $r_{CAN} = 12\%$, $r_{UK} = 9\%$, $S =$ CDN$1.50/£, $f =$ CDN$1.6/£, where S is the spot exchange rate and f is the forward exchange rate. Which of the two types of government securities would constitute a better investment?

CHAPTER 14

SOVEREIGN RISK

After studying this chapter you should be able to:

LO1 Discuss the difference between credit risk and sovereign risk.

LO2 Discuss the difference between debt repudiation and debt rescheduling.

LO3 Discuss and apply country risk evaluation models.

LO4 Discuss the secondary market for sovereign risk.

INTRODUCTION

worldbank.org
imf.org

In the 1970s, major international banks rapidly expanded their loans to Eastern European, Latin American, and other emerging market and less-developed countries (LDCs). This was largely to meet these countries' demand for funds beyond those provided by the World Bank and the International Monetary Fund (IMF) to aid their development. These loans allowed international banks to recycle "petrodollar" funds from huge U.S. dollar holders such as Saudi Arabia, dollars that helped to create the LIBOR market. Making LDC loans resulted in **sovereign risk** for the banks, the risk of a foreign government's limiting or preventing domestic borrowers in its jurisdiction from repaying the principal and interest on debt owed to external lenders. In many cases, these loans were made with little judgment regarding the credit quality of the sovereign country in which the borrower resided.

sovereign risk
The risk of a foreign government's limiting or preventing domestic borrowers in its jurisdiction from repaying amounts owed to external lenders.

debt moratorium
A delay in repaying interest and/or principal on a debt.

loan loss provision
An amount deducted from income and used to write off bad loans as the losses are realized.

Due to rapidly deteriorating macroeconomic conditions, in the fall of 1982, both the Mexican and Brazilian governments announced a **debt moratorium** (a delay in repaying interest and/or principal on debt) that had a major and long-lasting impact on the balance sheets and profits of internationally active banks. In 1987, the newly formed Office of the Superintendent of Financial Institutions (OSFI) required Canadian banks to increase their **loan loss provisions** to 30 to 40 percent of their loans outstanding to 34 countries, including Mexico, Argentina, and Brazil. The Canadian banks made combined provisions of \$8.5 billion on loans of \$20.5 billion. The net dollar exposure of \$12 billion (\$20.5 − \$8.5 billion) represented 66 percent of the Big Six Canadian banks' common equity. In 1989, Canadian Imperial Bank of Commerce (CIBC), which held \$1.17 billion in non-Mexican LDC debt, increased its loan loss provisions by \$525 million and took an after-tax charge to its 1989 earnings of \$300 million. CIBC also restructured its Mexican debt, which totalled \$604 million at the time. By comparison, the U.S. banks' average exposure to LDC debt in 1989 was 120 percent of total equity. Citicorp (now Citigroup) alone set aside US\$5 billion in loan loss reserves after Brazil declared a debt moratorium on its US\$68 billion commercial bank debt.

osfi-bsif.gc.ca
cibc.com

Notwithstanding their experience with LDC lending, international FIs began once again to invest considerable amounts in emerging-market (EM) countries in the late 1980s to early 1990s. The Basel I capital regulations (Chapter 20) came into effect for internationally active banks in the early 1990s, reducing the returns on bank loans. So rather than making loans, the FIs concentrated their investments in bond debt and equity claims. However, with rising trade deficits and declining foreign exchange (FX) reserves, the "tequila crisis" occurred and Mexico devalued its peso in December 1994, triggering a run on EM debt and equity markets. The U.S. government, the IMF, and the Bank for International Settlements (BIS) put together a US$50 billion international aid package, providing loan guarantees over three to five years to help restructure the debt. Mexican oil revenues were promised as collateral, and by January 1997, the Mexican economy had improved and the Mexican government paid back all of its loans.

However, EMs in Asia faltered again in 1997 when an economic and financial crisis in Thailand, a relatively small country in terms of financial markets, produced worldwide reactions. In early July, the devaluation of the Thai baht resulted in contagious devaluations of currencies throughout Southeast Asia (including those of Indonesia, Singapore, Malaysia, and South Korea), and the devaluations eventually spread to South America and Russia.

Possibly as a reaction to the events (losses) experienced with the Latin American countries in the 1980s or to improved sovereign risk assessment techniques (see later discussion), North American FIs held their exposure in Asia in the mid- and late 1990s to approximately one-third of the investment made by Japanese and European banks. They still experienced losses from these sovereign risks. In 1999, North American banks wrote off hundreds of millions of dollars as they accepted a payoff of less than five cents on the dollar for Russian securities. As Asian currencies collapsed, FIs such as Yamaichi Securities in Japan and Peregrine Investment Holdings in Hong Kong failed or were forced to merge or restructure. Commercial banks in Japan and Hong Kong that had lent heavily to other Southeast Asian countries failed in record numbers as well.

In the early 2000s, concerns were raised about the ability of Argentina and Turkey to meet their debt obligations and the effects this would have on other EM countries. For example, in December 2001, Argentina defaulted on US$130 billion in government-issued debt, and in 2002, passed legislation that led to defaults on US$30 billion of corporate debt owed to foreign creditors. The situation continued to deteriorate, and in November 2002 Argentina's government paid only US$79.5 million of a US$805 million repayment (that had become more than 30 days delinquent) due to the World Bank. As Argentina pulled out of its crisis, it offered debtholders only 25 cents on the dollar. In 2002, Scotiabank sold its subsidiary in Argentina and left a country where it had done business for 40 years, taking an after-tax charge against earnings of $540 million. Effective macroeconomic management played a key role in the recovery of the Argentinian economy. As a result, economic growth in the country averaged 9 percent during 2003–2005 and more than 8 percent in 2006 and 2007.

scotiabank.com

Finally, after 2008, economies plummeted worldwide as a result of the global financial crisis. The annualized gross domestic product in the first quarter of 2009 fell by 21.5 percent in Mexico, 15.2 percent in Japan, and 14.4 percent in Germany. The United Kingdom's economy saw its worst drop in GDP in 30 years, 7.6 percent; the value of German exports fell by 20.7 percent; and Spain's jobless rate soared to 17.3 percent. Globally, manufacturing output fell by 2.9 percent and world trade by nearly 10 percent from 2008 to 2009. GDP in developing countries fell sharply from 5.9 percent in 2008 to 1.2 percent in 2009. The World Bank projected that developing countries were likely to face a dramatic decrease in private capital flows and that many of these countries would find it difficult to meet their external financing needs, estimated to be $2 trillion. International organizations, such as the World Bank and the IMF, and national governments worldwide took steps to avoid the debt moratoria seen in the 1980s, 1990s, and early 2000s. Table 14–1 lists some of the actions taken by governments in developed countries to shore up their countries' banking systems (see also Table 1–2). Further, the IMF pledged to inject US$250 billion into the global economy to bolster countries' reserves, US$100 billion of which would be allocated to EM countries and LDCs. Additionally, the World Bank committed US$58.8 billion in fiscal year 2009 to help countries struggling amid the global economic crisis. Despite these efforts, in November 2009, Dubai World, the finance arm of Dubai, asked creditors for a six-month delay on interest payments due on US$60 billion of the country's debt. In the mid- and late 2000s, Dubai became a centre of investment and development, much of it funded by burgeoning oil wealth from neighbouring countries. But during the financial crisis, the Middle East nation was hard hit by a falling real estate market.

Throughout 2009–2012 Greece struggled with a severe debt crisis. Early on, some of the healthier European countries tried to step in and assist the debt-ridden country. Specifically, in March 2010 a plan led by Germany and France to bail out Greece with as much as US$41 billion in aid began to take shape. However, in

TABLE 14–1
Elements of Banking System Rescue Plans in Developed Economies

Source: *BIS Quarterly Review*, Bank for International Settlements, Basel, Switzerland, December 2008.

		Guarantee of Wholesale Liabilities*			
Country	Expansion of Retail Deposit Insurance	New Debt	Existing Debt	Capital Injections**	Asset Purchases
Australia	•	•	•		•
Austria	•	•		•	
Belgium	•	•			
Canada		•			•
Denmark	•	•	•		
Finland	•				
France		•		•	
Germany	•	•		•	•
Greece	•	•		•	
Ireland	•	•	•		
Italy		•		•	
Netherlands	•	•		•	
New Zealand	•				
Norway					•
Portugal	•	•			
Spain	•	•		•	•
Sweden	•	•		•	
Switzerland				•	•
United Kingdom	•	•		•	
United States	•	•		•	•

* Includes bond issuance, interbank lending, and other wholesale liabilities. Coverage of the guarantee on these items varies across countries.

** Refers to announced programs only (excluding stand-alone actions).

late April 2010, Greek bond prices dropped dramatically as traders began betting a debt default was inevitable, even if the country received a massive bailout. The selloff was the result of still more bad news for Greece, which showed that the 2009 budget deficit was worse than had been previously reported, and, as a result, politicians in Germany began to voice opposition to a Greek bailout. Further, Moody's Investors Service downgraded Greece's debt rating and warned that additional cuts could be on the way. The problems in the Greek bond market then spread to other European nations with fiscal problems, such as Portugal, Spain, and Italy. As a result, in May Eurozone countries and the IMF, seeking to halt a widening European debt crisis that had now threatened the stability of the euro, agreed to extend Greece an unprecedented US$147 billion rescue in return for huge budget cuts.

Additional rescue packages and promises of further austerity measures intended to cut the burgeoning Greek deficit occurred through 2012. Yet the European debt crisis continued. While Greece had not yet missed a bond payment, in March 2012 the International Swaps and Derivatives Association (ISDA), the trade group that oversees the market for credit default swaps, declared that Greece had undergone a "restructuring credit event," which triggered insurance policy payments. The restructuring event was a forced swap of old debt held by some of its private bondholders for new debt. The swap forced a 74 percent "haircut" on those creditors that held out, triggering the effective default. At one point, Greece seemed unable to form a government and the leader of one party rejected the country's bailout commitments. It seemed increasingly possible that Greece might have to leave the Eurozone. Economists estimated that a Greek exit from the Eurozone would cost the EU US$1 trillion, or about 5 percent of the EU's annual economic output. Yet the leaders of EU countries, particularly Germany and France, continued to work to keep Greek reform on track and the EU together. Through June 2012, the cost of bailouts required to do so totalled over US$480 billion, but the crisis in the EU was not over, as Spain and Italy required bailouts as well. Fears arose that keeping the EU together and the euro intact might actually draw sound countries into a crisis as they bailed out unhealthy countries to prevent them from leaving the currency union.

At the end of September 2010, the foreign claims reported by Canada's banks totalled US$5.1 billion to Ireland, US$0.1 billion to Portugal, US$4.0 billion to Spain, and a negligible amount to Greece. However, the risks posed to the international banking system from a Greek debt default and a contagion crisis in other Eurozone countries were huge. The United States had sovereign risk exposure of US$391.6 billion to Greece, Ireland, Portugal, and Spain. Worldwide, bank exposure to these four countries totalled US$2,512.3 billion. Table 14–2 shows the foreign exposure to these four countries by bank nationality. As the European debt crisis progressed, banks reduced their Greek exposure significantly. For example, by September 2012, Canadian banks reporting to the BIS showed no exposure to Greece, Ireland, and Portugal and only US$3.0 billion to Spain. However, Canadian banks had a total exposure of US$193.3 billion to the developed countries of Europe with 59.3 percent (US$114.6) to the United Kingdom. The U.S. Federal Reserve estimated that in March 2012, 35 percent of the holdings in U.S. money market funds represented European assets.

Thus, North American banks would feel the economic impact of the Greek debt crisis. A Greek debt default, or a default by any other country of Europe, including Cyprus, and the events that would follow, would mean a reduction in the size of

TABLE 14–2 Foreign Exposures to Greece, Ireland, Portugal, and Spain, End of Third Quarter, 2010 (in billions of U.S. $)

Exposure to	Germany	Spain	France	Italy	Other Euro Area	U.K.	U.S.	Rest of World	Total
Greece	$ 69.4	$ 1.5	$ 92.0	$ 6.5	$ 33.5	$ 20.4	$ 43.1	$ 11.5	$ 277.9
Ireland	208.3	17.5	78.1	24.4	67.2	224.6	113.9	79.8	813.8
Portugal	48.5	108.6	45.5	7.9	21.9	33.7	47.1	8.6	321.8
Spain	242.3	-	224.7	41.8	179.6	152.4	187.5	70.5	1,098.8
Total	$568.5	$127.6	$440.3	$80.6	$302.2	$431.1	$391.6	$170.4	$2,512.3

Source: BIS Quarterly Review, March 2011, *Bank for International Settlements*, www.bis.org.

the exports to Europe. Further, a freeze of financial markets resulting from the default of a European country on its debt could lead to a worldwide credit freeze and, in turn, a drop in worldwide equity prices, similar to that after the Lehman Brothers bankruptcy in September 2008. Thus, banks, in their role as lenders to businesses and as investors in securities issued by Eurozone countries and worldwide, would feel the effects of changes in economic conditions due to a European-based debt crisis from multiple fronts.

multiyear restructuring agreements (MYRAs)
The official terminology for a sovereign loan rescheduling.

These recurring experiences confirm the importance of assessing the country or sovereign risk of a borrowing country before making lending or other investment decisions such as buying foreign bonds or equities. In this chapter, we first compare credit risk and sovereign or country risk. We next look at measures of sovereign risk that FIs can use as screening devices before making loans or other investment decisions. Appendix 14A looks at ways FIs have managed sovereign risk problems, including entering into **multiyear restructuring agreements (MYRAs)**, debt–equity swaps, loan sales, and bond-for-loan swaps.

CREDIT RISK VERSUS SOVEREIGN RISK

LO1

rescheduling
Changing the contractual terms of a loan, such as its maturity and interest payments.

To understand the difference between the sovereign risk and the credit risk on a loan or a bond, consider what happens to a domestic firm that refuses to repay, or is unable to repay, its loans. The lender would probably seek to work out the loan with the borrower by **rescheduling** its promised interest and principal payments on the loan into the future. Ultimately, continued inability or unwillingness to pay would likely result in bankruptcy proceedings and eventual liquidation of the firm's assets. Consider next a dollar loan made by an FI to a private Greek corporation. Suppose that this first-class corporation always maintained its debt repayments in the past; however, the Greek economy and the Greek government's reserve position are in bad shape. As a result, the Greek government refuses to allow any further debt repayment to be made to outside creditors. This puts the Greek borrower automatically into default even though, when viewed on its own, the company is a good credit risk. The Greek government's decision is a *sovereign* or *country risk event* in large part independent of the credit standing of the individual loan to the borrower. Further, unlike the situation in Canada, where the lender might seek a legal remedy in the local bankruptcy courts, there is no international bankruptcy court to which the lender can take the Greek government. That is, the lender's legal remedies to offset a sovereign country's default or debt moratorium decisions are very limited. For example, lenders can seek legal remedies in Canadian courts, but such decisions pertain only to Greek government or Greek corporate assets held in Canada.

This situation suggests that making a lending decision to a party residing in a foreign country is a *two-step* decision. First, the lender must assess the underlying *credit quality* of the borrower, as it would do for a normal domestic loan, including setting an appropriate credit risk premium or credit limit (see Chapter 10). Second, the lender must assess the *sovereign risk quality* of the country in which the borrower resides. Should the credit risk or quality of the borrower be assessed as good but the sovereign risk be assessed as bad, the lender should not make the loan. When making international lending or foreign bond investment decisions, an FI manager should consider sovereign risk above considerations of private credit risk.

CONCEPT QUESTIONS

1. **What is the difference between credit risk and sovereign risk?**
2. **In deciding to lend to a party residing in a foreign country, what two considerations must an FI weigh?**

DEBT REPUDIATION VERSUS DEBT RESCHEDULING

LO2

A good deal of misunderstanding exists regarding the nature of a sovereign risk event. In general, a sovereign country's (negative) decisions on its debt obligations or the obligations of its public and private organizations may take two forms: repudiation and rescheduling.

repudiation
Outright cancellation of all current and future debt obligations by a borrower.

worldbank.org
imf.org

- *Debt repudiation.* **Repudiation** is an outright cancellation of all a borrower's current and future foreign debt and equity obligations. Since World War II, only China (1949), Cuba (1961), and North Korea (1964) have followed this course. The low level of repudiations partly reflects recent international policy toward the poorest countries in the world. Specifically, in the fall of 1996, the World Bank, the IMF, and major governments around the world agreed to forgive the external debt of the world's poorest, most heavily indebted poor countries (HIPCs). The HIPC initiative broke new ground by removing debt obligations from countries that pursue economic and social reform targeted at measurable poverty reduction. By 2012, 36 countries had received irrevocable debt relief under the HIPC initiative, 30 of them in Africa. Together, these countries had their outstanding debt reduced by US$76 billion. Repudiations on debt obligations were far more common before World War II, as we discuss later in this chapter.
- *Debt rescheduling.* Rescheduling has been the most common form of sovereign risk event. Specifically, a country (or a group of creditors in that country) declares a moratorium or delay on its current and future debt obligations and then seeks to ease credit terms through a rescheduling of the contractual terms, such as debt maturity and/or interest rates. Such delays may relate to the principal and/or the interest on the debt. (South Korea in January 1998, Argentina in 2001, and Greece in 2011–2012 are recent examples of debt reschedulings.)

One of the interesting questions in the provision of international financial services is why we have generally witnessed international debtor problems (of other than the most HIPCs) being met by reschedulings in the post–World War II period, whereas a large proportion of debt problems were met with repudiations before World War II. A fundamental reason given for this difference in behaviour is that until recently, most postwar international debt has been in *bank loans*, while before the war it was mostly in the form of *foreign bonds*.

International loan rather than bond financing makes rescheduling more likely for reasons related to the inherent nature of international loan versus bond contracts. First, there are generally fewer FIs in any international lending syndicate compared with the thousands of geographically dispersed bondholders. The relatively small number of lending parties makes renegotiation or rescheduling easier and less costly than when a borrower or a bond trustee has to get thousands of bondholders to agree to changes in the contractual terms on a bond.

Second, many international loan syndicates make up the same groups of FIs, which adds to FI cohesiveness in loan renegotiations and increases the probability of consensus being reached. For example, Citigroup was chosen the lead bank negotiator by other banks in five major loan reschedulings in the 1980s, as well as in the Mexican and South Korean reschedulings. JPMorgan Chase was the lead bank in Argentina's loan reschedulings.

Third, many international loan contracts contain cross-default provisions that state that if a country were to default on just one of its loans, all the other loans it has outstanding would automatically be put into default as well. Cross-default clauses prevent a country from selecting a group of weak lenders for special default treatment and make the outcome of any individual loan default decision potentially very costly for the borrower.

A further set of reasons that rescheduling is likely to occur on loans relates to the behaviour of governments and regulators in lending countries. One of the overwhelming public policy goals in recent years has been to prevent large FI failures in countries such as Canada, the United States, Japan, Germany, and the United Kingdom. Thus, government-organized rescue packages arranged either directly or indirectly via World Bank/IMF guarantees are ways of subsidizing large FIs and/or reducing the incentives for countries to default on their loans. To the extent that banks are viewed as special (see Chapter 1), domestic governments may seek political and economic avenues to reduce the probability of foreign sovereign borrowers defaulting on or repudiating their debt contracts. Governments and regulators appear to view the social costs of default on international bonds as less worrisome than those on loans. The reason is that bond defaults are likely to be more geographically and numerically dispersed in their effects, and bondholders do not play a key role in the provision of liquidity services to the domestic and world economy. It should also be noted that the tendency of the IMF/governments to bail out countries and thus, indirectly, FI lenders, such as the major North American, Japanese, and European FIs, has not gone without criticism. Specifically, it has been argued that unless FIs and countries are ultimately punished, they will have no incentives to avoid similar risks in the future. This is one reason sovereign debt crises keep recurring.

In the aftermath of the 2008 financial crisis and the failure of countries (Iceland) and large systemically important global FIs (AIG, Lehman Brothers), central banks and regulators worked to increase regulations on global FIs, including hedge funds. The Financial Stability Board (FSB), chaired by Mark Carney as Governor of the Bank of Canada and as head of the Bank of England since July 2013, published a framework for the resolution of troubled FIs in 2011. The new paradigm,

www.financialstabilityboard.org

which was partially implemented in Cyprus in 2013, expects uninsured depositors, bondholders, and shareholders of systemically important FIs to take "haircuts" prior to countries' obtaining support from governments. Chapter 20 deals with this issue in more depth.

CONCEPT QUESTIONS

1. **What is the difference between debt repudiation and debt rescheduling?**
2. **Provide four reasons we see sovereign loans being rescheduled rather than repudiated.**

COUNTRY RISK EVALUATION

LO3

In evaluating sovereign risk, an FI can use many methods, varying from the highly quantitative to the very qualitative. Moreover, as in domestic credit analysis, an FI may rely on outside evaluation services or develop its own internal evaluation or sovereign risk models. Of course, to make a final assessment, an FI may use models and sources together because different measures of country risk are not mutually exclusive.

We begin by looking at three country risk assessment services available to outside investors and FIs: the *Euromoney Country Risk* index, the *Economist Intelligence Unit*, and the *Institutional Investor* index. We then look at ways an FI manager might make internal risk assessments regarding sovereign risk.

Outside Evaluation Models

The Euromoney Country Risk Index

euromoney countryrisk.com
economist.com

The Euromoney Country Risk (ECR) index rates sovereign risk of over 180 countries based on the opinions of a global network of economists and policy analysts. The index is based on a large number of economic and political factors, including a country's economic characteristics, political characteristics, structural characteristics, access to capital and credit ratings, and debt indicators. ECR scores are scaled from 0 to 100 (100 = no risk, 0 = maximum risk) and are put into one of five tiers that are updated quarterly. ECR Tier 1 countries have a score between 80 and 100, which can be equated to a credit rating of AA and above; Tier 2 countries have a score between 65 and 79.9, which can be equated to a credit rating of A− to AA; Tier 3 countries have a score between 50 and 64.9, translated to a credit rating of BB+ to A−; Tier 4 countries have a score between 36 and 49.9, equivalent to a credit rating of B− to BB+; and Tier 5 countries have a score between 0 and 35.9, equivalent to a credit rating of D to B−. Table 14–3 reports ECR scores for several countries as of April 2012. As can be seen in this table, ECR ratings assess Norway as the country with the least chance of default and Somalia as the country with the highest chance of default. Canada ranks with Norway, Switzerland, Sweden, and Australia as a Tier 1 country but, because of the growing budget deficit, the United States has dropped to a Tier 2–rated country.

The Economist Intelligence Unit

A sister firm of *The Economist*, the *Economist Intelligence Unit* (EIU) rates country risk by combining economic and political risk on a 100-point (maximum) scale. The higher the number, the worse the sovereign risk rating of the country. The EIU country risk ratings reported as of 2012 are presented in Figure 14–1.

TABLE 14–3
ECR Ratings, April 2012

Source: Euromoney Country Risk, *Euromoney*, April 2012. euromoneycountryrisk.com.

Country	Tier	Score	Country	Tier	Score
Norway	1	90.69	Turkey	3	57.12
Switzerland	1	89.12	Portugal	3	52.17
Sweden	1	85.12	Venezuela	5	35.12
Canada	1	84.57	Greece	5	33.00
Australia	1	82.25	Iraq	5	29.85
United States	2	75.66	Sudan	5	26.98
United Kingdom	2	79.94	Iran	5	26.40
France	2	75.05	Syria	5	24.27
Italy	3	63.19	Libya	5	24.07
Spain	3	61.83	Zimbabwe	5	16.87
Ireland	3	57.28	Somalia	5	13.85

The Institutional Investor Index

Normally published twice a year, the *Institutional Investor* index is based on surveys of the loan officers of major multinational banks. These officers give subjective scores regarding the credit quality of given countries. Originally, the score was based on 10, but since 1980 it has been based on 100, with a score of 0 indicating certainty of default and 100 indicating no possibility of default. The *Institutional Investor* then weighs the scores received from the officers surveyed by the exposure

FIGURE 14–1
The EIU Country Risk Ratings

Source: Country Risk Service Risk Ratings, 2012, The *Economist*, www.eiu.com.

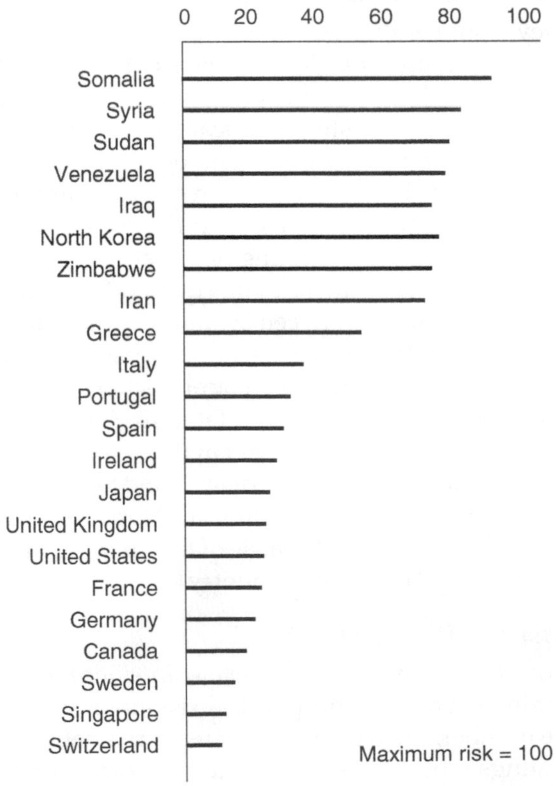

of each bank to the country in question. For a sampling of the *Institutional Investor's* country credit ratings as of March 2012, see Table 14–4 . For example, in March 2012, loan officers around the world assessed Norway as the country with the least chance of default, while they assessed Somalia as the country with the highest chance of default.

TABLE 14–4
***Institutional Investor's* 2012 Country Credit Ratings**

Source: *Institutional Investor,* March 2012, www.institutional-investor.com.

Rank					
March 2012	September 2011	Country	*Institutional Investor* Rank	Six-Month Change	One-Year Change
1	1	Norway	94.8	−0.7	−0.4
2	2	Switzerland	94.1	−0.8	0.0
3	7	Canada	93.1	0.7	0.0
4	4	Sweden	92.9	−0.4	0.3
5	5	Finland	92.5	−0.5	0.0
6	8	Singapore	92.4	0.2	−0.3
7	3	Luxembourg	91.6	−2.5	−0.9
8	9	Netherlands	90.8	−0.7	−0.2
9	6	Germany	89.8	−2.8	−3.5
10	11	Australia	89.7	−0.9	−1.2
11	12	United States	89.4	−1.1	−2.0
12	10	Denmark	89.1	−1.7	−2.1
13	13	Austria	88.2	−1.5	−1.9
14	16	Hong Kong	85.6	0.2	0.1
15	17	United Kingdom	85.6	0.8	−2.2
16	15	New Zealand	85.2	−1.1	−2.0
17	14	France	85.2	−2.7	−4.5
18	19	Chile	82.1	−0.5	2.6
19	18	Japan	81.1	−1.9	−4.2
20	25	Qatar	80.2	2.3	1.2
42	34	Italy	66.5	−5.9	−9.9
43	42	Spain	64.7	−2.6	−7.3
68	75	Ireland	51.9	2.9	−9.1
75	72	Portugal	46.5	−3.4	−18.9
151	131	Greece	19.6	−7.6	−27.3
168	170	Burundi	12.6	−1.7	−3.2
169	167	Comoros	12.5	−2.7	−2.3
170	173	Central African Republic	12.4	0.4	0.8
171	169	Democratic Republic of Congo	11.9	−2.4	−1.8
172	166	Guinea	11.8	−3.7	−0.3
173	172	Afghanistan	11.4	−1.1	−1.5
174	174	Sudan	10.4	−1.4	0.5
175	–	South Sudan	10.0	–	–
176	175	Myanmar	9.9	0.0	−2.7
177	178	North Korea	6.0	1.6	0.3
178	177	Zimbabwe	5.3	0.3	−0.5
179	176	Somalia	5.2	−0.7	1.3
		Global average rating	44.1	−1.6	−2.2

Internal Evaluation Models

Statistical Models

By far, the most common approach to evaluating sovereign country risk among large FIs has been to develop sovereign country risk–scoring models based on key economic ratios for each country, similar to the domestic credit risk–scoring models discussed in Chapter 10.

An FI analyst begins by selecting a set of macro- and microeconomic variables and ratios that might be important in explaining a country's probability of rescheduling. Then the analyst uses past data on rescheduling and nonrescheduling countries to see which variables best discriminate between those countries that rescheduled their debt and those that did not. This helps the analyst identify a set of key variables that best explain rescheduling and a group of weights indicating the relative importance of these variables. For example, domestic credit risk analysis can employ discriminant analysis to calculate a Z score rating of the probability of corporate bankruptcy. Similarly, in sovereign risk analysis we can develop a Z score to measure the probability that a country will reschedule (see Chapter 10 for discussion of the Z score model).[1]

The first step in this country risk analysis (CRA) is to pick a set of variables that may be important in explaining rescheduling probabilities. In many cases analysts select more than 40 variables. Here we identify the variables most commonly included in sovereign risk probability models.

The Debt Service Ratio

The debt service ratio (DSR) is

$$DSR = \frac{\text{Interest plus amortization on debt}}{\text{Exports}}$$

A country's exports are its primary way of generating hard currencies. The larger the debt repayments in hard currencies are in relation to export revenues, the greater the probability that the country will have to reschedule its debt. Thus, there should be a *positive* relationship between the size of the **debt service ratio** and the probability of rescheduling. Table 14–5 shows the scheduled DSRs of various countries. Note that Latvia is servicing debt obligations at almost one-third the level of its exports (e.g., Latvia's DSR is 30.81 percent).

debt service ratio
The ratio of a country's interest and amortization obligations to the value of its exports.

The Import Ratio

The import ratio (IR) is

$$IR = \frac{\text{Total imports}}{\text{Total FX reserves}}$$

Many countries must import manufactured goods since their inadequate infrastructure limits their domestic production. In times of famine, even food becomes a vital import. To pay for imports, the country must run down its stock of hard currencies—its FX reserves. The greater its need for imports—especially vital imports—the quicker a country can be expected to deplete its FX reserves. For example, Greece's import ratio was 1377.91 percent in 2011, implying that Greece

[1] Alternatively, analysts could employ linear probability, logit, or probit models.

TABLE 14–5
DSR for Various Countries

Source: 2012 "Data by Topic" World Bank website, worldbank.org.

Country	Debt Service Ratio %
Argentina	3.62%
Armenia	23.29
Brazil	5.71
Bulgaria	22.32
Chile	11.20
China	1.17
Colombia	4.58
El Salvador	14.76
Latvia	30.81
Mexico	1.60
Nicaragua	10.02
Romania	15.28
Russia	8.07
Serbia	23.96
Turkey	18.28
Ukraine	19.52
United States	15.98

imported more goods and services than it had foreign reserves to pay for them. In contrast, China's import ratio was 58.52 percent in 2011, implying that China imported fewer goods and services than it had foreign reserves to pay for them. Since the first use of reserves is to buy vital imports, the larger the ratio of imports to FX reserves, the higher the probability that the country will have to reschedule its debt repayments. This is so because these countries generally view repaying foreign debtholders as being less important than supplying vital goods to the domestic population. Thus, the **import ratio** and the probability of rescheduling should be *positively* related.

import ratio
The ratio of a country's imports to its total foreign currency reserves.

Investment Ratio

The investment ratio (INVR) is

$$INVR = \frac{\text{Real investment}}{\text{GNP}}$$

investment ratio
The ratio of a country's real investment to its GNP.

The **investment ratio** measures the degree to which a country is allocating resources to real investment in factories, machines, and so on, rather than to consumption. The higher this ratio, the more productive the economy should be in the future and the lower the probability that the country would need to reschedule its debt. This implies a *negative* relationship between INVR and the probability of rescheduling. An opposing view is that a higher INVR allows a country to build up its investment infrastructure. The higher ratio puts it in a stronger bargaining position with external creditors since the country would rely less on funds in the future and would be less concerned about future threats of credit rationing by FIs should it request a rescheduling. This view argues for a *positive* relationship between the INVR and the probability of rescheduling, especially if the country invests heavily in import competing industries. Just before the collapse of their economies in 2007, INVRs in Greece, Italy, and Portugal were 25.69, 22.12, and 22.83 percent, respectively. In contrast, China's INVR was 41.74 percent in 2011.

Variance of Export Revenue

The variance of export revenue (VAREX) is

$$VAREX = \sigma^2_{ER}$$

A country's export revenues may be highly variable as a result of two risk factors. *Quantity risk* means that the production of the raw commodities the country sells abroad—for example, coffee or sugar—is subject to periodic gluts and shortages. *Price risk* means that the international dollar prices at which the country can sell its exportable commodities are subject to high volatility as world demand for and supply of a commodity, such as copper, vary. The more volatile a country's export earnings, the less certain creditors can be that at any time in the future it will be able to meet its repayment commitments. That is, there should be a *positive* relationship between σ^2_{ER} and the probability of rescheduling.

Domestic Money Supply Growth

The domestic money supply growth (MG) is

$$MG = \frac{\Delta M}{M}$$

The faster the domestic growth rate of a country's money supply, $\Delta M/M$, which measures the change in the money supply (ΔM) over its initial level (M), the higher the domestic inflation rate and the weaker that country's currency becomes in domestic and international markets.[2] When a country's currency loses credibility as a medium of exchange, real output is often adversely impacted, and the country must increasingly rely on hard currencies for both domestic and international payments, a recent case being Venezuela in 2011 where MG was 54.40 percent and inflation was 26.09 percent. These inflation, output, and payment effects suggest a *positive* relationship between MG and the probability of rescheduling.

We can summarize the expected relationships among these five key economic variables and the probability of rescheduling (P) for any country as

$$P = f(\underset{+}{DSR}, \underset{+}{IR}, \underset{+\text{ or }-}{INVR}, \underset{+}{VAREX}, \underset{+}{MG}, \ldots)$$

For example, P is positively related (+) to MG. After selecting the key variables, the FI manager normally places countries into two groups or populations:

P_1 = Bad (reschedulers)
P_2 = Good (nonreschedulers)

Then the manager uses a statistical methodology such as discriminant analysis (see Chapter 10) to identify which of these variables best discriminates between the population of rescheduling borrowers and that of nonrescheduling borrowers. Once the key variables and their relative importance or weights have been identified, the discriminant function can classify as good or bad current sovereign loans or sovereign loan applicants using currently observed values for the DSR, IR, and so on. Again, the methodology is very similar to the credit scoring models discussed in Chapter 10.

[2] The purchasing power parity (PPP) theorem argues that high relative inflation rates lead to a country's currency depreciating in value against other currencies.

Problems with Statistical CRA Models

Even though this methodology has been one of the most common forms of CRA used by FIs, it is fraught with problems. This section discusses six major problems in using traditional CRA models and techniques. We do not imply in any way that these techniques should not be used but instead indicate that FI managers should be aware of the potential pitfalls in using such models.

Measurement of Key Variables Very often the FI manager's information on a country's DSR or IR is out of date because of delays in collection of data and errors in measurement. For example, the BIS collects aggregate loan volume data for countries; frequently, this information is six months old or more before it is published. This example illustrates the problem: Scotiabank may know today the current amount of its outstanding loans to Indonesia, but it is unlikely to know with any great degree of accuracy Indonesia's total outstanding external loans and debt with every other lender in the world.

bis.org

Moreover, these measurement problems are compounded by forecast errors when managers use these statistical models to predict the probabilities of rescheduling with future or projected values of key variables such as DSR and IR.

Population Groups Usually, analysts seek to find variables that distinguish between only two possible outcomes: reschedulers and nonreschedulers. In actuality, a finer distinction may be necessary—for example, a distinction between those countries announcing a moratorium on only interest payments and those announcing a moratorium on both interest and principal payments. Thus, Greece, which forced a 74 percent haircut on debt to private debtholders, should be viewed as a higher-risk country than a country such as Dubai, which delayed the interest payments on its debt for a few months in 2009 because of short-term FX shortages.

Political Risk Factors Traditionally, CRA statistical credit scoring models incorporate only economic variables. While there may be a strong correlation between an economic variable such as money supply growth and rescheduling, the model may not capture purely political risk events such as *strikes*, *elections*, *corruption*, and *revolutions* very well. For example, the election of a strongly nationalist politician may reduce the probability of repayment and increase the probability of rescheduling. Similarly, a considerable part of the debt repayment and banking crisis problems in Southeast Asia has been attributed to cronyism and corruption.

heritage.org

Since 1995, the *Index of Economic Freedom* (compiled by the Heritage Foundation) has provided a measure that summarizes the economic freedom of over 180 countries in the world. The Heritage Foundation defines economic freedom as "the absence of government coercion or constraint on the production, distribution, or consumption of goods and services beyond the extent necessary for citizens to protect and maintain liberty itself."

The index includes measures of trade policy, fiscal burden of government, government intervention in the economy, monetary policy, capital flows and foreign investment, banking and finance, wages and prices, property rights, regulation, and black market activities. Each country is assigned a score ranging from 0 to 100 for each of the 10 individual factors as well as an overall score based on the average of these factors. A score of 100 signifies the maximum economic freedom. Table 14–6 lists the economic freedom index for the 10 highest- and lowest-rated

TABLE 14–6
Economic Freedom Index for Various Countries

Source: The Heritage Foundation website, July 2012, heritage.org.

Country	Overall Economic Freedom Index
Hong Kong	89.9
Singapore	87.5
Australia	83.1
New Zealand	82.1
Switzerland	81.1
Canada	79.9
Chile	78.3
Mauritius	77.0
Ireland	76.9
United States	76.3
Equatorial Guinea	42.8
Iran	42.3
Congo	41.1
Burma	38.7
Venezuela	38.1
Eritrea	36.2
Libya	35.9
Cuba	28.3
Zimbabwe	26.3
North Korea	1.0

countries in 2012. An alternative quantitative measure of country risk is the *Corruption Perceptions Index*, produced by Transparency International. Figure 14–2 shows the corruption index for 22 out of 182 countries for 2012. The least-corrupt countries are assigned a score of 10, while the most-corrupt countries are assigned a score of 0.

Portfolio Aspects Traditional CRA considers each country separately. However, many large banks with sovereign risk exposures hold a portfolio of EM loans. In a portfolio context, the risk of holding a well-diversified portfolio of sovereign loans may be smaller than that of having a portfolio heavily concentrated in EM loans. In particular, the lender may distinguish between those key risk indicator variables having a *systematic* effect on the probability of repayment across a large number of sovereign countries and those variables having an *unsystematic* effect by impacting only one or a few countries.

One way to address this problem is to employ a portfolio framework (such as those discussed in Chapter 11) for sovereign risk analysis. Such an analysis would identify those indicator variables that have a *systematic* impact across all borrowers' probability of repayment and those that tend to be country specific (or *unsystematic*). The indicator variables that the FI manager should really be concerned with are the *systematic* variables, since they cannot be diversified away in a multisovereign loan portfolio. By comparison, unsystematic, or country-specific, risks can be diversified away. Consider the following model (see Chapters 10 and 11 for a discussion of the construction of these models):

$$X_i = a_i + b_i\overline{X} + e_i$$

FIGURE 14–2
Corruption Perceptions Index, 2012

Source: Transparency International, July 2012, www.transparency.org.

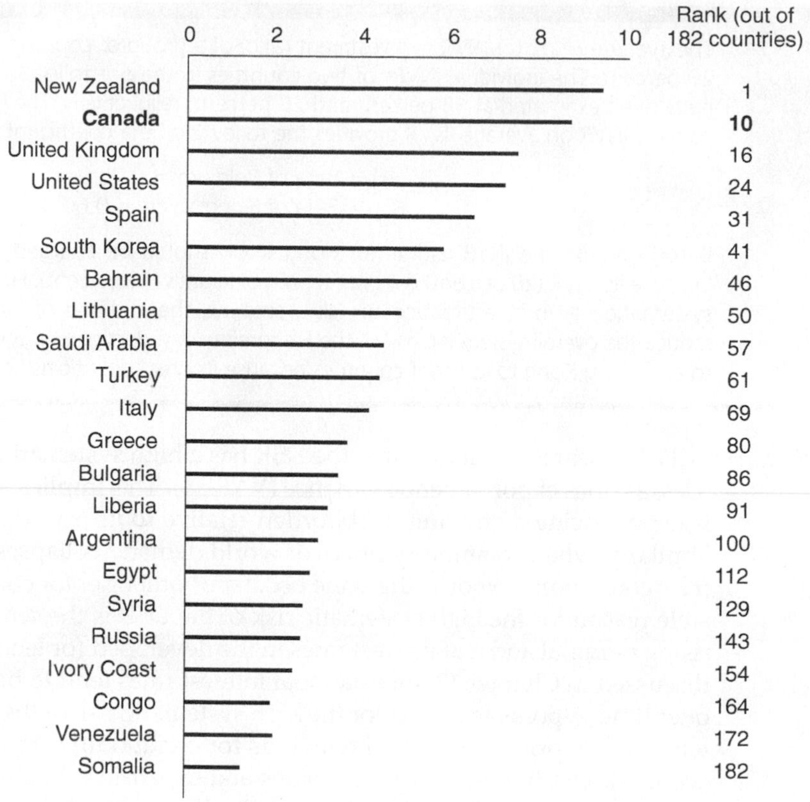

where

X_i = Key variable or country risk indicator for country *i* (e.g., the DSR for country *i*)

$\overline{X}$ = Weighted index of this key risk indicator across all countries to which the lender makes loans (e.g., the DSR for each country weighted by the shares of loans for each country in the FI's portfolio)

e_i = Other factors impacting X_i for any given country

Expressing this equation in variance terms, we get

$$\begin{array}{ccccc} VAR(X_i) & = & b_i^2 VAR(\overline{X}) & + & VAR\,(e_i) \\ \text{Total risk} & = & \text{Systematic risk} & + & \text{Unsystematic risk} \end{array}$$

From this equation, you can see that the total risk or variability of any given risk indicator for a country, such as the DSR for Nigeria, can be divided into a nondiversifiable *systematic* risk element that measures the extent to which that country's DSR moves in line with the DSRs of all other debtor countries and an unsystematic risk element that impacts the DSR for Nigeria independently. The greater the size of the *unsystematic* element relative to the systematic risk element, the less important this variable is to the lender since it can be diversified away by holding a broad array of sovereign loans.

EXAMPLE 14-1

Calculating Sovereign Risk for an FI's Portfolio

The average σ^2_{INVR} (or INVR = investment ratio) of a group of countries has been estimated at 20 percent. The individual INVRs of two countries in the portfolio, Belgium and Hong Kong, have been estimated at 10 percent and 20 percent, respectively. The regression of individual country INVR on average INVR provides the following beta coefficient estimates:

$$\beta_B = \text{Beta of Belgium} = 0.75$$
$$\beta_{HK} = \text{Beta of Hong Kong} = 0.60$$

Based only on the INVR estimates, Hong Kong should be charged a higher risk premium because its INVR (20 percent) is higher than is Belgium's (10 percent). However, if the FI includes systematic risk in its estimation of risk premiums, the addition of loans to Hong Kong will reduce the overall systematic risk of the FI's foreign loan portfolio. In this case, it benefits the FI to add Hong Kong to its list of countries because its unsystematic risk can be diversified away.

Past research has found that the DSR has a high systematic element across countries, as does export revenue variance (VAREX). This implies that when one country is experiencing a growing debt burden relative to its exports, so are all the others. Similarly, when commodity prices or world demand collapses for one debtor country's commodity exports, the same occurs for other debtor countries as well. A possible reason for the high systematic risk of the DSR is the sensitivity of this ratio to rising nominal and real interest rates in the developed (or lending) countries. As we discussed in Chapter 13, international interest rates tend to be positively correlated over time. A possible reason for the high systematic risk of the export variance is the tendency of prices and world demands for commodities to reflect simultaneously economic conditions such as recessions and expansions in developed countries.

By comparison, MG ($\Delta M/M$) and the IR appear to have low systematic elements. This is not surprising since control over the money supply and the use of domestic foreign currency reserves are relatively discretionary variables for governments. Thus, while Argentina may choose an MG rate of 50 percent per annum, the Chilean government may choose a target rate of 10 percent per annum. Similarly, the Argentinean and Chilean economies may have very different demands for imports, and the scale of vital imports may differ quite widely across countries. Using this type of analysis allows an FI manager to focus on relatively few variables such as the DSR and VAREX that affect the risk of the sovereign loan portfolio.

Incentive Aspects CRA statistical models often identify variables based on rather loose or often nonexistent analyses of the borrower's or lender's incentives to reschedule. Rarely are the following questions asked: What are the *incentives* or *net benefits* to a country seeking a rescheduling? What are the incentives or net benefits to an FI that grants a rescheduling? That is, what determines the demand for rescheduling by borrowers (countries) and the supply of rescheduling by lenders (FIs)? Presumably, only when the benefits outweigh the costs for both parties does rescheduling occur. Consider the following benefits and costs of rescheduling for borrowers on the one hand and FIs on the other.

Borrowers

Benefits:

- By rescheduling its debt, the borrower lowers the present value of its future payments in hard currencies to outside lenders. This allows it to increase its consumption of foreign imports and/or increase the rate of its domestic investment.

Costs:

- By rescheduling now, the borrower may close itself out of the market for loans in the future. As a result, even if the borrower encounters high-growth investment opportunities in the future, it may be difficult or impossible to finance them.
- Rescheduling may result in significant interference with the borrower's international trade since it would be difficult to gain access to instruments such as letters of credit (LCs), without which trade may be more costly.

Lenders (FIs)

Benefits:

- Once a loan has been made, a rescheduling is much better than a borrower default. With a rescheduling, the FI lender may anticipate some present value loss of principal and interest on the loan; with an outright default, the FI stands to lose all its principal and future interest repayments.
- The FI can renegotiate fees and various other collateral and option features into a rescheduled loan.
- There may be tax benefits to an FI's taking a recognized writedown or loss in value on a rescheduled sovereign loan portfolio.

Costs:

- Through rescheduling, loans become similar to long-term bonds or even equity, and the FI often becomes locked into a particular loan portfolio structure.
- Those FIs with large amounts of rescheduled loans are subject to greater regulatory attention. For example, in the United States, such FIs may be placed on the regulators' problem list of FIs.

All these relevant economic incentive considerations go into the demand for and the supply of rescheduling; however, it is far from clear how the simple statistical models just described incorporate this complex array of incentives. At a very minimum, statistical models should clearly reflect the underlying theory of rescheduling.

Stability A final problem with simple statistical CRA models is that of stability. The fact that certain key variables may have explained rescheduling in the past does not mean that they will perform or predict well in the future. Over time, new variables and incentives affect rescheduling decisions, and the relative weights on the key variables change. This suggests that the FI manager must continuously update the CRA model to incorporate all currently available information and ensure the best predictive power possible. This is particularly true in today's new global environment of enhanced trade and competition, with major changes in production technology taking place in countries such as China and India.

LO4

Using Market Data to Measure Risk: The Secondary Market for Sovereign Debt

Since the mid-1980s, shortly after the beginning of the debt crisis in Latin America, the LDC debt secondary market began to develop among large commercial banks in New York and London. Trading volume was initially small, around US$2 billion per year. However, trading volume increased significantly in the late 1980s as several LDC countries adopted debt-for-equity swap programs to restructure their debt, and implementation of programs that allowed for sovereign debt restructuring and trading of existing and proposed new debt. What started as a market of highly individualized loan sales transactions between a limited number of FIs developed into a large and sophisticated trading market, which became known in the early 1990s as the EM. By the mid-1990s, trading volume had topped US$4.5 billion.

Trading declined to US$4.2 billion in 1998 after the Russian debt defaults and again in 1999 after Ecuador's failure to pay interest on its already restructured bonds. Trading has also been adversely affected by schemes of the more successful EM countries to get investors to swap restructured bonds for domestic government bonds (see below). The early 2000s were characterized by increasing trading activity and growing investor confidence in EMs, sparked in large part by Brazil's rapid economic recovery, Mexico's credit rating upgrade to investment grade, and Russia's successful debt restructuring. By 2007 secondary-market LDC and EM trading volumes had grown to US$6.5 trillion. With the onset of the financial crisis and the worldwide recession, investors turned to more conservative, less risky investments. LDC and EM trading volume fell to US$4.173 trillion in 2008, the lowest level since 2003 (US$3.973 trillion). However, as worldwide economic conditions improved, trading volumes rebounded to US$6.765 trillion in 2010 and US$6.5 trillion in 2011.

The Structure of the Market

This secondary market in distressed sovereign debt has considerably enhanced the liquidity of these loans on bank and other FI balance sheets.[3] The following are the market players that sell and buy distressed loans and debt instruments.

Sellers:

- Large FIs willing to accept writedowns of loans on their balance sheets
- Small FIs wishing to disengage themselves from the sovereign loan market
- FIs willing to swap one country's debt for another's to rearrange their portfolios of country risk exposures

Buyers:

- Wealthy investors, hedge funds (see Chapter 5), FIs, and corporations seeking to engage in debt-for-equity swaps or speculative investments
- FIs seeking to rearrange their balance sheets by reorienting their debt concentrations

The Early Market for Sovereign Debt

Consider the quote sheet from Salomon Brothers, in Table 14–7, for May 2, 1988—a relatively early stage of sovereign loan market development. As indicated in Table 14–7, FIs such as investment banks and major commercial banks (e.g. ING, Citigroup, J.P. Morgan) acted as market makers, quoting two-way bid–ask prices for distressed sovereign debt. Thus, an FI or an investor could have bought US$100 of Peruvian loans from Salomon for US$9 in May 1988,

[3] Loans change hands when one creditor assigns the rights to all future interest payments and principal payments to a buyer. In most early market transactions, the buyer had to get the permission of the sovereign debtor country before the loan could be assigned to a new party. This was because the country might have concerns as to whether the buyer was as committed to any new money deals as part of restructuring agreements as the original lender. Most recent restructuring agreements, however, have removed the right of assignment from the borrower (the sovereign country). This has increased liquidity in the loan market.

TABLE 14–7 **Indicative Prices for LDC Bank Loans (U.S. $)**

	Indicative Cash Prices		Swap Index		
Country	Bid ($)	Offer ($)	Sell	Buy	Trading Commentary
Algeria	91.00	93.00	5.22	6.71	Longer-dated paper resurfacing as cash substitute in swaps.
Argentina	29.00	30.00	0.66	0.67	Less volume this period; consolidation exercise slows note trades.
Bolivia	10.00	13.00	0.52	0.54	Minimal current activity.
Brazil	53.00	54.00	1.00	1.02	Rally topping out as supply catches up with auction interest.
Chile	60.50	61.50	1.19	1.22	Market firm and rising as deal calendar fills.
Colombia	67.00	68.00	1.42	1.47	Resurgence of interest as high-quality exit.
Costa Rica	13.00	16.00	0.54	0.56	Market building reserves of patience to deal with this name again.
Dominican Republic	17.00	20.00	0.57	0.59	Trading picks up at lower levels.
Ecuador	31.00	33.00	0.66	0.70	Occasional swaps surfacing.
Honduras	25.00	28.00	0.63	0.65	Viewed as expensive on a relative value basis.
Ivory Coast	30.00	33.00	0.67	0.70	Newly sighted by fee swappers.
Jamaica	33.00	36.00	0.70	0.73	Slow but serious inquiry continues.
Mexico	52.50	53.50	0.99	1.01	Prices continue upward drift on lower, lumpy flow.
Morocco	50.00	51.00	0.94	0.96	Fee swappers oblige sellers by jumping into the wider breach versus Latins.
Nicaragua	3.00	4.00	0.48	0.49	Avoided by the surviving court tasters.
Nigeria	28.50	30.50	0.66	0.68	Retail stonewalls dealer interest.
Panama	20.00	23.00	0.59	0.61	Recent bidding stirs the mud.
Peru	7.00	9.00	0.51	0.52	Debt-for-debt workouts and debt-for-goods deals continue.
Philippines	52.00	53.00	0.98	1.00	Prices drift higher with good interest in non-CB* names.
Poland	43.25	44.50	0.83	0.85	Somewhat slower trading this period.
Romania	82.00	84.00	2.61	2.94	Bidding improves on expectations of 1988 principal payments.
Senegal	40.00	45.00	0.78	0.85	Trading talk more serious.
Sudan	2.00	10.00	0.48	0.52	Still on the mat.
Turkey	97.50	99.00	18.80	47.00	CTLDs** remain well bid.
Uruguay	59.50	61.50	1.16	1.22	Remains a patience-trying market.
Venezuela	55.00	55.75	1.04	1.06	Trading stronger as uptick in Chile brings swaps back into range.
Yugoslavia	45.50	47.00	0.86	0.89	More frequent trading.
Zaire	19.00	23.00	0.58	0.61	New interest develops.

*Central bank.
**Convertible Turkish lira deposits.
Source: Salomon Brothers Inc., May 2, 1988.

a 91 percent discount from face value. However, in selling the same loans to Salomon, the investor would have received only US$7 per US$100, a 93 percent discount. The bid–ask spreads for certain countries were very large in this period; for example, Sudan's US$2 bid and US$10 ask exemplified a serious lack of market demand for the sovereign loans of many countries.

Today's Market for Sovereign Debt

In recent years there have been many changes in the structure of the market. Initially, there were three market segments: sovereign bonds, performing loans, and nonperforming loans.

Sovereign Bonds The first segment of the market is that for sovereign bonds, i.e. government-issued debt. Sovereign bonds have historically been issued in foreign currencies, either U.S. dollars or euros. LDC and EM sovereign debt tends to have lower credit ratings than other sovereign debt because of the increased economic and political risks. Where most developed countries are AAA- or AA-rated, most LDC issuance is rated below investment grade, though a few countries that have seen significant improvements have been upgraded to BBB or A ratings, and a handful of LDCs have reached ratings levels equivalent to more-developed countries. Accordingly, sovereign bonds require higher interest spreads. For example, sovereign bonds are uncollateralized and their price or value reflects the credit risk rating of the country issuing the bonds. The US$2.8 billion June 1997 issue by Brazil of 30-year dollar-denominated bonds (rated BB grade by Standard & Poor's) was sold at a yield spread of nearly 4 percent over U.S. Treasuries at the time of issue.

In July 2001, Argentinian sovereign bonds were trading at spreads of over 15 percent above U.S. Treasury rates, with the J.P. Morgan *Emerging Market Bond Index* showing a spread of nearly 10 percent over U.S. Treasuries. This reflected the serious economic problems in Argentina and the contagious effects these were having on other sovereign bond markets. More recently, in September 2008, fears of the global economic crisis and falling commodity prices hit EM particularly hard: Mexico's sovereign debt spread jumped from 165 basis points (bp) to over 587 bp, Brazil's from 200 bp to over 586 bp, Chile's from 69 bp to over 322 bp, Colombia's from over 29 bp to more than 600 bp, and Argentina's and Venezuela's from 942 bp and 873 bp to over 4,019 bp and 2,325 bp, respectively. By the week of October 24, spread had tripled since early August 2008. However, it should also be noted that credit default spreads on 10-year U.S. Treasury debt rose to a record 29.2 bp: developed countries were not immune to the crisis.

Under the doctrine of sovereign immunity, the repayment of sovereign debt cannot be forced by the creditors and is thus subject to compulsory rescheduling, interest rate reduction, or even repudiation. The only protection available to the creditors is threat of the loss of credibility and lowering of the international standing (the sovereign debt rating of the country, which may make it much more difficult to borrow in the future).

Performing Loans The second category of the sovereign debt market is that for performing loans. Performing loans are original or restructured outstanding sovereign loans on which the sovereign country is currently maintaining promised payments to lenders or debtholders. Any discounts from 100 percent reflect expectations that these countries may face repayment problems in the future. Table 14–8 reports external bank loans outstanding for several countries in 2003 through 2011. Note the increase in bank loans throughout the period.

Nonperforming Loans The third segment of the sovereign debt market is that for nonperforming loans. Nonperforming loans reflect the secondary-market prices for the sovereign loans of countries where there are no interest or principal payments currently being made. These are normally traded at very deep discounts from 100 percent.

CONCEPT QUESTIONS

1. **Are the credit ratings of countries by *Institutional Investor* forward looking or backward looking?**
2. **What variables are commonly included in CRA? What does each measure?**
3. **What are the major problems involved with using traditional CRA models and techniques?**

TABLE 14–8
Bank Loans Outstanding, 2003 through 2012 (U.S. $ billions)

Source: World Bank website, January 2004, November 2006, August 2009, and July 2012, www.worldbank.org.

Country	2003	2006	2009	2011
Argentina	$ 25.0	$ 10.5	$ 14.0	$ 3.9
Brazil	58.2	57.5	92.8	138.2
Bulgaria	0.8	3.9	18.7	7.3
Costa Rica	3.0	2.9	5.5	2.3
Ecuador	1.8	2.2	2.1	1.0
Greece	35.4	90.4	162.6	118.0
Ireland	388.3	888.8	952.4	479.2
Italy	460.5	789.1	867.5	712.4
Mexico	45.7	38.9	72.9	22.0
Peru	4.2	4.7	12.5	10.3
Philippines	12.2	17.2	13.0	7.8
Poland	16.8	23.4	69.9	66.0
Portugal	479.2	820.3	1,127.8	927.0
Russia	35.3	87.6	147.7	160.7
Spain	155.8	202.1	269.7	174.4

Questions and Problems

1. What risks are incurred in making loans to borrowers based in foreign countries? Explain.
2. What is the difference between debt rescheduling and debt repudiation?
3. Identify and explain at least four reasons that rescheduling debt in the form of loans is easier than rescheduling debt in the form of bonds.
4. What three CRA models are available to investors? How is each model compiled?
5. What types of variables are normally used in a CRA *Z* score model? Define the following ratios and explain how each is interpreted in assessing the probability of rescheduling.
    a. DSR
    b. IR
    c. INVR
    d. VAREX
    e. MG
6. An FI manager has calculated the following values and weights to assess the credit risk and likelihood of having to reschedule the loan. From the *Z* score calculated from these weights and values, is the manager likely to approve the loan? Validation tests of the *Z* score model indicated that scores below 0.500 were likely to be nonreschedulers, while scores above 0.700 indicated a likelihood of rescheduling. Scores between 0.500 and 0.700 do not predict well.

Variable	Country Value	Weight
DSR	1.25	0.05
IR	1.60	0.10
INVR	0.60	0.35
VAREX	0.15	0.35
MG	0.02	0.15

7. Countries A and B have exports of US$2 billion and US$6 billion, respectively. The total interest and amortization on foreign loans for both countries are US$1 billion and US$2 billion, respectively.
    a. What is the DSR for each country?
    b. Based only on this ratio, to which country should lenders charge a higher risk premium?
    c. What are the shortcomings of using only these ratios to determine your answer in (b)?
8. How do price and quantity risks affect a country's VAREX?
9. Explain the following relationship:

$$P = f(IR, INVR)$$
$$+ \quad + \text{ or } -$$

where

P = Probability of rescheduling
IR = Total imports/Total FX reserves
$INVR$ = Real investment/GNP

10. What shortcomings are introduced by using traditional CRA models and techniques? In each case, what adjustments are made in the estimation techniques to compensate for the problems?
11. What is systematic risk in terms of sovereign risk? Which of the variables often used in statistical models tend to have high systematic risk? Which variables tend to have low systematic risk?
12. The average σ^2_{ER} (or VAREX) of a group of countries has been estimated at 20 percent. The individual VAREX of two countries in the group, Netherlands and Singapore, has been estimated at 15 percent and 28 percent, respectively. The regression of individual country VAREX on the average VAREX provides the following beta (coefficient) estimates:

$$\beta_H = \text{Beta of Netherlands} = 0.80$$

$$\beta_S = \text{Beta of Singapore} = 0.20$$

    a. Based only on the VAREX estimates, which country should be charged a higher risk premium? Explain.
    b. If FIs include unsystematic risk in their estimation of risk premiums, how would your conclusions to (a) be affected? Explain.
13. What are the benefits and costs of rescheduling to the following?
    a. A borrower
    b. A lender
14. Who are the primary sellers of LDC and EM debt? Who are the buyers? Why are FIs often both sellers and buyers of LDC and EM debt in the secondary markets?
15. Identify and describe the three market segments of the secondary market for LDC and EM debt.

Appendix 14A Mechanisms for Dealing with Sovereign Risk Exposure

View Appendix 14A on Connect.

CHAPTER 15

MARKET RISK

After studying this chapter you should be able to:

LO1 Discuss the impact of market risk on the operations of an FI.

LO2 Discuss the benefits of market risk measurement (MRM) for an FI.

LO3 Calculate the market risk exposure (VaR) for fixed-income securities, foreign exchange contracts, and equities.

LO4 Use the RiskMetrics Model to calculate the market risk exposure (VaR) for a portfolio.

LO5 Compare the historic (back simulation) approach with the RiskMetrics model.

LO6 Discuss the Monte Carlo simulation approach to measuring market risk.

LO7 Use the expected shortfall (ES) model to calculate market risk.

LO8 Discuss the BIS Standardized Framework and compare it with large bank internal models.

INTRODUCTION

LO1

Over the years, the trading activities of FIs have raised considerable concern among regulators and FI analysts. Some of these trading losses have been spectacular. For example, in 2008, "rogue trader" Jérôme Kerviel of French bank Société Générale lost US$7.1 billion in trading European stock index futures, and in July 2012, JPMorgan Chase reported a loss of US$5.8 billion from a trading position known as the "London Whale."

market risk
Risk related to the uncertainty of an FI's earnings on its trading portfolio caused by changes in market conditions.

Market risk can be defined as the risk related to the uncertainty of an FI's earnings on its trading portfolio caused by changes in market conditions, such as the price of an asset, interest rates, market volatility, and market liquidity.[1] Thus, risks such as interest rate risk (discussed in Chapters 8 and 9), credit risk (including credit risk from sovereign debt exposure, discussed in Chapters 10, 11, and 14), liquidity risk (discussed in Chapter 12), and foreign exchange (FX) risk (discussed in Chapter 13) affect market risk. However, market risk emphasizes the risks to FIs that actively trade assets and liabilities (and derivatives) rather than hold them for longer-term investment, funding, or hedging purposes.

Market risk was at the heart of much of the loss associated with the financial crisis. Signs of significant problems in the U.S. economy first arose in late 2006 and the first half of 2007 when house prices plummeted and defaults by subprime mortgage borrowers began to affect the U.S. mortgage lending industry. As mortgage

[1] Market risk used by FI managers and regulators is not synonymous with systematic market risk analyzed by investors in securities markets. Systematic (market) risk reflects the co-movement of a security with the market portfolio (reflected by the security's beta), although beta is used to measure the market risk of equities, as noted below.

borrowers defaulted on their mortgages, FIs holding and actively trading these mortgages and mortgage-backed securities started announcing huge losses. This soon became a global problem, and losses from the falling value of U.S. subprime mortgages and securities backed by these mortgages reached over US$1 trillion worldwide through mid-2009. Investment banks and securities firms were major traders of mortgage-backed securities and were particularly hard hit with huge losses on the mortgages and securities backing them.

A prime example of the losses incurred is that of Bear Stearns. In the summer of 2007, two Bear Stearns hedge funds suffered heavy market risk–related losses on investments in the subprime mortgage market. The two funds filed for bankruptcy in the fall of 2007. Bear Stearns's market value was hurt badly by these losses. The losses became so great that in March 2008 JPMorgan Chase and the U.S. Federal Reserve stepped in to rescue the then–fifth largest investment bank in the United States before it failed or was sold piecemeal to various FIs. The market risk meltdown continued through the summer and fall of 2008. On September 15, Lehman Brothers (the 158-year-old investment bank) filed for bankruptcy, Merrill Lynch was bought by Bank of America, AIG (one of the world's largest insurance companies) met with U.S. federal regulators to raise desperately needed cash, and Washington Mutual (the largest savings institution in the United States) was acquired by JPMorgan Chase. As news spread that Lehman Brothers would not survive, FIs moved to disentangle trades made with Lehman and tension mounted around the world. Stock markets saw huge swings in value as investors tried to sort out who might survive. Markets from Russia to Europe were forced to suspend trading as stock prices plunged. Financial markets froze and banks stopped lending to each other at anything but exorbitantly high rates. Market risk was the root cause of much of this market failure and the substantial losses incurred by FIs globally.

LO2

Conceptually, an FI's trading portfolio can be differentiated from its investment portfolio on the basis of time horizon and liquidity. The trading portfolio contains assets, liabilities, and derivative contracts that can be quickly bought or sold on organized financial markets (such as long and short positions in bonds, commodities, FX, equity securities, interest rate swaps, and options). Further, with the securitization of bank loans (e.g., mortgages), more and more assets have become liquid and tradable (e.g., mortgage-backed securities). Additionally, many large syndicated loans are often partly sold off (participations in loans; see Chapter 25). The lead bank usually retains a percentage (normally 15 to 30 percent). These syndicated loans can be viewed as held for sale and thus part of the trading book. The investment portfolio (or, in the case of banks, the banking book) contains assets and liabilities that are relatively illiquid and held for longer holding periods (such as consumer and business loans, retail deposits, and branches). Table 15–1 shows a breakdown between banking book and trading book assets and liabilities. Note that capital produces a cushion against losses on either the banking or trading books (see Chapter 20).

Income from trading activities is increasingly replacing income from traditional FI activities of deposit taking and lending. The resulting earnings uncertainty can be measured over periods as short as a day or as long as a year. Moreover, market risk can be defined in absolute terms as a *dollar* exposure amount or as a relative amount against some benchmark.

With time, every asset and liability can be sold. Bank regulators have normally viewed tradable assets as those being held for horizons of less than one year, and FIs take an even shorter term view. In particular, FIs are concerned about the fluctuation

TABLE 15–1
The Investment (Banking) Book and Trading Book of a Commercial Bank

	Assets	Liabilities
Banking Book	Cash Loans Premises and equipment Other illiquid assets	Deposits Other illiquid borrowed funds Capital
Trading Book	Bonds (long) Commodities (long) FX (long) Equities (long) Mortgage-backed securities (long)	Bonds (short) Commodities (short) FX (short) Equities (short)
	Derivatives* (long)	Derivatives* (short)

*Derivatives are OBS (as discussed in Chapter 7).

in value—or value at risk (VaR or VAR)—of their trading account assets and liabilities for periods as short as one day, especially if such fluctuations pose a threat to their solvency. So important is market risk in determining the viability of an FI that, since 1999, OSFI has included market risk in determining the required level of capital a federally regulated FI must hold. OSFI defines market risk for capital adequacy purposes as "the risk of losses in on- and off-balance-sheet positions arising from movements in market prices, including interest rates, exchange rates, and equity values."[2] OSFI applies this market risk framework to DTIs whose trading book assets or trading book liabilities (market value) represent 10 percent of total assets, or are greater than $1 billion.

Further, part of the U.S. Wall Street Reform and Consumer Protection Act, passed in 2010 in response to the financial crisis, is the Volcker Rule (to be implemented by U.S. banks by July 2014 at the earliest). The Volcker Rule prohibits U.S. depository institutions from engaging in proprietary trading (i.e., any transaction to purchase or sell as a principal for the trading account of the bank) and from investing in hedge funds or private equity funds. However, U.S. depository institutions may organize and offer a hedge fund or private equity fund if they do not have an ownership interest in the fund except for a seed investment that is limited to no more than 3 percent of total ownership interest of the fund within one year after the date of establishment of the fund. Additionally, the institution's overall investment in hedge funds or private equity funds may not exceed 3 percent of its Tier 1 capital. The rule was named after former U.S. Federal Reserve Chairman Paul Volcker, who had been outspoken in his claims that such activities played a major part in the financial crisis. The Volcker Rule is intended to restrict speculative trades made by depository institutions with their own money and, thus, is intended to reduce market risk at depository institutions. However, some have said the new rules are anti–bank specialness. This argument stems from the fact that the new rules on FIs' trading portfolios virtually force FIs to hold a matched maturity book. This limits the traditional specialness in bank maturity intermediation, i.e., borrow in the short-term funds market to lend in the long-term market.

Table 15–2 summarizes several benefits of measuring market risk, including providing management with information on the extent of market risk exposure, market risk limits, resource allocation, and performance evaluation, as well as information on how to protect banks and the financial system against failure due to

[2] OSFI, *Capital Adequacy Requirements A–Part I* (January 2001).

TABLE 15–2
Benefits of Market Risk Measurement (MRM)

1. *Management information.* MRM provides senior management with information on the risk exposure taken by FI traders. Management can then compare this risk exposure to the FI's capital resources.
2. *Setting limits.* MRM considers the market risk of traders' portfolios, which will lead to the establishment of economically logical position limits per trader in each area of trading.
3. *Resource allocation.* MRM involves the comparison of returns to market risks in different areas of trading, which may allow for the identification of areas with the greatest potential return per unit of risk into which more capital and resources can be directed.
4. *Performance evaluation.* MRM, relatedly, considers the return–risk ratio of traders, which may allow a more rational bonus (compensation) system to be put in place. That is, those traders with the highest returns may simply be the ones who have taken the largest risks. It is not clear that they should receive higher compensation than traders with lower returns and lower risk exposures.
5. *Regulation.* With the BIS and OSFI currently regulating market risk through capital requirements (discussed later in this chapter), private-sector benchmarks are important, since it is possible that regulators will overprice some risks. MRM conducted by the FI can be used to point to potential misallocations of resources as a result of prudential regulation. This is why, in certain cases, regulators are allowing banks to use their own (internal) models to calculate their capital requirements.

extreme market risk. The sections that follow concentrate on absolute dollar measures of market risk. We look at three major approaches that are being used to measure market risk: RiskMetrics, historic or back simulation, and Monte Carlo simulation. The link between market risk and required capital levels is also discussed in the chapter.

CALCULATING MARKET RISK EXPOSURE

Large banks, insurance companies, and mutual funds have all developed market risk models. In the development of these internal models four major approaches have been followed:

- RiskMetrics (or the variance/covariance approach)
- Historic or back simulation
- Monte Carlo simulation
- Expected shortfall (ES)

The first three models offer different methods of calculating VaR. We consider RiskMetrics[3] first and then compare it with other internal model approaches, such as historic or back simulation. The ES model (also called the conditional VaR) is an alternative to the traditional VaR measure that is more sensitive to the shape of the loss tail of the probability distribution of returns. Starting in January 2012, regulators replaced VaR as the main measure of market risk with the ES measure.

[3] J.P. Morgan first developed RiskMetrics in 1994. In 1998 the Corporate Risk Management Department that operated RiskMetrics was spun off from J.P. Morgan and became known as RiskMetrics Group. The company went public in January 2008 and was subsequently acquired, in June 2010, by MSCI. The material presented in this chapter is an overview of the RiskMetrics model. The details, additional discussion, and examples are found in *Return to RiskMetrics: The Evolution of a Standard,* April 2001, available at the JPMorgan Chase website, jpmorganchase.com, or at riskmetrics.com.

THE RISKMETRICS MODEL

LO3

The ultimate objective of MRM models can best be seen from the following statement from an FI manager: "I am X percent sure that the FI will not lose more than $VaR in the next T days." In a nutshell, the FI manager wants a single *dollar* number that indicates the FI's market risk exposure over the next T days—especially if those days turn out to be extremely "bad" days.

This can be nontrivial, given the extent of a large or or even mid-sized FI's trading business. When J.P. Morgan developed its RiskMetrics model in 1994 it had 14 active trading locations with 120 independent units trading fixed-income securities, FX, commodities, derivatives, emerging-market (EM) securities, and proprietary assets. In 2011, JPMorgan Chase operated worldwide and held a trading portfolio worth over US$444 billion. This scale and variety of activities is typical of the major U.S. banks, large overseas banks (e.g., Deutsche Bank and Barclays), major insurance companies, and investment banking companies.

Here, we will concentrate on measuring the market risk exposure of a major FI on a daily basis using the RiskMetrics approach. As will be discussed later, measuring the risk exposure for periods longer than a day (e.g., five days) is under certain assumptions a simple transformation of the one-day risk exposure number.

Essentially, the FI is concerned with how to preserve equity if market conditions move adversely tomorrow; that is,

$$\text{Market risk} = \text{Estimated potential loss under adverse circumstances}$$

one-day value at risk (one-day VaR)
The expected one-day loss at a given confidence level.

More specifically, the market risk is measured in terms of the FI's **one-day value at risk (one-day VaR)**[4] and has three components:

$$\begin{matrix}\text{One-day} & & \text{(Dollar market} & & \text{(Price} & & \text{(Potential} \\ \text{VaR} & = & \text{value of} & \times & \text{sensitivity of} & \times & \text{adverse move} \\ & & \text{the position)} & & \text{the position)} & & \text{in yield)}\end{matrix}$$

Since price sensitivity multiplied by adverse yield move measures the degree of price volatility of an asset, we can also write this equation as

$$\begin{matrix}\text{One-day} & & \text{(Dollar market} & & \text{(Price} \\ \text{VaR} & = & \text{value of} & \times & \text{volatility)} \\ & & \text{the position)} & & \end{matrix} \qquad (15.1)$$

How price sensitivity and an adverse yield move will be measured depends on the FI and its choice of a price-sensitivity model as well as its view of what exactly is a potentially adverse price (yield) move.

We concentrate on how the RiskMetrics model calculates one-day VaR in three trading areas—fixed income, FX, and equities—and then on how it estimates the aggregate risk of the entire trading portfolio to meet an FI manager's objective of a single aggregate dollar exposure measure across the whole bank on a given day.

[4] Although RiskMetrics calls market risk exposure *daily earnings at risk* (DEAR), we adopt the more common Canadian usage, *one-day value at risk*, also called *one-day VaR*, *one-day VaR*, or often shortened to *VaR* or *VaR*.

The Market Risk of Fixed-Income Securities

Suppose an FI has a $1 million market value position in zero-coupon bonds of seven years to maturity with a face value of $1,631,483. Today's yield on these bonds is 7.243 percent per year.[5] These bonds are held as part of the trading portfolio. Thus,

$$\text{Dollar market value of position} = \$1 \text{ million}$$

The FI manager wants to know the potential exposure the FI faces should interest rates move against the FI as a result of an adverse or reasonably bad market move the next day. How much the FI will lose depends on the bond's price volatility. From the duration model in Chapter 9 we know that

$$\begin{aligned}\text{Daily price volatility} &= (\text{Price sensitivity to a small change in yield}) \\ &\quad \times (\text{Adverse daily yield move}) \\ &= (MD) \times (\text{Adverse daily yield move}) \qquad (15.2)\end{aligned}$$

The modified duration (MD) of this bond is[6]

$$MD = \frac{D}{1+R} = \frac{7}{(1.07243)} = 6.527$$

given that the yield on the bond is $R = 7.243$ percent. To estimate price volatility, multiply the bond's MD by the expected adverse daily yield move.

EXAMPLE 15-1

Daily VaR on Fixed-Income Securities

Suppose we define bad yield changes such that there is only a 1 percent chance that the yield changes will exceed this amount in either direction—or, since we are concerned only with bad outcomes, and we are long in bonds, that there is 1 chance in 100 (or a 1 percent chance) that the next day's yield increase (or shock) will exceed this given adverse move.

If we assume that yield changes are normally distributed,[7] we can fit a normal distribution to the histogram of recent past changes in seven-year zero-coupon interest rates (yields) to estimate the size of this adverse rate move. From statistics, we know that (the middle) 98 percent of the area under the normal distribution is to be found within ± 2.33 standard deviations (σ) from the mean—that is, 2.33σ—and 2 percent of the area under the normal distribution is found beyond $\pm 2.33\sigma$ (1 percent under each tail, -2.33σ and $+2.33\sigma$, respectively).[8]

---

[5] The face value of the bonds is $1,631,483—that is, $\$1{,}631{,}483/(1.07243)^7 = \$1{,}000{,}000$ market value. In the original model, prices were determined using a discrete rate of return, R_j. In the document *Return to RiskMetrics: The Evolution of a Standard,* April 2001, prices are determined using a continuously compounded return, e^{-rt}. The change was implemented because continuous compounding has properties that facilitate mathematical treatment. For example, the logarithmic return on a zero-coupon bond equals the difference of interest rates multiplied by the maturity of the bond. That is,

$$\ln\left(\frac{e^{-\tilde{r}t}}{e^{-rt}}\right) = -(\tilde{r} - r)t$$

where $\tilde{r}$ is the expected return.

[6] Assuming annual compounding for simplicity.

[7] In reality, many asset return distributions—such as exchange rates and interest rates—have "fat tails." Thus, the normal distribution will tend to underestimate extreme outcomes. This is a major criticism of the RiskMetrics modelling approach and a major reason for regulators' move to the use of the ES from the traditional VaR measure of market risk. Further, the original CreditMetrics calculation incorporated a 5 percent chance that the next day's yield increase would exceed this given adverse move. The use of 1 percent to measure adverse moves produces a more conservative estimate of an FI's VaR.

[8] For 95 percent of the area under the normal distribution (2.5 percent under each tail), we use ± 1.96, and for 90 percent of the area (5 percent under each tail) we use ± 1.65.

Suppose that during the last year the mean change in daily yields on seven-year zero-coupon bonds was 0 percent[9] and the standard deviation was 10 basis points (bp) (or 0.001). Thus, 2.33σ is 23.3 bp.[10] In other words, over the last year, daily yields on seven-year, zero-coupon bonds have fluctuated (either positively or negatively) by more than 23.3 bp 2 percent of the time. Adverse moves in yields are those that decrease the value of the security (i.e., the yield increases). These occurred 1 percent of the time, or 1 in 100 days. This is shown in Figure 15–1.

We can now calculate the potential daily price volatility on seven-year discount bonds using equation 15.2 as

$$\begin{aligned}\text{Price volatility} &= MD \times (\text{Potential adverse move in yield})\\ &= (6.527) \times (0.00233)\\ &= 0.01521 \text{ or } 1.521\%\end{aligned}$$

Given the price volatility and initial market value of the seven-year bond portfolio, we drop the minus sign and use equation 15.1 to calculate the one-day VaR as

$$\begin{aligned}\text{One-day VaR} &= (\text{Dollar market value of position}) \times (\text{Price volatility})\\ &= (\$1{,}000{,}000) \times (0.01521)\\ &= \$15{,}210\end{aligned}$$

That is, the potential one-day loss on the $1 million position is $15,210 if the 1 bad day in 100 occurs tomorrow.

FIGURE 15–1
Adverse Rate Move, Seven-Year Rates

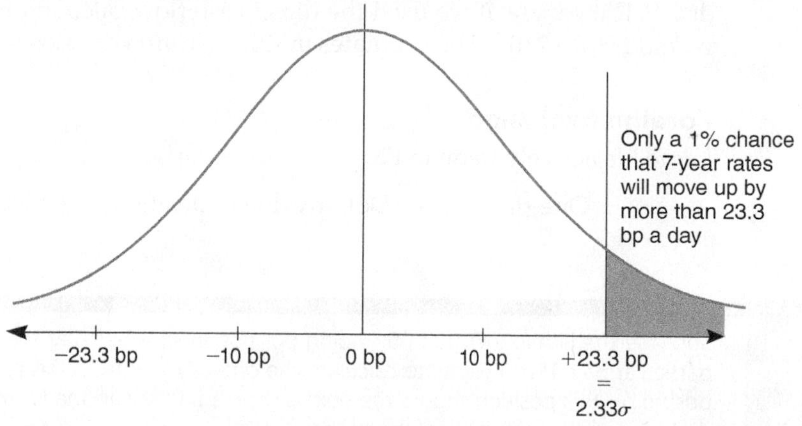

We can extend this analysis to calculate the potential loss over 2, 3, . . . , *N* days. If we assume that yield shocks are independent and daily volatility is approximately constant,[11] and that the FI is locked into holding this asset for *N* days, then

[9] If the mean were nonzero (e.g., −1 bp), this could be added to the 23.3 bp (i.e., 22.3 bp).

[10] RiskMetrics weights recent observations more than older observations (called *exponential weighting*) so recent news is more heavily reflected in the calculation of σ. Regular σ calculations weight all past observations equally.

[11] The assumptions that daily volatility is constant and that there is no autocorrelation in yield shocks are strong assumptions. Much recent literature suggests that shocks are autocorrelated in many asset markets over relatively long horizons. To understand why we take the square root of *N*, consider a five-day holding period. The σ_5^2, or five-day variance of asset returns, will equal the current one-day variance σ_1^2 times 5 under the assumptions of constant daily variance and no autocorrelation in shocks, or

$$\sigma_5^2 = \sigma_1^2 \times 5$$

The standard deviation of this equation is

$$\sigma_5 = \sigma_1 \times \sqrt{5}$$

or since the one-day VaR is measured in the same dimensions as a standard deviation (σ), in the terminology of RiskMetrics, the five-day value at risk (VaR_5) is

$$5\text{-day } VaR = \text{daily } VaR \times \sqrt{5}$$

the *N*-day market VaR is related to the one-day VaR by

$$N\text{-day } VaR = \text{One-day } VaR \times \sqrt{N} \tag{15.3}$$

That is, the earnings the FI has at risk, should interest rate yields move against the FI, are a function of the one-day VaR and the (square root of the) number of days that the FI is forced to hold the securities because of an illiquid market. Specifically, one-day VaR assumes that the FI can sell all the bonds tomorrow, even at the new lower price. In reality, it may take many days for the FI to unload its position. This relative illiquidity of a market exposes the FI to magnified losses (measured by the square root of *N*).[12] If *N* is five days, then

$$5\text{-day } VaR = \$15{,}210 \times \sqrt{5} = \$24{,}082 = \$34{,}011$$

If *N* is 10 days as required by BIS, then

$$10\text{-day } VaR = \$15{,}210 \times \sqrt{10} = \$34{,}057 = \$48{,}098$$

In the above calculations, we estimated price sensitivity using MD. However, the RiskMetrics model generally prefers using the present value of cash flow changes as the price-sensitivity weights over modified durations. Essentially, each cash flow is discounted by the appropriate zero-coupon rate to generate the one-day VaR measure. If we used the direct cash flow calculation in this case, the loss would be \$15,210.[13] The estimates in this case are very close.

Foreign Exchange

Large FIs actively trade in FX. Remember that

$$\text{One-day VaR} = (\text{Dollar value of position}) \times (\text{Price volatility})$$

EXAMPLE 15-2

One-Day VaR of FX Contracts

Suppose the FI had a €800,000 trading position in spot euros at the close of business on a particular day. The FI wants to calculate the one-day VaR from this position (i.e., the risk exposure on this position should the next day be a bad day in the FX markets with respect to the value of the euro against the dollar).

The first step is to calculate the dollar value of the position:

$$\begin{aligned}\text{Dollar equivalent value of position} &= (\text{FX position}) \times (\text{€/\$ spot exchange rate})\\ &= (\text{€1.6 million}) \times (\text{\$ per unit of foreign currency})\end{aligned}$$

Suppose for simplicity that the exchange rate is €0.8000/\$1 or \$1.25/€1 at the daily close; then

$$\begin{aligned}\text{Dollar value of position} &= (\text{€800,000}) \times (\$1.25/\text{€1})\\ &= \$1 \text{ million}\end{aligned}$$

[12] In practice, a number of FIs calculate *N* internally by dividing the position held in a security by the median daily volume of trading of that security over recent days. Thus, if trading volume is low because of a "one-way market," in that most people are seeking to sell rather than buy, then *N* can rise substantially; that is, *N* = (\$ position in security/median daily \$ volume of trading).

[13] The initial market value of the seven-year zero was \$1,000,000, or $\$1{,}631{,}483/(1.07243)^7$. The (loss) effect on each \$1 (market value) invested in the bond of a rise in rates by 1 bp from 7.243 percent to 7.253 percent is 0.00065277. However, the adverse rate move is 23.3 bp. Thus,

$$\text{One-day VaR} = (\$1 \text{ million}) \times (0.00065277) \times (23.3) = \$15{,}210$$

Suppose that, looking back at the daily percentage changes in the €/$ exchange rate over the past year, we find that the volatility, or standard deviation (σ), of daily changes in the spot exchange rate was 56.5 bp. However, suppose that the FI is interested in adverse moves—that is, bad moves that will not occur more than 1 percent of the time, or 1 day in every 100. Statistically speaking, if changes in exchange rates are historically "normally" distributed, the exchange rate must change in the adverse direction by 2.33σ (2.33×56.5 bp) for this change to be viewed as likely to occur only 1 day in every 100 days:[14]

$$\text{FX volatility} = 2.33 \times 56.5 \text{ bp} = 131.645 \text{ bp}$$

In other words, during the last year, the euro declined in value against the dollar by 131.645 bp 1 percent of the time. As a result:

$$\begin{aligned}\text{One-day VaR} &= (\text{Dollar value of position}) \times (\text{FX volatility})\\ &= (\$1 \text{ million}) \times (0.0136454)\\ &= \$13{,}164\end{aligned}$$

This is the potential one-day exposure to adverse euro-to-dollar exchange rate changes for the FI from the €800,000 spot currency holdings.

Equities

Many large FIs also take positions in equities. As is well known from the capital asset pricing model (CAPM), there are two types of risk to an equity position in an individual stock *i:*

$$\begin{matrix}\text{Total risk} & = & \text{Systematic risk} & + & \text{Unsystematic risk}\\ (\sigma_{it}^2) & = & (\beta_i^2\sigma_{mt}^2) & + & (\sigma_{eit}^2)\end{matrix} \qquad (15.4)$$

beta
Systematic (undiversifiable) risk reflecting the co-movement of the returns on a specific stock with returns on the market portfolio.

Systematic risk reflects the co-movement of that stock with the market portfolio reflected by the stock's **beta** (β_i) and the volatility of the market portfolio (σ_{mt}), whereas unsystematic risk is specific to the firm itself (σ_{eit}).

In a very well diversified portfolio, unsystematic risk (σ_{eit}^2) can be largely diversified away (i.e., will equal zero), leaving behind systematic (undiversifiable) market risk ($\beta_i^2\sigma_{mt}^2$). If the FI's trading portfolio follows (replicates) the returns on the stock market index, the β of that portfolio will be 1, since the movement of returns on the FI's portfolio will be one to one with the market,[15] and the standard deviation of the portfolio, σ_{it}, will be equal to the standard deviation of the stock market index, σ_{mt}.

EXAMPLE 15-3
One-Day VaR on Equities

Suppose the FI holds a $1 million trading position in stocks that reflect a stock market index (e.g., the S&P TSX Composite Index). Then $\beta = 1$ and the one-day VaR for equities is

$$\begin{aligned}\text{One-day VaR} &= (\text{Dollar market value of position}) \times (\text{Stock market return volatility})\\ &= (\$1{,}000{,}000) \times (2.33\ \sigma_m)\end{aligned}$$

[14] Technically, 98 percent of the area under a normal distribution lies between $\pm 2.33\sigma$ from the mean. This means that 1 percent of the time, daily exchange rate changes will increase by more than 2.33σ, and 1 percent of the time, will decrease by 2.33σ. This case concerns only adverse moves in the exchange rate of euros to dollars (i.e., a depreciation of 2.33σ).

[15] If $\beta \neq 1$, as in the case of most individual stocks, One-day VaR = Dollar value of position $\times\ \beta_i \times 2.33\ \sigma_m$, where β_i is the systematic risk of the *i*th stock.

If, over the last year, the σ_m of the daily returns on the stock market index was 200 bp, then $2.33\sigma_m$ = 466 bp (i.e., the adverse change or decline in the daily return on the stock market exceeded 466 bp only 1 percent of the time). In this case,

$$\text{One-day VaR} = (\$1{,}000{,}000) \times (0.0466) = \$46{,}600$$

That is, the FI stands to lose at least $46,600 in earnings if adverse stock market returns materialize tomorrow.[16]

In less well diversified portfolios or portfolios of individual stocks, the effect of unsystematic risk σ_{eit} on the value of the trading position needs to be added. Moreover, if the CAPM does not offer a good explanation of asset pricing compared with, say, multi-index arbitrage pricing theory (APT), a degree of error will be built into the one-day VaR calculation.[17]

Portfolio Aggregation

LO4

The preceding sections analyzed the one-day VaRs of individual trading positions. The examples considered a seven-year, zero-coupon, fixed-income security ($1 million market value); a position in spot euros ($1 million market value); and a position in the stock market index ($1 million market value). The individual one-day VaRs were:

1. Seven-year zero-coupon bonds = $15,210
2. Euro spot = $13,164
3. Equities = $46,600

However, senior management wants to know the aggregate risk of the entire trading position. To calculate this, we *cannot* simply sum the three VaRs—$15,210 + $13,164 + $46,600 = $74,974—because that ignores any degree of offsetting covariance or correlation among the fixed-income, FX, and equity trading positions. In particular, some of these asset shocks (adverse moves) may be negatively correlated. As is well known from portfolio theory, negative correlations and correlations less than one between asset shocks will reduce the degree of portfolio risk.

EXAMPLE 15–4

Calculation of the Daily VaR of a Portfolio

Table 15–3 shows a hypothetical correlation matrix between daily seven-year zero-coupon bond yield changes, €/$ spot exchange rate changes, and changes in daily returns on a stock market index. From Table 15–3, the correlation between the seven-year zero-coupon bonds and €/$ exchange rates, $\rho_{z,€}$, is negative (−0.2), while the seven-year zero-coupon yield changes with stock returns, $\rho_{z,m}$ (0.4), and €/$ shocks, $\rho_{m,€}$ (0.1), are positively correlated.

[16] If we consider a single-equity security with a beta (β) = 1.25 (i.e., one that is more sensitive than the market, such that as market returns increase [decrease] by 1 percent, the security's return increases [decreases] by 1.25 percent), then with a $1 million investment and the same (assumed) volatility (σ) of 2 percent, the FI would stand to lose at least $58,250 in daily earnings if adverse stock returns materialize (i.e., one-day VaR = $1,000,000 × 1.25 × 2.33 × 0.02 = $58,250).

[17] Derivatives are also used for trading purposes. In the calculation of its one-day VaR, a derivative has to be converted into a position in the underlying asset (e.g., bond, FX, or equity).

TABLE 15–3
Correlations (ρ_{ij}) among Assets

	Seven-Year Zero	€/$1	Stock Index
Seven-year zero	—	−0.2	0.4
€/$1		—	0.1
Stock index			—

Using this correlation matrix along with the individual asset one-day VaRs, we can calculate the risk or standard deviation of the whole (three-asset) trading portfolio as[18]

$$\text{One-day VaR portfolio} = \begin{bmatrix} (VaR_z)^2 + (VaR_€)^2 + (VaR_m)^2 \\ +(2 \times \rho_{z,€} \times VaR_z \times VaR_€) \\ +(2 \times \rho_{z,m} \times VaR_z \times VaR_m) \\ +(2 \times \rho_{m,€} \times VaR_m \times VaR_€) \end{bmatrix}^{1/2} \tag{15.5}$$

This is a direct application of modern portfolio theory (MPT), since one-day VaRs are directly similar to standard deviations. Substituting into this equation the calculated individual one-day VaRs (in thousands of dollars), we get

$$\begin{aligned}\text{One-day VaR portfolio} &= [(15{,}210)^2 + (13{,}164)^2 + (46{,}600)^2 + 2(-0.20)(15{,}210)(13{,}164) \\ &\quad + 2(0.4)(15{,}210)(46{,}600) + 2(0.1)(13{,}164)(46{,}600)]^{1/2} \\ &= \$56{,}443\end{aligned}$$

The equation indicates that considering the risk of each trading position as well as the correlation structure among those positions' returns results in a lower measure of portfolio trading risk ($56,433) than when risks of the underlying trading positions (the sum of which was $74,974) are added. A quick check will reveal that had we assumed that all three assets were perfectly positively correlated (i.e., $\rho_{ij} = 1$), the one-day VaR for the portfolio would have been $74,974 (i.e., equal to the sum of the three one-day VaRs). Clearly, even in abnormal market conditions, assuming that asset returns are perfectly correlated will exaggerate the degree of actual trading risk exposure.

Table 15–4 shows the type of spreadsheet used by FIs to calculate VaR. As you can see, in this example positions are taken in 13 different country (currency) bonds in eight different maturity buckets.[19] There is also a column for FX risk (and, if necessary, equity risk) in these different country markets, although in this example, the FI has no FX risk exposure (all the cells are empty).

In the example in Table 15–4, while the FI is holding offsetting long and short positions in both Danish and euro bonds, it is still exposed to trading risks of $48,000 and $27,000, respectively (see the column "Interest VaR"). This happens because the EU yield curve is more volatile than the Danish and shocks at different

[18] In modern portfolio theory (MPT), the standard deviation or risk of a portfolio of three assets is equal to the square root of the sum of the variances of returns on each of the three assets individually plus two times the covariances among each pair of these assets. With three assets there are three covariances. Here we use the fact that a correlation coefficient times the standard deviations on each pair of assets equals the covariance between each pair of assets. Note that one-day VaR is measured in dollars and has the same dimensions as a standard deviation.

[19] Bonds held with different maturity dates (e.g., six years) are split into two and allocated to the nearest two of the eight maturity buckets (here, five years and seven years) using three criteria: (1) The sum of the current market value of the two resulting cash flows must be identical to the market value of the original cash flow, (2) the market *risk* of the portfolio of two cash flows must be identical to the overall market risk of the original cash flow, and (3) the two cash flows have the same *sign* as the original cash flow. See J.P. Morgan, *RiskMetrics—Technical Document,* November 1994, and *Return to RiskMetrics: The Evolution of a Standard,* April 2001, msci.com.

TABLE 15-4 Portfolio One-Day VaR Spreadsheet

	Interest Rate Risk Notional Amounts (U.S. $ millions equivalents)									FX Risk		Total	
	1 Month	1 Year	2 Years	3 Years	4 Years	5 Years	7 Years	10 Years	Interest VaR	Spot FX	FX VaR	Portfolio Effect	Total VaR
Australia										AUD			
Brazil										BRL			
Canada										CAD			
Denmark	19			−30				11	48	DKK			48
European Union	−19			30				−11	27	EUR			27
Hong Kong										HKD			
Japan										YEN			
Mexico										MXN			
Singapore										SGD			
Sweden										SEK			
Switzerland										CHF			
United Kingdom										GBP			
United States					10			10	76	USD			76
Total					10			10	151				151
					Portfolio effect				(62)				(62)
					Total VaR ($000s)				89				89

maturity buckets are not equal. The VaR figure for a U.S. bond position of long $20 million is $76,000. Adding these three positions yields a VaR of $151,000. However, this ignores the fact that Danish, EU, and U.S. yield shocks are not perfectly correlated. Allowing for diversification effects (the portfolio effect) results in a total VaR of only $89,000. This would be the number reported to the FI's senior management. Most FIs establish limits for VaR, one-day VaR, position limits, and dollar trading loss limits for their trading portfolios. Actual activity compared with these limits is then monitored daily. Should a risk exposure level exceed approved limit levels, management must provide a strategy for bringing risk levels within approved limits. Table 15–5 reports the average, minimum, and maximum one-day VaR and the one-day stressed VaR (discussed below) that were reported by six large Canadian banks in 2012 for their trading portfolios.

bmo.com
cibc.com
nbc.ca
rbc.com
scotiabank.com
td.com

As an indication of the complexity of the calculations for a large FI, the number of markets covered by the U.S. bank Citigroup's traders and the number of correlations among those markets require the daily production and updating of over 250,000 volatility estimates (σ) and correlations (ρ). These data are updated daily, requiring a significant investment in computer technology and time.

CONCEPT QUESTIONS

1. **What is the ultimate objective of MRM models?**
2. **Refer to Example 15–1. What is the VaR for this bond if σ is 15 bp?**
3. **In Example 15–4, what is the portfolio's VaR if the asset returns are independent of each other?**

TABLE 15-5
Trading Portfolio One-Day VaR and Stressed VaR for Canadian Banks, 2012* ($ millions)

Source: 2012 annual reports.

Name	Average VaR 2012	Minimum VaR during 2012	Maximum VaR during 2012	Average Stressed VaR 2012
Bank of Montreal**	$15.4	$11.1	$22.6	$17.1
CIBC	4.9	3.3	7.0	6.5
National Bank	5.7	3.9	11.4	9.1
Royal Bank	52	43	66	78
Scotiabank	25.1	15.2	24.2	37.1
TD Bank	26.1	14.8	41.1	47.7

* The figures are based on the banks' internal models and may be based on methodologies that differ from RiskMetrics.
** Reported as pre-tax Canadian equivalent.

HISTORIC (BACK SIMULATION) APPROACH

LO5

A major criticism of VaR models is the need to assume a symmetric (normal) distribution for all asset returns.[20] Clearly, for some assets, such as options and short-term securities (bonds), this is highly questionable. For example, the most an investor can lose if he or she buys a call option on an equity is the call premium; however, the investor's potential upside returns are unlimited. In a statistical sense, the returns on call options are nonnormal since they exhibit a positive skew.[21]

Because of these and other considerations discussed below, the large majority of FIs (e.g., TD, RBC, CIBC, BNS, BMO, and National Bank) that have developed market risk models have employed a historic or back simulation approach. The advantages of this approach are (1) it is simple, (2) it does not require that asset returns be normally distributed, and (3) it does not require that the correlations or standard deviations of asset returns be calculated.

The essential idea is to take the current market portfolio of assets (FX, bonds, equities, etc.) and revalue them on the basis of the actual prices (returns) that existed on those assets yesterday, the day before that, and so on. Frequently, the FI will calculate the market or value risk of its current portfolio on the basis of prices (returns) that existed for those assets on each of the last 500 days. It will then calculate the 1 percent worst case—the portfolio value that has the fifth-lowest value out of 500. That is, only on 5 days out of 500, or 1 percent of the time, would the

[20] Another criticism is that VaR models like RiskMetrics ignore the (risk in the) payments of accrued interest on an FI's debt securities. Thus, VaR models will underestimate the true probability of default and the appropriate level of capital to be held against this risk. Also, because of the distributional assumptions, while RiskMetrics produces reasonable estimates of downside risk for FIs with highly diversified portfolios, FIs with small, undiversified portfolios will significantly underestimate their true risk exposure using RiskMetrics. Further, a number of authors have argued that many asset distributions have "fat tails" and that RiskMetrics, by assuming the normal distribution, underestimates the risk of extreme losses. One alternative approach to dealing with the "fat-tail" problem is extreme value theory. Simply put, one can view an asset distribution as being explained by two distributions. For example, a normal distribution may explain returns up to the 95 percent threshold, but for losses beyond that threshold another distribution, such as the generalized Pareto distribution, may provide a better explanation of loss outcomes such as the 99 percent level and beyond. In short, the normal distribution is likely to underestimate the importance and size of observations in the tail of the distribution, which is, after all, what VaR models are meant to be measuring. Finally, VaR models by definition concern themselves with risk rather than return. It should be noted that minimizing risk may be highly costly in terms of the return the FI gives up. Indeed, there may be many more return–risk combinations preferable to that achieved at the minimum risk point in the trading portfolio. Recent upgrades to RiskMetrics (see the RiskMetrics website at msci.com) allow management to incorporate a return dimension to VaR analysis so that management can evaluate how trading portfolio returns differ as VaR changes.

[21] For a normal distribution, its skew (which is the third moment of a distribution) is zero.

value of the portfolio fall below this number based on recent historic experience of exchange rate changes, equity price changes, interest rate changes, and so on.

Consider the simple example in Table 15–6, where an FI is trading two currencies: the Japanese yen and the Swiss franc. At the close of trading on December 1, 2015, it has a long position in Japanese yen of ¥500 million and a long position in Swiss francs of Sf20 million. It wants to assess its VaR. That is, if tomorrow is that 1 bad day in 100 (the 1 percent worst case), how much does it stand to lose on its total foreign currency position? As shown in Table 15–6, six steps are required to calculate the VaR of its currency portfolio. It should be noted that the same methodological approach would be followed to calculate the VaR of any asset, liability, or derivative (bonds, options, etc.) as long as market prices were available on those assets over a sufficiently long historic time period.

- *Step 1: Measure exposures.* Convert today's foreign currency positions into dollar equivalents using today's exchange rates. Thus, an evaluation of the FX position of the FI on December 1, 2015, indicates that it has a long position of $5,000,000 in yen (¥500,000,000/(¥100/$1))and $18,181,818 (Sf20,000,000/(Sf1.1/$1)) in Swiss francs.
- *Step 2: Measure sensitivity.* Measure the sensitivity of each FX position by calculating its delta, where delta measures the change in the dollar value of each FX position if the yen or the Swiss franc depreciates (declines in value) by 1 percent against the dollar.[22] As can be seen from Table 15–6, line 6, the delta for the Japanese yen position is −$49,505 (or ¥500,000,000/(¥101/$1) − ¥500,000,000/(¥100/$1)), and for the Swiss franc position, it is −$180,018 (or Sf20,000,000/(Sf1.111/$1) − Sf20,000,000/(Sf1.1/$1)).
- *Step 3: Measure risk.* Look at the actual percentage changes in exchange rates, ¥/$ and Sf/$, on each of the past 500 days. Thus, on November 30, 2015, the yen declined in value against the dollar over the day by 0.5 percent while the Swiss franc declined in value against the dollar by 0.2 percent. (It might be noted that if the currencies were to appreciate in value against the dollar, the sign against the number in row 7 of Table 15–6 would be negative; that is, it takes fewer units of foreign currency to buy a dollar than it did the day before.) As can be seen in row 8, combining the delta and the actual percentage change in each FX rate means a total loss of $60,756.1 if the FI had held the current ¥500,000,000 and Sf20,000,000 positions on that day (November 30, 2015).
- *Step 4: Repeat step 3.* Step 4 repeats the same exercise for the yen and Swiss franc positions but uses actual exchange rate changes on November 29, 2015; November 28, 2015; and so on. That is, we calculate the FX losses and/or gains on each of the past 500 trading days, excluding weekends and holidays, when the FX market is closed. This amounts to going back in time over two years. For each of these days the actual change in exchange rates is calculated (row 7) and multiplied by the deltas of each position (the numbers in row 6 of Table 15–6). These two numbers are summed to attain total risk measures for each of the past 500 days.

[22] That is, in the case of FX, delta measures the dollar change in FX holdings for a 1 percent change in the foreign exchange rate. In the case of equities, it would measure the change in the value of those securities for a 1 percent change in price, while for bonds, it measures the change in value for a 1 percent change in the price of the bond (note that delta measures the sensitivity of a bond's value to a change in yield, not price).

TABLE 15–6 **Hypothetical Example of the Historic, or Back Simulation, Approach Using Two Currencies, as of December 1, 2015**

	Yen	Swiss Franc
Step 1. Measure exposures		
1. Closing position on December 1, 2015	¥500,000,000	SF 20,000,000
2. Exchange rate on December 1, 2015	¥100/$1	SF 1.1/$1
3. Dollar equivalent position on December 1, 2015	$5,000,000	$18,181,818
Step 2. Measure sensitivity		
4. 1.01 × current exchange rate	¥101/$1	SF 1.111/$1
5. Revalued position in dollars	$4,950,495	$18,001,800
6. Delta of position ($) (measure of sensitivity to a 1% adverse change in exchange rate, or row 5 minus row 3)	−$49,505	−$180,018
Step 3. Measure risk of December 1, 2015, closing position using exchange rates that existed on each of the last 500 days		
November 30, 2015	**Yen**	**Swiss Franc**
7. Change in exchange rate (%) on November 30, 2015	0.5%	0.2%
8. Risk (delta × change in exchange rate)	−$24,752.5	−$36,003.6
9. Sum of risks = −$60,756.1		
Step 4. Repeat Step 3 for each of the remaining 499 days		
November 29, 2015		
:		
:		
April 15, 2014		
:		
:		
November 30, 2013		
:		
:		

Step 5. Rank days by risk from worst to best

Date	Risk ($)
1. May 6, 2014	−$119,096
2. January 27, 2015	−$116,703
3. December 1, 2013	$104,366
4. September 14, 2013	−$100,248
5. August 8, 2014	−$ 97,210
: :	
: :	
25. November 30, 2015	−$60,756.1
: :	
: :	
499. April 8, 2015	+$112,260
500. July 28, 2014	+$121,803

Step 6. VaR (5th-worst day out of last 500)

VaR = −$97,210 (August 8, 2014)

- *Step 5: Rank days by risk from worst to best.* These risk measures can then be ranked from worst to best. Clearly the worst-case loss would have occurred on this position on May 6, 2014, with a total loss of $119,096. Although this worst-case scenario is of interest to FI managers, we are interested in the 1 percent worst case, that is, a loss that does not occur more than 5 days out of the 500 days (5 ÷ 500 equals 1 percent). As can be seen, in our example, the 5th-worst loss out of 500 occurred on August 8, 2014. This loss amounted to $97,210.

- *Step 6:* VaR. If it is assumed that the recent past distribution of exchange rates is an accurate reflection of the likely distribution of FX rate changes in the future—that exchange rate changes have a stationary distribution—then the $97,210 can be viewed as the FX VaR exposure of the FI on December 1, 2014. That is, if tomorrow (in our case, December 2, 2015) is a bad day in the FX markets, and given the FI's position of long ¥500 million and long Sf20 million, the FI can expect to lose $97,210 (or more) with a 1 percent probability. This VaR measure can then be updated every day as the FX position changes and the delta changes. For example, given the nature of FX trading, the positions held on December 5, 2015, could be very different from those held on December 1, 2015.[23]

The Historic (Back Simulation) Model versus RiskMetrics

One obvious benefit of the historic, or back simulation, approach is that we do not need to calculate standard deviations and correlations (or assume normal distributions for asset returns) to calculate the portfolio risk figures in row 9 of Table 15–6.[24] A second advantage is that it directly provides a worst-case scenario number, in our example, a loss of $97,210—see step 5. Since it assumes asset returns are normally distributed—that returns can go to plus and minus infinity— RiskMetrics provides no such worst-case scenario number.[25]

The disadvantage of the back simulation approach is the degree of confidence we have in the 1 percent VaR number based on 500 observations. Statistically speaking, 500 observations are not very many, so there will be a very wide confidence band (or standard error) around the estimated number ($97,210 in our example). One possible solution to the problem is to go back in time more than 500 days and estimate the 1 percent VaR based on 1,000 past daily observations (the 10th-worst case) or even 10,000 past observations (the 100th-worst case). The problem is that as one goes back farther in time, past observations may become decreasingly relevant in predicting VaR in the future. For example, 10,000 observations may require the FI to analyze FX data going back 40 years. Over this period we have moved through many very different FX regimes: from relatively fixed exchange rates in the 1950–1970 period, to relatively floating exchange rates in the 1970s, to more managed floating rates in the 1980s and 1990s, to the abolition of exchange rates and the introduction of the euro in January 2002, to large fluctuations in exchange rates during the financial crisis of 2008–2009. Clearly, exchange rate behaviour and risk in a fixed exchange rate regime will have little relevance to an FX trader or market risk manager operating and analyzing risk in a floating exchange rate regime.

This seems to present the market risk manager with a difficult modelling problem. There are, however, at least two approaches to this problem. The first is to

[23] As in RiskMetrics, an adjustment can be made for illiquidity of the market, in this case, by assuming the FI is locked into longer holding periods. For example, if it is estimated that it will take five days for the FI to sell its FX position, then the FI will be interested in the weekly (i.e., five trading days) changes in FX rates in the past. One immediate problem is that with 500 past trading days, only 100 weekly periods would be available, which reduces the statistical power of the VaR estimate (see below).

[24] The reason is that the historic, or back simulation, approach uses actual exchange rates on each day that explicitly include correlations or co-movements with other exchange rates and asset returns on that day.

[25] The 1 percent in RiskMetrics tells us that we will lose more than this amount on 1 day out of every 100; it does not tell us the maximum amount we can lose. Theoretically, with a normal distribution, this could be an infinite amount.

weight past observations in the back simulation unequally, giving a higher weight to the more recent past observations. The second is to use a Monte Carlo simulation approach, which generates additional observations that are consistent with recent historic experience. The latter approach, in effect, amounts to simulating or creating artificial trading days and FX rate changes.

THE MONTE CARLO SIMULATION APPROACH

LO6

To overcome the problems imposed by a limited number of actual observations, we can generate additional observations (in our example, FX changes). Normally, the simulation or generation of these additional observations is structured using a Monte Carlo simulation approach so that returns or rates generated reflect the probability with which they have occurred in recent historic time periods. The first step is to calculate the historic variance–covariance matrix (Σ) of FX changes. This matrix is then decomposed into two symmetric matrices, A and A'.[26] This allows the FI to generate scenarios for the FX position by multiplying the A' matrix, which reflects the historic volatilities and correlations among FX rates, by a random number vector z:[27] 10,000 random values of z are drawn for each FX exchange rate.[28] This simulation approach results in realistic FX scenarios being generated as historic volatilities and correlations among FX rates are multiplied by the randomly drawn values of z. The VaR of the current position is then calculated as in Table 10–6, except that in the Monte Carlo approach, the VaR is the 100th worst simulated loss out of 10,000.

Monte Carlo simulation is, therefore, a tool for considering portfolio valuation under all possible combinations of factors that determine a security's value. The model generates random market values drawn from the multivariate normal distributions representing each variable. For example, BMO and the Scotiabank use Monte Carlo simulation as one of their models in estimating one-day VaR.

EXAMPLE 15-5

Calculating VaR Using Monte Carlo Simulation

Consider an FI with a long position in a one-year, zero-coupon NZ$1,000,000 bond. The current one-year interest rate on the bond is 10 percent. So, the present value of the one-year, NZ$1 million notional bond is NZ$909,091. The current $/NZ$ exchange rate is 0.65 (i.e., the NZ$/$ exchange rate is 1.538461). Thus, the FI has a long position of $590,909 in the bond. The FI wants to evaluate the VaR for this bond based on changes in interest rates and FX rates over the next 10 days.

The two underlying bond characteristics to be simulated are the $/NZ$ exchange rate and the one-year bond price for changes in one-year interest rates. Historical daily volatilities of the $/NZ$ exchange rate and the bond price are such that $\sigma_{FX} = 0.0042$ and $\sigma_B = 0.0008$. The historic correlation between the two is $\rho_{FX,B} = -0.17$. To generate 1,000 scenarios for values of the two underlying assets in 10 days, Monte Carlo analysis first generates 1,000 pairs of standard normal variates whose correlation is $\rho_{FX,B} = -0.17$. Label each pair z_{FX} and z_B. Histograms for the results are shown in Figure 15–2. Note that the distributions are essentially the same.

[26] The only difference between A and A' is that the numbers in the rows of A become the numbers in the columns of A'. The technical term for this procedure is the *Cholesky decomposition,* where $\sigma = AA'$.

[27] Here z is assumed to be normally distributed with a mean of zero and a standard deviation of 1 or $z \sim N(0, 1)$.

[28] Technically, let y be an FX scenario; then $y = A'z$. For each FX rate, 10,000 values of z are randomly generated to produce 10,000 values of y. The y values are then used to revalue the FX position and calculate gains and losses.

FIGURE 15–2
Frequency Distribution for z_{FX} and z_B (1,000 trials)

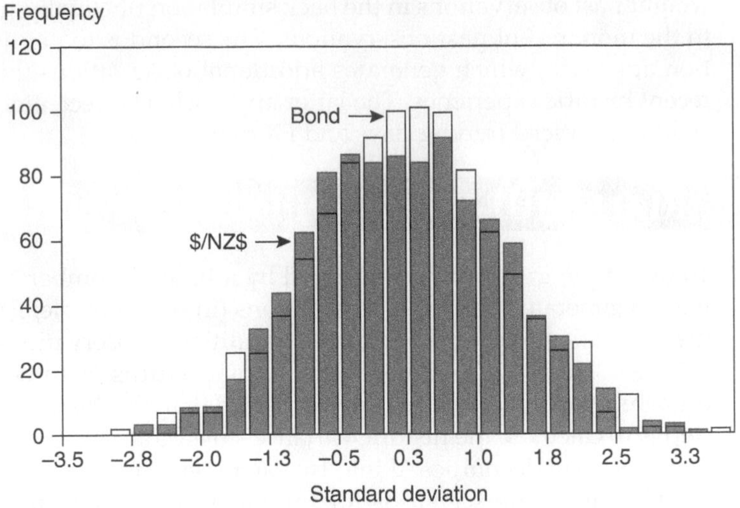

Next, Monte Carlo simulation creates the actual scenarios for the variables, FX and B. That is, for each pair z_{FX} and z_B, future values are created by applying

$$P_{FX} = 0.65e^{0.0042 \times \sqrt{5} \times z_{FX}} \quad (15.6)$$

and

$$P_B = \text{NZ\$}909{,}091e^{0.0008 \times \sqrt{5} \times z_B} \quad (15.7)$$

To express the bond price in dollars (accounting for both the exchange rate and interest rate risk for the bond), it is necessary to multiply the simulated bond price by the exchange rate in each scenario. Figures 15–3 and 15–4 show the distributions of future values, P_{FX} and P_B, respectively, obtained by 1,000 simulations. Note that the distributions are no longer normal, and for the bond price, the distribution shows a marked asymmetry. This is due to the transformation made from normal to lognormal variates by applying equations 15–6 and 15–7. Table 15–7 lists the first 10 scenarios generated from Monte Carlo analysis. The process would be repeated until the 10,000 random observations are generated. Then with the observations ranked from worst (biggest loss) to best (biggest gain), the VaR is the 100th-worst estimate out of 10,000.

FIGURE 15–3
Frequency Distribution for Bond Price (1,000 trials)

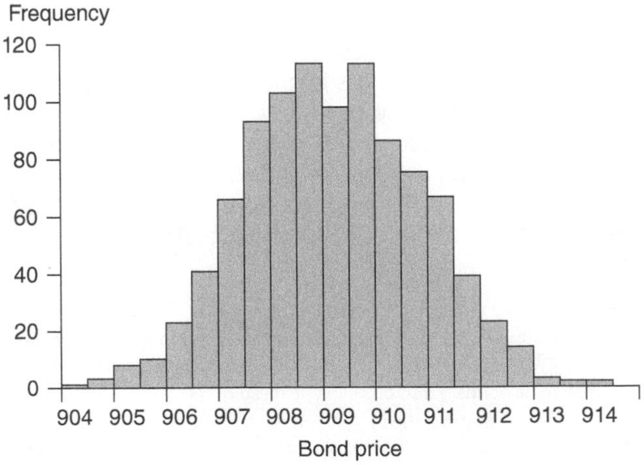

FIGURE 15–4

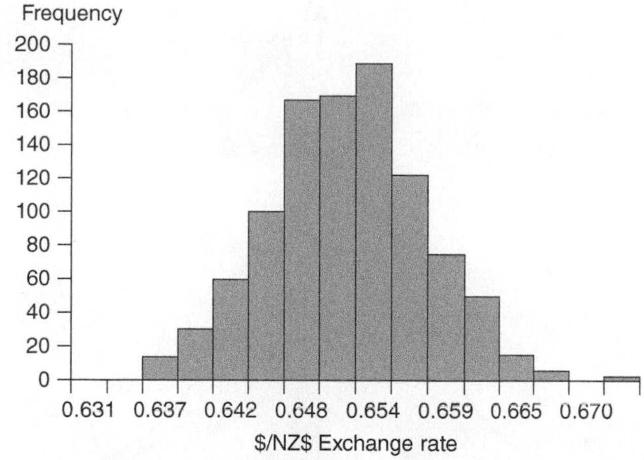

TABLE 15–7
Monte Carlo Scenarios (1,000 Trials)

$/NZ$	PV of Cash Flow (in NZ$)	PV of Cash Flow (in $)
0.6500	NZ$906,663	$589,350
0.6540	907,898	593,742
0.6606	911,214	601,935
0.6513	908,004	591,399
0.6707	910,074	610,430
0.6444	908,478	585,460
0.6569	908,860	597,053
0.6559	906,797	594,789
0.6530	906,931	592,267
0.6625	920,768	603,348

CONCEPT QUESTIONS

1. **What are the advantages of the historic approach over RiskMetrics to measure market risk?**
2. **What are the steps involved with the historic approach to measuring market risk?**
3. **What is the Monte Carlo simulation approach to measuring market risk?**

EXPECTED SHORTFALL APPROACH

LO7

As mentioned above, a criticism of VaR is that it tells the FI manager the level of possible losses that might occur with a given confidence level, i.e., 99th percentile, assuming a normally shaped return distribution. ES, also referred to as conditional VaR and expected tail loss, tells us the average of the losses in the tail of the distribution beyond the 99th percentile, i.e., if 1 in every 100 days there is a loss, ES tells us the average of those 1 in 100 day losses. For example, in Table 15–6, the FI's 99 percent confidence level VaR is $97,210. Thus, if tomorrow is a bad day, there is a 1 percent probability that the FI's losses will exceed $97,210 assuming a normal probability distribution. However, many return distributions have "fat tails." Consider Figure 15–5. The VaR of the probability distribution is $97,210; i.e., assuming a normal probability distribution, there is a 1 in 100 chance that the FI

FIGURE 15–5
Probability Distribution of Returns for a Security

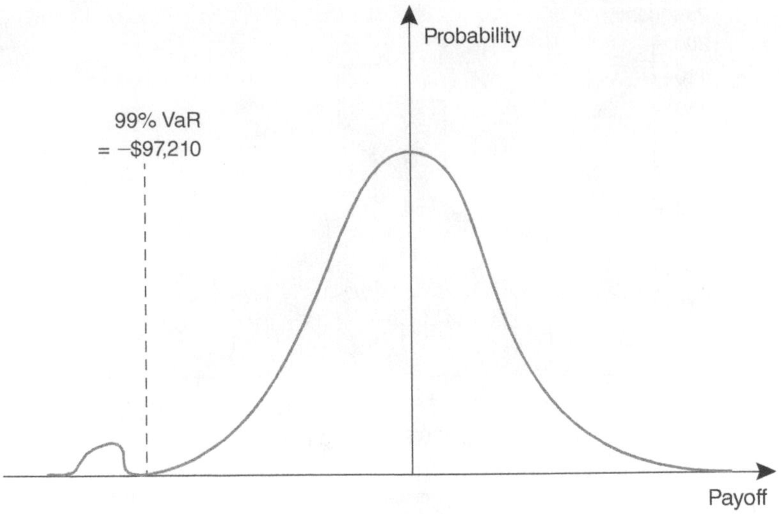

will lose $97,210. However, clearly the probability distribution is not normal, but has a fat tail loss. Thus, the average of the 1 in 100 day losses will be larger than $97,210.

VaR corresponds to a specific point of loss on the probability distribution. It does not provide information about the potential size of the loss that exceeds it; i.e., VaR completely ignores the patterns and the severity of the losses in the extreme tail. Thus, VaR gives only partial information about the extent of possible losses, particularly when probability distributions are nonnormal. The drawbacks of VaR became painfully evident during the financial crisis as asset returns plummeted into the "fat tail" region of nonnormally shaped distributions. FI managers and regulators were forced to recognize that VaR projections of possible losses far underestimated actual losses on extreme bad days.

ES is a measure of market risk that estimates the expected value of losses beyond a given confidence level; i.e., it is the average of VARs beyond a given confidence level. Specifically, for a confidence level *c*, ES can be solved using the following formula for a continuous probability distribution:

$$\text{ES}(c) = \frac{1}{1-c}\int_c^1 \text{VaR}(u)du$$

That is, for a confidence level of, say, 99 percent (i.e., *c*), we measure the area under the probability distribution from the 99th to the 100th percentile.

For a discrete distribution,

$$\text{ES} = -\text{E}(\Delta V|\Delta V < -\text{VaR})$$

That is, for a confidence level of, say, 99 percent, we sum the weighted value of any observation in the discrete probability distribution from the 99th to the 100th percentile.

In Figure 15–5, VaR tells the FI manager the loss at a particular point, *c*, on the probability distribution, i.e., 99th percentile. It fails, however, to incorporate information regarding the shape of the probability distribution below that particular point. ES is the average VaR to the left of the 99 percent confidence level. Thus, VaR is identical for both probability distributions. However, ES, which incorporates points to the left of VaR, is larger when the probability distribution exhibits fat tail losses. Accordingly, ES provides more information about possible market risk losses than VaR. For situations in which probability distributions exhibit fat tail losses, VaR may look relatively small, but ES may be very large.

EXAMPLE 15–6

Simple Example of VaR versus ES

Consider the following discrete probability distribution of payoffs for two securities, A and B, held in the trading portfolio of an FI (in millions of $):

Probability	A	Probability	B
50.00%	$100	50.00%	$100
49.00	80	49.00	92
1.00	−920	0.25	−920
		0.75	1,704

The FI wants to estimate which of the two securities will add more market risk to its trading portfolio according to both the VaR and ES measures. Values below are in millions of dollars:

$$\text{Expected return on security A} = 0.50(\$100) + 0.49(\$80) + 0.01(-\$920) = \$80$$

$$\text{Expected return on security B} = 0.50(\$100) + 0.49(\$92) + 0.0025(-\$920) + 0.0075(-\$1{,}704) = \$80$$

For a 99% confidence level, $VAR_A = VAR_B = -\$920$. Yet, for a 99% confidence level,

$$ES_A = -\$920, \text{ while } ES_B = 0.25(-\$920) + 0.75(-\$1{,}704) = -\$1{,}508$$

Thus, while the VaR is identical for both securities, the ES finds that security B has the potential to subject the FI to much greater losses than security A. Specifically, if tomorrow is a bad day, VaR finds that there is a 1 percent probability that the FI's losses will exceed $920 million on either security. However, if tomorrow is a bad day, ES finds that there is a 1 percent probability that the FI's losses will exceed $920 million if security A is in its trading portfolio, but losses will exceed $1,508 million if security B is in its trading portfolio.

For continuous probability distributions, ES uses a scaling factor based on a fat-tailed student-t distribution.[29] Thus, while the scaling factors for VaR are 2.33 for a 1 percent confidence level (and 1.65 for a 5 percent confidence level), ES scales up the risk factor to account for fat tails in the probability distribution, using 2.665 for a 1 percent confidence level (and 2.063 for a 5 percent confidence level).

[29] Specifically,

$$ES = \text{scale}^{ES} \times \sigma \times X$$

where

$$\text{scale}^{ES} = \frac{-N^{pdf}(N^{-1}(1-c))}{1-c}$$

EXAMPLE 15-7

Estimating VaR and ES of Trading Portfolio Securities

An FI has €1 million in its trading portfolio on the close of business on a particular day. The FI wants to calculate the one-day VaR and ES from this position.

The first step is to calculate the dollar value position.

Suppose the current exchange rate of euros for dollars is €0.7983/\$, or dollars for euros is \$1.2527, at the daily close. So

$$\text{Dollar value of position} = €1 \text{ million} \times 1.2527 = \$1{,}252{,}700$$

Suppose also that looking back at the daily percentage changes in the €/\$ exchange rate over the past year, we find that the volatility, or standard deviation (σ), of daily percentage changes in the spot exchange rate was 44.3 bp. However, the FI is interested in adverse moves—bad moves that will not occur more than 1 percent of the time, or 1 day in every 100.

VaR

Using VaR, which assumes that changes in exchange rates are normally distributed, the exchange rate must change in the adverse direction by 2.33σ (2.33×44.3 bp) for this change to be viewed as likely to occur only 1 day in every 100 days:

$$\text{FX volatility} = 2.33 \times 44.3 \text{ bp} = 103.219 \text{ bp}$$

In other words, using VaR during the last year, the euro declined in value against the dollar by 103.219 bp 1 percent of the time. As a result, the one-day VaR is

$$\text{VaR} = \$1{,}252{,}700 \times 0.0103219 = \$12{,}930$$

ES

Using ES, which assumes that changes in exchange rates are normally distributed but with fat tails, the exchange rate must change in the adverse direction by 2.665σ (2.665×44.3 bp) for this change to be viewed as likely to occur only 1 day in every 100 days:

$$\text{FX volatility} = 2.665 \times 44.3 \text{ bp} = 118.0595 \text{ bp}$$

In other words, using ES during the last year the euro declined in value against the dollar by 118.0595 bp 1 percent of the time. As a result, the one-day ES is

$$\text{ES} = \$1{,}252{,}700 \times 0.01180595 = \$14{,}789$$

The potential loss exposure to adverse euro to dollar exchange rate changes for the FI from the €1 million spot currency holdings are higher using the ES measure of market risk. ES estimates potential losses that are \$1,859 higher than VaR. This is because VaR focuses on the location of the extreme tail of the probability distribution. ES also considers the shape of the probability distribution once VaR is exceeded.

CONCEPT QUESTIONS

1. **What is the difference between VaR and ES?**
2. **Why is ES superior to VaR as a measure of market risk?**

REGULATORY MODELS: THE BANK FOR INTERNATIONAL SETTLEMENTS STANDARDIZED FRAMEWORK

LO8

The development of internal market risk models was partly in response to proposals by the BIS in 1993 to measure and regulate the market risk exposures of banks by imposing capital requirements on their trading portfolios. As noted in Chapter 7, the BIS is an organization encompassing the largest central banks in the world. After refining these proposals over a number of years, most recently in 2013, the BIS decided on a final approach to measuring market risk and the capital necessary for an FI to hold to withstand and survive market risk losses. These required levels of capital held to protect against market risk exposure are in addition to the minimum level of capital banks are required to hold for credit risk purposes (see Chapter 20). Since January 1998, banks in the countries that are members of the BIS can calculate their market risk exposures in one of two ways. The first is to use a simple standardized framework (to be discussed below). The second, with regulatory approval, is to use their own internal models, which are similar to the models described above. However, if an internal model is approved for use in calculating capital requirements for the FI, it is subject to regulatory audit and certain constraints. Before looking at these constraints, we examine the BIS standardized framework. Additional details of this model can be found at the BIS website.

bis.org

The financial crisis exposed a number of shortcomings in the way market risk was being measured in accordance with Basel II rules. Although the crisis largely exposed problems with the large-bank internal models approach to measuring market risk, the BIS also identified shortcomings with the standardized approach. These included a lack of risk sensitivity, a very limited recognition of hedging and diversification benefits, and an inability to sufficiently capture risks associated with more complex instruments. To address shortcomings of the standardized approach to measuring market risk, Basel III proposes a "partial risk factor" approach as a revised standardized approach. Basel III also introduces a "fuller risk factor" approach as an alternative to the revised partial risk factor standardized approach.

Partial Risk Factor Approach

The partial risk factor approach applies risk weights to the market values of trading portfolio securities, with enhancements to prudently reflect hedging of and diversification across securities. Particularly, the partial risk factor approach requires the following process be followed by FIs to determine capital requirements:

1. *Assign instruments to asset "buckets."* Instruments are placed in one of 20 asset buckets across each of five risk classes according to their risk similarity. The five risk classes are FX, interest rates, equities, credit (including securitizations), and commodities.
2. *Calculate each bucket's risk measure.* A risk measure is calculated for each bucket using a regulator-specified formula based on ES estimates. The market values of the assets in each bucket are then multiplied by the risk weight.
3. *Aggregate the buckets.* The risk measures of the individual asset buckets are aggregated to obtain the capital requirement for the trading portfolio. The formula used to aggregate is

$$Capital = \sqrt{\sum_{b=1}^{B} K_b^2 + \sum_{b=1}^{B}\sum_{c \neq b} \gamma_{bc} S_b S_c}$$

where

$$S_b = \sum_{i \in b} RW_i MV_i$$

and γ_{bc} is the correlation parameter between buckets b and c, defined by regulators. The first term in this formula aggregates risk across buckets without considering cross-bucket diversification (the "sum of squares"). The second term adjusts for the "same-direction" correlation between the asset types in b and c (i.e., long/long or short/short), γ_{bc}.

Fuller Risk Factor Approach

The fuller risk factor approach maps each trading portfolio security to a set of risk factors and associated shocks that explain the variation in the security values. The set of risk factors and shocks to the risk factors is established by regulators. The risk factors are organized in a hierarchy. Those risk factors listed at the top of the hierarchy impact the largest number of securities, and risk factors listed farther down in the hierarchy are more specific in nature. Thus, changes in these risk factors would impact a smaller number of instruments. Finally, risk factors listed at the bottom of the hierarchy are nonhedgeable risk factors (i.e., risk that cannot easily be hedged in periods of financial stress). Table 15–8 illustrates the order of risk factors proposed by the BIS for Basel III. FIs then apply BIS empirically estimated standard deviations of shocks to these underlying risk factors. The capital charge is then determined by converting the risk position to an ES similar to that described in the previous section. The fuller risk factor approach requires the following process be followed by FIs to determine capital requirements:

1. *Assign each instrument to applicable risk factors.* The BIS defines a set of risk factors and associated shocks that explain the variation in the value of an FI's trading portfolio securities. Using a BIS-provided description of the mapping of securities to each risk factor, FIs determine which risk factors influence the value of their trading portfolio securities.
2. *Determine the size of the net risk position in each risk factor.* Once the FI determines the risk factors that apply to each of its trading portfolio securities, it uses a pricing model to determine the size of the risk positions from each security with respect to the applicable risk factors. The size of the risk positions is based on the sensitivity of the instruments to the prescribed risk factors. The FI then aggregates all negative and positive gross risk positions to determine the net risk position. For nonhedgeable risk factors the gross risk position equals the net risk position.

TABLE 15–8 Hierarchy of Hedgeable Risk Factors under the Standardized Model Fuller Risk Factor Approach

Level	FX Risk	Interest Rate Risk	Equity Risk	Credit Risk	Commodity Risk
I	Exchange rate of domestic currency to worldwide currency basket	Wordwide interest rate index	Worldwide equity index	Worldwide credit spread index	Commodity price index
II	Exchange rate of worldwide currency basket to respective foreign currency	Level of money market/swap rate curve in respective currency	Equity index by broad industry category	Credit spread index by industry category	Price index for commodity type
III		Slope of money market/swap rate curve in respective currency	Price of individual equity	Credit spread for individual issuer	Price index for physical type of commodity
IV		Money market/swap rate between vertex points in respective currency (residual)			

Source: "Fundamental Review of the Trading Book," BIS Basel Committee on Banking Supervision, May 2012.

3. *Aggregate overall risk position across risk factors.* To compute the overall capital requirement for each risk factor class, the net risk positions determined in step 2 are aggregated. Regulators specify the distribution of the risk factors (i.e., the standard deviations to apply against each of the risk factors). One option offered by the BIS is to assume that all risk factors of the same risk factor class are independently distributed.[30] Thus, the overall portfolio standard deviation is calculated using a sum of squares multiplied by a scalar that approximates the average across the loss tail of the portfolio distribution (i.e., the ES). The ES scalar factor implemented by regulators in Basel III is four. Thus, the overall capital requirement is four times the overall portfolio standard deviation.

The following example is the BIS illustration of the fuller risk factor approach of the standardized model.[31]

EXAMPLE 15–8

Calculating Market Risk Capital Requirement Using the Fuller Risk Factor Approach

In its trading portfolio, an FI holds 1,000 Daimler shares at a share price of €101 and has sold 500 Volkswagen shares under a forward contract that matures in one year. The current share price for Volkswagen is €20. To calculate the market risk capital charge on these securities, the FI proceeds as follows.

Step 1. Assign each instrument to applicable risk factors. From Table 15–8, hedgeable risk factors for these equities include Level I movements in global equity markets (worldwide equity index), Level II movements in sectoral equity indices (equity index by broad industry category), and Level III movements in the prices of individual equity. Daimler and Volkswagen have the same hedgeable risk factors at Levels I and II, i.e., global and industry-specific equity indices. However, movements in the prices of the two firms are unique. Thus, they do not have the same risk factor at Level III and as a result they are mapped to different individual equity risk factors.[32] There is also a nonhedgeable risk factor for the Volkswagen equity price to capture basis risk from the forward contract.

Step 2. Determine the size of the net risk position in each risk factor. For each risk factor the FI determines a net risk position, calculated as the sum of gross risk positions for all instruments that are subject to that risk factor.[33] Table 15–9 shows the gross and net positions for Daimler and Volkswagen equities for the equity risk factor. The size of the gross position in Daimler for the three applicable risk factors is €101,000 (1,000 shares × €101) and for the short position in Volkswagen is –€10,000 (500 shares × €20). Note again that the two securities do not have the same risk factor at Level III. Thus, they are mapped to different individual equity risk factors. Further, to capture basis risk from the forward contract, there is a nonhedgeable risk factor for

[30] The BIS stated that to recognize diversification it would be necessary to impose a distribution on the risk factors. However, specifying a distribution of risk factors, with appropriate pairwise correlations between risk factors, is likely to be a burdensome and complex task for regulators and would also complicate FIs' calculations considerably. The simplest approach is to treat all risk factors of the same risk factor class as independently distributed.

[31] See "Fundamental Review of the Trading Book," BIS Basel Committee on Banking Supervision, May 2012.

[32] However, these risk factors can be hedged with other positions that shared this risk factor, such as Daimler equity options.

[33] For equities this is equivalent to assuming that equity betas are homogeneous and equal to one. For FX, the size of the gross risk position is the market value of the instrument converted to the reporting currency of the FI. For linear interest rate risk– and credit risk–related instruments the size of the gross risk position is determined by applying a small shift to the respective risk factor and determining the value change of the instrument in relation to the shift applied.

TABLE 15–9
Calculation of Gross and Net Risk Position

Source: "Fundamental Review of the Trading Book," BIS Basel Committee on Banking Supervision, May 2012.

Level	Equity Risk	Daimler Gross Risk Position	Volkswagen Gross Risk Position	Total Size of Net Risk Position
I	Worldwide equity index	€101,000	−€10,000	€91,000
II	Industry equity index	€101,000	−€10,000	€91,000
III	Daimler share price	€101,000	–	€101,000
	Volkswagen share price	–	−€10,000	−€10,000
N-h*	Volkswagen share price		−€10,000	−€10,000

* Nonhedgeable risk factor.

the Volkswagen equity price, −€10,000. The net risk position of the two securities for each risk factor, listed in the last column of Table 15–9, is the sum of the gross risk factors for the securities at each level, i.e., €91,000 for Levels I and II; €101,000 and −€10,000, respectively, for Level III; and −€10,000 for nonhedgeable risk.

Step 3. Aggregate overall risk position across risk factors. The net risk position is then converted into a capital charge by multiplying by regulator-specified standard deviations (i.e., shift risk factors). Table 15–10 shows the calculations of the capital charge for market risk. The net risk positions (listed in column 3 for each risk level) are multiplied by the standard deviations assigned for each level (column 4) to produce the standard deviations of the net risk position. For example, the standard deviation of the net risk position for the Level I worldwide equity index is equal to the net risk (€91,000) times the regulator-set shift risk factor (5%) to give the standard deviation associated with the Level I risk factor, (€4,550). The square of the standard deviation (the variance) is then listed in column 5 (i.e., €20,702,500 for Level I). Summing the squared standard deviations gives the portfolio variance (€164,299,400), and taking the square root of this gives the portfolio standard deviation (€12,818). Finally, this portfolio standard deviation is multiplied by a scalar (currently set at 4) to achieve the overall expected shortfall for the portfolio.

TABLE 15–10 Calculation of Market Risk Capital Charge

Level	Equity Risk: Portfolio	Net Risk Position (EUR)	Standard Deviation (i.e., Shift of Risk Factor)	Standard Deviation of Net Risk Position	Square the Standard Deviation of the Net Risk Position (i.e., Variance)
I	Worldwide equity index	91,000	5%	4,550	20,702,500
II	Industry equity index	91,000	7%	6,370	40,576,900
III	Price Daimler share	101,000	10%	10,100	102,010,000
III	Price of Volkswagen share	10,000	10%	1,000	1,000,000
N-h*	Volkswagen share price	10,000	1%	100	10,000
Portfolio	Sum the squared standard deviations (portfolio variance)				164,299,400
Portfolio	Take the square root (portfolio standard deviation)				12,818
Portfolio	Multiply by scalar to obtain expected shortfall				51,270

* Nonhedgeable risk factor.
Notes: E.S. Scalar Factor decided by regulators = 4 × standard deviation.
Correlation (ρ) between stocks = 0 is assumed by the model.
Source: "Fundamental Review of the Trading Book," BIS Basel Committee on Banking Supervision, May 2012.

THE BANK FOR INTERNATIONAL SETTLEMENTS REGULATIONS AND LARGE-BANK INTERNAL MODELS

As discussed above, the BIS capital requirement for market risk exposure introduced in January 1998 allows large banks (subject to regulatory permission) to use their own internal models to calculate market risk instead of the standardized framework. The initial market risk capital requirements were included as part of what became known as the Basel I capital rules. However, details of the capital calculations have been refined and revised over the years. Today, FIs' internal models are governed by Basel 2.5 rules, which were implemented in 2012, and Basel III rules, which are being phased in between 2013 and 2019.[34] We examine the initiatives taken by the BIS and the major central banks in controlling bank risk exposure through capital requirements in greater detail in Chapter 20. During the financial crisis, losses due to market risk were significantly higher than the minimum market risk capital requirements under BIS Basel I and II rules. As a result, in July 2009, the BIS announced Basel 2.5, a final version of revised rules for market risk capital requirements. Specifically, in addition to the risk capital charge already in place (steps 1 and 2 below), an incremental capital charge is assessed, which includes a "stressed VaR" capital requirement, taking into account a one-year observation period of significant financial stress relevant to the FI's portfolio (step 3 below). The introduction of stressed VaR in Basel 2.5 is intended to reduce the cyclicality of the VaR measure and alleviate the problem of market stress periods dropping out of the data period used to calculate VaR after some time. Basel 2.5 requires the following process to be followed by large FIs using internal models to calculate the market risk capital charge:

1. In calculating one-day VaR, the FI must define an adverse change as being in the 99th percentile (multiply σ by 2.33).
2. The FI must assume the minimum holding period to be 10 days (this means that one-day VaR has to be multiplied by $\sqrt{10}$).
3. The FI must add to this a stressed VaR that is intended to replicate a VaR calculation that would be generated on the FI's trading portfolio if the relevant market factors were experiencing a period of stress. The stressed VaR is based on the 10-day, 99th-percentile VaR of the trading portfolio, with model inputs incorporating historical data from a one-year period of significant financial stress. The period used must be approved by the supervisor and regularly reviewed. For example, a 12-month period relating to significant losses during the financial stress would adequately reflect a period of such stress.

The FI must consider its proposed capital charge or requirement as the *sum* of

1. The higher of the previous day's value at risk $\times \sqrt{10}$ and the average one-day VaR over the previous 60 business days times a multiplication factor with a minimum value of 3, i.e., capital charge = (avg. VaR) $\times$ ($\sqrt{10}$) $\times$ (3) (in general, the multiplication factor makes required capital significantly higher than VaR produced from private models), and

[34] Banks are allowed to vary from the Basel market risk regulations provided their capital calculations are at least as conservative as Basel and their regulator is satisfied that the approach is reasonable. See *Revisions to the Basel II Market Risk Framework*, Bank for International Settlements, January 2009.

2. The higher of its latest available stressed VaR and an average of the stressed VaR over the preceding 60 business days times a multiplication factor with a minimum value of 3 and a maximum of 4.

For example, suppose the FI's portfolio VaR over the previous 60 days was $10 million and stressed VaR over the previous 60 days was $25 million using the 1 percent worst case (or 99th percentile). The minimum capital charge would be[35]

$$\text{Capital charge} = [(\$10\text{ million}) \times (\sqrt{10}) \times (3)] + [(\$25\text{ million}) \times (\sqrt{10})) \times (3)]$$
$$= \$332.04\text{ million}$$

Basel III proposes to replace VaR models with those based on extreme value theory and ES. As discussed earlier, the ES measure analyzes the size and likelihood of losses above the 99th percentile in a crisis period for a traded asset and thus measures "tail risk" more precisely. Thus, ES is a risk measure that considers a more comprehensive set of potential outcomes than VaR. The BIS change to ES highlights the importance of maintaining sufficient regulatory capital not only in stable market conditions, but also in periods of significant financial stress. Indeed, it is precisely during periods of stress that capital is vital for absorbing losses and safeguarding the stability of the banking system. Accordingly, the Basel Committee intends to move to a framework that is calibrated to a period of significant financial stress.

Two methods of identifying the stress period and calculating capital requirements under the internal models are the direct method and the indirect method. The direct method is based on the approach used in the Basel 2.5 stressed VaR. The FI would search the entire historical period and identify the period that produces the highest ES result when all risk factors are included. However, Basel III would require the FI to determine the stressed period on the basis of a reduced set of risk factors. Once the FI has identified the stressed period, it must then determine the ES for the full set of risk factors for the stress period. The indirect method identifies the relevant historical period of stress by using a reduced set of risk factors. However, instead of calculating the full ES model for that period, the FI calculates a loss based on the reduced set of risk factors. This loss is then scaled using the ratio of the full ES model using current market data to the full ES model using the reduced set of risk factors using current market data.

Finally, it should be noted that the market risk framework discussed above is based on an assumption that an FI's trading book positions are liquid, i.e., that FIs can exit or hedge the trading book positions over a 10-day horizon. The financial crisis proved this to be false. Thus, under the new liquidity risk measures the 10-day liquidity metric as used in the VaR calculations above (i.e., VaR $\times \sqrt{10}$) is replaced with liquidity horizons based on a set of quantitative and qualitative criteria that allow for changes in market liquidity conditions. Specifically, FIs' exposures would be assigned to one of five liquidity horizon categories, ranging from 10 days to one year based on the time required to exit or hedge a risk position in a stressed market environment. Further, capital add-ons are included for jumps in liquidity premia. These add-ons would apply only to instruments that could become particularly illiquid to the extent that the market risk measures, even with

[35] The idea of a minimum multiplication factor of 3 is to create a scheme that is "incentive compatible." Specifically, if FIs using internal models constantly underestimate the amount of capital they need to meet their market risk exposures, regulators can punish those FIs by raising the multiplication factor to as high as 4. Such a response may effectively put the FI out of the trading business. The degree to which the multiplication factor is raised above 3 depends on the number of days an FI's model underestimates its market risk over the preceding year. For example, an underestimation error that occurs on more than 10 days out of the past 250 days will result in the multiplication factor being raised to 4.

TABLE 15–11 **Canadian Banks' Risk-Weighted Assets and Basel II Capital Ratios, 2012 ($ billions)**

	Credit Risk-Weighted Assets	Market Risk-Weighted Assets	Operational Risk-Weighted Assets	Total Risk-Weighted Assets	Total Regulatory Capital	Tier 1 Capital Ratio	Basel II Total Capital Ratio
BMO	$172.0	$ 7.6	$25.7	$205.2	$30.7	12.6%	14.9%
CIBC	93.4	3.0	18.8	115.2	19.9	13.8%	17.3%
National Bank	45.2	2.6	8.1	55.9	8.9	12.0%	15.9%
RBC	209.6	30.1	40.9	280.6	42.3	13.1%	15.1%
Scotiabank	210.0	13.8	29.5	253.3	42.2	13.6%	16.7%
TD	201.3	12.0	32.6	245.9	38.6	12.6%	15.7%

Source: Company annual reports, 2012.

extended liquidity horizons, would not sufficiently capture the risk to FI solvency from large fluctuations in liquidity premia on these securities.

Table 15–11 shows the dollar amounts of the risk-weighted assets calculated according to Basel II capital adequacy rules that were reported by the major Canadian banks in their 2012 annual reports. Notice how small the market risk–weighted assets are relative to the total risk–weighted assets. Since OSFI required these six banks to have a minimum Tier 1 capital ratio of 7 percent under Basel II, for its market risk–weighted assets of $7.6 billion, BMO must have Tier 1 capital of $0.532 billion (Tier 1 capital/Risk-weighted assets = 7 percent) and total capital of $0.76 billion to support its market risk. BMO's total Tier 1 capital was $25.9 billion at October 31, 2012, giving it a Tier 1 capital ratio of 12.6 percent, well above OSFI's Basel II requirement. The Canadian banks transitioned to IFRS for their 2012 annual reports and met Basel III Capital Requirements beginning January 1, 2013. Chapter 20 covers the Basel capital adequacy requirements in greater detail.

CONCEPT QUESTIONS

1. **What is the BIS standardized framework for measuring market risk?**
2. **How does using the 99th percentile (1 percent worst case) rather than the 95th percentile (5 percent worst case) affect the market risk exposure?**

Questions and Problems

1. What is meant by market risk?
2. Why is the measurement of market risk important to the manager of an FI?
3. What is meant by VaR? What are the three measurable components? What is the price volatility component?
4. Fundy Bank has a $1 million position in a five-year, zero-coupon bond with a face value of $1,402,552. The bond is trading at a yield to maturity of 7.00 percent. The historical mean change in daily yields is 0.0 percent and the standard deviation is 12 bp.
   a. What is the MD of the bond?
   b. What is the maximum adverse daily yield move given that we desire no more than a 1 percent chance that yield changes will be greater than this maximum?
   c. What is the price volatility of this bond?
   d. What is the one-day VaR for this bond?
5. How can one-day VaR be adjusted to account for potential losses over multiple days? What would be the VaR for the bond in problem 4 for a 10-day period? What statistical assumption is needed for this calculation? Could this treatment be critical?

6. The one-day VaR for a bank is $8,500. What is the VaR for a 10-day period? A 20-day period? Why is the VaR for a 20-day period not twice as much as that for a 10-day period?
7. The mean change in the daily yields of a 15-year, zero-coupon bond has been 5 bp over the past year with a standard deviation of 15 bp. Use these data and assume that the yield changes are normally distributed.
   a. What is the highest yield change expected if a 99 percent confidence limit is required, that is, adverse moves will not occur more than 1 day in 100?
   b. What is the highest yield change expected if a 95 percent confidence limit is required? Adverse moves will not occur more than one day in 20.
8. In what sense is duration a measure of market risk?
9. Bank Alpha has an inventory of AAA-rated, 15-year, zero-coupon bonds with a face value of $400 million. The bonds are currently yielding 9.5 percent in the over-the-counter (OTC) market.
   a. What is the MD of these bonds?
   b. What is the price volatility if the potential adverse move in yields is 25 bp?
   c. What is the one-day VaR?
   d. If the price volatility is based on a 99 percent confidence limit and a mean historical change in daily yields of 0.0 percent, what is the implied standard deviation of daily yield changes?
10. Bank Beta has an inventory of AAA-rated, 10-year, zero-coupon bonds with a face value of $100 million. The MD of these bonds is 12.5 years, the one-day VaR is $2,150,000, and the potential adverse move in yields is 35 bp. What is the market value of the bonds, the yield on the bonds, and the duration of the bonds?
11. Bank Two has a portfolio of bonds with a market value of $200 million. The bonds have an estimated price volatility of 0.95 percent. What are the one-day VaR and the 10-day VaR for these bonds?
12. Suppose that an FI has a €1.6 million long trading position in spot euros at the close of business on a particular day. Looking back at the daily percentage changes in the exchange rate in the €/$ for the past year, the volatility or standard deviation (σ) of daily percentage changes in the €/$ spot exchange rate was 62.5 bp. Calculate the FI's one-day VaR from this position (i.e., adverse moves in the FX markets with respect to the value of the euro against the dollar will not occur more than 1 percent of the time, or 1 day in every 100 days) if the spot exchange rate is €0.80/$1, or $1.25/€, at the daily close.
13. Bank Three has determined that its inventory of €20 million and £25 million is subject to market risk. The spot exchange rates are $1.25/€1 and $1.60/£1, respectively. The σ values of the spot exchange rates of the euro and pound, based on the daily changes of spot rates over the past six months, are 65 bp and 45 bp, respectively. Determine the bank's 10-day VaR for both currencies. Use adverse rate changes in the 99th percentile.
14. Bank of Bentley has determined that its inventory of yen (¥)- and Swiss franc (Sf)–denominated securities is subject to market risk. The spot exchange rates are ¥80.00/$1 and Sf0.9600/$1, respectively. The σ's of the spot exchange rates of the yen and Swiss franc, based on the daily changes of spot rates over the past six months, are 75 bp and 55 bp, respectively. Using adverse rate changes in the 99th percentile, the 10-day VARs for the two currencies, yen and Swiss franc, are $350,000 and $500,000, respectively. Calculate the yen- and Swiss franc–denominated value positions for Bank of Bentley.
15. Suppose that an FI holds a $15 million trading position in stocks that reflect the Canadian stock market index (e.g., the S&P TSX). Over the last year, the σ_m of the daily returns on the stock market index was 156 bp. Calculate the one-day VaR for this portfolio of stocks using a 99 percent confidence limit.
16. Bank Four's stock portfolio has a market value of $10 million. The beta of the portfolio approximates the market portfolio, whose standard deviation (σ_m) has been estimated at 1.5 percent. What is the five-day VaR of this portfolio using adverse rate changes in the 99th percentile?
17. Jeff Resnick, vice-president of operations of Choice Bank, is estimating the aggregate one-day VaR of the bank's portfolio of assets consisting of loans (L), foreign currencies (FX), and common stock (EQ). The individual one-day VaRs are $300,700, $274,000, and $126,700, respectively. If the correlation coefficients (ρ_{ij}) between L and FX, L and EQ, and FX and EQ are 0.3, 0.7, and 0.0, respectively, what is the one-day VaR of the aggregate portfolio?
18. Calculate the one-day VaR for the following portfolio, first with the correlation coefficients and then with perfect positive correlation between the various asset groups:

Assets	Estimated One-Day VaR	($\rho_{S,FX}$)	($\rho_{S,B}$)	($\rho_{FX,B}$)
Stocks (S)	$300,000	−0.10	0.75	0.20
Foreign Exchange (FX)	200,000			
Bonds (B)	250,000			

What is the amount of risk reduction resulting from the lack of perfect positive correlation between the various asset groups?

19. What are the advantages of using the back simulation approach to estimate market risk? Explain how this approach would be implemented.

20. Export Bank has a trading position in Japanese yen and Swiss francs. At the close of business on February 4, the bank had ¥300,000,000 and Sf10,000,000. The exchange rates for the most recent six days are given below.

Exchange Rates per Dollar at the Close of Business

	4/2	3/2	2/2	1/2	29/1	28/1
Japanese yen	80.13	80.84	80.14	83.05	84.35	84.32
Swiss francs	0.9540	0.9575	0.9533	0.9617	0.9557	0.9523

a. What is the FX position in dollar equivalents using the FX rates on February 4?

b. What is the definition of delta as it relates to the FX position?

c. What is the sensitivity of each FX position; that is, what is the value of delta for each currency on February 4?

d. What is the daily percentage change in exchange rates for each currency over the five-day period?

e. What is the total risk faced by the bank on each day? What is the worst-case day? What is the best-case day?

f. Assume that you have data for the 500 trading days preceding February 4. Explain how you would identify the worst-case scenario with a 99 percent degree of confidence.

g. Explain how the 1 percent VaR position would be interpreted for business on February 5.

h. How would the simulation change at the end of the day on February 5? What variables and/or processes in the analysis may change? What variables and/or processes will not change?

21. Export Bank has a trading position in euros and Australian dollars. At the close of business on October 20, the bank had €20 million and A$30 million. The exchange rates for the most recent six days are given below:

Exchange Rates per Canadian Dollar at the Close of Business

	20/10	19/10	18/10	17/10	16/10	15/10
Euros	0.8000	0.7970	0.7775	0.7875	0.7950	0.8115
Australian dollars	0.9700	0.9550	0.9800	0.9655	0.9505	0.9460

a. What is the FX position in dollar equivalents using the FX rates on October 20?

b. What is the sensitivity of each FX position; that is, what is the value of delta for each currency on October 20?

c. What is the daily percentage change in exchange rates for each currency over the five-day period?

d. What is the total risk faced by the bank on each day? What is the worst-case day? What is the best-case day?

22. What is the primary disadvantage of the back simulation approach in measuring market risk? What effect does the inclusion of more observation days have as a remedy for this disadvantage? What other remedies can be used to deal with the disadvantage?

23. How is Monte Carlo simulation useful in addressing the disadvantages of back simulation? What is the primary statistical assumption underlying its use?

24. What is the difference between VaR and ES as measure of market risk?

25. Consider the following discrete probability distribution of payoffs for two securities, A and B, held in the trading portfolio of an FI (amounts in $ millions):

Probability	A	Probability	B
50.00%	$80	50.00%	$80
49.00	60	49.00	68
1.00	−740	0.40	−740
		0.60	−1,393

Which of the two securities will add more market risk to the FI's trading portfolio according to the VaR and ES measures?

26. Consider the following discrete probability distribution of payoffs for two securities, A and B, held in the trading portfolio of an FI (amounts in $ millions):

Probability	A	Probability	B
55.00%	$120	55.00%	$120
44.00	95	44.00	100
1.00	−1,100	0.30	−1,100
		0.70	−1,414

Which of the two securities will add more market risk to the FI's trading portfolio according to the VaR and ES measures?

27. An FI has £5 million in its trading portfolio on the close of business on a particular day. The current exchange rate of pounds for dollars is £0.6400/$1, or dollars for pounds is $1.5625, at the daily close. The volatility, or standard deviation (σ), of daily percentage changes in the spot £/$ exchange rate over the past year was 58.5 bp. The FI is interested in adverse moves—bad moves that will not occur more than 1 percent of the time, or 1 day in every 100. Calculate the one-day VaR and ES from this position.
28. An FI has ¥500 million in its trading portfolio on the close of business on a particular day. The current exchange rate of yen for dollars is ¥80.00/$1, or dollars for yen is $0.0125, at the daily close. The volatility, or standard deviation (σ), of daily percentage changes in the spot ¥/$1 exchange rate over the past year was 121.6 bp. The FI is interested in adverse moves—bad moves that will not occur more than 1 percent of the time, or 1 day in every 100. Calculate the one-day VaR and ES from this position.
29. Bank of Victoria's stock portfolio has a market value of $250 million. The beta of the portfolio approximates the market portfolio, whose standard deviation (σ_m) has been estimated at 2.25 percent. What are the five-day VaR and ES of this portfolio using adverse rate changes in the 99th percentile?
30. Despite the fact that market risk capital requirements have been imposed on FIs since the 1990s, huge losses in value were recorded from losses incurred in FIs' trading portfolios. Why did this happen? What changes to capital requirements did regulators propose to prevent such losses from reoccurring?
31. In its trading portfolio, an FI holds 10,000 Agrium (AGU) shares at a share price of $86.50 and has sold 5,000 BlackBerry (BB) shares under a forward contract that matures in one year. The current share price for BB is $20.50. The shift risk factor (i.e., standard deviation) for Level I risk factor is 4 percent, for Level II risk factor is 6 percent, for Level III long positions is 9 percent, for Level III short positions is –9 percent, and for nonhedgeable risk is 1 percent. Using the risk factors listed in Table 15–8, calculate the market risk capital charge on these securities.
32. In its trading portfolio, a U.S. FI is long £20 million worth of pound FX forward contracts and has sold €40 million of euro FX forward contracts that mature in one year. The current exchange rate of U.S. dollars for pounds is $1.5625 and the exchange rate of euros for pounds is $1.25 at the daily close. The shift risk factor (i.e., standard deviation) for Level I risk factor is 5 percent, for Level II risk factor for pounds is 8 percent, and for Level II risk factors for euros is 12 percent. Using the risk factors listed in Table 15–8, calculate the market risk capital charge on these securities.
33. Suppose an FI's portfolio VaR for the previous 60 days was $3 million and stressed VaR for the previous 60 days was $8 million using the 1 percent worst case (or 99th percentile). Calculate the minimum capital charge for market risk for this FI.

CHAPTER 16

OFF-BALANCE-SHEET RISK

After studying this chapter you should be able to:

LO1 Discuss the effect of OBS activities on an FI's risk exposure, return, performance, and solvency.

LO2 Discuss the different types of OBS activities and the risks associated with each.

LO3 Discuss the role of OBS activities in reducing the risk of an FI.

INTRODUCTION

contingent assets and liabilities
Assets and liabilities off the balance sheet that can potentially produce positive or negative future cash flows for an FI.

One of the most important choices facing an FI manager is the relative scale of an FI's on- and off-balance-sheet activities. Most of us are aware of on-balance-sheet activities because they appear on an FI's published asset and liability balance sheets. For example, an FI's deposits and holdings of bonds and loans are on-balance-sheet activities. By comparison, off-balance-sheet (OBS) activities are less obvious and often are invisible to all but the best-informed investor or regulator. In accounting terms, OBS items usually appear "below the bottom line," frequently just as footnotes to financial statements. In economic terms, however, OBS items are **contingent assets and liabilities** that affect the future, rather than the current, shape of an FI's balance sheet. As such, they have a direct impact on the FI's future profitability and performance. Consequently, efficient management of these OBS items is central to controlling overall risk exposure in a modern FI.

From a valuation perspective, OBS assets and liabilities have the potential to produce positive or negative *future* cash flows. Fees from OBS activities provide a key source of noninterest income for many FIs, especially the largest and most creditworthy ones.[1] For example, Canadian domestic banks reported trading income of $4.0 billion to OSFI at the end of the fourth quarter of 2012 compared with a loss of $7.1 billion at the height of the financial crisis for the fourth quarter of 2008. The notional amount of derivative contracts reported to OSFI by domestic banks at Quarter 4, 2012, was $20.0 trillion, compared to on-balance-sheet assets of $3.8 trillion. FIs use some OBS activities (especially forwards, futures, options, and swaps) to reduce or manage their interest rate risk (see Chapters 8 and 9), FX risk (see Chapter 13), and credit risk (see Chapters 10 and 11) exposures in a manner superior to what would exist without these activities. However, OBS activities can involve risks that add to an FI's overall risk exposure. At the very heart of the financial crisis were losses associated with OBS mortgage-backed securities created and held by FIs. Losses resulted in the failure, acquisition, or bailout of some of the world's largest FIs and a near meltdown of the

[1] This fee income can have both direct (e.g., a fee from the sale of a letter of credit) and indirect (through improved customer relationships) effects that have a positive income impact in other product areas. In cases where customers feel aggrieved with respect to derivatives purchased from a dealer FI, OBS activities can have important negative reputational effects that have an adverse impact on the future flow of fees and other income.

TABLE 16–1
Major Types of OBS Activities

Loan commitment Contractual commitment to make a loan up to a stated amount at a given interest rate in the future.

Letters of credit (LCs) Contingent guarantees sold by an FI to underwrite the performance of the buyer of the guarantee.

Derivative contract Agreement between two parties to exchange a standard quantity of an asset at a predetermined price at a specified date in the future.

When-issued (WI) trading Trading in securities prior to their actual issue.

Loans sold Loans originated by an FI and then sold to other investors that (in some cases) can be returned to the originating institution in the future if the credit quality of the loans deteriorates.

Settlement risk Intraday credit risk, such as that associated with some wire transfer activities.

Affiliate risk Risk imposed on one holding company affiliate as a result of the potential failure of the other holding company affiliates.

world's financial and economic systems. As a result, the true value of an FI's capital or net worth is not simply the difference between the market values of assets and liabilities on its balance sheet today, but also reflects the difference between the current market values of its OBS or contingent assets and liabilities.

This chapter examines the various OBS activities (listed in Table 16–1) of FIs. We first discuss the effect of OBS activities on an FI's risk exposure, return performance, and solvency. We then describe the different types of OBS activities and the risks associated with each. Because OBS activities create solvency risk exposure, regulators impose capital requirements on these activities. These capital requirements are described in Chapter 20. While the discussion emphasizes that these activities may add to an FI's riskiness, the chapter concludes with a discussion of the role of OBS activities in reducing the risk of an FI.

OFF-BALANCE-SHEET ACTIVITIES AND FINANCIAL INSTITUTION SOLVENCY

LO1

OBS asset
An item or activity that, when a contingent event occurs, moves onto the asset side of the balance sheet.

OBS liability
An item or activity that, when a contingent event occurs, moves onto the liability side of the balance sheet.

An item or activity is an **OBS asset** if, when a contingent event occurs, the item or activity moves onto the asset side of the balance sheet. Conversely, an item or activity is an **OBS liability** if, when the contingent event occurs, the item or activity moves onto the liability side of the balance sheet. For example, as we discuss in more detail later, FIs sell various performance guarantees, especially guarantees that their customers will not default on their financial and other obligations. Examples of such guarantees include letters of credit (LCs) and standby letters of credit (SLCs). Should a customer default occur, the FI's contingent liability (its guarantee) becomes an actual liability and it moves onto the liability side of the balance sheet. FI managers and regulators are just beginning to recognize and measure the risk of OBS activities and their impact on the FI's value. While some part of OBS risk is related to interest rate risk, credit risk, and other risks, these items also introduce unique risks that must be managed by FIs. From the failure of U.K. investment bank Barings in 1995 to the failure or near failure of some of the largest U.S. FIs during the financial crisis (e.g., investment banks Lehman Brothers, Bear Stearns, and Merrill Lynch; savings institution Washington Mutual;

TABLE 16–2 Some Big Losses on Derivatives

- September–October 1994: Bankers Trust is sued by Gibson Greeting and Procter & Gamble over derivative losses that amounted to US$21 million for Gibson and a US$200 million settlement for Procter & Gamble.
- February 1995: Barings, Britain's oldest investment bank, announces a loss that ultimately totals US$1.38 billion, related to derivatives trading in Singapore by trader Nicholas Leeson.
- December 1996: NatWest Bank finds losses of £77 million caused by mispricing of derivatives in its investment banking arm. Former trader Kyriacos Papouis was blamed for the loss, caused by two years of unauthorized trading by him, but NatWest Markets chief Martin Owen resigned over the incident.
- March 1997: Damian Cope, a former trader at Midland Bank's New York branch, is banned by the U.S. Federal Reserve Board over the falsification of books and records relating to his interest rate derivatives trading activities. Midland parent HSBC says the amount of money involved is not significant.
- November 1997: Chase Manhattan is found to have lost up to US$200 million on trading emerging-market (EM) debt; part of the problem is reportedly due to debt and part is reportedly due to exposure to EMs through complex derivatives products.
- January 1998: Union Bank of Switzerland is reported to be sitting on unquantified derivatives losses; UBS pledges full disclosure at a later date.
- August–September 1998: Long-Term Capital Management, a hedge fund with an exposure exceeding US$1.25 trillion in derivatives and other securities, has to be rescued by a consortium of commercial and investment banks that infused an additional US$3.65 billion of equity into the fund.
- July 2001: Global banks are exposed to losses on credit derivatives issued to a failing Enron.
- December 2001–January 2002: Allied Irish Bank incurs a US$750 million loss from FX trades by rogue trader John Rusnak.
- September 2006: Amaranth Advisors loses US$6 billion on investments in natural gas futures. Total assets before loss were $9 billion.
- 2008: Rogue trader Jérôme Keviel of the French bank Société Générale loses US$7.2 billion trading European stock index futures.
- April 2011: Morgan Stanley loses US$1.75 billion from poorly hedged bets on interest rate and FX swaps.
- September 2011: UBS AG loses US$2 billion from unauthorized derivatives trading by Kweku Adoboli, which were unhedged and breached the bank's risk limits.
- May 2012: JPMorgan Chase loses more than US$2 billion in credit default swap (CDS) trading by Bruno Iksil, also known as the "London Whale."

Source: Dan Atkinson, "UBS Pledged Derivatives Explanation," *Manchester Guardian*, 1998; updated by authors.

insurance company AIG; commercial bank Citigroup; finance company CIT Group; and government-sponsored agencies Fannie Mae and Freddie Mac) can be attributed to risks associated with OBS activities. Losses from the falling value of subprime mortgages and OBS securities backed by these mortgages reached over US$1 trillion worldwide through mid-2009.

cibc.com
td.com
royalbank.com

While Canadian FIs escaped the financial crisis relatively unscathed, OBS activities can pose a significant risk. In 2005, CIBC's OBS deals with Enron affected its solvency by bringing its Tier 1 capital ratio to 7.5 percent, close to the 7 percent required by OSFI. As we discuss later in the chapter, FI OBS holdings and the collapse of the U.S. subprime mortgage market in the mid- and late 2000s, and the switch of Canadian FIs to IFRS, resulted in changes in the reporting of OBS activities by FIs. Table 16–2 lists some other notable losses for FIs from trading in derivatives. Derivative securities (futures, forwards, options, and swaps) are examined in detail in Chapters 22 through 24 and defined in Table 16–3.

delta of an option
The change in the value of an option for a unit change in the price of the underlying security.

Since OBS items are contingent assets and liabilities and move onto the balance sheet with a probability less than 1, their valuation is difficult and often highly complex. Because many OBS items involve option features, the most common methodology has been to apply contingent claims/option pricing theory models of finance. For example, one relatively simple way to estimate the value of an OBS position in options is by calculating the **delta of an option**—the sensitivity of an option's value to a unit change in the price of the underlying security, which is then

TABLE 16–3
Derivative Securities Held Off the Balance Sheet of FIs

Forward contract	An agreement between a buyer and a seller at time 0 to exchange a nonstandardized asset for cash at some future date. The details of the asset and the price to be paid at the forward contract expiration date are set at time 0. The price of the forward contract is fixed over the life of the contract.
Futures contract	An agreement between a buyer and a seller at time 0 to exchange a standardized asset for cash at some future date. Each contract has a standardized expiration, and transactions occur in a centralized market. The price of the futures contract changes daily as the market value of the asset underlying the futures fluctuates.
Option	A contract that gives the holder the right, but not the obligation, to buy or sell the underlying asset at a specified price within a specified period of time.
Swap	An agreement between two parties to exchange assets or a series of cash flows for a specific period of time at a specified interval.

notional value
The face value of an OBS item.

multiplied by the notional value of the option's position. (The delta of an option lies between 0 and 1.) Thus, suppose an FI has bought call options on bonds (i.e., it has an OBS asset) with a face or **notional value** of $100 million, and the delta is calculated[2] at 0.25. Then the contingent asset value of this option position would be $25 million:

$$d = \text{Delta of an option} = \frac{\text{Change in the option's price}}{\text{Change in price of underlying security}} = \frac{dO}{dS} = 0.25$$

$$F = \text{Notional or face value of options} = \$100 \text{ million}$$

The delta equivalent or contingent asset value = delta × face value of option = 0.25 × $100 million = $25 million. Of course, to determine the value of delta for the option, we need an option pricing model such as Black–Scholes or a binomial model. We provide a review of these models in Appendix 10B. In general, the delta of the option varies with the level of the price of the underlying security as it moves in and out of the money;[3] that is, $0 < d < 1$.[4] Note that if the FI sold options, they would be valued as a contingent liability.

Loan commitments and LCs are also OBS activities that have option features. Specifically, the holder of a loan commitment or credit line who decides to draw on that credit line is exercising an *option to borrow.* When the buyer of a guarantee defaults, this buyer is exercising a *default* option. Similarly, when the counterparty to a derivatives transaction is unable or unwilling to meet its obligation to pay (e.g., in a swap), this is considered an exercise of a default option.

With respect to swaps, futures, and forwards, a common approach is to convert these positions into an equivalent value of the underlying assets. For example, a $20 million, 10-year, fixed–floating interest rate swap in which an FI receives 20 semiannual fixed interest rate payments of 8 percent per annum (i.e., 4 percent per half year) and pays floating-rate payments every half year indexed to LIBOR can be viewed as the equivalent, in terms of valuation, of an

---

[2] A 1-cent change in the price of the bonds underlying the call option leads to a 0.25-cent change in the price of the option.

[3] For an in-the-money call option, the price of the underlying security exceeds the option's exercise price. For an out-of-the-money call option, the price of the underlying security is less than the option's exercise price. In general, the relationship between the value of an option and the underlying value of a security is nonlinear. Thus, using the delta method to derive the market value of an option is an approximation. To deal with the nonlinearity of payoffs on options, some analysts take into account the gamma as well as the delta of the option (gamma measures the change in delta as the underlying security price varies). The BIS standardized model used to calculate the market risk of options incorporates an option's delta, its gamma, and its vega (a measure of volatility risk).

[4] In the context of the Black–Scholes model, the value of the delta on a call option is $d = N(d_1)$, where $N(\cdot)$ is the cumulative normal distribution function and $d_1 = [\ln(S/X) + (r + \sigma^2/(2\tau))]/\sigma\sqrt{T}$.

on-balance-sheet position in two $20 million bonds. That is, the FI can be viewed as being long $20 million (holding an asset) in a 10-year bond with an annual coupon of 8 percent per annum and short $20 million (holding a liability) in a floating-rate bond of 10 years' maturity whose rate is adjusted every six months. The market value of the swap can be viewed as the present value of the difference between the cash flows on the fixed-rate bond and the expected cash flows on the floating-rate bond. This market value is usually a very small percentage of the notional value of the swap. In our example of a $20 million swap, the market value is about 3 percent of this figure, or $600,000. The BIS reported that the total notional value of over-the-counter (OTC) derivative securities was US$647.8 billion in June 2012, and the market value of these securities was US$27.3 billion (or 4.2 percent of notional value). In December 2008 (after the start of the financial crisis), the notional value was US$591.6 billion and the market value was US$33.89 billion (5.7 percent).

Given these valuation models, we can calculate an approximate current or market value of each OBS asset and liability and its effect on an FI's solvency. From both the stockholders' and regulators' perspectives, large increases in the value of OBS liabilities can render an FI economically insolvent just as effectively as can losses due to mismatched interest rate gaps and default or credit losses from on-balance-sheet activities. For example, during the financial crisis, losses on OBS collateralized debt obligations linked to U.S. mortgages were expected to reach US$260 billion.

CONCEPT QUESTIONS

1. **Define a contingent asset and a contingent liability.**
2. **How can option pricing theory be used to price OBS assets and liabilities?**

RETURNS AND RISKS OF OFF-BALANCE-SHEET ACTIVITIES

In the 1980s, rising losses on loans to less-developed and Eastern European countries, increased interest rate volatility, and squeezed interest margins for on-balance-sheet lending due to nonbank competition induced many large commercial banks to seek profitable OBS activities. By moving activities off the balance sheet, banks hoped to earn more fee income to offset declining margins or spreads on their traditional lending business. At the same time, they could avoid regulatory costs or taxes, since reserve requirements, deposit insurance premiums, and capital adequacy requirements were not levied on OBS activities. Thus, banks had both earnings and regulatory tax-avoidance incentives to move activities off their balance sheets.

bis.org

notional amount
The face value of a financial contract.

The dramatic growth in OBS activities caused OSFI to introduce a reporting system in 1996 to satisfy the BIS capital requirements. In 2008, Canadian banks replaced Basel I with Basel II reporting for OBS derivatives, which we discuss in further detail in Chapter 20. Table 16–4 shows the level of OBS activities of Canadian banks, reported quarterly to OSFI at their **notional amount**, which overestimates their current market, or contingent claims, value. The notional amount of OBS contracts reported for Quarter 4, 2012, is four times the 1996 figure, a phenomenal growth rate that reflects the global trend toward the provision of and exposure to OTC and exchange-traded derivatives contracts by FIs. The OBS derivatives exposure for Canadian banks comes from OTC interest rate contracts

TABLE 16–4
Notional Amounts of Derivatives Reported by Canadian Domestic Banks (Notional Amounts, $ billions)

Source: OSFI quarterly reports for all banks, osfi-bsif.gc.ca.

OBS Items	1996	2008*	2012*
Interest Rate Contracts			
OTC	2,717.0		13,711.9
Exchange-Traded	339.1		1,502.4
FX and Gold Contracts			
OTC	1,938.0	3,315.6	3,902.3
Exchange-Traded	9.3	35.5	52.8
Credit Derivative Contracts			
OTC		835.5	157.6
Equity-Linked Contracts			
OTC		225.5	284.3
Exchange-Traded		229.8	121.8
Other			
OTC	37.2	171.8	103.1
Exchange-Traded	6.0	242.8	192.5
Total Derivative Contracts	5,046.6	14,982.3	20,028.6

*2008 and 2012 results reported under Basel II rules.

followed by OTC FX and gold contracts. The total notional amount of derivative contracts of $20.0 trillion is over five times the $3.8 trillion of on-balance-sheet assets. Other OBS items (guarantees, SLCs, securities lending, documentary and commercial LCs, lease commitments, loan commitments, and loans sold) reported to OSFI under Basel I for 1996–2007 made up a small amount of risk exposure for Canadian banks relative to the notional amounts of derivatives. These items are reported with credit risk.

credit derivative contracts
Contracts that transfer credit risk from one party to another.

equity-linked contracts
Contracts with an option feature whose value depends in part on a stock, a basket of stocks, or an equity index such as the TSX.

As shown in Table 16–4, OTC **credit derivative contracts** and OTC and exchange-traded **equity-linked contracts** were reported separately for the first time in 2008, reflecting the growth in global markets for credit default swaps (CDSs) and equity-related forwards, swaps, and options. However, the notional amounts of CDSs globally declined from US$57 trillion in 2008 to US$27 trillion 2012, less than half the amount reported by global FIs at the end of 2007. These contracts had been largely unregulated and attracted the attention of regulators for their potential role in the credit crisis in 2007–2008.

The OBS picture for individual banks can be different since the notional amounts for derivatives overstate an FI's risk. CIBC reported a total notional derivative amount of $1.78 trillion in its 2012 annual report, with $1.51 trillion for trading purposes and $0.27 trillion for asset liability management. When converted for capital adequacy purposes as required by OSFI (discussed in Chapter 20), the credit equivalent is only $10.99 billion and the risk-weighted amount is only $2.48 billion. In addition to derivatives, CIBC also reports securitizations, guarantees, pledged assets, and credit-related arrangements. Table 16–5 shows a summary of the contract amounts of OBS credit-related arrangements reported by CIBC for 2012. These are discussed in the next section.

Other FIs engage in OBS activities as well. For example, Canadian insurance companies provide OBS variable annuities as well as guarantees on equities and debt in segregated funds that protect the investor from losses. In 2008, because of the decline in equity markets, Manulife increased its balance sheet reserves by $5.78 billion through a charge to operating income and raised additional capital of $4.3 billion in debt and equity.

TABLE 16–5
CIBC's 2011 and 2012 OBS Credit-Related Arrangements ($ millions, as at October 31)

Source: CIBC *Annual Accountability Report 2012*, p. 147.

	2011 Total	2012 Total
Securities lending[(1)]	$ 10,924	$ 15,396
Unutilized credit commitments[(2)]	140,338	148,957
Backstop liquidity facilities[(3)]	2,273	3,189
SLCs and performance LCs	6,323	7,504
Documentary and commercial LCs	312	449
Other	412	359
	$ 160,582	$ 175,854

[(1)] Excludes securities lending of $1.6 billion (October 31, 2011) for cash because it is reported on the consolidated balance sheet.
[(2)] Includes irrevocable lines of credit totalling $35.9 billion (October 31, 2011).
[(3)] Excluses backstop liquidity facilities provided to consolidated sponsored asset-backed commercial paper (ABCP) programs totalling $390 million October 31, 2011).

THE MAJOR TYPES OF OFF-BALANCE-SHEET ACTIVITIES

LO2

The major types of OBS activities for Canadian banks are

- Loan commitments
- SLCs and LCs
- Futures, forwards, swaps, and options
- When-issued (WI) securities
- Loans sold

This section analyzes these OBS activities in more detail and pays particular attention to the types of risk exposure an FI faces when engaging in such activities. As we discussed earlier, precise market valuation of these contingent assets and liabilities can be extremely difficult because of their complex contingent claim features and option aspects. At a very minimum, FI managers should understand not only the general features of the risk exposure associated with each major OBS asset and liability but also how each one can impact the return and profitability of an FI.

Loan Commitments

loan commitment agreement
A contractual commitment to make a loan up to a stated amount at a given interest rate in the future.

up-front fee
The fee charged for making funds available through a loan commitment.

back-end fee
The fee imposed on the unused balance of a loan commitment.

These days, most commercial loans are made by firms that take down (or borrow against) prenegotiated lines of credit or loan commitments rather than borrow spot loans (see Chapter 10's discussion on business loans). A **loan commitment agreement** is a contractual commitment by an FI to lend to a firm a certain maximum amount (say, $10 million) at given interest rate terms (say, 12 percent). The loan commitment agreement also defines the length of time over which the borrower has the option to take down this loan. In return for making this loan commitment, the FI may charge an **up-front fee** (or facility fee) of, say, ⅛ percent of the commitment size, or $12,500 in this example. In addition, the FI must stand ready to supply the full $10 million at any time over the commitment period—say, one year. Meanwhile, the borrower has a valuable option to take down any amount between $0 and $10 million. The FI also may charge the borrower a **back-end fee** (or commitment fee) on any unused balances in the commitment line at the end of the period. In this example, if the borrower takes down only $8 million in funds over the year and the fee on *unused* commitments is ¼ percent, the FI will generate additional revenue of ¼ percent times $2 million, or $5,000. Figure 16–1 summarizes the structure of this loan commitment.

FIGURE 16–1
Structure of a Loan Commitment

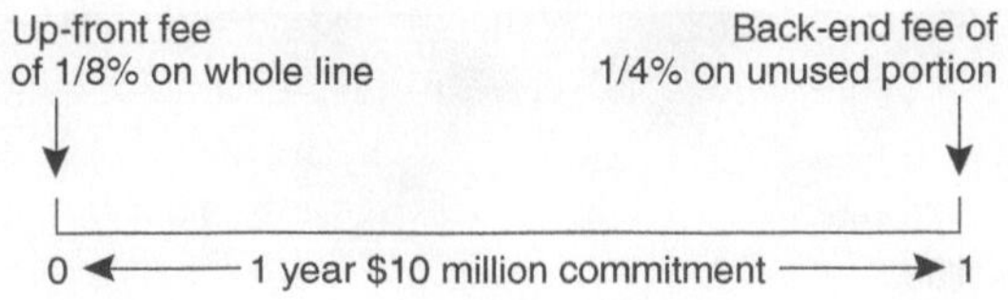

EXAMPLE 16–1

Calculation of the Promised Return on a Loan Commitment

It is quite easy to show how the unique features of loan commitments affect the promised return $(1 + k)$ on a loan. In Chapter 10 we developed a model for determining $(1 + k)$ on a spot loan. This can be extended by allowing for partial drawdown and the up-front and back-end fees commonly found in loan commitments. For a one-year loan commitment, let

BR = FI's base interest on the loan = 12%

m = Risk premium on the loan commitment = 2%

f_1 = Up-front fee on the whole commitment = ⅛%

f_2 = Back-end fee on the unused commitment = ¼%

td = Expected (average) drawdown rate ($0 < td < 1$) on the loan commitment = 75%

Then the general formula for the promised return $(1 + k)$ of the loan commitment is[5]

$$1 + k = 1 + \frac{f_1 + f_2(1 - td) + (BR + m)td}{td}$$

$$1 + k = 1 + \frac{0.00125 + 0.0025(0.25) + (0.12 + 0.02)0.75}{0.75}$$

$$1 + k = 1 + \frac{0.106875}{0.75} = 1.1425 \quad \text{or} \quad k = 14.25\%$$

Note that only when the borrower actually draws on the commitment do the loans made under the commitment appear on the balance sheet. Thus, only when the $8 million loan is drawn down does the balance sheet show a new $8 million loan being created. When the $10 million commitment is made at time 0, nothing shows on the balance sheet. Nevertheless, the FI must stand ready to make the full $10 million in loans on any day within the one-year commitment period; that is, at time 0 a new contingent claim on the resources of the FI was created.

This raises the following question: What contingent risks are created by the loan commitment provision? At least four types of risk are associated with the extension of loan commitments: interest rate risk, drawdown or takedown risk, credit risk, and aggregate funding risk.

Interest Rate Risk

Interest rate risk is a contingent risk emanating from the fact that the FI precommits to make loans available to a borrower over the commitment period at either (1) some fixed interest rate as a fixed-rate loan commitment or (2) some variable rate as a variable-rate loan commitment. Suppose the FI precommits to lend a maximum of $10 million at a fixed rate of 12 percent over the year, and its cost of funds rises. The cost of funds may well rise to a level that makes the spread between

[5] Note that for simplicity we have used undiscounted cash flows. Taking into account the time value of money means that we would need to discount both f_2 and $BR + m$ since they are paid at the end of the period. If the discount factor (cost of funds) is d = 10 percent, then k = 12.95 percent.

the 12 percent commitment rate and the FI's cost of funds negative or very small. Moreover, 12 percent may be much less than the rate the customer would have to pay if forced to borrow on the spot loan market under current interest rate conditions. When rates do rise over the commitment period, the FI stands to lose on its portfolio of fixed-rate loan commitments as borrowers exercise to the full amount their very valuable options to borrow at below-market rates.[6]

One way the FI can control this risk is by making commitment rates float with spot loan rates, for example, by indexing loan commitments to the prime or LIBOR rate. If the prime rate rises during the commitment period, so does the cost of commitment loans to the borrower—the borrower pays the market rate in effect when the commitment is drawn on. Nevertheless, this fixed formula rate solution does not totally eradicate interest rate risk on loan commitments. For example, suppose that the prime rate rises 1 percent but the cost of funds rises 1.25 percent; the spread between the indexed commitment loan and the cost of funds narrows by 0.25 percent. This spread risk is often called **basis risk.**[7]

basis risk
The variable spread between a lending rate and a borrowing rate or between any two interest rates or prices.

Drawdown or Takedown Risk

Another contingent risk is takedown risk. Specifically, in making the loan commitment, the FI must always stand ready to provide the maximum of the commitment line—$10 million in our example. The borrower has the flexible option to borrow anything between $0 and the $10 million ceiling on any business day in the commitment period, usually with a short notice period (e.g., three days). In fact, the borrower could come to the bank and borrow different amounts over the period ($1 million in month 1, $2 million in month 2, etc.) The only constraint is the $10 million ceiling. This exposes the FI to a degree of future liquidity risk or uncertainty (see Chapter 13). The FI can never be absolutely sure when, during the commitment period, the borrower will demand the full $10 million or some proportion thereof in cash. For example, in September and October 2008, the severe global liquidity crisis that dried up commercial paper and other short-term money market funds drove borrowers to draw down their credit lines at banks. To some extent, at least, the back-end fee on unused amounts is designed to create incentives for the borrower to take down lines in full to avoid paying this fee. However, in actuality, many lines are only partially drawn upon.

Credit Risk

FIs also face a degree of contingent credit risk in setting the interest or formula rate on a loan commitment. Specifically, the FI often adds a risk premium based on its current assessment of the creditworthiness of the borrower. For example, the borrower may be judged as an AA credit risk, paying 1 percent above prime rate. However, suppose that over the one-year commitment period the borrowing firm gets into difficulty; its earnings decline so that its creditworthiness is downgraded to BBB. The FI's problem is that the credit risk premium on the commitment had been preset to the AA level for the one-year commitment period. To avoid being exposed to dramatic declines in borrower creditworthiness over the commitment period, most FIs include a *material adverse change in conditions clause* by which the FI can cancel or reprice a loan commitment. For example, because of the deteriorating credit quality of businesses and household borrowers in late 2008, U.S.

[6] In an options sense, the loans are in the money to the borrower.

[7] Basis risk arises because loan rates and deposit rates are not perfectly correlated in their movements over time.

banks reduced or cancelled lines of credit to businesses and retail customers, as well as unused commitments to fund loans. However, exercising such a clause is really a last-resort tactic for an FI because it may put the borrower out of business and result in costly legal claims for breach of contract.[8]

Aggregate Funding Risk

Many large borrowing firms, such as Home Depot, Ford, and IBM, take out multiple commitment or credit lines with many FIs as insurance against future credit crunches. In a credit crunch, the supply of spot loans to borrowers is restricted, possibly as a result of restrictive monetary policy actions of the Bank of Canada. Another cause is an FI's increased aversion toward lending such as seen during the financial crisis when many banks were unwilling to lend to any but the most creditworthy loan applicants; that is, there is a shift to the left in the loan supply function at all interest rates.

bankofcanada.ca

In such credit crunches, borrowers with long-standing loan commitments are unlikely to be as credit constrained as those without loan commitments. However, this also implies that borrowers' aggregate demand to take down loan commitments is likely to be greatest when the FI's borrowing and funding conditions are most costly and difficult. In difficult credit conditions, this aggregate commitment takedown effect can increase the cost of funds above normal levels while many FIs scramble for funds to meet their commitments to customers. For example, in mid-September 2008, financial markets had frozen and banks stopped lending to each other at anything but exorbitantly high rates. The overnight LIBOR (a benchmark rate that reflects the rate at which banks lend to one another) more than doubled. Banks generally rely on each other for cash needed to meet their daily needs. Interest rates on this interbank borrowing are generally low because of the confidence that the FIs will repay each other. But confidence had broken down since August 2007 and had not been completely restored. This is similar to the *externality effect* common in many markets when all participants simultaneously act together and adversely affect the costs of each individual participant.

The four contingent risk effects just identified—interest rate risk, drawdown or takedown risk, credit risk, and aggregate funding risk—appear to imply that loan commitment activities increase the insolvency exposure of FIs that engage in such activities. However, an opposing view holds that loan commitment contracts may make an FI less risky than had it not engaged in them. This view maintains that to be able to charge fees and sell loan commitments or equivalent credit rationing insurance, the FI must convince borrowers that it will still be around to provide the credit needed in the *future.* To convince borrowers that an FI will be around to meet its future commitments, managers may have to adopt *lower*-risk portfolios *today* than would otherwise be the case. By adopting lower-risk portfolios, managers increase the probability that the FI will be able to meet all its long-term on- and off-balance-sheet obligations. Interestingly, empirical studies have confirmed that banks making more loan commitments have lower on-balance-sheet portfolio risk characteristics than those with relatively low levels of commitments; that is, safer banks have a greater tendency to make loan commitments.

---

[8] Potential damage claims can be enormous if the borrower goes out of business and attributes this to the cancellation of loans under the commitment contract. There are also important reputational costs to take into account in cancelling a commitment to lend.

Commercial LCs and SLCs

commercial letters of credit
Contingent guarantees sold by an FI to underwrite the trade or commercial performance of the buyer of the guarantee.

standby letters of credit
Guarantees issued to cover contingencies that are potentially more severe and less predictable than contingencies covered under trade-related or commercial letters of credit.

In selling **commercial letters of credit** (LCs) and **standby letters of credit** (SLCs) for fees, FIs add to their contingent future liabilities. Both LCs and SLCs are essentially *guarantees* sold by an FI to underwrite the *performance* of the buyer of the guarantee (such as a corporation). In economic terms, the FI that sells LCs and SLCs is selling insurance against the frequency or severity of some particular future occurrence. Further, similar to the different lines of insurance sold by property and casualty (P&C) insurers, LC and SLC contracts differ as to the severity and frequency of their risk exposures. We look next at an FI's risk exposure from engaging in LC and SLC OBS activities.

Commercial LCs

Commercial LCs are widely used in both domestic and international trade. For example, they ease the shipment of grain between a farmer in Saskatchewan and a purchaser in British Columbia or the shipment of goods between a foreign exporter and a Canadian importer. The FI's role is to provide a formal guarantee that payment for goods shipped or sold will be forthcoming regardless of whether the buyer of the goods defaults on payment. We show a very simple LC example in Figure 16–2 for an international transaction between a Canadian importer and a German exporter.

Suppose the importer sent an order for $10 million worth of machinery to a German exporter, as shown by arrow 1 in Figure 16–2. However, the German exporter may be reluctant to send the goods without some assurance or guarantee of being paid once the goods are shipped. The importer may promise to pay for the goods in 90 days, but the German exporter may feel insecure either because it knows little about the creditworthiness of the importer or because the importer has a low credit rating (say, B or BB). To persuade the German exporter to ship the goods, the importer may have to turn to a large Canadian FI with which it has developed a long-term customer relationship. In its role as a lender and monitor, the FI can better appraise the importer's creditworthiness. The FI can issue a contingent payment guarantee—that is, an LC to the German exporter on the importer's behalf—in return for an LC fee paid by the importer.[9] In our example,

FIGURE 16–2
Simple LC Transaction

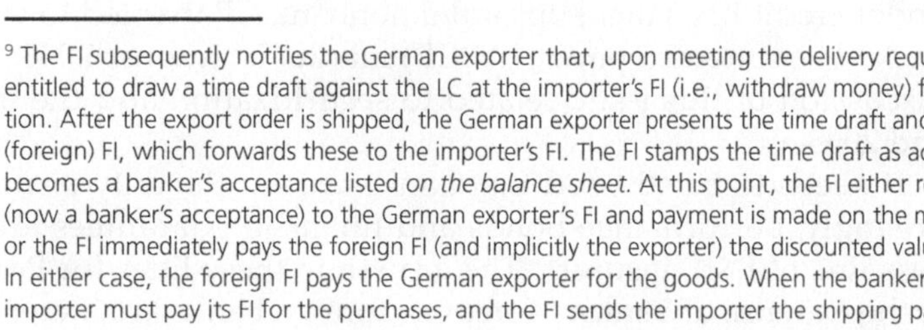

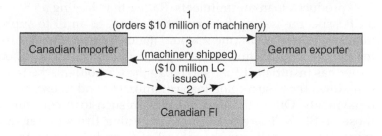

[9] The FI subsequently notifies the German exporter that, upon meeting the delivery requirements, the exporter is entitled to draw a time draft against the LC at the importer's FI (i.e., withdraw money) for the amount of the transaction. After the export order is shipped, the German exporter presents the time draft and the shipping papers to its own (foreign) FI, which forwards these to the importer's FI. The FI stamps the time draft as accepted and the draft becomes a banker's acceptance listed *on the balance sheet.* At this point, the FI either returns the stamped time draft (now a banker's acceptance) to the German exporter's FI and payment is made on the maturity date (e.g., in 90 days), or the FI immediately pays the foreign FI (and implicitly the exporter) the discounted value of the banker's acceptance. In either case, the foreign FI pays the German exporter for the goods. When the banker's acceptance matures, the importer must pay its FI for the purchases, and the FI sends the importer the shipping papers.

the FI would send to the German exporter an LC guaranteeing payment for the goods in 90 days regardless of whether the importer defaults on its obligation to the German exporter (see arrow 2 in Figure 16–2). Implicitly, the FI is replacing the importer's credit risk with its own credit risk guarantee. For this substitution to work effectively, in guaranteeing payment, the FI must have a higher credit standing or better credit quality reputation than the importer. Once the FI issues the LC and sends it to the German exporter, the exporter ships the goods to the importer, as shown by arrow 3. The probability is very high that in 90 days' time, the importer will pay the German exporter for the goods sent and the FI keeps the LC fee as profit. The fee is, perhaps, 10 bp of the face value of the LC, or $10,000 in this example.

A more detailed version of an LC transaction is presented in Appendix 16A.

SLCs

SLCs perform an insurance function similar to that of commercial and trade letters of credit. However, the structure and type of risks covered are different. FIs may issue SLCs to cover contingencies that are potentially more *severe*, less *predictable* or frequent, and not necessarily trade related. These contingencies include performance bond guarantees whereby an FI may guarantee that a real estate development will be completed in some interval of time. Alternatively, the FI may offer default guarantees to back an issue of commercial paper (CP) to allow issuers to achieve a higher credit rating and a lower funding cost than would otherwise be the case.

Without credit enhancements, for example, many firms would be unable to borrow in the CP market or would have to borrow at a higher funding cost. P1 borrowers, which offer the highest-quality commercial paper, normally pay 40 bp less than P2 borrowers, the next quality grade. By paying a fee of perhaps 25 bp to an FI, the FI guarantees to pay CP purchasers' principal and interest on maturity should the issuing firm itself be unable to pay. The SLC backing of CP issues normally results in the paper's placement in the lowest default risk class (P1) and the issuer's savings of up to 15 bp on issuing costs—40 bp (the P2–P1 spread) minus the 25 bp SLC fee equals 15 bp.

Note that in selling the SLCs, FIs are competing directly with another of their OBS products, loan commitments. Rather than buying an SLC from an FI to back a CP issue, the issuing firm might pay a fee to an FI to supply a loan commitment. This loan commitment would match the size and maturity of the CP issue, for example, a $100 million ceiling and 45-day maturity. If, on maturity, the CP issuer has insufficient funds to repay the CP holders, the issuer has the right to take down the $100 million loan commitment and to use those funds to meet CP repayments. Often, the up-front fees on such loan commitments are less than those on SLCs. Therefore, many CP-issuing firms prefer to use loan commitments. However, it was the refusal of Canadian banks to permit drawdowns under credit lines that supported nonbank CP that led to the freeze in the asset-backed commercial paper (ABCP) market in August 2008. See Chapter 26 for a discussion of this issue related to securitization and the market crises of 2007 and 2008.

It needs to be stressed that banks are not the only issuers of SLCs. Not surprisingly, performance bonds and financial guarantees are an important business line of P&C insurers. The growth in these lines for P&C insurers has come at the expense of banks. Moreover, foreign banks are increasingly taking a share of the market in SLCs. The reason for the loss in this business line by U.S. banks is that to sell guarantees such as SLCs credibly, the seller must have a better credit rating than the customer. In recent years, few U.S. banks or their parent holding companies have had AA ratings. Other domestic U.S. FIs and Canadian and other foreign banks and insurance companies (e.g., Manulife), on the other hand, have more often had AA ratings. High credit ratings not only make the guarantor more attractive from the buyer's perspective but also make the guarantor more competitive because its cost of funds is lower than that of less creditworthy FIs.

Risks Associated with LCs

The risk to an FI in selling an LC is that the buyer of the LC may fail to perform as promised under a contractual obligation. For example, with the commercial LC described above, there exists a small probability that the Canadian importer will be unable to pay the $10 million in 90 days and will default. Then the FI would be obliged to make good on its guarantee that the contractual obligation will be fulfilled. The cost of such a default would mean that the guaranteeing FI must pay $10 million to the German exporter, although it would have a creditor's claim against the importer's assets to offset this loss. Likewise, for the SLC, there is a small probability that the CP issuer will be unable to pay the CP holders the $100 million as promised at maturity. The FI would then be obliged to pay $100 million to the CP holders (investors) on the issuer's behalf. Clearly, the fee on LCs should exceed the expected default risk on the LC or SLC, which is equal to the probability of a default by a counterparty times the expected net payout on the LC, after adjusting for the FI's ability to reclaim assets from the defaulting importer/CP issuer and any monitoring costs.

Derivative Contracts: Futures, Forwards, Swaps, and Options

jpmorganchase.com
citigroup.com
bankofamerica.com

FIs can be either users of derivative contracts for hedging (see Chapters 22 through 24) and other purposes or dealers that act as counterparties in trades with customers for a fee. Of the notional derivatives amounts reported in Table 16–4 for Q4 2012, OTC contracts are by far the greater portion of OBS exposure for the banks on a notional basis. By comparison, although over 1,291 U.S. banks were users of derivatives in 2012, the big three dealer banks (JPMorgan Chase, Citigroup, and Bank of America) accounted for 75 percent of the US$227.982 trillion derivatives reported to the U.S. Office of the Comptroller of the Currency. However, as noted in Table 16–2 and the discussion throughout the chapter, risk on these securities can lead to large losses and even firm failure.

Contingent credit risk is likely to be present when FIs expand their positions in forwards, futures, swaps, and option contracts. This risk relates to the fact that the counterparty to one of these contracts may default on payment obligations, leaving the FI unhedged and having to replace the contract at today's interest rates, prices, or exchange rates. Further, such defaults are most likely to occur when the counterparty is losing heavily on the contract and the FI is in the money on the contract. This type of default risk is much more serious for forward (and swap) contracts than for futures contracts. This is so because **forward contracts** are nonstandard contracts entered into bilaterally by negotiating parties such as two FIs, and all cash flows are required to be paid at one time (on contract maturity). Thus, they are essentially OTC arrangements with no external guarantees should one or the other party default on the contract. For example, the contract seller

forward contracts
Nonstandard contracts between two parties to deliver and pay for an asset in the future.

might default on a forward FX contract that promises to deliver £10 million in three months' time at the exchange rate of $1.40 to £1 if the cost to purchase £1 for delivery is $1.60 when the forward contract matures. By contrast, **futures contracts** are standardized contracts guaranteed by organized exchanges such as the Montréal Exchange or the New York Futures Exchange (NYFE), a part of ICE Futures US (formerly the New York Board of Trade (NYBOT)). Futures contracts, like forward contracts, make commitments to deliver FX (or some other asset) at some future date. If a counterparty defaults on a futures contract, however, the exchange assumes the defaulting party's position and the payment obligations. For example, when Barings, the British merchant bank, was unable to meet its margin calls on Nikkei Index futures traded on the Singapore futures exchange (SIMEX) in 1995, the exchange stood ready to assume Barings' US$8 billion position in futures contracts and ensure that no counterparty lost money. Thus, unless a systematic financial market collapse threatens the exchange itself, futures are essentially default risk–free.[10] In addition, default risk is reduced by the daily marking to market of contracts. This prevents the accumulation of losses and gains that occurs with forward contracts. These differences are discussed in more detail in Chapter 22.

futures contracts
Standardized contracts guaranteed by organized exchanges to deliver and pay for an asset in the future.

www.theice.com
m-x.ca

An **option** is a contract that gives the holder the right, but not the obligation, to buy (a call option) or sell (a put option) an underlying asset at a prespecified price for a specified time period. Option contracts can also be purchased or sold by an FI, trading either OTC or bought/sold on organized exchanges. If the options are standardized options traded on exchanges, such as bond options, they are virtually default risk–free.[11] If they are specialized options purchased OTC such as interest rate caps (see Chapter 23), some element of default risk exists.[12]

option
A contract that gives the holder the right but not the obligation to buy (sell) an asset at a specified price for a specified time period.

A **swap** is an agreement between two parties (called *counterparties*) to exchange specified periodic cash flows in the future based on some underlying instrument or price (e.g., a fixed or floating rate on a bond or note). Conceptually, a swap contract can be viewed as a succession of forward contracts. Similar to options, swaps are OTC instruments susceptible to counterparty risk (see Chapter 24). If interest rates (or FX rates) move a lot, one party can be faced with considerable future loss exposure, creating incentives to default.

swap
An agreement to exchange specified periodic cash flows in the future.

Credit derivatives (including forwards, options, and swaps) allow FIs to hedge their credit risk. They can be used to hedge the credit risk on individual loans or bonds or portfolios of loans and bonds. For example, if a borrower files for bankruptcy, the FI can exercise its right to exchange its loan with the credit derivative seller for par, thereby protecting the FI from a loss on the notional amount. In return, the FI pays the seller an up-front fee as well as periodic payments to maintain the derivative protection. Credit derivatives, the newest of the derivative securities, have been growing in volume by over 5,000 percent per year since 1996.

---

[10] More specifically, there are at least four reasons that the default risk of a futures contract is less than that of a forward contract: (1) daily marking to market of futures, (2) margin requirements on futures that act as a security bond, (3) price limits that spread out over extreme price fluctuations, and (4) default guarantees by the futures exchange itself.

[11] Note that the options can still be subject to interest rate risk; see our earlier discussion of the delta on a bond option.

[12] Under an interest rate cap, in return for a fee, the seller promises to compensate the buyer if interest rates rise above a certain level. If rates rise a lot more than expected, the cap seller may have an incentive to default to limit losses. Thus, selling a cap is similar to selling interest rate risk insurance (see Chapter 23).

Many of the FIs that hold large amounts of these credit derivatives hold them in what are known as special purpose vehicles (SPV) or special investment vehicles (SIV), also known as shadow vehicles (see Chapter 21). SIVs and SPVs are fully described in Chapter 26. While SIVs are closely related to SPVs, they differ in the crucial extent of the mismatching of maturities of their liabilities (short-term CP) and assets (longer-term loans, mortgages, etc.). By contrast, SPVs generally match the maturities of their liabilities (bonds) to those of their assets (mortgages, long-term loans).

An SPV purchases the assets (newly originated loans) from the originating bank for cash generated from the sale of asset-backed securities. The SPV sells the newly created asset-backed securities (credit derivatives) to investors such as insurance companies and pension funds, earning a fee for the services. An SIV is a structured operating company that invests in assets that are designed to generate higher returns than the SIV's cost of funds. Rather than selling the asset-backed securities directly to investors in order to raise cash (as do SPVs), an SIV sells bonds or CP to investors in order to raise the cash to purchase the bank's assets. The SIV then holds the loans purchased from the banks on its own balance sheet until maturity. These loan assets held by the SIV back the debt instruments issued by the SIV to investors. The SIV pays a lower interest rate on the short-term debt that it issues than it earns on the mortgages and other longer-term assets in which it invests. However, the SIV's short-term funding must be rolled over fairly frequently to continue the financing of the SIV. This subjects it to both a liquidity risk (failure to roll over liabilities) and an interest rate risk (due to the mismatch of the durations of their assets and liabilities).

Most of the CP issued by SIVs is sold to institutional investors that require the SIV to have an investment grade credit rating from a credit rating agency such as Standard & Poor's Rating Service, Moody's Investors Service, or Fitch Ratings. The organization of an SIV as a separate entity appears to provide bankruptcy remoteness from the seller of the assets (often the bank). However, during the financial crisis, liquidity shortages made it virtually impossible for SIVs to roll over their CP and fund their assets. Since these SIVs had back-up lines of credit from the sponsoring bank (e.g., Citibank provided a line of credit to its OBS SIV), these lines were drawn down to prevent the SIV from becoming insolvent. However, in effect the SIV was reintermediated back into the bank and, effectively, what was an "OBS bank," the SIV, became an "on-balance-sheet bank."[13]

The emergence of these new derivatives is important since more FIs fail as a result of credit risk exposures than either interest rate or FX risk exposure. We discuss these derivatives in more detail in Chapters 22 through 24.

Credit Risk Concerns with Derivative Securities

In general, default risk on OTC contracts increases with the time to maturity of the contract and the fluctuation of underlying prices, interest rates, or exchange

---

[13] The adoption of IFRS by Canadian banks mitigates some of these issues by tightening the rules that allow FIs to report SIVs and special-purpose entities (SPEs) OBS. Many critics have argued that SIVs are virtual "OBS banks" and should be regulated just like banks since they have a similar short-term/long-term asset–liability structure.

rates.[14] Most empirical evidence suggests that derivative contracts have generally reduced FI risk or left it unaffected. However, the financial crisis clearly illustrates the magnitude of the risk that derivatives can impose on an FI and the world's financial system.

Credit risk occurs because of the potential for the counterparty to default on its payment obligations under a derivative contract, a situation that would require the FI to replace the contract at the current market prices and rates, potentially at a loss.[15] This risk is most prevalent in OTC rather than exchange-traded derivative contracts, e.g., collateralized debt obligations (CDOs or CMOs). OTC contracts are typically nonstandardized or unique contracts that do not have external guarantees from an organized exchange. Defaults on these contracts usually occur when the FI stands to gain and the counterparty stands to lose. Such was the case in the late 2000s.

Signs of significant problems in the U.S. economy first arose in late 2006 and the first half of 2007 when home prices plummeted and defaults by subprime mortgage borrowers began to affect the mortgage lending industry and other parts of the economy. Mortgage delinquencies, particularly on subprime mortgages, surged in the last quarter of 2006 through 2008, as home owners who stretched themselves financially to buy a home or refinance a mortgage in the early 2000s fell behind on their loan payments. As mortgage borrowers defaulted on their mortgages, FIs that held these mortgages and credit derivatives (in the form of mortgage-backed securities) started announcing huge losses on them. Since these securities had been purchased by global FIs and other investors, losses from the falling value of subprime mortgages and securities backed by these mortgages reached US$700 billion worldwide by early 2009.

Investment banks and securities firms were major purchasers of mortgage originators in the early 2000s, which allowed them to increase their business of packaging the loans as securities. As mortgage borrowers defaulted on their mortgages, investment banks were particularly hard hit with huge losses on the mortgages and securities backing them. A prime example of the losses incurred is that of Bear Stearns. In the summer of 2007, two Bear Stearns funds suffered heavy losses on investments in the subprime mortgage–backed securities market. The two funds filed for bankruptcy in the fall of 2007. The losses became so great that in March 2008 JPMorgan Chase and the U.S. Federal Reserve stepped in to rescue the then–fifth largest investment bank in the U.S. before it failed. September 2008 marked a crucial turning point in the financial crisis. On September 8, the U.S. government seized Fannie Mae and Freddie Mac, taking direct responsibility for the firms that provided funding for about three-quarters of new home mortgages written in the United States. Fannie Mae and Freddie Mac were particularly hard hit by the subprime mortgage market collapse in the mid-2000s as these U.S. government–sponsored agencies are deeply involved in the market that securitizes subprime mortgages. On September 15, Lehman Brothers (the 158-year-old investment bank) filed for bankruptcy, Merrill Lynch was bought by Bank of America, AIG (one of the world's largest insurance companies) met with U.S. regulators to raise desperately needed cash, and Washington Mutual (the

[14] Reputational considerations and the need for future access to markets for hedging deter the incentive to default.

[15] For instance, if the replacement contract has a less favourable price (e.g., the replacement interest rate swap requires the bank to pay a fixed rate of 10 percent to receive a floating-rate payment based on LIBOR rates) than, say, 8 percent before the counterparty (the original floating-rate payer) defaulted.

largest savings institution in the United States) sought a buyer to save it from failing. A financial crisis was at hand, a big part of which was the result of FI's dealings in OBS derivative securities.

In an attempt to unfreeze credit markets, then–U.S. Treasury Secretary Henry Paulson met with Congressional leaders to devise a plan to get bad mortgage loans and mortgage-backed securities off the balance sheets of FIs. After two weeks of debate (and one failed vote for passage), a US$700 billion rescue plan was passed and signed into law by President Bush on October 3, 2008. The bill established the Troubled Asset Relief Program (or TARP) that gave the U.S. Treasury the funds to buy "toxic" mortgages and other securities from FIs. The TARP plan was slow to be instituted, and not all FIs chose to participate in the program; better-capitalized FIs wanted to hold onto their troubled OBS securities rather than sell them and record losses.

The growth of the derivative securities markets was one of the major factors underlying the imposition of the BIS risk-based capital requirements (see Chapter 20). The fear then was that in a long-term derivative security contract, an out-of-the-money counterparty—that is, a counterparty that is currently at a disadvantage in terms of cash flows—would have incentives to default on such contracts to deter current and future losses. Consequently, the BIS imposed a required capital to be held by DTIs against their holdings of derivative securities. As discussed above, these capital requirements were not sufficient to insure solvency of some FIs against the extreme losses experienced during the financial crisis.

bis.org

Forward Purchases and Sales of WI Securities

when-issued (WI) trading
Trading in securities prior to their actual issue.

Very often banks and other FIs—especially investment banks—enter into commitments to buy and sell securities before issue. This is called **when-issued (WI) trading**. These OBS commitments can expose an FI to future or contingent interest rate risk. FIs often include these securities as a part of their holdings of forward contracts.

An example of a WI commitment is that taken on with new T-bills in the week prior to the announcement of T-bill auction results. The Bank of Canada releases a call for tenders for three-month, six-month, and one-year Government of Canada Treasury bills on Thursday afternoon and the auction is held the following Thursday afternoon, as shown in Figure 16–3. Secondary trading (the WI market) for these bills occurs until the settlement date, which is the day following the auction of the bills. There are 21 Government Securities Distributors (GSDs), of which 10 are primary dealers for Treasury bills and 12 are primary dealers for Government of Canada Bonds. The Bank of Canada provides details of the responsibilities of government securities distributors on its website.

bankofcanada.ca

FIGURE 16–3
T-Bill Auction Time-Line

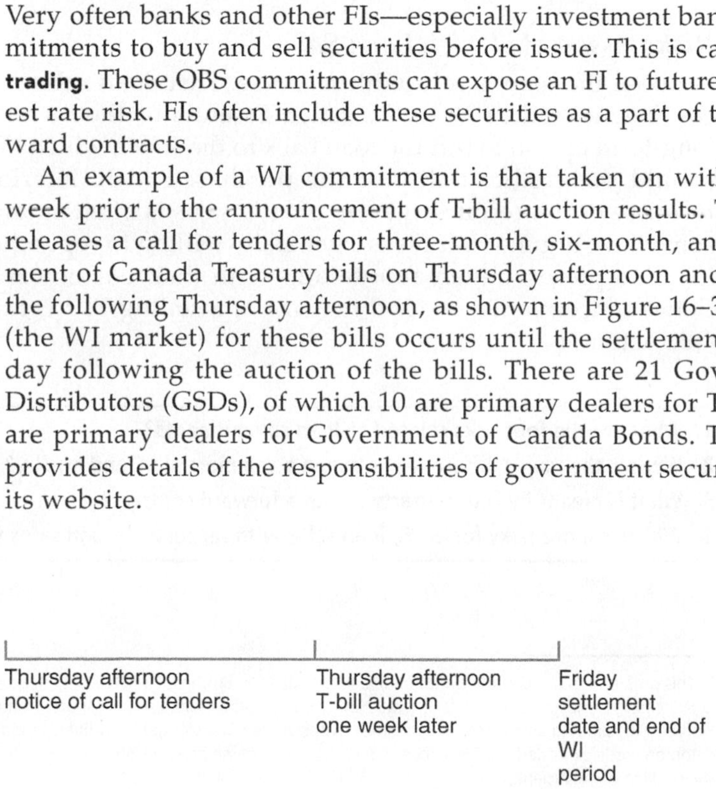

Risks Associated with WI Securities

Normally, primary dealers sell the yet-to-be-issued T-bills for forward delivery to customers in the secondary market at a small margin above the price they expect to pay at the primary auction. This can be profitable if the primary dealer gets all the bills needed at the auction at the appropriate price or interest rate to fulfill these forward WI contracts. A primary dealer that makes a mistake regarding the tenor of the auction (i.e., the level of interest rates) faces the risk that the commitments entered into to deliver T-bills in the WI market can be met only at a loss. For example, an overcommitted dealer may have to buy T-bills from other dealers at a loss right after the auction results are announced to meet the WI T-bill delivery commitments made to its customers.[16]

Loans Sold

In Chapter 25 we discuss in detail the types of loans FIs sell, the FIs' incentives to sell, and the way the loans can be sold. Increasingly, banks and other FIs originate loans on their balance sheets, but, rather than holding them to maturity, they quickly sell them to outside investors. These outside investors include other banks, insurance companies, mutual funds, and even corporations. In acting as loan originators and loan sellers, FIs are operating more in the fashion of loan brokers than as traditional asset transformers (see Chapter 1).

recourse
The ability to put an asset or loan back to the seller if the credit quality of that asset deteriorates.

When an outside party buys a loan with absolutely no **recourse** to the seller of the loan should the loan eventually go bad, loan sales have no OBS contingent liability implications for FIs. Specifically, *no recourse* means that if the loan the FI sells goes bad, the buyer of the loan must bear the full risk of loss. In particular, the buyer cannot put the bad loan back to the seller or originating bank.

Risks Associated with Loan Sales

Suppose the loan is sold with recourse. Then loan sales represent a long-term contingent credit risk to the seller. Essentially, the buyer of the loan holds a long-term option to put the loan back to the seller, which the buyer can exercise should the credit quality of the purchased loan deteriorate. In reality, the recourse or nonrecourse nature of loan sales is often ambiguous. For example, some have argued that FIs are generally willing to repurchase bad nonrecourse loans to preserve their reputations with their customers. Obviously, reputational concerns may extend the size of a selling FI's contingent liabilities for OBS activities.

CONCEPT QUESTIONS

1. **What are the four risks related to loan commitments?**
2. **What is the major difference between a commercial LC and an SLC?**
3. **What is meant by counterparty risk in a forward contract?**
4. **Which is more risky for an FI, loan sales with recourse or loan sales without recourse?**

[16] This problem occurred in the United States when Salomon Brothers cornered or squeezed the market for new two-year U.S. Treasury bonds in 1990. Under the auction rules, no bidder could bid for or attain more than 35 percent of an issue. However, by bidding using customers' names (without their knowledge) in addition to bidding under its own name, Salomon vastly exceeded the 35 percent limit. This put extreme pressure on other dealers, which were unable to meet their selling commitments.

OTHER OFF-BALANCE-SHEET RISKS

So far we have looked at five different OBS activities of banks that report to OSFI. Remember that many other FIs engage in these activities as well. Thus, credit unions and caisses populaires, insurance companies, and investment banks all engage in futures, forwards, swaps, and options transactions of varying forms. Life insurers are heavily engaged in making loan commitments in commercial mortgages, P&C companies underwrite large amounts of financial guarantees, and investment banks engage in WI securities trading. Moreover, the five activities just discussed are not the only OBS activities that can create contingent liabilities or risks for an FI. Next, we briefly introduce two other activities that can create them; we discuss the activities at greater length in later chapters.

Settlement Risk

cdnpay.ca

clearing
The exchange and reconciliation of payments in order to transfer funds from one FI to another.

settlement
The adjustment of financial positions of individual FIs at the Bank of Canada.

chips.org

settlement risk
Intraday credit risk associated with wire transfer activities.

Canadian FIs send their domestic Canadian and U.S. dollar payments via the systems operated by the Canadian Payments Association (CPA), which had 119 members in 2013, of which 12 FIs and the Bank of Canada are direct clearers. The Automated Clearing Settlement System (ACSS) is involved in **clearing** 99 percent of the daily volume of transactions in Canada, but this is only 12 percent of the total daily value cleared. The Large Value Transfer System (LVTS) clears 88 percent of the total daily value (an average of $149 billion per day in 2010) and is used for irrevocable payments. The LVTS is the first of its kind in the world and gives real time **settlement**, eliminating settlement risk for these types of transactions within Canada.

CHIPS is an international and private network owned by approximately 55 participating or member banks. Unlike the ACSS and the LVTS, funds or payment messages sent on the CHIPS network *within* the day are provisional messages that become final and are settled only at the end of the day, giving rise to an intraday, or within-day, **settlement risk** that does not appear on the FI's balance sheet. For example, Bank X sends a fund transfer payment message to Bank Z at 11 AM EST. The actual cash settlement and the physical transfer of funds between X and Z take place at the end of the day, normally by transferring cash held in reserve accounts at the U.S. Federal Reserve bank. Because the transfer of funds is not finalized until the end of the day, Bank Z—the message-receiving bank—faces an *intraday*, or within-day, settlement risk. Specifically, Bank Z assumes that the funds message received at 11 AM from Bank X will result in the actual delivery of the funds at the end of the day and may lend them to Bank Y at 11:15 AM. However, if Bank X does not deliver (settle) the promised funds at the end of the day, Bank Z may be pushed into a serious net funds deficit position and may therefore be unable to meet its payment commitment to Bank Y. Conceivably, Bank Z's net debtor position may be large enough to exceed its capital and reserves, rendering it technically insolvent. Such a disruption can occur only if a major fraud were discovered in Bank X's books during the day and bank regulators closed it the same day. That situation would make payment to Bank Z impossible to complete at the end of the day. Alternatively, Bank X might transmit funds it does not have in the hope of keeping its name in the market to be able to raise funds later in the day. However, other banks may revise their credit limits for this bank during the day, making Bank X unable to deliver all the funds it promised to Bank Z.

The essential feature of settlement risk is that an FI may be exposed to a within-day, or intraday, credit risk that does not appear on the balance sheet. The balance sheet at best summarizes only the end-of-day closing position or book of an FI. Thus, intraday settlement risk is an additional form of OBS risk for FIs participating on private wholesale wire transfer system networks. The payments system in Canada is discussed in more detail in Chapter 17.

Affiliate Risk

affiliate risk
The risk imposed on a parent company or holding company due to the potential failure of another unit in the group.

holding company
A corporation that owns the shares (normally more than 25 percent) of other corporations.

parent-subsidiary corporate structure
A corporate structure where the subsidiaries are owned and controlled by the parent and subject to the same level of regulatory oversight.

Affiliate risk is the risk imposed on the parent company group or holding company group due to the potential failure of another unit in the group. A **holding company** is a corporation that owns the shares (normally more than 25 percent) of other corporations. Under the Bank Act, federally regulated FIs are permitted to operate with a **parent-subsidiary company structure**, where each member of the group is subject to the same regulatory oversight as the parent, or in a holding company structure. Most developed countries allow bank holding company structures. For example, Citigroup is a one-bank U.S. holding company (OBHC) that owns all the shares of Citibank. Citigroup engages in certain permitted nonbank activities such as data processing through separately capitalized affiliates or companies that it owns. Similarly, a number of other holding companies are multibank holding companies (MBHCs) that own shares in a number of different banks. JPMorgan Chase is an MBHC that holds shares in banks throughout the United States. The organizational structures of these two types of holding companies are presented in Figure 16–4.

Legally, in the context of OBHCs, the bank and the nonbank affiliate are separate companies, as are Bank 1 and Bank 2 in the context of MBHCs. Thus, in Figure 16–4, the failure of the nonbank affiliate and Bank 2 should have no effect on the financial resources of the bank in the OBHC or Bank 1 in the MBHC. In reality, the failure of an affiliated firm or bank imposes affiliate risk on another bank in a holding company structure. Both creditors and regulators may look to the holding company (that is, the corporation that owns the shares of the affiliate) for support for a failed affiliate, particularly if they have similar names such as Town Bank and Town Bank Credit Card Company.

special-purpose entities (SPEs)
Separate companies or trusts created for the sale of specific assets.

At the present time, affiliate risk for FIs operating in Canada arises primarily from the use of **special-purpose entities** (SPEs, also called variable-interest entities or VIEs) that are created as vehicles for the securitization of assets such as residential mortgage loans, credit card receivables, and commercial mortgage loans. The risk arises when the assets have been removed from the bank's balance sheet but the bank retains an interest in the securitized assets. The mechanisms of securitization will be discussed in greater detail in Chapter 26.

FIGURE 16–4
OBHC and MBHC Structures

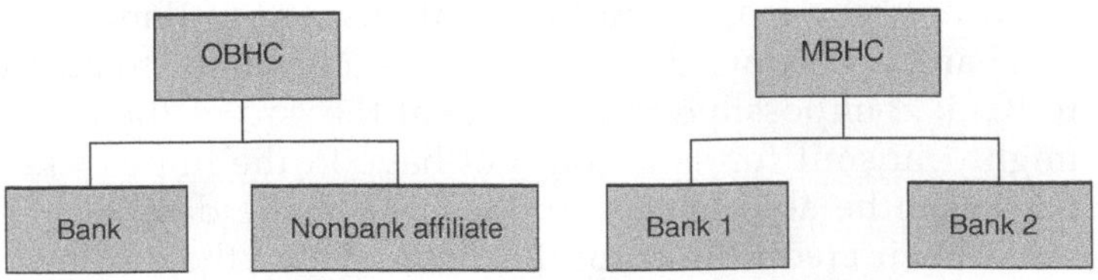

THE ROLE OF OFF-BALANCE-SHEET ACTIVITIES IN REDUCING RISK

LO3

This chapter has emphasized that OBS activities may add to the riskiness of an FI's activities. Indeed, most contingent assets and liabilities have various characteristics that may accentuate an FI's default and/or interest rate risk exposures. Even so, FIs use some OBS instruments—especially forwards, futures, options, and swaps—to reduce or manage their interest rate risk, FX risk, and credit risk exposures in a manner superior to what would exist in their absence. When used to hedge on-balance-sheet interest rate, FX, and credit risks, these instruments can actually work to reduce FIs' overall insolvency risk. Although we do not fully describe the role of these instruments as hedging vehicles in reducing an FI's insolvency exposure until Chapters 22 through 24, you can now recognize the inherent danger in the overregulation of OBS activities and instruments. For example, the risk that a counterparty might default on a forward FX contract is very small. It is probably much lower than the insolvency risk an FI faces if it does not use forward contracts to hedge its FX assets against undesirable fluctuations in exchange rates. (See Chapters 13 and 22 for some examples of this.)

Despite the risk-reducing attributes of OBS derivative securities held by FIs, the expanded use of derivatives has caused many regulators to focus on the risk-increasing attributes of these securities and the possible detrimental effect the risk may have on global financial markets. The result has been an increase in the amount of regulation proposed for these activities. In the wake of the market meltdown in 2008, for example, there have been proposals, notably by the Financial Stability Board (FSB), to move CDSs and other derivatives to organized exchanges or centralized clearing houses so that their risk to the global financial system is more transparent and regulated. Partially as a result of these concerns, the regulatory costs of hedging have risen (e.g., through the imposition of special capital requirements or restrictions on the use of such instruments [see Chapter 20]). As a result, FIs may have a tendency to underhedge, thereby increasing, rather than decreasing, their insolvency risk.

www.financialstabilityboard.org

Despite the risk, by allowing risk-averse managers to hedge risk, derivatives may induce the managers to follow more value-maximizing investment strategies. That is, derivatives may allow manager–stockholder agency conflicts over the level of risk-taking to be reduced. In addition, fees from OBS activities provide a key source of noninterest income for many FIs, especially the largest and most creditworthy ones. The importance of noninterest income for large banks is shown in Table 17–1 in Chapter 17. Thus, if managed carefully, increased OBS earnings can potentially compensate for increased OBS risk exposure and actually reduce the probability of insolvency for some FIs.

CONCEPT QUESTIONS

1. **Explain how OBS instruments can reduce the insolvency risk of FIs.**
2. **Other than hedging and speculation, what reasons do FIs have for engaging in OBS activities?**

Questions and Problems

1. Classify the following items as (1) on-balance-sheet assets, (2) on-balance-sheet liabilities, (3) OBS assets, (4) OBS liabilities, or (5) capital accounts.
   a. Loan commitments
   b. Allowance for loan losses
   c. LC
   d. Bankers' acceptance
   e. Rediscounted bankers' acceptance
   f. Loan sales without recourse
   g. Loan sales with recourse
   h. Forward contracts to purchase
   i. Forward contracts to sell
   j. Swaps
   k. Loan participations
   l. Securities borrowed
   m. Securities lent
   n. Loss-adjustment expense account (P&C insurers)
2. How does one distinguish between an OBS asset and an OBS liability?
3. Contingent Bank has the following balance sheet in market value terms ($ millions):

Assets		Liabilities	
Cash	$ 20	Deposits	$ 220
Mortgages	220	Equity	20
Total assets	$ 240	Total liabilities and equity	$ 240

   In addition, the bank has contingent assets with $100 million market value and contingent liabilities with $80 million market value. What is the true stockholder net worth? What does the term *contingent* mean?
4. Why are contingent assets and liabilities like options? What is meant by the delta of an option? What is meant by the term *notional value*?
5. An FI has purchased options on bonds with a notional value of $500 million and has sold options on bonds with a notional value of $400 million. The purchased options have a delta of 0.25, and the sold options have a delta of 0.30. What are (a) the contingent asset value of this position, (b) the contingent liability value of this position, and (c) the contingent market value of net worth?
6. What factors explain the growth of OBS activities in the 1980s through the early 2000s among FIs?
7. What are the characteristics of a loan commitment that an FI may make to a customer? In what manner and to whom is the commitment an option? What are the various possible pieces of the option premium? When does the option or commitment become an on-balance-sheet item for the FI and the borrower?
8. A FI makes a loan commitment of $2.5 million with an up-front fee of 50 bp and a back-end fee of 25 bp on the unused portion of the loan. The takedown on the loan is 50 percent.
   a. What total fees does the FI earn when the loan commitment is negotiated?
   b. What are the total fees earned by the FI at the end of the year, that is, in future value terms? Assume the cost of capital for the FI is 6 percent.
9. Use the following information on a one-year loan commitment to calculate the return on the loan commitment:

   BR = FI's base interest on the loans = 8%
   m = Risk premium on loan commitment = 2.5%
   f_1 = Up-front fee on the whole commitment = 25 bp
   f_2 = Back-end fee on the unused commitment = 50 bp
   td = Expected (average) takedown rate on the loan commitment = 70%

10. An FI has issued a one-year loan commitment of $2 million for an up-front fee of 25 bp. The back-end fee on the unused portion of the commitment is 10 bp. The FI's base rate on loans is 7.5 percent and loans to this customer carry a risk premium of 2.5 percent. The customer is expected to draw down 80 percent of the commitment at the beginning of the year.
   a. What is the expected return on the loan without taking future values into consideration?
   b. What is the expected return using future values? That is, the net fee and interest income are evaluated at the end of the year when the loan is due.
11. Suburb Bank has issued a one-year loan commitment of $10,000,000 for an up-front fee of 50 bp. The back-end fee on the unused portion of the commitment is 20 bp. The bank's base rate on loans is 7 percent, and loans to this customer carry a risk premium of 2 percent. The customer is expected to draw down 60 percent of the commitment.
   a. What is the expected return on this loan?
   b. What is the expected return per annum on the loan if the drawdown on the commitment does not occur until the end of six months?
12. How is an FI exposed to interest rate risk when it makes loan commitments? In what way can an FI control for this risk? How does basis risk affect the implementation of the control for interest rate risk?

13. How is an FI exposed to credit risk when it makes loan commitments? How is credit risk related to interest rate risk? What control measure is available to an FI for the purpose of protecting against credit risk? What is the realistic opportunity to implement this control feature?
14. How is an FI exposed to takedown risk and aggregate funding risk? How are these two contingent risks related?
15. Do the contingent risks of interest rate, takedown, credit, and aggregate funding tend to increase the insolvency risk of an FI? Why or why not?
16. What is an LC? How is an LC like an insurance contract?
17. A German bank issues a three-month LC on behalf of its customer in Germany, who is planning to import \$100,000 worth of goods from Canada. It charges an up-front fee of 100 bp.
    a. What up-front fee does the bank earn?
    b. If the exporter decides to discount this LC after it has been accepted by the German bank, how much will the exporter receive, assuming that the interest rate is 5 percent and that 90 days remain before maturity? (*Hint:* To discount a security, use the time value of money formula: $PV = FV[1 - \text{interest rate} \times (\text{days to maturity}/365)]$.)
    c. What risk does the German bank incur by issuing this LC?
18. How do SLCs differ from commercial LCs? With what other types of FI products do SLCs compete? What types of FIs can issue SLCs?
19. A corporation is planning to issue \$1,000,000 of 270-day CP for an effective annual yield of 5 percent. The corporation expects to save 30 bp on the interest rate by using either an SLC or a loan commitment as collateral for the issue.
    a. What are the net savings to the corporation if a bank agrees to provide a 270-day SLC for an up-front fee of 20 bp (of the face value of the loan commitment) to back the CP issue?
    b. What are the net savings to the corporation if a bank agrees to provide a 270-day loan commitment to back the issue? The bank will charge 10 bp for an up-front fee and 10 bp for a back-end fee for any unused portion of the loan. Assume the loan is not needed, and that the fees are on the face value of the loan commitment.
    c. Should the corporation be indifferent to the two alternative collateral methods at the time the CP is issued?
20. Explain how the use of derivative contracts such as forwards, futures, swaps, and options creates contingent credit risk for an FI. Why do OTC contracts carry more contingent credit risk than do exchange-traded contracts? How is the default risk of OTC contracts related to the time to maturity and the price and rate volatilities of the underlying assets?
21. What is meant by WI trading? Explain how forward purchases of WI government T-bills can expose FIs to contingent interest rate risk.
22. Distinguish between loan sales with and without recourse. Why would banks want to sell loans with recourse? Explain how loan sales can leave banks exposed to contingent interest rate risks.
23. The manager of Shakey Bank sends a \$2 million funds transfer payment message via CHIPS to the Trust Bank at 10 AM. Trust Bank sends a \$2 million funds transfer message via CHIPS to Hope Bank later that same day. What type of risk is inherent in this transaction? How might the risk become reality?
24. Explain how settlement risk may be incurred in the interbank payment mechanism and how it is another form of OBS risk. How does the LVTS eliminate this risk for some payments in Canada?
25. What is the difference between a parent–subsidiary structure and a holding company structure? Discuss how the failure of an affiliate might affect the holding company even if the affiliate were structured separately.
26. Defend the statement that although OBS activities expose FIs to several forms of risk, they can also alleviate the risks of FIs.

Appendix **16A** A Letter of Credit Transaction

View Appendix 16A on Connect.

CHAPTER 17

TECHNOLOGY AND OTHER OPERATIONAL RISKS

After studying this chapter you should be able to:

LO1 Discuss the sources of operational risk for an FI.

LO2 Discuss the impact of technological innovation on an FI's profitability.

LO3 Discuss the effects of technology on the wholesale and retail production of an FI.

LO4 Discuss the effect of technology on the revenues and costs of an FI.

LO5 Define economies of scale and economies of scope related to technology expenditures by FIs.

LO6 Discuss the impact of technology on the evolution of the payments system.

LO7 Discuss other operational risks for FIs.

LO8 Discuss the difference between the basic indicator approach and the advanced measurement approach.

INTRODUCTION

Chapters 7 through 16 concentrated on the financial risks that arise as FIs perform their asset-transformation and/or brokerage functions on or off the balance sheet. However, financial risk is only one part of a modern FI's risk profile. As with regular corporations, FIs have a real or production side to their operations that results in additional costs and revenues. This chapter focuses (1) on factors that impact the operational returns and risks of FIs (with an emphasis on technology) and (2) on the importance of optimal management and control of labour, capital, and other input sources and their costs. In particular, well-managed FIs can use operational cost savings to increase profits and thus reduce the probability of insolvency.

Central to FIs' decision-making processes is the cost of inputs, or factors used to produce services both on and off the balance sheet. Two important factors are labour (tellers, credit officers) and capital (buildings, machinery, furniture). Crucial to the efficient management and combination of these inputs to result in financial outputs at the lowest cost is technology. Technological innovation has been a major concern of FIs in recent years. Since the 1980s, banks, insurance companies, and other FIs have sought to improve operational efficiency with major investments in internal and external communications, computers, and an expanded technological infrastructure. Internet and mobile communications technologies are having a profound effect on financial services. These technologies are more than just new distribution channels—they are a completely different way of providing financial services. A global financial services firm such as the U.S.-based bank Citigroup has operations in more than 100 countries connected in real time by a proprietary satellite system. Operational risk is partly related to technology risk and can arise when existing technology malfunctions or back-office support systems break down. Further, back-office support systems combine labour and technology to provide clearance, settlement, and other services to back FIs' underlying on- and off-balance-sheet transactions.

According to Hitachi Data Systems, back-office system failures usually occur four times per year in the average firm. Recovery time from system failures averages 12 hours. The 2001 terrorist attacks on the World Trade Center and the Pentagon in the United States created back-office system failures of an unforeseen magnitude. For example, over a week after the attacks, Bank of New York was still having trouble with some crucial communications links. The risks of technological malfunctions for FIs were again highlighted in June 2004, when the Royal Bank of Canada (RBC) experienced a programming error that affected its main and backup computer systems. The problem, which lasted for a week, resulted in customers overdrawing their accounts when their paycheques were not deposited on time. This operational risk cost the bank the trust of their clients (**reputational risk**) and increased their noninterest expense by $11 million in 2004.

reputational risk
The potential for an FI's actions to cause a loss of trust of clients, the market, or regulators.

More recently, on May 6, 2010, FIs saw huge swings in the market values of their investment portfolios as financial markets experienced a brief but severe drop in prices, falling 998 points (more than 5 percent) in a matter of minutes, only to recover a short time later. The "flash crash" was attributed to trading by a little-known mutual fund—Asset Strategy Fund—located in Kansas City. A fund trader triggered the fall with the sale of US$4.1 billion of futures contracts linked to the S&P 500 Index. The trader used a computer algorithm that tied the sale to the market's overall volume. Trading volume soared on May 6, and the sell order was executed. While similar trades had taken several hours to execute, this trade was executed in 20 minutes. The initial trade triggered a pyramid effect from FIs' computerized trading programs, which are designed to sell when the market moves lower.

On a smaller, but more typical, scale, in August 2012 a computer malfunction caused by just one junior technician in India at the Royal Bank of Scotland (RBS) left 17 million customers unable to access their accounts. The inexperienced technician accidentally wiped out account information during a routine software upgrade. Deleted information had to be painstakingly rekeyed into the bank's computer system. The error created a backlog of more than 100 million transactions that were not paid in or out of customer accounts as they should have been. RBS reimbursed affected customers for the cost of any fines or late payment fees incurred from delays. It was estimated that the cost to RBS of dealing with the technology failure was likely between US$75 million and US$150 million. Also in August 2012, a software glitch at Knight Capital Group Inc. almost forced the company to close. Knight was holding about $7 billion of stocks at one point as a result of errant trades made when a computer software program failed. Knight's traders worked frantically to sell shares while trying to minimize losses due to the software problem. By the end of the day the position was down to US$4.6 billion. However, the US$4.6 billion position would have prevented Knight from opening for business the next day since the brokerage firm would have lacked the capital required by regulators to offset risks from holding the stocks. Knight avoided closure by agreeing to sell the portfolio to Goldman Sachs Group Inc. However, Knight ended up with a US$440 million loss.

As should already be apparent, technology and operational risks are closely related and in recent years have caused great concern to FI managers and regulators alike. The Bank for International Settlements (BIS), the principal organization of central banks in the major economies of the world, has defined operational risk (inclusive of technological risk) as "the risk of losses resulting from inadequate or failed internal processes, people, and systems or from external events."[1] A number of FIs add reputational risk and strategic risk (e.g., due to a failed merger) as part of a broader definition of **operational risk**. So significant has operational risk become that since the adoption of Basel II in 2008, Canadian banks have calculated a capital cushion against losses from this risk. We discuss this briefly in this chapter and in more detail in Chapter 20.

bis.org

operational risk
The potential for losses from failed systems, personnel, or external events.

WHAT ARE THE SOURCES OF OPERATIONAL RISK?

LO1

Controlling and reducing operational risks improves the operational efficiency of the FI. As seen in the following section, improvements in operational efficiency lead to increases in net income, return on assets (ROA), and other quantitative measures of FI performance. However, as we see throughout the chapter, operational risk is much less tangible and is often hard to quantify. There are at least five sources of operational risk:

1. Technology (e.g., technological failure and deteriorating systems)
2. Employees (e.g., human error and internal fraud)
3. Customer relationships (e.g., contractual disputes)
4. Capital assets (e.g., destruction by fire or other catastrophes)
5. External (e.g., external fraud)

Items 1 through 4 are internally controllable for an FI, while item 5 is an external, event-type risk that is relatively uncontrollable for an FI. A good example of internal operational risk related to employees (item 2 above) involves the US$7.2 billion in trading losses incurred by Société Générale's Jérôme Kerviel in February 2008. Mr. Kerviel started using futures on the European stock indexes to place huge bets that European markets would continue to rise. At the end of 2007 the trades were profitable. But at the beginning of 2008 the European markets turned against him, falling sharply and amounting to the largest market risk–related loss ever. Kerviel was able to circumvent any controls the bank had because he had worked in the back office and knew how trades were processed. (Note that this example involves market risk and OBS risk as well.)

A more recent example of internal operational risk is Barclays PLC, which admitted to, on numerous occasions over a four-year period between 2005 and 2009, manipulating and making false reports concerning the LIBOR to benefit its derivatives trading positions. Barclays made false LIBOR reports at the direction of members of senior management to protect its reputation during the global financial crisis. In addition, attempts to manipulate LIBOR included Barclays' traders asking other banks to assist in manipulating the global benchmark interest rate. As a result of the actions, Barclays was ordered to pay US$455 million in fines, cease

[1] See Basel Committee on Bank Supervision, *Overview of the New Basel Capital Accord*, Bank for International Settlements, April 2003, p. 120.

and desist from further violations as charged, and take specified steps to ensure the integrity and reliability of its LIBOR submissions. Further, senior executives and traders involved with the manipulation resigned or were suspended and some face criminal charges.

In 2013, RBC faced a different type of operational risk when it was revealed that it had been outsourcing its information technology (IT) functions to iGate, an Indian technology company. RBC's Canadian employees were made redundant but required to train their replacements brought in from India. The situation was a public relations nightmare for RBC, causing many customers to switch their accounts to other FIs and the Canadian government to investigate the use of short-term visas for foreign workers.

TECHNOLOGICAL INNOVATION AND PROFITABILITY

LO2

technology
Computers, audio and visual communication systems, and other information systems that can be applied to an FI's production of services.

Increasingly important to the profitability and riskiness of modern FIs has been item 1 in the list of sources of operational risk: technology. Broadly defined, **technology** includes computers, visual and audio communication systems, and other IT. The Canadian Bankers Association (CBA) reports that, between 2002 and 2012, the six largest Canadian banks spent $60.4 billion, an average of $5.5 billion per year, on technology, such as computer hardware and software, capital leases related to computer equipment, data and voice communication equipment, and development expenses related to these items.[2]

An efficient technological base for an FI can result in:

cba.ca

1. Lower costs, by combining labour and capital in a more efficient mix.
2. Increased revenues, by allowing a wider array of financial services to be produced or innovated and sold to customers.

The importance of an FI's operating costs and the efficient use of technology affecting these costs is clearly demonstrated by this simplified profit function:

$$\text{Earnings or profit before taxes} = (\text{Interest income} - \text{Interest expense})$$
$$- (\text{Charge for Impairment}) + (\text{Other income} - \text{Noninterest expense})$$

osfi-bsif.gc.ca

Table 17–1 breaks down the profit data for Canadian banks reporting to the Office of the Superintendent of Financial Services (OSFI) over the 1996–2012 period into the different components impacting profits. For example, at the end of quarter four of 2012, interest income of $99,382 million and interest expense of $37,353 million produced net interest income of $62,029 million. However, the banks also had total noninterest income of $50,684 million (including service charges on retail and commercial deposits of $5,524 million) and noninterest expenses of $66,571 million (including salaries, pensions, and employee benefits of $35,751 million and premises and equipment expenses of $10,916 million). Thus, banks' net noninterest income was −$15,887 million ($50,684 − $66,571). After

[2] A 2011 survey by CEB Tower Group found that more than half of banking executives expected technology investment over the next two years to increase by more than 6 percent, with 15 percent expecting greater than 20 percent increases. Only 6 percent expected IT investment to decline. The survey found that for commercial banking in particular, the increase in technology spending was driven as much by the goal to reduce the long-term operating costs and the costs of maintaining outdated and duplicative systems as it was to meet regulatory requirements and client demands for enhanced solutions.

TABLE 17–1 Earnings and Other Data for Domestic Banks Reporting to OSFI ($ millions)*

Financial Data	1996	2002	2004	2006	2008	2010	2012**
Interest income	63,383	69,592	65,141	95,307	113,542	83,505	99,382
Interest expense	−40,875	−36,091	−31,394	−61,537	−70,271	32,065	−37,353
Net interest income	22,508	33,501	33,747	33,770	43,272	51,439	62,029
Charge for impairment	−2,139	−9,719	−1,547	−2,538	−7,131	−8,363	−7,776
Deposit service charges	2,090	3,402	3,584	4,045	4,531	5,034	5,524
Credit and debit card fees	1,432	2,212	2,371	2,843	3,522	3,625	5,622
Loan fees	1,056	1,775	1,522	1,474	1,648	2,040	2,538
Mutual fund and underwriting fees	3,858	9,790	10,789	11,559	11,609	13,273	14,453
Trading account income and gains	1,029	3,259	4,438	7,664	−8,783	4,496	5,472
All other	3,836	10,842	11,621	15,255	17,358	19,956	17,075
Total noninterest income	13,301	31,280	34,325	42,840	29,884	45,485	50,684
Salaries, pensions, and benefits	−12,526	−23,826	−24,790	−26,645	−28,054	31,248	−35,751
Premises and equipment	−4,424	−7,907	−7,989	−8,134	−9,416	−9,196	−10,916
All other	−5,874	−12,693	−12,865	−12,522	−13,807	−17,367	−19,904
Noninterest expenses	−22,284	−44,427	−45,644	−47,301	−51,306	−57,811	−66,571
Income taxes	−4,080	−2,391	−5,631	−5,679	−1,142	−7,966	−7,263
Noncontrolling interests in subsidiaries	124	−508	−593	−488	−218	−501	−637
Extraordinary items	0	8	2	107	290	−235	–
Net income	6,640	7,745	14,659	20,710	13,649	22,519	30,540
Total assets ($ billions)	1,014.6	1,688.5	1,816.8	2,265.8	2,988.8	3,051.3	3,721.3
Return on assets (%)	0.65%	0.46%	0.81%	0.91%	0.46%	0.74%	0.82%

* Year to date as of the end of Quarter 4 of the relevant year.

**Data prepared using International Financial Reporting Standards (IFRS). All other years prepared using Canadian Generally Accepted Accounting Principles (GAAP).

Source: Office of the Superintendent of Financial Services, osfi-bsif.gc.ca.

considering charges for impaired loans of $7,776 million, noncontrolling interest in subsidiaries ($637 million), and taxes ($7,263 million), net income was $30,540 million. Underscoring the importance of operating costs is the fact that noninterest expenses amounted to 178 percent of interest expenses ($66,571 ÷ $37,353), reflecting the low interest paid on deposits versus the costs for salaries and premises, and were 218 percent of net income ($66,571 ÷ $30,540) for 2012.

net interest margin
Net interest income as a percentage of average interest-earning assets.

Technology is important because well-chosen technological investments have the potential to increase both the FI's **net interest margin**, defined as net interest income as a percentage of average interest-earning assets, and other net income. Therefore, technology can directly improve profitability, as the following examples show:

1. *Interest income* can increase if the FI sells a broader array of financial services as a result of technological developments. These may include cross-selling financial products by having the computer identify customers and then having the FI telemarket financial services products directly and electronically over the Internet and mobile devices. Additionally, the promise of additional revenue from investment in technology encourages an increase in the rate of innovation of new products and supports improvements in service quality and convenience. Many FIs use high-tech efforts to determine how they can reach more customers

with more products. As marketing lines are identified and defined, new product ideas emerge that further the usefulness of FI products to customers.

2. *Interest expense* can be reduced if access to markets for liabilities is directly dependent on the FI's technological capability. For example, the wire transfer systems linking domestic and international interbank lending markets are based on interlocking computer network systems. Moreover, an FI's ability to originate and sell commercial paper (CP) is increasingly computer-driven. Thus, failure to invest in the appropriate technology may lock an FI out of a lower-cost funding market.
3. *Other income* increases when fees for FI services, especially those from OBS activities, are linked to the quality of the FI's technology. For example, letters of credit (LCs) are now commonly originated electronically by customers; swaps, caps, options, and other complex derivatives are usually traded, tracked, and valued using high-powered computers and algorithms. FIs could not offer innovative derivative products to customers without investments in suitable IT. Further, new technology has resulted in an evolution of the payment systems (see below), which has increased the amount of fee income (noninterest income) as a percentage of total operating income (interest income plus noninterest income) for FIs. For example, referring again to Table 17–1, we see that noninterest income as a percentage of total income was 17 percent in 1996 and increased to 34 percent in 2012. Noninterest income declined significantly in 2008 from losses in the trading account as a result of the financial crisis.
4. *Noninterest expenses* can be reduced if the collection and storage of customer information as well as the processing and settlement of numerous financial products are computer based rather than paper based. This is particularly true of security-related back-office activities.

CONCEPT QUESTIONS

1. **What are some of the advantages of an efficient technological base for an FI? How can it be used to directly improve profitability?**
2. **Looking at Table 17–1, determine if noninterest expenses and noninterest income increased or decreased as a percentage of total bank costs over the 1996–2012 period.**

TECHNOLOGY AND FINANCIAL SERVICES

LO3

The previous discussion established that technology has the potential to directly affect an FI's profit-producing areas. The following discussion focuses on some specific technology-based products found in retail and wholesale operations of FIs. Note that this is far from a complete list.

Wholesale Financial Services

Probably the most important area in which technology has had an impact on wholesale or corporate customer services is an FI's ability to provide cash management or working capital services. Cash management services include collecting, disbursing, and transferring funds—on a local, regional, national, or international basis—and providing information about the location and status of those funds. Cash management service needs have largely resulted from (1) corporate recognition that excess cash balances result in a significant opportunity cost due to lost or forgone interest and (2) corporate need to know cash or working capital position on a real-time basis. More recently, FIs have used their own technological investments to help corporate customers improve the efficiency with which they incorporate technology into their business. Among the services FIs provide to improve the efficiency with which corporate clients manage their financial positions are the following:

1. *Controlled disbursement accounts.* An account feature that establishes in the morning almost all payments to be made by the customer in a given day. The FI informs the corporate client of the total funds it needs to meet disbursements, and the client wire-transfers the amount needed. These chequing accounts are debited early each day so that corporations can obtain an early insight into their net cash positions.
2. *Account reconciliation.* A chequing feature that records which of the firm's cheques have been paid by the FI.
3. *Wholesale and electronic lockbox.* A centralized or online collection service for corporate payments to reduce the delay in cheque clearing, or the **float**. In a typical lockbox arrangement, a local FI sets up a lockbox at the post office for a corporate client located outside the area. Local customers mail payments to the lockbox rather than to the out-of-town corporate headquarters. The FI collects these cheques several times per day and deposits them directly into the customer's account. Details of the transaction are wired to the corporate client. With electronic lockboxes, the FI receives online payments for public utilities and similar corporate clients.

float
The interval between the deposit of a cheque and when funds become available for depositor use, that is, the time it takes a cheque to clear at a bank.

4. *Funds concentration.* A system that redirects funds from accounts in a large number of FIs or branches to a few centralized accounts at one FI.
5. *Electronic funds transfer.* Overnight payments; automated payment of payrolls or dividends; and automated transmission of payment messages by SWIFT, an international electronic message service owned and operated by global FIs that instructs FIs to make specific payments.
6. *Cheque deposit services.* Encoding, endorsing, microfilming, and handling of customers' cheques.
7. *Electronic initiation of letters of credit.* A system that allows customers in a network to access FI computers to initiate letters of credit.
8. *Treasury management software.* Software that allows efficient management of multiple currency and security portfolios for trading and investment purposes.
9. *Electronic data interchange.* The exchange of structured information from one computer application to another by electronic means and with a minimum of human intervention. An electronic data exchange allows businesses to transfer and transact invoices, purchase orders, and shipping notices automatically, using FIs as clearinghouses.
10. *Electronic billing.* Presentment and collection services for companies that send out substantial volumes of recurring bills. FIs combine the email capability of the Internet to send out bills with their ability to process payments electronically through the interbank payment networks.
11. *Verification of identities.* The use of encryption technology by FIs to certify the identities of their own account holders and serve as the intermediary through which their business customers can verify the identities of account holders at other FIs.

12. *Assistance to small businesses entering into e-commerce.* Help for smaller firms in setting up the infrastructure—interactive website and payment capabilities—for engaging in e-commerce.
13. *Online customer-facing technologies.* Technologies that allow an FI's business clients to reach their customers more individually and efficiently across online channels, e.g., give business customers the technology to scan cheque and deposit images online, or the ability to provide online and mobile applications.
14. *Cloud computing.* Technologies that allow business clients to log into an FI-provided web-based service that hosts all software the business client needs, from email to word processing to complex data analysis programs.[3]
15. *Facilitation of business-to-business e-commerce.* A service offered by the largest FIs to automate the entire information flow associated with the procurement and distribution of goods and services among businesses.

Retail Financial Services

Retail customers have demanded efficiency and flexibility in their financial transactions. Using only cheques or holding cash is often more expensive and time-consuming than using retail-oriented electronic payments technology and, increasingly, the Internet and mobile devices. Further, securities trading has moved toward electronic platforms not tied to any specific location. Electronic trading networks have lowered the costs of trading and allowed for better price determination. For example, customers of a major bank can obtain information on their account balances, pay their bills online, and trade stocks in their brokerage accounts and their RRSP accounts from one website. An FI may charge the retail customer for a transaction conducted through a branch visit or phone call but the same transaction conducted online or through an ATM may be free. Some of the most important retail payment product innovations include:

credit card transaction
An extension of credit to a cardholder and a transfer of payment by the card issuer (e.g., bank, credit union) to the merchant.

debit card transaction
A withdrawal (debit) directly from a customer's account with an FI.

1. *Automated banking machines (ABMs)* (also called automated teller machines (ATMs) in the United States and Australia). Allow customers 24-hour access to their deposit accounts. Customers can pay bills as well as withdraw cash from these machines. In addition, if the FI's ABMs are part of a bank network (such as CIRRUS), retail depositors can gain direct nationwide—and in many cases international—access to their deposit accounts by using the ABMs of other banks in the network to draw on their accounts.[4]
2. *Point-of-sale (POS) debit cards.* Allow customers who choose not to use cash, cheques, or credit cards for purchases to buy merchandise using debit card/POS terminals. The merchant avoids the cheque float and any delay in payment associated with credit card receivables since the FI offers the debit card/POS service immediately and transfers funds directly from the customer's deposit account into the merchant's deposit account at the time of card use. Unlike cheque or **credit card transactions, debit card transactions** result in an

[3] Cloud computing differs from traditional hosting in that it is sold on demand rather than prearranged, it is variable in that the business client uses as little or as much of a service as it needs at any given time, the service is fully managed by the FI, and the business client needs only computer and Internet access to access the cloud.

[4] Using another FI's ABM usually results in an access fee to the customer.

immediate transfer of funds from the customers' account to the merchant's account.[5] Moreover, the customer never runs up a debit to the card issuer, as is common with a credit card.

3. *Preauthorized debits/credits.* Include direct deposits of payroll cheques into bank accounts as well as direct payments of mortgage and utility bills.
4. *Smart cards (store-value cards).* Allow the customer to store and spend money for various transactions using a card that has a chip storage device, usually in the form of a strip. These have become increasingly popular at universities.[6]
5. *Online banking.* Allows customers to conduct retail banking and investment services offered via the Internet. In some cases this involves building a new Internet-only "bank," such as ING Direct, a virtual bank that was purchased by the Bank of Nova Scotia in 2012.

ingdirect.ca

6. *Mobile banking.* Allows customers to acquire banking apps through Apple and Android marketplaces and/or by scanning promotional QR codes. Services provided over mobile devices include remote deposit capture and digital wallets in which bank customers can pay for items using smartphone apps.
7. *Tablet banking.* Similar to mobile banking, but allows customers access to bank services through the tablet format.
8. *FI social media sites.* Allow customers to comment, see promotional advertisements, or request services through the FI's social media site, e.g., Facebook.
9. *Integration of online, offline, and mobile channels.* Allows a customer to start a loan application online and later finish the application at a branch without having to start the process over.
10. *Financial planning services.* Allow customers to manage their finances and monitor spending through online, mobile, and tablet services.
11. *Instant "micro mobile loans."* Allow customers to apply for, get approval on, and receive disbursement of a loan via a mobile or tablet device.
12. *Loyalty programs.* Allow customers to receive benefits from retail, entertainment, travel, and vacation services through mobile and tablet devices.

Advanced Technology Requirements

The services mentioned above require FIs to continuously update and integrate their technology infrastructure. Some of the specific technological advances FIs must deal with include:

1. *Integration of online, mobile, and tablet technologies.* As revenue generators, FIs are welcoming the mobile and tablet channels for attracting and serving customers, while at the same time continuing to support the older technology of online banking. However, FIs have not fully integrated technologies used for the various ebanking methods. Advanced technology requires FIs to develop a single technology on which to run all of these ebanking channels. An interconnected

identity theft
The theft of electronic identification (debit or credit cards) to gain illegal access to customer accounts.

[5] In the case of bank-supplied credit cards, the merchant is normally compensated very quickly but not instantaneously by the credit card issuer (usually one or two days). The bank then holds an account receivable against the card user. However, even a short delay can represent an opportunity cost for the merchant.

[6] Associated with the increased use of electronic transfers is **identity theft**, the use of credit or debit cards illegally to access FIs' customers' accounts. The Bank Act limits credit card users to a maximum liability of $50 if their cards are used illegally, but debit cards are not covered by the same limits on illegal fund withdrawals or transfers. See the latest information on debit card liability at the Office of Consumer Affairs' (OCA) website at ic.gc.ca.

set of technologies will make mobile and tablet applications and online development easier for banks to manage and will lower the cost of their operation for FIs.

2. *Provision of integrated, multichannel business information*. To increase efficiency, lower operating costs, and satisfy regulations, FIs need advanced technologies that allow for enhanced methods of gathering and reporting data. Most FIs operate using multiple back-office systems that are not integrated. In fact, customer data across FIs are often managed and serviced by multiple business units within the FI or even by outsourcing data management. Advanced technology requires the integration of multiple sales channels and customer services into a single business process that allows for the sharing and collaborating of information across all organizational units within the FI. Data integration helps FIs obtain a more accurate picture of their customers, allowing them to break through data "silos" to look at all data on customers to get a more complete view of consumers' habits. Advanced technology in banking also provides FI employees organized and timely access to information they need to effectively and efficiently perform their jobs. While costly, this type of integrated and multichannel data organization increases revenues by targeting banking products and services to customers based on an analysis of their individual characteristics, needs, and activities. This process requires technology that provides data mining and analytical capabilities.
3. *Cloud computing*. Just as FIs provide cloud computing for their business customers, FIs use cloud computing to support their own business activities. Rather than run software applications on in-house computers with the staff to support them, they are run on a network of computers that constitute the cloud. Cloud computing systems allow for significant reductions in technology-related employee workloads and operating expenses; the FI needs only a computer that has interface software allowing access to the cloud, which can be as simple as a Web browser.
4. *Increased reliance on message centres to replace email communication*. FIs have virtually abandoned email for any customer communication containing sensitive or private information. Replacing email is the message centre. These message centres are dedicated web portals set up for secure communication between an FI and its customers. The increased incidence of email phishing scams targeting FI customers made it difficult for FI customers to differentiate between a legitimate email from their FI and a phishing email. Similarly, FI employees became the target of advanced attackers using phishing scams to compromise the FI. To avoid this security issue, FIs employ message centre technology to communicate with customers.
5. *Technology used for security issues*. The used of advanced technology brings with it increased potential for and more complex forms of fraud. Thus, FIs have an ever greater need for technology-based risk management systems. Such technology helps increase the efficiency and effectiveness of security monitoring efforts, using computers, rather than time- and labour-intensive manual processes, to detect theft, fraud, and other illegal activities. By electronically capturing and recording data across the FI, an automated technological approach to security issues can alert an FI to threats more quickly. Such a system can also track a trail of flagged activity to simplify the investigation process and reduce losses. The use of technology to identify security issues can also enable an FI to

assess risk more comprehensively, across the entire FI and in an integrated manner. Such a process promotes close operational synergy between the risk and finance functions of the FI.

A specific security issue arises as more FI customers conduct their banking on mobile and tablet devices. Mobile and tablet devices are more prone to security breaches since they are a relatively new technology. Further, mobile and tablet users do not always exercise the security precautions they would with their laptop computers. Thus, the increased use of these devices, particularly at wifi hotspots, has become the growing focus of hackers. FIs face an additional security threat as employees bring their own technology to work. FI employees who use tablet computers or other mobile devices for work purposes expose the FI to security breaches when they do not use the proper security precautions with the devices.

6. *Data backup and disaster recovery*. The extensive use of advanced technology by FIs creates a need for data backup systems used to save copies of all important data at least daily. By backing up its data, an FI can recover data virtually completely and quickly in the event of a disaster, data deletion, corruption, or fraud. Data backup systems allow an FI to upload to a remote server at least one copy of files and data, which is stored and accessed online and is safeguarded from anything that could compromise these files. The backed-up files are generally kept in a secret location far from the FI's branch or business locations. Thus, if a disaster happens in one part of the world, the FI has its data in a location that is unaffected. For large FIs, data backup storage requirements are substantial. Thus, organization of storage space and managing the backup process are complicated activities.

CONCEPT QUESTIONS

1. **Describe some of the wholesale financial services that have been improved by technology.**
2. **Describe some of the automated retail payment products available today. What advantages do these products offer the retail customer?**

THE EFFECT OF TECHNOLOGY ON REVENUES AND COSTS

LO4

The previous section presented an extensive list of current products or services being offered by FIs that are built around a strong technological base and, increasingly, the Internet. Technological advances allow an FI to offer such products to its customers and potentially to earn higher profits. The investment of resources in many of these products is risky, however, because product innovations may fail to attract sufficient business relative to the initial cash outlay and the future costs related to these investments once they are in place. In the terminology of finance, a number of technologically based product innovations may turn out to be *negative* net present value (NPV) projects because of uncertainties over revenues and costs and how quickly rivals will mimic or copy any innovation. Another factor is agency conflicts, in which managers undertake growth-oriented investments to increase an FI's size. Such investments may be inconsistent with stockholders' value-maximizing objectives. As a result, losses on technological innovations and new technology could weaken an FI because scarce capital resources are invested in value-decreasing products.

Standard capital budgeting techniques can be applied to technological innovations and new FI products. Let

I_0 = Initial capital outlay for developing an innovation or product at time 0
R_i = Expected net revenues or cash flows from product sales in future years i, $i = 1, \ldots, N$
d = FI's discount rate reflecting its risk-adjusted cost of capital

Thus, a negative NPV project would result if

$$I_0 > \frac{R_1}{(1+d)} + \cdots + \frac{R_N}{(1+d)^N}$$

Clearly, the profitability of any product innovation is negatively related to the size of the initial setup and development costs (I_0) and the FI's cost of capital (d), and positively related to the size of the stream of expected net cash flows (R_i) from selling the services.

This leads one to consider whether direct or indirect evidence is available that indicates whether technology investments to update the operational structure of FIs have increased revenues or decreased costs. Most of the direct or indirect evidence has concerned the effects of size on financial firms' operating costs, and it is the largest FIs that appear to be investing most in IT and other technological innovations.

We first discuss the evidence on the product revenue side and then discuss the evidence on the operating cost side. However, before looking at these revenue and cost aspects, we should stress that the success of technologically related innovation cannot be evaluated independently from regulation and regulatory changes. For example, while Canadians take their nationwide branch banking for granted, the introduction of full interstate banking in the United States in 1997, as well as the rapid consolidation in the U.S. financial services industry (e.g., as a result of mergers of large banks and the development of national branch systems), has created opportunities for Canadian FIs in the U.S. market. Product and geographic diversification, supported by technological advances, is discussed in more detail in Chapter 21.

Technology and Revenues

One potential benefit of technology is that it allows an FI to cross-market both new and existing products to customers. Such joint selling does not require the FI to produce all the services sold within the same branch or financial services outlet. For example, a bank may link up with an insurance company to jointly market each other's loan, credit card, and insurance products. This arrangement has proven popular in Germany, where some of the largest banks have developed sophisticated cross-marketing arrangements with large insurance companies. In the United States, Citicorp's merger with Travelers Group to create Citigroup was explicitly designed to cross-market banking, insurance, and securities products in over 100 countries. However, Citigroup management admitted after the completion of the merger that it could take 10 or more years to integrate computer systems to a sufficient degree to achieve this objective. Indeed, by 2005 Citigroup decided to sell its life insurance underwriting division to MetLife. Reasons cited for this divestiture included earnings on insurance underwriting being more seasonal and vulnerable to large disasters. Further, it was also difficult to sell this kind of insurance directly to customers since most industrial customers are accustomed to purchasing insurance through a broker. Citigroup still heavily sells all forms of insurance, but it no longer manufactures (i.e., underwrites) insurance.

Although there has been considerable cross-selling of retail banking and brokerage services, Canadian banks are not allowed to offer life insurance products through their branches. A merger of an insurance company and a bank requires the approval of the federal minister of finance. The bank–bank mergers and bank–insurance mergers could be addressed by the next review of the Bank Act. This issue is discussed in more detail in Chapter 21.

The rate of adoption of technology by consumers determines the profitability of the investment. For example, a survey conducted by the CBA in 2012 indicated that online banking continues to grow. Forty-seven percent of Canadians surveyed indicated that they conducted the majority of their banking online. The use of ABMs for deposits and bill payments decreased, as did cash withdrawals as retail customers increased their usage of debit cards for POS purchases. The CBA's 2012 statistics showed that 842 million transactions were carried out at bank-owned ABMs and 583.6 million transactions were conducted online at the six largest Canadian banks. However, we cannot ignore the issue of service quality and convenience. For example, while ABMs and Internet banking may potentially lower FI operating costs compared with employing full-service tellers, the inability of machines to address customers' concerns and questions flexibly may drive retail customers away and revenue losses may counteract any cost-savings effects. Customers still want to interact with a person for many transactions.

Technology and Costs

Traditionally, FIs have considered the major benefits of technological advances to be on the cost side rather than the revenue side. After a theoretical look at how technology favourably or unfavourably affects an FI's costs, we look at the direct and indirect evidence of technology-based cost savings for FIs. In general, technology may favourably affect an FI's cost structure by allowing it to exploit either economies of scale or economies of scope.

Economies of Scale

LO5

economy of scale
A drop in the average costs of production as the output of an FI increases.

As financial firms become larger, the potential scale and array of the technology in which they can invest generally expands. As noted above, the largest FIs make the largest expenditures on technology-related innovations. If improved technology lowers an FI's average costs of financial service production, larger FIs may have an **economy of scale** advantage over smaller financial firms. Economies of scale imply that the unit or average cost of producing FI services in aggregate (or some specific service such as deposits or loans) falls as the size of the FI expands. Thus, noninterest expenses per dollar of assets falls and ROA increases.

Figure 17–1 shows economies of scale for three different-sized FIs. The average cost of producing an FI's output of financial services is measured as

$$AC_i = \frac{TC_i}{S_i}$$

where

AC_i = Average costs of the *i*th FI
TC_i = Total costs of the *i*th FI
S_i = Size of the FI measured by on- and off-balance-sheet assets, deposits, or loans

FIGURE 17–1
Economies of Scale in FIs

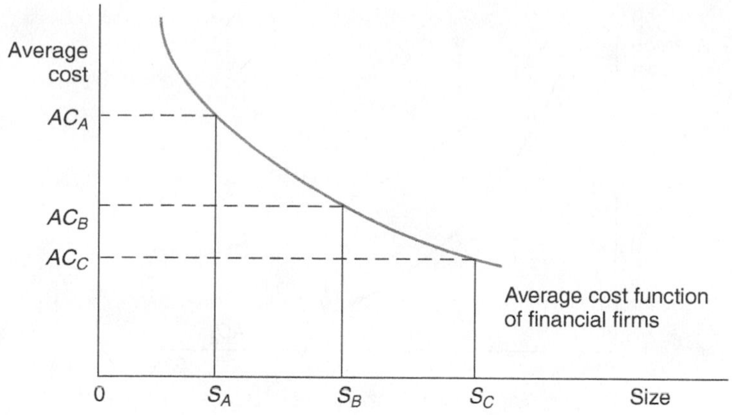

The largest FI in Figure 17–1 (of size S_C) has a lower average cost of producing financial services than do smaller firms S_B and S_A. This means that at any given price for financial service firm products, firm S_C can make a bigger profit than either S_B or S_A. Alternatively, firm S_C can undercut S_B and S_A in price and potentially gain a larger market share. For example, PNC Financial's US$3.62 billion acquisition of RBC's U.S. retail banking unit and credit card assets in 2012 was billed as a cost-saving acquisition. The combined company expected to realize US$230 million in annual cost savings (about 27 percent of RBC's noninterest expense) through operational and administrative efficiency improvements. Cost cutting was expected to come mainly from back-office positions in departments such as accounting, public relations, and data processing. In the framework of Figure 17–1, RBC, firm S_A, might be operating at AC_A and PNC Financial might be represented as firm S_B operating at AC_B. The consolidation of overlapping activities would lower the average costs for the combined (larger) bank S_C in Figure 17–1, operating at AC_C.

The long-run implication of economies of scale on the FI sector is that the larger and more cost-efficient FIs will drive out smaller FIs, leading to increased large-firm dominance and concentration in financial services production. Such an implication is reinforced if time-related operating or technological improvements increasingly benefit larger FIs more than smaller FIs. For example, satellite technology and supercomputers, in which enormous technological advances are being made, may be available to only the largest FIs. The effect of improving technology over time, which is biased toward larger projects, is to shift the *AC* curve downward over time but with a larger downward shift for large FIs (see Figure 17–2). In Figure 17–2, AC_1 is the hypothetical *AC* curve prior to cost-reducing technological innovations. AC_2 reflects the cost-lowering effects of technology on FIs of all sizes but with the greatest benefit accruing to those of the largest size.

As noted earlier, technological investments are risky. If their future revenues do not cover their costs of development, they reduce the value of the FI and its net worth to the FI's owners. On the cost side, large-scale investments may result in excess capacity problems and integration problems as well as cost overruns and cost control problems. Then small FIs with simple and easily managed computer systems and/or those leasing time on large FIs' computers (e.g., transaction processing for President's Choice Financial is done by CIBC) without bearing the fixed costs of installation and maintenance may have an average cost advantage.

FIGURE 17–2
Effects of Technological Improvement

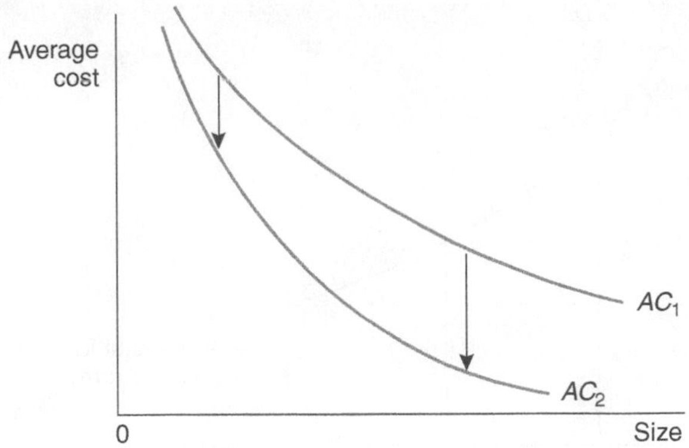

In this case, technological investments of large-sized FIs result in higher average costs of financial service production, causing the industry to operate under conditions of **diseconomies of scale**. Diseconomies of scale imply that small FIs are more cost-efficient than large FIs and that in a freely competitive environment for financial services, small FIs prosper.

diseconomies of scale
Increases in the average costs of production as the output of an FI increases.

Economies of Scope

Although technological investments may have positive or negative effects on FIs in general and these effects may well differ across FIs of different size, technology tends to be applied more in some product areas than in others. That is, FIs are multiproduct firms producing services involving different technological needs. Moreover, technological improvements or investments in one financial service area (such as lending) may have incidental and synergistic benefits in lowering the costs of producing financial services in other areas (such as securities underwriting and brokerage). Specifically, computerization allows the storage and joint use of important information on customers and their needs. The simple *economies of scale* concept ignores these interrelationships among products and the "jointness" in the costs of producing financial products. In particular, FIs' abilities to generate synergistic cost savings through joint use of inputs in producing multiple products is called *economies of scope* as opposed to economies of scale.

Technology may allow two FIs to jointly use their input resources, such as capital and labour, to produce a set of financial services at a lower cost than if financial service products were produced independently of one another. Specifically, let X_1 and X_2 be two financial products; each is produced by one firm as a specialized producer. That is, firm A produces only X_1 and no X_2, and firm B produces only X_2 and no X_1. The average cost functions (AC) of these firms are

$$AC_A[X_1, 0] \quad \text{and} \quad AC_B[0, X_2]$$

Economies of scope exist if these firms merge and jointly produce X_1 and X_2, resulting in

$$AC_{A+B}[X_1, X_2] < AC_A[X_1, 0] + AC_B[0, X_2]$$

That is, the cost of joint production via cost synergies is less than the cost of separate and independent production of these services.

economies of scope
The ability of FIs to generate synergistic cost savings through joint use of inputs in producing multiple products.

EXAMPLE 17-1

Calculation of Average Cost

Let TC_B be a bank's total cost of producing lending services to a corporate client. Suppose that the total operating costs of producing these services is \$50,000 for a loan volume (L_B) of \$10 million. Such costs include information collection and monitoring as well as account maintenance and processing. Thus, the average cost (AC_B) of loan production for the bank is

$$AC_B = \frac{TC_B}{L_B} = \frac{\$50{,}000}{\$10{,}000{,}000} = 0.005 = 0.5\%$$

At the same time, a specialized investment bank is selling CP for the same corporate customer. The investment bank's total cost (TC_S) of running the CP operation is \$10,000 for a \$1 million issue (P_S). These costs include the cost of underwriting the issue as well as placing the issue with outside buyers. Thus,

$$AC_S = \frac{TC_S}{P_S} = \frac{\$10{,}000}{\$1{,}000{,}000} = 0.01 = 1\%$$

Consequently, the total average cost (TAC) of separately producing the loan services through the bank and the CP issuance through the investment bank is

$$TAC = \frac{\$60{,}000}{\$11{,}000{,}000} = 0.54\%$$

Suppose, instead, a single FI produces both \$10 million of lending services and \$1 million in CP issuance services for the same customer (i.e., P_{FS} = \$11 million). Loans and CP are substitute sources of funds for corporate customers. For an FI to originate a loan and CP requires very similar expertise both in funding that issue and in credit risk assessment and monitoring. Common technologies in the loan and CP production functions suggest that a single FI simultaneously (or jointly) producing both loan and CP services for the same client at a total cost TC_{FS} should be able to do this at a lower average cost than could the specialized FIs that separately produce these services. That is, the single FI should be able to produce the \$11,000,000 (P_{FS}) of financial services at a lower cost (say TC_{FS} = \$51,000), than should two specialized FIs. Accordingly,

$$AC_{FS} = \frac{TC_{FS}}{P_{FS}} = \frac{\$51{,}000}{\$11{,}000{,}000} = 0.46\% < 0.54\%$$

Formally, if AC_{FS} is the total average cost of a nonspecialized financial services firm, then economies of scope imply that

$$AC_{FS} < TAC$$

diseconomies of scope
The costs of joint production of FI services are higher than they would be if they were produced independently.

Nevertheless, **diseconomies of scope** may occur instead. FIs might find costs actually higher from joint production of services than if they were produced independently. For example, suppose an FI purchases some very specialized information-based technology to ease the loan production and processing function. The FI could use any excess capacity this system has in other service areas. However, this process could be a relatively inefficient technology for other service areas and could add to the overall costs of production compared with using a specialized technology for each service or product area. Indeed, most studies find that cost-based economies of scope are negligible, although revenue-based economies of scope may arise for the largest FIs. It is unclear whether technological advances will make the production of financial services more efficient as financial service companies offer one-stop shopping to customers.

CONCEPT QUESTIONS

1. **What are two risk factors involved in an FI's investment in technological products?**
2. **Do economies of scale mean that in the long run, small FIs cannot survive?**
3. **With diseconomies of scope, do specialized FIs have a relative cost advantage over product-diversified FIs?**
4. **Make a list of the potential economies of scope or cost synergies if two Canadian FIs were allowed to merge. How would the merger of two large Canadian banks differ from the merger of a bank and an insurance company?**

TESTING FOR ECONOMIES OF SCALE AND ECONOMIES OF SCOPE

To test for economies of scale and economies of scope, FIs must clearly specify both the inputs to their production process and the cost of those inputs. Basically, the two approaches to analyzing the cost functions of FIs are the production and the intermediation approaches.

The Production Approach

The production approach views FIs' outputs of services as having two underlying inputs: labour and capital. If w = wage costs of labour, r = rental costs of capital, and y = output of services, the total cost function (C) for the FI is

$$C = f(y, w, r)$$

The Intermediation Approach

The intermediation approach views the output of financial services as being produced by labour and capital as well as funds that the intermediary uses to produce intermediated services. Thus, deposit costs would be an input in the banking and trust industries, while premiums or reserves would be inputs in the insurance industry, and

$$C = f(y, w, r, k)$$

where k reflects the cost of funds for the FI.

CONCEPT QUESTIONS

1. **Describe the production approach to testing for economies of scale and scope.**
2. **How does the intermediation approach differ from the production approach?**

EMPIRICAL FINDINGS ON ECONOMIES OF SCALE AND SCOPE

A large number of studies have examined economies of scale and scope in different financial services industry sectors. With respect to banks, most of the early studies failed to find economies of scale for any but the smallest banks.[7] More

[7] Good reviews are found in A. Berger, W. C. Hunter, and S. B. Timme, "The Efficiency of Financial Institutions: A Review and Preview of Research Past, Present and Future," *Journal of Banking and Finance* 17, 1993, pp. 221–49; R. DeYoung, Learning-by-Doing, Scale Efficiencies, and Financial Performance at Internet-Only Banks, Federal Reserve Bank of Chicago working paper, June 2002; and A. Berger and R. DeYoung, "Technological Progress and the Geographic Expansion of the Banking Industry," *Journal of Money, Credit, and Banking*, September 2006, pp. 1483–513. A. Berger, D. Humphrey, and L. B. Pulley, "Do Consumers Pay for One-Stop Banking? Evidence from an Alternative Revenue Function," *Journal of Banking and Finance* 20, 1996, pp. 1601–21, looks at revenue economies of scope (rather than cost economies of scope) between loans and deposits over the 1978–1990 period and finds no evidence of revenue economies of scope.

recently, better data sets and improved methodologies have suggested that economies of scale may exist for banks up to the $10 billion to $25 billion size range. With respect to economies of scope either among deposits, loans, and other traditional banking product areas or between on-balance-sheet products and OBS products such as loan sales, the evidence that cost synergies exist is at best very weak. Similarly, the smaller number of studies involving nonbank financial services firms such as savings and loans, co-ops, insurance companies, and securities firms almost always report neither economies of scale nor economies of scope.[8]

Economies of Scale and Scope and X-Inefficiencies

A number of studies that primarily use data for U.S. FIs have looked at the *dispersion* of costs in any given FI size class rather than the shape of the average cost functions. These efficiency studies find quite dramatic cost differences of 20 percent or more among banks and insurance companies in any given size class ($100 million asset size class, $200 million asset size class, etc.). Moreover, these studies find that only a small part of the cost differences among FIs in any size class can be attributed to economies of scale or scope.[9] This suggests that cost inefficiencies related to managerial performance and other hard-to-quantify factors (so-called **X-inefficiencies**) may better explain cost differences and operating cost efficiencies among financial firms than technology-related investments per se.[10]

X-inefficiencies
The production of less than efficient levels of output from a given level of input.

There is little strong, direct evidence that larger multiproduct financial services firms enjoy cost advantages over smaller, more specialized financial firms. Nor do economies of scope and scale explain many of the cost differences among FIs of the same size. These empirical findings raise questions about the benefits of technology investments and technological innovation. While a majority of the studies tested for economies of scope and scale rather than the benefits of technology, these results are consistent with the relatively low payoff from technological innovation. To the extent that large FIs obtain benefits, they may well be on the revenue generation/new product innovation side rather than on the cost side. Indeed, recent studies looking at output and input efficiencies for banks and insurance companies derived from revenue and profit functions found that large FIs tend to be more efficient in revenue generation than smaller FIs and that such efficiencies may well offset scope and scale cost inefficiencies related to size.[11]

Early studies, using data from the 1980s, failed to find scale economies in any except very small banks. However, more recent studies, using data from the 1990s and 2000s and more modern methods for modelling bank technology, find significant

[8] J. D. Cummins, S. Tennyson, and M. A. Weiss, "Consolidation and Efficiency in the U.S. Life Insurance Industry," *Journal of Banking and Finance* 23, 1999, pp. 325–57, finds that mergers and acquisitions (M&As) in the insurance industry do produce economies of scale, while efficiency gains are significantly smaller in non-M&A life insurers.

[9] See K. Mukherjee, S. C. Ray, and S. M. Miller, "Productivity Growth in Large U.S. Commercial Banks: The Initial Post-Deregulation Experience," *Journal of Banking and Finance* 25, 2001, pp. 913–39; and A. Akhigbe and J. E. McNulty, "The Profit Efficiency of Small U.S. Commercial Banks," *Journal of Banking and Finance* 27, 2003, pp. 307–25.

[10] See, for example, T. T. Milbourn, A. W. A. Boot, and A. V. Thakor, "Megamergers and Expanded Scope: Theories of Bank Size and Activity Diversity," *Journal of Banking and Finance* 23, 1999, pp. 195–214.

[11] See A. N. Berger and L. J. Mester, "Inside the Black-Box: What Explains Differences in the Efficiencies of Financial Institutions," *Journal of Banking and Finance* 21 (1997), pp. 895–947, for an extensive review of these efficiency studies. See also J. Cummins, S. Tennyson, and M. A. Weiss, "Efficiency, Scale Economies and Consolidation in the U.S. Life Insurance Industry," *Journal of Banking and Finance*, February 1999, pp. 325–57, and R. DeYoung and K. P. Roland, "Product Mix and Earnings Volatility at Commercial Banks: Evidence from a Degree of Total Leverage Model," *Journal of Financial Intermediation* 10, 2001, pp. 54–84.

scale economies at banks of all sizes. The difference in results between the earlier versus the more recent studies reflects improvements in the methods researchers used for measuring scale economies; geographic deregulation, which has led to larger efficient scale of banking production; and to a change in bank technology, such as the use of information technologies.[12]

The real benefits of technological innovation may be long term and dynamic, related to the evolution of the Canadian and U.S. payments systems away from cash and cheques and toward electronic means of payment. Such benefits are difficult to obtain in traditional economy of scale and scope studies, which are largely static and ignore the more dynamic aspects of efficiency gains. This dynamic technological evolution not only has affected the fundamental role of FIs in the financial system but also has generated some new and subtle types of risks for FIs and their regulators. In the next section we take a closer look at the effects of technology on the payments system.

CONCEPT QUESTION

What does the empirical evidence reveal about economies of scale and scope?

TECHNOLOGY AND THE EVOLUTION OF THE PAYMENTS SYSTEM

LO6

To better understand the changing nature of the payments system, look at Table 17–2. In Canada in 2011, nonelectronic methods—cheques—accounted for 8.9 percent of noncash transactions, but this represented 50.5 percent of the dollar *value* of noncash transactions. By comparison, while electronic methods of payment—credit cards, debit cards, and credit transfer systems and direct debits—accounted for 91.1 percent in volume, they accounted for only 49.5 percent in value.

As can be seen from Tables 17–3 and 17–4, the use of electronic methods of payment is higher in some major developed countries than in others. For example, in Canada, Germany, and the United Kingdom electronic transactions account for over 90 percent of total transactions measured by number of transactions.

Cheque writing lays the foundation of e-money. When a cheque is written and given to a person with an account at a different bank, the banks do not transfer currency. Rather, the banks use an electronic fund transfer. E-money removes the intermediary. Instead of requesting that the banks transfer funds, the e-money user transfers the money from his or her bank account to the account of the funds' receiver. The primary function of e-money is to facilitate transactions on the Internet. Many of these transactions may be small in value and would not be cost-efficient through other payment mediums such as credit cards. With e-money, the user can

[12] See J. P. Hughes and L. J. Mester, "Efficiency in Banking: Theory, Practice, and Evidence," Chapter 19 in *The Oxford Handbook of Banking*, edited by A.N. Berger, P. Molyneux, and J. Wilson, Oxford University Press (2010); J. P. Hughes, W. Lang, L. J. Mester, and C.-G. Moon, "Efficient Banking Under Interstate Branching," *Journal of Money, Credit, and Banking* 28 (1996), pp. 1045–71; J. P. Hughes and L. J. Mester, "Bank Capitalization and Cost: Evidence of Scale Economies in Risk Management and Signaling," *Review of Economics and Statistics* 80 (1998), pp. 314–25; J. P. Hughes and L. J. Mester, Who Said Large Banks Don't Experience Scale Economies? Evidence from a Risk-Return-Driven Cost Function, Working Paper, July 2011; D. C. Wheelock and P. W. Wilson, Are U. S. Banks Too Large? Working Paper 2009-054B, Federal Reserve Bank of St. Louis, December 2009; and J. P. Hughes, L. J. Mester, and C.-G. Moon, "Are Scale Economies in Banking Elusive or Illusive? Evidence Obtained by Incorporating Capital Structure and Risk-Taking into Models of Bank Production," *Journal of Banking and Finance* 25 (2001), pp. 2169–208.

TABLE 17–2
Canadian Cashless Payments: Volume, Value, and Average Transaction Amount, 2011

Source: Bank for International Settlements, *Statistics on Payment Systems in Selected Countries*, Basel, Switzerland, January 2013, bis.org.

	Volume (billions)	Percentage	Value ($ billions)	Percentage	Transaction Average Value ($)
Cheque	0.9	8.9	$2,993.4	50.5	$3,368
Debit card	4.1	42.2	182.7	3.2	44
Credit card	3.1	31.4	331.1	5.7	107
Credit transfers	1.0	10.6	1,774.5	30.6	1,700
Direct debits	0.7	6.9	581.6	10.0	863
	9.8		$5,803.3		

TABLE 17–3
Percentage of Total Volume of Noncash Paper and Electronic Transactions, 2011

Source: Bank for International Settlements, *Statistics on Payment Systems in Selected Countries*, Basel, Switzerland, January 2013, bis.org.

	Paper (Cheque)	Debit and Credit Cards	Credit Transfers	Direct Debits	Total Electronic
Canada	8.9	73.6	10.6	6.9	91.1
United States	18.6	64.1	6.9	10.3	81.3
Germany	0.2	16.6	34.3	48.7	99.6
United Kingdom	5.5	55.6	20.2	18.7	94.5
All countries	11.7	55.2	17.0	14.0	88.3

TABLE 17–4
Percentage of Total Value of Noncash Paper and Electronic Transactions, 2011

Source: Bank for International Settlements, *Statistics on Payment Systems in Selected Countries*, Basel, Switzerland, January 2013, bis.org.

	Paper (Cheque)	Debit and Credit Cards	Credit Transfers	Direct Debits	Total Electronic
Canada	50.5	8.9	30.6	10.0	49.5
United States	37.0	5.7	34.9	22.4	63.0
Germany	0.4	0.3	79.6	19.8	99.7
United Kingdom	1.4	0.7	96.4	1.5	98.6
All countries	60.6	7.8	n.a.*	31.6	n.a.*

*Country totals were not calculated because credit transfer data are not consistent across countries.

download money into his or her cyber-wallet in any currency desired. A merchant can accept any amount and currency and convert it into local currency when the cyber-cash is uploaded to a bank account. If a user wants e-money offline, all that is necessary is smart card technology. The money is loaded onto the smart card, and electronic wallets are used to offload the money onto other smart cards or directly to an online system. In essence, e-money transfers combine the benefits of other transaction methods. They are similar to debit/credit cards, but allow individuals to conduct transactions directly with each other. Like personal cheques, they are feasible for very small transactions. However, unlike deposits that are insured by CDIC, money stored in e-money accounts and cards is not covered by deposit insurance.

Canada has two systems for the clearing of noncash payments. As noted in Chapter 16, the **Large Value Transfer System (LVTS)** handles time-sensitive, large value transactions. The **Automated Clearing Settlement System (ACSS)** processes regular bill payments (e.g., debit card transactions, cheques, automatic bill payments). The LVTS thus operates essentially as a wholesale type of system while the ACSS is the system for smaller retail transactions.

Large Value Transfer System (LVTS)
The payment system operated by the Canadian Payments Association for time-sensitive, large value transactions that are irrevocable.

Automated Clearing Settlement System (ACSS)
The payment system for ordinary transactions operated by the Canadian Payments Association.

The payments system has been viewed in Canada as a source of systemic risk to the financial system. For this reason, in 1996, the Payment Clearing and Settlement Act gave the Bank of Canada responsibility for the payment systems that could put the overall financial system at risk including, since 1999, the LVTS. The focus has been to develop a system that serves Canadians nationally with the best technology and with a view to competition and economies of scale and scope. The additional focus has also been on cross-border transactions within North America, particularly the United States, but with a view to the internationalization of capital flows. James Dingle's history of the Canadian Payments Association (CPA) from 1980 to 2002 provides a view of the payments system in Canada.[13] As well, the BIS Committee on Payment and Settlement Systems (CPSS) has published several studies regarding the payment infrastructure of global financial markets. However, the difference in customs, regulations, and culture between countries, even between close neighbours such as Canada and the United States, is an issue in the globalization of payments systems.

Another way to see the enormous growth in the use of electronic transfers in Canada is to consider the percentage of electronic versus paper items flowing through the ACSS between 1990 and 2011. According to the CPA, the volume of electronic transactions grew from 13.4 percent in 1990 to 85.91 percent in 2011. On a dollar value basis, electronic transactions increased from 0.6 percent of the value of the transactions through the ACSS in 1990 to 46.16 percent in 2011. The volume of electronic transactions through the ACSS has exceeded the volume of paper transactions since 1997. The CPA's systems cleared an average daily value of $174.5 billion in 2012. The annual volume was 6.3 trillion items through the ACSS in 2011 and 7.0 million items through the LVTS in 2012.

According to the data in Table 17–5, Canada is not the only country in which wholesale wire transfer systems have come to dominate the payment systems. The United States, the European Union, the Netherlands, the United Kingdom, Switzerland, Hong Kong, Germany, and Japan also have very large wire transfer systems measured as a percentage of local gross domestic product (GDP). In 2001 as a result of the single currency (the euro) and the European Monetary Union, a single wholesale wire transfer system for Europe fully emerged, linking all countries that are members of the European Monetary Union. The transaction system is called TARGET (Trans-European Automated Real-Time Gross-Settlement Express Transfer).

Risks That Arise in an Electronic Transfer Payment System

At least six important risks have arisen along with the growth of wire transfer systems. We mentioned some of these while discussing OBS activities in Chapter 16; here, we go into more detail.

Settlement Risk

cdnpay.ca

The CPA operates the payment systems in Canada. Members of the CPA include the Bank of Canada, all of the domestic banks, and authorized foreign banks. In addition, other DTIs (credit unions, caisses populaires, savings and loans) as well as

[13] See J. Dingle, *Planning an Evolution: The Story of the Canadian Payments Association, 1980–2002,* May 2003, the Bank of Canada and the Canadian Payments Association, available at cdnpay.ca.

TABLE 17–5
Wholesale Wire Transfer Systems in Selected Countries 2011

Source: Bank for International Settlements, *Statistics on Payment Systems in Selected Countries*, Basel, Switzerland, January 2013, bis.org.

	Number of Transactions (millions)	Annual Value of Transactions (U.S. $ billions)	Value of Transactions as % of GDP
Germany			
TARGET2-BBk	43.85	$ 351,659	9,755.3
RPS	2690.1	$3,354.2	93.0
Hong Kong			
HKD CHATS	5.60	$ 17,103.2	6,879.5
USD CHATS	3.52	$ 3,503.1	1,409.1
Japan			
FXYCS	6.33	$ 35,399.2	599.5
BOJ-NET	12.93	311,549	5,276.2
Zengin System	1,394.8	32,204.2	545.4
Tokyo Clearing House	26.64	3,522.2	59.6
Netherlands			
Equens	4,021.4	$ 2,850.2	340.5
Target2-NL	8.35	110,129	13,157.7
Sweden			
E-RIX	n.a.	n.a.	n.a.
K-RIX	3.46	17,456.7	3,239
Bankgirot	791.1	1,263.3	234.4
Dataclearing	125.5	398.8	74
Switzerland			
SIC	402.5	70,802	10,699.8
United Kingdom			
CHAPS-Euro	n.a.	n.a.	n.a.
CHAPS-Sterling	34.02	102,393	4,227.1
BACS	2,394.6	6,994.1	288.7
Cheque/credit	62.4	1,166.1	48.1
United States			
Fedwire	127.0	663,838	4,403.4
CHIPS	95.06	403,349	2,675.5
European Union			
TARGET	88.88	906,309	6,932.3
Euro 1/STEP 1	62.32	89,015	680.9
Canada			
LVTS	6.61	40,003	2,299.3

insurance companies, securities dealers, and mutual funds are also eligible for membership. Clearing of accounts is done through the LVTS and the ACSS, as mentioned previously, and the settlement of accounts occurs through adjustments to the accounts of approximately 12 FIs that have settlement accounts at the Bank of Canada. If an FI is unable to cover its LVTS or ACSS obligations, the Bank of Canada lends funds to the FI on an overnight basis at the upper band of the bank rate. The Bank of Canada also settles obligations for the Government of Canada.

FIGURE 17–3 LVTS Daily Operating Schedule

12:30 AM–11 PM	12:30 AM–6 AM	6 AM–6 PM	6 PM–6:30 PM	6:30 PM–7:30 PM
CLS participants pledge collateral to the Bank of Canada, set debit caps for Tranche 1 activity, and set lines of credit for Tranche 2 activity.	CLS transactions. Participants may adjust debit caps, lines of credit, and collateral.	Other payments start. Non-CLS participants send debit caps, bilateral lines of credit, and collateral to the Bank of Canada between 7 AM and 8 AM. Participants can track their positions and adjust Tranche 1, Tranche 2, and collateral during the day.	LVTS closes. Transactions between participants occur to reduce the need for overnight borrowing from the Bank of Canada.	The Bank of Canada settles each participant's account irrevocably and releases unused collateral.

Source: Bank of Canada, *LVTS Operating Schedule*, bankofcanada.ca.

continuous linked settlement (CLS)
The method of settling global foreign exchange transactions used by CLS Bank to eliminate settlement risk.

www.cls-group.com

Since 2002, the LVTS has been used for the settlement of Canadian dollar transfers in FX transactions through a process called **continuous linked settlement (CLS)**. This process occurs between 1 AM and 6 AM, Monday through Friday, resulting in a 24-hour-a-day operation at the CPA, and has virtually eliminated settlement risk on FX transactions by providing real-time and irrevocable settlement across international time zones. The market turmoil of 2007 and 2008 raised concerns at the Bank of Canada about settlement risk arising on FX transactions for Canadian banks with international counterparties. While Canadian FIs were remarkably stable during this time period, global FIs (e.g., AIG, Fortis) were experiencing severe liquidity constraints. Canadian banks increased their use of CLS Bank for FX trades after Lehman Brothers, the U.S. investment bank, collapsed in September 2008. This episode illustrates the interconnection of risks (counterparty, FX, and operational risks) for major international FIs.[14]

Figure 17–3 illustrates the operations of the LVTS system on a daily basis. The settlement risk is virtually eliminated by the requirement that each direct participant in the LVTS be a member of the CPA, use the SWIFT network for telecommunications, and keep a settlement account at the Bank of Canada. In addition, there are limits on the net amount that each participant is able to owe, and each participant pledges collateral at the Bank of Canada, which provides liquidity to the system if one of the participants defaults. The participants have a choice between Tranche 1 payments, which are covered by the collateral pledged to the Bank of Canada, and Tranche 2 payments, which are bilateral lines of credit granted by each participant to every other participant. These are set daily and can be monitored and adjusted during the day. If the collateral is insufficient to settle the accounts when a participant fails, then the surviving FIs will absorb the losses, and, in the event of more than one participant failing, the Bank of Canada guarantees settlement. Participants with overdrafts at the Bank of Canada at the end of the day, either through their LVTS operations or through the ACSS, borrow overnight at the upper band of the bank rate.

chips.org

The payment systems in the United States (Fedwire, CHIPS) are operated differently and give rise to daylight overdraft risk for those FIs (including Canadian banks) with U.S. operations. Settlement, or daylight, overdraft risk is a source of instability

[14] CLS Bank eliminates the settlement risk of FX transactions by offsetting each party's account. The Bank of Canada acts as the banker for CLS Bank. J. Armstrong and G. Caldwell, "Liquidity Risk at Banks: Trends and Lessons Learned from the Recent Turmoil," Bank of Canada, *Financial System Review*, December 2008, pp. 47–52, analyzes the FX settlement risk for Canadian banks.

FIGURE 17–4
Daylight Overdrafts on Fedwire

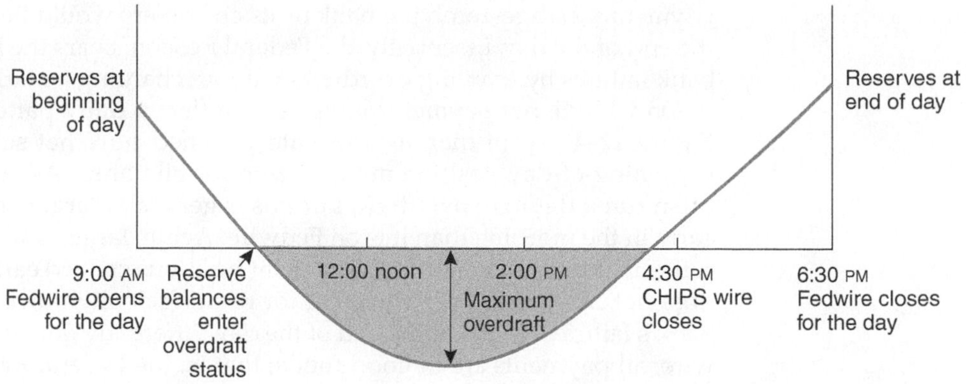

in the financial markets. To understand daylight overdrafts better, look at Figure 17–4. It shows a typical daily pattern of net wire payment transfers—payment messages sent (debits) minus payment messages received (credits)—for a large money centre bank using Fedwire (the U.S. Federal Reserve's wire transfer network).

Under the U.S. Federal Reserve Act, banks must maintain cash reserves on deposit at the Federal Reserve; Fedwire settlement occurs at the end of the banking day at 6:30 PM EST. At that time, the Federal Reserve adjusts each member bank's reserve account to reflect its net debit (credit) position with other banks. CHIPS transactions settle on Fedwire by 4:30 PM, before Fedwire closes. Under current regulations, the member bank's end-of-day reserve position cannot be negative. However, what is true at the end of the day is not true during the day; that is, the Federal Reserve allows banks to run real-time **daylight overdrafts** (or negative intraday balances) on their reserve accounts. These negative reserve balances occur under the current payments system because large banks and their customers often send payment messages repaying overnight loans and making interest payments at the beginning of the banking day and borrow funds and receive payment messages toward the end of the banking day. For periods during the day, banks frequently run daylight overdrafts on their reserve accounts at the Federal Reserve by having their payment outflow messages exceed their payment inflow messages (see Figure 17–4).

daylight overdrafts
Banks' negative intraday balances in their reserve account at the Federal Reserve.

In effect, the Federal Reserve is implicitly lending banks within-day reserves. This process involves two other important institutional factors. First, until 1993, the Federal Reserve did not charge banks an explicit interest rate or fee for these daylight overdrafts. As a result, neither banks nor their large corporate customers had any incentive to economize on these transactions. Daylight Fedwire overdrafts were effectively free and therefore oversupplied. The current daylight overdraft fee is 50 bp, quoted as an annual rate on the basis of a 24-hour day.[15] Second, under Regulation J, the Federal Reserve guarantees payment finality for every wire transfer message. Therefore, if the representative bank in Figure 17–4 were to fail at noon, the Federal Reserve would be liable for all of the bank's Fedwire transactions made that day by that bank until noon. This eliminates any risk that a

[15] The annual rate is converted to an effective annual rate by multiplying it by the fraction of the day that Fedwire is scheduled to be open, currently 21.5 hours out of 24, or 21.5/24. Thus, the current effective annual rate charged for overdrafts is 44.79 bp (50 bp × 21.5/24 hours). The effective annual rate is converted to an effective daily rate by multiplying it by 1/360. See *Guide to the Federal Reserve's Payments System Risk Policy on Daylight Credit*, Federal Reserve System, July 2012.

payment message–receiving bank or its customers would be left short of funds at the end of the day. Essentially, the Federal Reserve bears the Fedwire credit risk of bank failures by granting overdrafts without charging a market interest rate.

On CHIPS, net payment flows often reflect a daily pattern similar to that in Figure 17–4 except that, as a privately owned pure net settlement system, the beginning-of-day position must be zero for all banks. As on Fedwire, big banks often run a daylight overdraft, but this is generally larger and more pronounced early in the morning than it is on Fedwire. Again, large banks then seek to borrow funds in the afternoon to cover net debit positions created earlier in the day. CHIPS does not charge banks explicit fees for running daylight overdrafts, but it treats a bank's failure to settle at the end of the day differently than does Fedwire. On Fedwire, all payments are in good funds; that is, the Federal Reserve guarantees the finality of any wire transfer at the time it is made. By contrast, on CHIPS, US$3 billion in funds is made available to cover each day's payment transactions. These idle funds permit some 97 percent of CHIPS payments to be finally settled in real time and released to customers as no net debit is created. The 3 percent of payments that cannot be immediately settled are not released to customers until they are settled at the end of the day. Unlike previous arrangements used by CHIPS, because payments are not now released to receiving banks until adequate funds are in the sending bank's CHIPS account, there is no contractual provision for a payments unwind. However, there can be and has been a refusal of payment request on CHIPS. This last occurred in the wake of the 2001 terrorist attack in New York when some bank payment requests were not made because of insufficient funds (and the payment request was returned to the requesting bank).

Because of these concerns, the U.S. FDIC Improvement Act, passed in 1991, required the Federal Reserve to implement Regulation F, under which U.S. and non-U.S. banks must develop internal procedures or benchmarks to limit their settlement and other credit exposures to DTIs with which they do business (called *correspondent banks*). Accordingly, since December 1992, banks have been required to limit their exposure to an individual correspondent to no more than 25 percent of the correspondent bank's capital. However, for adequately capitalized banks, this can be raised to 50 percent, while no set benchmark is required for well-capitalized banks. Thus, it is now easier for the most solvent banks to transact on the wire transfer networks and run daylight overdrafts than for less well capitalized banks. In addition, as long as the benchmarks are adhered to, regulators' exposure to settlement risk is reduced.

International Technology Transfer Risk

In recent years Canada and the United States have been at the forefront in making technology investments and financial service innovations in the payments system. For example, North American FIs have been pioneers of ABMs, yet such networks have grown relatively slowly in countries such as Sweden and the Netherlands.

This suggests that financial service firms have often been unable to transfer profitably their domestic technological innovations to international markets to gain competitive advantage, at least in the short term. In contrast, foreign financial service firms entering the North American market gain direct access to, and knowledge of, technology-based products at a very low cost. For example, since the passage of the International Banking Act in the United States in 1978, foreign banks, including the Canadian banks, have had direct access to U.S. Fedwire.

Crime and Fraud Risk

The increased replacement of cheques and cash by electronic transfers as methods of payment or exchange has resulted in an increase in the efficiency of the execution of transactions, but it has also resulted in new problems regarding theft, data snooping, and white-collar crime. Because huge sums are transferred across the networks each day and some bank employees have specialized knowledge of personal identification numbers (PINs) and other entry codes, the incentive for white-collar crime appears to have increased. For example, a manager at the Sri Lankan branch of the now-defunct BCCI reportedly stole a computer chip from a telex machine in the bank's Oman branch and used it to transfer US$10 million from three banks in the United States and Japan to his own account in Switzerland.

Moreover, as described earlier in the chapter, considerable security problems exist in trying to develop the Internet as a form of electronic payment system. Internet transactions can be intercepted by third parties. FIs are accordingly concerned about open credit or debit card details on the Internet. Any version of electronic payment via the Internet must not only meet the requirements of recognition and acceptability associated with physical cash but also provide the same high level of security that is demanded of cash payments but that the Internet itself cannot guarantee. Further, penalties for cybercrimes are on the rise, and regulatory and legal requirements on data protection and data security at FIs are emerging. Government organizations are also becoming increasingly involved in cyber warfare. After the terrorist attacks on September 11, 2001, the U.S. Congress passed the U.S. Patriot Act of 2001. The act contains a number of specific amendments to existing criminal laws designed to streamline early detection and investigation of suspected terrorist activity conducted through FIs. In December 2005, the U.S. Federal Reserve and Treasury Department fined Dutch bank ABN Amro US$80 million for violating U.S. money-laundering laws and sanctions against Iran and Libya. The move came in response to nearly 10 years of violations involving billions of dollars in transactions that passed through the bank's offices in New York and Dubai, United Arab Emirates. The investigation found that bank employees falsified numerous wire transfer records to hide the identities of Iranian and Libyan companies and individuals sending money to the United States. More recently, in November 2009 the FBI successfully concluded an investigation of the simultaneous theft of money from over 2,100 ABMs in 280 different cities on three continents. The crime came about when a 28-year-old Moldovan man discovered a vulnerable computer network of an Atlanta-based major credit card processing company. He passed the information to a hacker in Estonia. The Estonian verified the network vulnerability and shared the information with a hacker in Russia. The Russian, with the help of the three other hackers, penetrated the electronic network, reverse-engineered the PINs from the encrypted system, and raised the limits on the amount of money that could be withdrawn from the prepaid payroll debit cards. Another hacker organized a network of thieves around the world, who used a total of 44 counterfeit cards to withdraw US$9 million within 12 hours. With international cooperation, the FBI was able to identify and charge all involved with the cybercrime.

In the future, greater bank and regulatory resources will have to be spent on surveillance and employee monitoring as well as on developing fail-safe and unbreakable entry codes to wire transfer accounts, especially as a number of countries have passed data privacy laws.

Financial Transactions and Reports Analysis Centre of Canada (FINTRAC)
A Government of Canada organization that tracks and analyzes money laundering, terrorist activity, and threats to Canadian security.

fintrac.gc.ca

The Patriot Act had unforeseen consequences for Canadian FIs. OSFI keeps an up-to-date list of suspected terrorist organizations on its website, and provides guidelines to DTIs regarding the Proceeds of Crime (Money Laundering) and Terrorism Financing Act introduced in 2003. All federally regulated FIs except property and casualty (P&C) insurance companies are required to implement programs to detect and prevent money laundering in order to protect their reputations and the stability of the financial system. OSFI works with the **Financial Transactions and Reports Analysis Centre of Canada** (FINTRAC) to counteract money laundering and terrorist activities, which come under the Criminal Code of Canada. The Royal Canadian Mounted Police (RCMP) may subpoena customer account information to investigate a crime. However, U.S. authorities have much broader powers to search under the Patriot Act; for example, Canadian FIs that outsource management of their credit card or other operations to companies in the United States leave their Canadian customers' transactions open to scrutiny by U.S. government agencies.

Regulatory Risk

The improvement in FIs' computer and telecommunications networks also enhances the power of FIs vis-à-vis regulators, effectively aiding regulatory avoidance. Thus, as implied earlier, regulation not only can affect the profitability of technological innovations but also can spur or hinder the rate and types of innovation. As a result of regulation in Canada and in the United States, banking in the relatively unregulated Cayman Islands has experienced considerable growth. The 500 or more FIs located there do most of their business via public and private telecommunications networks. The use of telecommunications networks and technological improvements has changed, perhaps irreversibly, the balance of power between large multinational FIs and governments—both local and national—in favour of the FIs. Such a shift in power may create incentives for countries to lower their regulations to attract entrants; that is, the shift may increase the incentives for competitive deregulation. This trend may be potentially destabilizing to the market in financial services, with the weakest regulators attracting the most entrants.

Tax Avoidance

The development of international wire networks as well as international financial service firm networks has enabled FIs to shift funds and profits by using internal pricing mechanisms, thereby minimizing their overall domestic tax burden and maximizing their foreign tax credits. For example, prior to 1986, many large Canadian and U.S. banks paid almost no corporate income taxes, despite large reported profits, by rapidly moving profits and funds across different tax regimes. This raised considerable public policy concerns and was a major reason for the 1987 tax reforms in Canada.

In the late 2000s, the U.S. government, including the Internal Revenue Service (IRS), took steps to get client names from foreign FIs. These client lists contained names of U.S. individuals and business that "hid" income in the foreign FIs to intentionally avoid paying U.S. taxes. In one case, UBS AG helped individuals hide income to avoid taxes. The tax scheme relied in part on channelling funds to a Swiss UBS account held in the name of a Hong Kong entity. The Hong Kong link was important because the Justice Department and IRS used that as a clue of wrongdoing as they investigated some 250 names that UBS turned over to the U.S. government.

Competition Risk

myctfs.com

As financial services become more technologically based, they are increasingly competing with nontraditional financial service suppliers. Also, once established, nonfinancial firms can easily purchase financial services technology. For example, Canadian Tire Financial Services offers credit cards and insurance. Thus, technology exposes existing FIs to the increased risk of erosion of their franchises as costs of entry fall and the competitive landscape changes.

CONCEPT QUESTIONS

1. **Describe the six risks faced by FIs with the growth of wire transfer payment systems.**
2. **What steps has the CPA taken to lower settlement risk for the LVTS?**

OTHER OPERATIONAL RISKS

LO7

While technology risk has become increasingly important to the profitability and riskiness of modern FIs, it is not the sole source of operational risk. Indeed, studies have found that the impact of an operational risk crisis (such as embezzlement and loan fraud) on the market value of a firm far exceeds (as much as 12 times) the actual cost. Early in the chapter we listed four other sources of operational risk. These are employees, customer relationships, capital assets, and external risks. For example, employee risk includes employee turnover and fraud, as well as programming errors by employees.

Table 17–6 summarizes the problems these sources of operational risk can create, including how the other sources of operational risk interact with technology risk. For example, while RBC may lose customers because of its outsourcing of Canadian jobs, the failure of a third-party technology provider to perform as promised, resulting in an FI's online banking services being interrupted, may also cause the FI to lose customers.

Like technology risk, these other sources of operational risk can result in direct costs (e.g., loss of income), indirect costs (e.g., client withdrawals and legal costs), and opportunity costs (e.g., forgone business opportunities) for an FI that reduce profitability and value. To offset these costs, FI managers spend considerable effort and resources to prevent, control, finance, and insulate the FI from losses due to operational risk. These efforts include:

1. *Loss prevention.* Training, development, and review of employees.
2. *Loss control.* Planning, organization, backup (e.g., computer systems).
3. *Loss financing.* External insurance (e.g., catastrophe insurance).
4. *Loss insulation:* FI capital.

Risk management efforts, of course, come at a cost to the FI. The greater the commitment of resources to risk management efforts, the lower the costs resulting from operational risks. However, the resources spent in preventing costs of operational risk may, at some point, be greater than the cost of the risk itself. In maximizing profits and value, FIs will invest in these risk management efforts until the costs of such efforts just offset operating losses from not undertaking such efforts.

TABLE 17–6
A Summary of Operational Risks Faced by FIs

Source: C. Marshall, *Measuring and Managing Operational Risks in Financial Institutions: Tools, Techniques and Other Resources*. Singapore: John Wiley and Sons, 2001.

Source of Risk	Specific Problem
Employee risk	Employee turnover Key personnel risk Fraud risk Error Rogue trading Money laundering Confidentiality breach
Technology risk	Programming error Model risk Mark-to-market error Management information IT systems outage Telecommunications failure Technology provider failure Contingency planning
Customer risk	Contractual disagreement Dissatisfaction Default
Capital asset risk	Safety Security Operating costs Fire/flood
External risk	External fraud Taxation risk Legal risk War Collapse of markets Reputation risk Relationship risk

CONCEPT QUESTIONS

1. **Give an example of operational risk from employees, customers, capital assets, and external risk.**
2. **What risk management efforts are involved in controlling operational risk?**

REGULATORY ISSUES AND TECHNOLOGY AND OPERATIONAL RISKS

LO8

As stated earlier, operational risk is the risk of direct or indirect loss resulting from inadequate or failed internal processes, people, or systems, and from external events. Certainly, as FIs' use of technology increases, operational risk increases as well. However, little has been done to oversee or regulate these increasing risks. In this section, we look at two areas that have been directly affected by the increase in operational risk.

1. *Operational risk and FI insolvency.* Research by Operational Research Inc., an operational risk consultancy firm, estimates that since 1980, FIs have lost over US$200 billion due to operational risk.[16] Regulators have recognized the significance of operational risk for FIs. Specifically, in 1999 the Basel Committee (of the BIS) on Banking Supervision said that operational risks "are sufficiently important

[16] See C. Smithson, "Measuring Operational Risk," *Risk*, March 2000, pp. 58–59.

for banks to devote necessary resources to quantify the level of such risks and to incorporate them (along with market and credit risk) into their assessment of their overall capital adequacy."[17] In its follow-up consultative documents released in January 2001 and April 2003, the Basel committee proposed three specific methods by which DTIs could calculate the required capital to protect themselves against operational risk. These methods are the basic indicator approach, the standardized approach, and the advanced measurement approach.[18] Banks are encouraged to move along the spectrum of available approaches as they develop more sophisticated operational risk measurement systems and practices. For example, for its 2012 annual reports, Bank of Montreal used the standardized approach while CIBC used the advanced measurement approach. Internationally active banks and banks with significant operational risk exposures (such as specialized processing banks) are expected to use an approach that is more sophisticated than the basic indicator approach and that is appropriate for the risk profile of the institution. A bank can be allowed to use the basic indicator or standardized approach for some parts of its operations and the advanced measurement approach for others provided certain minimum criteria are met. A bank is not allowed to choose to revert to a simpler approach once it has been approved for a more advanced approach without supervisor approval. Research has found that the amount of capital held for operational risk according to these models will often exceed capital held for market risk and that the largest banks could choose to allocate several billion dollars in capital to operational risk. We discuss each of the methods in more detail in Chapter 20.

2. *Consumer protection.* The KPMG *Information Security Survey 2000* reported that business customers hesitate to put their personal and financial information on the Internet for two reasons. First, they are worried about who has access to this information and how it will be used. Second, they worry that credit card or bank account details will be stolen or used fraudulently.

For example, in 2009 a 28-year-old American citizen, Albert Gonzalez, and two Russian accomplices were indicted for what prosecutors believed was one of the largest ever hacking and identity-theft crimes. U.S. federal prosecutors alleged the three devised a global scheme to hack into the computer systems of five major companies, including Hannaford Brothers supermarkets, 7-Eleven, and Heartland Payment Systems Inc., and steal data from over 130 million credit and debit cards. Gonzalez and his co-conspirators committed the crime on a network of computers located in New Jersey, California, Illinois, Latvia, the Netherlands, and Ukraine. The group was able to infiltrate the computer networks of the victim companies, access credit and debit card numbers, and install back doors in victims' computer networks that enabled them to steal more data in the future. They also installed "sniffer" programs to capture card data and send it to the hacker. The hackers made extensive efforts to conceal their activities, including registering the computers they used under false names and communicating online under a variety of screen names.

---

[17] See Basel Committee on Banking Supervision, *A New Capital Adequacy Framework*, Bank for International Settlements, Basel, Switzerland (bis.org), June 1999, p. 50.

[18] See Basel Committee on Banking Supervision, *The New Basel Capital Accord*, January 2001, and *Overview of The New Basel Capital Accord*, April 2003, Bank for International Settlements, Basel, Switzerland (bis.org). The advanced measurement approach offers three alternative methodologies for capital reserve calculations for the most sophisticated and largest banks in the world.

The advent of electronic banking is making consumer protection an increasingly important responsibility for regulators of FIs. Global standards and protocols that can be credibly enforced will become increasingly necessary to assure the customer's desired degree of privacy.

As mentioned earlier in the chapter, with respect to security risk, because Internet transactions involve open systems, they are susceptible to interception and fraud. Cryptographic techniques for ensuring transaction security are rapidly improving and are almost fully secure for consumer transactions. Further, technological developments are soon expected that will provide protection needed for large transactions as well. Availability of these technologies does not ensure that FIs will use them, especially if their costs are high. Consequently, regulators may need to oversee or even mandate the implementation of these technologies if FIs are slow to use them operationally.

CONCEPT QUESTION

What are the three approaches proposed by the Basel Committee on Banking Supervision for measuring capital requirements for operational risk?

Questions and Problems

1. Explain how technological improvements can increase an FI's interest and noninterest income and reduce interest and noninterest expenses. Use some specific examples.
2. Table 17–1 shows data on earnings, expenses, and assets for banks that report to OSFI. Calculate the annual growth rates in the various income, expense, earnings, and asset categories from 1996 to 2012. If part of the growth rates in assets, earnings, and expenses can be attributed to technological change, in what areas of operating performance has technological change appeared to have the greatest impact? What growth rates are more likely to be caused by economywide economic activity?
3. Compare the effects of technology on an FI's wholesale operations with the effects of technology on an FI's retail operations. Give some specific examples.
4. What are some of the risks inherent in being the first to introduce a financial innovation?
5. The operations department of a major FI is planning to reorganize several of its back-office functions. Its current operating expense is $1,500,000, of which $1,000,000 is for staff expenses. The FI uses a 12 percent cost of capital to evaluate cost-saving projects.
   a. One way of reorganizing is to outsource a portion of its data entry functions. This will require an initial investment of approximately $500,000 after taxes. The FI expects to save $150,000 in annual operating expenses after tax for the next seven years. Should it undertake this project, assuming that this change will lead to permanent savings?
   b. Another option is to automate the entire process by installing new state-of-the-art computers and software. The FI expects to realize more than $500,000 per year in after-tax savings, but the initial investment will be approximately $3,000,000. In addition, the life of this project is limited to seven years, at which time new computers and software will need to be installed. Using this seven-year planning horizon, should the FI invest in this project? What level of after-tax savings would be necessary to make this plan comparable in value creation to the plan in part (a)?
6. City Bank upgrades its computer equipment every five years to keep up with changes in technology. Its next upgrade is two years from today and is budgeted to cost $1,000,000. Management is considering moving up the date by two years to install some new computers with breakthrough software that could generate significant cost savings. The cost for this new equipment is also $1,000,000. What should be the savings per year to justify moving up the planned upgrade by two years? Assume a cost of capital of 15 percent.

7. Identify and discuss three benefits of technology in generating revenue for FIs.
8. Distinguish between economies of scale and economies of scope.
9. What information on the operating costs of FIs does the measurement of economies of scale provide? If economies of scale exist, what implications do they have for regulators?
10. What are diseconomies of scale? What are the risks of large-scale technological investments, especially to large FIs? Why are small FIs willing to outsource production to large FIs against which they are competing? Why are large FIs willing to accept outsourced production from smaller FI competition?
11. What information on the operating costs of FIs is provided by the measurement of economies of scope? What implications do economies of scope have for regulators?
12. Buy Bank had $130 million in assets and $20 million in expenses before the acquisition of Sell Bank, which had assets of $50 million and expenses of $10 million. After the merger, the bank had $180 million in assets and $35 million in costs. Did this acquisition generate either economies of scale or economies of scope for Buy Bank?
13. A bank with assets of $2 billion and costs of $200 million has acquired an investment banking firm subsidiary with assets of $40 million and expenses of $15 million. After the acquisition, the costs of the bank are $180 million and the costs of the subsidiary are $20 million. Does the resulting merger reflect economies of scale or economies of scope?
14. What are diseconomies of scope? How could diseconomies of scope occur?
15. A survey of a local market has provided the following average cost data: Mortgage Bank A (MBA) has assets of $3 million and an average cost of 20 percent. Life Insurance Company B (LICB) has assets of $4 million and an average cost of 30 percent. Corporate Pension Fund C (CPFC) has assets of $4 million and an average cost of 25 percent. For each firm, average costs are measured as a proportion of assets. MBA is planning to acquire LICB and CPFC with the expectation of reducing overall average costs by eliminating the duplication of services.
    a. What should be the average cost after acquisition for the bank to justify this merger?
    b. If MBA plans to reduce operating costs by $500,000 after the merger, what will be the average cost of the new firm?
16. What is the difference between the production approach and the intermediation approach to estimating cost functions of FIs?
17. What are some of the conclusions of empirical studies on economies of scale and scope? How important is the impact of cost reductions on total average costs? What are X-inefficiencies? What role do these factors play in explaining cost differences among FIs?
18. Why do some industrialized countries lag behind others in the proportion of annual electronic noncash transactions per capita? What factors could be important in causing the gap to decrease?
19. What are the differences between the LVTS and CHIPS payment systems?
20. What provision has been made by the members of the CPA to reduce the settlement risk problem in the LVTS?
21. What has been the impact of rapid technological improvements in the electronic payment systems on crime and fraud risk?
22. How does technology create regulatory risk?
23. How has technology altered the competition risk of FIs?
24. What actions has the BIS taken to protect DTIs from insolvency due to operational risk?

PART **3**

MANAGING RISK

18 ▸	Liability and Liquidity Management	413
19 ▸	Deposit Insurance and Other Liability Guarantees	431
20 ▸	Capital Adequacy	457
21 ▸	Product and Geographic Expansion	493
22 ▸	Futures and Forwards	528
23 ▸	Options, Caps, Floors, and Collars	563
24 ▸	Swaps	598
25 ▸	Loan Sales	622
26 ▸	Securitization	638

CHAPTER 18

LIABILITY AND LIQUIDITY MANAGEMENT

After studying this chapter you should be able to:

LO1 Discuss liquid asset management and describe the composition of the liquid asset portfolio for a DTI.

LO2 Discuss the risk–return trade-off for liquid assets.

LO3 Discuss liability management and the funding risk and cost for a DTI.

LO4 Discuss the choice of liability structure for a DTI.

LO5 Discuss the liquidity and liability structures for Canadian DTIs.

LO6 Discuss liability and liquidity risk management in insurance companies.

LO7 Discuss liability and liquidity risk management in other FIs.

LO8 Discuss the role of central banks and regulators in recognizing and controlling for liquidity risk.

INTRODUCTION

DTIs and insurance companies are especially exposed to liquidity risk (see Chapter 12) because the essential feature of this risk is that an FI's assets are relatively illiquid when liquid claims are suddenly withdrawn (or not renewed). The classic case is a bank run in which depositors demand cash as they withdraw their claims from a bank and the bank is unable to meet those demands because of the relatively illiquid nature of its assets. For example, the bank could have a large portfolio of nonmarketable small business or real estate loans.

To reduce the risk of a liquidity crisis, FIs can insulate their balance sheets from liquidity risk by efficiently managing their liquid asset positions or managing the liability structure of their portfolios. In reality, an FI manager can optimize over both liquid asset and liability structures to insulate the FI against liquidity risk. In this chapter, we consider how an FI can manage liquidity risk, and we discuss the various liquid assets an FI might use and the risk–return trade-offs across these assets. In addition to ensuring that FIs can meet expected and unexpected liability withdrawals, an additional motive for holding liquid assets is monetary policy implementation. The chapter concludes with a look at the specific issues associated with liquidity risk management in DTIs, insurance companies, and other FIs.

LIQUID ASSET MANAGEMENT

LO1

A liquid asset can be turned into cash quickly and at a low transaction cost with little or no loss in principal value (see the discussion on the liquidity index in Chapter 12). Specifically, a liquid asset is traded in an active market so that even large transactions in that asset do not move the market price or move it very little. Good examples of liquid assets are newly issued T-bills and other government debt. The ultimate liquid asset is, of course, cash. While it is obvious that an FI's liquidity risk can be reduced by holding large amounts of assets such as cash, T-bills, and Government of Canada bonds, FIs usually face a return or interest earnings penalty from doing this. Because of their high liquidity and low default risks, such assets often bear low returns that reflect their essentially risk free nature. By contrast, nonliquid assets must often promise additional returns or liquidity risk premiums to compensate an FI for the relative lack of marketability and often greater default risk of the instrument.

bankofcanada.ca

Holding relatively small amounts of liquid assets exposes an FI to enhanced illiquidity and risk of a bank run. Excessive illiquidity can result in an FI's inability to meet required payments on liability claims and, at the extreme, in insolvency. It can even lead to contagious effects that negatively impact other FIs (see Chapter 12). Consequently, regulators have often imposed minimum liquid asset reserve requirements. In general, these reserve requirements differ in nature and scope for various FIs and according to country. The requirements depend on the liquidity risk exposure perceived for the FI's type and other regulatory objectives. For example, the U.S. Federal Reserve Bank strengthens its monetary policy by setting a minimum ratio of liquid reserve assets to deposits that limits the ability of DTIs to expand lending.

A decrease in the reserve ratio means that DTIs are able to lend a greater percentage of their deposits, thus increasing credit availability in the economy. As new loans are issued and used to finance consumption and investment expenditures, some of these funds will return to the DTIs as new deposits. In turn, after deducting the appropriate reserve requirement, these new deposits can be used by DTIs to create additional loans, and so on. This process continues until the DTI's deposits have grown sufficiently large that the DTI willingly holds its reserve balance at the new lower reserve ratio. Thus, a decrease in the reserve requirements results in a multiplier effect on the supply of DTI deposits and thus the money supply.

Conversely, an increase in the reserve requirement results in a decrease in lending and subsequent decrease in the money supply. For example, in order to slow down its overheated economy, China has increased reserve requirements for its banks from time to time. Consequently, the banks are able to lend out a smaller percentage of their deposits than before, thus decreasing credit availability and lending and, eventually, leading to a multiple contraction in deposits and a decrease in the money supply. In this context, requiring DTIs to hold minimum ratios of liquid assets to deposits allows the central bank to gain greater control over deposit growth and thus over the money supply (of which bank deposits are a significant portion) as part of its overall macrocontrol objectives.

Another reason for minimum requirements on DTI liquid asset holdings is to force DTIs to invest in government financial claims rather than private-sector financial claims. That is, a minimum required liquid asset reserve requirement is an indirect way for governments to raise additional "taxes" from DTIs. While these reserves are not official government taxes, having DTIs hold cash in the vault or cash reserves at the central bank (when there is only a small interest rate compensation paid) requires DTIs to transfer a resource to the central bank. In fact, the profitability of many central banks is contingent on the size of the reserve requirement "tax," which can be viewed as the equivalent of a levy on DTIs under their jurisdiction. The tax or cost effect of low-interest reserve requirements is increased if inflation erodes the purchasing power value of those balances.

The Bank of Canada is one of several central banks (another example is the Reserve Bank of New Zealand) whose mandate is to control inflation. The Bank of Canada does this by setting a target for the overnight rate rather than by imposing reserve requirements. In effect, the Bank of Canada has set the reserve requirements for banks at zero since 1994. However, it still stands as the lender of last resort in providing overnight liquidity and emergency lending assistance to DTIs and other members of the Canadian Payments Association (CPA). The United Kingdom is another country that no longer imposes reserve requirements on its banks. Since the financial crisis in 2008, the Bank for International Settlements (BIS) has been working on liquidity principles and a liquidity ratio as part of the Basel capital adequacy regulations for internationally active banks. These will be discussed later in the chapter.

THE COMPOSITION OF THE LIQUID ASSET PORTFOLIO

LO1

The composition of an FI's liquid asset portfolio, especially among cash and government securities, is determined partly by earnings considerations and partly by the type of minimum liquid asset reserve requirements the central bank imposes. In many countries, such as the United Kingdom, reserve ratios were historically imposed to encompass both cash and liquid government securities such as T-bills. Thus, a 20 percent **liquid assets ratio** requires a DTI to hold $1 of cash plus government securities for every $5 of deposits. Many states in the United States impose liquid asset ratios on life insurance companies that require minimum cash and government securities holdings in their balance sheets. By contrast, the minimum liquid asset requirements on DTIs in the United States have been cash based and have excluded government securities. As a result, government securities are less useful because they are not counted as part of reserves held by DTIs and at the same time yield lower promised returns than loans. Nevertheless, many DTIs view government securities holdings as performing a useful **secondary** or **buffer reserve** function. In times of a liquidity crisis, when significant drains on cash reserves occur, these securities can be turned into cash quickly and with very little loss of principal value because of the deep nature of the markets in which these assets are traded.

liquid assets ratio
A minimum ratio of liquid assets to total assets set by the central bank.

secondary or buffer reserves
Nonreserve assets that can be quickly turned into cash.

CONCEPT QUESTION

Is it better to hold three-month T-bills or 10-year government bonds as liquid assets? Explain.

RETURN–RISK TRADE-OFF FOR LIQUID ASSETS

LO2

In optimizing its holdings of liquid assets, an FI must trade the benefit of cash immediacy for lower returns. In a jurisdiction that, like Canada and the United Kingdom, does not impose reserve requirements, an FI is able to optimize its liquid asset holdings by matching its assets holdings with the liquidity needs of its short-term liabilities, such as deposit withdrawals. A further consideration in the liquid asset mix for large Canadian FIs is the requirement for members of the Large Value Transfer System (LVTS; see Chapter 17) to provide collateral on a daily basis for the largest transaction that they expect to clear through the payment system. Since LVTS transactions are instantaneous and irrevocable, the collateral acts as a form of co-insurance to protect other LVTS participants and the Bank of Canada should a member experience liquidity difficulties during the day. If an LVTS participant were unable to make its payments, the Bank of Canada would sell the securities held as collateral to meet the FI's obligations. Thus, the collateral is highly liquid and is limited to securities issued or guaranteed by the Government of Canada or provincial governments, deposits held at the Bank of Canada, bankers' acceptances, commercial paper (CP), short-term paper or bonds issued by municipalities, and corporate bonds.

Chapter 12 discussed several models FIs use to measure liquidity risk, including models used to determine the FI's liquid asset needs over a future period of time. However, since cash is a nonearning asset, an FI will hold as little cash as possible to meet its liquid asset needs. The remaining liquid assets are generally stored in the FI's security portfolio (e.g., holding Treasury bills).

Managing the securities portfolio is an integral part of liquidity management for FIs. FI managers must determine the optimal combination of lower-yielding, liquid assets versus higher-yielding, less-liquid assets. Short-term marketable securities are held for immediate liquidity needs, and mortgage securities and other longer-term securities are held and can be sold if liquidity needs are larger than expected. Indeed, as discussed in Chapter 1, FIs are special in that they can mismatch the maturity of their assets and liabilities (issuing short-term deposits to fund long-term assets). FIs profit by performing this "special" service. However, during a liquidity crisis, such as that during the financial crisis of 2008–2009, the ability to liquidate these less-liquid assets may be severely constrained and may even affect the very solvency of the FI. In this respect, liquidity risk is related to operational risk (see Chapter 17); i.e., external liquidity events that are unforeseen and uncontrollable by the FI can affect the FI's ability to operate. Other ways of maintaining liquidity are loan sales and securitization (see Chapters 25 and 26). Briefly, FIs can sell loans (or securitized assets) for liquidity to long-term investors, such as insurance companies. These loan sales provide a stream of liquidity that can be used to fund new loan demand or deposit withdrawals. However, as seen during the financial crisis, these securities, like other long-term securities, may have to be liquidated at fire-sale prices. In addition, if the FI removes loans from its balance sheet, it can use the funds received from the sale of loans to pay off depositors and shrink the size of the balance sheet. With fewer assets, the FI's required capital can be reduced (see Chapter 20).

In summary, holding too many liquid assets penalizes a DTI's earnings and, thus, its stockholders. A DTI manager who holds excessive amounts of liquid assets is unlikely to survive long. Similarly, a manager who holds too small amounts of liquid assets faces enhanced risks of liquidity crises and regulatory intervention. Again, such a manager's tenure at the DTI may be relatively short.

LIABILITY MANAGEMENT

LO3

Liquidity and liability management are closely related. One aspect of liquidity risk control is the buildup of a prudential level of liquid assets. Another aspect is the management of the DTI's liability structure to reduce the need for large amounts of liquid assets to meet liability withdrawals. However, excessive use of purchased funds in the liability structure can result in a liquidity crisis if investors lose confidence in the DTI and refuse to roll over such funds.

As discussed in Chapter 17, improvements in technology and demand for efficiency and flexibility in the financial transactions of wholesale and retail customers have lowered the costs of holding deposits and changed the way FIs manage liquidity risk. Technologically oriented services (such as online banking) connect customers to their deposit and brokerage accounts via personal computers and mobile devices. These technologies also provide other services, such as electronic securities trading and bill paying. Likewise, preauthorized debits of payroll cheques get cash into FIs' deposit accounts faster and with more predictability. In doing so, cheque processing time and handling costs can be reduced significantly for FIs. Many FIs perform the payroll processing for customers for a fee as part of their cash management services. These types of activities have changed the way liquidity management is viewed by FIs.

Funding Risk and Cost

Guaranteed Investment Certificate (GIC)
A fixed-maturity instrument offered to retail clients that is nonredeemable, carries a term from 30 days to five years, and pays interest at a specified rate at the end of the term.

cdic.ca

Unfortunately, constructing a low-cost, low-withdrawal-risk liability portfolio is more difficult than it sounds. This is true because those liabilities, or sources of DTI funds, that are the most subject to withdrawal risk are often the least costly to the DTI. That is, a DTI must trade off the benefits of attracting liabilities at a low funding cost with a high chance of withdrawal against liabilities with a high funding cost and low liquidity. For example, demand deposits are relatively low funding cost vehicles for DTIs but can be withdrawn without notice.[1] By contrast, a five-year, fixed-rate **Guaranteed Investment Certificate (GIC)** may have a relatively high funding cost but can be withdrawn before the five-year maturity is up only after the deposit holder pays a substantial interest rate penalty. As well, Canadian dollar GICs are covered by deposit insurance with premiums that are paid by the DTI to Canada Deposit Insurance Corporation (CDIC).

Thus, in structuring the liability, or funding, side of the balance sheet, the DTI manager faces a trade-off along the lines suggested in Figure 18–1. That is, funding costs are generally inversely related to the period of time the liability is likely to remain on the DTI's balance sheet (i.e., to funding risk).

Although we have discussed DTIs' funding risk, other FIs face a similar trade-off. For example, investment banks can finance through overnight funds (repurchase agreements and brokered deposits) or longer-term sources such as notes and bonds. Finance companies have a choice between CP and longer-term notes and bonds.

In some respects, the management of funding risk and cost is similar to the treasury function of any other large corporation. However, the regulatory climate provides an added dimension to the "treasury" management of a large FI. The

[1] Depositors do not always exercise this option; therefore, some demand deposits behave like longer-term core deposits. In addition, many DTIs waive monthly fees when a depositor maintains a minimum monthly balance, creating an incentive to leave the funds on deposit.

FIGURE 18–1
Funding Risk versus Cost

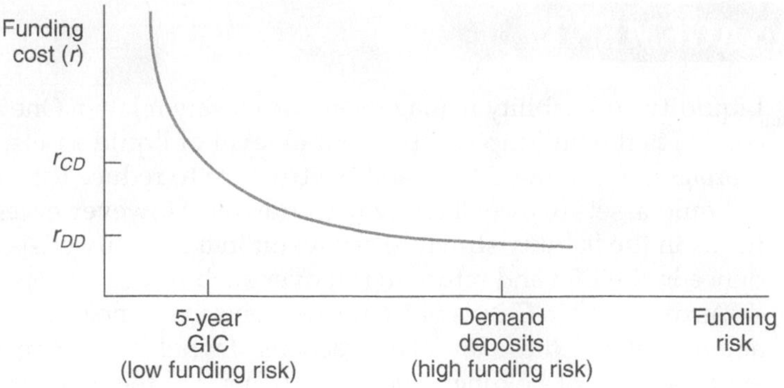

consequences for the FI of undershooting its liquidity needs and, as a result, being unable to settle its payments through the clearing system or meet its customers' deposit withdrawals are a loss of confidence by depositors and regulators; the potential for long-term damage to its reputation; and, in the worst-case scenario, insolvency. The renewed emphasis by BIS and OSFI on liquidity management for the FIs that they regulate is discussed at the end of the chapter. The next section looks at the spectrum of liabilities available to a DTI manager in seeking to actively impact liquidity risk exposure through the choice of liability structure.

CONCEPT QUESTIONS

1. **How are liquidity and liability management related?**
2. **Describe the trade-off faced by an FI in structuring the liability side of the balance sheet.**

CHOICE OF LIABILITY STRUCTURE

LO4

This section considers in more detail the withdrawal (or funding) risk and funding cost characteristics of the major liabilities available to a modern DTI manager.

Demand Deposits

Withdrawal Risk

Demand deposits issued by DTIs have a high degree of withdrawal risk. Withdrawals can be instantaneous and largely expected by the DTI manager, such as pre-weekend cash withdrawals, or unexpected, as occur during economic crisis situations and bank runs (see Chapter 17).

Costs

Demand deposits pay the lowest interest rates, making them a low-cost source of funds for DTIs. In addition, DTIs can adjust the levels of interest rates and fees charged in order to partially control for the withdrawal risk associated with these contracts. For example, it is common for deposit accounts at FIs to pay a higher interest rate depending on the amount kept on balance in the account, or to provide no-fee chequing if a minimum monthly balance is maintained. Very few bank deposits in Canada are non-interest-bearing. For example, a summary of average deposits and interest rates from CIBC's 2012 Annual Report is shown in Table 18–1. CIBC reported total foreign and domestic deposits of \$299.205 billion. Of this total, only \$32.3 billion of deposits (10.8 percent) were non-interest-bearing. The average

cibc.com

TABLE 18–1
Average Deposits and Interest Rates, CIBC, October 31, 2012

Source: 2012 CIBC Annual Report, cibc.com.

	Average Balance ($ millions)	Total Deposits (%)	Average Interest Rate (%)
Domestic deposits:			
Payable on demand:			
Personal	$ 7,481	2.5%	0.23%
Business and government	26,413	8.8	0.39
Bank	1,188	0.4	0.25
Payable after notice:			
Personal	64,549	21.6	0.62
Business and government	15,478	5.2	1.07
Bank	11	—	—
Payable on a fixed date:			
Personal	40,288	13.5	2.03
Business and government	47,111	15.7	1.63
Bank	424	0.1	0.94
Secured borrowings	51,975	17.4	2.15
Total domestic deposits	254,918	85.2	1.33
Total foreign deposits	44,287	14.8	0.53
Total deposits	299,205	100.0	1.21

rate paid on domestic deposits was 1.33 percent, with the highest average rate paid on secured borrowings (2.15 percent) and the lowest average rate on personal demand deposits (0.23 percent). At $118.2 billion, person retail deposits were CIBC's main source of funding in 2012. CIBC conducts stress testing to determine which are core deposits and so unlikely to be withdrawn during a liquidity crisis. A high level of core deposits reduces an FI's need to go to the wholesale markets for funding.

Competition among DTIs and other FIs has resulted in the payment of implicit interest, or payments of interest in kind, on chequing accounts. Specifically, in providing demand deposits that are chequable accounts, a DTI must provide a whole set of associated services such as providing chequebooks, clearing cheques, and sending out statements with cleared cheques or cheque images. Because such services absorb real resources of labour and capital, they are costly for DTIs to provide. DTIs can recapture these costs by charging fees, such as 10 cents per cheque cleared. To the extent that these fees do not fully cover the DTI's cost of providing such services, the depositor receives a subsidy or an implicit interest payment.

EXAMPLE 18–1

Calculation of Average Implicit Interest Rate

Suppose a DTI pays 15 cents to clear a cheque but charges a fee of only 10 cents per cheque cleared. The customer receives a 5 cent subsidy per cheque. We can calculate implicit yields for each service, or an average implicit interest rate (IIR), for each demand deposit account. For example, an average IIR for a DTI's demand deposits might be calculated as

$$\text{Average } IIR = \frac{\begin{array}{c}\text{Average management costs}\\ \text{per account per annum}\end{array} - \begin{array}{c}\text{Average fees earned per}\\ \text{account per annum}\end{array}}{\text{Average annual size of account}}$$

Suppose that

$$\text{Average management costs per account per annum} = \$150$$
$$\text{Average fees earned per account per annum} = \$100$$
$$\text{Average annual size of account} = \$1{,}200$$

Then

$$IIR = \frac{\$150 - \$100}{\$1,200} = 4.167\%$$

The payment of implicit interest means that the DTI manager is not absolutely powerless to mitigate deposit withdrawals, especially if rates on competing instruments are rising. In particular, the DTI could lower cheque-clearing fees, which in turn raises implicit interest payments to depositors. Such payments are *payments in kind* or *subsidies* that are not paid in actual dollars and cents, as is interest earned on competing instruments. Nevertheless, implicit payments of interest are tax-free to the depositor, but explicit interest payments are taxable.

Interest-Bearing Chequing Accounts

Withdrawal Risk

Canadian FIs offer chequable deposits that pay interest and are withdrawable on demand. The major distinction between these instruments and traditional demand deposits is that these instruments usually require the depositor to maintain a minimum account balance to earn interest. If the minimum balance falls below some level, such as $500, the account formally converts to a status equivalent to demand deposits and earns no interest. The payment of explicit interest and the existence of minimum balance requirements make these accounts potentially less prone to withdrawal risk than demand deposits. Nevertheless, they are still highly liquid instruments from the depositor's perspective.

Costs

As with demand deposits, the FI can influence the potential withdrawability of chequing accounts by paying implicit interest or fee subsidies such as not charging the full cost of cheque clearance. However, the manager has two other ways to influence the yield paid to the depositor. The first is by varying the minimum balance requirement. If the minimum balance requirement is lowered—say, from $500 to $250—a larger portion of the account becomes subject to interest payments and thus the explicit return and attractiveness of these accounts increase. The second is to vary the explicit interest rate payment itself, such as increasing it from 2 to 2¼ percent. Thus, the FI manager has three pricing mechanisms to increase or decrease the attractiveness, and therefore impact the withdrawal rate, of chequing accounts: implicit interest payments, minimum balance requirements, and explicit interest payments.

EXAMPLE 18-2

Gross Interest Return

Consider a depositor who holds on average $250 per month for the first three months of the year, $500 per month for the next three months, and $1,000 per month for the final six months of the year in a chequing account. The account pays 5 percent per year if the minimum balance is $500 or more, and it pays no interest if the account falls below $500. The depositor writes an average of 50 cheques per month and pays a service fee of 10 cents for each cheque although it costs the bank 15 cents to process each cheque. The account holder's gross interest return, consisting of implicit plus explicit interest, is

$$\begin{aligned}\text{Gross interest return} &= \text{Explicit interest} + \text{Implicit interest} = \$500(0.05)(0.25) \\ &\quad + \$1000(0.05)(0.5) + (\$0.15 - \$0.10)(50)(12) \\ &= \$6.25 + \$25 + \$30 = \$61.25\end{aligned}$$

Suppose the minimum balance was lowered from \$500 to \$250 and cheque service fees were lowered from 10 cents to 5 cents per cheque. Then

$$\begin{aligned}\text{Gross interest return} &= \$250(0.05)(0.25) + \$500(0.05)(0.25) + \$1{,}000(0.05)(0.5) \\ &\quad + (\$0.15 - \$0.05)(50)(12) \\ &= \$3.125 + \$6.25 + \$25 + \$60 \\ &= \$94.375\end{aligned}$$

Savings Accounts

Withdrawal Risk

Savings accounts are generally less liquid than demand deposits and chequing accounts for two reasons. First, they are nonchequable and may involve physical presence at the institution for withdrawal. Second, the FI has the legal power to delay payment or withdrawal requests. This is rarely done, and FIs normally meet withdrawal requests with immediate cash payment, but they have the legal right to delay, which provides important withdrawal risk control to FI managers.

Costs

Since these accounts are nonchequable, any implicit interest rate payments are likely to be small; thus, the principal costs to the FI are the explicit interest payments on these accounts. In recent years, FIs have normally paid slightly higher explicit rates on savings than on chequing accounts.

Retail Term Deposits and GICs

Withdrawal Risk

retail term deposits
Fixed-maturity instruments offered to retail clients for a term of one to five years with a guaranteed interest payment that is usually semiannual and carries an interest penalty for early withdrawal.

By contractual design, fixed-term deposits reduce the withdrawal risk to issuers. DTIs in Canada offer **retail term deposits**, which are redeemable prior to maturity subject to an interest penalty, and GICs, which are generally not redeemable prior to maturity to retail investors. Term deposits are straightforward deposits whose rates are generally set to be competitive, but fixed over the term of the deposit. The size, maturity, and rate on term deposits are usually standardized. GICs, on the other hand, come in many variations to appeal to retail customers as an alternative to other sources of investment, particularly for registered retirement savings plans (RRSPs) or registered retirement income funds (RRIFs). For example, the rate on GICs may be tied to money market rates (e.g., the FI's rate for bankers' acceptances) or, alternatively, may carry a rate tied to the S&P TSX60 Index or other market indices, which may change over the term of the deposit. In a world of no early withdrawal requests, the DTI knows the exact scheduling of interest and principal payments to depositors holding such deposit claims, since these payments are contractually specified. As such, the FI manager can directly control fund inflows and outflows by varying the maturities of the deposits offered to the public. In addition, since many GICs are held by depositors within an RRSP or RRIF, they may be less subject to withdrawal to another FI on rollover dates. At October 31, 2012, the domestic banks reported a total of \$91.6 billion of tax-sheltered fixed-term deposits to OSFI.

When depositors wish to withdraw before the maturity of a term deposit, FIs impose penalties on a withdrawing depositor, such as the loss of a certain number of months' interest depending on the maturity of the deposit. Although this does impose a friction or transaction cost on withdrawals, it is unlikely to stop withdrawals of term deposits when the depositor has exceptional liquidity needs. Also, withdrawals may increase if depositors perceive the DTI to be insolvent, despite interest penalties and deposit insurance coverage up to $100,000. Nevertheless, under normal conditions, these instruments have low withdrawal risk compared with chequing accounts and can be used as an important liability management tool to control withdrawal/liquidity risk.

Costs

tax-free savings account (TFSA)
A registered account that allows investors to accumulate and withdraw investment income tax-free on deposits of up to $5,000 per year.

tfsa.gc.ca

Similar to those of savings accounts, the major costs of these deposits are explicit interest payments. Short-term GICs are often competitive with money market instruments such as T-bills. Note that depositors who buy term deposits and GICs are subject to taxes on their interest payments, although those held within RRSPs are sheltered until withdrawn. As well, the **tax-free savings account (TFSA)** introduced by the Government of Canada in 2009 is registered. TFSAs allow contributions of up to $5,000 per year that can be held in GICs, mutual funds, and other investments such as bonds. The investment income is tax-free, as are withdrawals from the TFSA.

Wholesale Fixed-Term Deposits and CDs

Withdrawal Risk

wholesale CDs
Time deposits with a face value above US$100,000.

negotiable instruments
Instruments whose ownership can be transferred in the secondary market.

Wholesale CDs were innovated by U.S. banks in the early 1960s as a contractual mechanism to allow depositors to liquidate their positions in these CDs by selling them in the secondary market rather than settling up with the FI. A depositor can sell a relatively liquid instrument without causing adverse liquidity risk exposure for the FI. Thus, the unique feature of these wholesale CDs is not so much their large minimum denomination size of US$100,000 but the fact that they are **negotiable instruments.** That is, they can be resold by title assignment in a secondary market to other investors. This means, for example, that if IBM bought a US$1 million three-month CD from Citibank but for unexpected liquidity reasons needed funds after only one month had passed, it could sell this CD to another outside investor in the secondary market. This does not impose any obligation on Citibank in terms of an early funds withdrawal request. Thus, a depositor can sell a relatively liquid instrument without causing adverse withdrawal risk exposure for the FI. Essentially, the only withdrawal risk (which can be substantial) is that these wholesale CDs are not rolled over and reinvested by the holder of the deposit claim on maturity.

Canadian FIs operating in the United States are able to take advantage of the CD market. However, a similar active market does not exist in Canada. For Canadian FIs, most core wholesale deposits come from institutional investors (governments, other FIs) and corporate entities with which the FI may have a relationship. Wholesale fixed-term deposits are tailored to meet the cash management needs of the customer, and the rates are higher than those on retail GICs, although many FIs rely on asset-backed commercial paper (ABCP) for short-term funding (see Chapter 26).

Costs

The rates that FIs pay on these instruments are competitive with other wholesale money market rates, especially those on CP and T-bills. This competitive rate aspect is enhanced by the highly sophisticated nature of investors in CDs, such as money market mutual fund (MMMF) managers, and the fact that these deposits are covered by deposit insurance guarantees only up to the limit per investor, per institution (US$100,000). To the extent that these CDs are offered by large FIs perceived as being too big to fail, the required credit risk premium on CDs is less than that required for similar-quality instruments issued by the nonbank private sector (e.g., CP). In addition, required interest yields on CDs reflect investors' perceptions of the depth of the secondary market for CDs. In recent years, the liquidity of the secondary market in CDs appears to have diminished as dealers have withdrawn. This has increased FIs' relative cost of issuing such instruments.[2]

Interbank Funds

Withdrawal Risk

The liabilities just described are all deposit liabilities, reflecting deposit contracts issued by DTIs in return for cash. However, DTIs not only fund their assets by issuing deposits but also can borrow in various markets for purchased funds. Since the funds generated from these purchases are borrowed funds, not deposits, they are not subject to deposit insurance premium payments to the CDIC (as with all the domestic deposits described earlier).[3] The largest market available for purchased funds is the interbank market. While DTIs with excess cash can invest some of this excess in interest-earning liquid assets such as T-bills and short-term securities, an alternative is to lend excess cash for short intervals to other FIs seeking increased short-term funding. **Interbank funds** are short-term uncollateralized loans made by one FI to another; more than 90 percent of such transactions have maturities of one day. The FI that purchases funds shows them as a liability on its balance sheet, while the FI that sells them shows them as an asset. For example, as shown in Table 18–1, CIBC showed average demand deposits of $1.19 trillion from banks paying an average interest rate of 0.25 percent on its 2012 annual report.

interbank funds
Short-term uncollateralized loans made by one FI to another.

CIBC also reported **U.S. federal funds** purchased of $437 million at October 31, 2012. The largest market available for purchased funds for banks operating in the United States is the federal funds market.

U.S. federal funds
Short-term uncollateralized loans made by one U.S. DTI to another.

For the liability-funding FIs, there is no risk that the interbank funds they have borrowed can be withdrawn within the day, although there may be settlement risk at the end of each day (see Chapter 17). However, there is some risk that funds will not be rolled over by the lending bank the next day if rollover is desired by the borrowing FI. In reality, this has occurred only in periods of extreme crisis. Nevertheless, since interbank funds are uncollateralized loans, institutions selling interbank funds normally impose maximum bilateral limits or credit caps on borrowing institutions. This may constrain the ability of a bank to

---

[2] In addition, for all the liability instruments considered so far, a U.S.-based FI may have to pay an FDIC insurance premium depending on its perceived riskiness. For example, consider a bank issuing CDs in the United States at 3.26 percent, at which rate a depositor might just be indifferent to holding T-bills at 3.00 percent, given a local tax rate of 8 percent. However, the cost to the bank of the CD issue is not 3.26 percent but

$$\text{Effective CD cost} = 3.26\% + \text{Insurance premium} = 3.26\% + 0.27\% = 3.53\%$$

where 27 bp is the assumed size of the deposit insurance premium. Thus, deposit insurance premiums add to the cost of deposits as a source of funds.

[3] CDIC does not insure foreign deposits (e.g., U.S. dollar accounts) in Canada, so they are not subject to deposit insurance premiums.

expand its interbank funds-borrowing position very rapidly if this is part of its overall liability management strategy. During the financial crisis in 2008, interbank funds were scarce as FIs worried about the stability of other global banks.

Costs

The cost of interbank funds for the purchasing institution is the interbank rate. The rate is set by FIs (mostly banks) that trade in the market and can vary considerably both within the day and across days. Another interbank source of funding is the LIBOR market. The LIBOR market normally provides global banks with a low-cost source of funds, often in U.S. dollars, that FIs match with their borrowers who have LIBOR-based loans. The level of liquidity provided by the interbank market became evident during the subprime mortgage crisis in 2007 and the liquidity crisis in 2008. Global banks began to doubt each other's solvency after the failure of Bear Stearns in the United States and the bailout of AIG. The cost of LIBOR deposits, that is, the rate banks charge to lend to each other, increased. Market participants watched as the **TED spread**, which measures the difference between the three-month U.S. dollar T-bill rate and the three-month Eurodollar rate, peaked at 465 bp between September and November 2008. The average TED spread reached 150 to 300 bp during the economic crisis, up from its normal value of 30 to 50 bp.

TED spread
The difference between the three-month U.S. Treasury bill rate and the three-month Eurodollar rate.

Repurchase Agreements (Repos)

Withdrawal Risk

repurchase agreements (RPs or repos)
Agreements involving the sale of securities by one party (e.g., a DTI) to another with a promise to repurchase the securities at a specified date and price in the future.

Repurchase agreements (RPs or repos) can be viewed as collateralized interbank transactions. The FI with excess cash sells overnight funds for one day to the purchasing FI. The next day, the purchasing FI returns the funds plus one day's interest reflecting the Bank of Canada's overnight rate. Since a credit risk exposure exists for the selling FI because the purchasing FI may be unable to repay the funds the next day, the seller may seek collateral backing for the one-day loan. In a repo transaction, the funds-selling FI receives government securities as collateral from the funds-purchasing FI. That is, the funds-purchasing FI temporarily exchanges securities for cash. The next day, this transaction is reversed. The funds-purchasing FI sends back the overnight funds it borrowed plus interest (the repo rate); it receives in return (or repurchases) its securities used as collateral in the transaction.

As with the interbank market, the repo market is a highly liquid and flexible source of funds for FIs needing to increase their liabilities and to offset deposit withdrawals. Moreover, these transactions can be rolled over each day. The major liability management flexibility difference between interbank funds and repos is that an interbank funds transaction can be entered into at any time in the business day. In general, it is difficult to transact a repo borrowing late in the day since the FI selling the funds must be satisfied with the type and quality of the securities collateral proposed by the borrowing institution. This collateral is normally in the form of T-bills, T-notes, T-bonds, and mortgage-backed securities, but its maturity and other features, such as callability and coupons, may be unattractive to the funds seller. Negotiations over the collateral package can delay repo transactions and make them more difficult to arrange than simple uncollateralized loans.[4]

---

[4] The Bank of Canada participates in the overnight funds market via purchase and resale agreements (PRAs) in order to enact monetary policy by influencing the overnight rate. When overnight funds are trading below the target rate, the Bank of Canada will offer to sell Government of Canada securities overnight and buy them back at a set price the next day.

Costs

Because of their collateralized nature, repo rates normally lie below interbank rates. Also, repo rates generally show less interday fluctuation than do interbank rates. This is partly due to the lower intraday flexibility of repos relative to interbank transactions.

Other Borrowings

While interbank funds and repos have been a major source of borrowed funds, FIs have utilized a host of other borrowing sources to supplement their liability management flexibility. We describe these briefly in the following sections.

Bankers' Acceptances

Banks often convert off-balance-sheet (OBS) letters of credit (LCs) into on-balance-sheet bankers' acceptances (BAs) by discounting the LC the holder presents for acceptance (see Chapter 16). Further, these BAs may then be resold to money market investors. Thus, BA sales to the secondary market are an additional funding source.

CP

As noted previously, Canadian FIs have been active issuers in the CP market. Bank of Canada statistics show $53.3 billion of CP outstanding on December 2012, 81.3 percent issued by financial corporations. The $51.975 billion average total of secured borrowing shown for CIBC in Table 18–1 comprises liabilities related to securitization of residential mortgages, covered bonds, and other securitizations. Covered bonds are similar to securitizations, but the assets remain on the balance sheet since the debt is recourse to the issuer. CIBC's covered bonds are unsecured and unsubordinated and are backed by insured mortgages. Royal Bank of Canada (RBC) has issued covered U.S. dollar–denominated bonds in the United States as well as euro-denominated bonds in Europe.

Medium-Term and Long-Term Notes

A number of DTIs in search of more stable sources of funds with low withdrawal risk have begun to issue medium-term notes, often in the five- to seven-year range. These notes are additionally attractive because they are not subject to deposit insurance premiums.

Overnight Loans with the Bank of Canada

As discussed earlier, FIs facing temporary liquidity crunches can borrow from the central bank at the overnight rate. Direct participants in the LVTS may borrow directly from the Bank of Canada at the overnight rate through the Standing Liquidity Facility (SLF) as described in detail in Chapter 19. Advances from the Bank of Canada for domestic Canadian banks reporting to OSFI totalled $11.894 million at October 31, 2012.

CONCEPT QUESTIONS

1. **Describe the withdrawal risk and funding cost characteristics of the liabilities available to an FI.**
2. **Demand deposits are subject to deposit insurance premiums; interbank funds are not. Should an FI fund all its assets with interbank funds? Explain your answer.**

DEPOSIT-TAKING INSTITUTIONS AND LIQUIDITY RISK

LO5

We summarize the preceding discussion by considering some balance sheet data for Canadian banks. Table 18–2 shows the liquid asset–nonliquid asset composition of domestic Canadian banks in 1996, 2005, 2009, and 2012.

Although the level of cash has declined since 1996, total cash plus government securities plus other securities remained relatively stable at 28.4 percent of total assets in 1996, 31.4 percent in 2005, 29.2 percent in 2009, and 26.7 percent in 2012. Note that Canadian banks switched to IFRS in 2011 so the 2012 numbers may not be completely comparable with previous years' numbers, which were prepared using Canadian Generally Accepted Accounting Principles (GAAP). Loans as a percentage of total on-balance-sheet assets declined by almost 16 percentage points from 1996 to 2009, increasing to 61.6 percent in 2012. This could be a reflection of the funding cost, since loans must be supported by capital (see Chapter 20). As we discuss in Chapters 25 and 26, DTI loans have become significantly more liquid over this period. DTI loans are increasingly being securitized and/or sold in secondary markets. This has fundamentally altered the illiquidity of bank loan portfolios and has made them more similar to securities than in the past. The more liquid the loan portfolio, the less the need for large amounts of traditional liquid assets, such as cash and securities, to act as a buffer again unexpected liability withdrawals.

Table 18–3 presents the liability composition of domestic Canadian banks at March 31 of 1996, 2005, 2009, and 2012. The level of demand and notice deposits increased from 20.2 percent in 1996 to 30.6 percent in 2012. There has been a shift away from fixed-term deposits over which the FI has some control. Term deposits declined from 53.9 percent in 1996 to 31.6 percent in 2012. This could reflect the decline in interest rates, which may not have been sufficiently high to encourage depositors to lock up their funds in longer-term instruments. As discussed in Chapters 2 through 6, the increased competition among banks and other FIs for funds over this period certainly contributed to the change in the composition of the liabilities presented in Table 18–3. DTIs have intentionally managed liabilities, however, to reduce withdrawal risk. As implied in Figure 18–1, there is often a trade-off between withdrawal risk and funding cost. DTIs' attempts to reduce their withdrawal risk by relying more on borrowed and wholesale funds have added to their interest expense.

On an individual basis, the Canadian banks manage their liquidity risk on an enterprisewide scale and have placed more focus on liquidity since the financial crisis. Canadian banks monitor their core deposits and, as mentioned above, provide incentives such as the waiving of fees or interest rates based on deposit levels to

TABLE 18–2 Liquid Assets versus Nonliquid Assets for Domestic Canadian Banks, as at March 31, 1996, 2005, 2009, and 2012 (in percentages)

Assets	1996	2005	2009	2012*
Cash	9.2%	5.2%	4.4%	6.1%
Government securities	10.3	6.6	10.0	6.8%
Other securities	8.9	19.6	14.8	13.8%
Loans	67.4	55.2	51.8	61.6%
Other assets	4.3	13.4	19.0	11.7%
	100.0%	100.0%	100.0%	100.0%

*Prepared using IFRS accounting. Remaining years used Canadian GAAP.

Source: Office of the Superintendent of Financial Services, osfi-bsif.gc.ca.

TABLE 18–3
Liability Structure of Domestic Canadian Banks, as at March 31, 1996, 2005, 2009, and 2012 (in percentages)

Source: Office of the Superintendent of Financial Services, osfi-bsif.gc.ca.

Liabilities	1996	2005	2009	2012
Demand deposits	5.8%	10.6%	25.8%*	30.6%
Notice deposits	14.4	13.6	—	—
Fixed-term deposits	53.9	41.5	37.3	31.6
Borrowings and other liabilities	21.0	29.6	32.1	32.4
Bank capital	4.9	4.7	4.8	5.4
	100.0%	100.0%	100.0%	100.0%

* Includes demand and notice deposits.
** Prepared using IFRS accounting. Remaining years used Canadian GAAP.

encourage customers to leave their deposits in place. They also rely on diversified sources of wholesale funding and contingency risk planning, including stress testing to determine the impact of market disruptions on liquidity needs.

Finally, it should be noted that too heavy a reliance on borrowed funds can be a risky strategy in itself. Even though withdrawal risk may be reduced if lenders in the market for borrowed funds have confidence in the borrowing FI, perceptions that the FI is risky can lead to sudden nonrenewals of interbank and repo loans and the nonrollover of wholesale deposits and other purchased funds as they mature. Consequently, excessive reliance on borrowed funds may be as bad an overall liability management strategy as excessive reliance on chequing and savings deposits. Thus, a well-diversified portfolio of liabilities may be the best strategy to balance withdrawal risk and funding cost considerations.

CONCEPT QUESTIONS

1. **From Table 18–2, how has the ratio of traditional liquid to nonliquid assets changed between 1996 and 2012?**
2. **From Table 18–3, how have the liabilities changed from 1996 to 2012?**

INSURANCE COMPANIES AND LIQUIDITY RISK

LO6

Insurance companies use a variety of sources to meet liquidity needs. As discussed in Chapters 6 and 12, liquidity is required to meet claims on the insurance policies these FIs have written as well as unexpected surrenders of those policies. These contracts therefore represent a potential future liability to the insurance company. Ideally, liquidity management in insurance companies is conducted so that funds needed to meet claims on insurance contracts written can be met with premiums received on new and existing contracts. However, a high frequency of claims at a single point in time (e.g., an unexpectedly severe hurricane season) could force insurers to liquidate assets at something less than their fair market value.

Insurance companies can reduce their exposure to liquidity risk by diversifying the distribution of risk in the contracts they write. For example, P&C insurers can diversify across the types of disasters they cover (e.g., according to Best's Review for August 2012, in the late 2000s the top two U.S. P&C insurance companies [in terms of premiums sold] held policies for over 30 different lines—from auto physical damage, for which they wrote 29.9 percent of all industry premiums, to homeowners' multiple peril, for which they wrote 32.4 percent of all industry premiums).

Alternatively, insurance companies can meet liquidity needs by holding relatively marketable assets to cover claim payments. Assets such as government and corporate bonds and corporate stock can usually be liquidated quickly at close to their fair market values in financial markets to pay claims on insurance policies when premium income is insufficient. For example, on OSFI's website, as at Quarter 4, 2012, Consolidated Assets of Total Canadian Life Companies showed 51.9 percent of the assets (excluding segregated funds) in bonds and debentures and a further 5.3 percent in preferred and common shares. Similarly, as at Quarter 4, 2012, Total Canadian P&C Consolidated Assets showed 52.4 percent in bonds and debentures and 11.2 percent in preferred and common shares.

CONCEPT QUESTIONS

1. **Discuss two strategies insurance companies can use to reduce liquidity risk.**
2. **Do P&C insurers hold more short-term liquid assets than life insurers?**

OTHER FINANCIAL INSTITUTIONS AND LIQUIDITY RISK

LO7

Other FIs, such as securities firms, investment banks, and finance companies, may experience liquidity risk if they rely on short-term financing (such as CP or bank loans) and investors become reluctant to roll those funds over. Remember from Chapter 4 that the main sources of funding for securities firms are repurchase agreements; bank call loans, which a lending bank can "call" with very short notice; and short positions in securities. Liquidity management for these FIs requires the ability to have sufficient cash and other liquid resources at hand to underwrite (purchase) new securities from quality issuers before reselling these securities to other investors. Liability management also requires an investment bank or securities firm to act as a market maker, which requires the firm to finance an inventory of securities in its portfolio. As discussed in Chapter 2, finance companies fund assets mainly with CP and long-term debt. Liquidity management for these FIs requires the ability to fund loan requests and loan commitments of sufficient quality without delay.

The experience of Drexel Burnham Lambert in 1989 in the United States is a good example of a securities firm being subjected to a liquidity challenge. Throughout the 1980s, Drexel Burnham Lambert captured the bulk of the junk bond market by promising investors that it would act as a dealer for junk bonds in the secondary market. Investors were, therefore, more willing to purchase these junk securities because Drexel provided an implied guarantee that it would buy them back or find another buyer at market prices should an investor need to sell. However, the junk bond market experienced extreme difficulties in 1989 as its prices fell, reflecting the economy's move into a recession. Serious concerns about the creditworthiness of Drexel's junk bond–laden asset portfolio led creditors to deny Drexel extensions of its vital short-term CP financings. As a result, Drexel declared bankruptcy. Drexel's sudden collapse makes it very clear that access to short-term purchased funds is crucial to the health of securities firms.

CONCEPT QUESTIONS

1. **What are the main sources of funding for securities firms?**
2. **Give two reasons an investment bank needs liquidity.**

THE ROLE OF CENTRAL BANKS AND REGULATORS

LO8

Lehman Brothers' saga in September 2008 reenacted Drexel's story in 1989: the failure of an investment banking firm that relied on short-term funding. Canadian FIs felt the liquidity crunch through increased interbank costs, but their access to term purchase and resale agreements (PRAs) from the Bank of Canada through the LVTS, the expanded acceptable collateral for PRAs, and the government guarantees of bank liabilities (the Canadian Lenders Assurance Facility), as well as asset purchases through CMHC, helped to stabilize the Canadian markets. The liquidity crisis of 2008 eliminated the stand-alone investment banks in the United States. Bear Stearns was bought by JPMorgan Chase and Merrill Lynch by Bank of America. Goldman Sachs and Morgan Stanley applied to become bank holding companies in order to gain access to U.S. government funding. American International Group (AIG), an insurance company without access to the Federal Reserve window, was provided with a US$85 billion capital injection. The central banks of Canada, the United States, the United Kingdom, and the Eurozone injected liquidity, eased collateral requirements for borrowing from the central bank, expanded deposit insurance coverage, guaranteed bank liabilities, injected capital, and purchased assets. These extraordinary measures were intended to deal with and stabilize systemic risk to the domestic and global financial systems.

The severe market turmoil demonstrated the systemic risk to the global financial system posed by unregulated activities of FIs. Governments and regulators became the main providers of liquidity to the global financial system. In some cases, equity injections (the Troubled Asset Relief Program [TARP] provided to FIs in the United States, and the government takeover of Northern Rock in the United Kingdom) resulted in the nationalization of FIs.

The Basel Committee on Banking Supervision (BCBS) revised its principles for liquidity management and proposed 17 principles that put the onus on FIs and their supervisors to recognize, measure, and manage liquidity risk. OSFI updated Guideline B-6 to incorporate the BCBS principles in 2012. Basel III requires banks to meet two ratios that focus on liquidity risk, the liquidity coverage ratio (LCR) and the net stable funding ratio (NSFR). Both the Basel Committee on Banking Supervision and OSFI define the inputs that are included in calculating the ratios. We discussed the LCR and the NSFR in detail in Chapter 12.[5]

As noted previously, Canadian FIs already monitor and manage their liquidity risks. As well, they have contingency plans that incorporate the severe stress to the global financial system in 2008. These liquidity criteria put a greater onus on FIs and their regulators to measure and monitor liquidity risk and may influence an FI's choice of liquid asset and liability structure.

---

[5] See "Basel III: International Framework for Liquidity Risk Measurement, Standards, and Monitoring," December 2010, and "Monitoring Tools for Intraday Liquidity Management, Basel Committee on Banking Supervision," January 2013, at bis.org. See also Guideline B-6 Liquidity Principles, February 2012, at osfi-bsif.gc.ca.

Questions and Problems

1. What are the benefits and costs to an FI of holding large amounts of liquid assets? Why are Government of Canada and U.S. Treasury securities considered good examples of liquid assets?
2. How is an FI's liability and liquidity risk management problem related to the maturity of its assets relative to its liabilities?
3. Consider the assets (in millions) of two banks, A and B. Both banks are funded by $120 million in deposits and $20 million in equity. Which bank has the stronger liquidity position? Which bank probably has a higher profit?

Bank A Assets		Bank B Assets	
Cash	$ 10	Cash	$ 20
Govt. securities	40	Consumer loans	30
Commercial loans	90	Commercial loans	90
Total assets	$140	Total assets	$140

4. What concerns motivate regulators to require DTIs to hold minimum amounts of liquid assets?
5. Rank these financial assets according to their liquidity: cash, corporate bonds, TSX-traded stocks, and T-bills.
6. What is the relationship between funding cost and funding or withdrawal risk?
7. An FI has estimated the following annual costs for its demand deposits: management cost per account = $140, average account size = $1,500, average number of cheques processed per account per month = 75, cost of clearing a cheque = $0.10, fee charged to customer per cheque = $0.05, and average fee charged per customer per month = $8.
   a. What is the implicit interest cost of demand deposits for the FI?
   b. What should be the per cheque fee charged to customers to reduce the implicit interest cost to 3 percent?
8. A chequing account requires a minimum balance of $750 for interest to be earned at an annual rate of 4 percent. An account holder has maintained an average balance of $500 for the first six months and $1,000 for the remaining six months. She writes an average of 60 cheques per month and pays $0.02 per cheque, although it costs the bank $0.05 to clear a cheque.
   a. What average return does the account holder earn on the account?
   b. What is the average return if the bank lowers the minimum balance to $400?
   c. What is the average return if the bank pays interest only on the amount in excess of $400? Assume that the minimum required balance is $400.
   d. By how much should the bank increase its cheque-clearing fee to ensure that the average interest it pays on this account is 5 percent? Assume that the minimum required balance is $750.
9. Rank the following liabilities with respect, first, to funding risk and, second, to funding cost.
   a. Demand deposits.
   b. GICs.
   c. Interbank funds.
   d. Bankers' acceptances.
   e. Eurodollar deposits.
   f. Chequing accounts.
   g. Wholesale GICs.
   h. Savings accounts.
   i. Repos.
   j. CP.
10. How is the withdrawal risk different for interbank funds and repos?
11. How does the cash balance, or liquidity, of an FI determine the types of repos into which it will enter?
12. What characteristics of Bank of Canada funds may constrain a DTI's ability to use these funds to expand its liquidity quickly?
13. What trends have been observed between 1996 and 2012 in regard to liquidity and liability structures of large Canadian banks?
14. What are the primary methods that insurance companies can use to reduce their exposure to liquidity risk?

CHAPTER 19

DEPOSIT INSURANCE AND OTHER LIABILITY GUARANTEES

After studying this chapter you should be able to:

LO1 Discuss the Canadian regulatory system and the roles of OSFI, CDIC, and the Bank of Canada in ensuring the safety and soundness of the Canadian financial system.

LO2 Discuss the causes of deposit insurance insolvency.

LO3 Discuss the role of deposit insurance in panic prevention and moral hazard.

LO4 Discuss how deposit insurance can be structured to reduce moral hazard and risk-taking.

LO5 Discuss the Bank of Canada's role as lender of last resort.

LO6 Discuss how guarantee programs of insurance companies (Assuris, PACICC) and investment firms (CIPF) differ from deposit insurance.

INTRODUCTION

Chapter 12 discussed the liquidity risks faced by FIs, and Chapter 18 described ways FIs can better manage that risk. Because of concerns about the asset quality or solvency of an FI, liability holders such as depositors and life insurance policyholders (and, to a lesser extent, mutual fund shareholders) have incentives to engage in runs, that is, to withdraw all their funds from an FI. As we discussed in Chapter 12, the incentive to run is accentuated in banks, trusts, and insurance companies by sequential servicing to meet liability withdrawals. As a result, deposit and liability holders who are first in line to withdraw funds get preference over those last in line.

Although a run on an unhealthy FI is not necessarily a bad thing—it can discipline the performance of managers and owners—there is a risk that runs on bad FIs can become contagious and spread to good or well-run FIs. In contagious run or panic conditions, liability holders do not bother to distinguish between good and bad FIs but instead seek to turn their liabilities into cash or safe securities as quickly as possible. Contagious runs can have a major contractionary effect on the supply of credit as well as the money supply regionally, nationally, or internationally. The run on U.S. investment bank Bear Stearns in March 2008 is seen by many as the initial step into the worldwide financial market collapse.

Moreover, a contagious run on FIs can have serious social welfare effects. For example, a major run on banks can have an adverse effect on the level of savings in all types of FIs and therefore can inhibit the ability of individuals to transfer wealth through time to protect themselves against major risks such as future ill health and falling income in old age.

Because of such wealth, money supply, and credit supply effects, government regulators of financial service firms have introduced guarantee programs to deter runs by offering liability holders varying degrees of failure protection. Specifically, if a liability holder believes a claim is totally secure even if the FI is in trouble, there is no incentive to run. The liability holder's place in line no longer affects getting his or her funds back. Regulatory guarantee or insurance programs for liability holders deter runs and thus deter contagious runs and panics.

In Canada, insurance protection is provided by the Canada Deposit Insurance Corporation (CDIC), which was created in 1967 for eligible federally regulated DTIs (banks, trusts, and savings and loans) and federally regulated cooperative credit associations (interprovincial associations of credit unions [CUs]). Provincially incorporated CUs and caisses populaires (CPs) are covered by provincial stabilization funds or guarantee companies (e.g., Québec Deposit Insurance Board). Assuris covers life insurance policies, accident and sickness policies, and annuity contracts should an insurance company fail. The Property and Casualty Insurance Compensation Corporation (PACICC) provides coverage in the event of the failure of a property and casualty (P&C) insurance company. As noted in Chapter 4, the Canadian Investor Protection Fund (CIPF) provides coverage for investors through the Investment Industry Regulatory Organization of Canada (IIROC) and the stock exchanges.

cdic.ca
assuris.ca
pacicc.ca
cipf.ca

iiroc.ca
fdic.gov

In this chapter we look at the Canadian guarantee funds, as well as the experience in the United States with the Federal Deposit Insurance Corporation (FDIC), which has had a longer and more turbulent history since its creation in 1933. This chapter discusses deposit insurance for federally regulated DTIs, beginning with the history of these funds and including the problems experienced by these funds; the methods available to reduce risk-taking, thus reducing the probability that deposit holders must be paid off with deposit insurance; the Bank of Canada's overnight funds as a (limited) alternative to deposit insurance; and other guarantee programs, including those for insurance companies, securities firms, and pension funds.

The Canadian Experience with Deposit Insurance

LO1

Despite the similarities between Canada and the United States, these two North American countries have different histories with respect to deposit insurance. The number of failures of Canadian FIs has been small relative to the experience covered below for the United States. Canada managed to avoid the major bank failures of the Great Depression (which resulted in the creation of U.S. deposit insurance in 1933), the savings and loan failures of the 1980s, and the failures of investment and commercial banks in the subprime and liquidity crises in 2007 and 2008. CDIC was not formed until 1967 as support for the deposits of federally regulated DTIs. In fact, no Canadian bank failed from 1923 (the Home Bank) until 1985 (Canadian Commercial Bank and the Northland Bank of Canada). During that time period, when Canadian banks experienced financial difficulties, they were absorbed by other FIs, resulting in the concentrated banking system that Canada has today.

Although CDIC has not had extensive experience with bank failures, it has experienced trust and loan company failures, including Saskatchewan Trust Co. (1991; CDIC's total claim and loans of $64 million), Standard Loan Co./Standard

Trust Co. (1991; $1.164 billion), Shoppers Trust Co. (1992; $492 million), Adelaide Capital Corp. (1992; $1.588 billion), Central Guarantee Trust Co. (1992; $500 million), Confederation Trust Co. (1994; $680 million), Income Trust Co. (1995; $193 million), and Security Home Mortgage Corp. (1996; $42 million). The failures in the 1990s were partly caused by a recession in the late 1980s, as well as consolidation in the financial industry as the four pillars (see Chapter 1) broke down. Only 43 members of CDIC have failed and no member has failed since 1996.

However, as we discuss in Chapter 21, Canada's financial system is smaller and more concentrated than that of the United States, which has roughly 100 times the number of DTIs. At its largest in 1983, CDIC insured 188 DTIs. Of these, 39 (20 percent) have since failed. Nevertheless, the government of the day in the 1980s was sufficiently alarmed by the failures of weaker DTIs to form a Royal Commission chaired by W. Z. Estey to review deposit insurance and the regulatory structure. CDIC was given new risk minimization and early intervention policies. As well, a new regulator, the Office of the Superintendent of Financial Institutions (OSFI), was created to supervise federally regulated trusts, insurance companies, and banks.[1] At April 30, 2012, CDIC insured $622 billion in deposits at 84 banks, trust companies, loan companies, cooperative credit associations, and subsidiaries of foreign FIs.

The Bank of Canada does not directly supervise and audit federally regulated FIs (see Figure 2–2), but it does have a mandate to ensure the safety and soundness of the financial system, and therefore its monetary policy affects both OSFI and CDIC, which jointly have powers to examine, classify, and take action with respect to federally regulated FIs. The federal Department of Finance, the OSFI, and the Financial Consumer Agency of Canada (FCAC) report to the federal minister of finance. CDIC and the Bank of Canada report to Parliament through the minister of finance. Under the Bank of Canada Act (amended in 1981) and the Canadian Payments Act (1985, revised in 2007), members of CDIC are eligible to operate in the Large Value Transfer System (LVTS; see Chapter 17) and to borrow from the Bank of Canada. Banks that accept only wholesale deposits (greater than $150,000) may opt out of CDIC coverage but remain members of the LVTS and eligible to borrow from the Bank of Canada. As well, the Bank of Canada has responsibility for the Canadian Payments Association (CPA).

bankofcanada.ca
osfi-bsif.gc.ca
fcac-acfc.gc.ca
fin.gc.ca
cdnpay.ca

Failures of weaker institutions in the 1980s; concerns that the strong were subsidizing the weak; and developments in other jurisdictions, such as the United States, led to CDIC's adoption of risk-based or differential premiums, which are discussed in detail later in the chapter. The stability of the Canadian system was demonstrated during the financial crisis in 2008. CDIC did not increase its deposit insurance limits, but the U.S. FDIC raised its coverage to US$250,000. The Federal Services Compensation Scheme in the United Kingdom increased its coverage to £50,000, and the European Union increased its deposit insurance coverage to €50,000. CDIC played a lead role in establishing the International Association of

regulatory forbearance
Regulators' policy of allowing an FI to continue to operate even when it is in breach of regulations in hopes that the situation will correct itself over time.

[1] The difference in the Canadian and U.S. experiences of FI failures has been of interest to researchers. For example, see L. Kryzanowski and G. S. Roberts, "Canadian Banking Solvency, 1922–1940," *Journal of Money, Credit, and Banking*, August 1993, 25(3), pp. 361–76, for a review of the literature and the proposal that **regulatory forbearance** played a role, along with the Canadian branch banking system, in the stability of the Canadian financial system. For a detailed discussion of the bank failures of the 1980s, see W. Z. Estey, *Report of the Inquiry into the Collapse of the CCB and Northland Bank*, 1986, Supply and Services Canada, Ottawa, and also J. F. Dingle, "The Bank Failures of September 1985," in *Planning an Evolution: The Story of the Canadian Payments Association 1980–2002*, 2004, Bank of Canada and the Canadian Payments Association, pp. 25–30.

iadi.org Deposit Insurers (IADI), which along with the BIS, released a report outlining 18 principles for countries to follow regarding deposit insurance.[2] We turn now to the U.S. experience with FI guarantee funds.

The U.S. Experience with Bank Deposit Insurance

The FDIC was created in 1933 in the wake of the banking panics of 1930–1933, when some 10,000 commercial banks failed. The original level of individual depositor insurance coverage at commercial banks was US$2,500, which was increased to US$100,000 in 1980 and to US$250,000 in October 2008. Between 1945 and 1980, commercial bank deposit insurance clearly worked; there were no runs or panics, and the number of individual bank failures was very small (see Figure 19–1). Beginning in 1980, however, bank failures accelerated, with more than 1,039 failures in the decade ending in 1990, peaking at 221 in 1988. This number of failures was actually larger than that for the entire 1933–1979 period. Moreover, the costs of each of these failures to the FDIC were often larger than the total costs for the mainly small bank failures in 1933–1979. As the number and costs of these closures mounted in the 1980s, the FDIC fund, built up from premiums paid by banks (and the reinvestment income from those premiums), was rapidly drained. Any insurance fund becomes insolvent if the premiums collected and the reserves built up from investing premiums are insufficient to offset the cost of failure claims. The FDIC's resources were virtually depleted by early 1991, when it was given permission to borrow US$30 billion from the U.S. Treasury. Even then, it ended 1991 with a deficit of US$7 billion. In response to this crisis, the U.S. Congress passed the FDIC Improvement Act (FDICIA) in December 1991 to restructure the bank insurance fund and prevent its potential insolvency.

There was a dramatic turnaround in FDIC's finances and a drop in U.S. bank failures after 1991, partly in response to record profit levels in banks. As shown in Figure 19–1, three DTIs failed in 2007 but none in 2005 and 2006. However, the

FIGURE 19–1 **Number of Failed U.S. Banks by Year, 1934–2012**

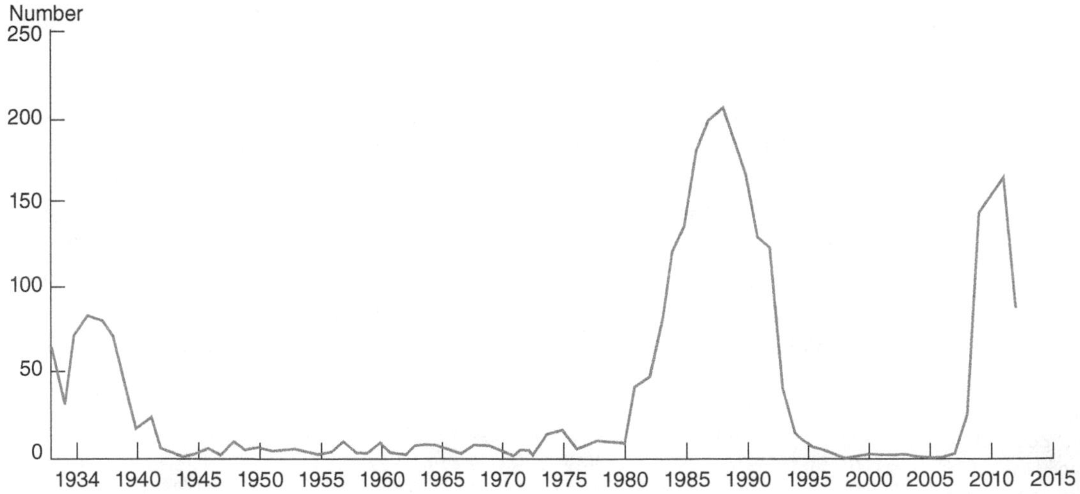

Source: FDIC annual reports and statistics on banking, fdic.gov.

[2] See Basel Committee on Banking Supervision and International Association of Deposit Insurers, *Core Principles for Effective Deposit Insurance Systems*, June 2009, at bis.org.

financial market crisis hit banks very badly. In 2008, 26 DTIs failed (at a cost to the FDIC of US$20 billion); in 2009, 140 additional failures occurred (at a cost of over US$36 billion); and in 2010, 157 failures occurred (at a cost of US$22.73 billion). Thus, during the worst of the financial crisis, 323 banks failed at a total cost to the FDIC of US$78.73 billion. By September 2009, the FDIC's reserves had fallen to –US$8.4 billion, less than zero for only the second time since its founding in 1933. The deficit peaked in the first quarter of 2010 at –US$20.86 billion. However, unlike the near bankruptcy of the FDIC in 1991, the negative balance in the FDIC's insurance fund did not result in talk of the insurer's possible failure. Rather, the FDIC and the federal government took several steps to ensure the fund would have sufficient resources to deal with any and all DI failures. To address the falling balance in the fund, the FDIC levied one special assessment in early 2009 and a second in the fall of 2009, in addition to raising the rates banks were charged for deposit insurance. Further, the agency took the unprecedented step of requiring banks to prepay US$45 billion of insurance premiums by the end of 2009. The premiums covered the fourth quarter of 2009 and all of 2010 through 2012. Finally, the FDIC was also given approval to tap US$500 billion in additional funding from the U.S. Treasury Department through the end of 2010. The actions of regulators (and the end of the crisis) proved successful as only 92 banks failed in 2011 (costing US$6.89 billion) and 12 banks failed through August 2012 (at a cost of US$2.08 billion). Further, FDIC reserves became positive (US$3.9 billion) in the first quarter of 2011 and rose to US$11.8 billion by March 2012.The FDIC maintains a list of failed banks at its website to provide information for depositors.

fdic.gov

CAUSES OF DEPOSIT INSURANCE INSOLVENCY

LO2

Deposit insurance provides support for DTIs and is therefore intended to contribute to the stability of the financial system. Canada has been fortunate that the impact of economic events in the 1980s and 1990s and in 2007–2009 did not test the deposit insurance fund provided by CDIC beyond its strength, although, as discussed below, Assuris required refunding after the collapse of Confederation Life in 1994. This means, however, that we need to look elsewhere for guidelines to failure. Therefore, the following discussion, although generalized for any deposit insurance system, draws heavily on the U.S. experience for examples and relevant research. There are at least two not necessarily independent views as to why deposit insurance funds can become economically insolvent.

The Financial Environment

One view of the cause of insolvency is that a number of external events or shocks can adversely affect DTIs. The dramatic rise in interest rates in the 1979–1982 period had a major negative effect on those FIs funding long-term, fixed-rate mortgages with short-term deposits. The second event was the collapse in oil, real estate, and other commodity prices, which particularly harmed oil, gas, and agricultural loans in the southwestern United States and in western Canada. The third event was increased financial service firm competition at home and abroad, which eroded the value of bank charters during the 1980s.[3] In the late 2000s, the collapse

[3] The value of a bank charter is the present value of expected profits from operating in the industry. As expected profits fall, so does the value of a bank charter.

of the U.S. housing market, and the resulting increase in the number of mortgage defaults, led to sharp declines in values of on- and off-balance-sheet assets held by FIs and an increase in their liabilities. These losses drove a few high-profile FIs (e.g., Bear Stearns, AIG, Lehman Brothers) into or near bankruptcy, which sent financial markets into steady declines and eventually sent the world economy into the worst recession since the Great Depression. DTIs, holding loans to and securities of these failed FIs, experienced large losses. Further, the rise in unemployment that accompanied the global recession meant consumer loan defaults rose significantly as well. Eventually, what began as a burst in the U.S. housing bubble resulted in large increases in the number of insolvent DTIs globally.

Moral Hazard

A second view is that these financial environment effects were catalysts for, rather than the causes of, economic crises. At the heart of the crises was deposit insurance itself, especially some of its contractual features. Although deposit insurance deters depositors and other liability holders from engaging in runs, in so doing it had also removed or reduced depositor discipline. Deposit insurance allows insured FIs to borrow at rates close to the risk-free rate and, if they choose, to undertake high-risk asset investments. The FI owners and managers know that insured depositors have little incentive to restrict such behaviour, either through fund withdrawals or by requiring risk premiums on deposit rates, since they are insured by deposit insurance if the FI fails. Given this scenario, losses on loans in the 1980s and real estate loans and mortgage-backed securities in 2007–2009 may be viewed as the outcome of bankers exploiting underpriced or mispriced risk under the deposit insurance contract. The provision of insurance that encourages rather than discourages risk-taking is called **moral hazard**. This is because, with deposit insurance, a highly leveraged bank whose debt holders need not monitor the FI's (borrower's) actions has a strong incentive to undertake excessively risky investment decisions, such as in its loan-generating activities.[4]

moral hazard
The loss exposure faced by an insurer when the provision of insurance encourages the insured to take more risks.

implicit premiums
Deposit insurance premiums or costs imposed on a DTI through activity constraints rather than direct monetary charges.

In the absence of depositor discipline (as will be explained below), regulators can price risk-taking either through charging explicit deposit insurance premiums linked to the FI's risk-taking or by charging **implicit premiums** through restricting and monitoring the risky activities of FIs. This could potentially have substituted for depositor discipline; those FIs that take more risk would pay directly or indirectly for this risk-taking behaviour. However, from 1933 until January 1, 1993, U.S. regulators based deposit insurance premiums on a deposit size rather than on risk, as did CDIC in Canada until 1999. The 1980s were a period of deregulation and capital adequacy forbearance rather than stringent activity regulation and tough capital requirements. Even with risk-based premiums and stricter capital adequacy requirements, it can be argued that FIs significantly increased their risks from 2000 to 2006, particularly their market risk exposure through their trading portfolios. Risk-based premiums for deposit insurance and capital adequacy requirements were insufficient to prevent the failure of many U.S. DTIs.

CONCEPT QUESTION

Why do deposit insurance funds become insolvent?

[4] The use of "bail-ins" as prescribed by the Financial Stability Board (FSB) for uninsured depositors and unsecured debtholders is an attempt to enforce discipline on the providers of funds for FIs. See "Key Attributes of Effective Resolution Regimes for Financial Institutions," October 2011, at www.financialstabilityboard.org.

PANIC PREVENTION VERSUS MORAL HAZARD

LO3

A great deal of attention has focused on the moral hazard reason for the collapse of the U.S. bank and savings and loans insurance funds in the 1980s and the strain placed on deposit insurance funds globally as a result of the financial crisis. The less FI owners have to lose from taking risks, the greater are their incentives to take excessively risky asset positions. When asset investment risks or gambles pay off, FI owners make windfall gains in profits. If they fail, however, the insurer bears most of the costs, given that owners—like owners of regular corporations—have limited liability. It's a "heads I win, tails I don't lose (much)" situation.

Note that even without deposit insurance, the limited liability of FI owners or stockholders always creates incentives to take risk at the expense of fixed claimants such as depositors and debt holders.[5] The difference between DTIs and other firms is risk-taking incentives induced by mispriced deposit insurance. That is, when risk-taking is not **actuarially fairly priced insurance**, this adds to the incentives to take additional risks.

actuarially fairly priced insurance
Insurance pricing based on the perceived risk of the insured.

Nevertheless, even though mispriced deposit insurance potentially accentuates risk-taking, deposit insurance effectively deterred panics and runs of the 1930–1933 kind in much of the postwar period. That is, deposit insurance has ensured a good deal of stability in the U.S. and Canadian credit and monetary system. During the financial crisis of 2008–2009, DTI deposits actually grew as risk-averse investors liquidated alternative investments and deposited the funds at DTIs, which were seen as a relatively safe haven.

This suggests that, ideally, regulators should design the deposit insurance contract with the trade-off between moral hazard risk and panic or run risk in mind. For example, by providing 100 percent coverage of all depositors and reducing the probability of runs to zero, the insurer may be encouraging certain DTIs to take a significant degree of moral hazard risk-taking behaviour. On the other hand, a very limited degree of deposit insurance coverage might encourage runs and panics, although moral hazard behaviour itself would be less evident.

Extensive insurance coverage for deposit holders and the resulting lack of incentive for deposit holders to monitor and restrict owners' and managers' risk-taking results in small levels of run risk but high levels of moral hazard risk.[6] By restructuring the deposit insurance contract, it may be possible to reduce moral hazard risk quite a bit without a very large increase in run risk.

---

[5] Thus, one possible policy to reduce excessive bank risk-taking is to eliminate limited liability for bank stockholders. A study by L. J. White found that bank failures in private banking systems with unlimited liability, such as what existed in 18th-century Scotland, were rare. In the United States, double liability existed for bank stockholders prior to the introduction of deposit insurance; that is, on failure, the stockholders would lose their initial equity contribution and be assessed by the receiver an extra amount equal to the par value of their stock, which would be used to pay creditors (over and above the liquidation value of the bank's assets). See L. J. White, "Scottish Banking and Legal Restrictions Theory: A Closer Look," *Journal of Money, Credit and Banking* 22 (1990), pp. 526–36. For a discussion of double liability in pre-1933 United States, see A. Saunders and B. Wilson, "If History Could Be Re-Run: The Provision and Pricing of Deposit Insurance in 1933," *Journal of Financial Intermediation* 4 (1995), pp. 396–413, and J. R. Macey and G. P. Miller, "Double Liability of Bank Shareholders: History and Implications," *Wake Forest Law Review* 27 (1992), pp. 31–62.

[6] Note that managers may not have the same risk-taking incentives as owners. This is especially true if managers are compensated through wage and salary contracts rather than through shares and share option programs. When managers are on fixed-wage contracts, they are risk averse. That is, they are unlikely to exploit the same type of moral hazard incentives that stock owner–controlled banks would. This is because managers have little to gain if their banks do exceptionally well (their salaries are fixed) but probably will lose their jobs and human capital investments if they fail.

CONTROLLING RISK-TAKING

LO4

There are three ways deposit insurance could be structured to reduce moral hazard behaviour:

1. Increase stockholder discipline.
2. Increase depositor discipline.
3. Increase regulator discipline.

Specifically, redesigning the features of the insurance contract can either directly or indirectly impact DTI owners' and stockholders' risk-taking incentives by altering the behaviour of depositors and regulators.

Stockholder Discipline

Insurance Premiums

One approach to making stockholders' risk-taking more expensive is to link insurance premiums to the risk profile of the DTI. Below we look at ways this might be done.

Theory A major feature of CDIC's deposit insurance contract from 1967 to 1998 was the flat deposit insurance premium levied on banks. Every bank paid the same premium to CDIC based on a fixed proportion of its deposits. The premium was 3.3 basis points (bp) per dollar of insured deposits from 1967 to 1985, increasing to 10 bp from 1986 to 1992 and to 12.5 bp in 1993 and 16.7 bp from 1994 to 1998.

To see why a flat or size-based premium schedule does not discipline risk-taking, consider two banks of the same domestic deposit size, as shown in Table 19–1. Banks A and B have domestic deposits of $100 million and in 1998 would pay the same premium to CDIC (0.00167 × $100 million = $167,000 per annum). However, their risk-taking behaviour is completely different. Bank A is excessively risky, investing all its assets in real estate loans. Bank B is almost risk free, investing all its assets in government T-bills. We graph the insurance premium rates paid by the two banks compared with their asset risk in Figure 19–2.

TABLE 19–1
Flat Deposit Insurance Premiums and Risk-Taking

Bank A				Bank B			
Assets		Liabilities		Assets		Liabilities	
Real estate loans	100	Domestic deposits	100	T-bills	100	Domestic deposits	100

FIGURE 19–2
Premium Schedules Relative to Risk

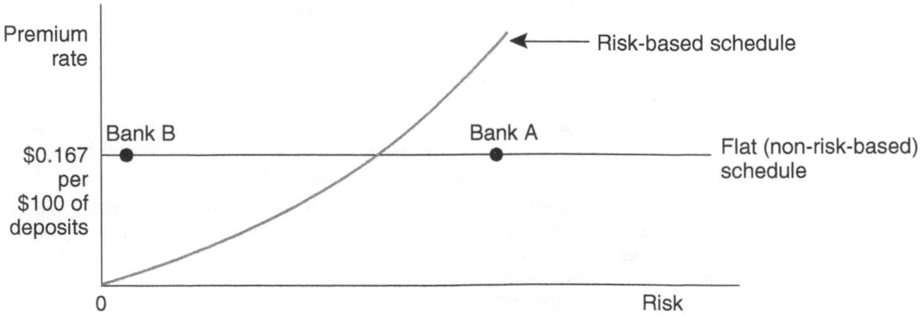

In Figure 19–2, note that under the flat premium schedule, banks A and B would have been charged the same deposit insurance premium based on a bank's domestic deposit size. Critics of flat premiums argue that a deposit insurance corporation should act more like a private P&C insurer. Under normal P&C insurance premium-setting principles, insurers charge those with higher risks higher premiums. That is, low-risk parties (such as Bank B) do not generally subsidize high-risk parties (such as Bank A). If premiums increased as bank risk increased, banks would have reduced incentives to take risks. Therefore, the ultimate goal might be to price risk in an actuarially fair fashion, similar to the process used by a private P&C insurer, so that premiums reflect the expected private costs or losses to the insurer from the provision of deposit insurance.

Note that there are arguments against imposing an actuarially fair risk-based premium schedule. If the deposit insurer's mandate is not to act as if it were a private cost-minimizing insurer such as a P&C insurance company because of social welfare considerations, some type of subsidy can be justified. Broader banking market stability concerns and savers' welfare concerns might arguably override private cost-minimizing concerns and require subsidies. Others have argued that if an actuarially fair premium is imposed on a banking system that is fully competitive, banking itself cannot be profitable. That is, some subsidy is needed for banks to exist profitably. However, while Canadian banking is competitive, it probably deviates somewhat from the perfectly competitive model.

Calculating the Actuarially Fair Premium Economists have suggested a number of approaches for calculating the fair deposit insurance premium that a cost-minimizing insurer such as CDIC should charge. One approach is to set the premium equal to the expected severity of loss times the frequency of losses due to failure plus some load or markup factor. This exactly mimics the approach toward premium setting in the P&C industry. However, the most common approach, the **option pricing model of deposit insurance** (OPM), has been to view the provision of deposit insurance as virtually identical to writing a put option on the assets of the FI that buys the deposit insurance. We depict the conceptual idea underlying the OPM approach in Figure 19–3.

option pricing model of deposit insurance
A model for calculating deposit insurance as a put option on the DTI's assets.

In this framework, CDIC charges a premium P to insure the FI's deposits (D). If the FI does well and the market value of the FI's assets is greater than D, its net worth is positive and it can continue in business. CDIC would face no charge against its resources and would keep the premium paid to it by the FI (P). If the FI

FIGURE 19–3
Deposit Insurance as a Put Option (D = DTI's deposits; A = DTI's assets; P = Premium paid by DTI)

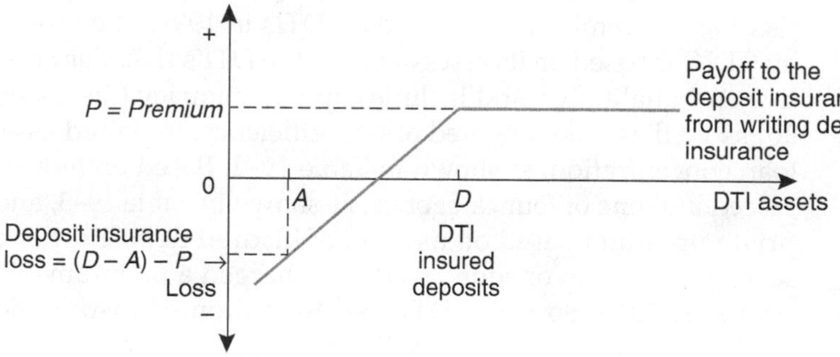

is insolvent, possibly because of a bad or risky asset portfolio, such that the value of the assets falls below D (say to A), and its net worth is negative, the owners will "put the bank" back to CDIC. If this happens, CDIC will pay out to the insured depositors an amount D and will liquidate the assets (A). As a result, CDIC bears the cost of the insolvency (or negative net worth) equal to ($D - A$) minus the insurance premiums paid by the FI (P).

When valued in this fashion as a simple European put option, the cost of providing deposit insurance increases with the level of asset risk (σ_A^2) and with the FI's leverage (D/A). That is, the actuarially fair premium (P) is equivalent to the premium on a put option and as such should be positively related to both asset risk (σ_A^2) and leverage risk (D/A). The value of a deposit insurance guarantee is shown to be the same as the Black–Scholes model for a European put option of maturity T, where T is the time period until the next premium assessment:

$$P(T) = De^{-rT}\,\phi(X_2) - A\phi(X_1)$$

where

$$X_1 = \{\log(D/A) - (r + \sigma_A^2/2)T\}/\sigma_A\sqrt{T}$$
$$X_2 = X_1 + \sigma_A\sqrt{T}$$

and ϕ is the standard normal distribution.

Even though the OPM is a conceptually and theoretically elegant tool, it is difficult to apply in practice—especially because an FI's asset value (A) and its asset risks (σ_A^2) are not directly observable. However, values of these variables can be extracted from the equity value and the volatility of equity value of the FI (see the discussion on the Moody's Analytics model in Chapter 10). Even so, the OPM framework is useful because it indicates that both leverage and asset quality (or risk) are important elements that should enter into any deposit insurance pricing model.

Next, we look at the risk-based deposit insurance premium scheme introduced by CDIC in 1999. It is directly linked to both bank leverage and asset quality.

CONCEPT QUESTIONS

1. **Bank A has a ratio of deposits to assets of 90 percent and a variance of asset returns of 10 percent. Bank B has a ratio of deposits to assets of 85 percent and a variance of asset returns of 5 percent. Which bank should pay the higher insurance premium?**
2. **If deposit insurance is similar to a put option, who exercises that option?**

Implementing Risk-Based Premiums

risk-based deposit insurance program
A program that assesses insurance premiums on the basis of capital adequacy and supervisory judgments on FI quality.

As DTIs were perceived to become more risky in the 1980s and 1990s, the FDIC adopted a **risk-based deposit insurance program** for U.S. FIs in 1993. CDIC established risk-based premiums for Canadian DTIs in 1999. The level of premiums charged by CDIC is based on its assessment of the DTI's risk. The criteria are both quantitative and qualitative, and include capital adequacy (discussed in detail in Chapter 20) as well as risk-weighted assets, efficiency, impaired assets, asset growth, and loan concentration, as shown in Table 19–2. Based on its score out of 100, the FI is placed into one of four categories, as shown in Table 19–3, and charged the appropriate premium based on its level of insured deposits. For example, an FI with a score greater than or equal to 80 was charged a premium of 2.8 bp of insured deposits in 2013. So if the DTI had \$1 billion of insured deposits, it would pay \$280,000 (\$1,000,000,000 × 0.00028) for deposit insurance. If its score was below 50,

TABLE 19–2
CDIC's Rating Criteria for Insured DTIs

Criteria or Factors	Maximum Score
Quantitative:	
Capital Adequacy	20
• Assets to capital multiple	
• Tier 1 risk-based capital ratio	
• Total risk-based capital ratio	
Other Quantitative	
• Return on risk-weighted assets	5
• Mean adjusted net income volatility	5
• Stress-tested net income	5
• Efficiency ratio	5
• Net impaired assets (including net unrealized losses on securities) to total capital	5
• Three-year moving average asset growth ratio	5
• Real estate asset concentration	5
• Aggregate commercial loan concentration ratio	5
Subtotal: Quantitative Score	60
Qualitative:	
• Examiner's rating	35
• Other information	5
Subtotal: Qualitative Score	40
Total Score	100

it would pay $2,220,000 ($1,000,000,000 × 0.00222), double the amount it would have been charged in 2009. Thus, the incentive is to maintain a high score so that the cost to the FI is minimized, since the insurance premium for deposits would be factored into an FI's cost of funds for loans and other services. The rates declined from 2002 to 2009, in line with decreased risk and low claims on the insurance corporation. In 2009–2010, CDIC premium rates increased by one-third over 2008–2009 rates, as shown in Table 19–3. Similar rate increases occurred in 2010–2011 and 2011/2012–2012/2013, doubling rates. An insured institution is notified each year of the rate that it will pay, but CDIC does not permit the FI to disclose its risk category, its total score, the examiner's rating, the premium rate that has been assigned, or any other information related to its premiums. The amount of insured deposits is calculated at April 30 each year.

TABLE 19–3 Premium Rates Charged by CDIC for Deposit Insurance, 1999–2013

Premium Categories and Rates								
Score	Premium Category	Premium Rate (bp % of insured deposits)						
		1999-2001	2001-2002	2002-2005	2005-2009	2009-2010	2010-2011	2011/2012-2012/2013
≥ 80	1 (best rated)	4.2	4.2	2.1	1.4	1.9	2.3	2.8
≥ 65 but < 80	2	8.3	8.3	4.2	2.8	3.7	4.6	5.6
≥ 50 but < 65	3	16.7	16.7	8.3	5.6	7.4	9.3	11.1
< 50	4 (worst rated)	16.7	33.3	16.7	11.1	14.8	18.5	22.2

Source: Canada Deposit Insurance Corporation, cdic.ca.

Increased Capital Requirements and Stricter Closure Rules

A second way to reduce stockholders' incentives to take excessive risks is to (1) require higher capital—lower leverage—ratios so that stockholders have more at stake in taking risky investments, and (2) impose stricter closure rules. The moral hazard risk-taking incentives of FI owners increase as their capital or net worth approaches zero and their leverage increases. For those U.S. thrifts allowed to operate in the 1980s with virtually no book equity capital and with negative net worth, the risk-taking incentives of their owners were enormous.

capital forbearance
Regulators' policy of allowing an FI to continue operating even when its capital funds are fully depleted.

By failing to close such FIs, regulators exhibited excessive **capital forbearance**. In the short term, forbearance may save the insurance fund some liquidation costs. In the long run, owners of bad DTIs have continuing incentives to grow and take additional risks in the hope of a large payoff that could turn the institution around. This strategy potentially adds to the future liabilities of the insurance fund and to the costs of liquidation. We now know that huge additional costs were the actual outcome of the regulators' policy of capital forbearance in the U.S. thrift industry in the 1980s.

As we discuss in Chapter 20, a system of risk-based capital requirements mandates that those FIs taking greater on- and off-balance-sheet, market, credit, operating, and interest rate risks must hold more capital. Thus, risk-based capital supports risk-based deposit insurance premiums by increasing the cost of risk-taking for FI stockholders.[7]

To the extent that the book value of capital approximates true net worth or the market value of capital, this enhances stockholder discipline by imposing additional costs on FI owners for risk-taking. It also increases the degree of co-insurance, in regard to risks taken, between FI owners and regulators such as CDIC.

CONCEPT QUESTIONS

1. **If you were managing an FI that is technically insolvent but has not yet been closed by the regulators, would you invest in Treasury bonds or real estate development loans? Explain your answer.**
2. **Do we need both risk-based capital requirements and risk-based insurance premiums to discipline shareholders?**

Depositor Discipline

An alternative, more indirect route to disciplining riskier FIs is to create conditions for a greater degree of depositor discipline. Depositors could either require higher interest rates and risk premiums on deposits or ration the amount of deposits they are willing to hold in riskier FIs.

Critics argue that under the current deposit insurance regulations, neither insured depositors nor uninsured depositors have sufficient incentives to discipline riskier DTIs. This is one of the reasons that the G20 leaders endorsed the Financial Stability Board's (FSB's) *Key Attributes of Effective Resolution Regimes for Financial Institutions* in November, 2011. To understand these arguments, we consider the risk exposure of both insured and uninsured depositors under the current deposit insurance contract.

www.financialstabilityboard.org

[7] On the assumption that new equity is more costly to raise than deposits for banks.

TABLE 19–4
CDIC's Deposit Insurance Coverage

Source: Canada Deposit Insurance Corporation, cdic.ca.

$100,000 DEPOSIT INSURANCE COVERAGE

What's Covered?

CDIC insures eligible deposits held in each member institution up to a maximum of $100,000 (principal and interest combined) per depositor, for each of the following deposits:

- Savings held in one name
- Savings held in trust for another person
- Savings held in Registered Retirement Savings Plans (RRSPs)
- Savings held in Registered Retirement Income Funds (RRIFs)
- Savings held for paying realty taxes on mortgaged property
- Savings held in more than one name (joint deposits)
- Savings held in Tax-Free Savings Accounts (TFSAs)

Depositors are responsible for ensuring that the member institution's records include all information required for the separate protection of these deposits. (See CDIC's website, cdic.ca, for details.)

What's an Eligible Deposit?

Eligible deposits include:

- Savings accounts and chequing accounts
- Guaranteed Investment Certificates (GICs) and other term deposits with an original term to maturity of five years or less
- Money orders, travellers' cheques and bank drafts issued by CDIC members, and cheques certified by CDIC members
- Debentures issued by loan companies that are CDIC members

Deposits must be payable in Canada, in Canadian currency.

What's Not Covered?

CDIC deposit insurance does not protect all accounts and financial products. For example, mutual funds, stocks, and foreign currency deposits, including those in U.S. dollars, are not covered by CDIC.

Insured Depositors

As noted above, CDIC is a Crown corporation that was created in 1967 to protect deposits held at banks, trust companies, and savings and loans. The level of coverage for a depositor increased from $60,000 to $100,000 effective February 2005. The $100,000 cap applies to a depositor's beneficial interest and ownership of deposited funds that are (1) made with an eligible member of CDIC, (2) in Canadian dollars payable in Canada, and (3) repayable within five years from the deposit date. The cap relates to deposits at a single member institution. Tax-free savings accounts (TFSAs) are subject to the same rules as other savings accounts. In actuality, by structuring deposit funds in a CDIC-insured institution in a particular fashion, a depositor can achieve many times the $100,000 cap on deposits. To see this, consider the different categories of deposit fund ownership (defined as savings and chequing accounts, term deposits, debentures issued by loan companies, money orders, drafts, certified cheques, and travellers cheques) available to an individual, shown in Table 19–4. Each of these categories represents a distinct accumulation of funds toward the $100,000 deposit insurance cap, the coverage ceiling per FI. We give an example of how depositors can raise the coverage level by adopting certain strategies.

EXAMPLE 19–1
Calculation of Insured Deposits

A married couple with one daughter, where both husband and wife have eligible funds in individual RRSPs, could accrue coverage at one CDIC-insured institution of $100,000 each for individual savings or chequing accounts ($300,000 total), $100,000 for each of three joint chequing accounts ($300,000), $100,000 each for trust deposits ($300,000), and $100,000 each for the husband and wife for five-year GICs in an RRSP ($200,000) for a total coverage cap of $1,100,000 as a family.

Note that the $100,000 coverage ceiling is per institution, not per branch. Wealthy and institutional investors can spread their funds over many DTIs up to the permitted cap insured by CDIC. In this way, all their deposits become explicitly insured. For example, a wealthy individual with $1 million in deposits could split the deposits between 10 of CDIC's members. In the United States, a wealthy individual with US$1 million in deposits could hire a deposit broker such as Bank of American Merrill Lynch to split the US$1 million into four parcels of US$250,000 and deposit those funds at four different banks. During the 1980s, the greatest purchasers of brokered deposits were the most risky banks that had no, or limited, access to the borrowed funds market. These risky banks attracted brokered deposits by offering higher interest rates than did relatively healthy banks. In fact, a high proportion of brokered deposits held by a bank became an early warning signal of its future failure risk. Neither the depositors nor the fund brokers were concerned about the risk of these funds because every parcel, including interest accrued up until the time of failure, was fully insured up to the US$100,000 ceiling. During the financial crisis of 2008–2009, in order to provide stability to the U.S. banking system, the deposit insurance limit was increased to $250,000 from $100,000 per person per institution.

deposit broker
A broker that breaks up large deposits into smaller units at different banks to ensure full coverage by deposit insurance.

Uninsured Depositors

The primary intention of deposit insurance is to deter runs and panics. A secondary and related objective has been to protect the smaller, less-informed saver against the reduction in wealth that would occur if that person were last in line when an FI fails. Under the current deposit insurance contract, the small, less-informed depositor is defined by the $100,000 ceiling. Theoretically at least, larger, more-informed depositors with more than $100,000 on deposit are at risk if an FI fails. As a result, these large uninsured depositors should be sensitive to risk and seek to discipline more risky FIs by demanding higher interest rates on their deposits or withdrawing their deposits completely. Until recently, the manner in which failures have been resolved meant that both large and small depositors were often fully protected against losses. This was especially so where large banks got into trouble and were viewed as **too big to fail (TBTF) banks**. That is, they were too big to be liquidated by regulators either because of the draining effects on the resources of the insurance fund or for fear of contagious or systemic runs spreading to other major banks. For example, in September 2008, the Irish government guaranteed all bank liabilities as it struggled to prevent a banking crisis. Thus, although uninsured depositors tended to lose in small-bank failures, in large-bank failures the failure resolution methods employed by regulators usually resulted in implicit 100 percent deposit insurance. As a result, for large banks in particular, neither small nor large depositors had sufficient incentives to impose market discipline on riskier banks.

too-big-to-fail (TBTF) banks
Banks that are viewed by regulators as being too big to be closed and liquidated without imposing a systemic risk to the banking and financial system.

In Canadian banking history, failing institutions have generally been absorbed by other institutions, such as the takeover of Central Guaranty Trust's assets by TD Bank in the early 1990s. In an effort to prevent the failure of the Canadian Commercial Bank and the Northland Bank of Canada in 1985, the federal regulators at the time (the Inspector General of Banks along with the Bank of Canada and the Department of Finance) arranged for support from the six large banks and government to provide liquidity to replace the banks' wholesale deposits that were maturing and not being renewed. In the fallout, Continental Bank of Canada became unable to renew its wholesale deposits, despite being declared solvent by the Big Six banks, which examined its loan portfolio. Continental was subsequently taken over by Hong Kong Bank of Canada.

Next, we look at three principal methods of failure resolution and their effect on depositors.

FEDERAL DEPOSIT INSURANCE CORPORATION POLICIES

least-cost resolution
A policy requiring that the lowest-cost method of closure be used for failing DTIs.

In the wake of the FDIC's growing deficit, the FDICIA of 1991 sought to pass more of the costs of insured DTI failures on to uninsured depositors, thereby enhancing their incentives to monitor DTIs and to control risk through requiring higher deposit rates and/or through their deposit placement decisions. The FDICIA required that a **least-cost resolution** (LCR) strategy be put in place by the FDIC. In applying the LCR strategy, the FDIC evaluates failure resolution alternatives on a present value basis and documents its assumptions in deciding which method to use.

However, there was a very important and controversial exemption to using LCR in all cases. Specifically, a *systemic risk* exemption applies where a large DTI failure could cause a threat to the whole financial system. Then methods that could involve the full protection of uninsured depositors as well as insured depositors could be used. However, the act has restricted the circumstances under which this systemic risk exemption can be used. Such an exemption is allowed only if a two-thirds majority of the boards of the Federal Reserve and the FDIC recommend it to the Secretary of the U.S. Treasury and if the Secretary of the U.S. Treasury, in consultation with the President of the United States, agrees. Further, any cost of such a bailout of a big DTI would have to be shared among all other DTIs by charging them an additional deposit insurance premium based on their size as measured by their total assets minus average tangible equity. Because large DTIs have more assets minus equity, they will have to make bigger contributions (per dollar of assets) than smaller DTIs to any future bailout of a large DTI.

bail-ins
The conversion of uninsured deposits and/or debt into equity when FIs get into trouble

bailouts
The provision of government funds as debt and/or equity to support troubled FIs

insured depositor transfer
A method of resolution in which uninsured depositors take a loss, or haircut, on failure equal to the difference between their deposit claims and the estimated value of the failed DTI's assets minus insured deposits.

Nevertheless, concerns have been raised about continuing the TBTF guarantee even in its more restricted form. With the growing wave of bank and financial service firm mergers, it is argued that more and more FIs are likely to be covered by TBTF guarantees. If we use the same asset-size cutoff (adjusted for inflation) that the U.S. Comptroller of the Currency used in specifying the 11 banks that were to be protected as being TBTF after the Continental Illinois failure in 1984, we find that today this amounts to an asset size of around US$45 billion. As of 2009, almost 34 banking organizations had assets exceeding this figure. During the financial crisis of 2008–2009, the Federal Reserve's rescue of FIs such as Bear Stearns, AIG, and Citigroup and the US$200 billion invested in over 630 banks through the Treasury Department's Capital Purchase Program (CPP) demonstrated that the TBTF bailouts reached much farther than anyone would have predicted, including FIs other than commercial banks and commercial bank deposits. By July 2012, 34 U.S. FIs had paid back more than US$192 billion of the US$205 billion lent out through the CPP plus an additional US$12 billion in interest and dividends. Thus, the BIS and the FSB focus on limiting and/or eliminating TBTF globally through **bail-ins** rather than **bailouts.**

With the exception of the systemic risk exemption, the LCR strategy requires the FDIC to employ the method that imposes the most failure costs on the uninsured depositors. To this end, the FDIC has been increasingly using an **insured depositor transfer** (IDT), or "haircut," method to resolve a number of post-1991 failures. Under the IDT method of resolution, the insured deposits of a closed DTI are usually transferred in full to another local DTI in the community to conduct a direct payoff of the depositors for the FDIC. By contrast, uninsured depositors must file a claim against the receiver of the failed DTI and share with the FDIC in any receivership distributions from the liquidation of the closed DTI's assets. This usually results in a loss for uninsured depositors (a haircut). For example, in 25 out of 323 failures in 2008–2012, the FDIC imposed initial losses, or haircuts, on uninsured depositors. The size of the haircut depends mostly on the FDIC-estimated value of the failed DTI's assets. During the financial crisis, to avoid an even larger collapse of the financial system, uninsured deposits were covered in over 90 percent of the DTI failures. However, the uninsured deposits were not paid off by the FDIC. Rather, the FDIC worked to have uninsured deposits transferred as part of the failure resolution. Further, the increase in the deposit insurance cap to $250,000 in 2009 meant that most deposits were insured. Thus, few uninsured deposits existed at many of the smaller failed banks, and the cost of covering them in the event of a failure was comparatively small.

Example 19–2 illustrates a simplified form of the IDT, or haircut, method that has been used by deposit insurers worldwide.

EXAMPLE 19-2

Liquidation and Payoff of a Failed Bank Using the IDT Method

In Table 19–5, a failed bank in Panel A has only $80 million in good assets to meet the $50 million in deposit claims of insured depositors and the $50 million in claims of the uninsured depositors. That is, it has $20 million negative net worth. Under an IDT, in Panel B, the deposit insurer would transfer the $80 million in assets to an acquiring bank along with the full $50 million in small insured deposits but only $30 million of the $50 million in uninsured deposits.[8] Notice that the uninsured depositors get protection against losses only up to the difference between the estimated value of the failed bank's assets and its insured deposits. In effect, the uninsured depositors are subject to a haircut to their original deposit claims of $20 million (or, as a percentage, 40 percent of the value of their deposit claims on the failed bank). After the IDT, the uninsured depositors own $30 million in deposits in the acquiring bank and $20 million in receivership claims on the bad assets of the failed bank. Only if the deposit insurer as a receiver can recover some value from the $20 million in bad assets will the loss to the uninsured be less than $20 million.

To summarize the losses of the three parties under the IDT:

		Loss ($ millions)
Insured depositors	=	0
Deposit insurer	=	0
Uninsured depositors	=	$20

TABLE 19–5 IDT Resolution ($ millions)

(a) Failed				(b) IDT			
Assets		**Liabilities**		**Assets**		**Liabilities**	
Good assets	$80	Insured deposits	$ 50	Good assets	$80	Insured deposits	$50 Merger → with good bank
		Uninsured deposits	50			Uninsured deposits	30
	$80		$100		$80		$80

purchase and assumption (P&A)
The merger of a failed DTI with a healthy FI.

[8] Unlike in a **purchase and assumption (P&A)**, it would not inject cash into the failed bank prior to a merger with the acquiring bank.

As you can see from this simple example, the uninsured depositors bear all the losses and now have a much stronger incentive than before to monitor and control the actions of FI owners through imposing market discipline via interest rates and the amount of funds deposited.

CONCEPT QUESTIONS

1. **Under current deposit insurance rules, how can depositors achieve more than the $100,000 CDIC cap on deposits?**
2. **Why do uninsured depositors benefit from a TBTF policy followed by regulators?**
3. **Construct a simple balance sheet to show how a deposit insurer can lose even when using an IDT to resolve a failed DTI.**

Regulatory Discipline

In the event that stockholder and deposit holder discipline does not reduce moral hazard–induced risk-taking, regulations can require regulators to act promptly and in a more consistent and predictable fashion to restrain FI risk-taking behaviour by (1) the frequency and thoroughness of examinations and (2) the forbearance shown to weakly capitalized FIs.

Examinations

As shown in Figure 2–2, the joint oversight by OSFI and CDIC provides the regulatory discipline for federally regulated banks, trusts, and loan companies in Canada. In addition to the monthly and quarterly reporting to OSFI, a federally regulated FI is inspected annually by OSFI, which may also conduct special examinations if desired. As well, CDIC provides oversight for provincially and territorially regulated DTIs and may conduct annual or special examinations of these FIs. Since 1987, CDIC has been able to act as a liquidator or receiver in the event of the failure of a CDIC member. In the United States, since 1992, every DTI must be examined annually on-site and is also subject to an audit by an independent private accountant. This is similar to the situation in the United Kingdom, where the 1987 Bank Act required an enhanced role for private auditors as a backup for regulatory examiners. After the financial crisis of 2008–2009 the Federal Reserve Bank of New York and the Office of the Comptroller of the Currency increased the number of examiners "embedded" in the big FIs they regulate, e.g., Bank of New York Mellon, Citigroup, and JPMorgan Chase. About 2,500 bank examiners work on location at these FIs, up almost 40 percent from 2006. In addition to policing the FIs for their maintenance of regulations, the examiners are charged with identifying vulnerabilities in the FIs early enough to head off major problems. However, it should be noted that, despite the presence of embedded examiners, JPMorgan Chase still managed to suffer over US$5 billion in losses in the bank's trading portfolio as certain credit risk limits were breached. Examiners failed to notice the complacency, poor judgment, and faulty risk controls of the bank as it tried to avoid showing the full amount of losses during the first quarter of 2012 by placing inaccurate prices on its positions.

Regulatory Forbearance

OSFI and CDIC jointly follow the *Guide to Intervention for Federal Financial Institutions* in dealing with a troubled FI, which, it can be argued, gives them more discretionary powers than the strict rules-based approach that has been adopted in the United States, which mandates "prompt corrective action" symptomatic of a movement toward a regulatory policy based on rules rather than on discretion. Such rules clearly direct regulators to act in a certain manner even if they are reluctant to do so out of self-interest or for other reasons. The weakness of such rules is that if a policy is bad, then bad policy becomes more effective.[9]

CONCEPT QUESTION

What additional measures can be taken by regulators to bolster stockholder and depositor discipline?

DEPOSIT INSURANCE SYSTEMS GLOBALLY

iadi.org

Deposit insurance systems are increasingly being adopted worldwide. The IADI has links to the websites of 112 countries that have some form of deposit insurance. Many countries offer quite different degrees of protection to depositors compared with the systems in Canada and the United States. For example, in response to the single banking and capital market in Europe, in 1994 the European Union (EU) issued a directive requiring insurance for deposit accounts in EU countries of at least €20,000. This was increased to a minimum of €50,000 in October 2008 and to €100,000 in 2010. The idea underlying the EU plan was to create a level playing field for banks across all EU countries, but the deposit insurance guarantees offered still vary across the EU. A common deposit insurance system would be a feature of the proposed European banking union, which is under discussion.

Japan established its deposit insurance system in 1971. In the late 1990s and early 2000s, the Japanese banking system was going through an experience similar to that of U.S. banks and thrifts in the 1930s and 1980s, with record bad debts and bank failures. Over the decade 1992–2002, Japanese banks had written off over US$650 billion in nonperforming loans. As of 2003, these banks still had over US$400 billion in bad loans on their balance sheets. The effect on Japan's deposit insurance fund was similar to that of the United States in the 1980s, with a rapidly declining reserve fund that limited its ability to deal with the crisis. These problems led to a government bailout to the tune of over US$500 billion and blanket protection, until April 2005, of all bank deposits. As of April 2005, deposits under full coverage have been limited to only those used for payment and settlement purposes that satisfy all three of the following conditions: deposits bearing no interest, being redeemable on demand, and providing normally required payment and settlement services. All other deposits (e.g., time and savings) are insured up to a maximum principal of ¥10 million (US$108,000) per account. Negotiable certificates of deposit have no insurance protection.

As early as 2000, China had proposed a deposit insurance system. It was shelved at the time because most local banks were state owned. Government-backed credit assured depositors that their savings would be protected from potential FI bankruptcies. In the mid-2000s, improved local financial conditions and fewer risks led the Peoples Bank of China to re-initiate its consideration of the

[9] L. Kryzanowski and G. S. Roberts, "Canadian Banking Solvency, 1922–1940," *Journal of Money, Credit, and Banking* (August 1993) 25(3), pp. 361–76, argues that regulatory forbearance allowed Sun Life to carry its securities at book value rather than at market value, keeping Sun Life from being declared insolvent and forcing the regulators to act to wind it up. Since the financial crisis in 2008, central bankers have increasingly worked together through the FSB to strengthen global financial markets.

system. Further, a growing number of small FIs were established to serve the small enterprises, rural areas, and midwest region. These institutions needed a deposit insurance system to avoid risks for the entire financial industry. In late 2009, China prepared a system to formally insure bank deposits. Officials of the China Banking Regulatory Commission planned to introduce a system like the FDIC that protects American depositors in case of a bank failure. The plan that was submitted was designed to insure about 98 percent of bank deposits in China by requiring FIs to buy deposit insurance from the Central Deposit Insurance Corporation, which would have held the right to borrow from the central bank and Ministry of Finance. The plan was to be financed by participating banks, and, in the event of an insured institution failing, the insurance corporation would compensate depositors. However, no plan was implemented, and, in October 2013, the central bank of China and the U.S. FDIC signed an agreement to develop a deposit insurance scheme for China's savers. China had US$27.9 trillion in yuan-denominated deposits in 2012. Over 98 percent of deposit accounts were less than 200,000 yuan (US$29,197).

IADI was formed in 2002 to encourage cooperation among global deposit insurers. In 2013, the IADI represented 67 deposit insurers.

The BIS and IADI released their report, *Core Principles for Effective Deposit Insurance Systems*, in June 2009. These core principles emphasized moral hazard and cross-border issues, as well as early detection, timely intervention, and effective resolution processes. After the global turmoil of 2008, regulators have discussed liquidity enhancements (Chapters 17 and 18), deposit insurance issues, and capital adequacy guidelines (Chapter 20). Best practices as well as increased regulatory oversight are on the agenda of policymakers worldwide. The FSB published *Key Attributes for Effective Resolution Regimes for Financial Institutions* in 2011. A review of the regimes in place to support and/or wind up troubled FIs, in particular, was released by IADI in 2013, and frameworks for resolving troubled FIs, including systemically important financial institutions (SIFIs; see Chapter 20) and nonbank FIs (e.g., investment banks and hedge funds) are being developed.

LENDER OF LAST RESORT

LO5

Deposit Insurance versus the Central Bank

The previous sections have described how a well-designed deposit insurance system might impose stockholder, depositor, and regulator discipline. Such a system can potentially stop runs and extreme liquidity problems arising in the banking system without introducing significant amounts of moral hazard risk-taking behaviour among insured institutions. However, deposit insurance is not the only mechanism by which regulators mitigate bank liquidity risk. A second mechanism has been the central banks' provision of a lender of last resort facility.

The Bank of Canada's Lender of Last Resort Policies

The Bank of Canada has the role of providing liquidity to the financial system. The Bank of Canada Act allows the Bank to provide loans secured by acceptable collateral (e.g., government securities, bankers' acceptances, and commercial paper (CP)) to solvent banks and members of the CPA. These functions come under the term "lender of last resort activities." As a result of foreign bank branches setting up in Canada in 1999 and expansion of the membership of the CPA in 2002, as well as the need of Canadian FIs for foreign liquidity, the Bank of Canada reviewed its policies in light of its role in providing stability to the financial system.[10] The Bank of Canada provides funds to the payments system in three ways:

1. *The Standing Liquidity Facility (SLF):* The SLF provides overnight, collateralized loans to those FIs that are direct participants in the LVTS (see Chapter 12) to handle temporary shortfalls in the day-to-day settlement of accounts. The borrowers must be solvent, and the collateral limits the amounts that may be borrowed, providing a curb on moral hazard, which would see a troubled FI transfer its risk to the central bank.
2. *Emergency lending assistance (ELA):* Through the ELA, the Bank of Canada provides longer-term assistance to DTIs that are solvent but illiquid. That is, they have illiquid assets supported by short-term highly liquid deposits.
3. *Forced LVTS loans:* In order to protect the payments system from systemic risk that could cause the whole system to fail, the Bank of Canada could be forced to lend to an insolvent DTI that failed to make its daily settlement. Since each LVTS participant pledges collateral (effectively co-insurance) in advance to cover its largest single expected daily settlement, the Bank of Canada's position would be protected. The Bank of Canada specifies the type of collateral and the margin requirements that are acceptable under the SLF.

As noted earlier in the chapter, the role of the Bank of Canada interconnects with the roles of OSFI and CDIC to provide a mechanism to ensure the safety and soundness of the Canadian financial system, including the payments system. Thus, Canada may be viewed as a stable link in global financial markets that are increasingly connected. During the liquidity crisis in the fall of 2008, the Bank of Canada increased the size of term purchase and resale agreements (PRAs), introduced a money market PRA facility and a term loan facility (TLF), broadened the type of collateral that it would accept, guaranteed bank liabilities through the Canadian Lenders Assurance Facility (CLAF), and agreed to up to $75 billion in asset purchases from CMHC-insured mortgage pools. The ability of LVTS participants to borrow from the Bank of Canada was a source of stability for banks and other FIs during the liquidity crisis of 2008.

The U.S. Federal Reserve

discount window
U.S. central bank lender of last resort facility.

federalreserve.gov

Traditionally, the U.S. Federal Reserve has provided a **discount window** facility to meet the short-term, nonpermanent liquidity needs of FIs. For example, suppose an FI has an unexpected deposit drain and cannot meet its reserve target. It can seek to borrow from the central bank's discount window facility. Normally, such loans are obtained by discounting short-term high-quality paper such as Treasury bills and bankers' acceptances with the central bank. The interest rate at which such securities are discounted is called the *discount rate* and is set by the central bank.

[10] For a detailed discussion of the Bank of Canada's role in ensuring the stability of the financial system, see F. Daniel, W. Engert, and D. Maclean, "The Bank of Canada as Lender of Last Resort," *Bank of Canada Review*, Winter 2004–2005, pp. 3–16, as well as "Bank of Canada Lender-of-Last-Resort Policies," Bank of Canada *Financial System Review*, December 2004.

In the United States, the central bank has historically set the discount rate below market rates, such as the overnight federal funds rates. The volume of outstanding discount loans was ordinarily small, however, because the Federal Reserve prohibited DTIs from using discount window loans to finance sales of Federal Reserve funds or to finance asset expansion. In January 2003, the Federal Reserve implemented changes to its discount window lending that increased the cost of borrowing but eased the terms. Specifically, three lending programs are now offered through the Federal Reserve's discount window. *Primary credit* is available to generally sound DTIs on a very short term basis, typically overnight, at a rate above the Federal Open Market Committee's (FOMC's) target rate for federal funds. Primary credit may be used for any purpose, including financing the sale of Federal Reserve funds. Primary credit may be extended for periods of up to a few weeks to DTIs in generally sound financial condition. *Secondary credit* is available to institutions that are not eligible for primary credit. It is extended on a very short term basis, typically overnight, at a rate that is above the primary credit rate. Secondary credit is available to meet backup liquidity needs when its use is consistent with a timely return to a reliance on market sources of funding or the orderly resolution of a troubled institution. Secondary credit may not be used to fund an expansion of the borrower's assets. *Seasonal credit* is available to institutions that can demonstrate a clear pattern of recurring intrayearly swings in funding needs. Eligible institutions are usually located in agricultural or tourist areas. These changes allow healthy banks to borrow from the Federal Reserve regardless of the availability of private funds.

In the wake of the terrorist attacks of September 11, 2001, the Federal Reserve's discount window supplied funds to the banking system in unprecedented amounts. The magnitude of destruction resulting from the attacks caused severe disruptions to the U.S. banking system, particularly in FIs' abilities to send payments. The physical disruptions caused by the attacks included outages of telephone switching equipment in Lower Manhattan's financial district, impaired records processing and communications systems at individual banks, the evacuation of buildings that were the sites for the payment operations of several large FIs, and the suspended delivery of cheques by air couriers. These disruptions left some FIs unable to execute payments to other FIs through the Federal Reserve's Fedwire system, which in turn resulted in an unexpected shortfall for other FIs. The Federal Reserve took several steps to address the problems in the payments system on and after September 11, 2001. Around noon on September 11, the Board of Governors of the Federal Reserve released a statement saying that it was open and operating, and that the discount window was available to meet liquidity needs of all DTIs. The Federal Reserve staff also contacted FIs often during the next few days, encouraging them to make payments and to consider the use of the discount window to cover unexpected shortfalls. Thus, the Federal Reserve's discount window was a primary tool used to restore payments coordination during this period.

The U.S. Federal Reserve took additional unprecedented steps, expanding the usual function of the discount window, to address the financial crisis. While the discount window had traditionally been available to DTIs, in March 2008 (as Bear Stearns nearly failed) investment banks gained access to the discount window through the Primary Dealer Credit Facility (PDCF). In the first three days, securities firms borrowed an average of US$31.3 billion per day from the Federal Reserve. The largest expansion of the discount window's availability to all FIs occurred in the wake of the Lehman Brothers failure, as a series of actions were taken in response to the increasingly fragile state of financial markets. In the fall of 2008, several new broad-based lending programs were implemented, providing funding to a wide array of new parties, including U.S. money market mutual funds (MMMFs), CP issuers, insurance companies, and others. These programs rapidly expanded the current lending programs offered via the Federal Reserve.

Also, in response to a weakening economy and a growing financial crisis, the Federal Reserve significantly reduced the level of short-term interest rates by lowering its target federal funds rate to near zero, down from 5.26 percent in September 2007. It also significantly reduced the spread (premium) between the discount rate and the federal funds target to just a quarter of a point, bringing the discount rate down to a half percent. With lower rates at the Federal Reserve's discount window, and interbank liquidity scarce as many lenders cut back their lending, more FIs chose to borrow at the window. The magnitude and diversity of nontraditional lending programs and initiatives developed during the crisis were unprecedented in Federal Reserve history. The lending programs were all designed to "unfreeze" and stabilize various parts of the credit markets, with the overall goal that parties receiving credit via these new Federal Reserve programs would, in turn, provide funding to creditworthy individuals and firms.

Despite the recent changes in the Federal Reserve's policy regarding discount window lending, there are a number of reasons that access to the discount window is unlikely to deter runs and panics to the extent that deposit insurance does. The first reason is that, to borrow from the discount window, an FI needs high-quality liquid assets to pledge as collateral. Failing, highly illiquid FIs are unlikely to have such assets available to discount. The second reason is that discount window borrowing, unlike deposit insurance coverage, is not automatic. That is, discount window loans are made at the discretion of the central bank. Third, discount window loans are meant to provide temporary liquidity for inherently solvent FIs, not permanent long-term support for otherwise insolvent FIs. Consequently, the discount window is a partial but not a full substitute for deposit insurance as a liquidity-stabilizing mechanism.

CONCEPT QUESTION

Is a DTI's access to central bank funds likely to be as effective as deposit insurance in deterring bank runs and panics? Why or why not?

OTHER GUARANTEE PROGRAMS

LO6

As discussed in Chapter 12, other FIs are also subject to liquidity crises and liability holder runs. To deter such runs and protect small claimholders, guarantee programs have appeared in other sectors of the financial services industry. We describe these programs and their similarities to and differences from deposit insurance next.

Autorité des Marchés Financiers (FMA)

CDIC provides protection for eligible members that are federally regulated (banks, trusts, and loan companies) as well as for eligible provincially and territorially incorporated DTIs (trusts and loan companies). The deposits of members of CDIC that are incorporated in the province of Québec are covered by the FMA for deposits in Québec and by CDIC for deposits made elsewhere in Canada.

www.lautorite.qc.ca

CUs/CPs

Since CUs and CPs are regulated at the provincial level in Canada, deposits are protected by the provincial deposit insurance fund or its equivalent. These funds have the ability to monitor their members and may levy premiums based on deposits, gross revenues, total assets, or some other measure. Because CUs and CPs hold many of their assets in government securities, as well as in residential mortgages and small consumer loans, often for amounts less than $10,000, they have a significant degree of risk diversification, which also lowers their risk of insolvency. Links to the provincial deposit insurers are provided at CDIC's website.

cdic.ca

Assuris

Although life insurers, like P&C insurers, and securities firms, including mutual funds, are subject to regulation, they are not supported by government-run guarantee funds like CDIC. These industries provide their own funds, supported by levies on their members.

Life insurance companies writing policies in Canada are required to become members of Assuris. If a life insurance company fails, Assuris covers policyholders for loss of benefits (e.g., health expenses, disability income, RRSPs, RRIFs, and death benefits). Assuris also covers savings benefits from policies. Details of the coverage provided by Assuris are shown in Table 19–6. The products covered reflect the range of consumer services provided by insurance companies in Canada and are similar in scope to the deposit coverage provided by CDIC.

assuris.ca

Assuris's current structure partially reflects a restructuring subsequent to the failure of three insurance companies (Les Coopérants, January 1992; Sovereign Life, December 1992; and Confederation Life, August 1994) in the 1990s, which brought into question the stability of the insurance industry and caused companies

TABLE 19–6
Benefits and Product Coverage Provided by Assuris

Source: Assuris, assuris.ca.

The following benefits are fully covered by Assuris up to

Monthly income	$2,000
Death benefit	$200,000
Health expense	$60,000
Cash value	$60,000

If total benefits exceed these amounts, Assuris covers 85% of the promised benefits, but not less than these amounts.

Accumulated value benefits are fully covered by Assuris up to $100,000. If accumulated value benefits are over $100,000, Assuris will ensure receipt of at least $100,000.

Coverage by Product

Assuris coverage applies to the benefits under a variety of products, including:

Individual Products

Life insurance	Long-Term Care Insurance
Critical illness	RRIFs
Health expense insurance	RRSPs
Disability income insurance	Accumulation Annuities
Payout annuities	Segregated Funds

Group Products

Group insurance	Group Retirement Plans

with group life and health insurance coverage to reconsider the protection from liability provided by Assuris under these policies. The federal government threatened to create a Crown corporation similar to CDIC for insurance companies, but Assuris increased its borrowing capabilities from members, established an independent board of directors, and put in place a plan for handling restructurings in order to keep control of its members out of government hands. Despite having to call on members for additional funds, Assuris provided 100 percent coverage in the case of Les Coopérants and Confederation Life, costing the industry $175 million and $5 million, respectively. Almost all of Sovereign Life's policyholders (96 percent) were covered 100 percent, with the remainder covered to 90 percent, costing the life insurance industry $25 million in the process. In the insurance company failures in Canada, the industry has worked to transfer policies to other insurers. For example, Confederation Life, which was the fourth-largest group life insurer in 1994, got into trouble by concentrating its investments in commercial real estate. After its failure, many of its policies were eventually taken over by other life insurers (e.g., Manulife, Maritime Life, Canada Life, Sun Life, Empire Life).

PACICC

pacicc.ca

P&C insurance companies in Canada have funded and operated a nonprofit fund, the PACICC, since 1989, which, in the event of the failure of one of its members, will automatically cover policyholders and claims. In order to sell P&C insurance in Canada, a company must be a member of PACICC, so all Canadian insurance policies are automatically covered. Policyholders are covered to a maximum of $250,000 for claims on most P&C policies. The P&C industry, as noted in Chapter 6, relies heavily on investments in bonds and other securities that have suffered lower returns over the past few years. The incentives for insurance policyholders to engage in a run if they perceive that an insurer has asset quality problems or insurance underwriting problems may be quite strong despite the presence of private guarantee funds. However, P&C insurers regulated by OSFI file a "prudent person" investment strategy that provides a measure of comfort that the industry is being monitored.

CIPF

cipf.ca

If an investment dealer becomes bankrupt, the CIPF, a private insurance fund founded in 1969, will cover the losses of eligible customers of the dealer members of the IIROC. Since its inception, the fund has had 17 insolvent members for whom it had paid out $37 million by 2011. In 2011, MF Global Canada Co. was declared insolvent following a filing for bankruptcy in the United States by MF Global's parent company; qualified investors were covered by CIPF. The coverage extends to securities, commodities and futures contracts, segregated funds (the insurance industry's equivalent of mutual funds, as explained in Chapter 6), and cash, up to a total of $1 million per account when a member becomes insolvent and a liquidator is appointed. Coverage is provided for each separate account (e.g., registered retirement plans, registered income plans, trusts), extending the coverage above the $1 million ceiling. Coverage may also exceed this amount if there are additional funds available upon liquidation. Only losses due to insolvency of a member of the CIPF are covered. CIPF's 2012 annual report showed a general fund of $425 million, an insurance policy up to $131 million, and lines of credit up to $125 million available at December 31, 2012. None of its members failed during the financial crisis.

CONCEPT QUESTIONS

1. **How do industry-sponsored guarantee funds for insurance companies differ from deposit insurance?**
2. **What specific protection against insolvencies does the CIPF provide to customers of securities firms?**

Questions and Problems

1. What is a contagious run? What are some of the potentially serious adverse social welfare effects of a contagious run? Do all types of FIs face the same risk of contagious runs?
2. How does deposit insurance help mitigate the problem of bank runs? What other elements of the safety net are available to FIs in Canada?
3. What is moral hazard?
4. How does a risk-based insurance program solve the moral hazard problem of excessive risk-taking by FIs? Is an actuarially fair premium for deposit insurance always consistent with a competitive banking system?
5. What are three suggested ways a deposit insurance contract could be structured to reduce moral hazard behaviour?
6. What are some ways of imposing stockholder discipline to prevent FI managers from engaging in excessive risk-taking?
7. How is the provision of deposit insurance similar to writing a put option on the assets of an FI that buys the insurance? What two factors drive the premium of the option?
8. What is capital forbearance? How does a policy of forbearance potentially increase the costs of financial distress to the insurance fund as well as the stockholders?
9. Under what conditions may the implementation of minimum capital guidelines, either risk based or non–risk based, fail to impose stockholder discipline as desired by regulators?
10. What has happened to the level of deposit insurance premiums since the risk-based program was implemented? Why?
11. Why did the fixed-rate deposit insurance system fail to induce insured and uninsured depositors in the United States to impose discipline on risky banks in the 1980s?
    a. How is it possible to structure deposits in an FI to reduce the effects of the insured ceiling?
    b. What has been the effect on FIs in Canada of the deposit insurance ceiling increasing to $100,000?
12. What is the TBTF doctrine? What factors caused regulators to act in a way that caused this doctrine to evolve?
13. The following is a balance sheet of a commercial bank ($ millions):

Assets		Liabilities and Equity	
Cash	$ 5	Insured deposits	$30
Loans	40	Uninsured deposits	10
		Equity	5
Total assets	$45	Total liabilities and equity	$45

The bank experiences a run on its deposits after it declares that it will write off $10 million of its loans as a result of nonpayment. The bank has the option of meeting the withdrawals by first drawing down its cash and then selling off its loans. A fire sale of remaining loans in one day can be accomplished at a 10 percent discount. They can be sold at a 5 percent discount if they are sold in two days. The full market value will be obtained if they are sold after two days.

    a. What is the amount of loss to the insured depositors if a run on the bank occurs on the first day? On the second day?
    b. What amount do the uninsured depositors lose if CDIC closes the bank immediately? The assets will be sold after the two-day period.

14. A bank with insured deposits of $55 million and uninsured deposits of $45 million has assets valued at only $75 million. What is the cost of failure resolution to insured depositors, uninsured depositors, and CDIC if an insured depositor transfer method is used?

15. A bank has $150 million in assets at book value. The insured and uninsured deposits are valued at $75 and $50 million, respectively, and the book value of equity is $25 million. As a result of loan defaults, the market value of the assets has decreased to $120 million. What is the cost of failure resolution to insured depositors, uninsured depositors, shareholders, and CDIC if an IDT method is used?
16. Match the following policies with their intended consequences:

    Policies:
    a. Lower CDIC insurance levels.
    b. Stricter reporting standards.
    c. Risk-based deposit insurance.

    Consequences:
    1. Increased stockholder discipline.
    2. Increased depositor discipline.
    3. Increased regulator discipline.
17. Why is access to the discount window of the U.S. Federal Reserve or the SLF of the Bank of Canada less of a deterrent to bank runs than deposit insurance?
18. How do insurance guarantee funds differ from deposit insurance? What impact do these differences have on the incentive for insurance policyholders to engage in a contagious run on an insurance company?

Appendix 19A Deposit Insurance Coverage for Commercial Banks in Various Countries

View Appendix 19A on Connect.

CHAPTER 20

CAPITAL ADEQUACY

After studying this chapter you should be able to:

LO1 Discuss the purpose of capital for a Canadian FI.

LO2 Discuss and illustrate how book value and market value of equity differ for an FI.

LO3 Discuss the Basel III Capital Accord and calculate the risk-weighted on-balance-sheet and off-balance-sheet assets, CET1 capital, Tier 1 capital, and Tier 2 capital for a Canadian bank as applied by OSFI.

LO4 Explain the concept of the capital conservation buffer.

LO5 Discuss the concepts of D-SIBs and G-SIBs.

INTRODUCTION

LO1

Chapters 7 through 17 examined the major areas of risk exposure facing a modern FI manager. These risks can emanate from both on- and off-balance-sheet activities and can be either domestic or international in source. To ensure survival, an FI manager needs to protect the institution against the risk of insolvency, that is, shield it from risks sufficiently large to cause the institution to fail. The primary means of protection against the risk of insolvency and failure is an FI's capital. This leads to the first function of capital, namely:

1. To absorb unanticipated losses with enough margin to inspire confidence and enable the FI to continue as a going concern.

In addition, capital protects nonequity liability holders—especially those uninsured by an external guarantor such as the CDIC—against losses. This leads to the second function of capital:

2. To protect uninsured depositors, bondholders, and creditors in the event of insolvency and liquidation.

When FIs fail, regulators have to intervene to protect insured claimants (see Chapter 19). The capital of an FI offers protection to insurance funds and ultimately the taxpayers who bear the cost of insurance fund insolvency. This leads to the third function of capital:

3. To protect FI insurance funds and the taxpayers.

By holding capital and reducing the risk of insolvency, an FI protects the industry from larger insurance premiums. Such premiums are paid out of the net profits of the FI. Thus, a fourth function of capital is as follows:

4. To protect the FI owners against increases in insurance premiums.

Finally, just as for any other firm, equity or capital is an important source of financing for an FI. In particular, subject to regulatory constraints, FIs have a choice between debt and equity to finance new projects and business expansion. Thus, the traditional factors that affect a business firm's choice of a capital structure—for instance, the tax deductibility of the interest on debt or the private costs of failure or insolvency—also interpose on the FI's capital decision. This leads to a fifth function of capital:

5. To fund the branch and other real investments necessary to provide financial services.

In the following sections, we focus on the first four functions of capital in reducing the risk of insolvency. We examine the different measures of capital adequacy used by FI owners, managers, and regulators, and the arguments for and against each. We then look at capital adequacy requirements for DTIs, securities firms, and insurance companies set by Canadian and, in some cases, international regulators. Appendix 20A describes the Bank for International Settlements (BIS) internal ratings–based (IRB) approach to measuring credit risk. Appendix 20B outlines the BIS capital surcharges required of global systemically important banks (G-SIBs).

CAPITAL AND INSOLVENCY RISK

LO2

Capital

To see how capital protects an FI against insolvency risk, we must define *capital* more precisely. The problem is that there are many definitions of capital: an economist's definition of capital may differ from an accountant's definition, which, in turn, may differ from the definition used by regulators. Specifically, the economist's definition of an FI's capital or owners' equity stake in an FI is the difference between the market values of its assets and its liabilities. This is also called the **net worth** of an FI. Although this is the *economic* meaning of capital, regulators have found it necessary to adopt definitions of capital that depart by a greater or lesser degree from economic net worth. The concept of an FI's economic net worth is really a *market value accounting concept*. With the exception of the investment banking industry, regulatory-defined capital and required leverage ratios are based in whole or in part on historical or **book value** accounting concepts.

net worth
A measure of an FI's capital that is equal to the difference between the market value of its assets and the market value of its liabilities.

book value
The historical cost basis for asset and liability values.

We begin by looking at the role of economic capital or net worth as an insulation device against two major types of risk: credit risk and interest rate risk. We then compare this market value concept with the book value concept of capital. Because it can actually distort the true solvency position of an FI, the book value of capital concept can be misleading to managers, owners, liability holders, and regulators. We also examine some possible reasons that FI regulators continue to rely on book value concepts in the light of such economic value transparency problems.

The Market Value of Capital

To see how economic net worth or equity insulates an FI against risk, consider the following example. Panel A of Table 20–1 presents a simple balance sheet where all the assets and liabilities of an FI are valued in **market value** terms at current prices on a **mark-to-market basis** (see Chapter 9). On a mark-to-market or market value basis, the economic value of the FI's equity is $10 million, which is the difference between the market values of its assets and liabilities. On a market value basis, the FI is economically solvent and would impose no failure costs on depositors or regulators if it were liquidated today. Let's consider the impact of a classic type of FI risk on this FI's net worth: credit risk.

market value or **mark-to-market basis**
Allowing balance sheet values to reflect current rather than historical prices.

TABLE 20–1
An FI's Market Value Balance Sheet ($ millions)

Panel A: Beginning Market Value Balance Sheet			
Assets		**Liabilities**	
Long-term securities	$ 80	Liabilities (short-term, floating-rate deposits)	$ 90
Long-term loans	20	Net worth	10
	$100		$100
Panel B: Market Value Balance Sheet after a $12 Million Decline in Loan Portfolio Value			
Long-term securities	$80	Liabilities	$90
Long-term loans	8	Net worth	−2
	$88		$88

Market Value of Capital and Credit Risk

In Panel A of Table 20–1, an FI has $20 million in long-term loans. (For simplicity, we drop the $ sign and "million" in the rest of the example.) Suppose that, because of a recession, a number of these borrowers get into cash flow problems and are unable to keep up their promised loan repayment schedules. A decline in the current and expected future cash flows on loans lowers the market value of the loan portfolio held by the FI below 20. Suppose that loans are really worth only 8 (the price the FI would receive if it could sell these loans in a secondary market at today's prices). This means the market value of the loan portfolio has fallen from 20 to 8. Look at the revised market value balance sheet in Panel B of Table 20–1.

This loss renders the FI insolvent; the market value of its assets (88) is now less than the value of its liabilities (90). The owners' net worth stake has been completely wiped out (reduced from 10 to −2), making net worth negative. As a result, liability holders are hurt, but only a bit. Specifically, the first 10 of the 12 loss in value of the loan portfolio is borne by the equity holders. Only after the equity holders are wiped out do the liability holders begin to lose. In this example, the economic value of their claims on the FI has fallen from 90 to 88, or a loss of 2. Note here that we are ignoring deposit insurance.[1]

This example clearly demonstrates the concept of net worth or capital as an insurance fund protecting liability holders, such as depositors, against insolvency risk. The larger the FI's net worth relative to the size of its assets, the more insolvency protection or insurance there is for liability holders and liability guarantors such as CDIC. This is why regulators focus on capital requirements such as the ratio of net worth to assets in assessing the insolvency risk exposure of an FI and in setting risk-based deposit insurance premiums (see Chapter 19).

The Book Value of Capital

We contrast market value or economic net worth with book value of capital or net worth. As we discuss in later sections, book value capital and capital rules based on book values are most commonly used by FI regulators. In Table 20–2, we use

[1] In the presence of deposit insurance, the insurer, such as the CDIC, would bear some of the depositors' losses; for details, see Chapter 19.

TABLE 20–2
Book Value of an FI's Assets and Liabilities ($ millions)

Assets		Liabilities	
Long-term securities	$80	Short-term liabilities	$90
Long-term loans	20	Net worth	10
	$100		$100

the same initial balance sheet we used in Table 20–1 but assume that assets and liabilities are now valued at their historical book values. That is, they reflect the values when the loans were made, the bonds were purchased, and the liabilities were issued, which may have been many years ago. The net worth or equity is now the book value of the stockholders' claims rather than the market value of those claims.

As the example in Table 20–2 is constructed, the book value of capital equals 10. However, invariably, the *book value of equity does not equal the market value of equity* (the difference between the market value of assets and that of liabilities). This inequality in book and market value of equity can be understood by examining the effects of the same credit risk shocks on the FI's capital position, but assuming book value accounting methods.

Book Value of Capital and Credit Risk

Suppose that some of the 20 in loans are in difficulty regarding repayment schedules. We assumed in Panel B of Table 20–1 that the revaluation of cash flows leads to an immediate downward adjustment of the loan portfolio's market value from 20 to 8, a market value loss of 12. By contrast, under historic book value accounting methods such as generally accepted accounting principles (GAAP), FIs have greater discretion in reflecting or timing problem loan loss recognition on their balance sheets and thus the impact of such losses on capital. The market value balance sheet is reflected in Panel B of Table 20–1, and the book balance sheet is reflected in Table 20–2. Notice that the book value balance sheet continues to list 10 of net worth, yet the true value is −2.

The Discrepancy between the Market and Book Values of Equity

The examples above show that market valuation of the balance sheet can produce more economically accurate picture of the net worth than book value accounting and, thus, the solvency position of an FI. Credit risk (and interest rate risk) shocks that result in losses in the market value of assets are borne directly by the equity holders in the sense that such losses are charges against the value of their ownership claims in the FI. As long as the owners' capital or equity stake is adequate, or sufficiently large, liability holders (and, implicitly, regulators that back the claims of liability holders) are protected against insolvency risk. That is, if an FI were closed by regulators before its economic net worth became zero, neither liability holders nor those regulators guaranteeing the claims of liability holders (e.g., CDIC) would stand to lose. Thus, many academics and analysts have advocated the use of market value accounting and market value of capital closure rules for all FIs.

fair value
A measure of market price for an asset or a liability.

International Financial Reporting Standards (IFRS) require financial instruments (assets or liabilities) that are classified as available-for-sale to be recorded at **fair value**, defined as the price market participants would pay for an asset or liability. Other assets, such as loans, are carried on the balance sheet at their amortized cost. Under IFRS 13 *Fair Value Measurement*, the fair value hierarchy uses Level 1 (using an observable market price), Level 2 (using observable inputs other than an active market price), and Level 3 (using unobservable inputs).

During a period of extreme market instability, the lack of market prices for assets greatly increases questions about the solvency of an FI. For example, for FIs with operations in the United States (e.g., TD, Manulife), the Financial Accounting Standards Board (FASB) Statement No. 115 technically requires securities classified as "available for sale" to be marked to market. By comparison, no similar marked-to-market requirement exists on the liabilities side of the balance sheet. In 2007, FAS 157 went into effect, which mandated that assets be measured at fair value. For DTIs, this meant that securities and loans held on the balance sheet had to be valued and reported according to prices being paid for similar instruments in the market. During the financial crisis, FASB clarified its position on the application of market value accounting where there are limited or no observable inputs for marking certain assets to market, as was the case with many of the mortgage-backed securities at the centre of the crisis. Specifically, FASB set its guidelines to allow for the valuation of assets to be based on a price that would be received in an orderly market rather than a forced liquidation. For DTIs, this means that some asset classes, such as derivatives and marketable equity securities, are required to be carried at fair value. Valuation of other types of assets, such as loans and debt securities, depend on whether the assets are held for trading or for investment. All trading assets are carried at fair value. Loans and debt securities that are held for investment or to maturity are carried at amortized cost. The guidance did not eliminate market value accounting, but it did provide management with much more discretion with respect to applying the convention when pricing illiquid assets. This discretion included the ability to use internal assumptions with respect to future cash flows, which would mean employing generally more benign estimates than what the "market" is currently imposing. The guidance specifically allows management to use internal cash flow models and assumptions to estimate fair value when there is limited market data available. This would be equivalent to the Level 3 market value under IFRS 13.

For large publicly traded FIs, we can get a good idea of the discrepancy between book values (*BV*) and market values (*MV*) of equity even when the FI itself does not mark its balance sheet to market. Specifically, in an efficient capital market, investors can value the shares of an FI by doing an as-if market value calculation of the assets and liabilities of the FI. This valuation is based on the FI's current and expected future net earnings or dividend flows. The stock price of the FI reflects this valuation and thus the market value of its shares outstanding. The market value of equity per share is therefore

$$MV = \frac{\text{Market value of equity ownership shares outstanding}}{\text{Number of shares}}$$

By contrast, the historical or book value of the FI's common equity per share (*BV*) is equal to

$$BV = \frac{\begin{matrix}\text{Common} \\ \text{shares}\end{matrix} + \begin{matrix}\text{Contributed} \\ \text{surplus}\end{matrix} + \begin{matrix}\text{Retained} \\ \text{earnings}\end{matrix} + \begin{matrix}\text{Net unrealized} \\ \text{gains (losses)}\end{matrix}}{\text{Number of common shares outstanding}}$$

market-to-book ratio
A ratio showing the discrepancy between the stock market value of an FI's equity and the book value of its equity.

The ratio *MV/BV* is often called the **market-to-book ratio** and shows the degree of discrepancy between the market value of an FI's equity capital as perceived by investors in the stock market and the book value of capital on its balance sheet.

The lower this ratio, the more the book value of capital *overstates* the true equity or economic net worth position of an FI as perceived by investors in the capital market.

Arguments against Market Value Accounting

The first argument against market value accounting is that it is difficult to implement. This may be especially true for smaller FIs with large amounts of nontraded assets such as small loans on their balance sheets. When it is impossible to determine accurate market prices or values for assets, marking to market may be done only with error. A counterargument to this is that the error resulting from the use of market valuation of nontraded assets is still likely to be less than that resulting from the use of original book or historical valuation since the market value approach does not require all assets and liabilities to be traded. As long as current and expected cash flows on an asset or liability and an appropriate discount rate can be specified, approximate market values can always be imputed (see CreditMetrics, described in Appendix 11A). Further, with the growth of loan sales and asset securitization (see Chapters 25 and 26), indicative market prices are available on an increasing variety of loans.

The second argument against market value accounting is that it introduces an unnecessary degree of variability into an FI's earnings—and thus net worth—because paper capital gains and losses on assets are passed through the FI's income statement. Critics argue that reporting unrealized capital gains and losses is distortionary if the FI actually plans to hold these assets to maturity. Insurers and FI managers argue that in many cases they do hold loans and other assets to maturity and, therefore, never actually realize capital gains or losses. Further, regulators have argued that they may be forced to close FIs too early—especially during periods of extreme market stress. For example, if an interest rate spike is only temporary, capital losses on securities can be quickly turned into capital gains as rates fall again (e.g., if interest rates are mean reverting, as much empirical evidence shows). Consistent with these arguments, as mentioned above, in April 2009 the U.S. FASB eased its stance on marking-to-market such that DTIs (as well as any firm) would not need to take earnings hits when asset markets were flawed. Specifically, the new FASB ruling allowed DTIs to avoid market losses by stating that they intend to hold the asset for the long term. The counterargument is that FIs are increasingly trading, selling, and securitizing assets rather than holding them to maturity.

The third argument against market value accounting is that FIs are less willing to accept longer-term asset exposures, such as mortgage loans and business loans, if these assets have to be continuously marked to market to reflect changing credit quality and interest rates. For example, as shown in Chapter 8, long-term assets are more interest rate sensitive than are short-term assets. The concern is that market value accounting may interfere with FIs' special functions as lenders and monitors (see Chapter 1) and may even result in or accentuate a major credit crunch. Of the three arguments against market value accounting, this one is probably the most persuasive to regulators concerned about small-business finance and economic growth.

Having discussed the advantages and disadvantages of book- and market-based measures of an FI's capital, we should note that most FI regulators have chosen some form of book value accounting standard. The major exception is the U.S. Securities and Exchange Commission (SEC). The SEC imposes on the NYSE and other major stock exchanges, as well as on securities firms, retail brokers, and

sec.gov

specialists, a capital or net worth rule that is, for all intents and purposes, a market value accounting rule.[2]

Next, we examine the capital adequacy rules imposed in two key FI sectors: (1) DTIs and (2) insurance companies. The capital adequacy rules currently differ considerably across these sectors. Nevertheless, there is a clear trend toward similar risk-based capital rules in the banking and insurance (both P&C and life) industries. We discuss this trend in more detail in the remainder of the chapter.

CONCEPT QUESTIONS

1. **Why is an FI economically insolvent when its net worth is negative?**
2. **Why does market value accounting produce a more accurate picture of a DTI's net worth than book value accounting?**
3. **What does a market-to-book ratio that is less than 1 imply about an FI's performance?**

CAPITAL ADEQUACY FOR DEPOSIT-TAKING INSTITUTIONS

The Assets to Capital Multiple

LO3

osfi-bsif.gc.ca

The assets to capital multiple (ACM) is reported to OSFI by banks and federally regulated trust and loan companies in Canada. It measures the ratio of the book value of assets to the book value of total capital. Total assets include off-balance-sheet (OBS) items as specified by OSFI. Total capital is the FI's risk-based capital and includes common equity (book value) plus qualifying cumulative perpetual preferred stock plus minority interests in equity accounts of consolidated subsidiaries. The ACM is calculated as follows:

$$ACM = \frac{\text{Total assets (including specified OBS items)}}{\text{Total capital}} \leq 20$$

where

Total assets = All on-balance-sheet assets plus notional amounts of selected OBS items (direct credit substitutes such as letters of credit (LCs) and guarantees, transaction-related contingencies, trade-related contingencies, and sale and repurchase agreements)

Total capital = Net Tier 1 capital + Net Tier 2 capital (described below)

The higher the ACM, the greater is the leverage, and therefore OSFI requires that the multiple be less than 20, but may set the multiple higher or lower for each DTI based on "such factors as operating and management experience, strength of parent, earnings, diversification of assets and appetite for risk." At year-end 2013, the ACM for Canadian banks ranged from 15.6 for Bank of Montreal to 18.4 for National Bank, as shown in Table 20–3. Note that the ACM does not take market value into account, nor does it adjust for the riskiness of assets. As well, only certain OBS items are included in the calculation of the ACM. We now turn to a different measure of capital adequacy. As well, we will discuss the leverage ratio which will be required under Basel III. Canadian DTIs will start reporting their leverage ratio to OSFI by 2015 and the ACM will be phased out.

[2] Canadian securities firms are regulated provincially/territorially (see Chapter 4) and therefore their regulations are not discussed here. The provincial/ territorial regulatory bodies and IIROC require their members to calculate regulatory capitals. IIROC's 196 members reported book value of shareholders' equity of $17.1 billion compared to regulatory capital of $34.3 billion in Q4, 2012.

TABLE 20–3
ACM for Canadian Banks as at October 31, 2013

Source: 2013 annual reports.

Name	ACM*
Bank of Montreal	15.6
Bank of Nova Scotia	17.1
CIBC	18.0
National Bank	18.4
Royal Bank	16.6
TD Bank	18.0

*Total assets and off-balance-sheet instruments as specified by OSFI, divided by total capital (adjusted net Tier 1 and adjusted Tier 2). Unless otherwise specified by OSFI, total assets can be a maximum of 20 times (20X) capital.

Risk-Based Capital Ratios: The Basel Agreement

Basel Agreement
The requirement to impose risk-based capital ratios on banks in major industrialized countries.

bis.org

Canadian and U.S. bank regulators formally agreed with other member countries of the BIS to implement two new risk-based capital ratios for all DTIs under their jurisdiction. The BIS phased in and fully implemented these risk-based capital ratios on January 1, 1993, under what has become known as the **Basel Agreement** (now called Basel I). The 1993 Basel Agreement explicitly incorporated the different credit risks of assets (both on and off the balance sheet) into capital adequacy measures. This was followed by a revision in 1998 in which market risk was incorporated into risk-based capital in the form of an add-on to the 8 percent (10 percent required by OSFI) ratio for credit risk exposure (see Chapter 10). In 2001, the BIS issued a consultative document, *The New Basel Capital Accord*, that proposed the incorporation of operational risk into capital requirements (see Chapter 17 and below) and updated the credit risk assessments in the 1993 agreement.

The new Basel Accord or Agreement (Basel II) was adopted by Canadian banks on November 1, 2008. Basel II consists of three mutually reinforcing pillars (illustrated in Figure 20–1), which together contribute to the safety and soundness of the financial system. Pillar 1 covered regulatory minimum capital requirements for credit, market, and operational risk. The measurement of market risk did not change from that adopted in 1998. In the 2006 Basel Accord, the BIS allowed for a range of options for addressing both credit and operational risk. Two options were allowed for the measurement of credit risk. The first was the standardized approach and the second was an IRB approach. The standardized approach was similar to that of the 1993 agreement, but it was more risk sensitive. Under the IRB approach, DTIs were allowed to use their internal estimates of borrower creditworthiness to assess credit risk in their portfolios (using their own internal rating systems and credit scoring models) subject to strict methodological and disclosure standards as well as explicit approval by the bank's supervising regulator (OSFI, in Canada). Three different approaches were available to measure operational risk: the basic indicator, standardized, and advanced measurement approaches. We discussed these briefly in Chapter 17 and will do so in more detail below.

In Pillar 2, the BIS stressed the importance of the regulatory supervisory review process as a critical complement to minimum capital requirements. Specifically, Basel II created procedures through which regulators ensure that each DTI has sound internal processes in place to assess the adequacy of its capital and set targets for capital that are commensurate with the DTI's specific risk profile. In Pillar 3 the BIS sought to encourage market discipline by developing a set of requirements on the disclosure of capital structure, risk exposures, and capital adequacy. Such disclosure requirements allow market participants to assess critical information describing the risk profile and capital adequacy of banks.

FIGURE 20–1
Basel II and Basel III Pillars of Capital Regulation

Basel II:

Pillar 1	**Pillar 2**	**Pillar 3**
Calculation of regulatory minimum capital requirements	Regulatory supervisory review so as to complement and enforce minimum capital requirements calculated under Pillar 1	Requirements on rules for disclosure of capital structure, risk exposures, and capital adequacy so as to increase FI transparency and enhance market/investor discipline
1. Credit risk: on balance sheet and off balance sheet (standardized vs. IRB approach)		
2. Market risk (standardized vs. IRB approach)		
3. Operational risk (basic indicator vs. standardized vs. advanced measurement approach)		

Basel III:

Enhanced minimum capital and liquidity requirement	Enhanced supervisory review for firmwide risk management and capital planning	Enhanced risk disclosure and market discipline
1. Liquidity risk		

The financial crisis of 2008–2009 revealed weaknesses with Basel II. For example, ratings of credit risk on various securities, such as credit default swaps (CDSs), were conducted by private companies without the supervision or review of official regulatory agencies. Further, the Basel II capital adequacy formula for credit risk was procyclical. Thus, as the financial crisis developed, the probability of borrower default and loss on default both increased, which meant that regulatory capital requirements increased. However, during the crisis, banks were unable to raise the required capital and, thus, had to turn to central banks for capital injections and liquidity support.

In response to these issues, Basel 2.5 was passed in 2009 (effective in 2013) and Basel III was passed in 2010 (fully effective in 2019). Basel 2.5 updated capital requirements on market risk from banks' trading operations (discussed in Chapter 15). The goal of Basel III is to raise the quality, consistency, and transparency of the capital base of banks to withstand credit risk and to strengthen the risk coverage of the capital framework. Specifically, as shown in Figure 20–1, Pillar 1 of Basel III calls for enhancements to both the standardized approach, discussed below, and the IRB approach, discussed in Appendix 20A on Connect, to calculating adequate capital. Changes to Pillar I include a greater focus on common equity, the inclusion of new capital conservation and countercyclical buffers (discussed below) to the minimum level of capital, significantly higher capital requirements for trading and derivatives activities, and a substantial strengthening of counterparty credit risk calculations in determining required minimum capital. Pillar 2 calls for enhanced bankwide governance and risk management to be put in place, such as enhanced incentives for banks to better manage risk and returns over the long term, more stress testing, and implementation of sound compensation practices. Pillar 3 calls for the enhanced disclosure of risks, such as those relating to securitization exposures and sponsorship of OBS vehicles.

Under Basel III, DTIs must calculate and monitor four capital ratios: common equity Tier 1 (CET1) risk-based capital ratio, Tier 1 risk-based capital ratio, total risk-based capital ratio, and Tier 1 leverage ratio. A liquidity ratio, a leverage ratio, and a net stable funding ratio will be required as well and will be phased in by each country according to their implementation plan. Basel III will be fully implemented by 2019 (see Table 20–4). OSFI accelerated this timetable for Canadian DTIs and required the Capital Adequacy Requirements (CAR) of Basel III to be followed by all Canadian banks, bank holding companies, federally regulated trust and loan companies, and cooperative retail associations as of January 1, 2013.[3]

total risk-weighted assets
On- and off-balance-sheet assets whose values are adjusted for approximate credit, market, and operational risk as defined by OSFI and the BIS.

Unlike the simple ACM ratio, the calculation of these risk-based capital adequacy measures is quite complex. Their major innovation is to distinguish among the different credit risks of assets on the balance sheet and to identify the credit risk inherent in instruments off the balance sheet by using **total risk-weighted assets** as the denominator in these capital adequacy ratios. In a very rough fashion, these capital ratios mark to market a DTI's on- and off-balance-sheet positions to reflect its credit risk. Further, additional capital charges must be held against market risk and operational risk.

common equity Tier 1 risk-based capital ratio
The ratio of the CET1 capital to the risk-weighted assets of the FI.

Tier 1 risk-based capital ratio
The ratio of the Tier 1 capital to the risk-weighted assets of the FI.

Under Basel III, the capital ratios used include:

i) **Common equity Tier 1 risk-based capital ratio** = CET1 capital/Credit risk–weighted assets

ii) **Tier 1 risk-based capital ratio** = Tier 1 capital (CET1 capital + additional Tier 1 capital)/Credit risk–weighted assets

TABLE 20–4 Phase-in of Basel III Capital Levels

	2011	2012	2013	2014	2015	2016	2017	2018	As of 1 January 2019
Leverage ratio	Supervisory monitoring		Parallel run 1 January 2013–1 January 2017 Disclosure starts 1 January 2015					Migration to Pillar 1	
Minimum CET1 capital ratio			3.5%	4.0%	4.5%	4.5%	4.5%	4.5%	**4.5%**
Capital conservation buffer						0.625%	1.25%	1.875%	**2.50%**
Minimum CET1 plus capital conservation buffer			3.5%	4.0%	4.5%	5.125%	5.75%	6.375%	**7.0%**
Minimum Tier 1 capital			4.5%	5.5%	6.0%	6.0%	6.0%	6.0%	**6.0%**
Minimum Tier 1 plus capital conservation buffer			4.5%	5.5%	6.0%	6.625%	7.25%	7.875%	**8.50%**
Minimum total capital			8.0%	8.0%	8.0%	8.0%	8.0%	8.0%	**8.0%**
Minimum total capital plus conservation buffer			8.0%	8.0%	8.0%	8.625%	9.25%	9.875%	**10.5%**
Maximum potential countercyclical capital buffer						0.625%	1.25%	1.875%	**2.50%**

Source: Basel Committee on Banking Supervision, *Basel III: A Global Regulatory Framework for More Resilient Banks and Banking Systems*, December 2010 (revised June 2011), bis.org.

[3] See *Capital Adequacy Requirements (CAR) 2013* at osfi-bsif.gc.ca.

total risk-based capital ratio
The ratio of the total capital to the risk-weighted assets of the FI.

iii) **Total risk-based capital ratio** = Total capital (Tier 1 + Tier 2)/Credit risk–weighted assets

iv) Tier 1 leverage ratio = Tier 1 capital/Total exposure

Once the ratios are fully phased in (in 2019; see Table 20–4), to meet Basel III requirements, a DTI must hold a minimum ratio of CET1 capital to risk-weighted assets of 4.5 percent, Tier 1 capital to risk-weighted assets of 6 percent, total capital to risk-weighted assets of 8 percent, and Tier 1 capital to total exposure of 4 percent.

In the measurement of a bank's risk-based capital adequacy, its capital is the standard by which each of these risks is measured.

Capital

OSFI requires all banks and federally regulated trust and loan companies to report their components of capital and capital adequacy ratios quarterly. Table 20–5 shows this information for all domestic banks as reported to OSFI at the end of the first quarter of 2013. Quarter 1, 2013, was the first time that Canadian FIs were required by OSFI to report using Basel III. Table 20–5 thus presents transitional data for domestic banks.

TABLE 20–5
Components of Capital and Capital Ratios for Total Domestic Banks, as at Q1, 2013 ($ thousands)

Source: OSFI, osfi-bsif.gc.ca.

CET1 Capital	
Common shares	70,599,458
Contributed surplus	1,094,559
Retained earnings	98,697,051
Adjustments	7,522,511
A Net CET1 Capital (after all deductions)	162,697,298
Additional Tier 1 capital:	
Noncumulative perpetual preferred shares	880,809
Other qualifying additional Tier 1 instruments	40,000
Other adjustments	1,631,408
Net additional Tier 1 capital	2,552,217
B Net Tier 1 capital	165,249,516
Tier 2 capital:	
Preferred shares	0
Subordinated debt	56,475
Adjustments	35,111,095
C Net Tier 2 capital	35,167,570
D Total capital	200,417,085
Risk-weighted assets	
Total credit risk	1,067,590,060
Market risk modelled	60,703,050
Market risk—standardized method	23,302,100
Operational risk	163,448,726
Adjustments	25,469,508
E Total risk-weighted assets	1,340,513,450
Capital ratios—transitional basis	
CET1 (A ÷ E)	12.14
Tier 1 (B ÷ E)	12.33
Total ratio (D ÷ E)	14.95
ACM	16.86

Under Basel III, a DTI's capital is divided into CET1, Additional Tier 1, and Tier 2. CET1 is primary or core capital of the DTI; Tier 1 capital is the primary capital of the DTI plus additional capital elements; Tier 2 capital is supplementary capital. The total capital that the FI holds is defined as the sum of Tier 1 and Tier 2 capital. The definitions of CET1, additional Tier 1 capital, and Tier II capital are listed in Table 20–6.

CET1 Capital CET1 capital is closely linked to an FI's book value of equity, reflecting the concept of the core capital contribution of an FI's owners. CET1 capital consists of the equity funds available to absorb losses. Basically, it includes the book value of common equity with adjustments required by OSFI, such as other comprehensive income, common equity issued by consolidated subsidiaries, and transitional amounts.

Tier 1 Capital Tier 1 capital is the sum of CET1 capital and additional Tier 1 capital. Included in additional Tier 1 capital are other options available to absorb losses of the bank beyond common equity. These consist of instruments with no maturity dates or incentives to redeem, e.g., noncumulative perpetual preferred stock. These instruments may be callable by the issuer after five years only if they are replaced with "better" capital.

Tier 2 Capital Tier 2 Capital is a broad array of secondary "equitylike"capital resources that includes nonperpetual preferred shares as well as subordinated debt and noncontrolling interests in subsidiaries.

We first look at how this capital is used as a cushion against credit risk using the BIS Standardized Approach described in Basel III as applied by OSFI.

Minimum Capital Requirements

Our approach below is intended to give a flavour of the capital requirements for Canadian federally regulated FIs. As shown in Table 20–6, there are many adjustments to capital and risk-weighted assets that make the calculations complex. As

TABLE 20–6
Definitions of Capital

Source: *Capital Adequacy Requirements (CAR) 2013*, OSFI, osfi-bsif.gc.ca

CET1 Capital
- Common shares issued by the bank and stock surplus that meet the criteria for classification as common shares for regulatory purposes
- Retained earnings
- Accumulated other comprehensive income and other disclosed reserves
- Common shares issued by consolidated subsidiaries of the bank and held by third parties (i.e., minority interest) that meet the criteria for inclusion in CET1 capital
- Less goodwill
- Regulatory adjustments applied in the calculation of CET1

Additional Tier 1 Capital
- Instruments with no maturity dates or incentives to redeem, but may be callable by issuer after five years only if replaced with instrument with "better" capital
- Noncumulative perpetual preferred stock and related surplus
- Tier 1 minority interest, not included in the banking organization's CET1 capital
- Regulatory adjustments applied in the calculation of additional Tier 1 capital

Tier 2 Capital
- Instruments subordinated to depositors and general creditors of the bank
- Subordinated debt and preferred stock
- Total capital minority interest, not included in the banking organization's Tier 1 capital
- Regulatory adjustments applied in the calculation of Tier 2 capital

osfi-bsif.gc.ca
bis.org

well, the regulatory system has been evolving since the 2007–2008 market. The reader is advised to visit OSFI's website as well as the BIS website for the latest capital rules.

In addition to their use to define adequately capitalized FIs, risk-based capital ratios—along with the ACM—also define the adequacy of capital in OSFI's assessment criteria. OSFI rates the adequacy of an FI's capital in four categories, from "Strong" to "Weak," as summarized in Table 20–7. In applying these criteria, OSFI also looks at the specific institution and whether its capital management policies are appropriate and have sufficient senior management and board of directors oversight.

Calculating Risk-Based Capital Ratios

Credit Risk–Weighted Assets

Under Basel capital adequacy rules, risk-weighted assets represent the denominator of the risk-based capital ratio. Two components make up credit risk–weighted assets: (1) credit risk–weighted on-balance-sheet assets, and (2) credit risk–weighted OBS assets.

Credit Risk–Weighted On-Balance-Sheet Assets under Basel III

A major criticism of the original Basel Agreement was that individual risk weights depend on the broad categories of borrowers (i.e., sovereigns, banks, or corporates). For example, under Basel I all corporate loans had a risk weight of 100 percent regardless of the borrowing firm's credit risk. The Basel II and III standardized approach aligns regulatory capital requirements more closely with the key elements of banking

TABLE 20–7
OSFI's Assessment Criteria for Rating Capital Adequacy

Source: OSFI, osfi-bsif.gc.ca.

ROLE OF CAPITAL

Capital is a source of financial support to protect an institution against unexpected losses, and is, therefore, a key contributor to its safety and soundness. Capital management is the ongoing process of raising and maintaining capital at levels sufficient to support planned operations. For complex institutions, it also involves allocation of capital to recognize the level of risk in its various activities. The assessment is made in the context of the nature, scope, complexity, and risk profile of an institution.

ADEQUACY OF CAPITAL

The following statements describe the rating categories used in assessing capital adequacy and capital management policies and practices of an institution. Capital adequacy includes both the level and quality of capital. The assessment is made in the context of the nature, scope, complexity, and risk profile of an institution.

Strong

Capital adequacy is strong for the nature, scope, complexity, and risk profile of the institution, and meets OSFI's target levels. The trend in capital adequacy over the next 12 months is expected to remain positive. Capital management policies and practices are superior to generally accepted industry practices.

Acceptable

Capital adequacy is appropriate for the nature, scope, complexity, and risk profile of the institution and meets OSFI's target levels. The trend in capital adequacy over the next 12 months is expected to remain positive. Capital management policies and practices meet generally accepted industry practices.

Needs Improvement

Capital adequacy is not always appropriate for the nature, scope, complexity, and risk profile of the institution and, although meeting minimum regulatory requirements, may not meet, or is trending below, OSFI's target levels. The trend in capital adequacy over the next 12 months is expected to remain uncertain. Capital management policies and practices may not meet generally accepted industry practices.

Weak

Capital adequacy is inappropriate for the nature, scope, complexity, and risk profile of the institution and does not meet, or marginally meets, minimum regulatory requirements. The trend in capital adequacy over the next 12 months is expected to remain negative. Capital management policies and practices do not meet generally accepted industry practices.

risk by introducing a wider differentiation of credit risk weights. The standardized approach of Basel III includes a greater number of exposure categories for the purpose of calculating total risk-weighted assets than Basel II, provides for greater recognition of financial collateral, and permits a wider range of eligible guarantors. Accordingly, compared with Basel I and II, the standardized approach of Basel III attempts to produce capital ratios more in line with the actual economic risks that FIs are facing.

Under the Basel III standardized approach, each bank assigns its assets to one of several categories of credit risk exposure. Table 20–8 lists the key categories and assets in these categories. The main features are that cash and claims on governments with a high credit rating (S&P rating AAA to AA− or an equivalent rating from another rating agency) attract a 0 percent risk weight. As well, National Housing Act (NHA) insured and NHA-mortgage-backed securities guaranteed by CMHC attract a 0 percent risk weight. The risk weights increase as the credit rating declines. So, for example, a loan to a corporation with an A+ to A− rating is given a 50 percent risk weighting, while a loan to a firm with a credit rating below BB− attracts a 150 percent risk weighting, making it costlier for the FI. However, the appropriateness of using rating agency credit ratings in assigning risk weights to sovereign debt and commercial loans has been criticized since the financial crisis. For example, during

TABLE 20–8
Summary of the Risk-Based Capital Standards for On-Balance-Sheet Items under Basel II & III

Source: OSFI, *Capital Adequacy Requirements (CAR) 2013*, osfi-bsif.gc.ca, and the Basel Committee on Banking Supervision (BCBS), *International Convergence of Capital Measurement and Capital Standards—June 2006* and *Basel III: A Global Regulatory Framework for More Resilient Banks and Banking Systems, December 2010* (revised June 2011), bis.org.

Risk Categories

Weight	Details
0%	Cash, gold bullion
	Claims on (or claims guaranteed by) sovereign governments and central banks with an external (e.g., S&P) credit rating of AAA to AA−
	Claims on provincial and territorial governments
	Claims on specified multilateral development banks (MDBs)
	NHA-insured residential mortgages and NHA mortgage-backed securities guaranteed by CMHC
20%	Claims on countries with credit ratings of A+ to A−
	Claims on banks and securities firms of countries with external credit ratings of AAA to AA−
	Claims on MDBs and corporate entities with external credit ratings of AAA to AA−
	Cheques and cash items in transit
35%	Residential mortgages (uninsured, maximum loan-to-value ratio of 80%)
	Mortgage-backed securities secured against qualifying residential mortgages
50%	Claims on countries with credit ratings of BBB+ to BBB−
	Claims on banks and securities firms of countries with credit ratings of A+ to A−
	Claims on MDBs with credit ratings from A+ to BBB−
	Claims on corporate entities with credit ratings of A+ to A−
75%	Claims on retail customers and small businesses
	Uninsured residential mortgages with a loan-to-value ratio > 80%
100%	Claims on countries with credit ratings of BB+ to B−
	Claims on banks and securities firms of countries with credit ratings of BBB+ to B−
	Claims on MDBs with credit ratings from BB+ to B−
	Claims on corporate customers with credit ratings of BBB+ to BB−
	Claims on governments, banks, securities firms, and corporate entities that are not rated
	Premises, plant, equipment, other fixed assets, real estate
	Future income taxes, prepaid expenses
150%	Claims on countries, MDBs, banks and securities firms below B−, and corporate entities with credit ratings below BB−
350%	Securitization tranches rated between BB+ and BB−
1250%	Securitization exposures rated B+ and below and unrated exposures; significant investments in commercial entities

Note: Claims on public-sector entities (PSEs) (e.g., school boards, hospitals, universities, municipalities) are ranked one category above the sovereign risk weight.

the financial crisis, the U.S. Congress characterized credit rating agencies as organizations whose activities are fundamentally commercial in character. Credit rating agencies played a critical "gatekeeper" role in the debt markets and performed evaluative and analytical services on behalf of clients. There were conflicts of interest of credit rating agencies in providing credit ratings to their clients. Further, by having these credit ratings incorporated into U.S. federal regulations, there was a perceived government "sanctioning" of the credit rating agencies' credit ratings. Thus, Basel III, as applied in the United States, no longer uses credit rating agencies' credit ratings. Instead, the OECD Country Risk Classification (CRC) is used for sovereign debt. The OECD is a noncommercial entity that does not produce credit assessments for fee-paying clients, nor does it provide the sort of evaluative and analytical services that credit rating agencies do.[4] The six largest Canadian banks use the IRB approach, which incorporates an internal credit risk model that has been approved by OSFI. Guidelines for the IRB approach are presented in Appendix 20A.

To calculate the credit risk–weighted assets of the bank (or trust and loan company), we multiply the dollar amount of assets it has in each category by the appropriate risk weight.

EXAMPLE 20-1

Calculation of On-Balance-Sheet Credit Risk–Weighted Assets under Basel III

Consider the bank's balance sheet in Table 20–9, categorized according to the risk weights of Basel III. Under the standardized approach of Basel III, the credit risk–weighted value of the bank's on-balance-sheet assets (in $ millions) would be as follows:

$$\text{Credit risk–weighted on-balance-sheet assets} = 0(8 + 13 + 60 + 50 + 42)$$
$$+ 0.2(10 + 10 + 20 + 55) + 0.35(342) + 0.5(75)$$
$$+ 1(390 + 108 + 22) + 1.5(10) = 711.2$$

The simple book value of on-balance-sheet assets is $1,215 million; its credit risk–weighted value under Basel III is $711.2 million using the standardized approach.

Credit Risk–Weighted OBS Activities

The credit risk–weighted value of on-balance-sheet assets is only one component of the capital ratio denominator. The other is the credit risk–weighted value of the bank's OBS activities. These OBS activities represent contingent rather than actual claims against DTIs (see Chapter 16). Thus, regulations require that capital be held not against the full face value of these items, but against an amount equivalent to any eventual on-balance-sheet credit risk these securities might create for a DTI. Therefore, in calculating the credit risk–weighted asset values of these OBS items we must first convert them into **credit-equivalent amounts**—amounts equivalent to an on-balance-sheet item. Further, the calculation of the credit risk–weighted values of the OBS activities involves some initial segregation of these activities. In particular, the calculation of the credit risk exposure or the credit risk–weighted asset amounts of contingent or guarantee contracts such as LCs differs from the calculation of the credit risk–weighted asset amounts for foreign exchange (FX) and interest rate forward, option, and swap contracts. We first consider the credit risk–weighted asset value of OBS guarantee-type contracts and contingent contracts and then derivative or market contracts.

credit-equivalent amount
The on-balance-sheet equivalent credit risk exposure of an OBS item.

[4] See Basel Committee on Banking Supervision, *Stocktaking on the Use of Credit Ratings*, June 2009. The OECD provides CRCs for more than 150 countries. Assessments are available at www.oecd.org.

TABLE 20–9 Bank's Balance Sheet under Basel III ($ millions)

Weight	Assets		Liabilities/Equity		Capital Class
0%	Cash, gold bullion	$ 8	Demand deposits	$ 150	
	Deposits with the Bank of Canada	13	Notice deposits	500	
	Securities issued or guaranteed by the Government of Canada	60	Fixed-term deposits	380	
	Securities issued or guaranteed by a Canadian province or territory or agents of the federal, provincial, or territorial governments	50	Advances from the Bank of Canada	80	
	Mortgage-backed securities with CMHC guarantee	42			
20	Cheques and items in transit	10	Noncontrolling interests in subsidiaries (subordinated)	15	Tier 2
	Loans to MDBs banks, AA− rated	10	Subordinated debt	15	Tier 2
	Securities issued or guaranteed by a Canadian municipal or school corporation	20	Preferred shares, nonperpetual	5	Tier 2
	Corporate loans, AAA− rated	55			
35	One-to-four-family residential mortgages (uninsured)	342	Common shares	30	CET1
			Contributed surplus	0	CET1
50	Corporate loans, A rated	75	Retained earnings	30	CET1
100	Corporate loans, BB+ rated	390	Noncumulative perpetual preferred shares	10	Additional Tier 1
	Loans to non-OECD countries, B+ rated	108	Noncontrolling Tier 1 interests in subsidiaries	0	Additional Tier 1
	Premises, equipment	22			
150	Corporate loans, CCC+ rated	10		$1215	
	Total assets	$1,215			

OBS Items	
	$80 million in two-year loan commitments to a large Canadian corporation rated BB+
100%	$10 million direct credit substitute SLCs issued to a Canadian corporation rated BBB−
	$50 million in commercial LCs issued to a Canadian corporation rated BBB−
50%	One fixed-floating interest rate swap for 4 years with notional dollar value of $100 million and replacement cost of $3 million
	One two-year euro$ contract for $40 million with a replacement cost of −$1 million

The Credit Risk–Weighted Asset Value of OBS Contingent Guarantee Contracts

Consider the appropriate conversion factors in Table 20–10. Note that under Basel III, direct credit substitute standby letter of credit (SLC) guarantees issued by banks have a 100 percent conversion factor rating or credit-equivalent amount. Similarly, sale and repurchase agreements and assets sold with recourse are also given a 100 percent conversion factor rating. Future performance–related SLCs and unused loan commitments of more than one year have a 50 percent conversion factor. Other loan commitments, those with one year or less to maturity, have a 20 percent credit conversion factor. Standard trade-related commercial LCs and bankers' acceptances sold have a 20 percent conversion factor.

Under Basel III, risk weights assigned to OBS contingent guarantee contracts are the same as if the bank had entered into the transactions as a principal. Thus, the credit ratings used to assign a credit risk weight for on-balance-sheet assets

TABLE 20–10 Credit Conversion Factors for OBS Contingent or Guarantee Contracts, Basel III

Conversion Factor	
100%	Direct credit substitutes (general guarantees of indebtedness and guarantee-type instruments, including SLCs serving as financial guarantees for, or supporting, loans and securities) Acquisitions of risk participation in bankers' acceptances and participation in direct credit substitutes (for example, SLCs) Sale and repurchase agreements Forward agreements (contractual obligations) to purchase assets, including financing facilities with certain drawdown Written put options on specified assets with the characteristics of a credit enhancement*
50%	Transaction-related contingencies (e.g., bid bonds, performance bonds, warranties, and SLCs related to a particular transaction) Commitments with an original maturity exceeding one year, including underwriting commitments and commercial credit lines Revolving underwriting facilities (RUFs), note issuance facilities (NIFs), and other similar arrangements
20%	Short-term, self-liquidating trade-related contingencies, including commercial/documentary LCs (Note: A 20% CCF is applied to both issuing and confirming banks.) Commitments with an original maturity of one year or less
0%	Commitments that are unconditionally cancellable at any time without prior notice.

*Written put options (where premiums are paid up-front) expressed in terms of market rates for currencies or financial instruments bearing no credit or equity risk are excluded from the framework.

Source: OSFI, osfi-bsif.gc.ca.

(listed in Table 20–8) are also used to assign credit risk weights on these OBS activities (e.g., issuing a commercial LC to a CCC-rated counterparty would result in a risk weight of 150 percent).

EXAMPLE 20–2

Calculating OBS Contingent or Guarantee Contracts' Credit Risk–Weighted Assets

To see how OBS activities are incorporated into the risk-based ratio, we can extend Example 20–1 for the bank in Table 20–9. Assume that in addition to having $711.2 million in credit risk–weighted assets on its balance sheet, the bank also has the following OBS contingencies or guarantees:

1. $80 million two-year loan commitments to a large Canadian corporation rated BB+
2. $10 million direct credit substitute SLCs issued to a Canadian corporation rated BBB
3. $50 million commercial LCs issued to a Canadian corporation rated BBB−

To find the risk-weighted asset value for these OBS items, we follow a two-step process.

Step 1. Convert OBS Values into On-Balance-Sheet Credit-Equivalent Amounts

In the first step we multiply the dollar amount outstanding of these items to derive the credit-equivalent amounts using the conversion factors listed in Table 20–10.

OBS Item	Face Value ($ millions)		Conversion Factor		Credit-Equivalent Amount ($ millions)
Two-year loan commitment	$80	×	0.5	=	$40
SLC	10	×	1.0	=	10
Commercial LC	50	×	0.2	=	10

Thus, the credit-equivalent amounts of loan commitments, SLCs, and commercial LCs are, respectively, $40 million, $10 million, and $10 million. These conversion factors convert an OBS item into an equivalent credit or on-balance-sheet item.

Step 2. Assign the OBS Credit-Equivalent Amount to a Risk Category

In the second step we multiply these credit-equivalent amounts by their appropriate risk weights. The appropriate risk weight in each case depends on the underlying counterparty to the OBS activity, such as a municipality, a government, or a corporation. In our example, because each of the contingent guarantee contracts involves a Canadian corporation with a credit rating between BBB+ and BB–, each is assigned a risk weight of 100 percent.

OBS Item	Credit-Equivalent Amount ($ millions)		Risk Weight (w_i)		Risk-Weighted Asset Amount ($ millions)
Two-year loan commitment	$40	×	1.0	=	$40
SLC	10	×	1.0	=	10
Commercial LC	10	×	1.0	=	10
					$60

The bank's credit risk–weighted asset value of its OBS contingencies and guarantees is $60 million.

The Credit Risk–Weighted Asset Value of OBS Market Contracts or Derivative Instruments In addition to having OBS contingencies and guarantees, modern FIs engage heavily in buying and selling OBS futures, options, forwards, swaps, caps, and other derivative securities contracts for interest rate and FX management and hedging reasons, as well as buying and selling such products on behalf of their customers (see Chapter 16). Each of these positions potentially exposes FIs to **counterparty credit risk**, that is, the risk that the counterparty (or other side of a contract) will default when suffering large actual or potential losses on its position. Such defaults mean that an FI would have to go back to the market to replace such contracts at (potentially) less favourable terms.

counterparty credit risk
The risk that the other side of a contract will default on payment obligations.

Under the risk-based capital ratio rules, a major distinction is made between exchange-traded derivative security contracts (e.g., the Montréal Exchange's exchange-traded options) and over-the-counter (OTC) traded instruments (e.g., forwards, swaps, caps, and floors). The credit or default risk of exchange-traded derivatives is approximately zero because when a counterparty defaults on its obligations, the exchange itself adopts the counterparty's obligations in full. However, no such guarantees exist for bilaterally agreed, OTC contracts originated and traded outside organized exchanges. Hence, most OBS futures and options positions have virtually no capital requirements for a bank, while most forwards, swaps, caps, and floors do.[5]

As with contingent or guarantee contracts, the calculation of the risk-weighted asset values of OBS market contracts requires a two-step approach. First, we calculate a conversion factor to create credit-equivalent amounts. Second, we multiply the credit-equivalent amounts by the appropriate risk weights.

[5] This may create some degree of preference among banks for using exchange-traded hedging instruments rather than OTC instruments, because using the former may save a bank costly capital resources. However, as we see in Chapters 22, 23, and 24, Canadian FIs trade mainly OTC contracts.

TABLE 20–11 Credit Conversion Factors for Calculating Potential Credit Exposure

Residual Maturity	Interest Rate Contracts	FX Rate and Gold Contracts	Credit Contract (Investment Grade)	Credit Contract (Noninvestment Grade)	Equity	Precious Metals Except Gold	Other Commodities
One year or less	0.0%	1.0%	5.0%	10.0%	6.0%	7.0%	10.0%
Over one year to five years	0.5%	5.0%	5.0%	10.0%	8.0%	7.0%	12.0%
Over five years	1.5%	7.5%	5.0%	10.0%	10.0%	8.0%	15.0%

Source: OSFI, *Capital Adequacy Requirements (CAR) 2013*, osfi-bsif.gc.ca.

Step 1. Convert OBS Values into On-Balance-Sheet Credit-Equivalent Amounts. We first convert the notional or face values of all non-exchange-traded swap, forward, and other derivative contracts into credit-equivalent amounts. The credit-equivalent amount itself is divided into a *potential exposure* element and a *current exposure* element. That is,

$$\text{Credit-equivalent amount of OBS derivative security items (\$)} = \text{Potential exposure (\$)} + \text{Current exposure (\$)}$$

potential exposure
The risk that a counterparty to a derivative securities contract will default in the future.

current exposure
The cost of replacing a derivative securities contract at today's prices.

The **potential exposure** component reflects the credit risk if the counterparty to the contract defaults in the *future*. The probability of such an occurrence depends on the future volatility of either interest rates for an interest rate contract or exchange rates for an exchange rate contract. Thus, the potential exposure conversion factors in Table 20–11 are larger for credit contracts than for interest rate contracts. Also, note the larger potential exposure credit risk for longer-term contracts.

In addition to calculating the potential exposure of an OBS market instrument, a bank must calculate its **current exposure** with the instrument. This reflects the cost of replacing a contract if a counterparty defaults *today*. The bank calculates this *replacement cost* or *current exposure* by replacing the rate or price initially in the contract with the current rate or price for a similar contract and recalculating all the current and future cash flows that would have been generated under current rate or price terms.[6] The bank discounts any future cash flows to give a current present value measure of the contract's replacement cost. If the contract's replacement cost is negative (i.e., the bank profits on the replacement of the contract if the counterparty defaults), regulations require the replacement cost (current exposure) to be set to zero. If the replacement cost is positive (i.e., the bank loses on the replacement of the contract if the counterparty defaults), this value is used as the measure of current exposure. Since each swap or forward is in some sense unique, calculating current exposure involves a considerable computer processing task for the bank's management information systems. Indeed, specialized service firms are likely to perform this task for smaller banks.

[6] For example, suppose a £1 million two-year forward FX contract was entered into in January 2015 at \$1.55/£1. In January 2016, the bank has to evaluate the credit risk of the contract, which now has one year remaining. To do this, it replaces the agreed forward rate \$1.55/£1 with the forward rate on current one-year forward contracts, \$1.65/£1. It then recalculates its net gain or loss on the contract if it had to be replaced at this price. If the spot rate in January 2016 is \$1.64/£1, then the replacement cost on this contract is (\$1.65 − \$1.55) × £1 million × \$1.64 = \$164,000.

Step 2. Assign the OBS Credit-Equivalent Amount to a Risk Category. Once the current and potential exposure amounts are summed to produce the credit-equivalent amount for each contract, we multiply this dollar number by a risk weight to produce the final credit risk–weighted asset amount for OBS market contracts.

Under Basel III the appropriate risk weight is generally 1.0, or 100 percent. That is,

$$\text{Credit risk–weighted value of OBS market contracts} = \text{Total credit-equivalent amount} \times 1.0\ (\text{risk weight})$$

EXAMPLE 20–3

Calculating OBS Market Contract Credit Risk–Weighted Assets

Suppose the bank in Examples 20–1 and 20–2 had taken one interest rate hedging position in the fixed–floating interest rate swap market for four years with a notional dollar amount of $100 million and one two-year forward FX contract for $40 million (see Table 20–9).

Step 1

We calculate the credit-equivalent amount for each item or contract as follows ($ amounts in millions):

			Potential Exposure + Current Exposure						
Type of Contract (Remaining Maturity)	**Notional Principal**	**×**	**Potential Exposure Conversion Factor**	**=**	**Potential Exposure**	**Replacement Cost**	**Current Exposure**	**=**	**Credit-Equivalent Amount**
Four-year fixed–floating interest rate swap	$100	×	0.005	=	**$0.5**	$3	**$3**		**$3.5**
Two-year forward FX contract	$ 40	×	0.050	=	**$2**	−$1	**$0**		**$2**

For the four-year fixed–floating interest rate swap, the notional value (contract face value) of the swap is $100 million. Since this is a long-term (one to five years to maturity) interest rate market contract, its face value is multiplied by 0.005 to get a potential exposure or credit risk equivalent value of $0.5 million (see row 2 of Table 20–11). We add this potential exposure to the replacement cost (current exposure) of this contract to the bank. The replacement cost reflects the cost of having to enter into a new four-year fixed–floating swap agreement at today's interest rates for the remaining life of the swap should the counterparty default. Assuming that interest rates today are less favourable, on a present value basis, the cost of replacing the existing contract for its remaining life would be $3 million. Thus, the total credit-equivalent amount—current plus potential exposures—for the interest rate swap is $3.5 million.

Next, look at the FX two-year forward contract of $40 million face value. Since this is an FX contract with a maturity of one to five years, the potential (future) credit risk is $40 million × 0.05, or $2 million (see row 2 in Table 20–11). However, its replacement cost is *minus* $1 million. That is, in this example our bank actually stands to gain if the counterparty defaults. Exactly why the counterparty would do this when it is in the money is unclear.

However, regulators cannot permit a bank to gain from a default by a counterparty since this might produce all types of perverse risk-taking incentives. Consequently, as in our example, current exposure has to be set equal to zero (as shown). Thus, the sum of potential exposure ($2 million) and current exposure ($0) produces a total credit-equivalent amount of $2 million for this contract. Since the bank has just two OBS derivative contracts, summing the two credit-equivalent amounts produces a total credit-equivalent amount of $3.5 million + $2 million = $5.5 million for the bank's OBS market contracts.

Step 2

The next step is to multiply this credit-equivalent amount by the appropriate risk weight. Specifically, to calculate the risk-weighted asset value for the bank's OBS derivative or market contracts, we multiply the credit-equivalent amount by the appropriate risk weight, which is generally 1.0 or 100 percent:

Credit risk–weighted asset value of OBS derivatives	=	$5.5 million (credit-equivalent amount)	×	1.0 (risk weight)	=	$5.5 million

Total Credit Risk–Weighted Assets under Basel III

Under Basel III, the total credit risk–weighted assets are $776.7 million ($711.2 million from on-balance-sheet activities, plus $60 million for the risk-weighted value of OBS contingencies and guarantees, plus $5.5 million for the risk-weighted value of OBS derivatives).

Netting under Basel III

One criticism of the above method is that it ignores the netting of exposures. In response, OSFI has adopted a proposal put forward by the BIS that allows netting of OBS derivative contracts as long as the bank has a bilateral netting contract that clearly establishes a legal obligation by the counterparty to pay or receive a single net amount on the different contracts. Provided that such written contracts (master netting agreements) are clearly documented by the bank, the new rules require the estimation of *net current exposure* and *net potential exposure* of those positions included in the bilateral netting contract. The sum of the net current exposure and the net potential exposure equals the total credit-equivalent amount.

The rules define net current exposure as the net sum of all positive and negative replacement costs (or mark-to-market values of the individual derivative contracts). If the sum of the replacement costs is positive, then the net current exposure equals the sum. If it is negative, the net current exposure is zero. The net potential exposure is defined by a formula that adjusts the gross potential exposure estimated earlier:

$$A_{net} = (0.4 \times A_{gross}) + (0.6 \times NPR \times A_{gross})$$

where A_{net} is the net potential exposure (or adjusted sum of potential future credit exposures), A_{gross} is the sum of the potential exposures of each contract, and NPR is the ratio of net current exposure or net replacement cost (NR) to gross current exposure. The 0.6 is the amount of potential exposure that is reduced as a result of netting.

The same example used in the previous section (without netting) will be used to show the effect of netting on the total credit-equivalent amount. *Here we assume that both contracts are with the same counterparty* ($ amounts in millions):

$$A_{gross} = \$2.5 \qquad \text{Net current exposure} = \$2 \qquad \text{Current exposure} = \$3$$

The net current exposure is the sum of the positive and negative replacement costs—that is, +\$3 and −\$1 = \$2. The gross potential exposure (A_{gross}) is the sum of the individual potential exposures = \$2.5. To determine the net potential exposure, the following formula is used:

$$A_{net} = (0.4 \times A_{gross}) + (0.6 \times NPR \times A_{gross})$$
$$NPR = \text{Net current exposure/Current exposure} = 2/3$$
$$A_{net} = (0.4 \times \$2.5) + (0.6 \times 2/3 \times \$2.5)$$
$$= \$2$$

$$\text{Total credit-equivalent amount} = \text{Net potential exposure} + \text{Net current exposure}$$
$$= \$2 + \$2 = \$4$$

$$\text{Risk-weighted asset value of OBS market contracts} = \text{Total credit-equivalent amount} \times 1.0 \text{ (risk weight)}$$
$$= \$4 \times 1.0 = \$4$$

As can be seen, netting reduces the credit risk–weighted asset value from \$5.5 million to \$4 million.

Calculating the Overall Risk-Based Capital Position

After calculating the risk-weighted assets for a DTI, the final step is to calculate the Tier 1 and total risk–based capital ratios.

EXAMPLE 20-4

Calculating the Overall Risk-Based Capital Position of a Bank

From Table 20–9, the bank's Tier 1 capital (common shares, retained earnings, noncumulative perpetual preferred shares) totals \$70 million. Tier 2 capital (subordinated noncontrolling interests in subsidiaries, subordinated debt, nonperpetual preferred shares) totals \$35 million. The resulting total Tier 1 and Tier 2 capital is, therefore, \$105 million.

We can now calculate our bank's capital adequacy Basel III risk-based capital requirements as (\$ amounts in millions)

$$\text{CET1 risk-based ratio} = \$60/\$776.7 = 7.72\%$$
$$\text{Tier 1 risk-based ratio} = \$70/\$776.7 = 9.01\%$$

and

$$\text{Total risk-based capital ratio} = \$105/\$776.7 = 13.52\%$$

The minimum CET1 capital ratio set by OSFI was 4.5 percent by the first quarter of 2013. The minimum total Tier 1 capital ratio was 6.0 percent, and the minimum total risk-based capital ratio required was 8.0 percent, both by the first quarter of 2014. Therefore, the bank in our example has adequate capital under all three capital requirement formulas.

Capital Conservation Buffer

LO4

In addition to revising the minimum capital ratio requirements for credit risk, Basel III introduced a capital conservation buffer designed to ensure that DTIs build up a capital surplus, or buffer, that can be drawn down as losses are incurred during periods of financial stress. The buffer requirements provide incentives for DTIs to build up a capital surplus by reducing discretionary

TABLE 20–12 Basel III Capital Conservation Buffer and Minimum Capital Ratio Plus Capital Conservation Buffer

Capital Conservation Buffer—Effective Q1 Each Year							
	2013	2014	2015	2016	2017	2018	2019
Capital conservation buffer				0.625%	1.25%	1.875%	2.50%
Minimum capital ratios plus capital conservation buffer							
CET 1	3.5%	4.0%	4.5%	5.125%	5.75%	6.375%	7.0%
Total Tier 1 capital	4.5%	5.5%	6.0%	6.625%	7.25%	7.875%	8.5%
Total capital	8.0%	8.0%	8.0%	8.625%	9.25%	9.875%	10.5%

Source: OSFI, *Capital Adequacy Requirements 2013*, Chapter 1, osfi-bsif.gc.ca

distributions of earnings such as dividends, share buybacks, and staff bonuses in order to reduce the risk that their capital levels will fall below the minimum requirements during periods of stress. The capital conservation buffer must be composed of CET1 capital and is held separately from the minimum risk-based capital requirements.

Under Basel III, a DTI would need to hold a capital conservation buffer of greater than 2.5 percent of total risk-weighted assets. The capital conservation buffer is being phased in between 2016 and 2019, when it will be set at 2.5 percent, as shown in Table 20–12. The minimum ratios for CET1, Total Tier 1 capital, and Total capital, inclusive of the capital conservation buffer, are also shown in Table 20–12. However, OSFI has required Canadian FIs to meet the "all-in" CET1 ratio (CET1 plus the capital conservation buffer) of 7 percent in Quarter 1, 2013, and the minimum all-in Tier 1 capital ratio (Tier 1 capital plus capital conservation buffer) of 8.5 percent, and the all-in total capital ratio (total capital plus capital conservation buffer) of 10.5 percent in Quarter 1, 2014, ahead of the Basel III schedule. Failure to meet the minimum all-in ratios would trigger OSFI's intervention. The guidelines for assessing capital adequacy (see Table 20–7) as well as the supervisory framework (updated in 2010) are provided at OSFI's website.

If an FI's capital buffer falls below 2.5 percent, constraints on *earnings payouts* (e.g., dividends, share buybacks, and "bonus" payments) will be imposed. Table 20–13 lists the capital conservation ratio as a percentage of distributable earnings that applies effective for all DTIs January 1, 2019. The capital conservation ratio is based on CET1. As can be seen, the closer the FI's CET1 plus capital conservation buffer is to the minimum, the greater the constraint on its discretionary payout of earnings. For example, a DTI with a CET1 capital ratio plus conservation buffer of

TABLE 20–13 Minimum Capital Conservation Ratios for Levels of CET1

Minimum Capital Conservation Ratios at Various Levels of CET1				
2016	**2017**	**2018**	**2019**	**Capital Conservation Ratio**
4.5%–4.656%	4.5%–4.813%	4.5%–4.969%	4.5%–5.125%	100%
> 4.656%–4.813%	> 4.813%–5.125%	> 4.969%–5.438%	> 5.125%–5.75%	80%
> 4.813%–4.969%	> 5.125%–5.438%	> 5.438%–5.906%	> 5.75%–6.375%	60%
> 4.969%–5.125%	> 5.438%–5.75%	> 5.906%–6.375%	> 6.375%–7.0%	40%
> 5.125%	> 5.75%	> 6.375%	> 7.0%	0%

Note: Capital conservation ratio is the percentage of earnings that must be retained when CET1 falls below the minimum required.

Source: OSFI, *Capital Adequacy Requirements 2013*, Chapter 1, osfi-bsif.gc.ca.

6.75 percent in Quarter 1, 2019, less than the minimum 7.0 percent required, would have to retain 40 percent of its net income in the following quarter and every quarter until it met the CET1 requirement, using the retained funds to build up its capital conservation buffer. In other words, its payout of dividend, share buybacks, or discretionary bonus payments is restricted to 60 percent of its earnings each quarter. Instead of increasing its retained earnings, an FI could also increase its CET1 capital by issuing common equity.

LO5

Systemically Important Financial Institutions

As a result of the financial crisis, Basel III recognizes that there are FIs that are too big to fail (TBTF) since their failure has the potential to cause significant disruption of the domestic and global financial systems. These FIs are required to have additional capital under Basel III. Domestic systemically important Banks (D-SIBS) have been identified by OSFI, and G-SIBS have been identified by the Basel Committe on Banking Supervision (BCBS).

D-SIBs

In March 2013, OSFI designated the six largest Canadian banks (Bank of Montreal, Bank of Nova Scotia, Canadian Imperial Bank of Commerce, National Bank of Canada, Royal Bank of Canada, and Toronto-Dominion Bank) as D-SIBs under Basel III. These banks were identified based on the following characteristics:

Size These six banks account for over 90 percent of total banking assets in Canada.

Interconnections The interconnectedness of the six banks to each other means that there is potential for the failure of one bank to cause problems for the others, weakening the Canadian financial system.

Substitutability In the Canadian financial system, the failure or distress of any one of the six banks would cause significant problems in finding another bank to take on their role. For example, payments transactions through the Large Value Transfer System (LVTS) or clearing and settling FX transactions could be interrupted if one of the large banks were to fail.

D-SIBs will be subject to the following requirements:

Capital Surcharge Beginning on January 1, 2016, the six D-SIBs will be required to hold a common equity surcharge equal to 1 percent of risk-weighted assets. This means that the CET1 target will be 8 percent. The mechanism used is the capital conservation buffer discussed previously. Table 20–14 shows the CET1 targets

TABLE 20–14 Minimum Capital Conservation Ratios for Levels of CET1 for D-SIBs

Minimum Capital Conservation Ratios for D-SIBs at Various Levels of Common Equity Tier 1 (CET1)				
2016	2017	2018	2019	Capital Conservation Ratio
5.5%-5.656%	5.5%-5.813%	5.5%-5.969%	5.5%-6.125%	100%
> 5.656%-5.813%	> 5.813%-6.125%	> 5.969%-6.438%	> 6.125%-6.75%	80%
> 5.813%-5.969%	> 6.125%-6.438%	> 6.438%-6.906%	> 6.75%-7.375%	60%
> 5.969%-6.125%	> 6.438%-6.75%	> 6.906%-7.375%	> 7.375%-8.0%	40%
> 6.125%	> 6.75%	> 7.375%	> 8.0%	0%

Note: Capital conservation ratio is the percentage of earnings that must be retained when CET1 falls below the minimum required.

Source: OSFI, *Domestic Systemic Importance and Capital Targets—DTIs*, March 2013, osfi-bsif.gc.ca.

for D-SIBs. The D-SIBs will be subject to greater restrictions on their payouts when they fail to meet CET1 requirements.

Higher Regulatory Supervision The size of the D-SIBs and their greater complexity means that they will be subject to higher and more frequent levels of monitoring by OSFI. As well, they will be expected to have more sophisticated risk management models (e.g., use the IRB approach to measuring credit risk; see Appendix 20A) and higher levels of internal control.

Information Disclosure The six banks are expected to provide more public information about their risk management practices and their models in order to increase confidence in the financial system.

G-SIBs

As part of Basel III, the BIS imposed an additional CET1 surcharge ("loss absorbency requirement") on G-SIBs: banking groups whose distress or disorderly failure would cause significant disruption to the wider financial system and economic activity. The basic idea is that since G-SIBs are TBTF banks (that would have to be bailed out by central governments and taxpayers), they need to lower their risk by increasing their tangible capital requirements even more than other banks. The surcharge ranges from 1 percent to 3.5 percent to be held over and above the 7 percent minimum CET1 plus conservation buffer requirement. The purpose of the additional capital requirement is twofold: (1) to reduce the probability of failure of a G-SIB by increasing its going-concern loss absorbency and (2) to reduce the extent or impact of the failure of a G-SIB on the financial system by improving global recovery and resolution frameworks.

G-SIBs are identified using a methodology developed by the BIS based on an indicator measurement approach that identifies factors that cause international contagion. The indicators were selected to capture the systemic impact of a bank's failure, rather than the probability that the bank will fail. The indicators include bank size, interconnectedness, cross-jurisdictional (global) activity, the lack of substitutes for their services, and complexity to rank their global systemic importance (see Appendix 20B on Connect). Using this methodology on an initial sample of 73 of the world's largest banks and year-end 2009 data for each indicator, the BIS designated 27 banks as G-SIBs. Two additional banks were added to this initial list based on the home supervisor's judgment, resulting in 29 G-SIBs headquartered in 12 countries. Table 20–15 lists the initial 29 G-SIBs. The number of G-SIBs can change over time, reflecting changes in the systemic importance of banks. The sample of banks to be assessed will be reviewed every three years, and the BIS anticipates eventually expanding the surcharge to a wider group of FIs, including insurance companies and other nonbank FIs.

The exact amount of the surcharge depends on a bank's placement in one of five "buckets" (requiring 1 percent, 1.5 percent, 2 percent, 2.5 percent, and 3.5 percent surcharges, respectively) based on the bank's score from the indicator measurement approach and may be met with CET1 capital only. The surcharge requirement will be phased in in parallel with the Basel III capital conservation and countercyclical buffers, beginning in 2016 and becoming fully effective in 2019.

Leverage Ratio

One of the features of the financial crisis of 2008–2009 was the accumulation of extreme on- and off-balance-sheet leverage throughout the banking system.

TABLE 20–15
G-SIBs

Bank	Country	Bank	Country
Groupe BPCE	France	Société Générale	France
Group Crédit Agricole	France	Deutsche Bank	Germany
Unicredit Group	Italy	Mitsubishi UFJ FG	Japan
Mizuho FG	Japan	Sumitomo Mitsui FG	Japan
ING Bank	Netherlands	Santander	Spain
Nordea	Sweden	Credit Suisse	Switzerland
UBS	Switzerland	Barclays	United Kingdom
HSBC	United Kingdom	Lloyds Banking Group	United Kingdom
Royal Bank of Scotland	United Kingdom	Bank of America	United States
Bank of New York Mellon	United States	Citigroup	United States
Goldman Sachs	United States	JPMorgan Chase	United States
Morgan Stanley	United States	State Street Bank	United States
Wells Fargo	United States	BBVA	Spain
Bank of China	China	Industrial and Commercial Bank of China Limited	China
BNP Paribas	France	Standard Chartered	United Kingdom

During the worst of the crisis, DTIs were forced by the market to reduce leverage to an extent that intensified falling asset prices, DTI losses, declines in DTI capital, and the reduction in credit availability. To prevent this cycle from reoccurring, Basel III introduced a leverage ratio requirement that is intended to discourage the use of excess leverage and to act as a backstop to the risk-based capital requirements described above.

The Basel III leverage ratio is defined as the capital measure (numerator) divided by the exposure measure (denominator):

$$\text{Leverage ratio} = \frac{\text{capital measure}}{\text{exposure measure}}$$

The capital measure is the Tier 1 capital as defined by Basel III. The exposure measure is the sum of on-balance-sheet exposures, derivative exposures, securities financing transaction exposures (SFTs), and off balance sheet items. A DTI must hold a minimum leverage ratio of 3 percent, which is less than the equivalent 5 percent (the inverse of the ACM) required by OSFI. Parallel testing of the minimum 3 percent leverage ratio for international DTIs started on January 1, 2013. DTIs will have to meet the 3 percent ratio starting January 1, 2018. OSFI will require Canadian FIs to meet the 3 percent and to start reporting their leverage ratio in 2015.[7]

Interest Rate Risk, Market Risk, and Risk-Based Capital

From a regulatory perspective, a credit risk–based capital ratio is adequate only as long as a DTI is not exposed to undue interest rate or market risk. The reason is that the risk-based capital ratio takes into account only the adequacy of a bank's

[7] See Basel Committee on Banking Supervision, Basel III leverage ratio framework and disclosure requirements, January 2014, www.bis.org, OSFI's guidelines are expected to be published in 2014.

capital to meet both its on- and off-balance-sheet credit risks. Not explicitly accounted for is the insolvency risk emanating from interest rate risk (duration mismatches) and market (trading) risk.

bis.org

To meet these criticisms, in 1993 the BIS developed additional capital requirements for interest rate risk (see Chapter 9) and market risk (see Chapter 15). As is discussed in Chapter 15, since 1998 DTIs have had to calculate an add-on to the risk-based capital ratio to reflect their exposure to market risk. There were two approaches available to DTIs to calculate the size of this add-on: (1) the standardized model proposed by regulators and (2) the DTI's own internal market risk model. As discussed in Chapter 15, the financial crisis exposed a number of shortcomings in the way market risk was being measured in accordance with Basel II rules. Although the crisis largely exposed problems with the large-bank internal models approach to measuring market risk, the BIS also identified shortcomings with the standardized approach. These included a lack of risk sensitivity, a very limited recognition of hedging and diversification benefits, and an inability to sufficiently capture risks associated with more complex instruments. To address shortcomings of the standardized approach to measuring market risk, Basel III proposes a partial risk factor approach as a revised standardized approach. Basel III also introduces a fuller risk factor approach as an alternative to the revised partial risk factor standardized approach. Both models are discussed and illustrated in Chapter 15. In addition, for large banks, which rely on internal based models to measure regulatory capital for market risk, a greater reliance is placed on the expected shortfall (ES) of capital that would likely result from a major shock rather than value-at-risk (VaR) (see Chapter 15). Moreover, the illiquidity measures to be used in internal model–based calculation are to be significantly increased.

To date, no formal add-on has been required for interest rate risk, although Basel II suggests a framework for a future capital ratio for interest rate risk similar to the original 1993 proposal. Specifically, Basel II states that banks should have interest rate risk measurement systems that assess the effects of interest rate changes on both earnings and economic value. These systems should provide meaningful measures of a bank's current levels of interest rate risk exposure and should be capable of identifying any excessive exposures that might arise.[8]

Operational Risk and Risk-Based Capital

Basel II implemented an additional add-on to capital for operational risk. Prior to this proposal, the BIS had argued that the operational risk exposures of banks were adequately taken care of by the total credit risk–weighted capital ratio. But increased visibility of operational risks in recent years (see Chapter 17) has induced regulators to propose a separate capital requirement for operational risks. As noted above, the BIS now believes that operational risks are sufficiently important for DTIs to devote resources to quantify such risks and to incorporate them separately into their assessment of their overall capital adequacy. In its 2001 and

[8] See Basel Committee on Banking Supervision, *Principles for the Management and Supervision of Interest Rate Risk*, July 2004, bis.org, and OSFI, *Guideline B-12, Interest Rate Risk Management—Sound Business and Financial Practices*, February 2005, osfi-bsif.gc.ca. See also *Principles for Sound Stress Testing Practices and Supervision*, May 2009, bis.org.

2003 *Consultative Documents* the Basel committee outlined three specific methods by which DTIs can calculate capital to protect against operational risk: the basic indicator approach, the standardized approach, and the advanced measurement approach.[9]

The basic indicator approach is structured so that banks, on average, will hold 12 percent of their total regulatory capital for operational risk. This 12 percent target was based on a widespread survey conducted internationally of current practices by large banks. To achieve this target, the basic indicator approach focuses on the gross income of the bank, that is, its net profits, or what is often called *value added*. This equals a bank's net interest income plus net noninterest income:

$$\text{Gross income} = \text{Net interest income} + \text{Net noninterest income}$$

According to BIS calculations, a bank that holds a fraction (alpha, α) of its gross income for operational risk capital, where alpha (α) is set at 15 percent, will generate enough capital for operational risk such that this amount will be 12 percent of its total regulatory capital holdings against all risks (i.e., credit, market, and operational risks). For example, under the basic indicator approach:

$$\text{Operational capital} = \alpha \times \text{Gross income}$$

or

$$= 0.15 \times \text{Gross income}$$

The problem with the basic indicator approach is that it is too aggregative, or top-down, and does not differentiate at all among areas in which operational risks may differ (e.g., Payment and Settlement may have a very different operational risk profile from Retail Brokerage).[10]

In an attempt to provide a finer differentiation of operational risks in a bank across different activity lines while still retaining a basically top-down approach, the BIS offers a second method for operational capital calculation. This second method, the standardized approach, divides activities into eight major business units and lines (shown in Table 20–16). Within each business line, there is a specified broad indicator (defined as beta, β) that reflects the scale or volume of a DTI's activities in that area. The indicator relates to the gross income reported for a particular line of business. It serves as a rough proxy for the amount of operational risk within each of these lines. A capital charge is calculated by multiplying the β for each line by the indicator assigned to the line and then summing these components. The βs reflect the importance of each activity in the average bank. The βs are set by regulators and are calculated from average industry figures from a selected sample of banks.

Suppose the industry β for corporate finance is 18 percent and gross income from the corporate finance line of business (the activity indicator) is $30 million for

[9] See Basel Committee on Banking Supervision, *International Convergence of Capital Measurement and Capital Standards*, June 2006, bis.org, and OSFI, *Capital Adequacy Requirements—Simpler Approaches*, Chapter 6, November 2007, February 2003, osfi-bsif.gc.ca.

[10] A second issue is that the α term implies operational risk that is proportional to gross income. This ignores possible economies of scale effects that would make this relationship nonlinear (nonproportional); that is, α might fall as bank profits and/or size grow.

TABLE 20–16
BIS Standardized Approach Business Units and Lines

Business Line	Indicator	Capital Factor
Corporate finance	Gross income*	$\beta_1 = 18\%$
Trading and sales	Gross income	$\beta_2 = 18\%$
Retail banking	Gross income	$\beta_3 = 12\%$
Commercial banking	Gross income	$\beta_4 = 15\%$
Payment and settlement	Gross income	$\beta_5 = 18\%$
Agency services	Gross income	$\beta_6 = 15\%$
Asset management	Gross income	$\beta_7 = 12\%$
Retail brokerage	Gross income	$\beta_8 = 12\%$

*The indicator relates to gross income reported for the particular line of business.

Source: OSFI, *Capital Adequacy Requirements (CAR)—Simpler Approaches*, November 2007, Chapter 6, p. 131, osfi-bsif.gc.ca.

the bank. Then the regulatory capital charge for this line for this year is

$$\begin{aligned} \text{Capital}_{\text{Corporate Finance}} &= \beta \times \text{Gross income from the corporate finance line of business for the bank} \\ &= 18\% \times \$30 \text{ million} \\ &= \$5{,}400{,}000 \end{aligned}$$

The total capital charge is calculated as the three-year average of the simple summation of the regulatory capital charge across each of the eight business lines.

The third method, the advanced measurement approach, allows individual banks to rely on internal data for regulatory capital purposes subject to supervisory approval. Under the advanced measurement approach, supervisors require the bank to calculate its regulatory capital requirement as the sum of the expected loss (EL) and unexpected loss (UL) for each event type, as listed in Table 20–17. Internally generated operational risk measures used for regulatory capital purposes must be based on a minimum three-year observation period of internal loss data, whether the internal loss data are used directly to build the loss measure or to validate it. A bank's internal loss data must be comprehensive in that the data capture all material activities and exposures from all appropriate subsystems and

TABLE 20–17
Operational Risk Loss Event Types

Internal fraud Losses due to acts of a type intended to defraud, misappropriate property, or circumvent regulations, the law, or company policy, excluding diversity/discrimination events, which involve at least one internal party.

External fraud Losses due to third-party acts of a type intended to defraud, misappropriate property, or circumvent the law.

Employment practices and workplace safety Losses arising from acts inconsistent with employment, health, or safety laws or agreements, from payment of personal injury claims, or from diversity/discrimination events.

Clients, products, and business practices Losses arising from an unintentional or negligent failure to meet a professional obligation to specific clients (including fiduciary and suitability requirements) or from the nature or design of a product.

Damage to physical assets Losses arising from loss or damage to physical assets from natural disaster or other events.

Business disruption and system failures Losses arising from disruption of business or system failures.

Execution, delivery, and process management Losses from failed transaction processing or process management or from relations with trade counterparties and vendors.

geographic locations. Risk measures for different operational risk estimates are added for the purpose of calculating the regulatory minimum capital requirement. FIs need OSFI's permission to use advanced measurement approaches. They also must conduct stress testing.

Criticisms of the Risk-Based Capital Requirements

The risk-based capital requirements seek to improve on a simple leverage ratio such as the ACM by (1) incorporating credit, market, and operational risks into the determination of capital adequacy; (2) more systematically accounting for credit risk differences among assets; (3) incorporating OBS risk exposures; and (4) applying a similar capital requirement across all the major DTIs (and banking centres) in the world. Unfortunately, the requirements have a number of conceptual and applicability weaknesses in achieving these objectives:

1. *Risk weights.* It is unclear how closely the risk weight categories in Basel III reflect true credit risk. For example, corporate loans have risk weights between 20 and 150 percent under Basel III. Taken literally, these relative weights imply that some corporate loans are exactly 7.5 times as risky as other loans.
2. *Risk weights based on external credit rating agencies.* While Basel II proposed reforms to improve on Basel I in measuring credit risk, that is, by replacing the single 100 percent risk weight for sovereign, bank, and corporate loans with different risk weights, depending on the loan's credit rating, it is unclear whether the risk weights accurately measure the relative (or absolute) risk exposures of individual borrowers. Moreover, Standard & Poor's and Moody's ratings are often accused of lagging behind rather than leading the business cycle. As a result, required capital may peak during a recession, when banks are least able to meet the requirements. Moreover, relying on rating agencies to determine a borrower's credit risk questions the specialness of banks as monitors—see Chapter 1.
3. *Portfolio aspects.* The BIS plans largely ignore credit risk portfolio diversification opportunities. As we discussed in Chapter 11, when returns on assets have negative or less than perfectly positive correlations, an FI may lower its portfolio risk through diversification. As constructed, the Basel III (standardized model) capital adequacy plan is essentially a linear risk measure that ignores correlations or covariances among assets and asset group credit risks—such as between residential mortgages and corporate loans. That is, the FI manager weights each asset separately by the appropriate risk weight and then sums those numbers to get an overall measure of credit risk. No account is taken of the covariances among asset risks between different counterparties (or risk weights).[11]
4. *Excessive complexity.* Basel III raises the cost of regulation by adding new levels of complexity. The cost of developing and implementing new risk management systems is significant, and the benefits may turn out to be small. As Andrew Haldane, Executive Director for Financial Stability at the Bank of England, pointed out, risk models have grown so complex that to have statistical confidence that a given set of formulas have captured true risks, you need 400 to 1,000 years of data.

---

[11] However, the more advanced IRB approach (see Appendix 20A) assesses correlations for borrower exposures. Currently, it is estimated that only the biggest banks will use the IRB approach.

5. *Loan-to-value ratio used for residential mortgages.* Basel III places a great reliance on the loan-to-value ratio for residential mortgages. During the financial crisis, property values used by DTIs were inflated by real estate appraisers. If this were to happen again, insufficient capital would be held against these mortgages.
6. *Pillar 2 may ask too much of regulators.* Pillar 2 of Basel III requires many very sensitive judgment calls from regulators that may be ill equipped to make them. This will particularly be a problem for less-developed country regulators. If Pillar 2 is taken seriously, supervisors may be exposed to a lot of criticism that most would rather avoid. However, in the wake of the financial meltdown of 2008–2009, the role of regulators is seen as central to financial stability as BIS guidelines for liquidity and capital are enhanced.
7. *Leverage, liquidity, and specialness.* Reducing bank leverage levels (through increased capital) will reduce DTI's returns on equity (ROEs) and make it harder for them to generate additional capital. Indeed, rather than earning traditional ROEs of over 15 percent, post-Basel III, many DTIs will see ROEs in the range of 8 to 10 percent. When added to the two new liquidity ratios introduced under Basel III (discussed in Chapter 12) that force DTIs to more closely match maturities of assets and liabilities rather than "borrowing short" and "lending long" as has traditionally been a special feature of DTIs, the special features of banking discussed in Chapter 1 will be reduced.

CONCEPT QUESTIONS

1. **What are the major strengths of the risk-based capital ratios?**
2. **You are a manager of a DTI with a CET1 ratio of 6 percent. Discuss four strategies to meet OSFI's required 7 percent ratio in a short period of time without raising new capital.**
3. **Why isn't a capital ratio levied on exchange-traded derivative contracts?**
4. **What is the difference between Tier 1 capital and Tier 2 capital?**
5. **Identify one asset in each of the credit risk weight categories for Basel III.**

CAPITAL REQUIREMENTS FOR OTHER FINANCIAL INSTITUTIONS

Securities Firms

Canadian securities firms are governed by provincial and territorial governments, as well as self-regulatory organizations (SROs) such as the Investment Industry Association of Canada (IIAC) and the stock exchanges (e.g., the TSX and the Montréal Exchange). While these SROs set their own requirements for capital for their members, there is no single national regulator, such as the SEC in the United States, of securities firms in Canada.

minimum continuing capital and surplus requirement (MCCSR)
The minimum capital required by OSFI for federally regulated life insurance companies operating in Canada.

Life Insurance Companies

Federally regulated life insurance companies (including branches of foreign life insurance companies operating in Canada) are required to maintain adequate levels of capital under the Insurance Companies Act (ICA). OSFI provides guidelines for the **minimum continuing capital and surplus requirements (MCCSR)** for life insurance companies that are risk based, and uses the concepts of Tier 1 (core) and Tier 2 (supplementary) capital as for federally regulated DTIs. Two MCCSR ratios apply. The Tier 1 ratio is calculated as

$$\text{Tier 1} = \text{Net Tier 1 capital/Total capital required} > 60 \text{ percent}$$

The total capital ratio is calculated as

$$\text{Total capital ratio} = \text{Total capital available/Total capital required} > 120 \text{ percent}$$

Table 20–18 shows the components and the calculations of the MCCSR ratios for Canadian life insurance companies as reported to OSFI at Quarter 1, 2013. Canadian life insurance companies regulated by OSFI are seen to be well above the minimum MCCSR ratios for Tier 1 (171.47 > 60) and total capital (219.15 > 120).

mortality risk
The risk of death.

morbidity risk
The risk of ill health.

As for the banks under its jurisdiction, OSFI requires an estimate of risk-weighted assets that encompasses (1) default (credit) and market risk, (2) insurance risks, (3) interest rate risk, (4) FX risk, and (5) other risks. Default and market risk are similar to the credit risk–weighted asset calculations for DTIs. Insurance risk captures the risk of adverse changes in **mortality risk** and **morbidity risk**. Interest rate risk in part reflects the liquidity of liabilities and their probability or ease of withdrawal as interest rates change.[12] Since 2007, representatives of OSFI, Assuris, and the Autorité des marchés financiers (FMA) have been working to update the MCCSR standard framework. Canadian and global regulators are concerned about the increasing complexity of insurance assets, as well as their exposure to market, credit, insurance, and operational risk. Life insurance companies' liabilities from exposure to segregated funds (discussed in Chapter 6) were of considerable concern to regulators during the 2008 market disruptions.

Property and Casualty Insurance Companies

minimum capital test (MCT)
The ratio of total capital available to minimum capital required for P&C companies regulated by OSFI in Canada.

Since 2003, federally regulated property and casualty (P&C) companies have been required to meet a **minimum capital test (MCT)**, which is defined as

$$\text{Total capital available/Minimum capital required} > 100 \text{ percent}$$

The minimum ratio is 100 percent, but P&C companies are expected to maintain capital at or above 150 percent, the supervisory target, in order to provide a buffer to deal with market volatility and other risks. Table 20–19 shows the MCT calculation for all Canadian federally regulated P&C companies as reported to OSFI as at Quarter 1, 2013. It can be seen that the ratio is simpler than that applied by OSFI under Basel III for Canadian banks, but it does consider some of the same components for capital that can be included in the numerator of the MCT. The denominator of the MCT establishes the minimum capital required for on- and off-balance-sheet assets, policy liabilities, and accident and sickness insurance, as well as for catastrophes, unearned premiums and unearned claims, and reinsurance. As seen in Table 20–19, the ratio of 243.92 for Canadian P&C companies is well above the 150 percent for individual companies. OSFI may set different targets based on the risk profile of the individual institution. P&C companies must notify OSFI if they expect to fall below their target ratio, and must also provide a plan for returning above their minimum.[13]

---

[12] For complete details, see Office of the Superintendent of Financial Institutions, *Minimum Continuing Capital And Surplus Requirements (MCCSR) for Life Insurance Companies—A*, December 2013, osfi-bsif.gc.ca.

[13] For complete details, see Office of the Superintendent of Financial Institutions, *Minimum Capital Test (MCT) for Federally Regulated Property and Casualty Insurance Companies—A*, January 2013, osfi-bsif.gc.ca.

TABLE 20–18
MCCSR for Canadian Life Insurance Companies as at Quarter 1, 2013 ($ thousands)

Source: Office of the Superintendent of Financial Institutions, osfi-bsif.gc.ca

Capital Available:		
Tier 1 Capital		
Common shares		$36,201,303
Contributed surplus		5,279,795
Retained earnings		23,228,020
Noncumulative perpetual preferred shares		861,498
Qualifying noncontrolling interests		401,071
Innovative instruments		1,811,232
Less: Adjustments and deductions		19,125,333
Adjusted Net Tier 1 Capital		**A $48,657,586**
Tier 2 Capital		
Tier 2A		1,153,950
Tier 2B allowed		4,719,271
Tier 2C		9,709,946
Net Tier 2 Capital		**13,527,462**
Total Capital Available		**B $62,185,048**
Capital Required:		
Assets Default & Market Risk		**15,444,981**
Insurance Risks		8,116,358
Changes in Interest Environment (C-3) Risk		4,676,981
FX Risk		137,510
Other		159
Total Capital Required		**C $28,375,989**
MCCSR Ratios:		
Tier 1	**(A/C) × 100**	171.47
Total	**(B/C) × 100**	219.15

TABLE 20–19
MCT for Canadian Insurance Companies as at Quarter 1, 2013 ($ thousands)

Source: Office of the Superintendent of Financial Institutions, osfi-bsif.gc.ca.

Capital Available	
Total equity less accumulated other comprehensive income	$26,345,402
Subordinated indebtedness and redeemable preferred shares	266,000
Accumulated other comprehensive income (loss) on:	
Available-for-sale equity securities	639,867
Available-for-sale debt securities	1,064,324
Foreign currency (net of hedging activities)	-33,526
Other additions	7,877
Other adjustments	-3,522,078
Total Capital Available	$24,767,866
Capital Required	
Balance sheet assets	3,135,568
Unearned premiums/unpaid claims/premium deficiencies	5,922,672
Catastrophes	296,512
Reinsurance ceded to unregistered insurers	44,605
Interest rate risk	683,700
Structured settlements, LCs, derivatives, and other exposures	71,169
Minimum Capital Required	$10,154,226
Excess Capital Available over Minimum Capital Required	$14,613,640
Total Capital Available as a % of Minimum Capital Required	243.92
Minimum Gross Capital Level	$1,466,083

CONCEPT QUESTIONS

1. **How do the capital requirements for life insurance firms differ from the capital rules for DTIs?**
2. **What types of risks are included in estimating the MCCSR of life insurance firms?**
3. **Why does the MCT for P&C companies differ from the MCCSR for life insurance companies?**

Questions and Problems

1. Identify and briefly discuss the importance of the five functions of an FI's capital.
2. Why are regulators concerned with the levels of capital held by an FI compared with those held by a non-FI?
3. What are the differences between the economic definition of capital and the book value definition of capital?
   a. How does economic value accounting recognize the adverse effects of credit risk?
   b. How does book value accounting recognize the adverse effects of credit risk?
4. Why is the market value of equity a better measure of an FI's ability to absorb losses than book value of equity?
5. Provincial Bank has the following year-end balance sheet ($ millions):

Assets	
Cash	$ 10
Loans	90
Total assets	$100
Liabilities and Equity	
Deposits	$ 90
Equity	10
Total liabilities and equity	$100

The loans are primarily fixed-rate, medium-term loans, while the deposits are either short-term or variable-rate deposits. Rising interest rates have caused the failure of a key industrial company, and, as a result, 3 percent of the loans are considered uncollectible and thus have no economic value. One-third of these uncollectible loans will be charged off. Further, the increase in interest rates has caused a 5 percent decrease in the market value of the remaining loans. What is the impact on the balance sheet after the necessary adjustments are made according to book value accounting? According to market value accounting?

6. What are the arguments for and against the use of market value accounting for DTIs?
7. How is the ACM for a Canadian bank defined?
8. Identify and discuss the weaknesses of the ACM as a measure of capital adequacy.
9. What is the Basel Agreement?
10. What are the major features of the Basel III capital requirements?
11. What are the definitional differences between CET1, Tier 1, and Tier 2 capital?
12. Under Basel III, what four capital ratios must DTIs calculate and monitor?
13. What are the credit risk–weighted assets in the denominator of the CET1 risk-based capital ratio, the Tier I risk-based capital ratio, and the total risk-based capital ratio?
14. Explain how OSFI evaluates the capital adequacy of an FI.
15. Explain the process of calculating risk-weighted on-balance-sheet assets.
16. Under Basel III, how are risk weights for sovereign exposures determined?
17. Halifax Bank has the following balance sheet ($ millions), has no OBS activities, and uses the standardized approach to calculate risk-weighted assets:

Assets	
Cash	$ 20
Treasury bills	40
Residential mortgages, uninsured	600
Sovereign loans, BB+ to B−	430
Total assets	$1,090
Liabilities and Equity	
Deposits	$ 980
Subordinated debentures	25
Common stock	45
Retained earnings	40
Total liabilities and equity	$1,090

a. What is the CET1 ratio?

b. What is the Tier 1 risk-based capital ratio?

c. What is the total risk-based capital ratio?

d. What is the ACM?

e. What is the leverage ratio?

f. How would OSFI categorize this bank's capital (Table 20–7)?

18. What is the capital conservation buffer? How would this buffer affect your answers to question 17?

19. What is the countercyclical capital buffer? If the home country set a countercyclical capital buffer of 1.5 percent, how would this buffer affect your answers to question 17?

20. Onshore Bank has $20 million in assets, with risk-weighted assets of $10 million. CET1 capital is $500,000, additional Tier 1 capital is $50,000, and Tier 2 capital is $400,000. How will each of the following transactions affect the value of the CET1, Tier 1, and total capital ratios? What will the new value of each ratio be?

a. The bank uses cash to repurchase $100,000 of common stock.

b. The bank issues $2,000,000 of fixed-term deposits and uses the proceeds for uninsured residential mortgages.

c. The bank receives $500,000 in deposits and invests them in T-bills.

d. The bank issues $800,000 in common stock and lends it to help finance a new shopping mall. The developer has an A+ credit rating.

e. The bank issues $1,000,000 in nonqualifying perpetual preferred stock and purchases provincial bonds.

f. Homeowners pay back $4,000,000 of uninsured residential mortgages, and the bank uses the proceeds to build new ABMs.

21. Explain the process of calculating risk-weighted OBS contingent guarantee contracts.

a. What is the basis for differentiating the credit-equivalent amounts of contingent guarantee contracts?

b. On what basis are the risk weights for the credit-equivalent amounts differentiated?

22. Explain how OBS market contracts, or derivative instruments, differ from contingent guarantee contracts.

a. What is counterparty credit risk?

b. Why do exchange-traded derivative contracts have no capital requirements?

c. What is the difference between the potential exposure and the current exposure of OTC derivative contracts?

d. Why are the credit conversion factors for the potential exposure of FX contracts greater than they are for interest rate contracts?

e. Why do regulators not allow banks to benefit from positive current exposure values?

23. What is the process of netting OBS derivative contracts under Basel III?

24. What are D-SIBs? What are G-SIBs? How do capital ratio requirements differ for these FIs?

25. Identify and discuss the problems in the risk-based capital approach to measuring capital adequacy.

26. What is the contribution to the credit risk–weighted asset base of the following items under the Basel III requirements using the standardized approach?

a. $10 million cash.

b. $50 million 91-day Treasury bills.

c. $25 million cash items in the process of collection.

d. $5 million U.K. government bonds, AAA rated.

e. $5 million Australian short-term government bonds, A− rated.

f. $1 million provincial government bonds.

g. $40 million repurchase agreements.

h. $500 million uninsured one-to-four-family-home mortgages.

i. $500 million corporate loans, BBB− rated.

j. $100,000 performance-related SLCs to an AAA-rated corporation.

k. $100,000 performance-related SLCs to a Canadian municipality issuing bonds.

l. $7 million commercial LC to a foreign, A-rated corporation.

m. $3 million five-year loan commitment to an OECD government.

n. $8 million bankers' acceptance conveyed to a Canadian corporation rated AA–.

o. $17 million three-year loan commitment to a private agent.

p. $17 million three-month loan commitment to a private agent.

q. $30 million SLC to back an A-rated corporate issue of CP.

r. $4 million five-year interest rate swap with no current exposure (the counterparty is a private agent).

s. $6 million two-year currency swap with $500,000 current exposure (the counterparty is a low credit risk entity).

27. Third Bank has the following balance sheet ($ millions) with the risk weights in parentheses:

Assets	
Cash (0%)	$ 20
OECD interbank deposits (20%)	25
Mortgage loans (50%)	70
Consumer loans (100%)	70
Total assets	$185
Liabilities and Equity	
Deposits	$175
Subordinated debt (5 years)	3
Cumulative preferred stock	2
Equity	5
Total liabilities and equity	$185

The cumulative preferred stock is qualifying and perpetual. In addition, the bank has $30 million in performance-related SLCs, $40 million in two-year forward FX contracts that are currently in the money by $1 million, and $300 million in six-year interest rate swaps that are currently out of the money by $2 million. Credit conversion factors follow:

Performance-related SLCs	50%
1- to 5-year FX contracts	5%
1- to 5-year interest rate swaps	0.5%
5- to 10-year interest rate swaps	1.5%

a. What are the risk-weighted on-balance-sheet assets of the bank as defined under the Basel Accord?

b. What are the CET1, Tier 1, and total capital required for both off- and on-balance-sheet assets?

c. Does the bank have enough capital to meet the Basel requirements? If not, what minimum CET1, additional Tier 1, or total capital does it need to meet the requirement?

d. Does the bank have enough capital to meet the Basel requirements, including the capital conservation buffer requirement? If not, what minimum CET1, additional Tier 1, or total capital does it need to meet the requirement?

28. Alberta Bank has the following balance sheet ($ millions) with the risk weights in parentheses:

Assets	
Cash (0%)	$ 20
Mortgage loans (35%)	50
Consumer loans (75%)	70
Total assets	$140
Liabilities and Equity	
Deposits	$120
Subordinated debt (> 5 years)	2
Equity	6
Total liabilities and equity	$128

In addition, the bank has $20 million in commercial direct credit substitute SLCs (AA rated) and $40 million in 10-year FX forward contracts that are in the money by $1 million.

a. What are the risk-weighted on-balance-sheet assets of the bank as defined under the Basel III Accord?

b. What are the CET1, Tier 1, and total capital required for both off- and on-balance-sheet assets?

c. Disregarding the capital conservation buffer, does the bank have sufficient capital to meet the Basel III requirements? How much in excess? How much short?

Appendix 20A Internal Ratings–Based Approach to Measuring Credit Risk–Weighted Assets

Appendix 20B Methodology Used to Determine G-SIBs Capital Surcharge

View Appendices 20A and 20B on Connect.

CHAPTER 21

PRODUCT AND GEOGRAPHIC EXPANSION

After studying this chapter you should be able to:

LO1 Discuss the issues considered by an FI in deciding to expand the products it offers.

LO2 Define shadow banking and discuss its impact on FIs and regulations.

LO3 Discuss the issue of competition for FIs and the impact of cross-pillar mergers in Canada.

LO4 Discuss the regulatory and economic issues that an FI uses when analyzing geographic expansions.

LO5 Discuss the advantages and disadvantages for a Canadian FI in expanding internationally.

INTRODUCTION

As we discovered in Chapter 20, an FI's capital, particularly its Tier 1 capital as defined by regulators, is extremely important to an FI and to the stability of the global financial system. Our concepts of what an FI should do—that is, what products it should offer—are tied to the regulatory capital required to undertake each activity. As a result, the investment decisions that drive the capital structure, dividend, and short-term financing decisions of an FI are motivated by profit as for any other company, but the risk of the activity is paramount. Since each product line undertaken by an FI has a risk component associated with it, domestic and global regulations are the starting point for an FI's strategy with respect to product and geographic expansion.

This chapter first examines product diversification. We analyze the problems and risks that can arise, and those that have arisen historically: FIs constrained to limited financial service sectors or franchises as well as the potential benefits from greater product expansion; the laws and regulations that have restricted product expansions for banks, insurance companies, and securities firms in Canada, the United States and elsewhere, as well as the recent modifications of many of these laws and regulations; barriers to product expansion between the financial sector and the real or commercial sector of the economy; and the advantages and disadvantages of allowing FIs to adopt more universal franchises. Second, we examine the potential benefits and costs to the risk management strategies considered by FI managers from domestic and international geographic expansion—especially through mergers and acquisitions (M&As). In particular, we examine the potential return–risk advantages and disadvantages of such expansions. We also present some evidence on the cost and revenue synergies as well as other market- and firm-specific factors impacting geographic expansion.

PRODUCT DIVERSIFICATION

LO1

universal FI An FI that can engage in a broad range of financial services activities.

The Canadian and U.S. financial systems were traditionally structured along segmented product lines. Regulatory barriers and restrictions have often inhibited the ability of an FI operating in one area of the financial services industry to expand its product set into other areas. This can be compared with FIs operating in Germany, Switzerland, and the United Kingdom, where a more **universal FI** structure has traditionally allowed individual financial services organizations to offer a far broader range of banking, insurance, securities, and other financial services products. In the late 1980s, both Canada and the United Kingdom underwent "big bangs" that revamped their regulatory systems and moved both countries toward universal banks. The revisions of the Bank Act in the 1980s and 1990s resulted in the Canadian banks absorbing and ultimately dominating the securities industry in Canada and eliminating the trust industry as a stand-alone function. The Canadian issues that remain to be resolved are cross-pillar mergers with insurance companies and mergers within the banking pillar.

On the asset side of the balance sheet, the business loans of banks have faced increased competition from the dynamic growth of the commercial paper (CP) market as an alternative source of short-term financing for large and medium-sized corporations. This trend mean that the economic value of narrowly defined bank franchises has declined. In particular, product line restrictions inhibit the ability of an FI to optimize the set of financial services it can offer, potentially forcing it to adopt a more risky set of activities than it would adopt if it could fully diversify.

Product restrictions also limit the ability of FI managers to adjust flexibly to shifts in the demand for financial products by consumers and to shifts in costs due to technology and related innovations. We analyze the advantages and disadvantages of increased product line diversification in more detail after we look more closely at the segmentation of the financial services industry.

SEGMENTATION IN THE FINANCIAL SERVICES INDUSTRY

Banking and Investment Banking

commercial banking Banking activity of deposit taking and lending.

investment banking Banking activity of underwriting, issuing, and distributing securities.

As noted above, Canadian banks have had investment banking arms since the 1990s. U.S. deregulation lagged behind. From 1933 to 1998, the United States was delayed in starting toward universal banking by the Glass–Steagall Act, which separated the functions of **commercial banking** and **investment banking**. After nearly 70 years of partial or complete separation between investment banking and commercial banking, the Financial Services Modernization Act of 1999 opened the door for the creation of full-service FIs in the United States similar to those that existed before 1933 and that exist in many other countries today. After implementation of the Financial Services Modernization Act, U.S. FIs swiftly caught up. A large number of M&As took place between 1997 and 2000, most notably the bank–insurance company merger between Citicorp and Travelers to create Citigroup. Citigroup was the second-largest universal bank in the world in 2004, as U.S. regulatory barriers receded and the globalization of financial services continued to move forward. However, the market meltdown in 2008 was particularly devastating to Citigroup, bringing its model of a universal bank into question. As well, the model of a large, stand-alone investment bank funded by short-term money market borrowing was eliminated in 2008, with only Goldman Sachs and Morgan Stanley left in the United States after the mergers of Bear Stearns with JPMorgan Chase and Merrill Lynch with Bank of America and the failure of Lehman Brothers. Goldman Sachs and Morgan Stanley both became bank holding companies, which are subject to stricter regulatory oversight. To address the crisis, one week after the closure of Lehman Brothers and the sale of Merrill Lynch to Bank of America, the Federal Reserve granted a request by the country's last two major investment banks, Goldman Sachs and Morgan Stanley, to change their status to bank holding companies. By becoming bank holding companies, the firms agreed to significantly tighter regulations and much closer supervision by bank examiners from several government agencies rather than only the Securities and Exchange Commission (SEC). With the conversion, the investment banks would look more like commercial banks, with more disclosure, higher capital, and less risk taking. Both banks already had limited retail deposit-taking businesses, which they planned to expand over time. In exchange for subjecting themselves to more regulation, the companies would have access to the full array of the Federal Reserve's lending facilities. For example, as bank holding companies, Morgan Stanley and Goldman Sachs now have greater access to the discount window of the Federal Reserve, which U.S. banks can use to borrow money from the central bank. These events on Wall Street—the failure or sale of three of the five largest independent investment banks and the conversion of the two remaining firms to commercial banks—effectively turned back the clock to the 1920s, when investment banks and commercial banks functioned under the same corporate umbrella.

As part of the increased authority given to the Federal Reserve in the 2010 Wall Street Reform and Consumer Protection Act, the Federal Reserve proposed in late 2011 that net credit exposures between any two of the nation's six largest financial firms would be limited to 10 percent of the company's regulatory capital. Other financial firms would be subject to a 25 percent limit, which was required by the 2010 act. The proposed Federal Reserve rule aims to reduce the interconnectedness of FIs in the U.S. financial system and reduce the ability of any single financial firm to damage the financial system and the broader economy—as happened when Lehman Brothers was allowed to fail. The result of the new rules is that big U.S. banks could be forced to return to a more traditional banking model that revolves around deposit taking and making loans. This could result in smaller capital markets and less securities lending.

Banking and Insurance

Certain types of insurance—for example, credit life insurance, mortgage insurance, and auto insurance—tend to have natural synergistic links to bank lending products. Moreover, we must make a distinction between a bank selling insurance as an agent by selling other FIs' policies for a fee and a bank acting as an insurance underwriter and bearing the direct risk of underwriting losses. In general, the risks of insurance agency activities are quite low in loss potential compared to insurance underwriting.

Canadian banks are permitted to sell some insurance products (e.g., travel insurance and credit life insurance to support mortgages and loans), but since 2001, have been unable to provide information about property and casualty (P&C) insurance or referrals in their branches. This is primarily because of concerns about consumer privacy and protection and the potential for tied selling. In 2009, OSFI permitted banks to sell insurance products online, but the finance minister asked them to remove these links from their websites. On the other hand, Canadian life insurance companies have expanded from annuity-type offerings into a full range of mutual fund and investment offerings related to RRSPs, RRIFs, and pensions, as well as segregated funds.

Canadian insurance companies, particularly Manulife and Sun Life, have expanded cross-border into the United States. The U.S. Financial Services Modernization Act of 1999 completely changed the landscape for insurance activities (and implicitly ratified the Citicorp–Travelers merger) as it allowed bank holding companies to open insurance underwriting affiliates and insurance companies to open commercial bank as well as securities firm affiliates through the creation of financial services holding companies (FSHCs). With the passage of this act, U.S. banks no longer have to fight legal battles to overcome restrictions on their ability to sell insurance. The insurance industry applauded the act, as it forced banks that underwrite and sell insurance to operate under the same set of state regulations (pertaining to their insurance lines) as insurance companies. Under the new act, an FSHC that engages in commercial banking, investment banking, and insurance activities is functionally regulated. This means that the holding company's banking activities are regulated by bank regulators, its securities activities are regulated by the SEC, and its insurance activities are regulated by up to 50 state insurance regulators.

Nonbank Financial Services Firms and Banking

LO2

In comparison with the barriers separating banking and securities, insurance, or commercial-sector activities, the barriers among nonbank financial services firms and banking are generally much weaker. Indeed, as mentioned above, the erosion of product barriers between commercial bank and other FI services firms has not been all one way. Nonbank financial services firms increasingly offer traditional banking services. For example, money market mutual funds offer chequing accounts; annuities are financial products issued by insurance companies that offer retirement income; and finance companies and industrial loan corporations provide commercial, real estate, and consumer loans that compete directly with the same services offered by commercial banks. These nonbank financial services firms provide credit, maturity, and liquidity intermediation without access to central bank liquidity provisions or deposit insurance. Their activities occur beyond the reach of existing government monitoring and regulation.

shadow banking
Activities of nonfinancial services firms that perform banking services.

More recently, activities of nonfinancial services firms that perform banking services have been termed **shadow banking.**[1] Beyond the examples listed above, new participants in the shadow banking system include structured investment vehicles (SIVs), special-purpose vehicles (SPVs), asset-backed paper vehicles, credit hedge funds, asset-backed commercial paper (ABCP) conduits, limited-purpose finance companies, and credit hedge funds. As of the end of 2011, worldwide total assets managed by the shadow banking system totalled US$67 trillion. In the shadow banking system, savers place their funds with money market mutual and similar funds, which invest these funds in the liabilities of shadow banks. Borrowers get

[1] The term "shadow banking system" is attributed to Paul McCulley, "Teton Reflections," *PIMCO Global Central Bank Focus* (2007), Federal Reserve Bank of Kansas City's Jackson Hole economic symposium.

loans and leases from shadow banks such as finance companies rather than from banks. Like the traditional banking system, the shadow banking system intermediates the flow of funds between net savers and net borrowers. However, instead of the bank serving as the intermediary, it is the nonbank financial services firm, or shadow bank, that intermediates. Further, unlike in the traditional banking system, where the complete credit intermediation is performed by a single bank, in the shadow banking system it is performed through a series of steps involving many nonbank financial services firms. For example, and as discussed in more detail in Chapter 26, the lending process might involve (1) loan originations performed by a finance company, (2) purchase and warehousing of these loans conducted by single and multiple SIVs funded through ABCP, and (3) purchase of ABCP by money market mutual funds (MMMFs). Thus, the shadow banking system decomposes the traditional process of deposit-funded, hold-to-maturity lending conducted by banks into a more complex, wholesale-funded, securitization-based lending process that involves multiple shadow banks that are not regulated by a specific regulatory body.

Because of the specialized nature involved in the credit intermediation process performed by shadow banks, these nonbank financial services firms can often perform the process more cost-efficiently than traditional banks. Further, because of the lower costs and lack of regulatory controls, shadow banks can take on risks that traditional banks either cannot or are unwilling to take. Thus, the shadow banking system allows credit to be available that might not otherwise have been generated through the traditional banking system. Moreover, because commercial banks and shadow banks are interrelated through the credit intermediation system, problems that arise in the shadow banking system can quickly spread to the traditional banking system. Indeed, by transforming the way the credit intermediation process works—from the traditional banking method to the multilayered process used by shadow banks—shadow banks fuelled much of the unprecedented growth in the real estate markets in the mid-2000s that eventually crashed and led to the financial crisis.

As of 2013, these shadow banks are unregulated in most jurisdictions globally, However, the Financial Stability Board (FSB), the Bank of Canada, and OSFI are involved in the global discussion of how to limit the systemic risk that these shadow banks pose to global financial stability. In the United States, the 2010 Wall Street Reform and Consumer Protection Act called for regulators to be given broad authority to monitor and regulate nonbank financial firms that pose risks to the financial system. As of the fall of 2012, U.S. regulators had outlined a process to identify nonbank financial services firms that should receive increased oversight. In the first stage of a proposed three-step process, regulators identify any nonbank financial service firm that has at least US$50 billion in assets and also meets one of five "quantitative" thresholds relating to interconnectedness, leverage, outstanding debt, and other risk factors that will be considered for increased scrutiny. In the second stage, regulators evaluate individual firms' potential riskiness using a variety of metrics. In the third stage, with a two-thirds vote, the Financial Stability Oversight Council (created as part of the 2010 act) can designate an individual firm as one that will receive additional regulation and monitoring. Regulators may also designate any nonbank FI that would not be captured by the three-step process as one that poses risks to the financial system and should receive additional regulatory oversight. The designated firms come under the supervision of the U.S. Federal Reserve and must comply with new rules, such as more stringent capital, risk management, and leverage standards. When implemented, the process is one tool by which the 2010 act will enable regulators to extend oversight and regulation to the shadow banking system.

DIVERSIFICATION IN OTHER COUNTRIES

In many cases, global competition has been reduced by the failure or takeover of FIs since 2008. But, as in most market disruptions, there are winners and losers. The global market share has shifted to the strongest FIs, as clients look for safer counterparties. As consolidation in the U.S. and global financial services industry proceeds, we may see the creation of very large, globally oriented, multiproduct financial services firms that will operate with a new set of risks and management strategies to handle these risks. Table 21–1 shows the largest financial services firms in the world (measured by assets) as of 2012 balance sheet information. Only one of the top 10, JPMorgan Chase, is headquartered in the United States. Royal Bank of Canada (RBC) and Toronto-Dominion (TD) Bank rank 37 and 38, respectively, based on asset size.

We have just described the barriers to product expansion and financial conglomeration in Canada and the United States. Although many of the barriers have eroded, those that remain fall most heavily on the banks. Product expansion and financial conglomeration are handled differently around the globe. Appendix 21A compares the range of product activities permitted for banks in other major industrialized countries and financial centres. Universal banks offer not only investment banking services, but also commercial lending, foreign exchange (FX), and custody and cash management services. Large universal banks that operate globally include Citigroup, JPMorgan Chase, UBS, Deutsche Bank, and Credit Suisse First Boston. With the possible exception of banks in Japan, U.S. banks are still the most constrained of all the major industrialized countries in terms of the range of nonbank product activities permitted. This has created continuing pressure to bring U.S. banks' activity powers in line with those of their global competitors and counterparts such as those in the EU and Switzerland. In the next section, we look at the issues that have been raised and will continue to be raised whenever the question of expanded product (or more universal) powers for banks and other FIs arise.

TABLE 21–1
The 10 Largest Banks in the World (in billions of U.S. dollars)

Source: relbanks.com June 2013.

	Total Assets
Industrial & Commercial Bank of China (ICBC) (China)	$2,811.3
HSBC Holdings (United Kingdom)	2,692.5
Deutsche Bank (Germany)	2,665.4
Credit Agricole Groupe (France)	2,660.9
Mitsubishi UFJ Financial Group (Japan)	2,594.8
BNP Paribas (France)	2,527.2
Credit Agricole SA (France)	2,441.2
Barclays PLC (United Kingdom)	2,401.8
JPMorgan Chase (United States)	2,359.1
Japan Post Bank (Japan)	2,291.4

ISSUES INVOLVED IN THE DIVERSIFICATION OF PRODUCT OFFERINGS

The economic value of narrowly defined bank franchises may decline over time. Product line restrictions can inhibit an FI's ability to optimize the set of financial services it offers, potentially forcing it to adopt a more risky set of activities than it would adopt if it could fully diversify. Product restrictions also limit the ability of FI managers to adjust flexibly to shifts in the demand for financial products by consumers and to shifts in costs due to technology and related innovations.

Whether the debate concerns existing activities or expansion into securities, insurance, or nonbank financial service firms' expansion into banking, similar issues arise. These include:

1. Safety and soundness issues.
2. Economy of scale and scope issues.
3. Conflict-of-interest issues.
4. Deposit insurance issues.
5. Regulatory oversight issues.
6. Competition issues.

Canadian banks have dominated the investment banking and securities industry in Canada since their takeover of the independent securities firms in the late 1980s and early 1990s, as discussed in Chapter 4. However, the regulation of banking functions is carried out by the OSFI, whereas securities regulation remains in the hands of the provincial and territorial regulators until the establishment of a national securities regulator. The six issues listed above are evaluated with a main focus on banks entering into securities activities, but can be extended to consider the last cross-pillar issue: the merger of banks and insurance companies.

osfi-bsif.gc.ca

Consider the three alternative organizational structures for linking banking and securities activities in Figure 21–1. In this figure, panel (a) shows the fully integrated universal bank, where banking and securities activities are conducted in different departments of a single organization. This is typical of how large banks in Germany, such as Deutsche Bank, engage in securities activities. Panel (b) shows the universal subsidiary model, where a bank engages in securities activities through a separately owned securities affiliate. This is typical of how banks in Canada (e.g., TD Bank) and in the United Kingdom (e.g., Barclays Bank)

FIGURE 21–1 **Alternative Organizational Forms for Nonbank Product Expansions of Banking Organizations**

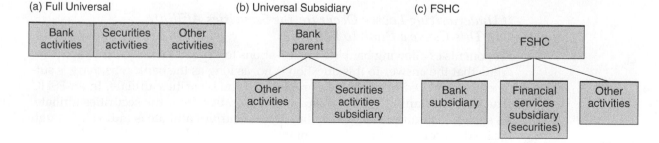

conduct their securities activities. This is also the model adopted to allow U.S. nationally chartered banks to expand their nonbank activities.

Note that the degree of bank–nonbank integration is much less with the FSHC model [panel (c)] than with either the full universal or universal subsidiary banking model. For example, in the universal subsidiary model, the bank holds a direct ownership stake in the securities subsidiary. By comparison, in the FSHC model, the bank and securities subsidiary are separate companies with their own equity capital; the link is that their equity is held by the same parent company, the FSHC.

Safety and Soundness

With respect to the securities activities of commercial banks and the possible effects on their safety and soundness, two key questions arise: How risky is securities underwriting? And if losses occur for a securities subsidiary, can this cause the affiliated bank to fail?

The Risk of Securities Underwriting

best-efforts offering
Securities sold by the distributing firm acting as agent for the issuing firm.

firm commitment offering
Securities offered from the issuing firm, purchased by an underwriter.

To understand the risk of securities underwriting, you must understand the mechanics of a best-efforts versus a firm commitment securities offering. With **best-efforts offering**, investment bankers act as *agents* on a fee basis related to their success in placing the issue. In a **firm commitment offering**, the underwriter purchases securities directly from the issuing firm (say, at $99 per share) and then reoffers them to the public or the market at large at a slightly higher price, say, $99.50. The difference between the underwriter's buy price ($99) and the public offer price ($99.50) is the spread that compensates the underwriter for accepting the principal risk of placing the securities with outside investors as well as any administrative and distribution costs associated with the underwriting. In our simple example of a $0.50 spread, the maximum revenue the underwriter can gain from underwriting the issue is $0.50 times the number of shares issued. Thus, if 1 million shares were offered, the maximum gross revenue for the underwriting would be $0.50 times 1,000,000, or $500,000. Note that once the public offering has been made and the price specified in the prospectus, the underwriter cannot raise the price over the offering period even if the market values the shares more highly.

The upside return from underwriting is normally capped, but the downside risk is not and can be very large. The downside risk arises if the underwriter overprices the public offering, setting the public offer price higher than outside investors' valuations. As a result, the underwriter will be unable to sell the shares during the public offering period and will have to lower the price to get rid of the inventory of unsold shares. In our example, suppose that the issue can be placed only at $97; the underwriter's losses will be $2 times 1,000,000 shares, or $2 million.

If Underwriting Losses Occur for the Securities Affiliate, Can This Cause a Bank to Fail?

Proponents of allowing banking organizations to expand their securities activities argue that the answer to this question is no, as long as the bank subsidiary is sufficiently insulated from the risk problems of the securities affiliate. In an FSHC structure, the bank is legally a separate corporation from the securities affiliate. As shown in Figure 21–2, its only link to its securities affiliate is indirect, through the holding company that owns a controlling equity stake in both the bank and the

FIGURE 21–2 The Role of Firewalls in Protecting Banks

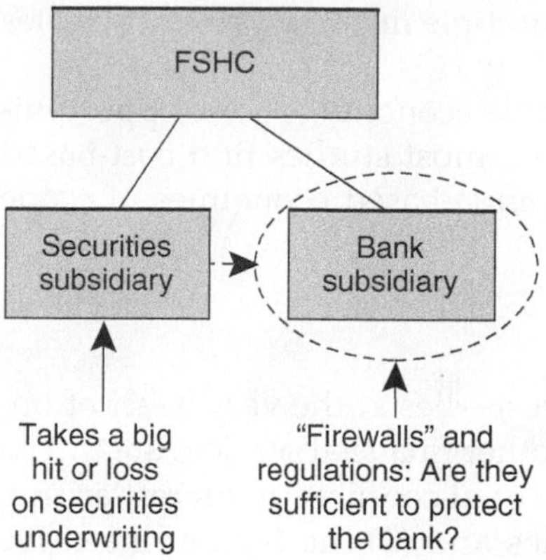

securities affiliate. However, even this indirect link raises the concern that the effects of losses by the securities affiliate could threaten the safety of the bank unless firewalls or regulatory barriers are introduced to insulate the bank against such losses (see Figure 21–2).

There are at least three ways a bank could be harmed by losses of a securities affiliate in a holding company structure. First, a holding company might be tempted to drain capital and funds from the bank by requiring excessive dividends and fees from the bank (this is called *upstreaming*). The holding company could then *downstream* these funds to protect the failing securities affiliate from insolvency. As a result, the bank would be weakened at the expense (or because) of the securities affiliate.

A second way in which a bank could be harmed is through interaffiliate loans. For example, the holding company may induce the bank to extend loans to the securities affiliate to keep it afloat even though such loans are excessively risky.

The third way in which a bank may be affected is through a contagious confidence problem. Specifically, difficulties at a securities firm subsidiary may result in a negative information signal to financial services consumers and investors regarding the quality of the management of the holding company and its bank affiliate. Such negative information can create incentives for large depositors and investors to withdraw their money from the bank in the manner described in Chapter 19. This bank-run possibility seems more likely to occur if the bank and its securities affiliate share similar names and logos, which in general they do.

Obviously, a big hit taken by the securities subsidiary can potentially threaten the safety and solvency of the affiliated bank, especially through the confidence effect. For example, the investment banking activities of CIBC World Markets in New York in providing "loans" to special-purpose entities (SPEs) of Enron led to CIBC's agreeing to pay US$2.4 billion to settle an Enron shareholders' class action lawsuit and an additional US$250 million to Enron in August 2005, amounts that represented one-tenth of CIBC's market capitalization at the time. This seriously weakened its balance sheet, affecting future growth. Analysts downgraded the company's ratings and CIBC's shares dropped from $80.64 to $74.55 in one day. Although CIBC admitted no wrongdoing, the damage was done to its reputation. However, at least two countervailing risk-reducing effects may enhance the safety and soundness of a bank indirectly linked to a securities subsidiary in a holding company framework. The first effect is a **product diversification benefit**. A well-diversified financial services firm (FSHC) potentially enjoys a far more stable earnings and profit stream over time than does a product-specialized bank. As demand and cost shifts reduce earnings in one activity area, such as banking, offsetting demand and cost shifts may take place in other activity areas, such as securities or insurance, increasing the holding company's earnings. A more stable and diversified earnings stream for the holding company enables it to act as a source of strength in keeping the affiliated bank well capitalized and thus reduces its bankruptcy risk.

product diversification benefit
Stabilization of earnings and profits resulting from a well-diversified FSHC.

Economies of Scale and Scope

A second issue concerning the expansion of banks into securities and other nonbank activities is the potential for additional economies of scale and scope. As financial firms become larger, the potential scale can lower an FI's average costs of financial services production. Thus, larger FSHCs may have an economy of scale advantage over smaller financial firms. Further, FSHCs' abilities to generate synergistic cost savings through joint use of inputs in producing multiple financial products creates economies of scope.

As we discussed in Chapter 17, there appear to be economy of scale opportunities for financial firms of all asset sizes. However, most studies find cost-based economies of scope are negligible, although revenue-based economies of scope may arise for the largest FIs.

Conflicts of Interest

A third issue—the potential for conflicts of interest—lies at the very heart of opposition to an expansion of banking powers into other financial services areas. The two principal questions that arise are (1) the potential conflicts of interest arising from the expansion of banks' securities activities and (2) the type of incentive structures that change *potential* conflicts into *actual* conflicts.

Six Potential Conflicts of Interest

Conflicts of interest that arise when commercial banks, investment banks, and insurance companies combine operations have been prominent in financial markets. In this section, we discuss the six most common potential conflicts of interest identified by regulators and academics.

Salesperson's Stake Critics argue that when banks have the power to sell nonbank products, bank employees no longer dispense dispassionate advice to their customers about which product to buy. Instead, they have a salesperson's stake in pushing the bank's own products, often to the disadvantage of the customer. Since the 2008 market meltdown, regulators and the public are increasingly interested in the bonuses paid to top performers at FIs during bad times. The issue of corporate governance and other ethical issues for FIs have arisen, particularly for investment advisors who continue to be paid large bonuses even when their clients have suffered huge losses in their retirement accounts and pension funds.

Stuffing Fiduciary Accounts Suppose a bank is acting as a securities underwriter and is unable to place these securities in a public offering. To avoid being exposed to potential losses, the bank may "stuff" these unwanted securities into accounts managed by its own trust department and over which it has discretionary investment powers. For example, a U.S. judge threw money manager Alan Bond, CIO of Albriond Capital, in jail after he was convicted on charges of allocating winning trades to his own brokerage account and saddling his clients' accounts with losers.

Bankruptcy Risk Transference Assume that a bank has a loan outstanding to a firm whose credit or bankruptcy risk has increased to the private knowledge of the banker. With this private knowledge, the banker may have an incentive to induce the firm to issue bonds underwritten by the bank's securities affiliate to an unsuspecting public. The proceeds of this bond issue could then be used to pay down the bank loan. As a result, the bank would have transferred the borrowing firm's credit risk from itself to less-informed outside investors, while the securities affiliate also earned an underwriting fee. For example, in 2002, CIBC, JPMorgan Chase, and Citigroup faced several investor lawsuits over funding deals for high-profile bankruptcies such as Enron. Investors say that because of their lending relationships, the banks knew or should have known of the problems at these companies when they sold the firm's bonds to the public. More recent is the 2010 case of investment banks' sales of mortgage-backed securities. A hearing of the U.S. Senate Permanent Subcommittee on Investigations (created with the broad mandate to determine whether any changes are required in U.S. law to better protect the public) focused on the role of investment banks in contributing to the financial crisis. U.S. investment banks frequently bundled toxic mortgages into complex financial instruments, many of which were rated AAA by credit rating agencies, and sold them to investors. Some of these banks, in an attempt to manage their own risk on these securities, reportedly shorted the mortgage market, setting themselves up for gains that would offset losses on the mortgage securities.

Third-Party Loans To ensure that an underwriting goes well, a bank may make cheap loans to third-party investors on the implicit condition that the loans be used to purchase securities underwritten by its securities affiliate.

Tie-Ins A bank may use its lending powers to coerce or "tie in" a customer to the products sold by its securities affiliate. For example, the bank may threaten to credit ration unless the customer agrees to let the bank's securities affiliate do its securities underwritings. In the early 2000s, CIBC's "loans" to Enron were in anticipation of other services the company might send its way.

Information Transfer In acting as a lender, the bank may become privy to certain inside information about its customers or rivals that it can use to set the prices or help the distribution of securities offerings by its affiliate. This information could also flow from the securities affiliate to the bank. Such conflicts are potentially present when M&A activity is involved along with new security issues and loan originations. Such was the case with JPMorgan Chase and Citigroup, two FIs involved as lead advisors *and* lead bankers in Enron's failed merger attempt with Dynegy in 2001. The two FIs had large balance sheets and boasted of their ability to provide both loans and advice in the merger. However, the FIs lost their bragging rights for pulling off a difficult deal as Dynegy pulled out of the merger, stating it was deprived of sufficient information on the deal and then learning that Enron had been hiding billions of dollars in debt and had been reporting exaggerated profits for years. Enron ended up declaring bankruptcy in December 2001, and JPMorgan Chase and Citigroup ended up losing between US$800 million and US$900 million each on loans to Enron.

Potential Conflicts of Interest and Their Actual Exploitation

On their own these conflicts appear to be extremely troublesome. Remember, however, that specific and general checks and balances limit their exploitation. Many of these conflicts are likely to remain potential rather than become actual conflicts of interest. Specifically, many of these conflicts, such as tie-ins and third-party loans, breach existing bank regulations and laws. Also, internal barriers or **Chinese walls** in most banks prohibit internal information transfers when they potentially conflict with the best interests of the customer. Further, sales of debt issues to a less-informed public to pay down bank loans may result in future lawsuits against the underwriter once investors discover their losses.[2]

Chinese wall
An internally imposed barrier within an organization that limits the flow of confidential client information among departments or areas.

[2] In particular, the underwriter may be accused of lack of due diligence in not disclosing information in the new issue's prospectus.

More generally, conflicts of interest are exploitable under only three conditions. First, markets for bank services are uncompetitive so that banks have monopoly power over their customers, for example, in making loans. Second, information flows between the customer and the bank are imperfect or asymmetric so that the bank possesses an information advantage over its customers. Third, the bank places a relatively low value on its reputation. The discovery of having exploited a client can result in considerable market and regulatory penalties.

Deposit Insurance

A traditional argument against expanded powers is that the explicit and implicit protection given to banks by deposit insurance coverage gives banks a competitive advantage over other financial services firms (see Chapter 19). For example, because bank deposits up to $100,000 are covered by explicit deposit insurance, banks are able to raise funds at subsidized, lower-cost rates than are available to other traditional financial services firms. This may allow them to pass on these lower costs in cheaper loans to their affiliates. This advantage may result if bank regulators regard certain large banking organizations as being too big to fail (TBTF), thereby encouraging these institutions to take excessive risks such as placing aggressive underwriting bids for new issues.

Regulatory Oversight

The regulation of integrated FIs in Canada is complex, involving both federal and provincial/territorial bodies, as discussed in Chapter 2 and shown in Appendix 2B. OSFI has been created as the primary prudential regulator for large federally regulated FIs (banks, savings and loans, life insurance, P&C insurance), but the regulation of securities activities is handled provincially and territorially. The creation of a national regulatory body for securities firms such as the U.S. SEC has been under discussion for quite some time now. As well, the regulatory issues regarding the deregulation of FI activities in individual countries are finding their way into the transnational regulations for internationally active banks through both the BIS and the FSB, as discussed in Chapter 20. CIBC's Enron payouts, with their impact on CIBC's Tier 1 capital and thus the safety and soundness of the Canadian financial system, triggered discussions of securities operations risks for integrated banks even though the impact came from operations within the ambit of the SEC.

The large Canadian banks and insurance companies have extensive operations in the United States and so are required to follow U.S. regulations. For example, the Dodd-Frank Wall Street Reform and Consumer Protection Act that became effective in 2010 has implications for Canadian FIs. Currently, most U.S. bank holding companies with extensive nonbank subsidiaries face a diffuse and multilayered regulatory structure that would potentially hinder the monitoring and control of conflict of interest abuses and excessive risk taking as banks are allowed to expand their securities activities further. Specifically, for an FSHC such as JPMorgan Chase, the Federal Reserve is the primary regulator. For its bank subsidiary, the Office of the Comptroller of the Currency, which is the charterer of national banks in the United States, shares regulatory oversight with the Federal Reserve and the FDIC. For JPMorgan Chase's securities subsidiary, the primary regulator is the SEC, although the Federal Reserve also has some oversight powers. Likewise, the Federal

Reserve coordinates its supervisory responsibilities with the state insurance authority when the bank holding company operates an insurance company subsidiary.

The Federal Reserve's role as the supervisor of a bank holding company is to review and assess the consolidated organization's operations, risk management systems, and capital adequacy to ensure that the holding company and its nonbank subsidiaries do not threaten the financial stability of the company's DTIs. In this role, the Federal Reserve serves as the umbrella supervisor of the consolidated organization. In fulfilling this role, the Federal Reserve relies to the fullest extent possible on information and analysis provided by the appropriate supervisory authority of the company's bank, securities, or insurance subsidiaries.

federalreserve.gov
occ.treas.gov
fdic.gov
sec.gov

U.S. financial regulatory overhaul legislation, passed in July 2010, calls for the Federal Reserve to receive new oversight powers. The proposals put the Federal Reserve in charge of monitoring the country's biggest financial firms—those considered critical to the health of the system as a whole. Those firms would also face new, stiffer requirements on how much capital and liquidity they keep in reserve. The overhaul also provides unprecedented powers to the Federal Reserve to step into any FIs—such as insurance giant AIG (whose main regulators include the New York State Department of Insurance and the Office of Thrift Supervision)—that are facing imminent collapse, in order to force an orderly bankruptcy that would protect the wider economy.

Competition

LO3

The final issue concerns the effects of bank activity expansions on competition in investment banking product lines. Since the Bank Act revisions of the 1980s, banks have come to dominate investment banking activities in Canada, as we discussed in Chapter 4. It could be argued that the banks have had greater monopoly power over capital markets in Canada, but this has been mitigated by the globalization of the investment banking industry, which allows Canadian companies to access international markets through cross-listing of shares on U.S. markets. In addition, large U.S. investment banking firms entered the Canadian market, providing

- Increased capital market access for large and small Canadian firms.
- Lowered commissions and fees as both Canadian bank-owned firms and international investment bankers compete for large securities issues such as TD Canada Trust's acquisition of BankNorth and the Molson and Coors breweries merger in 2004.
- A reduction in the degree of underpricing of new issues.

The greatest risk to the underwriter is to price a new issue too high relative to the market's valuation of that security. That is, underwriters stand to lose when they overprice new issues. Given this, underwriters have an incentive to underprice new issues by setting the public offer price (*OP*) below the price established for the security in the secondary market once trading begins (*P*). The investment banker stands to gain by underpricing as it increases the demand for the shares by investors and the probability of selling the whole issue to the public very quickly. Both the underwriter and the outside investor may benefit from underpricing. The loser is the firm issuing the securities because it obtains lower proceeds than if the offer price had been set at a higher price reflecting a more accurate market valuation.

IPO (initial public offering)
A corporate equity or debt security offered to the public for the first time through an underwriter.

If a major cause of **IPO (initial public offering)** underpricing is a lack of competition among existing investment banks, then bank entry and competition should lower the degree of underpricing and increase the new issue proceeds for firms.

Nevertheless, many economists argue that monopoly power is not the primary reason for the underpricing of new issues. In their view, underpricing reflects a risk premium that must be paid to investors and investment bankers for information imperfections. That is, underpricing is a risk premium for the information advantage possessed by issuers who better know the true quality of their firm's securities and its assets. If this is so, bank entry into securities underwriting may reduce the degree of underpricing only to the extent that it reduces the degree of information imperfection among issuers and investors. This might reasonably be expected, given the specialized role of banks as delegated monitors (see Chapter 1).

Anticompetitive Effects

With the revision of the Bank Act, the biggest Canadian banking organizations, measured by either capital or assets, were many times larger than the biggest securities firms. The Big Six Canadian banks, aided by the stock market crash of 1987, which weakened securities firms, particularly those that had underwritten the IPO of British Petroleum, absorbed the independent securities firms. The banks thus assumed quasi-oligopoly positions, causing market concentration to rise and perhaps long-run prices for investment banking services to rise also. One possible reason for the slow development of the German corporate bond market is that German universal banks wish to preserve their monopoly power over corporate debt. This may best be done by encouraging corporate loans rather than bond issues. This may be ascribed to the structure of the financial system in Germany, which historically did not have the strict separation of banking and securities functions found in Canada, the United Kingdom, and the United States.

Cross-Pillar Mergers: Banks and Insurance Companies

A cross-pillar issue in Canada that has yet to be resolved is the merger of banks and insurance companies. Banks and insurance companies have presented briefs to the federal government since the MacKay Commission report in 1998, and a review of the financial services legislation in Canada is conducted every five years. The six issues discussed with respect to banks and securities mergers are relevant to the insurance discussion and are discussed briefly below.

Safety and Soundness Issues Both the banks and the federally regulated life insurance companies and P&C insurance companies in Canada are already regulated by OSFI. It can be argued that the regulations for these FIs are converging since OSFI provides guidelines on capital adequacy, large exposure limits, and risk management for all of the FIs under its jurisdiction. Therefore, unlike the securities industry, which is governed by self-regulatory organizations (SROs) such as the exchanges and the Investment Industry Association of Canada (IIAC), the regulatory oversight is already in place for cross-pillar mergers of insurance companies and banks, and the safety and soundness of the financial system will not be threatened.

iiac.ca

Economies of Scale and Scope Issues The banks already possess a branch network that gives them the ability to sell mutual fund and other investment products in their branches. Therefore, the availability of insurance products, along with the banks' experience in creating innovative savings products, could allow them to offer insurance products at a competitive price to existing customers and to generate more profits for their investment in branches, savings that could be passed on to the consumer. If the finance minister allowed insurance products to be offered through existing bank websites, there could be additional cost savings for online consumers.

Conflict-of-Interest Issues Both banks and insurance companies already sell mutual fund and mutual fund–type (segregated funds) products by employees licensed to sell such products. Tied product selling and other legal and ethical issues are already addressed by such organizations as the Mutual Fund Dealers Association of Canada (MFDA).

mfda.ca

Deposit Insurance Issues To the extent that insurance companies would accept deposits similar to other deposit-taking FIs, they would be eligible for membership in the Canada Deposit Insurance Corporation (CDIC) and able to pay the risk-based premiums. This would add another layer of regulation to insurance-based companies and could increase their costs along with the additional annual regulatory evaluation that CDIC conducts to establish the insurance premiums (see Chapter 19).

cdic.ca

Regulatory Oversight Issues Regulation of insurance companies as part of a bank–insurance conglomerate should not be an issue for OSFI since banks already report their assets based on banking, trading, and insurance. No doubt there would be more discussion of the regulation of financial conglomerates, particularly those holding companies outside the banking sphere, such as Power Financial, which controls significant Canadian insurance (Great West Life, London Life, Canada Life) and mutual fund (IGM Financial, which includes Investors Group and Mackenzie Financial) assets.

Competition Issues The biggest barrier to bank–insurance mergers is the issue of competition in Canada. The banks held in excess of $3.0 trillion in on-balance-sheet assets in Canada in 2013, dwarfing the remaining FIs, including the insurance companies, even with the $7.3 billion merger of Sun Life and Clarica Life Insurance in 2003 and the Manulife and John Hancock of Boston $11 billion deal completed in 2004. There were rumours that Manulife was to merge with CIBC in 2003, but the federal Department of Finance was not open to that possibility. Since the template for bank–insurance mergers has not been established, it is difficult to speculate as to whether a cross-pillar merger would reduce competition and services for consumers. For example, sale of insurance products in bank branches and online might still be prohibited in order to protect the small insurance brokers. Similarly, banks could be required to keep branches open and staff levels up as a condition of mergers, either cross-pillar or bank–bank. Since 2001, and particularly throughout 2004 and 2005, various FIs have filed briefs with the federal Department of Finance outlining their positions on competition in the financial services industry. The final report of the Competition Policy Review Panel, filed in June 2008, concluded that the "widely held" rule controls the potential for self-dealing and poor corporate governance. The report thus recommended that the minister of finance allow cross-pillar mergers of large FIs that would be overseen by OSFI and the Competition Bureau. The financial markets upheaval in 2008 allowed the Bank of Montreal (BMO) to expand its insurance presence by acquiring the insurance assets of the U.S. insurer AIG in Canada. The large FIs in Canada appear to have adopted different strategies that, because of their strong capital positions, allow them to acquire assets domestically and internationally.

CONCEPT QUESTIONS

1. **What are some of the issues that arise in response to bank expansion into securities, insurance, and commercial activities?**
2. **Explain how firm commitment to underwriting of securities is similar to writing put options on assets.**
3. **Describe ways in which the losses of a securities affiliate could be transmitted to a bank.**
4. **In addition to the potential conflicts of interest discussed in this section, can you think of any additional possible conflicts that might arise when commercial banks are allowed to expand their investment banking or insurance activities?**

GEOGRAPHIC EXPANSIONS: CANADA AND THE UNITED STATES

LO4

Just as product expansion may enable an FI to reduce risk and increase returns, so may geographic expansion. Geographic expansions can have a number of dimensions. In particular, expansions can be either domestic or international.

Historically, the ability of FIs to expand domestically has been constrained by regulation. By comparison, no special regulations have inhibited the ability of commercial firms such as General Motors, IBM, and Walmart from establishing new or **de novo offices**, factories, or stores anywhere in the country. Nor have commercial firms been prohibited from acquiring other firms—as long as they are not banks. Although securities firms and insurance companies have faced relatively few restrictions in expanding their business domestically, other FIs, especially banks, have faced a complex and changing network of rules and regulations. Such regulations may inhibit expansions, but they also create potential opportunities to increase an FI's returns. In particular, regulations may create locally uncompetitive markets with monopoly economic rents that new entrants can potentially exploit. Thus, for the most innovative FIs, regulation can provide profit opportunities as well as costs. As a result, regulation both inhibits engaging in and creates incentives to engage in geographic expansions. It is rare that we see a hostile takeover or unfriendly merger in banking. Unlike the case of a merger or acquisition of commercial firms, the extensive review by regulators virtually forces the two parties in a bank merger to work together so that they can get through the review process successfully.

de novo office
A newly established office.

The economic factors that affect commercial firm expansion and acquisition decisions are likely to influence the decisions of FIs as well. Two major groups of factors are cost and revenue synergies and firm/market-specific attractions, such as the specialized skills of an acquired firm's employees and the markets of the firm to be acquired. Thus, the attractiveness of a geographic expansion, whether through acquisition, branching, or opening a new office, depends on a broad set of factors encompassing

1. Regulation and the regulatory framework.
2. Cost and revenue synergies.
3. Firm- or market-specific factors.

We start by considering how the first factor—regulation—influences an FI's geographic expansion decision.

CONCEPT QUESTIONS

1. **Explain why regulation both inhibits an FI from engaging in and provides incentives to an FI to engage in geographic expansion.**
2. **What three basic factors influence the attractiveness of geographic expansion to an FI?**

REGULATORY FACTORS IMPACTING GEOGRAPHIC EXPANSION

Insurance Companies

As discussed in Chapter 6, with the exception of the federally regulated life and P&C companies, insurance companies are regulated by the provinces and territories. By establishing a subsidiary in one province or territory, an insurance company normally has the opportunity to sell insurance anywhere in that jurisdiction and often to market the product nationally by Internet marketing, telemarketing, and direct sales. To deliver a financial service effectively, however, it is often necessary to establish a physical presence in a local market. To do this, insurance companies establish offices in other provinces and territories. Thus, most large insurance companies have a physical presence in virtually every Canadian province and territory.

Banks

Canadian banks can be chartered only federally and thus the industry is controlled by one federal regulator. This means that Canadian banks and Canadian consumers take the "sea-to-sea" nature of their banking system for granted. It can be argued that the absence of branching restrictions for domestic banks accelerated the introduction of the technology for interbranch banking and, as well, facilitated the development of the Large Value Transfer System (LVTS) for payments settlements (see Chapters 17 and 20). In a Canadian market that is roughly one-tenth the size of the U.S. market, the major considerations for a domestic expansion are cost and revenue synergies, as discussed below. However, regulatory restrictions on branches have been applied to Schedule II and Schedule III banks, as discussed in Chapter 2.

U.S. Commercial Banks

The U.S. market has provided many opportunities for growth and expansion for Canadian banks (e.g., BMO's acquisition of Harris Bank of Chicago in the 1990s and TD's acquisition of Banknorth in 2004). We next consider the U.S. situation in order to provide a North American perspective on the merger wave that has been ongoing since the passage of the Riegle–Neal Interstate Branching and Efficiency Act of 1994.

U.S. Restrictions on Intrastate Banking

unit bank
A bank with a single office.

For most of the early 1900s, most U.S. banks were **unit banks** with a single office. Improving communications and customer needs resulted in a rush to branching in the first two decades of the 20th century. Increasingly, this movement ran into opposition from the smallest unit banks and the largest money centre banks. The smallest unit banks perceived a competitive threat to their retail business from the larger branching banks; money centre banks feared a loss of valuable correspondent business such as cheque-clearing and other payment services. As a result, several states restricted the ability of banks to branch within the state.

U.S. Restrictions on Interstate Banking

The defining piece of legislation affecting interstate branching until 1997 was the McFadden Act, passed in 1927 and amended in 1933. The McFadden Act and its amendments restricted nationally chartered banks' branching abilities to the same extent allowed to state-chartered banks. Because states prohibit interstate banking for state-chartered banks in general, nationally chartered banks were similarly prohibited.

Between 1927 and 1997, bank organizations expanding across state lines largely relied on establishing subsidiaries rather than branches. Some of the biggest banking organizations established **multibank holding companies (MBHCs)** for that purpose. An MBHC is a parent company that acquires more than one bank as a direct subsidiary. While MBHCs had been around in the early part of the 20th century, the 1927 restrictions on interstate branching gave the bank acquisition movement an added impetus.

multibank holding company (MBHC)
A parent banking organization that owns a number of individual bank subsidiaries.

Riegle–Neal Interstate Banking and Branching Efficiency Act of 1994 It had long been recognized that nationwide banking expansion through MBHCs was potentially far more expensive than through branching. Separate corporations and boards of directors must be established for each bank in an MBHC, and it is hard to achieve the same level of economic and financial integration as with branches. Moreover, most major banking countries, such as Canada, Japan, Germany, France, and the United Kingdom, have nationwide branching.

In the fall of 1994, the U.S. Congress passed an interstate banking law that allows U.S. and non-U.S. banks to branch interstate by consolidating out-of-state bank subsidiaries into a branch network and/or acquiring banks or individual branches of banks by M&A. The effective date for these new branching powers was June 1, 1997. The implication of the Riegle–Neal Act is that full interstate banking—with the exception of de novo branching—became a reality in the United States in 1997. The relaxation of the branching restrictions, along with recognition of the potential cost, revenue, and risk benefits from geographic expansions (discussed next), set off a wave of consolidation in the U.S. banking system. This consolidation trend was particularly evident among the largest U.S. banks in a wave of **megamergers**, which reshaped the U.S. banking industry into a nationwide banking system along Canadian and European lines. As a result of mergers and acquisitions, 25 major U.S. banks in existence in 1995 became 4 by 2009.

megamerger
The merger of two large banks.

The 2008 global market crisis weakened some of the larger U.S. FIs, such as AIG and Citigroup. However, it sparked another reorganization of U.S. banking assets and provided opportunities for further expansion for the strongest, as the Federal Deposit Insurance Corporation (FDIC) looked for purchasers for failing FIs. For example, JPMorgan Chase purchased Washington Mutual's (WaMu's) bad loans and deposits from regulators in September 2008 for US$1.9 billion. WaMu was the largest bank failure in U.S. history. Wells Fargo purchased Wachovia's assets for US$12.7 billion in October 2008 and moved from 123rd to 6th place in *The Banker's* "Top 1000 World Banks" for 2009. Bank of America purchased Countrywide, a subprime lender, in July 2008 and also acquired Merrill Lynch's assets in September 2008. Many of these purchases proved to be strategic and profitable.

Canadian FIs have expanded geographically by purchasing assets in the United States. At year-end 2012, BMO had the highest concentration of U.S. assets with an average of $190.8 billion, 35.1 percent of its average total on-balance-sheet assets. Scotiabank had 14 percent of its average assets in the United States and over 25 percent in Mexico, Peru, and other international countries. These asset exposures are dwarfed by the 10 largest banks in the world. For example, China's ICBC has assets greater than U.S.$2.8 trillion, and JPMorgan Chase's total assets at year-end 2012 were over US$2.3 trillion. This compares with RBC's on-balance-sheet assets of US$842.0 billion (CDN$825.1 billion).

SYNERGIES OF GEOGRAPHIC EXPANSION

One reason for an FI deciding to expand (or not to expand) geographically by acquisition relates to the regulations defining its merger opportunities. Other reasons relate to the exploitation of potential cost and revenue synergies from merging (as well as the associated diversification of risk benefits). We look at these potential gains next.

Cost Synergies

X efficiencies
Cost savings due to the greater managerial efficiency of the acquiring bank.

A common reason given for bank mergers is the potential cost synergies that may result from economies of scale, economies of scope, or managerial efficiency sources (often called **X efficiencies**[3] because they are difficult to pin down in a quantitative fashion). For example, in 1996, Chase Manhattan and Chemical Bank merged, creating the (then) largest banking organization in the United States, with assets of US$300 billion. It was estimated that annual cost savings from the merger would be US$1.5 billion, to be achieved by consolidating certain operations and eliminating redundant costs, including the elimination of some 12,000 positions from a combined staff of 75,000 in 39 states and 51 countries.

While the mergers discussed above are interesting examples of megamergers, they are still essentially mergers in the same or closely related banking markets. By comparison, mergers such as Bank of America and FleetBoston and JPMorgan Chase and Bank One are clearly a geographic extension merger between two banks with little or no geographic overlap. By acquiring FleetBoston in 2003 for $43 billion, Bank of America added nearly 1,500 branches and 3,400 ABMs in the New England area. The combined banks projected annual cost savings to be US$1.1 billion, including consolidation of redundant technology systems.

In a recent study of nine megamergers by Rhoades (seven of the nine occurring since 1990), large cost savings were found. Specifically, four of the nine mergers showed significant cost efficiency gains relative to a peer group of nonmerged banks, and seven of the nine showed a significant improvement in their return on assets. In addition to the cutting of duplicate back-office operations, larger banks can also take more advantage of outsourcing these operations locally or abroad. It is estimated that, in 2011, 77 percent of U.S. retail banks outsourced at least one part of their business, reducing bank costs of these services by between 20 and 40 percent. Larger banks find it more cost effective to outsource a larger number of services and therefore experience the bigger costs savings from outsourcing. Interestingly, where cost efficiency gains were *not* realized, the major problems came from integrating data processing and operating systems.

Revenue Synergies

The revenue synergies argument has three dimensions. First, revenues may be enhanced by acquiring a bank in a growing market. For example, the 2009 merger of Wells Fargo and Wachovia was estimated to produce cost savings of

[3] X efficiencies are those cost savings not directly due to economies of scope or economies of scale. As such, they are usually attributed to superior management skills and other difficult-to-measure managerial factors. To date, the explicit identification of what composes these efficiencies remains to be established in the empirical banking literature.

US$5 billion per year. However, the success of the merger was attributed to revenue growth and synergies. By late 2009, the merged companies announced that business and revenue synergies were ahead of expectations and on track to realize annual revenue growth of US$5 billion upon full integration. The merged banks recorded broad-based revenue contribution from diverse businesses, with particular strength in regional banking, commercial banking, mortgage banking, investment banking, asset-based lending, auto lending, student lending, debit card, merchant card, wealth management, securities brokerage retirement services, and international operations. Shortly after the merger, over 40 percent of legacy Wells Fargo retail households had purchased over six Wachovia-based products, and one of every four retail households had at least eight products with the merged banks.

Second, the acquiring bank's revenue stream may become more stable if the asset and liability portfolio of the target institution exhibits different credit, interest rate, and liquidity risk characteristics from the acquirer. For example, U.S. real estate loan portfolios showed very strong regional cycles in the 1980s and again in the 2006–2008 period. Specifically, U.S. real estate declined in value in the southwest and then in California. Thus, a geographically diversified real estate portfolio may be far less risky than one in which both acquirer and target specialize in a single region. As a result, the potential revenue diversification gains for more geographically concentrated mergers are likely to be relatively low. As noted in Chapter 19, the failures of the Canadian Commercial Bank and the Northland Bank of Canada in 1985 were related to their undiversified loan portfolios, which concentrated on oil and gas and real estate loans in western Canada. Studies confirm risk diversification gains from geographic expansions.

Third, there is an opportunity for revenue enhancement by expanding into markets that are less than fully competitive. That is, banks may be able to identify and expand geographically into those markets where *economic rents* potentially exist, but where such entry will not be viewed as being potentially anticompetitive by regulators. Arguably, one of the great potential benefits of the JPMorgan Chase and Bank One merger was the potential for enhanced revenue diversification due to the lack of overlap of the branch networks of the two systems due to the merger.

Merger Guidelines

To the extent that geographic expansions are viewed as enhancing the monopoly power of an FI, regulators and governments may act to prevent a merger unless it produces potential efficiency gains that cannot be reasonably achieved by other means. In Canada, mergers of large FIs require the approval of the minister of finance. In 1998, RBC and BMO were set to merge, as were CIBC and TD Bank, but the mergers were not approved. Shortly after, the federal government started public consultations regarding large bank mergers in Canada and accepted submissions until December 31, 2003. The Competition Bureau's 2008 policy review paper recommended that bank mergers and cross-pillar mergers be allowed in Canada. However, the poor performance of many of the large global FIs has changed the appetite of many FIs and their regulators for consolidation of FIs except to prevent the failure of an FI that poses a systemic risk. Global sentiment has changed from "too big to fail" to "too big to bail." And it has been suggested that the world of

fin.gc.ca

TABLE 21–2
U.S. Department of Justice Horizontal Merger Guidelines

Source: Department of Justice, *Merger Guidelines*, 2010.

Postmerger Market Concentration	Level of HHI	Change in HHI and Likelihood of a Challenged Merger
Highly concentrated	Greater than 1,800	Greater than 100—likely to be challenged 50 to 100—depends on other factors* Less than 50—unlikely to be challenged
Moderately concentrated	1,000–1,800	Greater than 100—likely to be challenged; other factors considered* Less than or equal to 100—unlikely to be challenged
Unconcentrated	Less than 1,000	Any increase—unlikely to be challenged

*In addition to the postmerger concentration of the market and the size of the resulting increase in concentration, the department will consider the presence of the following factors in deciding whether to challenge a merger: ease of entry; the nature of the product and its terms of sale; market information about specific transactions; buyer market characteristics; conduct of firms in the market; and market performance.

1998, where bank mergers were necessary for Canadian FIs to compete globally, is gone forever.

usdoj.gov

Of importance to Canadian and other foreign banks seeking to expand in the United States, the U.S. Department of Justice has laid down guidelines regarding the acceptability or unacceptability of acquisitions based on the potential increase in concentration in the market in which an acquisition takes place.[4]

Herfindahl-Hirschman Index (HHI)
An index or measure of market concentration based on the squared market shares of market participants.

These merger guidelines are based on a measure of market concentration called the **Herfindahl-Hirschman Index (HHI)**. This index is created by taking the percentage market shares of all firms in a market, squaring them, and then adding these squared shares. Thus, in a market where a single firm had a 100 percent market share, the HHI would be

$$HHI = (100)^2 = 10{,}000$$

Alternatively, in a market in which there was an infinitely large number of firms of equal size, then

$$HHI = 0$$

Thus, the HHI must lie between 0 and 10,000.

Whether a merger will be challenged under the U.S. Department of Justice guidelines depends on the postmerger HHI level. As you can see in Table 21–2, the U.S. Department of Justice defines a *concentrated* market as having a postmerger HHI ratio of greater than 1,800, a moderately concentrated market as having a ratio of 1,000 to 1,800, and an unconcentrated market as having a ratio of less than 1,000. In either a concentrated or a moderately concentrated market, postmerger HHI increases of 100 or more may be challenged.[5]

[4] The Federal Reserve also has the power to approve or disapprove mergers among state member banks and bank holding companies. The Comptroller of the Currency has similar powers over nationally chartered banks. The Federal Reserve's criteria are similar to those of the Department of Justice in that they take into account the HHI (market concentration index). However, it also evaluates the risk effects of the merger. The Department of Justice has powers to review the decisions made by the bank regulatory agencies.

[5] In practice, it is only when the change exceeds 200 in banking that a challenge may occur. This is the case because banking is generally viewed as being more competitive than most industries. See U.S. Department of Justice, *Horizontal Merger Guidelines*. Systemic risk (TBTF) issues were more important to regulators than monopoly considerations during 2008–2009.

EXAMPLE 21-1

Calculation of Change in the HHI Associated with a Merger

Consider a market that has three banks with the following market shares:

Bank A = 50%
Bank B = 46%
Bank C = 4%

The premerger HHI for the market is

$$\text{HHI} = (50)^2 + (46)^2 + (4)^2 = 2{,}500 + 2{,}116 + 16 = 4{,}632$$

Thus, the market is highly concentrated according to the Department of Justice guidelines.

Suppose Bank A wants to acquire Bank C so that the postacquisition market would exhibit the following shares:[6]

$$A + C = 54\%$$
$$B = 46\%$$

The postmerger HHI would be

$$\text{HHI} = (54)^2 + (46)^2 = 2{,}916 + 2{,}116 = 5{,}032$$

Thus, the increase or change in the HHI (ΔHHI) postmerger is

$$\Delta\text{HHI} = 5{,}032 - 4{,}632 = 400$$

Since the increase is 400, which is more than the 100 benchmark defined in the Department of Justice guidelines, the market is heavily concentrated and the merger could be challenged.

There are two problems of interpretation of the HHI in the context of banking and financial services. First, what is the relevant geographic scope of the market for financial services—national, regional, or city? Second, once that market is defined, do we view banks, credit unions, savings and loan companies, and insurance companies as separate or unique lines of business, or are they competing in the same financial market? That is, what defines the institutional scope of the market? In the case of financial services, it has been traditional to define markets on functional, or line of business, criteria, so that commercial banking is a separate market from retail banking and other financial services. Further, the relevant market area has usually been defined as highly localized: the standard metropolitan statistical areas (SMSAs) or rural areas (non-SMSAs). Unfortunately, such definitions become increasingly irrelevant in a world of greater geographic and product expansions. Indeed, the use of HHIs should increasingly be based on regional or national market lines and include a broad financial services firm definition of the marketplace.

S. Claessens and L. Laeven evaluated the concentration of banking assets for 50 different countries using an H-statistic that has a value from 0 to 1, with 1 being the highest level of concentration. Table 21–3 summarizes H-statistic data for eight countries from their sample for the period from 1994 to 2001. As can be seen, Canada's H-statistic was 0.83, while the U.S. had the lowest H-statistic at 0.47, an indication of the difference in the level of banking concentration between Canada and its closest neighbour.[7]

---

[6] Here we consider the effect on the HHI of a within-market acquisition. Similar calculations can be carried out for between-market acquisitions.

[7] For details of the calculation of the H-statistic, see S. Claessens and L. Laeven, "What Drives Bank Competition? Some International Evidence, 2003," available at worldbank.org. C. A. Northcott, *Competition in Banking: A Review of the Literature*, 2004, Bank of Canada Working Paper 2004–24, available at bankofcanada.ca, compares and summarizes this study with others from a Canadian perspective on competition. S. Shaffer, "A Test of Competition in Canadian Banking," 1993, *Journal of Money, Credit, and Banking* 25(1), pp. 49–61, studied the Canadian banking system between 1965 and 1989 and concluded that the Canadian banking system was concentrated, but still competitive, over that time.

TABLE 21–3
H-Statistic Measures of Concentration for Selected Countries

Source: S. Claessens and L. Laeven, 2003, elibrary.worldbank.org/doi/book/10.1596/1813-9450-3113.

	H-Statistic	Number of Banks
Australia	0.94	26
Canada	0.83	49
Germany	0.65	2,226
France	0.81	355
Japan	0.53	44
Switzerland	0.74	227
United Kingdom	0.78	106
United States	0.47	1,135

A 2009 study prepared by Celent found that, despite the consolidation in the U.S. system in 2008, the United States and Germany each had an HHI below 500, indicating low bank concentration. Canada and Russia were highly concentrated, with an HHI above 1500. The problems with the Russian banking system versus the stability of the Canadian financial and regulatory system during the global meltdown make it clear that other criteria are needed to assess the stability of a country's financial system (see Chapter 20).[8]

Interestingly, comparing asset concentrations by bank size, the U.S. merger wave in banking appears to have decreased the national asset share of the very smallest banks (under $100 million) from 16.1 percent in 1984 to 0.9 percent in 2012, while the relative size of the very biggest banks (over $10 billion) has increased from 34.5 percent in 1984 to 82.1 percent in 2012. The relative market shares of intermediate-sized banks ($100 million to $10 billion) have decreased as well, falling from 49.4 percent in 1984 to 17.0 percent in 2012. However, even though the degree of concentration of assets among the largest banks has increased, the percentage share exhibited by the largest U.S. banks is still well below the shares attained by the largest Canadian and European banks in their domestic markets. Thus, mergers involving the largest U.S. banks will likely continue to be approved by the Department of Justice as well as other regulatory bodies.

CONCEPT QUESTIONS

1. **What recent U.S. bank mergers have been motivated by cost synergies?**
2. **What are the three dimensions of revenue synergy gains?**
3. **Suppose each of five firms in a banking market has a 20 percent share. What is the HHI?**
4. **What factors might sway Canada's minister of finance to allow large bank mergers?**

OTHER FACTORS IMPACTING GEOGRAPHIC EXPANSION

In addition to regulation and cost and revenue synergies, other factors may impact an acquisition decision. For example, an acquiring FI may be concerned about the solvency and asset quality of a potential target FI. Thus, important factors influencing the acquisition decision may include the target FI's leverage or capital ratio, and the amount of nonperforming loans in its portfolio.

merger bid premium
The ratio of the purchase price of a target bank's equity to its book value.

In a review of a number of U.S. studies that analyzed the determinants of **merger bid premiums** (the ratio of the purchase price of a target bank's equity to its book

[8] See B. Narter, "Too Big to Bail? Bank Concentration in the Developed World," *Celent,* June 22, 2009, at http://www.celent.com/reports/too-big-bail-bank-concentration-developed-world.

value), Darius Palia found that premiums are higher (1) in states with the most restrictive regulations and (2) for target banks with high-quality loan portfolios. Palia also concludes that the growth rate of the target bank has little effect on bid premiums, while the results for the effects on bid premiums of target bank profitability and capital adequacy are rather mixed. Brewer, Jackson, Jagtiani, and Nguyen found that, in the 1990s, higher-performing targets (as measured by both return on equity and return on assets) receive higher bids; the lower the capital-to-deposit ratio, the larger the bid the acquiring bank is willing to offer; larger targets' loan-to-assets ratios and bank size are positively related to bid premiums, and higher prices occurred in the post-Riegle–Neal environment.[9]

There is little research in the Canadian context. However, an event study of the 1998 failed Canadian bank mergers (RBC and BMO; CIBC and TD Bank) by Baltazar and Santos found that market power rather than scale, scope, or X-efficiency economies was important to shareholders and that event studies would be useful to regulators in discerning societal benefits. Another Canadian study by Ng found that investors do not necessarily react positively to the news of an acquisition or merger between FIs.[10]

CONCEPT QUESTIONS

1. **Suppose you are a manager of an FI looking at another FI as a target for acquisition. What three characteristics of the target FI would most attract you?**
2. **Given the same scenario as in question 1, what three characteristics would most discourage you?**

INTERNATIONAL EXPANSIONS

LO5

Many FIs can diversify domestically, but only the very largest can aspire to diversify beyond national frontiers. This section analyzes recent trends toward the globalization of FI franchises and examines the potential return–risk advantages and disadvantages of such expansions. While FIs from some countries are currently seeking to expand internationally, others are contracting their international operations. The extent to which an FI expands internationally is thus part of the overall risk management of the FI. Total assets of banks that report data to the BIS were US$33.8 trillion in 2012. The international banking market presents an opportunity for geographic expansion beyond what an FI can achieve domestically.

There are at least three ways an FI can establish a global or international presence: (1) selling financial services from its domestic offices to foreign customers, such as a loan originating in the Toronto office of Scotiabank made to a Mexican manufacturer; (2) selling financial services through a branch, agency, or representative office established in the foreign customer's country, such as making a loan to the Mexican customer through Scotiabank's branch in Mexico; and (3) selling financial services to a foreign customer through subsidiary companies in the foreign customer's country, such as Scotiabank buying a Mexican bank and using

[9] D. Palia, "Recent Evidence of Bank Mergers," *Financial Markets, Instruments, and Institutions* 3(5), 1994, pp. 36–59; and E. Brewer II, W. E. Jackson III, J. A. Jagtiani, and T. Nguyen, "The Price of Bank Mergers in the 1990s," Federal Reserve Bank of Chicago, *Economic Perspectives* 24(1), 2000, pp. 2–24.

[10] See R. Baltazar and M. Santos, "The Benefits of Banking Mega-Mergers: Event Study Evidence from the 1998 Failed Mega-Merger Attempts in Canada," *Canadian Journal of Administrative Sciences* 20(2), September 2003, pp. 196–208, and A. Ng, "Wealth Effects of Canadian Financial Services Takeovers: Consolidation, Diversification and Foreign Evidence," *American Journal of Finance and Accounting* 1(2), pp. 194–212.

that wholly owned bank to make loans to the Mexican customer. Note that these three methods of global activity expansion are not mutually exclusive; an FI could use all three simultaneously to expand the scale and scope of its operations.

Canadian and U.S. banks, insurance companies, and securities firms have expanded abroad in recent years, often through branches and subsidiaries. This has been reciprocated by the entrance and growth until recently of foreign FIs in Canadian and U.S. financial service markets. Of the top 30 global banks, no single country dominates. Canada, Ireland, the Netherlands, the United States, Austria, Germany, Spain, Switzerland and the United Kingdom each had banks with significant overseas business. The next section concentrates on the growth of global banking. It begins with Canadian and U.S. bank expansions into foreign countries and the factors motivating these expansions and then discusses foreign bank expansions into Canada and the United States.

Canadian and U.S. Banks Abroad

Serving an exporting nation, particularly in the resource sector, Canadian banks have a long history of international activities, maintaining representative offices for their Canadian clients abroad and networks of correspondent banks to support their exports. As well, Canadian banks are major participants in the global loan syndication markets. However, the level of international diversification varies among the largest banks, ranging from CIBC with just 14.4 percent of its average total balance sheet assets outside Canada to the BMO with 38.8 percent in 2012. For example, Scotiabank has always had a reputation as an international bank. As well as billing itself as "a local bank in 50+ countries" in its 1997 annual report, Scotiabank owned 10 percent of Mexico's Grupo Financiero Inverlat, increased the stake to 97.3 percent by 2004, and changed the name of the bank to Scotiabank Inverlat. A significant portion of the foreign assets of Canadian banks are located in the United States. This is particularly true for BMO, with Harris Bank in Chicago, and TD Bank, with a strong presence on the U.S. east coast. However, both CIBC and RBC have reduced their presence in the United States since the financial crisis.

While some U.S. banks, such as JPMorgan Chase, have had offices abroad since the beginning of the 20th century, the major phase of growth began in the early 1960s after the passage of the Overseas Direct Investment Control Act of 1964. This law restricted domestic U.S. banks' ability to lend to U.S. corporations that wanted to make foreign investments. The law was eventually repealed, but it created incentives for U.S. banks to establish foreign offices to service the funding and other business needs of their U.S. clients in other countries. This offshore funding and lending in dollars created the beginning of a market we now call the *eurodollar market*. The term **eurocurrency transaction** denotes any transaction in a currency that takes place outside of the country of origin. For example, a banking transaction booked externally to the boundaries of the United States, often through an overseas branch or subsidiary, is called a **eurodollar transaction.**[11]

eurocurrency transaction
Any transaction in a currency that takes place outside the country of origin.

eurodollar transaction
Any transaction involving U.S. dollars that takes place outside the United States.

As might be expected, large U.S. banks generally have significant foreign assets. Assets in U.S. bank foreign offices increased from US$353.8 billion in 1980 to US$1,542.6 billion in 2008, then increased to US$1,440.5 billion by March 2009 during the financial crisis. However, as a percentage of these banks' total assets,

[11] That is, the definition of a eurodollar transaction is more general than "a transaction booked in Europe." In fact, any deposit in dollars taken externally to the United States normally qualifies that transaction as a eurodollar transaction. The definition may be generalized to all currencies (e.g., euroyen, etc.).

assets in foreign offices fell from 32.4 percent in 1980 to 16.2 percent in 2009. By March 2012, U.S. bank assets in foreign offices had risen back to US$1,578.8 billion. However, as a percentage of total assets, assets in foreign offices remained at financial crisis levels, 16.2 percent.

U.S. Bank Expansions Abroad

While regulation of foreign lending was the original impetus for the early growth of the eurodollar market and the associated establishment of U.S. branches and subsidiaries outside the United States, other regulatory and economic factors have also impacted the growth of U.S. offshore banking. These factors are discussed next.

The U.S. Dollar as an International Medium of Exchange The growth of international trade after World War II and the use of the dollar as an international medium of exchange encouraged foreign corporations and investors to demand dollars. A convenient way to do this was by using U.S. banks' foreign offices to intermediate such fund flows between the United States and foreigners wishing to hold dollars. Today, trade-related transactions underlie much of the activity in the eurodollar market.

Political Risk Concerns Political risk concerns among savers in emerging-market (EM) countries have led to enormous outflows of dollars from those countries, often to banks with branches and subsidiaries in the Cayman Islands and the Bahamas, where there are very stringent bank secrecy rules. Because of the secrecy rules in some foreign countries and the possibility that these rules may result in money laundering and the financing of terrorist activities, the U.S. government enacted the USA Patriot Act of 2001. The act prohibits U.S. banks from providing banking services to foreign banks that have no physical presence in any country (so-called shell banks). The bill also added foreign corruption offences to the list of crimes that can trigger a U.S. money-laundering prosecution. Also, U.S. federal authorities have the power to subpoena the records of a foreign bank's U.S. correspondent account. Further, the bill makes a depositor's funds in a foreign bank's U.S. correspondent account subject to the same civil forfeiture rules that apply to depositors' funds in other U.S. accounts. Finally, the act requires U.S. banks to improve their due diligence reviews in order to guard against money laundering. In Canada, the OSFI maintains a list of suspected terrorist organizations and, under the United Nations Suppression of Terrorism Regulations (UNSTR), requires all Canadian banks and foreign bank subsidiaries to provide reports of accounts held for suspect individuals. Under the Proceeds of Crime (Money Laundering) and Terrorist Financing Act, reports must be sent to the Financial Transactions and Reports Analysis Centre of Canada (FINTRAC).

osfi-bsif.gc.ca
fintrac.gc.ca

Domestic Regulatory Restrictions/Foreign Regulatory Relaxations As discussed earlier in the chapter, prior to the 1999 Financial Services Modernization Act, U.S. banks faced considerable activity restrictions at home regarding their securities, insurance, and commercial activities. However, with certain exceptions, Federal Reserve regulations have allowed U.S. banking offices in other countries to engage in the permitted banking activities of the foreign country even if such activities were not permitted in the United States. For example, U.S. banks setting up foreign subsidiaries can lease real property, act as general insurance agents, and underwrite and deal in foreign corporate securities (up to a maximum commitment of US$2 million). Foreign activity regulations also encourage Canadian and U.S. bank expansion abroad. For example, in late 2003 the Chinese Banking Regulatory Commission signalled a shift in policy away from restricting overseas competition to one of cautiously embracing it when it announced a comprehensive plan to overhaul the country's shaky banking system. The plan gave foreign banks greater scope to operate in China, including increasing the ceiling on foreign ownership in Chinese FIs from 15 percent to 20 percent for a single investor, expanding the number of cities where foreign branches could do local currency business, and easing capital requirements for foreign branches.

Technology and Communications Improvements The improvements in telecommunications and other communications technologies such as CHIPS (the international payment system; see Chapter 17) and the development of proprietary communication networks by large FIs have allowed FIs to extend and maintain real-time control over their foreign operations at a decreasing cost. The decreasing operating costs of such expansions have made it feasible to locate offices in an even wider array of international locations.

Factors Deterring Expansions Abroad

A number of potential factors deter international expansion, as discussed next.

Capital Constraints The Basel II and III reforms of the BIS capital requirements raised the required capital needed to back loans to sovereign countries outside the Organisation for Economic Co-operation and Development (OECD). Under Basel III (see Chapter 20), risk weights for sovereign exposures are determined using OECD country risk classifications (CRCs), which assigns countries to one of eight risk categories (0–7). Countries assigned to categories 0–1 have the lowest possible risk assessment and are assigned a risk weight of 0 percent, while countries assigned to category 7 have the highest possible risk assessment and are assigned a risk weight of 150 percent. The strong capital positions of the Canadian banks since the financial crisis have allowed them to consider asset purchases in Canada and internationally. However, the strong Canadian dollar has worked against this, since, although asset prices decrease, revenues from foreign operations decline when the dollar strengthens.

EM and European Problems

The problems of other EM countries, such as Korea, Thailand, and Indonesia in 1997 and 1998 and Argentina in the early 2000s, have made many Canadian and U.S. banks more cautious in expanding outside traditional foreign markets. This is despite the existence of increasingly favourable regulatory environments. For example, the 1994 **NAFTA** agreement gave Canadian and U.S. banks greater powers to expand into Mexico. The December 1997 agreement by 100 countries, reached under the auspices of the World Trade Organization (WTO), was also an important step toward dismantling the regulatory barriers inhibiting the entry of North American FIs into EM countries.

NAFTA
The North American Free Trade Agreement.

The financial crisis spread to EMs in 2008 and 2009 and again led banks to be cautious about expansion into these areas. Even with the perceptions that EM economies were delinked from events in the developed world, in Eastern Europe, Latin America, and Asia the financial collapse was evident. Even China, the country most immune to contagion, saw its growth decline from 12 percent to 9 percent. Panic in global financial markets compelled the International Monetary Fund (IMF) to reinstate programs of lending and financial rescue. The

IMF engaged in talks with Hungary, Iceland, Ukraine, Pakistan, and other countries. Further, Canada, the United States, and their European partners began discussions about stepping in with credit lifelines to middle-income EM countries in need of loans to avoid default. Throughout the spring of 2010 Greece struggled with a severe debt crisis. Early on, some of the healthier European countries tried to step in and assist the debt-ridden country. However, in late April, Greek bond prices dropped dramatically as traders began betting a debt default was inevitable, even if the country received a massive bailout. The problems in the Greek bond market then spread to other European nations with fiscal problems, such as Portugal, Spain, and Italy. The risks posed to international banks and the global banking system from a Greek debt default and a contagion crisis in other Eurozone countries were significantly large. As the European debt crisis progressed, banks reduced their Greek exposure dramatically.

Competition Global banks face extensive competition for overseas business. For example, aiding the competitive position of European banks has been the passage of the European Community (EC) Second Banking Directive, which created a single banking market in Europe as well as the introduction of a single currency for much of Europe (the euro). Under the Directive, European banks are allowed to branch and acquire banks throughout the European Union—that is, they have a single EC passport.[12] Although the Second Banking Directive did not come fully into effect until the end of 1992, it was announced as early as 1988. As a result, there was a cross-border merger wave among European banks that paralleled the U.S. domestic M&A wave. In addition, a number of European banks formed strategic alliances that enabled retail bank customers to open new accounts, access account information, and make payments to third parties through any of the branches of the member banks in the alliance. This greater consolidation in European banking created more intense competition for Canadian and other foreign banks in European wholesale markets and made it more difficult for them to penetrate European retail markets.

Foreign Banks in North America

As discussed in Chapter 2, foreign banks in Canada are called Schedule II banks; are regulated by OSFI; and are subsidiaries of international FIs such as Citibank, the U.K.'s HSBC, and Germany's Deutsche Bank. OSFI lists 23 foreign bank subsidiaries in Canada, with total assets of $126 billion at April 30, 2013. This is a small amount compared to the total assets of Canadian banks of $3.87 trillion. Partly as a result of their strong capital positions since the financial crisis, Canadian banks have been able to purchase the assets of foreign banks that have exited the Canadian market as a result of problems in their home countries. For example, Scotiabank acquired the assets of ING bank in Canada.

Canadian banks hold many of their assets in the United States. Just as U.S. banks can profitably expand into foreign markets, Canadian and foreign banks have historically viewed the United States as an attractive market for entry. The following sections discuss foreign banks in the United States.

---

[12] Direct branching by non-EC banks into member states was not governed by the Second Banking Directive but by the laws of each member state. Currently, all EC countries allow foreign banks to branch.

Organizational Form

Foreign banks use five primary forms of entry into the U.S. market. The choice of which organizational form to use is a function of regulations in the bank's home country as well as the risk management strategies followed by the bank.

Subsidiary A foreign bank subsidiary has its own capital and charter; it operates in the same way as any U.S. domestic bank, with access to both retail and wholesale markets.

Branch A branch bank is a direct expansion of the parent bank into a foreign or U.S. banking market. As such, it is reliant on its parent bank, such as Sumitomo Mitsui Banking Corporation in Japan, for capital support; normally, it has access to both wholesale and retail deposit and funding markets in the United States.

Agency An agency is a restricted form of entry; this organizational form restricts access of funds to those funds borrowed on the wholesale and money markets (i.e., an agency cannot accept deposits).

Edge Act Corporation
Specialized organizational form open to U.S. domestic and foreign banks that specialize in international trade-related banking transactions or investments.

Edge Act Corporation An **Edge Act Corporation** is a specialized organizational form open to U.S. domestic banks since 1919 and to foreign banks since 1978. These banks specialize in international trade-related banking transactions or investments.

Representative Office Even though a representative office books neither loans nor deposits in the United States, it acts as a loan production office, generating loan business for its parent bank at home. This is the most limited organizational form for a foreign bank entering the United States.

Trends and Growth

Table 21–4 shows the expansion of foreign banks in the United States between 1980 and 2012. In 1980, foreign banks had US$166.7 billion in assets (10.8 percent of the size of total U.S. bank assets). This activity grew through 1992, when foreign banks had US$514.3 billion in assets (16.4 percent of the size of U.S. assets). In the mid-1990s, there was a modest retrenchment in the asset share of foreign banks in the United States. In 1994, their U.S. assets totalled US$471.1 billion (13.8 percent of the size of U.S. assets). This retrenchment reflected a number of factors, including the highly competitive market for wholesale banking in the United States; a

TABLE 21–4
U.S. and Foreign Bank Assets, 1980–2012

Source: *Assets and Liabilities of Commercial Banks in the United States*, Federal Reserve Board website, various dates, federalreserve.gov.

	Bank Assets Held in United States (US$ billions)	
	U.S.-Owned	Foreign-Owned
1980	$1,537.0	$ 166.7
1985	2,284.8	175.5
1990	3,010.3	389.6
1992	3,138.4	514.3
1994	3,409.9	471.1
1995	3,660.6	530.1
2000	5,366.0	863.9
2005	7,738.1	938.5
2008 (June)	10,689.6	1,333.8
2009 (September)	10,400.7	1,369.0
2010	10,417.4	1,539.9
2012 (September)	11,049.5	1,967.7

decline in average U.S. loan quality, capital constraints on Japanese banks at home and their poor lending performance at home; and the introduction of the Foreign Bank Supervision and Enhancement Act (FBSEA) of 1991, which tightened regulations on foreign banks in the United States (discussed below). However, as foreign banks adjusted to these developments and because of the strong U.S. economy in the late 1990s, activity of foreign banks in the United States grew, reaching 16.1 percent in 2000. The worldwide economic recession in the early 2000s again depressed the level of international activity in the United States. As the situation improved, the level of international activity in the United States accelerated. In September 2009 (late in the financial crisis) foreign bank assets in the United States were 13.2 percent the size of domestic bank assets. At year-end 2010 they were 14.8 percent the size of domestic assets, and in September 2012, foreign bank assets in the U.S. were 17.8 percent the size of domestic assets.

Regulation of Foreign Banks in the United States

Before 1978, foreign branches and agencies entering the United States were licensed mostly at the state level. As such, their entry, regulation, and oversight were almost totally confined to the state level. Beginning in 1978 with the passage of the International Banking Act (IBA) and the more recent passage of the FBSEA, Title II of the FDIC Improvement Act (FDICIA) of December 1991, federal regulators have exerted increasing control over foreign banks operating in the United States.

federalreserve.gov

The IBA of 1978

Before the passage in 1978 of the IBA, foreign agencies and branches entering the United States with state licences had some competitive advantages and disadvantages relative to most domestic banks.

The unequal treatment of domestic and foreign banks regarding federal regulation and lobbying by domestic banks regarding the unfairness of this situation provided the impetus for Congress to pass the IBA in 1978. The fundamental regulatory philosophy underlying the IBA was one of **national treatment**, a philosophy that attempted to create a level playing field for both domestic and foreign banks in U.S. banking markets. As a result of this act, foreign banks were required to hold Federal Reserve–specified reserve requirements if their worldwide assets exceeded US$1 billion, were subjected to Federal Reserve examinations, and were subjected to both the McFadden and Glass–Steagall acts.

national treatment
Regulating foreign banks in the same fashion as domestic banks or creating a level playing field.

The FBSEA of 1991 Along with the growth of foreign bank assets in the United States came concerns about foreign banks' rapidly increasing share of U.S. banking markets as well as about the weakness of regulatory oversight of many of these institutions. Three events focused attention on the weaknesses of foreign bank regulation. The first event was the collapse of the Bank of Credit and Commerce International (BCCI), which had a highly complex international organizational structure based in the Middle East, the Cayman Islands, and Luxembourg and had undisclosed ownership stakes in two large U.S. banks. BCCI was not subject to any consolidated supervision by a home-country regulator; this quickly became apparent after its collapse, when massive fraud, insider lending abuses, and money-laundering operations were discovered. The second event was the issuance of more than US$1 billion in unauthorized letters of credit (LCs) to Saddam Hussein's Iraq by the Atlanta agency of the Italian Banca Nazionale del Lavoro.

The third event was the unauthorized taking of deposit funds by the U.S. representative office of the Greek National Mortgage Bank of New York.

These events and related concerns led to the passage of the FBSEA of 1991. The objective of this act was to extend U.S. federal regulatory authority over foreign banking organizations in the United States, especially where these organizations entered using state licences. The act's five main features have significantly enhanced the powers of federal bank regulators over foreign banks in the United States.

1. *Entry.* Under FBSEA, a foreign banking organization must now have the Federal Reserve's approval to establish a subsidiary, branch, agency, or representative office in the United States. The approval applies to both a new entry and an entry by acquisition. To get Federal Reserve approval, the organization must meet a number of standards, two of which are mandatory. First, the foreign bank must be subject to comprehensive supervision on a consolidated basis by a home-country regulator. Second, that regulator must furnish all the information needed by the Federal Reserve to evaluate the application. Both standards are aimed at avoiding the lack of disclosure and lack of centralized supervision associated with BCCI's failure.
2. *Closure.* The act also gives the Federal Reserve authority to close a foreign bank if its home-country supervision is inadequate, if it has violated U.S. laws, or if it is engaged in unsound and unsafe banking practices.
3. *Examination.* The Federal Reserve has the authority to examine each office of a foreign bank, including its representative offices. Further, each branch or agency must be examined at least once a year.

fdic.gov

4. *Deposit taking.* Only foreign subsidiaries with access to FDIC insurance can take retail deposits under US$250,000. This effectively rolls back the provision of the IBA that gave foreign branches and agencies access to FDIC insurance.
5. *Activity powers.* Beginning on December 19, 1992, state-licensed branches and agencies of foreign banks could not engage in any activity that was not permitted to a federal branch.

Overall, the FBSEA considerably increased the Federal Reserve's authority over foreign banks and added to the regulatory burden or costs of entry into the United States.

CONCEPT QUESTIONS

1. **What were the major policy changes pertaining to bank expansion introduced by NAFTA?**
2. **What are the primary forms of entry by foreign banks into the U.S. market?**
3. **How did the IBA of 1978 and the FBSEA of 1991 affect foreign banks operating in the United States?**

ADVANTAGES AND DISADVANTAGES OF INTERNATIONAL EXPANSION

Historical and recent trends affecting the geographic expansion of FIs both into and outside North America have been discussed above. Here we summarize the advantages and disadvantages of international expansions to the individual FI seeking to generate additional returns or better diversify its risk.

Advantages

Below are the six major advantages of international expansion.

Revenue and Risk Diversification

As with domestic geographic expansions, an FI's international activities potentially enhance its opportunity to diversify the risk of its revenue flows. Often, domestic revenue flows from financial services are strongly linked to the state of the economy. Therefore, the less integrated the economies of the world, the greater is the potential for revenue diversification through international expansions.

Economies of Scale

To the extent that economies of scale exist, an FI can potentially lower its average operating costs by expanding its activities beyond domestic boundaries.

Innovations

An FI can generate extra returns from new product innovations if it can sell such services internationally rather than just domestically. For example, consider complex financial innovations, such as securitization, caps, floors, and options, that FIs have innovated in North America and sold to new foreign markets with few domestic competitors.

Funds Source

International expansion allows an FI to search for the cheapest and most available sources of funds. This is extremely important given the very thin profit margins in domestic and international wholesale banking. Also, it reduces the risk of fund shortages (credit rationing) in any one market.

Customer Relationships

International expansions also allow an FI to maintain contact with and service the needs of domestic multinational corporations. Indeed, one of the fundamental factors determining the growth of FIs in foreign countries has been the parallel growth of foreign direct investment and foreign trade by globally oriented multinational corporations from the FI's home country.

Regulatory Avoidance

To the extent that domestic regulations such as activity restrictions and reserve requirements impose constraints or taxes on the operations of an FI, seeking out low regulatory tax countries can allow an FI to lower its net regulatory burden and to increase its potential net profitability.

Disadvantages

Below are the three major disadvantages of international expansion.

Information/Monitoring Costs

Although global expansions give an FI the potential to better diversify its geographic risk, the absolute level of exposure in certain areas such as lending can be high, especially if the FI fails to diversify in an optimal fashion. For example, the FI may fail to choose a loan portfolio combination on the efficient lending frontier (see Chapter 11). Foreign activities may also be riskier for the simple reason that monitoring and information collection costs are often higher in foreign markets.

For example, Canadian firms adopted International Financial Reporting Standards (IFRS) in 2011, requiring those Canadian FIs with operations in the United States to report using both IFRS and U.S. generally accepted accounting principles (GAAP). In addition, language, legal, and cultural issues can impose additional transaction costs on international activities. Finally, because the regulatory environment is controlled locally and regulation imposes a different array of net costs in each market, a truly global FI must master the various rules and regulations in each market.

Nationalization/Expropriation

To the extent that an FI expands by establishing a local presence through investing in fixed assets such as branches or subsidiaries, it faces the political risk that a change in government may lead to the nationalization of those fixed assets, such as has occurred in Africa. Further, if foreign FI depositors take losses following nationalization, they may seek legal recourse from the FI in North American courts rather than from the nationalizing government. For example, it took many years to resolve the outstanding claims of depositors in Citicorp's branches in Vietnam following the Communist takeover and expropriation.

Fixed Costs

The fixed costs of establishing foreign organizations may be extremely high. For example, a Canadian FI seeking an organizational presence in the Tokyo banking market faces real estate prices significantly higher than those in Toronto, Vancouver, or New York. Such relative costs can be even higher if an FI chooses to enter by buying an existing bank rather than establishing a new operation. These relative cost considerations become even more important if there is uncertainty about the expected volume of business to be generated.

CONCEPT QUESTIONS

1. **What are the major advantages of international expansion to an FI?**
2. **What are the major disadvantages of international expansion to an FI?**

Questions and Problems

1. How does product segmentation reduce the profitability and risks of FIs? How does it increase the profitability and risks of FIs?
2. What is shadow banking? How does the shadow banking system differ from the traditional banking system?
3. What are the differences in the risk implications of a firm commitment securities offering versus a best-efforts offering?
4. An FI is underwriting the sales of 1 million shares of Ultrasonics Inc. and is quoting a bid–ask price of \$6.00–\$6.50.
   a. What are the fees earned by the FI if a firm commitment method is used to underwrite the securities?
   b. What are the fees if the FI uses the best-efforts method and a commission of 50 bp is charged?
   c. How would your answer be affected if the FI manages to sell the shares at only \$5.50 using the firm commitment method? The commission for best efforts is still 50 bp.
5. The investment arm of a large Canadian FI agrees to underwrite a debt issue for one of its clients. It has suggested a firm commitment offering for issuing 100,000 shares of stock. The FI quotes a bid–ask spread of \$97.00–\$97.50 to its customer on the issue date.
   a. What are the total underwriting fees generated if all the issue is sold? If only 60 percent is sold?

b. Instead of taking a chance that only 60 percent of the shares will be sold on the issue date, the FI suggests a price of $95 to the issuing firm. The FI quotes a bid–ask spread of $95.00–$95.40 and sells 100 percent of the issue. From the FI's perspective, which price is better if it expects to sell the remaining 40 percent at the bid price of $97 under the first quote?

6. How could the failure of a securities affiliate negatively affect a bank?
7. What role does bank activity diversification play in the ability of a bank to exploit economies of scale and scope? What remains as the limitation to creating potentially greater benefits?
8. What conflicts of interest have been identified as potential roadblocks to the expansion of banking powers into the financial services area?
9. What are some of the legal, institutional, and market conditions that lessen the likelihood that an FI can exploit conflicts of interest from the expansion of commercial banks into other financial services areas?
10. Under what circumstances could the existence of deposit insurance provide an advantage to banks in competing with other traditional securities firms?
11. In what ways does the current regulatory structure argue against providing additional insurance powers to the banking industry? Does this issue only concern banks?
12. What are the potential positive effects of allowing banks to enter more fully into insurance sales and underwriting? What is the anticompetitive argument or position?
13. How do limitations on geographic diversification affect an FI's profitability?
14. Bank mergers often produce hard-to-quantify benefits called *X efficiencies* and costs called *X inefficiencies*. Give an example of each.
15. What are the three revenue synergies that may be obtained by an FI from expanding geographically?
16. What is the HHI? How is it calculated and interpreted?
17. City Bank currently has a 60 percent market share in banking services, followed by Nations Bank with 20 percent and State Bank with 20 percent.
    a. What is the concentration ratio as measured by the HHI?
    b. If City Bank acquires State Bank, what will be the new HHI?
    c. Assume that the government will allow mergers as long as the changes in HHI do not exceed 1,400. What is the minimum amount of assets that City Bank will have to divest after it merges with State Bank?
18. A government has been asked to review a merger request for a market with the following four FIs:

Bank	Assets
A	$12 million
B	25 million
C	102 million
D	3 million

    a. What is the HHI for the existing market?
    b. If Bank A acquires Bank D, what will be the effect on the market's level of concentration?
    c. If Bank C acquires Bank D, what will be the effect on the market's level of concentration?
    d. What is likely to be the government's response to the two merger applications based on the HHI?
19. A government measures market concentration using the HHI of market share. What problems does this measure have for (a) multiproduct FIs and (b) FIs with global operations?
20. What factors other than market concentration should a government consider in determining the acceptability of a merger?
21. What are some of the important firm-specific financial factors that influence the acquisition of an FI?
22. What are some of the benefits for banks engaging in geographic expansion?
23. What are three ways in which an FI can establish a global or international presence?
24. What is a eurodollar transaction? What are eurodollars?
25. Identify and explain the impact of at least four factors that encourage global bank expansion.
26. What is the expected impact of the implementation of the revised BIS risk-based capital requirements on the international activities of major banks?
27. What is the European Community (EC) Second Banking Directive? What impact has the Second Banking Directive had on the competitive banking environment in Europe?
28. Identify and discuss the various ways in which foreign banks can enter the U.S. market. What are international banking facilities?

29. What are the major advantages of international expansion to FIs? Explain how each advantage can affect the operating performance of FIs.
30. What are the difficulties of expanding globally? How can each of these difficulties create negative effects on the operating performance of FIs?
31. The Canadian minister of finance has asked you to provide a recommendation regarding the merger of large FIs in Canada and to answer the following questions:
    a. What factors should be considered in evaluating the benefits of a merger?
    b. Should bank–bank and bank–insurance mergers be allowed in Canada?
    c. How would your response differ if you were preparing this report for the board of directors of a large Canadian bank or insurance company?

Appendix 21A EU and G-10 Countries: Regulatory Treatment of the Mixing of Banking, Securities, and Insurance Activities and the Mixing of Banking and Commerce

View Appendix 21A on Connect.

CHAPTER 22

FUTURES AND FORWARDS

After studying this chapter you should be able to:

LO1 Discuss the differences between futures and forward contracts.

LO2 Demonstrate how forward contracts can be used to hedge interest rate risk.

LO3 Use microhedging and macrohedging with futures contracts to hedge interest rate risk.

LO4 Discuss and demonstrate the effect of basis risk when hedging with futures.

LO5 Demonstrate hedging foreign exchange risk with futures and forward contracts.

LO6 Demonstrate how futures and forwards can be used to hedge credit risk.

LO7 Discuss the regulation of derivative securities.

INTRODUCTION

Chapter 16 describes the growth in FIs' off-balance-sheet (OBS) activities. A major component of this growth has been in futures and forward contracts. Although a significant amount of derivatives reflects the trading activity of large banks, FIs of all sizes have used these instruments to hedge their asset–liability risk exposures and thus reduce the value of their net worth at risk due to adverse events. Derivative securities generally involve an agreement between two parties to exchange a standard quantity of an asset or cash flow at a predetermined price and at a specified date in the future. As the value of the underlying security to be exchanged changes, the value of the derivative security changes. Derivatives involve the buying and selling, or transference, of risk. As such, they can involve profits and losses if a position is unhedged.

notional value of an OBS item
The face value of an OBS contract.

Table 22–1 lists the derivative holdings of the six major Canadian banks at October 31, 2012. Table 22–2 lists the derivative contract holdings of all U.S. commercial banks and, specifically, the 25 largest U.S. banks, as of June 2012 (in U.S. dollars). The tables show the breakdown of the derivatives positions into futures and forwards, swaps, options, credit derivatives, and other derivatives contracts (e.g., equity, commodity). The tables show that the **notional value** (dollar) contract volume for the Canadian banks was equal to $19.4 trillion, whereas the total for the top 25 U.S. banks, reflecting the size of the broader North American market for derivatives, was US$222.2 trillion. As can be seen, both in Canada and in the United States, swaps dominate, representing $13.4 trillion and US$134.5 trillion, respectively, of the total notional amount. Futures and forwards are in second place ($4.514 trillion and US$40.7 trillion), followed by options ($0.6 trillion and US$33.6 trillion). The replacement cost (current credit risk exposure) of these derivative contracts (expressed as the bilaterally netted current exposure as required

TABLE 22–1 Derivative Contracts: Notional Amount, Credit-Equivalent Amount, and Risk-Weighted Amount of the Six Major Canadian Banks, October 31, 2012 ($ billions)

Source: Bank annual reports, 2012.

		Notional Amount of Derivative Contracts								
Bank	Total Assets	Futures & Forwards	Total Swaps	Total Options	Credit Derivatives	Other Contracts	Total Derivatives	Replacement Cost of All Contracts	Credit-Equivalent Amount	Risk-Weighted Amount
BMO	$ 525.4	$ 1,030.5*	$ 2,249.6	$ n.a.	$ 35.8	$ 32.3	$ 3,348.2	$12.6	$ 21.0	$ 5.6
Scotiabank	668.0	667.8	1,845.6	74.5	68.4	109.8	2,766.1	7.0	19.6	5.6
CIBC	393.4	382.8	1,279.4	42.8	22.4	56.4	1,783.8	6.7	11.0	2.5
National	177.9	35.8	364.9	45.0	33.3**	57.9	536.9	2.5	5.6	2.0
RBC	825.1	1,583.4	4,960.7	332.3	17.1	270.3	7,163.8	21.9	33.4	11.9
TD Bank	811.1	813.4	2,730.1	133.5	8.7	105.6	3,791.3	6.4	28.7	7.4
Total	$3,400.9	$ 4,513.7	$13,430.3	$628.1	$185.7	$632.3	$19,390.1	$57.1	$119.3	$35.0
% of total derivatives		23.3%	69.3%	3.2%	0.9%	3.3%	100.0%			

Note: Replacement cost of all contracts, credit-equivalent amount, and risk-weighted amounts reported after master netting agreements as required by Basel II.

* Options included with futures and forwards.

** Equity, commodity, and precious metals contracts included with credit derivatives.

TABLE 22–2 Derivative Contracts: Notional Amount and Credit-Equivalent Exposure of the 25 U.S. Commercial Banks and Trust Companies with the Most Derivative Contracts, June 2012 (in millions of U.S. dollars)

Source: Office of the Comptroller of the Currency website, October 2012. www.occ.gov.

			Derivative Contracts								
Rank	Bank Name	Total Assets	Forwards & Futures	Total Swaps	Total Options	Credit Derivatives	Total Derivatives	Current Credit Exposure	Potential Future Exposure	Credit Exposure from All Contracts	Credit Exposure to Capital Ratio
1.	JPMorgan Chase Bank	$ 1,812,837	$13,242,193	$ 38,953,299	$11,025,862	$ 6,016,995	$ 69,238,349	$162,867	$181,892	$ 344,759	246
2.	Citibank NA	1,347,841	7,129,350	32,630,778	9,344,370	3,046,472	52,150,970	72,809	164,919	237,728	174
3.	Bank of America NA	1,445,093	11,440,172	26,283,299	3,291,616	3,390,285	44,405,372	66,064	139,939	206,003	141
4.	Goldman Sachs Bank	114,693	4,478,725	28,810,776	7,809,128	481,766	41,508,395	27,757	119,715	147,472	738
5.	HSBC Bank USA	193,995	896,034	2,793,846	270,043	575,870	4,535,794	7,015	30,086	37,101	172
6.	Wells Fargo Bank NA	1,180,190	1,096,881	1,914,889	512,720	66,360	3,590,850	29,613	19,656	49,269	42
7.	Morgan Stanley Bank NA	69,390	454,621	1,285,759	720,259	20,982	2,481,621	350	14,179	14,529	135
8.	Bank of New York Mellon	259,069	373,852	677,825	244,115	221	1,296,013	6,490	5,257	11,747	87
9.	State Street Bank & TC	196,960	795,187	2,930	69,005	28	867,150	4,821	7,374	12,195	90
10.	PNC Bank NA	291,824	82,410	224,863	81,543	3,415	392,231	3,304	850	4,154	12
11.	SunTrust Bank	172,028	43,307	161,771	64,398	4,507	273,983	2,868	1,539	4,407	25
12.	Northern Trust Co	94,216	215,280	10,310	104	76	225,770	2,462	2,322	4,785	61
13.	Standard Chartered Bank	48,377	134,888	2,566	7,930	0	145,384	0	0	0	0
14.	U.S. Bank National Assn	342,823	54,616	49,489	13,921	3,048	121,074	1,373	245	1,617	5
15.	Regions Bank	121,330	57,424	59,687	3,083	739	120,933	948	235	1,183	8
16.	Keybank National Assn	83,966	17,185	55,688	5,675	2,613	81,161	1,066	136	1,202	11
17.	Branch Banking and Trust	173,678	17,029	39,015	20,968	0	77,013	1,569	402	1,971	12
18.	Fifth Third Bank	115,041	14,586	33,068	23,527	1,317	72,498	1,714	711	2,425	17
19.	TD Bank National Assn	195,943	9,633	57,714	1,594	740	69,680	2,575	754	3,329	23
20.	Union Bank National Assn	87,275	7,384	36,655	14,715	35	58,790	1,036	525	1,561	15
21.	RBS Citizens National Assn	106,894	7,573	25,984	2,122	887	36,567	1,122	284	1,406	13
22.	Bank of Oklahoma NA	25,415	28,748	3,139	3,282	0	35,168	235	242	477	20
23.	Capital One NA	158,240	825	31,735	44	705	33,310	657	270	927	6
24.	BMO Harris Bank NA	92,222	1,294	26,670	2,905	90	30,959	621	318	939	9
25.	Ally Bank	87,336	8,239	13,216	7,383	0	28,838	139	177	316	2
Total 25 commercial banks		**$ 8,816,679**	**$40,607,436**	**$134,184,972**	**$33,540,312**	**$13,617,151**	**$221,949,873**	**$399,474**	**$692,028**	**$1,091,501**	**129[a]**
Other 1,332 commercial banks		**$ 3,525,137**	**$141,054**	**$297,514**	**$ 75,475**	**$ 7,622**	**$521,665**	**$10,240**	**$ 3,847**	**$14,087**	**4**
Total for all banks		**$12,341,817**	**$40,748,491**	**$134,482,486**	**$33,615,787**	**$13,624,773**	**$222,471,538**	**$409,714**	**$695,875**	**$1,105,589**	**90**

[a] Average.

by Basel II) for the Canadian banks is $57.1 billion, and the credit-equivalent amount is $119.3 billion compared with US$399.0 and US$1.1 billion for the top 25 U.S. banks. The risk-weighted amount is $35.0 billion for the Canadian banks, significantly smaller than the notional amount.[1]

Not only do FIs hold these contracts to hedge their own risk (interest rate, credit, etc.), but FIs also serve as the counterparty (for a fee) in these contracts for other (financial and nonfinancial) firms wanting to hedge risks on their balance sheets.

The rapid growth of derivatives use by both FIs and nonfinancial firms has been controversial. Critics charge that derivative contracts contain potential losses that can materialize to haunt their holders, particularly banks and insurance companies that deal heavily in these instruments. As will be discussed in this chapter and the following two chapters, when employed appropriately, derivatives can be used to hedge (or reduce) an FI's risk. However, when misused, derivatives can increase the risk of an FI's insolvency. A number of scandals involving FIs, firms, and municipalities (such as Bankers Trust and the Allied Irish Bank) led to a tightening of the accounting (reporting) requirements for derivative contracts.

fasb.org

Specifically, beginning in 2000, the Financial Accounting Standards Board (FASB) in the United States required all derivatives to be marked to market and mandated that losses and gains be immediately transparent on FIs' and other firms' financial statements. Then, in the late 2000s, billions of dollars of losses on derivative securities and the near collapse of the world's financial markets led to a call for major regulations to be imposed on the trading of derivative securities. The regulations intended to bring the many over-the-counter (OTC) derivative contracts made between FIs under federal regulation and empower securities and commodities regulators to police them.

frascanada.ca

In Canada, the Accounting Standards Board (AcSB, now Financial Reporting and Assurance Standards Canada), aware of the experience with derivative losses elsewhere in the world, produced new regulations for derivative instruments that combined U.S. generally accepted accounting principles (GAAP) and international accounting standards. These new regulations became mandatory for all companies, including FIs, that used derivative products after November 1, 2006. In order to be comparable with other international banks, in 2012, Canadian banks reported using IFRS for all of their operations.

In this chapter, we look at the role futures and forward contracts play in managing an FI's interest rate, foreign exchange (FX), and credit risk exposures, as well as their role in hedging natural catastrophes. We start with a comparison of forward and futures contracts to spot contracts. We then examine how forwards and futures can be used to hedge interest rate risk, FX risk, credit risk, and catastrophe risk. We look at option-type derivatives and swaps in Chapters 23 and 24.

FORWARD AND FUTURES CONTRACTS

LO1

To understand the essential nature and characteristics of forward and futures contracts, we can compare them with spot contracts. We show appropriate time lines for each of the three contracts using a bond as the underlying financial security to the derivative contract in Figure 22–1.

[1] See Chapter 20 for a discussion of how the credit exposure of derivatives is calculated for regulatory reporting.

FIGURE 22–1
Contract Time Lines

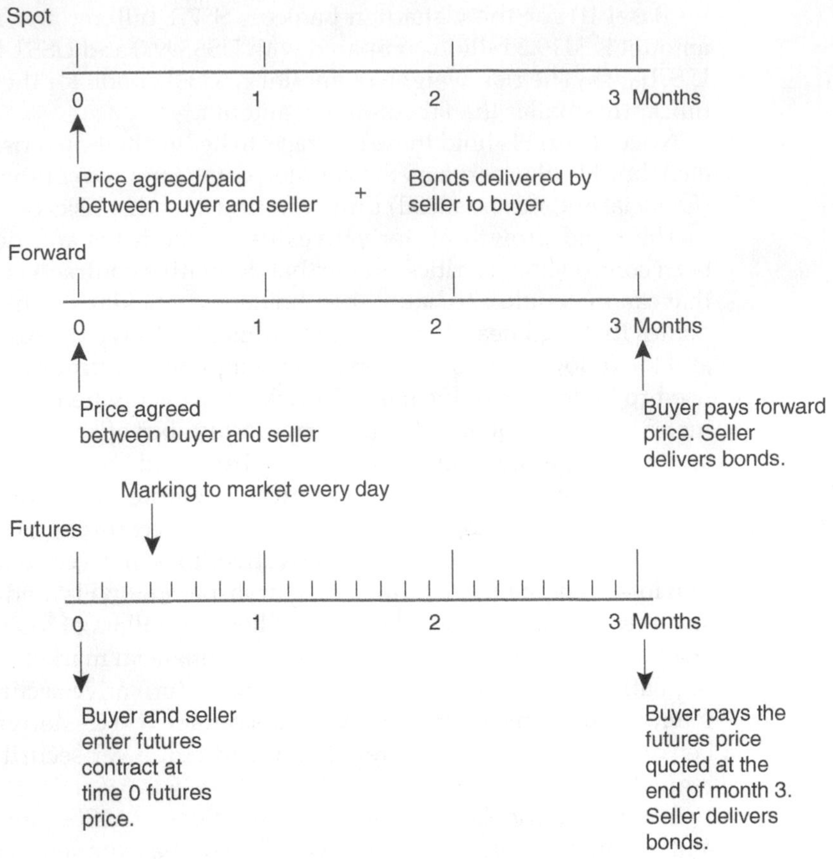

Spot Contracts

spot contract
An agreement involving the immediate exchange of an asset for cash.

A **spot contract** is an agreement between a buyer and a seller at time 0, when the seller of the asset agrees to deliver it immediately and the buyer of the asset agrees to pay for that asset immediately.[2] Thus, the unique feature of a spot market contract is the immediate and simultaneous exchange of cash for securities, or what is often called *delivery versus payment*. A spot bond quote of $97 for a 20-year-maturity bond is the price the buyer must pay the seller, per $100 of face value, for immediate (time 0) delivery of the 20-year bond.

Forward Contracts

forward contract
An agreement involving the exchange of an asset for cash at a fixed price in the future.

A **forward contract** is a contractual agreement between a buyer and a seller at time 0 to exchange a prespecified asset for cash at a later date. For example, in a three-month forward contract to deliver 20-year bonds, the buyer and seller agree on a price and quantity today (time 0), but the delivery (or exchange) of the 20-year bond for cash does not occur until three months hence. If the forward price agreed to at time 0 was $97 per $100 of face value, in three months' time the seller delivers $100 of 20-year bonds and receives $97 from the buyer. This is the price the buyer

[2] Technically, physical settlement and delivery may take place one or two days after the contractual spot agreement in bond markets. In equity markets, delivery and cash settlement normally occur three business days after the spot contract agreement.

must pay and the seller must accept no matter what happened to the spot price of 20-year bonds during the three months between the time the contract was entered into and the time the bonds are delivered for payment.

Commercial banks and investment banks and broker–dealers are the major forward market participants, acting as both principals and agents. These FIs make a profit on the spread between the prices at which they buy and sell the asset underlying the forward contracts. Each forward contract is originally negotiated between the FI and the customer, and therefore the details of each (e.g., price, expiration, size, delivery date) can be unique. As the forward market has grown over the last decade, however, traders have begun making secondary markets in some forward contracts, communicating the buy and sell prices on the contracts over computer networks.

Futures Contracts

futures contract
An agreement involving the future exchange of an asset for cash at a price that is determined daily.

m-x.ca

marked to market
The process by which the prices on outstanding futures contracts are adjusted each day to reflect current futures market conditions.

A **futures contract** is normally arranged through an organized exchange (in Canada, the Montréal Exchange). It is an agreement between a buyer and a seller at time 0 to exchange a standardized, prespecified asset for cash at a later date. As such, a futures contract is very similar to a forward contract. However, there are four major differences between a futures contract and a forward contract. The first difference relates to the price, which in a forward contract is fixed over the life of the contract ($97 per $100 of face value for three months), but in a futures contract is **marked to market** daily. This means the contract's price is adjusted each day as the futures price for the contract changes. Therefore, actual daily cash settlements occur between the buyer and seller in response to this marking-to-market process. This can be compared to a forward contract, where the whole cash payment from buyer to seller occurs at the end of the contract period.

A second difference between futures and forward contracts is that forwards are tailor-made contracts that are negotiated between two parties, while futures contracts are standardized because they are offered by and traded on an exchange. Third, because they are exchange-traded securities (see below), the exchange itself guarantees the performance of the futures contract. Thus, the risk of default by either party is minimized since the exchange will step in and take over the defaulting counterparty's position. No such guarantee exists for a forward contract. Finally, delivery of the underlying asset almost always occurs for forward contracts, but seldom occurs for futures contracts. Instead, an offsetting or reverse futures transaction occurs through the exchange prior to the maturity of the contract.

Futures trading occurs on organized exchanges—for example, the Montréal Exchange in Canada. The Montréal Exchange and TSX Group Inc. joined in 2008 to create the TMX Group. The Montréal Exchange provides futures and options trading in Canada for interest rate, index, and equity contracts. The Canadian Derivatives Clearing Corporation (CDCC) is a self-regulatory organization (SRO) that is wholly owned by the Bourse de Montréal Inc. CDCC issues, clears, and guarantees the contracts traded on the Montréal Exchange.

cmegroup.com

Canadian FIs also trade futures on U.S. exchanges—for example, the Chicago Board of Trade (CBOT) and the Chicago Mercantile Exchange (CME). Financial futures market trading was introduced in the United States in 1972 with the establishment of FX futures contracts on the International Money Market (IMM). By the mid-1990s, five major exchanges existed in the United States,[3] and several exchanges existed outside the United States.[4] The terms of futures contracts (e.g., contract size, delivery month, trading hours, minimum price fluctuation, daily price limits, and process used for delivery) traded in the United States are set by the exchange and are subject to the approval of the Commodity Futures Trading Commission (CFTC), the principal U.S. regulator of futures markets. In recent years, "off-market" trading systems have sprung up in which institutional investors and money managers can continue to trade during, as well as after, futures exchange operating hours. Indeed, it is estimated that trading volume in off-market currencies, interest rate swaps, and eurodollars has grown three to ten times as fast as trading volume on futures exchanges.

cftc.gov

CONCEPT QUESTIONS

1. **What is the difference between a futures contract and a forward contract?**
2. **What are the major differences between a spot contract and a forward contract?**

FORWARD CONTRACTS AND HEDGING INTEREST RATE RISK

LO2

naive hedge
When a cash asset is hedged on a direct dollar-for-dollar basis with a forward or futures contract.

To see the usefulness of forward contracts in hedging the interest rate risk of an FI, consider a simple example of a **naive hedge** (the hedge of a cash asset on a direct dollar-for-dollar basis with a forward or futures contract). Suppose an FI portfolio manager holds a 20-year, $1 million face value bond on the balance sheet. At time 0, these bonds are valued by the market at $97 per $100 face value, or $970,000 in total. Assume the manager receives a forecast that interest rates are expected to rise by 2 percent from their current level of 8 to 10 percent over the next three months. Knowing that rising interest rates mean that bond prices will fall, the manager stands to make a capital loss on the bond portfolio. Having read Chapters 8 and 9, the manager is an expert in interest rate risk and has calculated the 20-year-maturity bonds' duration to be exactly 9 years. Thus, the manager can predict a capital loss, or change in bond values (ΔP), from equation 9.5:[5]

$$\frac{\Delta P}{P} = -D \times \frac{\Delta R}{1 + R}$$

where

ΔP = Capital loss on bonds = ?
P = Initial value of bond position = \$970,000
D = Duration of the bonds = 9 years
ΔR = Change in forecast yield = 0.02
$1 + R$ = 1 plus the current yield on 20-year bonds = 1.08

$$\frac{\Delta P}{\$970{,}000} = -9 \times \left[\frac{0.02}{1.08}\right]$$

$$\Delta P = -9 \times \$970{,}000 \times \left[\frac{0.02}{1.08}\right] = -\$161{,}667$$

[3] These include the CBOT, the CME, the Intercontinental Exchange, and the Kansas City Board of Trade. The CBOT and the CME merged in 2007 to become the CME Group.

[4] These include the London International Financial Futures Exchange (LIFFE, part of NYSE Euronext), the Singapore Exchange Limited, and the Montréal Exchange.

[5] For simplicity, we ignore issues relating to convexity here.

As a result, the FI portfolio manager expects to incur a capital loss on the bond portfolio of $161,667 (as a percentage loss ($\Delta P/P$) = 16.67%) or as a drop in price from $97 per $100 face value to $80.833 per $100 face value. To offset this loss—in fact, to reduce the risk of capital loss to zero—the manager may hedge this position by taking an OBS hedge, such as selling $1 million face value of 20-year bonds for forward delivery in three months' time.[6] Suppose at time 0 the portfolio manager can find a buyer willing to pay $97 for every $100 of 20-year bonds delivered in three months' time.

Now consider what happens to the FI portfolio manager if the gloomy forecast of a 2 percent rise in interest rates proves to be true. The portfolio manager's bond position has fallen in value by 16.67 percent, equal to a capital loss of $161,667. After the rise in interest rates, the manager can buy $1 million face value of 20-year bonds in the spot market at $80.833 per $100 of face value, a total cost of $808,333, and deliver these bonds to the forward contract buyer. Remember that the forward contract buyer agreed to pay $97 per $100 of face value for the $1 million of face value bonds delivered, or $970,000. As a result, the portfolio manager makes a profit on the forward transaction of

$970,000	−	$808,333	=	$161,667
(price paid by forward buyer to forward seller)		(cost of purchasing bonds in the spot market at t = month 3 for delivery to the forward buyer)		

As you can see, the on-balance-sheet loss of $161,667 is exactly offset by the off-balance-sheet gain of $161,667 from selling the forward contract. In fact, for any change in interest rates, a loss (gain) on the balance sheet is offset by a gain (loss) on the forward contract. Indeed, the success of a hedge does not hinge on the manager's ability to accurately forecast interest rates. Rather, the reason for the hedge is the lack of ability to perfectly predict interest rate changes. The hedge allows the FI manager to protect against interest rate changes even if they are unpredictable. Thus, the FI's net interest rate exposure is zero; in the parlance of finance, the FI has **immunized** its assets against interest rate risk.

immunized
Describes an FI that is fully hedged or protected against adverse movements in interest rates (or other asset prices).

CONCEPT QUESTIONS

1. **Explain how a naive hedge works.**
2. **What does it mean to say that an FI has immunized its portfolio against a particular risk?**

HEDGING INTEREST RATE RISK WITH FUTURES CONTRACTS

LO3

Even though some hedging of interest rate risk does take place using forward contracts—such as forward rate agreements commonly used by insurance companies and banks prior to mortgage loan originations—many FIs hedge interest rate risk either at the micro level (called *microhedging*) or at the macro level (called *macrohedging*) using futures contracts. Before looking at futures contracts, we explain

[6] Since a forward contract involves delivery of bonds in a future time period, it does not appear on the balance sheet. Thus, forwards are an example of off-balance-sheet items (see Chapter 16).

the difference between microhedging and macrohedging and between routine hedging and selective hedging.

Microhedging

microhedging
Using a futures (forward) contract to hedge a specific asset or liability.

An FI is **microhedging** when it employs a futures or a forward contract to hedge a particular asset or liability risk. For example, earlier we considered a simple example of microhedging asset-side portfolio risk, where an FI manager wanted to insulate the value of the institution's bond portfolio fully against a rise in interest rates. An example of microhedging on the liability side of the balance sheet occurs when an FI, attempting to lock in a cost of funds to protect itself against a possible rise in short-term interest rates, takes a short (sell) position in futures contracts on T-bills. In microhedging, the FI manager often tries to pick a futures or forward contract whose underlying deliverable asset is closely matched to the asset (or liability) position being hedged. The earlier example, where we had an exact matching of the asset in the portfolio with the deliverable security underlying the forward contract (20-year bonds), was unrealistic. Such exact matching cannot be achieved often; this produces a residual unhedgeable risk termed **basis risk**. We discuss basis risk in detail later in this chapter; it arises mainly because the prices of the assets or liabilities that an FI wishes to hedge are imperfectly correlated over time with the prices on the futures or forward contract used to hedge risk.

basis risk
A residual risk that arises because the movement in a spot (cash) asset's price is not perfectly correlated with the movement in the price of the asset delivered under a futures or forward contract.

Macrohedging

macrohedging
Hedging the entire duration gap of an FI.

Macrohedging occurs when an FI manager uses futures or other derivative securities to hedge the entire balance sheet duration gap. This contrasts with microhedging, where an FI manager identifies specific assets and liabilities and seeks individual futures and other derivative contracts to hedge those individual risks. Note that macrohedging and microhedging can lead to quite different hedging strategies and results. In particular, a macrohedge takes a whole-portfolio view and allows for individual asset and liability interest rate sensitivities or durations to net each other out. This can result in a very different aggregate futures position than when an FI manager disregards this netting or portfolio effect and hedges individual asset and liability positions on a one-to-one basis.

Also, to dynamically hedge the entire portfolio, the assets must be marked-to-market on a daily basis, and the portfolio rebalanced. The futures and forwards markets may not be sufficiently liquid to permit this, or a Canadian FI may resort to using U.S. contracts to achieve its goal of being fully hedged.

Routine Hedging versus Selective Hedging

routine hedging
Seeking to hedge all interest rate risk exposure.

Routine hedging occurs when an FI reduces its interest rate or other risk exposure to the lowest possible level by selling sufficient futures to offset the interest rate risk exposure of its whole balance sheet or cash positions in each asset and liability. For example, this might be achieved by macrohedging the duration gap, as described next. However, since reducing risk also reduces expected return and thus shareholder wealth, not all FI managers seek to do this. Indeed, a manager would follow this strategy only if the direction and size of interest rate changes were extremely unpredictable to the extent that the manager was willing to forgo return

FIGURE 22–2
The Effects of Hedging on Risk and Expected Return

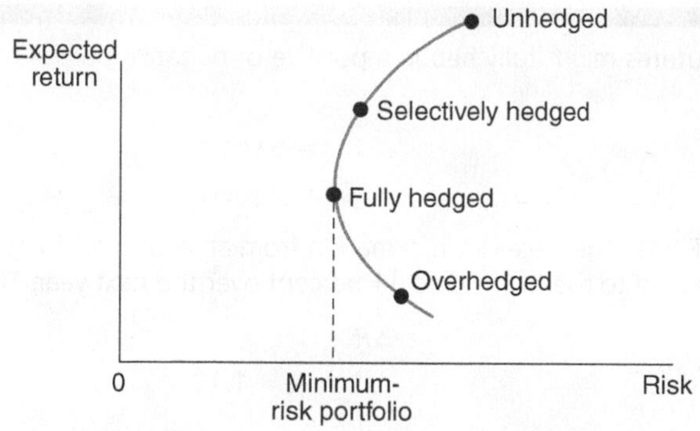

to hedge this risk. Figure 22–2 shows the trade-off between expected return and risk and the minimum-risk fully hedged portfolio.[7]

hedging selectively
Only partially hedging the duration gap or individual assets and liabilities.

Rather than a fully hedged position, most FIs choose to bear some interest rate risk as well as credit and FX risks because of their comparative advantage as FIs (see Chapter 1). One possibility is that an FI may choose to **hedge selectively** its portfolio. For example, an FI manager may generate expectations regarding future interest rates before deciding on a futures position. As a result, the manager may selectively hedge only a proportion of its balance sheet position. Alternatively, the FI manager may decide to remain unhedged or even to overhedge by selling more futures than required by the cash position, although regulators may view this as speculative. Thus, the fully hedged position—and the minimum-risk portfolio—become one of several choices depending, in part, on managerial interest rate expectations, managerial objectives, and the nature of the return–risk trade-off from hedging. Finally, an FI may selectively hedge in an attempt to arbitrage profits between a spot asset's price movements and movements in a futures price.

Macrohedging with Futures

The number of futures contracts that an FI should buy or sell in a macrohedge depends on the size and direction of its interest rate risk exposure and the return–risk trade-off from fully or selectively hedging that risk. Chapter 9 showed that an FI's net worth exposure to interest rate shocks was directly related to its leverage-adjusted duration gap as well as its asset size. Again, this is

$$\Delta E = -(D_A - kD_L) \times A \times \frac{\Delta R}{1 + R}$$

where

ΔE = Change in an FI's net worth
D_A = Duration of its asset portfolio
D_L = Duration of its liability portfolio
k = Ratio of an FI's liabilities to assets (L/A)
A = Size of an FI's asset portfolio
$\frac{\Delta R}{1 + R}$ = Shock to interest rates

[7] The minimum-risk portfolio is not shown as zero here because of basis risk (discussed below), which prevents perfect hedging. In the absence of basis risk, a zero-risk position becomes possible.

EXAMPLE 22-1

Calculation of Change in FI Net Worth as Interest Rates Rise

To see how futures might fully hedge a positive or negative portfolio duration gap, consider the FI where

$$D_A = 5 \text{ years}$$
$$D_L = 3 \text{ years}$$

Suppose the FI manager receives information from an economic forecasting unit that interest rates are expected to rise from 10 to 11 percent over the next year. That is,

$$\Delta R = 1\% = 0.01$$
$$1 + R = 1.10$$

The FI's initial balance sheet follows:

Assets ($ millions)	Liabilities ($ millions)
$A = \$100$	$L = \$\ 90$
	$E = \ \ 10$
$100	$100

so that $k = L/A = 90/100 = 0.9$.

The FI manager wants to calculate the potential loss to the FI's net worth (E) if the forecast of rising rates proves to be true. As we showed in Chapter 9,

$$\Delta E = -(D_A - kD_L) \times A \times \frac{\Delta R}{1 + R}$$

so that

$$\Delta E = -[5 - (0.9)(3)] \times \$100 \times \frac{0.01}{1.1} = -\$2.091$$

The FI could expect to lose $2.091 million in net worth if the interest rate forecast turns out to be correct. Since the FI started with a net worth of $10 million, the loss of $2.091 million is almost 21 percent of its initial net worth position. Clearly, as this example illustrates, the effect of the rise in interest rates could be quite threatening to the FI and its insolvency risk exposure.

The Risk-Minimizing Futures Position

The FI manager's objective to fully hedge the balance sheet exposure would be fulfilled by constructing a futures position such that if interest rates do rise by 1 percent to 11 percent, as in the prior example, the FI will make a gain on the futures position that just offsets the loss of balance sheet net worth of $2.091 million.

When interest rates rise, the price of a futures contract falls since its price reflects the value of the underlying bond that is deliverable against the contract. The amount by which a bond price falls when interest rates rise depends on its duration. Thus, we expect the price of the 20-year T-bond futures contract to be more sensitive to interest rate changes than the price of the 3-month T-bill futures contract, since the former futures price reflects the price of the 20-year T-bond deliverable on contract maturity. Thus, the sensitivity of the price of a futures contract depends on the duration of the deliverable bond underlying the contract, or

$$\frac{\Delta F}{F} = -D_F \times \frac{\Delta R}{1 + R}$$

where

ΔF = Change in dollar value of futures contracts
F = Dollar value of the initial futures contracts
D_F = Duration of the bond to be delivered against the futures contracts, such as a 20-year, 8 percent coupon T-bond
ΔR = Expected shock to interest rates
$1 + R$ = 1 plus the current level of interest rates

This can be rewritten as

$$\Delta F = -D_F \times F \times \frac{\Delta R}{1 + R}$$

The left side of this expression (ΔF) shows the dollar gain or loss on a futures position when interest rates change.

To see this dollar gain or loss more clearly, we can decompose the initial dollar value position in futures contracts, F, into its two component parts:

$$F = N_F \times P_F$$

The dollar value of the outstanding futures position depends on the number of contracts bought or sold (N_F) and the price of each contract (P_F). N_F is positive when the futures contracts are bought and is assigned a negative value when contracts are sold.

Futures contracts are homogeneous in size. Thus, futures exchanges sell U.S. T-bond futures in minimum units of \$100,000 of face value; that is, one T-bond future ($N_F = 1$) equals US\$100,000. U.S. T-bill futures are sold in larger minimum units: one T-bill future ($N_F = 1$) equals US\$1,000,000. The quote for each contract reported is the price per \$100 of face value for delivering the underlying bond. *The Wall Street Journal Online* reports end-of-day information for those futures contracts that are nearest to maturity and the most recent quotes for each type of interest rate futures contract. See, for example, the part of an interest rate futures quote retrieved from the website on September 21, 2012, shown in Figure 22–3. Looking at Figure 22–3, a price quote, or settle, of 146 28/32 on September 21, 2012, for the T-bond futures contract maturing in December 2012 means that the buyer locks in a purchase price for the underlying T-bonds of \$146,875 for one contract. That is, at maturity (in December 2012), the futures buyer would pay \$146,875 to the futures seller and the futures seller would deliver one \$100,000, 20-year, 8 percent T-bond to the futures buyer.[8] The subsequent profit or loss from a position in the December 2012 T-bond taken on September 21, 2012, is graphically described in Figure 22–4. A short position in the futures contract will produce a profit when interest rates rise (meaning that the value of the underlying T-bond decreases). Therefore, a short position in the futures market is the appropriate hedge when the FI stands to lose on the balance sheet if interest rates are expected to rise (e.g., the FI has a positive duration gap). A long position in the futures market produces a profit when interest rates fall (meaning that the value of the underlying T-bond increases).[9] Therefore,

---

[8] In practice, the futures price changes day to day, and gains or losses would be generated for the seller/buyer over the period between when the contract is entered into and when it matures. See our later discussion of this unique marking-to-market feature. Note that the FI could sell contracts in T-bonds maturing at later dates. However, while contracts exist for up to two years into the future, longer-term contracts tend to be infrequently traded and therefore relatively illiquid.

[9] Notice that if rates move opposite from that expected, losses are incurred on the futures position. That is, if rates rise and futures prices drop, the long hedger loses. Similarly, if rates fall and futures prices rise, the short hedger loses. However, such losses are offset by gains on their cash market positions. Thus, the hedger is still protected.

FIGURE 22–3 U.S. Futures Contracts on Interest Rates

Interest Rate Futures | Index | Agricultural | Currency | Metals & Petroleum

Friday, September 21, 2012

Treasury Bonds (CBT)-$100,000; pts 32nds of 100%

	OPEN	HIGH	LOW	SETTLE	CHG	LIFETIME HIGH	(▲▼)	LIFETIME LOW	OPEN INT
Dec 12	146–270	147–040	146–100	146–280	+5.0	154–170		133–200	544,847
Mar 13	145–060	145–210	145–060	145–190	+1.0	152–000		143–080	88

Eurodollar (CME)-$1,000,000; pts of 100%

	OPEN	HIGH	LOW	SETTLE	CHG	LIFETIME HIGH	(▲▼)	LIFETIME LOW	OPEN INT
Oct 12	99.6575	99.6650	99.6575	99.6625	+.0050	99.6800		99.3300	43,053
Nov 12	99.6600	99.6750	99.6600	99.6700	+.0050	99.6850		99.4350	6,159
Dec 12	99.6600	99.6800	99.6500	99.6750	+.0150	99.7100		99.2300	975,691
Mar 13	99.6500	99.6650	99.6400	99.6600	+.0100	99.7100		99.2350	843,769
Jun 13	99.6350	99.6450	99.6250	99.6350	...	99.6900		99.2250	716,912
Sep 13	99.6200	99.6300	99.6100	99.6200	...	99.6700		99.1700	646,903
Dec 13	99.5950	99.6050	99.5850	99.5950	...	99.6450		99.0500	689,197
Mar 14	99.5700	99.5800	99.5600	99.5750	+.0050	99.6200		98.9300	618,685
Jun 14	99.5300	99.5400	99.5150	99.5350	+.0050	99.5750		98.7950	479,843
Sep 14	99.4800	99.5000	99.4650	99.4900	+.0050	99.5250		98.6350	420,306
Dec 14	99.4200	99.4400	99.4050	99.4350	+.0100	99.4650		98.4400	421,721
Mar 15	99.3650	99.3900	99.3500	99.3800	+.0100	99.4150		98.2450	399,149
Jun 15	99.2850	99.3100	99.2650	99.3050	+.0150	99.3350		98.0350	499,138

Eurodollar (CME)-$1,000,000; pts of 100%

	OPEN	HIGH	LOW	SETTLE	CHG	LIFETIME HIGH	(▲▼)	LIFETIME LOW	OPEN INT
Sep 15	99.1750	99.2100	99.1450	99.2000	+.0200	99.2350		97.8400	315,681
Dec 15	99.0400	99.0800	99.0150	99.0650	+.0200	99.1050		97.6550	251,377
Mar 16	98.9000	98.9500	98.8800	98.9300	+.0200	98.9800		97.4400	178,599
Jun 16	98.7450	98.7950	98.7150	98.7800	+.0250	98.8350		97.3250	132,677
Sep 16	98.5850	98.6350	98.5550	98.6200	+.0300	98.6800		97.1700	114,475
Dec 16	98.4100	98.4650	98.3850	98.4500	+.0300	98.5350		97.0050	94,904
Mar 17	98.2600	98.3150	98.2250	98.2950	+.0300	98.4200		96.8700	75,633
Jun 17	98.1050	98.1550	98.0650	98.1350	+.0300	98.3050		96.7700	45,180
Sep 17	97.9550	98.0050	97.9200	97.9850	+.0250	98.1800		96.6250	28,478
Dec 17	97.8050	97.8500	97.7650	97.8300	+.0200	98.0600		96.5100	14,887

Source: The Wall Street Journal Online, September 21, 2012.

a long position is the appropriate hedge when the FI stands to lose on the balance sheet if interest rates are expected to fall (e.g., has a negative duration gap).

In actuality, the seller of the futures contract has a number of alternatives other than an 8 percent coupon, 30-year bond that can be delivered against the T-bond futures contract. If only one type of bond could be delivered, a shortage or squeeze might develop, making it very hard for the short side or seller to deliver. In fact, the seller has quite flexible delivery options; apart from delivering the 30-year, 8 percent coupon bond, the seller can deliver bonds that range in maturity from 15 years upward. Often, up to 25 different bonds may qualify for delivery. However, as futures markets grow, a shortage of deliverable bonds can occur. When a bond other than the 30-year benchmark bond is delivered, the buyer pays a different invoice price for the futures contract based on a **conversion factor** that calculates the price of the deliverable bond if it were to yield 8 percent divided by face value. Suppose $100,000 worth of 18-year, 6 percent semiannual coupon Treasury bonds were valued at a yield of 5.5 percent. This would produce a fair present value of the bond of approximately $105,667. The conversion factor for the bond would be 1.057 (or $105,667/$100,000). This means the buyer would have to pay the seller the

conversion factor
A factor used to figure out the invoice price on a futures contract when a bond other than the benchmark bond is delivered to the buyer.

FIGURE 22–4
Profit or Loss on a Futures Position in Treasury Bonds Taken on September 21, 2012

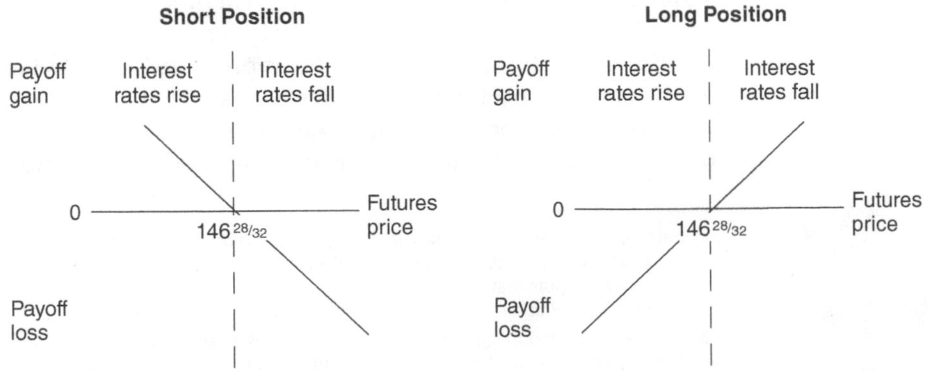

conversion factor of 1.057 times the published futures price of \$146,875. That is, the futures price would be \$155,198.41.[10]

We can now solve for the number of futures contracts to buy or sell to fully macrohedge an FI's on-balance-sheet interest rate risk exposure. We have shown the following:

1. *Loss on balance sheet.* The loss of net worth for an FI when rates rise is equal to

$$\Delta E = -(D_A - kD_L)A\frac{\Delta R}{1 + R}$$

2. *Gain off balance sheet on futures.* The gain off balance sheet from selling futures is equal to[11]

$$\Delta F = -D_F(N_F \times P_F)\frac{\Delta R}{1 + R}$$

Fully hedging can be defined as buying or selling a sufficient number of futures contracts (N_F) so that the loss of net worth on the balance sheet (ΔE) when interest rates change is just offset by the gain from OBS buying or selling of futures (ΔF), or

$$\Delta F + \Delta E = 0$$

Substituting in the appropriate expressions for each,

$$\left[-D_F(N_F \times P_F)\frac{\Delta R}{1 + R}\right] + \left[-(D_A - kD_L)A\frac{\Delta R}{1 + R}\right] = 0$$

Cancelling $\Delta R/(1 + R)$ on both sides,[12]

$$D_F(N_F \times P_F) + (D_A - kD_L)A = 0$$

Solving for N_F (the number of futures to sell),

$$N_F = \frac{-(D_A - kD_L)A}{D_F \times P_F}$$

Appendix 22A derives the equation and provides an example for the number of futures contracts to buy or sell for a microhedge.

For a microhedge, this equation becomes

$$N_F = \frac{-D \times P}{D_F \times P_F}$$

where P is the price of the asset or liability being hedged and D is its duration.

Short Hedge

An FI takes a short position in a futures contract when rates are expected to rise; that is, the FI loses net worth on its balance sheet if rates rise, so it seeks to hedge the value of its net worth by selling an appropriate number of futures contracts.

---

[10] In practice, the seller exploits the delivery option by choosing the cheapest bond to deliver, that is, bonds whose conversion factor is most favourable (being based on an 8 percent yield) relative to the true price of the bond to be delivered (which reflects the actual level of yields).

[11] When futures prices fall, the buyer of the contract compensates the seller, here the FI. Thus, the FI gains when the prices of futures fall.

[12] This amounts to assuming that the interest changes of the cash asset position match those of the futures position; that is, there is no basis risk. This assumption is relaxed later.

EXAMPLE 22-2

Macrohedge of Interest Rate Risk Using a Short Hedge

From the equation for N_F, we can now solve for the correct number of futures positions to sell (N_F) in the context of Example 22–1, where the FI was exposed to a balance sheet loss of net worth (ΔE) amounting to \$2.091 million when interest rates rose. In that example,

$$D_A = 5 \text{ years}$$
$$D_L = 3 \text{ years}$$
$$k = 0.9$$
$$A = \$100 \text{ million}$$

Suppose the current futures price quote is \$97 per \$100 of face value for the benchmark 20-year, 8 percent coupon bond underlying the nearby futures contract; the minimum contract size is \$100,000; and the duration of the deliverable bond is 9.5 years. That is,

$$D_F = 9.5 \text{ years}$$
$$P_F = \$97{,}000$$

Inserting these numbers into the expression for N_F, we can now solve for the number of futures to sell:[13]

$$N_F = \frac{-[5 - (0.9)(3)] \times \$100 \text{ million}}{9.5 \times \$97{,}000}$$
$$= \frac{-\$230{,}000{,}000}{\$921{,}500}$$
$$= -249.59 \text{ contracts}$$

When $N_F < 0$, then contracts should be shorted, or sold.

Since the FI cannot sell a part of a contract, the number of contracts should be rounded down to the nearest whole number, or 249 contracts.[14] Note that the hedging formula simply gives the number of futures contracts to use in the hedge. If the FI is hedging a loss on the balance sheet as interest rates rise, the futures position to take is a short one (i.e., $N_F < 0$). As interest rates rise (and losses occur on the balance sheet, the value of the futures contracts falls and the FI makes a profit on the short position to offset the on-balance-sheet losses. If the Fi is hedging a loss on the balance sheet as interest rates fall, the futures position to take is a long one (i.e., $N_F > 0$). As interest rates fall (and losses occur on the balance sheet), the value of the futures contracts rises, and the FI makes a profit on the long position to offset the on-balance-sheet losses.

Next, we verify that selling 249 T-bond futures contracts will indeed hedge the FI against a sudden increase in interest rates from 10 to 11 percent, or a 1 percent interest rate shock.

On Balance Sheet

As shown above, when interest rates rise by 1 percent, the FI loses \$2.091 million in net worth (ΔE) on the balance sheet:

$$\Delta E = -(D_A - kD_L)A\frac{\Delta R}{1 + R}$$
$$= -[5 - (0.9)(3)] \times \$100{,}000{,}000 \times \left(\frac{0.01}{1.1}\right)$$
$$= -\$2{,}091{,}000$$

[13] Also note that if the FI intends to deliver any bond other than the 20-year benchmark bond, the P_F has to be multiplied by the appropriate conversion factor (c). If c = 1.19, then $P_F = 97 \times 1.19 = \$115.43$ per \$100 of face value and the invoice price per contract is \$115,430.

[14] The reason for rounding down rather than rounding up is technical. The target number of contracts to sell is that which minimizes interest rate risk exposure. By slightly underhedging rather than overhedging, the FI can generate the same risk exposure level but the underhedging policy produces a slightly higher return (see Figure 22–2).

TABLE 22–3 On- and Off-Balance-Sheet Effects of a Microhedge Hedge

	On Balance Sheet	Off Balance Sheet
Begin hedge t = 0	Equity value of \$10 million exposed to impact of rise in interest rates.	Sell 249.59 T-bond futures contracts at \$97,000. Underlying T-bond coupon rate is 8%.
End hedge t = 1 day	Interest rates rise on assets and liabilities by 1%.	Buy 249.59 T-bond futures (closes out futures position).
	Opportunity loss on balance sheet:	Real gain on futures hedge:
	$\Delta E = -[5 - 0.9(3)] \times \$100{,}000{,}000 \times \frac{0.01}{1.1}$	$\Delta F = -9.5 \times (-249.59 \times \$97{,}000) \times \frac{0.01^{*}}{1.1}$
	$= -\$2.091$ million	$= \$2.091$ million

*Assuming no basis risk and no contract "rounding."

Off Balance Sheet

When interest rates rise by 1 percent, the change in the value of the futures position is

$$\Delta F = -D_F(N_F \times P_F)\frac{\Delta R}{1 + R}$$

$$= -9.5(-249 \times \$97{,}000)\left(\frac{0.01}{1.1}\right)$$

$$= \$2{,}086{,}000$$

The value of the OBS futures position (ΔF) falls by \$2.086 million when the FI sells 249 futures contracts in the T-bond futures market. Such a fall in value of the futures contracts means a positive cash flow to the futures seller as the buyer compensates the seller for a lower futures price through the marking-to-market process. This requires a cash flow from the buyer's margin account to the seller's margin account as the price of a futures contract falls.[15] Thus, as the seller of the futures, the FI gains \$2.086 million. As a result, the net gain/loss on and off the balance sheet is

$$\Delta E + \Delta F = -\$2.091 \text{ million} + \$2.086 \text{ million} = -\$0.005 \text{ million}$$

This small remaining net loss of \$0.005 million to equity or net worth reflects the fact that the FI could not achieve the perfect hedge—even in the absence of basis risk—as it needed to round down the number of futures to the nearest whole contract from 249.59 to 249 contracts. Table 22–3 summarizes the key features of the hedge (assuming no rounding of futures contracts).

Suppose instead of using the 20-year T-bond futures to hedge, it had used the three-month eurodollar futures. We can use the same formula to solve for N_F in the case of eurodollar futures:

$$N_F = \frac{-(D_A - kD_L)A}{D_F \times P_F}$$

$$= \frac{-[5 - (0.9)(3)]\ \$100 \text{ million}}{D_F \times P_F}$$

[15] An example of marking to market might clarify how the seller gains when the price of the futures contract falls. Suppose on day 1 the seller entered into a 90-day contract to deliver 20-year T-bonds at $P = \$97$. The next day, because of a rise in interest rates, the futures contract, which now has 89 days to maturity, is trading at \$96 when the market closes. Marking to market requires the prices on all contracts entered into on the previous day(s) to be marked to market at each night's closing (settlement) price. As a result, the price of the contract is lowered to \$96 per \$100 of face value, but in return for this lowering of the price from \$97 to \$96, the buyer has to compensate the seller to the tune of \$1 per \$100 of face value. Thus, given a \$100,000 contract, there is a cash flow payment of \$1,000 on that day from the buyer to the seller. Note that if the price had risen to \$98, the seller would have had to compensate the buyer \$1,000. The marking-to-market process goes on until the futures contract matures. If, over the period, futures prices have mostly fallen, then the seller accumulates positive cash flows on the futures position. It is this accumulation of cash flows that can be set off against losses in net worth on the balance sheet.

Assume that P_F = \$97 per \$100 of face value or \$970,000 per contract (the minimum contract size of a eurodollar future is \$1,000,000) and $D_F = 0.25$ (the duration of a three-month eurodollar deposit, that is, the discount instrument deliverable under the contract).[16] Then

$$N_F = \frac{-[5 - (0.9)(3)]\,\$100{,}000{,}000}{0.25 \times \$970{,}000} = \frac{-\$230{,}000{,}000}{\$242{,}500}$$

$$N_F = -948.45 \text{ contracts, or sell } 948.45 \text{ contracts}$$

Rounding down to the nearest whole contract, $N_F = 948$.

As this example illustrates, we can hedge an FI's on-balance-sheet interest rate risk when its $D_A > kD_L$ by shorting or selling either T-bond or eurodollar futures. In general, fewer T-bond than eurodollar contracts need to be sold—in our case, 948 eurodollar versus 249 T-bond contracts. This suggests that on a simple transaction cost basis, the FI might normally prefer to use T-bond futures. However, other considerations can be important, especially if the FI holds the futures contracts until the delivery date. The FI needs to be concerned about the availability of the deliverable set of securities and any possible supply shortages or squeezes. Such liquidity concerns may favour eurodollars.[17]

The Problem of Basis Risk

LO4

Because spot bonds and futures on bonds are traded in different markets, the shift in yields, $\Delta R/(1 + R)$, affecting the values of the on-balance-sheet cash portfolio may differ from the shift in yields, $\Delta R_F/(1 + R_F)$, affecting the value of the underlying bond in the futures contract; that is, changes in spot and futures prices or values are not perfectly correlated. This lack of perfect correlation is called *basis risk*. In the previous section, we assumed a simple world of no basis risk in which $\Delta R/(1 + R) = \Delta R_F/(1 + R_F)$.

Basis risk occurs for two reasons. First, the balance sheet asset or liability being hedged is not the same as the underlying security on the futures contract. For instance, in Example 22–2 we hedged interest rate changes on the FI's entire balance sheet with T-bond futures contracts written on 20-year-maturity bonds with a duration of 9.5 years. The interest rates on the various assets and liabilities on the FI's balance sheet and the interest rates on 20-year T-bonds do not move in a perfectly correlated (or one-to-one) manner. The second source of basis risk comes from the difference in movements in spot rates versus futures rates. Because spot securities (e.g., government bonds) and futures contracts (e.g., on the same bonds) are traded in different markets, the shift in spot rates may differ from the shift in futures rates (i.e., they are not perfectly correlated).

To solve for the risk-minimizing number of futures contracts to buy or sell, N_F, while accounting for greater or less rate volatility and hence price volatility in the

---

[16] We assume the same futures price (\$97) here for purposes of comparison. Of course, the actual prices of the two futures contracts are very different.

[17] However, when rates change, the loss of net worth on the balance sheet and the gain on selling the futures are instantaneous; therefore, delivery need not be a concern. Indeed, because of the daily marking-to-market process, an FI manager can close out a futures position by taking an exactly offsetting position. That is, a manager who had originally sold 100 futures contracts could close out a position on any day by buying 100 contracts. Because of the unique marking-to-market feature, the marked-to-market price of the contracts sold equals the price of any new contracts bought on that day.

futures market relative to the spot or cash market, we look again at the FI's on-balance-sheet interest rate exposure:

$$\Delta E = -(D_A - kD_L) \times A \times \Delta R/(1 + R)$$

and its OBS futures position:

$$\Delta F = -D_F(N_F \times P_F) \times \Delta R_F/(1 + R_F)$$

Setting

$$\Delta E + \Delta F = 0$$

and solving for N_F, we have

$$N_F = \frac{-(D_A - kD_L) \times A \times \Delta R/(1 + R)}{D_F \times P_F \times \Delta R_F/(1 + R_F)}$$

Let *br* reflect the relative sensitivity of rates underlying the bond in the futures market relative to interest rates on assets and liabilities in the spot market; that is, $br = [\Delta R_F/(1 + R_F)]/[\Delta R/(1 + R)]$. Then the number of futures contracts to buy or sell is

$$N_F = \frac{-(D_A - kD_L)A}{D_F \times P_F \times br}$$

The only difference between this and the previous formula is an adjustment for basis risk (*br*), which measures the degree to which the futures price (yield) moves more or less than spot bond price (yield).

EXAMPLE 22-3

Macrohedging Interest Rate Risk When Basis Risk Exists

From Example 22–2, let $br = 1.1$. This means that for every 1 percent change in discounted spot rates $[\Delta R/(1 + R)]$, the implied rate on the deliverable bond in the futures market moves by 1.1 percent. That is, futures prices are more sensitive to interest rate shocks than are spot market prices. Solving for N_F, we have

$$N_F = \frac{-[5 - (0.9)(3)] \times \$100 \text{ million}}{9.5 \times \$97{,}000 \times 1.1}$$

$$= -226.9 \text{ contracts, or sell 226.9 contracts}$$

or 226 contracts, rounding down. This compares to 249 when we assumed equal rate shocks in both the cash and futures markets $[\Delta R/(1 + R) = \Delta R_F/(1 + R_F)]$. Here we need fewer futures contracts than was the case when we ignored basis risk because futures rates and prices are more volatile, so that selling fewer futures is sufficient to provide the same ΔF (the value of the futures position) than before when we implicitly assumed $br = 1$. Note that if futures rates or prices had been less volatile than spot rates or prices, we would have had to sell more than 249 contracts to get the same dollar gain in the futures position as was lost in net worth on the balance sheet so that $\Delta E + \Delta F = 0$.

An important issue FIs must deal with in hedging interest rate and other risks is how to estimate the basis risk adjustment in the preceding formula. One method is to look at the ratio between $\Delta R/(1 + R)$ and $\Delta R_F/(1 + R_F)$ today. Since this is only one observation, the FI might better analyze the relationship between the two interest rates by investigating their relative behaviour in the recent past. We can do this by running an ordinary least-squares (OLS) linear regression of implied futures rate changes on spot rate changes with the slope coefficient of this regression giving an estimate of the degree of comovement of the two rates over time. We discuss this regression procedure in greater detail next in connection with calculating basis risk when hedging with FX futures.[18]

CONCEPT QUESTIONS

1. **Compare microhedging to macrohedging and routine hedging to selective hedging.**
2. **In Example 22–2, suppose the FI had the reverse duration gap; that is, the duration of its assets was shorter (D_A = 3) than the duration of its liabilities (D_L = 5). (This might be the case of a bank that borrows with long-term notes or time deposits to finance floating-rate loans.) How should it hedge using futures?**
3. **In Example 22–3, how many futures contracts should have been sold using the 20-year bond and 3-month eurodollar contracts, if the basis risk measured *br* = 0.8?**

HEDGING FOREIGN EXCHANGE RISK

LO5

Just as forwards and futures can hedge an FI against losses due to interest rate changes, they also can hedge against FX risk.

Forwards

Chapter 13 analyzed how an FI uses forward contracts to reduce the risks due to FX fluctuations when it mismatches the sizes of its foreign asset and liability portfolios. That chapter considered the simple case of an FI that raised all its liabilities in dollars while investing half of its assets in U.K. pound sterling–denominated loans and the other half in dollar-denominated loans. Its balance sheet looks as follows:

Assets	Liabilities
CDN loans ($) $100 million	CDN GICs $200 million
U.K. loans (£) $100 million	

All assets and liabilities are of a one-year maturity and duration. Because the FI is net long in pound sterling assets, it faces the risk that over the period of the loan, the pound will depreciate against the dollar so that the proceeds of the pound loan (along with the dollar loan) will be insufficient to meet the required payments on the maturing dollar GICs. Then the FI will have to meet such losses out of its net worth; that is, its insolvency risk will increase.

Chapter 13 showed that by selling both the pound loan principal and interest forward one year at the known forward exchange rate at the beginning of the year, the FI could hedge itself against losses on its pound loan position due to changes in the dollar/pound exchange rate over the succeeding year. Note the strategy for hedging (£100 million) of U.K. pound sterling loans with forwards in Figure 22–5.

[18] Another problem with the simple duration gap approach to determining N_F is that it is assumed that yield curves are flat. This could be relaxed by using duration measures that allow for nonflat yield curves (see Chapter 9).

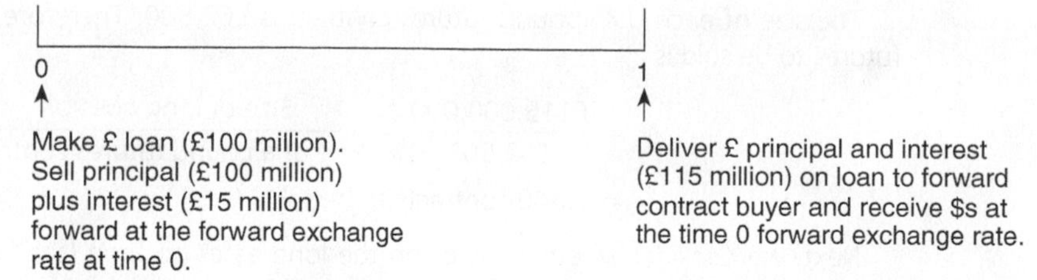
0
1
Make £ loan (£100 million).
Sell principal (£100 million)
plus interest (£15 million)
forward at the forward exchange
rate at time 0.
Deliver £ principal and interest
(£115 million) on loan to forward
contract buyer and receive $s at
the time 0 forward exchange rate.

FIGURE 22–5
Hedging a Long Position in Pound Assets through Sale of Pound Forwards

Futures

Instead of using FX forward contracts to hedge FX risk, the FI could use FX futures contracts. Consider an FI wishing to hedge a one-year U.K. pound loan of £100 million principal plus £15 million interest (or £115 million) against the risk of the pound falling in value against the dollar over the succeeding year. Suppose the FI wished to hedge this loan position on September 24, 2014, via the futures markets. How many futures should it sell? The answer to this question is that it should sell the amount that produces a sufficient profit on the pound futures contracts to just offset any exchange rate losses on the pound loan portfolio should the pound fall in value relative to the dollar. There are two cases to consider:

1. The futures dollar/pound price is expected to change in exactly the same fashion as the spot dollar/pound price over the course of the year. That is, futures and spot price changes are perfectly correlated; there is no basis risk.
2. Futures and spot prices, though expected to change in the same direction, are not perfectly correlated (there is basis risk).

EXAMPLE 22–4

Hedging FX Risk Assuming Perfect Correlation between Spot and Futures Prices

Suppose on September 24, 2014,

S_t = Spot exchange rate (\$/£): \$1.6230 per £1

f_t = Futures price (\$/£) for the contract expiring in September 2015 (in approximately one year): \$1.6215 per £1

Suppose the FI made a £100 million loan at 15 percent interest and wished to fully hedge the risk that the dollar value of the proceeds would be eroded by a declining U.K. pound sterling over the year. Also suppose that the FI manager receives a forecast that in one year's time the spot and futures will be

$$S_{t+1} = \$1.5730 \text{ per } £1$$
$$f_{t+1} = \$1.5715 \text{ per } £1$$

so that over the year,

$$\Delta S_t = -5 \text{ cents}$$
$$\Delta f_t = -5 \text{ cents}$$

For a manager who believes this forecast of a depreciating pound against the dollar, the correct full-hedge strategy is to cover the £115 million of expected earnings on the U.K. loan by selling, or shorting, £115 million of U.K. pound futures contracts on September 24, 2014. We assume here that the FI manager continuously rolls over the futures position into new futures contracts and will get out of futures on September 24, 2015.

The size of each U.K. pound futures contract is £62,500. Therefore, the number (N_F) of futures to be sold is

$$N_F = \frac{£115{,}000{,}000}{£62{,}500} = \frac{\text{Size of long position}}{\text{Size of a pound futures contract}}$$
$$= 1{,}840 \text{ contracts to be sold}$$

Next, we consider whether losses on the long asset position (the U.K. loan) would just offset gains on the futures should the FI sell 1,840 U.K. pound futures contracts if spot and futures prices change in the direction and amount expected.

Loss on U.K. Pound Loan

The loss on the U.K. pound loan in dollars would be

$$[£ \text{ Principal} + \text{Interest}] \times \Delta S_t = [£115 \text{ million}] \times [\$1.6230/£ - \$1.5730/£]$$
$$= \$5.75 \text{ million}$$

That is, the dollar value of the U.K. pound loan proceeds would be $5.75 million less should the pound depreciate from $1.6230/£1 to $1.5730/£1 in the spot market over the year.

Gain on Futures Contracts

The gain on the futures contracts would be

$$[N_F \times £62{,}500] \times \Delta f_t = [1{,}840 \times £62{,}500] \times [\$1.6215/£ - \$1.5715/£]$$
$$= \$5.75 \text{ million}$$

By selling 1,840 futures contracts of 62,500 each, the seller makes $5.75 million as the futures price falls from $1.6215/£ at the contract initiation on September 24, 2014, to $1.5715/£ at the futures position termination on September 24, 2015. This cash flow of $5.75 million results from the marking to market of the futures contract. As the futures price falls, due to the daily marking to market, the pound futures contract buyer has the contract repriced to a lower level in dollars to be paid per pound. But the seller must be compensated from the buyer's margin account for the difference between the original contract price and the new lower marked-to-market contract price. Thus, over the one year, the buyer compensates the seller by a net of 5 cents per £1 of futures purchased, that is, $1.6215/£ minus $1.5715/£ as the futures price falls, or a total of 5 cents × the number of contracts (1,840) × the pound size of each contract (£62,500). Note that on September 24, 2015, when the principal and interest on the pound loan are paid by the borrower, the FI seller of the pound futures terminates its position in 1,840 short contracts by taking an opposing position of 1,840 long in the same contract. This effectively ends any net cash flow implications from futures positions beyond this date.

tail the hedge
Reduce the number of futures contracts that are needed to hedge a cash position because of the interest income that is generated from reinvesting the marked-to-market cash flows generated by the futures contract.

Finally, in this example, we have ignored the interest income effects of marking to market. In reality, the $5.75 million from the futures position would be received by the FI seller over the course of the year. As a result, this cash flow can be reinvested at the current short-term dollar interest rate to generate a cash flow of more than $5.75 million. Given this, an FI hedger can sell slightly fewer contracts in anticipation of this interest income. The number of futures that could be sold, below the 1,840 suggested, would depend on the level and pattern of short-term rates over the hedging horizon as well as the precise expected pattern of cash flows from marking to market. In general, the higher the level of short-term interest, the more an FI manager could **tail the hedge** in this fashion.[19]

[19] One way to do this is to discount the calculated hedge ratio (the optimal number of futures to sell per $1 of cash position) by a short-term interest rate such as the Bank of Canada's overnight rate.

EXAMPLE 22-5

Hedging FX Risk Assuming Imperfect Correlation between Spot and Futures Prices (Basis Risk)

Suppose, instead, the FI manager did not believe that the spot exchange rate and futures price on the dollar/pound contract would fall by exactly the same amount. Instead, let the forecast for one year's time be

$$S_{t+1} = 1.5730/£$$
$$f_{t+1} = \$1.5915/£$$

Thus, in expectation, over the succeeding year,

$$\Delta S_t = -5 \text{ cents}$$
$$\Delta f_t = -3 \text{ cents}$$

This means that the dollar/pound futures price is expected to depreciate less than the spot dollar/pound. This basis risk arises because spot and futures contracts are traded in different markets with different demand and supply functions. Given this, even though futures and spot prices are normally highly correlated, this correlation is often less than 1.

Because futures prices and spot prices do not always move exactly together, this can create a problem for an FI manager seeking to hedge the long position of £115 million with pound futures. Suppose the FI manager ignored the fact that the spot pound is expected to depreciate faster against the dollar than the futures price for pounds and continued to believe that selling 1,840 contracts would be the best hedge. That manager could be in for a big (and nasty) surprise in one year's time. To see this, consider the loss on the cash asset position and the gain on the futures position under a new scenario where the dollar/pound spot rate falls by 2 cents more than dollar/pound futures over the year.

Loss on U.K. Pound Loan

The expected fall in the spot value of the pound by 5 cents over the year results in a loss of

$$[£115 \text{ million}] \times [\$1.6230/£ - \$1.5730/£] = \$5.75 \text{ million}$$

Gain on Futures Position

The expected gain on the futures position is

$$[1{,}840 \times £62{,}500] \times [\$1.6215/£ - \$1.5915/£] = \$3.45 \text{ million}$$

Thus, the net loss to the FI is

$$\text{Net loss} = \text{Loss on U.K. pound loan} - \text{Gain on U.K. pound futures}$$
$$\text{Net loss} = \$5.75 \text{ million} - \$3.45 \text{ million}$$
$$\text{Net loss} = \$2.3 \text{ million}$$

Such a loss would have to be charged against the FI's profits and implicitly its net worth or equity. As a result, the FI manager needs to take into account the lower sensitivity of futures prices relative to spot exchange rate changes by selling more than 1,840 futures contracts to fully hedge the U.K. pound loan risk.

To see how many more contracts are required, we need to know how much more sensitive spot exchange rates are than futures prices. Let h be the ratio of ΔS_t to Δf_t:

$$h = \frac{\Delta S_t}{\Delta f_t}$$

Then, in our example,

$$h = \frac{\$0.05}{\$0.03} = 1.66$$

hedge ratio
The dollar value of futures contracts that should be sold per dollar of cash position exposure.

That is, spot rates are 66 percent more sensitive than futures prices, or—put slightly differently—for every 1 percent change in futures prices, spot rates change by 1.66 percent.[20] An FI manager could use this ratio, *h*, as a **hedge ratio** to solve the question of how many futures should be sold to hedge the long position in the U.K. pound when the spot and futures prices are imperfectly correlated. Specifically, the value of *h* means that for every £1 in the long asset position, £1.66 in futures contracts should be sold. To see this, look at the FI's losses on its long asset position in pound loans relative to the gains on its selling pound futures.

Loss on U.K. Pound Loans
As before, its losses are

$$[£115 \text{ million}] \times [\$1.6230/£ - \$1.5730/£] = \$5.75 \text{ million}$$

Gains on U.K. Pound Futures Position
Taking into account the degree to which spot exchange rates are more sensitive than futures prices—the hedge ratio (*h*)—we can solve for the number of futures (N_F) to sell as

$$N_F = \frac{\text{Long asset position} \times h}{\text{Size of one futures contract}}$$

$$N_F = \frac{£115 \text{ million} \times 1.66}{£62{,}500} = 3{,}054.4 \text{ contracts}$$

or, rounding down to the nearest whole contract, 3,054 contracts. Selling 3,054 U.K. pound futures results in expected profits of

$$[3{,}054 \times £62{,}500] \times [\$1.6215/£ - \$1.5915/£] = \$5.73 \text{ million}$$

The difference of $0.02 million between the loss on British pound loans and the gain on the pound futures is due to rounding.

Estimating the Hedge Ratio

The previous example showed that the number of FX futures that should be sold to fully hedge FX rate risk exposure depends crucially on expectations regarding the correlation between the change in the dollar/pound spot rate (ΔS_t) and the change in its futures price (Δf_t). When

$$h = \frac{\Delta S_t}{\Delta f_t} = \frac{\$0.05}{\$0.05} = 1$$

there is no basis risk. Both the spot and the futures are expected to change together by the same absolute amount, and the FX risk of the cash position should be hedged dollar for dollar by selling FX futures. When basis risk is present, the spot and future exchange rates are expected to move imperfectly together:

$$h = \frac{\Delta S_t}{\Delta f_t} = \frac{\$0.05}{\$0.03} = 1.66$$

The FI must sell a greater number of futures than it has to when basis risk is absent.

Unfortunately, without perfect foresight, we cannot know exactly how exchange rates and futures prices will change over some future time period. If we did, we

[20] Expressed the other way around: A 1 percent change in spot prices leads, on average, to only a 0.6 percent change in futures prices.

FIGURE 22–6
Hypothetical Monthly Changes in ΔS_t and Δf_t in 2016

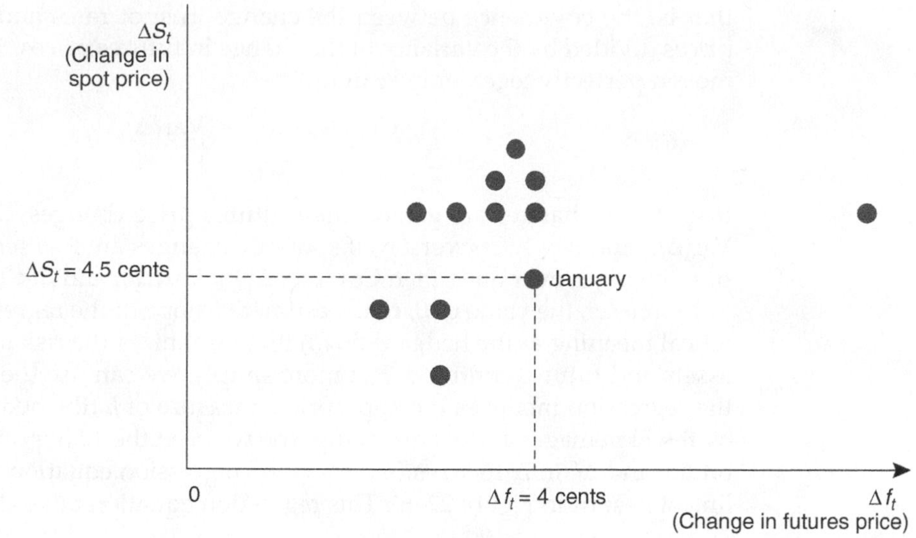

would have no need to hedge in the first place! Thus, a common method to calculate h is to look at the behaviour of ΔS_t relative to Δf_t over the *recent past* and to use this past behaviour as a prediction of the appropriate value of h in the future. One way to estimate this past relationship is to run an OLS regression of recent changes in spot prices on recent changes in futures prices.[21]

Consider Figure 22–6, where we plot hypothetical monthly changes in the spot pound/dollar exchange rate (ΔS_t) against monthly changes in the futures pound/dollar price (Δf_t) for 2016. Thus, we have 12 observations from January through December. For information purposes, the first observation (January) is labelled in Figure 22–6. In January, the dollar/pound spot rate rose by 4.5 cents and the dollar/pound futures price rose by 4 cents. Thus, the pound appreciated in value over the month of January but the spot exchange rate rose by more than the futures price did. In some other months, as implied by the scatter of points in Figure 22–6, the futures price rose by more than the spot rate did.

An OLS regression fits a line of best fit to these monthly observations such that the sum of the squared deviations between the observed values of ΔS_t and its predicted values (as given by the line of best fit) is minimized. This line of best fit reflects an intercept term α and a slope coefficient β. That is,

$$\Delta S_t = \alpha + \beta\, \Delta f_t + u_t$$

where the u_t are the regression's residuals (the differences between actual values of ΔS_t and its predicted values based on the line of best fit).

By definition, β, or the slope coefficient, of the regression equation is equal to

$$\beta = \frac{\text{Cov}(\Delta S_t, \Delta f_t)}{\text{Var}(\Delta f_t)}$$

[21] When we calculate h (the hedge ratio), we could use the ratio of the most recent spot and futures price changes. However, this would amount to basing our hedge ratio estimate on one observation of the change in S_t and f_t. This is why the regression model, which uses many past observations, is usually preferred by market participants.

that is, the covariance between the change in spot rates and change in futures prices divided by the variance of the change in futures prices. Suppose ΔS_t and Δf_t moved perfectly together over time. Then

$$\text{Cov}(\Delta S_t, \Delta f_t) = \text{Var}(\Delta f_t)$$
$$\text{and } \beta = 1$$

If spot rate changes are greater than futures price changes, then $\text{Cov}(\Delta S_t, \Delta f_t) > \text{Var}(\Delta f_t)$ and $\beta > 1$. Conversely, if spot rate changes are less sensitive than futures price changes over time, then $\text{Cov}(\Delta S_t, \Delta f_t) < \text{Var}(\Delta f_t)$ and $\beta < 1$.

Moreover, the value of β, or the estimated slope of the regression line, has theoretical meaning as the hedge ratio (h) that minimizes the risk of a portfolio of spot assets and futures contracts. Put more simply, we can use the estimate of β from the regression model as the appropriate measure of h (the hedge ratio) to be used by the FI manager. For example, suppose we used the 12 hypothetical observations on ΔS_t and Δf_t in 2016 to estimate an OLS regression equation (the equation of the line of best fit in Figure 22–6). This regression equation takes the form

$$\Delta S_t = 0.15 + 1.2\,\Delta f_t$$

Thus,

$$\alpha = 0.15$$
$$\beta = 1.2$$

Using $\beta = 1.2$ as the appropriate risk-minimizing hedge ratio h for the portfolio manager, we can solve our earlier problem of determining the number of futures contracts to sell to protect the FI from FX losses on its £115 million loan:

$$N_F = \frac{\text{Long position in £ assets} \times \beta \text{ (estimated value of the hedge ratio } h \text{ using past data)}}{\text{Size of one £ futures contract}}$$

$$N_F = \frac{\text{£115 million} \times 1.2}{\text{£62,500}} = 2{,}208 \text{ contracts}$$

Thus, using the past relationship between ΔS_t and Δf_t as the best predictor of their future relationship over the succeeding year dictates that the FI manager sell 2,208 contracts.

The degree of confidence the FI manager may have in using such a method to determine the appropriate hedge ratio depends on how well the regression line fits the scatter of observations. The standard measure of the goodness of fit of a regression line is the R^2 value of the equation, or the square of the correlation coefficient between ΔS_t and Δf_t:

$$R^2 = \rho^2 = \left\{ \frac{[\text{Cov}(\Delta S_t, \Delta f_t)]}{\sigma_{\Delta S_t} \times \sigma_{\Delta f_t}} \right\}^2$$

The term in curly brackets is the statistical definition of a correlation coefficient. If changes in the spot rate (ΔS_t) and changes in the futures price (Δf_t) are perfectly correlated, then

$$R^2 = \rho^2 = (1)^2 = 1$$

and all observations between ΔS_t and Δf_t lie on a straight line. By comparison, an $R^2 = 0$ indicates that there is no statistical association at all between ΔS_t and Δf_t.

hedging effectiveness
The (squared) correlation between past changes in spot asset prices and futures prices.

Since we are using futures contracts to hedge the risk of loss on spot asset positions, the R^2 value of the regression measures the degree of **hedging effectiveness** of the futures contract. A low R^2 means that we might have little confidence that the slope coefficient β from the regression is actually the true hedge ratio. As the value of R^2 approaches 1, the degree of confidence increases in the use of futures contracts, with a given hedge ratio (h) estimate, to hedge our cash asset–risk position.

CONCEPT QUESTIONS

1. **Identify an observation in Figure 22–6 that shows futures price changes exceeding spot price changes.**
2. **Suppose that $R^2 = 0$ in a regression of ΔS_t on Δf_t. Would you still use futures contracts to hedge? Explain your answer.**
3. **In running a regression of ΔS_t on Δf_t, the regression equation is $\Delta S_t = 0.51 + 0.95\Delta f_t$ and $R^2 = 0.72$. What is the hedge ratio? What is the measure of hedging effectiveness?**

HEDGING CREDIT RISK WITH FUTURES AND FORWARDS

LO6

Chapter 11 demonstrated that by diversifying their loan portfolios across different borrowers, sectors, and regions, FIs can diversify away much of the borrower-specific or unsystematic risk of the loan portfolio. Of course, the ability of an FI manager to diversify sufficiently depends in part on the size of the loan portfolio under management. Thus, the potential ability to diversify away borrower-specific risk increases with the size of the FI.

In recent years, however, new types of derivative instruments have been developed (including forwards, options, and swaps) to better allow FIs to hedge their credit risk. Credit derivatives can be used to hedge the credit risk on individual loans or bonds or on portfolios of loans and bonds. The credit derivative market, while still relatively young, has already gained a reputation as an early warning signal for spotting corporate debt problems. As shown in Table 22–1, at October 31, 2012, the notional amount of credit derivatives reported by the Big Six Canadian banks was equal to $185.7 billion. This is a significant decline from 2008 when credit derivatives represented 6.0 percent of the total notional amount of $14,378.1 billion, reflecting a decline in the use of these derivatives globally since the financial crisis. As shown in Table 22–2, U.S. banks had over US$13.6 trillion of notional value in credit derivatives outstanding in June 2012 and an estimated more than US$24.9 trillion worldwide. This is down from the US$54.6 trillion in credit derivatives outstanding in July 2008, just before the worst of the financial crisis.

The emergence of these new derivatives is important since more FIs fail due to credit risk exposure than to either interest rate or FX risk exposures. Credit derivatives, such as credit default swaps (CDSs), allow FIs to separate the credit risk exposure from the lending process itself. That is, FIs can assess the creditworthiness of loan applicants, originate loans, fund loans, and even monitor and service loans without retaining exposure to loss from credit events, such as default or missed payments. This decoupling of the risk from the lending activity allows the market to efficiently transfer risk across counterparties. However, it also loosens the incentives to carefully perform each of the steps of the lending process and can result in poor loan underwriting, shoddy documentation and due diligence, failure to monitor borrower activity, and fraudulent activity on the part of both lenders and borrowers. This loosening of incentives was an important factor leading to the global financial crisis of 2008–2009. Further, although the credit protection buyer hedges exposure to default risk, there is still counterparty credit risk in the event that the seller fails to perform its obligations under the terms of the contract (as was the concern in September 2008 with regard to AIG, an active CDS seller[22]).

Typically, banks, securities firms, and corporates are net buyers of credit protection, whereas insurance companies, hedge funds, mutual funds, and pension funds are net sellers. However, some financial firms are market makers in the market for credit derivatives, and therefore take both long and short positions. We discuss credit forward contracts below (less than 1 percent of all credit derivatives outstanding). In Chapter 23 we discuss credit options (less than 0.02 percent of all credit derivatives outstanding), and in Chapter 24 we discuss credit swaps (over 98 percent of all credit derivatives outstanding).

Credit Forward Contracts and Credit Risk Hedging

credit forward
An agreement that hedges against an increase in default risk on a loan after the loan terms have been determined and the loan has been issued.

A **credit forward** is a forward agreement that hedges against an increase in default risk on a loan (a decline in the credit quality of a borrower) after the loan rate is determined and the loan is issued. Common buyers of credit forwards are insurance companies, and common sellers are banks. The credit forward agreement specifies a credit spread (a risk premium above the risk-free rate to compensate for default risk) on a benchmark bond issued by an FI borrower. For example, suppose the benchmark bond of a bank borrower was rated BBB at the time a loan was originated. Further, at the time the loan was issued, the benchmark bonds had a 2 percent interest rate or credit spread (representing default risk on the BBB bonds) over a government security (bond) of the same maturity. To hedge against an increase in the credit risk of the borrower, the bank enters into (sells) a credit forward contract when the loan is issued. We define CS_F as the credit spread over the government security (bond) rate on which the credit forward contract is written (equals 2 percent in this example). Table 22–4 illustrates the payment pattern resulting from this credit forward. In Table 22–4, CS_T is the actual credit spread on the bond when the credit forward matures, for example, one year after the loan was originated and the credit forward contract was entered into; *MD* is the modified duration on the benchmark BBB bond; and *A* is the principal amount of the forward agreement.

From the payment pattern established in the credit forward agreement, Table 22–4 shows that the credit forward buyer (an insurance company) bears the risk of an increase in default risk on the benchmark bond of the borrowing firm, while the credit forward seller (the bank lender) hedges itself against an increase in the borrower's default risk. That is, if the borrower's default risk increases so that

TABLE 22–4
Payment Pattern on a Credit Forward

Credit Spread at End of Forward Agreement	Credit Spread Seller (Bank)	Credit Spread Buyer (Counterparty)
$CS_T > CS_F$	Receives $(CS_T - CS_F) \times MD \times A$	Pays $(CS_T - CS_F) \times MD \times A$
$CS_F > CS_T$	Pays $(CS_F - CS_T) \times MD \times A$	Receives $(CS_F - CS_T) \times MD \times A$

[22] Indeed, under the U.S. government's bailout of AIG, the largest component was to satisfy counterparty claims in AIG CDSs. Under AIG CDS programs, if AIG was downgraded (e.g., from AAA to BB), then the CDS contracts had to be marked to market. Any marking-to-market losses of AIG had to be paid to the CDS counterparties. Since AIG was close to insolvent, these losses were borne by the U.S. government as part of the AIG bailout.

when the forward agreement matures the market requires a higher credit spread on the borrower's benchmark bond, CS_T, than that originally agreed to in the forward contract, CS_F (i.e., $CS_T > CS_F$), the credit forward buyer pays the credit forward seller, which is the bank, $(CS_T - CS_F) \times MD \times A$. For example, suppose the credit spread between BBB bonds and government bonds widened to 3 percent from 2 percent over the year, the modified duration (MD) of the benchmark BBB bond was five years, and the size of the forward contract A was $10,000,000. Then the gain on the credit forward contract to the seller (the bank) would be $500,000 [(3% − 2%) × 5 × $10,000,000]. This amount could be used to offset the loss in market value of the loan due to the rise in the borrower's default risk. However, if the borrower's default risk and credit spread decrease over the year, the credit forward seller pays the credit forward buyer $(CS_F - CS_T) \times MD \times A$. (However, the maximum loss on the forward contract (to the bank seller) is limited, as will be explained below.)

Figure 22–7 illustrates the effect on the bank of hedging the loan. If the default risk on the loan increases, the market or present value of the loan falls below its value at the beginning of the hedge period. However, the bank hedged the change in default risk by selling a credit forward contract. Assuming the credit spread on the borrower's benchmark bond also increases (so that $CS_T > CS_F$), the bank receives $(CS_T - CS_F) \times MD \times A$ on the forward contract. If the characteristics of the benchmark bond (i.e., change in credit spread, modified duration, and principal value) are the same as those of the bank's loan to the borrower, the loss on the balance sheet is offset completely by the gain (off the balance sheet) from the credit forward (i.e., in our example, a $500,000 market value loss on the loan would be offset by a $500,000 gain from selling the credit forward contract).

If the default risk does not increase or decreases (so that $CS_T < CS_F$), the bank selling the forward contract will pay $(CS_F - CS_T) \times MD \times A$ to the credit forward buyer (the insurance company). However, importantly, this payout by the bank is limited to a maximum. This is when CS_T falls to zero, that is, the default spread on BBB bonds falls to zero or the original BBB bonds of the borrower are viewed as having the same default risk as government bonds (in other words,

FIGURE 22–7
Effect on a Bank of Hedging a Loan with a Credit Forward Contract

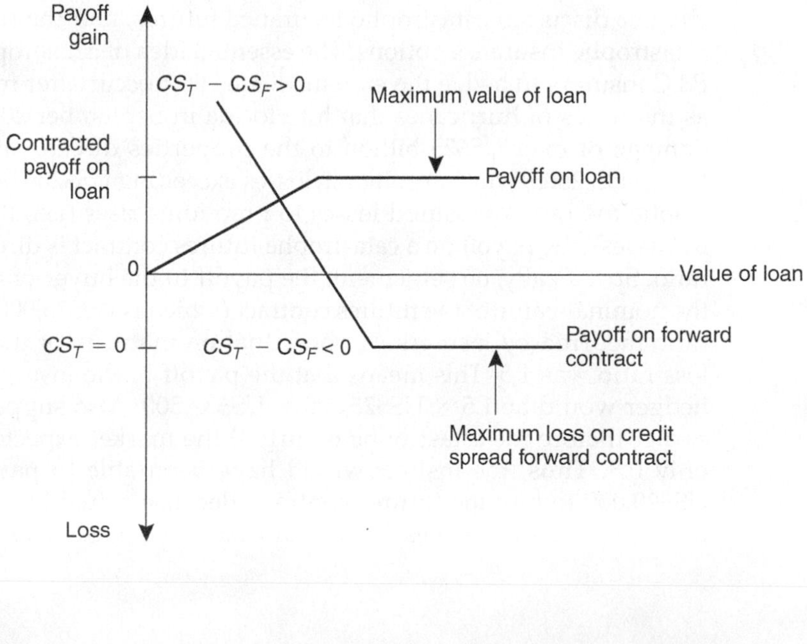

the credit spread or rate on the benchmark bond cannot fall below the risk-free rate). In this case, the maximum loss on the credit forward $[CS_F - (0)] \times MD \times A$ mirrors (offsets) the maximum and limited upside gain (return) on the loan. Anyone familiar with options will recognize that (as was discussed in Chapter 10) when the bank makes a loan, it is similar to writing a put option. In selling a credit forward, the payoff is similar to buying a put option (see Chapter 23 as well).

EXAMPLE 22-6

Hedging Credit Risk with Credit Spread Forward Contract

A bank issues a $5 million loan to a firm with an A– credit rating. The modified duration on the loan is 4.5 years. At the time of issue, the credit spread between A– bonds and government bonds is 2 percent (CS_F). The bank believes that the borrower's credit rating may fall during the period of the loan. To hedge this credit risk, the bank enters (or sells) a $5 million credit spread forward contract. Subsequently, at the end of the forward period, the borrower's credit rating does indeed drop, to BB (CS_T). The credit spread between BB-rated bonds and government bonds is 5 percent (or $CS_T > CS_F$). Thus, the change in the market value of the loan to the bank, from the duration model, is

$$\Delta L = L \times D \times [\Delta R_L/(1 + R_L)] = L \times D/(1 + R_L) \times \Delta R_L = L \times MD \times \Delta R_L$$

or

$$\Delta L = \$5{,}000{,}000 \times 4.5 \times (0.03) = \$675{,}000$$

However, the bank hedged this risk with a credit spread forward and receives, from the credit spread buyer,

$$(5\% - 2\%) \times 4.5 \times \$5{,}000{,}000 = \$675{,}000$$

Thus, the loss in the value of the loan due to a drop in the credit rating of the borrower is completely offset by the gain from the credit spread forward contract.

Futures Contracts and Catastrophe Risk

www.cmegroup.com

The CBOT has introduced futures and options for catastrophe insurance. This chapter discusses catastrophe insurance futures, and the next chapter discusses catastrophe insurance options. The essential idea of catastrophe futures is to allow P&C insurers to hedge the extreme losses that occur after major hurricanes, such as the series of hurricanes that hit Florida in September 2004, which resulted in damage of over US$25 billion to the properties directly affected, or Hurricane Katrina in 2005, which resulted in losses exceeding US$200 billion. Since in a catastrophe the ratio of insured losses to premiums rises (i.e., the so-called loss ratio increases), the payoff on a catastrophe futures contract is directly linked to the loss ratio. Specifically, on settlement, the payoff to the buyer of the futures is equal to the nominal value of the futures contract (which is US$25,000) times the actual loss ratio incurred by insurers. Suppose that on maturity of the futures contract the loss ratio was 1.5. This means that the payoff to the insurance company futures hedger would be 1.5 × US$25,000 = US$37,500. Also suppose that three months earlier (before the catastrophe occurred) the market expected the loss ratio to be only 0.8. Thus, the insurer would have been able to pay 0.8 × US$25,000 = US$20,000 to buy the futures contract. Because actual losses exceeded expected losses, the insurer makes a profit of US$37,500 − $20,000 = US$17,500 on each contract. These profits on futures contracts can be used to help offset the huge payouts on hurricane insurance contracts.

REGULATION OF DERIVATIVE SECURITIES

LO7 m-x.ca

In Canada, derivative contracts are traded on the Montréal Exchange, which is responsible for the regulation of trading. The Montréal Exchange determines which contracts will trade as well as who may trade. The Montréal Exchange also establishes other rules regarding futures contracts, such as price reporting requirements, antimanipulation regulations, position limits, audit trail requirements, and margin requirements.

osfi-bsif.gc.ca

The OSFI requires federally regulated FIs (domestic and foreign banks, trust and loans, cooperatives, life insurance companies, and P&C insurance companies) to follow its *Derivatives Best Practices Guideline B-7*, effective since May 1995. Banks are required to report on their derivative positions quarterly as well as to follow the guidelines for best practices regarding capital adequacy, innovative instruments, large exposure limits, and derivative best practices, as well as specific guidelines with respect to interest rate risk and accounting guidelines regarding the disclosure of derivative positions. Overall, the policy of OSFI is to encourage appropriate risk management practices at the FIs under its jurisdiction. As well, the AcSB required all FIs (and nonfinancial firms) to adopt IFRS, which require derivative contracts to be reported at their marked-to-market value in the financial statements. As noted in Chapter 20, exchange-traded derivative securities such as futures contracts are subject to nominal risk-based capital requirements. This is because the credit or default risk of exchange-traded derivatives is approximately zero: when a counterparty defaults on its obligations, the exchange itself adopts the counterparty's obligations in full. By contrast, no such guarantees exist for bilaterally agreed, OTC contracts originated and traded outside organized exchanges. Other things being equal, the risk-based capital requirements favour the use of futures over forwards.

acsbcanada.org

In the United States, derivative contracts are subject to three levels of institutional regulation. First, regulators of derivatives specify "permissible activities" that institutions may engage in. Second, once permissible activities have been specified, institutions engaging in those activities are subjected to supervisory oversight. Third, regulators attempt to judge the overall integrity of each institution engaging in derivative activities by assessing the capital adequacy of the institutions and by enforcing regulations to ensure compliance with those capital requirements. The SEC and the CFTC are often viewed as "functional" regulators. The SEC regulates all securities traded on national securities exchanges, including several exchange-traded derivatives. The CFTC has exclusive jurisdiction over all exchange-traded derivative securities. It therefore regulates all national futures exchanges, as well as all futures and options on futures. The CFTC's regulations include minimum capital requirements for traders, reporting and transparency requirements, antifraud and antimanipulation regulations, and minimum standards for clearinghouse organizations.This means that U.S. FIs must immediately recognize all gains and losses on such contracts and disclose those gains and losses to shareholders and regulators. Further, firms must show whether they are using derivatives to hedge risks connected to their business or whether they are just taking an open (risky) position. Overall, the policy

sec.gov
cftc.gov

of regulators is to encourage the use of futures for hedging and discourage their use for speculation, although on a practical basis, it is often difficult to distinguish between the two.

www.financialstabilityboard.org

Finally, as noted in Chapter 20, exchange-traded futures contracts are not subject to risk-based capital requirements; by contrast, OTC forward contracts are potentially subject to capital requirements. Other things being equal, the risk-based capital requirements favour the use of futures over forwards. However, because of their lack of regulation and because of the significant negative role that OTC derivative securities played during the financial crisis, in 2010, the FSB made recommendations to the G20 to regulate OTC derivatives to reduce their risk to the global financial system. These recommendations included a plan to regulate OTC derivatives according to internationally agreed standards. The plan, first, called for most of the OTC derivatives to trade on regulated exchanges that would guarantee trades and help cushion against potential defaults. This change would make it easier for participants to see market prices of these securities and make the markets more transparent. Second, like exchange-traded derivatives, the previous OTC-traded securities would now come under the authority of bank regulators, who would oversee banks that deal in derivatives and would apply increased capital requirements for derivatives. Thus, the proposed changes would result in OTC derivative securities being regulated in a similar fashion as exchange-traded securities.

Questions and Problems

1. What are derivative contracts? What is the value of derivative contracts to the managers of FIs? Which type of derivative contracts had the highest value among Canadian banks as of October 2012?
2. What are some of the major differences between futures and forward contracts? How do these contracts differ from spot contracts?
3. What is a naive hedge? How does a naive hedge protect an FI from risk?
4. An FI holds a 15-year, par value, $10,000,000 bond that is priced at 104 with a yield to maturity of 7 percent. The bond has a duration of eight years, and the FI plans to sell it after two months. The FI's market analyst predicts that interest rates will be 8 percent at the time of the desired sale. Because most other analysts are predicting no change in rates, two-month forward contracts for 15-year bonds are available at 104. The FI would like to hedge against the expected change in interest rates with an appropriate position in a forward contract. What will this position be? Show that if rates rise 1 percent as forecast, the hedge will protect the FI from loss.
5. Contrast the position of being short with that of being long in futures contracts.
6. Suppose an FI purchases a bond futures contract at 95.
   a. What is the FI's obligation at the time the futures contract is purchased?
   b. If an FI purchases this contract, in what kind of hedge is it engaged?
   c. Assume that the bond futures price falls to 94. What is the loss or gain?
   d. Assume that the bond futures price rises to 97. Mark to market the position.
7. Long Bank has assets that consist mostly of 25-year mortgages and liabilities that are short-term demand deposits and GICs. Will an interest rate futures contract the bank buys add to or subtract from the bank's risk?
8. In each of the following cases, indicate whether it would be appropriate for an FI to buy or sell a forward contract to hedge the appropriate risk.
   a. A bank plans to issue GICs in three months.
   b. An insurance company plans to buy bonds in two months.

c. A credit union is going to sell Government of Canada securities next month.

d. A Canadian bank lends to a French company: The loan is payable in euros.

e. A finance company has assets with a duration of 6 years and liabilities with a duration of 13 years.

9. The duration of a 20-year, 8 percent coupon government bond selling at par is 10.292 years. The bond's interest is paid semiannually, and the bond qualifies for delivery against a government bond futures contract.

   a. What is the modified duration of this bond?

   b. What is the effect on the bond price if market interest rates increase 50 bp?

   c. If you sold a government bond futures contract at 95 and interest rates rose 50 bp, what would be the change in the value of your futures position?

   d. If you purchased the bond at par and sold the futures contract, what would be the net value of your hedge after the increase in interest rates?

10. What are the differences between a microhedge and a macrohedge for an FI? Why is it generally more efficient for FIs to employ a macrohedge than a series of microhedges?

11. What are the reasons that an FI may choose to selectively hedge its portfolio?

12. Hedge Row Bank has the following balance sheet ($ millions):

Assets	$150	Liabilities	$ 135
		Equity	$ 15
Total	$150	Total	$ 150

The duration of the assets is six years, and the duration of the liabilities is four years. The bank is expecting interest rates to fall from 10 percent to 9 percent over the next year.

   a. What is the duration gap for Hedge Row Bank?

   b. What is the expected change in net worth for Hedge Row Bank if the forecast is accurate?

   c. What will be the effect on net worth if interest rates increase 110 bp?

   d. If the existing interest rate on the liabilities is 6 percent, what will be the effect on net worth of a 1 percent increase in interest rates?

13. For a given change in interest rates, why is the sensitivity of the price of a government bond futures contract greater than the sensitivity of the price of a government T-bill futures contract?

14. What is the meaning of the government bond futures price quote 101–13?

15. What is meant by fully hedging the balance sheet of an FI?

16. Tree Row Bank has assets of $150 million, liabilities of $135 million, and equity of $15 million. The asset duration is six years, and the duration of the liabilities is four years. Market interest rates are 10 percent. Tree Row Bank wishes to hedge the balance sheet with eurodollar futures contracts, which currently have a price quote of $96 per $100 face value for the benchmark three-month eurodollar CD underlying the contract. The current rate on three-month eurodollar CDs is 4.0 percent and the duration of these contracts is 0.25 years.

   a. Should the bank go short or long on the futures contracts to establish the correct macrohedge?

   b. Assuming no basis risk, how many contracts are necessary to fully hedge the bank?

   c. Verify that the change in the futures position will offset the change in the cash balance sheet position for a change in market interest rates of plus 100 bp and minus 50 bp.

   d. If the bank had hedged with Treasury bond futures contracts that had a market value of $95 per $100 of face value, a yield of 8.5295 percent, and a duration of 10.3725 years, how many futures contracts would have been necessary to fully hedge the balance sheet? Assume no basis risk.

   e. What additional issues should be considered by the bank in choosing between eurodollar and T-bond futures contracts?

17. What is basis risk? What are the sources of basis risk?

18. How would your answers for part (b) in problem 16 change if the relationship of the price sensitivity of futures contracts to the price sensitivity of underlying bonds was $br = 0.92$?

19. Reconsider Tree Row Bank in problem 16 but assume that the cost rate on the liabilities is 6 percent. On-balance-sheet rates are expected to increase by 100 bp. Further, assume there is basis risk such that rates on three-month eurodollar CDs are expected to change by 0.10 times the rate change on assets and liabilities, i.e., $\Delta R_F = 0.10 \times \Delta R$.

   a. How many contracts are necessary to fully hedge the bank?

   b. Verify that the change in the futures position will offset the change in the cash balance sheet position for a change in market interest rates of plus 100 bp and minus 50 bp.

   c. If the bank had hedged with Treasury bond futures contracts that had a market value of $95 per $100 of face value, a yield of 8.5295 percent, and a duration of 10.3725 years, how many futures contracts would have been necessary to fully hedge the balance sheet? Assume there is basis risk such that rates on T-bonds are expected to change by 0.75 times the rate change on assets and liabilities, i.e., $\Delta R_F = 0.75 \times \Delta R$.

20. A mutual fund plans to purchase $500,000 of 30-year government bonds in four months. These bonds have a duration of 12 years and are priced at 96.25 (percent of face value). The mutual fund is concerned about interest rates changing over the next four months and is considering a hedge with government bond futures contracts that mature in six months. The bond futures contracts are selling for 98.75 (percent of face value) and have a duration of 8.5 years.
    a. If interest rate changes in the spot market exactly match those in the futures market, what type of futures position should the mutual fund create?
    b. How many contracts should be used?
    c. If the implied rate on the deliverable bond in the futures market moves 12 percent more than the change in the discounted spot rate, how many futures contracts should be used to hedge the portfolio?
    d. What causes futures contracts to have a different price sensitivity than assets in the spot markets?
21. Consider the following balance sheet ($ millions) for an FI:

Assets		Liabilities	
Duration = 10 years	$950	Duration = 2 years	$860
		Equity	90

    a. What is the FI's duration gap?
    b. What is the FI's interest rate risk exposure?
    c. How can the FI use futures and forward contracts to put on a macrohedge?
    d. What is the impact on the FI's equity value if the relative change in interest rates is an increase of 1 percent? That is, $\Delta R/(1 + R) = 0.01$.
    e. Suppose that the FI in part (c) macrohedges using government bond futures that are currently priced at 96. What is the impact on the FI's futures position if the relative change in all interest rates is an increase of 1 percent? That is, $\Delta R/(1 + R) = 0.01$. Assume that the deliverable government bond has a duration of nine years.
    f. If the FI wants a perfect macrohedge, how many government bond futures contracts does it need?
22. Refer again to problem 21. How does consideration of basis risk change your answers?
    a. Compute the number of futures contracts required to construct a perfect macrohedge if

$$\frac{\Delta R_F/(1 + R_F)}{\Delta R/(1 + R)} = br = 0.90$$

    b. Explain what is meant by $br = 0.90$.
    c. If $br = 0.90$, what information does this provide on the number of futures contracts needed to construct a perfect macrohedge?
23. An FI is planning to hedge its US$100 million bond instruments with a cross hedge using eurodollar interest rate futures. How would the FI estimate

$$br = \frac{\Delta R_F/(1 + R_F)}{\Delta R/(1 + R)}$$

to determine the exact number of eurodollar futures contracts to hedge?
24. Village Bank has $240 million worth of assets with a duration of 14 years and liabilities worth $210 million with a duration of 4 years. In the interest of hedging interest rate risk, Village Bank is contemplating a macrohedge with interest rate futures contracts now selling for 102.65625 (percent of face value). The T-bond underlying the futures contract has a duration of nine years. If the spot and futures interest rates move together, how many futures contracts must Village Bank sell to fully hedge the balance sheet?
25. Assume that an FI has assets of $250 million and liabilities of $200 million. The duration of the assets is six years, and the duration of the liabilities is three years. The price of the futures contract is $115,000, and its duration is 5.5 years.
    a. What number of futures contracts is needed to construct a perfect hedge if $br = 1.10$?
    b. If $\Delta R_F/(1 + R_F) = 0.0990$, what is the expected $\Delta R/(1 + R)$?
26. Suppose an FI purchases a US$1 million 91-day eurodollar futures contract trading at 98.50.
    a. If the contract is reversed two days later by selling the contract at 98.60, what is the net profit?
    b. What is the loss or gain if the price at reversal is 98.40?
27. Dudley Hill Bank has the following balance sheet:

Assets (in millions)		Liabilities (in millions)	
A	$425	*L*	$380
	—	*E*	45
			$425

Further,

$D_A = 6$ years
$D_L = 2$ years

The bank manager receives information from an economic forecasting unit that interest rates are expected to rise from 8 to 9 percent over the next six months.

a. Calculate the potential loss to Dudley Hill's net worth (E) if the forecast of rising rates proves to be true.

b. Suppose the manager of Dudley Hill Bank wants to hedge this interest rate risk with T-bond futures contracts. The current futures price quote is $122.03125 per $100 of face value for the benchmark 20-year, and the minimum contract size is $100,000, so P_F equals $122,031.25. The duration of the deliverable bond is 14.5 years, that is, $D_F = 14.5$ years. How many futures contracts will be needed? Should the manager buy or sell these contracts? Assume no basis risk.

c. Verify that selling T-bond futures contracts will indeed hedge the FI against a sudden increase in interest rates from 8 to 9 percent, or a 1 percent interest rate shock.

d. If the bank had hedged with eurodollar futures contracts that had a market value of $98 per $100 of face value, how many futures contracts would have been necessary to fully hedge the balance sheet?

e. How would your answer for part (b) change if the relationship of the price sensitivity of futures contracts to the price sensitivity of underlying bonds was $br = 1.15$?

f. Verify that selling T-bond futures contracts will indeed hedge the FI against a sudden increase in interest rates from 8 to 9 percent, or a 1 percent interest rate shock. Assume the yield on the T-bond underlying the futures contract is 8.45 percent as the bank enters the hedge and rates rise by 1.154792 percent.

28. An FI has an asset investment in euros. The FI expects the exchange rate of $/€ to increase by the maturity of the asset.

a. Is the dollar appreciating or depreciating against the euro?

b. To fully hedge the investment, should the FI buy or sell euro futures contracts?

c. If there is perfect correlation between changes in the spot and futures contracts, how should the FI determine the number of contracts necessary to hedge the investment fully?

29. What is meant by tailing the hedge? What factors allow an FI manager to tail the hedge effectively?

30. What does the hedge ratio measure? Under what conditions is this ratio valuable in determining the number of futures contracts necessary to fully hedge an investment in another currency? How is the hedge ratio related to basis risk?

31. What technique is commonly used to estimate the hedge ratio? What statistical measure is an indicator of the confidence that should be placed in the estimated hedge ratio? What is the interpretation if the estimated hedge ratio is greater than 1? Less than 1?

32. An FI has assets denominated in U.K. pounds sterling of $125 million and pound liabilities of $100 million.

a. What is the FI's net exposure?

b. Is the FI exposed to a dollar appreciation or depreciation?

c. How can the FI use futures or forward contracts to hedge its FX rate risk?

d. If a futures contract is currently trading at $1.55/£, what is the number of futures contracts that must be utilized to fully hedge the FI's currency risk exposure? Assume the contract size on the U.K. pound futures contract is £62,500.

e. If the U.K. pound falls from $1.60/£ to $1.50/£, what will be the impact on the FI's cash position?

f. If the U.K. pound futures price falls from $1.55/£ to $1.45/£, what will be the impact on the FI's futures position?

g. Using the information in parts (e) and (f), what can you conclude about basis risk?

33. An FI is planning to hedge its one-year 100 million Swiss francs (Sf)–denominated loan against exchange rate risk. The current spot rate is $0.60/Sf. A one-year Swiss franc futures contract is currently trading at $0.58/Sf. Swiss franc futures are sold in standardized units of Sf125,000.

a. Should the FI be worried about the Swiss franc appreciating or depreciating?

b. Should the FI buy or sell futures to hedge against exchange rate exposure?

c. How many futures contracts should the FI buy or sell if a regression of past changes in spot prices on changes in future prices generates an estimated slope of 1.4?

d. Show exactly how the FI is hedged if it repatriates its principal of Sf100 million at year-end, the spot price of Swiss francs at year-end is $0.55/Sf, and the forward price is $0.5443/Sf.

34. An FI has a long position in £75,500,000 assets funded with dollar-denominated liabilities. The FI manager is concerned about the U.K. pound appreciating relative to the dollar and is considering a hedge of this FX risk using pound futures contracts. The manager has regressed recent changes

in the spot pound exchange rate on changes in pound futures contracts. The resulting regression equation is $\Delta S_T = 0.09 + 1.5\Delta F_T$. Further, the $\text{Cov}(\Delta S_t, \Delta F_t)$ was found to be 0.06844, $\sigma_{\Delta S_t} = 0.3234$, and $\sigma_{\Delta F_t} = 0.2279$. Pound futures contracts are sold in standardized units of £62,500. Calculate the number of futures contracts needed to hedge the risk of the £75,500,000 asset. Calculate the hedging effectiveness of these futures contracts. To what extent can the manager have confidence that the correct hedge ratio is being used to hedge the FI's FX risk position?

35. An FI has made a loan commitment of Sf10 million that is likely to be drawn down in six months. The current spot rate is $0.60/Sf.
    a. Is the FI exposed to the dollar's depreciating or appreciating? Why?
    b. If the spot rate six months from today is $0.64/Sf, what dollar amount is needed if the loan is drawn down and the FI is unhedged?
    c. If the FI decides to hedge using Swiss franc futures, should it buy or sell Swiss franc futures?
    d. A six-month Swiss franc futures contract is available for $0.61/Sf. What net amount would be needed to fund the loan at the end of six months if the FI had hedged using the Sf10 million futures contract? Assume that futures prices are equal to spot prices at the time of payment (i.e., at maturity).
36. An FI has assets denominated in Swiss francs (Sf) of 75 million and liabilities denominated in Swiss francs of 125 million. The spot rate is $0.6667/Sf, and one-year futures are available for $0.6579/Sf.
    a. What is the FI's net exposure?
    b. Is the FI exposed to dollar appreciation or depreciation?
    c. If the Sf spot rate changes from $0.6667/Sf to $0.6897/Sf, how will this affect the FI's currency exposure? Assume no hedging.
    d. What is the number of futures contracts necessary to fully hedge the currency risk exposure of the FI? The contract size is Sf125,000 per contract.
    e. If the Swiss franc futures price falls from $0.6579/Sf to $0.6349/Sf, what will be the effect on the FI's futures position?
37. What is a credit forward? How is it structured?
38. What is the gain on the purchase of a $20 million credit forward contract with a modified duration of seven years if the credit spread between a benchmark government bond and a borrowing firm's debt decreases 50 bp?
39. How is selling a credit forward similar to buying a put option?
40. A P&C insurance company purchased catastrophe futures contracts to hedge against loss during the hurricane season. At the time of purchase, the market expected a loss ratio of 0.75. After processing claims from a severe hurricane, the P&C actually incurred a loss ratio of 1.35. What amount of profit did the P&C make on each $25,000 futures contract?
41. What is the primary goal of regulators in regard to the use of futures by FIs? What guidelines have regulators given to banks for trading in futures and forwards?

Appendix 22A Microhedging with Futures

View Appendix 22A on Connect.

CHAPTER 23

OPTIONS, CAPS, FLOORS, AND COLLARS

After studying this chapter you should be able to:

- **LO1** Discuss the basic features of buying/writing a put/call option on a bond.
- **LO2** Describe the mechanics of hedging a bond or a bond portfolio.
- **LO3** Demonstrate how options can be used to hedge interest rate risk on an FI's balance sheet.
- **LO4** Demonstrate how options can be used to hedge FX risk.
- **LO5** Demonstrate how an FI can use options to hedge credit risk.
- **LO6** Demonstrate how catastrophe risk can be hedged with call spread options.
- **LO7** Demonstrate the use of caps, floors, and collars to hedge interest rate risk.

INTRODUCTION

Just as there is a wide variety of forward and futures contracts available for an FI to use in hedging, there is an even wider array of option products, including exchange-traded options; over-the-counter (OTC) options; options embedded in securities; and caps, collars, and floors. As we saw with futures contracts (in Chapter 22), the use of options can protect an FI against a loss of net worth due to unexpected changes in interest rates, credit risk, FX risk, and so forth. Not only has the range of option products increased in recent years, but also the use of options has increased as well. However, like forwards, futures, and swaps, options can also lead to huge losses for FIs.

This chapter starts with a review of the four basic options strategies: buying a call, writing a call, buying a put, and writing a put. We then look at economic and regulatory reasons FIs choose to buy versus write (sell) options. The chapter then concentrates on the use of fixed-income or interest rate options to hedge interest rate risk. We also discuss the role of options in hedging FX and credit risks as well as catastrophe risk. The chapter concludes with an examination of caps, floors, and collars. As with futures and forwards, discussed in Chapter 22, options, caps, floors, and collars are held by FIs not only to hedge their own risk, but also to serve as counterparties (for a fee) for other financial and nonfinancial firms wanting to hedge risk on their own balance sheets.

option
A contract that gives the holder the right but not the obligation to buy or sell the underlying asset at a specified price within a specified period of time.

BASIC FEATURES OF OPTIONS

LO1

An **option** is a contract that gives the holder the right, but not the obligation, to buy or sell an underlying asset at a prespecified price for a specified time period. Options are classified as either call options or put options. We discuss both of these below, highlighting their profits in terms of price movements on the underlying asset. The Chicago Board of Options Exchange (CBOE), opened in 1973, was the first exchange devoted solely to the trading of stock options. In 1982, financial futures options contracts (options on financial futures contracts, e.g., Treasury bond futures contracts) started trading. Options markets have grown rapidly since the mid-1980s.

The trading process for options is the same as that for futures contracts. An FI desiring to take an option position places an order to buy or sell a stated number of call or put option contracts with a stated expiration date and exercise price. The order is directed to a representative on the appropriate exchange for execution. Trading on the largest exchanges, such as the CBOE, takes place in trading pits, where traders for each delivery date on an option contract informally group together. As with futures contracts, options trading can occur electronically or by open-outcry auction method. Once an option price is agreed on in a trading pit, the two parties send the details of the trade to the option clearinghouse (the Options Clearing Corporation), which breaks up trades into buy and sell transactions and takes the opposite side of each transaction—becoming the seller for every option contract buyer and the buyer for every option contract seller. The broker on the floor of the options exchange confirms the transaction with the investor's broker.

In the early 2000s, the CBOE increased the speed at which orders can be placed, executed, and filled by equipping floor brokers with hand-held touch-screen computers that allow them to route and execute orders more easily and efficiently. For example, when a broker selects an order from the workstation, an electronic trading card appears on his or her computer screen. The electronic card allows the broker to work the order and enter necessary trade information (e.g., volume, price, opposing market makers). When the card (details of the transaction) is complete, the broker can execute the trade with the touch of a finger. Once the broker has submitted the trade, the system simultaneously sends a "fill" report to the customer and instantaneously transmits the data to traders worldwide.

While the CBOE is the biggest options exchange, Canadian FIs are also able to buy and sell options on the Montréal Exchange. As noted in Chapter 22, the Montréal Exchange, part of the TMX Group since 2008, provides options trading in Canada for interest rate, index, and equity contracts. The Canadian Derivatives Clearing Corporation (CDCC), a self-regulatory organization (SRO) wholly owned by the Bourse de Montréal Inc., issues, clears, and guarantees the contracts traded on the Montréal Exchange. The Montréal Exchange offers index options (e.g., S&P/TSX 60 Index Options), **exchange-traded funds (ETFs)** (e.g., Horizons BetaPro S&P/TSX 60 Bear Plus Fund), equity options (e.g., Suncor Energy Inc.), and U.S. dollar currency options.

exchange-traded funds (ETFs)
Funds that track a specific index or basket of shares and trade like shares on a stock exchange. They can be bought and sold at any time during a trading day.

In describing the features of the four basic option strategies FIs might employ to hedge interest rate risk, we discuss their return payoffs in terms of interest rate movements. Specifically, we consider bond options whose payoff values are inversely linked to interest rate movements in a manner similar to bond prices and interest rates in general (see Chapter 8).

Buying a Call Option on a Bond

The first strategy of buying (or taking a long position in) a call option on a bond is shown in Figure 23–1. A **call option** gives the purchaser the right (but not the obligation) to buy the underlying security—a bond—at a prespecified

call option
Gives a purchaser the right (but not the obligation) to buy the underlying security from the writer of the option at a prespecified exercise price on a prespecified date.

FIGURE 23–1
Payoff Function for the Buyer of a Call Option on a Bond

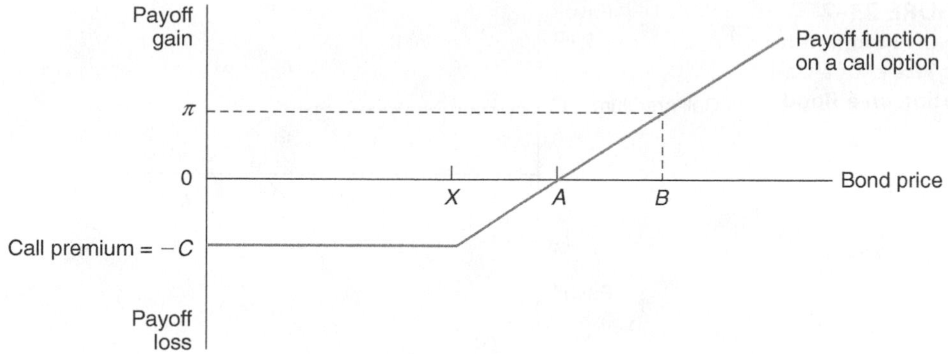

exercise or *strike price* (*X*). In return, the buyer of the call option must pay the writer or seller an up-front fee known as a *call premium* (*C*). This premium is an immediate negative cash flow for the buyer of the call, who potentially stands to make a profit if the underlying bond's price rises above the exercise price by an amount exceeding the premium. If the price of the bond never rises above *X*, the buyer of the call never exercises the option (i.e., buying the bond at *X* when its market value is less than *X*). In this case, the option matures unexercised. The call buyer incurs a cost, *C*, for the option, and no other cash flows result.

As shown in Figure 23–1, if the price of the bond underlying the option rises to price *B*, the buyer makes a profit of π, which is the difference between the bond price (*B*) and the exercise price of the option (*X*) minus the call premium (*C*). If the bond price rises to *A*, the buyer of the call has broken even in that the profit from exercising the call ($A - X$) just equals the premium payment for the call (*C*).

Notice two important things about bond call options in Figure 23–1:

1. As interest rates fall, bond prices rise and the call option buyer has a larger profit potential; the more rates fall, the higher bond prices rise and the larger the profit on the exercise of the option.
2. As interest rates rise, bond prices fall and the potential for a negative payoff (loss) for the buyer of the call option increases. If rates rise so that bond prices fall below the exercise price *X*, the call buyer is not obliged to exercise the option. Thus, the losses of the buyer are truncated by the amount of the up-front premium payment (*C*) made to purchase the call option.

Thus, buying a call option is a strategy to take when interest rates are expected to fall. Notice that unlike interest rate futures, whose prices and payoffs move symmetrically with changes in the level of rates, the payoffs on bond call options move asymmetrically with interest rates.

Writing a Call Option on a Bond

The second strategy is writing (or taking a short position in) a call option on a bond. In writing a call option on a bond, the writer or seller receives an up-front fee or premium (*C*) and must stand ready to sell the underlying bond to the purchaser of the option at the exercise price, *X*. Note the payoff from writing a call option on a bond in Figure 23–2.

FIGURE 23–2
Payoff Function for the Writer of a Call Option on a Bond

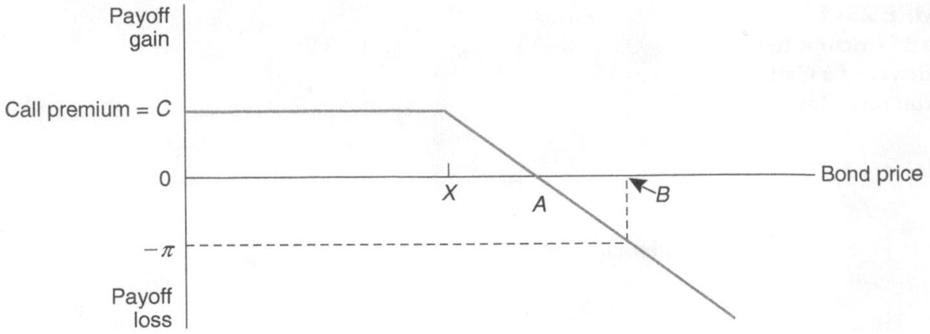

There are two important things to notice about this payoff function:

1. When interest rates rise and bond prices fall, there is an increased potential for the writer of the call to receive a positive payoff or profit. The call buyer is less likely to exercise the option, which would force the option writer to sell the underlying bond at the exercise price. However, this profit has a maximum equal to the call premium (C) charged up-front to the buyer of the option.
2. When interest rates fall and bond prices rise, the writer has an increased potential to take a loss. The call buyer will exercise the option, forcing the option writer to sell the underlying bonds. Since bond prices are theoretically unbounded in the upward direction, although they must return to par at maturity, these losses could be very large.

Thus, writing a call option is a strategy to take when interest rates are expected to rise. Caution is warranted, however, because profits are limited but losses are potentially large if rates fall. In Figure 23–2, a fall in interest rates and a rise in bond prices to B results in the writer of the option losing π.

Buying a Put Option on a Bond

The third strategy is buying (or taking a long position in) a put option on a bond. The buyer of a **put option** on a bond has the right (but not the obligation) to sell the underlying bond to the writer of the option at the agreed exercise price (X). In return for this option, the buyer of the put option pays a premium to the writer (P). We show the potential payoffs to the buyer of the put option in Figure 23–3. Note the following:

put option
Gives a purchaser the right (but not the obligation) to sell the underlying security to the writer of the option at a prespecified exercise price on a prespecified date.

1. When interest rates rise and bond prices fall, the buyer of the put has an increased probability of making a profit from exercising the option. Thus, if bond prices fall to D, the buyer of the put option can purchase bonds in the bond market at that price and put them (sell them) back to the writer of the put at the higher exercise price (X). As a result, the buyer makes a profit, after deducting the cost of the put premium (P), of πp in Figure 23–3.
2. When interest rates fall and bond prices rise, the probability that the buyer of a put will lose increases. If rates fall so that bond prices rise above the exercise price (X), the put buyer does not have to exercise the option. Thus, the maximum loss is limited to the size of the up-front put premium (P).

Thus, buying a put option is a strategy to take when interest rates are expected to rise.

FIGURE 23–3
Payoff Function for the Buyer of a Put Option on a Bond

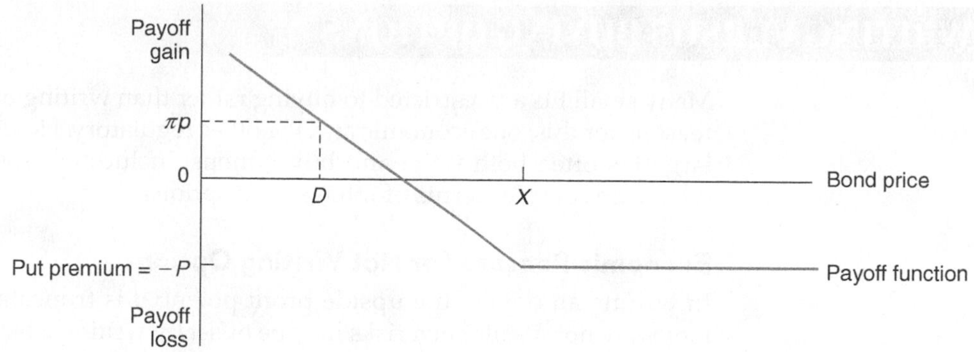

FIGURE 23–4
Payoff Function for the Writer of a Put Option on a Bond

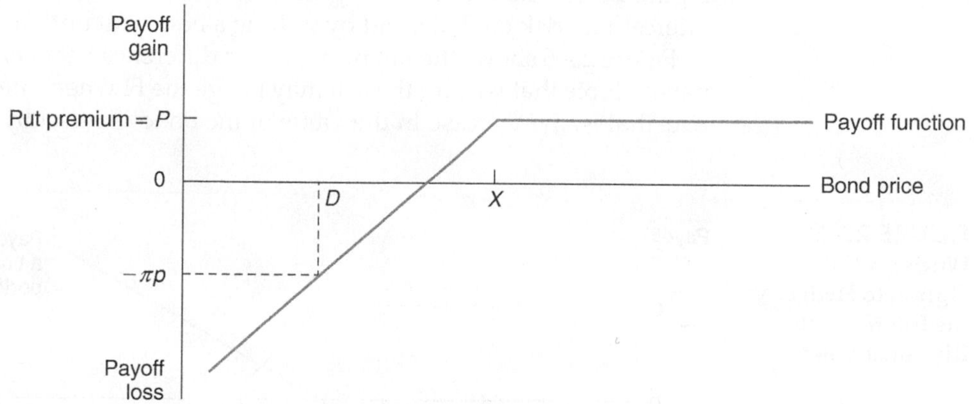

Writing a Put Option on a Bond

The fourth strategy is writing (or taking a short position in) a put option on a bond. In writing a put option on a bond, the writer or seller receives a fee or premium (P) in return for standing ready to buy bonds at the exercise price (X) if the buyer of the put chooses to exercise the option to sell. See the payoff function for writing a put option on a bond in Figure 23–4. Note the following:

1. If interest rates fall and bond prices rise, the writer has an enhanced probability of making a profit. The put buyer is less likely to exercise the option, which would force the option writer to buy the underlying bond. However, the writer's maximum profit is constrained to be equal to the put premium (P).
2. If interest rates rise and bond prices fall, the writer of the put is exposed to potentially large losses (e.g., $-\pi p$, if bond prices fall to D in Figure 23–4).

Thus, writing a put option is a strategy to take when interest rates are expected to fall. However, profits are limited and losses are potentially unlimited.

CONCEPT QUESTIONS

1. **How do interest rate increases affect the payoff from buying a call option on a bond? How do they affect the payoff from writing a call option on a bond?**
2. **How do interest rate increases affect the payoff from buying a put option on a bond? How do they affect the payoff from writing a put option on a bond?**

WRITING VERSUS BUYING OPTIONS

Many small FIs are restricted to buying rather than writing options. There are two reasons for this, one economic and the other regulatory. However, as we note later, large FIs often both write and buy options, including caps, floors, and collars, which are complex forms of interest rate options.

Economic Reasons for Not Writing Options

In writing an option, the upside profit potential is truncated, but the downside losses are not. While such risks may be offset by writing a large number of options at different exercise prices and/or hedging an underlying portfolio of bonds, the downside risk exposure of the writer may still be significant. To see this, look at Figure 23–5, where an FI is long in a bond in its portfolio and seeks to hedge the interest rate risk on that bond by writing a bond call option.

Figure 23–6 shows the net profit, or the difference between the bond and option payoff. Note that writing the call may hedge the FI when rates fall and bond prices rise; that is, the increase in the value of the bond is offset by losses on the written

FIGURE 23–5
Writing a Call Option to Hedge the Interest Rate Risk on a Bond

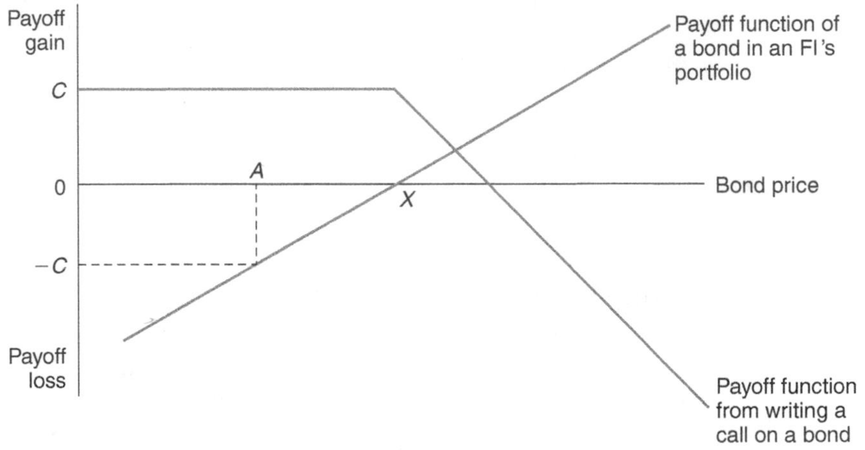

FIGURE 23–6
Profit from Writing a Call Option and Investing in a Bond

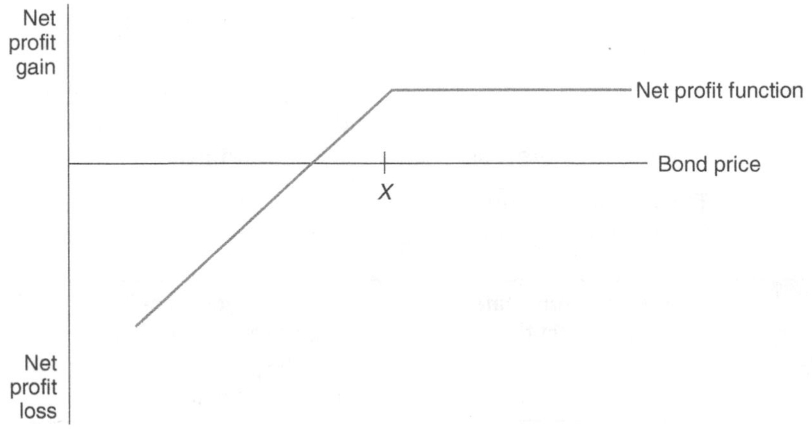

call. When the reverse occurs and interest rates rise, the FI's profits from writing the call may be insufficient to offset the loss on its bonds. This occurs because the upside profit (per call written) is truncated and is equal to the premium income (*C*). If the decrease in the bond value is larger than the premium income (to the left of point *A* in Figure 23–5), the FI is unable to offset the associated capital value loss on the bond with profits from writing options.

By contrast, hedging the FI's risk by buying a put option on a bond offers the manager a much more attractive alternative. Figure 23–7 shows the gross payoff of the bond and the payoff from buying a put option on a bond. In this case, any losses on the bond (as rates rise and bond values fall) are offset with profits from the put option that was bought (points to the left of point *X* in Figure 23–7). If rates fall, the bond value increases, yet the accompanying losses on the purchased put option positions are limited to the option premiums paid (points to the right of point *X*). Figure 23–8 shows the net payoff or the difference between the bond and option payoff.

Note the following:

1. Buying a put option truncates the downside losses on the bond following interest rate rises to some maximum amount and scales down the upside profits by the cost of bond price risk insurance—the put premium—leaving some positive upside profit potential.
2. The combination of being long in the bond and buying a put option on a bond mimics the payoff function of buying a call option (compare Figures 23–1 and 23–8).

FIGURE 23–7
Buying a Put Option to Hedge the Interest Rate Risk on a Bond

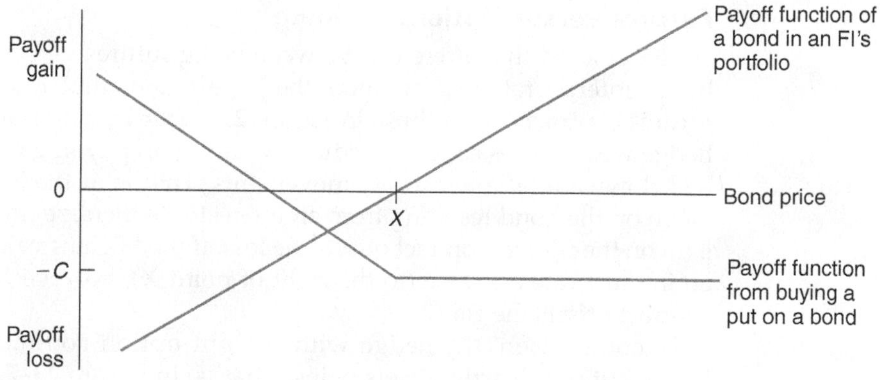

FIGURE 23–8
Net Payoff of Buying a Bond Put and Investing in a Bond

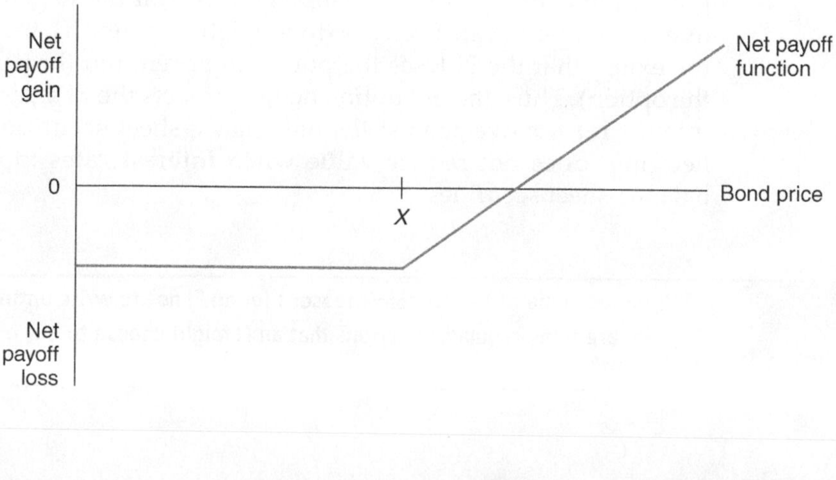

FIGURE 23–9
Buying a Futures Contract to Hedge the Interest Rate Risk on a Bond

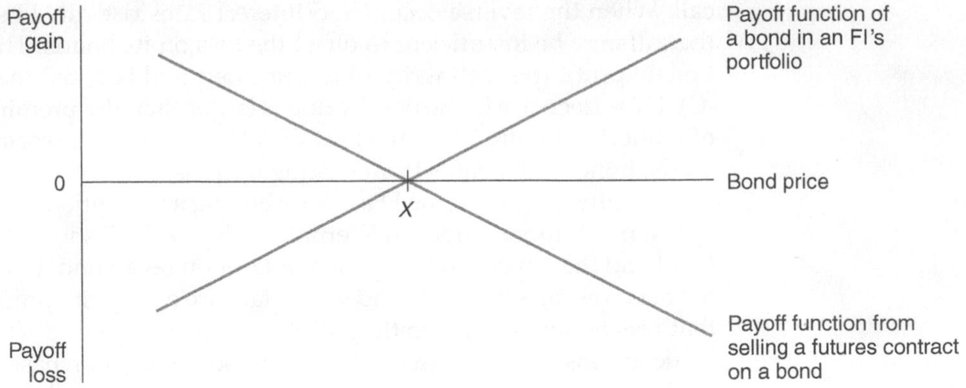

Regulatory Reasons

There are also regulatory reasons that FIs buy options rather than write options. Regulators view writing options, especially **naked options**, which do not identifiably hedge an underlying asset or liability position, to be risky because of the large loss potential. In some countries, regulators prohibit banks from writing puts or calls in certain areas of risk management.

naked options
Option positions that do not identifiably hedge an underlying asset or liability.

Futures versus Options Hedging

To understand the differences between using futures versus options contracts to hedge interest rate risk, compare the payoff gains illustrated in Figure 23–9 (for futures contracts) with those in Figure 23–7 (for buying put option contracts). A hedge with futures contracts reduces volatility in payoff gains on both the upside and downside of interest rate movements. That is, if the FI in Figure 23–9 loses value on the bond resulting from an interest rate increase (to the left of point *X*), a gain on the futures contract offsets the loss. If the FI gains value on the bond due to an interest rate decrease (to the right of point *X*), however, a loss on the futures contract offsets the gain.

In comparison, the hedge with the put option contract completely offsets losses but only partly offsets gains. That is, in Figure 23–7, if the FI loses value on the bond due to an interest rate increase (to the left of point *X*), a gain on the put option contract offsets the loss. However, if the FI gains value on the bond due to an interest rate decrease (to the right of point *X*), the gain is offset only to the extent that the FI loses the put option premium (because it never exercises the option). Thus, the put option hedge protects the FI against value losses when interest rates move against the on-balance-sheet securities but, unlike futures hedging, does not reduce value when interest rates move in favour of on-balance-sheet securities.

CONCEPT QUESTIONS

1. **What are some of the economic reasons for an FI not to write options?**
2. **What are some regulatory reasons that an FI might choose to buy options rather than write options?**

THE MECHANICS OF HEDGING A BOND OR BOND PORTFOLIO

LO2

We have shown how buying a put option on a bond can hedge the interest rate risk of an FI that holds bonds as part of its investment portfolio. In this section, we demonstrate the mechanics of buying a put option as a hedging device and show how an FI can calculate the fair premium value for a put option on a bond.

In calculating the fair value of an option, two alternative models can be used: the binomial model and the Black–Scholes model. The Black–Scholes model produces a closed-form solution to the valuation of call and put options. Appendix 23A shows how to calculate the value of an option using the Black–Scholes model. Although it works well for stocks, the Black–Scholes model has two major problems when employed to value bond options. First, it assumes that short-term interest rates are constant, which they generally are not. Second, it assumes a constant variance of returns on the underlying asset.[1] The application of the Black–Scholes formula to bonds is problematic because of the way bond prices behave between issuance and maturity.[2] This is shown in Figure 23–10, where a bond is issued at par, that is, the price of the bond is 100 percent times its face value at time of issue. If interest rates fall, its price

FIGURE 23–10
The Variance of a Bond's Price

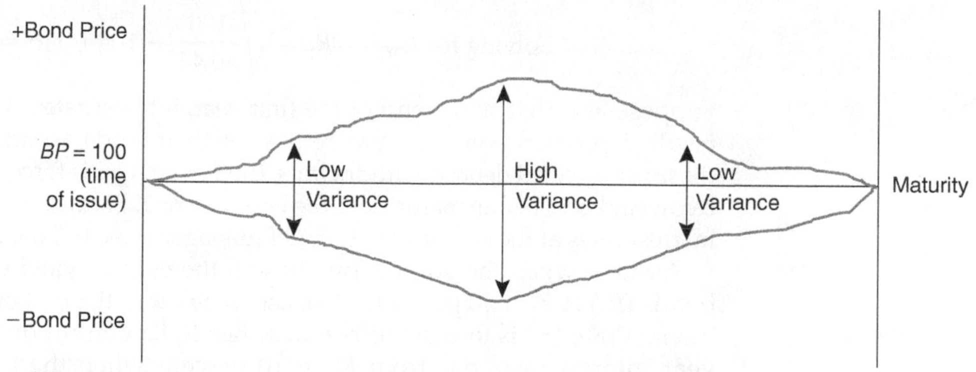

[1] The Black–Scholes formulas for a put and a call are

$$P = Xe^{-rT}N[-D + \sigma\sqrt{T}] - SN[-D]$$
$$C = SN[D] - Xe^{-rT}N[D - \sigma\sqrt{T}]$$

where

S = Price of the underlying asset
X = Exercise price
T = Time to option expiration
r = Instantaneous riskless interest rate
$D = \dfrac{ln(S/X) + (r + \sigma^2/2)T}{\sigma\sqrt{T}}$
$ln[\,.\,]$ = Natural logarithm
σ = Volatility of the underlying asset
$N[\,.\,]$ = Cumulative normal distribution function, that is, the probability of observing a value less than the value in brackets when drawing randomly from a standardized normal distribution

[2] There are models that modify Black–Scholes to allow for nonconstant variance. These include Merton, who allows variance to be time-dependent; Ball and Tourous, who allow bond prices to change as a stochastic process with a variance that first increases and then decreases (the Brownian bridge process); and the Schaefer–Schwartz model, which assumes that the standard deviation of returns is proportional to a bond's duration. See R. C. Merton, "On the Pricing of Corporate Debt: The Risk Structure of Interest Rates," *Journal of Finance* 29, 1974, pp. 449–470; C. Ball and W. N. Tourous, "Bond Price Dynamics and Options," *Journal of Financial and Quantitative Analysis* 18, 1983, pp. 517–531; and S. Schaefer and E. S. Schwartz, "Time Dependent Variance and the Pricing of Bond Options," *Journal of Finance* 42, 1987, pp. 1113–1128.

may rise above 100 percent, and if interest rates rise, its price may fall below 100 percent. However, as the bond approaches maturity, all price paths must lead to 100 percent of the face value of the bond or principal paid by the issuer on maturity. Because of this **pull-to-par**, the variance of bond prices is nonconstant over time, rising at first and then falling as the bond approaches maturity. We evaluate the mechanics of hedging using bond put options in a simple binomial framework next.

pull-to-par
The tendency of the variance of a bond's price or return to decrease as maturity approaches.

Hedging with Bond Options Using the Binomial Model

Suppose that an FI manager has purchased a \$100 zero-coupon bond with exactly two years to maturity. A zero-coupon bond, if held to maturity, pays its face value of \$100 on maturity in two years. Assume that the FI manager pays \$80.45 per \$100 of face value for this zero-coupon bond. This means that if held to maturity, the FI's annual yield to maturity (R_2) from this investment would be

$$BP_2 = \frac{100}{(1 + R_2)^2}$$

$$80.44 = \frac{100}{(1 + R_2)^2}$$

$$\text{Solving for } R_2, \qquad R_2 = \sqrt{\frac{100}{80.44}} - 1 = 0.115 = 11.5\%$$

Suppose also that, at the end of the first year, interest rates rise unexpectedly. As a result, depositors, seeking higher returns on their funds, withdraw deposits. To meet these unexpected deposit withdrawals, the FI manager is forced to liquidate (sell) the two-year bond before maturity, at the end of year 1. Because of the unexpected rise in interest rates at the end of year 1, the FI manager must sell the bond at a low price.

Assume when the bond is purchased, the current yield on one-year discount bonds (R_1) is $R_1 = 10$ percent. Also, assume that at the end of year 1, the one-year interest rate (r_1) is forecast to rise to either 13.82 percent or 12.18 percent. If one-year interest rates rise from $R_1 = 10$ percent when the bond is purchased to $r_1 = 13.82$ percent at the end of year 1, the FI manager will be able to sell the zero-coupon bond with one year remaining to maturity for a bond price, BP, of

$$BP_1 = \frac{100}{(1 + r_1)} = \frac{100}{1.1382} = \$87.86$$

If, on the other hand, one-year interest rates rise to 12.18 percent, the manager can sell the bond with one year remaining to maturity for

$$BP_1 = \frac{100}{(1 + r_1)} = \frac{100}{(1.1218)} = \$89.14$$

In these equations, r_1 stands for the two possible one-year rates that might arise one year into the future.[3] That is,

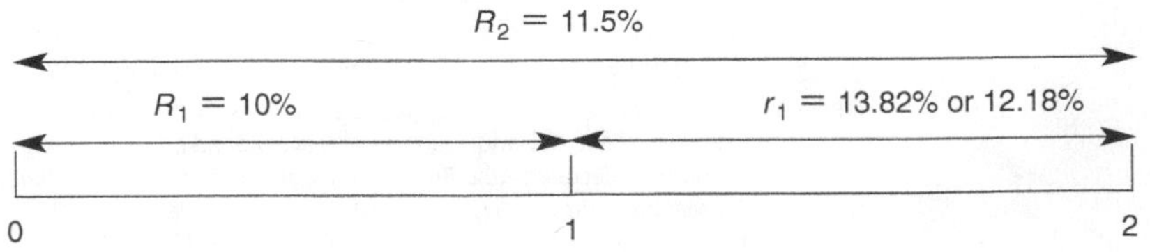

[3] If one-year bond rates next year equalled the one-year bond rate this year, $R_1 = r_1 = 10$ percent, then the bond could be sold for $BP_1 = \$90.91$.

FIGURE 23–11
Binomial Model of Bond Prices: Two-Year Zero-Coupon Bond

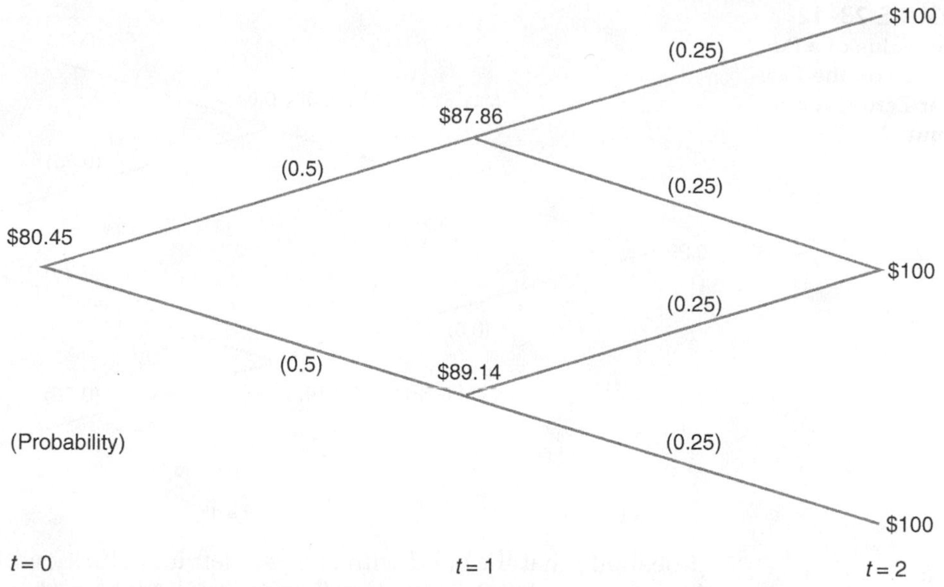

Assume the manager believes that one-year rates (r_1) one year from today will be 13.82 percent or 12.18 percent with an equal probability. This means that the expected one-year rate one year from today would be

$$E(r_1) = 0.5(0.1382) + 0.5(0.1218) = 0.13 = 13\%$$

Thus, the expected price if the bond has to be sold at the end of the first year is[4]

$$E(P_1) = \frac{100}{(1.13)} = \$88.50$$

Assume that the FI manager wants to ensure that the bond sale produces at least $88.50 per $100; otherwise the FI has to find alternative and very costly sources of liquidity (for example, the FI might have to borrow from the central bank's discount window and incur the direct and indirect penalty costs involved; see Chapter 19). One way for the FI to ensure that it receives at least $88.50 on selling the bond at the end of the year is to buy a put option on the bond at time 0 with an exercise price of $88.50 at time (year) 1. If the bond is trading below $88.50 at the end of the year—say, at $87.86—the FI can exercise its option and put the bond back to the writer of the option, who will have to pay the FI $88.50. If, however, the bond is trading above $88.50—say, at $89.14—the FI does not have to exercise its option and instead can sell the bond in the open market for $89.14.

The FI manager will want to recalculate the fair premium to pay for buying this put option or bond insurance at time 0. Figure 23–11 shows the possible paths (i.e., the binomial tree or lattice) of the zero-coupon bond's price from purchase to maturity over the two-year period. The FI manager purchased the bond at $80.45 with two years to maturity. Given expectations of rising rates, there is a 50 percent

---

[4] The interest rates assumed in this example are consistent with arbitrage-free pricing under current term structure conditions. That is, the expectations theory of interest rates implies that the following relationship must hold:

$$(1 + R_2)^2 = (1 + R_1) \times [1 + E(r_1)]$$

As you can easily see, when the interest rates from our example are inserted, $R_1 = 10\%$, $R_2 = 11.5\%$, $E(r_1) = 13\%$, this equation holds. Also, the two interest rates (prices) imply that the current volatility of one-year interest rates is 6.3 percent. That is, from the binomial model, $\sigma = 1/2 ln[r_u/r_d]$, such that $\sigma = 1/2 ln[13.82/12.18] = 0.063$ or 6.3%.

FIGURE 23–12
The Value of a Put Option on the Two-Year Zero-Coupon Bond

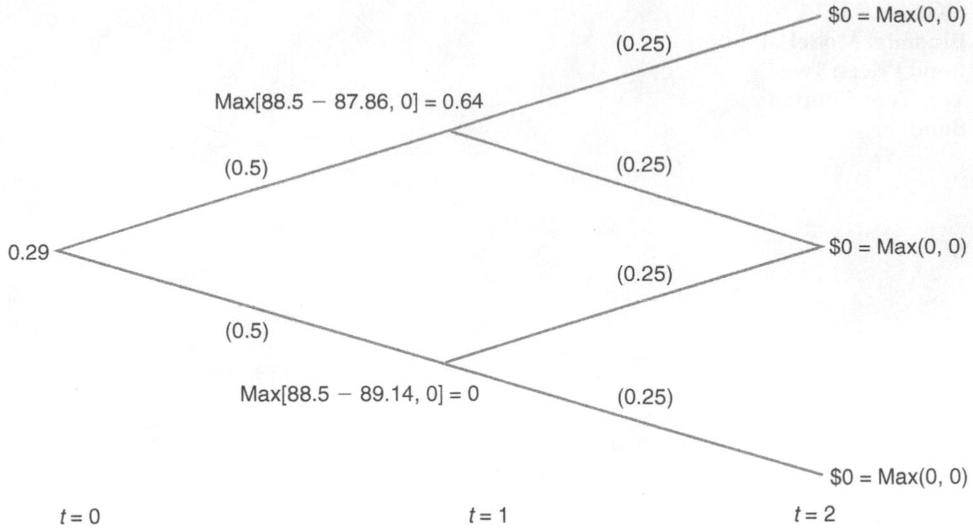

probability that the bond with one year left to maturity will trade at \$87.86 and a 50 percent probability that it will trade at \$89.14. Note that between $t = 1$, or one year left to maturity, and maturity ($t = 2$), there must be a pull-to-par on the bond; that is, all paths must lead to a price of \$100 on maturity.

The value of the option is shown in Figure 23–12. The option in Figure 23–12 can be exercised only at the end of year 1 ($t = 1$). If the zero-coupon bond with one year left to maturity trades at \$87.86, the option is worth \$88.50 − \$87.86 in time-1 dollars, or \$0.64. If the bond trades at \$89.14, the option has no value since the bond could be sold at a higher value than the exercise price of \$88.50 on the open market. This suggests that in time-1 dollars, the option is worth

$$0.5(\$0.64) + 0.5(\$0) = \$0.32$$

However, the FI is evaluating the option and paying the put premium at time $t = 0$, that is, one year before the date when the option might be exercised. Thus, the fair value of the put premium (P) the FI manager should be willing to pay is the discounted present value of the expected payoff from buying the option. Since one-year interest rates (R_1) are currently 10 percent, this implies

$$P = \frac{\$0.32}{1 + R_1} = \frac{\$0.32}{(1.1)} = \$0.29$$

or a premium, P, of approximately 29 cents per \$100 bond option purchased.

Further, as you can easily see, the option becomes increasingly valuable as the variability of interest rates increases. Conceptually, the branches of the binomial tree diagram become more widely dispersed as variability increases. For example, suppose one-year interest rates on the upper branch were expected to be 14.82 percent instead of 13.82 percent. Then the price on a one-year, zero-coupon bond associated with a one-year yield of 14.82 percent is \$87.09 and the option is worth \$88.50 − \$87.09 in time-1 dollars, or \$1.41. Thus, the value of the put option (P) with the same exercise price of \$88.50 is

$$P = \frac{0.5(\$1.41) + 0.5(\$0)}{1.1}$$
$$= 64 \text{ cents}$$

Notice the familiar result from option pricing theory holds:

$$\frac{\delta P}{\delta \sigma} > 0$$

That is, the value of the put option increases with an increase in underlying variance of asset returns.

CONCEPT QUESTIONS

1. **What are two common models used to calculate the fair value of a bond option? Which is preferable, and why?**
2. **In the example above, calculate the value of the option if the exercise price (*X*) = \$88. (*P* = \$0.064)**

ACTUAL BOND OPTIONS

m-x.ca
cboe.com

open interest
The outstanding stock of put or call contracts.

futures option
An option contract that, when exercised, results in the delivery of a futures contract as the underlying asset.

We have presented a simple example of how FIs may use bond options to hedge exposure to liability withdrawal and forced liquidation of assets in a world of interest rate variability. In actuality, FIs have a wide variety of OTC and exchange-traded options available. Interest rate options are listed on the Montréal Exchange in Canada and on the CBOE. However, these contracts are rarely traded. For example, in September 2012 there was no trading of any of the four interest rate option contracts (13-week U.S. T-bill, U.S. T-yield 5 year, 10-year U.S. T-notes, and U.S. T-yield 30 year) on the CBOE. In actual practice, most pure bond options trade OTC. This is not because interest rate or bond options are not used, although the **open interest** is relatively small, but because the preferred method of hedging is an option on an interest rate futures contract.

A **futures option** is a contract in which the underlying asset is a futures contract (e.g., \$100,000 Treasury bond futures). The buyer of a call (put) option on a futures contract has the right to buy (sell) the underlying futures contract before expiration (i.e., an American option). The seller of a call (put) option on a futures contract creates the obligation to sell (buy) the underlying futures contract on exercise by the option buyer. If exercised, a call (put) option holder can buy (sell) the underlying futures contract at the exercise price. Options on futures can be more attractive to FIs than options on an underlying asset when it is cheaper or more convenient to deliver futures contracts on the asset rather than the actual asset. For example, trading options on T-bond futures contracts rather than options on T-bonds ensures that a highly liquid asset will be delivered and that problems associated with accrued interest and the determination of which long-term bond to deliver are avoided. Another advantage is that price information about futures contracts (the underlying asset on the option) is generally more readily available than price information on the T-bonds themselves (T-bond price information can be obtained only by surveying bond dealers).

Finally, bond or interest rate futures options are generally preferred to options on the underlying bond because they combine the favourable liquidity, credit risk, homogeneity, and marking-to-market features of futures with the same asymmetric payoff functions as regular puts and calls. Figure 23–13 lists settle prices for some of the futures options (i.e., an option contract that, when exercised, results in the delivery of a futures contract as the underlying asset) on bonds for trading on September 21, 2012.

FIGURE 23–13
Futures Options on Interest Rates and Currencies, September 21, 2012

Source: *The Wall Street Journal Online*, September 21, 2012, online.wsj.com. Reprinted by permission of *The Wall Street Journal*. All prices are settlement prices. Volume and open interest are from the previous trading day.

Interest Rate Futures Options

U.S. Treasury Bonds (CBOT)
$100,000, pts & 64ths of 100 pct

	CALLS			PUTS		
Strike Price	**Oct**	**Dec**	**Mar**	**Oct**	**Dec**	**Mar**
15000	0-01	1-20	2-09	3-09	4-28	6-34
15100	0-01	1-02	1-52	4-09	5-10	7-13
15200	0-01	0-51	1-34	5-09	5-59	7-59
15300	0-01	0-39	1-18	6-09	6-46	8-42
15400	0-01	0-30	1-04	7-09	7-37	9-28
15500	0-01	0-23	0-56	8-09	8-30	10-16
15600	0-01	0-18	0-45	9-09	9-25	11-05
15700	0-01	0-14	0-36	10-09	10-21	11-60
15800	0-01	0-11	0-29	11-09	11-18	12-53
15900	0-01	0-09	0-23	12-09	12-16	13-46
Open Interest		**CALLS**	**259,217**		**PUTS**	**297,542**

10-Yr. Treasury (CBOT)
$100,000, prin, pts & 64ths of 100 pct

Strike Price	**Oct**	**Dec**	**Mar**	**Oct**	**Dec**	**Mar**
15000	0-01	0-01	0-01	17-22	17-21	17-58
15050	0-01	0-01	0-01	17-54	17-53	18-26
15100	0-01	0-01	0-01	18-22	18-21	18-58
15150	0-01	0-01	0-01	18-54	18-53	19-26
15200	0-01	0-01	0-01	19-22	19-21	19-58
15250	0-01	0-01	0-01	19-54	19-53	20-26
15300	0-01	0-01	0-01	20-22	20-21	20-58
15350	0-01	0-01	0-01	20-54	20-53	21-26
Open Interest		**CALLS**	**775,688**	**PUTS**	**1,037,195**	

Eurodollars (CME)
$1 million, pts of 100 pct

	CALLS			PUTS		
Strike Price	**Oct**	**Dec**	**Mar**	**Oct**	**Dec**	**Mar**
981250	155.00	155.00	153.75	-	0.25	0.25
982500	142.50	142.50	141.25	-	0.25	0.25
983750	130.00	130.00	128.75	-	0.25	0.25
985000	117.50	117.50	116.25	-	0.25	0.25
986250	105.00	105.00	104.00	-	0.25	0.50
987500	92.50	92.50	91.50	0.25	0.25	0.50
988750	80.00	80.00	79.25	0.25	0.25	0.75
990000	67.50	67.50	66.75	0.25	0.25	0.75
991250	55.00	55.00	54.50	0.25	0.25	1.00
992500	42.50	42.75	42.25	0.25	0.25	1.25
993750	30.00	30.25	30.25	0.25	0.25	1.75
995000	17.50	18.00	18.50	0.25	0.50	2.50
996250	5.25	7.00	8.25	0.25	2.00	4.75
997500	0.25	1.00	2.00	7.75	8.50	11.00
998750	0.25	0.25	0.50	20.00	20.00	22.00
1000000	-	0.25	0.25	32.50	32.50	34.00
1001250	-	-	-	45.00	45.00	46.50
1002500	-	-	-	57.50	57.50	59.00
Open Interest	**CALLS**	**2,086,816**		**PUTS**		**3,843,362**

Currency Futures Options

Japanese Yen (CME)
12,500,000 yen, cents per 100 yen

Strike Price	**Oct**	**Dec**	**Mar**	**Oct**	**Dec**	**Mar**
1260	1.17	2.11	3.20	0.04	0.94	1.89
1265	0.67	1.80	2.91	0.09	1.13	2.10
1270	0.17	1.52	2.64	0.19	1.35	2.33
1275	0.36	1.27	2.38	0.33	1.60	2.57
1280	0.16	1.04	2.14	0.83	1.87	2.83
1285	0.06	0.84	1.93	1.33	2.17	3.12
1290	0.01	0.67	1.73	1.83	2.50	3.41
Open Interest		**CALLS**	**26,801**	**PUTS**		**44,440**

Swiss Franc (CME)
125,000 francs, cents per franc

Strike Price	**Oct**	**Dec**	**Mar**	**Oct**	**Dec**	**Mar**
1060	1.71	2.56	3.58	0.01	0.85	1.70
1065	1.21	2.22	3.26	0.04	1.01	1.88
1070	0.71	1.91	2.97	0.12	1.20	2.08
1075	0.21	1.62	2.68	0.29	1.41	2.29
1080	0.17	1.36	2.41	0.29	1.65	2.52
1085	0.06	1.13	2.17	0.79	1.92	2.78
1090	0.02	0.93	1.94	1.29	2.22	3.05
Open Interest		**CALLS**	**2,381**	**PUTS**		**1,786**

Canadian Dollar (CME)
100,000 dollars, cents per dollar

Strike Price	**Oct**	**Dec**	**Mar**	**Oct**	**Dec**	**Mar**
1000	1.98	2.47	2.97	-	0.49	1.23
1005	1.48	2.09	2.65	0.02	0.61	1.40
1010	0.98	1.74	2.33	0.06	0.76	1.58
1015	0.48	1.42	2.03	0.17	0.94	1.78
1020	0.18	1.14	1.76	0.02	1.16	2.01
1025	0.05	0.89	1.51	0.52	1.41	2.26
1030	0.01	0.68	1.29	1.02	1.70	2.54
Open Interest		**CALLS**	**30,756**	**PUTS**		**40,678**

British Pound (CME)
62,500 pounds, cents per pound

Strike Price	**Oct**	**Dec**	**Mar**	**Oct**	**Dec**	**Mar**
1580	3.38	3.97	4.90	0.01	0.60	1.57
1590	2.38	3.20	4.21	0.01	0.82	1.88
1600	1.38	2.50	3.56	0.02	1.12	2.23
1610	0.38	1.89	2.98	0.11	1.51	2.64
1620	2.29	1.38	2.45	0.62	2.00	3.11
1630	0.06	0.96	2.00	0.62	2.58	3.65
1640	0.01	0.66	1.60	2.62	3.28	4.25
Open Interest		**CALLS**	**23,236**	**PUTS**		**23,592**

When the FI hedges by buying put options on bond futures, if interest rates rise and bond prices fall, the exercise of the put causes the FI to deliver a bond futures contract to the writer at an exercise price higher than the cost of the bond future currently trading on the futures exchange. The futures price itself reflects the price of the underlying deliverable bond, such as a 15-year, 8 percent coupon T-bond; see Figure 23–13. As a result, a profit on futures options may be made to offset the loss on the market value of bonds held directly in the FI's portfolio. If interest rates fall and bond and futures prices rise, the buyer of the futures option will not exercise the put, and the losses on the futures put option are limited to the put premium. Thus, if on September 21, 2012, the FI had bought one US$100,000 December 2012 T-bond futures put option at a strike price of US$154 but did not exercise the option, the FI's loss equals the put premium of 7 32/64 per US$100, or US$7,578.125 per US$100,000 contract. Offsetting these losses, however, would be an increase in the market value of the FI's underlying bond portfolio. Unlike futures positions in Chapter 22, an upside profit potential remains when interest rates fall and FIs use put options on futures to hedge interest rate risk. We show this in the next section.

CONCEPT QUESTIONS

1. **Why are bond or interest rate futures options generally preferred to options on the underlying bond?**
2. **If an FI hedges by buying put options on futures and interest rates rise (i.e., bond prices fall), what is the outcome?**

HEDGING INTEREST RATE RISK WITH OPTIONS

LO3

Our previous simple example showed how a bond option could hedge the interest rate risk on an underlying bond position in the asset portfolio. Next, we determine the put option position that can hedge the interest rate risk of the overall balance sheet; that is, we analyze macrohedging rather than microhedging.

Chapter 9 showed that an FI's net worth exposure to an interest rate shock could be represented as

$$\Delta E = -(D_A - kD_L) \times A \times \frac{\Delta R}{1+R}$$

where

ΔE = Change in the FI's net worth

$(D_A - kD_L)$ = FI's leverage-adjusted duration gap

A = Size of the FI's assets

$\frac{\Delta R}{1+R}$ = Size of the interest rate shock

k = FI's leverage ratio (L/A)

Suppose the FI manager wishes to determine the optimal number of put options to buy to insulate the FI against rising rates. An FI with a positive duration gap (see Figure 23–14) would lose on-balance-sheet net worth when interest rates rise. In this case, the FI manager would buy put options.[5] That is, the FI manager

[5] Conversely, an FI with a negative duration gap would lose on-balance-sheet net worth when interest rates fall. In this case, the FI manager would buy call options to generate profits to offset the loss in net worth due to an interest rate shock.

FIGURE 23–14
Buying Put Options to Hedge the Interest Rate Risk Exposure of the FI

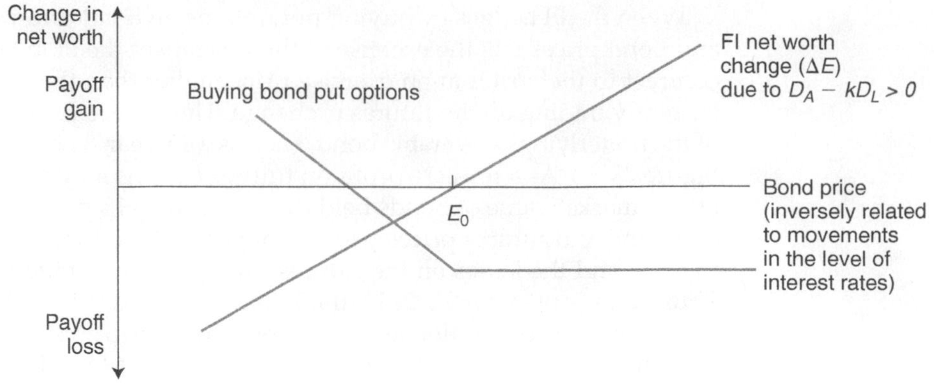

would adopt a put option position to generate profits that just offset the loss in net worth due to an interest rate shock (where E_0 is the FI's initial equity (net worth) position in Figure 23–14).

Let ΔP be the total change in the value of the put option position in T-bonds. This can be decomposed into

$$\Delta P = (N_p \times \Delta p) \tag{23.1}$$

where N_p is the number of \$100,000 put options on T-bond contracts to be purchased (the number for which we are solving) and Δp is the change in the dollar value for each \$100,000 face value T-bond put option contract.

The change in the dollar value of each contract (Δp) can be further decomposed into

$$\Delta p = \frac{dp}{dB} \times \frac{dB}{dR} \times \Delta R \tag{23.2}$$

This decomposition needs some explanation. The first term (dp/dB) shows the change in the value of a put option for each \$1 change in the underlying bond. This is called the *delta of an option* (δ) and lies between 0 and 1. For put options, the delta has a negative sign since the value of the put option falls when bond prices rise.[6] The second term (dB/dR) shows how the market value of a bond changes if interest rates rise by 1 bp. This value of 1 bp can be linked to duration. Specifically, we know from Chapter 9 that

$$\frac{dB}{B} = -MD \times dR \tag{23.3}$$

That is, the percentage change in the bond's price for a small change in interest rates is proportional to the bond's modified duration (MD). Equation 23.3 can be rearranged by cross-multiplying as

$$\frac{dB}{dR} = -MD \times B \tag{23.4}$$

[6] For call options, the delta has a positive sign since the value of the call rises when bond prices rise. As we proceed with the derivation, we examine only the case of a hedge using a put option contract (i.e., the FI has a positive duration gap and expects interest rates to rise). For a hedge with a call option contract (i.e., the FI has a negative duration gap), the derivation below changes only in that the sign on the delta is reversed (from negative to positive).

Thus, the term dB/dR is equal to minus the modified duration on the bond (MD) times the current market value of the T-bond (B) underlying the put option contract. As a result, we can rewrite equation 23.2 as

$$\Delta p = [(-\delta) \times (-MD) \times B \times \Delta R] \tag{23.5}$$

where ΔR is the shock to interest rates (i.e., the number of basis points by which rates change). Since from Chapter 9 we know that $MD = D/(1 + R)$, we can rewrite equation 23.5 as

$$\Delta p = \left[(-\delta) \times (-D) \times B \times \frac{\Delta R}{1 + R}\right] \tag{23.6}$$

Thus, the change in the total value of a put position[7] (ΔP) is

$$\Delta P = N_p \times \left[\delta \times D \times B \times \frac{\Delta R}{1 + R}\right] \tag{23.7}$$

The term in brackets is the change in the value of one $100,000 face value T-bond put option as rates change, and N_p is the number of put option contracts.

To hedge net worth exposure, we require the profit on the off-balance-sheet put options (ΔP) to just offset the loss of on-balance-sheet net worth ($-\Delta E$) when interest rates rise (and thus bond prices fall). That is,

$$\Delta P + \Delta E = 0$$

$$N_p \times \left[\delta \times D \times B \times \frac{\Delta R}{1 + R}\right] + \left[-[D_A - kD_L] \times A \times \frac{\Delta R}{1 + R}\right] = 0$$

Multiplying through by $(1 + R)/\Delta R$, we get

$$N_p \times [\delta \times D \times B] + [-[D_A - kD_L] \times A] = 0$$

Solving for N_p—the number of put options to buy—we have[8]

$$N_p = \frac{[D_A - kD_L] \times A}{[\delta \times D \times B]} \tag{23.8}$$

Appendix 23B derives the equation for the number of option contracts to buy or sell for a microhedge.[9]

---

[7] Note that since both the delta and D values of the put option and bond have negative signs, their product will be positive. Thus, these negative signs are not shown in the equation to calculate N_p.

[8] For a hedge involving a call option, the formula is

$$N_C = \frac{[D_A - kD_L] \times A}{-[\delta \times D \times B]}$$

[9] For a microhedge, this equation becomes

$$N_O = \frac{D \times P}{\delta \times D \times B}$$

where P is the price of the asset or liability being hedged and D is its duration.

EXAMPLE 23–1

Macrohedge of Interest Rate Risk Using a Put Option

Suppose, as in Example 22–1, an FI's balance sheet is such that $D_A = 5$, $D_L = 3$, $k = 0.9$, and $A = \$100$ million. Rates are expected to rise from 10 to 11 percent over the next six months, which would result in a \$2.09 million loss in net worth to the FI. Suppose also that δ of the put option is 0.5, which indicates that the option is close to being in the money; $D = 8.82$ for the bond underlying the put option contract; and the current market value of \$100,000 face value of long-term Treasury bonds underlying the option contract, B, equals \$97,000. Solving for N_p, the number of put option contracts to buy is

$$N_p = \frac{[5 - 0.9 \times 3] \times \$100 \text{ million}}{[0.5 \times 8.82 \times \$97{,}000]} = \frac{\$230{,}000{,}000}{\$427{,}770}$$
$$= 537.672 \text{ contracts}$$

If the FI slightly underhedges, this will be rounded down to 537 contracts. If rates increase from 10 to 11 percent, the value of the FI's put options will change by

$$\Delta P = 537 \times \left[0.5 \times 8.82 \times \$97{,}000 \times \frac{0.01}{1.1}\right] = \$2.09 \text{ million}$$

just offsetting the loss in net worth on the balance sheet.

The total premium cost to the FI of buying these puts is the price (premium) of each put times the number of puts:

$$\text{Cost} = N_p \times \text{Put premium per contract}$$

Suppose that T-bond put option premiums are quoted at \$2½ per \$100 of face value for the nearby contract or \$2,500 per \$100,000 put contract; then the cost of macrohedging the gap with put options will be

$$\text{Cost} = 537 \times \$2{,}500 = \$1{,}342{,}500$$

or over \$1.3 million. Remember, the total assets of the FI were assumed to be \$100 million.

Figure 23–15 summarizes the change in the FI's overall value from a 1 percent increase in interest rates and the offsetting change in value from the hedge in the put option market. If rates increase as predicted, the FI's gap exposure results in a decrease in net worth of \$2.09 million. This decrease is offset with a \$2.09 million

FIGURE 23–15 Buying Put Options to Hedge an FI's Interest Rate Gap Risk Exposure

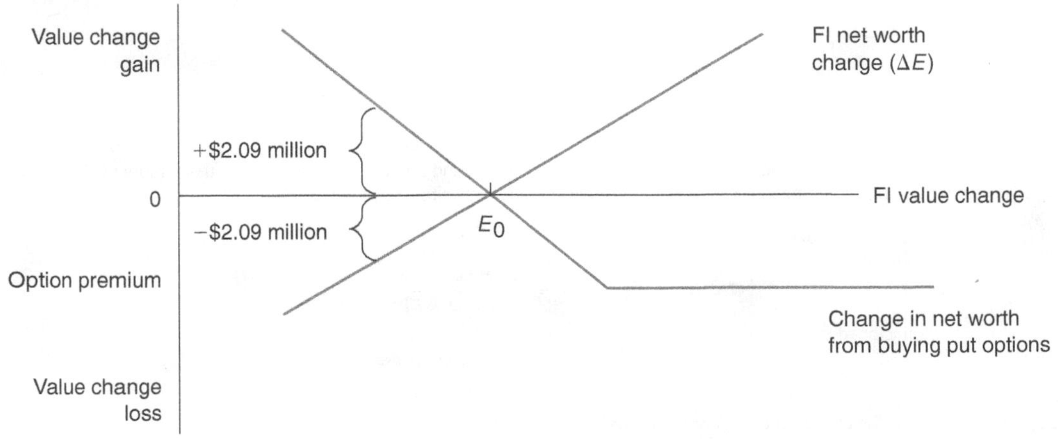

gain on the put option position held by the FI. Should rates decrease, however, the resulting increase in net worth is not offset by a decrease in an out-of-the-money put option.

Appendix 23B illustrates how these options can be used to microhedge a specific asset or liability on an FI's balance sheet against interest rate risk.

Basis Risk

It is again important to recognize that in the previous examples, the FI hedged interest rate risk exposure perfectly because basis risk was assumed to be zero. That is, we assumed the change in interest rates on the balance sheet is equal to the change in the interest rate on the bond underlying the option contract [i.e., $\Delta R/(1 + R) = \Delta R_b/(1 + R_b)$]. As discussed in Chapter 22, the introduction of basis risk means that the FI must adjust the number of option contracts it holds to account for the degree to which the rate on the option's underlying security (i.e., T-bond) moves relative to the spot rate on the asset or liability the FI is hedging.

Allowing basis risk to exist, the equation used to determine the number of put options to buy to hedge interest rate risk becomes

$$N_p = \frac{(D_A - kD_L) \times A}{\delta \times D \times B \times br}$$

where br is a measure of the volatility of interest rates (R_b) on the bond underlying the options contract relative to the interest rate that impacts the bond on the FI's balance sheet (R). That is,

$$br = \frac{\dfrac{\Delta R_b}{1 + R_b}}{\dfrac{\Delta R}{1 + R}}$$

EXAMPLE 23–2

Put Option Macrohedge with Basis Risk

Refer to Example 23–1. Suppose that basis risk, br, is 0.92 (i.e., the rate on the option's underlying bond changes by 92 percent of the spot rate change on the balance sheet being hedged). In Example 23–1, with no basis risk, the number of options needed to hedge interest rate risk on the bond position is 537.672 put option contracts. Introducing basis risk, $br = 0.92$:

$$N_p = \frac{\$230{,}000{,}000}{0.5 \times 8.82 \text{ years} \times \$97{,}000 \times 0.92} = 584.4262 \text{ put option contracts}$$

Additional put option contracts are needed to hedge interest rate risk because interest rates on the bond underlying the option contract do not move as much as interest rates on the bond held as an asset on the balance sheet.

As described in Chapter 22, the FI can analyze the relationship between interest rates on the security underlying the futures option contract (e.g., T-bond) and the security being hedged on the FI's balance sheet by investigating their relative behaviour in the recent past. This can be done by running an ordinary least-squares (OLS) linear regression of T-bond rate changes on spot rate changes with the slope coefficient of this regression giving an estimate of the degree of comovement of the two rates over time, or basis risk.

CONCEPT QUESTIONS

1. **If interest rates fall, are you better off purchasing call or put options on bonds, and why?**
2. **In the example above, what number of put options should you purchase if $\delta = 0.25$ and $D = 6$? ($N_p = 1{,}718.213$)**

HEDGING FOREIGN EXCHANGE RISK WITH OPTIONS

LO4

Just as an FI can hedge a long position in bonds against interest rate risk through bond options or futures options on bonds, a similar opportunity is available to microhedge long or short positions in a foreign currency asset against FX rate risk. To see this, suppose that a U.S.-based FI bought, or is long in, a Canadian dollar (CDN$) asset in September 2012. This CDN$ asset is a two-month T-bill paying CDN$100 million in December 2012. Since the FI's liabilities are in U.S. dollars, it may wish to hedge the FX risk that the Canadian dollar will depreciate over the two months. Suppose that if the CDN$ were to fall from the current exchange rate of US$1.0217/CDN$, the FI would make a loss on its Canadian T-bill investment when measured in U.S. dollar terms. For example, if the CDN$ depreciated from US$1.0217/CDN$ in September 2012 to US$1.0037/CDN$ in December 2012, the C$100 million asset would be worth only US$100.37 million on maturity instead of the expected US$102.17 million when it was purchased in September. If the FX rate depreciation is sufficiently severe, the FI might be unable to meet its dollar liability commitments used to fund the T-bill purchase. To offset this exposure, the FI may buy three-month put options on Canadian dollars at an exercise price of US$1.015/CDN$. Thus, if the exchange rate does fall to US$1.0037/CDN$ at the end of three months, the FI manager can put the CDN$100 million proceeds from the T-bill on maturity to the writer of the option. Then the FI receives US$101.5 million instead of the US$100.37 million if the Canadian dollars were sold at the open market spot exchange rate at the end of the two months. If the CDN$ actually appreciates in value, or does not depreciate below US$1.015/CDN$, the option expires unexercised and the proceeds of the CDN$100 million asset will be realized by the FI manager by a sale of Canadian dollars for U.S. dollars in the spot FX market one month into the future (see Figure 23–16).

cme.com

As with bonds, the FI can buy put options on foreign currency futures contracts to hedge this currency risk. The futures option contracts for foreign currencies traded on the Chicago Mercantile Exchange (CME) are shown in Figure 23–13. A

FIGURE 23–16
Hedging FX Risk by Buying a Put Option on Canadian Dollars

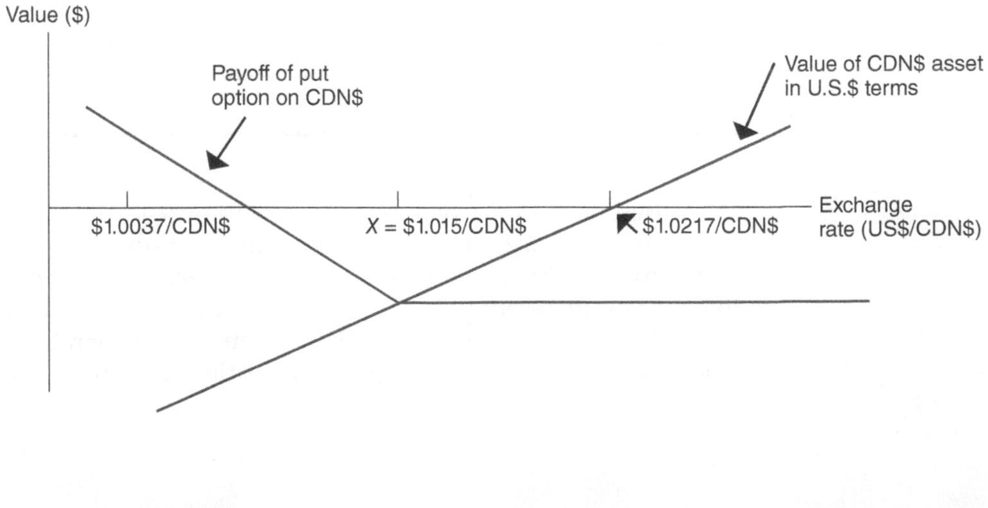

put position in one foreign currency futures contract with expiration in December 2012 and exercise price of US$1.015/CDN$ would have cost the FI a premium of US$0.0094/CDN$ on September 21, 2012. Since each Canadian dollar futures option contract is CDN$100,000 in size, the cost would have been US$940 per contract. If we ignore the question of basis risk—that is, the imperfect correlation between the US$/CDN$ exchange rate on the spot and futures in options markets—the optimal number of futures options purchased is

$$\frac{\text{C\$100,000,000}}{\text{C\$100,000}} = 1{,}000 \text{ contracts}$$

with a total premium cost of US$940,000.

CONCEPT QUESTIONS

1. **What is the difference between options on foreign currency and options on foreign currency futures?**
2. **If an FI has to hedge a US$5,000,000 liability exposure in Swiss francs (Sf), what options should it purchase to hedge this position? Using Figure 23–13, how many contracts of Swiss franc futures options should it purchase (assuming no basis risk) if it wants to hedge against the Swiss franc falling in value against the U.S. dollar given a current exchange rate of US$1.0755/Sf (or 0.9298 Sf/US$). (Buy 37.192 call options on Sf futures.)**

HEDGING CREDIT RISK WITH OPTIONS

LO5

Options also have a potential use in hedging the credit risk of an FI. Relative to their use in hedging interest rate risk, option use to hedge credit risk is a new phenomenon. Although FIs are always likely to be willing to bear some credit risk as part of the intermediation process (i.e., exploit their comparative advantage to bear such risk), options may allow them to modify that level of exposure selectively. In Chapter 22 we stated that an FI could seek an appropriate credit risk hedge by selling credit forward contracts. Rather than using credit forwards to hedge, an FI has at least two alternative credit option derivatives with which it can hedge its on-balance-sheet credit risk.

credit spread call option
A call option whose payoff increases as a yield spread increases above some stated exercise spread.

A **credit spread call option** is a call option whose payoff increases as the (default) risk premium or yield spread on a specified benchmark bond of the borrower increases above some exercise spread, *S*. An FI concerned that the risk on a loan to that borrower will increase can purchase a credit spread call option to hedge the increased credit risk.

Figure 23–17 illustrates the change in the FI's capital value and its payoffs from the credit spread call option as a function of the credit spread. As the credit

FIGURE 23–17
Buying Credit Spread Call Options to Hedge Credit Risk

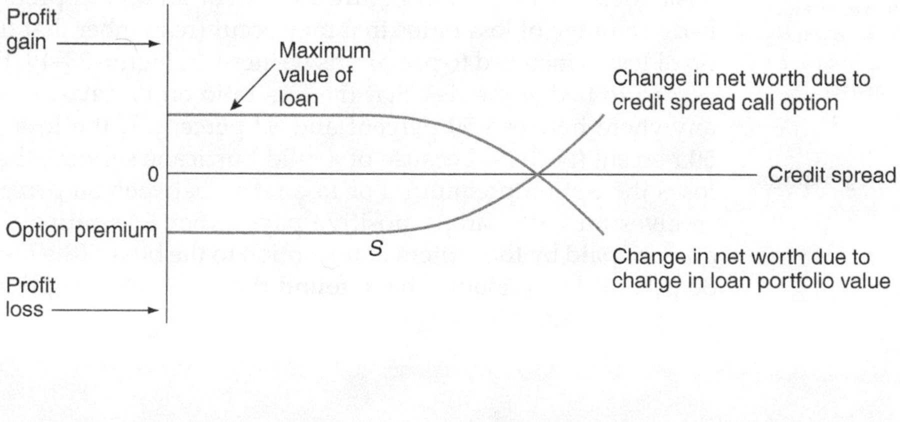

FIGURE 23–18
Buying a Digital Default Option to Hedge Credit Risk

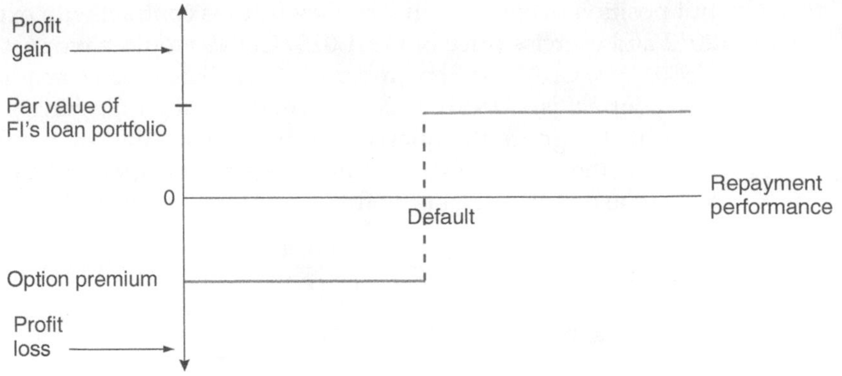

spread increases on an FI's loan to a borrower, the value of the loan, and consequently the FI's net worth, decreases. However, if the credit risk characteristics of the benchmark bond (i.e., change in credit spread) are the same as those on the FI's loan, the loss of net worth on the balance sheet is offset with a gain from the credit spread call option. If the required credit spread on the FI's loan decreases (perhaps because the credit quality of the borrower improves over the loan period), the value of the FI's loan and net worth increases (up to some maximum value), but the credit spread call option will expire out of the money. As a result, the FI will suffer a maximum loss equal to the required (call) premium on the credit option, which will be offset by the market value gain of the loan in the portfolio (which is reflected in a positive increase in the FI's net worth).

digital default option
An option that pays the par value of a loan in the event of default.

A **digital default option** is an option that pays a stated amount in the event of a loan default (the extreme case of increased credit risk). As shown in Figure 23–18, the FI can purchase a default option covering the par value of a loan (or loans) in its portfolio. In the event of a loan default, the option writer pays the FI the par value of the defaulted loans. If the loans are paid off in accordance with the loan agreement, however, the default option expires unexercised. As a result, the FI will suffer a maximum loss on the option equal to the premium (cost) of buying the default option from the writer (seller).

HEDGING CATASTROPHE RISK WITH CALL SPREAD OPTIONS

LO6

catastrophe (CAT) call spread
A call option on the loss ratio incurred in writing catastrophe insurance with a capped (or maximum) payout.

www.cmegroup.com

In 1993 the Chicago Board of Trade (CBOT) introduced **catastrophe (CAT) call spread** options to hedge the risk of unexpectedly high losses being incurred by property and casualty (P&C) insurers as a result of catastrophes such as hurricanes. The basic idea can be seen in Figure 23–19. For an option premium, the insurer can hedge a range of loss ratios that may occur (remember that the loss ratio is the ratio of losses incurred to premiums written). In Figure 23–19, the insurer buys a call spread to hedge the risk that the loss ratio on its catastrophe insurance may be anywhere between 50 percent and 80 percent. If the loss ratio ends up below 50 percent (perhaps because of a mild hurricane season), the insurance company loses the option premium. For loss ratios between 50 percent and 80 percent, it receives an increasingly positive payoff. For loss ratios above 80 percent, the amount paid by the writers of the option to the buyer (the insurer) is capped at the 80 percent level. Studies have found that catastrophe options can be used effectively by insurers to hedge catastrophe risk.

FIGURE 23–19
Catastrophe Call Spread Options

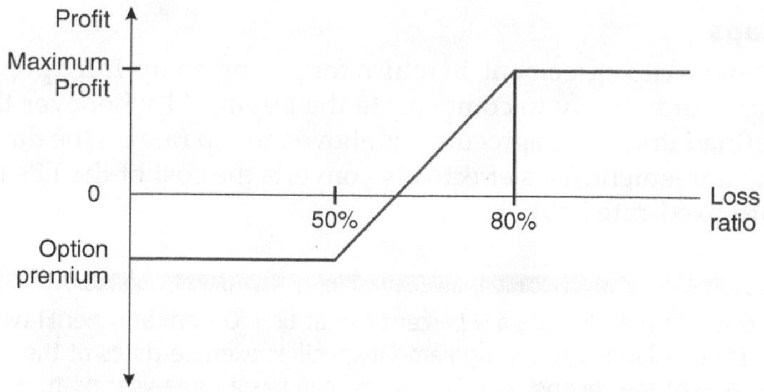

CONCEPT QUESTIONS

1. **What is the difference between a credit spread call option and a digital default option?**
2. **What is the difference between the profit on the catastrophe call spread option in Figure 23–19 and the profit of a standard call option on a stock?**

CAPS, FLOORS, AND COLLARS

LO7

cap
A call option on interest rates, often with multiple exercise dates.

floor
A put option on interest rates, often with multiple exercise dates.

collar
A position taken simultaneously in a cap and a floor.

Caps, floors, and collars are derivative securities that have many uses, especially in helping an FI hedge interest rate risk exposure as well as risk unique to its individual customers. Buying a **cap** means buying a call option or a succession of call options on interest rates. Specifically, if interest rates rise above the cap rate, the seller of the cap—usually a bank—compensates the buyer—for example, another FI—in return for an up-front premium. As a result, buying an interest rate cap is like buying insurance against an (excessive) increase in interest rates. A cap agreement can have one or many exercise dates.

Buying a **floor** means buying a put option on interest rates. If interest rates fall below the floor rate, the seller of the floor compensates the buyer in return for an up-front premium. As with caps, floor agreements can have one or many exercise dates.

A **collar** occurs when an FI takes a simultaneous position in a cap and a floor, such as buying a cap and selling a floor. The idea here is that the FI wants to hedge itself against rising rates but wants to finance the cost of the cap. One way to do this is to sell a floor and use the premiums on the floor to pay the premium on the purchase of the cap. Thus, these three OTC instruments are special cases of options; FI managers use them like bond options and bond futures options to hedge the interest rate risk of an FI's portfolios.

In general, FIs purchase interest rate caps if they are exposed to losses when interest rates rise. Usually, this happens if they are funding assets with floating-rate liabilities such as notes indexed to LIBOR (or some other cost of funds) and they have fixed-rate assets or they are net long in bonds, or—in a macrohedging context—their duration gap is $D_A - kD_L > 0$. By contrast, FIs purchase floors when they have fixed costs of debt and have variable rates (returns) on assets, are net short in bonds, or $D_A - kD_L < 0$. Finally, FIs purchase collars when they are concerned about excessive volatility of interest rates and to finance cap or floor positions.

Caps

Under a cap agreement, in return for paying an up-front premium, the seller of the cap stands ready to compensate the buying FI whenever the interest rate index defined under the agreement is above the cap rate on the dates specified under the cap agreement. This effectively converts the cost of the FI's floating-rate liabilities into fixed-rate liabilities.

EXAMPLE 23-3
Illustration of a Cap Used to Hedge Interest Rate Risk

Assume that an FI buys a 9 percent cap at time 0 from another FI with a notional face value of $100 million. The cap agreement specifies exercise dates at the end of the first year and the end of the second year. That is, the cap has a three-year maturity from initiation until the final exercise dates, with exercise dates at the end of year 1 and year 2.[10]

Thus, the buyer of the cap would demand two cash payments from the seller of the cap if rates lie above 9 percent at the end of the first year and at the end of the second year on the cap exercise dates. In practice, cap exercise dates usually closely correspond to payment dates on liabilities, for example, coupon dates on floating-rate notes. Consider one possible scenario in Figure 23–20.

In Figure 23–20, the seller of the cap has to pay the buyer of the cap the amount shown in Table 23–1. In this scenario, the cap-buying FI would receive $3 million (undiscounted) over the life of the cap to offset any rise in the cost of liability funding or market value losses on its bond/asset portfolio. However, the interest rates in Figure 23–20 are only one possible scenario. Consider the possible path to interest rates in Figure 23–21. In this interest scenario, rates fall below 9 percent at the end of the first year to 8 percent, and at the end of the second year to 7 percent on the cap exercise dates. Thus, the cap seller makes no payments.

FIGURE 23–20
Hypothetical Path of Interest Rates

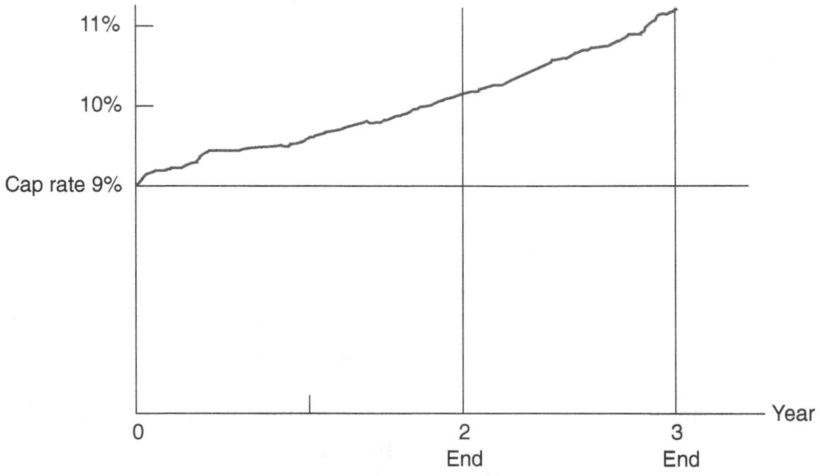

TABLE 23–1
Payments under the Cap

End of Year	Cap Rate	Actual Interest Rate	Interest Differential	Payment by Seller to Buyer
2	9%	10%	1%	$1 million
3	9	11	2	$2 million
Total				$3 million

[10] There is no point exercising the option at the end of year 1 (i.e., having three exercise dates) since interest rates for year 1 are set at the beginning of that year and are contractually set throughout. As a result, the FI does not bear interest rate uncertainty until the end of year 1 (i.e., interest uncertainty exists only in years 2 and 3).

FIGURE 23–21
Hypothetical Path of Interest Rates

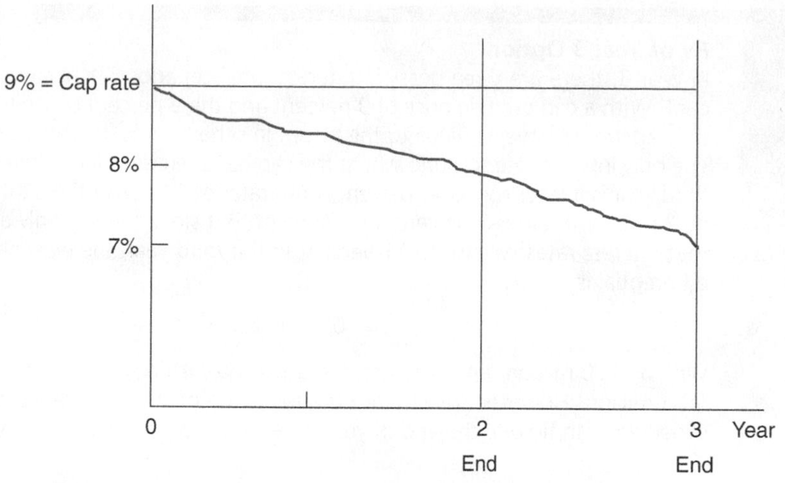

This example makes it clear that buying a cap is similar to buying a call option on interest rates in that when the option expires out of the money, because the interest rate is below the cap level, the cap seller makes no payments to the buyer. Conceptually, buying this cap is like buying a complex call option on an interest rate or a put option on a bond price with a single exercise price or interest rate and two exercise dates: the end of year 1 and the end of year 2.

The problem for the FI manager is to calculate the fair value of this 9 percent cap in the face of interest rate uncertainty. In particular, the FI manager does not know whether interest rates will be 10 percent at the end of year 1 or 8 percent. Similarly, the manager does not know whether interest rates will be 11 percent or 7 percent at the end of year 2. Nevertheless, to buy interest rate risk insurance in the form of a cap, the manager has to pay an up-front fee or premium to the seller of the cap. Next, we solve for the fair value of the cap premium in the framework of the binomial model introduced earlier to calculate the premium on a bond option.

Consider Figure 23–22, the binomial tree for the cap contract entered into at time 0. The cap can be exercised at the end of the first year and the end of the second year.[11] The current (time 0) value of the cap or the fair cap premium is the sum of the present value of the cap option exercised at the end of year 1 plus the present value of the cap option exercised at the end of year 2:

$$\text{Fair premium} = P = PV \text{ of year 1 option} + PV \text{ of year 2 option}$$

FIGURE 23–22
Interest Rate Cap with a 9 Percent Cap Rate

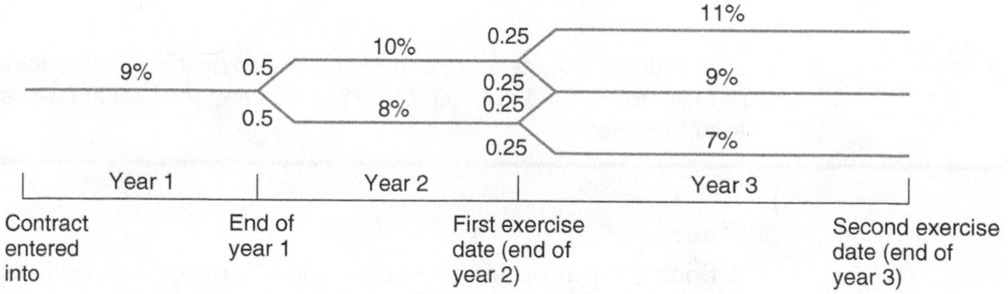

[11] Interest rates are normally set at the *beginning* of each period and paid at the *end* of each period.

EXAMPLE 23-4

Calculating the Premium on an Interest Rate Cap

***PV* of Year 3 Option**

In year 3, there are three possible interest rate scenarios: 11 percent, 9 percent, and 7 percent. With a cap exercise price of 9 percent and the 9 percent or 7 percent scenarios realized, the cap would have no value to the buyer. In other words, it would expire out of the money. The only interest rate scenario where the cap has exercise value to the buyer at the end of the third year is if rates rise to 11 percent. With rates at 11 percent, the interest differential would be 11 percent minus 9 percent, or 2 percent. But since there is only a 25 percent probability that interest rates will rise to 11 percent in the third year, the expected value of this interest differential is

$$0.25 \times 2\% = 0.5\%$$

With a $100 million cap, therefore, the expected cash payment at the end of year 3 would be $0.5 million. However, to calculate the fair value of the cap premium in current dollars, the expected cash flow at the end of year 3 has to be discounted back to the present (time 0):

$$PV_3 = \frac{0.5}{(1.09)\,(1.1)\,(1.11)} = 0.3757$$

where 9 percent, 10 percent, and 11 percent are the appropriate one-year discount rates for payments in years 1, 2, and 3. Thus, the fair present value of the option at the end of year 3 is 0.3757, or $375,700, given the $100 million face value of the cap.

***PV* of Year 2 Option**

In year 2, there are two interest rate scenarios: interest rates could rise to 10 percent or fall to 8 percent. If rates fall to 8 percent, the 9 percent cap has no value to the buyer. However, if rates rise to 10 percent, this results in a positive interest differential of 1 percent at the end of year 2. However, the expected interest differential is only 0.5 of 1 percent since this is the probability that rates will rise from 9 percent to 10 percent in year 2:

$$0.5 \times 1\% = 0.5\%$$

In dollar terms, with a $100 million cap, the expected value of the cap at the end of year 2 is $0.5 million. To evaluate the time 0 or present value of a cap exercised at the end of time period 2, this expected cash flow has to be discounted back to time 0 using the appropriate one-year discount rates. That is,

$$PV_2 = \frac{0.5}{(1.09)(1.1)} = 0.417$$

or $417,000, given the $100 million face value of the cap. As a result, the fair value of the premium the FI should be willing to pay for this cap is

$$\begin{aligned} \text{Cap premium} &= PV_2 + PV_3 \\ &= \$417{,}000 + 375{,}700 \\ &= \$792{,}700 \end{aligned}$$

That is, under the interest rate scenarios implied by this simple binomial model, the FI should pay no more than $792,700, or 0.7927 percent of notional face value, in buying the cap from the seller.

Floors

A floor is a put option or a collection of put options on interest rates. Here the FI manager who buys a floor is concerned about falling interest rates. Perhaps the FI is funding liabilities at fixed rates and has floating-rate assets, or maybe it is short in some bond position and will lose if it has to cover the position with higher-priced bonds after interest rates fall. In a macrohedging sense, the FI could face a duration gap where the duration of assets is less than the leverage-adjusted duration of liabilities ($D_A - kD_L < 0$).

EXAMPLE 23-5

Illustration of a Floor Used to Hedge Interest Rate Risk

Consider the profit from buying a floor depicted in Figure 23–23. In this simple example, the floor is set at 4 percent and the buyer pays an up-front premium to the seller of the floor. While caps can be viewed as buying a complex call option on interest rates, a floor can be viewed as buying a complex put option on interest rates. In our example, the floor has two exercise dates: the end of year 2 and the end of year 3.

If the interest scenario in Figure 23–23 is the actual interest rate path, the payments from the seller to the buyer would be as shown in Table 23–2.

FIGURE 23–23
Interest Rate Floor with a 4 Percent Floor

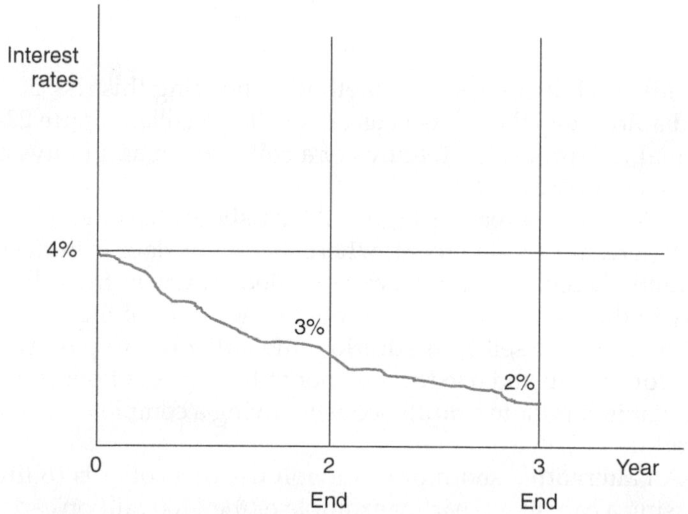

TABLE 23–2
Hypothetical Floor Payments

End of Year	Cap Rate	Actual Interest Rate	Interest Differential	Payment by Seller to Buyer
2	4%	3%	1%	\$1 million
3	4	2	2	\$2 million
Total				\$3 million

Since the buyer of the floor is uncertain about the actual path of interest rates—rates could rise and not fall—such profits are only probabilistic. That is, the buyer would have to use a model similar to the binomial model for caps to calculate the fair up-front premium to be paid for the floor at time 0.

Collars

FI managers who are very risk averse and overly concerned about the exposure of their portfolios to increased interest rate volatility may seek to protect the FI

FIGURE 23–24
Payoffs from a Collar

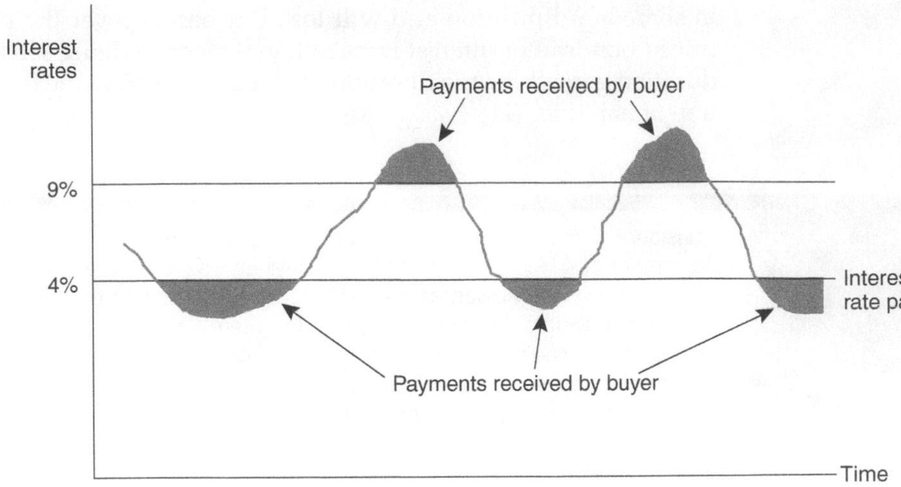

against such increases. One method of hedging this risk is through buying a cap and a floor together. This is usually called a collar. Figure 23–24 illustrates the essential risk-protection features of a collar when an FI buys a 9 percent cap and a 4 percent floor.

The shaded areas in Figure 23–24 show the interest rate payment regions (> 9 percent or < 4 percent) where the cap or floor is in the money and the buyer potentially receives either a cap or a floor payment from the seller. If interest rates stay in the 4 through 9 percent range, the buyer of the collar receives no compensation from the seller. In addition, the buyer has to pay two up-front premiums: one for the cap and one for the floor to the cap and floor sellers. As is clear, buying a collar is similar to simultaneously buying a complex put and call bond option, or straddle.

An alternative and more common use of a collar is to finance the cost of purchasing a cap. In our earlier example of the $100 million cap, the fair cap premium (pc) was $792,700, or 0.7927 percent of the notional face value (NV_c) of the cap. That is, the cost (C) of the cap is

$$\begin{aligned} C &= NV_c \times pc \\ &= \$100 \text{ million} \times 0.007927 \\ &= \$792{,}700 \end{aligned}$$

To purchase the cap, the FI must pay this premium to the cap seller in up-front dollars.

Many large FIs, more exposed to rising interest rates than falling interest rates—perhaps because they are heavily reliant on interest-sensitive sources of liabilities—seek to finance a cap by selling a floor at the same time.[12] In so doing, they generate up-front revenues; this floor premium can finance the cost of the cap purchase or the cap premium. Nevertheless, they give up potential profits if rates fall rather than rise. Indeed, when rates fall, the floor is more likely to be triggered and the FI must compensate the buyer of the floor.

[12] In this context, the sale of the floor is like the sale of any revenue-generating product.

After an FI buys a cap and sells a floor, its net cost of the cap is

$$C = (NV_c \times pc) - (NV_f \times pf)$$
$$C = \text{Cost of cap} - \text{Revenue on floor}$$

where

NV_f = Notional principal of the floor
pf = Premium rate on the floor

EXAMPLE 23–6

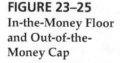

Calculating the Cost of a Collar

Suppose that, in Example 23–3, while buying the cap the FI sold a two-year $100 million notional face value floor at a premium of 0.75 percent. The net up-front cost of purchasing the cap is reduced to

$$C = (\$100{,}000{,}000 \times 0.007927) - (\$100{,}000{,}000 \times 0.0075) = \$42{,}700$$

Note that if the FI is willing to raise the floor exercise interest rate, thereby exposing itself to increasing losses if rates fall, it can generate higher premiums on the floor it sells. Like any option, as the exercise price or rate moves from being out of the money, when current rates are above the floor, to being in the money, when current rates are below the floor, the floor buyer would be willing to pay a higher premium to the writer (the FI). Given this, the buyer of the cap could set the floor rate with notional face values of $100 million each so that the floor premium earned by the FI just equals the cap premium paid:

$$C = (\$100{,}000{,}000 \times 0.007927) - (\$100{,}000{,}000 \times 0.007927)$$
$$= 0$$

When $pc = pf$, the cap buyer–floor seller can reduce the cap's net cost of purchase to zero.

Indeed, if the cap buyer bought a very out of the money cap and sold a very in the money floor, as shown in Figure 23–25, the net cost of the cap purchase could actually be negative. In Figure 23–25, the current interest rate is 7 percent while the cap rate is 10 percent. Thus, rates would have to rise at least 3 percent for the cap buyer to receive a payment at the end of year 1. By contrast, the 8 percent floor is already 1 percent above the current 7 percent rate. If rates stay at 7 percent until the end of year 1, the FI seller of the floor is already exposed to a 1 percent notional face value loss in writing the floor.

If the out-of-the-money cap can be bought at a premium of 0.7927 percent, but the in-the-money floor is sold at a premium of 0.95 percent, the (net) cost of the cap purchase is

$$C = (NV_c \times pc) - (NV_f \times pf)$$
$$= \$792{,}700 - \$950{,}000$$
$$= -\$157{,}300$$

FIGURE 23–25
In-the-Money Floor and Out-of-the-Money Cap

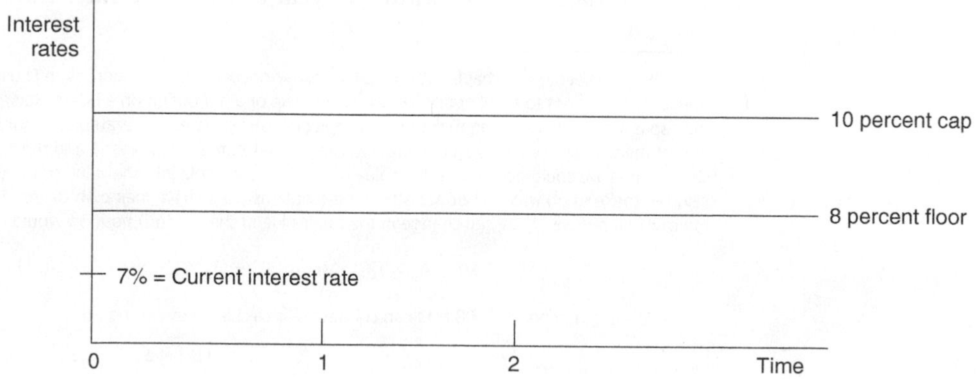

Raising the floor exercise rate and thus the floor premium can also be combined with mismatching the notional principal amounts of the cap and the floor to produce a zero net cost financing for the cap. That is, there is no reason that both the floor and cap agreements have to be written against the same notional face values ($NV_c = NV_f =$ \$100 million).

Suppose the out-of-the-money cap can be bought at a premium of 0.7927 percent and the in-the-money floor can be sold at a 0.95 percent premium. An FI manager might want to know what notional principal on the floor (or contract size) is necessary to finance a \$100 million cap purchase at zero net up-front cost. That is,

$$C = (NV_c \times pc) - (NV_f \times pf) = 0$$
$$= (\$100 \text{ million} \times 0.007927) - (NV_f \times 0.0095) = 0$$

Solving for NV_f:

$$NV_f = \frac{(\$100 \text{ million} \times 0.007927)}{0.0095} = \frac{(NV_c \times pc)}{pf}$$
$$= \$83.44 \text{ million}$$

Clearly, the higher premium rate on the floor requires a lower notional face value floor amount to generate sufficient premium income up-front to finance the cap's purchase. In general, to fully fund the cap purchase ($C = 0$), the relationship between premium rates and notional value should be[13]

$$\frac{NV_f}{NV_c} = \frac{pc}{pf}$$

Caps, Floors, Collars, and Credit Risk

One important feature of buying caps, collars, and floors for hedging purposes is the implied credit risk exposure involved that is absent for exchange-traded futures and options. Since these are multiple exercise OTC contracts, the buyer of these instruments faces a degree of counterparty credit risk. To see this, consider the cap example just discussed. Suppose the writer of the cap defaulted on the \$1 million due at the end of the first year if interest rates rose to 10 percent. The buyer not only would fail to collect on this in-the-money option but also would lose a potential payment at the end of year 2. In general, a default in year 1 would mean that the cap buyer would have to find a replacement contract for year 2 (and any succeeding years thereafter) at the cap rate terms or premiums prevailing at the end of year 1 rather than at the beginning of year 0. These cap rates may be far less favourable

---

[13] As shown earlier in this chapter, it is possible to macrohedge a gap position of an FI using put options. A cap is economically equivalent to a call option on an interest rate or a put option on a bond. However, the major difference is that the cap is a complex option in that there are multiple exercise dates. For example, in our simple model of the determination of the fair cap premium, there were two exercise dates: the end of year 1 and the end of year 2. However, we showed that we could decompose the value of the cap as a whole into the value of the (end of) year 1 option and the value of the (end of) year 2 option. Both of these options would have their own deltas (δ) because of the different maturity of these options. Thus, the change in the total value of the cap (ΔC) position would equal

$$\Delta C = N_c \times \{[\delta_1 \times (D_1 \times B)] + [\delta_2 \times (D_2 \times B)]\} \times \Delta R/(1 + R)$$

where N_c—the number of \$100,000 cap contracts—is calculated by solving

$$N_c = \frac{[D_A - kD_L] \times S}{[\delta_1 \times (D_1 \times B)] + [\delta_2 \times (D_2 \times B)]}$$

than those under the original cap contract (reflecting the higher interest rate levels at the end of year 1). In addition, the buyer could incur further transaction and contracting costs in replacing the original contract. Because of the often long term nature of cap agreements, occasionally extending up to 10 years, only FIs that are the most creditworthy are likely to be able to write and run a large cap/floor book without the backing of external guarantees such as standby letters of credit (SLCs). As we discuss in the next chapter, swaps have similar credit risk exposures due to their long-run contractual nature and their OTC origination.

CONCEPT QUESTIONS

1. **In Example 23–4, suppose that in year 3 the highest and lowest rates were 12 percent and 6 percent instead of 11 percent and 7 percent. Calculate the fair premium on the cap. ($980,500)**
2. **Assume two exercise dates at the end of year 2 and the end of year 3. Suppose the FI buys a floor of 4 percent at time 0. The binomial tree suggests that rates at the end of year 2 could be 3 percent (p = 0.5) or 5 percent (p = 0.5) and at the end of year 3 rates could be 2 percent (p = 0.25), 4 percent (p = 0.5), or 6 percent (p = 0.25). Calculate the fair value of the floor premium. Assume the notional face value of the floor is $100 million. ($792,700)**
3. **An FI buys a $100 million cap at a premium of 0.75 percent and sells a floor at a 0.85 percent premium. What size floor should be sold so that the net cost of the cap purchase is zero? ($88,235,394)**
4. **Why are only the most creditworthy FIs able to write a large cap/floor book without external guarantees?**

Questions and Problems

1. How does using options differ from using forward or futures contracts?
2. What is a call option?
3. What must happen to interest rates for the purchaser of a call option on a bond to make money? How does the writer of the call option make money?
4. What is a put option?
5. What must happen to interest rates for the purchaser of a put option on a bond to make money? How does the writer of the put option make money?
6. Consider the following:
   a. What are the two ways to use call and put options on government bonds to generate positive cash flows when interest rates decline? Verify your answer with a diagram.
   b. Under what balance sheet conditions would an FI use options on government bonds to hedge its assets and/or liabilities against interest rate declines?
   c. Is it more appropriate for FIs to hedge against a decline in interest rates with long calls or short puts?
7. In each of the following cases, identify what risk the manager of an FI faces and whether that risk should be hedged by buying a put or a call option.
   a. A commercial bank plans to issue GICs in three months.
   b. An insurance company plans to buy bonds in two months.
   c. A credit union plans to sell Government of Canada securities next month.
   d. A U.S. bank lends to a French company with a loan payable in euros.
   e. A mutual fund plans to sell its holding of stock in a British company.
   f. A finance company has assets with a duration of 6 years and liabilities with a duration of 13 years.
8. Consider an FI that wishes to use bond options to hedge the interest rate risk in the bond portfolio.
   a. How does writing call options hedge the risk when interest rates decrease?
   b. Will writing call options fully hedge the risk when interest rates increase? Explain.

c. How does buying put options reduce the losses on the bond portfolio when interest rates rise?

d. Diagram the purchase of a bond call option against the combination of a bond investment and the purchase of a bond put option.

9. What are the regulatory reasons that FIs seldom write options?

10. What are the problems of using the Black–Scholes option pricing model to value bond options? What is meant by the term *pull-to-par*?

11. An FI has purchased a two-year, $1,000 par value zero-coupon bond for $867.43. The FI will hold the bond to maturity unless it needs to sell the bond at the end of one year for liquidity purposes. The current one-year interest rate is 7 percent, and the one-year rate in one year is forecast to be either 8.04 percent or 7.44 percent with equal likelihood. The FI wishes to buy a put option to protect itself against a capital loss if the bond needs to be sold in one year.

a. What was the yield on the bond at the time of purchase?

b. What is the market-determined, implied one-year rate one year before maturity?

c. What is the expected sale price if the bond has to be sold at the end of one year?

d. Diagram the bond prices over the two-year horizon.

e. If the FI buys a put option with an exercise price equal to your answer in part (c), what will be its value at the end of one year?

f. What should be the premium on the put option today?

g. Diagram the values of the put option on the two-year, zero-coupon bond.

h. What would have been the premium on the option if the one-year interest rates at the end of one year were expected to be 8.14 percent and 7.34 percent?

12. A pension fund manager anticipates the purchase of a 20-year, 8 percent coupon U.S. Treasury bond at the end of two years. Interest rates are assumed to change only once every year at year-end, with an equal probability of a 1 percent increase or a 1 percent decrease. The Treasury bond, when purchased in two years, will pay interest semiannually. Currently the Treasury bond is selling at par.

a. What is the pension fund manager's interest rate risk exposure?

b. How can the pension fund manager use options to hedge that interest rate risk exposure?

c. What prices are possible on the 20-year T-bonds at the end of year 1 and year 2?

d. Diagram the prices over the two-year period.

e. If options on US$100,000, 20-year, 8 percent coupon Treasury bonds (both puts and calls) have a strike price of 101, what are the possible (intrinsic) values of the option position at the end of year 1 and year 2?

f. Diagram the possible option values.

g. What is the option premium? (Use an 8 percent discount factor.)

13. Why are options on interest rate futures contracts preferred to options on cash instruments in hedging interest rate risk?

14. Consider Figure 23–13. What are the prices paid for the following futures option?

a. March T-bond calls at $157.00.

b. March 10-year T-note puts at $151.50.

c. December eurodollar calls at 99.50%.

15. Consider Figure 23–13. What happens to the price of the following?

a. A call when the exercise price increases.

b. A call when the time until expiration increases.

c. A put when the exercise price increases.

d. A put when the time to expiration increases.

16. An FI manager writes a call option on a T-bond futures contract with an exercise price of 11400 at a quoted price of 0–55.

a. What type of opportunities or obligations does the manager have?

b. In what direction must interest rates move to encourage the call buyer to exercise the option?

17. What is the delta of an option (δ)?

18. An FI has a US$100 million portfolio of six-year eurodollar bonds that have an 8 percent coupon. The bonds are trading at par and have a duration of five years. The FI wishes to hedge the portfolio with T-bond options that have a delta of -0.625. The underlying long-term Treasury bonds for the option have a duration of 10.1 years and trade at a market value of US$96,157 per US$100,000 of par value. Each put option has a premium of US$3.25 per US$100 of face value.

a. How many bond put options are necessary to hedge the bond portfolio?

b. If interest rates increase 100 bp, what is the expected gain or loss on the put option hedge?

c. What is the expected change in market value on the bond portfolio?

d. What is the total cost of placing the hedge?

e. Diagram the payoff possibilities.
f. How far must interest rates move before the payoff on the hedge will exactly offset the cost of placing the hedge?
g. How far must interest rates move before the gain on the bond portfolio will exactly offset the cost of placing the hedge?
h. Summarize the gain, loss, and cost conditions of the hedge on the bond portfolio in terms of changes in interest rates.

19. Corporate Bank has US$840 million of assets with a duration of 12 years and liabilities worth US$720 million with a duration of 7 years. The bank is concerned about preserving the value of its equity in the event of an increase in interest rates and is contemplating a macrohedge with interest rate options. The call and put options have delta (δ) values of 0.4 and −0.4, respectively. The price of an underlying T-bond is 104.53125 (104 68/128), its duration is 8.17 years, and its yield to maturity is 7.56 percent.
a. What type of option should Corporate Bank use for the macrohedge?
b. How many options should be purchased?
c. What will be the effect on the economic value of the equity if interest rates rise 50 bp?
d. What will be the effect on the hedge if interest rates rise 50 bp?
e. What will be the cost of the hedge if each option has a premium of US$0.875 per $100 face value?
f. Diagram the economic conditions of the hedge.
g. How much must interest rates move against the hedge for the increased value of the bank to offset the cost of the hedge?
h. How much must interest rates move in favour of the hedge, or against the balance sheet, before the payoff from the hedge will exactly cover the cost of the hedge?
i. Formulate a management decision rule regarding the implementation of the hedge.

20. An FI has a US$200 million asset portfolio that has an average duration of 6.5 years. The average duration of its US$160 million in liabilities is 4.5 years. The FI uses put options on T-bonds to hedge against unexpected interest rate increases. The average delta (δ) value of the put options has been estimated at −0.3, and the average duration of the T-bonds is 7 years. The current market value of the T-bonds is US$96,000.
a. What is the modified duration of the T-bonds if the current level of interest rates is 10 percent?
b. How many put option contracts should it purchase to hedge its exposure against rising interest rates? The face value of the T-bonds is US$100,000.
c. If interest rates increase 50 bp, what will be the change in value of the equity of the FI?
d. What will be the change in value of the T-bond option hedge position?
e. If put options on T-bonds are selling at a premium of US$1.25 per face value of US$100, what is the total cost of hedging using options on T-bonds?
f. Diagram the spot market conditions of the equity and the option hedge.
g. What must be the change in interest rates before the change in value of the balance sheet (equity) will offset the cost of placing the hedge?
h. How much must interest rates change before the payoff of the hedge will exactly cover the cost of placing the hedge?
i. Given your answer in part (g), what will be the net gain or loss to the FI?

21. A mutual fund plans to purchase US$10,000,000 of 20-year T-bonds in two months. These bonds have a duration of 11 years. The mutual fund is concerned about interest rates changing over the next four months and is considering a hedge with a two-month option on a T-bond futures contract. Two-month calls with a strike price of 105 are priced at 1–25, and puts of the same maturity and exercise price are quoted at 2–09. The delta of the call is 0.5 and the delta of the put is −0.7. The current price of a deliverable T-bond is US$103.2500 per US$100 of face value, its duration is nine years, and its yield to maturity is 7.68 percent.
a. What type of option should the mutual fund purchase?
b. How many options should it purchase?
c. What is the cost of those options?
d. If rates change ±50 bp, what will be the effect on the price of the desired T-bonds?
e. What will be the effect on the value of the hedge if rates change ±50 bp?
f. Diagram the effects of the hedge and the spot market value of the desired T-bonds.
g. What must be the change in interest rates to cause the change in value of the purchased T-bond to exactly offset the cost of placing the hedge?

22. An FI must make a single payment of 500,000 Swiss francs (Sf) in six months at the maturity of a CD (certificate of deposit). The FI's in-house analyst expects the spot price of the franc to remain stable at

the current \$0.80/Sf. But the analyst is concerned that it could rise as high as \$0.85/Sf or fall as low as \$0.75/Sf. Because of this uncertainty, the analyst recommends that the FI hedge the CD payment using either options or futures. Six-month call and put options on the Swiss franc with an exercise price of \$0.80/Sf are trading at 4 cents and 2 cents, respectively. A six-month futures contract on the Swiss franc is trading at \$0.80/Sf.

a. Should the analysts be worried about the dollar depreciating or appreciating?
b. If the FI decides to hedge using options, should the FI buy put or call options to hedge the CD payment? Why?
c. If futures are used to hedge, should the FI buy or sell Swiss franc futures to hedge the payment? Why?
d. What will be the net payment on the CD if the selected call or put options are used to hedge the payment? Assume the following three scenarios: the spot price in six months will be \$0.75, \$0.80, or \$0.85/Sf. Also assume that the options will be exercised.
e. What would the net payment have been if futures had been used to hedge the CD payment? Use the same three scenarios as in part (a).
f. Which method of hedging is preferable after the fact?

23. A U.S.-based insurance company issued \$10 million of one-year, zero-coupon GICs (guaranteed investment contracts) denominated in Swiss francs (Sf) at a rate of 5 percent. The insurance company holds no Sf-denominated assets and has neither bought nor sold francs in the FX market.
    a. What is the insurance company's net exposure in Swiss francs?
    b. What is the insurance company's risk exposure to FX rate fluctuations?
    c. How can the insurance company use futures to hedge the risk exposure in part (b)? How can it use options to hedge?
    d. If the strike price on Swiss franc options is US\$0.6667/Sf and the spot exchange rate is US\$0.6452/Sf, what is the intrinsic value (on expiration) of a call option on Swiss francs? What is the intrinsic value (on expiration) of a Swiss franc put option? (*Note:* Swiss franc futures options traded on the CME are set at Sf125,000 per contract.)
    e. If the June delivery call option premium is US0.32 cent per Swiss franc and the June delivery put option is US10.7 cents per Swiss franc, what is the dollar premium cost per contract? Assume that today's date is April 15.
    f. Why is the call option premium lower than the put option premium?

24. An FI has made a loan commitment of Sf10 million that is likely to be drawn down in six months. The current spot rate is \$0.60/Sf.
    a. Is the FI exposed to the dollar depreciating or the dollar appreciating? Why?
    b. If the FI decides to hedge using Swiss franc futures, should it buy or sell Swiss franc futures?
    c. If the spot rate six months from today is \$0.64/Sf, what dollar amount is needed in six months if the loan is drawn?
    d. A six-month Swiss franc futures contract is available for \$0.61/Sf. What is the net amount needed at the end of six months if the FI has hedged using the Sf10 million of futures contracts? Assume that futures prices are equal to spot prices at the time of payment, that is, at maturity.
    e. If the FI decides to use options to hedge, should it purchase call or put options?
    f. Call and put options with an exercise price of \$0.61/Sf are selling for \$0.02 and \$0.03, respectively. What would be the net amount needed by the FI at the end of six months if it had used options instead of futures to hedge this exposure?

25. What is a credit spread call option?
26. What is a digital default option?
27. How do the cash flows to the lender differ for a credit spread call option hedge from the cash flows for a digital default option?
28. What is a catastrophe call option? How do the cash flows of this option affect the buyer of the option?
29. What are caps? Under what circumstances would the buyer of a cap receive a payoff?
30. What are floors? Under what circumstances would the buyer of a floor receive a payoff?
31. What are collars? Under what circumstances would an FI use a collar?
32. How is buying a cap similar to buying a call option on interest rates?
33. Under what balance sheet circumstances would it be desirable to sell a floor to help finance a cap? When would it be desirable to sell a cap to help finance a floor?
34. Use the following information to price a three-year collar by purchasing an in-the-money cap and writing an out-of-the-money floor. Assume a binomial options pricing model with an equal probability of

interest rates increasing 2 percent or decreasing 2 percent per annum. Current rates are 7 percent, the cap rate is 7 percent, and the floor rate is 4 percent. The notional value is $1 million. All interest payments are annual payments as a percentage of notional value, and all payments are made at the end of year 2 and the end of year 3.

35. Use the following information to price a three-year collar by purchasing an out-of-the-money cap and writing an in-the-money floor. Assume a binomial options pricing model with an equal probability of interest rates increasing 2 percent or decreasing 2 percent per annum. Current rates are 4 percent, the cap rate is 7 percent, and the floor rate is 4 percent. The notional value is $1 million. All interest payments are annual payments as a percentage of notional value, and all payments are made at the end of year 2 and the end of year 3.

36. Contrast the total cash flows associated with the collar position in question 34 against the collar in question 35. Do the goals of FIs that utilize the collar in question 34 differ from those that put on the collar in question 35? If so, how?

37. An FI has purchased a $200 million cap (i.e., call options on interest rates) of 9 percent at a premium of 0.65 percent of face value. A $200 million floor (i.e., put options on interest rates) of 4 percent is also available at a premium of 0.69 percent of face value.
    a. If interest rates rise to 10 percent, what is the amount received by the FI? What are the net savings after deducting the premium?
    b. If the FI also purchases a floor, what are the net savings if interest rates rise to 11 percent? What are the net savings if interest rates fall to 3 percent?
    c. If, instead, the FI sells (writes) the floor, what are the net savings if interest rates rise to 11 percent? What if they fall to 3 percent?
    d. What amount of floors should it sell to compensate for its purchase of caps, given the above premiums?

38. What credit risk exposure is involved in buying caps, floors, and collars for hedging purposes?

Appendix 23A Black–Scholes Option Pricing Model

Appendix 23B Microhedging with Options

View Appendices 23A and 23B on Connect.

CHAPTER 24

SWAPS

After studying this chapter you should be able to:

LO1 Identify the potential for an interest rate swap and calculate the cash flows for each participant.

LO2 Calculate the cash flows for a macrohedge conducted using swaps.

LO3 Calculate the cash flows for a fixed–fixed currency swap and fixed–floating currency swap.

LO4 Discuss the role of credit swaps in the financial crisis of 2008–2009.

LO5 Discuss swaps and credit risk concerns.

INTRODUCTION

swap
An agreement between two parties to exchange assets or a series of cash flows for a specified period of time at a specified interval.

A **swap** is an agreement between two parties (called *counterparties*) to exchange specified periodic cash flows in the future based on some underlying instrument or price (e.g., a fixed or floating rate on a bond or note). Like forward, futures, and option contracts, swaps allow firms to better manage their interest rate, FX, and credit risks. However, swaps can also result in large losses. At the heart of the financial crisis in 2008–2009 were derivative securities, mainly credit swaps, held by FIs. Losses on these derivatives led to the failure or near failure of some of the largest FIs in the United States (e.g., Lehman Brothers, Washington Mutual, and Merrill Lynch), the U.S. federal government takeover of mortgage giants Fannie Mae and Freddie Mac and insurance giant AIG, and the near collapse of the world's financial system. More recently, in 2012 JPMorgan Chase lost $2 billion on credit default swap (CDS) contracts it held in its trading portfolio. Using CDS contracts as a bet that the U.S. economy would improve, JPMorgan Chase incurred the massive losses when the markets moved against this bet.

Swaps were first introduced in the early 1980s, and the market for swaps has grown enormously. The notional value of swap contracts outstanding for the six large Canadian banks was $13.4 trillion in 2012 (see Chapter 22), and worldwide over US$450 trillion in swap contracts were outstanding. Commercial banks and investment banks are major participants in the market as dealers, traders, and users for proprietary hedging purposes. Insurance companies have also adopted hedging strategies using swaps, and their interest in this market is growing quickly. A swap dealer can act as an intermediary or third party by putting a swap together and/or creating an OTC secondary market for swaps for a fee.

Even before the financial crisis, the massive growth of the swap market had raised regulatory concerns regarding the credit risk exposures of FIs engaging in this market. This growth was one of the motivations behind the introduction of the Bank for International Settlements (BIS)–sponsored risk-based capital adequacy reforms described in Chapter 20. In addition, the enormous sums of money in the swap markets mean that large events such as problems in the CDS markets can have implications for the global financial system. For example, in the late 2000s, FIs such as Lehman Brothers and AIG had written and (in the case of AIG) insured billions of dollars of CDS contracts. When mortgages underlying these contracts fell drastically in value, CDS writers found themselves unable to make good on their promised payments to CDS holders. The result was a significant increase in risk and decrease in profits for the FIs that had purchased these CDS contracts. To prevent a massive collapse of the financial system, the U.S. government had to step in and bail out several of these FIs. The CDS case demonstrates the potentially devastating problems the swap market can create for FIs as well as the financial system as a whole.

The five generic types of swaps, in order of their quantitative importance, are interest rate swaps, currency swaps, credit swaps, commodity swaps, and equity swaps.[1] While the instrument underlying the swap may change, the basic principle of a swap agreement is the same in that there is a restructuring of asset or liability cash flows in a preferred direction by the transacting parties. Next, we consider the role of the two major generic types of swaps—interest rate and currency—in hedging FI risk. We then go on to examine the newest and fastest-growing type of swap: the credit swap.

SWAP MARKETS

In some ways a swap is similar to a forward or futures contract. That is, a forward or futures contract requires delivery or taking delivery of some commodity or financial security at a specified time in the future at a price specified at the time of origination. In a swap, each party promises to deliver and/or receive a prespecified series of payments at specific intervals over a specified time horizon. In this way, a swap can be considered to be the same as a series of forward or future contracts. Although similar in many ways, swaps are different from other derivative securities. First, a swap can be viewed as a portfolio of forward contracts with different maturity dates. Since cash flows on forward contracts are symmetric, the same can be said of swaps. This is in contrast to options, whose cash flows are asymmetric (truncated either on the positive or negative side depending upon the position). Second, the introduction of a swap dealer or intermediary—which stands between the two swap parties—can reduce the credit risk exposure and the information and monitoring costs that are associated with a portfolio of individual forward contracts. Indeed, most swaps are intermediated through a third-party dealer. Third, while futures and options are marked to market continuously and swaps are marked to market at coupon payment dates, forward contracts are settled only upon delivery (at maturity). Therefore, the credit risk exposure is greatest under a forward contract, where no third-party guarantor exists as in options (the options clearing corporation for exchange-traded options) and swaps (the swap intermediary). Fourth, transaction costs are highest for the option (the nonrefundable option premium), next for the swap (the swap intermediary's fee), and finally for

[1] There are also swaptions, which are options to enter into a swap agreement at some pre-agreed contract terms (e.g., a fixed rate of 10 percent) at some time in the future in return for the payment of an up-front premium.

the forward (which has no up-front payment). Finally, swaps have a longer maturity than any other derivative instruments and provide an additional opportunity for FIs to hedge longer-term positions at lower cost.

Swap transactions are generally heterogeneous in terms of maturities, indexes used to determine payments, and timing of payments—there is no standardized contract. Commercial and investment banks have evolved as the major swap dealers, mainly because of their close ties to the financial markets and their specialized skills in assessing credit risk. Each swap market dealer manages a portfolio of swaps and, as a result, can diversify some of the swap risk exposure away. Swap dealers exist to serve the function of taking the opposite side of each transaction in order to keep the swap market liquid by locating or matching counterparties or, in many cases, taking one side of the swap themselves. In a direct swap between two counterparties, each party must find another party having a mirror-image financing requirement—for example, an FI in need of swapping fixed-rate payments (for floating-rate payments) made quarterly for the next 10 years on $25 million in liabilities must find a counterparty in need of swapping $25 million in floating-rate payments (for fixed-rate payments) made quarterly for the next 10 years. Without swap dealers, the search costs of finding such counterparties to a swap can be significant.

Swap dealers also generally guarantee swap payments over the life of the contract. If one of the counterparties defaults on a direct swap, the other counterparty is no longer adequately hedged against risk and may have to replace the defaulted swap with a new swap at less favourable terms (so-called replacement risk). By booking or engaging in a swap through a swap dealer as the intermediary, a default by one counterparty will not affect the other counterparty since the swap dealer incurs any costs associated with the default by replacing the defaulting party on the same terms as the original swap.[2] However, if an extreme number of defaults occurs such that the swap dealer cannot honour the terms of the swap agreement, both counterparties are exposed to risk. Such was the case with CDSs written by AIG in 2008. At the time, AIG had more than US$440 billion in CDS contracts outstanding. FIs all over the world bought CDS protection from AIG. A major customer was Lehman Brothers. When Lehman declared bankruptcy on September 15, 2008, AIG was exposed to US$9 billion in losses on CDS contracts with Lehman. This exposure was so large that AIG could not cover or meet all of the CDS obligations, and many FIs had to buy replacement coverage at dramatically higher swap rates.

INTEREST RATE SWAPS

LO1

interest rate swap
An exchange of fixed interest payments for floating interest payments by two counterparties.

By far the largest segment of the global swap market is composed of **interest rate swaps**. Conceptually, an interest rate swap is a succession of forward contracts on interest rates arranged by two parties.[3] As such, it allows an FI to put in place a long-term hedge, sometimes for as long as 15 years. This hedge reduces the need to roll over contracts if reliance had been placed on futures or forward contracts to achieve such long-term hedges.

[2] The fee or spread charged by the swap dealer to each party in a swap incorporates this credit risk.

[3] For example, a four-year swap with annual swap dates involves four net cash flows between the parties to a swap. This is essentially similar to arranging four forward contracts: a one-year, a two-year, a three-year, and a four-year contract.

swap buyer
By convention, makes the fixed-rate payments in an interest rate swap transaction.

swap seller
By convention, makes the floating-rate payments in an interest rate swap transaction.

In a swap, the **swap buyer** agrees to make a number of fixed interest rate payments on periodic settlement dates to the **swap seller**. The seller of the swap in turn agrees to make floating-rate payments to the swap buyer on the same periodic settlement dates. The fixed-rate side—by convention, the swap buyer—generally has a comparative advantage in making fixed-rate payments, whereas the floating-rate side—by convention, the swap seller—generally has a comparative advantage in making variable or floating-rate payments. In undertaking this transaction, the FI that is the fixed-rate payer is seeking to transform the variable-rate nature of its liabilities into fixed-rate liabilities to better match the fixed returns earned on its assets. Meanwhile, the FI that is the variable-rate payer seeks to turn its fixed-rate liabilities into variable-rate liabilities to better match the variable returns on its assets.

To explain the role of a swap transaction in hedging FI interest rate risk, we use a simple example. Consider two FIs: The first is a bank that has raised $100 million of its funds by issuing four-year, medium-term notes with 10 percent annual fixed coupons rather than relying on short-term deposits to raise funds (see Panel A of Table 24–1). On the asset side of its portfolio, the bank makes business loans whose rates are indexed to annual changes in the London Interbank Offered Rate (LIBOR). As we discussed in Chapter 10, banks currently index most large business loans to the Canadian Dealer Offered Rate (CDOR) or LIBOR.

As a result of having floating-rate loans and fixed-rate liabilities in its asset–liability structure, the bank has a negative duration gap; the duration of its assets is shorter than that of its liabilities:

$$D_A - kD_L < 0$$

One way for the bank to hedge this exposure is to shorten the duration or interest rate sensitivity of its liabilities by transforming them into short-term floating-rate liabilities that better match the duration characteristics of its asset portfolio. The bank can make changes either on or off the balance sheet. On the balance sheet, the bank could attract an additional $100 million in short-term deposits that are indexed to the LIBOR rate (say, LIBOR plus 2.5 percent) in a manner similar to its loans. The proceeds of these deposits can be used to pay off the medium-term notes. This reduces the duration gap between the bank's assets and liabilities. Alternatively, the bank could go off the balance sheet and sell an interest rate swap—that is, enter into a swap agreement to make the floating-rate payment side of a swap agreement.

The second party in the swap is a credit union (CU) that has invested $100 million in fixed-rate residential mortgages of long duration. To finance this residential mortgage portfolio, the CU has had to rely on short-term guaranteed investment certificates (GICs) with an average duration of one year (see Panel B of Table 24–1). On maturity, these GICs have to be rolled over at the current market rate.

TABLE 24–1
Balance Sheets Of Swap Participants

Assets		Liabilities	
Panel A: Bank's Balance Sheet (Swap Seller)			
Business loans (rate indexed to LIBOR)	$100 million	Medium-term notes (coupons fixed)	$100 million
Panel B: Credit Union's Balance Sheet (Swap Buyer)			
Fixed-rate mortgages	$100 million	Short-term GICs (one year)	$100 million

Consequently, the CU's asset–liability balance sheet structure is the reverse of the bank's; that is,

$$D_A - kD_L > 0$$

The CU could hedge its interest rate risk exposure by transforming the short-term floating-rate nature of its liabilities into fixed-rate liabilities that better match the long-term maturity/duration structure of its assets. On the balance sheet, the CU could issue long-term notes with a maturity equal or close to that on the mortgages (at, say, 12 percent). The proceeds of the sale of the notes can be used to pay off the GICs and reduce the duration gap. Alternatively, the CU can buy a swap—take the fixed-payment side of a swap agreement.

The opposing balance sheet and interest rate risk exposures of the bank and the CU provide the necessary conditions for an interest rate swap agreement between the two parties. This swap agreement can be arranged directly between the parties. However, it is likely that an FI—another bank or an investment bank—would act as either a broker or an agent, receiving a fee for bringing the two parties together or intermediating fully by accepting the credit risk exposure and guaranteeing the cash flows underlying the swap contract. By acting as a principal as well as an agent, the FI can add a credit risk premium to the fee. However, the credit risk exposure of a swap to an FI is somewhat less than that on a loan (this is discussed later in this chapter). Conceptually, when a third-party FI fully intermediates the swap, that FI is really entering into two separate swap agreements: one with the bank and one with the CU.

plain vanilla
A standard agreement without any special features.

For simplicity, we consider a **plain vanilla** fixed–floating rate swap where a third-party intermediary acts as a simple broker or agent by bringing together two FIs with opposing interest rate risk exposures to enter into a swap agreement or contract.

EXAMPLE 24–1

Expected Cash Flows on an Interest Rate Swap

Suppose the notional value of a swap is $100 million—equal to the assumed size of the bank's medium-term note issue—and the maturity of four years is equal to the maturity of the bank's note liabilities. The annual coupon cost of these note liabilities is 10 percent, and the bank's problem is that the variable return on its assets may be insufficient to cover the cost of meeting these coupon payments if market interest rates, and therefore asset returns, *fall*. By comparison, the fixed returns on the CU's mortgage asset portfolio may be insufficient to cover the interest cost of its GICs if market rates *rise*. As a result, a feasible swap agreement might dictate that the CU send fixed payments of 10 percent per annum of the notional $100 million value of the swap to the bank to allow the bank to fully cover the coupon interest payments on its note issue. In return, the bank sends annual payments indexed to one-year LIBOR to help the CU cover the cost of refinancing its one-year renewable GICs. Suppose that one-year LIBOR is currently 8 percent and the bank agrees to send annual payments at the end of each year equal to one-year LIBOR plus 2 percent to the CU.[4] We depict this fixed–floating rate swap transaction in Figure 24–1; the expected net financing costs for the FIs are listed in Table 24–2.

As a result of the swap, the bank has transformed its four-year, fixed-rate interest payments into variable-rate payments, matching the variability of returns on its assets. Further, through the interest rate swap, the bank effectively pays LIBOR plus 2 percent for its financing.

[4] These rates implicitly assume that this is the cheapest way each party can hedge its interest rate exposure. For example, LIBOR + 2 percent is the lowest-cost way in which the bank can transform its fixed-rate liabilities into floating-rate liabilities.

FIGURE 24–1
Fixed–Floating Rate Swap

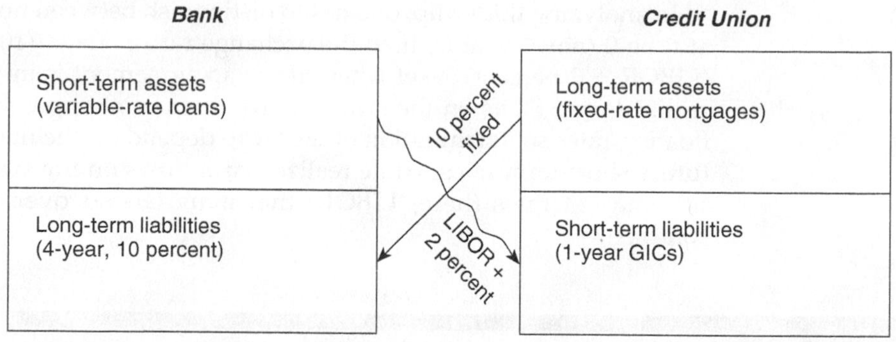

TABLE 24–2
Financing Cost Resulting from Interest Rate Swap ($ millions)

	Bank	Credit Union
Cash outflows from balance sheet financing	−10% × $100	−(GIC) × $100
Cash inflows from swap	10% × $100	(LIBOR + 2%) × $100
Cash outflows from swap	−(LIBOR + 2%) × $100	−10% × $100
Net cash flows	−(LIBOR + 2%) × $100	−(8% + GIC Rate − LIBOR) × $100
Rate available on:		
Variable-rate debt	LIBOR + 2½%	
Fixed-rate debt		12%

Had it gone to the debt market, we assume that the bank would pay LIBOR plus 2.5 percent (a savings of 0.5 percent with the swap). Further, the CU has transformed its variable-rate interest payments into fixed-rate payments, plus a "small" variable component (GIC rate − LIBOR), similar to those received on its assets. Had it gone to the debt market, we assumed that the CU would pay 12 percent (a savings of 4 percent + GIC rate − LIBOR with the swap).

Note in Example 24–1 that in the absence of default/credit risk, only the bank is really fully hedged. This happens because the annual 10 percent payments it receives from the CU at the end of each year allow it to meet the promised 10 percent coupon rate payments to its note holders regardless of the return it receives on its variable-rate assets. By contrast, the CU receives variable-rate payments based on LIBOR plus 2 percent. However, it is quite possible that the GIC rate the CU has to pay on its deposit liabilities does not exactly track the LIBOR-indexed payments sent by the bank. That is, the CU is subject to basis risk exposure on the swap contract. There are two possible sources of this basis risk. First, GIC rates do not exactly match the movements of LIBOR rates over time since the former are determined in the domestic money market and the latter in the eurodollar market. Second, the credit/default risk premium on the CU's GICs may increase over time; thus, the +2 percent add-on to LIBOR may be insufficient to hedge the CU's cost of funds. The CU might be better hedged by requiring the bank to send it floating payments based on domestic GIC rates rather than LIBOR. To do this, the bank would probably require additional compensation since it would then be bearing basis risk. Its asset returns would be sensitive to LIBOR movements, while its swap payments were indexed to GIC rates.

In analyzing this swap, one has to distinguish between how it should be priced at time 0 (now) [that is, how the exchange rate of fixed (10 percent) for floating (LIBOR + 2 percent) is set when the swap agreement is initiated] and the actual realized cash flows on the swap. As we discuss in Appendix 24A, the fixed and floating rates set on initiation of the swap depend on the market's expectations of future short-term rates, while realized cash flows on the swap depend on the actual market rates (here, LIBOR) that materialized over the life of the swap contract.

EXAMPLE 24–2

Calculation of Realized Cash Flows

We assume that the realized or actual path of interest rates (LIBOR) over the four-year life of the contract would be as follows:

End of Year	LIBOR
1	9%
2	9
3	7
4	6

The bank's variable payments to the CU were indexed to these rates by the formula

$$(\text{LIBOR} + 2\%) \times \$100 \text{ million}$$

By contrast, the fixed annual payments that the CU made to the bank were the same each year: 10% × $100 million. We summarize the actual or realized cash flows among the two parties over the four years in Table 24–3. The CU's net gains from the swap in years 1 and 2 are $1 million per year. The enhanced cash flow offsets the increased cost of refinancing its GICs in a higher interest rate environment—that is, the CU is hedged against rising rates. By contrast, the bank makes net gains on the swap in years 3 and 4 when rates fall; thus, it is hedged against falling rates. The positive cash flow from the swap offsets the decline in the variable returns on the bank's asset portfolio. Overall, the bank made a net dollar gain of $1 million in nominal dollars; its true realized gain would be the present value of this amount.

TABLE 24–3
Realized Cash Flows on the Swap Agreement ($ millions)

End of Year	One-Year LIBOR	One-Year LIBOR + 2 percent	Cash Payment by Bank	Cash Payment by CU	Net Payment Made by Bank
1	9%	11%	$11	$10	$+1
2	9	11	11	10	+1
3	7	9	9	10	−1
4	6	8	8	10	−2
Total			$39	$40	$−1

Realized Cash Flows on an Interest Rate Swap

off-market swaps
Swaps that have nonstandard terms that require one party to compensate another.

Swaps can always be moulded or tailored to the needs of the transacting parties as long as one party is willing to compensate the other party for accepting nonstandard terms or **off-market swap** arrangements, usually in the form of an up-front fee or payments. Relaxing a standardized swap can include special interest rate terms and indexes as well as allowing for varying notional values underlying the swap.

FIGURE 24–2
Inverse Floater Swap–Structured Note

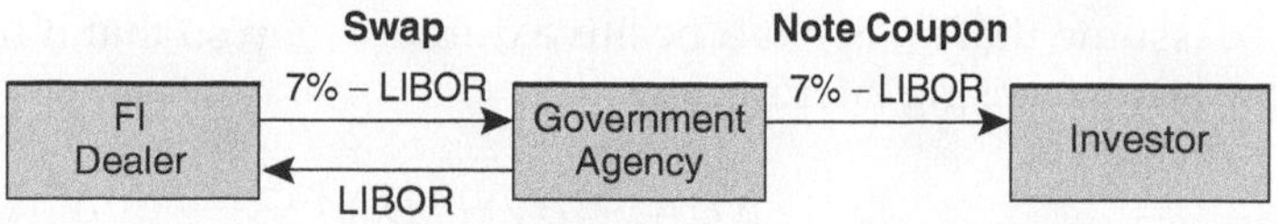

For example, in the case we just considered, the notional value of the swap was fixed at $100 million for each of the four annual swap dates. However, swap notional values can be allowed either to decrease or to increase over a swap contract's life. This flexibility is useful when one of the parties has heavy investments in mortgages (in our example, the CU) and the mortgages are **fully amortized**, meaning that the annual and monthly cash flows on the mortgage portfolio reflect repayments of both principal and interest such that the periodic payment is kept constant. Fixed-rate mortgages normally have larger payments of interest than principal in the early years, with the interest component falling as mortgages approach maturity. One possibility is for the CU to enter into a mortgage swap to hedge the amortizing nature of the mortgage portfolio or alternatively to allow the notional value of the swap to decline at a rate similar to the decline in the principal component of the mortgage portfolio.

fully amortized mortgages
Mortgage portfolio cash flows that have a constant payment.

Another example of a special type of interest rate swap is the inverse floater swap, which was engineered by major FIs as part of structured note financing deals to lower the cost of financing to various government agencies. Such arrangements have resulted in enormous problems in the United States for investor groups such as municipal authorities and corporations that are part of the overall swap deal.

A structured note–inverse floater swap arrangement is shown in Figure 24–2. In this arrangement, a government agency issues notes (say, $100 million) to investors with a coupon that is equal to 7 percent minus LIBOR—that is, an (inverse) floating coupon. The novel feature of this coupon is that when market rates fall (and thus LIBOR is low), the coupon received by the investor is large. The government agency then converts this spread liability (7 percent − LIBOR) into a LIBOR liability by entering into a swap with an FI dealer (e.g., a bank). In effect, the cost of the $100 million note issue is LIBOR to the agency plus any fees relating to the swap.

The risk of these notes to the investor is very clear. If LIBOR is 2 percent, then the investor will receive coupons of 7 percent − 2 percent = 5 percent, which is an excellent spread return if the investor can borrow at close to LIBOR (or 2 percent in this case). However, consider what happens if interest rates rise. If LIBOR rises from 2 to 8 percent, the promised coupon becomes 7 percent − 8 percent = −1 percent. Since negative coupons cannot be paid, the actual coupon paid to the investor is 0 percent. However, if the investor borrowed funds to buy the notes at LIBOR, the cost of funds is 8 percent in this case. Thus, the investor is facing an extremely large negative spread and loss.

Macrohedging with Swaps

LO2

The duration model shown in Chapters 22 and 23 to estimate the optimal number of futures and options contracts to hedge an FI's duration gap can also be applied to estimate the optimal number of swap contracts. For example, an FI manager might wish to know how many 10-year (or 5-year) swap contracts are needed to hedge its overall risk exposure. The optimal notional value of swap contracts should be set so that the gain on swap contracts entered into off the balance sheet just offsets any loss in net worth on the balance sheet when interest rates change.

Assume that an FI has a positive duration gap so that it has positive net worth exposure to rising interest rates:

$$\Delta E = -(D_A - kD_L)A\frac{\Delta R}{1 + R} > 0$$

As discussed above, the FI can seek to hedge by paying fixed and receiving floating payments through an interest rate swap. However, many different maturity swaps are available. As will be shown below, the size of the notional value of the interest rate swaps entered into will depend on the maturity (duration) of the swap contract. Suppose the FI manager chooses to hedge with 10-year swaps.

In terms of valuation, a 10-year swap arrangement can be considered in terms of bond-equivalent valuation. That is, the fixed-rate payments on a 10-year swap are formally equivalent to the fixed payments on a 10-year government bond. Similarly, the floating-rate payments on a 10-year swap with *annual* payments can be viewed as equivalent to floating coupons on a bond where coupons are repriced (to LIBOR) every year. That is, the change in the value of the swap (ΔS) when interest rates $[\Delta R/(1 + R)]$ rise will depend on the relative interest sensitivity of 10-year bonds to 1-year bonds, or in duration terms, $(D_{10} - D_1)$.[5] In general,

$$\Delta S = (D_{fixed} - D_{float}) \times N_S \times \frac{\Delta R}{1 + R}$$

where

ΔS = Change in the market value of the swap contract

$(D_{fixed} - D_{float})$ = Difference in durations between a government bond that has the same maturity and coupon as the fixed-payment side of the swap and a government bond that has the same duration as the swap-payment interval (e.g., annual floating payments)

N_S = Notional value of swap contracts

$\frac{\Delta R}{1 + R}$ = Shock to interest rates

Note that as long as $D_{fixed} > D_{float}$, when interest rates rise, the market (present) value of fixed-rate payments will fall by more than the market (present) value of floating-rate payments; in market (or present) value terms, the fixed-rate payers gain when rates rise and lose when rates fall.

To solve for the optimal notional value of swap contracts,[6] we set

$$\Delta S + \Delta E = 0$$

[5] Although principal payments on bonds are not swapped on maturity, this does not matter since the theoretical payment and receipt of principal values cancel each other out.

[6] Note that the FI wants to enter swaps to protect itself against rising rates. Thus, it will pay fixed and receive floating. In the context of swap transactions, when an FI pays fixed, it is said to be "buying swaps." Thus, we are solving for the optimal number of swaps contracts the FI should buy in this example.

The gain on swap contracts entered into off the balance sheet just offsets the loss in net worth on the balance sheet when rates rise. Substituting values for ΔS and ΔE:

$$\left[(D_{fixed} - D_{float}) \times N_S \times \frac{\Delta R}{1+R}\right] + \left[-(D_A - kD_L) \times A \times \frac{\Delta R}{1+R}\right] = 0$$

Cancelling out the common terms:

$$[(D_{fixed} - D_{float}) \times N_S] + [-(D_A - kD_L) \times A] = 0$$

Solving for N_S:

$$N_S = \frac{(D_A - kD_L) \times A}{D_{fixed} - D_{float}}$$

EXAMPLE 24-3

Calculating the Notional Value of Swaps in a Macrohedge

Suppose $D_A = 5$, $D_L = 3$, $k = 0.9$, and $A = \$100$ million. Also, assume the duration of a current 10-year, fixed-rate government bond with the same coupon as the fixed rate on the swap is seven years, while the duration of a floating-rate bond that reprices annually is one year:[7]

$$D_{fixed} = 7 \quad \text{and} \quad D_{float} = 1$$

Then

$$N_S = \frac{(D_A - kD_L) \times A}{D_{fixed} - D_{float}} = \frac{\$230{,}000{,}000}{7-1} = \$38{,}333{,}333$$

If each swap contract is \$100,000 in size,[8] the number of swap contracts into which the FI should enter will be \$38,333,333/\$100,000 = 383.33, or 383 contracts, rounding down. Table 24–4 summarizes the key features of the hedge assuming that the initial rate on the T-bond is 10 percent and is expected to rise by 1 percent. As shown in Table 24–4, the loss of \$2.09 million in net worth on the balance sheet is exactly offset by a gain off the balance sheet on the swap hedge.

If the FI engaged in a longer-term swap—for example, 15 years—such that $D_{fixed} = 9$ and $D_{float} = 1$, then the notional value of swap contracts will fall to \$230,000,000/(9 − 1) = \$28,750,000. If each swap contract is \$100,000 in size, the FI should enter into 287 swap contracts.

TABLE 24–4
On- and Off-Balance-Sheet Effects of a Swap Hedge

	On Balance Sheet	Off Balance Sheet
Begin hedge, $t = 0$	Equity exposed to impact of rise in interest rates	Sell interest rate swap
End hedge, $t = 1$	Interest rates rise on assets and liabilities by 1%	Buy interest rate swap
Opportunity loss on balance sheet: $\Delta E = -[5 - 0.9(3)] \times \$100 \text{ million} \times (0.01/1.1)$ $= -\$2.09$ million		Gain on interest rate swap: $\Delta S = (7 - 1) \times \$38{,}333{,}333 \times (0.01/1.1)$ $= \$2.09$ million

While it may seem logical that fewer contracts are preferable in the sense of saving on fees and other related costs of hedging, this advantage is offset by the fact that longer-term swaps have greater counterparty default or credit risk (discussed later in this chapter).

[7] See Chapter 8 for a discussion of the duration on floating-rate bonds.

[8] The notional value of swap contracts can take virtually any size since they are individually tailored OTC contracts.

CONCEPT QUESTIONS

1. **In Example 24–2, which of the two FIs has its liability costs fully hedged and which is only partially hedged? Explain your answer.**
2. **What are some nonstandard terms that might be encountered in an off-market swap?**
3. **In Example 24–3, what is the notional size of swap contracts if D_{fixed} = 5 and swap contracts require payment every six months? (N_S = \$51,111,111)**

CURRENCY SWAPS

LO3

currency swap
A swap used to hedge against exchange rate risk from mismatched currencies on assets and liabilities.

Just as swaps are long-term contracts that can hedge interest rate risk exposure, they can also be used to hedge currency risk exposures of FIs. The following section considers a simple, plain vanilla example of how **currency swaps** can immunize FIs against exchange rate risk when they mismatch the currencies of their assets and liabilities.

Fixed-Fixed Currency Swaps

Consider the Canadian FI in Panel A of Table 24–5 with all of its fixed-rate assets denominated in dollars. Assume that the dollar–pound exchange rate is fixed at \$1.6/£. It is financing part of its asset portfolio with a £50 million issue of four-year, medium-term U.K. pound notes that have a fixed annual coupon of 10 percent. By comparison, the U.K. FI in Panel B of Table 24-5 has all its assets denominated in pounds; it is partly funding those assets with an \$80 million issue of four-year, medium-term dollar notes with a fixed annual coupon of 10 percent.

These two FIs are exposed to opposing currency risks. The Canadian FI is exposed to the risk that the dollar will depreciate against the pound over the next four years, making it more costly to cover the annual coupon interest payments and the principal repayment on its pound-denominated notes. On the other hand, the U.K. FI is exposed to the dollar appreciating against the pound, making it more difficult to cover the dollar coupon and principal payments on its four-year \$80 million note issue out of the sterling cash flows on its assets.

The FIs can hedge the exposures either on or off the balance sheet. On the balance sheet, the Canadian FI can issue \$80 million in four-year, medium-term dollar notes (at, say, 10.5 percent). The proceeds of the sale can be used to pay off the £50 million of four-year, medium-term pound notes. Similarly, the U.K. FI can issue £50 million in four-year, medium-term pound notes (at, say, 10.5 percent), using the proceeds to pay off the \$80 million of four-year, medium-term dollar notes. Both FIs have taken actions on the balance sheet so that they are no longer exposed to movements in the exchange rate between the two currencies.

TABLE 24–5
Balance Sheets of Currency Swap Participants

Assets	Liabilities
Panel A: Canadian FI	
\$80 million Canadian loans (4-year) in dollars, 11%	£50 million U.K. GICs or CDs (4-year) in pounds, 10%
Panel B: U.K. FI	
£50 million U.K. loans (4-year) in pounds, 11%	\$80 million Canadian notes (4-year) in dollars, 10%

EXAMPLE 24–4

Expected Cash Flows on Fixed–Fixed Currency Swap

Rather than make changes on the balance sheet, a feasible currency swap into which the U.K. and Canadian FIs can enter is one under which the U.K. FI sends annual payments in pounds to cover the coupon and principal repayments of the Canadian FI's pound sterling note issue, and the Canadian FI sends annual dollar payments to the U.K. FI to cover the interest and principal payments on its dollar note issue.[9] We summarize the currency swap in Figure 24–3 and Table 24–6. As a result of the swap, the U.K. FI transforms fixed-rate dollar payments into fixed-rate pound payments that better match the pound fixed-rate cash flows from its asset portfolio. Similarly, the Canadian FI transforms fixed-rate pound payments into fixed-rate dollar payments that better match the fixed-rate dollar cash flows from its asset portfolio. Further, both FIs transform the pattern of their payments at a lower rate than if they had made changes on the balance sheet. Both FIs effectively obtain financing at 10 percent while hedging against exchange rate risk. Had they gone to the market, we assumed above that they would have paid 10.5 percent to do this. In undertaking this exchange of cash flows, the two parties normally agree on a fixed exchange rate for the cash flows at the beginning of the period.[10] In this example, the fixed exchange rate would be $1.6/£.

FIGURE 24–3
Fixed–Fixed Pound/Dollar Currency Swap

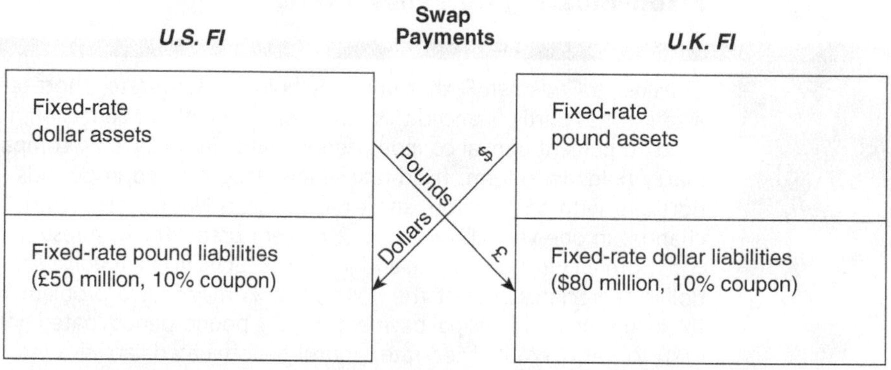

TABLE 24–6
Financing Costs Resulting from the Fixed–Fixed Currency Swap Agreement ($ and £ millions)

	Canadian FI	U.K. FI
Cash outflows from balance sheet financing	−10% × £50	−10% × $80
Cash inflows from swap	10% × £50	10% × $80
Cash outflows from swap	−10% × $80	−10% × £50
Net cash flows	−10% × $80	−10% × £50
Rate available on:		
Dollar-denominated notes	10.5%	
Pound-denominated notes		10.5%

In this example, both liabilities bear a fixed 10 percent interest rate. This is not a necessary requirement for the fixed–fixed currency swap agreement. For example, suppose that the Canadian FI's note coupons were 5 percent per annum, while the U.K. FI's note coupons were 10 percent. The swap dollar payments of the Canadian FI would remain unchanged, but the U.K. FI's sterling payments would be

[9] In a currency swap, it is usual to include both principal and interest payments as part of the swap agreement. For interest rate swaps, it is usual to include just interest rate payments. The reason for this is that both principal and interest are exposed to FX risk.

[10] As with interest rate swaps, this exchange rate reflects the contracting parties' expectations in regard to future exchange rate movements.

reduced by £2.5 million (or $4 million) in each of the four years. This difference could be met either by some up-front payment by the U.K. FI to the Canadian FI, reflecting the difference in the present value of the two fixed cash flows, or by annual payments that result in zero net present value differences among the fixed–fixed currency swap participants' payments. Also note that if the exchange rate changed from the rate agreed in the swap ($1.6/£), either one or the other side would be losing in the sense that a new swap might be entered into at an exchange rate more favourable to one party. Specifically, if the dollar were to appreciate (rise in value) against the pound over the life of the swap, the agreement would become more costly for the Canadian FI. If, however, the dollar were to depreciate (fall in value), the U.K. FI would find the agreement increasingly costly over the swap's life.

By combining an interest rate swap of the fixed–floating type described earlier with a currency swap, we can also produce a fixed–floating currency swap that is a hybrid of the two plain vanilla swaps we have considered so far.

Fixed–Floating Currency Swaps

EXAMPLE 24-5

Financing Costs Associated with a Fixed–Floating Currency Swap

Consider a Canadian FI that primarily holds floating-rate, short-term, dollar-denominated assets. It has partly financed this asset portfolio with a £50 million, four-year note issue with fixed 10 percent annual coupons denominated in pounds. By comparison, a U.K. FI that primarily holds long-term, fixed-rate assets denominated in pounds has partly financed this portfolio with $80 million, short-term, dollar-denominated euro CDs whose rates reflect changes in one-year LIBOR plus a 2 percent premium. As a result, the Canadian FI is faced with both an interest rate risk and an FX risk. Specifically, if dollar short-term rates fall and the dollar depreciates against the pound, the FI may face a problem in covering its promised fixed-coupon and principal payments on the pound-denominated note. Consequently, it may wish to transform its fixed-rate, pound-denominated liabilities into variable-rate, dollar-denominated liabilities. The U.K. FI also faces interest rate and FX rate risk exposures. If Canadian interest rates rise and the dollar appreciates against the pound, the U.K. FI will find it more difficult to cover its promised coupon and principal payments on its dollar-denominated CDs out of the cash flows from its fixed-rate pound asset portfolio. Consequently, it may wish to transform its floating-rate, short-term, dollar-denominated liabilities into fixed-rate pound liabilities.

Both FIs can make changes on the balance sheet to hedge the interest rate and FX rate risk exposure. The Canadian FI can issue $80 million, dollar-dominated, floating-rate, short-term debt (at, say, LIBOR plus 2.5 percent), the proceeds of which can be used to pay off the existing £50 million four-year note. The U.K. FI can issue £50 million in four-year notes (at, say, 11 percent) and use the proceeds to pay off the $80 million in short-term euro CDs. By changing the financing used on the balance sheet, both FIs hedge both the interest rate and the FX rate risk. We again assume that the dollar/pound exchange rate is $1.6/£.

Alternatively, each FI can achieve its objective of liability transformation by engaging in a fixed–floating currency swap. A feasible swap would be one in which each year, the two FIs swap payments at some prearranged dollar/pound exchange rate, assumed to be $1.6/£. The U.K. FI sends fixed payments in pounds to cover the cost of the Canadian FI's pound-denominated note issue, while the Canadian FI sends floating payments in dollars to cover the U.K. FI's floating-rate dollar CD costs. The resulting expected financing costs are calculated in Table 24–7. As a result of the fixed–floating currency swap, both FIs have hedged interest rate and FX rate risk and have done so at a rate below what they could have achieved by making on-balance-sheet changes. The Canadian FI's net financing cost is LIBOR plus 2 percent with the swap, compared to LIBOR plus 2.5 percent in the debt market. The U.K. FI's financing cost is 10 percent with the swap, compared to 11 percent had it refinanced on the balance sheet.

TABLE 24–7 Financing Costs Resulting from the Fixed–Floating Currency Swap ($ and £ millions)

	Canadian FI	U.K. FI
Cash outflows from balance sheet financing	−10% × £50	−(LIBOR + 2%) × $80
Cash inflows from swap	10% × £50	(LIBOR + 2%) × $80
Cash outflows from swap	−(LIBOR + 2%) × $80	−10% × £50
Net cash outflows	−(LIBOR + 2%) × $80	−10% × £50
Rate available on:		
Dollar-denominated variable-rate debt	LIBOR + 2½%	
Pound-denominated fixed-rate debt		11%

Given the realized LIBOR rates in column (2), we show the relevant payments among the contracting parties in Table 24–8. The realized cash flows from the swap result in a net nominal payment of $1.6 million by the Canadian FI to the U.K. FI over the life of the swap.

TABLE 24–8 Realized Cash Flows on a Fixed–Floating Currency Swap ($ and £ millions)

Year	LIBOR	LIBOR + 2 percent	Floating-Rate Payment by Canadian Bank ($)	Fixed-Rate Payment by U.K. FI (£)	Fixed-Rate Payment by U.K. FI ($ at $1.6/£1)	Net Payment by Canadian FI ($)
1	9%	11%	$ 8.8	£ 5	$ 8	$+0.8
2	7	9	7.2	5	8	−0.8
3	8	10	8	5	8	0
4	10	12	89.6	55	88	+1.6
Total net payment						$+1.6

CONCEPT QUESTIONS

1. **Referring to the fixed–fixed currency swap in Table 24–6, if the net cash flows on the swap are zero, why does either FI enter into the swap agreement?**
2. **Referring to Table 24–8, suppose that the Canadian FI had agreed to make floating payments of LIBOR + 1 percent instead of LIBOR + 2 percent. What would its net payment have been to the U.K. FI over the four-year swap agreement? (−$1.6 million)**

CREDIT SWAPS

LO4

In recent years the fastest-growing types of swaps have been those developed to better allow FIs to hedge their credit risk, *credit swaps* or *CDSs*. In 2001, the total notional principal for outstanding credit derivative contracts reported to the BIS was US$698 billion. By December 2008, this amount had risen to US$41.9 trillion. However, this amount declined to US$26.9 trillion by June 2012. Credit swaps are important for two reasons. First, credit risk is still more likely to cause an FI to fail than is either interest rate risk or FX risk. Second, CDSs allow FIs to maintain long-term customer lending relationships without bearing the full credit risk exposure from those relationships. Indeed, then Federal Reserve Board Chairman Alan Greenspan has credited this market with helping the banking system maintain its strength through the economic recession in the early 2000s. He argued that credit swaps were effectively used to shift a significant part of banks' risk from their corporate loan portfolios.[11] For example, significant exposures to telecommunications firms were hedged by banks through credit swaps. However, the Federal Reserve chairman also commented that these derivative securities are prone to induce speculative excesses that need to be contained through regulation, supervision, and private-sector action. While banks have been buyers of credit risk protection through CDSs, insurance companies (such as AIG) and reinsurance companies (such as Munich Re) have been net sellers of credit risk protection. Thus, they have been more willing than banks to bear credit risk. The result is that the FI bearing the credit risk of a loan (a bank) is often different from the FI that issued the loan. In some recessionary periods, insurance companies suffered large losses as buyers of credit risk, and banks have been well protected. And as discussed above and below, during the financial crisis of 2008–2009 insurance or reinsurance company losses from credit swaps were so large that some could not pay the promised obligations and, as a result, banks (and other buyers of credit swaps) were exposed to significantly higher credit risk.

The buyer of a CDS makes periodic payments to the seller until the end of the life of the swap or until the credit event specified in the contract occurs. These payments are typically made every quarter, six months, or year. The settlement of the swap in the event of a default involves either physical delivery of the bonds (or loans) or a cash payment. Generally, a CDS specifies that a number of different bonds (loans) can be delivered in the event of a default. The bonds (loans) typically have the same seniority, but they may not sell for the same percentage of face value immediately after a default. This gives the holder of a CDS a cheapest-to-deliver option. When a default happens, the buyer of protection will review alternative deliverable bonds (or loans) and choose the one that can be purchased most cheaply for delivery.

In contrast to actual insurance policies, there is no requirement that the CDS buyer actually own the underlying reference securities, and therefore the notional value of CDS contracts in recent years has exceeded the total value of the outstanding debt instruments. As of 2012, the BIS estimated total global corporate debt instruments (bonds plus loans) outstanding at US$10.7 trillion. In contrast, the BIS reported that single-name CDSs outstanding in 2012 had a total notional value exceeding US$16.9 trillion.[12] This has implications for both settlement of the CDS contract and systemic risk exposure.

Similar to options, but different from noncredit-related swaps, the risks on a credit swap are not symmetrical. That is, the protection buyer receives a payment upon the occurrence of a credit event trigger, but the swap "expires worthless" if no trigger occurs.[13] In that event, the protection seller keeps the periodic premiums paid for the swap, similar to the cash flows that characterize options. Thus, the protection buyer transfers the credit risk to the protection seller in exchange for a premium. Although the credit protection buyer hedges exposure to default

---

[11] Much of this risk exposure was absorbed by domestic and foreign insurance and reinsurance companies.

[12] Single-name CDSs specify a single reference security. In contrast, multiname CDSs reference more than one name, as in a portfolio or basket CDS or CDS index, such as the Dow Jones CDX. Baskets are credit derivatives based on a small portfolio of loans or bonds, such that all assets included in the underlying pool are individually listed. In contrast, the contents of larger portfolios are described by their characteristics. A basket CDS, also known as a first-to-default swap, is structured like a regular CDS, but the reference security consists of several securities. The first reference entity to default triggers a default payment of the par value minus the recovery value and then all payments end. As of 2012, there was an additional US$11.8 trillion notional value in multiname CDSs.

[13] In contrast, an interest rate swap (fixed-for-floating-rate swap) will entail symmetric payments such that the swap buyer (the fixed-rate leg of the swap) earns positive cash flows when interest rates increase and the swap seller (the floating-rate leg) earns positive cash flows when interest rates decrease.

risk, there is still counterparty credit risk in the event that the seller fails to perform its obligations under the terms of the contract (as was the concern in September 2008 with regard to AIG, an active CDS seller).

Below we look at two types of credit swaps: (1) the total return swap and (2) the pure credit swap. We then look at credit risk concerns with the swaps themselves.

Total Return Swaps

total return swap
A swap involving an obligation to pay interest at a specified fixed or floating rate for payments representing the total return on a specified amount.

Although FIs spend significant resources attempting to evaluate and price expected changes in a borrower's credit risk over the life of a loan, a borrower's credit situation (credit quality) sometimes deteriorates unexpectedly after the loan terms are determined and the loan is issued. A lender can use a total return swap to hedge this possible change in credit risk exposure. A **total return swap** involves swapping an obligation to pay interest at a specified fixed or floating rate for payments representing the total return on a loan or a bond (interest and principal value changes) of a specified amount.

EXAMPLE 24-6

Calculation of Cash Flows on a Total Return Swap

Suppose that an FI lends US$100 million to a Brazilian manufacturing firm at a fixed rate of 10 percent. If the firm's credit risk increases unexpectedly over the life of the loan, the market value of the loan and consequently the FI's net worth will fall. The FI can hedge an unexpected increase in the borrower's credit risk by entering into a total return swap in which it agrees to pay a total return based on an annual fixed rate (f) plus changes in the market value of Brazilian (U.S. dollar–denominated) government debt (changes in the value of these bonds reflect the political and economic events in the firm's home country and thus will be correlated with the credit risk of the Brazilian borrowing firm). Also, the bonds are in the same currency (U.S. dollars) as the loans. In return, the FI receives a variable market rate payment of interest annually (e.g., one-year LIBOR rate). Figure 24–4 and Table 24–9 illustrate the cash flows associated with the typical total return swap for the FI.

FIGURE 24–4
Cash Flows on a Total Return Swap

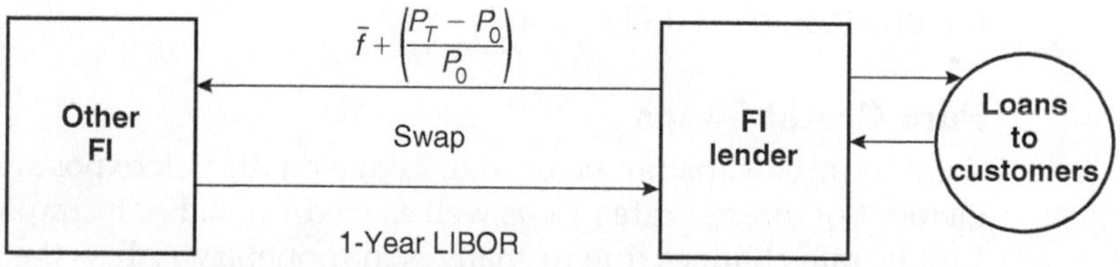

TABLE 24–9 Cash Flows on a Total Return Swap

	Annual Cash Flow for Year 1 through Final Year	Additional Payment by FI	Total Return
Cash inflow on swap to FI lender	1-year LIBOR (11%)	–	1-year LIBOR (11%)
Cash outflow on swap to other FI	Fixed rate ($\bar{f}$) (12%)	$P_T - P_0$ (90 – 100)	$\left[\bar{f} + \frac{P_T - P_0}{P_0}\right]$
			$\left(12\% + \frac{90 - 100}{100} = 12\% - 10\% = 2\%\right)$
		Net profit	9%

Using the total return swap, the FI agrees to pay a fixed rate of interest annually and the capital gain or loss on the market value of the Brazilian (U.S. dollar) bond over the period of the hedge. In Figure 24–4, P_0 denotes the market value of the bond at the beginning of the swap period and P_T represents the market value of the bond at the end of the swap period. If the Brazilian bond decreases in value over the period of the hedge ($P_0 > P_T$), the FI pays a relatively small (possibly negative) amount to the counterparty equal to the fixed payment on the swap minus the capital loss[14] on the bond. For example, suppose the Brazilian (U.S. dollar) bond was priced at par ($P_0 = 100$) at the beginning of the swap period. At the end of the swap period or the payment date, the Brazilian bond had a secondary-market value of 90 ($P_T = 90$) due to an increase in Brazilian country risk. Suppose that the fixed-rate payment ($\bar{f}$) as part of the total return swap was 12 percent; then the FI would send to the swap counterparty the fixed rate of 12 percent minus 10 percent (the capital loss on the Brazilian bond), or a total of 2 percent, and would receive in return a floating payment (e.g., LIBOR = 11 percent) from the counterparty to the swap. Thus, the net profit on the swap to the FI lender is 9 percent (11 percent minus 2 percent) times the notional amount of the swap contract. This gain can be used to offset the loss of market value on the loan to the Brazilian firm. This example is illustrated in Table 24–9.

Thus, the FI benefits from the total return swap if the Brazilian bond value deteriorates as a result of a political or economic shock. Assuming that the Brazilian firm's credit risk deteriorates along with the local economy, the FI will offset some of this loss of the Brazilian loan on its balance sheet with a gain from the total return swap.

Note that hedging credit risk in this fashion allows the FI to maintain its customer relationship with the Brazilian firm (and perhaps earn fees from selling other financial services to that firm) without bearing a large amount of credit risk exposure. Moreover, since the Brazilian loan remains on the FI's balance sheet, the Brazilian firm may not even know its loan is being hedged. This would not be the case if the FI sought to reduce its risk by selling all or part of the loan (see Chapter 25). Finally, the swap does not completely hedge credit risk in this case. Specifically, basis risk is present to the extent that the credit risk of the Brazilian firm's dollar loan is imperfectly correlated with Brazilian country risk reflected in the price of the Brazilian (U.S. dollar) bonds.[15]

Pure Credit Swaps

Total return swaps can be used to hedge credit risk exposure, but they contain an element of interest rate risk as well as credit risk. For example, in Table 24–9, if the LIBOR rate changes due to changes in monetary policy, the *net* cash flows on the total return swap will also change—even though the credit risks of the underlying loans (and bonds) have not changed.

pure credit swap
A swap by which an FI receives the par value of the loan on default in return for paying a periodic swap fee.

To strip out the "interest rate"–sensitive element of total return swaps, an alternative swap has been developed called a **pure credit swap**. In this case, as shown in Figure 24–5, the FI lender will send (each swap period) a fixed fee or payment (like an insurance premium) to the FI counterparty. If the FI lender's loan or loans do not default, it will receive nothing back from the FI counterparty. However, if the loan or loans default, the FI counterparty will cover the default loss by making a

---

14 Total return swaps are typically structured so that the capital gain or loss is paid at the end of the swap. However, an alternative structure does exist in which the capital gain or loss is paid at the end of each interest period during the swap.

15 In many swaps, the total return on a loan (rather than a bond as in this example) is swapped for a floating payment such as LIBOR. In this case, $\bar{f}$ would equal any fees paid for loan origination and $[(P_T - P_0)/P_0]$ would reflect the estimated change in market value of the loan as perceived by brokers/traders in the secondary market for loan sales. The secondary market for loans is described in Chapter 25.

FIGURE 24–5
A Pure Credit Swap

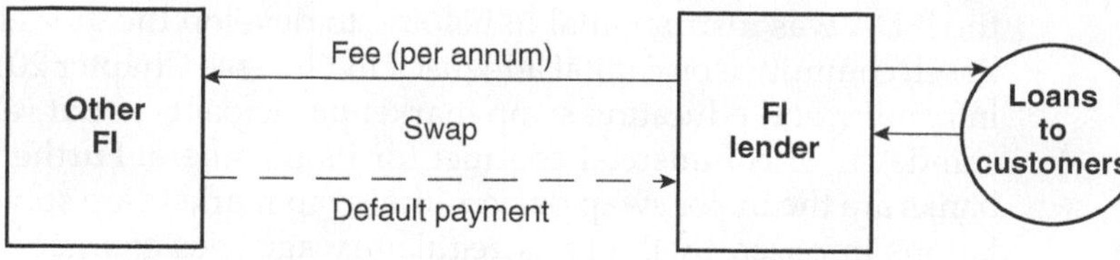

default payment that is often equal to the par value of the original loan (e.g., P_0 = \$100) minus the secondary-market value of the defaulted loan (e.g., P_T = \$40); that is, the FI counterparty will pay $P_0 - P_T$ (or \$60, in this example).[16] Thus, a pure credit swap is like buying credit insurance and/or a multiperiod credit option.

CDS Indexes

In September 2003, the Dow Jones CDX (DJ CDX) North American Investment Grade Index was introduced. In November 2004, Markit initiated a credit index data service, which included the DJ CDX (which also includes indexes covering emerging-market credit derivatives) and the International Index Company's (IIC) iTraxx (which covers the EU, Japan, and non-Japan Asia). Both sets of indexes are made up of 125 of the most-liquid, investment-grade credits in the form of CDSs. For example, the DJ CDX consists of a basket of 125 CDS contracts on U.S. firms with liquid, investment-grade corporate debt. The identity of the components in the index changes every six months—every March and September for the DJ CDX. Companies may be dropped from the index if they are downgraded or become illiquid. For example, Ford and General Motors were dropped from the DJ CDX in September 2005 when their debt fell below investment grade. The index is equally weighted, and so each CDS component makes up 0.8% of the index value. Using indexed CDSs to hedge credit risk may be less expensive because of the liquidity of these instruments, although it does expose the hedger to basis risk.[17]

SWAPS AND CREDIT RISK CONCERNS

LO5

In contrast to futures and options markets, swap markets are governed by very little regulation—there is no central governing body overseeing swap market operations. Indeed, it is not entirely clear who the proper regulator of the swap market is. The International Swaps and Derivatives Association (ISDA) is a global trade association with over 840 members (including most of the world's major FIs) from some 59 countries on six continents that sets codes and standards for swap markets. Established in 1985, the ISDA establishes, reviews, and updates the code of standards (the language and provisions) for swap documentation. The ISDA also acts as the spokesgroup for the industry on regulatory changes and issues, promotes the development of risk management practices for swap dealers (for example,

isda.org

[16] While a pure credit swap is like a default option (e.g., the digital default option in Chapter 23), a key difference is that the fee (or premium) payments on the swap are paid over the life of the swap, whereas for a default option the whole fee (premium) is paid up-front.

[17] Basis risk results when the fluctuations in the value of the reference security underlying the derivative do not move in lock step with the hedge position. For example, there is basis risk if an indexed CDS is used to hedge a portfolio of loans to firms that are not identical to the 125 firms in the index.

the ISDA was instrumental in helping to develop the guidelines set by the BIS, or Basel, committee on capital adequacy in FIs—see Chapter 20), provides a forum for informing and educating swap market participants about relevant issues, and sets standards of commercial conduct for its members. Further, because commercial banks are the major swap dealers, the swap markets are subject, indirectly, to regulations imposed by the bank regulatory agencies charged with monitoring bank risk. For example, commercial banks must include swap risk exposure when calculating risk-based capital requirements (see Chapter 20). To the extent that swap activity is part of a bank's overall business, swap markets are monitored for abuses. Investment banks and insurance companies have become bigger players in the swap markets, however, and these dealers are subject to few regulations on their swap dealings. As well, many hedge funds and investment banks with questionable credit ratings participated in the CDS markets in 2007 and 2008. This increased the counterparty risk and the systemic risk to the global financial system during the financial crisis.

The financial crisis showed just how much risk the swap market can present to FIs and the global financial system. Specifically, as the subprime mortgage market began to fail in the summer of 2008, subprime mortgage pools that FIs bought ended up falling precipitously in value as defaults and foreclosures rose on the underlying mortgage pools. Many CDSs were written on these subprime mortgage securities. Thus, as mortgage security losses started to rise, buyers of the CDS contracts wanted to be paid for these losses. AIG was a major writer of these CDS securities. As of June 30, 2008, AIG had written US$441 billion worth of swaps on corporate bonds and mortgage-backed securities (MBSs). And, when MBSs started to fall in value, AIG had to make good on billions of dollars of CDSs. The problem was exacerbated by the fact that so many FIs were linked to each other through these deals. Lehman Brothers alone had more than US$700 billion worth of swaps outstanding, and many of them were backed by AIG. As the value of these subprime CDSs fell, AIG had to post more collateral against these swaps. Soon it became clear that AIG was not going to be able to cover its CDS market losses. The result was a significant increase in the risk exposure of banks, investment banks, and insurance companies that had purchased AIG CDS contracts. Indeed, the reason the U.S. government stepped in and bailed out AIG was that the insurer was a dominant player in the CDS market. While banks and hedge funds were playing both sides of the CDS business—buying and trading them and thus offsetting whatever losses they took—AIG was simply selling the CDSs. Had AIG defaulted, every FI that had bought a CDS contract from the company would have suffered substantial losses.

Global funding and risk pressures were also evident in the FX swap market during the financial crisis. This risk was driven by demand for U.S. dollars from global FIs, particularly Canadian and European FIs. As many of these institutions increasingly struggled to obtain funding in the unsecured cash markets, they turned to the FX swap market as a primary channel for raising dollars. This extreme demand for dollar funding led a sizeable shift in FX forward prices, with the implied dollar funding rate observed in FX swaps on many currencies rising sharply above that suggested by the other relative interest measures such as the dollar overnight index swap (OIS) rate and the U.S. dollar LIBOR. Dealers reported that bid–ask spreads on FX swaps increased to as much as 10 times the levels that had prevailed before August 2007. During the last quarter of 2008, the spread of the three-month FX swap-implied dollar rate from euro and pound—U.S. dollar

FX forward rate—over the dollar LIBOR fixed rate widened to around 330 and 260 bp, respectively.

Given the role that swaps played in the financial crisis, the U.S. government has started regulating them more heavily. Specifically, in October 2009, the Over-the-Counter Derivatives Market Act was passed. This was followed by the Wall Street Reform and Consumer Protection Act of 2010. The acts established a framework for the comprehensive regulation of OTC derivatives. The regulations require central clearing and exchange trading for specified swaps and established rules for disclosure, reporting, and recordkeeping of all swaps. Among other things, the act requires swap dealers and major swap participants to register with either the Commodity Futures Trading Commission (CFTC) or the Securities and Exchange Commission (SEC). The CFTC has jurisdiction over swaps. Swaps are defined as (1) options or other contracts involving the exchange of payments that are linked to, among other things, interest rates, currencies, securities, commodities, instruments of indebtedness, and quantitative measures; (2) event-based contracts providing for purchase, sale, payment, or delivery dependent on event or contingency associated with a potential financial, economic, or commercial consequence; (3) contracts commonly known to the trade as swaps; or (4) any combination or permutation of the above. These includes interest rate swaps, FX or currency swaps, total return swaps, and CDSs that are not security based (i.e., multiname CDSs). The SEC has jurisdiction over security-based swaps. A security-based swap is defined as any agreement, contract, or transaction that would be a swap and that (1) is based on a narrow-based security index, (2) is based on a single security or loan, or (3) is a CDS linked to a single issuer of a security or the issuers of securities in a narrow-based security index. Further, the acts grant authority to U.S. federal financial regulators (including the SEC, the CFTC, the Federal Deposit Insurance Corporation (FDIC), the Board of Governors of the Federal Reserve System, the National Credit Union Administration, the Office of the Comptroller of the Currency, the Office of Thrift Supervision, and all other federal agencies that have authority under law to regulate FIs or financial instruments) to oversee any agreements.

Given the events surrounding the financial crisis, and the role that swaps played in the crisis, it is critical that both regulators and market participants have a heightened awareness of credit risks. If the transaction is not structured carefully, it may pass along unintended risks to participants, exposing them to higher frequency and severity of losses than if they had held an equivalent cash position.

This raises a question: Is credit or default risk on swaps the same as or different from the credit or default risk on loans? In fact, there are three major differences between the credit risk on swaps and the credit risk on loans. As a result, the credit risk on a swap is generally considered to be much less than that on a loan. We discuss these differences next.

Netting and Swaps

One factor that mitigates the credit risk on swaps is the netting of swap payments. On each swap payment date, a fixed payment is made by one party and a floating payment is made by the other. However, in general, each party calculates the net difference between the two payments, and a single payment for the net difference is made by one party to the other. This netting of payments implies that the default exposure of the in-the-money party is limited to the net payment rather than either the total fixed or the total floating payment. Further, when two parties have large numbers of contracts outstanding against each other, they tend to net across contracts. This process, called *netting by novation*—often formalized through a master netting agreement—further reduces the potential risk of loss if some contracts are in the money and others are out of the money to the same counterparty.[18]

Payment Flows Are Interest and Not Principal

While currency swaps involve swaps of interest and principal, interest rate swaps involve swaps of interest payments measured only against some notional principal value. This suggests that the default risk on such swaps is less than that on a regular loan, where both interest and principal are exposed to credit risk.

Standby Letters of Credit

In cases where swaps are made between parties of different credit standing, such that one party perceives a significant risk of default by the other party, the poor-quality-credit-risk party may be required to buy a standby letter of credit (SLC, or another form of performance guarantee) from a third-party high-quality (AA) FI such that if default occurs, the SLC will provide the swap payments in lieu of the defaulting party. Further, low-quality counterparties are increasingly required to post collateral in lieu of default. This collateral is an incentive mechanism working to deter swap defaults.

CONCEPT QUESTIONS

1. **What is the link between preserving "customer relationships" and credit derivatives such as total return swaps?**
2. **Is there any difference between a digital default option (see Chapter 23) and a pure credit swap?**
3. **Are swaps as risky as equivalent-sized loans?**

[18] Since 1995, the BIS has allowed banks to use bilateral netting of swap contracts in calculating their risk-based capital requirements (see Chapter 20). It is estimated that this reduces banks' capital requirements against swaps by up to 40 percent.

Questions and Problems

1. Explain the similarity between a swap and a forward contract.
2. Forwards, futures, and options contracts had been used by FIs to hedge risk for many years before swaps were invented. If FIs already had these hedging instruments, why did they need swaps?
3. Distinguish between a swap buyer and a swap seller. In which markets does each have the comparative advantage?
4. An insurance company owns $50 million of floating-rate bonds yielding LIBOR plus 1 percent. These loans are financed by $50 million of fixed-rate GICs costing 10 percent. A bank has $50 million of car loans with a fixed rate of 14 percent. The loans are financed by $50 million in GICs at a variable rate of LIBOR plus 4 percent.
   a. What is the risk exposure of the insurance company?
   b. What is the risk exposure of the bank?
   c. What would be the cash flow goals of each company if they were to enter into a swap arrangement?
   d. Which FI would be the buyer and which FI would be the seller in the swap?
   e. Diagram the direction of the relevant cash flows for the swap arrangement.
   f. What are reasonable cash flow amounts, or relative interest rates, for each of the payment streams?

5. In a swap arrangement, the variable-rate swap cash flow streams often do not fully hedge the variable-rate cash flow streams from the balance sheet due to basis risk.
   a. What are the possible sources of basis risk in an interest rate swap?
   b. How could the failure to achieve a perfect hedge be realized by the swap buyer?
   c. How could the failure to achieve a perfect hedge be realized by the swap seller?
6. A bank has $200 million of four-year-maturity floating-rate loans yielding the T-bill rate plus 2 percent. These loans are financed by $200 million of four-year-maturity fixed-rate deposits costing 9 percent. The bank can issue four-year variable-rate deposits at the T-bill rate plus 1.5 percent. A CU has $200 million of four-year-maturity mortgages with a fixed rate of 13 percent. They are financed by $200 million in four-year-maturity GICs with a variable rate of the T-bill rate plus 3 percent. The CU can issue four-year long-term debt at 12.5 percent.
   a. Discuss the type of interest rate risk each FI faces.
   b. Propose a swap that would result in each FI having the same type of asset and liability cash flows.
   c. Show that this swap would be acceptable to both parties.
   d. The realized T-bill rates over the four-year contract period are as follows:

End of Year	T-bill Rate
1	1.75%
2	2.00
3	2.25
4	2.50

   Calculate the realized cash flows on the swap and the net interest yield for the CU and the bank over the contract period.
   e. What are some of the practical difficulties in arranging this swap?
7. Bank 1 can issue five-year GICs at an annual rate of 11 percent fixed or at a variable rate of LIBOR plus 2 percent. Bank 2 can issue five-year GICs at an annual rate of 13 percent fixed or at a variable rate of LIBOR plus 3 percent.
   a. Is a mutually beneficial swap possible between the two banks?
   b. Where is the comparative advantage of the two banks?
   c. What is an example of a feasible swap?
8. First Bank can issue one-year floating-rate GICs at prime plus 1 percent or fixed-rate GICs at 12.5 percent. Second Bank can issue one-year floating-rate GICs at prime plus 0.5 percent or fixed-rate GICs at 11 percent.
   a. What is a feasible swap with all the benefits going to First Bank?
   b. What is a feasible swap with all the benefits going to Second Bank?
   c. Diagram each situation.
   d. What factors will determine the final swap arrangement?
9. Two multinational FIs enter their respective debt markets to issue $100 million of two-year notes. FI A can borrow at a fixed annual rate of 11 percent or a floating rate of LIBOR plus 50 bp, repriced at the end of the year. FI B can borrow at a fixed annual rate of 10 percent or a floating rate of LIBOR, repriced at the end of the year.
   a. If FI A is a positive duration gap insurance company and FI B is a money market mutual fund, in what market(s) should each firm borrow to reduce its interest rate risk exposure?
   b. In which debt market does FI A have a comparative advantage over FI B?
   c. Although FI A is riskier than FI B and therefore must pay a higher rate in both the fixed-rate and floating-rate markets, there are possible gains to trade. Set up a swap to exploit FI A's comparative advantage over FI B. What are the total gains from the swap trade? Assume a swap intermediary fee of 10 bp.
   d. The gains from the swap trade can be apportioned between FI A and FI B through negotiation. What terms of trade would give all the gains to FI A? What terms of trade would give all the gains to FI B?
   e. Assume swap pricing that allocates all the gains from the swap to FI A. If A buys the swap from B and pays the swap intermediary's fee, what are the end-of-year net cash flows if LIBOR is 8.25 percent?
   f. If A buys the swap in part (e) from B and pays the swap intermediary's fee, what are the end-of-year net cash flows if LIBOR is 11 percent? Be sure to net swap payments against cash market payments for both firms.
   g. If all barriers to entry and pricing inefficiencies between FI A's debt markets and FI B's debt markets were eliminated, how would that affect the swap transaction?
10. What are off-market swap arrangements? How are these arrangements negotiated?

11. Describe how an inverse floater works to the advantage of an investor who receives coupon payments of 10 percent minus LIBOR if LIBOR is currently at 4 percent. When is it a disadvantage to the investor? Does the issuing party bear any risk?
12. An FI has $500 million of assets with a duration of nine years and $450 million of liabilities with a duration of three years. The FI wants to hedge its duration gap with a swap that has fixed-rate payments with a duration of six years and floating-rate payments with a duration of two years. What is the optimal amount of the swap to effectively macrohedge against the adverse effect of a change in interest rates on the value of the FI's equity?
13. A Canadian FI has most of its assets in the form of Swiss franc–denominated floating-rate loans. Its liabilities consist mostly of fixed-rate dollar-denominated CDs. What type of currency risk and interest rate risk does this FI face? How might it use a swap to eliminate some of those risks?
14. A Swiss bank issues a $100 million, three-year eurodollar CD at a fixed annual rate of 7 percent. The proceeds of the CD are lent to a Swiss company for three years at a fixed rate of 9 percent. The spot exchange rate is Sf1.50/$.
    a. Is this expected to be a profitable transaction?
    b. What are the cash flows if exchange rates are unchanged over the next three years?
    c. What is the risk exposure of the bank's underlying cash position?
    d. How can the Swiss bank reduce that risk exposure?
    e. If the dollar is expected to appreciate against the Swiss franc to Sf1.65/$, Sf1.815/$, and Sf2.00/$ over the next three years, what will be the cash flows on this transaction?
    f. If the Swiss bank swaps dollar payments for Swiss franc payments at the current spot exchange rate, what are the cash flows on the swap? What are the cash flows on the entire hedged position? Assume that the dollar appreciates at the rates in part (e).
    g. What are the cash flows on the swap and the hedged position if actual spot exchange rates are as follows:

       End of year 1: Sf1.55/$

       End of year 2: Sf1.47/$

       End of year 3: Sf1.48/$
    h. What would be the bank's risk exposure if the fixed-rate Swiss loan was financed with a floating-rate $100 million, three-year eurodollar CD?
    i. What type(s) of hedge is (are) appropriate if the Swiss bank in part (h) wants to reduce its risk exposure?
    j. If the annual eurodollar CD rate is set at LIBOR, and LIBOR at the end of years 1, 2, and 3 is expected to be 7 percent, 8 percent, and 9 percent, respectively, what will be the cash flows on the bank's unhedged cash position? Assume no change in exchange rates.
    k. What are the cash flows on the bank's unhedged cash position if exchange rates are as follows:

       End of year 1: Sf1.55/$

       End of year 2: Sf1.47/$

       End of year 3: Sf1.48/$
    l. What are both the swap and the total hedged position cash flows if the bank swaps out its floating-rate dollar CD payments in exchange for 7.75 percent fixed-rate Swiss franc payments at the current spot exchange rate of Sf1.50/$?
    m. If forecast annual interest rates are 7 percent, 10.14 percent, and 10.83 percent over the next three years, respectively, and exchange rates over the next years are those in part (k), calculate the cash flows on an 8.75 percent fixed–floating rate swap of dollars to Swiss francs at Sf1.50/$.
15. Bank A has the following balance sheet information ($ millions):

Assets	
Rate-sensitive assets	$ 50
Fixed-rate assets	150
Total assets	$200
Liabilities and Equity	
Rate-sensitive liabilities	$ 75
Fixed-rate liabilities	100
Net worth	25
Total liabilities and equity	$200

    Rate-sensitive assets are repriced quarterly at the 91-day Treasury bill rate plus 150 bp. Fixed-rate assets have five years until maturity and are paying 9 percent annually. Rate-sensitive liabilities are repriced quarterly at the 91-day Treasury bill rate plus 100 bp. Fixed-rate liabilities have two years until maturity and are paying 7 percent annually. Currently, the 91-day Treasury bill rate is 6.25 percent.
    a. What is the bank's current net interest income? If Treasury bill rates increase 150 bp, what will be the change in the bank's net interest income (NII)?
    b. What is the bank's repricing or funding gap? Use the repricing model to calculate the change in the bank's NII if interest rates increase 150 bp.
    c. How can swaps be used as an interest rate hedge in this example?
16. Use the following information to construct a swap of asset cash flows for the bank in problem 15. The bank is a price taker in both the fixed-rate market at 9 percent and the rate-sensitive market at the

T-bill rate plus 1.5 percent. A securities dealer has a large portfolio of rate-sensitive assets funded with fixed-rate liabilities. The dealer is a price taker in a fixed-rate asset market paying 8.5 percent and a floating-rate asset market paying the 91-day T-bill rate plus 1.25 percent. All interest is paid annually.

a. What is the interest rate risk exposure to the securities dealer?

b. How can the bank and the securities dealer use a swap to hedge their respective interest rate risk exposures?

c. What are the total potential gains to the swap trade?

d. Consider the following two-year swap of asset cash flows: an annual fixed-rate asset cash flow of 8.6 percent in exchange for a floating-rate asset cash flow of T-bill plus 125 bp. The total swap intermediary fee is 5 bp. How are the swap gains apportioned between the bank and the securities dealer if they each hedge their interest rate risk exposures using this swap?

e. What are the swap net cash flows if T-bill rates at the end of the first year are 7.75 percent and at the end of the second year are 5.5 percent? Assume that the notional value is $107.14 million.

f. What are the sources of the swap gains to trade?

g. What are the implications for the efficiency of cash markets?

17. Consider the following currency swap of coupon interest on the following assets:

5 percent (annual coupon) fixed-rate $1 million bond

5 percent (annual coupon) fixed-rate bond denominated in Swiss francs (Sf)

The spot exchange rate is Sf1.5/$.

a. What is the face value of the Swiss franc bond if the investments are equivalent at spot rates?

b. What are the realized cash flows, assuming no change in spot exchange rates? What are the net cash flows on the swap?

c. What are the cash flows if the spot exchange rate falls to Sf0.50/$? What are the net cash flows on the swap?

d. What are the cash flows if the spot exchange rate rises to Sf2.25/$? What are the net cash flows on the swap?

e. Describe the underlying cash position that would prompt the FI to hedge by swapping dollars for Swiss francs.

18. Consider the following fixed–floating rate currency swap of assets: 5 percent (annual coupon) fixed-rate $1 million bond and floating-rate Sf1.5 million bond set at LIBOR annually. Currently LIBOR is 4 percent. The face value of the swap is Sf1.5 million. The spot exchange rate is Sf1.5/$.

a. What are the realized cash flows on the swap at the spot exchange rate?

b. If the 1-year forward rate is Sf1.538/$, what are the end-of-year net cash flows on the swap? Assume LIBOR is unchanged.

c. If LIBOR increases to 6 percent, what are the end-of-year net cash flows on the swap? Evaluate at the forward rate.

19. Give two reasons credit swaps have been the fastest-growing form of swaps in recent years.

20. What is a total return swap?

21. How does a pure credit swap differ from a total return swap? How does it differ from a digital default option?

22. Why is the credit risk on a swap lower than the credit risk on a loan?

23. What is netting by novation?

24. What role did the swap market play in the financial crisis of 2008–2009?

The following problem refers to material in Appendix 24A.

25. The following information is available on a three-year swap contract. One-year-maturity notes are currently priced at par and pay a coupon rate of 5 percent annually. Two-year-maturity notes are currently priced at par and pay a coupon rate of 5.5 percent annually. Three-year-maturity notes are currently priced at par and pay a coupon rate of 5.75 percent annually. The terms of a three-year swap of $100 million notional value are 5.45 percent annual fixed-rate payments in exchange for floating-rate payments tied to the annual discount yield.

a. If an insurance company buys this swap, what can you conclude about the interest rate risk exposure of the company's underlying cash position?

b. What are the realized cash flows expected over the three-year life of the swap?

c. What are the realized cash flows that occur over the three-year life of the swap if d_2 = 4.95 percent and d_3 = 6.1 percent?

Appendix 24A Setting Rates on an Interest Rate Swap

View Appendix 24A on Connect.

CHAPTER 25

LOAN SALES

After studying this chapter you should be able to:

LO1 Define recourse and nonrecourse loan sales and demonstrate their impact on the balance sheet of an FI.

LO2 Discuss the types of loan sales contracts.

LO3 Identify the buyers and sellers of loans and discuss why an FI participates in this activity.

LO4 Demonstrate how a good bank–bad bank structure is used.

LO5 Discuss why banks and other FIs sell loans.

LO6 Discuss the factors affecting the growth of the loan sales market.

INTRODUCTION

Traditionally, banks and other FIs have relied on a number of contractual mechanisms to control the credit risks of lending. These have included (1) requiring higher interest rate spreads and fees on loans to more risky borrowers; (2) restricting or rationing loans to more risky borrowers; (3) requiring enhanced seniority (collateral) for the bank over the assets of risky borrowers; (4) diversifying across different types of risky borrowers; and (5) placing more restrictive covenants on risky borrowers' actions, such as restrictions on the use of proceeds from asset sales, new debt issues, and dividend payments. These traditional mechanisms for controlling or managing credit risk were described in Chapters 10 and 11.

Additionally, in Chapters 22 through 24 we discussed the increasing use of credit derivatives in the forward, options, and swaps markets to manage credit risk—for example, the use of credit default swaps (CDSs, or put options) to control the credit risk of an individual loan or portfolio of loans. In addition, FIs may require borrowers to hedge their own risks, especially when the FI makes floating-rate loans to borrowers. When interest rates rise, the borrower of a floating-rate loan may have greater difficulty meeting interest rate payments. However, if the borrower has hedged the risk of rising rates in the derivatives market (e.g., by selling interest rate futures or receiving floating payments—paying fixed payments in an interest rate swap), the borrower is in a far better position to meet its contractual payments to the FI. As a result, the credit risk exposure of the FI is reduced.

This and the following chapter on securitization describe the role of loan sales and other techniques (such as the good bank–bad bank structure) used by FI managers to control credit risk. Although loan sales have been in existence for many years, the use of loan sales (by removing existing loans from the balance sheet) is increasingly being recognized as a valuable additional tool in an FI manager's portfolio of credit risk management techniques. Indeed, it has been found that new loan announcements are associated with a positive stock price announcement effect even when a borrower's loans trade on the secondary market. Moreover, when a borrower's existing loans trade for the first time in the secondary loan market, this elicits a positive stock price response. The chapter begins with an overview of the loan sales market. We define and look at the types of loan sales and summarize who are the buyers and sellers of loans. We then discuss why banks and other FIs would sell loans, as well as the factors that deter and encourage loan sales.

THE BANK LOAN SALES MARKET

Definition of a Loan Sale

LO1

The credit derivatives (such as credit swaps) discussed in Chapters 22 through 24 allow FIs to reduce credit risk without physically removing assets from their balance sheet. Loan sales allow FIs to reduce credit risk by removing the loan from the balance sheet. Specifically, a **bank loan sale** occurs when an FI originates a loan and sells it either with or without recourse to an outside buyer. Many loan agreements contain a clause that allows an FI to sell the loan to another buyer, sometimes without having to notify the borrower of the sale. This facilitates the legal transfer of ownership of the financial asset and provides increased flexibility for an FI to adjust its balance sheet.

bank loan sale
The sale of a loan originated by an FI with or without recourse to an outside buyer.

If a loan is sold without recourse, not only is it removed from the FI's balance sheet but also the FI has no explicit liability if the loan eventually goes bad. Panel A of Table 25–1 shows an FI's balance sheet before and after a $20 million loan sale. The buyer (and not the FI that originated the loan) bears all the credit risk. If, however, the loan is sold with **recourse**, under certain conditions the buyer can put the loan back to the selling FI; therefore, the FI retains a contingent credit risk liability. Panel B of Table 25–1 shows the FI's balance sheet, including the contingent liability from the loan sale held off the balance sheet. In practice, most loans are sold without recourse because a loan sale is technically removed from the balance sheet only when the buyer has no future credit risk

recourse
The ability of a loan buyer to put the loan back to the originator if it goes bad.

TABLE 25–1 **FI Balance Sheet before and after a $20 Million Loan Sale ($ millions)**

Panel A: Loan Sale without Recourse							
Before Loan Sale				**After Loan Sale**			
Assets		**Liabilities/Equity**		**Assets**		**Liabilities/Equity**	
Cash assets	$ 10	Deposit	$ 90	Cash assets	$ 10	Deposits	$ 90
				Loans	70		
Loans	90	Equity	10	New investments	20	Equity	10
	$100		$100		$100		$100
Panel B: Loan Sale with Recourse							
Before Loan Sale				**After Loan Sale**			
Assets		**Liabilities/Equity**		**Assets**		**Liabilities/Equity**	
Cash assets	$ 10	Deposit	$ 90	Cash assets	$ 10	Deposits	$ 90
				Loans	70		
Loans	90	Equity	10	New investments	20	Equity	10
	$100		$100		$100		$100
				Off balance sheet: Loan sale (contingent liability)			$ 20

claim on the FI. Importantly, loan sales involve no creation of new types of securities such as the pass-throughs, collateralized mortgage obligations (CMOs), and mortgage-backed securities (MBSs) described in Chapter 26. As such, loan sales are a primitive form of securitization in that loan selling creates a secondary market for loans in which ownership of the loan is simply transferred to the loan buyer.

Types of Loan Sales

LO2

The loan sales market has three segments: two involve the sale and trading of domestic loans, while the third involves sovereign debt loan sales and trading. Since we described sovereign debt loan sales in Chapter 15 on sovereign risk, we concentrate on the North American loan sales market here.

Traditional Short-Term Loan Sales

In the traditional short-term segment of the market, FIs sell loans with short maturities, often one to three months. This market has characteristics similar to those of the market for commercial paper (CP) issued by corporations in that loan sales have similar maturities and issue size. Loan sales, however, usually have yields that are 1 to 10 basis points (bp) above those of CP of a similar rating. In particular, the loan sales market in which an FI originates and sells a short-term loan of a corporation is a close substitute for the issuance of CP. The key characteristics of the short-term loan sales market are as follows:

- They are secured by assets of the borrowing firm.
- They are made to investment-grade borrowers or better.
- They are issued for a short term (90 days or less).
- They have yields closely tied to the CP rate.
- They are sold in units of $1 million and up.

highly leveraged transaction (HLT) loan
A loan made to finance a merger and acquisition: a leveraged buyout results in a high leverage ratio for the borrower.

Until 1984 and the emergence of the **highly leveraged transactions (HLTs)** and emerging-market (EM) loan markets, traditional short-term loan sales dominated the loan sales market. The growth of the CP market, as well as the increased ability of banks to underwrite CP (see Chapter 21), also reduced the importance of this market segment.

HLT Loan Sales

With the growth in mergers and acquisitions (M&As) and leveraged buyouts (LBOs) via HLTs, especially during the period 1985–1989, a new segment in the loan sales market appeared.

What constitutes an HLT loan has often caused dispute. However, in October 1989 the three U.S. federal bank regulators adopted a definition of an HLT loan as one that (1) involves a buyout, acquisition, or recapitalization and (2) doubles the company's liabilities and results in a leverage ratio higher than 50 percent, results in a leverage ratio higher than 75 percent, or is designated as an HLT by a syndication agent. HLT loans mainly differ according to whether they are nondistressed (bid price exceeds 90 cents per $1 of loans) or distressed (bid price is less than 90 cents per $1 of loans or the borrower is in default).

Virtually all HLT loans have the following characteristics:

- They are term loans (TLs).
- They are secured by assets of the borrowing firm (usually given senior secured status).
- They have a long maturity (often three- to six-year maturities).
- They have floating rates tied to LIBOR, the prime rate, or a CD rate (normally 200 to 275 bp above these rates).
- They have strong covenant protection.

Nevertheless, HLTs tend to be quite heterogeneous with respect to the size of the issue, the interest payment date, interest indexing, and prepayment features. After origination, some HLT borrowers, such as Macy's and El Paso Electric, suffered periods of **financial distress**. As a result, a distinction is usually made between the markets for distressed and nondistressed HLTs. Spreads on HLT loans behave more like investment-grade bonds than like high-yield bonds. A possible reason for this is that HLT loans tend to be more senior in bankruptcy and to have greater collateral backing than do high-yield bonds.

financial distress
A period when a borrower is unable to meet a payment obligation to lenders and other creditors.

Approximately 100 banks and securities firms make a market in this debt either as brokers or (less commonly) as broker–dealers, including Bank of America, JPMorgan Chase, Citigroup, CIBC, and Wells Fargo. Most of these FIs view trading in this debt as similar to trading in junk bonds.

Types of Loan Sales Contracts

There are two basic types of loan sales contracts or mechanisms by which loans can be transferred between seller and buyer: participations and assignments. Currently, assignments make up the bulk of loan sales trading.

Participations

The unique features of **participation in a loan** are as follows:

participation in a loan
Buying a share in a loan syndication with limited contractual control and rights over the borrower.

- The holder (buyer) is not a party to the underlying credit agreement so that the initial contract between loan seller and borrower remains in place after the sale.
- The loan buyer can exercise only partial control over changes in the loan contract's terms. The holder can vote only on material changes to the loan contract, such as the interest rate or collateral backing.

The economic implication of these features is that the buyer of the loan participation has a double risk exposure: a risk exposure to the borrower and a risk exposure to the loan-selling FI. Specifically, if the selling FI fails, the loan participation bought by an outside party may be characterized as an unsecured obligation of the FI rather than as a true sale if there are grounds for believing that some explicit or implicit recourse existed between the loan seller and the loan buyer. Alternatively, the borrower's claims against a failed selling FI may be set off against its loans from that FI, reducing the amount of loans outstanding and adversely impacting the buyer of a participation in those loans. As a result of these exposures, the buyer bears a double monitoring cost as well.

Assignments

assignment
Buying a share in a loan syndication with some contractual control and rights over the borrower.

Because of the monitoring costs and risks involved in participations, loans are sold on an assignment basis in more than 90 percent of the cases on the North American market. The key features of an **assignment** are as follows:

- All rights are transferred on sale, meaning the loan buyer now holds a direct claim on the borrower.
- Transfer is normally associated with legal proof that a change of ownership has occurred.

Although ownership rights are generally much clearer in a loan sale by assignment, contractual terms frequently limit the seller's scope regarding to whom the loan can be sold. In particular, the loan contract may require either the FI agent or the borrower to agree to the sale. The loan contract may also restrict the sale to a certain class of institutions, such as those that meet certain net worth/net asset size conditions. (An *FI agent* is an FI that distributes interest and principal payments to lenders in loan syndications with multiple lenders.) Assignments are common in loan syndications, discussed in Chapter 11. In a syndicated loan, two or more banks agree to jointly make a loan to a borrower. The syndicate is formed around the arrangers, which generally include the borrower's relationship banks, which retain a portion of the loan and look for junior participants (e.g., smaller banks).

accrued interest
The loan seller's claim to part of the next interest payment on the loan.

Currently, the trend appears to be toward loan contracts being originated with very limited assignment restrictions. This is true in both the North American domestic and the international loan sales markets. The most tradable loans are those that can be assigned without buyer restrictions. Even so, one has to distinguish between floating-rate and fixed-rate assignment loans. For floating-rate loans, most loan sales by assignment occur on the loan's repricing date (which may be two or four times a year), due to complexities for the agent FI in calculating and transferring accrued interest—especially given the heterogeneous nature of floating-rate loan indexes such as LIBOR. In addition, the nonstandardization of **accrued interest** payments in fixed-rate loan assignments (trade date, assignment date, coupon payment date) adds complexity and friction to this market. Moreover, while the FI agent may have a full record of the initial owners of the loans, it does not always have an up-to-date record of loan ownership changes and related transfers following trades. This means that great difficulties can occur for the borrower, FI agent, and loan buyer in ensuring that the current holder of the loan receives the interest and principal payments due. Finally, the buyer of the loan often needs to verify the original loan contract and establish the full implications of the purchase regarding the buyer's rights to collateral if the borrower defaults.

Because of these contractual problems, trading frictions, and costs, some loan sales take as long as three months to complete; reportedly, up to 50 percent eventually fail to be completed at all. In many cases, the incentive to renege on a contract arises because market prices move away from those originally agreed upon so that the counterparty finds reasons to delay the completion of a loan sale and/or eventually refuses to complete the transaction.[1]

---

[1] However, in recent years, completion of a trade within 10 days (or $T + 10$) has become an increasing convention.

TRENDS IN LOAN SALES

correspondent banking
A relationship entered into between a small bank and a big bank in which the big bank provides a number of deposit, lending, and other services to the small bank.

project finance loans
Loans made to a single-purpose entity where principal and interest are paid from the cash flows of the project.

Banks and other FIs have sold loans among themselves for over 100 years. In fact, a large part of **correspondent banking** involves small banks making loans that are too big for them to hold on their balance sheets—for lending concentration, risk, or capital adequacy reasons—and selling parts of these loans to large banks with which they have a long-term deposit-lending correspondent relationship. In turn, the large banks often sell parts of their loans called *participations* to smaller banks. Even though this market has existed for many years, it grew slowly until the early 1980s, when it entered a period of spectacular growth, largely due to expansion in **project finance loans** as well as HLT loans to finance LBOs and M&As. Specifically, the volume of loans sold by North American banks grew from less than US$20 billion in 1980 to US$285 billion in 1989. Between 1990 and 1994 the volume of loan sales fell almost equally dramatically, along with the decline in LBOs and M&As as a result of the credit crunch associated with the 1990–1991 recession. In 1994, the volume of loan sales had fallen to approximately US$20 billion.

In the late 1990s, the volume of loan sales expanded again, partly due to an expanding economy and a resurgence in M&As. For example, the loan market research firm Loan Pricing Corporation reported that secondary loan trading volume in 1999 was more than US$77 billion. Loan sales continued to grow to over US$175 billion in 2005 and US$238 billion in 2006 as FIs sold distressed loans (loans trading below 90 cents on the dollar). Triggered by an economic slowdown, distressed loan sales jumped from 11 percent of total loan sales in 1999 to 36 percent in 2001 and 42 percent in 2002. As the North American economy improved in the early and mid-2000s, the percentage of distressed loan sales fell to 17 percent in 2006. Even as the economy slowed in 2007 and 2008, while loan sales surged to over US$500 billion, distressed loan sales remained low. In 2007 distressed loans were just 9 percent of total loan sales and in 2008 they were under 8 percent of all loan sales. Loan sales fell only slightly (to US$474 billion) in 2009, during the worst of the financial crisis. However, as might be expected during a recession, the percentage of distressed loans increased significantly, to almost 30 percent. Loan sales decreased slightly in 2010, as the economy began to improve. However, distressed loan sales remained high, over 20 percent. In 2011, the U.S. economy continued to struggle and loan sales increased slightly. However, the percentage of distressed loans decreased significantly, to 8.7 percent, as many FIs had already sold off their marketable distressed loans in 2009 and 2010. Figure 25–1 shows the growth in loan sales over the 1991–2011 (second-quarter) period.

Many of these loans are syndicated, involving many sponsoring banks. For example, in the first three quarters of 2011 the Loan Pricing Corporation reported that JPMorgan Chase was the leading loan syndicator in the worldwide secondary loan market, sponsoring 951 deals worth US$1.096 trillion. Yet JPMorgan Chase retained risk for only US$257 billion of these loans. JPMorgan Chase, Bank of America Merrill Lynch (US$1.096 trillion), Citigroup (US$877 billion), BNP Paribas (US$670 billion), and RBS (US$633 billion) were the top five secondary-market loan syndicators in the first three quarters of 2012.

The Canadian debt market plays a minor role in loan sales in North America. All of the six major Canadian banks use syndications and loan sales for credit risk management, but when loan defaults are low and banks have sufficient

FIGURE 25–1
U.S. Secondary Loan Market Volume, Trading 1991–Q3 2011 (U.S. $ billions)

Source: Thomson Reuters LPC website, 2012, loanpricing.com.

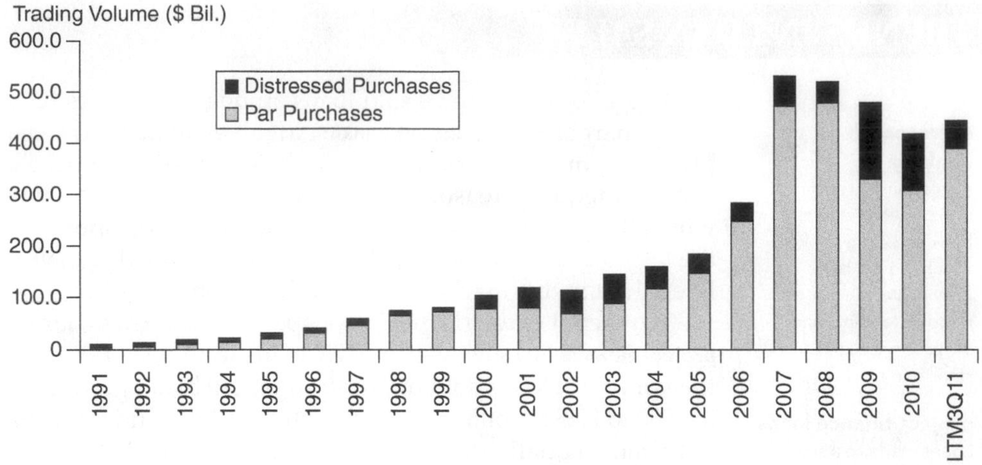

scotiabank.com

capital, there is little need for a bank to sell its loans other than to adjust its risk exposure to different industries or countries. For example, Scotiabank reported loan sales of $649 million in 2012, less than 1 percent of its total average daily loans to businesses and governments. As well, Canadian banks (e.g., RBC) report using syndication groups to increase their fee income and enhance their global presence.

The Buyers and the Sellers

The Buyers

LO3

vulture funds
Specialized hedge funds that invest in distressed loans.

Of the wide array of potential buyers, some are concerned with only a certain segment of the market for regulatory and strategic reasons. In particular, an increasingly specialized group of buyers of distressed HLT loans includes investment banks, **vulture funds**, and other banks.

Investment Banks Investment banks are predominantly buyers of HLT loans because (1) analysis of these loans utilizes investment skills similar to those used in junk bond trading and (2) investment banks were often closely associated with the HLT distressed borrower in underwriting the original junk bond/HLT deals. As such, large U.S. investment banking operations—for example, Bank of America Merrill Lynch and Goldman Sachs—are relatively more informed agents in this market, either by acting as market makers or in taking short-term positions on movements in the discount from par.

Vulture Funds Vulture funds are specialized hedge funds established to invest in distressed loans, often with an agenda that may not include helping the distressed firm to survive (see Chapter 5 for a discussion of hedge funds). These investments can be active, especially for those seeking to use the loans purchased for bargaining in a restructuring deal; this generates restructuring returns that strongly favour the loan purchaser. Alternatively, such loans may be held as passive investments, such as high-yield securities in a well-diversified portfolio of distressed securities. Many vulture funds are in fact managed by investment banking firms.

For the nondistressed HLT market and the traditional loan sales market, the major buyers are other domestic or foreign banks, insurance companies and pension funds, closed-end bank loan mutual funds, and nonfinancial corporations.

Other Banks Interbank loan sales are at the core of the traditional market and have historically revolved around correspondent banking relationships and, in the United States, regional banking/branching restrictions. Restrictions on nationwide banking have often led U.S. banks to originate regionally undiversified and borrower-undiversified loan portfolios. Small U.S. banks often sell loan participations to their large correspondents to improve regional/borrower diversification and to avoid regulatory-imposed, single-borrower loan concentration ceilings. U.S. regulations require that credit exposure to a single borrower not exceed 10 percent of a bank's capital. This arrangement can also work in the other direction, with the larger banks selling participations to smaller banks.

The traditional U.S. interbank market, however, has been shrinking. This is due to at least three factors. First, the traditional correspondent banking relationship is breaking down in a more competitive and increasingly consolidated U.S. banking market. Second, concerns about counterparty risk and moral hazard have increased. In particular, moral hazard is the risk that the selling bank will seek to offload its "bad" loans (via loan sales), keeping the "good" loans in its portfolio. Third, the barriers to U.S. nationwide banking were largely eroded with the passage of the Riegle–Neal Interstate Branching and Efficiency Act of 1994. Nevertheless, some small banks find the loan sales market enormously useful as a way to regionally diversify their loan portfolios.

osfi-bsif.gc.ca

In Canada, FIs (banks, authorized foreign banks, and trust and loan companies) regulated by the Office of the Superintendent of Financial Services (OSFI) are subject to the "prudent person approach" and so must have written internal policies regarding large exposures to any one customer, country, or other FI. These FIs are limited to 25 percent of capital to any one entity and, in the normal course of business, are expected to be below this limit. Thus, large loans may be originated with the intention of syndication to other banks. Foreign bank subsidiaries are limited to 100 percent of their total capital to any one entity, and so may be both buyers and sellers of loans. Foreign banks thus are able to diversify their North American loan portfolios without having a banking network in either Canada or the United States and so, in some years, purchased over 40 percent of the loans sold in the United States. However, asset **downsizing**, as a result of the global financial market turmoil in 2008, has caused this source of demand for loan sales to contract.

downsizing
Shrinking the asset size of an FI.

Insurance Companies and Pension Funds Subject to meeting liquidity and quality or investment-grade regulatory restrictions, insurance companies and pension funds are important buyers of long-term maturity loans.

Closed- and Open-End Bank Loan Mutual Funds First established in the United States in 1988, these leveraged mutual funds, such as Highland Capital Management of Dallas, Texas, invest in domestic U.S. bank loans. While they purchase loans on the secondary market, such as loan resales, the largest funds have also moved into primary loan syndications because of the attractive fee income available. That is, these mutual funds participate in funding loans originated by commercial banks. The mutual fund, in turn, receives a fee or part of the interest payment. Indeed, some U.S. money centre banks, such as JPMorgan Chase, have actively encouraged closed-end fund participation in primary loan syndications. The first bank loan mutual fund (Trimark Floating Rate Income Fund) was created by AIM Trimark in 2005. Since then, other Canadian FIs (e.g., BMO, Manulife) and U.S. FIs (e.g., AGF, Trimark) have offered floating-rate income funds to Canadian investors. These funds invest primarily in the floating-rate loans of U.S. and international companies.

Nonfinancial Corporations There are some corporations that buy loans, but this activity is limited mostly to the financial services arms of the very largest U.S. and European companies (e.g., GE Capital and ITT Financial) and amounts to no more than 5 percent of total U.S. domestic loan sales.

The Sellers

LO4

The sellers of domestic loans and HLT loans in North America are major banks, foreign banks, investment banks, and the U.S. government and its agencies, particularly the FDIC.

Major Banks In the United States, loan selling has been dominated by the largest money centre banks. In recent years, market concentration on the loan-selling side has been accentuated by the growth of HLTs (and the important role major money centre banks have played in originating loans in HLT deals) as well as the growth in real estate loan sales. Large U.S. money centre banks have engaged in large (real estate) loan sales directly or have formalized such sales through the mechanism of a "good bank–bad bank" structure.

Good Bank–Bad Bank Bad banks are special-purpose banks that hold portfolios of distressed assets and that are organized to liquidate portfolios of nonperforming loans. As such, their sources of financing can be debt or equity. As the assets are liquidated, the bad bank shrinks and eventually disappears as it pays off debtholders and equityholders from the cash flows on the liquidated "bad" assets. The principal objective in their creation is to maximize asset values by separating good loans (in the "good bank") from bad loans (in the "bad bank"). For example, U.S. Mellon Bank wrote down the face value of US$941 million in real estate loans and sold them to a specially created bad-bank subsidiary—Grant Street National Bank—for US$577 million. This special-purpose bad bank was funded by bond issues and common and preferred stock. Managers of the bad bank were given equity (junior preferred stock) as an incentive mechanism to generate maximum values in liquidating the loans purchased from Mellon (i.e., achieving a market resale value greater than US$577 million). More recently, the good bank–bad bank model was proposed as a way of removing toxic assets from the balance sheets of FIs during the financial crisis. The good bank–bad bank proposal called for the use of U.S. tax money to buy the toxic assets and put them in a new nationalized FI (the bad bank) that would operate under U.S. federal government control. The toxic assets would be sold off over time. The good bank would be left with the good assets and could then operate free from concerns about troubled assets. Similarly, Spain used this same concept during its banking crisis in 2012. A bad bank, known as SAREB, was set up as a condition of a European aid package received by the country in June 2012. Spanish government debt was used to finance less than 50 percent of the bank. Private investors (such as Deutsche Bank of Germany, British bank Barclays, and French insurer Axa) provided the remaining financing. The bad bank bought billions of euros worth of distressed loans and foreclosed property from Spanish banks for approximately half their book value. The program was expected to remove €60 billion (US$77 billion) of toxic assets from banks' balance sheets. All Spanish banks that received European aid were obligated to transfer assets to the bad bank.

Table 25–2 illustrates the sale of nonperforming loans from a good bank to a subsidiary bad bank. In Panel A of Table 25–2, the good bank has $950 million of nonperforming loans along with $2,500 million in performing loans and $500 million in cash assets on its balance sheet before the loan sale. The assets are financed with

TABLE 25–2 **Good Bank–Bad Bank Balance Sheets before and after a Loan Sale ($ millions)**

Panel A: Good Bank							
Before Loan Sale				**After Loan Sale**			
Assets		**Liabilities/Equity**		**Assets**		**Liabilities/Equity**	
Cash assets	$ 500	Deposits	$2,500	Cash assets	$ 500	Deposits	$2,500
Loans		Purchased		Loans		Purchased	
Performing	2,500	funds	750	Performing	2,500	funds	170
Nonperforming	950	Equity	700	Nonperforming	0	Equity	330
	$3,950		$3,950		$3,000		$3,000
Panel B: Bad Bank							
Before Loan Sale				**After Loan Sale**			
Assets		**Liabilities/Equity**		**Assets**		**Liabilities/Equity**	
Cash assets	$ 600	Bonds	$300	Cash assets	$ 20	Bonds	$300
Loans	0	Preferred stock	100	Loans	580	Preferred stock	100
		Common stock	200			Common stock	200
	$ 600		$600		$600		$600

$2,500 million in deposits, $750 million in purchased funds, and $700 million in equity. If the bad bank, in Panel B, buys the nonperforming loans (with the proceeds of bond, preferred stock, and common stock financing) for $580 million, the good bank gets these loans off its balance sheet, incurring a $370 million loss in equity (i.e., $950 million face value of loans minus $580 million received in their purchase). The proceeds of the loan sale are then used to pay off purchased funds, bringing their balance down to $170 million, or $750 million minus $580 million. The bad bank now has the $950 million face value loans (for which it paid $580 million) on its balance sheet. These loans can be restructured or disposed of. If the loans realize more than $580 million, additional returns can be passed through to the bad bank common stockholders in dividends or used to repurchase bonds or preferred stock.

There are at least five reasons for believing that loan sales through a bad bank vehicle will be value enhancing compared to the originating bank itself retaining (and eventually selling) these loans:

1. The bad bank enables bad assets to be managed by loan workout specialists.
2. The good bank's reputation and access to deposit and funding markets tend to be improved once bad loans are removed from the balance sheet.
3. Because the bad bank does not have any short-term deposits (i.e., is a self-liquidating entity), it can follow an optimal disposition strategy for bad assets, as it is not overly concerned with liquidity needs.
4. As in the case of Mellon's bad bank, contracts for managers can be created to maximize their incentives to generate enhanced values from loan sales.
5. The good bank–bad bank structure reduces information asymmetries about the value of the good bank's assets (the so-called lemons problem), thus potentially increasing its attractiveness to risk-averse investors.

Foreign Banks To the extent that foreign banks are sellers rather than buyers of loans, these loans come out of branch networks such as Japanese-owned banks in

California or through their market-making activities selling loans originated in their home country in the North American loan sales markets. One of the major market makers in the North American loan sales market (especially the HLT market) is the Dutch FI ING Bank. Barclays Bank, BNP Paribas, Deutsche Bank, and Royal Bank of Scotland also participate in this market.

rbc.com

Investment Banks Investment banks, such as Merrill Lynch (a subsidiary of Bank of America) and RBC's U.S. investment and corporate banking arm, act as loan sellers either as part of their market-making function (selling loans they have originated) or as active traders. Again, these loan sales are are often confined to large HLT transactions.

fdic.gov

The U.S. Government and Its Agencies In the recent credit crisis, the U.S. government and its agencies have shown an increased willingness to engage in loan sales. In 2009, the FDIC and U.S. Treasury began operating the Legacy Loans Program to remove distressed loans from FIs' balance sheets through public–private investment funds (PPIFs). As well, as part of the process of winding up failed FIs, the FDIC offers packages of loans for sale to qualified buyers.

CONCEPT QUESTIONS

1. **Which loans have the highest yields: loans sold with recourse or loans sold without recourse?**
2. **Which have higher yields, junk bonds or HLT loans? Explain your answer.**
3. **Describe the two types of contracts by which loans can be transferred between seller and buyer.**
4. **What institutions are the major buyers in the traditional North American loan sales market? What institutions are the major sellers in this market?**

WHY BANKS AND OTHER FINANCIAL INSTITUTIONS SELL LOANS

LO5

The introduction to this chapter stated that one reason that FIs sell loans is to manage their credit risk better. Loan sales remove assets (and credit risk) from the balance sheet and allow an FI to achieve better asset diversification. However, other than credit risk management, there are a number of economic and regulatory reasons that encourage FIs to sell loans. These are discussed below.

Reserve Requirements

Regulatory requirements such as reserve requirements (e.g., those imposed on banks operating in the United States), which a bank has to hold at the central bank, are a form of tax that adds to the cost of funding the loan portfolio. Regulatory taxes such as reserve requirements create an incentive for banks to remove loans from the balance sheet by selling them without recourse to outside parties. Such removal allows banks to shrink both their assets and their deposits and, thus, the amount of reserves they have to hold against their deposits.

Fee Income

An FI can often report any fee income earned from originating (and then selling) loans as current income, whereas interest earned on direct lending can be accrued (as income) only over time. As a result, originating and quickly selling loans can boost an FI's reported income.

Capital Costs

Like reserve requirements, the capital adequacy requirements imposed on FIs are a burden as long as required capital exceeds the amount the FI believes to be privately beneficial. For tax reasons, debt is a cheaper source of funds than equity capital. Thus, FIs struggling to meet a required assets (A) to capital (K) ratio can reduce this ratio by reducing assets (A) rather than boosting capital (K) (see Chapter 20). One way to downsize or reduce A and reduce the A/K ratio is through loan sales.

Liquidity Risk

In addition to credit risk and interest rate risk, holding loans on the balance sheet can increase the overall illiquidity of an FI's assets. This illiquidity is a problem because FI liabilities tend to be highly liquid. Asset illiquidity can expose an FI to harmful liquidity squeezes whenever liability holders unexpectedly liquidate their claims. To mitigate a liquidity problem, an FI's management can sell some of its loans to outside investors. Thus, the loan sales market has created a secondary market in loans that has significantly reduced the illiquidity of FI loans held as assets on the balance sheet.

CONCEPT QUESTIONS

1. **What are some of the economic and regulatory reasons that FIs choose to sell loans?**
2. **How can an FI use its loans to mitigate a liquidity problem?**

FACTORS AFFECTING LOAN SALES GROWTH

LO6

The loan sales market has gone through a number of up and down phases in recent years (as discussed above). However, notwithstanding the value of loan sales as a credit risk management tool, there remain a number of factors that will both spur and deter the market's growth and development in future years. We first discuss factors that may deter the market's growth.

Access to the CP Market

More and more smaller middle market firms are gaining direct access to the CP market. As a result, they have less need to rely on bank loans to finance their short-term expenditures. However, banks often provide credit commitments to customers as backup lines to CP. Drawdowns of these during times of market turmoil can result in severe liquidity stress for an FI.

Customer Relationship Effects

As the FI industry consolidates and expands the range of financial services sold, customer relationships are likely to become even more important than they are today. To the extent that a loan customer (borrower) views the sale of its loan by its FI as an adverse statement about the customer's value to the FI, loan sales can harm revenues generated by the FI as current and potential future customers take their business elsewhere.

Legal Concerns

A number of legal concerns hamper the loan sales market's growth, especially for distressed HLT loans. In particular, while banks are normally secured creditors,

fraudulent conveyance
When a transaction such as a sale of securities or transference of assets to a particular party is ruled illegal.

this status may be attacked by other creditors if the firm enters bankruptcy. For example, **fraudulent conveyance** proceedings have been brought in the United States against the secured lenders to Revco, Circle K, Allied Stores, and RJR Nabisco. More recently, in October 2012 the U.S. Justice Department filed a complaint against Bank of America claiming that the bank and its Countrywide Financial unit generated thousands of defective loans and sold them to Fannie Mae and Freddie Mac. If such legal moves are upheld, then the sale of loans to a particular party may be found to be illegal. Such legal suits represent one of the factors that have slowed the growth of the distressed loan market. Indeed, in many recent sales, loan buyers have demanded a put option feature that allows them to put the loan back to the seller at the purchase price if a transaction is proven to be fraudulent. Further, a second type of distressed-firm risk may result if, in the process of a loan workout, the FI lender acts more like an equity owner than an outside debtor. For example, the FI may get involved in the day-to-day running of the firm and make strategic investment and asset sales decisions. This could open up claims that the FI's loans should be treated like equity rather than secured debt. That is, the FI's loans may be subordinated in the claims priority ranking or be subject to lender liability.

There are at least six factors that point to an increasing volume of loan sales in the future. These are in addition to the credit risk "hedging" value of loan sales.

BIS Capital Requirements

bis.org

The Bank for International Settlements (BIS) risk-based capital rules (see Chapter 20) mean that bankers will continue to have strong incentives to sell commercial loans to other FIs and investors to downsize their balance sheets and boost bank capital ratios.

Market Value Accounting

sec.gov
fasb.org

The U.S. Securities and Exchange Commission (SEC) and the Financial Accounting Standards Board (FASB) have advocated the replacement of book value accounting with market value accounting for financial services firms (see Chapter 20). In addition, capital requirements for interest rate risk and market risk have moved banks toward a market value accounting framework (see Chapter 10). The trend toward the marking to market of assets will make bank loans look more like securities and thus make them easier to sell and/or trade.

Asset Brokerage and Loan Trading

The emphasis of large banks on trading and trading income suggests that significant attention will still be paid to those segments of the loan sales market where price volatility is high and thus potential trading profits can be made. Most HLT loans have floating rates so that their underlying values are in large part insulated from swings in the level of interest rates (unlike fixed-income securities such as government bonds). Nevertheless, the low credit quality of many of these loans and their long maturities create an enhanced potential for credit risk volatility. As a result, a short-term, three-month secured loan to an AAA-rated company is unlikely to show significant future credit risk volatility compared to an eight-year HLT loan to a distressed company. This suggests that trading in loans to below-investment-grade companies will always be attractive for FIs that use their specialized credit monitoring skills as asset traders rather than as asset transformers in participating in the market.

Government Loan Sales

With the increased involvement of the U.S. federal government in the loan sales market (through its direct purchases of distressed loans held by FIs and its takeover of mortgage giants Fannie Mae and Freddie Mac) during the financial crisis, there is a strong likelihood that the sale of loans by the U.S. government and its agencies will increase in the future.

Credit Ratings

There is a growing trend toward the "credit rating" of loans offered for sale. Unlike bonds, a loan credit rating reflects more than the financial soundness of the underlying borrowing corporation. In particular, the value of the underlying collateral can change a loan's credit rating up to one full category above a standard bond rating. As more loans are rated, their attractiveness to secondary-market buyers is likely to increase.

Purchase and Sale of Foreign Bank Loans

With over US$1,200 billion in doubtful and troubled loans on their books in the early 2000s, Japanese banks presented a huge potential market for the sale of distressed loans. A number of commercial and investment banks established funds to buy up some of the bad loans. For example, in 2003 Goldman Sachs announced a US$9.3 billion fund to buy troubled loans from Japan's second-largest bank, SMFG. This fund represented the first transfer of a bad loan package of this size to a non-government-affiliated entity in Japan. This deal provided banks with a way of removing bad loans from their balance sheets while still retaining control over the corporate restructuring process. More recently, during the early 2010s, inadequate capital levels were such that European banks would need to have decreased in size by over US$2.4 trillion to be adequately capitalized. As such, loan sales increased significantly. For example, in 2012 European banks sold a record US$61 billion in loans, after US$44 billion sold in 2011. Most of these loans have stopped generating their expected interest streams, and working out how to restructure or dispose of them costs banks significant time and money. The buyers are often large asset managers, such as "vulture" hedge funds or private equity firms that specialize in generating profits from distressed debts, or buying performing debts at a discount from banks that just want to trim their balance sheets.

THE GLOBAL CREDIT AND LIQUIDITY CRISIS, 2008–2009

The secondary loan market was impacted by the credit and liquidity crisis that hit global financial markets in 2008 and 2009. There was a decline in trading volume for both distressed and nondistressed loans. The Loan Pricing Corporation reported that total loan issuance in the United States declined by 55 percent from US$1.7 trillion in 2007 to US$764 billion in 2008. FIs globally were burdened with toxic assets, nonperforming loans, and a global liquidity crisis that shut down the interbank market as well as the money markets in the third and fourth quarters of 2008. This meant that borrowers were looking to replace CP and other short-term market funds with bank loans at a time when banks were writing off loans and therefore in need of raising capital or selling assets in order to meet their regulatory capital requirements. The inability to remove loans, both performing and nonperforming, from an FI's balance sheet, either through loan sales or securitization (see Chapter 26), resulted in government programs to provide liquidity and to purchase assets, as we discussed in Chapter 1.

The 2008–2009 financial crisis illustrates how quickly our view of global financial markets can change. In 2002, loan sales were seen as a valid risk management technique likely to pose a minor systemic risk to the markets, and, according to Alan Greenspan, the then Federal Reserve chairman, there was "no evidence of anything remotely resembling the credit crunch we had a decade ago, where you just could not get a loan out of a commercial bank no matter what your creditworthiness. . . ." However, by September 2008, credit markets were disrupted and it was difficult for even a highly creditworthy borrower to draw down existing loan commitments or to increase its credit facilities. The deleveraging process of FIs, nonfinancial firms, and consumers in 2008 and 2009 resulted in a slowdown in the global economy. The "originate-to-distribute model" that drove the loan sales and securitization markets was being questioned, and the future of loan sales, other than syndications, was not clear. As well, the concern of regulators, particularly the BIS, resulted in new regulations (see Chapter 20) that affected bank strategies.

CONCEPT QUESTIONS

1. **What are some of the factors that are likely to deter the growth of the loan sales market in the future?**
2. **What are some specific legal concerns that have hampered the growth of the loan sales market?**
3. **What are some of the factors that are likely to encourage loan sales growth in the future?**
4. **Why would accounting organizations recommend that FIs replace book value accounting with market value accounting?**

Questions and Problems

1. What is the difference between loans sold with recourse and loans sold without recourse from the perspective of both sellers and buyers?
2. A bank has made a three-year, $10 million loan that pays annual interest of 8 percent. The principal is due at the end of the third year.
   a. The bank is willing to sell this loan with recourse at an interest rate of 8.5 percent. What price should it receive for this loan?
   b. The bank has the option to sell this loan without recourse at a discount rate of 8.75 percent. What price should it receive for this loan?
   c. If the bank expects a 0.5 percent probability of default on this loan, is it better to sell this loan with or without recourse? It expects to receive no interest payments or principal if the loan is defaulted.
3. What are some of the key features of short-term loan sales?
4. Why are yields higher on loan sales than on CP issues with similar maturity and issue size?
5. What are HLTs? What is the regulatory definition of an HLT?
6. How do the characteristics of an HLT loan differ from those of a short-term loan that is sold?
7. What is a possible reason that the spreads on HLT loans perform differently than do the spreads on junk bonds?
8. City Bank has made a 10-year, $2 million HLT loan that pays annual interest of 10 percent. The principal is expected to be paid at maturity.
   a. What should City Bank expect to receive from the sale of this loan if the current market interest rate on loans of this risk is 12 percent?
   b. The price of loans of this risk is currently being quoted in the secondary market at bid–offer prices of 88–89 cents (on each dollar). Translate these quotes into actual prices for the above loan.

c. Do these prices reflect a distressed or a nondistressed loan? Explain.

9. What is the difference between loan participations and loan assignments?
10. What are the difficulties in completing a loan assignment?
11. Who are the buyers of loans, and why do they participate in this activity?
    a. What are vulture funds?
    b. What are the reasons that the interbank market for loan sales has been shrinking?
    c. What are reasons that a small FI would be interested in participating in a loan syndication?
12. Who are the sellers of loans, and why do they participate in this activity?
    a. What is the purpose of a bad bank?
    b. What are the reasons that loan sales through a bad bank will be value enhancing?
13. In addition to managing credit risk, what are some other reasons for the sale of loans by FIs?
14. What are factors that may deter the growth of the loan sales market in the future? Discuss.
15. An FI is planning the purchase of a \$5 million loan to raise the existing average duration of its assets from 3.5 years to 5 years. It currently has total assets worth \$20 million, \$5 million in cash (0 duration), and \$15 million in loans. All the loans are fairly priced.
    a. Assuming it uses the cash to purchase the loan, should it purchase the loan if its duration is seven years?
    b. What asset duration loans should it purchase to raise its average duration to five years?
16. In addition to hedging credit risk, what factors can be expected to encourage loan sales in the future? Discuss the impact of each factor.

CHAPTER 26

SECURITIZATION

After studying this chapter you should be able to:

LO1 Discuss the mechanisms used to convert on-balance-sheet assets to a securitized asset.

LO2 Discuss and provide examples of the three major forms of asset securitization.

LO3 Discuss the benefits and costs of securitization for an FI.

INTRODUCTION

asset securitization
The packaging and selling of loans and other assets backed by securities.

Along with futures, forwards, options, swaps, and loan sales, **asset securitization**—the packaging and selling of loans and other assets backed by securities—is a mechanism that FIs use to hedge their interest rate exposure gaps. Securitization involves a change of strategy from a traditional FI's policy of holding the loans it originates on its balance sheet until maturity. Instead, securitization consists of packaging loans or other assets into newly created securities and selling these asset-backed securities (ABSs) to investors. By packaging and selling loans to outside parties, the FI removes considerable liquidity, interest rate, and credit risk from its asset portfolio. Rather than holding loans on the balance sheet until maturity, shortly after origination the originate-to-distribute model entails the FI's sale of the loan and other ABSs for cash, which can then be used to originate new loans/assets, thereby starting the securitization cycle over again. Thus, the process of securitization allows FI asset portfolios to become more liquid; provides an important source of fee income (with FIs acting as servicing agents for the assets sold); and helps reduce the effects of regulatory taxes such as capital requirements, reserve requirements (for bank lenders in the United States), and deposit insurance premiums.

The Canadian and U.S. securitization markets have evolved differently. Thus, while mortgage-backed securities (MBSs) became a big market in the United States, a small amount of Canadian residential mortgages were securitized. In Canada, short-term commercial borrowing dominates the ABS market, led by credit card receivables. As of 2012, over 66 percent of all U.S. residential mortgages were securitized, compared with less than 15 percent in 1980. In 2012, in Canada, less than 5 percent of residential mortgages were securitized compared to 11 percent in 2003. In this chapter we discuss the market for asset-backed commercial paper (ABCP) and asset-backed term notes in Canada, followed by a discussion of MBSs in a global context.

Credit derivatives, such as asset securitization and credit default swaps (CDSs), allow investors to separate the credit risk exposure from the lending process itself. That is, FIs can assess the creditworthiness of loan applicants, originate loans, fund loans, and even monitor and service loans without retaining exposure to loss from credit events, such as default or missed payments. This decoupling of the risk from the lending activity allows the market to efficiently transfer risk across counterparties. However, it also loosens the incentives to carefully perform each of the steps of the lending process and can lead to poor loan underwriting, inferior documentation and due diligence, failure to monitor borrower activity, and fraudulent activity on the part of both lenders and borrowers. This loosening of incentives was an important factor leading to the global financial crisis of 2008–2009. Although bank regulators attempt to examine the off-balance-sheet (OBS) activities of banks to ascertain their safety and soundness, there is far less scrutiny off the balance sheet than there is for on-balance-sheet activities (i.e., traditional lending and deposit taking). To the extent that counterparty credit risk is not fully disclosed to, or monitored by, regulators, the increased use of these innovations transfers risk in ways that are not necessarily scrutinized or understood. It is in this context of increased risk and inadequate regulation that the credit crisis developed.

This chapter investigates the role of securitization in affecting the return–risk trade-off for FIs. We first describe the mechanisms used by FIs to convert an on-balance-sheet asset to a securitized asset. We then describe the three major forms of asset securitization and analyze their unique characteristics. The major forms of asset securitization are the pass-through security, the collateralized mortgage obligation (CMO), and the mortgage-backed bond (MBB). Chapter 25 dealt with a more primitive form of asset securitization—loan sales—whereby loans are sold or traded to other investors and no new securities are created. In addition, although all three forms of securitization originated in the real estate lending market, these techniques are also applied to loans other than mortgages—for example, credit card loans, car loans, consumer loans, and business loans. We end the chapter with a discussion of the Canadian market for ABSs.

CONVERTING ON-BALANCE-SHEET ASSETS TO A SECURITIZED ASSET

LO1

The basic mechanism of securitization is accomplished via removal of assets (e.g., loans) from the balance sheets of the FIs. This is often done by creating OBS subsidiaries, such as a special-purpose vehicle (SPV, also known as an SPE, or special-purpose entity) or a structured investment vehicle (SIV). As discussed in Chapter 21, these shadow banks provide credit, maturity, and liquidity intermediation without access to central bank liquidity provisions or deposit insurance. Further, their activities occur beyond the reach of existing regulation and monitoring.

Typically, the SPV is used in the more traditional form of securitization. In this form, an FI selects a pool of loans and sells them to an OBS SPV—a company that is created by an arranger for the purpose of issuing the new securities (see Figure 26–1).[1] The SPV packages the loans together and creates new securities

[1] The arranger purchases the assets to be placed in the pool, obtains the credit rating, structures the deals, files with the securities regulator, and underwrites the ABSs to be issued by the SPV. Thus, the arranger must fund the loans over the period (typically three months or less) after origination and before the ABSs are issued. Bank arrangers use their own funds to finance the loans over this period, but nonbank arrangers typically use third-party warehouse lenders. Indeed, an early step in the credit crisis in the United States occurred in January 2007 when warehouse lenders pulled back and demanded more collateral to finance the loans of nonbank arrangers.

FIGURE 26–1
The Traditional Securitization Process Using an SPV

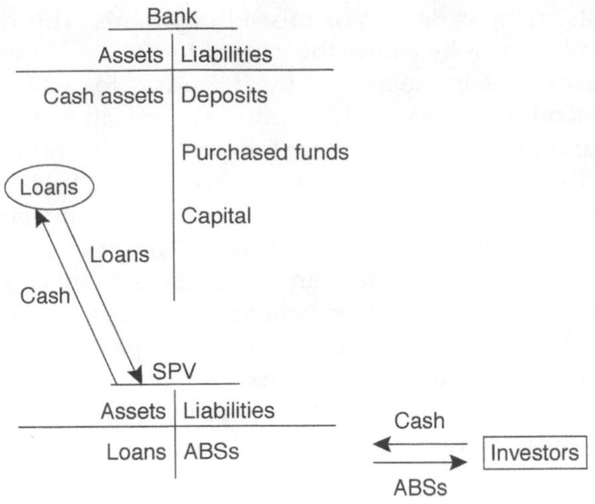

backed by the cash flows from the underlying loan pool (i.e., ABSs). The SPV sells the newly created ABSs to investors such as insurance companies and pension funds and uses the proceeds to pay the loan-originating FI for the loans. The SPV earns fees from the creation and servicing of the newly created ABSs. However, the underlying loans in the asset pool belong to the ultimate investors in the ABSs. All cash flows from the loans are passed through the SPV and allocated according to the terms of the ABS contract to the ultimate investors. Thus, the SPV acts as a conduit, selling the ABSs to investors and passing the cash back to the originating bank. It is then the ABS security investor that has direct rights to the cash flows on the underlying assets. The life of the SPV is limited to the maturity of the ABS. That is, when the last cash flows of the ABS are paid off, the SPV ceases to exist.

While this method of securitization was lucrative, financial intermediaries soon discovered another method that was even more lucrative. For this form of securitization, an SIV is created. In contrast to the SPV, the SIV's lifespan is not tied to any particular security. Instead, the SIV is a structured operating company that invests in assets that are designed to generate higher returns than the SIV's cost of funds. Rather than selling the ABSs directly to investors in order to raise cash (as do SPVs), the SIV sells commercial paper (CP, or bonds) to investors in order to raise the cash to purchase the bank's loans. The SIV then holds the loans purchased from the banks on its own balance sheet until maturity. These loan assets held by the SIV back the debt instruments issued by the SIV to investors. Thus, in essence the SIV itself becomes an ABS, and the SIV's CP liabilities are considered ABCP. The SIV acts similarly to a traditional bank, holding loans or other assets until maturity and issuing short-term debt instruments (such as ABCP) to fund its asset portfolio. The major difference between an SIV and a traditional bank is that the SIV cannot issue deposits to fund its asset base (i.e., it is not technically a "bank"; rather it is a shadow bank).

Figure 26–2 shows the structure of the SIV method of asset securitization. Investors buy the liabilities (most often ABCP) of the SIV, providing the

FIGURE 26–2
Securitization Process Using an SIV

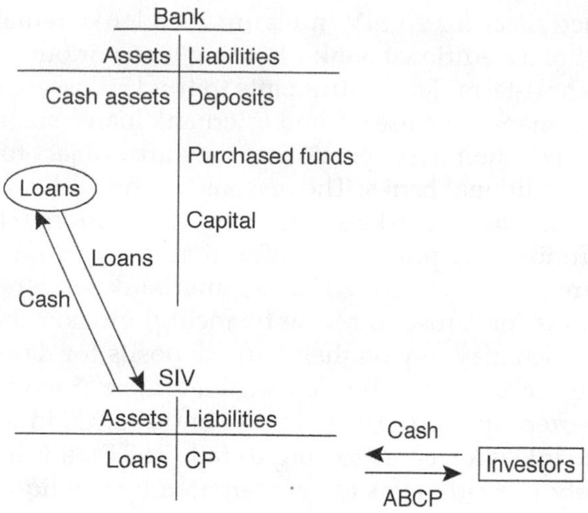

proceeds for the purchase of loans from originating banks. The SIV's debt (or ABCP) is backed by the loan or asset portfolio held by the SIV. However, the SIV does not simply pass through the payments on the loans in its portfolio to the ABCP investors. Indeed, investors have no direct rights to the cash flows on the underlying loans in the portfolio; rather, they are entitled to the payments specified on the SIV's debt instruments. That is, the SIV's ABCP obligations carry interest obligations that are independent of the cash flows from the underlying loan/asset portfolio. Thus, in the traditional form of securitization, the SPV pays out only what it receives from the underlying loans in the pool of assets backing the ABS. In the newer form of securitization, the SIV is responsible for payments on its ABCP obligations whether or not the underlying pool of assets generates sufficient cash flow to cover those costs. Of course, if the cash flows from the asset pool exceed the cost of ABCP liabilities, then the SIV keeps the spread and makes an additional profit. However, if the assets in the underlying pool do not generate sufficient cash flows, the SIV is still obligated to make interest and principal payments on its debt instruments. In such a situation the SIV usually has lines of credit or loan commitments from the sponsoring bank. Thus, ultimately, the loan risk would end up back on the sponsoring bank's balance sheet.

Because of the greater expected return on this newer form of securitization, the SIV became very popular in the years leading up to the financial crisis. Whereas an SPV earns the fees only for the creation of the ABSs, the SIV also earns an expected spread between high-yielding assets (such as commercial loans) and low-cost CP, as long as the yield curve is upward sloping and credit defaults on the asset portfolio are low. Indeed, because of these high potential spreads, hedge funds owned by Citigroup, Bear Stearns, and others adopted this investment strategy. Until the financial crisis, these instruments appeared to offer investors a favourable return–risk trade-off, i.e., a positive return and an apparently small risk given the asset backing of the security.

The balance sheet for an SIV in Figure 26–2 looks remarkably similar to the balance sheet of a traditional bank—holding loans or other assets until maturity and issuing short-term debt instruments to fund its asset portfolio. However, to the extent that many SIVs use CP and interbank loans (such as repurchase agreements) to finance their asset portfolios, they are subject to even more liquidity risk than are traditional banks. The reasons for the added liquidity risk are twofold. First, in financial markets, sophisticated lenders (so-called suppliers of "purchased funds") are prone to "run" at the first sign of trouble, whereas small depositors are slower to react. That is, interbank lenders and CP buyers will withdraw funds (or refuse to renew financing) quicker than traditional "core" depositors, which may rely on their bank deposits for day-to-day business purposes or may be protected by deposit insurance. Second, bank deposits are explicitly insured up to $100,000 in Canada ($250,000 in the United States) and for those in banks viewed as too big to fail (TBTF), a full implicit 100 percent. Thus, liquidity risk problems are exacerbated by the liquidity requirements of the SIVs that rely on short-term sources of funding, such as CP, which have to be renewed within a short period of time, i.e., every nine months, and repurchase agreements, which must be fully backed by collateral at all points in time in the absence of a deposit insurance umbrella. Consequently, if the value of the SIV's portfolio declines due to deterioration in credit conditions, the SIV is forced to sell long-term, illiquid assets in order to meet its short-term liquid debt obligations.

Regardless of the form of the OBS subsidiary used (SPV or SIV), after the subsidiary is formed, the securitization of loans and the sale of ABSs to investors involves the following steps:

1. The loans are transferred from the originating FI to the SPV or SIV.
2. The SPV or SIV securitizes the loans (either directly or through the issuance of ABCP) and then sells the resulting ABSs to investors.
3. The proceeds of the ABS sale are paid to the FI that originates the loans.

The profitability of securitized assets is largely determined by the SPV or SIV having a high credit rating, since most investors consist of institutional investors who, because they are financial fiduciaries of others, demand or are legally compelled to buy only investment-grade securities. Credit rating agencies review all documents of the SPV or SIV before assigning a rating. While the credit rating agency is not a legal party to any of the agreements for setting up the subsidiary, it is listed in all documents as the credit rating agency. Further, once the SPV or SIV is formed, information must be provided to the credit rating agency continually to ensure that the proper procedures are being followed to maintain credit quality, and that credit quality is actually being maintained.

Asset securitization through the use of these OBS subsidiaries played a prominent role in the U.S. subprime mortgage crisis, where critics say these securities hid the underlying risk in mortgage investments because the ratings on various securities were based on misleading or incorrect information about the creditworthiness of the borrowers. For a variety of reasons, market participants did not accurately measure the risk inherent with the ABSs or understand the impact of this risk on the overall stability of the financial system. As financial assets became more and more complex, and harder and harder to value, investors were reassured by the fact that both the international bond rating agencies and bank regulators, who came to rely on the rating agencies, accepted as valid some complex mathematical models that theoretically showed the risks of the ABSs were much smaller than they actually proved to be in practice. The new products became so complicated that the regulators could no longer calculate the risks and started relying on the risk management methods of the banks themselves. Similarly, the rating agencies relied on the information provided by the originators of synthetic products: a massive abdication of responsibility.

THE PASS–THROUGH SECURITY

LO2

FIs frequently pool mortgages and other assets they originate and offer investors an interest in the pool in the form of *pass-through securities*. Pass-through mortgage securities "pass through" promised payments by households of principal and interest on pools of mortgages created by FIs to secondary-market investors (MBS bondholders) holding an interest in these pools. After an FI accepts mortgages, it pools them and sells interests in these pools to pass-through security holders. Each pass-through mortgage security represents a fractional ownership share in a mortgage pool. Thus, a 1 percent owner of a pass-through mortgage security issue is entitled to a 1 percent share of the principal and interest payments made over the life of the mortgages underlying the pool of securities. The originating FI (e.g., bank or mortgage company) or third-party servicer receives principal and interest payments from the mortgage holder and passes these payments (minus a servicing fee) through to the pass-through security holders.

While many different types of loans and assets on FIs' balance sheets can be securitized, the original use of securitization is a result of government-sponsored programs to enhance the liquidity of the residential mortgage market. These programs indirectly subsidize the growth of home ownership in Canada and the United States. Given this, we begin by analyzing the government-sponsored securitization of residential mortgage loans. Four government agencies or government-sponsored enterprises are directly involved in the creation of mortgage-backed, pass-through securities in North America. They are Canada Mortgage and Housing Corporation (CMHC), and, in the United States, Ginnie Mae (GNMA), Fannie Mae (FNMA), and Freddie Mac (FHLMC).

CMHC

cmhc.ca

Most of the residential MBSs in Canada are sold by CMHC, a Crown corporation. In addition to fully insuring mortgages, CMHC guarantees all payments to the security holders under the National Housing Act (NHA), and so an NHA MBS is the equivalent of a Government of Canada bond that is also secured by residential property. These securities are thus default-free for the purchasers and have served as substitutes for fixed-income government securities for institutional investors such as pension funds. As well, the securities are eligible for the registered retirement savings plans (RRSPs) and registered retirement income funds (RRIFs) of individual investors and so are sold by Canadian banks and trusts for this purpose. Issuers of NHA MBSs are FIs that are approved lenders of NHA-insured mortgages. These include insurance companies, banks, trust and loan companies, credit unions (CUs), and caisses populaires (CPs), as well as investment dealers that are not originators of mortgages, but that may be approved by CMHC. The issuer pays a fee for the NHA guarantee and generally lists the security in the name of the issuer, or "street name" so that they are liquid and may be sold by the investor at any time.

The markets for MBSs have developed differently in the United States and Canada. In the United States, savings and loan companies (S&Ls) were the chief supplier of mortgages that, in the 1980s, were based on fixed-rate, 25- or 30-year terms. Because of ceilings on the rates that the S&Ls could pay on their deposits, these FIs mismatched their long-term mortgage assets with short-term deposits. The creation of MBSs resolved this issue and, in the process, created three large government agencies to provide funding for the housing industry. These three organizations provide residential MBSs in the United States. They have grown so that FNMA was the third-largest FI by asset size in the United States. The same level of MBS market development did not occur in Canada because by the 1960s, Canadian fixed-rate mortgages, while amortized over 25-year periods, had their rates reset every five years or less and so could be matched more easily with five-year deposits. By mid-2013, a cumulative amount of over $1 trillion in NHA MBSs had been issued in Canada with $403 billion remaining principal balance.

GNMA

ginniemae.gov

The Government National Mortgage Association (GNMA), or "Ginnie Mae," began in 1968 when it split off from the FNMA. GNMA is a U.S. government–owned agency with two major functions. The first is sponsoring MBS programs by FIs such as banks, thrifts (S&Ls), and mortgage bankers. The second is acting as a guarantor to investors in MBSs regarding the timely pass-through of principal and interest payments on their sponsored bonds. In other words, GNMA provides **timing insurance**. We describe this more fully later in the chapter. In acting as a sponsor and payment-timing guarantor, GNMA supports only those pools of mortgage loans whose default or credit risk is insured by one of four U.S. government agencies: the Federal Housing Administration (FHA), the Veterans Administration (VA), the Department of Housing and Urban Development's Office of Indian and Public Housing, and the USDA Rural Development. Mortgage loans insured by these agencies target groups that might otherwise be disadvantaged in the housing market, such as low-income families, young families, and veterans. As such, the maximum mortgage under the GNMA securitization program is capped.

timing insurance
A service provided by a sponsor of pass-through securities (such as CMHC or GNMA) guaranteeing the bondholder interest and principal payments at the calendar date promised.

FNMA

fanniemae.com

Originally created in 1938, the Federal National Mortgage Association (FNMA), or "Fannie Mae," is the oldest of the three U.S. MBS-sponsoring agencies. While it is now a private corporation owned by shareholders, in the minds of many investors it still has implicit government backing that makes it equivalent to a government-sponsored enterprise (GSE). Indeed, supporting this view is the fact that FNMA has historically had a secured line of credit available from the U.S. Treasury should it need funds in an emergency. Furthermore, and as discussed in more detail below, on September 7, 2008, the Federal Housing Finance Agency (FHFA) placed

Fannie Mae (and Freddie Mac; see below) in conservatorship. As conservator, the FHFA was given full powers to control the assets and operations of the firms. Dividends to common and preferred shareholders were suspended, but the U.S. Treasury put in place a set of financing agreements to ensure that the GSEs continue to meet their obligations to bondholders. This means that U.S. taxpayers basically were the guarantors behind about US$5 trillion of GSE debt. This step was taken because a default by either Fannie Mae or Freddie Mac, which had been battered by the downturn in housing and credit markets, could have caused severe disruptions in global financial markets, made U.S. home mortgages more difficult and expensive to obtain, and had negative repercussions throughout the U.S. economy.

FNMA is a more active agency than GNMA in creating pass-through securities. GNMA merely sponsors such programs. FNMA actually helps create pass-throughs by buying and holding mortgages on its balance sheet. It also issues bonds directly to finance those purchases. Specifically, FNMA creates MBSs by purchasing packages of mortgage loans from banks and thrifts. It finances such purchases by selling MBSs to outside investors such as life insurers and pension funds. In addition, FNMA engages in swap transactions whereby it swaps MBSs with an FI for original mortgages. Since FNMA guarantees securities as to the full and timely payment of interest and principal, the FI receiving the MBSs can then resell them on the capital market or hold them in its portfolio. Unlike GNMA, FNMA securitizes conventional mortgage loans as well as FHA/VA-insured loans, as long as the conventional loans have acceptable loan-to-value or collateral ratios normally not exceeding 80 percent. Conventional loans with high loan-to-value ratios usually require additional private-sector credit insurance before they are accepted into FNMA securitization pools.

FHLMC

www.freddiemac.com

The FHLMC, or "Freddie Mac," performs a function similar to that of FNMA except that its major securitization role has historically involved savings institutions. Like FNMA, FHLMC is a stockholder-owned corporation, yet it is currently in conservatorship with the FHFA, as noted above. Further, like FNMA, it buys mortgage loan pools from FIs and swaps MBSs for loans. FHLMC sponsors conventional loan pools, as well as pools of U.S. government-sponsored mortgage loans, and guarantees timely payment of interest and ultimate payment of principal on the securities it issues.

The Incentives and Mechanics of Pass-Through Security Creation

In order to analyze the securitization process, we trace through the mechanics of an NHA MBS securitization to provide insights into the return–risk benefits of this process to the originating FI in enhancing return on equity, as well as the attractiveness of these securities to investors. The focus for an FI in creating an ABS is to forecast the projected cash flow that determines the yield and depends on the prepayment model assumed. For an MBS, contraction risk arises when mortgage rates decline and borrowers speed up their prepayments. Similarly, extension risk arises when mortgage rates rise and prepayments slow down, leading to a decline in market price of the security. This instability in the cash flows makes pass-through securities unsuitable as an investment vehicle for asset–liability management for certain FIs such as pension funds, which have long-term liabilities.

FIGURE 26–3
Summary of an NHA MBS

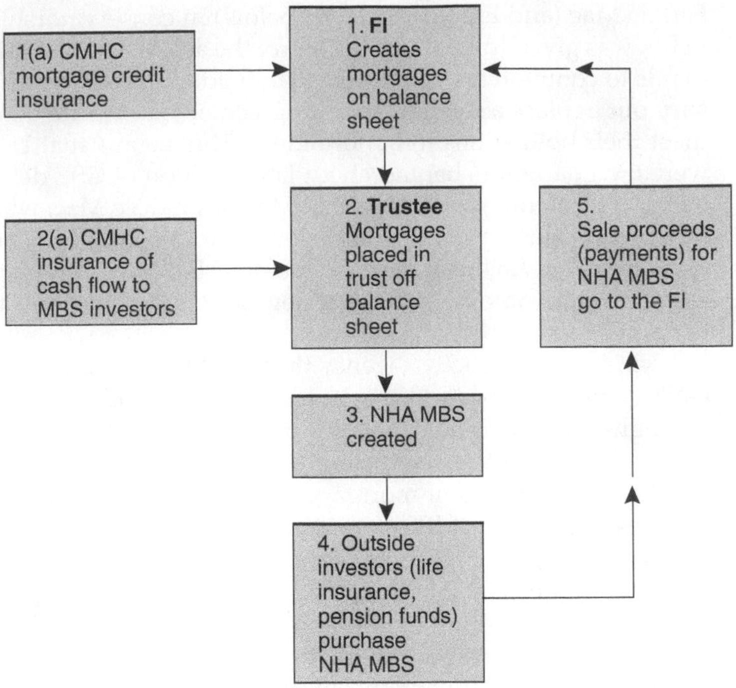

Thus, our discussion focuses on the prepayment models used to structure an ABS, followed by a discussion of CMOs and other innovations in securitization.[2]

Suppose a bank has just originated 1,000 new residential mortgages (box 1 in Figure 26–3). The average size of each mortgage is \$100,000. Thus, the total size of the new mortgage pool is

$$1{,}000 \times \$100{,}000 = \$100 \text{ million}$$

We assume that half of the mortgages (\$50 million) are high-ratio mortgages (loan to value greater than 80 percent) insured by CMHC mortgage insurance (Box 1(a) in Figure 26–3). The remaining \$50 million are low-ratio mortgages that are uninsured. In addition, each of these new mortgages has an initial stated maturity of 25 years and a mortgage rate—often called the mortgage coupon—of 12 percent per annum.[3] Suppose the bank originating these loans relies mostly on liabilities such as demand deposits as well as its own capital or equity to finance its assets. Under current capital adequacy requirements, each \$1 of the new uninsured residential mortgage loans (\$50 million) has to be backed by some capital. Since uninsured

---

[2] We assume CMHC mortgage insurance in the discussion that follows. By law, all high-ratio mortgages in Canada (loan to value greater than 80 percent) must carry mortgage insurance. Low-ratio mortgages are not required to carry mortgage insurance but CMHC will provide insurance for low-ratio mortgages (loan to value less than 75 percent) in order to facilitate securitization for the FI and to make the NHA MBS essentially risk-free for the investor. Private insurance may also be provided. See cmhc.ca for up-to-date regulations. See also *Standard Terminology and Calculations for MBS* at http://www.cmhc-schl.gc.ca/en/hoficlincl/mobase/stteca/index.cfm for sample calculations on prices and prepayment assumptions for Canadian MBSs adopted by Canadian securities dealers. Nonbank-sponsored MBSs are rated by a bond rating agency such as DBRS, so other mechanisms may be put in place to improve the quality of the credit to make it marketable and to protect the investor from default. The federal government's 2013 budget proposed prohibiting the use of government-insured mortgages as collateral for nonbank-sponsored securitizations.

[3] In Canada, by law, mortgage rates are quoted with semiannual compounding. For simplicity, unless otherwise stated, mortgage rates used in this chapter are effective annual rates; that is, the quoted rates have been adjusted to reflect annual compounding.

TABLE 26–1
Bank Balance Sheet ($ millions)

Assets		Liabilities	
Cash	$ 0.00	Demand deposits	$ 98.775
Long-term mortgages	100.00	Capital	1.225
	$100.00		$100.00

residential mortgages fall into the 35 percent risk weight in the Basel risk-based capital standards (see Chapter 20), and we assume the risk-based Tier 1 capital requirement is 7 percent, the bank capital needed to back the $50 million uninsured mortgages in the portfolio is

$$\text{Capital requirement} = \$50 \text{ million} \times 0.35 \times 0.07 = \$1.225 \text{ million}$$

We assume that the remaining $98.775 million needed to fund the mortgages comes from the issuance of demand deposits.

Given these considerations, the bank's initial postmortgage balance sheet may look like that in Table 26–1. In addition to the capital requirement, the bank has to pay an annual insurance premium to CDIC based on the risk of the bank. Assuming a deposit insurance premium of 22.2 bp (for the lowest-quality FI), the fee would be[4]

$$\$98.775 \text{ million} \times 0.00222 = \$219{,}280$$

Although the bank is earning a 12 percent mortgage coupon on its mortgage portfolio, it is facing two levels of regulatory costs:

1. Capital requirements.
2. CDIC insurance premiums.

Thus, one incentive to securitize is to reduce the regulatory burden on the FI to increase its after-tax return.[5] In addition to facing regulatory costs on its residential mortgage portfolio earnings, the bank in Table 26–1 has two risk exposure problems: gap exposure and illiquidity exposure.

Gap Exposure or $D_A > kD_L$

The FI funds the 25-year mortgage portfolio with short-term demand deposits; thus, it has a duration mismatch.[6] This is true even if the mortgage assets have been funded with short-term GICs, time deposits, or other purchased funds.

Illiquidity Exposure

The bank is holding a very illiquid asset portfolio of long-term mortgages and no excess cash; as a result, it is exposed to the potential liquidity shortages discussed in Chapter 12, including the risk of having to conduct mortgage asset fire sales to meet large unexpected demand deposit withdrawals.

One possible solution to these duration mismatch and illiquidity risk problems is to lengthen the bank's on-balance-sheet liabilities by issuing longer-term deposits or

---

[4] In 2013, the deposit insurance premium was 2.8 bp for the highest-quality banks (see Chapter 19).

[5] Other reasons for securitization include greater geographic diversification of the loan portfolio. Specifically, many FIs originate mortgages from the local community; the ability to securitize facilitates replacing them with MBSs based on mortgages from other cities and regions.

[6] As we discuss in Chapters 8 and 9, core demand deposits usually have a duration of less than three years. Depending on prepayment assumptions, mortgages normally have durations of at least 4.5 years.

other liability claims, such as medium-term notes. Another solution is to engage in interest rate swaps to transform the bank's liabilities into those of a long-term, fixed-rate nature (see Chapter 24). These techniques do not resolve the problem of regulatory costs and the burden they impose on the FI's returns.

By contrast, creating NHA pass-through securities can largely resolve the duration and illiquidity risk problems on the one hand and reduce the burden of regulatory costs on the other. This requires the bank to securitize the $100 million in residential mortgages by issuing NHA pass-through securities. In our example, the bank can do this since the 1,000 underlying mortgages have the same stated mortgage maturity of 25 years and coupons of 12 percent. Therefore, they are eligible for securitization under the NHA program if the bank is an approved lender (which we assume it is).

The bank begins the securitization process by packaging the $100 million in mortgage loans and removing them from the balance sheet by placing them with a third-party trustee in an SPV off the balance sheet. This third-party trustee may be another bank of high creditworthiness or a legal trustee.[7] Next, the bank determines that (1) CMHC will guarantee, for a fee, the timing of interest and principal payments on the securities issued to back the mortgage pool and (2) the bank itself will continue to service the pool of mortgages for a fee, even after they are placed in trust. Then CMHC issues pass-through securities backed by the underlying $100 million pool of mortgages. These NHA CMHC MBSs are sold to outside investors in the capital market, and the proceeds (net of any underwriting fees) go to the originating bank. Large purchasers of these securities include insurance companies and pension funds.

Before we examine the mechanics of the repayment on a pass-through security, we consider the attractiveness of these bonds to investors. In particular, investors in these bonds are protected against two levels or types of default risk: that of the mortgagee and that of the bank/trustee.

Default Risk by the Mortgagee

Suppose that because of rapidly falling house prices, a homeowner walks away from a mortgage, leaving behind a low-valued house to be foreclosed at a price below the outstanding mortgage. This might expose the MBS to losses unless there are external guarantors. Through CMHC housing insurance, government agencies bear the risk of default, thereby protecting the NHA MBS holders against such losses.

Default Risk by Bank/Trustee

Suppose the bank that had originated the mortgages goes bankrupt or the trustee absconds (this would occur only with non-NHA MBSs) with the mortgage interest and principal due to the MBS holders. Because it guaranteed the prompt timing of interest and principal payments on NHA CMHC securities, CMHC would bear the cost of making the promised payments in full and on time to MBS holders.

Given this default protection, the returns for Canada Mortgage Bond holders (or investors) from holding these securities would be the monthly repayments of interest and principal on the 1,000 mortgages in the pool, after the deduction of a mortgage-servicing fee by the mortgage-originating bank and a monthly timing insurance fee to be paid to CMHC. If we assume that the total of these fees is around 50 bp, or ½ percent, the stated coupons on the NHA MBS bonds would be

---

[7] For Canada Mortgage Bonds, which are AAA-rated, the trustee is Canada Housing Trust.

set at approximately ½ percent below the coupon rate on the underlying mortgages. In our example:

Mortgage coupon rate	12.00%
Minus	
Servicing fee	−0.50
NHA MBS coupon	11.50%

Suppose that CMHC issues $100 million face value NHA MBSs at par to back the pool of mortgage loans. The minimum size of a single MBS is $5,000; each investor gets a pro rata monthly share of all the interest and principal received by the bank minus servicing costs and insurance fees. Thus, if a life insurance company bought 25 percent of the NHA MBS issue (or 1,000 bonds × $5,000 each = $5 million), it would get a 25 percent share of the 300 promised monthly payments from the mortgages making up the mortgage pool.

Every month, each mortgagee makes a payment to the bank. The bank aggregates these payments and passes the funds through to NHA MBS investors via the trustee net of servicing fee. To make things easy, most fixed-rate mortgages are **fully amortized** over the mortgage's life. This means that as long as the mortgagee does not seek to prepay the mortgage early within the 25-year period, either to buy a new house or to refinance the mortgage should interest rates fall, investors can expect to receive a constant stream of payments each month analogous to the stream of income on other fixed-coupon, fixed-income bonds. In reality, however, mortgagees do not act in such a predictable fashion. For a variety of reasons, they relocate (sell their house) or refinance their mortgages (especially when current mortgage rates are below mortgage coupon rates). This propensity to **prepay** early, before a mortgage matures, and then refinance with a new mortgage means that *realized* coupons/cash flows on pass-through securities can often deviate substantially from the stated or expected coupon flows in a no-prepayment world. This unique prepayment risk provides the attraction of pass-throughs to some investors but leads other, more risk averse, investors to avoid these instruments. Before we analyze in greater detail the unique nature of prepayment risk, we summarize the steps followed in the creation of a pass-through in Figure 26–3. Then we analyze how this securitization has helped solve the duration, illiquidity, and regulatory cost problems of the FI manager.

fully amortized loan
A loan with periodic repayments that include both interest and principal over the life of the loan.

prepay
To pay back a loan before maturity to the FI that originated the loan.

In the previous discussion we traced the securitization process, the origination of mortgages on the balance sheet (Figure 26–3, Box 1) through to the sale of NHA MBSs to outside investors (Box 4). To close the securitization process, the cash proceeds of the sale of NHA MBS (Box 5) net of any underwriting fees go to the originating bank. As a result, the bank has substituted cash for long-term mortgages by using the securitization mechanism. Abstracting from the various fees and underwriting costs in the securitization process, the balance sheet of the bank might look like the one in Table 26–2 immediately after the securitization has taken place. Under International Financial Reporting Standards (IFRS), which

TABLE 26–2
The Bank's Balance Sheet after Securitization ($ millions)

Assets		Liabilities	
Cash (proceeds from mortgage securitization)	$100.00	Demand deposits	$ 98.775
Mortgages	0.00	Capital	1.225
	$100.00		$100.00

Canadian banks adopted in 2011, securitized assets are not removed from the FI's balance sheet until the risks, rewards, and control have been transferred. Securitized assets may be carried on the balance sheet as secured loans since they may not be immediately removed from the balance sheet as would occur under the generally accepted accounting principles (GAAP) used in the United States.

Assuming control and the risks and rewards have been transferred, there has been a dramatic change in the balance sheet exposure of the bank. First, $100 million in illiquid mortgage loans has been replaced by $100 million in cash. Second, the duration mismatch has been reduced since both D_A and D_L are now low. Third, the bank has an enhanced ability to deal with and reduce its regulatory costs. Specifically, it can reduce its capital since capital standards require none be held against cash on the balance sheet compared to uninsured residential mortgages. Deposit insurance premiums are also reduced if the bank uses part of the cash proceeds from the NHA MBS sale to pay off or retire demand deposits and downsize its balance sheet.

Of course, keeping a highly liquid asset portfolio and/or downsizing is a way to reduce regulatory costs, but these strategies are hardly likely to enhance an FI's profits. The real logic of securitization is that the cash proceeds from the mortgage/NHA MBS sale can be reused to create or originate new mortgages, which in turn can be securitized. In so doing, the FI is acting more like an asset (mortgage) broker than a traditional asset transformer, as we discussed in Chapter 1. The advantage of being an asset broker is that the FI profits from mortgage pool servicing fees plus up-front fees from mortgage origination. At the same time, the FI no longer has to bear the illiquidity and duration mismatch risks and regulatory costs that arise when it acts as an asset transformer and holds mortgages to maturity on its balance sheet. Put more simply, the FI's profitability becomes more fee dependent than interest rate spread dependent.

The limits of this securitization process clearly depend on the supply of mortgages (and other assets such as credit card receivables, car loans, business loans, etc.) that can be securitized and the demand by investors for pass-through securities. As was noted earlier, the unique feature of pass-through securities from the demand-side perspective of investors is prepayment risk. To understand the unique nature of this risk and why it might deter or limit investments by other FIs and investors, we next analyze the characteristics of pass-through securities more formally.

CONCEPT QUESTIONS

1. **What is a pass-through security?**
2. **Should an FI with $D_A > kD_L$ seek to securitize its assets? Why or why not?**

Prepayment Risk on Pass-Through Securities

To understand the effects of prepayments on pass-through security returns, it is necessary to understand the nature of the cash flows received by investors from the underlying portfolio of mortgages. Most conventional mortgages are fully amortized. This means that the mortgagee pays back to the mortgage lender (mortgagor) a constant amount each month that contains some principal and some interest. While the total monthly promised payment remains unchanged, the interest component declines throughout the life of the mortgage contract and the principal component increases.

The problem for the FI is to figure a constant monthly payment that exactly pays off the mortgage loan at maturity. This constant payment is formally equivalent to a monthly "annuity" paid by the mortgagee. Consider our example of 1,000 mortgages making up a \$100 million mortgage pool that is to be paid off monthly over 300 months at an annual mortgage coupon rate of 12 percent:

Size of pool	= \$100,000,000
Maturity	= 25 years ($n = 25$)
Number of monthly payments	= 12 ($m = 12$)
r	= Annual mortgage coupon rate = 12 percent
PMT	= Constant monthly payment to pay off the mortgage over its life

Thus, we solve for *PMT* from the following equation:

$$\$100{,}000{,}000 = \left[PMT\left(1+\frac{r}{m}\right)^{-1} + PMT\left(1+\frac{r}{m}\right)^{-2} + \cdots + PMT\left(1+\frac{r}{m}\right)^{-300}\right]$$

$$= PMT\left[\left(1+\frac{r}{m}\right)^{-1} + \left(1+\frac{r}{m}\right)^{-2} + \cdots + \left(1+\frac{r}{m}\right)^{-300}\right]$$

The term in square brackets is a geometric expansion that in the limit equals

$$100{,}000{,}000 = \left[\frac{1-\dfrac{1}{\left(1+\dfrac{r}{m}\right)^{mn}}}{\dfrac{r}{m}}\right] \times PMT$$

The new term in brackets is the present value of the annuity factor, *PVAF,* or 100,000,000 = *PMT*[*PVAF*]. Rearranging to solve for *PMT,* the required equal monthly payment on the mortgages, we have

$$PMT = \frac{100{,}000{,}000}{PVAF}$$

$$= \frac{100{,}000{,}000}{\left[\dfrac{1-\dfrac{1}{\left(1+\dfrac{r}{m}\right)^{nm}}}{\dfrac{r}{m}}\right]}$$

$$= \frac{100{,}000{,}000}{\left[\dfrac{1-\dfrac{1}{\left(1+\dfrac{0.12}{12}\right)^{300}}}{\dfrac{0.12}{12}}\right]} = \$1{,}053{,}224$$

TABLE 26–3
Fully Amortized Mortgages

Month	Outstanding Balance Payment	Fixed Monthly Payment (*PMT*)	Interest Component	Principal Component	Principal Remaining
1	$100,000,000	$1,053,220	$1,000,000	$53,220	$99,946,780
2	99,946,780	1,053,220	999,468	53,752	99,893,028
.	.	.	.	.	.
.	.	.	.	.	.
.	.	.	.	.	.
.	.	.	.	.	.
300	.	.	.	.	.

As a result, PMT = $1,053,224, or, given 1,000 individual mortgages, $1,053.22 per mortgage, rounding to the nearest cent. Thus, payments by the 1,000 mortgagees of an average monthly mortgage payment of $1,053.22 will pay off the mortgages outstanding over 25 years, assuming no prepayments.

The aggregate monthly payments of $1,053,224 comprise different amounts of principal and interest each month.[8] Table 26–3 breaks down the aggregate monthly amortized mortgage payments of PMT = $1,053,220 into their interest and principal components. In month 1, the interest component is 12 percent divided by 12 (or 1 percent) times the outstanding balance on the mortgage pool ($100 million). This comes to $1,000,000, meaning that the remainder of the aggregate monthly payment, or $53,224, can be used to pay off outstanding principal on the pool. At the end of month 1, the outstanding principal balance on the mortgages has been reduced by $53,224 to $99,946,776. In month 2 and thereafter, the interest component declines and the principal component increases, but the two still sum to $1,053,220. Thus, in month 2, the interest component has declined to $999,468 (or 1 percent of the outstanding principal at the beginning of month 2) and the principal component of the payment has increased to $53,752.

Although 12 percent is the coupon or interest rate the house buyers pay on the mortgages, the rate passed through to NHA MBS investors is 11½ percent, reflecting an average 50-bp fee paid to the originating bank. The servicing fees are normally paid monthly rather than as lump-sum single payments up-front to create the appropriate collection/servicing incentives over the life of the mortgage for the originating bank. For example, the bank's incentive to act as an efficient collection/servicing agent over 300 months would probably decline if it received a single large up-front fee in month 1 and nothing thereafter. The effect of the ½ percent fee is to reduce the cash flows passed through to the MBS investors from $1,053,224 ($100,000,000 amortized at 12 percent) to $1,016,469 (11.5 percent amortization).

As we have shown so far, the cash flows on the pass-through directly reflect the interest and principal cash flows on the underlying mortgages minus service fees. However, over time, mortgage rates change. Let Y be the current annual mortgage coupon rate, which could be higher or lower than 12 percent, and let y be the yield on

[8] Because of the rounding of each monthly payment to the nearest cent, we assume that aggregate monthly cash flows are 1,000 × $1,053.22 = $1,053,220. As well, in Canada, the annual percentage rate (APR) is based on semiannual compounding.

newly issued par value NHA MBSs. With no prepayments, the market value of the 12 percent mortgage coupon pool (11½ percent actual coupons) could be calculated as

$$V = \frac{\$1{,}016{,}469}{\left(1 + \frac{y}{12}\right)^1} + \frac{\$1{,}016{,}469}{\left(1 + \frac{y}{12}\right)^2} + \cdots + \frac{\$1{,}016{,}469}{\left(1 + \frac{y}{12}\right)^{300}}$$

If y is less than 11½ percent, the market value of the pool will be greater than its original value; if y is greater than 11½ percent, the pool will decrease in value. However, valuation is more complex than this since we have ignored the prepayment behaviour of the 1,000 mortgages. In effect, prepayment risk has two principal sources: refinancing and housing turnover.

Refinancing

As coupon rates on new mortgages fall, there is an increased incentive for individuals in the pool to pay off old, high-cost mortgages and refinance at lower rates. However, refinancing involves transaction costs and recontracting costs. Many FIs charge prepayment penalty fees on the outstanding mortgage balance prepaid. In addition, there are often origination costs for new mortgages to consider along with the cost of appraisals and credit checks. As a result, mortgage rates may have to fall by some amount below the current coupon rate before there is a significant increase in prepayments in the pool.

Housing Turnover

The other factor that affects prepayments is the propensity of the mortgagees in the pool to move before their mortgages reach maturity. The decision to move or turn over a house may be due to a complex set of factors, such as the level of house prices, the size of the underlying mortgage, the general health of the economy, and even the season (e.g., spring is a good time to move). In addition, if the existing mortgage is an **assumable mortgage**, the buyer of the house takes over the outstanding mortgage's payments. Thus, the sale of a house in a pool does not necessarily imply that the mortgage has to be prepaid. By contrast, nonassumability means a one-to-one correspondence between sale of a house and mortgage prepayment.

assumable mortgage
The mortgage contract is transferred from the seller to the buyer of a house.

Figure 26–4 plots the prepayment frequency of a pool of mortgages in relation to the spread between the current mortgage coupon rate (Y) and the mortgage coupon rate (r) in the existing pool (12 percent in our example). Notice when the current mortgage rate (Y) is above the rate in the pool ($Y > r$), mortgage prepayments are small, reflecting monthly forced turnover as people have to relocate

FIGURE 26–4
The Prepayment Relationship

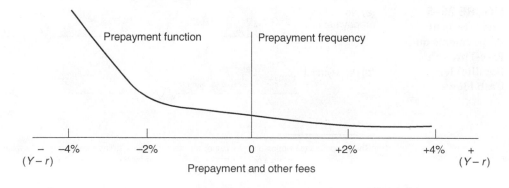

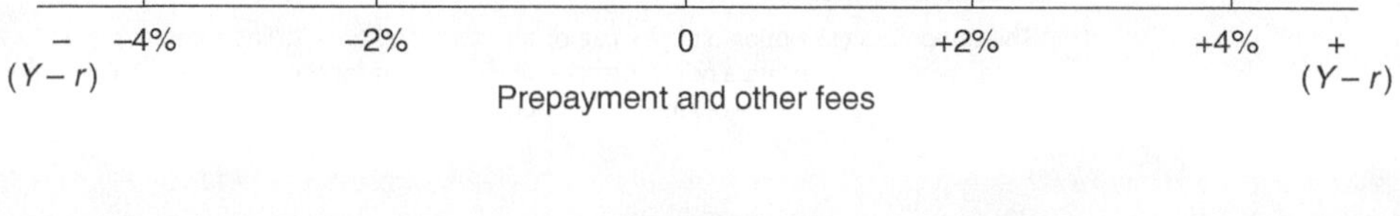

because of jobs, divorces, marriages, and other considerations. Even when the current mortgage rate falls below *r*, those remaining in the mortgage pool do not rush to prepay because up-front refinancing, contracting, and penalty costs are likely to outweigh any present value savings from lower mortgage rates. However, as current mortgage rates continue to fall, the propensity for mortgage holders to prepay increases significantly. Conceptually, mortgage holders have a very valuable call option on the mortgage when this option is in the money.[9] That is, when current mortgage rates fall sufficiently low so that the present value savings of refinancing outweigh the exercise price (the cost of prepayment penalties and other fees and costs), the mortgage will be called.

Since the bank has sold the mortgage cash flows to investors and must by law pass through all payments received (minus servicing fees), investors' cash flows directly reflect the rate of prepayment. As a result, instead of receiving an equal monthly cash flow, *PMT*, as is done under a no-prepayment scenario, the actual cash flows (*CF*) received on these securities by investors fluctuate monthly with the rate of prepayments (see Figure 26–5).

In a no-prepayment world, each month's cash flows are the same: $PMT_1 = PMT_2 = \cdots = PMT_{300}$. However, in a world with prepayments, each month's realized cash flows from the mortgage pool can differ. In Figure 26–5 we show a rising level of cash flows from month 2 onward, peaking in month 60, reflecting the effects of early prepayments by some of the 1,000 mortgagees in the pool. This leaves less outstanding principal and interest to be paid in later years. For example, if 300 mortgagees fully prepay by month 60, only 700 mortgagees will remain in the pool at that date. The effect of prepayments is to lower dramatically the principal and interest cash flows received in the later months of the pool's life. For instance, in Figure 26–5, the cash flow received by MBS holders in month 300 is very small relative to month 60 and even months 1 and 2. This reflects the decline in the pool's outstanding principal.

The lowering of current mortgage interest rates and faster prepayments have some good news and bad news effects on the current market valuation of the 12 percent mortgage pool, that is, the 11½ percent NHA MBSs.

Good News Effects First, lower market yields reduce the discount rate on any mortgage cash flow and increase the present value of any given stream of cash flows. This would also happen for any fixed-income security. Second, lower yields lead to faster prepayment of the mortgage pool's principal. As a result, instead of principal payments being skewed toward the end of the pool's life, the principal is received (paid back) much faster.

FIGURE 26–5
The Effects of Prepayments on Pass-Through Bondholders' Cash Flows

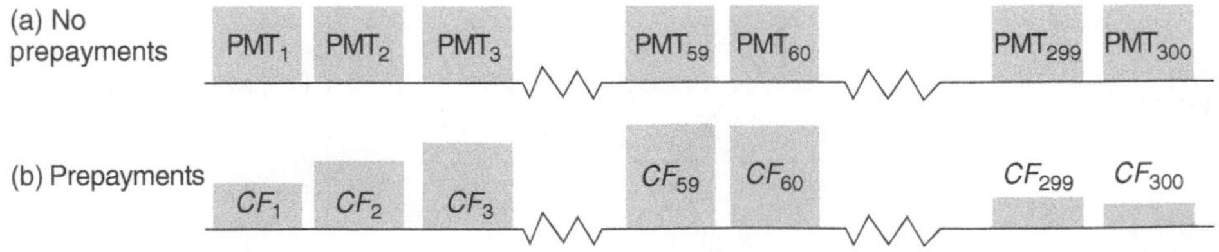

[9] The option is a call option on the value of the mortgage since falling rates increase the value of calling the old mortgage and refinancing a new mortgage at lower rates for the owner of the call option, who is the mortgagee. This option can also be viewed as a put option on interest rates.

Bad News Effects First, with early prepayment come fewer interest payments in absolute terms. Thus, instead of receiving scheduled interest payments over 300 months, some of these payments are irrevocably lost as principal outstanding is paid early. That is, mortgage holders are not going to pay interest on mortgage loans they no longer have outstanding. Second, faster cash flow due to prepayments induced by interest rate falls can be reinvested only at lower interest rates when they are received. That is, instead of reinvesting monthly cash flows at 12 percent, investors may reinvest only at lower rates such as 8 percent.

CONCEPT QUESTIONS

1. **What are the two sources of cash flows on a pass-through security?**
2. **What two factors can cause prepayments on the mortgages underlying pass-through securities?**

Prepayment Models

Clearly, managers running FI investment portfolios need to factor in assumptions about the prepayment behaviour of mortgages before they can assess the fair value and risk of their MBS portfolios. Next, we consider three alternative ways to model prepayment effects using the Securities Industry and Financial Markets Association (SIFMA) prepayment model, other empirical models, and option valuation models.

sifma.org

To begin, we look carefully at the results of one prepayment model. The weighted-average life (WAL) of an MBS reflects an assumed prepayment schedule. This WAL is not the same as duration, which measures the weighted-average time to maturity based on the relative present values of cash flows as weights. Instead, it is a significant simplification of the duration measure seeking to concentrate on the expected timing of payments of principal. Technically, **weighted-average life (WAL)** is measured by

weighted-average life (WAL)
The sum of the products of the time when principal payments are received and the amount of principal received all divided by total principal outstanding.

$$WAL = \frac{\sum(\text{Time} \times \text{Expected principal received})}{\text{Total principal outstanding}}$$

For example, consider a loan with two years to maturity and $100 million in principal. Investors expect $40 million of the principal to be repaid at the end of year 1 and the remaining $60 million to be repaid at maturity.

Time	Expected Principal Payments	Time × Principal
1	$ 40	$ 40
2	60	120
	$100	$160
	$WAL = \frac{160}{100} = 1.6$ years	

PSA Model

The prepayment model developed by the Public Securities Association (renamed the Bond Market Association in 1997 and merged with the Securities Industry Association in 2006 to form the Securities Industry and Financial Markets Association) is an empirically based model that reflects an average rate of prepayment based on

FIGURE 26–6
PSA Prepayment Model

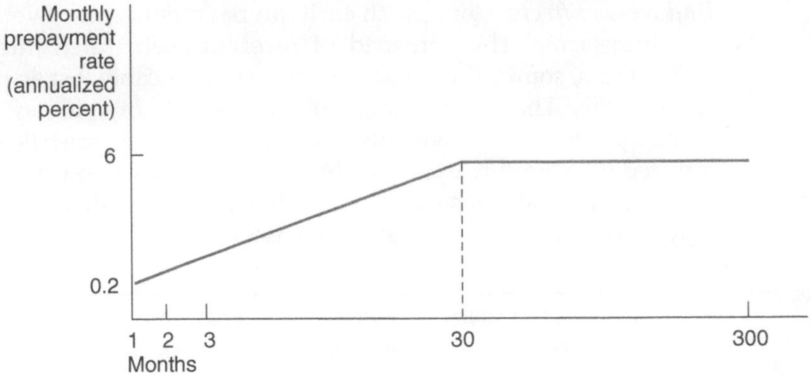

past experience. Essentially, the PSA model assumes that the prepayment rate starts at 0.2 percent (per annum) in the first month, increasing by 0.2 percent per month for the first 30 months, until the annualized prepayment rate reaches 6 percent. This model assumes that the prepayment rate then levels off at a 6 percent annualized rate for the remaining life of the pool[10] (see Figure 26–6). Issuers or investors who assume that their mortgage pool prepayments exactly match this pattern are said to assume 100 percent PSA behaviour. Realistically, the actual prepayment rate on any specific mortgage pool backing a specific pass-through security may differ from PSA's assumed pattern for general and economic reasons, including

1. The level of the pool's coupon relative to the current mortgage coupon rate (the weighted-average coupon).
2. The age of the mortgage pool.
3. Whether the payments are fully amortized.
4. Assumability of mortgages in the pool.
5. Size of the pool.
6. Conventional or nonconventional mortgages.
7. Geographic location.
8. Age and job status of mortgagees in the pool.

One approach would be to approximately control for these factors by assuming some fixed deviation of any specific pool from PSA's assumed average or benchmark pattern. For example, one pool may be assumed to be 75 percent PSA, and another 125 percent PSA. The former has a slower prepayment rate than historically experienced; the latter, a faster rate. Note these values in Figure 26–7 relative to 100 percent PSA.

Other Empirical Models

FIs that are trading, dealing, and issuing pass-throughs have also developed their own proprietary empirical models of prepayment behaviour to get a pricing edge on other issuers/investors. Clearly, the FI that can develop the best, most accurate prepayment model stands to make large profits either in originating and issuing such securities or in trading such instruments in the secondary market. As a wide variety of empirical models have been developed, we briefly look at the types of methodology followed.

---

[10] Or, after month 30, prepayments are made at approximately ½ percent per *month*.

FIGURE 26–7
Deviations from 100 Percent PSA

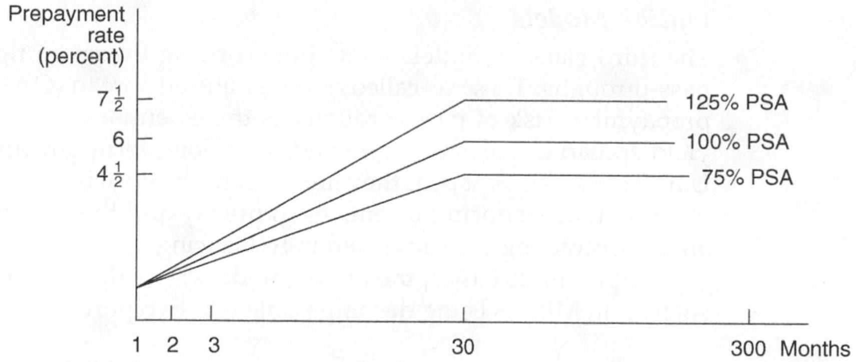

Specifically, most empirical models are proprietary versions of the PSA model in which FIs make their own estimates of the pattern of monthly prepayments. From this modelling exercise, an FI can estimate either the fair price or the fair yield on the pass-through. Of course, those FIs that make the most profits from buying and selling pass-throughs over time are the ones that have most accurately predicted actual prepayment behaviour.

In constructing an empirical valuation model, FIs begin by estimating a prepayment function from observing the experience of mortgage holders prepaying during any particular period on mortgage pools similar to the one to be valued. This is conditional, of course, on the mortgages not having been prepaid prior to that period. These conditional prepayment rates in month i (p_i) for similar pools would be modelled as functions of the important economic variables driving prepayment—for example, $p_i = f$(mortgage rate spread, age, collateral, geographic factors, **burn-out factor**).[11] This modelling should take into account the idiosyncratic factors affecting this specific pool, such as its age and burn-out factor, as well as market factors affecting prepayments in general, such as the mortgage rate spread. Once the p_i frequency distribution is estimated, as shown in Figure 26–8, the FI can calculate the expected cash flows on the mortgage pool under consideration and estimate its fair yield given the current market price of the pool.

burn-out factor
The aggregate percentage of the mortgage pool that has been prepaid prior to the month under consideration.

FIGURE 26–8
Estimated Prepayment Function for a Given Pool

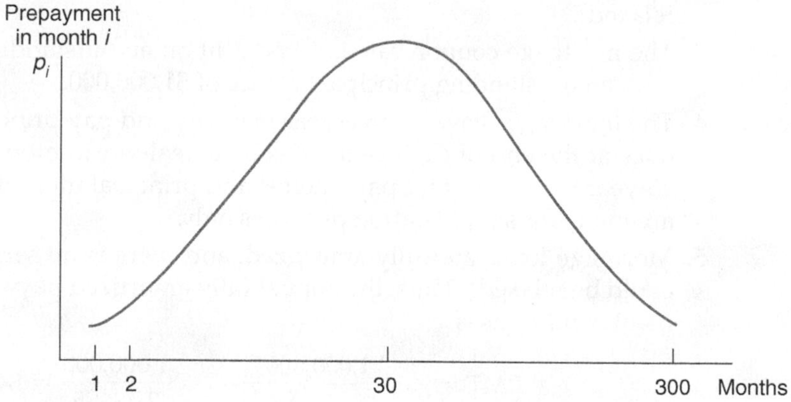

[11] A burn-out factor is a summary measure of a pool's prepayments in total prior to month *i*. As such, it is meant to capture the heterogeneity of prepayment behaviour within any given pool rather than between pools.

Option Models

The third class of models uses option pricing theory to figure the fair yield on pass-throughs. These so-called option-adjusted spread (OAS) models focus on the prepayment risk of pass-throughs as the essential determinant of the required yield spread of pass-through bonds over long-term government securities (e.g., U.S. Treasuries). As such, they are open to the criticism that they fail to properly include nonrefinancing incentives to prepay and the variety of transaction costs and recontracting costs involved in refinancing.

Stripped to its basics, the option model views the fair price on a pass-through such as an MBS as being decomposable into two parts:

$$P_{MBS} = P_{TBOND} - P_{PREPAYMENT\ OPTION}$$

That is, the value of an MBS to an investor (P_{MBS}) is equal to the value of a standard noncallable Treasury bond of the same duration (P_{TBOND}) minus the value of the mortgage holder's prepayment call option ($P_{PREPAYMENT\ OPTION}$). Specifically, the ability of the mortgage holder to prepay is equivalent to the bond investor writing a call option on the bond and the mortgagee owning or buying the option. If interest rates fall, the option becomes more valuable as it moves into the money and more mortgages are prepaid early by having the bond called or the prepayment option exercised. This relationship can also be thought of in the yield dimension:

$$Y_{MBS} = Y_{TBOND} + Y_{OPTION}$$

The investors' required yield on an MBS should equal the yield on a similar-duration T-bond plus an additional yield for writing the valuable call option. That is, the fair yield spread or **option-adjusted spread (OAS)** between MBS and T-bonds should reflect the value of this option.

option-adjusted spread (OAS)
The required interest spread of a pass-through security over a Treasury when prepayment risk is taken into account.

To gain further insight into the option model approach and the OAS, we can develop an example showing how to calculate the value of the OAS on MBSs. To do this, we make a number of simplifying assumptions indicative of the restrictive nature of many of these models:

1. The only reason for prepayment is refinancing mortgages at lower rates; there is no prepayment for turnover reasons.
2. The current discount (zero-coupon) yield curve for T-bonds is flat (this could be relaxed).
3. The mortgage coupon rate is 10 percent on an outstanding pool of mortgages with an outstanding principal balance of $1,000,000.
4. The mortgages have a three-year maturity and pay principal and interest only once at the end of each year. Of course, real-world models would have 15- or 25-year maturities and pay interest and principal monthly. These assumptions are made for simplification purposes only.
5. Mortgage loans are fully amortized, and there is no servicing fee (again, this could be relaxed). Thus, the annual fully amortized payment under no prepayment conditions is

$$PMT = \frac{1{,}000{,}000}{\left[\dfrac{1 - \dfrac{1}{(1+0.10)^3}}{0.1}\right]} = \frac{1{,}000{,}000}{2.48685} = \$402{,}114$$

In a world with no prepayments, no default risk, and current mortgage rates (y) of 9 percent, we would have the MBS selling at a premium over par:

$$P_{MBS} = \frac{PMT}{(1+y)} + \frac{PMT}{(1+y)^2} + \frac{PMT}{(1+y)^3}$$

$$P_{MBS} = \frac{\$402{,}114}{(1.09)} + \frac{\$402{,}114}{(1.09)^2} + \frac{\$402{,}114}{(1.09)^3}$$

$$P_{MBS} = \$1{,}017{,}869$$

6. Because of prepayment penalties and other refinancing costs, mortgagees do not begin to prepay until mortgage rates, in any year, fall 3 percent or more below the mortgage coupon rate for the pool (the mortgage coupon rate is 10 percent in this example).
7. Interest rate movements over time change a maximum of 1 percent up or down each year. The time path of interest rates follows a binomial process.
8. With prepayments present, cash flows in any year can be the promised payment PMT = \$402,114, the promised payment (PMT) plus repayment of any outstanding principal, or zero if all mortgages have been prepaid or paid off in the previous year.

In Figure 26–9 we show the assumed time path of interest rates over the three years with associated probabilities (p).

End of Year 1 Since rates can change up or down by only 1 percent per annum, the farthest they can be expected to fall in the first year is to 8 percent. At this level, no mortgage holder would prepay since any mortgage rate savings would be offset by the penalty costs of prepayment; that is, by the assumption it is worth prepaying only when the mortgage rate falls at least 3 percent below its 10 percent coupon rate. As a result, the MBS pass-through investor could expect to receive PMT = \$402,114 with certainty. Thus, CF_1 = \$402,114.

FIGURE 26–9
Mortgage Rate Changes: Assumed Time Path

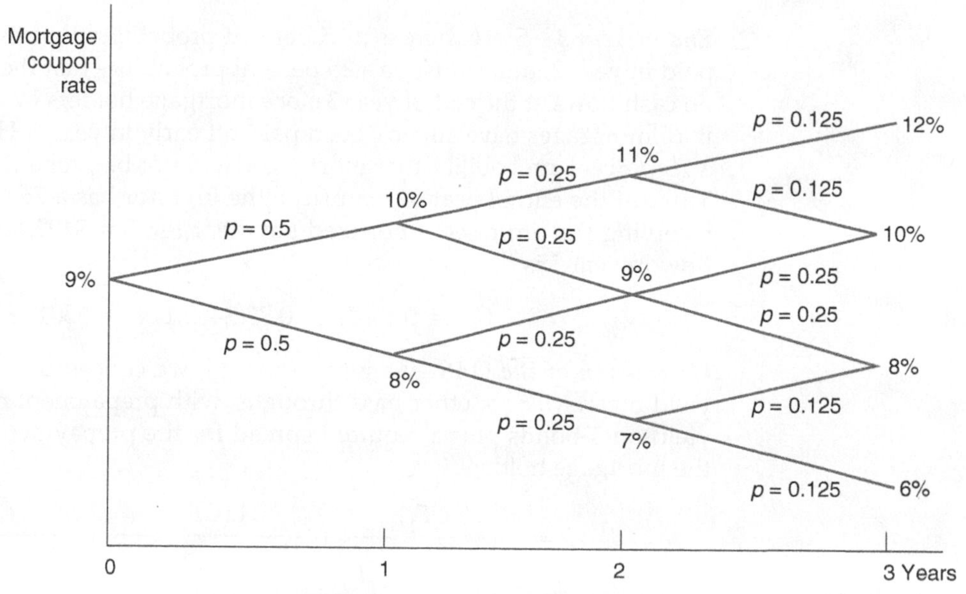

End of Year 2 In year 2, there are three possible mortgage interest rate scenarios. However, the only one that triggers prepayment is when mortgage rates fall to 7 percent (3 percent below the 10 percent mortgage coupon rate of the pool). According to Figure 26–9, this occurs with only a 25 percent probability. If prepayment does not occur with 75 percent probability, the investor receives PMT = \$402,114. If prepayment occurs with 25 percent probability, the investor receives

$$PMT + \text{Principal balance remaining at end of year 2}$$

We can calculate the principal balance remaining at the end of year 2 as follows. At the end of the first year, we divide the amortized payment, PMT = \$402,114, into a payment of interest and a payment of principal. With a 10 percent mortgage coupon rate, the payment of interest component would be 0.10 × \$1,000,000 = \$100,000, and the repayment of principal component = \$402,114 − \$100,000 = \$302,114. Thus, at the beginning of the second year, there would be \$1,000,000 − \$302,114 = \$697,886 principal outstanding. At the end of the second year, the promised amortized payment of PMT = \$402,114 can be broken down to an interest component of 10 percent × \$697,886 = \$69,788.6, and a principal component amount of \$402,114 − \$69,788.6 = \$332,325.4, leaving a principal balance at the end of year 2 of \$1,000,000 − \$302,114 − \$332,325.4 = \$365,560.6.

Consequently, if yields fall to 7 percent, the cash flow received by the investor in year 2 would be

$$\begin{aligned} &PMT + \text{Principal balance outstanding at end of year 2} \\ &= \$402{,}114 + \$365{,}560.6 = \$767{,}674.6 \end{aligned}$$

Thus, expected cash flows at the end of year 2 would be

$$\begin{aligned} CF_2 &= 0.25(\$767{,}674.6) + 0.75(\$402{,}114) \\ &= \$191{,}918.65 + \$301{,}585.5 \\ &= \$493{,}504.15 \end{aligned}$$

End of Year 3 Since there is a 25 percent probability that mortgages will be prepaid in year 2, there must be a 25 percent probability that the investor will receive no cash flows at the end of year 3 since mortgage holders owe nothing in this year if all mortgages have already been paid off early in year 2. However, there is also a 75 percent probability that mortgages will not be prepaid at the end of year 2. Thus, at the end of year 3 (maturity), the investor has a 75 percent probability of receiving the promised amortized payment PMT = \$402,114. The expected cash flow in year 3 is

$$CF_3 = 0.25(0) + 0.75(\$402{,}114) = \$301{,}585.5$$

Derivation of the OAS As just discussed, we conceptually divide the required yield on an MBS, or other pass-throughs, with prepayment risk, into the required yield on T-bonds plus a required spread for the prepayment call option given to the mortgage holders:

$$P = \frac{E(CF_1)}{(1 + d_1 + O_s)} + \frac{E(CF_2)}{(1 + d_2 + O_s)^2} + \frac{E(CF_3)}{(1 + d_3 + O_s)^3}$$

where

P = Price of MBS
d_1 = Discount rate on one-year, zero-coupon Treasury bonds
d_2 = Discount rate on two-year, zero-coupon Treasury bonds
d_3 = Discount rate on three-year, zero-coupon Treasury bonds
O_S = OAS on MBS

Assume that the T-bond yield curve is flat, so that

$$d_1 = d_2 = d_3 = 8\%$$

We can now solve for O_S:

$$1{,}017{,}869 = \frac{\$402{,}114}{(1 + 0.08 + O_s)} + \frac{\$493{,}504.15}{(1 + 0.08 + O_s)^2} + \frac{\$301{,}185.5}{(1 + 0.08 + O_s)^3}$$

Solving for O_S, we find that

$$\begin{aligned} O_S &= 0.96\% \text{ (to two decimal places)} \\ Y_{MBS} &= Y_{TBOND} + O_S \\ &= 8\% + 0.96\% \\ &= 8.96\% \end{aligned}$$

Notice that when prepayment risk is present, the expected cash flow yield at 8.96 percent is 4 bp less than the required 9 percent yield on the MBS when no prepayment occurs. The slightly lower yield results because the positive effects of early prepayment (such as earlier payment of principal) dominate the negative effects (such as loss of interest payments). Note, however, that this result might well be reversed if we altered our assumptions by allowing a wider dispersion of possible interest rate changes and having heavier penalties for prepayment.

Nevertheless, the OAS approach is useful for FI managers in that they can place lower bounds on the yields they are willing to accept on MBSs and other pass-through securities before they place them in their portfolios. Realistically, some account has to be taken of nonrefinancing prepayment behaviour and patterns; otherwise significant mispricing may occur.

CONCEPT QUESTIONS

1. **Should an FI with $D_A < kD_L$ seek to securitize its assets? Why or why not?**
2. **In general terms, discuss the three approaches developed by analysts to model prepayment behaviour.**
3. **In the context of the option model approach, list three ways in which transaction and other contracting costs are likely to interfere with the accuracy of its predictions regarding the fair price or interest spread on a pass-through security.**

NHA MBS Pools

All NHA MBS issues are pooled according to mortgage type and the prepayment provisions of the original mortgages. Table 26–4 lists the numbers and the definitions of some of the pool types available. New pools have been created to allow for the types of mortgages that are issued in Canada and the conditions that they must meet in order to be eligible for mortgage insurance. For example, the 970 pool type

TABLE 26–4
NHA MBS Mortgage Pool Classifications

Source: Canada Mortgage and Housing Corporation (CMHC). *The NHA Mortgage-Backed Securities Guide*, cmhc.ca/en/.

a)	**Homeowner:** **964**—Exclusive homeowner mortgage pools, which are classified as prepayable because the borrowers within this type of pool have the option to prepay their mortgage (often at a penalty) in accordance with the specific terms of the mortgage. The appropriate penalty interest payment (PIP) is passed through to the investors. **967**—Exclusive homeowner mortgage pools, which are classified as prepayable because the borrowers within this type of pool have the option to prepay their mortgage. However, the PIP is not passed through to the investor. **970**—Offers investors an indemnity where mortgages are renegotiated during the closed period of the loan. Penalty interest payments are retained by the issuer. For all prepayments in circumstances other than those permitted in the *Information Circular*, an indemnity is passed through.
b)	**Multiples:** **966**—Multifamily pool type, which is composed exclusively of multiple family loans, and is not prepayable.
c)	**Social housing:** NHA-insured mortgages issued to finance low-cost housing for senior citizens, the disabled, and the economically disadvantaged. Typically, such housing is sponsored by government housing agencies, other social service organizations, and private nonprofit organizations. **99**—Special category of NHA MBS pool created to allow exclusive pools of "social housing mortgages." The key feature of social housing pools is the absence of prepayment at the option of the borrower on the underlying mortgages; this makes them more attractive to investors who seek predictable cash flow.
d)	**Mixed** **965**—Mixed pools, which are composed of a combination of homeowner, multiple, or social housing mortgages. These also consist of prepayable multifamily pools.
Other:	**975**—Similar to 970 but with prepayments allowed up to five years; introduced December 29, 2000. **985**—Backed by variable rate mortgages; introduced November 26, 2004. **980**—Backed by adjustable rate mortgages with a one-month interest rate reset; introduced May 31, 2005. **987**—Backed by floating-rate mortgages with a coupon rate that is a weighted-average of the pooled mortgages; introduced September 1, 2005. **990**—Nonrepayable mortgages.

allows for prepayments up to the third anniversary of the mortgage and the 975 type up to the fifth anniversary. As can be seen in Table 26–5, which shows the percentage share of the market by pool type in May 2013, the largest pools dollar-wise and in total are the 975 and 985 types, which are single-family mortgages issued according to the standard NHA mortgage provisions. The 966 and 990 pools are backed by nonrepayable mortgages and make up less than 2.5 percent of the total MBSs outstanding. As of May 2013, there was a total of 10,363 pools with a remaining principal balance of $402.7 billion.

The NHA MBSs provide a cheaper source of funds for FIs, and the benefits are passed on to homebuyers in lower mortgage rates. There are different issuers, including trust companies (Equitable Trust, Home Trust), CUs and CPs (Vancouver City Savings, Caisse centrale Desjardins du Québec) and investment firms (Merrill Lynch Canada Inc.). As might be expected, the largest issuers of these types of securities are the major banks. The Basel Liquidity Coverage Ratio (LCR; see Chapter 12) also provides an incentive for banks to insure their on-balance-sheet mortgages and to create NHA MBSs. NHA MBSs are considered Level 1 assets in the calculation of the LCVR, which can result in lower capital requirements.

TABLE 26–5
NHA MBS Issued Amounts, May 2013.

Pool Type	Number of Pools	Issued Amount	% of Total
867	846	48,267,446,957.95	4.3%
880	148	6,754,500,946.39	0.6%
885	65	4,505,306,676.78	0.4%
964	1,740	23,476,965,642.87	2.1%
965	886	27,000,245,678.70	2.4%
966	303	5,754,625,599.48	0.5%
967	244	2,296,096,018.71	0.2%
970	1,022	72,166,157,840.21	6.5%
975	10,240	653,098,627,641.01	58.4%
980	1,773	49,033,584,162.88	4.4%
985	1,336	169,828,032,351.20	15.2%
987	806	34,906,354,798.73	3.1%
990	1,047	20,826,286,029.87	1.9%
Grand Total	**20,456**	**1,117,914,230,344.78**	**100.0%**

Source: Canada Mortgage and Housing Corporation (CMHC). *NHA Mortgage-Backed Securities, Daily Status*, MBS-R303A, p. 7.

U.S. Government Sponsorship and Oversight of FNMA and FHLMC

Together FNMA and FHLMC represent a huge presence in the financial system as they have over 65 percent of the single-family mortgage pools in the United States. Some regulators and politicians have argued that these two government-sponsored enterprises have gained too much of a market share. Underlying the concerns about the actions of these two GSEs was the widespread perception among investors that neither would be allowed to fail if they got into trouble. This perception created a subsidy for the agencies and allowed them to borrow more cheaply than other firms with similar balance sheets. The fear was that the two agencies used their implicit federal backing to assume more risk and finance expansion through increased debt. Such actions created a source of systematic risk for the U.S. financial system. These fears and concerns became reality during the financial crisis. The turmoil in the housing and credit markets that began in 2007 put extreme financial pressure on Fannie Mae and Freddie Mac. The value of their mortgage assets fell, but the debt they issued to purchase those assets remained on their balance sheets. To maintain a positive net worth in the face of falling asset values, financial firms have several options to raise capital, none of which were readily available to Fannie or Freddie. If they sold assets, they would depress the prices of mortgage loans and MBSs even further, worsening both their own balance sheet positions and those of many other financial firms. They could not use retained earnings to increase capital because their operations had not earned a profit since 2006. Finally, rapidly falling share prices made it difficult to raise capital by selling new common stock.

GSE status, however, enabled them to continue to fund their operations by selling debt securities, because the market believed that Fannie and Freddie debt was implicitly guaranteed by the U.S. government. In July 2008, however, Fannie and Freddie's share prices fell sharply, resulting in the possibility that market participants might refuse to extend credit to Fannie and Freddie under any terms. Even though Fannie and Freddie maintained access to the debt markets (albeit at higher than usual interest rates), their inability to raise new capital cast doubts on their long-term viability. As a result, the federal government concluded that "the companies cannot continue to operate safely and soundly and fulfill their critical public mission, without significant action" to address their financial weaknesses.

The U.S. Housing and Economic Recovery Act of 2008, enacted July 30, 2008, gave the authority for the U.S. government's takeover of the GSEs. The act created a new GSE regulator, the FHFA, with the authority to take control of either GSE to restore it to a sound financial condition. The Act also gave the Treasury emergency authority to purchase an unlimited amount of GSE debt or equity securities if necessary to provide stability to the financial markets, prevent disruptions in the availability of mortgage finance, and protect the taxpayer. On September 7, 2008, the FHFA established a conservatorship for both Fannie and Freddie. As conservator, the FHFA took over the assets and assumed all the powers of the shareholders, directors, and officers. Shareholders' voting rights were suspended during the conservatorship, and both firms replaced their CEOs. Dividends on common and preferred shares were suspended, although the shares continued to trade. (However, in June 2010 the NYSE, through the FHFA, notified Fannie and Freddie that they no longer met NYSE listing standards. The FHFA ordered the two GSEs to delist their common and preferred shares from the NYSE to the OTC market.) The conservatorship will end when the FHFA finds that a safe and solvent condition has been restored.

The takeover of Fannie and Freddie, and specifically the commitment to meet all of the firms' obligations to debtholders, exposes the U.S. government to a potentially large financial risk. At the time the FHFA took over, debt issued or guaranteed by the GSEs totalled more than US$5 trillion. The risks of not acting, however, clearly appeared intolerable to the government. A failure or default by either Fannie or Freddie would have severely disrupted financial markets around the world. If the GSE portfolios of mortgage loans and MBSs had to be liquidated, prices would have plunged even further, the secondary market for mortgages would have been decimated, and the supply of new mortgage credit would have been severely restricted.

THE COLLATERALIZED MORTGAGE OBLIGATION

While pass-throughs are still the primary mechanism for securitization, the CMO is a second and growing vehicle for securitizing FI assets. Innovated in 1983 by the U.S. FHLMC and First Boston, the CMO is a device for making MBSs more attractive to investors. The CMO does this by repackaging the cash flows from mortgages and pass-through securities in a different fashion to attract different types of investors. While a pass-through security gives each investor a pro rata share of any promised and prepaid cash flows on a mortgage pool, the CMO is a multiclass pass-through with a number of different investor classes or tranches. Unlike a pass-through, each class has a different guaranteed coupon, just like a regular T-bond. But, more important, the allocation of early cash flows due to mortgage prepayments is such that at any one time, all prepayments go to retiring the principal outstanding of only one class of bondholders, leaving the other classes' prepayment protected for a period of time. Thus, a CMO serves as a way to mitigate or reduce prepayment risk.

FIGURE 26–10
The Creation of a CMO

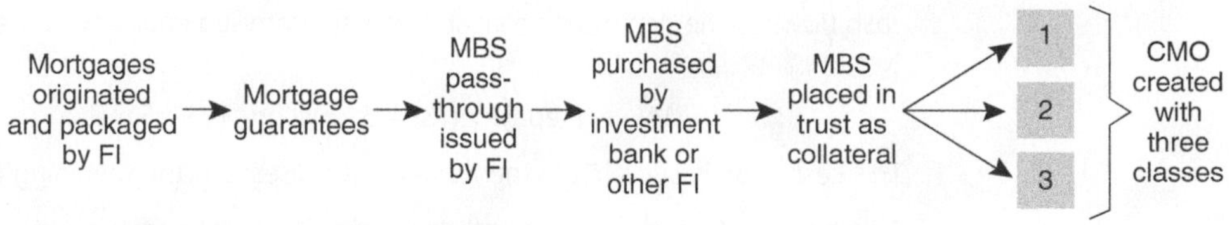

Creation of CMOs

collateralized mortgage obligation (CMO)
A mortgage-backed bond issued in multiple classes or tranches.

A **collateralized mortgage obligation (CMO)** can be created either by packaging and securitizing whole mortgage loans or, more usually, by placing existing pass-throughs in a trust off the balance sheet. The trust or third-party FI holds the pass-through as collateral against issues of new CMO securities. The trust issues these CMOs in three or more different classes. We show a three-class or tranche CMO in Figure 26–10.

Issuing CMOs is often equivalent to double securitization. Mortgages are packaged, and a pass-through is issued. An investment bank or a savings institution may buy this whole issue or a large part of the issue and then place these MBSs as collateral with a trust and issue three new classes of bonds backed by the MBSs as collateral. As a result, the investors in each CMO class have a sole claim to the MBS collateral if the issuer fails. The investment bank or other issuer creates the CMO to make a profit by repackaging the cash flows from the single-class MBS pass-through into cash flows more attractive to different groups of investors. The sum of the prices at which the three CMO bond classes can be sold normally exceeds that of the original pass-through:

$$\sum_{i=1}^{3} P_{i,CMO} > P_{MBS}$$

To understand the gains from repackaging, it is necessary to understand how CMOs restructure prepayment risk to make it more attractive to different classes of investors. We explain this in the following simple example.

EXAMPLE 26–1
The Value Additivity of CMOs

Suppose an investment bank buys a $150 million issue of MBSs and places them in trust as collateral. It then issues a CMO with these three classes:

Class A: Annual fixed coupon 7 percent, class size $50 million

Class B: Annual fixed coupon 8 percent, class size $50 million

Class C: Annual fixed coupon 9 percent, class size $50 million

Under the CMO, each class has a guaranteed or fixed coupon. By restructuring the MBSs as a CMO, the investment bank can offer investors who buy bond Class C a higher degree of mortgage prepayment protection compared to a pass-through. Those who buy bond Class B receive an average degree of prepayment protection, and those who take Class A receive virtually no prepayment protection.

Each month, mortgagees in the pool pay principal and interest on their mortgages; each payment includes the promised amortized amount (*PMT*) plus any additional payments as some of the mortgage holders prepay principal to refinance their mortgages or because they have sold their houses and are relocating. These cash flows are passed through to the owner of the MBSs. The CMO issuer uses the cash flows to pay promised coupon interest to the three classes of CMO bondholders. Suppose that in month 1 the promised amortized cash flows (*PMT*) on the mortgages underlying the pass-through collateral are $1 million, but an additional $1.5 million cash flow results from early mortgage prepayments. Thus, the cash flows in the first month available to pay promised coupons to the three classes of investors are

$$PMT + \text{Prepayments} = \$1 \text{ million} + \$1.5 \text{ million} = \$2.5 \text{ million}$$

This cash flow is available to the trustee, who uses it in the following fashion:

1. *Coupon payments.* Each month (or, more commonly, each quarter or half year), the trustee pays out the guaranteed coupons to the three classes of investors at annualized coupon rates of 7 percent, 8 percent, and 9 percent, respectively. Given the stated principal of $50 million for each class, the Class A (7 percent coupon) investors receive approximately $291,667 in coupon payments in month 1, the Class B (8 percent coupon) receive approximately $333,333 in month 1, and the Class C (9 percent coupon) receive approximately $375,000 in month 1. Thus, the total promised coupon payments to the three classes amount to $1,000,000 (equal to *PMT*, the no-prepayment cash flows in the pool).
2. *Principal payments.* The trustee has $2.5 million available to pay out as a result of promised mortgage payments plus early prepayments, but the total payment of coupon interest amounts to $1 million. The remaining $1.5 million has to be paid out to the CMO investors. The unique feature of the CMO is that the trustee would pay this remaining $1.5 million only to Class A investors to retire these investors' principal. This retires early some of these investors' principal outstanding. At the end of month 1, only $48.5 million ($50 million − $1.5 million) of Class A bonds remains outstanding, compared to $50 million Class B and $50 million Class C. These payment flows are shown graphically in Figure 26–11.

Let's suppose that in month 2 the same thing happens. The cash flows from the mortgage pool exceed the promised coupon payments to the three classes of bondholders. Again, the trustee uses any excess cash flows to pay off or retire the principal of Class A bondholders. If the excess cash flows again amount to $1.5 million, at the end of month 2 there will be only $47 million ($48.5 million − $1.5 million) of Class A bonds outstanding. Given any positive flow of prepayments, it is clear that within a few years the Class A bonds will be fully retired. In practice, this often occurs between 1.5 and 3 years after issue. After the trustee retires Class A, only Classes B and C remain.

As before, out of any cash flows received from the mortgage pool, the trustee pays the bondholders their guaranteed coupons, C_B = $333,333 and C_C = $375,000, for a total of $708,333. Suppose that total cash flows received by the trustee are $1,208,333 in the first month after the total retirement of Class A bonds, reflecting amortized mortgage payments by the remaining mortgagees in the pool plus any new prepayments. The excess cash flows of $500,000 ($1,208,333 − $708,333) then go to retire the principal outstanding of CMO bond Class B. At the end of that month, there is only $49.5 million in Class B bonds outstanding. This is shown graphically in Figure 26–12.

FIGURE 26–11 Allocation of Cash Flows to Owners of CMO Tranches

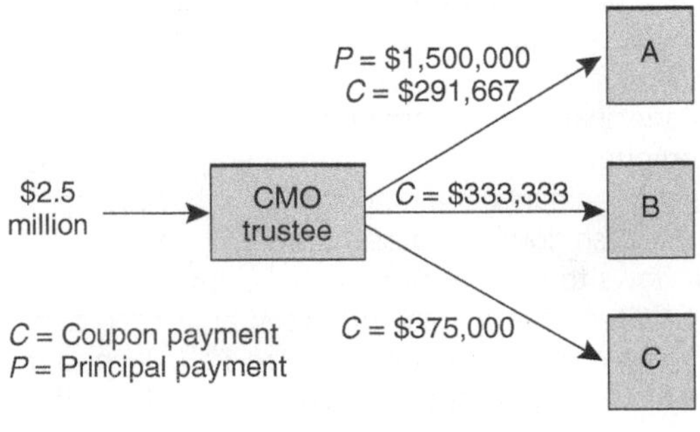

FIGURE 26–12 Allocation of Cash Flows to Remaining Tranches of CMO Bonds

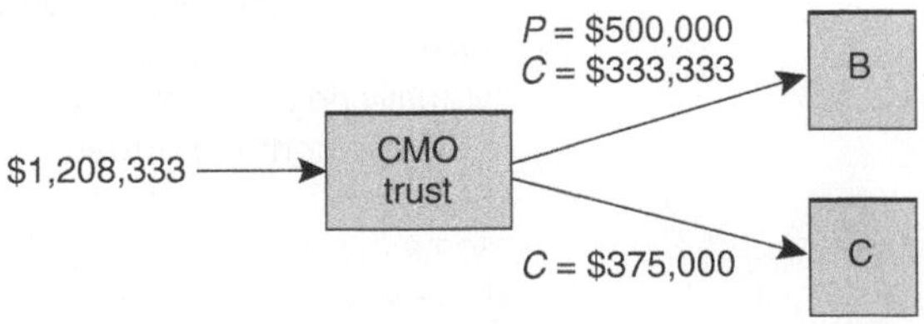

As the months pass, the trustee will use any excess cash flows over and above the promised coupons to investors of Class B and C bonds to retire bond Class B's principal. Eventually, all of the $50 million principal on Class B bonds will be retired—in practice, five to seven years after the CMO issue. After Class B bonds are retired, all remaining cash flows will be dedicated to paying the promised coupon of investors of Class C bonds and retiring the $50 million principal on Class C bonds. In practice, Class C bonds can have an average life as long as 20 years.

Class A, B, and C Bond Buyers

Class A

These bonds have the shortest average life with a minimum of prepayment protection. They are, therefore, of great interest to investors seeking short-duration mortgage-backed assets to reduce the duration of their mortgage-related asset portfolios.

Class B

These bonds have some prepayment protection and expected durations of five to seven years depending on the level of interest rates. Pension funds and life insurance companies would purchase these bonds, although some deposit-taking institutions (DTIs) would buy this bond class as well.

Class C

Because of their long expected duration, Class C bonds are highly attractive to insurance companies and pension funds seeking long-duration assets to match their long-duration liabilities. Indeed, because of their failure to offer prepayment protection, regular pass-throughs may not be very attractive to these institutions. Class C CMOs, with their high but imperfect degree of prepayment protection, may be of greater interest to the FI managers of these institutions.

In summary, by splitting bondholders into different classes and by restructuring cash flows into forms more valued by different investor clienteles, the CMO issuer stands to make a profit.

Other CMO Classes

CMOs can always have more than the three classes described in the previous example. Indeed, issues of up to 17 different classes have been made. Clearly, the 17th-class bondholders would have an enormous degree of prepayment protection since the first 16 classes would have had their bonds retired before the principal outstanding on this bond class would be affected by early prepayments. In addition, trustees have created other special types of classes as products to attract investor interest; we discuss these classes next.

Class Z

Z class
An accrual class of a CMO that makes a payment to bondholders only when preceding CMO classes have been retired.

Frequently, CMO issues contain a **Z class** as the last regular class. The Z implicitly stands for zero, but these are not really zero-coupon bonds. This class has a stated coupon, such as 10 percent, and accrues interest for the bondholder on a monthly basis at this rate. The trustee does not pay this interest, however, until all other classes of bonds are fully retired. When the other classes have been retired, the Z-class bondholder receives the promised coupon and principal payments plus accrued interest payments. Thus, the Z class has characteristics of both a zero-coupon bond (no coupon payments for a long period) and a regular bond.

Class R

In placing the MBS collateral with the trustee, the CMO issuer normally uses very conservative prepayment assumptions. If prepayments are slower than expected, there is often collateral left over in the pool when all regular classes have been retired. Further, trustees often reinvest funds or cash flows received from the underlying instrument (MBS) in the period prior to paying interest on the CMOs. In general, the size of any excess collateral and interest on interest gets bigger when rates are high and the timing of coupon intervals is semiannual rather than monthly. This residual **R class** or "garbage class" is a high-risk investment class that gives the investor the rights to the overcollateralization and reinvestment income on the cash flows in the CMO trust. Because the value of the returns in this bond class increases when interest rates increase, while normal bond values fall with interest rate increases, Class R often has a negative duration. Thus, it is potentially attractive to DTIs seeking to hedge their regular bond and fixed-income portfolios.[12]

R class
The residual class of a CMO giving the owner the right to any remaining collateral in the trust after all other bond classes have been retired plus any reinvestment income earned by the trust.

CONCEPT QUESTIONS

1. **Would insurance companies prefer Z-class CMOs? Explain your answer.**
2. **Are Z-class CMOs exactly the same as T-bond strips? If not, why not?**
3. **In our example, the coupon on the Class C bonds was assumed to be higher than that on the Class B bonds and the coupon on Class B bonds was assumed to be higher than that on Class A bonds. Under what term structure conditions might this not be the case?**

THE MORTGAGE-BACKED (COVERED) BOND

Mortgage (asset)-backed bonds (MBBs) (called *covered bonds* in Canada and Europe) are the third asset securitization vehicle. These bonds differ from pass-throughs and CMOs in two key dimensions. First, while pass-throughs and CMOs help DTIs remove mortgages from their balance sheets as forms of OBS securitization, MBBs normally remain on the balance sheet. Second, pass-throughs and CMOs have a direct link between the cash flows on the underlying mortgages and the cash flows on the bond vehicles. By contrast, the relationship for MBBs is one of collateralization—there is no direct link between the cash flow on the mortgages backing the bond and the interest and principal payments on the MBB.

mortgage (asset)-backed bonds (MBBs)
Bonds collateralized by a pool of assets.

An FI issues an MBB to reduce risk to the MBB bondholders, who have a first claim to a segment of the FI's mortgage assets. Practically speaking, the FI segregates a group of mortgage assets on its balance sheet and pledges this group as collateral against the MBB issue. A trustee normally monitors the segregation of assets and ensures that the market value of the collateral exceeds the principal owed to MBB holders. That is, FIs back most MBB issues by excess collateral. This excess collateral backing of the bond, in addition to the priority rights of the bondholders, generally ensures that these bonds can be sold with a high credit rating, such as AAA. In contrast, the FI, when evaluated as a whole, could be rated BBB or even lower. A high credit rating results in lower coupon payments than would be required if significant default risk had lowered the credit rating (see Chapter 10). To explain the potential benefits and the sources of any gains to an FI from issuing MBBs, we examine the following simple example.

[12] Negative duration implies that bond prices increase with interest rates. That is, the price–yield curve is positively sloped.

EXAMPLE 26–2

Gains to an FI from Issuing MBBs

Consider an FI with $20 million in long-term mortgages as assets. It is financing these mortgages with $10 million in short-term uninsured deposits (e.g., wholesale deposits over $100,000) and $10 million in insured deposits (e.g., retail deposits of $100,000 or less). In this example, we ignore the issues of capital and reserve requirements. Look at the balance sheet structure in Table 26–6.

This balance sheet poses problems for the FI manager. First, the FI has a positive duration gap ($D_A > kD_L$). Second, because of this interest rate risk and the potential default and prepayment risk on the FI's mortgage assets, uninsured depositors are likely to require a positive and potentially significant risk premium to be paid on their deposits. By contrast, the insured depositors may require approximately the risk-free rate on their deposits as they are fully insured by CDIC (see Chapter 19).

To reduce its duration gap exposure and lower its funding costs, the FI can segregate $12 million of the mortgages on the asset side of its balance sheet and pledge them as collateral backing a $10 million long-term MBB issue. Because of this overcollateralization, the MBB issued by the FI may cost less to issue, in terms of required yield, than uninsured deposits; that is, it may well be rated AAA while uninsured deposits might be rated BBB. The FI can therefore use the proceeds of the $10 million bond issue to retire the $10 million of uninsured deposits.

Consider the FI's balance sheet after the issue of the MBBs in Table 26–7. It might seem that the FI has miraculously engineered a restructuring of its balance sheet that has resulted in a better matching of D_A to D_L and a lowering of funding costs. The bond issue has lengthened the average duration of liabilities by replacing short-term deposits with long-term MBBs and lowered funding costs because AAA-rated bond coupon rates are below BBB-rated uninsured deposit rates. However, this outcome occurs only because the insured depositors do not worry about risk exposure since they are 100 percent insured by CDIC. The result of the MBB issue and the segregation of $12 million of assets as collateral backing the $10 million bond issue is that the $10 million insured deposits are now backed only by $8 million in free or unpledged assets. If smaller depositors were not insured by CDIC, they would surely demand very high risk premiums to hold these risky deposits. The implication of this is that the FI gains only because CDIC is willing to bear enhanced credit risk through its insurance guarantees to depositors.[13] As a result, the FI is actually gaining at the expense of CDIC. Consequently, it is not surprising that CDIC and OSFI are concerned about the growing use of this form of securitization by risky DTIs.

TABLE 26–6
Balance Sheet of Potential MBB Issuer ($ millions)

Assets		Liabilities	
Long-term mortgages	$20	Insured deposits	$10
		Uninsured deposits	10
	$20		$20

TABLE 26–7
FI's Balance Sheet after MBB Issue ($ millions)

Assets		Liabilities	
Collateral (market value of segregated mortgages)	$12	MBB issue	$10
Other mortgages	8	Insured deposits	10
	$20		$20

[13] As well, CDIC does not make the risk-based deposit insurance premium to banks and other deposit-taking FIs sufficiently large to reflect this risk.

The transfer of risk from the DTI to CDIC was considered by OSFI when it allowed Canadian FIs to issue limited amounts of covered bonds in June 2007. The issue of covered bonds by Canadian DTIs is limited to 4 percent of the total assets of the DTI, where *total assets* is defined as the numerator of the asset-to-capital multiple (see Chapter 20). In 2008, RBC had two covered bond issues for a total of €4.5 billion, BMO issued €1.0 billion, and CIBC had two issues totalling €2.32 billion. CIBC's issues were backed by residential mortgages insured by CMHC. In May 2013, the total covered bond debt outstanding reported by DBRS was $60 billion. Covered bond issues in Canadian dollars are called **Maple covered bonds.**

Maple covered bonds
Covered bonds issued in Canadian dollars.

Other than regulatory discouragement and the risk of regulatory intervention, there are private return reasons that an FI might prefer the pass-through/CMO forms of securitization to issuing MBBs. First, MBBs tie up mortgages on the FI's balance sheet for a long time. This increases the illiquidity of the asset portfolio. Second, the amount of mortgages tied up is enhanced by the need to overcollateralize to ensure a high-quality credit risk rating for the bond issue; in our example, the overcollateralization was $2 million. Third, by keeping mortgages on the balance sheet, the FI continues to be liable for capital adequacy requirement. Because of these problems, MBBs are the least used of the three basic vehicles of securitization in the United States. However, German and Danish banks use covered bonds extensively. Recently, after the MBS crisis, some U.S. regulators have reconsidered their opposition to these types of bonds because of their greater security for investors. The difference between U.S. GAAP and the IFRS used by Canadian and European banks may create different incentives. IFRS rules require banks to report securitized mortgages with loans on the balance sheet until the FI has transferred control and the risks and rewards to the SIV. The MBS under IFRS is reported as a secured borrowing, whereas loan sales under U.S. GAAP would be reported as a sale, providing immediate removal from the balance sheet.

CONCEPT QUESTION

Would a large Canadian FI issue covered bonds? Explain your answer.

INNOVATIONS IN SECURITIZATION

We now turn our attention to the growing innovations in FIs' asset securitization. We discuss two major innovations and their use in return–risk management by FIs: mortgage pass-through strips and the extension of the securitization concept to other assets.

Mortgage Pass-Through Strips

The mortgage pass-through strip is a special type of CMO with only two classes. The fully amortized nature of mortgages means that any given monthly payment, *PMT*, contains an interest component and a principal component. Beginning in 1987, investment banks and other FI issuers stripped out the interest component from the principal component and sold each payment stream separately to different bond class investors. They sold an interest-only (IO) class and a principal-only (PO) class. These two bond classes have very special cash flow

FIGURE 26–13
IO/PO Strips

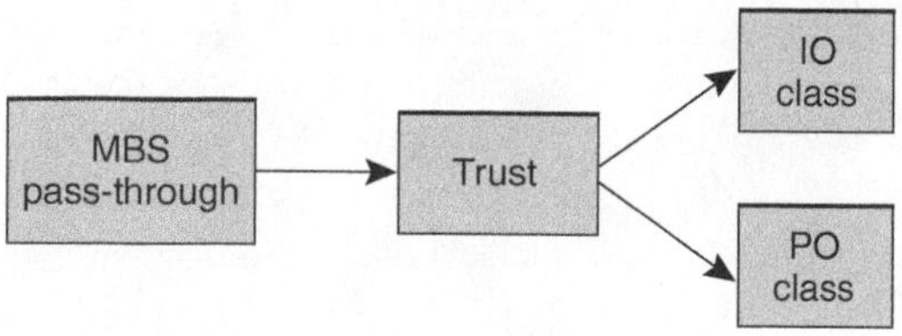

characteristics, especially regarding the interest rate sensitivity of these bonds. We show this stripping of the cash flows in Figure 26–13 and consider the effects of interest rate changes on the value of each of these stripped instruments below.

IO Strips

IO strip
A bond sold to investors whose cash flows reflect the monthly interest payments received from a pool of mortgages.

The owner of an **IO strip** has a claim to the present value of interest payments made by the mortgage holders in the pool, that is, to the IO segments of each month's cash flow received from the underlying mortgage pool:

$$P_{IO} = \frac{IO_1}{\left(1 + \frac{y}{12}\right)} + \frac{IO_2}{\left(1 + \frac{y}{12}\right)^2} + \frac{IO_3}{\left(1 + \frac{y}{12}\right)^3} + \cdots + \frac{IO_{300}}{\left(1 + \frac{y}{12}\right)^{300}}$$

When interest rates change, they affect the cash flows received on mortgages. We concentrate on two effects: the discount effect and the prepayment effect on the price or value of IOs, denoted by P_{IO}.

Discount Effect As interest rates (y) fall, the present value of any cash flows received on the strip—the IO payments—rises, increasing the value (P_{IO}) of the bond.

Prepayment Effect As interest rates fall, mortgagees prepay their mortgages. In absolute terms, the number of IO payments the investor receives is likely to shrink. For example, the investor might receive only 100 monthly IO payments instead of the expected 300 in a no-prepayment world. The shrinkage in the size and value of IO payments reduces the value (P_{IO}) of the bond.

Specifically, one can expect that as interest rates continue to fall below the mortgage coupon rate of the bonds in the pool, the prepayment effect gradually dominates the discount effect, so that over some range the price or value of the IO bond falls as interest rates fall. Note the price–yield curve in Figure 26–14 for an IO strip on a pass-through bond with 10 percent mortgage coupon rates. The price–yield curve slopes upward in the interest rate range below 10 percent. This means that as current interest rates rise or fall, IO values or prices rise or fall. As a result, the IO is a rare example of a **negative-duration** asset that is very valuable as a portfolio-hedging device for an FI manager when included with regular bonds whose price–yield curves show the normal inverse relationship. That is, even though as interest rates rise the value of the regular bond portfolio falls, the value of an IO portfolio may rise. Note in Figure 26–14 that at rates above the pool's mortgage coupon of 10 percent, the price–yield curve changes shape and tends to perform like any regular bond. In recent years, FIs have purchased IOs to hedge the interest rate risk on the mortgages and other bonds held as assets in their portfolios. We depict the hedging power of IOs in Figure 26–15.

negative duration
A relationship in which the price of a bond increases or decreases as yields increase or decrease.

FIGURE 26–14
Price–Yield Curve of an IO Strip

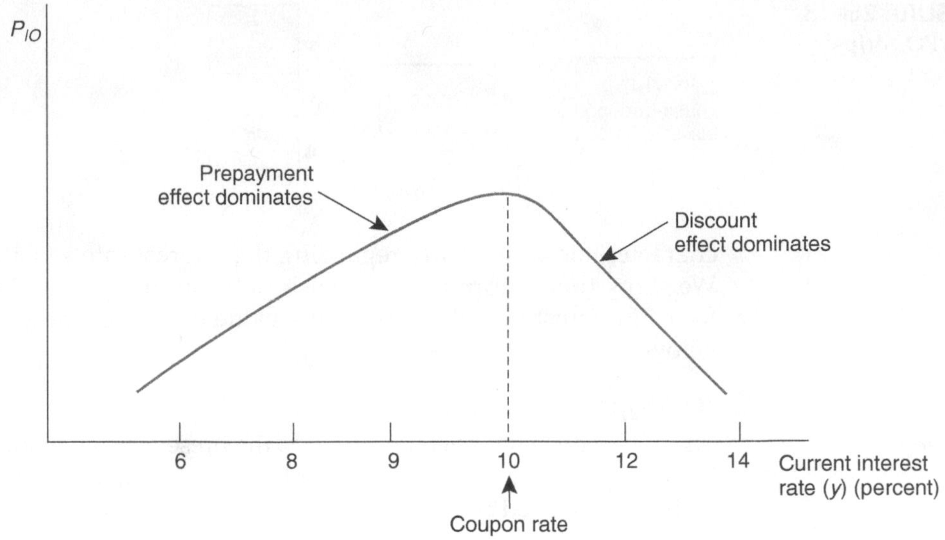

FIGURE 26–15
Hedging with IOs

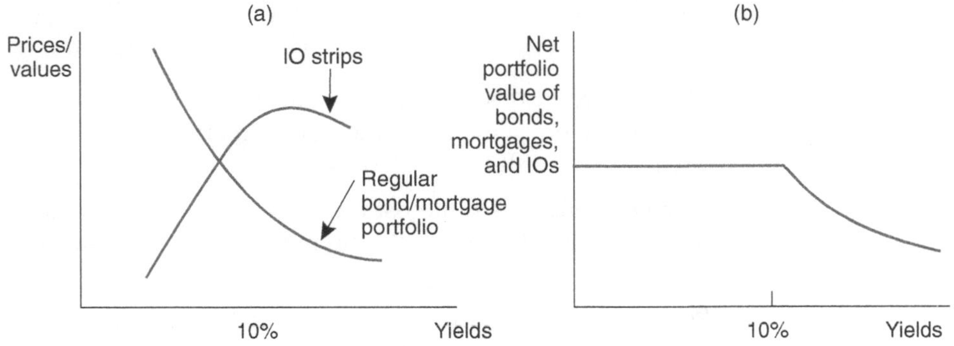

PO Strips

PO strip
A bond whose cash flows to investors reflect the monthly principal payments received from a pool of mortgages.

The value of the **PO strip** (P_{PO}) is defined by

$$P_{PO} = \frac{PO_1}{\left(1 + \frac{y}{12}\right)} + \frac{PO_2}{\left(1 + \frac{y}{12}\right)^2} + \frac{PO_3}{\left(1 + \frac{y}{12}\right)^3} + \cdots + \frac{PO_{300}}{\left(1 + \frac{y}{12}\right)^{300}}$$

where the PO_i ($i = 1$ to 300) represent the mortgage principal components of each monthly payment by the mortgage holders. This includes both the monthly amortized payment component of *PMT* that is principal and any early prepayments of principal by the mortgagees. Again, we consider the effects on a PO's value (P_{PO}) of a change in interest rates.

Discount Effect As yields (y) fall, the present value of any principal payments must increase and the value of the PO strip rises.

Prepayment Effect As yields fall, the mortgage holders pay off principal early. Consequently, the PO bondholder receives the fixed principal balance outstanding on the pool of mortgages earlier than stated. Thus, this prepayment effect must also work to increase the value of the PO strip.

FIGURE 26–16
Price–Yield Curve of a PO Strip

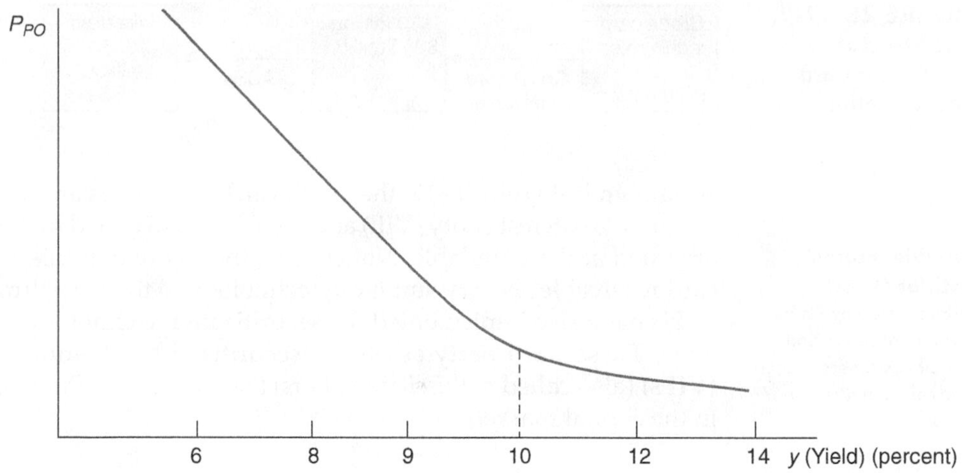

As interest rates fall, both the discount and prepayment effects point to a rise in the value of the PO strip. The price–yield curve reflects an inverse relationship, but with a steeper slope than for normal bonds. That is, PO strip bond values are very interest rate sensitive, especially for yields below the stated mortgage coupon rate. We show this in Figure 26–16 for a 10 percent PO strip. (Note that a regular coupon bond is affected only by the discount effect.) As you can see, when yields fall below 10 percent, the market value or price of the PO strip can increase very quickly. At rates above 10 percent, it tends to behave like a regular bond (as the incentive to prepay disappears).

The IO–PO strip is a classic example of financial engineering. From a given pass-through bond, two new bonds have been created: the first with an upward-sloping price–yield curve over some range and the second with a steeply downward-sloping price–yield curve over some range. Each class is attractive to different investors and investor segments. The IO is attractive to DTIs as an on-balance-sheet hedging vehicle. The PO is attractive to FIs that wish to increase the interest rate sensitivity of their portfolios and to investors or traders who wish to take a naked or speculative position regarding the future course of interest rates. This high and complex interest sensitivity has resulted in major traders such as JPMorgan Chase and Bank of America Merrill Lynch, as well as many investors such as hedge funds, suffering considerable losses on their investments in these instruments when interest rates have moved unexpectedly against them.

Securitization of Other Assets

Although a major use of the three securitization vehicles—pass-throughs, CMOs, and MBBs—has been for packaging residential mortgages, the techniques have been adapted and used for FIs' other assets, such as car loans and leases, credit card receivables, commercial mortgages, equipment leases and loans, lines of credit, trade receivables, and corporate loans.

In addition to securitizing their residential mortgages, Canadian banks as well as retail stores Canadian Tire (Canadian Tire Bank) and Sears Canada (Sears Canada Bank) have been active in securitizing their credit card receivables. Credit card securitization is very similar in technology to pass-through mortgage securities.

FIGURE 26–17
The Structure of a Credit Card Securitization

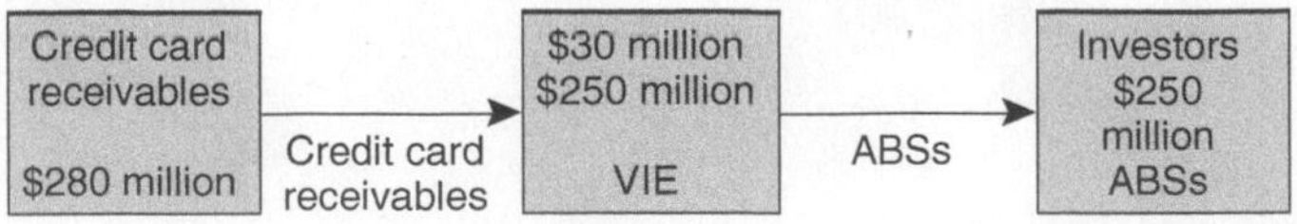

As shown in Figure 26–17, the credit card receivables are sold to a trust company or variable-interest entity (VIE) and then ABSs are issued in the form of notes, which are rated and are tradable. Notice from the figure that this securitization of credit card receivables is very similar in technology to the pass-through mortgage bond.

variable-interest entities (VIEs)
SPEs created by FIs for the securitization and sale of customers' assets; also called *multiseller conduits*.

FIs have also implemented the securitization technology for their customers for a fee. These third-party assets are securitized by creating **variable-interest entities (VIEs)** (also called *multiseller conduits*) that create ABCP that is rated and then sold in the capital markets.

CAN ALL ASSETS BE SECURITIZED?

LO3

The extension of securitization technology to other assets raises questions about the limits of securitization and whether all assets and loans can be securitized. Conceptually the answer is that they can, as long as it is profitable to do so or the benefits to the FI from securitization outweigh the costs of securitization. In Table 26–8, we summarize the benefits versus the costs of securitization.

From Table 26–8, given any set of benefits, the more costly and difficult it is to find asset packages of sufficient size and homogeneity, the more difficult and expensive it is to securitize. For example, corporate and other business loans have maturities running from a few months up to eight years; further, they have varying interest rate terms (fixed, LIBOR floating, prime rate floating) and fees. In addition, they contain differing covenants and are made to firms in a wide variety of industries. Despite this, FIs have still been able to issue securitization packages called collateralized loan obligations (CLOs), containing high-quality, low-default-risk loans, and collateralized debt obligations (CDOs), containing a diversified collection of loans and other assets. The interest and principal payments on a CDO are linked to the timing of default losses and repayments on a pool of underlying loans or bonds. The riskiest of the CDOs, sometimes called "toxic waste," pay out only if everything goes right. The best CDOs will pay out unless the entire portfolio defaults. A synthetic CDO is a type of CDO in which the underlying credit exposures are CDSs rather than a pool of loans or bonds. Thus, the periodic payments are linked to the cash flows from the CDSs. If the credit event occurs in the

TABLE 26–8
Benefits versus Costs of Securitization

Benefits	Costs
1. New funding source (bonds versus deposits)	1. Cost of public/private credit risk insurance and guarantees
2. Increased liquidity of FI loans	2. Cost of overcollateralization
3. Enhanced ability to manage the duration gap of $(D_A - kD_L)$	3. Valuation and packaging costs (the cost of asset heterogeneity)
4. If off balance sheet, the issuer saves on deposit insurance premiums and capital adequacy requirements	

underlying portfolio, the synthetic CDO (and any investors) become responsible for the losses. Synthetic CDOs are securitized securities that can offer extremely high returns to investors. However, investors can lose more than their initial investments if several credit events occur in the underlying portfolio.

The volume of CDO issues in the United States grew from US$10 billion in 1995 to over US$500 billion in 2006, before the financial crisis. As discussed below, CDOs were at the very heart of the financial crisis, and this market has decreased in size significantly as a result, to US$31.1 billion in 2011 and US$39.5 billion in the first three quarters of 2012. The major sellers of CDOs are U.S. commercial and investment banks, through their SIVs or SPVs (discussed above). The major buyers are hedge funds, commercial banks, investment banks, and pension funds. While the banks that create and sell the CDOs distribute the cash flows from the underlying assets to the CDO buyers, the valuation of these credit derivatives is not based solely on the estimated cash flows from underlying assets. Rather, the valuation of CDOs involves the use of metrics and algorithms developed by traders and mathematicians. Generally, it has been much harder to securitize low-quality loans into CDOs. Specifically, the harder it is to value a loan or asset pool, the greater the costs of securitization due to the need for overcollateralization or credit risk insurance.

Of all of the instruments that caused damage to SIVs (and SPVs), the FIs that owned them, and the world's financial markets in general during the financial crisis, the most damaging was the cash flow CDOs backed by subprime and Alt-A CMO tranches. Alt-A mortgages are rated lower than prime quality, but are generally higher quality than subprime mortgages. Many SIVs had invested heavily in these CDOs. Cash flow CDOs have as their underlying collateral real securities, such as bonds, CMO tranches, and ABS tranches. The most naive investors simply looked at the ratings on these CDO tranches and then bought the tranche if they liked the rating. They did not attempt or did not have the models to confirm if the price they were asked to pay was a fair value.[14] Other investors accepted what CDO arrangers and rating agencies recommended for valuation technology. However, these models consistently underestimated the worst-case scenario and overvalued CDO tranches.[15] The best practice in valuing cash flow CDOs is to simulate the performance of the mortgage loans underlying the CMO tranches, loan by loan, then simulate the losses and cash flows of the CMO tranches in the CDO structure. Most investors until recently have done no analysis—because they did not have such software capabilities at their disposal. As a result, they consistently overpaid for cash flow CDO tranches, and they took on risk that they did not understand.

By mid-2009, regulators were looking at Basel II, domestic and international accounting standards, and the role and responsibilities of credit agencies for ways to better understand and to control the risks of securitization. Global FIs and their regulators were acting to prevent a repeat of the market disruptions experienced in 2008. The question asked is now more along the lines of: *Should* all assets be

[14] These investors ignored the fact that the rating agencies are paid by the CDO arranger and that they have a bias in favour of a rating that is better than the real risk level. Unless CDO tranches were rated favourably, arrangers could not make money by packaging securities freely available in the market and then reselling them at a higher price in the form of tranches.

[15] Note that this technique also maximizes CDO arrangers' profits by getting investors to buy CDO tranches that they would not purchase if they had accurately measured value.

securitized? The potential boundary to securitization may well be defined by the relative degree of heterogeneity and credit quality of an asset type or group. It is not surprising that fixed-rate residential mortgages were the first assets to be securitized since they are the most homogeneous of all assets on FI balance sheets. For example, the existence of secondary markets for houses provides price information that allows reasonably accurate market valuations of the underlying asset to be made, and extensive data are available on mortgage default rates by locality.

CONCEPT QUESTION

Can all assets and loans be securitized? Explain your answer.

THE CANADIAN MARKET FOR ASSET-BACKED SECURITIES

asset-backed commercial paper (ABCP)
Short-term debt issued by commercial firms that is backed by collateral such as inventory and account receivables.

capital markets
The market for all short-term and long-term financial securities.

money market
The market for short-term financial securities with maturities of less than one year.

Through securitization, credit risk is transferred from the balance sheets of FIs into financial markets. This unmonitored credit risk was a major cause of disruption during the financial turmoil that hit global markets in mid-2007. In particular, U.S. subprime mortgage loans were the source of instability that started the global deleveraging process and led to the liquidity and credit crisis that brought down many global FIs. However, Canadian markets and their financial intermediaries were remarkably stable during this time period, with the exception of one portion of the markets: the market for **asset-backed commercial paper (ABCP). Capital markets** include both short- and long-term financial securities. The **money market** refers to the part of the capital markets composed of short-term instruments with a maturity of less than one year. In December 2007, Canadian capital markets totalled \$6.3 trillion, with the money market making up \$363 billion (5.8 percent) of this amount. The money markets provided \$76 billion in ABCP sponsored by banks and \$32 billion sponsored by nonbanks.

ABCP Market Freeze: August 2007

dbrs.com

conduit
A trust created to purchase assets from FIs and corporations and issue ABSs to investors.

When global investors lost confidence in the markets starting in June 2007, the fear spread to Canada. Borrowers became unable to roll over their ABCP. The bank-sponsored ABCP was supported by backup lines of credit that the issuers were able to draw down. However, under the market disruption clause of the contracts, nonbank issuers of ABCP were unable to draw down their backup credit lines. In August 2007, under the Montréal Accord, investors and issuers of ABCP in Canada agreed to a freeze on the approximately \$32 billion in nonbank CP representing 22 **conduits**. The freeze lasted until early 2009, when the Pan-Canadian ABCP Committee Restructuring Plan allowed small investors to receive some of their capital back and large investors to convert to longer-term notes.

The Canadian Securitization Market

ABSs outstanding in Canada are divided into two types: term ABSs for longer maturities, and ABCP for shorter maturities. Total ABS market outstandings grew from less than \$70 billion in January 2000 to a maximum of \$177.6 billion in August 2007. However, the market for CP worldwide declined following Lehman Brothers' failure in September 2008 and the freezing of some segments of the

TABLE 26–9
Outstanding Canadian ABSs, March 31, 2013

Author's note: Outstanding Amount in the Market Share section includes publicly rated issues only. It may be different from the total market size mentioned elsewhere, which includes both publicly rated and privately rated issues.

Source: DBRS Limited, *Canadian Securitization Market Overview,* March 2013. dbrs.com.

Dealer/Administrator	Outstanding Amount	Market Share
BlackRock Asset Management Canada Limited	$26,340,193,743	27.3%
TD Securities Inc.	17,969,035,053	18.6
RBC Capital Markets Inc.	16,893,824,150	17.5
CIBC World Markets Inc.	12,031,411,742	12.5
BMO Capital Markets	7,286,224,627	7.6
Merrill Lynch Canada Inc.	4,966,848,743	5.1
Scotia Capital Inc.	3,445,876,630	3.6
National Bank Financial Inc.	3,173,105,366	3.3
Bank of Montreal (BMO)	2,187,168,817	2.3
Credit Suisse	562,953,093	0.6
Dundee Securities Corporation	550,000,000	0.6
Other	378,365,194	0.4
Canadian Imperial Bank of Commerce (CIBC)	300,000,000	0.3
HSBC Securities (Canada) Inc.	193,922,492	0.2
Canadian Tire Bank	119,220,058	0.1
Deutsche Bank Securities Limited	46,436,030	0.0
Total	**$96,444,585,738**	**100.0%**

money markets. The total ABSs (excluding private placements) was reported at $96.4 billion by DBRS at March 31, 2013, as shown in Table 26–9. Figure 26–18 shows the type of assets securitized in the Canadian ABS and ABCP markets. The market was dominated by credit cards (38.6 percent), followed by commercial mortgage-backed securities (CMBSs, 15.1 percent). Residential mortgages totalled 21.8 percent (insured mortgages at 10.5 percent, conventional mortgages at 1.7 percent, and home equity lines of credit (HELOCs) at 9.6 percent).

Canadian banks have been active in securitizing their own credit card receivables as a means of managing their capital and as a source of funding. In addition, Canadian Tire Corporation formed Canadian Tire Bank and Sears Canada Inc. created Sears Canada Bank, both of which are regulated by OSFI; the purpose of both is to manage these retail firms' credit card receivables via securitization vehicles. In addition, Canadian banks manage the securitizations of the trade receivables, credit cards, and mortgages of other firms via SPEs or VIEs and receive a fee to administer them.

FIGURE 26–18
Asset Composition of the ABS and ABCP Market in Canada, March 31, 2013

Source: DBRS Limited, *Canadian Securitization Market Overview,* March 2013. dbrs.com.

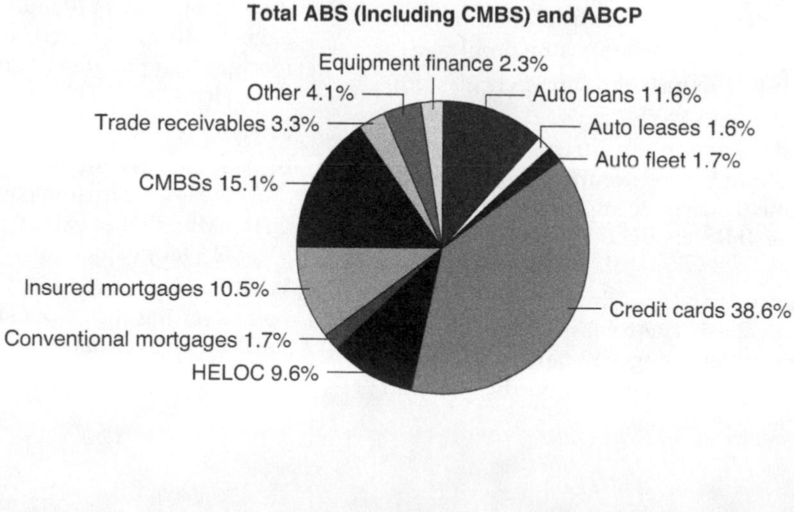

www.financialstabilityboard.org
bankofcanada.ca

As they have developed, the North American and global markets for securitizations have undergone a convergence in regulations in order to increase the transparency of the deals for investors and, through standardization of these transactions, to reduce the costs for FIs that originate these securities. As noted in Chapter 20, global regulators are concerned with credit risk transfer mechanisms and their effects on the stability of global capital markets, particularly in light of fears about market systemic risk from unregulated FIs and securities, i.e., the shadow banking sector, in 2007 and 2008. The Financial Stability Board, the Bank of Canada, and other central banks are providing policy recommendations that are intended to result in lower systemic risk to the global financial system.

Questions and Problems

1. What has been the effect of securitization on the asset portfolios of FIs?
2. What regulatory costs do FIs face when making loans? How does securitization reduce the levels of cost?
3. An FI is planning to issue $100 million in BB-rated commercial loans. The FI will finance the loans by issuing demand deposits.
   a. What is the minimum amount of capital required by Basel III?
   b. What is the amount of demand deposits needed to fund this loan, assuming the bank is based in Canada, where there are no reserve requirements on demand deposits?
   c. Show a simple balance sheet with total assets, total liabilities, and equity if this is the only project funded by the bank.
4. Consider the FI in problem 3.
   a. What additional risk exposure problems does the FI face?
   b. What are some possible solutions to the duration mismatch and the illiquidity problems?
   c. What advantages does securitization have in dealing with the FI's risk exposure problems?
5. How are investors in pass-through securities protected against default risk?
6. What specific changes occur on the balance sheet at the completion of the securitization process? What adjustments occur to the risk profile of the FI? How have IFRS changed the accounting for Canadian FIs?
7. Consider the mortgage pass-through example presented in Table 26–3. The total monthly payment by the borrowers reflecting a 12 percent mortgage rate is $1,053,220. The payment passed through to the ultimate investors reflecting an 11.5 percent return is $1,016,469. Who receives the difference between these two payments? How are the shares determined?
8. Consider a mortgage pool with principal of $20 million. The maturity is 25 years with a monthly mortgage payment of 10 percent per annum. Assume no prepayments.
   a. What is the monthly mortgage payment (100 percent amortizing) on the pool of mortgages?
   b. If the servicing fee is 45 bp, what is the yield on the MBS pass-through?
   c. What is the monthly payment on the MBS in part (b)?
   d. Calculate the first monthly servicing fee paid to the originating FIs.
9. Calculate the value of (a) the mortgage pool and (b) the MBS pass-through in question 8 if market interest rates increase 50 bp. Assume no prepayments.
10. What would be the impact on MBS pricing if the pass-through was not fully amortized? What is the present value of a $10 million pool of 15-year mortgages with an 8.5 percent per annum monthly mortgage coupon if market rates are 5 percent? The FI servicing fee is 44 bp.
    a. Assume that the MBS is fully amortized.
    b. Assume that the MBS is only half amortized. There is a lump-sum payment at the maturity of the MBS that equals 50 percent of the mortgage pool's face value.
11. What is prepayment risk? How does prepayment risk affect the cash flow stream on a fully amortized mortgage loan? What are the two primary factors that cause early payment?

12. Under what conditions do mortgage holders have a call option on their mortgages? When is the call option in the money?
13. What are the benefits of market yields that are less than the average rate in the NHA MBS mortgage pool? What are the disadvantages of this rate inversion? To whom does the good news and the bad news accrue?
14. What is the WAL of a mortgage pool supporting pass-through securities? How does WAL differ from duration?
15. If 150 $200,000 mortgages in a $60 million 15-year mortgage pool are expected to be prepaid in three years and the remaining 150 $200,000 mortgages are to be prepaid in four years, what is the WAL of the mortgage pool? Mortgages are fully amortized, with mortgage coupon rates set at 10 percent to be paid annually.
16. An FI originates a pool of 500 25-year mortgages, each averaging $150,000 with an annual mortgage coupon rate of 8 percent. Assume that the CMHC insurance fee is 20 bp and the FI's servicing fee is 55 bp.
    a. What is the present value of the mortgage pool?
    b. What is the monthly mortgage payment?
    c. For the first two payments, what portion is interest and what portion is principal repayment?
    d. What are the expected monthly cash flows to each MBS investor?
    e. What is the present value of the MBS? Assume that the risk-adjusted market annual rate of return is 8 percent compounded monthly.
    f. Would actual cash flows to MBS investors deviate from expected cash flows as in part (d)? Why or why not?
    g. What are the expected monthly cash flows for the FI?
    h. If all the mortgages in the pool are completely prepaid at the end of the second month, what is the pool's WAL? *Hint:* Use your answer to part (c).
    i. What is the price of the NHA MBS pass-through security if its WAL is equal to your solution for part (h)? Assume no change in market interest rates.
    j. What is the price of the MBS with a WAL equal to your solution for part (h) if market yields decline 50 bp?
17. What is the difference between the yield spread to average life and the OAS on MBSs?
18. Explain precisely the prepayment assumptions of the PSA prepayment model.
19. What does an FI mean when it states that its mortgage pool prepayments are assumed to be 100 percent PSA equivalent?
20. What factors may cause the actual prepayment pattern to differ from the assumed pattern? How would an FI adjust for the presumed occurrence of some of these factors?
21. What is the burnout factor? How is it used in modelling prepayment behaviour? What other factors may be helpful in modelling the prepayment behaviour of a given mortgage pool?
22. What is the goal of prepayment models that use option pricing theory? How do these models differ from the PSA or empirical models? What criticisms are often directed toward these models?
23. How does the price on an MBS relate to the yield on an MBS option from the perspective of the investor? What is the OAS?
24. Use the options prepayment model to calculate the yield on a $30 million three-year fully amortized mortgage pass-through where the mortgage coupon rate is 6 percent paid annually. Market yields are 6.4 percent paid annually. Assume that there is no servicing or guarantee fee.
    a. What is the annual payment on the MBS?
    b. What is the present value of the MBS?
    c. Interest rate movements over time are assumed to change a maximum of 0.5 percent per year. Both an increase of 0.5 percent and a decrease of 0.5 percent in interest rates are equally probable. If interest rates fall 1.0 percent below the current mortgage coupon rates, all of the mortgages in the pool will be completely prepaid. Diagram the interest rate tree and indicate the probability of each node in the tree.
    d. What are the expected annual cash flows for each possible situation over the three-year period?
    e. The government yield curve is flat at a discount yield of 6 percent. What is the OAS on the MBS?
25. Use the options prepayment model to calculate the yield on a $12 million, five-year, fully amortized mortgage pass-through where the mortgage coupon rate is 7 percent paid annually. Market yields are 8 percent paid annually. Assume that there is no servicing or guarantee fee.
    a. What is the annual payment on the MBS?
    b. What is the present value of the MBS?

c. Interest rate movements over time are assumed to change a maximum of 1 percent per year. Both an increase of 1 percent and a decrease of 1 percent in interest rates are equally probable. If interest rates fall 3 percent below the current mortgage coupon rates, all mortgages in the pool will be completely prepaid. Diagram the interest rate tree and indicate the probability of each node in the tree.

d. What are the expected annual cash flows for each possible situation over the five-year period?

e. The Treasury yield curve is flat at a discount yield of 6 percent. What is the OAS on the MBS?

26. What conditions would cause the yield on pass-through securities with prepayment risk to be less than the yield on pass-through securities without prepayment risk?

27. What is a CMO? How is it similar to a pass-through security? How does it differ? In what way does the creation of a CMO use market segmentation to redistribute prepayment risk?

28. Consider $200 million of 25-year mortgages with a coupon of 10 percent per annum paid quarterly.

a. What is the quarterly mortgage payment?

b. What are the interest repayments over the first year of life of the mortgages? What are the principal repayments?

c. Construct a 25-year CMO using this mortgage pool as collateral. The pool has three tranches, where tranche A offers the least protection against prepayment and tranche C offers the most protection against prepayment. Tranche A of $50 million receives quarterly payments at 9 percent per annum, tranche B of $100 million receives quarterly payments at 10 percent per annum, and tranche C of $50 million receives quarterly payments at 11 percent per annum. Diagram the CMO structure.

d. Assume nonamortization of principal and no prepayments. What are the total promised coupon payments to the three classes? What are the principal payments to each of the three classes for the first year?

e. If, over the first year, the trustee receives quarterly prepayments of $10 million on the mortgage pool, how are these funds distributed?

f. How are the cash flows distributed if prepayments in the first half of the second year are $20 million quarterly?

g. How can the CMO issuer earn a positive spread on the CMO?

29. Consider $100 million of 30-year mortgages with a coupon of 5 percent per year paid quarterly.

a. What is the quarterly mortgage payment?

b. What are the interest and principal repayments over the first year of life of the mortgages? What are the principal repayments?

c. Construct a 30-year CMO using this mortgage pool as collateral. The pool has three tranches, where tranche A offers the least protection against prepayment and tranche C offers the most protection against prepayment. Tranche A of $25 million receives quarterly payments at 4 percent per year, tranche B of $50 million receives quarterly payments at 5 percent per year, and tranche C of $25 million receives quarterly payments at 6 percent per year.

d. Assume nonamortization of principal and no prepayments. What are the total promised coupon payments to the three classes? What are the principal payments to each of the three classes for the first year?

e. If, over the first year, the trustee receives quarterly prepayments of $5 million on the mortgage pool, how are these funds distributed?

f. How are the cash flows distributed if prepayments in the first half of the second year are $10 million quarterly?

30. How does a Class Z tranche of a CMO differ from a Class R tranche? What causes a Z class to have characteristics of both a zero-coupon bond and a regular bond? What factors can cause an R class to have a negative duration?

31. Why would buyers of Class C tranches of CMOs be willing to accept a lower return than purchasers of Class A tranches?

32. What are MBBs? How do MBBs differ from pass-through securities and CMOs?

33. From the perspective of risk management, how does the use of MBBs by an FI assist the FI in managing credit and interest rate risk?

34. Consider a bank with $50 million in long-term mortgages as assets. It is financing these mortgages with $30 million in short-term uninsured deposits and $20 million in insured deposits. To reduce its interest rate risk exposure and to lower its funding costs, the bank can segregate $35 million of the mortgages on the asset side of its balance sheet and pledge them as collateral backing a $30 million long-term MBB issue. Because the $30 million in MBBs is backed by mortgages worth $35 million, the MBB issued by the bank costs less to issue, in

terms of required yield, than uninsured deposits. Thus, the FI can then use the proceeds of the $30 million bond issue to replace the $30 million of uninsured deposits. Show the bank's balance sheet before and after the issue of the MBB.

35. What are four reasons that an FI may prefer the use of either pass-through securities or CMOs to the use of MBBs?

36. What is an IO strip? How do the discount effect and the prepayment effect of an IO create a negative-duration asset? What macroeconomic effect is required for this negative-duration effect to be possible?

37. What is a PO strip? What causes the price–yield profile of a PO strip to have a steeper slope than that of a normal bond?

38. An FI originates a pool of short-term real estate loans worth $20 million with maturities of 10 years and paying interest rates of 9 percent per annum.
    a. What is the average payment received by the FI, including both principal and interest, if no prepayment is expected over the life of the loan?
    b. If the loans are converted into pass-through certificates and the FI charges a servicing fee of 50 bp, what is the payment amount expected by the holders of the pass-through securities if no prepayment is expected?
    c. Assume that the payments are separated into IO and PO payments, that prepayments of 5 percent occur at the end of years 3 and 4, and that the payment of the remaining principal occurs at the end of year 5. What is the expected annual payment for each instrument? Assume discount rates of 9 percent.
    d. What is the market value of IOs and POs if the market interest rates for instruments of similar risk decline to 8 percent?

39. What are the factors that, in general, allow assets to be securitized? What are the costs involved in the securitization process?

40. How does an FI use loan sales and securitization to manage interest rate, credit, and liquidity risks? Summarize how each of the possible methods of securitization affects the balance sheet and profitability of an FI in the management of these risks.

INDEX

7-Eleven, 409
9/11 terrorist attacks, 403

ABN Amro, 405
Absolute dollar measures of market risk
  historic (back simulation) approach, 337–341
  Monte Carlo simulation, 341
  RiskMetrics model, 329–336
Abu Dhabi Investment Authority, 100
Accident and health insurance, 107–108
Account reconciliation, 386
Accounting, 458, 460–462, 634
Accounting standards and practices, 164, 458, 460, 531, 557, 634
Accounting Standards Board (AcSB), 531, 557
Accounts receivable, 45
Accrued interest, **626**, **627**
Acquisitions. *See* Mergers and acquisitions
Actual capital rules, 467–468
Actuarial liabilities, life insurance, 108–110
Actuarially fair premium, calculating, 439–440
Actuarially fair price, 11*n*
Actuarially fairly priced insurance, 437
Actuarially priced insurance premium, **105**
Adelaide Capital Corp., 433
Adjustable rate mortgages (ARMs), 16, 199
Adoboli, Kweku, 359*t*
Advanced measurement approach, to capital requirement, 485–486
Adverse material change, 365
Adverse selection problem, **105**
Affiliate risk, 358*t*, **376**
Agency, 521
Agency conflicts, 389
Agency costs, **5**–6
Agency transactions, 62
Agency, organizational form, 521
Agent, 4
AGF Funds/Investments Inc, 79, 85, 629
Aggregate funding risk, 366
Aggressive growth funds, 90
Agrifinance, 36
AIC, 85
AIG. *See* American International Group Inc. (AIG)
AIM Trimark, 629
Air Canada, 40, 99, 130
Akhigbe, A., 397*n*
Albriond Capital, 502
Allen, L., 215*n*, 217*n*, 223*n*, 240*n*
Allianz, 113, 123*t*
Allied Irish Bank, 359*t*, 531
Allied Stores, 634
Allstate, 113
Ally Bank, 530*t*
Ally Credit Canada Limited, 44
Ally Financial, 41, 43, 44
Alpha, 484
Alt-A mortgages, 675
Alternative Investment Management Association (AIMA), 88
Altman's discriminant function, 213
Altman's Z score, 213–214, 219*n*, 312
Altman, E.I., 213*n*, 217*n*, 218*n*, 222*n*, 243*n*
Amaranth Advisors, 359*t*
American Express, 51
American International Group Inc. (AIG), 18, 102, 104*t*, 123, 136, 270–271, 308, 326, 359, 372, 402, 424, 429, 436, 445, 505, 507, 510, 554, 598, 599, 600, 612, 613, 616
Amortization, 199
AMR Corp., 231
Angel venture capitalists, **62**
Annual all-in-spread (AIS), 242
Annual report, mutual fund, 80
Annuities, 107
Annuity, future value, 179*n*
Appreciation, 279
  currency, Switzerland, 283–284
Arbitrage, 88, 296
  interest rate parity theorem, 296, 297
Arbitrage-free pricing, 573*n*
Arbitrage funds, 91
Arbitrage pricing theory (APT), 334
Argentina
  debt default, 134–135, 303
  debt rescheduling, 307
  domestic money supply growth, 318
  external debt outstanding, 303
  loan default, 303
  sovereign bonds, 322
Armstrong, J., 402*n*
Asia, 303, 405
Aspinwall, R.C., 213*n*
Asset-backed commercial paper (ABCP), 16, 422, 425, 638, 640, 641, **676**
  market freeze of 2007, 676
Asset-backed financing (ABF), **41**
Asset-backed paper vehicles, 16
Asset-backed securities (ABS). *See also* Asset securitization; Securitization
  Canada, 676–678
  CDOs, 674–675
  collateralized loan obligation (CLO), 674
  collateralized mortgage obligation (CMO), 664–668
  commercial mortgages (CMBS), 639
  commercial paper, 199, 425, 638
  credit card receivables, 638, 673–674
  mortgage-backed (covered) bond (MBB), 668–670
  pass-through security, 643–663
  pass-through strips, 670–673
  residential mortgages, 638–639
Asset-based financing (ABF)/asset-based lending (ABL), **41**
Asset-based lending (ABL), **41**
Asset brokerage, 634
Asset liquidity, 633
Asset purchases, 18*t*
Asset risk, 463, 487–489
Asset securitization, 16, **638**. *See also* Securitization
Asset transformation, **5**
Asset-side liquidity risk, 252–253, 257–259
Assets, 162–165
  banks, of, 25–28
  credit unions, of, 35
  finance companies, of, 45–49
  financial intermediaries, of, 2
  life insurance companies, of, 108
  off-balance-sheet (OBS), 28–30, 358
  rate-sensitive, 150–151
  securitization of, 638, 673–674
Assets to capital multiple (ACM), 463–464
Assicurazioni Generali, 123*t*
Assignment, **626**
  defined, **626**
  loan, 626
Assumable mortgage, **653**
Assuris, 32, 111, 432, 435, 453–454, 488
Automated clearing houses, 139, 399
Automated Clearing Settlement System (ACSS), 139, 375, 399, 400, 402
Automated teller machines (ATMs), 387
Automobile finance companies, 45–47
Automobile insurance, 113. *See also* Property and casualty (P&C) insurance
Automobile liability and physical damage insurance, 113
Autorité des Marchés Financiers (FMA), 452, 488
Available stable funding (ASF), 265
Available-for-sale securities, 459
Average cost, 395
Average implicit interest rate, 419
Aviva Canada, 112*t*, 123*t*
AXA Group/Canada, 110, 112*t*, 123*t*, 630

Back simulation, 328
Back-end fee, **363**
Back-end load, 82
Back-office functions, 65, 381
Back-office support, 19
  labour, 3
  systems, 3
  technology, 3
Backward pricing, **85**
Bad banks, 630–631
Bad debt loans, 627
Bahamas, 518
"Bail-ins," 436*n*, **445**
Bailout effect, 39
Bailouts, **445**
Balance sheets, 66–69
  securities firms, 66–69
  using options to hedge interest rate risk on, 577–582
Balanced funds, **79**
Ball, C., 571*n*
Baltazar, R., 516
Banca Nazionale del Lavoro, 522

Bank Act (Canada), **2**, 13, 21, 31, 77, 376, 388*n*, 494, 505, 506
Bank failure resolution, least-cost resolution, 445
Bank for International Settlements (BIS), 31, 139, 249, 262, 281, 305, 361, 408, 415, 458, 464, 519, 611, 612, 616. *See also* Basel I; Basel II; Basel III
- capital requirements, 634
- duration model and, 186
- fixed-income trading portfolio, risk measurement of, 346–350
- foreign loans and, 303
- fuller risk factor approach, 348
- large bank internal models and, 351–353
- liquidity coverage ratio (LCR), 262–264
- liquidity planning, 262–266
- liquidity risk management, 262–266
- market risk capital requirements, 346–350, 361, 634
- market risk framework, 346–350
- moral hazard issues, 447
- operational risks for, 139, 382
- risk-based capital adequacy reforms of, 519, 598–599
- risk-based capital requirements, 373
- standardized approach, 468–487
- standardized framework, 346–350

Bank holding companies, 495
Bank loan mutual funds, 629
Bank loan sale. *See* Loan sale(s)
Bank loans, 6, 308, 624–625
Bank mergers, 24
Bank of America Corporation, 23, 49, 56, 72, 85, 136, 226*n*, 326, 369, 372, 429, 482*t*, 495, 511, 530*t*, 625, 632
Bank of America Merrill Lynch, 285*t*, 444, 627, 628, 632, 673
Bank of British Columbia, 24
Bank of Canada, 24, 31, 37, 51, 63, 147, 211, 245–246, 262, 268*n*, 308, 366, 400, 401, 402, 678
- lender of last resort, 449–450
- liquidity risk management, 256
- moral hazard, 449
- overnight rate, 424
- transmission of monetary policy from, 12

Bank of Canada Act, 433
Bank of China, 482*t*
Bank of Credit and Commerce International (BCCI), collapse of, 522
Bank of East Asia Ltd., 37
Bank of England, 19, 37, 73, 308, 486
Bank of Japan, 37
Bank of Montreal, 22, 31, 56, 132, 147, 286*t*, 337, 341, 353*t*, 409, 480, 507, 510, 512, 516, 517, 529*t*, 670
Bank of New York, 381
Bank of New York Mellon, 447, 482*t*, 530*t*
Bank of New Zealand, 415
Bank of Nova Scotia, 22, 23*t*, 30, 56, 132, 281, 286*t*, 303, 337, 388, 463, 480, 517, 529*t*, 628. *See also* Scotiabank
Bank of Nova Scotia Trust Company, 30
Bank of Oklahoma, 530*t*
Bank One Corporation, 511, 512
Bank panics, 268*n*, **269**, 434. *See also* Bank runs
Bank rate, **148**
Bank reserves, 12, 203, 415
Bank run liquidity risk, 268–269
Bank runs, **268**, 413, 431, 434
Bank(s), 2, 23–39. *See also* Commercial banks; Geographic expansion; Investment banks
- assets of, 25–28
- bad, 630–631
- balance sheet and recent trends, 25–30
- bank–bank mergers, 494–495, 507, 511
- bank–finance company consolidation, 50–51
- bank–insurance company mergers, 103, 391–392, 495–496, 506–507
- Big Six, 22, 24, 33, 72, 77, 302, 480, 506, 553
- branch, 521
- Canadian, 21–22, 23–24, 495, 509, 511, 516, 517–520, 529
- central, 148–150
- China, 36
- correspondent, 31
- country-wide, 509
- credit quality problems, 195
- defined, 23
- domestic, 627–628
- equity of, 28
- European, 37
- failures, 10, 24, 140–141, 434, 435, 445–446, 522
- foreign, 635
- foreign, in North America, 520–523
- German, 37
- global issues, 36–39
- global market crisis (2008), 510, 531
- good–bad, 630–631
- home, 388
- industry performance, 33, 528–531
- insurance products, 495–496
- insurance subsidiaries, 24
- integrated bank-owned security firms, 56, 63
- investment, 55, 58–60, 494
- investment banks, subsidiaries of Canadian banks, 58
- Islamic banking, 37
- Japanese, 37, 303
- leverage, 27–28
- liabilities of, 28
- liability composition of domestic Canadian, 426–427
- loan companies, and, 30–31
- measuring liquidity exposure, 259–267
- nonbank, 496*n*
- off-balance-sheet activities, 28–30, 358–360, 361–363, 369
- online banking, 33
- operating costs, 383
- product diversification, 499–507
- reasons for selling loans, 632–633
- regulations for, 31–32
- reserve requirements, 12, 203, 415
- risk-taking behaviour, 435–436
- Schedule I, 23
- Schedule II, 23, 520
- Schedule III, 23
- shell, 518
- size, structure, and composition of industry, 23–25
- spreads, 24
- subprime crisis, 17–19, 200
- too-big-to-fail, 444, 445, 480, 481, 642
- total daily value at risk, 329
- trust services, 30
- U.S. and Canada abroad, 517
- unit, 509

Bank-supplied credit cards, 388*n*
Bank/trustee, default risk by, 648–650
Bankers acceptances, 153, 425, 638
Bankers Trust, 223, 359*t*, 531
Bankers' acceptances, 472
Banking. *See* Bank(s); Commercial banks; Investment banks
Banking Act (1933), 494
Banking book, 128–129
Banking crisis of 2012, Spain, 630
Banking industry, 2, 463–487
Banking panics of 1930–1933, 434
Banking services, 60
BankNorth, 505, 509
Bankruptcy, rates, 195
Bankruptcy risk transference, 502–503
Barclays Bank, 73, 203, 285*t*, 329, 382, 482*t*, 498*t*, 499, 630, 632
Barclays Capital Inc., 73
Barclays PLC, 382
Barings Bank, 358, 359*t*, 370
Base lending rate, 203
Basel Agreement (Basel I), 32, 464
- credit-risk-adjusted on-balance-sheet assets under, 464–465

Basel Agreement (Basel II), 464
Basel Agreement (Basel III), 463, **464**
Basel Agreement. *See* Basel I; Basel II; Basel III
Basel Committee, 243
Basel Committee on Banking Supervision (BCBS), 408, 480
Basel I, 303, 361, 362, 464
- capital rules, 351

Basel II
- capital adequacy requirements, 353
- capital rules, 353, 361, 464–465
- credit risk-weighted on-balance-sheet assets, 464–465
- pillars of capital regulation, 464
- tiered division of capital, 466

Basel III, 347, 348, 351, 352, 353, 429
- bank lending, and, 486
- capital requirements, 353
- capital rules, 519
- credit risk-adjusted asset off-balance-sheet derivative instruments with netting, 477–478
- credit risk-adjusted on-balance-sheet assets under, 469–471
- criticisms of, 486–487
- excessive complexity, 486
- impact on capital requirements, 486
- netting, 477–478
- other risks exposure, and, 486
- portfolio aspects, 486
- risk weights for off-the-sheet contingent guarantee contract, 472–474
- risk-based capital standards, 647
- risk-weighted asset value of off-the-sheet market contracts, 474–477
- total credit risk-weighted assets, 477

Basel Liquidity Coverage Ratio (BLCR), 662
Basic indicator approach, capital requirement, 484
Basis points, 624
Basis risk, **365**, **536**, 544–546, 581, 615*n*
Basket CDS, 612*n*

BBVA, 482*t*
BCCI, 405
Bear Stearns, 273, 326, 358, 372, 424, 429, 431, 436, 445, 495, 641
Bear Stearns High Grade Structured Credit Fund, 88, 93–94
Bears Stearns, 56
Belgium, investment ratio, 318
Berger, A.N., 396*n*, 397*n*, 398*n*
Berkshire Hathaway Inc., 104*t*, 123*t*
Bermuda, offshore financial centre, 94
Bernard L. Madoff Investment Securities, 86
Best-efforts offering, **500**
Beta, 325*n*, **333**, 484, 485
Bid–ask (buy–sell) spreads, 7, 62, 291
  foreign exchange, 286
"Big bangs," 72, 494
Big Six banks, 22, 24, 33, 72, 77, 302, 480, 506, 553
Bill payment via telephone, 388
Binomial model, hedging with bond options, 360, 571–575
Binomial tree diagram, 574, 576
Black, F., 226
Black–Scholes model, 360, 571
Black–Scholes option pricing model, 360, 571–572, 597
BlueGold Global Fund, 91
BMO, 260, 509, 529*t*, 629, 670
BMO Capital Markets, 281
BMO Financial Group, 25*t*, 123
BMO Harris Bank, 530*t*
BMO Investments, 77
BMO Life Assurance Company, 123
BMO Nesbitt Burns, 56
BNP Paribas, 482*t*, 498*t*, 627, 632
Bond, Alan, 502
Bond contracts, 6
Bond financing, 308
Bond funds, **79**
Bond Market Association, 655
Bond options, 572–575
Bond portfolio, mechanics of hedging, 571–575
Bond rating agencies, 643
Bond(s), 564–567
  catastrophe, 118
  consol, 171
  covenants, 208–209
  covered, 668–670
  credit risk, 129–130
  fixed-income coupon, 129–130
  junk, 195
  mechanics of hedging, 571–575
  mortgage, 210
  put option, 566–567
  ratings, 216
  treasury strips, 216
  valuation, 193
  zero-coupon, 170–171, 216
Book value, **458**, 459–460
  capital of, 460–462
  defined, **458**
  discrepancy between market value of equity, and, 460–462
Book value accounting, **164**, 634
Boot, A.W.A., 397
Borrower specific factors, 209
  default risk, 209
Borrowers, 209
Bourse de Montréal Inc., 533, 564
Bradford & Bingley, 37
Branch bank, 521
Branch Banking and Trust, 530*t*
Brazil
  debt moratorium, 302
  sovereign bonds, 322
Breach of fiduciary responsibility, 13
Brewer, W., II, 516
British North America Act (BNA), 32
British Petroleum, 506
Broker-dealers, **55**
  forward market, 533
Brokerage function, 4–5
Brokerage funds, 2
Brokers, 4–5
Brownian bridge process, 571*n*
Bubble, 16
Buffer reserves, **415**
Burn-out factor, **657**
Business credit institutions, **44**, 45
Business cycle, 210–211
Business Development Bank of Canada, 52
Business Development Corporation (BDC), 62
Business loans, 48–49, 197–199, 206–208
Business risk in life insurance, 487–488
Business-to-business e-commerce, 387

Caisse Centrale Desjardins du Québec, 662
Caisse populaires, 34
  guarantee system, 453
  size, structure and composition, 34–36
Caldwell, G., 402*n*
Call loan, 202
Call options, 230*n*, 370, 577*n*, 578*n*, 579*n*
  buying, on bond, 564–565
  caps, 585–588
  defined, **564**
  hedging catastrophe risk with, 584–585
  strike price, 565
  writing, on bond, 565–566
Call premium, 565
Canada
  asset-backed securities, 676–678
  banking industry, 21–22, 23–25, 36–37, 493–494, 509, 511, 517–520, 528
  Crown corporations, 41
  deposit insurance, 432–434
  foreign bank branches in, 520
  insurance industry, 103–106, 107
  regulatory system for financial institutions, 433
  securitization market, 676–678
Canada Deposit Insurance Corporation (CDIC), 10, 11, **28**, 32, 399, 417, 423, 432–434, 436, 438, 439, 440, 441, 443, 444, 447, 449, 507, 647
Canada Life, 79, 103, 454, 507
Canada Life and Health Insurance Compensation Corporation (Assuris), 32, 111, 432, 435, 453–454, 488
Canada Life Assurance Company, 112*t*
Canada Life Insurance Company, 112*t*
Canada Mortgage and Housing Corporation (CMHC), 9, 47, 53, 429, 470, 643–644, 670
Canada Pension Plan, 95
Canada Pension Plan Investment Board (CPPIB), 283
Canada Revenue Agency (CRA), 107
Canada Trust, 30
Canadian and British Insurance Companies Act, 103
Canadian Banking Association (CBA), 33, 200, 383, 392
Canadian Commercial Bank, 24, 140, 141, 262, 432, 444
Canadian Dealer Offered Rate (CDOR), **24**, **203**, 601
Canadian Derivatives Clearing Corporation (CDCC), 533, 564
Canadian Finance and Leasing Association (CFLA), 49
Canadian Foreign Exchange Committee (CFEC), 281
Canadian Hedge Fund Performance Index, 88
Canadian Imperial Bank of Commerce (CIBC), 23*t*, 25*t*, 33, 56, 81, 140, 260, 286*t*, 302, 337, 353*t*, 359, 362, 363*t*, 393, 409, 418–419, 423, 425, 480, 502, 503, 504, 507, 512, 516, 517, 529*t*, 670
Canadian Investment Funds Standards Committee (CIFSC), 79
Canadian Investor Protection Fund (CIPF), 70, 432, 454–455
Canadian Lenders Assurance Facility (CLAF), 429, 450
Canadian Life and Health Insurance Association Inc. (CLHIA), 105, 107
Canadian Life and Health Insurance Compensation Corporation. *See* Assuris
Canadian Payday Loan Association (CPLA), 47
Canadian Payments Act, 433
Canadian Payments Association (CPA), 9, 31, 32, 139, 375, 400, 402, 415, 433, 449
Canadian Securities Administrators, 69
Canadian Tire Bank, 673, 677
Canadian Tire Corporation, 81, 200, 673, 677
Canadian Venture Capital and Private Equity Association (CVCA), 62
Canadian Western Bank, 23*t*
Canwest Global, 194
Capital, 380
  book value of, 459–460
  discrepancy between market and book values of equity, 460–462
  economic net worth, 458
  functions of, 457–458
  insolvency risk, 459
  market value of, 458–459
  regulatory-defined concept of, 348
  Tier I, Tier II, 466
Capital (net worth) ratio, 185
Capital adequacy, 457–490, 557. *See also* Risk-based capital; Risk-based capital ratios
  actual capital rules, 463
  commercial banking and thrift industry, in, 463–487
  deposit-taking institutions, for, 463–487
  life insurance companies, for, 487–488
  minimum capital requirements, 465–466
  property and casualty insurance companies, for, 488
  requirements, 29
  risk-based capital ratios, 466–468
  securities firms, for, 487
Capital adequacy requirements (CAR), **29**, 466

Capital asset pricing model, 333–334
Capital conservation buffer, 478–480
Capital constraints, 519
Capital costs, 633
Capital forbearance, **442**
Capital gain effect, 188
Capital gains and losses, 462
Capital injection, 18*t*
Capital loss effect, 188
Capital loss/gain effect, 188
Capital markets, **676**
Capital One, 530*t*
Capital Purchase Program (CPP), 445
Capital ratios, risk-based, 464–466
Capital requirements, 638
Capital requirements for financial intermediaries, 487–489
Capital structure, 209
Capital surcharge, 480–481
Caps, **585**, 586–588
Captive finance companies, **44**
Carney, Mark, 19, 308
Carry trades, **283**
Cash flows from off-balance-sheet activities, 159–160
Cash management, 385
Cash reserves, 414
Catastrophe bond, 118
Catastrophe call spread, **584**
Catastrophe risk, 556–557
  hedging, with call spread options, 584
Cayman Islands, 518
CDOR. *See* Canadian Dealer Offered Rate
CDOs. *See* Collateralized debt obligations (CDOs)
CDS Indexes, 615
CEB Tower Group, 383*n*
Celent, 515
Central bank, 148–150. *See also* Federal Reserve
Central Deposit Insurance Corporation, 449
Central Guaranty Trust, 433, 444
Centre for Financial Services Ombudsnetwork (CFSON), 70
Cerberus Capital Management LP, 41, 43, 44
Certificates of deposit (CDs), 153
CGAP effects, **155**, 156
Charles Schwab, 85
Charter value, 13
Chartered banks. *See* Banks
Chase Manhattan Corp., 359*t*, 511, 512
Chegue deposit services, 386
Chemical Bank, 511
Cheque-clearing, 9
Cheques, 398–400
Chequing accounts, interest bearing, 420
Chicago Board of Options Exchange (CBOE), 564, 575
Chicago Board of Trade (CBOT), 533, 534*n*, 556
Chicago Mercantile Exchange (CME), 533, 534*n*, 582
Chile
  domestic money supply growth, 318
  sovereign bonds, 322
China
  banking industry, 36
  debt repudiation, 307
  import ratio, 313
  investment ratio, 313
  production technology, 319
China Banking Regulatory Commission, 449, 519
China Life Insurance, 123*t*
China, depository institutions in, 34
Chinese walls, **503**
CHIPS, 375, 402, 403, 404, 519
Chrysler, 211
CI Mutual Funds, 85
CIBC. *See* Canadian Imperial Bank of Commerce
CIBC Asset Management, 77, 78
CIBC Capital Markets, 516
CIBC Mellon Trust Company, 30
CIBC World Markets, 56, 63, 65, 281, 501
Circle K, 634
CIT Business Credit Canada, 49
CIT Group, 41, 44, 51, 359
Citibank, 33, 45, 103, 371, 376, 422, 494, 520, 530*t*
Citicorp, 302, 391, 491, 494, 496, 510
Citigroup, 23, 30, 33, 45, 72, 85, 141, 285*t*, 286, 302, 308, 320, 336, 359, 369, 376, 381, 391, 392, 445, 447, 482*t*, 494, 496, 498, 502, 510, 625, 627, 641
Claessens, S., 514
Claims ratio, **114**. *See also* Loss ratio
Clarica Life Insurance, 103, 507
Class A bond buyers, 665–667
Class B bond buyers, 665–667
Class C bond buyers, 665–667
Clearing, 375
Clearing House Interbank Payments Systems (CHIPS), 402
Clone funds, **77**
  pension funds, 96
Closed-end bank loan mutual funds, 629
Closed-end fund, **271**
Closed-end investment companies, **81**
Cloud computing, 387, 389
CLS bank, 402
Co-operative financial institutions, **34**
Co-operative Trust Company of Canada, 36
Co-operators Group Limited, 36, 112*t*
Collars, **585**, 589–592
Collateral, 210
Collateral changes, 18*t*
Collateralized debt obligations (CDOs), 93–94, 372, 674–675
  fair value, 675
  rating agencies, 675
  synthetic, 674, 675
  tranches, 675
Collateralized loan obligations (CLOs), 674
Collateralized mortgage obligations (CMOs), 372, 639, 664, **665**, 666–668
  bond classes, 667–668
  creation of, 665
  prepayment risk, 666–667
Colombia, sovereign bonds, 322
Combined ratio, **118**
Commercial and industrial (C&I) loans, 494, 517
Commercial banks, 494
  CDOs, as purchasers, 675
  forward market, 533
  geographic expansion of, 509–510
  loans of, 44
Commercial letter of credit, **137**
Commercial letters of credit, **367**–**368**
Commercial mortgage-backed securities (CMBSs), 638, 677
Commercial multiple peril insurance, 113–114
Commercial paper (CP), 14–15, 153, **199**, 425, 494, 624, 638, 640. *See also* Asset-backed securities
  market for, 25–26, 633
Commerzbank, 38
Commission costs, 118
Commission fees, 58
Commissions, 5
Commitment fee. *See* Back-end fee
Committee on Payment and Settlement Systems (CPSS), 400
Commodity Futures Trading Commission (CFTC), 534, 557, 617
Common equity Tier 1 (CET1), risk-based capital ratio, 466, 468
Companies' Creditors Arrangement Act, **49**
Compensating balances, **203**
Competition, 2, 505–507
Competition Bureau, 512
Competition Policy Review Panel, 507
Competition risk, 407
Comptroller of the Currency, 445, 447, 504, 513*n*, 617
Concentration limits, **238**
Conduit, 643, **676**
Confederation Life, 103, 435, 453, 454
Confederation Trust Co., 433
Conflict of interest, 15, 502–504, 507
  credit ratings agencies, 471
  management fees, 85
Consol bond (perpetuities), 171
Consumer loans, 44, 45–47, 200
  short-term, 153
Consumer price index (CPI), **148**
Consumer privacy, 495
Consumer protection, 12–13, 409
Contagion, **24**, 268*n*
Contagion crisis, 520
Contagion effect, 10*n*, **24**
Continental Bank of Canada, 24, 262, 444, 445
Continental Illinois National Bank and Trust company, 445
Contingent assets and liabilities, **357**
  defined, **357**
  valuation, 358–360
Contingent credit risk, 369
Continuous linked settlement, **402**
Contraction risk, 645
Contractually promised return on loan, 202–205
Controlled disbursement accounts, 386
Conversion factor, **540**–541
Convexity, 187–189
Convexity, incorporating, into duration model, 193
Cooperants, Les, 453
Coors, 505
Cope, Damian, 359*t*
Core deposits, **154**, **254**

Correlation, 243–244
Correlation coefficient, 240*n*
Correspondent banks, 31, 403
Corruption, 315
Corruption Perceptions Index, 316
Cost of funds, **24**, 27
Cost synergies, 511
Costs of trading, 5
Costs, technology and, 392–396
Counterparty, 554*n*, 639
Counterparty credit risk, **474**, 592, 639
Counterparty risk, 370, 629
Country risk, **134**. *See also* Sovereign risk
  analysis (CRA), 312
  classification (CRC), 519
  evaluation, 309–323
  event, 306
Countrywide Financial, 50, 51, 131, 268*n*, 510, 634
Coupon bond, five-year duration, 178–179
Coupon interest, duration and, 173
Covariance, 240*n*
Covenants, **208**–209
  loan sales, 625
Credit Agricole Group, 38, 498*t*
Credit allocation, 3, 9, 12, 194
Credit Analysis, 237
Credit card debt, 200–202
Credit card securitization, 638–639, 673–674
Credit card transactions, **387**
Credit cards, 388*n*, 398
Credit cooperatives, 34
Credit crisis. *See* Global credit crisis; Subprime crisis
Credit crunch of 1990–1991, 627
Credit default swaps (CDSs), 93–94, 102, 271, 362, 553, 598, 638. *See also* Credit swaps
Credit derivative contracts, **362**, 370, 553, 638
Credit equivalent amounts, **471**
Credit exposure, 626
Credit forward, **554**
  modified duration, 555
  put option, 556
Credit forward contracts, **554**
Credit guarantees, 3, 19
  off balance sheet (OBS), 3
Credit hedge funds, 16
Credit intermediation process, 497
Credit life insurance, 106
Credit line, 200
Credit quality, 195–197, 307
Credit rating, 635
  sovereign debt, 471
Credit rating agencies, 642
  conflict of interest, 471
Credit rationing, **206**, 524
Credit risk, 16, 29, 30, 126, 129–130, 365–366. *See also* Default risk; Loan(s); Sovereign risk
  adjusted on-balance-sheet assets under Basel I, 464
  book value of capital and, 460
  counterparty, 592, 639
  Credit Risk+, 237
  defined, **129**
  derivative securities, 371–373
  diversification, 130, 424
  firm-specific, 130
  five Cs of credit, 211
  hedging, 553–557, 583–584
  individual loan risk, 194–232
  calculating return on loan, 202–206
  credit quality problems, 195–197
  default models, 209–215
  newer models of measurement and pricing, 215–232
  retail *vs.* wholesale credit decisions, 206–208
  types of loans, 197–202
  loan commitments, 365–366
  loan concentration risk, 237–239
  loan portfolio and concentration risk, 237–238
  market value of capital and, 458–459
  measurement of, 208–209
  mortality rate derivation of, 221–223
  premium, 205, 206
  "prudent person approach," 239
  risk distribution, 130
  sovereign risk *vs.*, 306–307
  swaps and concerns of, 615–618
  systematic, 130
  term structure derivation of, 215–221
Credit risk exposure, 27, 130
Credit risk management, 627
Credit Risk+, 237
Credit risk-adjusted asset value of off-balance-sheet derivative instruments with netting under Basel III, 477–478
Credit risk-adjusted assets, 466
Credit risk-adjusted off-balance-sheet activities, 471–477
Credit risk-based capital ratio, 477–478
Credit risk-weighted assets, 466
Credit risk-weighted default risk models
  linear discriminant models, 213–215
  linear probability model, 212–215
  logit model, 212–213
Credit risk-weighted off-balance-sheet activities
  contingent guarantee contracts, 472–474
  market contracts or derivative instruments, 474–477
Credit risk-weighted on-balance-sheet assets under Basel II, 464–466
Credit scoring models, 211–215
Credit spread call option, **583**
Credit spread forward contract, 556
Credit Suisse, 285*t*, 482*t*
Credit Suisse First Boston (CSFB), 498
Credit swaps, 611–615
  insurance companies and, 598, 612
  pure, 614–615
  total return, 613–614
Credit Union Central of Canada (CUCC), 35
Credit unions, 2, **34**–36
  balance sheets, 35
  cooperative credit movement, 34
  guarantee system, 453
  industry performance, 36
  primary objective of, 34
  recent trends, 34–36
  regulation, 36
  size, structure and composition, 34–36
Credit, installment, 44
CreditMetrics, 237, 242, 251, 462
Creditor proofing, **108**
  life insurance, 108
CreditRisk+, 242, 251
Crime and fraud risk, 405–406
Criminal Code of Canada, 12, 406
Criminal rate, **47**
Crisis of confidence, 17
Cross-border issues, 15–17
Cross-border trading, 70
Cross-default clauses, 308
Cross-exchange trading, 278, 279
Cross-pillar, 2
Cross-pillar diversification, 27
Cross-pillar mergers, 494, 506
Cross-selling, **30**
Crown corporation, 52, 443, 454
Cryptographic techniques, 410
Cuba, debt repudiation, 307
Cummins, J.D., 397*n*
Cumulative default probability, **218**
Cumulative gap (CGAP), 152, 155, 156–157
Currency swaps, **608**–611
  exchange rate, 609–610
  fixed–fixed, 608–610
  fixed–floating, 610–611
  LIBOR, 610, 611
Current exposure, **475**–477
Customers, 62
Cyber-wallet, 399

Dai-ichi Life Insurance, 123*t*
Daily earnings at risk (DEAR), 329*n*
Daily price volatility, 329
Daily value at risk (daily VaR), 329. *See also* RiskMetrics
Daimler, 349
Daniel, F., 450*n*
Daylight overdrafts, 402–**403**
De novo branching, 508
De novo office, **508**
DealScan, 246
Debit card transactions, **387**
Debit cards, 398
Debt ceiling, 280
Debt holder's payoff from loans, 227
Debt moratoria, **302**
Debt repayment problems, 302
Debt repudiation, debt rescheduling *vs.*, 307–309
Debt rescheduling, debt repudiation *vs.*, 307–309
Debt service ratio (DSR), **312**
Debt-for-debt swaps, 318
Debt-for-equity swaps, 306
Deep discount bond. *See* Zero-coupon bond
Default option, 360
Default risk, **205**, 648–650
  bank/trustee, by, 648–650
  borrower specific factors, 209
  credit scoring models, 211–212
  defined, **205**
  financial theory, 215
  market-specific factors, 209
  measurement of, 208–209
  models for, 209–215

mortality rate approach, 221–223
mortgagees, by, 648
option models, 226–231
option models of, 226–231
qualitative models, 209–211
RAROC models, 223–226
recovery rate on defaulted debt, 217
swaps, on, 617
term structure of credit risk approach, 215–221
Default risk exposure, 27
Defined benefit plan, **96**
Defined contribution plan, **96**
Delegated monitor, **6**
Deleveraging, **17**, 18
Delivery *vs.* payment, 532
Delta method, 360*n*
Delta of option, **359**, 578
Demand deposit contract, **28**, 268, 418–420
Demutualization, 103
Denomination intermediation, 3, 9, 15
Department of Finance, 433, 444
Department of Insurance, 31
Department of Treasury (U.S.), 272
Deposit brokers, 444
Deposit drains, 268–269
interest rate fluctuations, 257–258
managing, 254–257
net deposit drains, 254
unexpected, 268–269
Deposit insurance, 18*t*, 268*n*, 269, 417, 422–423, 431–455, 459*n*, 638. *See also* Liability guarantee programs
Canadian experience, 432–434
central bank, *vs.*, 449
controlling risk-taking, 438–445
depositor discipline, 442–445
discount window *vs.*, 450
explicit, 436
FDIC and, 434–435
global systems, 448–449
guarantee programs and, 452–455
implicit premiums, 436
increased capital requirements, 442
insolvency, 434–435, 435–436
insurance premiums, 438–440
insured depositors, 443–444
option pricing model of, 439–440
panic prevention *vs.* moral hazard, 437
product diversification and, 504
regulatory discipline, 447–448
risk-based deposit insurance program, 440–441
risk-based premiums, 436
stockholder discipline, 438–442
stricter closure rules, 442
U.S. experience, 434–435
uninsured depositors, 444–445
Deposit notes, 425
Deposit rates, 8
Deposit-taking institutions. *See* Banks; Credit unions; Caisse populaires
Depositor discipline in controlling deposit insurance risk taking, 442–445
Depository fund insolvencies, causes of, 435–436
Depository institutions, 9, 10, 21–23
controlling risk taking, 438–445
decline in total share of, 14
liquidity and liability structures for Canada, 426–427
liquidity risk at, 253–269
Deposits
retail term, 421
wholesale fixed-term, 422–423
Depreciation, 279
Derivative contracts, 29, 358*t*, 360, 369–371, 528–531. *See also* Forwards; Futures contracts; Over-the-counter (OTC) derivatives; Swaps
accounting requirements, 531
credit derivatives, 371
credit risk, 371–372
forward foreign exchange transactions, 280, 282
loans sold, 374
notional value, 528, 531
off-the-balance-sheet credit risk-weighted asset, value of, 474–477
regulation of, 557–558
when-issued securities, 373–374
Derivative markets, growth of, 528
Derivative securities, credit risk, 371–373
Derivatives Best Practices Guideline B-7, 557
Derivatives trading, 88
Desjardins Financial Security Life Assurance, 112*t*
Desjardins Group Inc., 22, 23*t*, 34, 662
Desmarais family, 78
Deutsche Bank, 49, 57, 72, 73, 223, 285*t*, 329, 482*t*, 498, 499, 520, 630, 632
Deutsche Bank Securities, 57
Devaluation, 303
Dexia, 37
DeYoung, R., 396*n*, 397*n*
Digital default option, **584**
Dingle, J.F., 400, 433*n*
Direct branching, 520*n*
Direct brokerage fees, 83, 85
Direct financial markets, evolution of, 14
Direct quote, **277**
Direct securities markets, 14
Directed brokerage, 85
Directed brokerage fees, **85**
Directors and Officers (D&O) insurance, **123**
Disclosure, 13
Discount bonds, five-year maturity, 178–179
Discount brokers, 5, **58**
Discount effect, 671, 672
Discount rate, 8, 450
Discount window, **450**, 495
Discover Financial, 51
Discrete risks, 130
Discriminant analysis model, 213
Diseconomies of scale, **384**
Diseconomies of scope, **395**
Disintermediation, **26**
Diversification, **7**
credit risk, 130, 424
geographic, 508–525
loan portfolio, 7, 239–249
maturity intermediation, 7–8
product of, 499–507
product offerings, of, 499–507
Diversification of product offerings, 499–507
competition issues, 505–506
conflict of interest issues, 502–504, 507
deposit insurance issues, 504, 507
economy of scale and scope issues, 500–501
regulatory oversight issues, 504–505
safety and soundness issues, 500–501
Documentary letter of credit, 137. *See also* Commercial letter of credit
Dodd-Frank, 71, 111, 504
Dollar as international medium of exchange, 518
Dollar duration, **175**
Domestic banks, 627–628
Domestic credit analysis, 309
Domestic money supply growth, 314
Domestic systematically important banks (D-SIBs), 480
Dominion Bond Rating Service (DBRS), 195, 237, 670, 677
Dominion of Canada General, 112*t*
Dow Jones CDX, 612*n*, 615
Downsizing, **629**
Downstream, 501
Drawndown risk. *See* Takedown risk
Drexel Burnham Lambert, 428
Dubai, debt delay, 315
Dubai World, 38, 304
interest rate delay, 304
Dublin, offshore financial centre, 94
Due diligence, 503*n*, 518, 553, 639
DuPont analysis, 25
Duration, **164**
consol bond (perpetuities), of, 171
cost concerns, 186
coupon bonds, 176–177, 178–181
coupon interest, and, 173
defined, **165**
difficulties in applying, 186–189
dollar, 175
economic meaning of, 173–177
features of, 171–173
general formula for, 167–171
immunization and, 177–185
interest-bearing bonds, of, 168–170
interest elasticity, 174
interest rate risk and, 164–189
interest rate shocks, 183–185
large interest rate changes, 187–189
market-based model, 164
maturity, and, 172
modified, 175
negative, 671
price sensitivity of bond, 173–175
price–yield curve, 188
risk management, 165, 176–185
semiannual coupon bonds, 176–177
single security, risk management on, 178–181
small interest rate changes, 174
whole balance sheet, risk management on, 181–185
yield, and, 172–173
zero-coupon bond, of, 170–171
Duration gap, **181**, 184
financial institution, for, 181–185
hedging, 536
leverage adjusted, 183
negative, 577
Duration matching, 186–187
Duration model
difficulties in applying, 186–189
duration analysis, 164–167

Duration model—*Cont.*
incorporating convexity into, 193
Macauley, 167–168
Dynegy, 503

E*Trade, 5
E-commerce, assistance to small businesses entering into, 387
E-mail billing, 388
E-money, 398–399
Earned loss ratio, 118
Earnings, volatility of, 147, 210
East Europe, debt repayment problems in, 303
Economic freedom index, 315, 316
Economic rents, 512
Economical Insurance Group, 112*t*
Economies of scale, 3*t*, **5**, 6, **139**, **392**–394, 511*n*, 524
defined, **392**–394
diversification of product offerings, 501–502
empirical findings on costs, and implications for technology, 396–398
international expansion of financial institutions, 524
scope and, 501–502, 506–507
technology, and, 392–394
testing for, 396
transaction costs, 7
Economies of scope, **139**, **394**–395, 397–398, 511*n*
defined, **394**
diversification of product offerings, 501–502
testing for, 396
Economist Intelligence Unit (EIU), 309–310
Economist, The, 309
Ecuador, debt default, 320
EDF (expected default frequency) models, 227
Edge Act Corporation, **521**
Efficiency, 5
Efficient frontier, 241*n*
Efficient portfolio composition, 248
Eisenbeis, R.A., 213*n*
El Paso Electric, 625
Elasticity, interest, 174
Elections, 315
Electronic billing, 386
Electronic data interchange, 386
Electronic data software, 386
Electronic funds transfer, 386, 398–402
Electronic initiation of letters of credit, 386
Electronic lockbox, 386
Electronic trading networks, 386
Electronic trading securities firms, specialized, 58
Electronic transfer payment system, risks that arise in, 400–407
Emergency Lending Assistance (ELA), 269, 450
Emerging market countries, 302–303, 518
Emerging-market crisis of 1997–1998, 303
Emerging market funds, 90
Empire Life, 454
Encana, 81, 198–199
Encryption technology, 386
Endowment life policy, 106
Engert, W., 450*n*
Enron Corp., 70, 333, 359, 501, 502, 503
Enterprise wide risk management, 126
Entry regulation, 13
Environment Canada, 116
Equipment leasing, 44
Equipment loans, 48
Equitable Life, 103
Equitable Trust, 662
Equities, 333–334
bank, 28
discrepancy between market and book values of, 460–462
finance companies, for, 49–50
Equity capital, 55
Equity funds, **79**
Equity-linked contracts, 29, **362**
Estey Royal Commission, 433
Estey, W.Z., 433
Ethics
banks, 33
corporate governance scandals, 70
direct brokerage fees, 83, 85
due diligence, 95
forward pricing, 85
hedge funds, 95
late trading, 85
market timing, 85
Mutual Fund Dealers Association of Canada (MFDA), 70
mutual funds trading, 33
public trust, and, 15
securities fraud, 70–71
unapproved business, 70
Euro, 286
Eurobond markets, 169
Eurocurrency transaction, **517**
Eurodollar market, 517
Eurodollar transaction, **517**
Euromoney Country Risk (ECR) index, 309
Euromoney Index, 309
European Community-located banks, 448
European Community Second Banking Directive, 520
European debt crisis (2012), 305
European Monetary Union, 400
Event-driven strategy, **92**
Event risks. *See* Discrete risks
Exchange rate
currency swaps, 609–610
interest rate, 294–297
monetary policy, 277
Exchange-traded derivatives, 361–362, 474
Exchange-traded funds (ETFs), **564**
Exercise price, 360*n*, 565
Expectations theory of interest rates, 573*n*
Expected inflation, 293
Expected inflation rate, 293
Expected loss, 485
Expected return on loan, 205–206
Expected shortfall approach, 343–346
Expected shortfall of capital, 483
Expense risk, 118–119
Explicit deposit insurance, 436
Exponential weighting, 331*n*
Export Development Corporation (EDC), 553
Expropriation, 525
Extension risk, 645
External fraud, 485*t*
Externalities, negative, **10**
Externality effect, 366

Facebook, 388
Facility fee. *See* Up-front fee
Factoring, **44**
Fair premium, 587, 590
Fair value, **460**, 461
Fair Value Measurement, 460
Fannie Mae. *See* Federal National Mortgage Association (FNMA)
Farm Credit Canada (FCC), 9, 53
FBI, 406
FDIC Improvement Act (FDICIA) (1991) (U.S.), 404, 434, 445, 522
Federal Deposit Insurance Corporation (FDIC), 10, 43, 432, 434–435, 445–448, 504, 510, 617, 630, 632
Federal Deposit Insurance Corporation Improvement Act (FDICIA) (1991), 434
Federal funds rate, **148**
Federal Home Loan Mortgage Corporation (FHLMC), 359, 372, 598, 634, 635, 645, 663–664
Federal Housing Administration (FHA), 644
Federal Insurance Office (FIO) (U.S.), 111
Federal National Mortgage Association (FNMA), 359, 372, 598, 634, 635, 644–645, 663–664
Federal Open Market Committee (FOMC), 451
Federal Reserve, 51, 95, 148–149, 256, 260, 271, 305, 326, 327, 359*t*, 372, 375, 403–404, 450–452, 495, 497, 504, 505, 513*n*, 523, 611, 612, 617, 636
Fedwire system of, 402, 403, 404, 451
monetary policy, 414
Federal Reserve Act (U.S.), 403
Federal Reserve Bank of New York, 447
Federal Services Compensation Scheme, 433
Fedwire, 402, 403, 404, 451
Fee income, 632
Fees, 5
Fidelity Investments Canada, 79
Fiduciary accounts, stuffing, 502
Fifth Third Bank, 530*t*
Finance companies, 41–45
assets, 45–49
captive companies, 44
funding risk and cost, 417
historical perspective, 41–44
industry performance, 50–51
regulation, 51–52
size, structure, and composition of industry, 41–45
Financial Accounting Standards Board (FASB), 461, 462, 634
on derivatives, 531
Financial Consumer Agency of Canada (FCAC), 12–13, 32, 433
Financial crisis of 2007–2009, 293–294, 308, 494, 495, 612, 616, 636, 639, 675, 678
Financial distress, **625**
Financial environment as cause of depository fund, insolvencies, 435–436
Financial innovations, 2
Financial institutions (DIs), universal, 494
Financial institutions (FIs), 2–19, 181–185. *See also* Geographic expansion; specific type of financial institution
ability to diversify, 7
asset-transformation function, 5
bankruptcies, 268*n*
brokerage function, 5

consolidation in financial sector, 14, 16, 24–25, 103–104
corporate equity and debt, 4
credit allocation, 9
delegated monitor, 6
denomination intermediation, 9, 15
economic function, 3–4
four pillars, 2, 24, 465
global issues for, 17–19
government bailout of, 531
information producer, as, 6
level of fund flows, 4
liability and liquidity risk management in other, 426–427
liquidity and price risk, 6–7
maturity intermediation, 7–8
off-balance-sheet activities and solvency of, 358–361
opening cost risk of, 3
operational risk and insolvency of, 407
product diversification, 499–507
product expansion and financial conglomeration, 493–494, 508
public trust, 15
reasons for selling loans, 632–633
reduced transaction costs, 7, 16
regulation of, 9–13
specialness, 2–19
time intermediation, 9
transmission of monetary policy, 8
Financial institutions agent, 626
Financial Institutions and Deposit Insurance Amendment Act (Canada), 31
Financial intermediation. *See also* Risk(s), 126–142
Financial market flows, globalization of, 149–150
Financial Reporting and Assurance Standards Canada, 531
Financial services holding companies (FSHCs), 496
Financial services industry, 2, 40–54. *See also* Finance companies; Investment banks; Mutual funds; Securities firms
asset-based financing (ABF)/asset-based lending (ABL), 41
assets, 45–49
balance sheet, 45–50
bank–finance company consolidation, 50–51
business loans, 48–49
consumer loans, 45–47
criminal rate, 47
factoring, 44
global liquidity crisis, 40–41
liabilities and equity, 49–50
mortgages, 47–48
products sold by, 22*t*
segmentation in, 494–496
size, structure and composition, 41–45
subprime crisis, 200
Financial Services Modernization Act (1999) (FSMA) (U.S.), 15, 72, 494, 496, 518
Financial Services Oversight Council, 71
Financial Services Regulatory Overhaul Bill, 51–52
Financial Stability Board (FSB), 19, 308, 377, 436*n*, 442, 497, 558, 678
Financial Stability Oversight Council (FSOC) (U.S.), 111, 497
Financial statement analysis, return on equity (ROE), framework for, 39
Financial theory, 215
Financial Transactions and Reports Analysis Centre of Canada (FINTRAC), 32, **406**, 518
Financing gap, **261**–262
Financing requirements, 261–262
Fire insurance, 113
Fire-sale prices, 131, **253**, 260, 416
Firewalls, 501
Firm commitment offering, **500**
Firm-specific credit risk, **130**
First-to-default swap, 612*n*
Fisher equation, 293*n*
Fisher, Irving, 293*n*
Fitch Ratings, 371
Fixed–fixed currency swaps, 608–610
Fixed–floating currency swaps, 610–611
Fixed-income coupon bond, 129–130
Fixed-income securities, market risk of, 330–332
Fixed-rate loan, 198
Fixed term deposits, **28**
"Flash crash," 381
FleetBoston, 511
Float, **386**
Floating rate loans, 198
Floating rate mortgages, 153
Floors, **585**, 588–589
Flow of funds, 8
Fonds Desjardins, 79
Forced LVTS loans, 450
Ford Motor Canada/Credit Co./Corp., 41, 44, 48, 366, 615
Foreclosure, mortgages, 17
Foreign Bank Supervision Enhancement Act (FBSEA) (1991), 522–523
Foreign banks, 631–632
purchase and sale of loans, 635
subsidiaries of, 521
Foreign bonds, 308
Foreign currency, inflation rate, 293
Foreign currency trading, 284–286
Foreign exchange, 332–333
agent, financial institution as, 285
bid–ask spread, 286
carry trade strategy, 283
direct quote, 277
European Union, 286
forward foreign exchange, 281
forward transaction, 280
indirect quote, 278
interest rate parity theorem, 296–297
long position, 285
momentum trading, 283
net exposure, 281
profitability of trading, 285–286
purchasing power parity, 294–296
rates, 277–280
return on transactions, calculating, 287–289
short position, 285
speculative trades, 285
spot foreign exchange, 281
spot transactions, 278, 285
trading activities, 285
Foreign exchange rate volatility, FX exposure and, 283–284
Foreign exchange risk, 29, 30, 126, 132–134, 277–297, 334–337
asset and liability positions, 286–294
currency trading, 284–286
defined, **133**
exchange rate volatility, 283–284, 286–287
hedging, 133, 289–293, 546–553, 582–583
multicurrency foreign asset-liability positions, 293–294
open positions, 285
return and risk of foreign investments, 287–289
RiskMetrics model, 332–333
sources of exposure, 280–284
sources of risk exposure, 280–284
using options to hedge, 582–583
Foreign investments, return and risk of, 287–289
Fortis NV, 37, 402
Forward contracts, 360*t*, **369**, 528, 532–533, 546
hedging credit risks with, 553–557
hedging interest rate risk and, 534–535
hedging with, 291–293
Forward exchange rate, **291**
Forward foreign exchange, **281**
Forward foreign exchange transaction, **280**
Forward market for FX, 280
Forward priced, **85**
Forward purchases, 369–370
Forward rate, **219**
Forwards, 357, 360, 369–370, 531–533. *See also* Derivative contracts
credit forward contracts, 553–557
defined, 532
foreign exchange risk, hedging, 546
interest rate risk, hedging, 532–533
regulation of, 557–558
Four Pillars, **2**, 24
Franklin Templeton Investments, 79
Fraud, 70–71, 142, 405–406, 553
Fraudulent conveyances, **634**
Freddie Mac. *See* Federal Home Loan Mortgage Corporation
Frequency of loss, **116**–117
Front-end load, 82
Full-line firms, 56
Full-service industry, 2
Full service retail, **58**
Full-service retail securities firm, 58
Full-service securities firm, 4–5, 58
Fully amortized mortgages, 605, **649**
Fund, **75**. *See also* Mutual funds; Pension funds
defined, **75**
economies of scale, 75
risks, 75
Funds concentration, 386
Funds management, objective of, 58
Funds of funds, **77**, 90
FundSERV, 85
Future payments, duration and immunizing, 178–181
Futures, 360
Futures contracts, 360*t*, **370**, 528, **532**, 533–534, 547–550. *See also* Derivative contracts
catastrophe risk, and, 556–557
conversion factor, 540–541
defined, **532**
hedging credit risks with, 553–557

Futures contracts—*Cont.*
hedging interest rate risk with, 535–546
macrohedging, 535–546
marked to market, 533
microhedging, 536
regulation of, 557–558
Futures options, **575**
FX exposure, foreign exchange rate volatility and, 283–284

G-SIBs, 481
G20, 19
Gamma, 360*n*
Gamma of option, 360*n*
Gap analysis. *See* Repricing model
Gap ratio, 155
GE Aviation, 43
GE Capital. *See* General Electric Capital Corp.
GE Commercial Finance, 49, 50
General Electric Capital Corp. (GECC), 40–42, 43, 44, 45, 50, 51, 630
General Electric Credit Corporation (GECC), 45
General Motors Acceptance Corp. (GMAC), 43, 44
General Motors Corporation (GMC), 41, 43, 44, 51, 211, 244*n*, 508, 615
Generally accepted accounting principles (GAAP), 25, 104, 460, 525, 531, 670. *See also* Accounting standards and practices
Genworth MI Canada, 47
Geographic diversification, 33
cost and revenue synergies, 511–512
global and international, 516–523
international, advantages and disadvantages of expansion, 523–525
regulatory factors, 509–510
Geographic expansion
advantages of international expansion, 524
Canadian and U.S. banks abroad, 517–520
Canadian banks, domestic expansion of, 509
capital constraints, 519
disadvanatages of international expansion, 524–525
domestic expansions, 508
emerging market problems, 519
factors deterring expansion abroad, 519–520
firm-specific factors and, 515–516
foreign banks in North America, 520–523
global and international expansions, 517–520
insurance companies, 509
international competition, 520
merger guidelines, 512–515
political risk concerns, 518
regulatory factors, 509–510, 518–519
regulatory factors impacting, 509–510
technology and communications improvement, 519
U.S. bank expansions abroad, 517–523
U.S. commercial banks, 509–510
Germany
capital outflow, 293
electronic transactions, 398
real interest rates, 293
universal FI structure, 494
Germany, depository institutions in, 37
Gibson Greeting Cards, 359*t*
GICs, 153
Ginnie Mae. *See* Government National Mortgage Association
Glass-Steagall Act (1993) (U.S.), 72, 494, 522
Global capital flows, hedge funds and, 86
Global credit crisis, 33, 66, 72–73, 93, 100, 142, 149, 256–257, 635–636
Global Crossings, 70
Global deposit insurance systems, 448–449
Global market/financial crisis of 2008–2009, 252, 510, 531, 554
Global issues/globalization
depository institutions, for, 36–39
financial intermediaries, for, 17–19
financial markets, 286–287
insurance companies, for, 122–123
Global liquidity crisis, 40–41, 93, 122, 256, 429, 451, 635–636
Globally systematically important banks (G-SIBs), 458
Globefunds, 79
GMAC, 51
GMAC Financial Services, 41, 51
Goldman Sachs Group Inc., 51, 55, 56, 65*t*, 141, 381, 429, 482*t*, 495, 530*t*, 628, 635
Gonzalez, Albert, 409
Good bank–bad bank, 630–631
Government loan sales, 635
Government National Mortgage Association (GNMA) (Ginnie Mae), 644
Government of Canada bonds, 373. *See also* Treasury bills
Government Securities Distributors (GSDs), 373
Grameen Bank, 34
Grant Street National Bank, 630
Great Depression, 19
Great West Life/Lifeco/Assurance Company, 78–79, 103, 104, 112t, 507
Greece
debt crisis, 38, 304, 305, 520
debt delay, 315
debt rescheduling, 307
import ratio, 313
investment ratio, 313
Greek National Mortgage Bank (New York), 523
Greenspan, Alan, 611, 636
Gross interest return, 420
Group Credit Agricole, 482*t*
Group life insurance, 106
Groupe BPCE, 482*t*
Grupo Financiero Inverlat, 132, 517
Guarantee programs. *See* Liability guarantee programs
Guaranteed Investment Certificate (GIC), **417**, 421
Guaranteed programs. *See* Deposit insurance
Guarantees, 18*t*, 367
guarantee funds, provision of, 11
guarantee programs, 452–455
Guide to Intervention for Federal Financial Institutions, 447
Guideline B-6, 429
Gulf Bank, 37

H-statistic, 514
"Haircut," 307, 445–446
Haldane, Andrew, 486
Halliburton, 117
Hannaford Brothers, 409
Harris Bank, 509, 517
Hartford Financial Services, 104*t*
Heartland Payment Systems Inc., 409
Heavily indebted poor countries (HIPCs), 307–308
Hedge funds, 13*n*, **75**, 86–95, 273, 641
absence of regulatory oversight, 85
aggressive growth funds, 90
aggressive strategies, 90
CDOs, as purchasers, 675
defined, 75
distressed securities funds, 90
emerging market funds, 90
event-driven, 92
fees on, 94
funds of funds, 90
global credit and liquidity crisis, 93, 94
history, size, structure and composition of industry, 86–89
largest funds by asset, 92
macro funds, 90
management fees, 94
market neutral-arbitrage funds, 91
market neutral-hedging funds, 91
moderate risk funds, 90
multistrategy funds, 91
non-directional, 89
offshore funds, 94
opportunistic funds/strategy, 90–91, 92
performance benchmarks, 94
performance fees, 94
performance of, 94
regulation, 95
risk-avoidance funds, 91
short-selling funds, 90
special-situation funds, 91
trading abuses and scandals, 93–94
types of, 89–94
value funds, 91
vulture funds, 628
Hedge ratio, 548*n*, **550**, 551*n*, 552, 553
estimating, 550–553
Hedging, 134*n*, 536. *See also* Macrohedging; Microhedging
binomial model, 571–575
bond options using binomial model, with, 572–575
bond or bond portfolio, 571–575
catastrophe with call spread options, of, 584
credit risk, 553–557
duration gap, 536
effectiveness, 553
foreign exchange risk, 546–553, 582–583
forwards, with, 291–293, 532–533, 554–556
futures *vs.* options, 570
futures, with, 536–546, 575–577
interest rate risk, 534–546, 577–581
interest rate risk with futures contracts, of, 535–546
marked-to-market, 536
mechanics of, for bond or bond portfolio, 571–575
naive hedge, 534
off-balance sheet, 289
on-balance sheet, 289–291
return-risk trade-off, 537

risk and, 289–293
routine *vs.* selective, 536–537
short option, 541–544
use of options in, for foreign exchange risks, 582–583
Hedging effectiveness, **553**
Herfindahl-Hirschman Index (HHI), **513**–515
Heritage Foundation, 315
High-ratio mortgage, 646
High ratio residential mortgages, **47**
High-water mark, 94
High yield bonds, 216
Highland Capital Management, 629
Highly leveraged transaction (HLT) loans, 624–625, 633–634
Historic (back simulation) approach, 328, 337–341
Historic approach to market risk, 337–341
advantages, 340
concept, 337–338
method, 338–340
RiskMetrics *vs.*, 340–341
Historic simulation, 328
Hitachi Data Systems, 381
HLT loan sales, 624–625
Holding companies, **376**
Home Bank, 24, 432
Home banking, 388
Home Depot, 366
Home equity lines of credit (HELOCs), 677
Home equity loans, 48
Home Trust, 662
Homeowners multiple peril (MP) insurance, 113
Hong Kong, investment ratio, 318
Hong Kong Bank of Canada, 445
Hong Kong Monetary Authority, 37
Hong Kong, pegging of currency in, 303
Horizons BetaPro, 564
Horvath, R., 294*tn*
Household Financial, 118
Household International, 50
Housing and Economic Recovery Act of 2008 (U.S.), 664
Housing bubble, 196
Housing market, 16
Housing turnover, 653–655
HSBC Bank Canada/Finance/Holdings, 23, 23*t*, 44, 49, 50, 285*t*, 359*t*, 482*t*, 498*t*, 520, 530*t*
Hudson's Bay Company, 49
Hughes, J.P., 398*n*
Human error, 140
Humphrey, D.B., 396*n*
Hunter, W.C., 396*n*
Hurdle rate, 94
Hurricane Katrina (2005), 121, 194, 556
Hurricane Rita, 194
Hybrid funds, 79
Hypo Real Estate, 37

IBM, 63, 244, 366, 508
ICBC (China), 510
ICE Futures US, 370
Ice storm of 1998, 120
Iceland, financial crisis, 308
ICICI Bank, 37
Identity theft, **388***n*
IFRS. *See* International Financial Reporting Standards
IG Investment Management, 85
iGate, 383
IGM Financial Inc., 78, 79, 507
Iksil, Bruno, 140, 359*t*
Immunization, 177–185
assets against interest rate risk, of, 535
defined, 535
dynamic problem, as, 187
regulatory considerations and, 185–186
Implicit contract, **210**
Implicit premiums, **436**
Import ratio, 312, **313**
In-the-money call option, 360*n*
Income Tax Act (Canada), 107
Income Trust Co., 433
Incomplete information, 6
Index of Economic Freedom, 315
India, production technology, 319
Indirect quote, **278**
Individual life insurance, 105–106
Individual loans, 200
Industrial Alliance Insurance & Financial Services, 112*t*
Industrial and Commercial Bank of China Limited, 482*t*, 498*t*
Industrial life insurance, 106
Industrial loans, 197–199
IndyMac, 10, 131
Inflation, 8, 17
expected, 293
interest rate, 148, 294–297
loss risk, 117
purchasing power parity, 294–296
Inflation rate
expected, 293
foreign currency, 293
Information asymmetries, 631
Information asymmetry, 6
Information costs, 3, 6, 14
Information producer, financial institutions as, 6
Information Security Survey 2000, 409
Information services, 15
Information transfer, 503
ING Bank/Canada/Direct/Group, 119, 123, 320, 388, 482*t*, 520, 632
Initial public offerings (IPOs), **58**, **505**–506
Innovations in securitization, 670–674
Inside money, **12**
Inside trading, 13
Insolvencies, depository fund, 435–436
Insolvency, deposit insurance, 435–436
Insolvency risk, 140–141, 458–463
function of capital and, 458
Inspector General of Banks, 24, 444
Installment credit, 44
Institutional firms, **57**
Institutional Investor Index, 309–310
Institutional securities firms, 57–58
Institutional venture capital firm, **62**
Insurance
9/11 terrorist attacks, 121
accident and health, 107–108
actuarial liabilities, 108
actuarially priced insurance premium, 105
adverse selection, 105
banking industry, and, 24
demutualization, 103
globalization, 122–123
life insurance companies, 112
major groups of, 102
moral hazard, 105
mutual insurer *vs.* stock company, 103
online sales, 24
property and casualty (P&C), 110–121
Quebec ice storm (1998), 120
surrender value of policies, 110
terrorist attacks, 117
top ten countries, for insurance premiums written, 122
top ten global insurance companies, 123
underwriting cycle, 120–121
Insurance Bureau of Canada (IBC), 112, 116
Insurance companies, 2, 102–123, 629. *See also* Life insurance companies; Property-casualty insurance
failures of, 10
geographic expansion of, 509
liability and liquidity risk management in, 427–428
Insurance Companies Act (Canada), 77, 103, 110
Insurance risk in life insurance, 488
Insured depositor transfer, **445**
Insured depositors, 443–444
Intact Financial, 112*t*
Integrated firms, **56**
Integrated securities firms, 56–57
Interbank borrowing, **28**
Interbank funds, **423**–424
Interbank market, 24, 629
Intercontinental Exchange, 534*n*
Interest elasticity, **174**
Interest expense, 385
Interest income, 384–385
Interest rate caps, 370*n*
Interest rate options, 577
Interest rate parity, 295, 296–297
Interest rate parity theorem, 293–295, **296**–297
Interest rate restrictions, 12
Interest rate risk, 3, 8, 16, 19, 29, 30, **127**–129, 147–160, 164–189, 364–365, 482–483. *See also* Duration; Repricing model
Bank of Canada and, 148–150
book value of capital and, 460
central bank and, 148–150
defined, **127**
duration and, 164–189
forward contracts and hedging, 534–535
futures contacts, hedging with, 535–546
hedging, with futures contracts, 535–546
life insurance, in, 488
loan commitments, 363–366
market value of capital and, 460–461
market value risk, 128
matching maturities, 128–129
maturity model, 150, 163
mismatched maturities, 128–129
prepayment risk, 128*n*
refinancing risk, 127, 151
repricing model, 150–157
risk-based capital, and, 482–483
using options to hedge, on balance sheet, 577–582
weaknesses of repricing model, 158–160
whole balance sheet, hedging on, 577–581

Interest rate swaps, 73, **600**–608
  balance sheet of participants, 601
  expected cash flows, 602–603
  fixed-floating rate swap, 605–606
  inverse floater swap, 605
  LIBOR, 601, 603
  macrohedging, 605–607
  mortgage swap, 605
  off-market swap, 604
  payment flows, 618
  realized cash flows, 604
Interest rate(s)
  bank rate, 148
  base lending rate, 203
  comparison of Canadian and U.S. rates, 149
  deficit reduction, and, 148
  equilibrium rate, 148
  exchange rate, 294–297
  expectation theory of, 573*n*
  federal funds rate, 148
  global credit crisis and, 149
  inflation, 294–297
  inflation and, 148
  large changes in, and convexity, 187–189
  level and movement, 148–150, 211
  operating band, 148
  overnight rate, 8, 148
  prime lending rate, 203
  promised loan rate *vs.* expected return, 205–206
  purchasing power parity, 294–296
  qualitative default risk models, 211
  real rate of interest, 293
  shock, 183, 577
  term structure of, 163
  uncertainty, 586*n*
  volatility of, 150
Interest, accrued, 626
Interest-bearing bonds, duration of, 168–170
Interest-bearing checking accounts, 420
Intergenerational wealth transfers, 3, 9. *See also* Time intermediation
Intermediating, 4
Intermediation approach, 396
Internal fraud, 485*t*
Internal market risk models, 343
Internal ratings-based (IRB) approach, 458, 464
Internal Revenue Service (IRS), 406
International Association of Deposit Insurers (IADI), 433–434, 448, 449
International Bank for Reconstruction and Development (IBRD), 54
International Banking Act (1978) (IBA), 403, 522
International Centre for Settlement of Investment Disputes (ICSID), 54
International Development Association (IDA), 54
International Finance Corporation (IFC), 54
International Financial Reporting Standards (IFRS), 25, 104, 353, 371*n*, 460–461, 525, 531, 557, 670
International Index Company, 615
International loan, 307
International loan syndicates, 308
International Monetary Fund (IMF), 38, 135, 302–303, 303–305, 307–308, 519, 520
International Money Market (IMM), 533
International Organization of Securities Commissions (IOSCO), 95
International Swaps and Derivatives Association (ISDA), 305, 398, 615, 616
International technology transfer risk, 404
Internet, 380
Inverse floater swaps, 605
Invesco Trimark, 79
Investing, 58–60
Investment
  life insurance companies, 107
  property and casualty (P&C) insurance companies, 119–120
  research, 5
Investment advisor, **83**
Investment banking, **55**, 58–60, **494**
  initial public offerings, 58–59
  mergers and acquisitions, 64–65
  private placement, 60
  public offering, 58, 59
Investment banks, 56–65, **494**, 628, 632
  CDOs, as purchasers, 675
  forward market, 533
  functions of, 55, 58–65
  funding risk and cost, 417–418
  global issues, 72–73
  highly leveraged transaction (HLT) loans, 624–625, 628
  recent trends, 66–69
  regulation, 69–71
  size, structure, and composition of, 56–65
  subsidiaries of Canadian banks, 58
  ten largest mergers and acquisitions firms, 65*t*
Investment companies, rising share of, 14
Investment dealers, 2
Investment Dealers Association of Canada (IDA), 56–**57**, 85
Investment funds, 14–15
Investment Funds Institute of Canada, 76
Investment Industry Association of Canada (IIAC), 32, 56–**57**, 69, 77, 95, 487, 506
Investment Industry Regulatory Organization of Canada (IIROC), 70, 432
Investment Planning Counsel Group of Funds, 79
Investment portfolio, 129
Investment ratio (INVR), **313**
Investment research, 5
Investment yield/return risk, 119–120
Investor protection regulation, 13
Investor reaction to geographic expansion, 516
Investor returns from mutual fund ownership, 80–81
Investors Group, 79, 507
IO strips, 671
Ireland
  banking crisis, 444
  restructuring credit event, 305, 306
Italian Banca Nazionale del Lavoro, 522
Italy, investment ratio, 313
iTRADE, 58
iTraxx, 615
ITT Finance, 630

J.P. Morgan. *See* JPMorgan (JPM); JPMorgan Chase
J.P. Morgan Emerging Market Bond Index, 322
Jackson, W.E., III, 516
Jagtiani, J.A., 516
Japan
  bad loans, 303
  banking industry, 37
  deposit insurance, 448
  European Union, 448*n*
Japan Post Bank, 498*t*
Japan Post Holdings, 123*t*
Japan, depository institutions in, 37
Jayanti, S.V., 232*n*
Jayhawk Acceptance Corporation, 47
John Hancock, 104, 507
JPMorgan (JPM), 23, 55, 65*t*, 140, 286, 320, 322, 328*n*, 329, 359*t*, 495, 510, 625
JPMorgan Chase, 23, 33, 56, 65*t*, 72, 136, 141, 273, 285*t*, 286, 308, 325, 326, 329, 359*t*, 369, 372, 376, 429, 447, 482*t*, 495, 498, 502, 503, 504, 512, 517, 530*t*, 598, 625, 627, 629, 673
Junk bonds, **195**, 216, 625
Justice, U.S. Department of, 513

Kansas City Board of Trade, 534*n*
Kerviel, Jerome, 325, 359*t*, 382
Keybank National Association, 530*t*
KMV Corporation, 227
KMV option model, 227
KMV portfolio manager model, 242
Knight Capital Group Inc., 381
KPMG, 409
Kryzanowski, L., 433*n*, 448*n*
Kuehne, B.J., 222*n*

Labour, 380
  back-office support, 3
Laeven, L., 514
Lang, W., 398
Large bank internal models, BIS regulations and, 351–353
Large exposure limits, **239**
Large Value Transfer System (LVTS), 9, 139, 256, 375, 400, 416, 433, 480, 509
Late trading, **33**, **85**
Laurentian Bank Canada, 23*t*
Law of one price, 296*n*
Least-cost resolution (LCR) model, 445–446
Leeson, Nicholas, 359
Legacy Loans Program, 632
Lehman Brothers, 18, 51, 56, 136, 141, 253, 272, 306, 308, 326, 358, 372, 402, 429, 436, 451–452, 495, 598, 599, 600, 616, 676
Lemons problem, 631
Lender of last resort, **269**, 449–450
  Bank of Canada, 449–450
Les Cooperants, 453, 454
Letters of credit (LCs), 29, **31**, 137, 321, 358, 367–369, 385, 386, 425
  commercial, 367–368
  electronic initiation of, 386
  standby, 368–369, 618
Leverage, 17, 88, 210, 287*n*, 463, 487
  banks, 27–28
Leverage mutual funds, 629
Leverage ratio, 481–482
Leveraged buyouts (LBOs), 210, 624
Levy, C.B., 398*n*
Liabilities, 153–154
  banks, for, 28
  credit unions, for, 35
  finance companies, for, 49–50

life insurance companies, for, 108–110
off-balance-sheet (OBS), 28–30, 358
Liability and liquidity management, 413–429
central banks and regulators, 429
choice of liability structure, 418–425
composition of liquid asset portfolio, 415
funding risk and cost, 417–418
liability management, 417–418
liquid asset management, 414–415
Liability and liquidity risk management
insurance companies, in, 427–428
securities firms, in, 428
Liability guarantee programs. *See also* Deposit insurance
Assuris, 453–454
Canadian Investor Protection Fund, 454–455
credit unions and caisse populaires, 453
Property and Casualty Insurance Compensation Corporation, 454
Quebec Deposit Insurance Board, 452
Liability insurance, 113–114. *See also* Property and casualty (P&C) insurance
Liability management, 417–418
Liability structure, choice of, 418–425
demand deposits, 418–420
interest-bearing checking accounts, 420
repurchase agreements, 424
Liability withdrawal, 3
Liability-side liquidity risk, 253–257
LIBOR, **24**, 73, 198, **203**, 252, 302, 360, 365, 366, 382–383, 424, 585, 674
currency swaps, 610, 611
interest rate swaps, 601, 603
swaps, 605, 606
U.S. dollar, 616, 617
Liens, **48**
Life insurance, 103–111, 487–488
actuarial liabilities, 108
annuity premiums, 107
classes of, 105–106
credit, 106
credit life, 106
creditor proofing, 108
endowment, 106
group, 106
individual, 105–106
industrial, 106
industrial life, 106
other investments, 107
registered retirement income funds, 107
registered retirement savings plans, 107
surrender values of policies, 110
term, 105
types of, 105–106
universal, 106
variable, 106
variable universal, 106
whole, 106
Life insurance companies, 103–111, 453–454
accident and health insurance, 107–108
assets, 108
balance sheet, 108–110
balance sheet and recent trends, 108–110
capital requirements for, 487–488
function of, 103
global consolidation, 103–104
investment, 107
liabilities, 108–110
liquidity risk, 269–270, 427–428
regulation, 110–111
size, structure, and composition of industry, 103–108
top ten North American companies, 104
Limited purpose finance companies, 16
Lincoln National Corporation, 104*t*
Linear discriminant models, 213–215
Linear probability, 312*n*
Linear probability model, 212
Linearity, 188
Liquid asset management, 414–415
Liquid asset portfolio, composition of, 415
Liquid assets
management of, 414–415
non-liquid assets, *vs.*, 415
portfolio, 415
return-risk trade off for, 416–417
Liquid assets ratio, **415**
Liquid assets, return-risk trade-off for, 416
Liquidity, **4**, 6–7, 12, 203*n*, 259–261, 487, 639, 643
liability structure for Canadian DTIs, and, 426–427
management, 417–418
market risk, 326
price risk and, 3, 6–7
purchased liquidity management, 255–256
sources of, 259
stored liquidity management, 256–257
Liquidity and liability structures for U.S. depository institutions, 426–427
Liquidity costs, 4
Liquidity coverage ratio (LCR), 262–264, 429
Liquidity crisis, 136, 413
Liquidity index, **260**–261
Liquidity injection, 18*t*
Liquidity planning, 262–266
Liquidity risk, 3, 16, 19, 126, **131**–132, 252–273, 413, 633, 642. *See also* Global liquidity crisis
asset side, 256–257
bank runs, 269
causes of, 253
defined, 252
deposit-taking institutions, at, 253–269
depository institutions, at, 253–269
insurance companies, 269–270
investment funds, 271–273
liability side, 253–257
market rates, 256
mutual funds, 271–273
off-balance-sheet (OBS) loans, 253
property-casualty insurers and, 270–271
seasonality, 254*n*
unexpected deposit drains, 268–269
Liquidity risk exposure, 259–267
financing gap, 261–262
financing requirement, 261–262
liquidity index, 260–261
liquidity planning, 262–266
net liquidity statement, 259
net stable funding ratio (NSFR), 262
peer group ratio comparisons, 259–260
Liquidity services, 16
Liquidity shortages, 371
Lloyd's, 112*t*
Lloyds Bank International, 262
Lloyds Banking Group, 482*t*
Load fund, **82**
Loan allocation deviation, 247–248
Loan assignment, 626
Loan commitment agreement, **363**
Loan commitments, 29, **198**–199, 358*t*, 360–361, 363–364, 472
aggregate funding risk, 366
agreement, 363
back-end fee, 363
credit risk, 365–366
drawndown risk, 365
interest rate risk, 364–365
promised return, 364
up-front fee, 363
Loan companies, 30–31, 432
Loan concentration risk
concentration limits, 238–239
migration analysis, 237–238
models of, 237
Loan concentrations, 246
Loan drawdowns, 259
Loan loss provisions. *See* Provisions for loan losses
Loan loss ratio-based models, 248–249
Loan loss ratios, 248
Loan loss reserves, **302**
Loan migration matrix, **237**
Loan origination fee, 203
Loan portfolio diversification
KMV Portfolio Manager model, 242–245
loan concentration risk, 237–239
loan loss ratio-based models, 248–249
loan volume-related models, 245–248
modern portfolio theory (MPT) and, 239–241
portfolio diversification models, 239–241
regulatory models, 249
Loan Pricing Corporation, 627, 635
Loan rates, 8
Loan sale(s), 306, 623, 625
access to commercial paper market, 633
asset brokerage and loan trading, 634
bad debt loans, 627
bank loan sales market, 623–626
buyers, 628–630
Canadian financial institutions, 627–628
correspondent banking, 627
covenants, 625
credit ratings, 635
customer relations effect, 633
defined, 623–624
double monitoring costs, 625
factors affecting loan sales growth, 633–635
factors deterring growth in future, 633–635
factors encouraging growth in future, 633–635
foreign bank subsidiaries, 629
global credit and liquidity crisis and, 634–636
good bank–bad bank structure, 630–631
highly leveraged transactions (HLT) loans, 624–625, 628, 633–634
insurance companies and pension funds, 629
investment banks, 628
legal concerns, 633–634
monitoring costs, 625, 626
reasons for selling loans, 632–633
recourse, 623, 625
risks, 626

Loan sale(s)—*Cont.*
secondary market loan syndicators, 627
sellers, 630–632
traditional short-term market, 624
trends in, 627–632
types of contracts, 625–626
U.S. banks, 629
Loan sales contracts, 625–626
buyers, 628–630
sellers, 630–632
Loan shark, **47**
Loan syndication, 16
Loan trading, 634
Loan volume-based models, 245–248
Loan(s). *See also* Credit risk; Mortgage(s); Sovereign risk
bank, 6, 49
business, 48–49, 197–199, 206–208
calculating return on, 202–206
call, 202, 428
commercial, 197–199
commercial and industrial, 494, 517
consumer, 44, 45–47, 153, 200
credit cards, 200–202
credit decisions, 206–208
expected return, 205–206
fees and charges, 203
fixed rate, 198
floating rate, 198
governments, to, 202
home equity, 48, 199
international, 308
investment dealers, to, 202
less developed countries (LDC), to, 195
nonperforming, 195, 322
originating, 16
overnight, 425
payday loans, 47
performing, 322
personal lines of credit, 200
policy, 108
public corporations, to, 202
reasons for selling, 632–633
return on, 202–204
revolving, 200
secured call, 202
secured, unsecured, 198
short-term, 153, 624
spot, **198**–199
syndicated loan, 197
third-party, 503
types of, 197–202
warehousing, 16
Loan-for-bond restructuring programs, 320
Loans sold, 358*t*, 374
Logit model, 212, 312*n*
London Interbank Offer Rate (LIBOR), **203**
London International Financial Futures and Options Exchange (LIFFE), 534*n*
London Life Insurance Company, 79, 103, 112*t*, 507
"London Whale," 140, 325, 359*t*
Long position, foreign exchange, 285
Long-tail loss, **117**
Long-Term Capital Management (LTCM), 13*n*, 88, 92–93, 359*t*
Long-term mortgage loans, 8
Long-term notes, 425
Loss absorbency requirement, 481
Loss adjustment expenses (LAE), 118
Loss control, 407
Loss distribution approach, 481
Loss financing, 407
Loss given default, 217*n*
Loss insulation, 407
Loss prevention, 407
Loss ratio, **118**, 556
Loss risk, 75, 116–117, 118–119
actuarial predictability, 116–117
combined ratio, 118
expense risk, 118–119
investment yield/return risk, 119–120
long tail *vs.* short tail, 117
loss ratio, 118
measuring, 118
product inflation *vs.* social inflation, 117
property *vs.* liability, 116
severity *vs.* frequency, 116–117
Loyalty programs, 388
Luxembourg, offshore financial centre, 94
LVTS participants, **256**

M1, 8
M1+, 8*n*
M1+ (gross), 8
M1, M2, and M3, 8
M2, 8
M2 (gross), 8*n*
M3, 8
M3 (gross), 8*n*
Macauley duration model, 167–168
Macey, J.R., 437*n*
MacKay Commission Report, 506
Mackenzie Financial, 79, 507
Maclean, D., 450*n*
Macrohedging, 535–**536**, 577–581
basis risk, 544–546
changes in net worth as interest rate rise, 538
defined, **536**
futures, with, 537–544
interest rate risk using put option, 577
put options, 577–581
risk-minimizing futures position, 538–541
short hedge, with, 541–544
swaps with, 605–607
Macy's, 625
Maison Placements Canada Inc., 57
Major money center banks, 630
Malfeasance, 13
Man Group, 92
Management expense ratio (MER), **83**
Management fees, **83**
hedge funds, 94
mutual funds, 82
Management information, market risk measurement, and, 328
Manufacturers Life Insurance Co., 103, 112*t*
Manulife, 454, 461, 496, 629
Manulife Asset Management, 78
ManuLife Financial Corporation, 95, 104, 110, 121, 362, 507
Manulife Investment, 78, 79
ManuLife Securities International Ltd., 95
Maple covered bonds, **670**
Marginal default probability, **218**
Marginal mortality rate (MMR), **221**
Marginal risk contribution, 244*n*
Maritime Life, 454
Mark-to-market basis, 458
Marked-to-market, **80**, **533**, 544*n*
Marked-to-market basis, **80**, 599
Marked-to-market requirement, 461
Market benchmarks, 246
Market conduct regulator, **32**
Market crisis of 2007–2008, 268*n*
Market data, using, to measure risk, 316–318
Market failure, 10
Market making, 62–63
Market meltdown of 2008, 494
Market neutral-arbitrage funds, 91
Market neutral-hedging funds, 91
Market rates, liquidity risk, 256
Market risk, 126, 135–136, 325–353, 482–483
benefits of measurement, 328
BIS standardized framework, 346–350
defined, **325**
expected shortfall, 343–346
fixed-income securities, of, 330–332
historic (back simulation) approach, 337–341
large bank internal models, 351–353
liquidity, 326
measurement of, 328
Monte Carlo simulation approach, 341–343
regulatory models for, 346–350
risk-based capital, and, 482–483
risk level limits, 328
RiskMetrics model, 329–336
systematic market risk, *vs.*, 325*n*
Market-specific factors, default risk, 209
Market timing, **33**, **85**
Market to book ratio, **461**
Market value, **458**–459, 463
capital, of, 458–459
defined, **458**
discrepancy between book value and, 460–462
off-the-book activities, 360–361
swaps, futures and forwards, 360
Market value accounting, **164**, 458, 461, 634
arguments against, 462–463
Market value effects, 158
Market value exposure, 147
Market value risk, 128
Marking-to-market, **164**, 462, 543*n*, 544*n*
Marking-to-market process, 539*n*
Markit, 615
MasterCard, 200
Matching maturities, 128–129
Maturity buckets, 150, 336
Maturity intermediation, 3, 7–8
Maturity model, 163
Maturity transformation, 14–15
Maturity, duration and, 172
McCulley, Paul, 496*n*
McFadden Act (1927), 509–510, 522
McNulty, J.E., 397*n*
Medium-term notes, 425
Megamergers, **510**
Meiji Yasuda Life Insurance, 123*t*
Mellon Bank, 630
Merger bid premiums, **515**
Merger premium, 515

Mergers
bank–bank, 495, 510
bank–insurance company, 103, 391–392, 496, 506–507
consolidation in financial sector, 14, 16, 24–25, 103–104
guidelines, 512–515
Mergers and acquisitions, 55, 64–65
advising on, 55
Canadian bank investment firms acquisitions, 56*t*
financing, 624
geographic expansion by, 511–512
guidelines for acceptability, 512–515
investment banks, 55, 64–65
megamergers, 510
ten largest merger and acquisition firms, 65*t*
Merkel, Angela, 39
Merrill Lynch, 56, 72, 85, 326, 358, 372, 429, 495, 598, 627, 632, 662, 673
Merton, R.C., 226, 228*n*, 571*n*
Message centres, 388
Mester, L.J., 397*n*, 398*n*
Metlife Inc./Metropolitan Life, 103, 104*t*, 110, 123*t*, 391
Mexico
currency devaluation, 303
debt moratorium, 302
economy in, 320
sovereign bonds, 322
Mexico, economy in, 302–303
Mezzanine capital, **61**
MF Global Canada Co., 454
Microhedging, 535–**536**, 578*n*, 579*n*
futures, with, 562
options, with, 579, 597
Midland Bank, 359*t*
Migration analysis, **237**
Milbourn, T.T., 397*n*
Miller, G.P., 437*n*
Miller, S.M., 397*n*
Minimum capital test (MCT), **488**, 489*t*
Minimum continuing capital and surplus requirements (MCCSR), **487**, 489*t*
Minimum-risk portfolio, **241**, 537*n*
Mitsubishi UFJ FG, 72, 482*t*, 498*t*
Mizuho FG, 482*t*
Mobile banking, 388
Modern Portfolio Theory (MPT)
diversification and, loan portfolio, 239–241
KMV Portfolio Manager model, 245–248
loan portfolio diversification and, 240–241
loan volume-based models, 245–248
standard deviation of trading portfolio, 335*n*
Modified duration (MD), **175**, 330–332
bonds, 577–578
credit forward, 555
options, 578
put option, 556
Molson, 505
Molyneux, P., 398
Momentum trading, **283**
Monetary policy, 8, 12, 148–150, 366
aim of, 8
exchange rates, 277
Federal Reserve, 414
liability and liquidity management and, 415
regulation, 12
transmission, 8
updates, 150
Money laundering, 32, 71, 405–406, 518, 522
Money market, **676**
Money market mutual funds (MMMFs), 6–7, 16, 75, 79, 272, 273, 422–423, 452, 496, 497
Money Mart, 47
Monitoring, 6, 7, 11
Monitoring costs, 4
Monoline insurers, **123**
Monte Carlo simulation approach, 328, 341–343
Montréal Accord, 676
Montréal Exchange, 70, 370, 487, 533, 534*n*, 557, 564, 575
Moody's Analytics, 237
Moody's Analytics model, 227, 230–231
Moody's Analytics Portfolio Manager, 242–245
Moody's Investors Service, 38, 195, 237, 305, 371, 486
Moon, C.-G., 398*n*
Moral hazard, 11*n*, **105**, **436**–437, 449, 629. *See also* Risk-taking
Morbidity risk, **488**
Morgan Stanley, 51, 56, 72, 285*t*, 359*t*, 429, 482*t*, 495, 530*t*
Morningstar, 79
Mortality rate, **221**–223
Mortality rate derivation, of default risk, 221–223
Mortality risk, **488**
Mortgage-backed (covered) bond (MBB), 639, **668**–670
Mortgage-backed securities (MBSs), 470, 616, 638, 643
Mortgage bonds, 210
Mortgage broker, 47
Mortgage loans, 199
Mortgage pass-through strips, 670–673
Mortgage swap, 605
Mortgage(s), 47–48. *See also* Asset-backed securities; Subprime crisis
Alt-A, 675
amortization, 199
assumable, 653
credit risk, 199–200, 200–202
default, 17
foreclosure, 17, 199
fully amortized, 605, 649
high-ratio, 646
high-ratio residential, 47
home equity loans, 48, 199
investment securities, as, 110
liens, 48
low-ratio, 646
prepayment risk, 128*n*, 650–653
rates, 199
residential, 2, 676, 677
securitized mortgage assets, 48
subprime, 16–17
variable rate mortgages (VRMs), 199
Mortgagees, default risk by, 648
Motor vehicle loans, 44, 47. *See also* Automobile loans
leases and, 45–47
MS&AD Insurance Group Holdings, 123*t*
MSCI, 328*n*
Mukherjee, K., 397*n*
Multibank holding companies (MBHC), 376, **510**
Multicurrency foreign asset-liability positions, 293–294
Multilateral Investment Guarantee Croup (MIGA), 54
Multiperiod debt instrument, probability of, default on, 218–221
Multistrategy funds, 91
Multiyear restructuring agreements (MYRAs), **306**
Munich Re Group, 123*t*, 612
Munich Reinsurance, 113
Munich Reinsurance Co., 112*t*, 117, 118
Mutual Fund Dealers Association of Canada (MFDA), 33, 70, 85, 507
Mutual funds, 2, 76–86, 271–273
annual reports, 80
back-end loads, 82
balanced funds, 79
bank loan funds, 629
bond funds, 79
clone funds, 75
closed-end investment companies, 81
costs of, 82–84
different types, 79
direct brokerage fees, 83, 85
equity funds, 79
foreign content in RRSPs, 77, 133
forward pricing, 85
fund operating expenses, 82–84
funds of funds, 77
global issues, 86
growth of, 14–15, 79, 86–87
historical trends, 76–79
income trusts, 81
investor returns, 80–81
investor returns from ownership, 80–81
late trading, 85
liquidity risk, 271–273
load *vs*. no-load funds, 82
management expense ratio (MER), 83
management fee, 82–83
marked-to-market, 80
market timing, 85
money market, 75
net asset value (NAV), 80
net asset value per share (NAVPS), 80
objectives of, 80
open-end, 80, 81
performance data, 83
prospectus, 80
real estate investment trusts (REITs), 81
regulation, 76–79, 84–86
RRSP-eligible, 77
size, structure and composition of industry, 76–96
top investment management companies, 78–79
trading at a discount, 81
trading at a premium, 81
trailer fee, 83
types of, 79
Mutual of Canada, 103
Mutual organizations, **34**

Naive hedge, **534**
Naked options, **570**
Narter, B., 515*n*
National Bank Financial, 56
National Bank of Canada, 22, 23*t*, 25*t*, 56, 260, 281, 286*t*, 337, 353*t*, 480, 529*t*
National Bank Securities, 78
National Credit Union Administration, 617
National debt ceiling, 280
National Hockey League, 41
National Housing Act (NHA), 53, 471
National Housing Act mortgage-back securities pools, 643–644, 661–663
National treatment, **522**
Nationalization, 525
NatWest Bank, 359*t*
Negative duration, **671**
Negative externalities, **10**
Negotiable instruments, **422**
Net asset value (NAV), **80**, **271**, 272
Net asset value per share (NAVPS), **80**
Net deposit drains, **254**
Net exposure, 282
Net interest income (NII), **33**, 147, 151, 155, 156, 157
Net interest income exposure, 151
Net interest margin (NIM), 33, **384**
Net liquidity statement, 259
Net long in a currency, **282**
Net premiums written, **113**
Net regulatory burden, **10**, 11, 13
Net short in foreign currency, **282**
Net stable funding ratio (NSFR), 264–266, 429
Net worth, **147**, 287*n*, **458**. *See also* Capital; Capital (net worth) ratio
Net write offs, 197*n*
Netting, 617–618
Netting by novation, 618
New York Board of Trade (NYBOT), 370
New York Futures Exchange (NYFE), 370
New York Life, 104
New York State Department of Insurance, 505
New York Stock Exchange (NYSE), 63, 284, 462, 664
New Zealand earthquake (2011), 121, 122, 270
Ng, A., 516
Nguyen, T., 516
NHA mortgage-backed securities, 643–644, 662–663
Nigeria, domestic money supply growth, 317
Nikkei Index, 370
Nikko Asset Management, 72
NikkoCiti Trust and Banking Corp., 72
Nippon Life Insurance, 123*t*
NKSJ Holdings, 123*t*
No arbitrage, **219**, 296, 297
No-load fund, **82**
No recourse, 374
Nomura Trust & Banking Co., 72
Non-deposit-taking institutions. *See* Finance companies; Insurance companies; Investment banks; Mutual funds; Securities firms
Non-performing loans, **195**
Nonbank banks, 496
Nonbank financial service firms and commerce, 496–498
Nondirectional strategy, **89**
Nonfinancial corporations, 630
Noninterest expenses, 385
Nonperforming loans, **195**, 322
Nordes, 482*t*
Nortel Networks, 99, 194
North American Free trade Agreement (NAFTA), 519
North American Investment Grade Index, 615
North American Life Insurance, 103
North Korea, debt repudiation, 307
Northcott, C.A., 514*n*
Northern Rock, 131, 268*n*, 429
Northland Bank of Canada, 24, 140, 141, 262, 432, 444
Northwest Mutual, 104
Nothern Trust Co., 530*t*
Notice deposits, **28**
Notional amount, **361**
Notional value, **360**, **528**, 590
  swap contract, 607*n*
NYSE Euronext, 534*n*

OECD Country Risk Classification (CRC), 471
Off-balance-sheet (OBS) activities, 463, 639
  banks, 28–30, 358–360, 361–363
  cash flows from, 159–160
  commercial letter of credit, 137, 367–368
  credit guarantees, 3
  credit risk-weighted activities, 471–477
  derivative contracts, 369–371
  fees, 357
  financial intermediaries (FI) solvency and, 358–361
  forward contracts/purchases, 369–370, 373–374
  growth in, 528
  loan commitments, 363–366
  loans sold, 374
  regulation, 361
  returns and risks of, 361–363
  risk reduction, and, 377
  role of, in reducing risk, 377
  standby letter of credit, 137, 368–369
  types of, 363–374
  valuation of contingent assets and liabilities, 358–360
Off-balance-sheet (OBS) assets, **29**
Off-balance-sheet (OBS) credit risk-weighted asset value
  contingent guarantee contracts, of, 472–474
  counterparty credit risk, 474
  credit-equivalent amount, 471
  current exposure, 475
  market contracts or derivatives, of, 474–477
  potential exposure, 475
Off-balance-sheet (OBS) hedging, 289, 291
Off-balance-sheet (OBS) liabilities, **29**
Off-balance-sheet (OBS) loans, liquidity risk, 253
Off-balance-sheet (OBS) risks, 126, **137**–138, 357–377
  affiliate risk, 376
  contingent liability, 357–358, 361
  defined, 137
  derivative securities, 373–374
  letters of credit, 369
  loan commitments, 364–366
  returns and, 361–363
  role of, in reducing risk, 377
  settlement risk, 375–376
  when-issued securities, 373–374
Off-market swap, 604
Office of Consumer Affairs (OCA), 388*n*
Office of the Comptroller of the Currency. *See* Comptroller of the Currency
Office of the Inspector General of Banks, 31
Office of the Superintendent of Financial Institutions (OFSI, 24, 26, 27, 31, 32, 33, 99, 103, 110–111, 121, 147, 237, 239, 245–246, 249, 302, 327, 328, 353, 357, 361, 383, 406, 433, 499, 507, 557, 629
  banking industry, 23, 24, 28, 30, 31, 32, 36, 506
  capital rules, 327
  countering money laundering activities, 405–406, 518
  credit risks, 237–239
  federally regulated financial institutions, 504
  futures and forward regulation, 557–558
  gap analysis, 147
  life insurance industry, 103, 110
  loan concentration limits, 238
  pension funds, 99
  property and casualty (P&C) insurance, 121
  reducing moral hazard-induced risk-taking, 447–448
  reporting buckets, 150*n*
  securities industry, 506
Office of Thrift Supervision, 505, 617
Offshore financial centres, 94
OmbudService for Life & Health Insurance (OLHI), 111
On-balance-sheet credit risk-weighted assets under Basel II, 464–466
On-balance-sheet foreign assets, 281
On-balance-sheet hedging, 289–291
One-bank holding company (OBHC), 376
One-period debt instrument, probability of default on, 216–218
OneWest Bank Group, 131
Online banking, **33**, 388
Ontario Securities Commission (OSC), 33, 77, 84
Open-end bank loan mutual funds, 629
Open-end mutual funds, 14–15, **80**, **271**
Open interest, **575**
Open market operations, 8
Open positions, **285**
Operating band, **148**
Operating cost risks, 3, 19
Operating ratio, **120**
Operating risk, 3
Operational Research Inc., 408
Operational risk, 126, 139–140, 381, 382. *See also* Technology risk
  capital requirement for, 483–486
  consumer protection, and, 409
  defined, 140
  financial institution insolvency and, 407, 408–409
  loss event types, 485
  management of, 407–408
  regulatory issues, 408–409
  risk-based capital and, 483–486
  sources of, 382–383, 383–384, 408
Opportunistic funds, 90

Option adjusted spread (OAS), 175*n*, **658**, 659, 660–661
defined, **658**
models, 658–661
Option contracts, 370
Option models of default risk, 226–231
borrower's payoff on loans, 227
debt holder's payoff on loans, 228
default risk premiums, calculation of, 228–230
KMV option model, 227
Option pricing model, 230–231
Option pricing model of deposit insurance, **439**
Option to borrow, 360
Option-adjusted spread models, 658
Options, **370**. *See also* Call options; Derivative contracts; Put options
basic features of, 563–567
bond, 572–575
calculating fair value of, 571–575
call, 564–567
call spread, 583–584
catastrophe risk, hedging, 584–585
credit risk, hedging, 583–584
defined, 360*t*, **370**, **563**
delta of, 359–360, 578
economic reasons for not writing, 568–569
foreign exchange risk, hedging, 582–583
futures *vs.* options hedging, 570
futures, on, 575
gamma of, 360*n*
hedging credit risk with, 583–584
hedging, mechanics of, 571–575
interest rate, 577
naked, 570
put, 566–567
trading process for, 564
using, 577–582
vega of, 360*n*
writing *vs.* buying, 568–570
Options Clearing Corporation, 564
Ordinary life insurance, 105–106
Organization for Economic Cooperation and Development (OECD), 519
Originate-and-distribute model, 16, 638
Originate-and-hold model, 16
Origination fee, 203
OSFI. *See* Office of the Superintendent of Financial Institutions
Out-of-the-money call option, 360*n*
Outside money, **12**
Over-the counter swap market, growth of, 617
Over-the-counter (OTC) derivatives, 361, 369–370, 474, 597
derivative-related credit risk, 617
derivative-related market risk, 617
fair value, 617
fair value option, 617
Over-the-counter derivatives market, 281
Over-the-Counter Derivatives Market Act (U.S.), 617
Overaggregation, 158
Overhedging, 542*n*
Overnight index swap (OIS), 616
Overnight loans, 425
Overnight rate, 8, **148**, 415, 424, 548*n*
Overseas Direct Investment Control Act (1964), 517
Owen, Martin, 359
Palia, D., 516*n*
Pan-Canadian ABCP Committee Restructuring Plan, 676
Panic prevention, moral hazard *vs.*, 437
Papouis, Kyriacos, 359*t*
Paradox of credit, 240*n*
Parent-subsidiary company structure, **376**
Participations, **625**
Pass-through securities, 643–663
cash flows from investors, 654–655
default risk, 648–650
Federal Home Loan Mortgage Corporation (FHLMC), 645
Federal National Mortgage Association (FNMA), 644–645
gap exposure, 647
Government National Mortgage Association (GNMA), 644
government-sponsored securitization of residential mortgages, 643–645
incentives and mechanics of, 645–650
prepayment models, 655–661
prepayment risk on, 650–653
Pass-through strips, 670–673
IO strips, 671
PO strips, 672–673
Patriot Act (U.S.), 70, 71
Paulson, Henry, 373
Payday loans, **47**
Payment Clearing and Settlement Act (Canada), 400
Payment of bills, via telephone, 388
Payment services, 3, 9, 14
Payment systems
clearing of non-cash payments, 399–400
e-money, 400
evolution of, 398–402
Payments system, technology and evolution of, 398–407
Payoff method of closure, 442
Peer group ratio comparisons, 259–260
Pension Benefits Standards Act (1985), 99
Pension funds, 30, **75**, 95–99, 629
asset mix, 97
balance sheet, 97–99
CDOs, as purchasers, 675
clone funds, 96
defined, 75
defined benefit plan, 96
defined contribution plan, 96
foreign content, 97, 133
global credit crisis and, 100
global issues, 100
investment income, 99
liquidity risk, 271–273
recent trends, 97–99
regulation, 99
retirement savings, 95
size, composition and structure, 95–96
sponsored plans, 95
top funds in Canada, 96
top money managers, 98
trusteed, 95
vested assets/vesting, 96
People's Insurance Co. of China, 123*t*
Peoples Bank of China, 448
Peregrine Investment Holding Ltd., 303
Performance evaluation, market risk measurement, 328
Performance fees, 94
Performing loans, 322
Permissible activities, 557
Perpetuities, 171
Personal identification numbers, 405
Personal lines of credit, **200**
Personal loan plans, **200**
Personal loans. *See* Consumer loans
Pierce, Jim, 260
Plain vanilla fixed–floating rate swap, 602
PNC Bank/Financial, 393, 530*t*
PO strips, **672–673**
Point-of-sale debit cards, 387–388
Poison pill provisions, 64
Poldauf, P., 294*tn*
Policy loans, **108**
Policy reserves, 116
Political risk, 315, 518
Portfolio aggregation, 334–336
Portfolio effect, 336
Portfolio manager, 242
Portfolio Manager model. *See* KMV Portfolio Manager model
Portfolio risk, 7. *See also* Loan portfolio diversification
diversification, 486
sovereign risk evaluation, 316–318
Portfolio theory, loan volume-based models, 245–248
Portugal
investment ratio, 313
restructuring credit event, 305
Portus Alternative Asset Management, 95
Position trading, 63
Potential exposure, **475**
Power Corporation, 78
Power Financial, 507
Preauthorized debits/credits, 388
Premiums earned, **118**
Prepayment effect, **649**, 671
Prepayment models, 655–661
burn-out factor, 657
option-adjusted spread models, 658–661
proprietary empirical models, 656–657
PSA model, 655–656
weighted average life (WAL), 655
Prepayment risk, 128*n*, 650–653
collateralized mortgage obligation (CMO), 666–667
housing turnover, 653–655
NHA mortgage-backed securities pools, 661–663
pass-through securities, 653–655
refinancing, 653
Prepayment risk on pass-through securities, 650–653
President's Choice Financial, 393
Price risk, 3, 3*t*, **4**, 6–7, 314
Price-risk protection, 16
Primary credit, 451
Primary Dealer Credit Facility (PDCF), 451
Primary insurers, **112**
Primary securities, **5**
Prime lending rate, **203**
Prime rate, 365
Principal Financial Group Inc., 104*t*

Principal transactions, 62
Private banking, 64
Private costs, 10
Private equity, **61**
Private pension funds, 107
Private pension plans. *See* Registered retirement savings plans (RRSPs)
Private placement, **60**
Probit model, 312*n*
Proceeds of Crime (Money Laundering) and Terrorist Financing Act, 71, 406, 518
Procter & Gamble (P&G), 359*t*
Product diversification, 499–507
  benefit, 501
  offerings, of, 499–507
  risks of segmentation, 494–496
  segmentation in U.S. financial services industry, 494–495
Product inflation, 117
Product offerings, diversification of, 499–507
Product segmentation, risks of, 494–496
Production approach, 396
Profitability, technological innovation and, 383–385
Program trading, 63, 88
Project finance loans, **627**
Property and casualty (P&C) insurance, 102, 111–121, 454
  automobile insurance, 113
  balance sheet, 114–121, 115*t*
  capital requirements, 488
  claims ratio, 114, 118
  directors and officers (D&O) insurance, 123
  global liquidity crisis, 122
  leading companies, 112
  liability insurance (other than auto), 113–114
  liquidity risk, 270–271
  loss risk, 116–117
  major lines of, 113–114
  net premiums written (NPW), 113
  property insurance, 113
  recent trends, 120–121
  regulation, 121
  reinsurance, 112, 117–118
  size, structure and composition of industry, 112–114
  underwriting risk, 114–121
Property and Casualty Insurance Compensation Corporation (PACICC), 32, 121, 432, 454
Property insurance. *See* Property and casualty (P&C) insurance
Prospectus, mutual fund, 80
Provision for loan losses, **33**, 302
"Prudent person" approach/investment strategy, 283*n*, 454, 629
Prudential Assurance, 111
Prudential Financial Inc., 104*t*, 123*t*
Prudential regulator, **32**
Public offer price, 505
Public offering, 58, 59
Public Securities Association (PSA), 655
model, 655–656
Public trust, weakening of, 15
Public–private investment funds (PPIFs), 632
Pull-to-par, **572**
Pulley, L.B., 396*n*
Purchase and assumption resolutions, 446*n*
Purchase and resale agreements (PRAs), 424*n*, 450
Purchased liquidity management, 255–**256**
Purchasing power parity (PPP), 294, **295**, 296, 296*n*
theorem, 314*n*
Pure arbitrage, 63
Pure credit swaps, **614**–615
Put option, 370, 566–567, 577–581, 578*n*, 579*n*, 584. *See also* Option(s)
  credit forward, 556

QR codes, 388
Qualitative default risk models, 209–211
  borrower-specific factors, 210
  business cycle, 210–211
  collateral, 210
  interest rates, 211
  leverage, 210
  market-specific factors, 210–211
  reputation of borrower, 210
  volatility of earnings, 210
Qualitative models, 209–211
Quantity risk, 314
Quebec Deposit Insurance Board, 432, 452
Quebec ice storm (1998), 120
Quebec Pension Plan, 95

R class, **668**
RAROC (risk-adjusted return on capital) models, 223–226
  duration method, 223–226
  loan default rates approach, 226
Rate sensitivity, **150**–157
  assets, of, 153–154, 155–156
  equal changes in rates on RSAs and RSLs, 154–155
  liabilities (RSLs), of, 153–154, 155–156
  rate-sensitive asset (RSAs), 153
  unequal changes in rates on RSAs and RSLs, 155–157
Ray, S.C., 397*n*
RBC Capital Markets, 55, 281
RBC Dominion Securities, 4, 56
RBC Financial Group, 25*t*
RBC Global Asset Management, 77–78
RBS. *See* Royal Bank of Scotland
RBS Citizens National Association, 530*t*
Real estate investment trust, **81**
Real estate loans, 199
Real interest rate, **293**
Recourse, **374**, 472, **623**, 625, 632
Reduced transaction costs, 7, 16
Refinancing, 653
Refinancing risk, **127**, **151**
Regions Bank, 530*t*
Registered Education Savings Plans (RESPs), **75**
Registered retirement income funds (RRIFs), **107**
Registered retirement savings plans (RRSPs), **75**, 77, 95, **107**
Regulation
  banks, 31–32
  Canadian regulatory system for financial institutions, 433
  consumer protection, 13
  credit allocation, 12
  credit unions, 36
  entry, 13
  foreign banks in United States, 521–523
  futures and forwards, 557–558
  geographic expansion of financial institutions, 509–510
  hedge funds, 95
  investor protection, 13
  life insurance companies, 121
  market failure, 10
  market risk measurement, 327
  monetary policy, 12
  mutual funds, 76–77, 84–86
  off-balance-sheet activities, 361
  pension funds, 99
  safety and soundness, 11
  securities firms, 69–71
  securities industry, 69–70
  specialness, 9–13
Regulation F, 404
Regulation J, 403
Regulators, futures and forward policies of, 557–558
Regulatory Analysis of Hedge Funds, 95
Regulatory barriers, 2, 501
Regulatory burden, 10
Regulatory capital, **56**
Regulatory considerations, immunization and, 185–186
Regulatory factors impacting geographic expansion, 509–510
Regulatory forbearance, **433*n***
Regulatory models, 249, 346–350
Regulatory oversight, 504–505
Regulatory risk, 406
Reinsurance, **112**, 117–118
Reinvestment income, 180*n*
Reinvestment risk, **128**, **151**
Repricing gap, 147, **150**, 157
Repricing model, 150–157
  cash flows from off-balance-sheet activities, 159–160
  equal changes in rates on RSAs and RSLs, 154–155
  market value effects, 158
  maturity buckets, 150–151
  OSFI, 147
  overaggregation, 158
  rate-sensitive assets (RSAs), 153, 154–155
  rate-sensitive liabilities (RSLs), 153–154
  runoffs, 159
  unequal changes in rates on RSAs and RSLs, 155–157
  weaknesses of, 158–160
Repudiation, **307**
Repurchase agreements (RPs), 66, **424**, 642
Reputational risk, **381**
Required stable funding (RSF), 265
Rescheduling, **306**, 307, 318–319
Research, investment, 5
Reserve Bank of New Zealand, 415
Reserve Primary Fund, 272
Reserve requirements, 11, 12, 203, 415, 632, 638
Residential mortgages, 2, 676, 677

Residential real estate, 9
ResMor Trust Company, 44
Resource allocation, market risk measurement and, 327
"Restructuring credit event," 305
Retail credit decisions, 206
Retail financial services, impact of technology on, 387–388
Retail firms, **58**
Retail GICs, 421
Retail introducer, **58**
Retail securities firms, 58
Retail term deposits and GICs, 421–422
Return on assets (ROA), 24–25, 202
Return on assets approach (loan), 202–204
Return on equity (ROE), 24–25, 39
Return–risk trade-offs, 16, 416, 641
Revco, 634
Revenue synergies, 511–512
Revenues, 524
Reverse repurchase agreements (reverse repos), **66**
Revolutions, 315
Revolvers, **49**
Revolving loan, **200**, 201
Rhoades, S.A., 511
Riegle-Neal Interstate Branching and Efficiency Act (1994), 509, 510, 516, 629
Risk adjusted return on capital (RAROC) models, 223–226
Risk arbitrage, 63
Risk diversification, international expansion, 523–525
Risk Management Association (RMA), 211
Risk(s), 2. *See also* under specific type of risk
  affiliate, 376
  aggregate funding, 366
  asset, 463, 487–489
  asset-side liquidity, 252–253, 257–259
  bank run liquidity, 268–269
  basis, 365, 536, 544–546, 581
  catastrophe, 556–557, 584–585
  competition, 407
  contingent credit, 369
  counterparty credit, 474, 592
  credit, 126, 129–130
  decoupling of, 639
  expense, 118–119
  financial institutions, 2
  foreign exchange, 132–134
  hedging and, 289–293
  identified by Canadian financial institutions, 126
  insolvency, 126, 140–141
  interaction of, 141–142
  interest rate, 127–129, 147–160
  letters of credit, 369
  liquidity, 126, 131–132
  loss, 116–117
  market, 126, 135–136
  market value, 128
  off-balance-sheet, 126, 137–138
  operational, 126, 139–140, 381, 382, 407–408, 483–486
  political, 315, 518
  price, 4, 6–7, 314
  refinancing, 127, 150
  regulatory, 406
  settlement, 375
  strategic, 381
  technology, 64, 126, 139–140, 407
  using market data to measure, 316
Risk-avoidance funds, 91
Risk-based capital, 478
  interest rate risk and, 482–483
  market risk and, 482–483
  operational risk and, 483–486
Risk-based capital ratios, 463–487
  calculating, 471–478
  Common equity Tier 1 (CET1), 466, 468
  credit risk-weighted off-balance-sheet activities, 471–477
  criticisms of, 486–487
  netting under Basel III, 477–478
  overall risk-based capital positions, 478–480
  Tier 1 (core) capital ratio, 466
  total credit risk-weighted assets under Basel III, 477
  total risk-based capital ratio, 467
Risk-based capital requirements, 373, 616
Risk-based deposit insurance program, **440**
Risk-based premiums, deposit insurance, 436
Risk-based premiums, implementing, 440–441
Risk-increasing behaviour, 11*n*
Risk-minimizing futures position, 538–541
Risk-taking, controlling, 438–445
RiskMetrics model, 328, 328*n*, 329–336
  criticisms of value at risk (VaR) models, 340
  equities, 333–334
  fixed-income securities, 330–332
  foreign exchange, 332–333
  historic (back simulation) model *vs.*, 340–341
  historic approach, *vs.*, 340–341
  portfolio aggregation, 334–336
RJR Nabisco, 634
Roberts, G.S., 433*n*, 448*n*
Rogue trader, 325
Roland, K.P., 397*n*
Routine hedging, **536**
Royal Bank of Canada, 22, 23*t*, 41, 44, 56, 140, 260, 281, 286*t*, 337, 353*t*, 381, 383, 393, 407, 425, 480, 498, 510, 512, 516, 517, 529*t*, 628, 632, 670
Royal Bank of Scotland, 38, 73, 285*t*, 381, 482*t*, 627, 632
Royal Canadian Mounted Police, 406
RRSP-eligible funds, **77**
Runoffs, **159**
Rusnak, John, 359*t*
Russia
  debt default, 303, 320
  economy in, 303

SAC Capital Partners, 94
Safety and soundness regulation, 10–12
Sale and repurchase agreements (SRAs), 424*n*, 472
Sales finance institutions, **44**
Salesperson's stake, 502
Salomon Brothers, 320–321, 374*n*
Santander, 482*t*
Santos, M., 516*n*
Sarbanes-Oxley Act (2002), 70, 85
SAREB, 630
Sarkozy, Nicolas, 39
Saskatchewan Trust Co., 432
Saunders, A., 217*n*, 223*n*, 227*n*, 240*n*, 437*n*
Saver withdrawal risk, 19
Savings account, 421
Savings and loan (S&L) crisis, 24
Schaefer, S., 571*n*
Schaefer-Schwartz model, 571*n*
Schedule B bank, 262
Schedule I banks, **23**
Schedule II banks, **23**, 262
Schedule III banks, **23**
Scholes, M., 226
Schwartz, E.S., 571*n*
Scotia Asset Management, 77
Scotia Capital, 55, 56, 88
Scotiabank, 25*t*, 58, 123, 159–160, 341, 353*t*, 510, 516, 517, 520, 529*t*, 628. *See also* Bank of Nova Scotia
Scotiabank Inverlat, 132, 517
Sears, 200
Sears Canada, 673, 677
Sears Canada Bank, 673, 677
Seasonal credit, 451
Secondary credit, 451
Secondary market trading, 4
Secondary markets, 316–318
Secondary reserves, **415**
Secondary securities, **5**
Secured call loans, 202
Secured loan, **198**
Securities
  asset valuation, 461
  book value of capital, 460–462
Securities and Exchange Commission (SEC), 85, 462, 495, 557, 617, 634
  regulation of mutual funds by, 85–86
  regulation of securities industries, in, 69–71
Securities firms, 56–65
  activities, areas of, 58–65
  back-office and other service functions, 65
  balance sheets, 66–69
  capital requirements for, 487
  cash management and banking services, 64
  clearance and settlement services, 65
  custody and escrow services, 65
  discount brokers, 58
  full-service, 4
  full-service retail, 58
  global issues, 72–73
  institutional, 57–58
  integrated, 56, 65
  investing, 58
  investment banking, 58–60
  liability and risk management, 428
  market-making, 62–63
  mergers and acquisitions, 55, 64–65
  purely electronic firms, 64
  recent trends, 66–69
  regulation, 69–71
  research and advisory services, 65
  retail introducer firms, 58
  retail securities firms, 58
  size, structure, and composition of, 56–65
  trading, 58, 63
  venture capital firms, 61–62

Securities industry
  2007–2008 global credit crisis, 66, 72–73
  broker-dealers, 55
  commission income, 66
  common equity financings (2001–2012), 59*t*
  consolidation, 56
  employment by sector, 57*t*
  fraud, 70–71
  global issues, 72–73
  investment banks, 55
  operating profits and revenues (1987–2012), 66–68
  recent trends, 66–69
  size, structure and composition, 56–65
  stock market crash of 1987, 66
  top underwriters, 60*t*
  total operating revenue by source (1987–2012), 67
Securities Industry and Financial Markets Association (SIFMA), 655
Securities Industry Association, 655
Securities services, 55
Securities trading, 55
Securities underwritings, 60, 500
Securitization, 17, **26**, 48, 376, 643–663
  assets, of, 638, 673–674
  Canadian market for asset-backed securities, 638
  collateralized mortgage obligation (CMO), 664–668
  convergence in regulations, 678
  credit card receivables, 638–639, 673–674
  credit cards, 677
  Federal Home Loan Mortgage Corporation (FHLMC), 645
  Federal National Mortgage Association (FNMA), 644–645
  Government National Mortgage Association (GNMA) (Ginnie Mae), 644
  incentives and mechanics of, 645–650
  innovations in, 670–674
  limits of, 674–676
  mortgage-backed (covered) bond (MBB), 668–670
  mortgages, of, 47–48, 677
  pass-through security, 643–663
  prepayment models/risk on, 650–653, 655–661
  regulation, 677, 678
  trade receivables, 677
Securitized mortgage assets, 47–48
Security Home Mortgage Corporation, 433
Security National Insurance, 112*t*
Security risks, 409
SEDAR. *See* System for Electronic Document Analysis and Retrieval
Segmentation in United States financial services industry, 494–495
Segregated funds, **108**
Selective hedging, **537**
Self-liquidating entity, 631
Self-regulatory organizations (SROs), **32**, 70, 75, 85, 487, 506, 533, 564
Semiannual coupon, 176–177
Sensitivity analysis, 147
September 11, 2001, terrorist attacks, 71, 381, 451
Service functions, back-office and other, 65
Settlement, 278*n*, **375**
Settlement risk, 358*t*, **375**, 400–404
Severity of loss, **116**–117
Shadow bank, 16, 497, 640
Shadow banking, **496**, 678
Shadow banking system, 496*n*
Shadow vehicles, 371
Shaffer, S., 514*n*
Sharpe ratio, 91, 241*n*
Shell banks, 518
Shoppers Trust Co., 433
Short hedge, 541–544
Short position, foreign exchange, 285
Short selling, 88
Short-selling funds, 90
Short-term commercial borrowing, 638
Short-term debt instruments, 640
Short-term liability contracts, 8
Short-term loans, 153, 624
Shortages of funds, 2
Simulations, 147
Singapore Exchange Limited, 534*n*
Singapore futures exchange (SIMEX), 370
Smart cards, 388
SMFG, 635
Smithson, C.W., 408*n*
"Sniffer" programs, 409
Social benefit, 11*n*
Social cost, 11*n*
Social inflation, 117
Social media, 388
Social welfare benefits, 10
Social welfare costs, 10
Social welfare effects, 431
Société Générale, 325, 359*t*, 382, 482*t*
"Sophisticated" investors, 13*n*
"Sophisticated" lenders, 642
South Korea, debt rescheduling, 307
Southeast Asia, devaluations of currency in, 303
Sovereign bonds, 321–322
Sovereign debt, 280, 321–322
  bank loans, 322
  country risk analysis, 321–322
  credit rating, 471
  secondary market for, 318–320
  sovereign bonds, 321–322
  structure of market for, 319–320
Sovereign debt crisis, 18
Sovereign Life, 453, 454
Sovereign risk, 126, **134**–135, **302**–323
  country evaluation, 309–323
  credit risk *vs.*, 306–307
  debt repudiation, 307
  debt repudiation *vs.* debt rescheduling, 307–309
  debt rescheduling, 306, 307, 318–319
  defined, **134**, **302**
  emerging market countries, 302–303
  less-developed countries, 302
Sovereign risk evaluation
  credit quality, 307
  debt service ratio (DSR), 312, 317–318
  domestic money supply growth (MG), 314, 317
  Economist Intelligence Unit (EIU), 309–310
  Euromoney Index, 309
  import ratio (IR), 312–313
  Institutional Investor Index, 309–310
  investment ratio (INVR), 313
  measurement of key variables, 315–321
  outside evaluation models, 309–311
  political risk factors, 315–316
  population groups, 315
  portfolio framework, 316–318
  problems with statistical models, 315–321
  sovereign risk quality, 306–307
  statistical models, 312
  variance of export revenue (VAREX), 314, 318
Sovereign risk event, 306
Sovereign risk quality, 307
Sovereign wealth funds, **100**
Spain
  banking crisis of 2012, 630
  debt rescheduling, 305, 306
Special investment vehicles (SIVs), 371
Special Purpose Entities (SPEs), **376**, 501, 639
Special situation funds, 91
Special-purpose vehicles (SPVs), 16, 371, 639, 640
Specialness, 2–19
  changing dynamics of, 14–16
  future trends, 14–15
  global issues, 17–19
  regulation, and, 9–13
  trends in Canada, 14–15
Speculative trades, 285
Spot contracts, 531–**532**
Spot currency trades, 285
Spot foreign exchange, **281**
Spot foreign exchange transaction, **278**
Spot loan, **198**–199
Spot market for FX, **282**
Spot market risk, 297
Spread effect, **156**
Spread risk, 365
Spreads, **24**, 641
Standard & Poor's (S&P) Rating Service, 39, 195, 237, 271, 280, 371, 470, 486
Standard & Poor's (S&P) 500 Index, 76, 322
Standard Chartered Bank, 482, 530*t*
Standard Industrial Classification (SIC) codes, 246
Standard Life Investment Inc., 99
Standard Loan Co., 432
Standard Loan/Standard Trust Co., 432–433
Standard portfolio theory, 335*n*
Standard Trust Co., 432–433
Standardized Approach, 466
Standardized approach, to capital requirement, 483–486
Standby letters of credit, **137**, **367**, 368–369, 472, 618
Standing Liquidity Facility (SLF), 425, 450
State Farm Insurance Companies/Mutual Auto, 112*t*, 123*t*
State Street Bank, 482*t*, 530*t*
State Street Global Advisors Ltd., 99
Statistical CRA models, problems with, 315–321
Statistical models, 312
Statistics Canada, 148
Stelco, 49
Stochastic process, 571*n*
Stock market crash (October 19, 1987), 63
Stockbroker, 63
Stockholder discipline in controlling depository, institution risk taking, 438–442
Store-value cards, 388
Stored liquidity management, **256**–257

Strategic risk, 381
Stress testing, 147
Stressed VaR, 351
Strike price, 565
Strikes, 315
Structural models. *See* Option models of default risk
Structured finance, 44
Structured investment vehicle (SIV), 16, 639, 640, 641
Stuffing fiduciary accounts, 502
Subprime crisis, 17–19, 200, 322, 435–436, 644–645
Subprime lender, **47**
Subprime mortgage crisis, 372, 642
Subprime mortgage market, 273
Subprime mortgages, 16–17, 325–326
Subsidiary banks, 510, 521
Subsidiary, foreign bank, 521
Sumitomo Mitsui FG, 482*t*
Sumitomo Mitsui Financial Group, 72
Sun Life Assurance/Insurance/Financial, 78, 103, 104, 104*t*, 110, 112*t*, 132, 448*n*, 454, 496
Sun Trust Bank, 530*t*
Suncor Energy Inc., 564
Suppliers of funds,/Surplus funds, 2
Surrender values of policies, **110**, **270**
Surveillance. *See* Monitoring
Swap buyer, **601**
Swap contract, 370
Swap dealer, 599, 600
Swap seller, **601**
Swaps, 305, 360, **370**, **598**–618. *See also* Derivative contracts
  credit, 598–599, 611–615
  credit risk concerns and, 615–618
  currency, 608–611
  default risk, 617, 618
  interest rate, 600–608
  inverse floater, 605
  LIBOR, 605, 606
  macrohedging with, 605–607
  markets, 599–600
  netting and, 617–618
  pure credit, 614–615
  total return, 613–614
  transaction costs, 599
Swaptions, 599*n*
SWIFT, 402
Swiss National Bank, 37, 283–284
Swiss RE, 113
Switzerland
  currency appreciation, 283–284
  universal bank, 494
Syndicated loan, **197**
Synergy. *See* Economies of scope
Synthetic CDOs, 674, 675
System for Electronic Document Analysis and Retrieval (SEDAR), 77, 78, 79, 86
Systematic/systemic risks, 15, 513*n*
credit risk, **130**
  emerging-market loans, 316–317
  equity position, 333–334
  exemption, 445
  loan loss risk, **248**
  market risk, 325*n*

T-bills. *See* Treasury bills
Tablet banking, 388
Tail the hedge, **548**
Takedown risk, 365
TARGET (Trans-European Automated Real-Time Gross-Settlement Express Transfer), 400
Target overnight rate, 8, 148, 415
Tax avoidance, 406
Tax-free savings account (TFSA), **422**, 443
Taxation, liability and liquidity management, 415
TD Asset Management, 77
TD Asset Management Group, 99
TD Bank, 23*t*, 56, 140, 286*t*, 444, 461, 463, 480, 498, 499, 509, 529*t*
TD Bank Financial Group, 25*t*
TD Bank National Association, 530*t*
TD Canada Trust, 23, 23*t*, 30, 56, 132, 140, 353*t*, 480, 498, 505, 509, 512, 516, 529*t*
TD Securities, 56, 281
TD Waterhouse, 30
Teaser rates, 16
Technological innovation, 380, 383–385
Technology, 2, 380–410
  advanced integration, 388–390
  back-office support, 3
  costs, 392–396
  data backup/data recovery, 390
  defined, **383**
  diseconomies of scale, 394
  economies of scale, 392–394
  effect of, on revenues and costs, 390–396
  electronic methods of payment, 398–402
  empirical findings on cost economies of scale and scope, 397–398
  evolution of payments system and, 398–407
  impact of wholesale financial services on, 385–387
  impact of, on retail financial services, 387–388
  interest expense, and, 385
  interest income, and, 384–385
  message centres, 389
  non-interest expenses, amd, 385
  operational risks and, 139–140
  other income, and, 385
  profitability, and, 383–385
  retail financial services, 387–388
  revenues, and, 391–392
  security issues, 389–390
  wholesale services, 385–387
Technology risk, 64, 126, 139–140, 407
  back-office system failures, 380–381
  crime and fraud risk, 405–406
  defined, 139
  failure of third party technology provider, 408
  international technology transfer risk, 404
  regulatory issues, 408–409
  settlement risk, 400–404
TED spread, 423
Temporary Guarantee Program, 272–273
Temporary Liquidity Guarantee Program (TLGP), 43
Tennyson, S., 397*n*
"Tequila crisis," 303
Term deposit, 153
  fixed-term, 421
  retail, 421
  wholesale fixed, 422–423
Term life insurance, 105
Term life policy, 105
Term loan facility (TLF), 450
Term loans, **49**
Term structure, 163
  derivation of credit risk, 217
  derivation of default risk, 215–221, 219*n*
  multi-period debt instrument, on, 218–221
  one-period debt instrument, on, 216–218
Term structure of interest rates, 163
Terrorism, 32, 71, 405–406, 518
Terrorist attacks, 117, 121, 403, 404
Thailand, currency devaluation, 303
Thakor, A.V., 397*n*
The Economist, 309
The Wall Street Journal Online, 539
Thin markets, 131
Third-party loans, 503
Third-party warehouse lenders, 639*n*
Tie-ins, 503
Tied selling, 496, 507
Tier 1 capital, 327, 466, 468
Tier 1 capital ratio, 359
Tier 2 Capital, 466, 468
Tier I capital, 466, 467
Tier II capital, 466
Time deposits, 153
Time intermediation, 9
Timme, S.B., 396*n*
TMX Group, 533
Tokio Marine Holdings, 123*t*
Tombstone advertisement, 59
Too-big-to-fail (TBTF) banks, **444**, 445, 480, 481, 642
Too-big-to-fail guarantee, 504
Toronto Stock Exchange (TSE/TSX), 2
Toronto-Dominion (TD) Bank. *See* TD Bank/TD Canada Trust
Total credit risk-weighted assets, under Basel III, 477
Total return swaps, **613**–614
Total risk-based capital ratio, **467**
Tourous, W.N., 571*n*
Toxic assets, 136, 322
Toxic credit derivatives, 30
Toxic mortgages, 30, 503
Toxic waste, 674
Toyota, 211
Trading, 63–64, 81
  costs of, 5
Trading friction, 627
Trading portfolio, 130
Trading securities, 460–462
Trailer fee, **83**
Tranche 1 payments, 402
Tranche 2 payments, 402
Trans-European Automated Real-Time Gross Settlement Express Transfer (TARGET), 400
Transaction account deposit contracts, 6–7
Transaction cost services, 14
Transaction costs, 3, 4, 7
Transaction needs, 12
Transmission of monetary policy/supply, 3, 3*t*, 8
Transparency International, 316

Travelers Group, 103, 391, 494, 495, 496
Treasury bills, 14–15, 153, 373, 414, 422
Treasury bonds, 414
Treasury management software, 386
Treasury notes, 153, 414
Treasury strips and zero-coupon corporate bonds, 216
Trimark Floating Rate Income Fund, 629
Troubled Assets Relief Program (TARP), 18, 373, 424, 429
Trust and Loans Companies Act, 30, 77
Trust companies, 2, 24, 30, 432–433
Trust services, 30
Trusteed pension funds, **95**
TSX Group Inc., 70, 487, 533
Turkey
  debt default, 303
  debt obligations, 303
Tyco, 70

U.S. Federal funds, **423**
U.S. Federal Reserve. *See* Federal Reserve
U.S. Government agencies, 632
U.S. National Bank Association, 530*t*
U.S. savings and loan crisis, 24
U.S. Senate Permanent Subcommittee on Investigations, 503
U.S. sovereign debt, 280
U.S. Steel Corp., 49
U.S. Treasury, 632
U.S. Treasury bonds, 374*n*
U.S. Treasury Department, 405
UBS AG, 285*t*, 406, 482*t*, 498
Underhedging, 542*n*
Underwriting, 55, **56**, 114
  defined, 56
  investment banking, 58–60
  loan, 553
  risk in, 3
  top underwriters, 60*t*
Underwriting cycle, 120–121
Underwriting risk, 19
  expense risk, 118–119
  investment yield/return risk, 119–120
  loss risk, 116–117
  reinsurance, 112, 117–118
  securities, 500–501
Unearned premiums, **116**
Unexpected loss, 485
Unicredit Group, 482
Uninsured depositors, 444–445
Union Bank National Association, 530*t*
Union Bank of Switzerland (UBS), 359*t*
United Kingdom
  electronic payment methods, 398
  universal bank, 494
United Nations Suppression of Terrorism Regulations (UNSTR), 518
United States
  bank failures, 434, 435, 522
  banking industry, 24
  corporate governance scandals, 70
  deposit insurance insolvency, 435–436
  dollar, 284, 517–523
  foreign banks in, 520–523
  interstate banking, 509–510
  mortgage-backed securities, 643–646
  securities frauds, 70–71
Universal banks, **2**, 494, 498
Universal financial institutions, 494
Universal life, 106
Unsecured loan, **198**
Unsystematic risks
  emerging-market loans, 316–317
  equity position, 333–334
Up-front fee, **363**
Upstreaming, 501
USA Patriot Act (2001), 70, 405–406, 518
Users of funds. *See* Shortages of funds
Usury ceilings. *See* Criminal Code of Canada

Value funds, 91
Value-at-risk (VaR), 147, 327, 483. *See also* Historic approach to market risk; RiskMetrics
Vancouver City Savings, 22, 23*t*, 34, 662
Variable-interest entities (VIEs), **674**. *See also* Special-purpose entities
Variable life insurance, 106
Variable rate mortgages (VRMs), 16, **199**
Variable universal life, 106
Variance of export revenue (VAREX), 314
Vega of option, 360*n*
Venezuela
  domestic money growth, 314
  sovereign bonds, 322
Venture capital, **52**, **61**
Venture capital firms, 61–62
Verification of identities, 386
Vested assets/Vesting, **96**
Visa, 200
Volatility of earnings, 210
Volatility risk, 360*n*
Volcker Rule, 21, 327
Volcker, Paul, 327
Vulture funds, **628**, 635

Wachovia, 510, 511
Wall Street Reform and Consumer Protection Act (U.S.), 70, 71, 111, 327, 495, 497, 504, 617
Washington Mutual, 10, 50, 51, 136, 141, 326, 358, 372, 510, 598
Watson Wyatt, 100
Wawanesa Mutual, 112*t*
Wealth management, **76**
Web fraud, 409
Weighted average life (WAL), **655**
Weiss, M.A., 397*n*
Wells Fargo, 23, 50, 482*t*, 510, 511, 530*t*
Wheelock, D.C., 398*n*
When-issued (WI) trading/securities, 358*t*, **373–374**
White, L.J., 437*n*
Whole life policy, 106
Wholesale CDs, 422–423
Wholesale credit decisions, 206–208
Wholesale financial services, impact of technology on, 385–387
Wholesale fixed term deposits, 422–423
Wholesale lockbox, 386
Wilson, B., 437*n*
Wilson, J., 398
Wilson, P.W., 398*n*
Wire transfer services, 9, 400
Wireless communications, 380
Withdrawal risks
  bankers' acceptances, 425
  commercial paper, 425
  demand deposits, 418
  GICs, 421–422
  interbank funds, 422–423
  interest-bearing chequing accounts, 420
  medium-term and long-term notes, 425
  overnight loans, 425
  repurchase agreements, 424
  retail term deposits, 421–422
  savings accounts, 421
  wholesale CDs, 422–423
  wholesale fixed-term deposits and CDs, 422–423
World Bank, 302, 303, 304, 307–308
World Bank Group, 54
World Trade Centre, 381
World Trade Organization (WTO), 519
WorldCom, 70, 223
Writing options
  buying *vs.*, 568–570
  calls, 565–566
  puts, 567

X-Inefficiencies, **397–398**, **511**, 511*n*

Yamaichi Securities, 303
Yield, duration and, 172–173
Yield curves, 546*n*

Z class, **667**
Z Score model, 213–214, 219*n*
Z score rating, 312
Z score. *See* Altman's Z score
Zaik, E., 226*n*
Zero-coupon bond
  defined, **216**
  duration, 170–171
Zero-coupon government debt. *See* Treasury strips
Zurich Financial Services, 123*t*